W9-ABK-458

McGRAW-HILL
SCIENCE

Macmillan/McGraw-Hill Edition
Teacher's Edition

Richard Moyer • Lucy Daniel • Jay Hackett

H. Prentice Baptiste • Pamela Stryker • JoAnne Vasquez

**NATIONAL
GEOGRAPHIC
SOCIETY**

On the Cover:

The Slberian, or Amur, tiger lives primarily in the forests of eastern Russia. Some are also found in China and northern North Korea. Only about 400 of these beautiful animals still exist in the wild. About 500 captive Siberian tigers are in wildlife conservation programs. The survival of Siberian tigers in the wild depends on preserving their habitat and protecting them from poachers.

**Macmillan
McGraw-Hill**

New York   Farmington

PROGRAM AUTHORS

Dr. Lucy H. Daniel
Teacher, Consultant
Rutherford County Schools,
North Carolina

Dr. Jay Hackett
Professor Emeritus of Earth Sciences
University of Northern Colorado

Dr. Richard H. Moyer
Professor of Science Education
University of Michigan-Dearborn

Dr. H. Prentice Baptiste
Professor of Science and Multicultural Education
New Mexico State University
Las Cruces, New Mexico

Pamela Stryker, M.Ed.
Elementary Educator and Science Consultant
Eanes Independent School District
Austin, Texas

Dr. JoAnne Vasquez
Elementary Science Education Consultant
Mesa Public Schools, Arizona
NSTA Past President

NATIONAL
GEOGRAPHIC
SOCIETY
Washington, D.C

The features in this textbook entitled "Invitation to Science," "Amazing Stories," and "People in Science," as well as the unit openers, were developed in collaboration with the National Geographic Society's School Publishing Division. Copyright © 2002 National Geographic Society. All rights reserved.

The name "National Geographic" and the Yellow Border are registered trademarks of the National Geographic Society.

Macmillan/McGraw-Hill

A Division of The McGraw-Hill Companies

Published by Macmillan/McGraw-Hill, of McGraw-Hill Education, a division of The McGraw-Hill Companies, Inc., Two Penn Plaza, New York, New York 10121. Copyright © 2002 by Macmillan/McGraw-Hill. All rights reserved. No part of this publication may be reproduced or distributed in any form or by any means, or stored in a database or retrieval system, without the prior written consent of The McGraw-Hill Companies, Inc., including, but not limited to, network storage or transmission, or broadcast for distance learning.

Printed in the United States of America

3 4 5 6 7 8 9 073/046 07 06 05 04 03 02

McGRAW-HILL
science
Macmillan/McGraw-Hill Edition
TEACHER'S EDITION

Table of Contents

Kindergarten

LIFE SCIENCE

Unit 2 - *Learn About Plants*
1 Living Things
2 Parts of Plants
3 Plants with Flowers
4 Seeds, Seeds, Seeds
5 How Plants Grow
6 Plants We Use

Unit 3 - *Learn About Animals*
1 Our Pets
2 Animals that Fly
3 Animals that Swim
4 Animals that Walk
5 Animal Babies
6 People and Animals

EARTH SCIENCE

Unit 4 - *A Home Called Earth*
1 Look Around You (landforms)
2 Rocks Everywhere
3 The Soil Under Your Feet
4 Water All Around
5 What Living Things
   Get from Earth
6 Take Care of Earth

Unit 5 - *Weather and Seasons*
1 All Kinds of Weather
2 Hot and Cold
3 The Sun
4 The Wind
5 Watch the Weather
6 The Seasons

PHYSICAL SCIENCE

Unit 1 - *Learn About Your World*
1 Use Your Eyes
2 Use Your Ears
3 Smell, Touch, and Taste
4 Tell About It
5 Same or Different
6 Make Groups

Unit 6 - *Make Things Move*
1 Move Along
2 Push and Pull
3 Slide and Roll
4 Wheels
5 Magnets
6 Float or Sink

Grade 1

Unit A - *Plants Are Living Things*
1 Your Senses
2 Living and Nonliving Things
3 Plants Are Living Things
4 Plants Have Parts
5 Roots
6 Stems and Leaves
7 Seeds
8 Plants Grow and Change

Unit B - *Animals Are Living Things*
1 Animals Are Living Things
2 Mammals
3 More Animal Groups
4 Grow and Change
5 Getting Food
6 Where Animals Live
7 Staying Safe

Unit C - *The Sky and Weather*
1 The Sun
2 The Moon and Stars
3 The Planets
4 Weather
5 Weather Changes
6 Spring and Summer
7 Fall and Winter

Unit D - *Caring for Earth*
1 Rocks and Minerals
2 Soil
3 Water
4 Air
5 Living Things
   Are Resources
6 Pollution
7 Caring for Earth's Resources

Unit E - *Matter, Matter Everywhere*
1 Properties of Matter
2 Solids
3 Liquids
4 Gases
5 Solids in Mixtures
6 Solids and Liquids in Water
7 Heat Changes Matter

Unit F - *On the Move*
1 Things Move
2 Measure Movement
3 The Ways Things Move
4 Things Magnets Move
5 A Magnet's Poles
6 Things Magnets Pull Through
7 Moving Things Make Sound
8 Explore Different Sounds

Grade 2

Unit A - *Plants and Animals*
1 Plants Are Living Things
2 Parts of Plants
3 Plants Make New Plants
4 Everyone Needs Plants
5 All Kinds of Animals
6 Animals Meet Their Needs
7 Animals Grow and Change

Unit B - *Homes for Plants and Animals*
1 Where Plants and Animals Live
2 Life in a Woodland Forest
3 Life in a Rain Forest
4 Life in a Desert
5 Life in the Arctic
6 Life in a Fresh Water Habitat
7 Life in a Salt Water Habitat
8 Caring for Earth's Habitats

Unit C - *Changes on Earth*
1 Water and Our Weather
2 Earth Can Change Slowly
3 Earth Can Change Quickly
4 Clues in Rocks
5 Putting the Clues Together
6 Life on Earth Changes

Unit D - *The Sun and Its Family*
1 Day and Night
2 Seasons
3 The Moon
4 The Moon Changes
5 Stars
6 Planets

Unit E - *Matter and Energy*
1 Matter All Around
2 Three States of Matter
3 Changing Matter
4 Heat
5 Light
6 Sound

Unit F - *Watch It Move*
1 Pushes and Pulls
2 Forces and Change
3 Levers
4 Ramps
5 All About Magnets
6 Everyday Magnets

Grade 3

Unit A - *Looking at Plants and Animals*
1 How Living Things Are Alike
2 The Needs of Plants
3 The Life Cycle of a Plant
4 The Needs of Animals
5 How Animals Grow
6 Parts of Animals
7 Kinds of Animals

Unit B - *Where Plants and Animals Live*
1 Ecosystems
2 Food Chains and Food Webs
3 Roles for Plants and Animals
4 Competition Among Living Things
5 Adaptations for Survival
6 Changing Ecosystems

Unit C - *Our Earth*
1 Minerals and Rocks
2 Kinds of Soils
3 Fossils and Fuels
4 Water in Sea, Land, and Sky
5 Saving Our Resources
6 Landforms
7 Slow Changes on Land
8 Fast Changes on Land

Unit D - *Cycles on Earth and in Space*
1 The Weather
2 The Water Cycle
3 Describing Weather
4 How Earth Moves
5 Phases of the Moon
6 The Sun and Its Planets

Unit E - *Forces and Motion*
1 Motion and Speed
2 Forces
3 Changes in Motion
4 Doing Work
5 Levers and Pulleys
6 More Simple Machines

Unit F - *Looking at Matter and Energy*
1 Properties of Matter
2 Comparing Solids, Liquids, and Gases
3 Building Blocks of Matters
4 How Heat Travels
5 How Light Travels
6 Properties of Sound
7 Paths for Electricity

Grade 4	Grade 5	Grade 6

LIFE SCIENCE

Grade 4

Unit A - *The World of Living Things*
1 The Cells in Living Things
2 Classifying Organisms
3 Organisms of the Past
4 Organisms and Where They Live
5 Changes in Ecosystems
6 Plant Parts
7 Plant Growth and Reproduction

Unit B - *Animals as Living Things*
1 Animal Characteristics
2 Animals Without Backbones
3 Animals with Backbones
4 Organ Systems
5 Development and Reproduction
6 Animal Survival

Grade 5

Unit A - *Structures of Plants and Animals*
1 Classifying Living Things
2 Roots, Stems, and Leaves
3 The Importance of Plants (photosynthesis)
4 Plants Without Seeds
5 Plants with Seeds
6 Flowers and Seeds
7 Plant Responses and Adaptations
8 Animal Structure and Function
9 Animal Adaptation

Unit B - *Interactions of Living Things*
1 Living Things and Their Environment
2 Food Chains and Food Webs
3 Cycles of Life
4 How Populations Survive
5 Biomes
6 How Ecosystems Change

Grade 6

Unit A - *Classifying Living Things*
1 The Kingdoms of Life
2 Classifying Plants
3 Invertebrates
4 Vertebrates
5 Reproduction and Growth

Unit B - *Organization of Living Things*
1 From Cells to Ecosystems
2 Comparing Earth's Biomes
3 Parts of a Cell
4 Movement and Nutrition in Cells
5 Cells Divide and Grow
6 The History of Genetics
7 Predicting Traits
8 How DNA Controls Traits
9 Using Genetics

EARTH SCIENCE

Grade 4

Unit C - *Earth and Beyond*
1 What You Can Learn from Rocks
2 Clues from Fossils
3 Shaping Earth's Surface
4 The Story of Soil
5 Inside Earth
6 Earth, the Moon, and the Sun
7 The Solar System and Beyond

Unit D - *Water and Weather*
1 Water, Water Everywhere
2 Follow the Water (water cycle)
3 Motions in the Oceans
4 Go with the Flow (groundwater)
5 Water Please! (conservation)
6 Air, Wind, and the Atmosphere
7 Weather and Climate

Grade 5

Unit C - *Earth and Its Resources*
1 Earth and Its Neighbors
2 Earth's Changing Crust
3 Minerals of Earth's Crust
4 Earth's Rocks and Soil
5 Earth's Atmosphere
6 Earth's Fresh Water
7 Earth's Oceans
8 Energy Resources

Unit D - *Weather and Climate*
1 Atmosphere and Air Temperature
2 Water Vapor and Humidity
3 Clouds and Precipitation
4 Air Pressure and Wind
5 Air Masses and Fronts
6 Severe Storms
7 Climate

Grade 6

Unit C - *Observing the Sky*
1 The Tools of Astronomers
2 Earth and the Sun
3 The Moon in Motion
4 The Inner Solar System
5 The Outer Solar System
6 Stars
7 Galaxies and Beyond

Unit D - *The Restless Earth*
1 Moving Plates
2 Earthquakes
3 Volcanoes
4 Making Mountains and Soil
5 Erosion and Deposition
6 The Rock Cycle
7 Geologic Time

PHYSICAL SCIENCE

Grade 4

Unit E - *Matter*
1 Matter (properties, states)
2 Measuring Matter
3 What Matter Is Made Of
4 Physical Changes
5 Chemical Changes

Unit F - *Energy*
1 Motion, Forces, and Energy
2 Energy and Tools
3 Heat
4 Light
5 Sound
6 Static Electricity
7 Current Electricity
8 Electricity and Magnetism

Grade 5

Unit E - *Properties of Matter and Energy*
1 Physical Properties
2 Elements and Compounds
3 Solids, Liquids, and Gases
4 Mixtures and Solutions
5 Chemical Changes
6 Acids and Bases
7 How Matter and Energy Interact

Unit F - *Motion and Energy*
1 Newton's First Law
2 Newton's Second and Third Laws
3 Newton's Law of Gravitation
4 Sound Waves
5 Pitch and Loudness
6 Reflection and Absorption
7 Light and Mirrors
8 Light and Lenses
9 Light and Color
10 Invisible Light

Grade 6

Unit E - *Interactions of Matter and Energy*
1 Physical Properties of Matter
2 Elements and Atoms
3 Chemical Changes
4 Temperature and Heat
5 How Heat Affects Matter
6 Sources of Energy
7 Static Electricity
8 Circuits
9 Electromagnets
10 Using Electricity

Unit F - *Motion, Work, and Machines*
1 Speed and Distance
2 Forces and Motion
3 Acceleration and Momentum
4 Energy and Work
5 How Levers Work
6 How Inclined Planes Work

Meeting National Science Standards

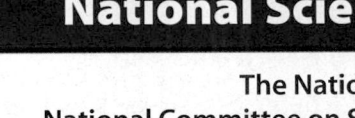

National Science Education Standards

The National Research Council set up a
National Committee on Science Education Standards and Assessment
to develop national standards in science education.
The Standards are summarized in these categories:

- Science as Inquiry
- Physical Science Content
- Life Science Content
- Earth and Space
  Science Content
- Science and Technology

- Science in Personal
  and Social Perspectives
- Nature and History of Science
- Unifying Concepts
  and Processes
- Fair, Consistent Assessment
  in a Variety of Contexts

Benchmarks for Science Literacy

The groundbreaking Project 2061 as presented in a report of the
American Association for the Advancement of Science,
the Benchmarks for Science Literacy,
provides teachers with common goals without requiring
uniform curricula and methods.

The Benchmarks can be summarized by:

- The Nature of Science
- The Nature of Technology
- The Physical Setting

- The Living Environment
- The Human Organism
- Common Themes

McGraw-Hill Science was developed to enable teachers to implement
these national science standards within the context of their
own state and local science criteria by focusing on three major aspects:

- **the tools and processes of inquiry in every lesson**
- **grade-level sequenced content**
  with life, earth, and physical sciences
  taught at each grade
- **assessment in a variety of contexts**

Pages TR2–TR3 in the Teacher Reference Section present a
correlation of the units of this grade level to both sets of these national standards.

Assessment in *McGraw-Hill Science*

McGraw-Hill Science provides a variety of contexts for assessment while students are learning and at ends of lessons, chapters, and units.

The assessment is student-centered, encompassing a four-fold assessment plan:

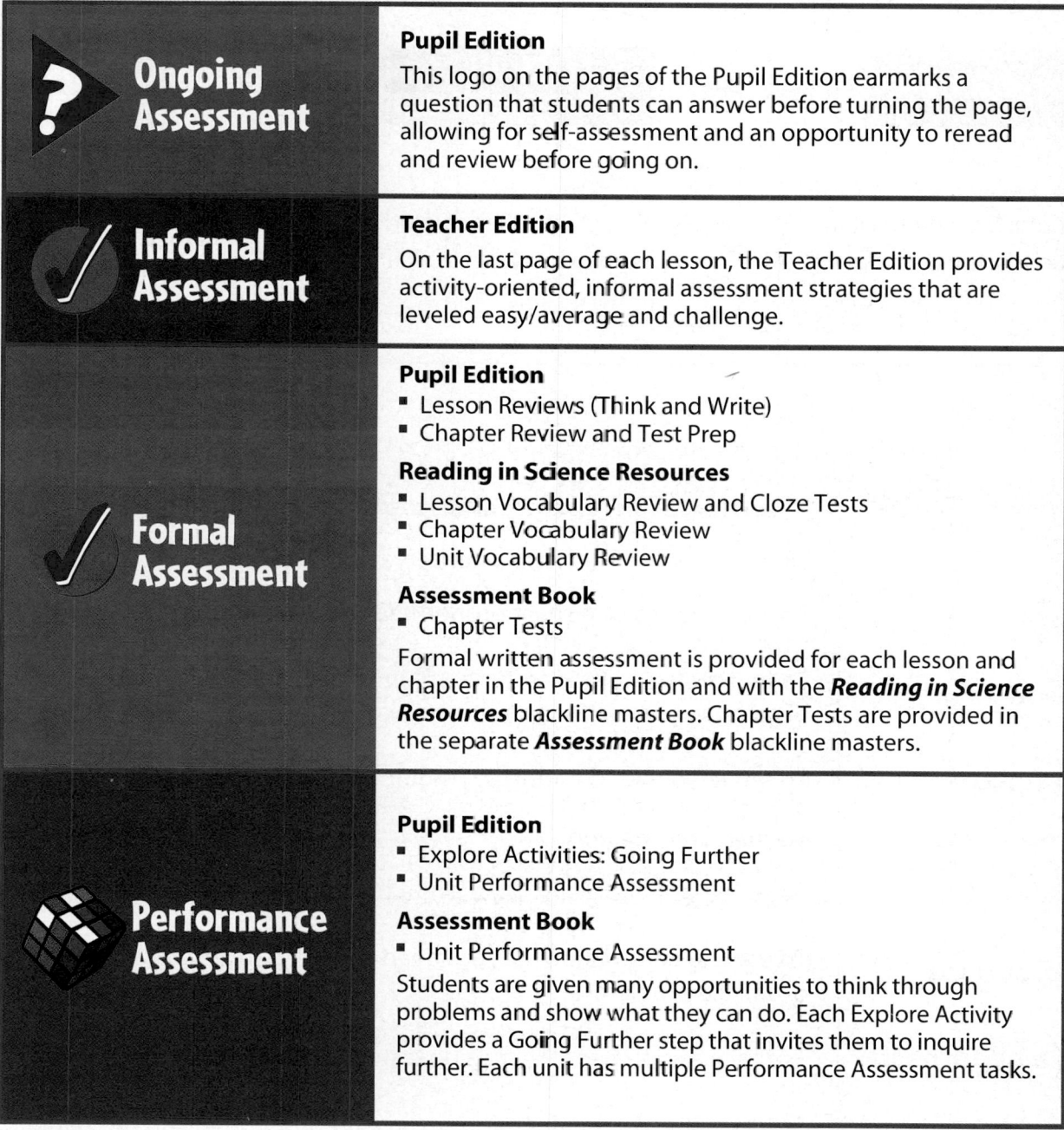

Ongoing Assessment

Pupil Edition
This logo on the pages of the Pupil Edition earmarks a question that students can answer before turning the page, allowing for self-assessment and an opportunity to reread and review before going on.

Informal Assessment

Teacher Edition
On the last page of each lesson, the Teacher Edition provides activity-oriented, informal assessment strategies that are leveled easy/average and challenge.

Formal Assessment

Pupil Edition
- Lesson Reviews (Think and Write)
- Chapter Review and Test Prep

Reading in Science Resources
- Lesson Vocabulary Review and Cloze Tests
- Chapter Vocabulary Review
- Unit Vocabulary Review

Assessment Book
- Chapter Tests

Formal written assessment is provided for each lesson and chapter in the Pupil Edition and with the *Reading in Science Resources* blackline masters. Chapter Tests are provided in the separate *Assessment Book* blackline masters.

Performance Assessment

Pupil Edition
- Explore Activities: Going Further
- Unit Performance Assessment

Assessment Book
- Unit Performance Assessment

Students are given many opportunities to think through problems and show what they can do. Each Explore Activity provides a Going Further step that invites them to inquire further. Each unit has multiple Performance Assessment tasks.

Portfolio Assessment

McGraw-Hill Science provides blackline masters (*Activity Resources*)
to accompany all activities in the Pupil Editions,
and Chapter Graphic Organizers (*Reading in Science Resources*)
as well as *School to Home Activities* and *Cross Curricular Projects* blackline masters
from which students can select items to build a portfolio.

Building Science Process Skills in McGraw-Hill Science

Building the skills of inquiry empowers students to solve problems, to evaluate their solutions, and to plan and implement their own investigations.

McGraw-Hill Science has a three-fold plan for building science process skills:

Introduction

Invitation to Science
Pupil Editions open with skill instruction in the real-life context of a working scientist.

Skill Instruction

Process Skill Builders
Special activities teach students how to use a process skill to accomplish a task.

Consistent Practice

Explore Activities Quick Labs
When students use a process skill in an activity, the step is labeled and highlighted.

The Process Skills taught in *McGraw-Hill Science Grades 3 to 6* are:

Observe	To use one or more of the senses to identify or learn about an object or event
Infer	To form an idea from facts or observations
Classify	To place things that share properties together in groups
Measure	To find the size, distance, time, volume, area, mass, weight, or temperature of an object or event
Use numbers	To order, count, add, subtract, multiply, and divide to explain data
Communicate	To share information
Predict	To state possible results of an event or experiment
Interpret data	To use the information that has been gathered to answer questions or solve a problem
Form a hypothesis	To make a statement that can be tested to answer a question
Use variables	To identify and separate things in an experiment that can be changed or controlled
Experiment	To perform a test to support or disprove a hypothesis
Make a model	To make something to represent an object or event
Define based on observations	To put together a description that is based on observations and experience

Developing Reading Skills in McGraw-Hill Science

Before– and After–Reading Questions

- **Before Reading**
  All Pupil Edition headings are questions that students can try to answer before reading.

- **After Reading**
  A corresponding question is provided at the end of each page or two-page spread to allow students to assess their comprehension.

Developing Vocabulary

- **Preview**
  The Teacher Edition provides a Chapter Vocabulary Preview on each Chapter Opener spread. The Pupil Edition previews vocabulary on the opening spread of each lesson.

- **Point of Instruction**
  Each vocabulary word is highlighted in yellow at the point where it is taught. At point of appearance the side column of the Teacher Edition provides a vocabulary teaching strategy for each vocabulary word.

Reading Strategy

The Teacher Edition provides additional opportunities for students to develop and apply reading skills. A listing on each Chapter Opener shows where the following skills are taught.

- **Cause and Effect**
- **Compare and Contrast**
- **Draw Conclusions**
- **Find the Main Idea**
- **Sequence of Events**
- **Summarize**
- **Ask Questions**

- **Reread**
- **Retell (paraphrase)**
- **Interpret Graphic Sources of Information**
- **Build on Prior Knowledge**
- **Organize Information**

Reading MiniLesson

Throughout the lessons, the Teacher Edition provides Reading Skill MiniLessons. Each MiniLesson is a brief tutorial and an activity for students to practice a specific reading skill for each chapter. One of the following skills is developed in each chapter:

- **Compare and Contrast**
- **Find the Main Idea**
- **Cause and Effect**
- **Draw Conclusions**
- **Sequence of Events**
- **Summarize**

Reading in Science Resources

Throughout the Teacher Edition, reductions of blackline masters for:

- Lesson Outlines
- Interpret Illustrations

from the **Reading in Science Resources** are provided at point of use.

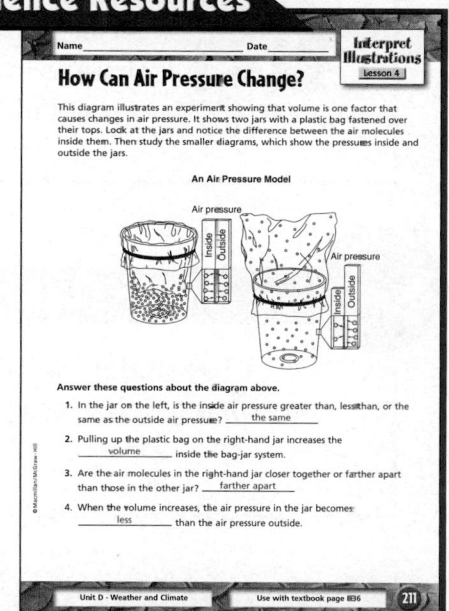

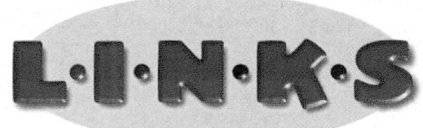

L·I·N·K·S

to Reading, Writing, Arithmetic, and More

McGraw-Hill Science is linked to all parts of your daily curriculum.
Students can integrate what they learn in science with what they learn throughout the day.

L·I·N·K·S

LESSON LINKS
At the end of each lesson students will find a Links column:

You will find Links to:

LITERATURE LINK

Additional outside reading for science and across the curriculum

Grade-Level Science Books
Three Grade-Level Science Books, complete with student activities, for each unit.

Cross Curricular Books
In each unit one book per chapter from the Reading and Social Studies curricula is pictured in the Teacher Edition at point of suggested use.

MATH LINK

The student will find activities involving graphs, measurements, problem solving, and shapes.

SOCIAL STUDIES LINK

Students will find activities involving map skills, cultural perspectives, and more.

MUSIC/ART LINK

Students will find activities making drawings, posters, models, as well as composing songs. In addition, opportunities to draw and create models abound in Explore Activities and Unit Performance Assessments.

HEALTH LINK

Students will find activities involving growing and staying healthy.

WRITING LINK

Students will have opportunities to write paragraphs, poems, stories, and skits.

TECHNOLOGY LINK

Students can find
- links on the Internet
- research projects on the Internet
- opportunities to use the Science Newsroom CD-ROMs

CROSS CURRICULAR PROJECTS

This blackline master booklet provides cross curricular projects organized into easy to use activities for each unit, complete with a Unit Culminating Activity.

Materials

Consumable materials (based on six groups)

Materials	Quantity Needed per group	Kit Quantity	Unit/Lesson
Ammonia solution		100 mL	E/6
Animals, pill bugs or sow bugs	8	coupon for 50	A/9
Animals, bugs, sow; earthworms; snail (pond)	4, 2, 8	coupons for 12 of each	B/1
Animal, snail, helix	2	coupon for 18	B/1
Antacid		2 tablets	E/6
Bag, plastic sandwich	4	80	C/2, D/4, F/8
Bag, plastic zip lip, 6" x 8"	1	12	C/4
Bag, plastic zip lip, 4" x 6"	1	6	F/4
Bag, specimen	1	12	D/2
Baking powder		7 oz	E/5
Baking soda		454 g	E/5, 6
Balloon, round, 5"	1	35	E/1
Balloon, long, 18"	1	10	F/2
Batteries, D-cell	12	24	E/7; F/7, 8, 9
Battery, 1.5 V alkaline, D-cell	1	6	E/7
Bottle, plastic, with cap	1		E/3
Bulb, 100 W	3	6	B/3, D/1, E/3
Cards, index		100	F/8
Cardboard sheet	6		A/5
Cardboard strip, 12 cm long	12		C/5
Cardboard tubes, long	2		F/6
Carton, small milk	4		B/4
Chalk	1 stick	12	C/5
Clay (cream)		2 lb	C/1, D/1
Clay (red, blue, green, yellow)		4 lb	C/2
Conifer, small pine seedling, or other	1		A/5
Crayons			E/5, F/9
Cup, foam, 8 oz	1	25	C/3, 4; F/4
Cups, paper, 100 mL, 200 mL	6, 2	50, 25	E/5
Cup, paper, 360 mL	1	25	A/7
Cup, plastic clear, 9 oz		150	B/5; C/4, 5, 6; D/2,3; E/3, 4, 6; F/8, 9
Detergent, powdered			E/6
Filters, coffee	1	100	E/4
Fingernail polish, clear			A/5
Foil, aluminum, 12" x 25'		1 roll	A/3; E/1; F/8, 10
Food coloring, dark red, 30 mL		2 bottles	A/1; D/2, 3; F/8
Food coloring, red, yellow, blue and green, 8 mL/ea		2 pkg	C/6,7;F/9
Food, banana, graham cracker crumbs, hazelnut, peanut butter			C/2
Food, beverage, carbonated			E/6
Food, celery stalk, piece of moss, or edible leaves			A/1, A/2
Food, cornstarch		500 g	E/5
Food, juice, grape, orange			E/6
Food, juice, lemon		15 oz	E/6
Food, marshmallows, large and small			E/2
Food, sugar cube	3	96	E/4
Food, tea bag	1	24	C/6, E/6
Food, vinegar		500 mL	C/5; E/5, 6
Food, whipping cream			E/4
Gloves, disposable		50 pair	E/6

Materials	Quantity Needed per group	Kit Quantity	Unit/Lesson
Gravel/pebbles		3 kg	B/1
Hydrogen peroxide, 3%, 230 mL		1 bottle	B/5
Iodine solution		100 mL	E/5
Iron filings		8 oz	E/4
Knives, plastic	3	24	A/1; C/2, 5
Microscope cover slip	3	100	A/1, 4; B/5
Paper, black	2 sheets		D/1
Paper, graph			C/1, D/1 E/4, F/1
Paper, wax, 75 sq ft	1	1 roll	C/2, E/5, F/8
Pen, marking	1		A/7
Pencil, wax marking	1	3	A/7
Petroleum jelly		4 oz	C/5
pH paper, blue and red litmus test	9	100 each	E/6
pH paper, wide range		100	E/6
Plant, cactus	1		A/2
Plant, duckweed, *Lemna minor*		coupon for 1 class package	B/1
Plant, *Elodea*	2	coupon for 12 sprigs	A/1, 2; B/1
Plant, fern, not w/spore cases	2		A/1
Plant, fern, w/spore cases		1 coupon	A/4
Plant, flowers, several large, from different plants	1		A/1, 2, 5, 6
Plant, garden or house, such as geranium	1		A/5, 7; D/2
Plant, grass	1		A/5
Plant, ivy	1		A/7
Plant, moss	2		A/1, 4
Plant, window or aquarium	1		A/3
Plastic wrap, 50 sq ft		1 roll	B/1, C/5
Rubber bands, medium		100	C/5; D/3, 4
Rubber bands, short	1	1 oz	F/1
Rubber bands, 5", long	1	approx. 80	F/2, 4
Salt		1,474 g	C/7; E/4, 5
Salt, kosher		2 lb	C/3
Salt, rock		1 lb	C/3
Sand, fine		2.5 kg	B/5, C/4, E/4
Sandpaper, 8½" x 11"	2 pieces	3 sheets	E/5, 7
Seeds, corn; lima bean		30 g; 2 oz	A/6
Seed, grass		60 g	A/7, B/1
Seeds, pinto bean	44	1 lb	A/7, B/4
Soil, clay		10 kg	B/3, D/7
Soil, potting		24 lb	A/7; B/1, 4, 5; C/4, 6
Sound maker (clicker or timer)	1		F/6
Spoons, plastic	10	24	B/5; C/3, 4; E/4, 5
Straws, plastic		200	F/2, 5, 10
Straws, wrapped		50	C/7
String		200 ft	throughout
Swabs, cotton		72	E/6
Toothpicks		3 boxes	A/4, 6; D/1; E/2, 4, 5
Vinegar		3 bottles	C/5

Materials

Non-consumable materials (based on six groups)

Materials	Quantity Needed per group	Kit Quantity	Unit/Lesson
Apron	5		E/6
Balance, double pan, w/masses	2	1	C/4, E/1
Ball, golf	2	6	E/1, F/3
Ball, table tennis	1	6	F/3
Battery holder w/ Fahnestock clips	2	6	E/7
Blocks, triangular; 30°, 60°, 90°	1 of each	6 of each	D/1
Books, research			B/6
Bottle, 1 qt	1		A/1
Bottle, 2-L plastic	2		D/6
Bottle, spray	1	6	D/7
Bowl, foam, 12 oz	1	25	D/1
Bowl, plastic, 40 oz	1	12	E/4
Bowl, squat, 8 oz	1	6	C/6
Box, sealed, opaque	3		E/2
Box, shoe	1		E/1
Box, small cardboard with lid	1		F/7
Calculator	2		B/4, C/4
Camera (optional)	2		A/7, B/2
Can, empty	1		B/3
Car, toy	1	6	F/2
Chart, pH color	1	6	E/6
Clock, wind-up	1		E/3, F/4
Clock, with second hand	1		F/1
Collecting net (optional)	1		B/2
Cloth, cotton, 18" x 22"	1	1	D/3
Compass	1	6	E/7
Container, clear, w/drilled hole	1	6	D/4
Container, plastic clear, 2 qt	1	6	B/3
Container, plastic, with lid	3		B/5
Cube-O-Grams		100	C/2
Cup, graduated plastic clear, 10 oz	2	6	E/3, 4
Dropper	5	18	A/1, 4, 6; B/5; E/5
Fishbowl, 1 gal	2	2	B/1
Flashlight	4	6	D/1; F/7, 8, 9
Forceps	7	6	A/4, 6
Goggles	5		B/5, C/1, 3, 5; D/2, E/4, 5, 6; F/2, 3, 4, 9
Hand lens	12	6	A/1, A/2, 4, 5, 6; C/3, 4, 5; E/4; F/8
Hook, screw, small brass	2	12	F/2
Jar, plastic, wide-mouthed, tall, 12 oz, w/lid	6	6	C/7
Light socket, mini, w/Fahenstock Clips	2	6	E/7
Light socket, porcelain	4	6	B/3; D/1, 7; E/3
Magnet	1	6	E/4
Marbles		80	E/2
Materials, hard and soft; such as book, wood block, cloth, metal sheet, sponge, towel			F/6
Microscope	1	3	A/1, 4, 5; B/5
Microscope slide	7	72	A/1, 4, 5; B/5

Materials	Quantity Needed per group	Kit Quantity	Unit/Lesson
Mineral collection		7 specimens/ 6 each	C/3
Mirror, plastic	1	6	F/7
Meterstick	4		B/4; C/1; F/2, 6, 10
Mug	1		D/3
Object, small, to put inside box	1		F/7
Nails		15	C/3, E/5
Pail	4	6	E/1, 3
Pan, aluminum, 8" x 8" x $\frac{1}{4}$"	2	12	D/7
Pan, aluminum, 13" x 10" x 2"	3	12	C/6
Pan, aluminum, 31 cm x 22 cm x 3 cm	1	6	A/9, F/10
Paper clips	20	200	F/10
Paper clips, jumbo		300	E/1, 2
Peanuts, foam packaging		200	C/6
Petri dish	2	6	A/7, C/6
Plastic, red, blue, green, yellow, 3" x 3" sheets	1 of each	6 of each	F/9
Rock samples		14 specimens/ 6 each	C/4, 5
Ruler	4		B/1, D/1, E/1, F/4
Ruler, metric	4		C/4, 5, 7; D/1; F/5
Stopwatch	2	6	D/1, F10
Streak plate	2	8	C4
Strip, metal	1	6	F/1
Thermometer	7	18	D/1, 2, 3, 7; E/3
Thumbtack	1	100	C/7
Tornado Tube	1	6	D/6
Washers	3	18	F/1
Whisk	1	3	E/4
Wire, copper, 16 gauge		20 in.	C/3, 4
Wire, copper, 22 gauge, plastic coated		100 ft	E/7
Wire, copper, 24 gauge, enamel coated		4 oz	E/7
Wood, block, 3" x 4" x $\frac{3}{4}$"	2	12	F/2

Consultants

LIFE SCIENCES

Dr. Carol Baskin
University of Kentucky, Lexington, KY

Dr. Joe W. Crim
University of Georgia, Athens, GA

Dr. Marie DiBerardino
Allegheny University of Health Sciences
Philadelphia, PA

Dr. R. E. Duhrkopf
Baylor University, Waco, TX

Dr. Dennis L. Nelson
Montana State University, Bozeman, MT

Dr. Fred Sack
Ohio State University, Columbus, OH

Dr. Martin VanDyke
Denver, CO

Dr. E. Peter Volpe
Mercer University, Macon, GA

EARTH SCIENCES

Dr. Clarke Alexander
Skidaway Institute of Oceanography,
Savannah, GA

Dr. Suellen Cabe
Pembroke State University, Pembroke, NC

Dr. Thomas A. Davies
Texas A & M University, College Station, TX

Dr. Ed Geary
Geological Society of America, Boulder, CO

Dr. David C. Kopaska-Merkel
Geological Survey of Alabama, Tuscaloosa, AL

PHYSICAL SCIENCES

Dr. Bonnie Buratti
Jet Propulsion Lab, Pasadena, CA

Dr. Shawn Carlson
Society of Amateur Scientists, San Diego, CA

Dr. Karen Kwitter
Williams College, Williamstown, MA

Dr. Steven Souza,
Williamstown, MA

Dr. Joseph P. Straley
University of Kentucky, Lexington, KY

Dr. Thomas Troland
University of Kentucky , Lexington, KY

Dr. Josephine Davis Wallace
University of North Carolina, Charlotte, NC

CONSULTANT FOR PRIMARY GRADES
Donna Harrell Lubcker
East Texas Baptist University, Marshall, TX

• TEACHER PANELISTS

Newark, NJ
First Avenue School
Jorge Alameda
Concetta Cioci
Neva Galasso
Bernadette Kazanjian - reviewer
Janet Mayer - reviewer
Toby Marks
Maria Tutela

Brooklyn, NY
P.S. 31
Paige McGlone
Janet Mantel
Madeline Pappas
Maria Puma - reviewer

P.S. 217
Rosemary Ahern
Charles Brown
Claudia Deeb - reviewer
Wendy Lerner

P.S. 225
Christine Calafiore
Annette Fisher - reviewer

P.S. 250
Melissa Kane

P.S. 277
Erica Cohen
Helena Conti
Anne Marie Corrado
Deborah Scott-DiClemente
Jeanne Fish
Diane Fromhartz
Tricia Hinz
Lisa Iside
Susan Malament
Joyce Menkes-reviewer
Elaine Noto
Jean Pennacchio

Jeffrey Hampton
Mwaka Yavana

Elmont, NY
Covert Avenue School
Arlene Connelly

Mt. Vernon, NY
Holmes School
Jennifer Cavallaro
Lou Ciofi
George DiFiore
Brenda Durante
Jennifer Hawkins - reviewer
Michelle Mazzotta
Catherine Moringiello
Mary Jane Oria - reviewer
Lucille Pierotti
Pia Vicario - reviewer

Ozone Park, NY
St. Elizabeth School
Joanne Cocchiola - Reviewer
Helen DiPietra - Reviewer
Barbara Kingston
Madeline Visco

St. Albans, NY
Orvia Williams

• TEACHER REVIEWERS

Peoria, IL
Rolling Acres Middle School
Gail Truho

Rockford, IL
Rockford Public Schools
Dr. Sharon Wynstra
Science Coordinator

Newark, NJ
Alexander Street School
Cheryl Simeonidis

Albuquerque, NM
Jackie Costales
Science Coordinator,
Montgomery Complex

Poughkeepsie, NY
St. Peter's School
Monica Crolius

Columbus, OH
St. Mary's School
Linda Cotter
Joby Easley

Keizer, OR
Cummings Elementary
Deanna Havel

McMinnville, OR
McMinnville School District
Kristin Ward

Salem, OR
Fruitland Elementary
Mike Knudson

Four Corners Elementary
Bethany Ayers
Sivhong Hanson
Cheryl Kirkelie
Julie Wells

Salem-Keizer Public Schools
Rachael Harms
Sue Smith,
Science Specialist

Yoshikai Elementary
Joyce Davenport

Norristown, PA
St. Teresa of Avila
Fran Fiordimondo

Pittsburgh, PA
**Chartiers Valley
Intermediate School**
Rosemary Hutter

Memphis, TN
Memphis City Schools
Quincy Hathorn
District Science Facilitator

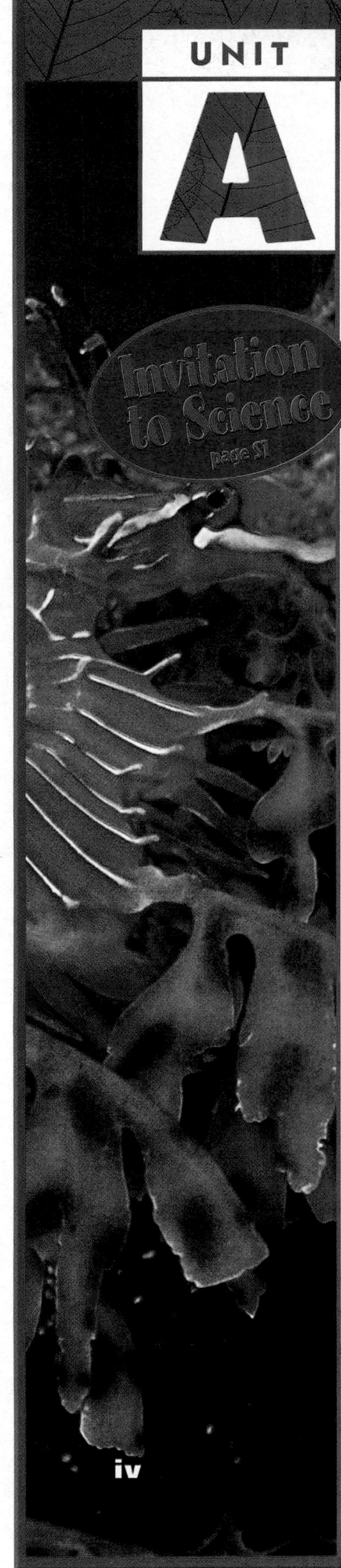

Life Science

Structures of Plants and Animals PAGE A1

UNIT C Earth Science

Earth and Its Resources PAGE C1

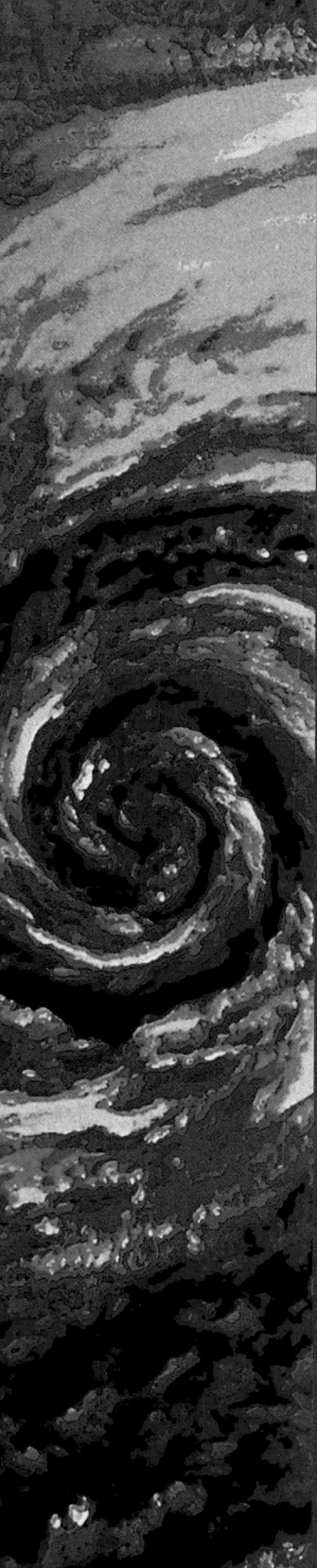

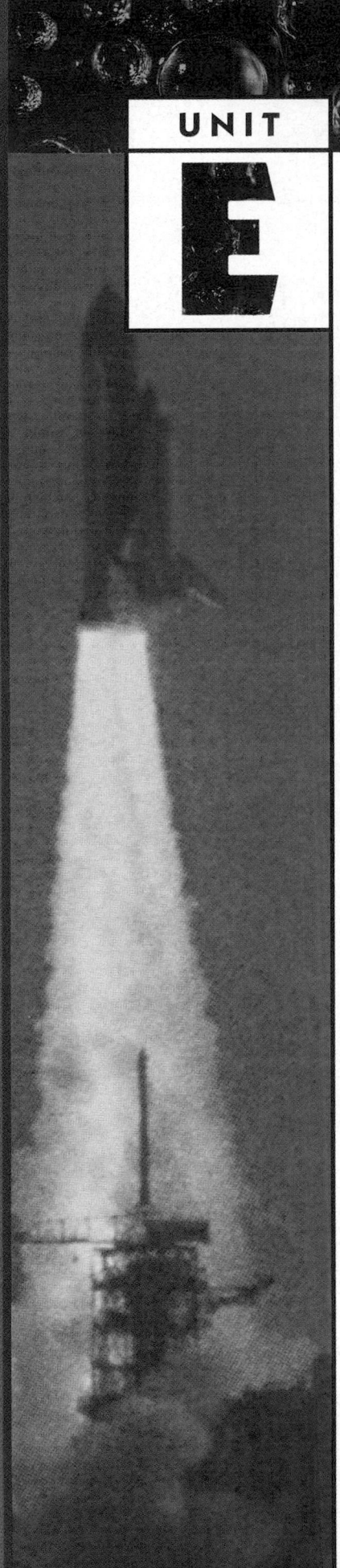

Physical Science

Properties of Matter and Energy PAGE E1

UNIT **F**

Physical Science
Motion and Energy PAGE F1

Activities

UNIT A

Explore Activities

What Do Plants Have in Common? **A5**

How Do a Plant's Parts Help
It Survive? **A19**

What Does Light Do for a Plant? **A31**

How Do Mosses Get Water? **A47**

How Do Seed Plants Differ? **A57**

How Do Flowers Differ? **A69**

How Do Roots Grow? **A79**

How Are Animals Classified? **A93**

How Do Sow Bugs Adapt
to Their Environment? **A105**

Quick Labs

Tubelike Plant Parts **A9**

Leaves **A25**

Ferns **A50**

Inside a Seed **A74**

Plants Compete for Light **A83**

Find the Hybrid Cat **A113**

Process Skill Builders

Experiment: Why Leaves
Change Color **A35**

Observe: Flowering Plants **A63**

Classify: Using a Key **A100**

UNIT B

Explore Activities

What Do Living Things Need
to Survive? **B5**

How Do Populations Interact? **B17**

What Happens to Water? **B31**

What Controls the Growth
of Populations? **B49**

Why Is Soil Important? **B63**

How Do Ecosystems Change? **B79**

Quick Labs

Getting Food **B19**

Soil Sample **B35**

Playground Space **B51**

Freshwater Communities **B72**

Predicting Succession **B85**

Process Skill Builders

Use Variables: Vanishing Bald Eagles **B13**

Infer: Comparing Ecosystems
in Volcanic Areas **B87**

UNIT C

Explore Activities

How Are Earth and the Sun
Held Together? **C5**

What Makes the Crust Move? **C17**

How Can You Identify a Mineral? **C31**

How Are Rocks Alike and Different? **C41**

What Makes Air Dirty? **C61**

How Can Salt Water Be Made Usable?
C71

How Do Ocean and Fresh Water
Compare? **C83**

How Do People Use Energy? **C99**

Quick Labs

Orbit Times **C7**

Model of Earth **C19**

Growing Crystals **C37**

Acids **C65**

Salt Water and Fresh Water **C85**

Fuel Supply **C103**

Process Skill Builders

Define Based on Observations:
Define Soil **C48**

Form a Hypothesis: How Do Wastes from
Land Get into Lakes and Rivers? **C77**

UNIT D

UNIT E

UNIT F

Reading In SCIENCE

As you study science, you will learn many new words. You will read about many new ideas. Read these pages. They will help you understand this book.

1. The **Vocabulary** list has all the new words you will learn in the lesson. The page numbers tell you where the words are taught.

2. The name tells you what the lesson is about.

3. Get Ready uses the picture on the page to help you start thinking about the lesson.

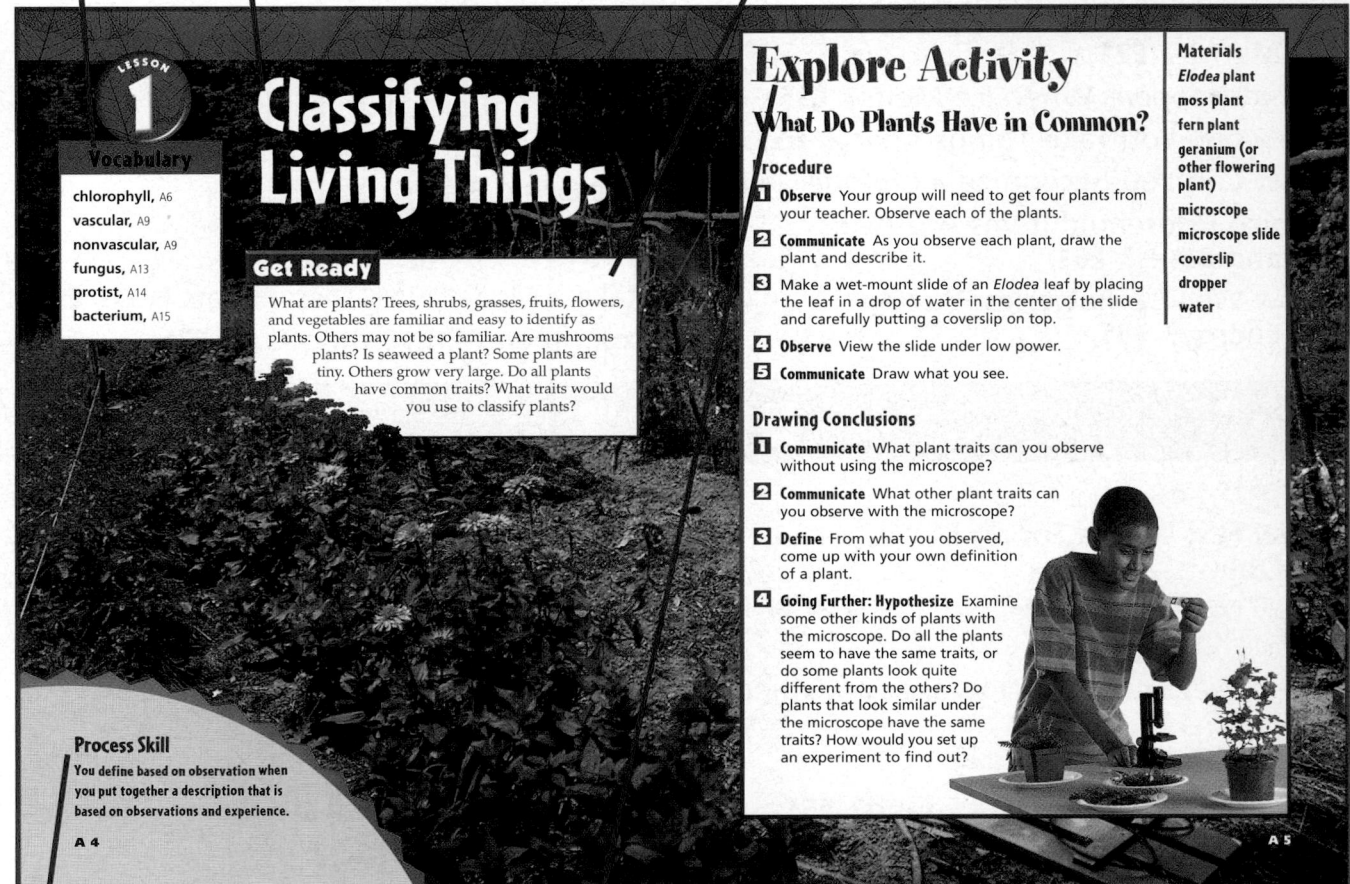

LESSON 1

Vocabulary

chlorophyll, A6
vascular, A9
nonvascular, A9
fungus, A13
protist, A14
bacterium, A15

Classifying Living Things

Get Ready

What are plants? Trees, shrubs, grasses, fruits, flowers, and vegetables are familiar and easy to identify as plants. Others may not be so familiar. Are mushrooms plants? Is seaweed a plant? Some plants are tiny. Others grow very large. Do all plants have common traits? What traits would you use to classify plants?

Process Skill

You define based on observation when you put together a description that is based on observations and experience.

A 4

Explore Activity

What Do Plants Have in Common?

Procedure

1 Observe Your group will need to get four plants from your teacher. Observe each of the plants.

2 Communicate As you observe each plant, draw the plant and describe it.

3 Make a wet-mount slide of an *Elodea* leaf by placing the leaf in a drop of water in the center of the slide and carefully putting a coverslip on top.

4 Observe View the slide under low power.

5 Communicate Draw what you see.

Drawing Conclusions

1 Communicate What plant traits can you observe without using the microscope?

2 Communicate What other plant traits can you observe with the microscope?

3 Define From what you observed, come up with your own definition of a plant.

4 Going Further: Hypothesize Examine some other kinds of plants with the microscope. Do all the plants seem to have the same traits, or do some plants look quite different from the others? Do plants that look similar under the microscope have the same traits? How would you set up an experiment to find out?

Materials

Elodea plant
moss plant
fern plant
geranium (or other flowering plant)
microscope
microscope slide
coverslip
dropper
water

A 5

4. This **Process Skill** is used in the Explore Activity.

5. The **Explore Activity** is a hands-on way to learn about the lesson.

As you read a lesson, follow these three steps. They will help you to understand what you are reading.

1. This box contains the **Main Idea** of the lesson. Keep the main idea of the lesson in mind as you read.

2. **Before Reading** Read the large red question before you read the page. Try to answer this question from what you already know.

3. **During Reading** Look for new **Vocabulary** words in yellow. Look at the pictures. They will help you understand what you are reading.

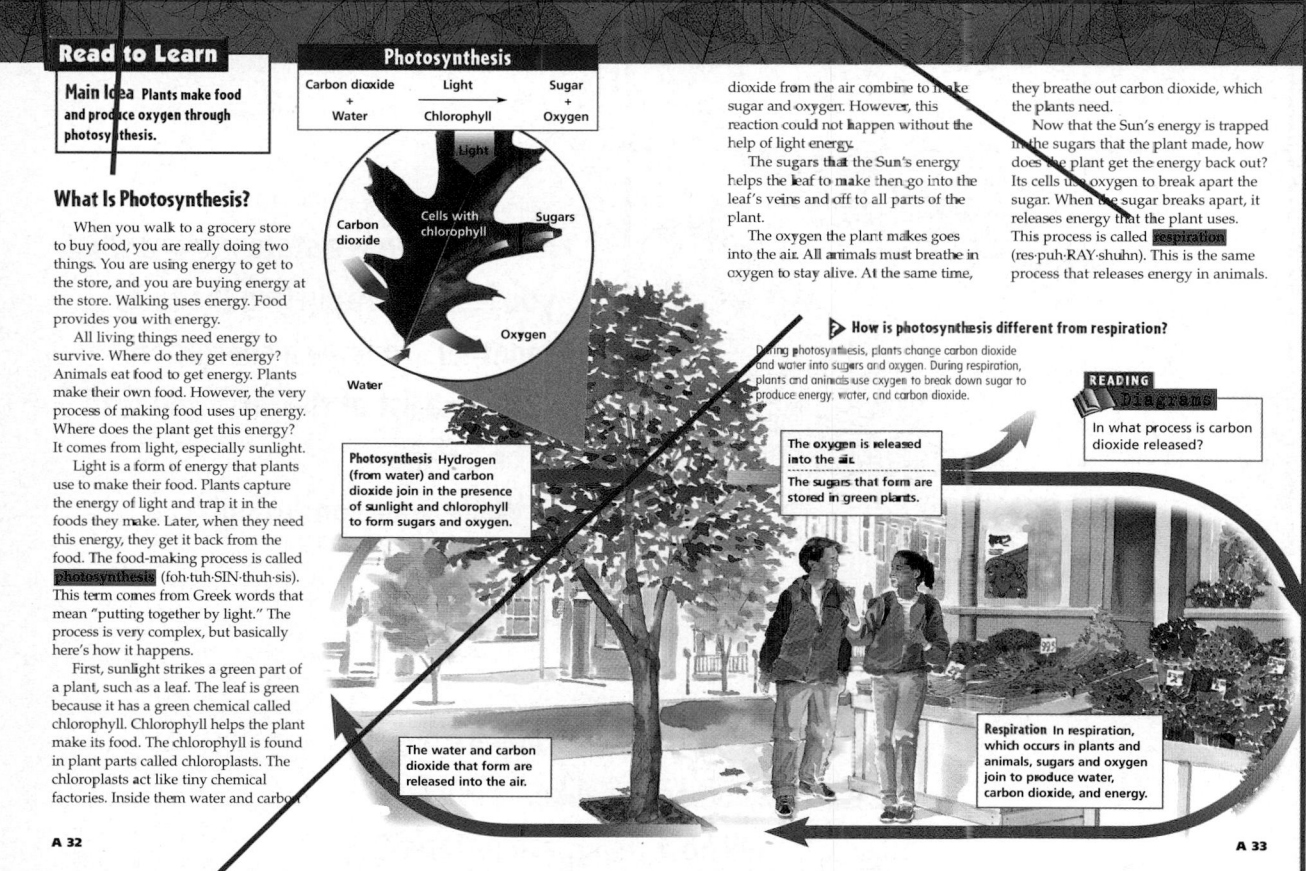

Read to Learn

Photosynthesis

Carbon dioxide + Water → Light / Chlorophyll → Sugar + Oxygen

Main Idea Plants make food and produce oxygen through photosynthesis.

What Is Photosynthesis?

When you walk to a grocery store to buy food, you are really doing two things. You are using energy to get to the store, and you are buying energy at the store. Walking uses energy. Food provides you with energy.

All living things need energy to survive. Where do they get energy? Animals eat food to get energy. Plants make their own food. However, the very process of making food uses up energy. Where does the plant get this energy? It comes from light, especially sunlight.

Light is a form of energy that plants use to make their food. Plants capture the energy of light and trap it in the foods they make. Later, when they need this energy, they get it back from the food. The food-making process is called **photosynthesis** (foh·tuh·SIN·thuh·sis). This term comes from Greek words that mean "putting together by light." The process is very complex, but basically here's how it happens.

First, sunlight strikes a green part of a plant, such as a leaf. The leaf is green because it has a green chemical called chlorophyll. Chlorophyll helps the plant make its food. The chlorophyll is found in plant parts called chloroplasts. The chloroplasts act like tiny chemical factories. Inside them water and carbon

dioxide from the air combine to make sugar and oxygen. However, this reaction could not happen without the help of light energy.

The sugars that the Sun's energy helps the leaf to make then go into the leaf's veins and off to all parts of the plant.

The oxygen the plant makes goes into the air. All animals must breathe in oxygen to stay alive. At the same time, they breathe out carbon dioxide, which the plants need.

Now that the Sun's energy is trapped in the sugars that the plant made, how does the plant get the energy back out? Its cells use oxygen to break apart the sugar. When the sugar breaks apart, it releases energy that the plant uses. This process is called **respiration** (res·puh·RAY·shuhn). This is the same process that releases energy in animals.

Cells with chlorophyll

Light

Carbon dioxide

Sugars

Oxygen

Water

Photosynthesis Hydrogen (from water) and carbon dioxide join in the presence of sunlight and chlorophyll to form sugars and oxygen.

How is photosynthesis different from respiration?

During photosynthesis, plants change carbon dioxide and water into sugars and oxygen. During respiration, plants and animals use oxygen to break down sugar to produce energy, water, and carbon dioxide.

The oxygen is released into the air.
The sugars that form are stored in green plants.

READING Diagrams

In what process is carbon dioxide released?

The water and carbon dioxide that form are released into the air.

Respiration In respiration, which occurs in plants and animals, sugars and oxygen join to produce water, carbon dioxide, and energy.

A 32

A 33

4. **After Reading** ▷ This arrow points to a question. It will help you check that you understand what you have read. Try to answer the question before you go to the next large red question.

On one page in each lesson, you will find a question that practices the Chapter Reading Skill. In any chapter you will find one of these skills:

Main idea and supporting details
The *main idea* is what the reading is about. To find the main idea:
- Answer the red question on a page.
- Look for facts that tell more about the main idea. Pictures on the page can add supporting details.

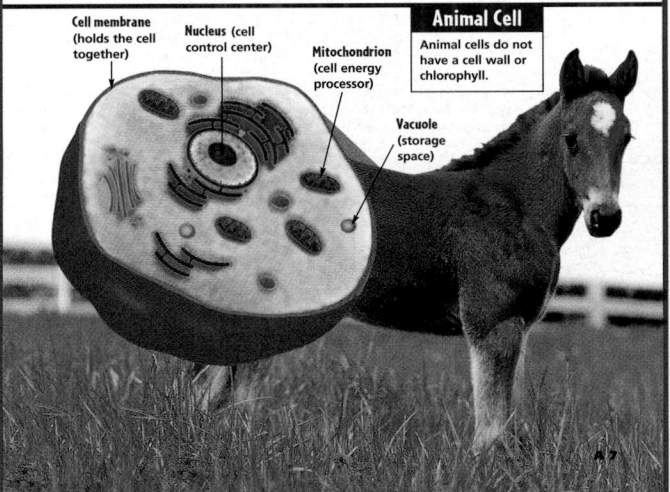

tree must be made of rigid building blocks—rigid cells that support it.

Under the microscope, *Elodea* cells look like boxes. What is one characteristic of boxes? They have walls, which keep them from collapsing into a heap. All plant cells have walls. That's why an oak tree can stand tall and strong.

The cells of all plants work together to keep the plants alive. Different kinds of cells do different kinds of jobs. Each job contributes to the health and survival of the plant. For example, in a tree, cells in leaves make the plant's food. Cells in stems, branches, roots, and the trunk form tubes through

which the food or water is moved, or *transported* (trans·PAWRT·uhd). Other cells may form flowers, fruits, and seeds that allow the tree to reproduce.

Cells are organized into *tissues* (TISH·ewz). The "strings" in celery stalks and the flesh of fruits are examples of plant tissues. Some tissues carry water and minerals to various parts of the plant. Some tissues support the plant.

READING Draw Conclusions
What is one of the things plants have in common that helps an oak tree stand tall and strong?

Cell membrane (holds the cell together)
Nucleus (cell control center)
Mitochondrion (cell energy processor)

Animal Cell
Animal cells do not have a cell wall or chlorophyll.

Vacuole (storage space)

A 7

Draw conclusions
A *conclusion* is a statement of what you learned by putting the facts together. To draw a conclusion:
- Make a list of the facts you read on a page.
- Write your conclusion.

Compare and contrast *Compare* means "to tell how things are alike." *Contrast* means "to tell how things are different."

Sequence of events The *sequence* is the order in which things happen. To find the sequence:

- Ask yourself: "What happened first?" Write it down.
- Then make a list of each thing that happened after that – in order.

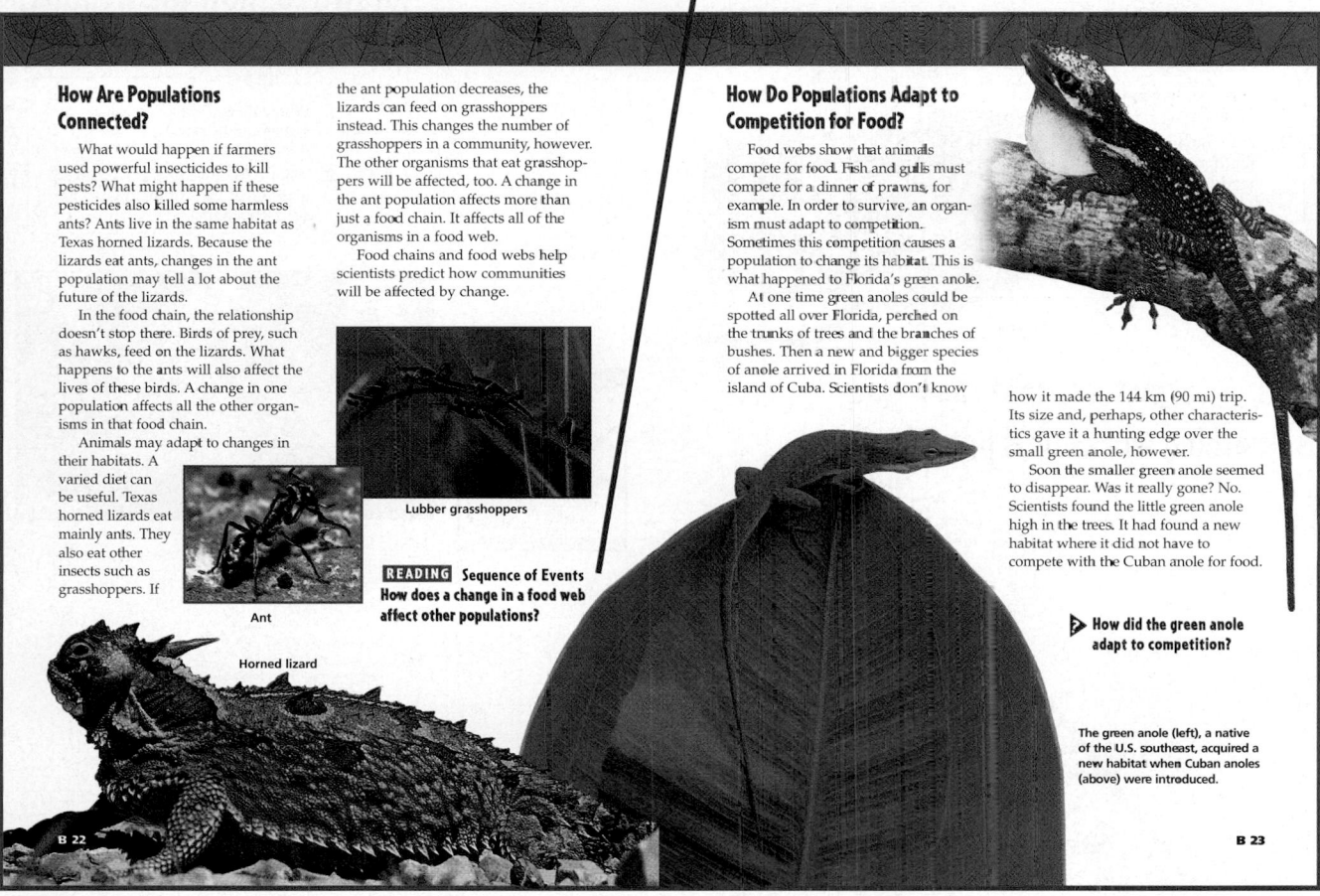

How Are Populations Connected?

What would happen if farmers used powerful insecticides to kill pests? What might happen if these pesticides also killed some harmless ants? Ants live in the same habitat as Texas horned lizards. Because the lizards eat ants, changes in the ant population may tell a lot about the future of the lizards.

In the food chain, the relationship doesn't stop there. Birds of prey, such as hawks, feed on the lizards. What happens to the ants will also affect the lives of these birds. A change in one population affects all the other organisms in that food chain.

Animals may adapt to changes in their habitats. A varied diet can be useful. Texas horned lizards eat mainly ants. They also eat other insects such as grasshoppers. If

the ant population decreases, the lizards can feed on grasshoppers instead. This changes the number of grasshoppers in a community, however. The other organisms that eat grasshoppers will be affected, too. A change in the ant population affects more than just a food chain. It affects all of the organisms in a food web.

Food chains and food webs help scientists predict how communities will be affected by change.

Lubber grasshoppers

READING Sequence of Events
How does a change in a food web affect other populations?

Ant

Horned lizard

How Do Populations Adapt to Competition for Food?

Food webs show that animals compete for food. Fish and gulls must compete for a dinner of prawns, for example. In order to survive, an organism must adapt to competition. Sometimes this competition causes a population to change its habitat. This is what happened to Florida's green anole.

At one time green anoles could be spotted all over Florida, perched on the trunks of trees and the branches of bushes. Then a new and bigger species of anole arrived in Florida from the island of Cuba. Scientists don't know how it made the 144 km (90 mi) trip. Its size and, perhaps, other characteristics gave it a hunting edge over the small green anole, however.

Soon the smaller green anole seemed to disappear. Was it really gone? No. Scientists found the little green anole high in the trees. It had found a new habitat where it did not have to compete with the Cuban anole for food.

▷ How did the green anole adapt to competition?

The green anole (left), a native of the U.S. southeast, acquired a new habitat when Cuban anoles (above) were introduced.

B 22

B 23

Cause and effect When you read about something that happened, ask yourself: "What made it happen?"

- A *cause* makes something happen. Beating a drum is a cause.
- The thing that happens is the *effect*. The effect is the sound.

Summarize To summarize:

- Ask yourself what the page you read is about.
- State it in your own words in a sentence or two.

Reading In SCIENCE

GRAPHICS

Throughout all chapters of this book, you will get information by reading graphics. Graphics are pictures that are drawn to show information.

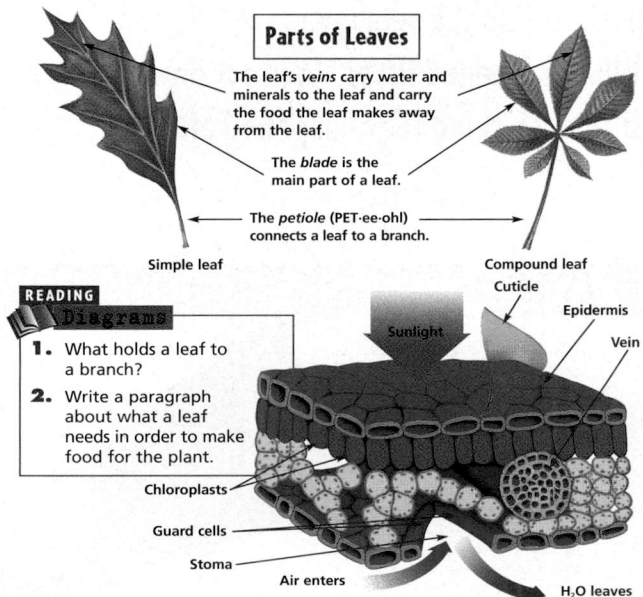

Parts of Leaves

The leaf's *veins* carry water and minerals to the leaf and carry the food the leaf makes away from the leaf.

The *blade* is the main part of a leaf.

The *petiole* (PET·ee·ohl) connects a leaf to a branch.

Simple leaf

Compound leaf

READING Diagrams

1. What holds a leaf to a branch?

2. Write a paragraph about what a leaf needs in order to make food for the plant.

Cuticle
Sunlight
Epidermis
Vein
Chloroplasts
Guard cells
Stoma
Air enters
H_2O leaves

diagrams: pictures that show how something works or is put together

maps: drawings that show features of places on Earth's surface. Some maps are drawn to show the weather.

READING Maps

1. Where do you see low pressure systems in the satellite picture? What do the clouds appear to be doing?

2. What kind of weather is happening in different parts of the country in each map? Explain.

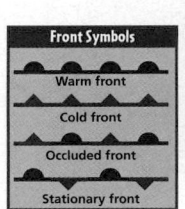

Front Symbols

Warm front
Cold front
Occluded front
Stationary front

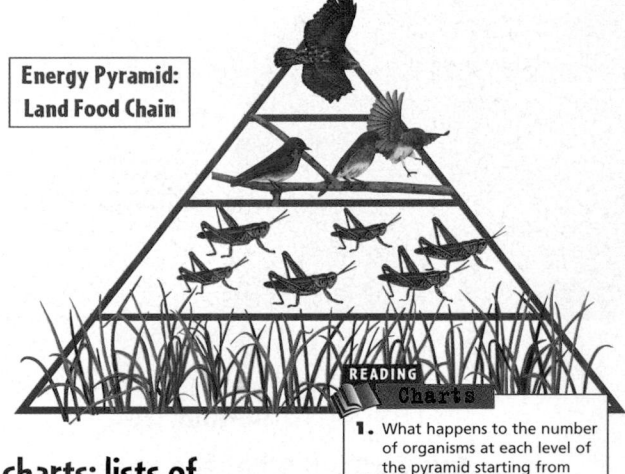

Energy Pyramid: Land Food Chain

READING Charts

1. What happens to the number of organisms at each level of the pyramid starting from the base?

2. How much more energy from the Sun was available to the grass than to the bluebirds?

charts: lists of information in tables with pictures

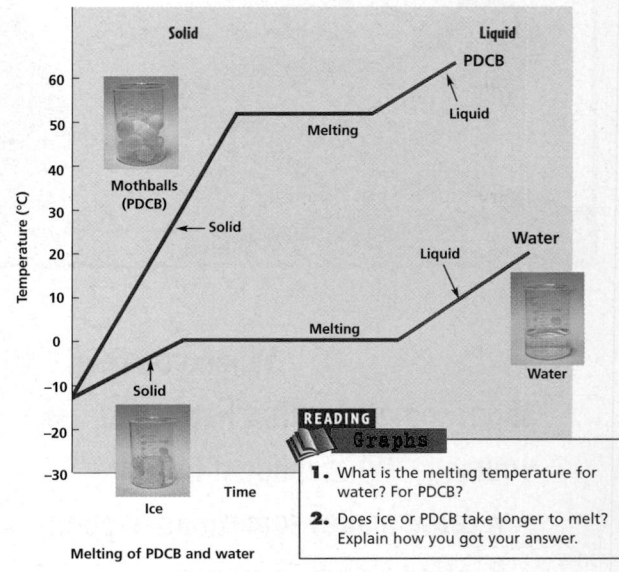

Solid
Liquid
PDCB
Melting
Liquid
Mothballs (PDCB)
Solid
Liquid
Water
Melting
Water
Solid
Ice
Time
Temperature (°C)

READING Graphs

1. What is the melting temperature for water? For PDCB?

2. Does ice or PDCB take longer to melt? Explain how you got your answer.

Melting of PDCB and water

graphs: lines, bars, or symbols drawn to help you compare amounts

Invitation to Science

- learn about the process science skills used throughout this book

- find out how a real-life scientist uses these skills to solve problems

Grade 3
Shirley Mah Kooyman, botanist

Grade 4
Eugenie Clarke, marine biologist

Grade 5
Walter Alvarez, geologist

Grade 6
Neil deGrasse Tyson, astrophysicist

Invitation to Science

There are many kinds of scientists. You can be one, too.

A Scientist:

- Observes
- Infers
- Classifies
- Measures
- Uses numbers
- Communicates
- Predicts
- Interprets data
- Forms hypotheses
- Uses variables
- Experiments
- Makes models
- Defines terms based on observations

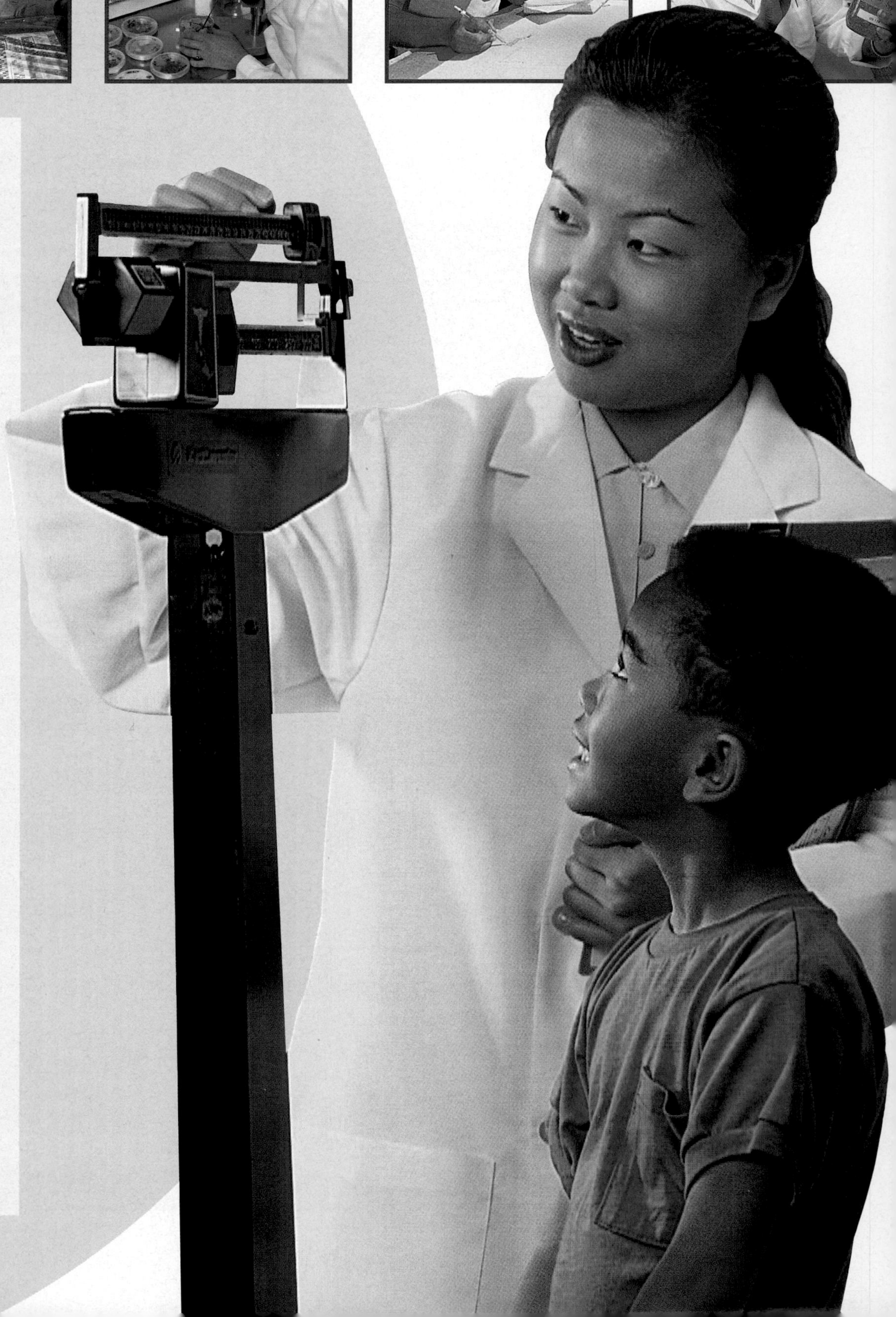

Invitation to Science

Some were bigger than a school bus. Some were fierce hunters, armed with giant hooked claws and teeth as long as dinner knives. Some defended themselves with spiked tails. No human ever saw them alive, but their bones are scattered over Earth. What were these creatures? They were dinosaurs, of course. They lived for millions of years. Today they are all gone. Why did the dinosaurs disappear?

Read about a scientist who may have found the answer. As you read, you'll learn about the **Methods of Science**—steps scientists follow to solve problems. Also watch for important science skills shown in **red**.

Dr. Walter Alvarez studies rock layers for clues to the disappearance of the dinosaurs.

S 1

Science Background

Dr. Alvarez's Impact Hypothesis

Dinosaurs were not the only living things to undergo mass extinction at the end of the Cretaceous period. The fossil record shows that, about 65 million years ago, 75 percent of the flora and fauna that coexisted with dinosaurs suddenly disappeared. This sudden, worldwide, extensive death of most of Earth's organisms supports what has become known as Dr. Alvarez's Impact Hypothesis.

Invitation to Science

Objective

- Describe how scientists use the methods of science in their work.

Build on Prior Knowledge

Ask students to explain how scientists do their work. What steps might scientists go through when they work? Write the possible steps on the board. Call students' attention to the skill words in red in the text. Remind students that these are the steps that scientists complete to do their jobs.

Developing the Main Idea

After students read the page ask them to discuss what they think might have happened to the dinosaurs. Ask:

- **Where might scientists look for clues to the disappearance of the dinosaurs?** (Possible answers: fossils, rocks, outer space)

Using the Illustrations

Introduce students to Dr. Walter Alvarez by drawing their attention to the photograph and having them read the caption. Ask students to speculate about what kinds of clues Dr. Alvarez might find.

Question

Developing the Main Idea

Ask students whether they think all science experiments are performed in a laboratory or classroom. Have them explain their answers. Guide students to recognize that science can be done anywhere people ask questions and then do something to find an answer. Ask:

- **When Dr. Alvarez found a layer of red rock sandwiched between ancient, fossil-rich rock and the newer rock that did not contain fossils, what questions did he form?** (Was the red rock deposited on Earth's crust at the time dinosaurs were dying? Could the red rock provide clues about what caused dinosaurs to become extinct?)

Question

One day in the 1970s, Walter Alvarez was digging in a rocky hillside in Italy. Alvarez was **observing** rocks because he is a geologist. A geologist is a scientist who studies Earth's crust. That day Dr. Alvarez found something surprising. He found a layer of ancient rock full of fossils. Above this layer, he found a layer of rock with no fossils in it. Between those two layers, there was a thin, red layer.

Dr. Alvarez knew that the rock layer with the fossils was formed millions of years ago when dinosaurs roamed Earth. The rock layer without fossils formed after the dinosaurs died. What about the red rock layer? As Dr. Alvarez held some of the red rock, many questions came to his mind. Was it deposited on Earth's crust just as the dinosaurs were dying? Could it provide clues about what killed them? Such questions are important. Scientific discovery always starts with good questions about how things work.

The impact of a huge meteorite created Meteor Crater in Arizona.

S 2

Science Background

Scientific Method
Most scientists use a series of planned steps called the scientific method to solve problems. This begins with a clear, testable hypothesis. Then scientists design an experiment in which they use the correct tools, make careful measurements, and record observations. After the experiment, scientists determine whether the results support the hypothesis.

Hypothesis

D r. Alvarez **communicated** with other scientists. Scientists communicate to share ideas and to work together. The others helped Dr. Alvarez **measure** the red rock's age. They found that the rock layer was 65 million years old. That means it formed just about the time the dinosaurs became extinct. The scientific team tested the red rock layer further. They discovered that it contained a lot of iridium. Iridium is a metal that is rare on Earth. However, iridium is found in large amounts on meteorites. Meteorites are rocky chunks of matter that travel through space and reach the surface of Earth.

Dr. Alvarez formed an idea based on facts and observations. He **inferred** that the iridium-rich rock came from a meteorite that smashed into Earth about the time the dinosaurs died. When you infer, you reason from evidence. Next Dr. Alvarez formed an important **hypothesis**. He stated that the meteorite was so big that it caused a huge explosion when it struck Earth. The explosion—and all its effects—killed the dinosaurs.

What is a hypothesis? A hypothesis is a possible answer to a question or puzzle. A good hypothesis must do three things.

- It must explain observations.
- It must be testable.
- It must predict new findings.

A **prediction** states possible results of an event or experiment. Dr. Alvarez's hypothesis did predict new findings. You might think of a hypothesis as an "If … then …" statement. For example, if a meteorite killed the dinosaurs, then there should be evidence of its impact somewhere on Earth. Dr. Alvarez's hypothesis also explained observations—such as the reason for the mysterious layer of red rock. Now, could Dr. Alvarez's hypothesis be tested?

This meteorite is on display at the Rose Center for Earth and Space in New York City.

S 3

Hypothesis

Developing the Main Idea

Explain that the long-held view was that ancient changes were similar to the gradual changes we observe today. See *Science Background* below. Ask:

- **What forces change the surface of the Earth today?** (Possible answers: earthquakes, volcanoes, floods)

- **Why did Dr. Alvarez hypothesize that the red rock found during his 1970s excavation originated from a meteorite?** (The rock contained iridium, a metal that is rare on Earth but abundant in meteorites.)

- **How did Dr. Alvarez form his hypothesis? What did he hypothesize?** (After gathering information, making careful measurements, communicating with other scientists, and making inferences, he hypothesized that an meteorite struck Earth, causing the extinction of dinosaurs.)

- **How do you think Dr. Alvarez's hypothesis challenged the long-held view?** (He believed that the crashing of a large meteorite into Earth's surface created an explosion that caused mass extinction.)

- **What did Dr. Alvarez's hypothesis predict?** (It predicted that evidence of the meteorite's impact must exist on Earth.)

Experiment

Developing the Main Idea
Challenge students to consider the ways in which Dr. Alvarez tested his hypothesis. Ask:

- **In the absence of an actual meteorite, how could Dr. Alvarez test his hypothesis?** (He could work with other scientists to create computer models representing real objects to show how real objects would react to changes in the environment.)

- **What did the models demonstrate?** (They showed that a large meteorite could, indeed, have caused changes that would result in the death of dinosaurs and other species.)

Exploring the Main Idea
Encourage students to use library or Internet resources to learn more about the Alvarez Hypothesis and *catastrophism*, the belief that cataclysmic events, such as meteorite strikes, caused massive changes to Earth and its life. Challenge students to write brief papers describing the evidence that has been found to support Dr. Alvarez's hypothesis.

Experiment

A scientific test of a hypothesis is called an experiment. Scientists **use variables** in their experiments. A variable is one of the things in an experiment that can be changed or controlled.

A good experiment must follow certain rules.

- It must be repeatable.
- It must test only one variable at a time.

![This scientist is working with a computer model to study tsunamis, or tidal waves.]

This scientist is working with a computer model to study tsunamis, or tidal waves.

Dr. Alvarez and others did many experiments to test his hypothesis. They calculated that the meteorite would need to be about ten kilometers (six

miles) wide to leave so much iridium on Earth. Could a meteorite that size cause enough damage to destroy the dinosaurs? To find out, the scientists used computer **models**. Models represent real objects. Models can show how real objects react to changes in their environment.

The computer models provided the answer. The models showed it would have been possible for a large meteorite to kill the dinosaurs. How? There would have been severe earthquakes around the world. Huge tidal waves—walls of water over 1.6 kilometers (1 mile) high—would have crashed along the coasts. Shock waves would have brought hurricane-like gusts of wind. Wildfires, ignited by the meteorite's debris, would have swept across the globe. The friction between the air and the rocky fragments would have made the air as hot as a furnace. Toxic gases could have formed. After the fires, tidal waves, and earthquakes stopped, temperatures would have dropped far below freezing as dust from the explosion blocked the Sun.

S 4

Science Background

Experimentation
An effective experiment must meet several criteria. First, it must state the question that is to be tested. Then, it must include a brief, clear, testable hypothesis that answers the question. The experimental variables must be identified, and the one best suited to test the hypothesis must be isolated. How the variable will be manipulated in the experiment must be decided. Finally, how the results will be measured must be determined.

English Language Learners

Experiment "Steps"
Encourage students to write brief outlines describing each of the steps of an effective experiment. A large index card can be used to display each of the steps. Ask students to say aloud one or two key words in each step. Finally, ask students to summarize how Dr. Alvarez's work met the requirements of good experimental technique.
Linguistic; Logical

Observation

Scientists around the world began making careful **observations** to look for clues to support Dr. Alvarez's hypothesis. A meteorite big enough to kill the dinosaurs would have left a huge crater when it struck Earth. That impact crater would have been hundreds of kilometers wide. Some traces would still exist. The scientists knew there were some huge craters on Earth. However, none they knew of were the right size and age to have been formed by Dr. Alvarez's meteorite.

Finally, in the 1980s, a huge crater about 200 kilometers (124 miles) wide was identified as an impact crater. Materials in the crater were later found to match those in the layer that Dr. Alvarez had found. The impact crater is off the tip of Mexico's Yucatan Peninsula. Scientists collected and interpreted data about the crater. When scientists **interpret data**, they analyze information that has been gathered. The nature of the crater, its age, and location fit Dr. Alvarez's theory perfectly. Most scientists now believe that the meteorite that made the giant crater also killed the dinosaurs.

This computer image shows the crater scientists believe was created by the meteorite that killed the dinosaurs.

Conclusion

The results of a good experiment should either clearly support or not support the hypothesis. If the results support the hypothesis, then it is possible to state a conclusion, or general rule. If results do not support the hypothesis, then a scientist needs to change the hypothesis or form a new one. New experiments must be done to test the new hypothesis. Through repeated testing, a hypothesis can be improved and refined. Even if the original hypothesis was flawed, it might eventually lead to one that is correct.

Dr. Alvarez used computer models to test his hypothesis. However, his theory was not widely accepted until there was clear evidence from the real world that his theory could be true. Today computer modeling is often used. Still, there is no substitute for solid evidence and experimentation in the real world.

The scientific method is used in simple experiments. It is also used in complex scientific studies that last a long time. Scientists around the world worked for more than 20 years to investigate Walter Alvarez's hypothesis. They made many predictions, measurements, and observations. Today scientists generally agree. A giant, burning meteorite, hurtling to Earth at a terrific speed, is what doomed the dinosaurs 65 million years ago.

S 5

Science Background

Walter Alvarez

Walter Alvarez was born in Berkeley, California, in 1940. After earning a Ph.D. in geology at Princeton University, he returned to the University of California at Berkeley as Professor of Geology and Geophysics. His 1973 discovery of the mysterious red rock led to experiments that while initially controversial, ultimately changed the way scientists view Earth's history.

Observation and Conclusion

Developing the Main Idea
Review Dr. Alvarez's experiment. Point out that, even after his experiments using computer models validated the plausibility of the hypothesis, a piece of the puzzle remained missing. Also discuss with students how a hypothesis may be strong or weak and why a scientist might need to repeat an experiment. Ask:

- **What evidence was needed to convince skeptical scientists of the validity of Dr. Alvarez's hypothesis?** (evidence of a crater large enough and old enough to have come from the hypothetical meteorite)

- **When the crater in the Yucatan Peninsula was discovered in the 1980s, how did scientists determine whether it was the scar left by the meteorite that killed off the dinosaurs?** (They analyzed the nature of the crater, its age, and its location.)

- **Do experimental results ever fail to support the hypothesis? Why would this happen?** (Yes. It happens because the experimenter is not always aware of all the factors that can affect the experiment.)

- **Why would anyone share the results of an experiment that did not work out as expected?** (Others could still learn from what happened and design new experiments to figure out the answer to the question.)

- **Why would someone repeat an experiment that worked as expected?** (to make sure it works that way every time and was not a fluke or "accident")

Thinking Further: *Inferring*
Remind students that the experiments that Walter Alvarez carried out involved the use of computer models. Ask:

- **Since Dr. Alvarez's experiments confirmed his hypothesis, why do you think it was important to locate the crater that the hypothetical meteorite left?** (The presence of the crater provided clear, real-world evidence that Dr. Alvarez's hypothesis was valid.)

Methods of Science

Here is a chart that shows the steps scientists such as Dr. Walter Alvarez follow when solving a problem in science. Scientists don't always follow the steps in the order shown.

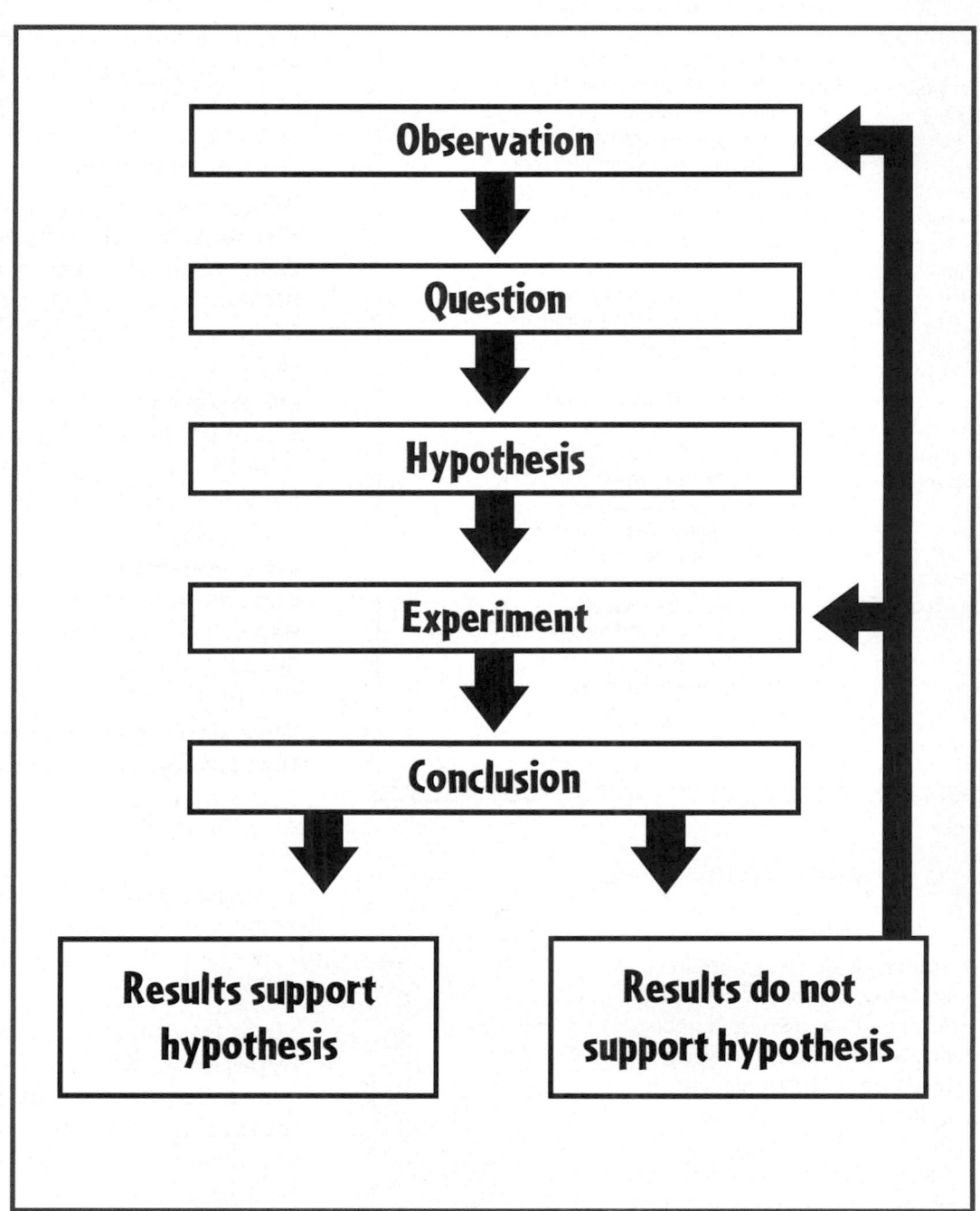

Observation

Question

Hypothesis

Experiment

Conclusion

Results support hypothesis

Results do not support hypothesis

Science Process Skills

Observe to use one or more of the senses to identify or learn about an object or event

Infer to form an idea from facts or observations

Classify to place things that share properties together in groups

Measure to find the size, distance, time, volume, area, mass, weight, or temperature of an object or event

Use numbers to order, count, add, subtract, multiply, and divide to explain data

Communicate to share information

Predict to state possible results of an event or experiment

Interpret data to use the information that has been gathered to answer questions or solve a problem

Form a hypothesis to make a statement that can be tested to answer a question

Use variables to identify things in an experiment that can be changed or controlled

Experiment to perform a test to support or disprove a hypothesis

Make a model to make something to represent an object or event

Define based on observations to put together a description that is based on observations and experience

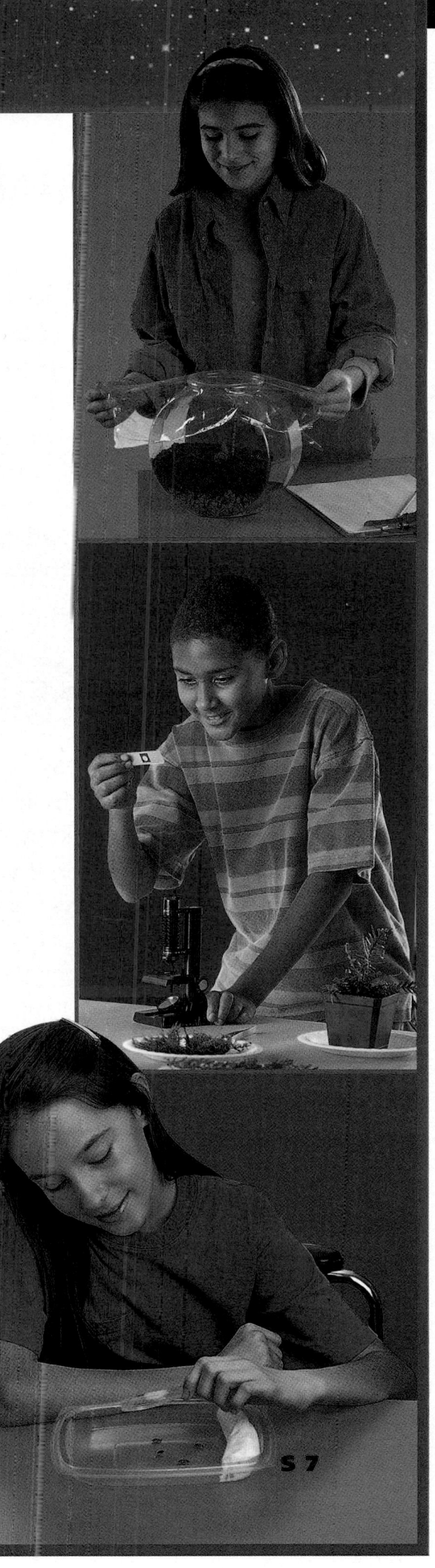

Science Safety Tips

In the Classroom

- Read all directions. Make sure you understand them. When you see **BE CAREFUL!**, be sure to follow the safety rule.
- Listen to your teacher for special safety directions. If you don't understand something, ask for help.
- Wash your hands with soap and water before an activity.
- Wear safety goggles when your teacher tells you to wear them. Wear them when working with anything that can fly into your eyes or when working with liquids.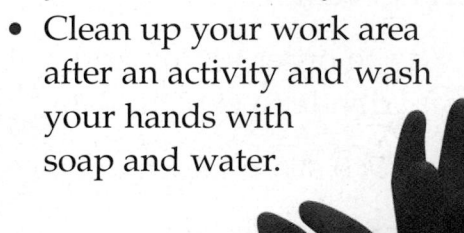
- Wear a safety apron if you work with anything messy or anything that might spill.
- Wipe up a spill right away or ask your teacher for help.
- Tell your teacher if something breaks. If glass breaks, do not clean it up yourself.
- Keep your hair and clothes away from open flames. Tie back long hair, and roll up long sleeves.
- Be careful around a hot plate. Know when it is on and when it is off. Remember that the plate stays hot for a few minutes after it's turned off.

- Keep your hands dry around electrical equipment.
- Don't eat or drink anything during an experiment.
- Put equipment back the way your teacher tells you.
- Dispose of things the way your teacher tells you.
- Clean up your work area after an activity and wash your hands with soap and water.

In the Field

- Go with a trusted adult—such as your teacher or a parent or guardian.
- Do not touch animals or plants without an adult's approval. The animal might bite. The plant might be poison ivy or another dangerous plant.

Responsibility

- Treat living things, the environment, and one another with respect.

S 8

Earth Science

UNIT
C

Earth and Its Resources

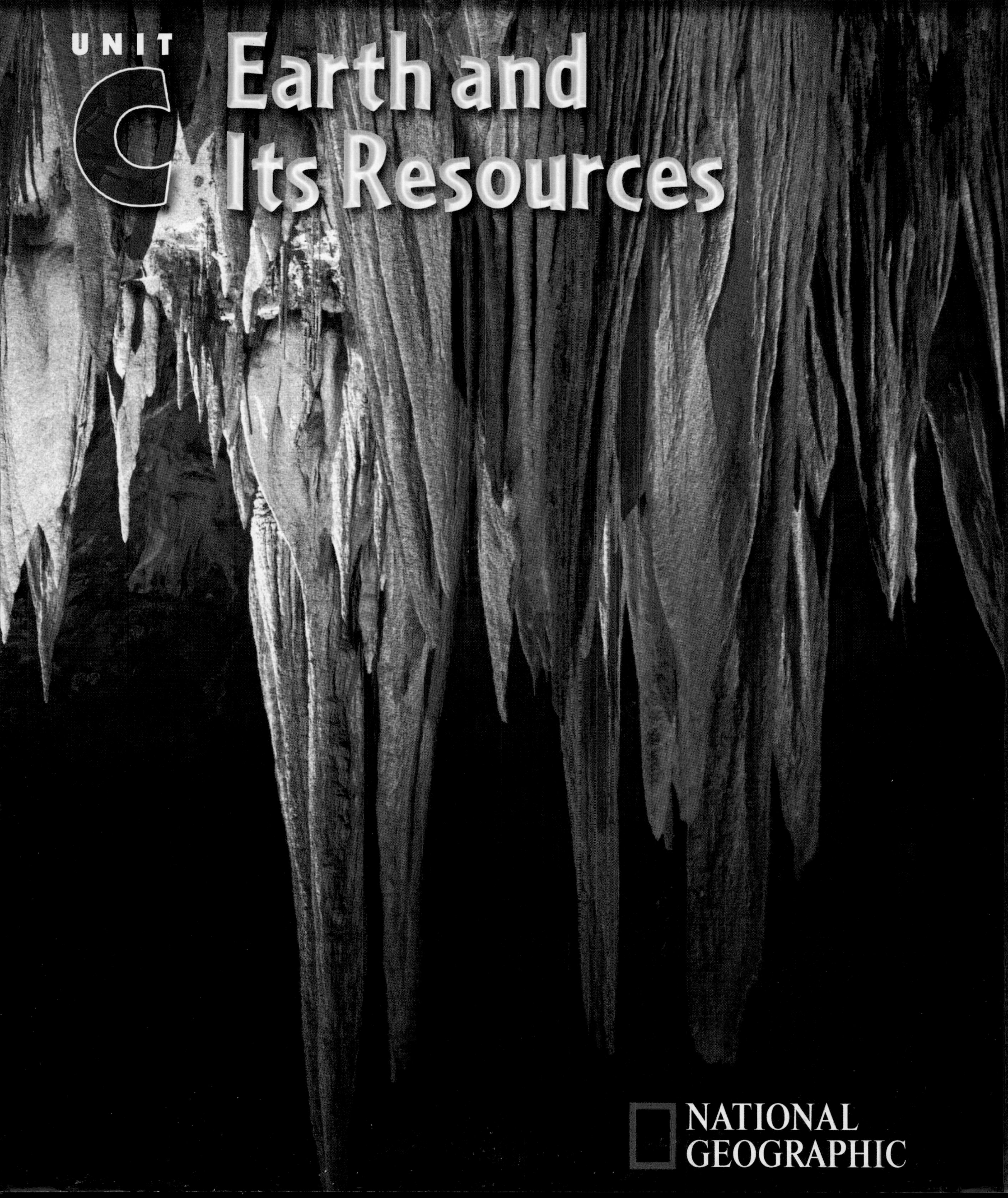

NATIONAL
GEOGRAPHIC

Earth and Its Resources

UNIT C

Main Idea: Among the planets of the solar system, Earth is uniquely equipped to support life. Resources of rocks, soil, water, and air make up Earth's surface. The surface is in constant change, being reshaped by natural forces. The resources are becoming all the more precious as humans use up many of those that are nonrenewable.

Unit Organizer

CHAPTER 6 Rocks and Minerals, *pp. C2–C57*

Main Idea: Gravity affects Earth, defining its position and movement in relation to its neighbors. The rocks and minerals of Earth's crust are in constant change by destructive and constructive forces, as well as by human use.

CHAPTER 7 Air, Water, and Energy *pp. C58–C109*

Main Idea: Earth's air, water, and energy resources are all necessary for life. Each must be kept clean and used efficiently to prevent the degradation and pollution of this planet.

LESSON 1 Earth and Its Neighbors, *pp. C4–C15*
Main Idea: The solar system consists of nine planets, many moons, and many other bodies orbiting the Sun.

LESSON 2 Earth's Changing Crust, *pp. C16–C27*
Main Idea: Forces on and under Earth shape its surface.

LESSON 3 Minerals of Earth's Crust, *pp. C30–C39*
Main Idea: Earth's crust contains many types of minerals with important uses.

LESSON 4 Earth's Rocks and Soil, *pp. C40–C53*
Main Idea: Rocks can be classified according to their composition and properties.

LESSON 5 Earth's Atmosphere, *pp. C60–C67*
Main Idea: Earth's atmosphere supports life on Earth.

LESSON 6 Earth's Water, *pp. C70–C79*
Main Idea: Fresh water is constantly renewed by the water cycle.

LESSON 7 Earth's Oceans, *pp. C82–C95*
Main Idea: Ninety–seven percent of Earth's water comes from oceans. Oceans are an important natural resource.

LESSON 8 Energy Resources, *pp. C98–C107*
Main Idea: Some energy resources are inexhaustible, while others will run out eventually.

Grade-Level Science Books

EASY	EASY	CHALLENGE

2061: PHOTOGRAPHING MARS Read about a teacher's trip to Mars. This futuristic adventure seems not so far away as it may once have.

OUR RIVERKEEPER One day when Carmen and her friends are picnicking along the river bank, they notice a strong smell coming from a drainpipe and report it to Riverkeeper Skip Johns. They learn all about pollution and its effect on their river and its resources.

QUINTO'S VOLCANO A boy overcomes his fear of the sea and saves his whole village from the eruption of a volcano. It is a story of courage in the face of an unstoppable natural force.

To order from Macmillan/McGraw-Hill, call 800-442-9685.

Cross Curricular Books from Macmillan/McGraw-Hill

Apple, Gary. **All About Islands.**

Spirn, Michele. **Raising the Wrecks.**

To order, call 800-442-9685.

Student Bibliography

Carr, Terry. **Spill! The Story of the Exxon Valdez**. New York: Franklin Watts, 1991.

Clifford, Nick. **Incredible Earth**. New York: Dorling Kindersley, Inc., 1996.

Dyson, Marianne J. **Space Station Science: Life in Free Fall.** New York: Scholastic Reference, 1999.

Fraser, Mary A. **In Search of the Grand Canyon**. New York: Henry Holt and Company, 1995.

Hyscock, Bruce. **The Big Rivers: The Missouri, the Mississippi, and the Ohio**. New York: Atheneum, 1998.

Malam, John. **Highest, Lowest, Deepest, Longest**. New York: Simon & Schuster Books for Young Readers, 1996.

Petty, Kate. **I Didn't Know That the Sun Is a Star and Other Amazing Facts About the Universe**. New York: Holiday House, 1998.

Robbins, Ken. **Earth**. New York: Henry Holt and Company, Inc., 1995.

Reading in Science

McGraw-Hill Science

Teacher Editions provide point-of-use strategies and resource support for students to practice reading skills as they read their science texts.

- **Reading MiniLessons**
- **Reduced Blackline Masters** from *Reading in Science Resources*
- **Additional Reading Strategies**

Reading in Science Resources

Boxes beneath the reduced Pupil Edition pages identify specific places in a lesson where students can complete worksheets from the *Reading in Science Resources* blackline masters. Reduced worksheets for this unit are found on the following pages of this Teacher Edition.

Lesson Outlines: pp. C6, C18, C32, C42, C62, C72, C84, C100

Interpret Illustrations: pp. C9, C11, C19, C20, C33, C35, C47, C49, C62, C63, C74, C78, C86, C88, C100, C102

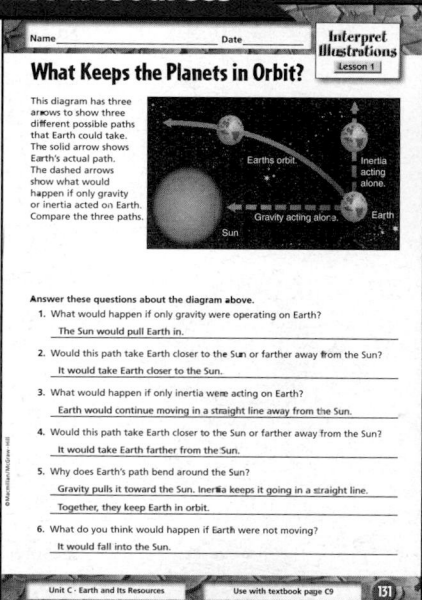

What Keeps the Planets in Orbit?

This diagram has three arrows to show three different possible paths that Earth could take. The solid arrow shows Earth's actual path. The dashed arrows show what would happen if only gravity or inertia acted on Earth. Compare the three paths.

Answer these questions about the diagram above.

1. What would happen if only gravity were operating on Earth?
   The Sun would pull Earth in.
2. Would this path take Earth closer to the Sun or farther away from the Sun?
   It would take Earth closer to the Sun.
3. What would happen if only inertia were acting on Earth?
   Earth would continue moving in a straight line away from the Sun.
4. Would this path take Earth closer to the Sun or farther away from the Sun?
   It would take Earth farther from the Sun.
5. Why does Earth's path bend around the Sun?
   Gravity pulls it toward the Sun. Inertia keeps it going in a straight line. Together, they keep Earth in orbit.
6. What do you think would happen if Earth were not moving?
   It would fall into the Sun.

Unit C · Earth and Its Resources — Use with textbook page C9 — 131

Reading in Science Resources, p. 131

Reading MiniLesson

Reading MiniLessons provide a brief tutorial and activity for students to practice a specific reading skill for each chapter. In this unit, the chapter reading skills are:

Sequence of Events: pp. C12, C25, C37, C52

Draw Conclusions: pp. C65, C73, C89, C106

Reading Strategy

Additional opportunities for students to develop and apply reading skills are provided in this unit as follows:

- **Cause and effect:** pp. C21, C22, C28, C86
- **Compare and contrast:** pp. C85, C87
- ○ **Draw conclusions**
- **Find the main idea:** p. C93
- **Sequence of events:** p. C47
- **Summarize:** pp. C15, C27, C29, C53, C55, C67, C69, C79, C81, C95, C97, C107
- **Ask questions:** p. C76
- ○ **Reread**
- **Retell (paraphrase):** pp. C13, C25, C26, C36, C51, C54, C64

- **Interpret graphic sources of information:** pp. C6, C8, C10, C20, C33, C34, C35, C43, C47, C49, C63, C72, C74, C78, C86, C91, C103
- **Build on prior knowledge:** pp. C4, C16, C28, C30, C38, C54, C60, C68, C70, C80, C82, C96, C98, C110
- **Organize information:** pp. C30, C42, C66, C68, C84, C92, C98

CROSS CURRICULUM IDEAS for integrating science

L·I·N·K·S

Meeting Individual Needs

McGraw-Hill Science includes all students in the learning process by providing a variety of strategies in this unit.

 **English Language Learners**

Volcanic Display

Challenge students to make a display of models or drawings of the different types of volcanoes and eruptions. They can use clay or papier mâché for models and can make little flags out of toothpicks and post-it notes. The flags can be used to label features. Students can then present their work in their own words. **Kinesthetic; Spatial**

 **Advanced Learners**

Space Probes

Challenge one group of students to find out more about the search for extraterrestrial life in our solar system as conducted by SETI (Search for Extraterrestrial Intelligence). Ask another group to research the Voyager probes (both launched in 1977) that traveled through the solar system. Ask them to find out what these probes discovered about atmospheres, surface temperatures, and chemicals on various planets. Then discuss with the class how the findings of both groups might be interrelated. **Linguistic**

 **Inclusion**

A Body in Motion

Ask students to draw an X on an index card and put a coin on top of the X. Invite them to move and then stop the card and observe what happens to the coin. (It will keep moving due to inertia.) They might try to push the card quickly across the table and then stop it suddenly, start the card with a jerk, or turn the card quickly. Ask them to relate what they observe with how they feel when riding in a car that makes a quick stop or a fast turn. How do their bodies act like the coin? **Kinesthetic**

For additional support, see pp. C8, C9, C11, C21, C23, C24, C29, C33, C36, C38, C43, C44, C45, C51, C55, C63, C64, C75, C78, C80, C82, C85, C87, C88, C90, C91, C94, C96, C101, C103, C105, C111

Learning Styles

Students acquire knowledge in a variety of ways that reflect different, often distinct, learning styles. The seven learning styles are:

- **Kinesthetic** pp. C5, C9, C17, C21, C31, C43, C44, C45, C61, C80, C88, C90, C91,
- **Social** pp. C36, C41, C51, C78, C81, C94, C99
- **Intrapersonal** p. C75
- **Linguistic** pp. C8, C11, C13, C14, C22, C23, C24, C29, C30, C33, C36, C38, C43, C51, C55, C60, C67, C72, C75, C78, C79,
- C80, C81, C85, C87, C90, C91, C94, C96, C101, C102, C105, C111
- **Logical** pp. C21, C42, C52, C55, C61, C63, C71, C81, C103
- ○ **Auditory/Musical**
- **Visual/Spatial** pp. C17, C21, C22, C29, C30, C31, C33, C38, C42, C45, C55, C71, C82, C83, C85, C88, C90, C91, C99, C103

Technology for McGRAW-HILL SCIENCE

CD-ROMs

Science Newsroom CD-ROM

Student-directed computer activities

Chapter 7: Sea to Shining Sea

Explore the water cycle.

Chapter 7: Fuels Rush In

Explore fossil fuels and alternative energy sources.

Join me in the Science Newsroom

Videotapes

Explore Activity Videos

All Explore Activities are available on videotape. Introduce lessons with Explore Activity Videos.

MindJogger Videos

Stage a quiz show in your classroom!

Science Experiences Videotapes

Chapter 6:

Lesson 1 Earth and Its Neighbors
Space Camp: A Week of Surprises (Package 5)
A Journey Through the Universe (Package 8)

Lesson 2 Earth's Changing Crust
Volcanoes: Churning and Burning (Package 5)

Chapter 7:

Lesson 7 Earth's Oceans
Life in a Coral Reef (Package 2)
Staying Alive: Adaptations for Survival (Package 4)
Researching the Ocean Depths (Package 7)

Lesson 8 Energy Resources
Environmentally Friendly Transportation (Package 8

Transparencies

Visual Aid Transparencies

- **9–12** Building a Water Cycle
- **17** The Solar System
- **18** The Rock Cycle
- **19** Desalination Plant
- **20** Ocean Currents
- **21** How Fuels Form

Reading Aid Transparencies

- C1–C8

Internet Resources

McGRAW-HILL SCIENCE is online at *www.mhscience02.com* with projects and activities for students, teachers, and parents.
Internet Research Projects pp. C15, C67
Links pp. C15, C27, C39, C53, C67, C79, C95, C107
Science Magazines and Features pp. C29, C55, C57, C69, C81, C97, C109, C111

AMERICAN MUSEUM OF NATURAL HISTORY

Visit www.amnh.org/resources/mhscience for a behind-the-scenes look at the exhibitions, collections, and research of the Museum. You'll find resources for teachers and students, such as online expeditions, profiles of scientists, interactives, links to professional development courses and more.

AVIATION WEEK'S THE NEXT CENTURY OF FLIGHT

LIFTOFF! with *AVIATION WEEK*.
Visit *www.AviationNow.com/LIFTOFF* for lessons, activities, and videos on Weather and Climate.

NATIONAL GEOGRAPHIC

* To order National Geographic Products, visit us online at *www.nationalgeographic.com/education* or call 1-800-368-2728. To order NGS Picture Show and NGS Picture Pack, call Macmillan/McGraw-Hill at 1-800-442-9685.

National Geographic Society Videos
- **Sun, Earth, Moon**
- **Our Dynamic Earth**
- **Atmosphere:** On the Air
- **Nuclear Energy:** The Question Before Us

NGS Picture Show CD-ROMs
- **Dynamic Earth**
- **Geology**

NGS Picture Pack Transparencies
- **Rocks and Minerals**
- **Solar System**

Process Skills

Science Process Skills	Explore Activities (Pupil Edition)	Quick Labs (Pupil Edition)	Process Skill Builders
Observe	pp. C5, C31, C61, C71, C83	pp. C37, C65, C85, C103	Pupil Edition p. C48
Infer	pp. C5, C41, C71, C99	pp. C19, C103	
Classify	p. C41		
Measure	p. C61	p. C85	
Use Numbers	pp. C41, C99		
Communicate	pp. C17, C31, C41, C61, C71, C83, C99	pp. C7, C103	
Predict	p. C83	p. C85	
Interpret Data	p. C61	p. C7	
Form a Hypothesis	p. C99		Pupil Edition pp. C77 Teacher Edition (MiniLesson) p. C77 Activity Resources pp. 108–109
Use Variables	pp. C5, C61, C71	pp. C7, C65	Pupil Edition p. C48
Experiment	pp. C5, C17, C31, C83		Pupil Edition pp. C48, C77
Make a Model	pp. C5, C17, C71	p. C19	Pupil Edition pp. C77
Define Based on Observations			Pupil Edition p. C48 Teacher Edition (MiniLesson) p. C48 Activity Resources pp. 98–99

Materials

Consumable materials (based on six groups)

Materials	Quantity Needed per group	Kit Quantity	Lesson
Bag, plastic sandwich	4	80	2
Bag, plastic zip lip, 1 qt	1	12	4
Cardboard strips, 12 cm long	12		5
Chalk	1 stick	12	5
Clay (cream)		2 lb	1
Clay (red, blue, green, yellow)		4 lb	2
Cup, clear plastic, 9 oz		150	5, 6
Cup, foam, 6 oz	1	25	3, 4
Food, banana			2
Food, graham cracker crumbs			2
Food, hazelnut			2
Food, peanut butter			2
Food, vinegar, 500 mL		1 bottle	5
Food coloring, blue, 8 mL		2 packages	7
Food coloring, green, 8 mL		2 packages	6, 7
Knife, plastic	3	24	2, 5
Marker	1		5
Marker, red	2		3, 4
Paper, graph			1
Paper, wax, 75 sq ft		1 roll	2, 7
Pen, marking	1		7
Petroleum jelly		4 oz	5
Plastic wrap, 50 sq ft.		1 roll	5
Rubber bands, medium		100	5
Salt		1,474 g (2 containers)	7
Salt, kosher		2 lbs	3
Salt, rock		1 lb	3
Sand, fine		5 kg	4
Soil, potting		24 lbs	4, 6
Spoon, plastic	10	24	3, 4
Straw, plastic drinking, wrapped	1	50	7
String		200 ft	1, 3, 5
Tape, clear			3, 4, 5
Tea bag	1	24	6

Non-consumable materials (based on six groups)

Materials	Quantity Needed per group	Kit Quantity	Lesson
Balance, double pan, w/masses	2	1	4
Bowl, squat, 8 oz	1	6	6
Calculator	2		4
Cube-O-Grams		100	2
Cup, foam, 6 oz	1	25	3
Goggles			1, 3, 5
Hand lens	3	6	3, 4, 5
Jar, plastic wide-mouthed, tall, 12 oz, w/lid	1	6	7
Meterstick	1		1
Mineral collection	1	1 kit, 7 specimens (6 each)	3
Nails		15	3
Pan, aluminum, 13" × 10" × 2"	3	12	6
Peanuts, foam packaging		200	6
Petri dish	1	6	6
Rock samples	3	1 kit, 14 specimens (6 each)	4, 5
Ruler, metric	2		4, 5, 7
Scissors	1		1
Streak plate	2	8	3, 4
Thumbtacks	1	100	7
Wire, bare copper, 16 gauge		20"	3, 4

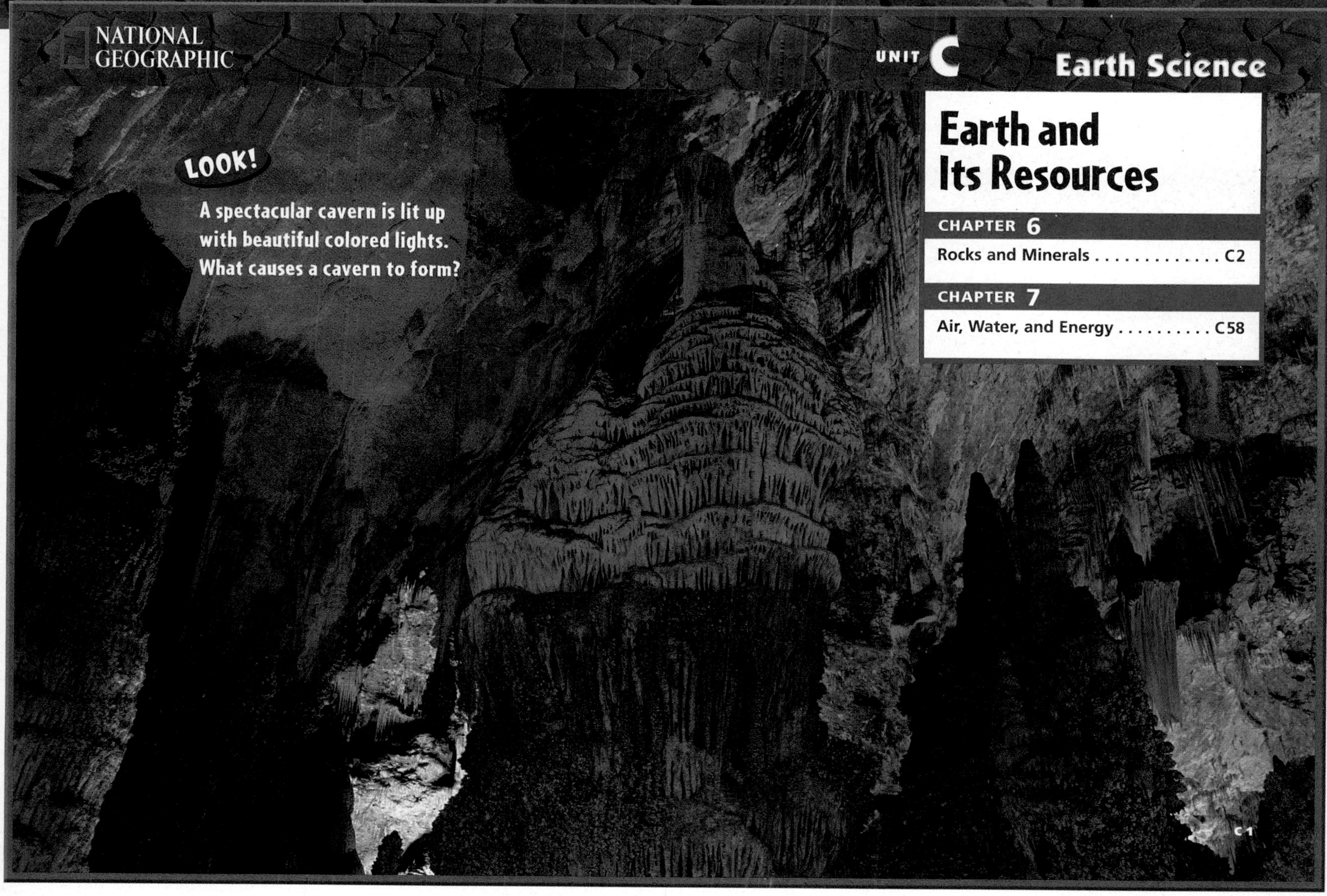

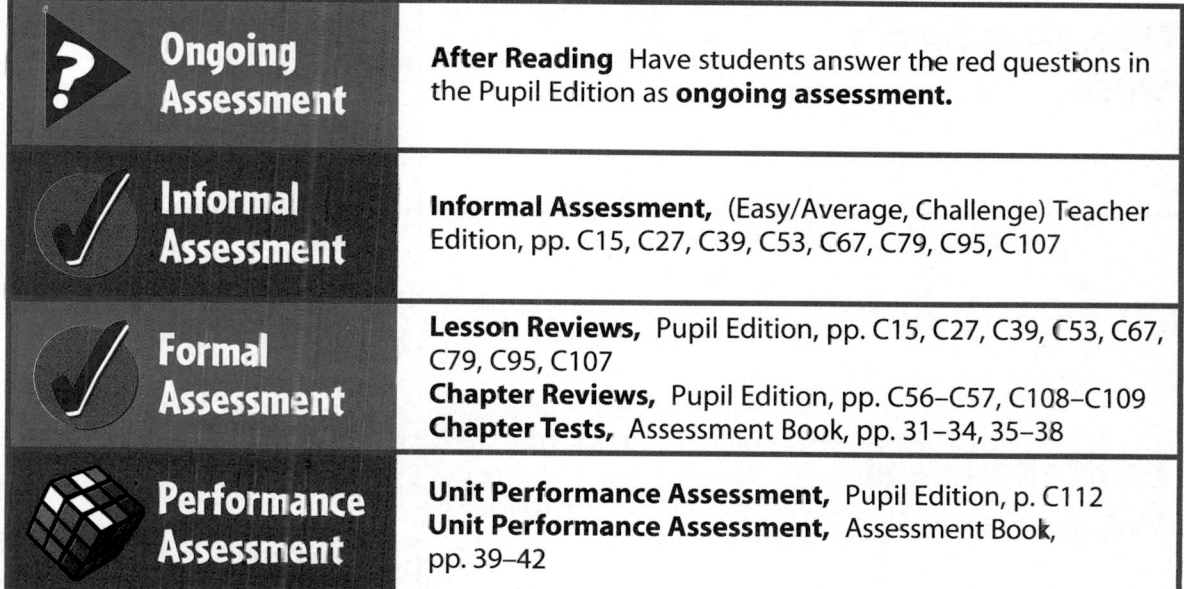

NATIONAL GEOGRAPHIC

UNIT **C**   **Earth Science**

Earth and Its Resources

LOOK!

A spectacular cavern is lit up with beautiful colored lights. What causes a cavern to form?

C1

Resources

- Reading in Science Resources, Unit Vocabulary, pp. 185–187
- School to Home Activities, pp. 15–22
- Cross Curricular Projects, pp. 17–24

Answers to

LOOK!

Groundwater contains carbonic acid, which reacts with the calcite in limestone. The acidic groundwater follows lines of weakness in the rock, creating cavities and eventually caverns.

Assessment Strand

McGraw-Hill Science provides a variety of strategies for assessing students' learning and progress, including ongoing assessment, informal assessment, formal assessment, and performance assessment.

? **Ongoing Assessment**	**After Reading** Have students answer the red questions in the Pupil Edition as **ongoing assessment.**
✓ **Informal Assessment**	**Informal Assessment,** (Easy/Average, Challenge) Teacher Edition, pp. C15, C27, C39, C53, C67, C79, C95, C107
✓ **Formal Assessment**	**Lesson Reviews,** Pupil Edition, pp. C15, C27, C39, C53, C67, C79, C95, C107 **Chapter Reviews,** Pupil Edition, pp. C56–C57, C108–C109 **Chapter Tests,** Assessment Book, pp. 31–34, 35–38
▦ **Performance Assessment**	**Unit Performance Assessment,** Pupil Edition, p. C112 **Unit Performance Assessment,** Assessment Book, pp. 39–42

Lesson Planner

Lesson	Objectives	Vocabulary	Pacing	Resources and Technology
LESSON 1 **Earth and Its Neighbors,** pp. C4–C15	■ Explore the orbit of a planet around the Sun. ■ Describe the effect of gravity between objects in the solar system. ■ Identify the effects of the Sun on Earth. ■ Compare the Moon's surface to Earth's.	solar system planet gravity inertia lithosphere crust hydrosphere atmosphere constellation	4 days	■ Activity Resources, pp. 79–83 ■ Reading in Science, pp. 129–134 ■ Vocabulary Cards ■ Grade-Level Science Book, *2061: Photographing Mars* ■ Transparencies C1, 17 ■ **Explore Activity Video** ■ **Science Experiences Videotapes** *Space Camp A Journey Through the Universe*
LESSON 2 **Earth's Changing Crust,** pp. C16–C27	■ Explore forces that build Earth's landforms. ■ Compare the effect of forces that build Earth's landforms. ■ Examine the effects of weathering and erosion. ■ Identify geologic forces on other bodies of the solar system.	fault geologist magma lava weathering erosion deposition meteorite	3 days	■ Activity Resources, pp. 84–88 ■ Reading in Science Resources, pp. 135–140 ■ Vocabulary Cards ■ School to Home Activities, p. 16 ■ Grade-Level Science Book, *Quinto's Volcano* ■ Reading Aid Transparency C2 ■ **Explore Activity Video** ■ **Science Experiences Videotapes** *Volcanoes: Churning and Burning*
LESSON 3 **Minerals of Earth's Crust,** pp. C30–C39	■ Explore ways to distinguish between minerals. ■ List and compare properties of minerals. ■ Contrast ways minerals form. ■ Relate uses and properties of minerals.	mineral luster streak hardness cleavage ore gem	3 days	■ Activity Resources, pp. 89–94 ■ Reading in Science Resources, pp. 141–146 ■ Vocabulary Cards ■ Reading Aid Transparency C3 ■ **Explore Activity Video**
LESSON 4 **Earth's Rocks and Soil,** pp. C40–C53	■ Explore ways to classify rocks. ■ Compare and contrast properties and uses of rocks. ■ Define soil as a resource with many properties. ■ Trace the steps of the rock cycle, including human-made rocks.	rock igneous rock sedimentary rock fossil metamorphic rock humus pollution rock cycle	4 days	■ Activity Resources, pp. 95–99 ■ Reading in Science Resources, pp. 147–152 ■ Vocabulary Cards ■ School to Home Activities, pp. 17–18 ■ Reading Aid Transparency C4 ■ Visual Aid Transparency 18 ■ **Explore Activity Video**

Activity Planner

Activity	Process Skills	Materials	Plan Ahead
1 Explore Activity **How Are Earth and the Sun Held Together?** p. C5	make a model, observe, experiment, infer, use variables	clay, string, scissors, meterstick, goggles	No advance planning is needed.
2 Explore Activity **What Makes the Crust Move?** p. C17	make a model, experiment, communicate	4–6 matching books (optional), layers of clay or modeling compound (optional), plastic knife, cubes, wax paper	Construct each model in advance and be prepared to assist students in constructing theirs. Math manipulative kits are a good source for the cubes students need.
QUICK LAB **FOR SCHOOL OR HOME** **Model of Earth** p. C19	infer, make a model, draw conclusions	mashed ripe banana (in a plastic bag), peanut butter, hazelnut, graham cracker crumbs (in a plastic bag), wax paper	You may want to prepackage the materials needed by each team. Provide an open area covered with newspaper for students to work.
3 Explore Activity **How Can You Identify a Mineral?** p. C31	communicate, observe, experiment	mineral samples, clear tape, red marker, copper penny or wire, porcelain tile, hand lens, nail	No advance planning is needed.
4 Explore Activity **How Are Rocks Alike and Different?** p. C41	classify, use numbers, communicate, infer	samples of rocks, clear tape, red marker, hand lens, copper wire, streak plate, balance, metric ruler, calculator	Rock samples should include granite, gabbro, basalt, shale with layers, conglomerate, sandstone, siltstone, gneiss with banding, and schist.
Process Skill **BUILDER** **Defining Soil** p. C48	define based on observations, observe, use variables, experiment	moist soil sample in plastic bag, sand sample in plastic bag, hand lens, 2 cups, 2 plastic spoons	Prepare a work space by spreading newspapers over a table or on desks.

Additional Quick Labs are found on pp. C7, C37.

Reading in Science Resources

McGraw-Hill Science **Reading in Science Resources** provides the following **Blackline Master** worksheets for this chapter.

Chapter Graphic Organizer

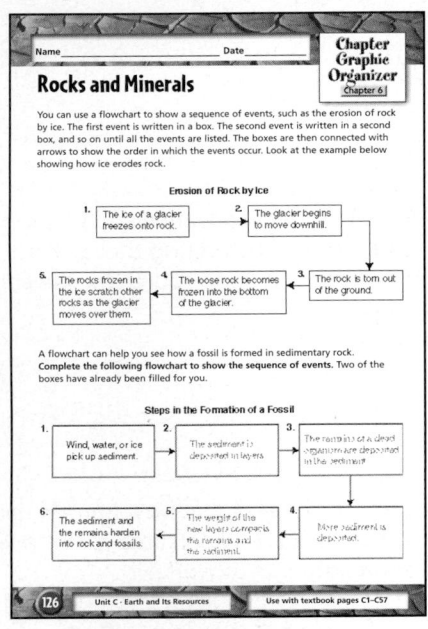

Reading in Science Resources,
p. 126

Chapter Reading Skill

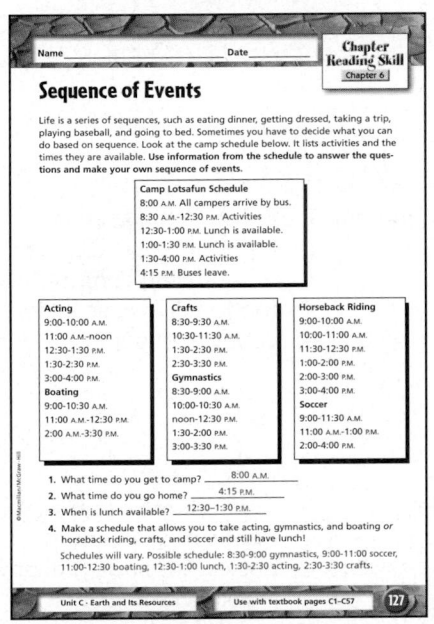

Reading in Science Resources,
pp. 127–128

Chapter Vocabulary

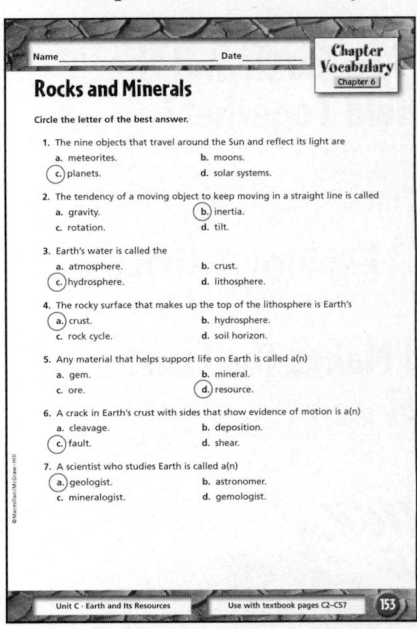

Reading in Science Resources,
pp. 153–154

McGraw-Hill Science **Reading in Science Resources** provides the following **Blackline Master** worksheets for every lesson in this chapter.

Lesson Outline

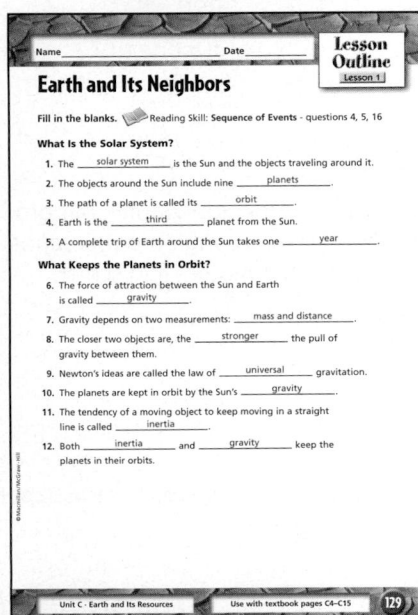

Reading in Science Resources,
pp. 129–130, 135–136, 141–142,
147–148

Interpret Illustrations

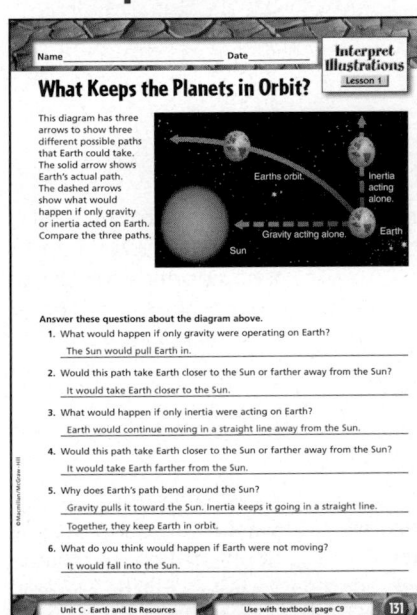

Reading in Science Resources,
pp. 131–132, 137–138, 143–144,
149–150

Lesson Vocabulary and Cloze Test

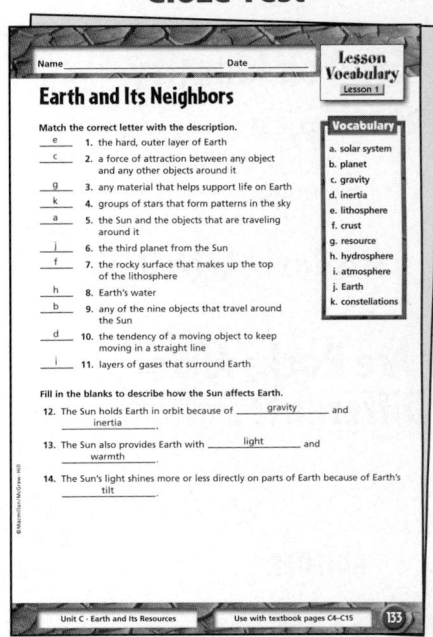

Reading in Science Resources,
pp. 133–134, 139–140, 145–146,
151–152

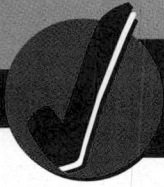

Activities and Assessment

McGraw-Hill Science **Activity Resources** provides the following **Blackline Master** worksheets for every lesson in this chapter.

Explore Activity and Alternative Explore Activity

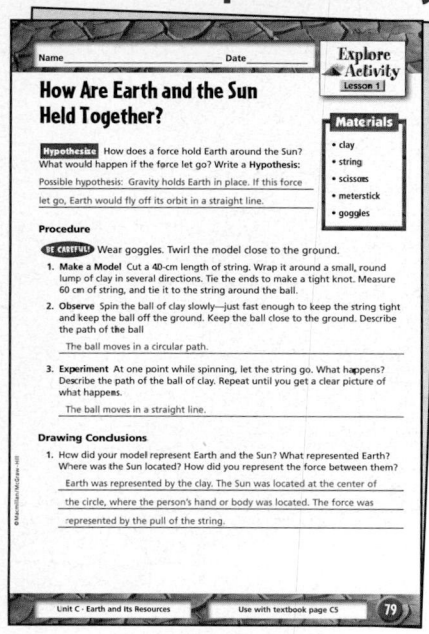

Activity Resources, pp. 79–81, 84–86, 89–92, 95–97

Quick Lab for School or Home

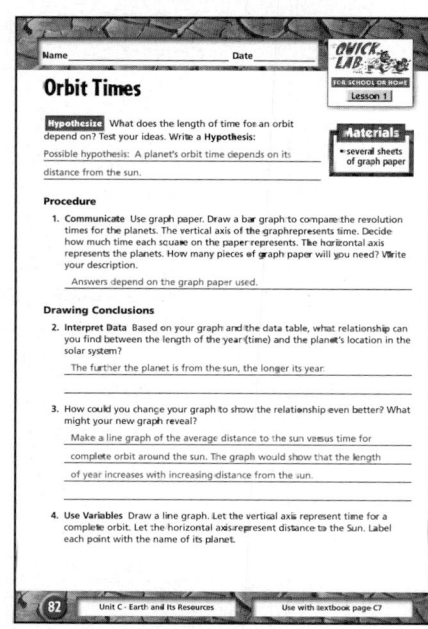

Activity Resources, pp. 82–83, 87–88, 93–94

Process Skill Builder

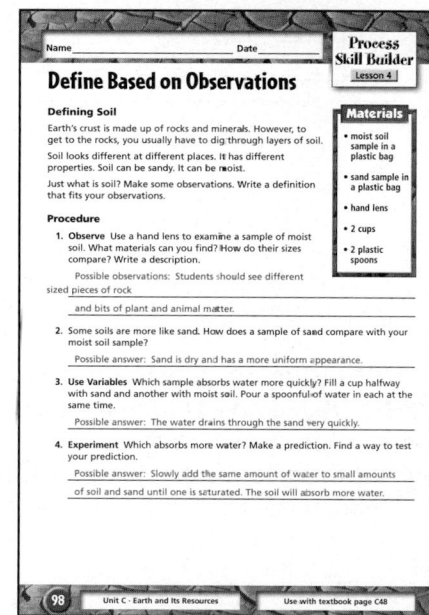

Activity Resources, pp. 98–99

McGraw-Hill Science **Assessment Book** provides the following **Blackline Master** worksheets for this chapter.

Chapter Test

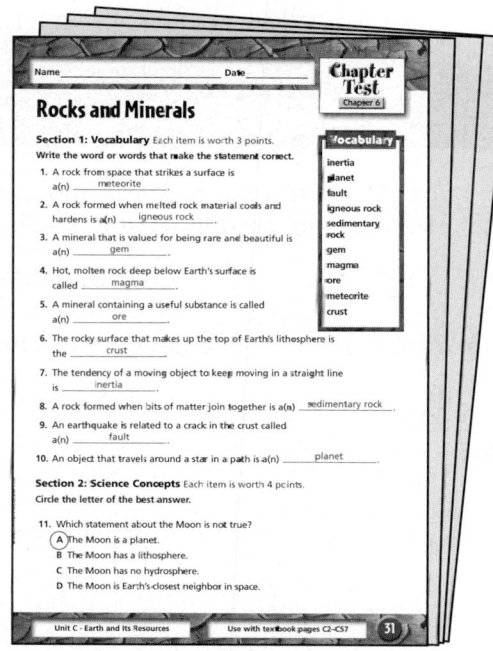

Assessment Book, pp. 31–34

6 Rocks and Minerals

Resources

- Reading in Science Resources, pp. 126–155
- Assessment Book, pp. 31–34

Did You Ever Wonder?

The stone structures of Zion National Park, in Springdale, Utah, started forming 250 million years ago when volcanoes spewed ash and sediment throughout the area. Continual weathering and erosion contributed to the formations seen today.

CHAPTER

6 Rocks and Minerals

Did You Ever Wonder?

What is this strange-looking rock formation? Did someone build it here in Zion National Park? No. This fantastic shape is a natural rock formation called a hoodoo. What natural processes could have produced a hoodoo and other unusual rock formations?

C 2

SCIENCE Reading Strategy

This chapter provides MiniLessons and other opportunities for developing and practicing the following reading skills:

- ◉ **Cause and Effect:** pp. C21, C22, C28
- ○ **Compare and Contrast**
- ○ **Draw Conclusions**
- ○ **Find the Main Idea**
- ◉ **Sequence of Events:** pp. C12, C25, C37, C47, C52
- ◉ **Summarize:** pp. C15, C27, C29, C39, C53, C55
- ○ **Ask Questions**
- ○ **Reread**

- ◉ **Retell (paraphrase):** pp. C13, C25, C26, C36, C51, C54
- ◉ **Interpret Graphic Sources of Information:** pp. C6, C8, C10, C34, C35, C43, C47
- ◉ **Build on Prior Knowledge:** pp. C4, C16, C28, C30, C40, C54
- ◉ **Organize Information:** pp. C14, C30, C42

C 3

Encourage students to keep a Science Dictionary. Remind them to add the Vocabulary words for each lesson in this chapter to their Dictionary as they complete each lesson.

solar system, C6	**meteorite,** C26
planet, C6	**mineral,** C32
gravity, C8	**luster,** C33
inertia, C9	**streak,** C34
lithosphere, C12	**hardness,** C34
crust, C12	**cleavage,** C34
hydrosphere, C12	**ore,** C38
atmosphere, C12	**gem,** C38
constellation, C14	**rock,** C42
fault, C18	**igneous rock,** C43
geologist, C18	**sedimentary rock,** C44
magma, C21	**fossil,** C45
lava, C21	**metamorphic rock,** C46
weathering, C22	**humus,** C49
erosion, C22	**pollution,** C50
deposition, C25	**rock cycle,** C52

AMERICAN MUSEUM ᴼᶠ NATURAL HISTORY

Visit www.amnh.org/resources/mhscience to discover more about Earth's crust, rocks, and soil.

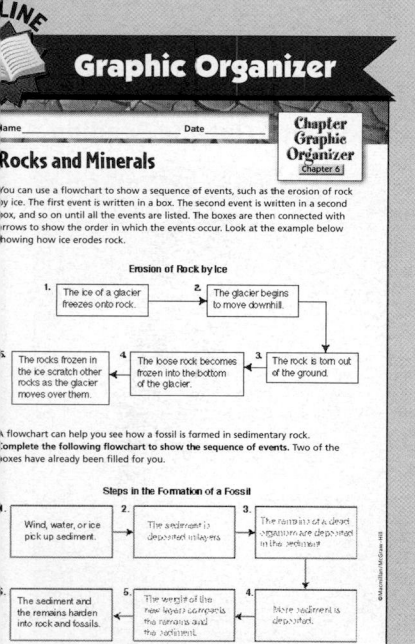

Graphic Organizer

Reading in Science Resources, p. 126

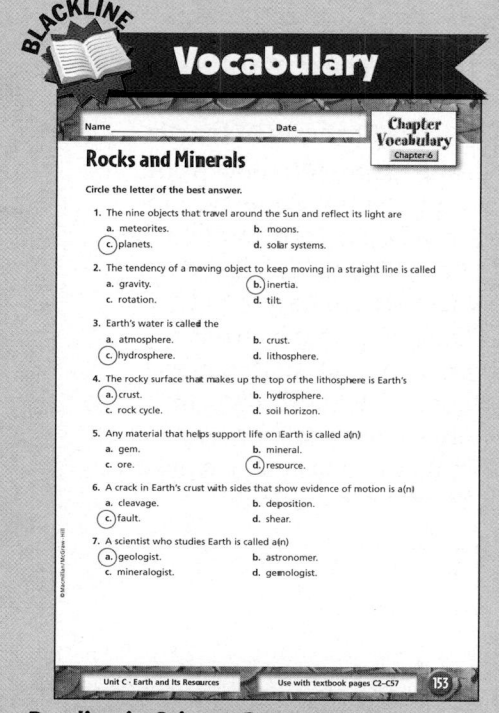

Vocabulary

Reading in Science Resources, pp. 153–154

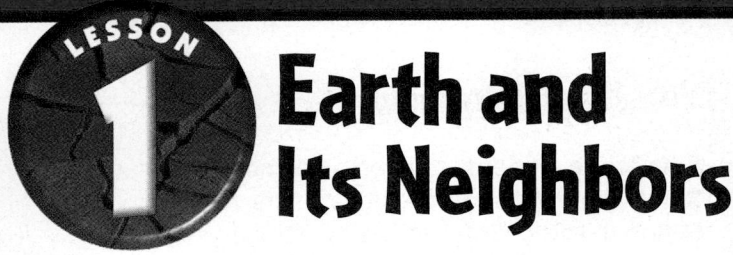

LESSON 1 Earth and Its Neighbors

Objectives

- Explore the orbit of a planet around the Sun.
- Describe the effect of gravity between objects in the solar system.
- Identify the effects of the Sun on Earth.
- Compare the Moon's surface to Earth's.

Resources

- Activity Resources, pp. 79–83
- Reading in Science Resources, pp. 129–134
- Vocabulary Cards
- Reading Aid Transparency C1
- Visual Aid Transparency 17
- Grade-Level Science Book, *2061: Photographing Mars*

Build on Prior Knowledge

Have students discuss what they know about Earth's relationship with the Sun. Ask students whether they have ever been spun around while holding hands with a friend. Then ask:

- **What would happen if your friend let go as you were spinning?** (You would fly off away from your friend.)

- **Why does this happen?** (An object in motion moves in a straight line unless acted on by an outside force.)

1 Get Ready

Developing the Main Idea

Ask students why Earth isn't pulled into the Sun. (Earth and all objects have the property of inertia—a moving object will tend to continue in a straight line—which together with gravity, keep earth in its orbit.)

LESSON 1 Earth and Its Neighbors

Vocabulary

- **solar system,** C6
- **planet,** C6
- **gravity,** C8
- **inertia,** C9
- **lithosphere,** C12
- **crust,** C12
- **hydrosphere,** C12
- **atmosphere,** C12
- **constellation,** C14

Get Ready

Saturn is not standing still in one spot. It is moving around the Sun in an almost circular path. What holds Saturn, and all the other planets, near the Sun? What keeps each planet on its path?

Process Skill

You use variables when you identify and separate things in an experiment that can be changed or controlled.

C 4

Science Background

The Property of Inertia Addressing Misconceptions

Inertia works with gravity to keep Earth in orbit around the Sun. Students may assume that inertia is a force as is gravity. Emphasize that inertia is a *property* of all matter. Inertia not only tends to keep an object in motion moving, it also makes an object at rest resist being set in motion.

Cross Curricular Books

Additional Outside Reading

All About Islands

written by Gary Apple
illustrated by Tom Leonard

To order, see page C1·b.

Explore Activity

How Are Earth and the Sun Held Together?

Materials
clay
string
scissors
meterstick
goggles

Procedure

 **BE CAREFUL!** Wear goggles. Twirl the model close to the ground.

1 Make a Model Cut a 40-cm length of string. Wrap it around a small, round lump of clay in several directions. Tie the ends to make a tight knot. Measure 60 cm of string, and tie it to the string around the ball.

2 Observe Spin the ball of clay slowly—just fast enough to keep the string tight and keep the ball off the ground. Keep the ball close to the ground. Describe the path of the ball.

3 Experiment At one point while spinning, let the string go. What happens? Describe the path of the ball of clay. Repeat until you get a clear picture of what happens.

Drawing Conclusions

1 How did your model represent Earth and the Sun? What represented Earth? Where was the Sun located? How did you represent the force between them?

2 Infer Explain what happened when you let the string go. Why do you think this happened?

3 Going Further: Use Variables How would your results change if the mass of the clay was doubled? Tripled? How does the mass affect the pull on the string? Make a prediction. Try it.

C 5

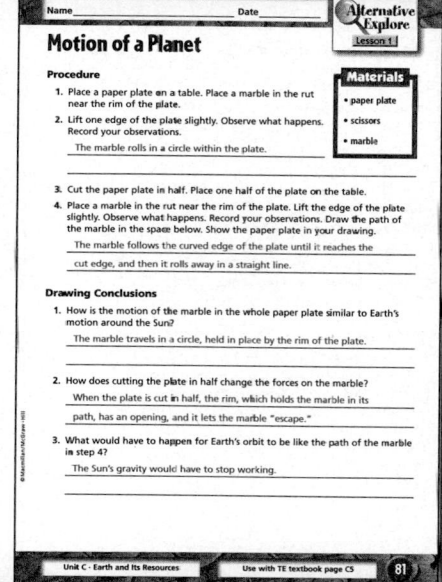 

Alternative Explore Activity

Materials paper plate, scissors, marble

Motion of a Planet Have each student cut a plate in half, lay it on a table, put a marble in the rut near the plate's rim, and lift the rim. The marble will roll in the rut until it rolls off the plate. Ask students to compare this to how Earth orbits the Sun. (The marble follows a curve because the plate holds it in place, like the Sun holds Earth in orbit. Once the marble leaves the plate, it moves in a straight line.)
Kinesthetic

Name_____ Date_____

Motion of a Planet

Alternative Explore
Lesson 1

Procedure

1. Place a paper plate on a table. Place a marble in the rut near the rim of the plate.
2. Lift one edge of the plate slightly. Observe what happens. Record your observations.
   The marble rolls in a circle within the plate.

3. Cut the paper plate in half. Place one half of the plate on the table.
4. Place a marble in the rut near the rim of the plate. Lift the edge of the plate slightly. Observe what happens. Record your observations. Draw the path of the marble in the space below. Show the paper plate in your drawing.
   The marble follows the curved edge of the plate until it reaches the
   cut edge, and then it rolls away in a straight line.

Drawing Conclusions

1. How is the motion of the marble in the whole paper plate similar to Earth's motion around the Sun?
   The marble travels in a circle, held in place by the rim of the plate.

2. How does cutting the plate in half change the forces on the marble?
   When the plate is cut in half, the rim, which holds the marble in its
   path, has an opening, and it lets the marble "escape."

3. What would have to happen for Earth's orbit to be like the path of the marble in step 4?
   The Sun's gravity would have to stop working.

Materials
• paper plate
• scissors
• marble

Unit C - Earth and Its Resources | Use with TE textbook page C5 | 81

Activity Resources, p. 81

Explore Activity

How Are Earth and the Sun Held Together?

Science Process Skills *make a model, observe, experiment, infer, use variables*

Resources Activity Resources, pp. 79–80

Pacing 20–30 minutes

Grouping individuals

Procedure

Be Careful! Caution students to twirl the clay ball close to the ground so that it will not fly off and strike any person or object. Stress the need to protect eyes by wearing goggles.

2 To spin the ball of clay, students should make the ball swing in a circle, with the student's hand at the center and the ball "orbiting" around it. (The ball moves in a circular path.)

3 Students should find that the ball flies off from the circle, traveling in a straight line.

Answers to Drawing Conclusions

1 Earth was represented by the clay, and the Sun was located at the center of the circle, where the person's hand or body was located. The force was represented by the pull of the string.

2 The clay flew off in a straight-line trajectory because the string no longer connected the spinner and the clay. The force between the Sun and Earth was removed.

3 Students may predict that the clay would fly off with double or triple the force but in the same direction if the clay's mass were doubled or tripled. The greater the mass, the stronger the pull on the string.

Inquiry Students can ask their own questions to explore, such as how the length of the string affects what happens to the clay.

Technology

■ When time is short, preview the activity with the **Explore Activity Video.**

2 Read to Learn

What Is the Solar System?

Before Reading
Have students try to answer the red question at the top of the page.

Developing the Main Idea
Tell students that you will use a flashlight to represent the Sun and a ball or globe to represent Earth. Show how sunlight reflects off Earth. Ask:

- **Does the sunlight reflect off the whole planet at once?** (No.)
- **Which part of the planet reflects light?** (The part turned toward the Sun.)

Using the Illustrations
Make sure students can identify Earth and its orbit. Point out the other objects in the illustration. Emphasize that the solar system contains more than just the Sun and the planets.

READING Diagrams

Pluto most of the time; no; Neptune's orbit sometimes extends beyond that of Pluto.

Technology

- Visual Aid Transparency 17: *The Solar System*

Developing Vocabulary

solar system Remind students that the word *solar* comes from a Latin word meaning "sun".

planet Ask students how many planets they can name. Tell them the sentence that helps remember the order of the planets from the Sun outward: Mother Very Easily Made a Jam Sandwich Using No Paprika.

Read to Learn

Main Idea The solar system consists of nine planets, many moons, and many other bodies orbiting the Sun.

What Is the Solar System?

If you were traveling in a spaceship through space as fast as light, you would be passing stars. Perhaps in time you would approach one star in particular, the star you know as the Sun. If so, you would be approaching your home address, the **solar system**. The solar system is the Sun and the objects that are traveling around it.

Our Sun is a star similar to other stars in the night sky. It appears so large and bright to us because it is much closer to Earth. The Sun is composed mostly of hydrogen and helium. The formation of helium from hydrogen is what generates light and heat from the Sun.

The objects around the Sun include nine **planets**. Planets are objects that travel around a star in a path. That path is called an *orbit*. The planets are held in orbit around the Sun. The planets do not give off light, as stars do. They reflect light from their star, the Sun.

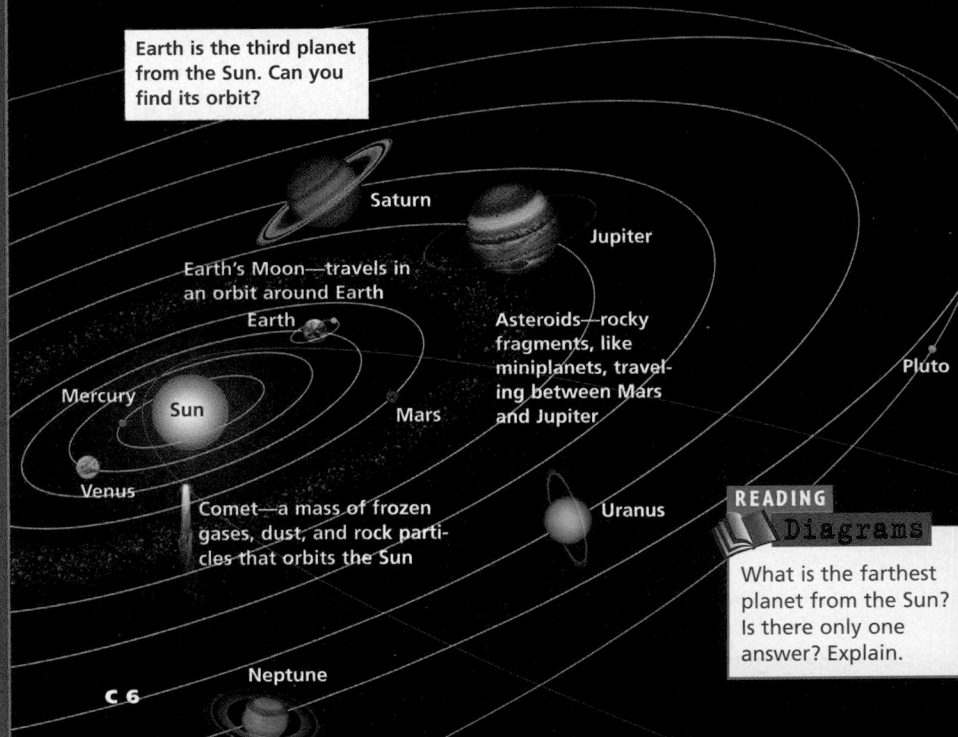

Earth is the third planet from the Sun. Can you find its orbit?

Saturn

Jupiter

Earth's Moon—travels in an orbit around Earth

Earth

Asteroids—rocky fragments, like miniplanets, traveling between Mars and Jupiter

Mercury

Sun

Mars

Pluto

Venus

Comet—a mass of frozen gases, dust, and rock particles that orbits the Sun

Uranus

READING Diagrams
What is the farthest planet from the Sun? Is there only one answer? Explain.

C 6

Neptune

Lesson Outline

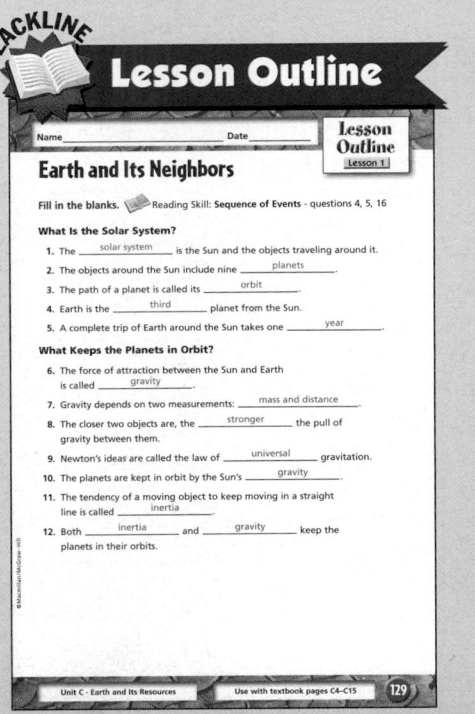

Name _____ Date _____

Lesson Outline Lesson 1

Earth and Its Neighbors

Fill in the blanks. Reading Skill: Sequence of Events - questions 4, 5, 16

What Is the Solar System?

1. The ___solar system___ is the Sun and the objects traveling around it.
2. The objects around the Sun include nine ___planets___.
3. The path of a planet is called its ___orbit___.
4. Earth is the ___third___ planet from the Sun.
5. A complete trip of Earth around the Sun takes one ___year___.

What Keeps the Planets in Orbit?

6. The force of attraction between the Sun and Earth is called ___gravity___.
7. Gravity depends on two measurements: ___mass and distance___.
8. The closer two objects are, the ___stronger___ the pull of gravity between them.
9. Newton's ideas are called the law of ___universal___ gravitation.
10. The planets are kept in orbit by the Sun's ___gravity___.
11. The tendency of a moving object to keep moving in a straight line is called ___inertia___.
12. Both ___inertia___ and ___gravity___ keep the planets in their orbits.

Unit C · Earth and Its Resources   Use with textbook pages C4–C15   129

Reading in Science Resources, p. 129

Science Background

The Asteroid Belt
Most asteroids orbit the Sun between Mars and Jupiter in the asteroid belt. Scientists have catalogued thousands of asteroids, but thousands more exist. The largest is Ceres—578 miles in diameter. Some asteroids cross Earth's orbit and present a threat of collision. Scientists believe that one did strike Earth, causing changes that led to the extinction of the dinosaurs and about 70 percent of life forms on Earth.

Except for Pluto, the orbit of each planet is almost a circle. Each orbit is slightly oval. What effect does an orbit of this shape have on the distance from a planet to the Sun?

One complete trip of an object in its orbit around the Sun takes one *year*. A year is different from planet to planet. For Earth one year is 365.25 days. The table shows how long a year takes for each planet. The time is given in days as days are timed on Earth.

▷ **What are the parts of the solar system?**

The solar system consists of the Sun and the objects that travel around it: planets, asteroids, and comets.

Planet	Average Distance to the Sun (million km)	Year Time for complete orbit around the Sun (in Earth days)
Mercury	57.9	88 days
Venus	108.2	224 days
Earth	149.6	365 days
Mars	227.9	687 days
Jupiter	778.3	4,333 days
Saturn	1,427	10,759 days
Uranus	2,870	30,685 days
Neptune	4,497	60,188 days
Pluto	5,900	90,700 days

QUICK LAB
FOR SCHOOL OR HOME
Orbit Times

1. **Communicate** Use graph paper. Draw a bar graph to compare the revolution times for the planets. The vertical axis of the graph represents time. Decide how much time each square on the paper represents. The horizontal axis represents the planets. How many pieces of graph paper will you need?

2. **Interpret Data** Based on your graph and the data table, what relationship can you find between the length of the year (time) and the planet's location in the solar system?

3. How could you change your graph to show the relationship even better? What might your new graph reveal?

4. **Use Variables** Draw a line graph. Let the vertical axis represent time for a complete orbit. Let the horizontal axis represent distance to the Sun. Label each point with the name of its planet.

Developing the Main Idea
Make sure students understand the concept of a year as the length of time an orbit takes and how the length of a year varies for each planet. Have some students ask and others answer questions based on the table. Ask:

■ **Which planet has the longest year and how many days is it? Which has the shortest and how many days is that?** (Pluto, 90,700 days; Mercury, 88 days)

■ **Using calculators, figure out how many Earth years the years of some other planets equal.** (Sample answers: A year on Neptune equals 164.9 Earth years; a year on Venus equals 0.3 Earth years.)

▶ **After Reading**
Have students answer the red question in the student book as **ongoing assessment**.

QUICK LAB
FOR SCHOOL OR HOME

Materials several sheets of graph paper

Science Process Skills *communicate, interpret data, use variables*

Resources Activity Resources, pp. 82–83

Step 1 Review with students how to construct a bar graph. Students may need to use several sheets of graph paper to fit all the values on the graph.

Step 2 The farther away a planet is from the Sun, the longer it takes to orbit the Sun, and the longer its year.

Step 3 You could change the scale along the vertical axis to show years instead of days. This change would make it easy to compare other orbits to Earth's.

Step 4 The line should increase its height with distance to confirm the relationship from step 2.

What Keeps the Planets in Orbit?

Before Reading
Have students try to answer the red question at the top of the page.

Exploring the Main Idea
Invite students to model gravity by playing tug-of-war in an open area. Begin with two volunteers. Add more students to one side until that side wins. Remind students not to pull abruptly so as to knock anyone over. Ask:

- **How strong was the force of attraction between the first two volunteers?** (It was strong enough to hold the two together.)

- **What happened when more mass was added to one side?** (That side was able to pull the lesser mass toward it.)

READING
Diagrams

Ask students to compare and contrast the mass of the rockets in each pair and their distance from the planet.

1. The rockets in A differ in distance from the planet. The rockets in B differ in mass.

2. In A, Rocket 1 is closer to the planet than Rocket 2, so it experiences a greater pull, shown by the bigger arrow. In B, Rocket 2 has more mass than Rocket 1, so it experiences a greater pull, indicated by the bigger arrow.

Technology

- **Science Experiences Videotapes**
  Space Camp: A Week of Surprises
  (Package 5)

Developing Vocabulary

gravity Have students list ways they notice gravity at work around their homes. For example, branches and leaves fall from trees, light fixtures and fans must be secured so they won't fall, and things piled too high may fall over.

What Keeps the Planets in Orbit?

Earth travels around the Sun, but you won't find a string connecting them! What is it that holds Earth in its path around the Sun? What keeps Earth from flying off into space?

This question once puzzled scientists, too. They knew that everything in the solar system orbits the Sun. What holds it all together?

Gravity

One scientist who lived about 300 years ago, Sir Isaac Newton, had some ideas to explain this. He described an invisible force holding the Sun and a planet together. He called the invisible force **gravity**. He described gravity as a property of all matter. It is a force of attraction, or pull, between any object and any other objects around it.

Gravity depends on two measurements—mass and distance. The more matter, or mass, in an object, the greater the pull in the object's direction. The closer two objects are, the stronger the pull of gravity between them.

When Newton's ideas are applied to the world around us, we find that they can explain how most objects behave. In fact, Newton extended his ideas to include all objects on Earth, in the solar system, and beyond. His ideas are called the law of universal gravitation.

READING
Diagrams

1. What are the differences between the objects in part A and part B?

2. Why is one arrow wider in part A? In part B?

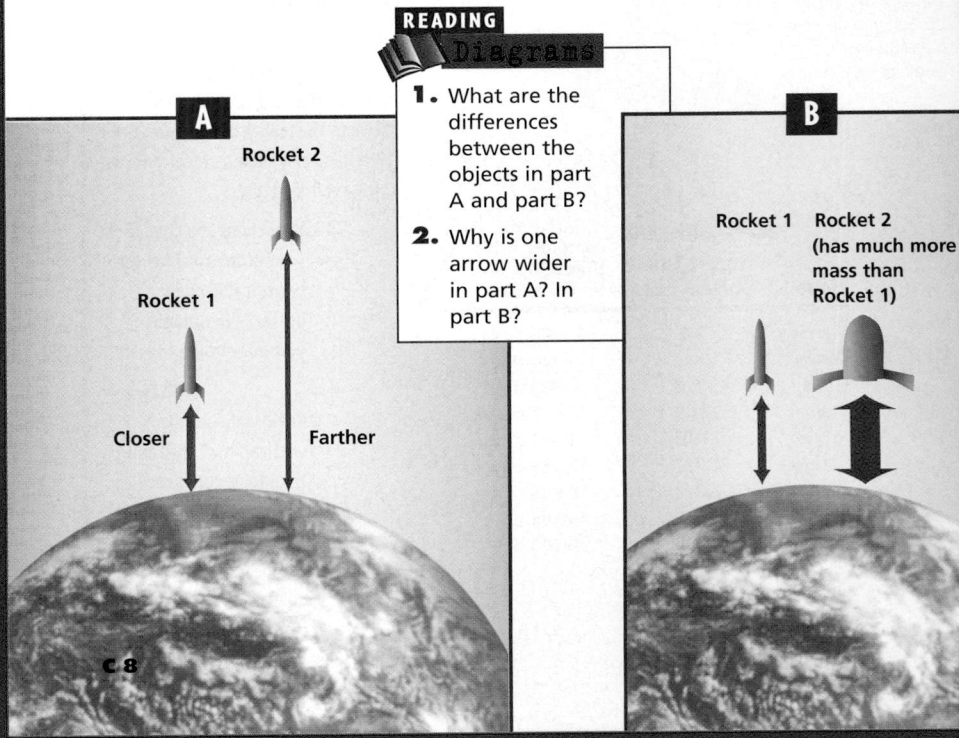

A
Rocket 2
Rocket 1
Closer   Farther
C 8

B
Rocket 1   Rocket 2 (has much more mass than Rocket 1)

Science Background

Gravity—The Weak Force
Although most people consider gravity to be a powerful force, scientists view it as weak compared to other basic forces, such as the force of electromagnetism and the force that holds atoms together. However, gravity acts over much longer distances than these other forces.

Advanced Learners

Great Thinkers
Invite students to write a report about scientists who worked to understand gravity. They include Galileo, Newton, and Einstein. **Linguistic**

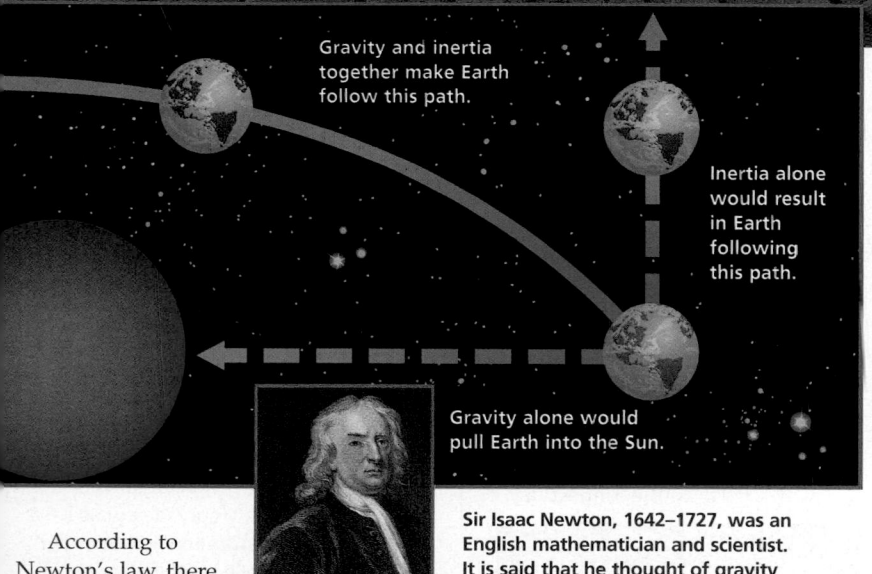

Gravity and inertia together make Earth follow this path.

Inertia alone would result in Earth following this path.

Gravity alone would pull Earth into the Sun.

Sir Isaac Newton, 1642–1727, was an English mathematician and scientist. It is said that he thought of gravity when an apple dropped on his head.

According to Newton's law, there is a force of attraction between you and Earth. Earth pulls you. You pull Earth. When you stumble, why do you fall down? Why doesn't Earth fall up?

Compared with Earth, you have a very small amount of mass. As a result, your gravity is very weak. Earth's gravity, however, is very strong because Earth is so massive. Earth's pull is strong enough to make everything near it move in its direction, including you. That's why you fall "down" if you stumble.

The Sun has far more mass than Earth or any other planet. Since it is much more massive than Earth, its gravity is much stronger, too. The Sun's gravity holds all of the objects in the solar system together. Without gravity, Earth and all of the other objects orbiting the Sun would go flying off into space.

Inertia

Gravity is not the only reason why the planets stay in their orbits. Gravity alone would pull Earth into the Sun, because the Sun is so massive. That doesn't happen because the planets are moving. The planets, as do all objects, have a property called **inertia** (i·NUR·shuh). Inertia is the tendency of a moving object to keep moving in a straight line.

The planets would move in straight lines without gravity because of their inertia. Gravity "steers" the planets in their oval paths around the Sun. It is gravity and inertia that keep the planets in their orbits.

 **How do gravity and inertia keep a planet in orbit?**

Gravity is an attraction that pulls a planet toward the Sun. Inertia is the tendency of a moving object to keep moving in a straight line. Combined, these forces make the planet travel in a curved path around the Sun.

C 9

Developing the Main Idea

Remind students that in the Explore Activity they experienced how inertia and the force of gravity interact—the pull by the person on the string holding the ball of clay and the tendency of the ball of clay to keep moving in a straight line. A planet's orbit is also a balance between a property of matter and a force acting on it—inertia and gravity. Ask:

- **What did the string in the Explore Activity represent?** (the force of gravity)
- **In what direction was gravity operating?** (Gravity was pulling the clay and the person toward each other.)
- **In what direction was inertia operating?** (Inertia was pulling the clay away from the person.)
- **How would you describe the pull of the clay away from the person in terms of inertia?** (The clay tends to move in a straight line but is being acted on by gravity. Gravity keeps it in orbit around the person.)

▶ **After Reading**

Have students answer the red question in the student book as **ongoing assessment**.

Developing Vocabulary

inertia Use the illustration to reinforce the concept of inertia which may be unfamiliar to the students. Emphasize that inertia is a property of matter, not a force that acts on it.

BLACKLINE — Interpret Illustrations

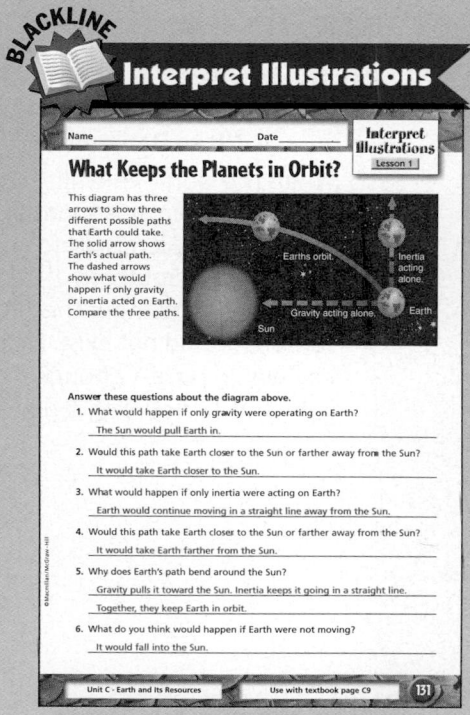

Reading in Science Resources, p. 131

SCIENCE FOR ALL — Inclusion

A Body in Motion

Ask students to draw an X on an index card and put a coin on top of the X. Invite them to move and then stop the card and observe what happens to the coin. (It will keep moving due to inertia.) They might try to push the card quickly across the table and then stop it suddenly, start the card with a jerk, or turn the card quickly. Ask them to imagine riding in a car that makes a quick stop. How would their bodies act like the coin? **Kinesthetic**

What Makes a Day?

Before Reading
Have students try to answer the red question at the top of the page.

Exploring the Main Idea
Ask a volunteer to hold a globe tilted at a 23 degree angle and slowly turn it counterclockwise. Ask another volunteer to shine the flashlight on it from several feet away so the class can investigate night and day. Ask:

■ **How does the rate of rotation affect the length of the day?** (A day is defined as one rotation of the planet.)

Identify where you live on the globe and ask students to describe what happens during the course of one day. Challenge students to use the globe to model a day for another planet. (A planet with a longer day would turn at a slower rate.)

READING Tables

Jupiter, Saturn, Neptune, Uranus, Earth, Mars, Pluto, Mercury, Venus.

▶ **After Reading**
Have students answer the red question in the student book as **ongoing assessment**.

What Makes a Day?

The Sun does more than just hold the planets in their orbits in the solar system. It also provides them with light and warmth. The Sun is the reason for day and night. All planets spin, or *rotate*, like huge spinning tops.

READING Tables

Make a list of planets in order from the shortest day to the longest day.

Length of Day	
Planet	**Day = time for complete spin (in Earth hours or days)**
Mercury	59 days
Venus	243 days
Earth	24 hours
Mars	24 hours 30 minutes
Jupiter	9 hours 56 minutes
Saturn	10 hours 40 minutes
Uranus	17 hours 14 minutes
Neptune	16 hours 6 minutes
Pluto	6.39 days

At any point in time, half of a planet is facing the Sun—it has daylight on that half. At the same time, half is facing away from the Sun—that half is in darkness, night.

As a planet rotates, places that are in darkness eventually turn to face the Sun, and those in daylight eventually turn away. Each planet makes one complete spin in its day. Each planet has its own speed of turning. The length of a day (that is, one complete day-night cycle) is different for each planet.

How much light and warmth a planet receives depends on how far it is from the Sun. Light spreads out as it travels outward from the Sun. An area of one square meter on the planet Mercury receives much more energy than an area of one square meter on a farther planet—such as Pluto. That is why Mercury is much hotter than Pluto.

 What is a day?
A day is the amount of time it takes a planet to complete one spin.

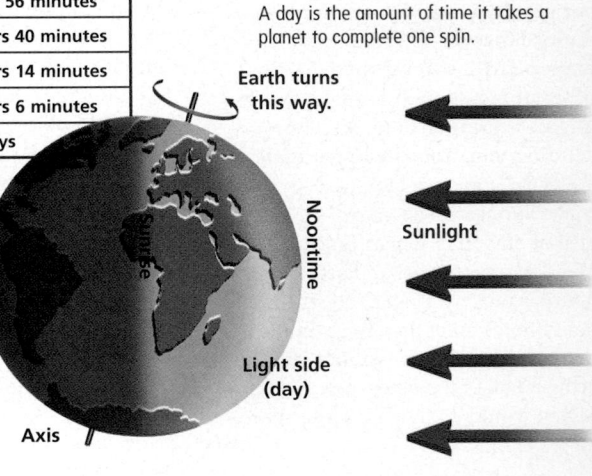

Earth turns this way.

Noontime

Sunlight

Dark side (night)

Light side (day)

Axis

Math | MiniLesson

Elapsed Times

Develop Find the elapsed time: 9:35 P.M. to 11:18 P.M. Subtract the minutes. Change units if needed.

```
      10   78
    11 h 18 min
  −  9 h 35 min
          43 min
```

Subtract the hours.

```
      10   78
    11 h 18 min
  −  9 h 35 min
       1 h 43 min
```

The elapsed time is 1h 43 min.

Practice Find the elapsed time.
1. 3:42 P.M. to 6:25 P.M.
   (2h 43 min)
2. 8:45 A.M. to 11:03 A.M.
   (2 h 18 min)

Activity Have students read the clock to find the present time. Have them find how much time has passed since they eat breakfast in the morning.

Science Background

A Tilt to Remember
When the North Pole tilts toward the Sun, it is summer in the Northern Hemisphere and winter in the Southern Hemisphere. Without this tilt, seasons would not exist. Each day would have 12 hours of light and 12 hours of darkness.

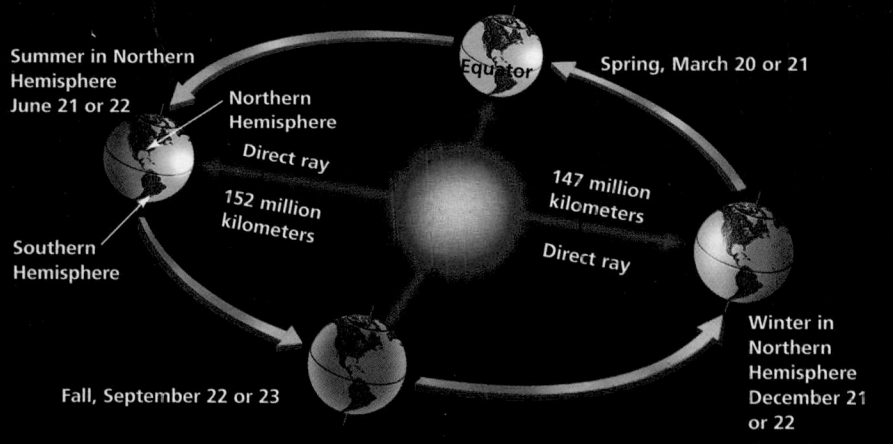

Summer in Northern Hemisphere June 21 or 22

Northern Hemisphere

Direct ray

152 million kilometers

Southern Hemisphere

Fall, September 22 or 23

Equator

Spring, March 20 or 21

147 million kilometers

Direct ray

Winter in Northern Hemisphere December 21 or 22

What Causes Earth's Seasons?

As the third planet from the Sun, Earth is at a location where it receives just the right amount of energy to provide living things with the warmth and light they need.

Different animals and plants live in different temperatures, in different climates, and at different heights above sea level on Earth.

Why are places generally cooler in winter than in summer? Earth's orbit is like a slightly stretched circle—an oval. This shape brings Earth slightly closer to the Sun during part of the year and farther away during other parts of the year. In the Northern Hemisphere, Earth is actually slightly closer to the Sun during winter than during summer. Then what causes colder winters and warmer summers?

The answer is Earth's tilt as it travels around the Sun. During the winter the Northern Hemisphere is tilted away from the Sun. The winter Sun stays low in the sky in the Northern Hemisphere. Temperatures are cooler. During the summer, the Northern Hemisphere is tilted toward the Sun. The midday summer Sun is higher in the sky in the Northern Hemisphere. Temperatures are warmer.

The closer a place is to the equator, the less change there is in temperatures from season to season. Why? The mid-day Sun is high in the sky all year round.

Also, some surfaces warm up more than others when bathed in sunlight. Land heats up more than water. Dark soils heat up more than light-colored sands. As a result, Earth ends up with a whole range of temperatures, which can support the many different kinds of life on Earth.

▷ **How does Earth's tilt bring about the seasons?**

C 11

What Causes Earth's Seasons?

Before Reading
Have students try to answer the red question at the top of the first text column.

Exploring the Main Idea
Ask volunteers to use the globe and flashlight to demonstrate the seasons. Remind students that the globe must be tilted at a 23 degree angle from vertical. Ask the volunteer with the globe to walk around the stationary flashlight. Observe the Northern Hemisphere during one orbit, the Southern Hemisphere during another, and the equatorial region during a third. Ask:

■ **Why is it summer in the Southern Hemisphere when it is winter in the Northern Hemisphere?** (At that time of year, more direct light shines on the Southern Hemisphere because it is tilted toward the Sun. The North end of Earth's axis points away from the Sun.)

■ **How do the seasons in the United States compare with those in Australia?** (Since the United States is in the Northern Hemisphere and Australia is in the Southern Hemisphere, their seasons are opposite. When it is autumn in the United States, it is spring in Australia.)

▶ After Reading
Have students answer the red question in the student book as **ongoing assessment.**

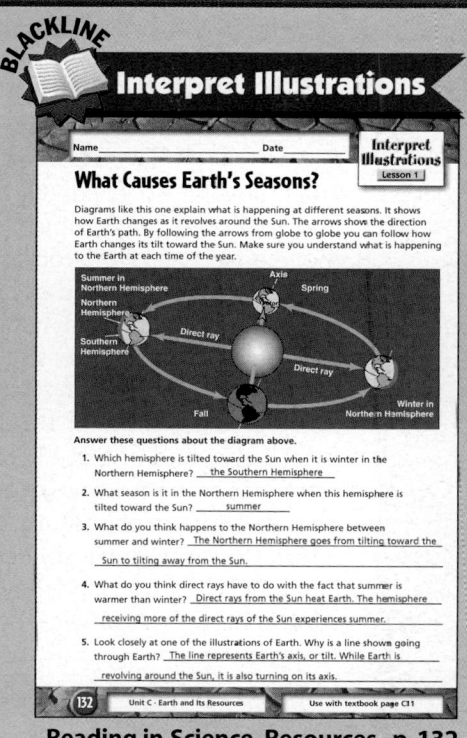

Reading in Science Resources, p. 132

Interpret Illustrations

What Causes Earth's Seasons?

Advanced Learners

Space Probes
Challenge one group of students to find out more about the search for extraterrestrial life in our solar system as conducted by SETI (Search for Extraterrestrial Intelligence). Ask another group to research the Voyager probes (both launched in 1977) that traveled through the solar system. Ask them to find out what was discovered about various planets. Then discuss how the findings of both groups might be interrelated. **Linguistic**

What Is Planet Earth Like?

Before Reading
Have students try to answer the red question at the top of the first text column.

Exploring the Main Idea
Show students a globe. Ask:

- **Where is the solid surface layer of Earth?** (All landforms make up the solid surface layer.)

- **Is there a part of the solid surface layer you cannot see?** (Yes.) **Where is it?** (Under the oceans and other bodies of water.)

- **What makes up the water layer on Earth?** (Oceans, lakes, rivers, ponds, and other bodies of water.)

▶ After Reading
Have students answer the red question in the student book as **ongoing assessment**.

Developing Vocabulary

lithosphere The root of this word is derived from the Greek *litho-* meaning "stone."

crust The outermost layer of Earth is the crust—like the outermost layer of bread.

hydrosphere The Greek root of this word, *hydro-*, means "water."

atmosphere The Greek *atmos-* means "vapor."

Atmosphere

Sea level

Lithosphere

Hydrosphere

Earth

What Is Planet Earth Like?

Is Earth a solid planet? Liquid? Gas? Earth is all of these. It has a solid surface layer, mostly covered by a layer of water, all surrounded by layers of gases. The Sun interacts with all of these layers of Earth.

- The **lithosphere** (LITH·uh·sfeer) is the hard, outer layer of Earth, about 100 km (62.14 mi) thick. The rocky surface that makes up the top of the lithosphere is the **crust**. The crust includes the continents and the ocean floors.

    The crust includes the soil and many other *resources*. Earth's resources are materials that help support life on Earth. Earth has high mountains, like the Rockies. It also has low valleys, like those of the ocean bottoms.

- The **hydrosphere** (HIGH·druh·sfeer) is Earth's water—trillions of liters of water. Earth's waters are another valuable resource. There is so much water that it covers most of the lithosphere. Most of this water is called the ocean. It is salty because of minerals that have been washed into it over the ages. The

hydrosphere also includes all of Earth's lakes, rivers, streams, underground water, and ice. Most of this is fresh water, which we use for drinking, cooking, and bathing.

The hydrosphere acts as a big heat absorber. Water changes temperature slowly compared to land. The oceans keep temperatures on Earth from changing too drastically.

- Pictures of Earth taken from space show lots of white clouds swirling in the **atmosphere**. The atmosphere is many layers of gases that surround Earth. The atmosphere contains oxygen needed for living things on Earth. It also contains other gases that help protect Earth from forms of harmful energy from the Sun. These gases are more of Earth's precious resources.

Earth consists first of the lithosphere, then the hydrosphere, then the atmosphere.

READING Sequence of Events
What is the order of Earth's layers?

C 12

Reading | MiniLesson

Sequence of Events

Develop Discuss with students that everything happens in an order, or sequence, including their daily schedule at school, and that knowing a sequence can help us make sense out of things. Point out that by writing about Earth's layers in sequence, the authors help us visualize the buildup of layers around and above us.

Practice Remind students that one way to show a sequence of events is in a flowchart on which each step is written inside a circle that's connected to the next circle by an arrow. Suggest that students make upside-down flowcharts to show the sequence of Earth's layers, beginning at the bottom of a page with *lithosphere* in the first circle, then an arrow leading up to *hydrosphere* in the next circle, and from there an arrow leading up to *atmosphere* in the top circle.

Science Background

Earth Layers

The lithosphere is divided into about 12 rigid plates, which move on a layer of hot rock and carry the continents and ocean floor with them. More than 97% of the hydrosphere is salt water, about 2% is ice in the polar ice caps, less than 1% is fresh water, and $\frac{1}{1000}$ of 1% is water vapor in the atmosphere. The atmosphere ends at about 95 km (60 miles) and is divided into four layers: troposphere, stratosphere, mesosphere, and thermosphere.

What Is the Moon Like?

With a telescope you can take a close look at Earth's nearest neighbor in the solar system. "Only" 384,000 km (240,000 mi) from Earth, the Moon's surface does not look at all like Earth's surface. You won't see clouds or oceans. There are no hills covered with forests—in fact there are no signs of life at all.

The Moon has no hydrosphere. It has no atmosphere to speak of. There is no water to drink, no air to breathe. There is no weather. Without the atmosphere to trap heat and the hydrosphere to circulate it, temperatures change greatly during a Moon day.

The Moon has a lithosphere, a rocky surface. With a telescope you can see features of the surface—such as dark-colored regions called *maria* (MAHR·ee·uh). *Maria* is Latin for "seas." In the past these areas were thought to be seas. They are really dry, flat land surrounded by mountains and ridges. The Moon has no atmosphere or hydrosphere. Temperatures vary greatly. It has a rocky surface with dark maria and craters.

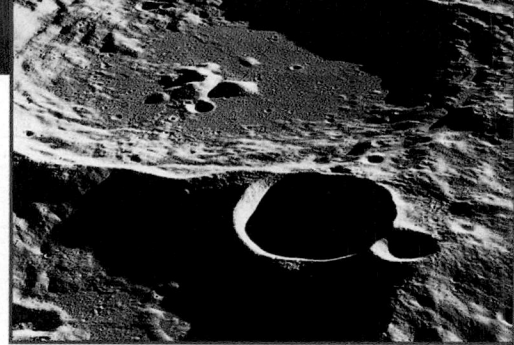
Earth's nearest neighbor looks nothing much like Earth.

Much of the Moon's surface is covered with huge dents, called craters. Trails of rock and dust extend out from them. They reflect sunlight and look like rays coming out of the crater.

The Moon is not a planet. It travels in an orbit around Earth. "Moon" light is actually "Sun" light. Your part of Earth is not facing the Sun at night. However, the Sun's light reaches the Moon and bounces into space. Some of this reflected light reaches Earth.

▷ **What are conditions on the Moon like?**

Astronauts landed in the Sea of Tranquility on their first visit to the Moon.

C 13

Before Reading
Have students try to answer the red question at the top of the page.

Exploring the Main Idea
Show students pictures of the Moon's surface taken by astronauts. Have them identify some of the features. Ask:

- **What "sphere" are you looking at: lithosphere, hydrosphere, or atmosphere?** (lithosphere.)

Point out one of the lunar "seas." Ask:

- **Do you think you would find water in a lunar sea?** (No.) **Why not?** (The Moon has no hydrosphere.)

- **Why did astronauts have to wear helmets and air tanks on the surface of the Moon?** (The Moon has no atmosphere; they needed the equipment so they could breathe.)

Using the Illustrations
Locate the Sea of Tranquility on a map of the Moon. Help students find a way to identify that spot when they look at the real Moon.

▶ **After Reading**
Have students answer the red question in the student book as **ongoing assessment**.

Technology

- **Science Experiences Videotapes**
  A Journey Through the Universe (Package 8)

Science Background

Moon Cycles
The Moon rotates on its axis once every 27.3 days. Because it also makes one revolution around Earth in the same amount of time, we see only one side of the Moon. Scientists think these cycles were different early in the Moon's history, but that gravity has probably slowed the Moon down.

What Are Constellations?

Before Reading
Have students try to answer the red question at the top of the page.

Developing the Main Idea
Show students a star map of the sky for the current date. Point out the Big Dipper and explain how Polaris, the pole star, always points north in the Northern Hemisphere. Explain that all the other stars revolve around Polaris. Ask

- **What stars do you think can always be seen in the Northern Hemisphere?** (those nearest Polaris)

- **Point out a constellation that may not be seen in all seasons.** (any that are near the horizon)

- **Do you think all the stars in a constellation are the same distance from us?** (No; on another planet or in another solar system, they would all appear quite different.)

Using the Illustrations
Have students pick one of the constellations in the bottom picture and find out what its name means and how the configuration of stars reflects that meaning.

▶ After Reading
Have students answer the red question in the student book as **ongoing assessment**.

Developing Vocabulary

constellation The Latin root of this word means "starry," reminding us that a constellation always contains at least three and usually more stars.

What Are Constellations?

When you look into the night sky, what else can you see besides the Moon? If the sky is dark enough, you can also see the stars. What are stars? A star is a large, hot ball of gas that is held together by gravity and gives off its own light. Stars look like points of light in the night sky. Unlike the Moon, stars are far outside the solar system.

In the past people looked at the stars and saw them arranged in groups that formed patterns in the sky. These patterns are called **constellations**. To these people the patterns looked like pictures of animals or people.

How can you find a star like Rigel in the night sky? The easiest way is by looking for its constellation. Rigel, for example, is a star in the constellation Orion, the hunter.

The pattern of stars in a constellation always looks the same even though the constellations appear to move across the sky. As Earth travels in its orbit around the Sun, its night side faces different

Rigel

The constellation Orion

directions. You see only the constellations that are in that direction. The constellation Orion, for example, is a winter constellation. We see it from the Northern Hemisphere in the winter months.

▶ **Why do constellations appear to move across the sky?**

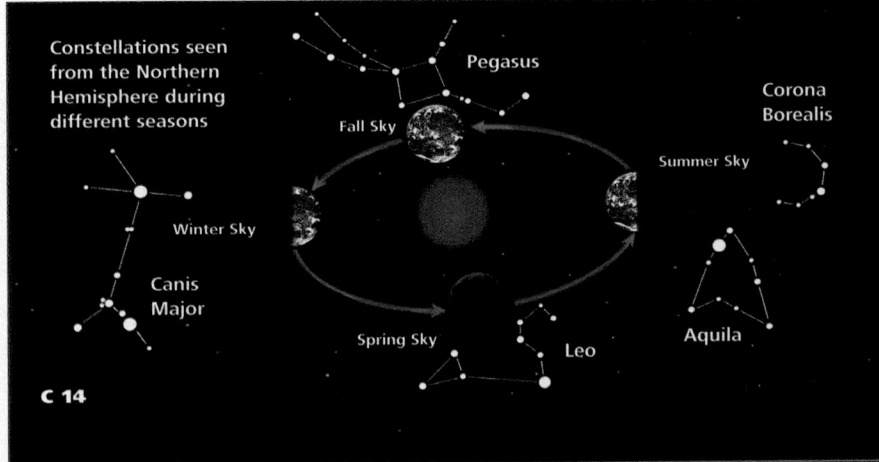

Constellations seen from the Northern Hemisphere during different seasons

Pegasus

Fall Sky

Corona Borealis

Summer Sky

Winter Sky

Canis Major

Spring Sky

Leo

Aquila

C 14

Why It Matters

Earth is teaming with life and movement. The Sun's energy helps produce seasons, day-to-day weather, and climates.

When astronauts first visited the Moon in 1969, they faced a tough problem. How do you survive in such a place? They had to bring all of the things they needed to stay alive all the way from Earth.

Earth is the only member of the solar system that supports life as we know it.

Visit **www.mhscience02.com** to do a research project on the solar system.

Think and Write

1. How would you state your address in space? Explain your answer.

2. How is gravity important for Earth?

3. How does the Sun affect life on Earth?

4. Why is the Moon unlivable compared with Earth?

5. **Critical Thinking** Would you weigh the same on all of the planets? Explain your answer.

L·I·N·K·S

ART LINK

Construct a mobile. Make a model of the solar system. Use a hanger, string, and construction paper or clay. Be sure to include all the planets.

SOCIAL STUDIES LINK

Research the planets. Learn more about Earth's neighbors. Which planets have moons? Rings? Which planets are most likely to support life? Use the Internet or an encyclopedia.

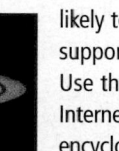

LITERATURE LINK

Read *2061: Photographing Mars* to learn about a teacher's trip to Mars. Try the activities at the end of the book.

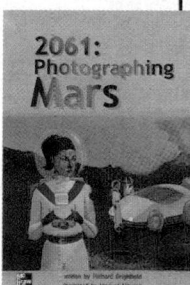

2061: Photographing Mars

TECHNOLOGY LINK

At the Computer Visit **www.mhscience02.com** for more links.

C 15

Informal Assessment

Easy/Average Ask students to list and explain ten ways the Sun and Moon affect Earth. Ask them to write a paragraph that describes how Earth differs from other planets.

Challenge Invite students to write a 10- to 20-question quiz for this lesson and to include the answers. Challenge them to give their quizzes to each other and then correct them.

Answers to Think and Write

1. An address for Earth would be "third planet from the Sun." This describes Earth's position relative to the Sun and other planets. (p. C6)

2. The Sun's gravity keeps Earth in orbit close enough to the Sun so that we have enough light and heat for life. (pp. C8–C9, C12)

3. The Sun provides Earth with heat and light, keeps us in orbit, and drives the water cycle, seasons, and climates. (pp. C8–C13)

4. The Moon has no air, food, or water; its surface temperatures vary. (p. C13)

5. **Critical Thinking** No; weight depends on the force of gravity, which depends on the mass of the planet. (p. C8)

Summarize

Check students' understanding by having them write a brief summary of the lesson in their own words.

ART LINK

Students' models must include all nine planets with the Sun at the center. Students may choose to make the model to scale in terms of planet size or distance from the Sun. Point out that they must use different scales for the size and distance.

SOCIAL STUDIES LINK

Students' research should include all planets with rings or moons. (moons—all planets except Mercury and Venus; rings—all four gas giants)

LITERATURE LINK

Have students read the Grade-Level Science Book, *2061: Photographing Mars*. For additional books to read, see page C1·b.

Technology

Internet Research Project Have students visit **www.mhscience02.com** to conduct a research project on the solar system. They will find a suggested outline for the project, questions to research, and links to Internet reference sites.

LESSON 2 Earth's Changing Crust

Objectives

- Explore forces that build Earth's landforms.
- Compare the effect of forces that build Earth's landforms.
- Examine the effects of weathering and erosion.
- Identify geologic forces on other bodies of the solar system.

Resources

- Activity Resources, pp. 84–88
- Reading in Science Resources, pp. 135–140
- Vocabulary Cards
- Reading Aid Transparency C2
- Grade-Level Science Book, *Quinto's Volcano*
- School to Home Activities p. 16

Build on Prior Knowledge

Have students discuss what they know about earthquakes. Ask them to describe experiences in which doors, windows, or buildings shook. Ask:

■ **Do earthquakes always cause destruction?**
(Though students may believe this is true, many small-scale quakes cause no damage and often are not even felt.)

1 Get Ready

Developing the Main Idea

Ask students if they know why earthquakes happen along the cracks in Earth's crust. Explain that the crust can move on either side of the crack. The movement causes the ground to shake.

LESSON 2 Earth's Changing Crust

Vocabulary

fault, C18
geologist, C18
magma, C21
lava, C21
weathering, C22
erosion, C22
deposition, C25
meteorite, C26

Get Ready

What causes an earthquake? An earthquake seems to happen without warning. The ground shakes suddenly, often with enough power to damage objects on the surface.

Where do earthquakes happen? Earthquakes are common in places where the crust is "cracked." One such crack extends through much of the state of California. Why do you think earthquakes happen along this crack?

Process Skill

You experiment when you perform a test to support or disprove a hypothesis.

C 16

 Science Background

Plate Movements

The movements of Earth's lithospheric plates are responsible for earthquakes and volcanic eruptions. Plates scrape by each other, or one plate plunges beneath another into the mantle. The many volcanoes at the plates bordering the Pacific Ocean are called the Ring of Fire.

Science Background

Earthquake Frequency
Addressing Misconceptions

Earthquakes occur all over the world almost continuously. Most are too small to be felt except by sensitive instruments. A great earthquake occurs about once a year somewhere in the world. Some small earthquakes are caused by human activities, such as explosions and nuclear tests.

Explore Activity

What Makes the Crust Move?

Procedure: Design Your Own

1 Make a Model Work with a partner to model layers of rock. You may use books, clay, or other materials to represent rock layers. Build your model on wax paper. Include a "crack" down through the layers. Stack cubes on the top of the model to represent buildings and other surface features.

2 Experiment Find as many ways of moving the model as you can to show how the crust may move during an earthquake. What happens to the surface features as you move the model each way? Draw and describe each.

3 Experiment How can you show movement without causing any visible effect on the surface features?

Drawing Conclusions

1 How many different ways could you move your model? How were they different?

2 Communicate How did each way you moved the model affect the surface features? How did each way change the positions of the layers? Explain.

3 Communicate How did you move the model without moving the surface features? Did the model change in any way? Explain.

4 Going Further: Experiment How can you use your model to show how a mountain might rise up high above sea level? Explain and demonstrate.

Materials

4–6 matching books (optional)

layers of clay or modeling compound (optional)

plastic knife

cubes

wax paper

C 17

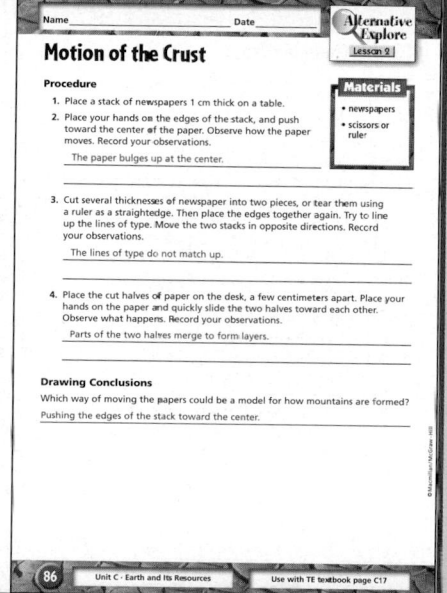

Alternative Explore Activity

Materials newspapers, scissors or ruler

Motion of the Crust Students can model movements of Earth's crust by using newspaper to simulate the effects. They can model folding by stacking wet newspapers on a table and pushing them together. They can model faulting by tearing the papers in half, then pressing them together. They can model tilting by quickly moving half of the papers against the other half. **Spatial; Kinesthetic**

Activity Resources, p. 86

Explore Activity

What Makes the Crust Move?

Science Process Skills *make a model, experiment, communicate*

Resources Activity Resources, pp. 84–85

Pacing 20–30 minutes

Grouping small groups

Plan Ahead Construct each model in advance and be prepared to assist students in constructing theirs. Math manipulative kits are a good source for the cubes students need.

Procedure: Design Your Own

2 Students might try shifting or sliding the model side to side, bouncing or bumping it up and down, and tilting it.

3 Possible answer: Slowly pull apart the bottom layers of clay.

Answers to Drawing Conclusions

1 Students can move the model three ways: up and down (a fault); sideways (a tilt); or toward each other (a fold). The different movements went in different directions.

2 Each way the layers moved caused the surface features to move. When the model moved up, the layers were no longer lined up. When the model moved sideways, the layers tilted against each other. When the model folded, the layers appeared bent.

3 If the model is moved slightly, the surface features will not move. The model itself will change only slightly.

4 Any of these movements can form a mountain if the movement is great enough. If the crust is under the ocean, the new mountain may rise above sea level.

 **Inquiry** Students can ask their own questions to explore, such as how the mountains on Earth's surface were formed in each of the three types of movement they demonstrated.

Technology

- When time is short, preview the activity with the **Explore Activity Video**.

What Makes the Crust Move?

Before Reading
Have students try to answer the red question at the top of the page.

Exploring the Main Idea
In an actual seismograph the paper, not the pen, moves. You can make a simple seismograph by suspending a spring from a ring stand and clamp and attaching a felt-tip pen to the bottom of the spring with clay, so the pen is parallel with the table. Prop a piece of white cardboard so the pen can write on it. Ask a volunteer to slam a book or other heavy object near the seismograph. Show students how the movement is recorded on the cardboard. Then experiment by slamming the book at different distances from the seismograph. Ask:

■ **What makes the pen move?** (Vibrations from the table, which are caused by the movement of the book.)

■ **What happens as the movement gets farther from the seismograph?** (The spring and pen do not move as much.)

■ **Can you slam the book far enough from the seismograph that the spring does not move?** (Yes.)

Developing Vocabulary

fault A fault is a break or a defect. To reinforce the concept of a geologic fault ask students if they have heard of the San Andreas Fault.

geologist Remind students that geology is the study of Earth's outer layer or crust. The suffix *-ist* refers to a person who knows about a particular branch of science.

Read to Learn

Main Idea Forces on and under Earth shape its surface.

What Makes the Crust Move?

Earth's crust is constantly moving, if not in one place then in another. Sometimes it moves quickly enough to be seen and felt. People who have been through an earthquake tell of seeing the ground heave up and down like an ocean wave.

Earthquakes are related to cracks in the crust called **faults**. These faults may have formed from earlier earthquakes. Sometimes they form while the earthquake happens. During an earthquake the crust on either side, or on both sides, of a fault is in motion.

During an earthquake vibrations travel through the crust. The farther away people are from the earthquake, the harder it is for them to feel the vibrations. However, delicate devices called *seismographs* (SIGHZ·muh·grafs)

Fossils in mountain areas

can record this motion at locations all around the crust.

Most of the time, however, the crust moves very slowly. Rocks can move slowly on either side of a fault over centuries. People realize there is movement only when something visibly changes position. Not all motion happens along faults, either. Often, layers of the crust bend, as shown in the picture below. Bending, like motion along a fault, may happen gradually over time.

To measure crust movement, *surveyors* (suhr·VAY·uhrz) measure *elevation*—how high a place is above sea level. They leave plaques called *bench marks* that tell the exact location and elevation of a place. When some bench marks are remeasured, they are found to have risen or sunk.

Geologists (jee·AHL·uh·jists), scientists who study Earth, place sensitive devices all along faults, such as the San Andreas Fault in California. They hope that records of tiny movements can be used to predict an earthquake.

Remains of ancient sea life are sometimes found in rock layers high up in mountains.

C 18

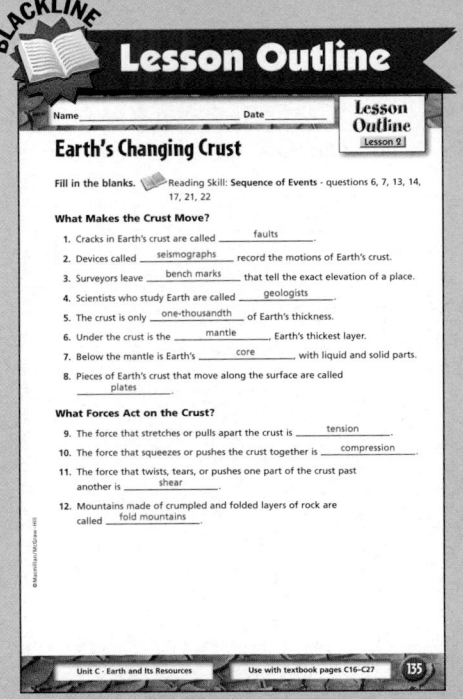

Lesson Outline

Name_____ Date_____

Lesson Outline Lesson 2

Earth's Changing Crust

Fill in the blanks. Reading Skill: Sequence of Events - questions 6, 7, 13, 14, 17, 21, 22

What Makes the Crust Move?

1. Cracks in Earth's crust are called _____faults_____
2. Devices called _____seismographs_____ record the motions of Earth's crust.
3. Surveyors leave _____bench marks_____ that tell the exact elevation of a place.
4. Scientists who study Earth are called _____geologists_____
5. The crust is only _____one-thousandth_____ of Earth's thickness.
6. Under the crust is the _____mantle_____ Earth's thickest layer.
7. Below the mantle is Earth's _____core_____ with liquid and solid parts.
8. Pieces of Earth's crust that move along the surface are called _____plates_____

What Forces Act on the Crust?

9. The force that stretches or pulls apart the crust is _____tension_____
10. The force that squeezes or pushes the crust together is _____compression_____
11. The force that twists, tears, or pushes one part of the crust past another is _____shear_____
12. Mountains made of crumpled and folded layers of rock are called _____fold mountains_____

Unit C · Earth and Its Resources | Use with textbook pages C16–C27 | 135

Reading in Science Resources, p. 135

Science Background

The First Seismograph
Almost 2,000 years ago, a Chinese astronomer named Chang Heng made the first seismograph. He balanced bronze balls on the sides of a jar with a pendulum inside it. The balls fell off if the ground shook because the jar moved more than the heavy pendulum. That seismograph, like modern ones, worked because of inertia—an object tends to stay at rest until acted on by a force.

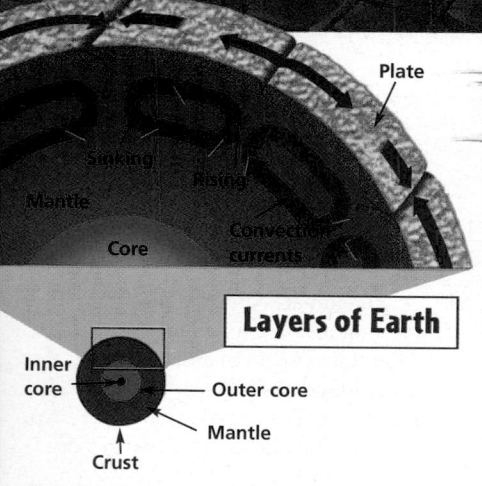

Layers of Earth

Inner core
Outer core
Mantle
Crust

Plate Tectonics

The crust is Earth's hard surface. Compared with the distance to Earth's center, it is very thin. It is only about one-thousandth of Earth's thickness.

Under the crust is the mantle, Earth's thickest layer. The rock material here is solid. However, it can flow like a liquid—as putty can "flow" when you squeeze it between your hands. Below the mantle is Earth's core. It is in two parts, a liquid outer core and a solid inner core.

The rock material in the mantle is in motion, something like heated water in a pot. It rises and pushes against the bottom of the crust. This movement causes the thin, brittle crust at the surface to break into pieces, or *plates*. The plates themselves can move along Earth's surface. Earthquakes and the slow motions of the crust all result from moving plates.

▶ **How are earthquakes related to faults and plates in the crust?**
Plates are the pieces of crust on either side of a fault. During an earthquake the plate on one or both sides of a fault is in motion.

QUICK LAB

FOR SCHOOL OR HOME

Model of Earth

BE CAREFUL! Students who are allergic to peanuts should not do this activity.

1. Infer You will use four materials to make a model of Earth on wax paper. Each material is one of Earth's layers. Read step 2. Decide which material represents which layer. Decide how thick each layer needs to be.

2. Make a Model Wash your hands. Cover a hazelnut with a layer of peanut butter. Put the covered nut in a plastic bag of mashed banana so that banana covers it completely. Roll the result into graham cracker crumbs on wax paper.

3. Draw Conclusions How does each material represent a different layer?

4. How thick did you decide to make each layer? Explain your reasoning.

C 19

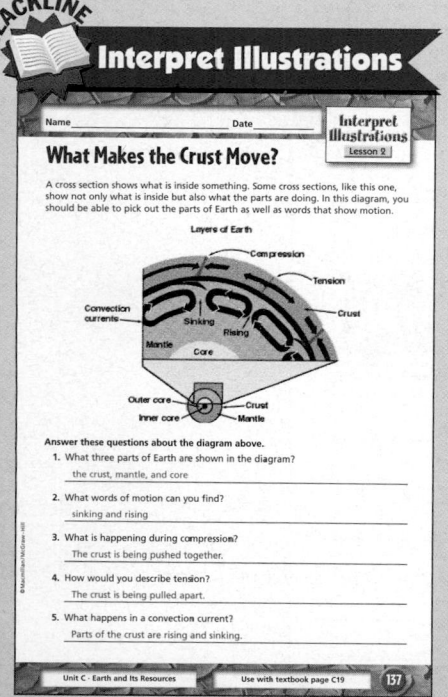
Science Background

Layers in Upheaval

At one time, the area where the fossils are found was under the sea. As Earth moved, that area was pushed up above water. Finding fossils of sea life above the sea shows how far up the layer of Earth was pushed.

Developing the Main Idea

Model the inside of Earth by showing students an apple cut in half lengthwise. Tell students that if Earth were the size of this apple, the crust would be about as thick as the skin. The seeds represent the hard core and the flesh represents the softer mantle.

▶ **After Reading**
Have students answer the red question in the student book as **ongoing assessment**.

QUICK LAB

FOR SCHOOL OR HOME

Materials mashed ripe banana (in a plastic bag), peanut butter, hazelnut, graham cracker crumbs (in a plastic bag), wax paper

Science Process Skills *infer, make a model*

Resources Activity Resources, pp. 87–88

Plan Ahead You may want to prepackage the materials needed by each team. Provide an open area covered with newspaper for students to work.

Be Careful! Determine if any students are allergic to peanut butter. Allow any such students to do the activity without including the peanut butter layer or with an alternative material.

Step 3 The hazelnut stands for Earth's solid core, peanut butter for the liquid part of the core, banana for the mantle, and graham cracker crumbs for the crust.

Step 4 The graham cracker crumbs had to make a thin layer because the crust is a thin layer; the mashed banana was much thicker to match the thick mantle. Both parts of the core are small.

What Forces Act on the Crust?

Before Reading
Have students try to answer the red question at the top of the page.

Developing the Main Idea
Ask:

- **What movement stretches the crust?** (tension)
- **What movement squeezes the crust?** (compression)
- **What movement twists the crust?** (shear)

Exploring the Main Idea
Illustrate these three types of movement with modeling clay as students go through the text and identify the action you are demonstrating with the clay. Ask:

- **When compression bunches layers together, what landform results?** (fold mountains)

Tell them that the whole subcontinent containing India and Pakistan has been pushing against Asia for eons. Ask:

- **What feature do you think resulted from this massive push?** (the fold mountains of the Himalayas, the highest mountain range in the world.)

What Forces Act on the Crust?

As the plates of the crust move, they can collide. They can pull away from each other. They can also slide past each other. These movements cause three kinds of forces to act on the crust.

- *Tension* stretches or pulls apart the crust.
- *Compression* squeezes or pushes together the crust.
- *Shear* twists, tears, or pushes one part of the crust past another.

Each of these forces can cause a fault to form in the crust. Each can cause movement along a fault. These forces can also result in other kinds of motion in the crust.

As forces inside Earth cause the crust to move upward, the land is built up. Compression can crumple rock layers into wavy folds. Mountains can be formed when two pieces of crust crash together.

The impact squeezes the crust, causing it to crumple into huge folds. Mountains made of crumpled and folded layers of rock are called *fold mountains*. The Appalachians, the Alps, and the Himalayas are all ranges of fold mountains.

Tension and shear can also build up the crust. Mountains can be formed as the crust is pulled apart. How?

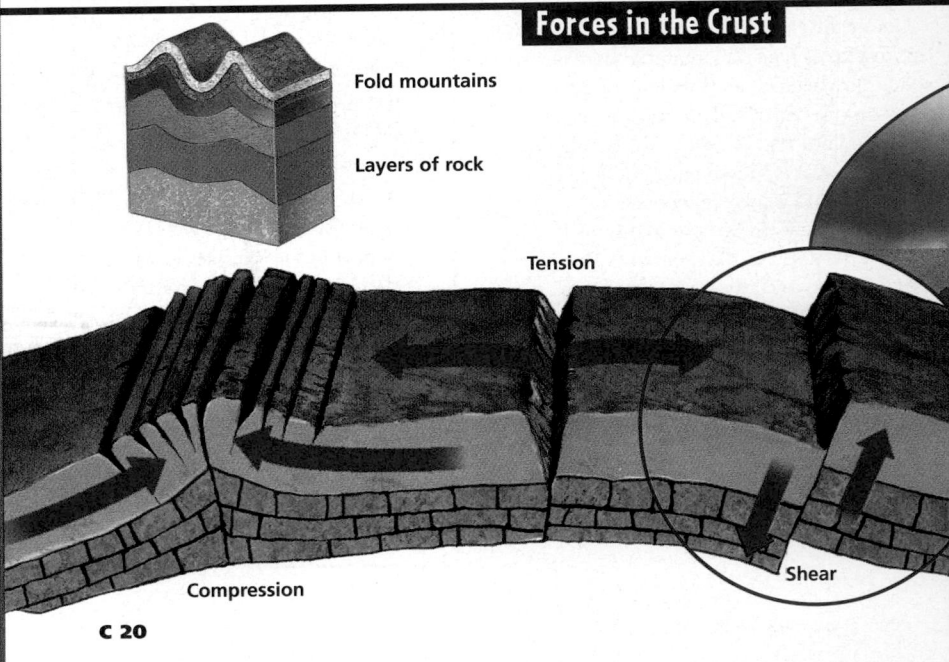

Forces in the Crust

Fold mountains

Layers of rock

Tension

Compression

Shear

C 20

BLACKLINE Interpret Illustrations

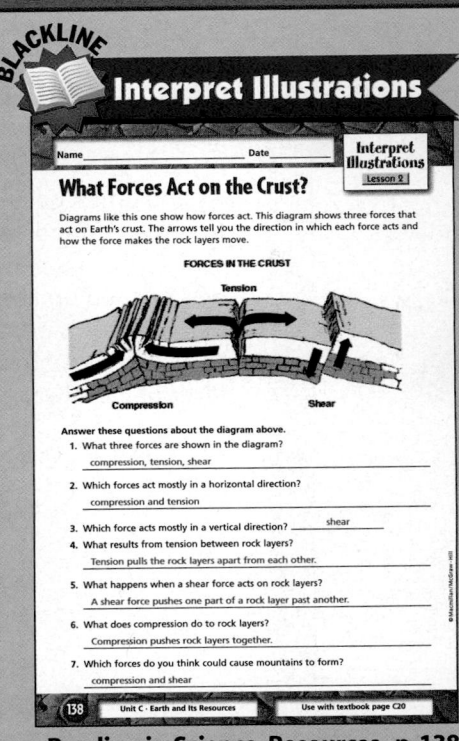

Reading in Science Resources, p. 138

Hot molten rock deep below Earth's surface, called **magma**, rises upward. If magma reaches the surface, it may flow out as **lava**.

Lava flows out or is hurled out when a volcano erupts. A volcano is building a new island off the coast of Iceland. Its lava is gushing up through a crack between two pieces of crust that are being pulled apart.

Tension and shear also cause great blocks of crust to break apart cleanly and move along faults. Blocks of crust moving along a fault can form *fault-block mountains*. A vast region of fault-block mountains known as the Basin and Range Province blankets several western states (see map).

Surtsey, an island near Iceland, is forming from an undersea volcano.

▶ **What are three forces that act on Earth's crust?**

Tension is a force that pulls the crust apart; compression is a force that pushes the crust together; shear is a force that pushes one part of the crust past another.

Fault-block mountains

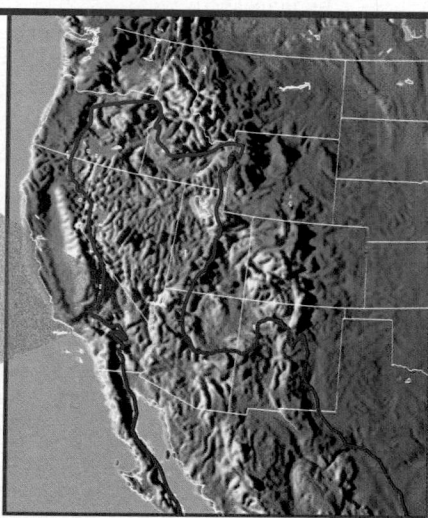

Basin and Range Province

C 21

 English Language Learners

Volcanic Display

Challenge students to make a display of models or drawings of the different types of volcanoes and eruptions. They can use clay or papier mâché for models and can make little flags out of toothpicks and post-it notes. The flags can be used to label features. Students can then present their work in their own words. **Kinesthetic; Spatial**

 **Reading Strategy**

Cause and Effect

Developing Reading Skills
Ask students to write a brief outline to explain what causes a volcano to erupt. They can also create a flow chart of the steps involved, with arrows going from the cause to the effect. **Logical**

Exploring the Main Idea

Use a half-filled tube of toothpaste to model a volcano. Press hard enough on the tube for the toothpaste to ooze out the top. Ask:

- **If this toothpaste tube acts as a model of a volcano, what does the toothpaste inside the tube represent?** (magma)
- **What does the toothpaste that comes out of the tube represent?** (lava)

Push on the tube hard enough to hurl the toothpaste out of the tube and onto a surface. Discuss the explosive power of volcanoes.

Students may find it interesting to learn that many formulas of toothpaste contain volcanic rock. Pumice from volcanoes is used as a mild abrasive.

▶**After Reading**

Have students answer the red question in the student book as **ongoing assessment**.

 **Technology**

- **Science Experiences Videotapes**
  Volcanoes: Churning and Burning
  (Package 5)

Developing Vocabulary

magma The word comes from a Greek root, meaning "thick ointment," and refers to molten rock before it has reached the surface.

lava Ask students if they have seen news photographs of volcanoes erupting. Explain that the material flowing out of a volcano is *lava*. Point out that *magma* and *lava* are the identical substances. Their different names refer solely to whether they are above or below Earth's surface.

What Other Forces Shape Earth's Surface?

Before Reading
Have students try to answer the red question at the top of the page.

Exploring the Main Idea
Have a student demonstrate how rocks can weather by using two pieces of chalk to model limestone. Tell students that limestone and chalk are both made from the same material. Then ask the student to rub the two pieces together until a pile of chalk dust forms. (The "rubbing" should be done in a large, clear plastic bag or box. Hold the bag open while the student rubs the chalk together.) Ask:

- **What process is being modeled here?** (weathering)

Now ask a volunteer to blow on the pile of dust. (Close the bag or box so that the chalk dust does not spread into the room.) Ask:

- **What agent of erosion is being demonstrated?** (wind)

Now take a piece of chalk and drop some vinegar on it. Ask:

- **What do you observe?** (bubbling)

- **What process is this modeling?** (acid eating away at limestone rock)

Developing Vocabulary

weathering Water, air, and temperature changes create *weathering*. The name for this process can be easily remembered if students think of an old building or signboard from which the paint is peeling. Ask students to look for examples of weather-beaten structures in their own neighborhood.

erosion This word comes from a Latin root meaning "a gnawing away." Tell students that while *weathering* may imply a gradual breaking down or wearing out, *erosion* actually suggests the "gnawing away" of a landscape. Ask students to look for places in their neighborhood where erosion needs to be controlled and then propose a solution to the problem.

What Other Forces Shape Earth's Surface?

While movements of the crust are building up Earth's surface, other forces are at work breaking it down. These processes are known as **weathering** (WETH·uhr·ing) and **erosion** (i·ROH·zhuhn). Weathering is the breaking down of the materials of Earth's crust into smaller pieces. Erosion is the picking up and carrying away of the pieces. Weathering and erosion have been going on for billions of years. They both happen in many ways.

Physical Weathering

Weathering happens when the crust is exposed to water, air, and changes in temperature. How do these break down rocks?

Water can break down the crust in many ways. Water can dissolve some minerals right out of the crust. Moving water can make pieces of rock bang into each other. Small chips can break

Rounded pebbles near a churning river

off the surface of the rock. This causes the rock to get smaller and rounder. The churning waters of a stream can wear down big pieces of rock into small rounded pebbles.

Wind is moving air. The wind blows sand and other broken bits of rock over Earth's surface. These particles also wear away rock.

If the temperature drops low enough, water can freeze. When water freezes it expands, or takes up more space. Water freezing in cracks in rocks expands against the rock. The force of the expanding water is so great that it can split the rock apart.

Limestone cavern

Rock formation carved by wind-blown sand

C 22

Reading Strategy

Cause and Effect
Developing Reading Skills
Ask students to write a brief outline to explain what causes weathering of Earth's surface. Students can summarize their answer by making a graphic organizer, with two columns, Physical and Chemical, and facts about each kind of weathering under the appropriate heading. **Linguistic; Spatial**

Science Background

Limestone Caverns
Underground caverns are formed when water eats away at underground limestone. Even though water can dissolve only a tenth of an inch of limestone in a year, these caverns can be enormous. Inside the cavern, formations called stalagmites and stalactites can often be found.

The action of plant roots also causes rocks to weather and erode.

Changes in temperature also cause rock to expand and contract. A rock may be made of a number of different materials. Sometimes one part of a rock expands or contracts more than another part. This difference can cause one part of the rock to push or pull against another part of the rock. Some geologists think that this eventually can cause the rock to break.

Chemical Weathering

Air contains gases that react chemically to form new substances. Oxygen in air reacts with iron to form rust. Carbon dioxide and sulfur dioxide in air react with rain to form acids. These acids eat away at limestone rocks. A limestone cavern was once solid rock. Acid rainwater seeping through the rock dissolved part of it. It "ate away" a huge hole—the cavern.

Houses near the shore may be affected by erosion.

Erosion

Erosion is the carrying away of pieces of weathered rock by gravity, water, wind, and ice. Piece by piece erosion can carry away a boulder, a hill, or even a whole mountain range!

The greatest agent of erosion is water. From the moment a drop of water falling from the sky first hits the ground, it erodes the land.

It may not seem like much, but think of how many raindrops fall in a rainstorm. Altogether they can move a lot of soil.

Once water reaches the ground, it begins to flow downhill. Moving water can push and carry things along with it. Water running downhill picks up pieces of rock and carries them downhill. The faster the water is moving, the bigger the pieces of rock it can move.

 **How do weathering and erosion work together to shape Earth's surface?**

Weathering breaks down Earth's surface, and erosion carries away the broken-down pieces.

C 23

Developing the Main Idea

Encourage students to recall cracks or potholes they have seen in sidewalks or roads. Note that ice can cause cracks in these surfaces in the same way that it breaks apart natural rocks.

Exploring the Main Idea

Model splash erosion by filling a small dish with loose soil. Put the dish on a piece of white paper. Use a dropper to drop water from about three feet above the soil. Ask a volunteer to measure how far the soil splashed from the dish. Then repeat from six feet. Ask:

- **When did the soil splash more?** (When the water was dropped from a greater distance.)

- **From what you observed, what is one way to help prevent splash erosion?** (Do something to keep the water from falling a great distance.)

Thinking Further: *Inferring*
Ask:

- **How do you think plants can help prevent splash erosion?** (Rainwater bounces off the plants before it hits the soil. The water travels just a short distance from the plant to the soil, which lessens the amount of splash erosion.)

▶After Reading

Have students answer the red question in the student book as **ongoing assessment**.

How Can Wind and
Ice Erode Rock?

Before Reading
Have students try to answer the red question at the top of the page?

Exploring the Main Idea
Use an ice cube, some sand, and a bar of soap to perform the demonstrations described in the text. Then let the ice cube melt in a dish. Ask:

- **What happens to the rocks in a glacier after the ice melts?** (The rocks will be left at the place to which they were carried by the glacier.)

▶**After Reading**
Have students answer the red question in the student book as **ongoing assessment**.

How Can Wind and
Ice Erode Rock?

Wind is moving air. Wind can push things along with it, just like moving water. Wind does not exert as hard a push as water moving at the same speed, however. Therefore, wind mostly erodes pieces of rock that are the size of sand particles or smaller.

Ice also causes a lot of erosion. The Margerie Glacier in Alaska is a moving river of ice. It may not move as quickly as water, but don't underestimate its power. When the ice of a glacier freezes onto rock and then the glacier moves downhill, the rock is torn right out of the ground. This glacier can carry chunks of rock bigger than your house with ease.

Glaciers also wear away the land as they flow over it. Place an ice cube in some sand for a minute or two. Then look at the bottom of the ice cube. What has become frozen into the bottom of the ice cube? Now rub the bottom of the ice cube on a bar of soap. What happens to the surface of the bar of soap?

Rocks of all sizes become frozen into the bottom of a glacier. As the glacier moves, the rock beneath it is scratched and worn down.

▷ **How do wind and ice cause erosion?**
Wind picks up small particles and moves them; ice freezes onto rock and scrapes away surfaces; glaciers tear rocks from the ground as they move.

The Margerie Glacier in Alaska

C 24

Math MiniLesson

Divide by Decimals

Develop Suppose a glacier moves 1.5 m each year. How many years will it take the glacier to move a distance of 43.5 m? You can divide to solve the problem.

Find: 43.5 ÷ 1.5

Multiply both the dividend and divisor by 10 to make the divisor a whole number.

$$1.5\overline{)43.5}$$

Place the decimal point in the quotient. Divide.

```
      29.
 15 )435.
     30
     135
     135
       0
```

Practice Divide.

1. 53.5 ÷ 8.2 (6.5)
2. 741.15 ÷ 40.5 (18.3)

Activity Have students use multiplication to check their answers for exercises 1 and 2.

Inclusion

Crumbling Glaciers
Have students research glaciers in Antarctica that are currently breaking off and crumbling into the ocean. The largest one so far was the size of Rhode Island. Ask students to find out if scientists think this is a normal process or is something new. Is a similar process occurring in the Arctic? Have students report and discuss their findings with the class.
Linguistic

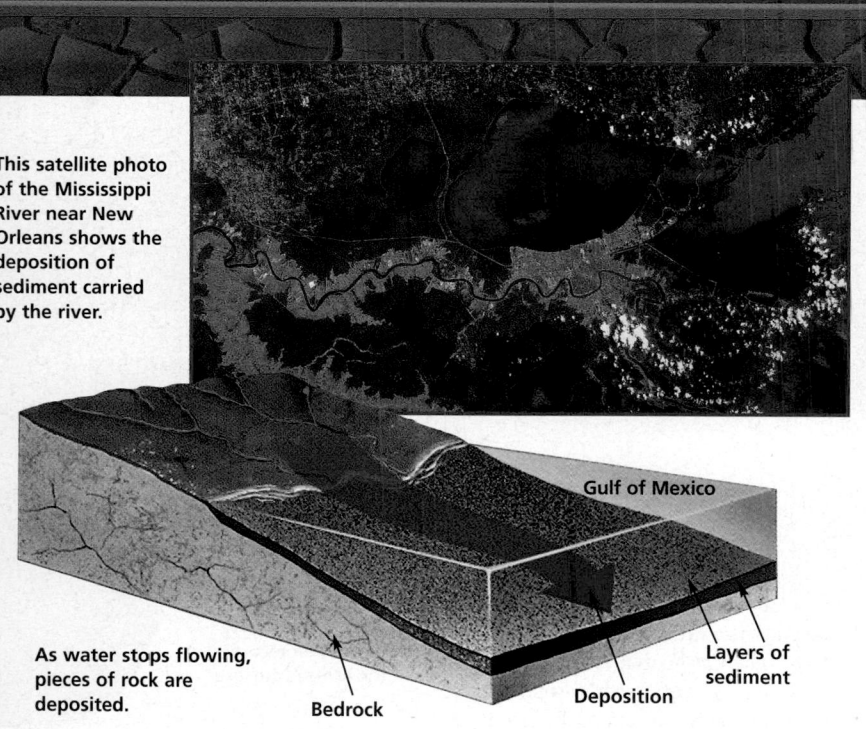

This satellite photo of the Mississippi River near New Orleans shows the deposition of sediment carried by the river.

Gulf of Mexico

Layers of sediment

Deposition

Bedrock

As water stops flowing, pieces of rock are deposited.

Where Do Eroded Rocks Go?

What happens to pieces of rock that are carried along by wind, moving ice, or moving water? A fast wind eventually slows down. A glacier stops moving and eventually melts at its front end and sides. All streams eventually slow down and end when they flow into a large body of water, such as a lake or ocean.

When water stops moving, it also stops carrying along bits and pieces of rock. The pieces of rock are dropped to the bottom of the stream, lake, or ocean. The dropping off of bits of eroded rock is called **deposition** (dep·uh·ZISH·uhn).

Deposition also takes place when glaciers melt and winds stop blowing. Layer by layer, pile after pile, bits and pieces of rock deposited by water, wind, and ice build up Earth's surface.

Very slowly deposition may fill up depressions, or basins, in Earth's surface. It can build up land along shorelines and at the end of rivers. Deposition does not seem as dramatic as colliding continents. However, the slow, steady work of deposition is one of the greatest constructive actions on Earth.

READING Sequence of Events
What happens to rocks after they break down?

Rocks erode and are then deposited.

C 25

Where Do Eroded Rocks Go?

Before Reading
Have students try to answer the red question above the text on this page.

Developing the Main Idea
Ask students to visualize the process of deposition as they read through the text. They can think about a beach, where the waves are constantly depositing sand, gravel, crushed seashells, and other organic materials. They can think about the "mighty Mississippi," slowing down as it reaches the Gulf of Mexico. Encourage them to picture the motion involved with deposition.

▶ After Reading
Have students answer the red question in the student book as **ongoing assessment**.

Developing Vocabulary

deposition Tell students that the word-parts in this word literally refer to taking something "out of position." Ask students if they can describe places of deposition along river banks, streambeds, or the ocean shore.

Reading MiniLesson

Sequence of Events

Develop Have volunteer students act out a simple sequence of events by picking up a book, carrying it a given distance, then setting it down. Ask other class members to describe the events in order, focusing on action verbs and modifiers. (picked up, carried, put down)

Practice Have students reread the first two paragraphs, name the events by looking for action verbs, and list those verbs in order. (carried along, slows down) To reinforce the time order, ask students to reread paragraph 3 and describe where they'd find the oldest rocks. (bottom layer)

Reading Strategy

Paraphrase
Developing Reading Skills
Ask students to write paragraphs that explain in their own words what the following terms mean: *weathering, erosion,* and *deposition.* Have students share and compare their writings.

What Forces Shape the Moon's Surface?

Before Reading
Have students try to answer the red question at the top of the first text column.

Developing the Main Idea
Ask students to review what they have learned in this lesson as they begin thinking about the Moon. Ask:

- **What factors are needed for erosion and weathering to happen?** (water, air, ice, changes in temperature, or chemicals in the atmosphere)

- **What preconditions make it likely that earthquakes will occur?** (The movement of plates in Earth's crust.)

- **What conditions precede the eruption of volcanoes?** (Hot molten rocks underneath Earth's surface begin to rise upward.)

▶ After Reading
Have students answer the red question in the student book as **ongoing assessment**.

Developing Vocabulary

meteorite Rhymes help to remember three related words that are easy to confuse. A mete**OR** is any body entering Earth from space. (Down they **POUR**.) While it is still in the sky (in the **VOID**) it is a meteor**OID**. When it lands (on a **SITE**) it is a meteor**ITE**.

What Forces Shape the Moon's Surface?

Earth's Moon, our nearest neighbor in space, is a far different place from Earth. There is no evidence of earthquake faults as on Earth's crust. There are no erupting volcanoes. In fact, there is no evidence of any of the kinds of motion that Earth's crust has.

Without air and water, there can be very little weathering or erosion. The Moon has almost no air or water. There are no streams, no glaciers, and no wind. The only weathering and erosion is due to the impact of rocks from space hitting the Moon's surface.

These rocks from space that strike a surface are called **meteorites**. Some craters formed by the impact of meteorites are big enough to be seen from Earth. Others are so tiny the entire crater is on a single mineral crystal.

Can meteorites also strike Earth's surface and produce craters? Yes. However, Earth's atmosphere protects its surface from many such impacts.

Meteorite impacts have been recorded on the Moon's surface.

Rocks from space "burn up" as they pass through Earth's atmosphere. The Moon has little atmosphere. How does that fact affect the Moon's surface?

Meteorite impacts shatter rocks on the Moon and also create a lot of heat. The heat melts the rock. Pieces of rock may melt together, and droplets and globs of molten rock can splatter outward. Over time continual meteorite impacts break down the rock. The end result is a mixture of shattered pieces of rock, rock droplets, and melted-together bits of rock.

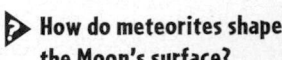 **How do meteorites shape the Moon's surface?**

Meteorites strike the Moon and create craters. They also create heat, which breaks apart and melts rocks on the Moon's surface.

C 26

 Reading Strategy

Paraphrase
Developing Reading Skills
Ask students to use their own words in paraphrasing an explanation of the difference between the Moon's surface and Earth's. Students can present their paraphrases orally within small groups. Group members can help modify the statements for clarity and conciseness.

Science Background

Extraterrrestrial Geology
Other planets may have features similar to Earth's, but the features may not be formed in the same way. For example, Mars has a single plate, so volcanoes and hills cannot be explained in terms of plates moving against each other or cracks forming between plates.

Lesson Review

Why It Matters

Natural forces change Earth and the other planets in our solar system. As the solar system has been explored, evidence of surface changes and erosion has been found on other worlds. There are perhaps thousands of volcanoes on Venus. The largest volcano in the solar system is Mars's Olympus Mons. It is 24 km (15 mi) high and 550 km (344 mi) across.

Some of Jupiter's moons also show evidence of constructive and destructive forces. The *Voyager* and *Galileo* spacecraft even sent back pictures showing some of Io's volcanoes erupting. The moons Ganymede, Callisto, and Europa have water and ice. The presence of water, organic compounds, and internal heat mean life may be possible on Europa.

Think and Write

1. What are some types of evidence that show Earth's crust has moved?

2. What are three types of forces acting on Earth's crust?

3. How are earthquakes measured?

4. What is the difference between weathering and erosion?

5. **Critical Thinking** How do fault-block mountains compare with fold mountains?

L·I·N·K·S

SOCIAL STUDIES LINK

Research earthquakes. Learn more about earthquakes in the United States. Where are they most common? What happened to the cities where they occurred? How did people overcome these disasters and plan for the future? Write a report to share what you have learned.

LITERATURE LINK

Read *Quinto's Volcano* to learn about a boy who overcomes his fear of the sea and saves his village. Try the activities at the end of the book.

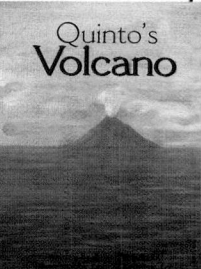

WRITING LINK

Write a paragraph. How can people plan ahead to prepare for an earthquake or other force that can change the crust suddenly?

TECHNOLOGY LINK

At the Computer Visit **www.mhscience02.com** for more links.

C 27

---

3 Lesson Review

Answers to Think and Write

1. earthquakes, volcanoes, mountains, and even the movement of instruments (pp. C18–C19)

2. tension, compression, and shear (p. C20)

3. They are measured with seismographs. (p. C18)

4. Weathering is the breaking down of materials into smaller pieces; erosion is the picking up and carrying away of the rock pieces. (p. C22)

5. **Critical Thinking** Fault-block mountains are formed by blocks of crust moving along a fault. Fold mountains are formed when compression pushes pieces of the crust together, folding rock layers. (pp. C20–C21)

Summarize

Check students' understanding by having them write a brief summary of the lesson in their own words.

SOCIAL STUDIES LINK

Students' research should concentrate on areas of the West Coast of the United States where most of the country's earthquakes occur. Students may focus on recent earthquakes in San Francisco, Los Angeles, and Seattle.

LITERATURE LINK

Have students read the Grade-Level Science Book, *Quinto's Volcano*. For additional books to read, see page C1·b.

WRITING LINK

Students should write about a variety of preparedness techniques, such as rehearsing building evacuation, having emergency food and water supplies, keeping a flashlight with batteries, and so on. Besides earthquakes, some other crust-changing forces are mudslides, rockfalls, and sinkholes.

Science, Technology, and Society

Waves of Erosion

Objective

■ Weigh the effects of shoreline damage due to erosion.

Build on Prior Knowledge

Ask students if they think we will always have beaches at the ocean. Will they always be the same beaches? Why or why not? (Encourage a lively discussion.)

Waves of Erosion

Developing the Main Idea

Focus on the nature of scientific inquiry by asking such questions as:

■ **Is a high cliff safer from erosion than a low cliff? Why or why not?** (Neither one is safe if waves can reach it. Waves can wear away the base of a cliff no matter how high it is.)

■ **Would you expect to see more erosion at a beach during the summer or winter? Why?** (During winter storms have more force, and waves are stronger.)

■ **What are some factors that affect the rate of erosion at the shore?** (the weather, seasons, the kind of rock in cliffs, the presence of break-waters)

Have you ever stood by the ocean and felt a wave pull the sand from under your feet? Waves constantly carry sand away from a beach, bit by bit.

People who live by beaches can watch their "front yards" slowly disappear. Many beach homes are built on stilts. That puts the buildings above water during high tides and storms. However, if the sand supporting the stilts washes away, the houses fall!

If there are cliffs on a shoreline, the pounding waves can wear away the lowest parts. Eventually the cliffs collapse and fall into the water. Then waves slowly break the rocks into smaller pieces. In time the cliffs will become sand.

Stormy winter weather increases erosion. Fierce winds push the waves, giving them the strength to pick up and carry small stones. The stones pound cliffs along with the waves and help to break the rocks. The stronger wind also pushes waves farther inland.

Some towns truck in sand to replace what's lost. Other towns build breakwaters close to shore. The stone and concrete breakwaters reduce the force of the waves before they reach shore. An island or a sandbar close to shore serves as a natural breakwater.

Nearly all sand and rock removed by wave erosion is deposited elsewhere. Only a small percentage is carried out to sea.

Waves can wear away the sand that supports a beachfront home.

C 28

Reading Strategy

Cause and Effect

Developing Reading Skills
Have students recall places where they have observed erosion and relate those observations to the material presented on pp. C28–C29. In each case they recall ask them what the landscape looked like before the erosion occurred, what caused it, and what the effect of the erosion was.

Science Background

Currents and Erosion
The shoreline is affected by two types of currents, and both cause erosion. Longshore currents move parallel to the shoreline on long, straight beaches. Fast-moving longshore currents pick up sand and carry it down the shore, dropping it when something slows them down. Nearshore or riptide currents hit the beach at a perpendicular angle. Strong and narrow, they, too, can carry off large amounts of sand.

People sometimes build sea walls to try to protect the beaches from pounding waves.

What Did I Learn?

1. Beach homes may be protected from high tides by
   A sea walls
   B stilts
   C breakwaters
   D all of the above

2. The main idea of this story is that
   F people should not live near the beach
   G beaches are affected by erosion
   H towns should build sea walls to protect beaches
   J all of the above

AT THE COMPUTER Visit www.mhscience02.com to learn more about erosion.

C 29

Developing the Main Idea

Explain that plant roots help to slow erosion in fields and along stream beds. Ask students:

■ **Would it be a good idea to plant grass and trees on a cliff overlooking the ocean?** (Probably not. Waves are much stronger and constant than rain and would tear out the plants. Plants above the level of the waves will fall into the ocean anyway when the cliff collapses.)

■ **What would be the best way to protect your home from erosion?** (build it far from the shoreline, where the waves cannot reach it or the ground under it at any time of the year)

■ **How could weathering increase erosion?** (Freezing and thawing could crack rocks in cliffs and make them more likely to break off. It could also weaken them by dissolving minerals in them.)

Test Prep:  What Did I Learn?

1. D

2. G

Summarize

Check students' understanding by having them write a brief summary of this article on erosion in their own words.

 Science Background

Wave Action

Waves not only erode cliffs, but they also create caves, rock arches, and platforms on rocky shorelines. By depositing sand, waves form sand dunes on beaches. If the waves are not strong enough to bring the sand to shore, they drop it in the water, forming sandbars. Sometimes the sand accumulates until it is above water, creating barrier beaches, such as those at Atlantic City in New Jersey, Miami Beach in Florida, and Coney Island in New York.

SCIENCE FOR ALL Advanced Learners

Waves

Have students research how ocean waves are similar to sound waves, light waves, radio waves, and seismic waves. They might make diagrams showing the similarities and differences and then share what they have learned with the class. **Spatial; Linguistic**

LESSON 3
Minerals of Earth's Crust

Objectives

- Explore ways to distinguish between minerals.
- List and compare properties of minerals.
- Contrast ways minerals form.
- Relate uses and properties of minerals.

Resources

- Activity Resources, pp. 89–94
- Reading in Science Resources, pp. 141–146
- Vocabulary Cards
- Reading Aid Transparency C3

Build on Prior Knowledge

Have students discuss what they know about minerals. Ask students to name as many minerals as they can. Make a list on the board. Have students describe each of the minerals. Help students to see that they are describing properties of the minerals.

1 Get Ready

Using the Illustrations

Ask students to discuss the characteristics of the minerals as shown in the picture. Ask how minerals in their natural state appear different from those we see every day. Discuss the *Science Background* at the right and be sure to include precious, semiprecious, and organic gems in the discussion.

LESSON 3
Minerals of Earth's Crust

Vocabulary

mineral, C32
luster, C33
streak, C34
hardness, C34
cleavage, C34
ore, C38
gem, C38

Get Ready

How many substances do you think make up Earth's solid surface, the crust? Would you believe about 2,000? The substances that make up Earth's crust are minerals. The formations you see here at Mono Lake in California are made entirely of a mineral called calcium carbonate. How can you tell one mineral from another?

Process Skill

You observe when you use one or more of the senses to identify or learn about an object or event.

C 30

Science Background

Gems

Gems are minerals that are beautiful, rare, and durable. Precious gems include diamonds, rubies, sapphires, and emeralds. Semiprecious gems include opals, jade, topaz, garnets, aquamarines, zircons, and quartz. Organic gems, made by organisms, include pearls, coral, and amber.

SCIENCE Reading Strategy

Organize Information
Developing Reading Skills
As students read this lesson, ask them to make a chart to organize information about ways to identify minerals.
Spatial; Linguistic

Explore Activity

How Can You Identify a Mineral?

Materials

mineral samples

clear tape

red marker

copper penny or wire

porcelain tile

hand lens

nail

Procedure

1 **Communicate** Use tape and a marker to label each sample with a number. Make a table with the column headings shown. Fill in numbers under "Mineral" to match your samples.

2 **Observe** Use the table shown as a guide to collect data on each sample. Fill in the data in your table. Turn to the table on page C35 for more ideas to fill in "Other."

Drawing Conclusions

1 Use your data and the table below to identify your samples. Were you sure of all your samples? Explain.

2 Which observations were most helpful? Explain.

3 **Going Further: Experiment** How could you make a better Scratch (Hardness) test?

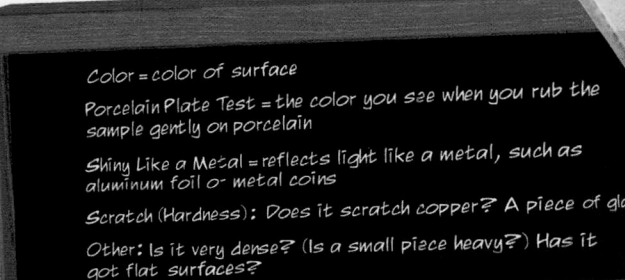

Color = color of surface

Porcelain Plate Test = the color you see when you rub the sample gently on porcelain

Shiny Like a Metal = reflects light like a metal, such as aluminum foil or metal coins

Scratch (Hardness): Does it scratch copper? A piece of glass?

Other: Is it very dense? (Is a small piece heavy?) Has it got flat surfaces?

Mineral	Color	Shiny Like a Metal (Yes/No)	Porcelain Plate Test	Scratch (Hardness)	Other
1.					
2.					

C 31

Alternative Explore Activity

Materials samples of minerals, poster board, scale, measuring cup, water

Classifying Minerals Have students work in small groups to develop ways to classify the mineral samples. They may use color, feel, density, and shape. They may also brainstorm other ways to test the samples. Then ask them to make a poster to describe their results and share their thinking with others.

Spatial; Kinesthetic

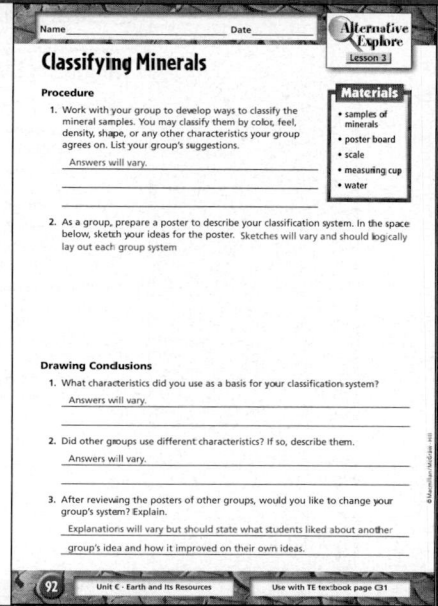

Name_____ Date_____

Alternative Explore
Lesson 3

Classifying Minerals

Procedure

Materials
• samples of minerals
• poster board
• scale
• measuring cup
• water

1. Work with your group to develop ways to classify the mineral samples. You may classify them by color, feel, density, shape, or any other characteristics your group agrees on. List your group's suggestions.

Answers will vary.

2. As a group, prepare a poster to describe your classification system. In the space below, sketch your ideas for the poster. Sketches will vary and should logically lay out each group system

Drawing Conclusions

1. What characteristics did you use as a basis for your classification system?

Answers will vary.

2. Did other groups use different characteristics? If so, describe them.

Answers will vary.

3. After reviewing the posters of other groups, would you like to change your group's system? Explain.

Explanations will vary but should state what students liked about another group's idea and how it improved on their own ideas.

92   Unit C · Earth and Its Resources   Use with TE textbook page C31

Activity Resources, p. 92

Explore Activity

How Can You Identify a Mineral?

Science Process Skills *communicate, observe, experiment*

Resources Activity Resources, pp. 89–91

Pacing 30–40 minutes

Grouping pairs

Procedure

Be Careful! Place the porcelain tile flat on a desk or table when testing for hardness. Do not allow students to lick or taste the samples.

2 When doing the scratch test, guide students to note whether the mineral they are testing is harder or softer than other minerals. They can do this by scratching one against the other. The softer one will get scratched.

Answers to Drawing Conclusions

1 Students' answers will vary depending on the sample. They may not be able to identify all of the samples and may want to do further testing.

2 The porcelain tile test and the hardness test give very specific results. Color was least reliable because a mineral can often come in many colors.

3 Students may say that the scratch test could include other materials, such as various types of nails and files.

Inquiry Students can ask their own questions to explore such as what other methods could be used to identify minerals.

Technology

■ When time is short, preview the activity with the **Explore Activity Video.**

How Can You Identify a Mineral?

Before Reading
Have students try to answer the red question at the top of the page.

Exploring the Main Idea
Pass around labeled samples of minerals, including copper wire, talcum powder, aluminum foil, table salt, and rock salt. Use these samples as models when discussing the properties of minerals.

Developing the Main Idea
Invite students to investigate how minerals are important to human life. Ask them to find a definition of *mineral* in a biology or health book and compare it with the one they are learning here. Challenge them to list the minerals important for life, how they are used, and where they come from.

Developing Vocabulary

mineral Point out that this word can refer to anything that is mined (salt, sulfur, sand, petroleum, water, or natural gas). It can, however, also refer to gemstones and jewelry such as turquoise or diamonds.

Read to Learn

Main Idea Earth's crust contains many types of minerals with important uses.

How Can You Identify a Mineral?

What do diamond rings, talcum powder, and aluminum foil have in common? They are made from minerals. So are copper wire, teeth fillings, china dishes, and table salt.

With so many differences in minerals, what can they have in common? Minerals are solid materials of Earth's crust. Like all matter they are made of elements. Some minerals, like gold, silver, copper, and carbon, are made of one element. Most minerals are chemical compounds, that is, two or more elements joined together.

Whether it is an element or a compound, each mineral has a definite chemical composition. Scientists can classify minerals by identifying the elements or compounds they are made of.

As minerals form, their atoms and molecules fall into fixed patterns. These patterns cause minerals to form geometric shapes, called *crystals*. Different patterns form different crystal shapes. You can see the six main crystal shapes on these pages.

No two minerals are exactly alike. Each mineral has a different composition. Each has its own set of properties

Crystal Shapes

Hexagonal	Tetragonal	Cubic

 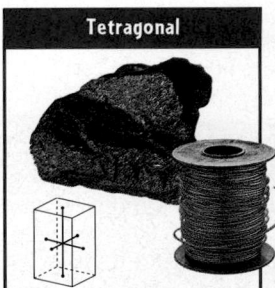 

The "lead" in a lead pencil is not the metal element lead at all. It is the mineral graphite (GRAF·ight), which is a form of the element carbon.

The mineral chalcopyrite (kal·kuh·PIGH·right) is a compound made of the elements copper, iron, and sulfur. It is where much of our copper comes from. Copper is used for wire, coins, pots, and pans.

Rock salt, which is used to melt ice, is the mineral halite (HAL·ight). It is a compound made of the elements sodium and chlorine.

C 32

Math | MiniLesson

Sums of Angles in Triangles and Quadrilaterals

Develop If one angle of a triangle is 75° and another angle is 45°, what is the measure of the unknown angle?

The sum of the angle measures of any triangle is 180°.

$75° + 45° + n = 180°$

$n = 180° - 75° - 45°$

$n = 60°$

The unknown angle measures 60°.

The known angles in a quadrilateral are 120°, 32° and 45°, what is the measure of the unknown angle?

The sum of the angle measures of any quadrilateral is 360°.

$120° + 30° + 45° + n = 360°$

$n = 360° + 120° - 30° + 45°$

$n = 165°$

The unknown angle measures 165°.

Practice Solve.

1. $90° + 30° + n = 180°$
   $(n = 60°)$

2. $150° + 95° + 75° + n = 360°$
   $(n = 40°)$

Lesson Outline

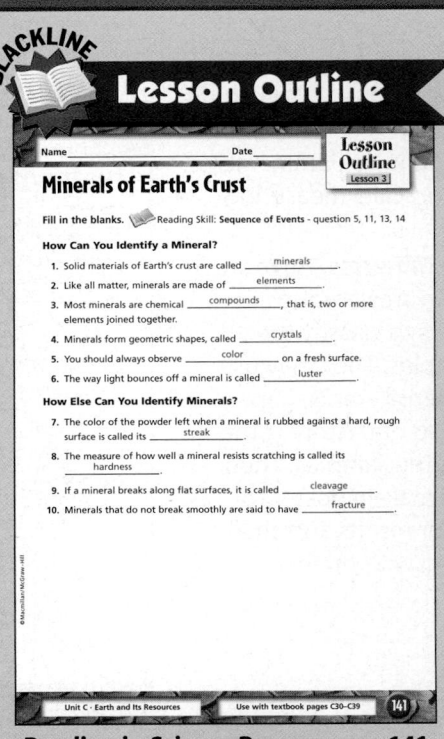

Reading in Science Resources, p. 141

that you can use to tell them apart. Crystal shape is one property. However, telling the exact chemical composition of most minerals or their crystal shape isn't easy. This requires special instruments.

Here are some simpler properties to use.

- The color of the outer surface of the mineral is the first thing you see. However, if a mineral is exposed to weather, it can become discolored. Therefore, you should always observe color on a fresh surface. Color alone cannot be used to identify most minerals. Why not? Some minerals come in a variety of colors, and some colors are common to many minerals.

- **Luster** is the way light bounces off a mineral. Minerals with a metallic luster are shiny, like metals. Graphite has a metallic luster.

  Minerals with a nonmetallic luster may look shiny or dull. Nonmetallic luster can be described as glassy, waxy, pearly, earthy, oily, or silky. Talc has a nonmetallic luster often described as oily.

▷ **What are the characteristics of a mineral?**

A mineral is a solid material of Earth's crust, and can be made of one or more elements with a definite chemical composition. Minerals form into six main crystal shapes.

Orthorhombic

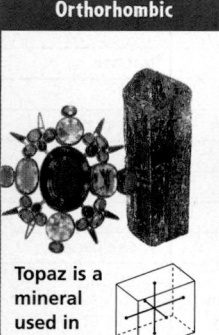

Topaz is a mineral used in many kinds of jewelry. It comes in many colors—pink, pale blue, and even yellow or white.

Monoclinic

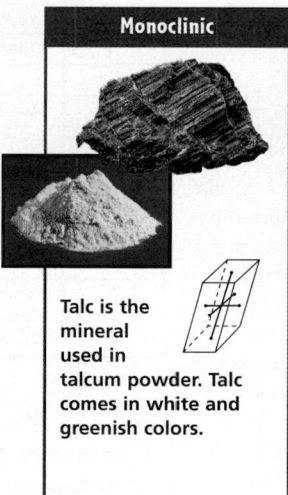

Talc is the mineral used in talcum powder. Talc comes in white and greenish colors.

Triclinic

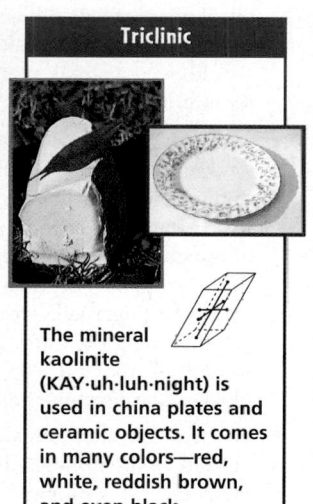

The mineral kaolinite (KAY·uh·luh·night) is used in china plates and ceramic objects. It comes in many colors—red, white, reddish brown, and even black.

C 33

Using the Illustrations
Students can compare the solid geometrical shapes in the crystal shapes examples. They can compare number, length, and position of axes and faces.

Developing the Main Idea
Show students as many samples or pictures of minerals as possible and ask them to classify the minerals. Ask:

■ **What properties can you use to classify these minerals?** (Answers should include the properties mentioned in the text.)

▶ **After Reading**
Have students answer the red question in the student book as **ongoing assessment.**

Developing Vocabulary

luster While this word specifically refers to the brightness with which a mineral shines, it also has a more general reference to brightness as such, as in *the luster of her eyes.*

Interpret Illustrations

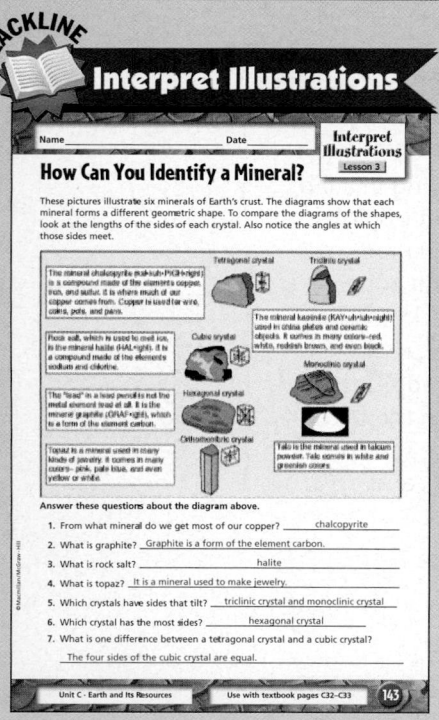

Reading in Science Resources, p. 143

English Language Learners

Crystal Shapes
Review the names of crystal shapes with students: *tetragonal, hexagonal, cubic, monoclinic, triclinic, orthorhombic.* Challenge them to find the meaning of each name. Ask them to find the meanings of the prefixes: *tetra-* (4), *hexa-* (6), *mono-* (1), *tri-* (3), and *ortho-* (8). Challenge them to find other words that begin with these prefixes. Also ask them to find out what *-gonal* (angle), *-clinic* (incline), and *-rhombic* (turn) mean. Invite them to find other words with those terms. **Linguistic**

Inclusion

Mineral Displays
Invite students to start a collection of the minerals they consider attractive. They might create posters to display the samples. Ask them to label each sample and to note how the mineral is used. Also ask students to describe why they picked the samples they did. **Spatial**

How Else Can You Identify Minerals?

Before Reading
Have students try to answer the red question at the top of the page.

Exploring the Main Idea
Demonstrate the value of the streak test by testing various colored samples of quartz (clear, purple, rose, milky). Show how the streak is always white or colorless.

Developing the Main Idea
Tell students that the color of the mineral is not as accurate in identifying the mineral as the streak color. Nonmetallic minerals usually leave a pale or colorless streak. Metallic minerals leave a dark streak. Ask:

- **Do you think the streak color is always the same color as the powdered mineral?** (Yes.)

Point out that we cannot use a streak test on minerals that are too hard to leave a powdery residue when tested.

READING

Tables

A fingernail scratches talc and gypsum; a glass plate scratches apatite, fluorite, calcite, gypsum, and talc.

Developing Vocabulary

streak Point out that the streak on the plate can be thought of as similar to a streak of lightning.

hardness Have students notice that hardness cannot be judged by eye; the mineral must be scratched in some way to determine the nature of this property.

cleavage From an Old English word meaning "to split," this word emphasizes the charateristic way that minerals split apart.

Reinforce the vocabulary words by actually demonstrating their meaning, using appropriate minerals.

Hematite has a blackish color but a reddish streak.

Galena has three cleavage planes. It breaks into cubes.

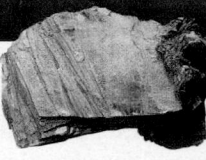
Mica has one cleavage plane. It breaks into sheets.

How Else Can You Identify Minerals?

Here are three other ways to identify a mineral.

- **Streak** is the color of the powder left when a mineral is rubbed against a hard, rough surface. Rub it against a porcelain streak plate. The streak is always the same for a given mineral, even if the mineral varies in color.

  The streak may not be the color of the outer surface of the mineral. Fool's gold, pyrite, is brassy yellow, but it has a greenish black streak. Gold has a yellow streak. You would need a streak plate to identify real gold.

- **Hardness** is a measure of how well a mineral resists scratching. Soft minerals are easily scratched. Mohs' scale of hardness is a numbered list of minerals. Talc, number 1, is the softest mineral. It can be scratched with your fingernail. Any item on the list, including the tools, can scratch something above it. You can use the tools to help find the hardness.

- The way a mineral breaks is also helpful. Some minerals have **cleavage**. This property is the tendency of a mineral to break along flat surfaces. Cleavage is described by the number of directions, or planes, along which the mineral breaks.

C 34

READING

Tables

Which mineral does a fingernail scratch? Which does a glass plate scratch?

Mohs' Scale of Hardness		
Hardness	Sample Mineral	Tool
1	Talc	
2	Gypsum	
		Fingernail
3	Calcite	
		Copper penny/wire
4	Fluorite	
		Iron nail
5	Apatite	
		Glass plate
6	Feldspar	
		Steel file
7	Quartz	
		Streak plate
8	Topaz	
9	Corundum	
10	Diamond	

Science Background

Mohs' Scale

Mineralogists working in a lab will often have a set of Mohs minerals for determining where a test mineral appears on the Mohs' scale. In the field, they may use other, more common, materials. In addition to those mentioned in the text, they can use coarse sandpaper (9), a penknife (5.5), and a #2 pencil (1).

A form of calcite shows double image because it refracts light twice as you look through it.

How is hornblende different from quartz? From feldspar? From mica?

Properties of Minerals

Mineral	Color(s)	Luster (Shiny as Metals)	Porcelain Plate Test (Streak)	Cleavage (Number)	Hardness (Tools Scratched By)	Density (Compared with Water)
Gypsum	colorless, gray, white, brown	no	white	varies	2 (all six tools)	2.3
Quartz	colorless, various colors	no	none	no	7 (streak plate)	2.6
Pyrite	brassy, yellow	yes	greenish black	no	6 (steel file, streak plate)	5.0
Calcite	colorless, white, pale blue	no	colorless, white	yes—3	3 (all but fingernail)	2.7
Galena	steel gray	yes	gray to black	yes—3 (cubes)	2.5 (all but fingernail)	7.5
Feldspar	gray, green, yellow, white	no	colorless	yes—2	6 (steel file, streak plate)	2.5
Mica	colorless, silvery, black	no	white	yes—1 (thin sheets)	2–3 (all but fingernail)	3.0
Hornblende	green to black	no	gray to white	yes—2	5–6 (steel file, streak plate)	3.4
Bauxite	gray, red, brown, white	no	gray	no	1–3 (all but fingernail)	2.0 – 2.5
Hematite	black, gray, red-brown	yes	red or red-brown	no	1–6 (all)	5.3

Many minerals do not break smoothly. They are said to have *fracture*. Quartz, for example, shows jagged edges when it breaks.

Some minerals have special properties that help you identify them. Magnetite, for example, is attracted by a magnet. Some minerals are more *dense* than others. That means they have a lot of mass packed into a given volume. *Density* makes a sample feel quite heavy. Gold, silver, and galena are examples of dense minerals.

▷ **How do tests for streak, hardness, and cleavage help you tell minerals apart?**

The streak test shows the color a mineral makes on a plate; the hardness test shows how hard it is compared with other minerals; the cleavage test shows whether a mineral breaks along flat surfaces. **C 35**

Developing the Main Idea

Ask students to compare the colors of the minerals with their streak. Ask:

- **Would any of these minerals float on water?** (No.) **Why not?** (They all have densities that are greater than that of water.)
- **Which mineral in the table is the hardest?** (quartz) **Why?** (It has the highest rating on the Mohs' scale.)

Remind students that metallic minerals usually have darker streak colors than nonmetallic minerals.

- **Which minerals in the table do you think are metallic?** (pyrite, galena, hematite) **Why?** (They have dark streak colors; they are shiny.)

- Differences from quartz: Hornblende has a darker color, leaves a streak, cleaves into two directions (or planes), is not as hard, but is more dense.
- Differences from feldspar: It leaves a gray to white streak and is more dense.
- Differences from mica: It cleaves into two directions and is harder and denser.

▶**After Reading**
Have students answer the red question in the student book as **ongoing assessment.**

Interpret Illustrations

Name_____ Date_____

Interpret Illustrations Lesson 3

How Else Can You Identify Minerals?

This table shows calcite and its properties. Read about each of the properties of calcite.

MINERAL	COLOR(S)	LUSTER (Shiny as Metals)	PORCELAIN PLATE TEST (Streak)	CLEAVAGE (Number)	HARDNESS (Tools scratched by)	DENSITY (Compared with water)
Calcite	colorless, white, pale blue	no	colorless, white	yes—3	3 (all but fingernail)	2.7

Answer these questions about the table above.

1. Why is the color of calcite listed as colorless, white, or pale blue?
   There are different colors of calcite.

2. What does it mean that calcite has no luster?
   It does not shine.

3. What would be a good title for this table?
   Properties of Calcite

4. How would you test for hardness?
   You would try to scratch it with various tools and then compare against a scale.

5. What does a density of 2.7 mean?
   The sample is 2.7 times as dense as water.

144 Unit C - Earth and Its Resources   Use with textbook page C35

Reading in Science Resources, p. 144

Math | MiniLesson

Compare and Order Decimals

Develop Order from least to greatest:

1.3121, 1.29, 1.315

You can order decimals by comparing their digits.

First, line up the decimal points. Start at the left. Compare the digits.

1.**3**121   1.**2**9   1.**3**15

3 > 2, So, 1.29 is the least.

Now compare 1.3121 and 1.315

1.3**1**21   1.3**1**5

5 > 2, So, 1.315 is the greatest.

The decimals from least to greatest are: 1.29, 1.3121, 1.315

Practice Order from least to greatest.

1. 40.9, 40.88, 41.2
   (40.88, 40.9, 41.2)

2. 0.3, 0.306, 0.293, 0.36
   (0.293, 0.3, 0.306, 0.36)

Activity Have students list 3 decimals that are between 5 and 5.1.

How Do Minerals Form?

Before Reading
Have students try to answer the red question at the top of the page.

Exploring the Main Idea
Show students some rock samples. Pass them around with a hand lens and ask students to pick out the minerals. Chip some of the rocks apart and compare the pieces with the rest of the rock. Pass these pieces and the rock around in a dish.

Developing the Main Idea
Point out that some of the most common rock-forming minerals include quartz, feldspars, mica, calcite, hematite, and gypsum.

How Do Minerals Form?

Where do you find minerals? The answer is simple—in the ground. Minerals make up the rocks of the crust. If you examine rocks with a hand lens, you can often find some of the most common rock-forming minerals in the rock.

How do minerals form? Many form when hot liquid rock, or magma, cools and hardens into a solid. Magma is very hot, and its molecules move very fast. When magma cools, its molecules slow down and get closer together. Then they connect into a pattern, forming crystals. The longer it takes magma to cool, the more time the crystals have to grow, and the larger they get.

Some of the rarest minerals form deep within the Earth. The temperatures are high at great depths. The weight of rocks overhead presses down on rocks below, like a huge pressure cooker. The heat and pressure produce minerals such as diamonds. Movements of Earth's crust then bring the minerals near the surface, where they can be mined.

Diamond

Crystals can form from the cooling of hot water. Water heated by magma inside the Earth is rich in dissolved minerals. Hot water can hold more dissolved minerals than cold water. As the water cools, it is able to hold less of the dissolved minerals. The minerals that can no longer stay dissolved form crystals. The huge quartz crystal shown below formed in this way.

The specks you see in this rock include minerals such as quartz, feldspar, hornblende, and mica.

Granite quarry

Quartz crystal

C 36

The piles of brightly colored minerals in this hot spring form when the heated water cools as it is exposed to the air.

These crystals then slowly settle to the bottom of the water.

Minerals can also form from evaporation. Ocean water contains many dissolved substances. As the ocean water evaporates, the substances that were dissolved form crystals. Common table salt is mined in areas that were once covered with salt water. The salt is a mineral, halite. It was left behind when an ancient sea evaporated.

READING Sequence of Events
In what ways do minerals form?

Answers may include: when magma cools and crystals form; when rocks are put under great pressure and heat and are then brought near the surface; when hot water cools and minerals settle out and crystallize; when water evaporates and minerals that were dissolved form crystals.

QUICK LAB

FOR SCHOOL OR HOME

Growing Crystals

Your teacher will put a cup of hot water onto a counter for you.

BE CAREFUL! Wear goggles. Use a kitchen mitt if you need to hold or move the cup. Don't touch the hot water.

1. Use a plastic spoon to gradually add small amounts of salt to the water. Stir. Keep adding and stirring until no more will dissolve.

2. Tie one end of a 15-cm piece of string to a crystal of rock salt. Tie the other end to a pencil. Lay the pencil across the cup so that the crystal hangs in the hot salt water without touching the sides or bottom.

3. **Observe** Observe the setup for several days. Record what you see.

4. Did any crystals grow? If so, did they have many shapes or just one? Explain your answer. If not, how would you change what you did if you tried again?

C 37

SCIENCE Reading MiniLesson

Sequence of Events

Develop Discuss with students how words like *when* and *then* are clues to readers that a time sequence is being described. Action words, such as *form*, also signal a sequence of events is underway. Have students browse pages C36 and C37 to look for these clue words in the heading, text, and captions.

Practice Challenge students to make flowcharts listing the sequence of events that occurred to produce the brightly colored minerals shown in the picture on page C37. (Flowchart steps should include magma heats mineral-rich water inside Earth, hot water dissolves minerals, water comes to surface in a hot spring, water cools, minerals form crystals.)

Exploring the Main Idea

Put some salt in a small amount of water in a beaker and heat over a hot plate. Show students how the salt is left over. Point out that heating is a fast way to evaporate water. After the beaker cools, have students look at the salt with a hand lens. Ask:

■ **Where did the crystals come from?** (The salt was dissolved in the water. As the water evaporated, the crystals formed.)

▶**After Reading**
Have students answer the red question in the student book as **ongoing assessment**.

QUICK LAB

FOR SCHOOL OR HOME

Materials foam cup half-filled with hot water, 2 plastic spoons, granulated table salt, 15-cm piece of string, pencil, goggles, oven mitt, crystal of rock salt

Science Process Skills *observe*

Resources Activity Resources, pp. 93–94

Plan Ahead You may wish to use 8-ounce or larger foam cups instead of drink-size cups. Adjust the length of the string as necessary. Use kosher salt if possible. Students will need a hand lens to examine the crystals.

Be Careful! Pour the hot water into the cups at the students' work stations so that it will not be necessary to move the cups. Stress the need to wear goggles and use a mitt.

Step 3 Salt crystals deposit on the suspended crystal of rock salt.

Step 4 Crystals of one shape should have formed but many sizes. Students may suggest cooling the water more slowly. The longer it takes for the water to cool, the more time the crystals have to grow and the larger they get.

What Are Minerals Used For?

Before Reading
Have students try to answer the red question at the top of the page.

Developing the Main Idea
Ask students to help you list the uses of minerals on the board. Then discuss how a day might be different if we did not have enough minerals.

Using the Illustrations
Ask students to name their birthstones. See if the class can name all twelve. Then tell the class that the origin of the twelve birthstones dates back to the first century A.D. It was linked to the twelve stones worn in the breastplate of the High Priest of Israel. In the 18th century, people in Poland started wearing birthstones. The practice spread throughout the world.

▶ After Reading
Have students answer the red question in the student book as **ongoing assessment**.

Developing Vocabulary

ore You may wish to spell and pronounce three homonyms (or, oar, ore) to contrast meanings

gem Compare the science meaning with the noun used to describe a person or thing considered valuable or talented.

What Are Minerals Used For?

Can you find minerals being used at home or school? Minerals are used to make many products, from steel to electric light bulbs.

Some of the most useful minerals are called **ores** (AWRZ). An ore is a mineral that contains a useful substance. Ores contain enough useful substances to make them valuable to mine.

For example, iron comes from the mineral hematite (HEE·muh·tight). Iron is used to make nails, buildings, and even ships. Aluminum comes from the mineral bauxite. It is used for food-wrap foil, soft-drink cans, and pie tins, just to name a few uses.

The iron and aluminum that come from these two ores are *metals*. Metals

Gemstones mark special occasions—such as weddings and birthdays. What is your birthstone? Birthstones are gemstones.

Gypsum is used in drywall, or wallboard, for construction of buildings.

have many useful properties. Metals conduct electricity and can be stretched into wires. The metal copper, for example, comes from a mineral ore. It is used to make electrical wires.

Aluminum is lightweight and strong. It shares these properties with another metal that comes from an ore, magnesium. These metals are ideal for use in building jets and spacecraft.

If you look in a jewelry store window, you'll probably see some minerals called **gems**. Gems are minerals that are valued for being rare and beautiful. You may have seen diamond rings. Rubies and sapphires are other gemstones.

▷ **What are two types of useful minerals?**

Gems are minerals that are used in jewelry; ores are used as a source of metals.

C 38

C 38

Science Background

Piezoelectricity
Pierre Curie (husband of Marie) and his brother Jacques discovered piezoelectricity in 1880. They found that pressure on a quartz crystal produced electric charges. Later, it was found that an electric current makes a crystal vibrate, which makes it useful for keeping time in watches.

Inclusion

Mohs' Art
Invite students to make a poster or display that shows samples of each level of the Mohs' scale. They may include everyday objects in addition to minerals. They may also include pictures of where each mineral is used in the community. Invite them to include whatever information they want, such as discovery, prevalence, location, and value. **Spatial; Linguistic**

Science Background

Other Mineral Properties
Tell students that we also use other properties to identify minerals, such as elasticity and strength, specific gravity, radioactivity, luminescence, and thermal, electrical, and magnetic properties. We can identify crystal shape by watching the cleavage of a mineral.

Why It Matters

Minerals are nonrenewable resources. They cannot be replaced as trees can be, for example. They take so long to form that they cannot be replaced in your lifetime.

Because minerals are nonrenewable, they must be *conserved*. To *conserve* means to "use wisely or avoid waste." One way people can conserve minerals is by recycling them—finding ways to treat them or use them again. Researchers can also come up with substitutes to use in place of natural minerals. Many diamonds used in industry for cutting stone, for example, are not natural diamonds.

Think and Write

1. Which properties are most useful to identify a mineral? Explain your answer.

2. What if you had two white samples of talc and gypsum? How could you tell them apart in one step?

3. How does time affect crystals?

4. How useful are metallic ores? Give some ways you use them.

5. **Critical Thinking** How could you avoid the mistake that miners made, thinking fool's gold was real gold? What are all the observations you might make to tell them apart?

L·I·N·K·S

SOCIAL STUDIES LINK

Research minerals. Learn about ways to conserve and recycle minerals. Use the Internet or an encyclopedia.

ART LINK

Make a collage. Cut pictures from magazines of household items that are made from minerals. Paste your pictures on a board.

MATH LINK

Think about shapes. You have learned about the three-dimensional shapes of minerals. How many other regular 3-D shapes do you know? Make a poster illustrating different 3-D shapes.

TECHNOLOGY LINK

 **At the Computer** Visit **www.mhscience02.com** for more links.

C 39

---

3 Lesson Review

Answers to Think and Write

1. No single physical property is best for identifying mineral samples. Check at least two or three properties to be sure. (pp. C33–C35)

2. Both minerals are soft and can be scratched with a fingernail. Gypsum can scratch talc. (pp. C33–C35)

3. The longer a crystal takes to form, the larger it can become. (p. C36)

4. We use metallic ores to construct many things: iron—building materials, vehicle bodies, and wires; aluminum—foil, cans, pie tins, and spacecraft; silver and gold—jewelry. (p. C38)

5. **Critical Thinking** Pyrite (that is, fool's gold) has a greenish black streak; gold has a yellow streak. You could also measure their hardness and density, which are different, to tell them apart. (pp. C33–C35)

Summarize
Check students' understanding by having them write a brief summary of the lesson in their own words.

SOCIAL STUDIES LINK
Students' research should focus on ways to conserve and recycle minerals such as aluminum and other scrap metal such as copper and iron.

ART LINK
Review the picture boards to be sure that students understand the concept of minerals and have chosen appropriate items.

MATH LINK
Check that students choose 3D rather than 2D shapes. (Possible answers: pyramids, cones, and spheres)

✓ Informal Assessment

Easy/Average Have students title three pieces of paper with the following headings: Properties of Mineral and Tests, Formation of Minerals, and Uses of Minerals. Ask them to work in teams to fill in the pages and then share their ideas with the other teams.

Challenge Invite teams of students to choose three minerals and describe their properties, how to test for these properties, and the minerals' uses. Then ask them to draw a diagram to describe how minerals are formed.

LESSON 4
Earth's Rocks and Soil

Objectives

- Explore ways to classify rocks.
- Compare and contrast properties and uses of rocks.
- Define soil as a resource with many properties.
- Trace the steps of the rock cycle, including human-made rocks.

Resources

- Activity Resources, pp. 95–99
- Reading in Science Resources, pp. 147–152
- Vocabulary Cards
- Reading Aid Transparency C4
- Visual Aid Transparency 18
- School to Home Activities, pp. 17–18

Build on Prior Knowledge

Have students discuss what they know about rocks. Ask students to name as many rocks as they can think of and list them on the board. Show students a varied collection of rocks and have them describe each of the rocks. Help students see that they are describing the rocks' colors, textures, hardness, and so on.

1 Get Ready

Using the Illustrations

Discuss the characteristics of the rock formations shown in the picture. Then ask:

- **How are the rocks shown in the picture the same or different from any other rocks?** (All rocks are made up of one or more minerals; rocks differ in that they have different colors, hardnesses, and minerals.)

- **How do we use rocks?** (Rocks can be used as building material, in pavement, in statues, as fuel, and so on.)

LESSON 4
Earth's Rocks and Soil

Vocabulary

rock, C42

igneous rock, C43

sedimentary rock, C44

fossil, C45

metamorphic rock, C46

humus, C49

pollution, C50

rock cycle, C52

Get Ready

What do we walk on, sail over, climb, fly over, live in, and even sit on?

Rocks! Rocks make up Earth's crust. Are all rocks the same? Are the rocks shown here just like any other rocks? How can we tell one rock from another?

Process Skill

You infer when you form an idea from facts or observations.

C 40

 **Math** | **MiniLesson**

Use a Formula

Develop An object has a metric mass of 3.5 g. The volume of the object is 5 cm³. What is the density of the object? You can use a formula to solve the problem.

A *formula* is an equation with at least two variables.

Use the formula for density.

Density = mass ÷ volume

Let d = density, m = mass, v = volume

Substitute the mass and volume in the formula.

d = 3.5 g ÷ 5 cm³

d = 0.7 g/cm³

The density of the object is 0.7 g/cm³

Practice Solve each equation.

1. $4t = 5$
   $(t = 1\frac{1}{4})$

2. $\frac{m}{2} = 3$
   $(m = 6)$

Activity Have students write a problem in words where the solution is found using the equation $2n + 1 = 4$. (Sample response: The double of a number n plus 1 is 4.)

C40 UNIT C *Earth and Its Resources*

Explore Activity

How Are Rocks Alike and Different?

Materials
- samples of rocks
- clear tape
- red marker
- hand lens
- copper wire
- streak plate
- balance
- metric ruler
- calculator

Procedure: Design Your Own

1 Use the tape to number each sample in a group of rocks.

2 **Classify** Find a way to sort the group into smaller groups. Determine what properties you will use. Group the rocks that share one or more properties. Your fingernail, the copper wire, and the edge of a streak plate are tools you might use. Scratch gently. Record your results.

3 **Use Numbers** You might estimate the density of each sample. Use a balance to find the mass. Use a metric ruler to estimate the length, width, and height.
Length × width × height = volume
Density = mass ÷ volume

Drawing Conclusions

1 How were you able to make smaller groups? Give supporting details from the notes you recorded.

2 Could you find more than one way to sort the rocks into groups? Give examples of how rocks from two different smaller groups may have a property in common.

3 **Communicate** Share your results with others. Compare your systems for sorting the rocks.

4 **Going Further: Infer** How might a sample be useful based on the properties that you observed?

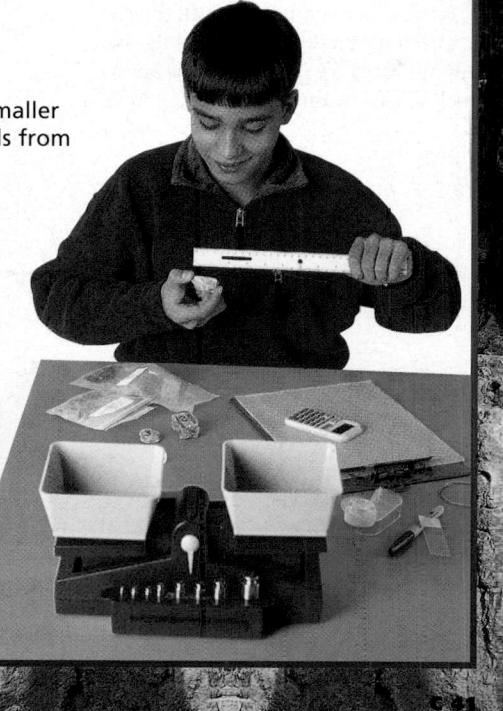

Alternative Explore Activity

Materials rock samples, poster board, art supplies, hand lens

Display Types of Rocks Invite teams of students to make a display or poster that features different types of rocks. Ask them to examine the rock samples and to decide how to group them. Have them label each group with its common characteristics. **Spatial; Social**

Activity Resources, p. 97

Explore Activity

How Are Rocks Alike and Different?

Science Process Skills classify, use numbers, communicate, infer

Resources Resource Activities pp. 95–96

Pacing 30–40 minutes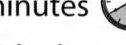

Grouping individual

Plan Ahead Rock samples should include granite, gabbro, basalt, shale with layers, conglomerate, sandstone, siltstone, gneiss with banding, and schist.

Procedure: Design Your Own

2 Stress that there are many ways that the rocks can be classified. Encourage students to use several criteria to sort the rocks. Refer students to the Mohs' scale of hardness on p. C34 as a way to compare rock samples.

3 Students could estimate the mass in an alternative way, such as with dried peas. They could hang plastic bags on either side of a metal coat hanger, add peas to one bag until they balance the rock in the other bag, and then count the peas.

Answers to Drawing Conclusions

1 Students may have made groups according to color, hardness, size, pattern, or density.

2 Students should determine that rocks can be sorted in a number of ways. Rocks from different groups may have different colors but the same hardness.

3 Students will use different methods.

4 Possible answers: Hardness can make a rock a useful building material; color can make a rock useful for decorating.

Inquiry Students can ask their own questions to explore such as how else can we classify rocks. (by their use as building materials or decorations)

Technology

- When time is short, preview the activity with the **Explore Activity Video.**

2 Read to Learn

How Are Rocks Alike and Different?

Before Reading
Have students try to answer the red question at the top of the page.

Exploring the Main Idea
Pass around pieces of granite or another igneous rock and hand lenses. Encourage students to identify the minerals they see. Have students compare textures as well as densities of rocks of similar sizes.

▶ After Reading
Have students answer the red question in the student book as **ongoing assessment**.

Developing Vocabulary

rock Brainstorm descriptive words to describe rocks. For each word, research a type of rock that fits the description.

Read to Learn

Main Idea Rocks can be classified according to their composition and properties.

How Are Rocks Alike and Different?

Rocks are mineral treasure chests. A rock is any naturally formed solid in the crust made up of one or more kinds of minerals. You can often see mineral crystals in a rock. Sometimes the crystals are too small to see easily.

Look with a hand lens at a piece of granite. You can often find crystals of quartz (whitish), feldspar (pink), mica (black), and even hornblende (black).

Each mineral in a rock has its own streak, hardness, or crystal shape. A rock with several minerals may have a mixture of properties. For example, it may have both hard and soft minerals. It may make both light and dark streaks.

The most exact way to identify a rock is to name the minerals it contains. However, color, density, and the way the rock's surface feels, or its *texture*, are also identifying features. The texture comes from the size, shape, and arrangement of the mineral crystals or grains in a rock. Are the grains large (coarse) or small (fine)? Do they interlock, or can you see each clearly? Are they soft edged or jagged?

A rock's color, density, and texture result from how the rock was formed. Rocks are grouped into three types according to how they were formed.

▷ What are the characteristics of rocks?
Rocks are naturally formed solids that are made up of one or more minerals. Each mineral adds its own properties to a rock. Rocks have different textures, densities, and colors.

Igneous Rocks

Extrusive—Cooled Above Ground

Rhyolite (RIGH·uh·light) has a fine texture and is light colored.

Obsidian (uhb·SID·ee·uhn) has no mineral grains and is dark colored.

Basalt (buh·SAWLT) has a fine texture and is dark colored.

C 42

What Are Igneous Rocks?

All the rocks on these two pages were at one time deep below Earth's surface. There it is hot enough for some rocks to be melted, or molten. Molten rock material deep below the surface is called magma.

Magma is less dense than the material surrounding it, so it rises toward the surface. Before magma reaches the surface, however, it may cool and harden into solid rock. Rocks that form when melted rock material cools and hardens are called igneous rocks.

Often magma makes it to the surface before hardening. Magma reaching the surface is called *lava*. Exposed to the air above ground, lava, too, hardens and cools, forming igneous rocks.

Below ground magma cools slowly. Crystals take a long time to grow. They grow to large (coarse) sizes.

Above ground cooling is much quicker. Crystals are smaller. Lava may cool so quickly that no crystals have a chance to form. What results is obsidian, a solid piece of volcanic glass.

The granite and gabbro shown on this page formed below ground. They both have large mineral crystals. However, granite contains lighter-colored minerals than gabbro.

All the rocks on page C42 formed above ground. They have small crystals or no crystals at all. How do they differ in color?

The texture and color make a difference in how an igneous rock is used. If you were making a monument, which of these rocks might you choose?

▶ **How are igneous rocks formed?**
Igneous rocks are formed when melted rock material, such as magma or lava, cools and hardens.

READING
Charts

How could you classify the rocks shown on these two pages? Show your results by making a table with two or three columns and rows. Use the properties as headings, and fill in the table with rock names.

Intrusive—Cooled Below Ground

Granite has a coarse texture. The crystals are large enough to be seen. It is a light-colored rock.

Gabbro (GAB·roh) has a coarse texture, but it is dark colored.

C 43

What Are Igneous Rocks?

Before Reading
Have students try to answer the red question at the top of the page.

Exploring the Main Idea
Ask students to recall from the last lesson how a half-filled tube of toothpaste modeled magma (when it is in the tube) and lava (when it comes out). Squeeze a bit of toothpaste onto a surface, preferably a cold surface. Ask:

■ **What do you think will happen to the toothpaste?** (It will harden.)

Tell students that this demonstration models one way igneous rock is formed. (Note one difference, that the toothpaste is drying out, rather than cooling down from a high temperature.) Let the toothpaste harden and draw students' attention to it as they go through the lesson.

READING
Charts

Rock	Where formed	Texture	Color
rhyolite	above ground	fine	light
obsidian	above ground	smooth	dark
basalt	above ground	fine	dark
granite	below ground	coarse	light
gabbro	below ground	coarse	dark

▶ **After Reading**
Have students answer the red question in the student book as **ongoing assessment**.

Developing Vocabulary

igneous rock Point out a similar word that starts with the same letters, *ignite*, which means "to set on fire." Both igneous and ignite come from the Latin for "fire." Discuss why this is an appropriate name for igneous rocks. (They are formed from molten rock.)

English Language Learners

Rock Words
Ask students to look through the text and find pairs of words that are both used to describe the same thing. (For example, large and coarse, small and fine, melted and molten, and surface feel and texture.) Point out that two words that mean the same thing are called synonyms. Challenge students to find synonyms for other words in the text, such as *small, large, hard, soft, light,* and *dark*. Model how they can use a thesaurus to find synonyms. **Linguistic**

Inclusion

Materials half of a chocolate bar, marshmallow, cooking pot, refrigerator, wax paper, plate

Make an Igneous Rock As a home activity, ask students to put the chocolate bar and marshmallow in the pot and heat them (with adult supervision). Then they pour the mixture onto the wax paper on the plate, let it cool a minute, fold the paper over the mixture, and put the mixture and wax paper in the freezer. Have students check the next day and discuss how this models the formation of igneous rock. **Kinesthetic**

What Are Sedimentary Rocks?

Before Reading
Have students try to answer the red question at the top of the page.

Exploring the Main Idea
Pass around as many samples of sedimentary rock as possible. As these circulate, show students a peanut butter and jelly sandwich in a plastic sandwich bag. Show students how the pieces are joined together. Use this image to help students think about sedimentary rocks when they compare them to igneous and metamorphic rocks.

Developing Vocabulary

sedimentary rock Sedimentary rocks as a type of rock can be reinforced to students by passing around sample of rocks—some containing fossils, if possible.

▶ After Reading
Have students answer the red question in the student book as **ongoing assessment.**

What Are Sedimentary Rocks?

How do the rocks here compare with igneous rocks? These rocks are **sedimentary rocks** . Sedimentary rocks are made of small bits of matter joined together. These bits of matter, or sediments, may be bits of weathered rocks. They may be shells or other remains of living things. Long ago water, wind, and ice picked up sediment and carried it. Eventually they dropped the sediment in places where it collected into layers.

Most common sedimentary rocks are formed when sediment is compacted or cemented together. The weight of layer upon layer of sediment on top of each other compacts or squeezes sediment together.

Coarser sediments are cemented by bits of minerals that "glue" the sediments together. Water that contains dissolved minerals seeps between the coarse pieces of sediment. The water evaporates, and mineral crystals form. These crystals hold together the coarse sediment, turning it into a solid rock.

You can see the pieces of sediment that make up these rocks. These rocks are named by the kind of sediment they contain.

Some sedimentary rocks are made of crystals of minerals that were once dissolved in water. The crystals were left behind when the water evaporated. Halite, the rock salt that is used to melt snow and ice, is formed this way.

A type of limestone consists mostly of a mineral called calcite. The mineral was dissolved in ocean water. As the water evaporated in certain areas, the calcite was left behind as solid limestone.

Some sedimentary rocks are made of substances that were once part of, or made by, living things. Cemented-together shells form *coquina* (koh·KEE·nuh). Coral skeletons form coral limestone. Sedimentary rocks are formed when small bits of matter are compacted or cemented together

▷ **How are sedimentary rocks formed?**

Coquina

C 44

Sediment (Small to Large)	Rock
Clay	Shale
Silt	Siltstone
Sand	Sandstone
Gravel	Conglomerate

How Are Sedimentary Rocks Useful?

They may be just clumps of bits and pieces, but sedimentary rocks are very useful. Sandstone, for example, is used for buildings and trim. Limestone is used for buildings, trim, monuments, and even park benches. Shale is often broken into pieces that are mixed with other materials to make concrete and cement.

Sedimentary rocks are very useful in helping to piece together Earth's history. They often contain clues, called fossils, to life long ago. Fossils are the remains or imprints of living things of the past.

The remains of dead organisms were often covered with mud, sand, or other sediment. Sometimes a living thing left an imprint, such as a footprint, in soft mud. Over centuries of time, the sediment and the remains or imprint hardened into rock. Almost all fossils are found in sedimentary rocks. Why do you think fossils could not be found in an igneous rock?

A type of coal is a sedimentary rock. This coal is called bituminous (bigh·TEW·muh·nuhs) coal, or soft coal. Earth's supplies of coal were formed millions of years ago from dead plants buried in ancient swamps and forests. Coal today is a source of energy, the energy that comes from those ancient forms of life.

▷ **What are some ways sedimentary rocks are used?**

Sedimentary rocks are used in buildings, in uncovering history through fossils, and as an energy source.

Fossils

Limestone blocks

Bituminous coal lights quickly and provides much energy, but it burns with a lot of soot and yellow smoke.

C 45

How Are Sedimentary Rocks Useful?

Before Reading
Have students try to answer the red question at the top of the page.

Developing the Main Idea
Ask students to think about the differences between sedimentary and igneous rocks as they read through the text. Ask:

- **Which type of rock is formed slowly by layers adding on top of each other and squeezing materials together?** (sedimentary)

- **Which type of rock is formed quickly by a material cooling and hardening?** (igneous)

Exploring the Main Idea
Invite students to find out more about the Grand Canyon in Arizona. They may want to learn about John Wesley Powell and his pioneering exploration of the Colorado River, what scientists have discovered about Earth's history by examining the layers of the canyon, and the cultures of people who have lived near and in the canyon. Challenge them to find out about other features, especially other canyons, in the surrounding area.

▶**After Reading**
Have students answer the red question in the student book as **ongoing assessment.**

Developing Vocabulary

fossil Point out to students that the Latin root for this word means "dug up," reminding us that fossils are often found in layers of rock, underground or lifted above ground by mountain building forces.

SCIENCE FOR ALL

Inclusion

Materials modeling clay, paper plate, seashell, cooking oil, plaster of Paris, spoon, paper cup, water

Make a Fossil Ask students to put a thick disk of clay on the plate, coat the shell with oil, press it into the clay to make a clear impression, and remove it. Have them mix four spoonfuls of plaster with two of water in the cup, pour the mixture into the impression, and discard the cup. (Don't pour excess plaster mixture down the sink, as it will clog.) Have students let this sit for about 20 minutes and then carefully separate the clay from the mold. The clay represents a cast fossil and the plaster a mold fossil. **Kinesthetic; Spatial**

What Are Metamorphic Rocks?

Before Reading
Have students try to answer the red question at the top of the page.

Exploring the Main Idea
Model the formation of metamorphic rock by bending some toothpicks into "V" shapes and standing them on a surface. Place a piece of paper on top. Then place some paper clips on top of the paper. Tell students this represents the minerals in a rock. Then ask a volunteer to place a book on top so everything is pushed together. Ask:

- **What happened to the minerals?** (They changed position and shape.)
- **How does the new rock look different from the original rock?** (It is different in size, texture, and appearance.)
- **What caused the rock to change?** (Pressure.)

▶ After Reading
Have students answer the red question in the student book as **ongoing assessment**.

Developing Vocabulary

metamorphic rock Show students a piece of marble as an example of metamorphic rock, although it may be difficult for students to understand the amount of heat and pressure necessary to change limestone into marble.

What Are Metamorphic Rocks?

Deep below Earth's surface, rocks can undergo great change. They are heated by the high temperatures at great depths. They are under pressure from the rocks lying above.

Great heat and pressure can change one rock into another rock. A rock formed under heat and pressure from another kind of rock is called a **metamorphic** (met·uh·MAWR·fik) **rock**. In the process the original rock does not melt under heat and pressure. If it did, it would become an igneous rock. Instead the original rock remains solid, but

- the mineral grains in the original rock may flatten and line up

- the minerals may change their identity; substances in a mineral may be exchanged with substances in surrounding minerals
- the minerals in the original rock may separate into layers of different densities

In each case the result is a rock different from the original.

Original Rock	Metamorphic Rock
Granite (igneous rock)	gneiss (NIGHS)
Shale (sedimentary rock)	slate
Sandstone (sedimentary rock)	quartzite
Limestone (sedimentary rock)	marble
Slate (metamorphic rock)	schist

 How are metamorphic rocks made from other rocks? Heat and pressure can change a rock into a new rock.

Pressure — Limestone — Marble — Heat

Pressure — Granite — Gneiss — Heat

C 46

🦉 Science Background

Marble Made in a Foundry
The root word for *metamorphic* means "to change." Both igneous and sedimentary rocks can be changed into metamorphic rocks, usually by intense heat and pressure underground. To prove that limestone, a sedimentary rock, can be changed into marble, a metamorphic rock, Sir James Hall (1761–1832) sealed powdered limestone in a gun barrel and heated it in a foundry. Crystalline marble came out.

✋ Cultural Perspective

Building Stones of Old
The great pyramids of Egypt are built of limestone. Some of the blocks of Stonehenge in England are made of gray sandstone. Concrete, a mixture of limestone, sand, gravel, and water, was invented by the Romans and used to build the Coliseum. Many Greek temples are made of granite.

How Are Metamorphic Rocks Used?

Metamorphic rocks are "rock makeovers." In their remade form, these rocks have new properties that are very useful.

Slate, for example, breaks into thin sheets. The minerals in slate are so tightly packed together that water cannot seep through this rock. This makes slate useful as roofing shingles as well as stepping stones and outdoor floors.

Marble is often shiny. It often contains minerals that give it brilliant colors, from greenish to red. It is easy to carve. It is often a first choice for making statues, floors, countertops, and monuments.

One kind of coal is a metamorphic rock. It is called anthracite, or hard coal. Anthracite is formed from soft coal.

▷ **Where might you find metamorphic rocks used in your community?**
Metamorphic rocks may be found on roofs or in monuments. **Anthracite, hard coal, burns cleaner and longer than soft coal, but does not provide as much energy.**

The Story of Coal

Millions of Years Ago					
300	280	220	150	10	Present
A forest swamp	Plants die and sink to the bottom.	A thick layer of peat, partly decayed plants, builds up.	The swamp dries up. Buried under layers of sediment, the peat changes to a sedimentary rock called lignite (LIG·night).	Buried by more and more layers of sediment, the lignite becomes more compacted. It forms bituminous coal.	Buried even deeper, bituminous coal is changed by great heat and pressure. It forms anthracite, a metamorphic rock.

Peat

Lignite

Bituminous (soft) coal (sedimentary rock)

Anthracite (hard) coal (metamorphic rock)

READING Diagrams

1. How is the position of the fuel layer changing from picture to picture?
2. How does this position affect what happens to the layer?

C 47

How Are Metamorphic Rocks Used?

Before Reading
Have students try to answer the red question at the top of the page.

Developing the Main Idea
Ask students to think about how metamorphic rock is formed, especially as they learn about how coal is formed.

READING Diagrams

Ask students to consider how long this process takes and why we must be careful using our natural resources.

1. The layer is getting deeper and deeper.
2. Because more material is on top, this layer gets more and more pressure.

▶ After Reading
Have students answer the red question in the student book as **ongoing assessment**.

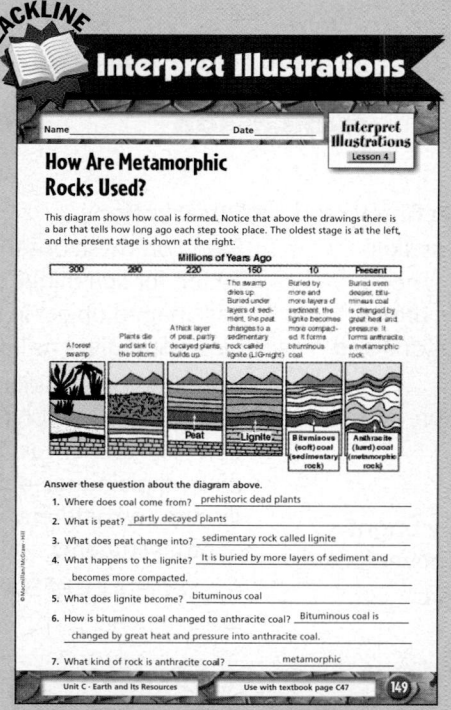
SCIENCE Reading Strategy

Sequence of Events

Develop Reading Skills Using the diagram on page C47, list the steps involved in the formation of coal by asking students to paraphrase what happens first, second, and so on. Then list the steps in numerical order.

Coal Formation in a Swamp
1. Plants grow in a swamp.
2. Plants die and sink.
3. Peat forms; layers of peat accumulate.
4. The swamp dries up; peat changes to lignite.
5. Compaction forms bituminous coal, a sedimentary rock.
6. Heat and pressure form anthracite, a metamorphic rock.

Process Skill
BUILDER

Defining Soil

Science Process Skills *define based on observations, observe, use variables, experiment*

Resources Activity Resources, pp. 98–99

Pacing 30–40 minutes

Grouping individuals

Plan Ahead Prepare a work space by spreading newspapers over a table or on desks.

Procedure

Be Careful! Remind students to wash their hands and wipe up their desks when they finish the activity.

1 Possible answer: pieces of rock, bits of plant and animal matter; varied sizes

2 Possible answer: Sand is dry and has a more uniform appearance.

3 Possible answer: Water drains through the sand very quickly.

4 Students might try putting equal-sized samples of sand and soil in two cups, each with a hole in the bottom. They can see how much water they can add before water starts draining out the holes. (Soil absorbs more water.)

5 Possible answer: Sand looks like tiny rock pieces; while soil consists of a variety of materials.

Answers to Drawing Conclusions

1 pieces of rock, water, and decayed plant and animal material

2 color, texture, and composition

3 Soil is a mixture of water, rock pieces, and decayed plant and animal pieces.

Process Skill
BUILDER

SKILL Define Based on Observations

Defining Soil

Earth's crust is made up of rocks and minerals. However, to get to the rocks, you usually have to dig through layers of soil.

Soil looks different at different places. It has different properties. Soil can be sandy. It can be moist.

Just what is soil? Make some observations. Write a definition that fits your observations.

Materials

moist soil sample in plastic bag

sand sample in plastic bag

hand lens

2 cups

2 plastic spoons

Procedure

1 **Observe** Use a hand lens to examine a sample of moist soil. What materials can you find? How do their sizes compare? Write a description.

2 Some soils are more like sand. How does a sample of sand compare with your moist soil sample?

3 **Use Variables** Which sample absorbs water more quickly? Fill a cup halfway with sand and another with moist soil. Pour a spoonful of water in each at the same time.

4 **Experiment** Which absorbs more water? Make a prediction. Find a way to test your prediction.

5 **Experiment** Make any other observations. Look for other differences.

Drawing Conclusions

1 Based on your observations, what is soil made up of?

2 How may soils differ?

3 **Define** Write a definition for *soil*. Take into account all your observations.

C 48

Process Skills
MiniLesson

Define Based on Observations

Develop This process skill involves putting together a description based on direct and indirect observations and experiences.

To define the term *Sun*, for example, list:

- It looks like a ball.
- It glows and is very bright. (Students should never look directly at the Sun.)
- It is in the sky.
- It gives us light and heat.

Based on these observations, a definition for *Sun* might be "a bright, ball-shaped object in the sky that glows and gives us light and heat."

Practice Have students define the term *Earth* based on their observations or experiences. Then have them explain their definitions and discuss any differences with those of other students.

A complete list of Science Process Skills appears on p. S7.

Where Does Soil Come From?

Under a hand lens, you can see that any soil shows that it is a mixture of many things. The main ingredient in soil is weathered rock. Soil may also contain water, air, bacteria, and **humus**. Humus is decayed plant or animal material.

Where does soil come from? A layer of solid rock weathers into chunks. The chunks weather into smaller pieces. Living things die and decay and form humus.

Gradually layers of soil, or soil horizons, develop. If you dig down through soil, you can see many layers and the solid rock, bedrock, beneath it. How do the horizons differ?

Soils differ in different locations. In polar deserts there is no A horizon at the top. However, grassland and forest soils can have very thick A horizons. Why do you think this is so? Some soils are very sandy. Why? How would they differ from soils in many farms?

Sometimes the materials in soil match the bedrock below it. Sometimes they do not match. Can you explain why?

Soil is Earth's greatest treasure. Most plants need soil to grow. Therefore, almost all living things depend on soil for food—and survival. One of the most important uses of soil is farming. All of the food you eat depends on soil.

▶ What is soil made up of?

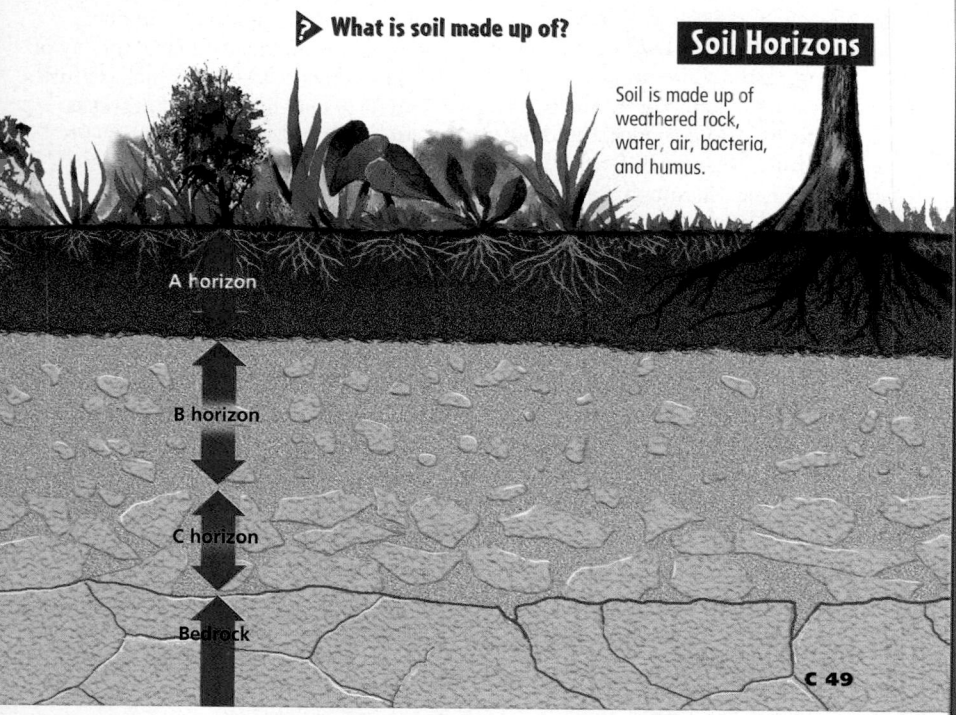

Soil Horizons

Soil is made up of weathered rock, water, air, bacteria, and humus.

A horizon

B horizon

C horizon

Bedrock

C 49

Where Does Soil Come From?

Before Reading
Have students try to answer the red question at the top of the page.

Developing the Main Idea
Encourage students to discuss the questions asked in the text. From their discussion, challenge them to describe the different horizons in their own words. Ask:

- **Where would you expect to find the most humus?** (The A horizon.)
- **Where would you expect to find the biggest rocks?** (The C horizon, or bedrock.)

▶ After Reading
Have students answer the red question in the student book as **ongoing assessment**.

Developing Vocabulary

humus Show students decaying leaf material as a sample of humus. The word comes from a Latin root meaning "ground, earth, soil," and refers to one of the most important substances that make up good farming soil.

BLACKLINE
Interpret Illustrations

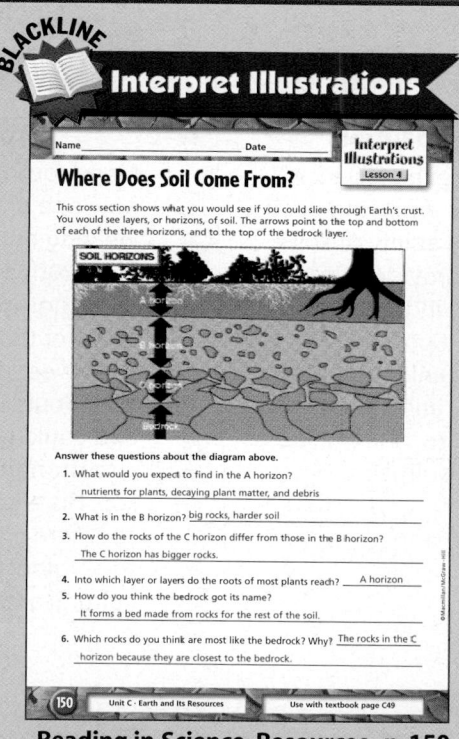

Reading in Science Resources, p. 150

Science Background

Roots as Rock Breakers
The soil-making process begins when plants take root in weathered rock. Mosses and lichens penetrate hard rock and are often the first sign of life in a barren, rocky area. As the plants grow, cracks in the rock get wider. This process of turning rock to soil takes tens of thousands of years.

How Can People Ruin Soil?

Before Reading
Have students try to answer the red question at the top of the page.

Developing the Main Idea
Ask students to discuss how often they see activities that hurt the soil. Ask:

■ **What part of the soil do these activities hurt the most?** (the A horizon, or topsoil)

■ **Why is it harmful to waste the top layer of soil?** (This is the layer that contains plant and animal material needed for plant growth.)

Using the Illustrations
Ask:

■ **What are some ways that you can reduce or prevent garbage pollution?** (reduce consumption, waste less, recycle)

■ **If a dump site such as the one shown existed in your community, what could you do about it?** (get volunteers to team up, collect the trash, and recycle it)

▶After Reading
Have students answer the red question in the student book as **ongoing assessment**.

Developing Vocabulary

pollution This word's Latin root means "to defile" and *pollution* suggests that something pure has been made completely filthy or debased. Students may have seen examples of soil pollution. For example, litter, strewn trash and garbage, or hazardous materials incorrectly disposed of. Have students share their observations.

How Can People Ruin Soil?

People depend on soil. Would you believe people ruin and waste soil? That might include you! It may be people in general or industries—such as factories or farms.

People often get rid of garbage and hazardous wastes by burying them in soil. Hazardous wastes are wastes that may be poisonous or cause diseases, such as cancer.

Spraying chemicals on soil to kill unwanted animals and plants also affects the soil. These chemicals become a part of the soil.

Tossing foam cups, plastic wrappers, and materials onto the ground, instead of using trash baskets, harms the soil. They do not decay. They remain as wastes in the soil. They may build up and make the soil unusable.

All these materials add up to **pollution**. *Pollution* means adding any harmful substances to Earth's land, water, or air. The substances are called *pollutants*. When people cause pollution, we say they *pollute* soil, water, or air.

Not only do people pollute soil, but they often waste it, too. For example, soil needs plants. When plants die and decay, they add valuable substances back into the soil. When a crop is harvested, the plants are removed. They do not decay and return nutrients back into the soil. Growing the same crop year after year uses up the nutrients in soil. Plants don't grow well in nutrient-poor soil.

Plant roots hold soil particles together. They protect soil from being blown away by wind or washed away by water. If plants are removed or if weak, sickly plants are growing in an area, the soil is exposed to erosion by wind and rain.

Letting cattle graze in the same area for a long time also exposes soil. Cutting down forests for lumber exposes soil, too. As a result of any of these practices, soil that took centuries to form may be removed in weeks.
People bury garbage in the ground, spray chemicals on soil, harvest too many plants, let cattle overgraze, and cut down forests.

▷ **How do people pollute and waste the soil?**

Each piece of garbage was thrown away by somebody. It takes people to make garbage. What are some ways to prevent this kind of pollution?

Science Background

People Pollution
People damage the soil in a variety of ways. Applying pesticides limits the ability of soil organisms to provide nutrients in the soil. Burying wastes in the ground can pollute groundwater. Building more houses, stores, and roads limits the amount of topsoil available for plants and animals.

Cultural Perspective

Crop Rotation
Many southern states grew only one or two crops for years, wearing out their soil. In the early 20th century, George Washington Carver found hundreds of uses for the peanut and sweet potato, two crops that would do well in the South and could replace crops such as cotton that had depleted the soil. His efforts transformed southern agriculture and made the region an important agricultural area once again.

By building terraces people in Bali have been able to farm steep hillsides.

Contour means "shape." How does contour plowing prevent water from running downhill?

How Can People Protect the Soil?

People need to take care of soil. We have to protect it from being polluted and wasted. Farmers take care of soil by

- *adding fertilizers and humus.* After growing crops, farmers add these materials to replace minerals removed by crops.
- *using crop rotation.* Each year farmers grow different crops. In this way the soil does not use up the same kinds of minerals year after year. Crops from one year may help replace minerals in the soil that are used up another year.
- *strip farming.* Many crops have stems spaced far apart. Rainwater can run off between the stems and wash soil away. In strip farming strips of tightly growing grasses are grown between more widely spaced crops. The grasses trap runoff and the soil it carries. The next year the position of the strips is switched.

- *contour plowing.* Farmers plow furrows across a slope rather than up and down a slope. Each furrow traps rainwater and keeps it from eroding the soil.
- *terracing.* A hillside is shaped into a series of steps. Runoff water and eroded soil get trapped on the steps. Planting rows of trees to block the wind prevents soil from being blown away.

What can you do to prevent soil from being polluted or wasted? Think about what you toss away as garbage. Is there any way to throw it away to make sure it does not simply end up in the soil? Is there any way to keep from throwing as much garbage away each day as you might?

Answers may include: by rotating crops, adding fertilizers to the soil, contour plowing, and terracing.

 **What are two ways people can protect the soil?**

C 51

Before Reading
Have students try to answer the red question at the top of the first text column.

Developing the Main Idea
Discuss with students how each of us can protect the soil. Ask:

- **Do you know anybody who composts their grass clippings and yard waste?** Explain that compost can help add nutrients back into the soil.

- **Are there any bare spots on the ground where you live where you could plant seeds?** Remind students that plants can help keep soil from washing away.

- **What can students do to clean up any trash that may have accumulated in their neighborhoods?** (organize weekend clean up teams and bag trash in accordance with sanitation regulations)

- **What do you think the school could do to protect the soil around it?** (replanting)

▶**After Reading**
Have students answer the red question in the student book as **ongoing assessment**.

 **Reading Strategy**

Paraphrase
Developing Reading Skills
Ask students to paraphrase the text concerning ways to protect the soil. They might list the main methods and describe each or they may paraphrase the topic as a whole. Have them read their paraphrases aloud to a partner to determine whether he or she can understand the main idea of soil conservation. **Linguistic; Social**

Advanced Learners

Toxic Dump Sites
Have students find information on one of the early cases of toxic dumps such as Love Canal. Ask students to find out what was done about that example of pollution and whether the site has actually been cleaned up after all this time. Have them report their findings to the class. **Linguistic**

What Is the Rock Cycle?

Before Reading
Have students try to answer the red question at the top of the page.

Developing the Main Idea
Ask students to recall how each type of rock forms. Begin a discussion of how one rock can turn into another by reviewing how sedimentary rock can turn into metamorphic. Recall the activities with the peanut butter and jelly sandwiches. Build the rock cycle on the board bit by bit as students discuss each idea.

▶ After Reading
Have students answer the red question in the student book as **ongoing assessment**.

Technology

- Visual Aid Transparency 18: *Rock Cycle*

Developing Vocabulary

rock cycle Discuss two meanings for *cycle*: a series of steps or events that can occur in a certain order, as well as over and over again. Have students explain how rock-forming processes fit both meanings of the word.

What Is the Rock Cycle?

Where do rocks and soil come from? Igneous rocks come from magma or lava. However, where did the magma and lava come from?

Sedimentary rock is made of broken-up pieces of rock. However, where did the pieces of rock come from?

All rocks come from other rocks. Rocks are constantly changing from one rock into another. They change in a never-ending series of processes called the **rock cycle**. Part of this cycle is the weathering of rocks into bits and pieces—some of which may eventually become soil.

Rocks are constantly forming—one changing into another. However, any rock takes a really long time to form. When we dig up a deposit of sandstone or use up the coal in an area, it cannot be replaced. Rocks are a *nonrenewable* resource.

People get into the rock-making process, too. Concrete, porcelain, and brick are all artificial rocks.

Answers for all rocks should include: exposure, weathering, erosion, and deposition, or dissolving in and evaporating from water.

READING Sequence of Events
What is the path of a rock through the rock cycle?

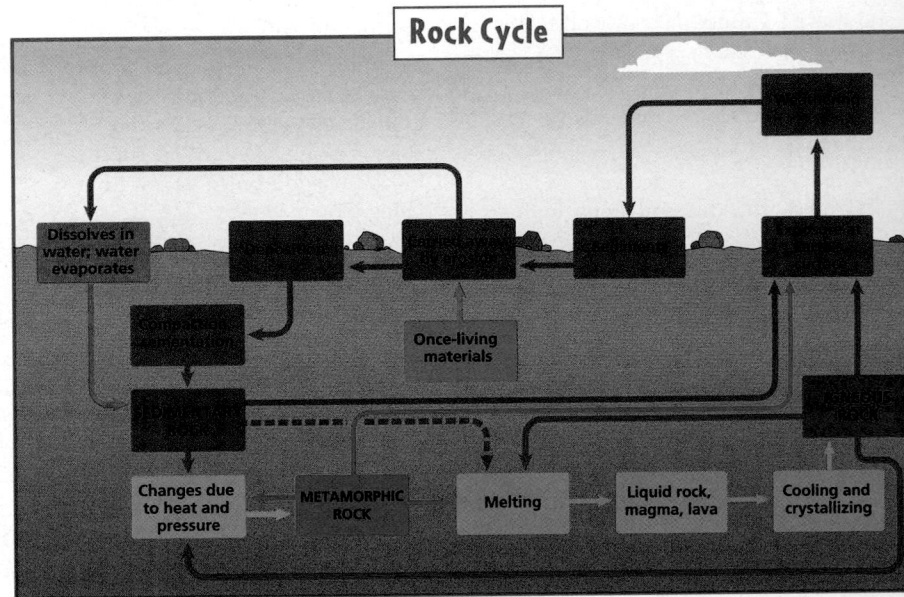

Rock Cycle

Dissolves in water; water evaporates

Once-living materials

Changes due to heat and pressure

METAMORPHIC ROCK

Melting

Liquid rock, magma, lava

Cooling and crystallizing

C 52

Reading MiniLesson

Sequence of Events

Develop Discuss with students how the word *cycle* in the title of page C52 is a clue that the written material will explain events in sequence because a cycle is a series of steps. Have students note other clue words in the text, such as *forming* (paragraph 4, line 1), that signal a sequence of events is being discussed.

Practice Discuss how the diagram on page C52 is constructed like a flowchart. Then challenge students to make flowcharts explaining how a huge boulder could become a tiny speck of soil. (Flowcharts might include weathering and erosion of the large rock until it becomes small enough to be deposited in a stream and dissolved, then evaporated to end up as a speck of soil.) **Logical**

Science Background

The Rock Cycle
We can view the rock cycle as one of many circular processes in nature. The rock cycle is a long cycle and takes millions of years, but it is happening every day in a way that students can see. Students even take part in the rock cycle when they break a soft rock into pieces.

Why It Matters

It is important to be able to tell one type of rock from another. Just think of all the ways you use rocks. What would life be like without them? There would be no mountains to climb, no beaches to walk on. There would be no soil—so that means no food, or forests, or fields. There would be no metals, because metals come from mineral ores that are found in rocks. There would be no bricks, no concrete, no buildings, no . . .

Think and Write

1. How are soils alike? How are they different?

2. How can you tell igneous rocks apart?

3. You pick up a rock. How can you tell if it is a sedimentary rock?

4. Define How can you tell rocks apart? Why are they identified in a different way from minerals?

5. Critical Thinking How can an igneous rock become a metamorphic rock? Think of three different ways.

WRITING LINK

Write a paragraph. Even if you don't live anywhere near a farm, you depend on soil. Explain how soil is important to everyone.

SOCIAL STUDIES LINK

Investigate building materials. Observe the buildings and streets in your neighborhood. How many are constructed with the help of rocks? How many different rocks can you identify?

ART LINK

Make a diagram. Where do igneous rocks come from? Draw a picture to show how igneous rocks form.

TECHNOLOGY LINK

At the Computer Visit **www.mhscience02.com** for more links.

C 53

Answers to Think and Write

1. All soils are made of broken-down rocks, minerals, and sometimes air, humus, bacteria, and water. Soils differ in composition, color, and texture. (p. C49)

2. by crystal size and type of minerals (p. C43)

3. Some sedimentary rocks have layers and in many you can identify individual crystals cemented together. (p. C44)

4. Define Rocks can be identified by the minerals they contain and by differences in color, texture, and density; they differ from minerals because they may contain more than one mineral. (p. C42)

5. Critical Thinking An igneous rock can become a metamorphic rock when its grains change shape and align, when minerals in it change their composition, or when minerals separate into layers of different densities. (p. C46)

Summarize
Check students' understanding by having them write a brief summary of the lesson in their own words.

WRITING LINK
Students' paragraphs may note that soil is necessary to grow crops that we all eat and to grow plants that contribute oxygen to our atmosphere.

SOCIAL STUDIES LINK
Students' research should state that almost all buildings, unless constructed from wood, are constructed with the help of rocks. The type of rock material may include granite, limestone, marble, and concrete.

ART LINK
Diagrams should show how both intrusive and extrusive igneous rocks form. They should include the steps of rock melting, rising toward or onto the surface, then cooling and hardening into solid rock.

✓ Informal Assessment

Easy/Average Ask students to make a chart that describes the three types of rocks. They should include how each type is formed, how the rocks are used, and how the rocks can turn into each of the other types. Students should also write a paragraph telling what soil is and why it's important.

Challenge Invite students to reproduce the diagram of the rock cycle. They should add information about each type of rock, including how it is formed and how it is used. Challenge them to include soil in their diagram.

Objective

■ Describe the use of silicon chips to operate computers.

Build on Prior Knowledge

Ask students to define *element* (a substance which cannot be broken down into smaller parts) and *mineral* (solid material of Earth's crust with a definite composition). Ask:

■ **Is silicon an element or mineral?** (element)

■ **Is quartz an element or mineral?** (mineral)

Silicon Rules!

Developing the Main Idea

Discuss what everyday life would be like without the use of silicon chips. Ask:

■ **Why is the use of silicon chips necessary to building today's computers?** (The chips can be made so tiny yet hold millions of pieces of information.)

■ **For what two reasons is silicon useful in making the chips?** (It's easy to control how silicon carries an electric current, and there's a huge supply of silicon.)

Amazing Stories

Silicon Rules!

It's the second most common element in Earth's crust after oxygen. It's found in almost all rocks, as well as in sand and clay. For centuries, it has been used to make glass. What element is it? It's silicon. Today, silicon is the most important material in computers and many other electronic devices.

Computers are made up of very small electronic circuits called chips. Almost all the chips are made from silicon. A computer chip is only the size of a fingernail but it can contain millions of pieces of information! Some chips carry instructions that tell the computer what to do. Other chips store data.

Silicon is used in computer chips for two reasons. First, it has excellent insulating properties that can endure high temperatures. Second, there's a huge supply of silicon!

Silicon chips are not just in computers. There are probably about 40 things in your home that contain chips! Chips control your video game and CD player. They make telephones and televisions work better.

Chips in some microwave ovens and washing machines "sense" when food is done or when clothes are clean. Your family car probably contains about 12 chips. One day, the car may drive itself using computer chips!

A silicon chip sits on a human fingertip to give an idea of its size.

C 54

Reading Strategy

Paraphrase

Developing Reading Skills

Ask students to paraphrase the current and future uses of silicon chips. (Possible answer: Silicon chips are now used in computers, video games, CD players, telephones, TVs, microwaves, washers, and cars. Future uses may include implants to help people who are blind, deaf, or paralyzed and making household appliances respond to voice commands.)

In the future, chips may be implanted in the eyes of blind people to help them see. Special chips may help deaf people hear. Chips will control many devices around your home and may even respond to voice commands. If you want to turn a light off, for example, you will speak and your chip-controlled lamp will obey your command. If the telephone rings, you will just start talking!

Sometimes, it's hard to see how valuable Earth's resources can be. Desert sand doesn't look useful, but the silicon in it has changed our lives!

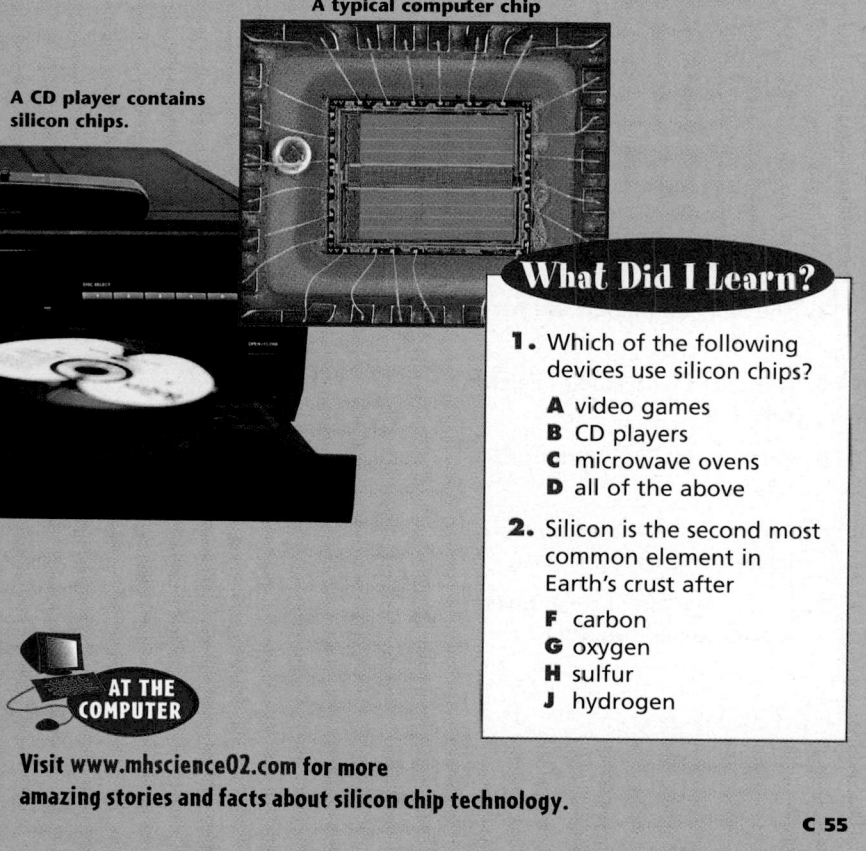

A CD player contains silicon chips.

A typical computer chip

AT THE COMPUTER

Visit www.mhscience02.com for more amazing stories and facts about silicon chip technology.

What Did I Learn?

1. Which of the following devices use silicon chips?

   A video games
   B CD players
   C microwave ovens
   D all of the above

2. Silicon is the second most common element in Earth's crust after

   F carbon
   G oxygen
   H sulfur
   J hydrogen

C 55

Developing the Main Idea

Quartz consists of only silicon and oxygen. Point out that the silicon is derived from heating quartz sand with another substance. The oxygen is burned off, leaving the silicon. Then ask:

■ **Is silicon a renewable or nonrenewable resource? Why?** (Nonrenewable, because, like all minerals, once the quartz sand is used up, it cannot be replaced.)

■ **Is quartz an ore? Why or why not?** (Possible answers: yes, because it is a mineral that contains a useful substance; no, because it doesn't have to be mined.)

Thinking Further: *Making Generalizations*
Ask:

■ **What if another substance could be used to make smaller, higher-capacity chips, but there was not very much of this substance. What might be the advantages of this chip? Disadvantages?** (Advantages: smaller chips that hold more information could be used in tinier devices; to make computers smaller and faster; as implants in humans; disadvantages: more expensive since it's rarer; fewer chips able to be made; might be depleted more quickly.)

Test Prep:  **What Did I Learn?**

1. D

2. G

Summarize
Check students' understanding by having them write a brief summary of the amazing story in their own words.

Inclusion

Elements of Earth's Crust
Have students make a circle graph or bar graph showing the percentages of different elements in Earth's crust. They are as follows: oxygen: 46.6, silicon: 27.7, aluminum: 8.1, iron: 5, calcium: 3.6, sodium: 2.8, potassium 2.6, magnesium: 2.1, other: 1.5. Ask:

■ **How can you tell that silicon is the second most common element?** (It is the second largest pie piece/bar.) **Spatial; Logical**

Advanced Learners

Periodic Table
Invite students to look up silicon in the periodic table. They can make a diagram of the silicon box showing the atomic symbol (Si), atomic number (14), and atomic weight (28.0855). They can then explain the diagram and the information it contains to the rest of the class. **Linguistic**

Chapter Review and Test Preparation

Resources

- Reading in Science Resources, pp. 153–154
- Assessment Book, pp. 31–34

Answers to Vocabulary

1. metamorphic rock
2. hydrosphere
3. solar system
4. geologist
5. planet
6. fossil
7. Sedimentary rock
8. lithosphere
9. mineral
10. Ore

Answers to Test Prep

11. D
12. F
13. A
14. H
15. B

Chapter 6 Review

Vocabulary

Fill each blank with the best word or words from the list.

erosion, C22
fossil, C45
geologist, C18
hydrosphere, C12
igneous rock, C43
lithosphere, C12
metamorphic rock, C46
mineral, C32
ore, C38
planet, C6
sedimentary rock, C44
solar system, C6

1. Rock that changes due to heat and pressure is _____.

2. The oceans are part of Earth's _____.

3. The Sun and planets are part of the _____.

4. A scientist who studies Earth is called a(n) _____.

5. Earth is a(n) _____ that orbits the Sun.

6. A(n) _____ is the imprint of a living thing from the past.

7. _____ is made of small bits of matter joined together.

8. The _____ is the hard outer layer of Earth.

9. A solid material in Earth's crust is called a(n) _____.

10. _____ is a mineral containing a useful substance.

Test Prep

11. The Moon is unlivable compared with Earth because _____.
    A there is no air to breathe
    B there is no water to drink
    C the surface temperature can be hotter than boiling water
    D all of the above

12. Earth's thickest layer is called the _____.
    F mantle
    G crust
    H inner core
    J outer core

13. Fossils are most often found in _____.
    A sedimentary rock
    B lava
    C sand
    D igneous rock

C 56

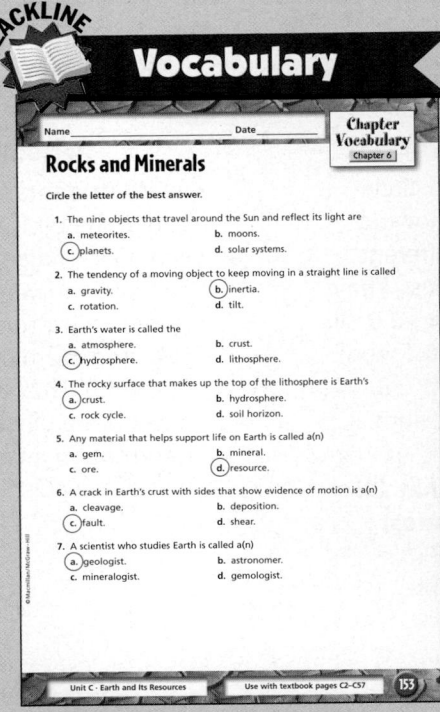

Reading in Science Resources, p. 153

14. Igneous rock is formed from

_____.

F crystals left behind when water evaporated

G meteorites that fell to Earth

H melted rock material that cooled and hardened

J layers of sediment that were squeezed together

15. The main ingredient in soil is

_____.

A bacteria

B weathered rock

C decayed animal material

D decayed plant material

16. Process Skills: Define You find a rock that is made up of different-colored layers. It seems to be made of different-sized grains. Some of it looks as though it is made of tiny seashells glued together. What type of rock is it?

17. Critical Thinking Describe two tests you can use to determine what minerals a rock is made of.

18. Reading in Science Explain the sequence of events that would happen if the force that keeps the planets orbiting the Sun did not exist.

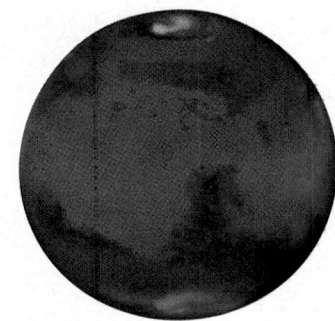

19. Scientific Methods Why is it unlikely we will find life on other planets in our solar system?

20. Decision Making What would you need to bring along on a space mission to another planet? Explain your choices.

Boost *your test scores!*

Be Smart!

Visit www.mhscience02.com

C 57

Answers to Concepts and Skills

16. Process Skills: Define sedimentary rock

17. Critical Thinking Luster is the way light bounces off a mineral and can be used to identify what minerals a rock is made of. Streak is the color of the powder left when a mineral is rubbed against a hard, rough surface and is always the same for a given mineral. Hardness and cleavage are also tests for identifying minerals.

18. Reading in Science Gravity is the force that holds all of the objects in the solar system together. Without gravity, Earth and all of the other objects orbiting the Sun would go flying off into space.

19. Scientific Methods The conditions that make life possible on Earth, just the right amount of energy to provide living things with warmth and light, do not exist in sufficient amounts on other planets in the solar system.

20. Decision Making food, oxygen, water—all the things that do not exist in space or on the other planet

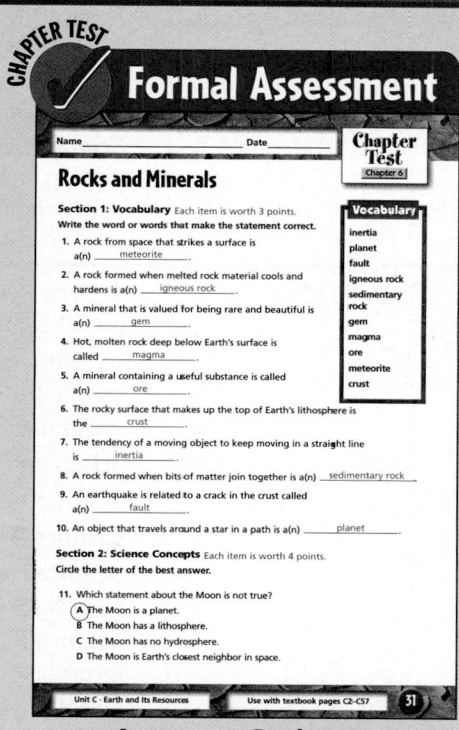

Assessment Book, p. 31

Lesson Planner

Lesson	Objectives	Vocabulary	Pacing	Resources and Technology
LESSON 5 **Earth's Atmosphere,** pp. C60–C67	■ Explore evidence of air pollution. ■ Identify air as a resource we need to survive. ■ Identify sources of air pollution. ■ Identify ways to clean up the air.	**renewable resource** **ozone layer** **fossil fuel** **nonrenewable resource** **smog** **acid rain**	3 days	■ Activity Resources, pp. 100–104 ■ Reading in Science Resources, pp. 159–164 ■ Vocabulary Cards ■ Reading Aid Transparency C5 ■ **Explore Activity Video**
LESSON 6 **Earth's Water Supply,** pp. C70–C79	■ Explore how salt water can be used to make fresh water. ■ Compare salt water and fresh water sources. ■ Recognize how water can become polluted. ■ Identify ways to clean up and conserve water.	**desalination** **water cycle** **groundwater** **water table** **aquifer** **spring** **well** **reservoir**	4 days	■ Activity Resources, pp. 105–109 ■ Reading in Science Resources, pp. 165–170 ■ Vocabulary Cards ■ Grade-Level Science Book, *Our Riverkeeper* ■ Reading Aid Transparency C6 ■ Visual Aid Transparencies 9, 10, 11, 12, 19 ■ **Explore Activity Video**
LESSON 7 **Earth's Oceans,** pp. C82–C95	■ Explore the difference between ocean water and fresh water. ■ Understand that oceans have many valuable resources. ■ Understand what causes currents, waves, and tides. ■ Describe the topography of the ocean floor.	**basin** **current** **continental shelf** **continental slope** **continental rise** **abyssal plain** **seamount** **trench** **mid-ocean ridge**	4 days	■ Activity Resources, pp. 110–114 ■ Reading in Science Resources, pp. 171–176 ■ Vocabulary Cards ■ Reading Aid Transparency C7 ■ Visual Aid Transparency 20 ■ **Explore Activity Video** ■ **Science Newsroom CD-ROM** *Sea to Shining Sea* ■ **Science Experiences Videos** *Staying Alive* *Researching the Ocean Depths* *Life in a Coral Reef*
LESSON 8 **Energy Resources,** pp. C98–C107	■ Explore ways that people use energy each day. ■ Compare and contrast fossil fuel use with world reserves. ■ Identify alternative energy sources. ■ Identify ways to use energy more wisely.	**alternative energy source** **geothermal energy** **biomass**	3 days	■ Activity Resources, pp. 115–119 ■ Reading in Science Resources, pp. 177–182 ■ Vocabulary Cards ■ School to Home, pp. 20–22 ■ Transparencies C8, 21 ■ **Explore Activity Video** ■ **Science Newsroom CD-ROM** *Fuels Rush In* ■ **Science Experiences Videos** *Environmentally Friendly Transportation*

Activity Planner

Activity	Process Skills	Materials	Plan Ahead
LESSON 5 Explore Activity **What Makes Air Dirty?** p. C61	use variables, observe, measure, interpret data, communicate	12 cardboard strips, petroleum jelly, plastic knife, transparent tape, string, hand lens, metric ruler, marker	No advance planning is needed.
LESSON 6 Explore Activity **Investigate How to Make Salt Water Usable** p. C71	make a model, observe, infer, use variables, communicate	tea bag; deep pan; plastic cup; saucer (or petri dish); large, clear bowl or container; water	No advance planning is needed.
Process Skill **BUILDER** **How Do Wastes From Land Get Into Lakes and Rivers?** p. C77	form a hypothesis, make a model, experiment	soil, food color, foam bits, 2 aluminum pans, water, 2 textbooks	Using diatomaceous earth (available from pool supply stores) rather than regular soil will show the results more clearly and make cleanup easier.
LESSON 7 Explore Activity **How Do Ocean and Fresh Water Compare?** p. C83	predict, experiment, observe, communicate	3 small plastic cups, "ocean water," "fresh water," clear-plastic straw, waterproof marking pen, wax paper, ruler	Make ocean water by placing several drops of food coloring and 3 teaspoons of salt in a cup of water. Stir until salt is dissolved. Fill another cup with fresh water and add several drops of a different color food coloring.
QUICK LAB FOR SCHOOL OR HOME **Salt Water and Fresh Water** p. C85	observe, measure, predict	jar, fresh water, salt water, thumbtack, pencil with eraser, waterproof marker, paper towel, metric ruler	No advance planning is needed.
LESSON 8 Explore Activity **How Do People Use Energy?** p. C99	communicate, infer, use numbers, hypothesize	none	No advance planning is needed.

Reading in Science Resources

McGraw-Hill Science **Reading in Science Resources** provides the following **Blackline Master** worksheets for this chapter.

Chapter Graphic Organizer

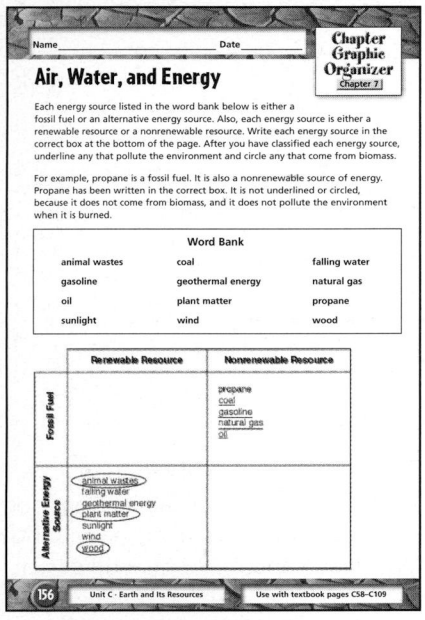

Reading in Science Resources,
p. 156

Chapter Reading Skill

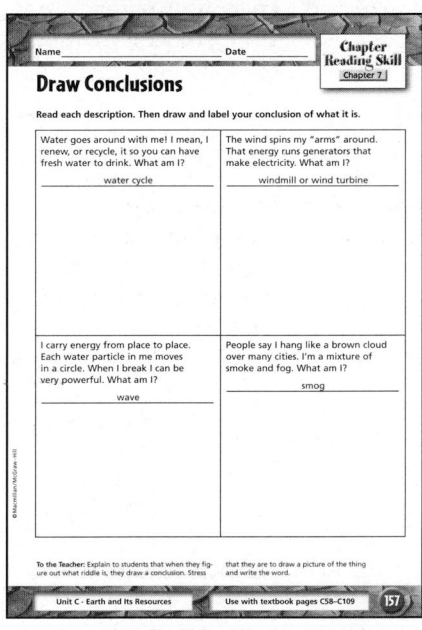

Reading in Science Resources,
pp. 157–158

Chapter Vocabulary

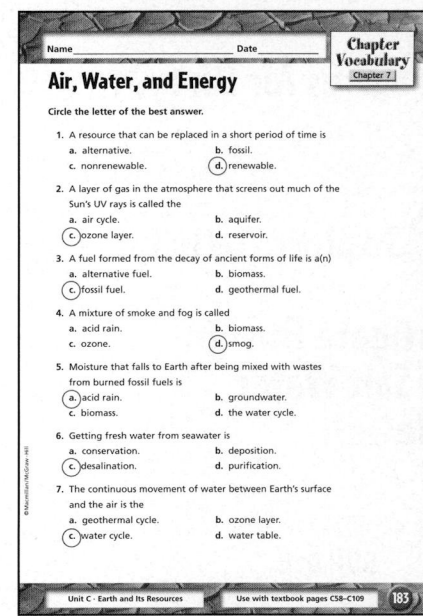

Reading in Science Resources,
pp. 183–184

McGraw-Hill Science **Reading in Science Resources** provides the following **Blackline Master** worksheets for every lesson in this chapter.

Lesson Outline

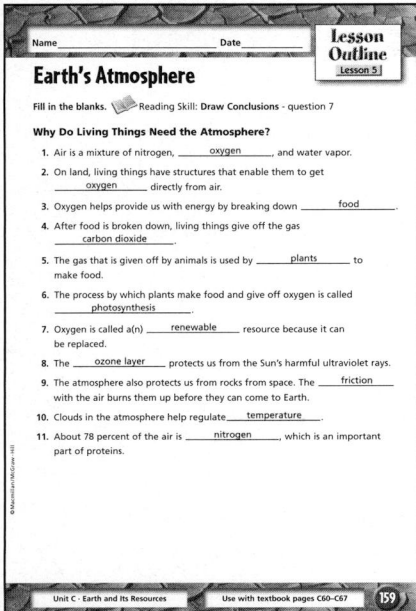

Reading in Science Resources,
pp. 159–160, 165–166, 171–172,
177–178

Interpret Illustrations

Reading in Science Resources,
pp. 161–162, 167–168, 173–174,
179–180

Lesson Vocabulary and Cloze Test

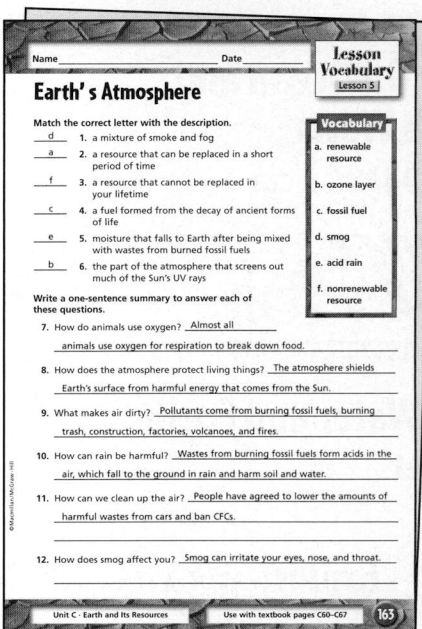

Reading in Science Resources,
pp. 163–164, 169–170, 175–176,
181–182

Activities and Assessment

McGraw-Hill Science **Activity Resources** provides the following **Blackline Master** worksheets for every lesson in this chapter.

Explore Activity and Alternative Explore Activity

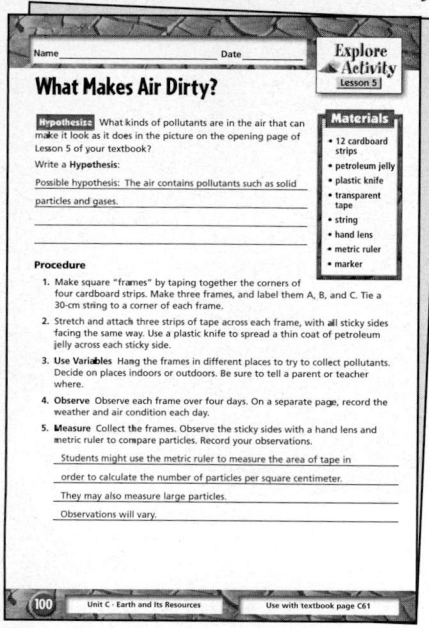

Activity Resources, pp. 100–102, 105–107, 110–112, 115–117

Quick Lab for School or Home

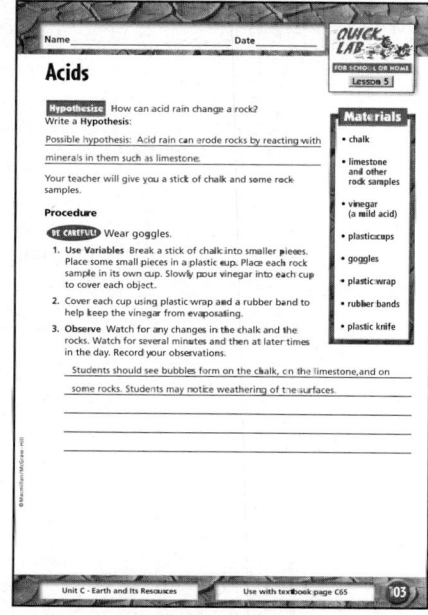

Activity Resources, pp. 103–104, 113–114, 118–119

Process Skill Builder

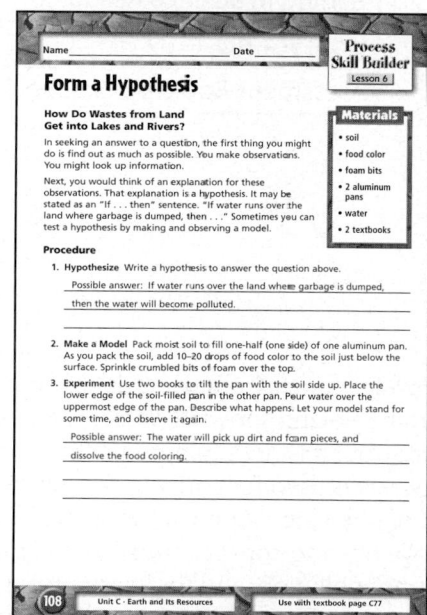

Activity Resources, pp. 108–109

McGraw-Hill Science **Assessment Book** provides the following **Blackline Master** worksheets for this chapter.

Chapter Test

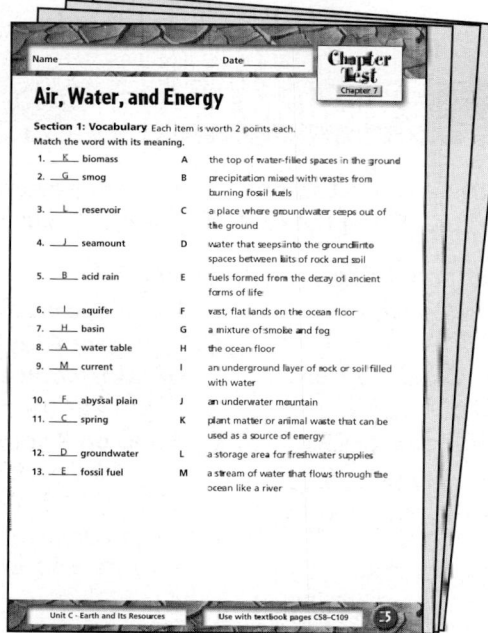

Assessment Book, pp. 35–38

CHAPTER 7 Air, Water, and Energy

Did You Ever Wonder?

Fresh water comes from rivers, lakes, and streams, and from rain and snowfall. Water is a renewable resource, but it is not unlimited. Much of the world's fresh water is used for agriculture. Pollution renders much of our water supply undrinkable, if not unusable. We need to conserve fresh water, protect supplies from pollution, and find better ways to reuse it. Students may or may not know if their water comes from wells or reservoirs. You may wish to have them do a research project to find out where the school's water comes from.

CHAPTER 7 Air, Water, and Energy

Did You Ever Wonder?

Where does Earth's freshwater supply come from? When you look at the spectacular waterfalls of Iguazu in Argentina, you might think that there is an endless supply of fresh water on Earth. Is this true? Might we run out of clean drinking water? Where does your drinking water come from?

C 58

Reading Strategy

This chapter provides MiniLessons and other opportunities for developing and practicing the following reading skills:

- ◉ **Cause and Effect:** p. C86
- ◉ **Compare and Contrast:** pp. C85, C87, C91
- ◉ **Draw Conclusions:** pp. C65, C73, C89, C106
- ◉ **Find the Main Idea:** p. C93
- ○ **Sequence of Events**
- ◉ **Summarize:** pp. C67, C79, C81, C95, C97, C107
- ◉ **Ask Questions:** p. C76

- ○ **Reread**
- ◉ **Retell (paraphrase):** p. C64
- ◉ **Interpret Graphic Sources of Information:** pp. C63, C72, C86, C91, C103
- ◉ **Build on Prior Knowledge:** pp. C60, C68, C70, C80, C82, C96, C98, C110
- ◉ **Organize Information:** pp. C66, C68, C84, C92, C98

C-59

Vocabulary Preview

Encourage students to keep a Science Dictionary. Remind them to add the Vocabulary words for each lesson in this chapter to their Dictionary as they complete each lesson.

renewable resource, C62

ozone layer, C63

fossil fuel, C64

nonrenewable resource, C64

smog, C64

acid rain, C65

desalination, C73

water cycle, C74

groundwater, C74

water table, C75

aquifer, C75

spring, C75

well, C75

reservoir, C75

basin, C84

current, C86

continental shelf, C90

continental slope, C90

continental rise, C90

abyssal plain, C90

seamount, C90

trench, C91

mid-ocean ridge, C91

alternative energy source, C104

geothermal energy, C104

biomass, C106

AMERICAN MUSEUM OF NATURAL HISTORY

Visit www.amnh.org/resources/mhscience to discover more about Earth's atmosphere, water, and resources.

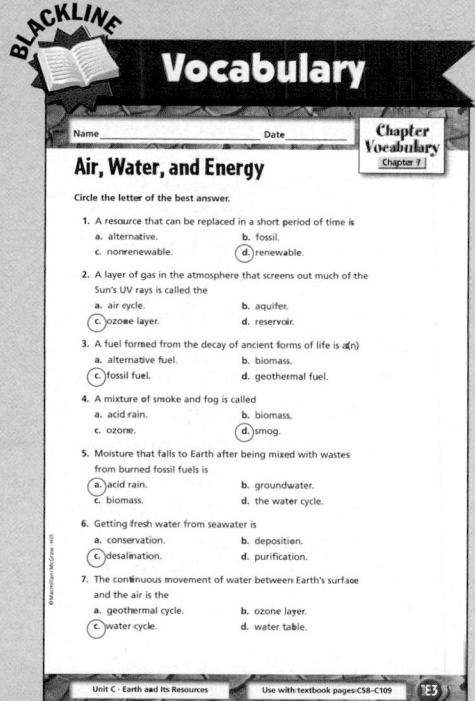

Graphic Organizer

Vocabulary

Reading in Science Resources, p. 156

Reading in Science Resources, pp. 183–184

Earth's Atmosphere

Objectives

- Explore evidence of air pollution.
- Identify air as a resource we need to survive.
- Identify sources of air pollution.
- Identify ways to clean up the air.

Resources

- Activity Resources, pp. 100–104
- Reading in Science Resources, pp. 159–164
- Vocabulary Cards
- Reading Aid Transparency C5

Build on Prior Knowledge

Have students discuss what they know about air as a resource. Ask:

- **How do we use air?** (We breathe it into our lungs.)
- **Can we use up Earth's air?** (Possible answers: No, plants put in the oxygen we take out; yes, if we get it too dirty.)

Discuss all answers but lead students to the idea that air is renewable.

1 Get Ready

Developing the Main Idea

Ask students how burning gasoline and other pollutants affect Earth's air, land, and water. (These things add impurities and make resources unusable) Discuss what kind of damage pollution can cause to our atmosphere and how that damage might affect us.

LESSON 5 Earth's Atmosphere

Vocabulary

renewable resource, C62
ozone layer, C63
fossil fuel, C64
nonrenewable resource, C64
smog, C64
acid rain, C65

Get Ready

From space Earth's atmosphere appears as a thin blue layer surrounding the planet. From the ground the air may appear different from day to day.

The air may seem clear and clean on some days. If you live in or near a big city, you may have days when the air seems smoky, or "hazy." Why? What kinds of pollutants are in the air that can make it look that way?

Process Skill

You interpret data when you use the information that has been gathered to answer questions or solve a problem.

C 60

Science Background

Pollution Sources

In the United States, major sources of pollution include power plants that burn fossil fuels; industrial boilers; home furnaces; cars and trucks; iron and steel mills; zinc, lead and copper smelters; incinerators; petroleum refineries; and cement plants. Have students pick one of these potential polluters and find information on what kind of problems and solutions there are for that form of pollution. **Linguistic**

Science Background

Making Coal Burn Cleaner
Addressing Misconceptions

Since one of the major concerns of this lesson is the burning of fossil fuels, stress early on how much air pollution could be reduced by burning cleaner coal. Point out, however, that "clean coal" does not mean the coal is washed in soap and water. New technologies exist that remove the sulfur chemically before or after the coal is burned. Direct interested students to research this topic on the Internet. **Linguistic**

Explore Activity

What Makes Air Dirty?

Procedure

1 Make square "frames" by taping together the corners of four cardboard strips. Make three frames, and label them A, B, and C. Tie a 30-cm string to a corner of each frame.

2 Stretch and attach three strips of tape across each frame, with all sticky sides facing the same way. Use a plastic knife to spread a thin coat of petroleum jelly across each sticky side.

3 **Use Variables** Hang the frames in different places to try to collect pollutants. Decide on places indoors or outdoors. Be sure to tell a parent or teacher where.

4 **Observe** Observe each frame over four days. Record the weather and air condition each day.

5 **Measure** Collect the frames. Observe the sticky sides with a hand lens and a metric ruler to compare particles.

Drawing Conclusions

1 **Interpret Data** How did the frames change over time? How did the hand lens and ruler help you describe any pollution?

2 **Communicate** Present your data in a graph to show differences in amounts.

3 **Going Further: Use Variables** What kinds of pollutants would your frames not collect? How might you design a collector for them? How might you extend this activity over different periods of time?

Materials

12 cardboard strips

petroleum jelly

plastic knife

transparent tape

string

hand lens

metric ruler

marker

C 61

Alternative Explore Activity

Materials wide-mouth gallon containers, water

Water Collector Have students put a little water in their containers. Direct them to place their uncovered containers where they won't be disturbed and leave them there until the water evaporates. Suggest both indoor and outdoor locations. After the water has evaporated, have students collect and examine the residue and compare the solid residues from all the containers. Have them consider where the matter comes from. (from the air) **Kinesthetic; Logical**

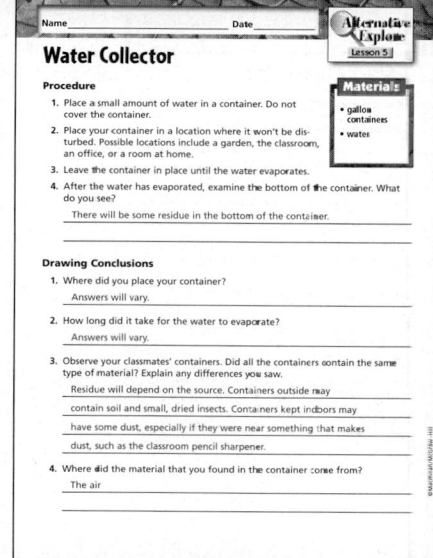

Activity Resources, p. 102

Explore Activity

What Makes Air Dirty?

Science Process Skills *use variables, observe, measure, interpret data, communicate*

Resources Activity Resources, pp. 100–101

Pacing 30–40 minutes

Grouping pairs

Procedure

Be Careful! Caution students to be careful not to get petroleum jelly on clothing, books, or furniture, and to wash their hands after using it.

1 Be sure students tape the strip together securely.

3 Advise students to place their frames where they won't be disturbed.

4 Remind students to make daily checks of their frames.

5 Students might note the size of larger particles, how plentiful they are, and how densely collected the particles are.

Answers to Drawing Conclusions

1 Various kinds of particles collected on the tape. The hand lens makes the matter more visible. The ruler may be used to measure the size of the particles and the area of the tape affected.

2 Students might graph the number of particles per square centimeter of tape and/or the number of particles of different sizes (in millimeters).

3 The frames did not collect gaseous pollutants. A collector design might include a way to trap gases using a special filtering device. The periods of time for collection could be lengthened or limited to only certain times of day. An alternate plan would be to replace the frames periodically for varying lengths of time.

Inquiry Students can ask their own questions to explore, such as what the particles are or where do they come from.

Technology

■ When time is short, preview the Activity with the **Explore Activity Video.**

2 | Read to Learn

Why Do Living Things Need the Atmosphere?

Before Reading
Have students try to answer the red question at the top of the page.

Developing the Main Idea
Use a pie chart to show that air is made up of about 21% oxygen; 78% nitrogen; 1% argon, carbon dioxide, water vapor, and other gases. Then invite students to inhale then exhale. Ask:

■ **What did you take in when you inhaled?** (air containing oxygen)

People take in oxygen when they inhale with their lungs. Fish have gills; insects have air tubes; reptiles, birds, and mammals have lungs. Plants take in oxygen through tiny openings in their leaves.

Using the Illustrations
Have students trace the path that oxygen takes when it is given off by a plant until it is returned to the plant within carbon dioxide. Point out that during photosynthesis, plants take in more carbon dioxide than oxygen.

Developing Vocabulary

renewable resource Students can discuss that *renew* means "to make new again," to start or open again." Discuss why "renew" begins the first word of this term. Remind students that oxygen is recycled in the Earth's atmosphere making it a renewable resource.

ozone layer Students may be familiar with the importance of the ozone layer from news reports. Have them describe why it is so important.

Read to Learn

Main Idea Earth's atmosphere supports life on Earth.

Why Do Living Things Need the Atmosphere?

Why couldn't humans live on a planet that does not have an atmosphere as on Earth? Every minute of every day, you need air.

Air is a mixture of nitrogen, oxygen, and a few traces of other gases, including water vapor. This mixture is a vital resource. It supports and protects life on Earth in many ways.

Almost all organisms need air to live. Actually, they need oxygen, one of the gases that is in air. On land living things have structures that enable them to get oxygen directly from the air. Living things in water habitats take in oxygen that is dissolved in the water.

What is oxygen for? Living things take in oxygen for respiration. In this process oxygen is used to break down food so that energy can be gotten from it. As a result of this process, living things give off wastes, including the gas carbon dioxide.

Why doesn't the atmosphere fill up with carbon dioxide? Plants and other producers, living things that have the green substance chlorophyll, take in carbon dioxide. They use it for making food. In the presence of light, these organisms carry on the process called photosynthesis. In this process they make food and give off oxygen.

Producers range in size from green plants to one-celled algae. They replace oxygen in the atmosphere. This makes oxygen a naturally renewable resource. A renewable resource is one that can be replaced. It can be replaced in a short enough period of time, such as a human lifetime, to support life on Earth.

Protection
The atmosphere also acts as a protective shield. It shields Earth's surface from harmful energy that comes from

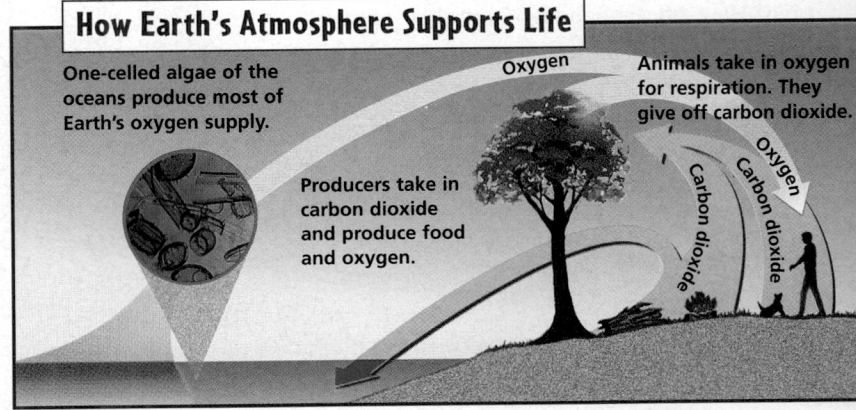

How Earth's Atmosphere Supports Life

One-celled algae of the oceans produce most of Earth's oxygen supply.

Producers take in carbon dioxide and produce food and oxygen.

Oxygen

Animals take in oxygen for respiration. They give off carbon dioxide.

Oxygen

Carbon dioxide

Carbon dioxide

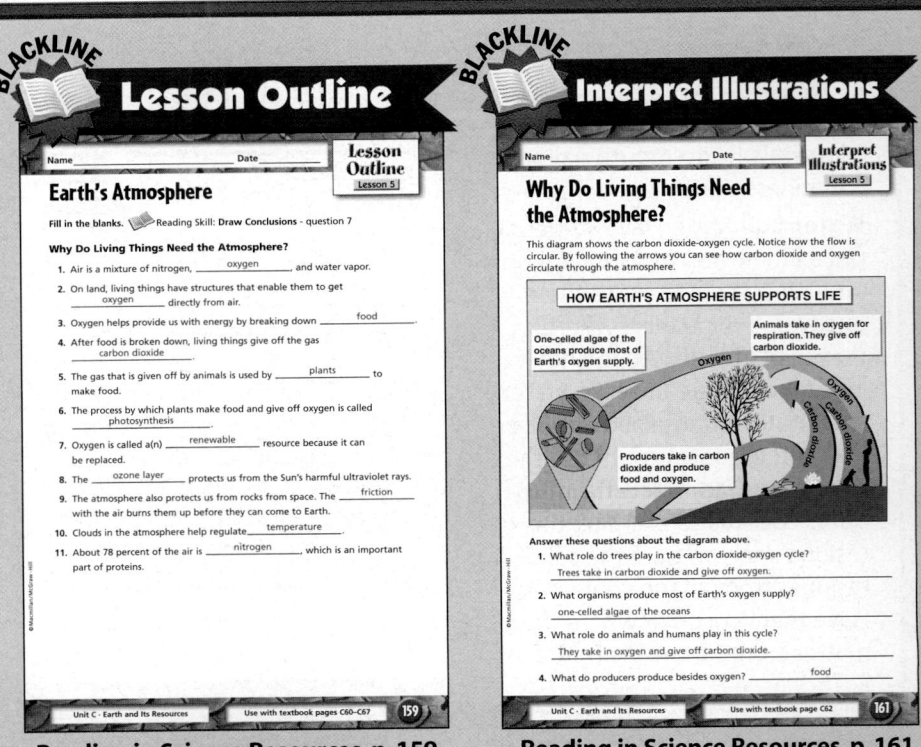

Air circulates in patterns called convection currents.

Warm air rising

Cold air sinking

the Sun. The atmosphere helps screen out harmful ultraviolet rays (UV rays) from the Sun. About 30 km (18.6 mi) above your head is a layer of gas called ozone (OH·zohn). This ozone layer screens out from 95 to 99 percent of the Sun's UV rays.

The atmosphere also shields Earth from rocks from space. The "shooting stars" you see on a clear night are not stars. They are rocks from space that burn up due to friction with the air as they speed through the atmosphere.

The atmosphere also protects life from extremes of temperature. Clouds block sunlight during the day. At night they keep much of the heat from escaping into space, so that the planet does not "cool off." Whenever one part of the atmosphere gets hotter than another, the air moves, or circulates, and spreads the heat around.

Most of the air, about 78 percent, is nitrogen. Nitrogen is an important ingredient in food,

namely proteins. How does it get into proteins? Nitrogen is taken from the air by certain kinds of bacteria. These bacteria change the nitrogen into a form that stays in the soil.

Plants use this nitrogen in the soil to make proteins. As living things eat the plants, nitrogen is passed along. It is returned to the soil when living things die.

▷ **What does the atmosphere provide for living things?**

The atmosphere provides important gases, oxygen and nitrogen, and protects us from the Sun's rays, space rocks, and extreme temperatures.

READING
Diagrams

1. Do you see any cycles in this diagram? Cycles are continuous processes, where one thing happens after another over and over in the same order.

2. Explain any cycles you see.

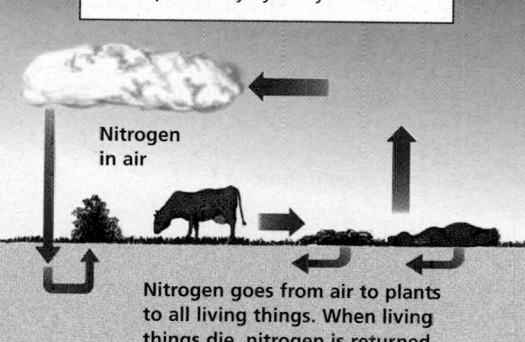

Nitrogen in air

Nitrogen goes from air to plants to all living things. When living things die, nitrogen is returned to the soil.

C 63

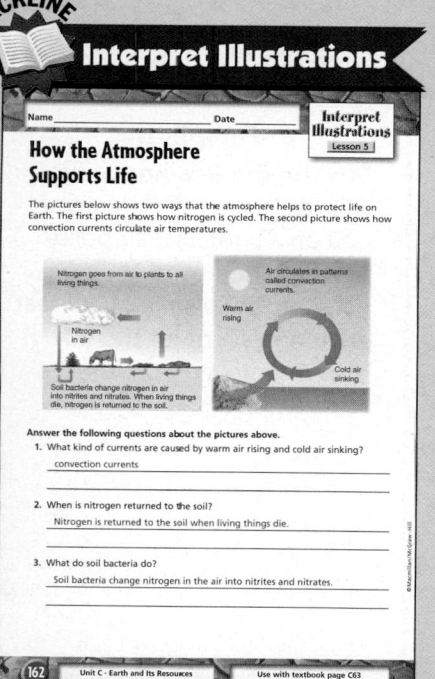

Inclusion

SCIENCE FOR ALL

SPF

Remind students that the atmosphere does not shield out all ultraviolet radiation, so wearing sunscreen is important for protecting their skin. Explain that *SPF* stands for *Sun Protection Factor*. A sunscreen rated as SPF 30 means that this sunscreen will protect the skin 30 times longer than if no sunscreen were used at all. Students should be advised to apply sunscreen *before* going into the sun, giving it time to react with the skin. **Logical**

Developing the Main Idea.
Ask:

■ **What have you heard in the news recently about the ozone layer?** (A hole has developed at the South Pole, causing a depletion of ozone that can lead to increases in skin cancers; most recently, the hole has begun to shrink again.)

■ **Why do you think hospitals remove flowers in patients' rooms during the night?** (They give off oxygen during the day, but at night, they give off carbon dioxide instead, which makes the air less fresh.)

■ **Are convection currents responsible for land and sea breezes as well as other winds?** (yes)

Exploring the Main Idea
Use a lamp like a spotlight or projection lamp to simulate the sun. Place a sieve in front of the lamp to illustrate the screening effect of the sun on a partly cloudy day. Have students note that visible light still comes through, and note that invisible radiation, such as ultraviolet light, also comes through. Ask a student to try holding the sieve and slowly move it in front of the lamp and then slowly remove it. Ask:

■ **What does the moving of the sieve represent?** (The movement of the day's cloud cover.)

READING
Diagrams

1. Yes; students might answer this question using the diagram at the bottom of the page—but might also look at the diagram at the top.

2. ■ A cycle involving nitrogen that goes from the air to soil—bacteria to plants to animals and back to the air. (diagram at the bottom)

   ■ A cycle involving air circulation, as warm air rises, cools, sinks, and is heated again. (diagram at the top)

▶ **After Reading**
Have students answer the red question in the student book as **ongoing assessment**.

What Causes Pollution?

Before Reading

Have students try to answer the red question at the top of the first text column.

Developing the Main Idea

Have students classify sources of air pollution as being natural or human-activity-generated. Explain that even natural air pollutants, such as dust, ash, and pollen, can be dangerous to health in high concentrations.

Exploring the Main Idea

Light a candle inside a heat-proof beaker. Completely cover the beaker with a square of glass as the candle is burning. Ask:

- **What collects on the glass?** (droplets of water)
- **What happens once the beaker fills with carbon dioxide gas?** (the candle goes out, since no more oxygen is available)

Emphasize that when fossil fuels are burned, they give off gases that enter the atmosphere. Remind students that all fossil fuels contain carbon and hydrogen. Ask:

- **What gases do you think are given off when fossil fuels are burned?** (Possible answers: carbon dioxide, carbon monoxide, and water vapor)

▶ After Reading

Have students answer the red question in the student book as **ongoing assessment**.

Developing Vocabulary

fossil fuel Students can see the word *fossil* in this term. Discuss that the fuels themselves are fossils. They are remains of ancient forms of life.

nonrenewable resource Have students recall the definition of *renewable resource* on p. C62. Then have them add the prefix *non-* to give their own definition. Discuss the use of this prefix with other words. (*nonstop, nonfiction*)

smog Students can assemble this word by breaking off pieces of *smoke* and *fog* and putting them together. Discuss why this is an appropriate name for these clouds.

Natural events can add to air pollution.

Industries produce wastes that add to air pollution.

Wearing a mask helps when smog is very heavy.

What Causes Pollution?

Many of the things humans do add pollution to the air. There are harmful solids, gases, and liquids in the air. Where do they come from?

Many pollutants get into the air from burning fossil fuels. These fuels were formed from the decay of ancient forms of life. Fossil fuels are nonrenewable resources. They cannot be replaced in your lifetime. Fossil fuels include coal, oil, and natural gas. Cars, buses, trucks, and planes burn these fuels, as do many homes and power plants. The wastes from burning these fuels add pollution to the air.

Burning trash adds smoke to the air. Dust comes from plowed fields. It comes from construction sites and from mines. Factories add chemical wastes to the air.

Other events also add to air pollution. Volcanoes erupt and shoot gases and particles into the air. Forest fires and grass fires can spread smoke over great distances.

All these pollutants can build up into thick clouds called smog. Smog is a mixture of smoke and fog. It forms when smoke and fumes collect in moist, calm air. Smog irritates the eyes, nose, and throat. People with breathing problems have died from heavy smog.

Smog hangs like a brown cloud over many cities. Why do you think it is most common in big coastal cities like Los Angeles?

Sometimes ozone can form in smog. High up in the atmosphere, remember, ozone protects Earth from UV radiation. However, at ground level this gas can make people sick.

 burning fossil fuels, volcanic eruptions, forest fires, dust from plowed fields, chemical wastes from factories, burning trash

▶ **What are five sources of air pollution?**

C 64

SCIENCE FOR ALL — Advanced Learners

Units of Measure

Invite students to look in an encyclopedia or other resource to find out what units are used to measure the amount of pollution in the air and what amounts are considered safe for health. Challenge students to explain the different measurements used for solids and for gases. (Concentrations of solid particles are usually measured in mass or weight per cubic meter; gas concentrations are usually given in parts per million — *ppm* — or parts per billion — *ppb*.)

SCIENCE — Reading Strategy

Paraphrase

Developing Reading Skills

Ask students to find information on a particular air pollutant and then write a paragraph explaining how that pollutant is formed and how it can be removed from the atmosphere.

What Is Acid Rain?

What can destroy forests, kill animals and plants in lakes, and even eat away at buildings? Part of the answer comes from power plants that burn coal to produce energy. Another part comes from motor vehicles that burn gasoline.

Wastes that come from burning these fossil fuels travel into the air. In the air the wastes mix with moisture. They can form chemicals called acids in the moisture. The moisture with acids can eventually fall to Earth's surface as **acid rain**. This term includes all forms of precipitation—rain, snow, hail, and sleet.

Acid rain can harm soil and water supplies. Some trees sicken and die if there is too much acid in the soil. Fish die when water in lakes contains too much acid. The acid weathers away statues and buildings. It can cause metal surfaces on cars to crumble.

READING Draw Conclusions
Why is acid rain harmful?

Acid rain is harmful because it can destroy water and soil supplies, kill living things, and weather statues, buildings, and cars, causing them to crumble.

Trees yellow and die due to acid rain.

QUICK LAB

FOR SCHOOL OR HOME

Acids

Your teacher will give you a stick of chalk and some rock samples.

BE CAREFUL! Wear goggles.

1. **Use Variables** Break a stick of chalk into smaller pieces. Place some small pieces in a plastic cup. Place each rock sample in its own cup. Slowly pour vinegar into each cup to cover each object.

2. Cover each cup using plastic wrap and a rubber band to help keep the vinegar from evaporating.

3. **Observe** Watch for any changes in the chalk and the rocks. Watch for several minutes and then at later times in the day. Record your observations.

4. Vinegar is a mild acid. How did it change the chalk?

5. Do all rocks change the same way? Explain based on your results.

C 65

Reading MiniLesson

Draw Conclusions

Develop Discuss with students that to draw a conclusion, we must look at all the facts, or clues, and use our common sense to figure things out. Stress that it's easy to draw a conclusion that acid rain is harmful when we have facts such as dead trees and fish and acid-eaten buildings and cars.

Practice Ask students to find evidence in the first two paragraphs of page C65 to support the conclusion that both factories and automobiles are responsible for acid rain. (Answers should include that coal-burning power plants and gas-burning cars produce wastes that mix with moisture in the air to form acid rain.)

What Is Acid Rain?

Before Reading
Have students try to answer the red question at the top of the page.

Using the Illustrations
Call students' attention to the photograph. Clarify that it shows the effect of acid rain on the trees but does not show harm done to water and soil.

▶ After Reading
Have students answer the red question in the student book as **ongoing assessment**.

QUICK LAB

FOR SCHOOL OR HOME

Materials stick of chalk, limestone and other rock samples, plastic cups, vinegar, plastic wrap, rubber bands, goggles, plastic knife

Resources Activity Resources, pp. 103–104

Science Process Skills *use variables, observe*

Plan Ahead You may wish to break the chalk into small pieces ahead of time by wrapping it in cloth and hitting it with the side of a hammer on a sturdy surface. Limestone or marble samples are usually available at building supply stores or garden centers

Be Careful! Stress the importance of safety goggles whenever chemicals are being used.

Step 3 Students might look for color changes, the production of gas bubbles, and the gradual deterioration of the samples.

Step 4 The chalk bubbled in the vinegar and the size of the chalk decreased.

Step 5 Results depend on the rock samples. Coquina (soft limestone composed of shell fragments) will show similar results as chalk. Limestone rock will react more slowly than chalk. Rocks that are not similar to limestone, such as feldspar, will not react with the vinegar (acid).

Developing Vocabulary

acid rain Students can describe common acids such as vinegar or lemon juice by listing their properties—sour taste, strong smell.

How Can We Clean Up the Air?

Before Reading
Have students try to answer the red question at the top of the page.

Developing the Main Idea
Emphasize the global nature of air pollution. Ask:

- **Why must all nations work together to clean up the air?** (Air moves all over the Earth and does not stay confined within national boundaries.)

- **What do you think Earth Day celebrations accomplish?** (Keeping people aware of environmental problems helps them to continue working for laws to protect the environment and to change their own habits to decrease pollution.)

You might want to discuss the Clean Air Act of 1967. This act set the first standards for air quality. The Act of 1970 established the EPA as the agency responsible for making sure that air quality standards are enforced. The amendments of 1990 identified major air pollution problems.

▶ After Reading
Have students answer the red question in the student book as **ongoing assessment**.

How Can We Clean Up the Air?

Cleaning up the air is a job that takes all nations to work on. That is why the Congress of the United States passed laws to protect the air. It passed the Clean Air Act in 1967 and added more parts in 1970, 1977, and 1990.

As a result of these laws, cars now have lowered amounts of harmful wastes that are released. "Clean coal" methods were introduced to lower the amount of harmful wastes that result in acid rain. Power plants that burn coal can wash coal before burning it, to remove sulfur. Sulfur can result in acid rain when the coal burns.

In 1970 the first Earth Day was celebrated. People were becoming very concerned about the health of planet Earth. That year the Environmental Protection Agency (EPA) was formed. The EPA is part of the United States government. It has the job of checking that laws are being followed. It investigates new dangers and offers solutions and guidelines.

The photographs show "holes" in the ozone layer. The ozone layer, remember, is a layer high up in the atmosphere that protects Earth from harmful UV radiation. However, it seems humans have caused holes to form in this layer. The holes are letting UV radiation through.

How did the holes get there? Scientists are not totally sure. Much evidence points to substances that

Satellite photos of Earth's ozone layer

people have been using a lot. These substances are called CFCs, which is short for chlorofluorocarbons (klawr·oh·floor·oh·KAHR·buhnz). They are gases used in such things as refrigerators, freezers, and air conditioners. CFCs were also used in many aerosol spray cans. Spray paints, hair sprays, and even shaving foams released CFCs. When the CFCs leak out from these products, they rise into the atmosphere. There they can affect the ozone layer.

In 1990 a group of representatives from around the world met in London. They signed an agreement to ban the use of CFCs worldwide in just ten years.

Aerosol spray cans can now use substitutes. Just read the label on a spray can, and you can see for yourself.

We can buy cars that release less waste, burn less fuel, and use products that don't release harmful chemicals into the atmosphere.

> **What are some ways we can reduce air pollution?**

C 66

Reading Strategy

Organize Information
Developing Reading Skills
Have students assemble a timeline of events based on the dates in the first paragraph, as well as the events described in paragraphs 3 and 6.

L·I·N·K·S

Why It Matters

Air pollution harms trees, lakes, and buildings. It can also affect you directly. Air pollution can make people sick. It can make your eyes and nose feel like they are burning. It can make your throat feel itchy and irritated.

Laws help to protect the air. However, it takes people to save the air. The Clean Air Act can work only if people work together. For example, using less electricity can save fuel. Finding ways to cut down on using cars saves fuel, too. Cutting down on burning fuel lowers air pollution.

Visit **www.mhscience02.com** to do a research project on the EPA.

Think and Write

1. Why is air important to living things?

2. How does the atmosphere protect Earth?

3. How do people pollute the air?

4. What causes acid rain? How does acid rain affect land and water?

5. **Critical Thinking** How can using less electricity cut down on the use of fossil fuels?

MATH LINK

Make a graph. Air samples are graded according to how many parts per million (ppm) of various pollutants they contain. Watch the news or read the newspaper every night for one week. Note the air quality for each day. Show the range of air quality in your community with a bar graph.

Pollutants	Air Quality
0–50 ppm	good
50–100 ppm	moderate
100–200 ppm	unhealthy
200–300 ppm	very unhealthy
300–500 ppm	hazardous

WRITING LINK

Write a paragraph. How can you cut down on using electricity and fuel? Be specific. Think about things you, your family, and your friends can do.

SOCIAL STUDIES LINK

Conduct research. Learn more about the Clean Air Act. Use the Internet or an encyclopedia.

TECHNOLOGY LINK

At the Computer Visit **www.mhscience02.com** for more links.

C 67

3 Lesson Review

Answers to Think and Write

1. Living things need oxygen from air for respiration and nitrogen from air directly or indirectly to make proteins. Plants use carbon dioxide from air for photosynthesis. (pp. C62–63)

2. The atmosphere shields Earth from harmful radiation. It also protects Earth against rocks from space and from extreme temperatures. (p. C63)

3. Most air pollution comes from burning fossil fuels. Other sources are dust from plowing fields and burning trash. (p. C64)

4. Acid rain falls as a result of wastes from burning fossil fuels combining with moisture in the air. Acid rain can harm soil and water, causing trees and aquatic life to die. (p. C65)

5. **Critical Thinking** Using less electricity would require less burning of fossil fuels at power plants. (pp. C64, C67)

Summarize
Check students' understanding by having them write a brief summary of the lesson in their own words.

MATH LINK
Students should write the ppm scale along one axis and the Days of the Week along the other axis. Suggest a scale in increments of 50 ppm. Discuss the air quality over the course of the week.

WRITING LINK
Students may suggest that they can turn off lights when leaving a room or turn off TVs when not in use. They may suggest that to cut back on fuel they can bike, walk, or use public transportation.

SOCIAL STUDIES LINK
Students' research should focus on how the EPA sets and enforces the standards that control air pollution. Students' ideas on how to help clean the air may include buying "environmentally friendly" products.

Technology

Internet Research Project Have students visit **www.mhscience02.com** to conduct a research project on the EPA. They will find a suggested outline for the project, questions to research, and links to Internet reference sites.

Science Magazine

Objective

- Compare atmospheres on other planets and moons with that of Earth.

Build on Prior Knowledge

Ask students if they think Jupiter has weather. If so, what kind? (Accept all answers.)

Planetary Weather

Developing the Main Idea

Have students focus on the nature of scientific inquiry by asking such questions as:

- **How does carbon dioxide in the atmosphere affect the climate on Venus? On Earth?** (In both cases, carbon dioxide traps the Sun's heat and raises surface temperatures.)

- **What factor increases the carbon dioxide on Earth that is not a factor on Venus?** (The amount of carbon dioxide in Earth's atmosphere has increased because of burning fossil fuels. There are no fossil fuels burned on Venus.)

- **How might Venus be different if it had Earth's atmosphere?** (An atmosphere like that on Earth would not trap as much heat. Temperatures might be much lower, leading to many other changes.)

Science Magazine

PLANETARY WEATHER

What's the weather like on other planets? Knowing about the atmosphere on other planets tells us more about our entire solar system.

Over the years scientists have learned that Venus's atmosphere is 97 percent carbon dioxide. A greenhouse effect occurs when the layer of carbon dioxide traps the Sun's heat, making Venus's average temperature 460°C (860°F).

Like Earth, Jupiter has storms. The Sun heats our atmosphere which creates conditions that cause storms. But Jupiter receives less of the Sun's heat than Earth. Scientists believe that storms on Jupiter might originate with heat rising from the planet's own hot interior. When it rains on Jupiter it rains liquid helium!

Venus has yellow clouds of sulfuric acid. Precipitation from these clouds is like acid rain on Earth, only worse.

C 68

Reading Strategy

Organize Information
Developing Reading Skills
Have students organize information about the similarities and differences of the planets mentioned on pp. C68–C69 in a chart.

Science Background

More on Venus's Atmosphere
Besides being mostly carbon dioxide, Venus's atmosphere is 90 times as dense as Earth's. At Venus's surface, the atmosphere exerts pressure equal to that at 1,000 m (3,300 ft) under Earth's oceans. An unprotected human body would implode under these conditions. Where did all that carbon dioxide come from? (Eruptions of Venus's volcanoes sent carbon dioxide into the atmosphere. With no oceans to absorb the carbon dioxide, it accumulated in the air.)

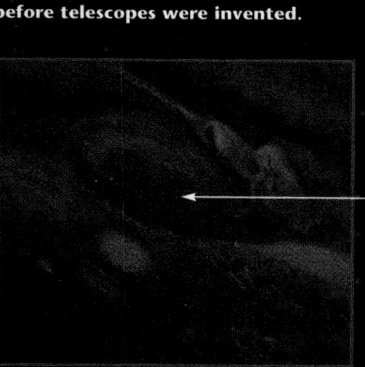

One of Jupiter's storms, the Great Red Spot, is about two times the size of Earth. It began before telescopes were invented.

Saturn has three cloud layers—water clouds, ammonia clouds, and ammonium hydrosulfide clouds. Together they form smog!

There is lightning on Venus, Jupiter, and Saturn. Uranus and Neptune are believed to have lightning as well. The lightning is from electrical discharges. Flashes on Jupiter may be 500 kilometers (310 miles) across.

Pluto has the greatest atmospheric changes of all the planets. That's because its orbit is irregular.

When Pluto is at its closest position to the Sun, the heat turns the frozen nitrogen on Pluto into a gas. This gives Pluto an atmosphere and weather to go with it. As Pluto moves farther from the Sun, the gas freezes.

Write ABOUT IT

1. Why should the atmosphere on Venus be a warning to us on Earth?

2. What forms of weather do we share with other planets?

AT THE COMPUTER

Visit www.mhscience02.com to learn more about weather on other planets.

C 69

Science Background

More About Jupiter

Scientists believe that Jupiter probably has a core of rock and metal about the size of Earth. In fact, Jupiter may be more like a star, with a hot inner core, than a planet. Jupiter has the same main components as the Sun, hydrogen and helium, and sends out 1.6 times as much energy as it receives from the Sun. It is this internal heat that stirs up Jupiter's atmosphere. However, Jupiter does not have enough mass to start hydrogen fusion reactions at its core, as stars do.

Developing the Main Idea
- **How much do you think the atmospheres on Venus and on Jupiter affect the conditions on those planets?** (totally)
- **Why does Pluto only have an atmosphere and weather some of the time?** (Pluto's orbit is irregular. When it is close to the Sun, gaseous nitrogen gives Pluto an atmosphere and weather.)

Thinking Further: *Compare and Contrast*
Ask:

- **How is Jupiter's weather similar to Earth's weather?** (Both Jupiter and Earth experience storms and lightning)
- **What is different about the heat that causes storms on Earth as compared to those on Jupiter?** (Scientists believe that the heat that causes storms on Jupiter is its own internal heat. Heat that causes storms on Earth is from the Sun.)

Answers to  **Write ABOUT IT**

1. Venus is very hot because it has so much carbon dioxide in its atmosphere. The amount of carbon dioxide is also increasing in Earth's atmosphere, which could cause Earth to warm up too much.
2. acid rain, clouds, storms, lightning

LESSON 6 — Earth's Fresh Water

Objectives

- Explore how salt water can be used to make fresh water.
- Compare salt water and fresh water sources.
- Recognize how water can become polluted.
- Identify ways to clean up and conserve water.

Resources

- Activity Resources, pp. 105–109
- Reading in Science Resources, pp. 165–170
- Vocabulary Cards
- Reading Aid Transparency C6
- Visual Aid Transparencies 9–12, 19
- Grade-Level Science Book, *Our Riverkeeper.*

Build on Prior Knowledge

Have students list nearby sources of fresh water, such as lakes, rivers, and reservoirs. Ask:

- **Do you think our supply of fresh drinkable water is limited?** (In spite of the water cycle and its natural recycling processes, our fresh water supplies are limited. Desalination of salt water and melting of glacial ice [poles] have practical limits.)

Ask if there has been a water shortage alert in their area recently.

1 Get Ready

Developing the Main Idea

Have students discuss where they think their tap water comes from. (Possible answers: wells, reservoirs, and nearby freshwater sources) Ask:

- **Why can't you drink salt water?** (Possible answers: It tastes bad; it makes you sick.)

LESSON 6 — Earth's Fresh Water

Vocabulary

- **desalination,** C73
- **water cycle,** C74
- **groundwater,** C74
- **water table,** C75
- **aquifer,** C75
- **spring,** C75
- **well,** C75
- **reservoir,** C75

Get Ready

Where do you get a drink when you are thirsty? Where does that water really come from?

Most of Earth's fresh water was once part of the ocean. How does salt water become fresh?

Process Skill

You communicate when you share information.

C 70

Science Background

Great Lakes

Five lakes—Superior, Huron, Michigan, Erie, and Ontario—are large freshwater lakes connected by waterways. The Great Lakes contain about 20 percent of Earth's aboveground fresh water. The Caspian Sea is the largest saltwater lake—about five times the size of Lake Superior, the world's largest freshwater lake. The Caspian Sea, while filled with salt water, is actually a landlocked lake.

Cross Curricular Books

Additional Outside Reading

Raising THE Wrecks

written by Michele Spirn
illustrated by Henry Levine

To order, see page C1·b.

Explore Activity

Investigate How to Make Salt Water Usable

Materials
tea bag

deep pan

plastic cup

saucer (or petri dish)

large, clear bowl or container

water

Procedure

1 Make a Model Keep a tea bag in a cup of water until the water is orange.

2 Make a Model Place a pan where there is strong light (sunlight, if possible). Pour some tea water into the saucer. Put the saucer in the pan. Cover the saucer with a large bowl.

3 Observe Look at the bowl and pan several times during the day and the next day. Note any water you see on the bowl or in the pan. Record your observations.

Drawing Conclusions

1 How was the water that collected in the bowl or pan different from the tea water?

2 Infer What do you think caused the water to collect in the bowl and pan?

3 How does this model represent what might happen to salt water, the water of Earth's oceans?

4 Use Variables How long did it take for water to collect in the bowl and pan? How might this process be speeded up?

5 Going Further: Communicate Do you think this model shows a useful way of turning ocean water into fresh water? Explain.

C 71

Alternative Explore Activity

Materials saltwater solution, flat dish or pie pan, heat source, hand lens, goggles

What's Left? Have students pour some saltwater solution into the dish and place it in sunlight or under a strong lamp. After the water evaporates, have them examine the residue and try to identify it. Discuss that salt remains when ocean water evaporates and the water that evaporates and condenses is fresh. **Logical; Spatial**

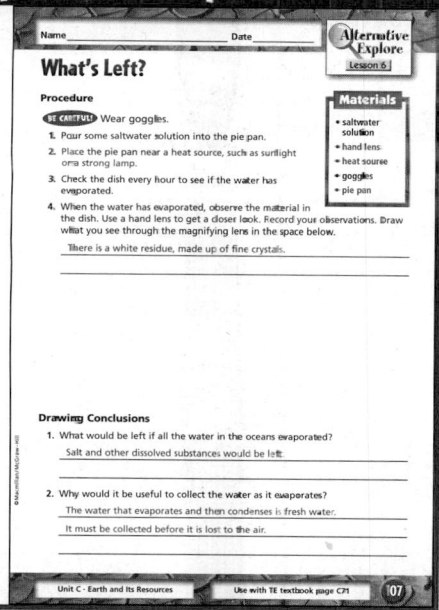

Activity Resources, p. 107

Explore Activity

Investigate How to Make Salt Water Usable

Science Process Skills *make a model, observe, infer, use variables, communicate*

Resources Activity Resources, pp. 105–106

Pacing 20–30 minutes

Grouping individual

Procedure

3 Water collects on the underside of the pan. It then drips or runs down onto the pan.

Answers to Drawing Conclusions

1 It does not have the color of tea. It appears to be fresh.

2 It evaporated from the saucer and condensed on the underside of the bowl.

3 Ocean water evaporates and then condenses as clouds. The clouds may eventually produce rain. The water that condenses does not have salt in it.

4 Times will vary. You might put the pan and bowl in a cool place after several hours to speed up condensation.

5 Students can discuss whether this is "useful," that is, practical, on a large scale.

 Inquiry Students can ask their own questions to explore, such as: Do I get the same results when I dissolve sugar in water? (Yes.)

Technology

■ When time is short, preview the activity with the **Explore Activity Video**.

How Do We Use Earth's Oceans?

Before Reading
Have students try to answer the red question at the top of the page.

Exploring the Main Idea
Distribute blank decimal cards or 10-cm by 10-cm square grids. Have students color 97 squares green to represent salt water and 3 squares blue to represent other water sources. Stress that fresh water is a precious resource.

Developing the Main Idea
Ask students what it's like to swim in an ocean compared to a pool or lake.

Using the Illustrations
Point out how the graph compares the percent of salt water to fresh water and how fresh water is distributed. Note that frozen water is not readily available for use.

READING Graphs

1. salt water, fresh water in icecaps and glaciers, surface water and groundwater, lakes and streams, water vapor in the atmosphere.
2. icecaps and glaciers

Developing Vocabulary

desalination This word contains the root *saline* which means "of salt." The prefix *de-* means "removed from," and the suffix -tion means "the act of." Thus the whole word refers to "the act of removing salt from" water or another substance.

Read to Learn

Main Idea Fresh water is constantly renewed by the water cycle.

How Do We Use Earth's Oceans?

If all the water in Earth's hydrosphere was represented by 100 cents, not even 3 cents would represent fresh water. Over 97 cents would be salt water. Salt water is water in the oceans as well as saltwater lakes and inland seas.

Much of the salt in salt water is halite, common rock salt. Salt water has seven times more salt than a person can stand. A person cannot survive drinking it. However, Earth's oceans and inland seas are still useful for the resources they contain.

- **Seafood** What kinds of seafood do you eat? Why are these foods healthful? The oceans support many forms of life. The water has dissolved gases, oxygen, and carbon dioxide, as well as minerals. Plants and other producers of the sea are able to get sunlight so that they can make food. They become food for other forms of sea life, which become food for us.

- **Minerals** Almost everything dissolves in water, at least a little. A pail of seawater contains almost every known element. It contains more minerals than just rock salt.

Hot water bubbling out of underwater volcanoes is especially mineral rich. It leaves rich deposits of minerals on the sea floor. Nodules, or lumps, of minerals can be picked up from the sea floor. They contain manganese and iron. Metals such as tin and gold are also found on the sea floor.

Earth's Water Supply

Fresh water: 2.8%

Salt water: 97.2%

Lakes and streams: 0.01%

Surface water and groundwater: 0.6%

Ice caps and glaciers: 2.2%

Water vapor in atmosphere: 0.001%

C 72

READING Graphs

1. Order the items in the bar graph from greatest to least.
2. Where is most of Earth's fresh water found?

BLACKLINE Lesson Outline

Name _____ Date _____

Lesson Outline Lesson 6

Earth's Fresh Water

Fill in the blanks. Reading Skill: Draw Conclusions - questions 5, 7, 9, 11, 15

How Do We Use Earth's Oceans?

1. The oceans provide us with food we call _____ seafood _____ and minerals.
2. Nodules, or lumps, of _____ minerals _____ can be picked up from the sea floor.
3. Offshore rigs pump _____ oil _____ and natural gas from beneath the ocean floor.
4. The process by which we get fresh water from seawater is called _____ desalination _____
5. Water leaves dissolved materials behind when it _____ evaporates _____

Where Is Fresh Water From?

6. Fresh water is constantly renewed in the _____ water cycle _____
7. Water is on the move–as a liquid that changes to a _____ gas _____ and then back to a _____ liquid _____
8. The main source of water in the water cycle is the _____ oceans _____
9. The main sources of fresh water on land are _____ rain _____ and _____ snow _____ which fall as _____ precipitation _____
10. Plants give off _____ water vapor _____

Unit C · Earth and Its Resources   Use with textbook pages C70–C79   165

Reading in Science Resources, p. 165

Science Background

Magnesium

Most magnesium comes from sea water. The water is treated with oyster shells, a source of lime. Magnesium in the water reacts with lime to form a compound that can be filtered out and dissolved in acid. Electricity is used to separate the magnesium from the solution. Have students research the products for which magnesium is needed and report their findings to the class. **Linguistic**

Then the water starts to back up and fill the spaces in the soil and rocks above. The top of the water-filled spaces is called the water table. If the water table reaches above the surface, a pond, a lake, or a stream forms.

Ponds and lakes are still bodies of water. They form where water fills up low-lying places. Streams, however, flow downhill. As they flow, they join with other streams, becoming a river. Eventually rivers reach the oceans or other large bodies of water.

An underground layer of rock or soil that is filled with water is called an aquifer (AK·wuh·fuhr). Water can move through an aquifer for great distances.

Some groundwater seeps out of the ground in a spring. Springs occur where the water table meets the surface. They feed water into streams and lakes long after it stops raining.

Long ago people learned to tap into groundwater by digging wells. Wells are holes dug below the water table. The water seeps into the hole. In some wells people get the water out of the hole with pumps. Wells can also be dug deep into aquifers that are sandwiched between tightly packed layers of rock. Water spouts up in these wells because it is being squeezed by the rock layers.

Most supplies of fresh water for large towns and cities come from reservoirs (REZ·uhr·vwahrz). Reservoirs are storage areas for freshwater supplies. They may be human-made or natural lakes or ponds. Pipelines transport the water from reservoirs.

Groundwater is an important part of the water cycle because it provides us with much of Earth's freshwater supply.

▷ **Why is groundwater an important part of the water cycle?**

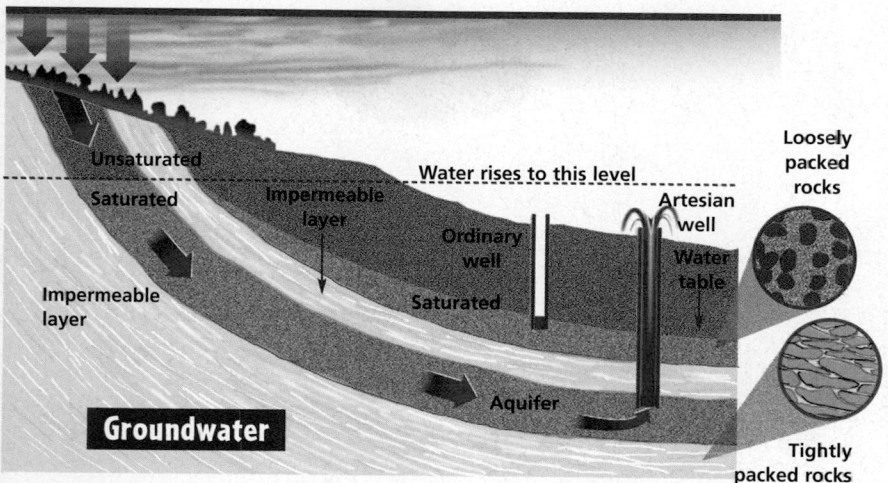

Groundwater

Unsaturated
Saturated
Impermeable layer
Impermeable layer
Water rises to this level
Ordinary well
Saturated
Artesian well
Water table
Aquifer
Loosely packed rocks
Tightly packed rocks

C 75

Model how groundwater seeps into pore spaces. Place an almost dry sponge in a pie pan. Slowly pour water onto the sponge. Ask:

- **What do you observe is happening?** (The sponge absorbs the water.)

- **Where does the water go?** (into the holes in the sponge)

Continue to pour water onto the sponge until it can't hold anymore and a pool of water starts to form in the pie pan. Direct students' attention to the part of the diagram showing the water table. Ask:

- **Where is the water table in this model?** (The surface of the water, within and around the sponge, is the water table.)

Squeeze the sponge to simulate tightly packed layers of rock forcing water upward in a well. Ask students to describe what happens.

Using Illustrations
Ask:

- **How is groundwater a part of the water cycle?** (Some precipitation that falls to Earth becomes stored as groundwater under the surface. Eventually this water works its way back to the ocean, or it is brought to the surface by way of wells and springs, where it can evaporate and continue through the water cycle.)

▶ **After Reading**
Have students answer the red question in the student book as **ongoing assessment**.

Developing Vocabulary

water table Have students think of the flat level surface of a tabletop. The water table is the top of the level of water-filled pore spaces.

aquifer Point out that this word is built from two Latin words for "water carrier." Similarly, the English word refers to a layer in Earth that "carries" water.

spring Discuss other meanings of this word (a coil, a season) and that "to spring" means "to surge forward," just as this kind of spring surges up from the ground.

well This comes from an old English word *wella*, which means "pit dug to get water."

reservoir Students might name related words, *reserve* and *reservation*, which both have to do with saving something.

Advanced Learners

Osmosis
The movement of water molecules across a membrane from a place of higher water concentration to a place of lower water concentration is called osmosis. Water enters and leaves the body's cells by osmosis; water also enters the root hairs of plants by osmosis. Invite interested students to find out how seawater can be desalinated by a process called reverse osmosis and explain it to the class. **Linguistic; Intrapersonal**

Science Background

Evaporation
Many inland bodies of water have little or no drainage. Water that flows into them is lost primarily through evaporation. These bodies of water include: Aral Sea in Central Asia, Caspian Sea in southeastern Europe, Chad Lake in central Africa, Crater Lake in Oregon, Dead Sea in Asia, Great Salt Lake in Utah, and Salton Sea in California.

How Can Fresh Water Be Polluted?

Before Reading
Have students try to answer the red question at the top of the page.

Developing the Main Idea
Water pollution can cause health problems for humans. Use the text to indicate the sources of water pollution. When pollutants enter the water system and are ingested by humans they present problems ranging from diarrhea to organ dysfunction.

Help students understand how they contribute to water pollution. Ask:

■ **What kinds of wastes do bath water, laundry water, and dishwater contain?** (dirt and soap residues)

Thinking Further: *Drawing Conclusions*
Ask:

■ **Why is it important to use biodegradable cleaning agents?** (These substances dissolve in water and break down into harmless chemicals.)

Explain that wastewater from homes is carried through pipes to treatment plants where the water is cleaned.

▶After Reading
Have students answer the red question in the student book as **ongoing assessment**.

How Can Fresh Water Be Polluted?

Oceans are polluted by people dumping wastes and spilling chemicals. Fresh water can be polluted, too, in many ways.

- **Precipitation** Rain or snow may pick up pollutants from the air. Some chemicals in the air make the rain turn into an acid. Acid rain harms living things and property.
- **Runoff water** Fresh water also gets polluted as it runs off over the land. Water that runs over dumped garbage can end up in streams and lakes. In some cases garbage is dumped into rivers.

  runoff water that picks up garbage, groundwater that picks up pesticides, industrial waste, and household waste

- **Groundwater** As water soaks down through the soil, it can pick up chemicals, such as pesticides.
- **Industry** Water used by industry gets polluted as it is used. For example, water that is used to help produce paper is filled with fibers and chemicals.
- **Household waste** You pollute water, too. Every time you flush the toilet, take a bath, brush your teeth, or wash dishes or clothes, water is polluted with wastes. Where do you think this water ends up?

Because of local pollution, many families use water-treatment devices in their faucets. Some families have to use bottled water for cooking and drinking.

▷ **What are four sources of water pollution?**

C 76

Science Background

Incinerators
Addressing Misconceptions
Landfills are not the only alternative for disposal of solid wastes. Modern incinerators burn almost all the combustible materials. The heat produced by the incinerator may be used as an energy supply. Scrubbing can remove toxic gases and fly ash, preventing them from polluting the atmosphere. The unburned materials and fly ash occupy considerably less space than the original refuse and can be disposed of in a landfill.

SCIENCE Reading Strategy

Ask Questions
Developing Reading Skills
Ask students to draw on their experience to ask questions based upon what they read above. How does acid rain harm property? What happens to the pesticides that get picked up by the groundwater? Interested students can research these questions and report to the class.

Science Background

Solid Waste
The two main categories of household solid waste are garbage and rubbish. Garbage is primarily made of decomposable materials like food wastes. Rubbish is made of non-decomposable materials like glass, metal, and wood. In 1990, the average citizen in the United States produced almost 1,600 pounds of solid waste per year—much more than Canada (1,300 pounds per year), Japan (900 pounds per year), or Great Britain (800 pounds per year).

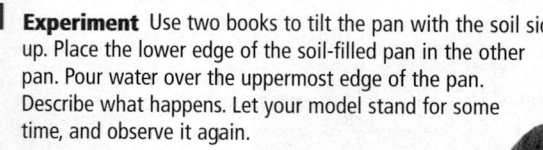

Process Skill
BUILDER

SKILL Form a Hypothesis

How Do Wastes from Land Get into Lakes and Rivers?

In seeking an answer to a question, the first thing you might do is find out as much as possible. You make observations. You might look up information.

Next, you would think of an explanation for these observations. That explanation is a hypothesis. It may be stated as an "If . . . then" sentence. "If water runs over land where garbage is dumped, then . . ." Sometimes you can test a hypothesis by making and observing a model.

Materials
soil

food color

foam bits

2 aluminum pans

water

2 textbooks

Procedure

1 **Hypothesize** Write a hypothesis to answer the question above.

2 **Make a Model** Pack moist soil to fill one-half (one side) of one aluminum pan. As you pack the soil, add 10–20 drops of food color to the soil just below the surface. Sprinkle crumbled bits of foam over the top.

3 **Experiment** Use two books to tilt the pan with the soil side up. Place the lower edge of the soil-filled pan in the other pan. Pour water over the uppermost edge of the pan. Describe what happens. Let your model stand for some time, and observe it again.

Drawing Conclusions

1 How does this model represent wastes on land?

2 Based on the model, how do wastes from land get into water? Does the model support your hypothesis? Explain.

3 **Hypothesize** How can some wastes be removed from water? Form a hypothesis, and test your ideas.

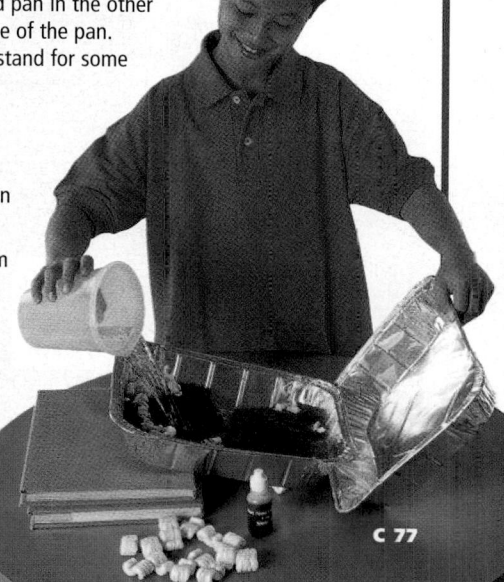

C 77

Process Skills
MiniLesson

Form a Hypothesis

Develop A hypothesis is a reasonable, testable statement that expresses an "if ... then" situation. The conditions to be tested are in the "if" part of the statement.

Example: A student wonders "does the mass of a marble change its speed as it rolls down a ramp?" A possible hypothesis might be "If I roll marbles of different masses down the same ramp, then they will travel at the same speed."

Practice Have students form a hypothesis for each question.

■ **How can grasses be used to slow rainwater from eroding a hillside?**

■ **How can you tell if ocean water has salt in it?**

■ **Can contour plowing help prevent soil erosion on a steep hillside?**

A complete list of Science Process Skills appears on p. S7.

Process Skill
BUILDER

How Do Wastes from Land Get into Lakes and Rivers?

Science Process Skills *form a hypothesis,* make a model, experiment

Resources Activity Resources, pp. 108–109

Pacing 30–40 minutes

Grouping pairs

Procedure

Plan Ahead Using diatomaceous earth (available from pool supply stores) rather than regular soil will show the results more clearly and make cleanup easier.

1 Students might suggest that wastes get into lakes and rivers by flowing through the ground or along a surface where wastes have been dumped.

3 Demonstrate how to trickle the water over the soil. Students should observe colored water draining out of the soil and some foam bits flowing to the newly formed pool of water in the empty half of the tray.

Answers to Drawing Conclusions

1 The water represents groundwater. The soil represents land. The foam bits used in the model stand for garbage that is thrown away on land; the food coloring stands for chemicals that seep into the soil.

2 Like the foam bits, garbage may be carried downhill with runoff water into lakes and streams. Like the food coloring, chemicals can seep into the soil and be mixed with water that runs through the soil. Students may find that their models support their hypotheses.

3 Students may suggest wastes can be removed by filtration, skimming, or chemical treatment. Testing may or may not support their hypotheses.

How Can We Purify Water?

Before Reading
Have students try to answer the red question at the top of the page.

Developing the Main Idea
Stress that the water cycle is a natural way that water is cleaned. Ask:

- **What are the major steps in the water cycle?** (evaporation, condensation, and precipitation)

- **During which parts of the cycle are substances removed from water?** (when water evaporates and when it seeps through the ground)

- **What kinds of materials might not be removed by water seeping through the ground?** (possible answers: dissolved substances, very small particles, germs)

Using the Illustration
Help students understand the different stages in water purification. Ask:

- **Why is the water treated with chemicals?** (to make particles clump together so they will sink)

- **What is the function of the gravel and sand?** (to filter out smaller particles)

- **Why is chlorine added to the water?** (to kill bacteria)

▶ After Reading
Have students answer the red question in the student book as **ongoing assessment**.

How Can We Purify Water?

Can polluted water be cleaned up? Yes, it can be—in many ways. For example, the water cycle helps clean water. Remember that when water evaporates, it leaves behind materials it contained. The water vapor and eventually the rain that forms no longer contain those materials.

When water seeps into the ground, the ground acts as a fine screen, or filter.

Most dirt particles in water are trapped, or filtered out, as water seeps down through the ground. As a result, a well that is dug down deep in the ground collects water that has been filtered.

Freshwater supplies for large areas can be cleaned on a large scale. Follow the steps in the process.

▷ What are three ways that water is purified?
the water cycle, filtration through the ground, and large-scale water purification.

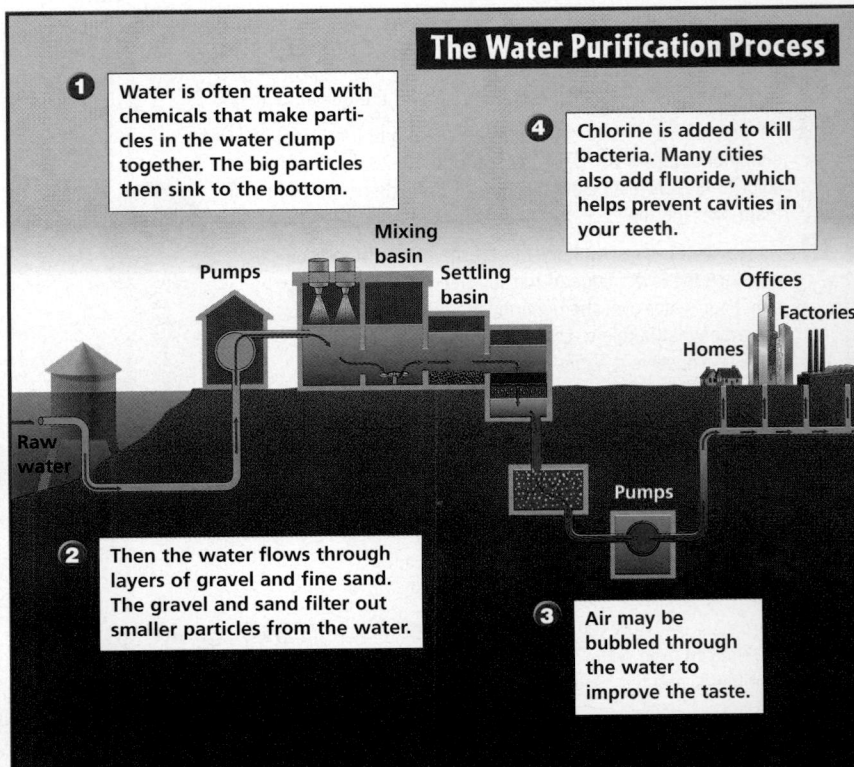

The Water Purification Process

1 Water is often treated with chemicals that make particles in the water clump together. The big particles then sink to the bottom.

4 Chlorine is added to kill bacteria. Many cities also add fluoride, which helps prevent cavities in your teeth.

Pumps — Mixing basin — Settling basin — Offices — Factories — Homes

Raw water

Pumps

2 Then the water flows through layers of gravel and fine sand. The gravel and sand filter out smaller particles from the water.

3 Air may be bubbled through the water to improve the taste.

C 78

BLACKLINE — Interpret Illustrations

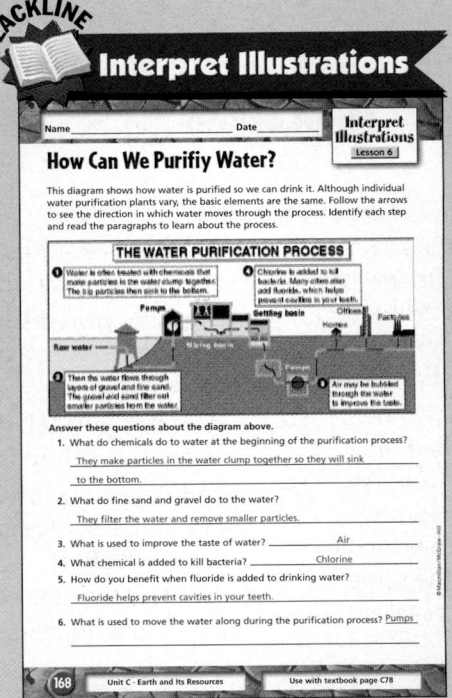

Reading in Science Resources, p. 168

Why It Matters

The United States Congress has passed laws such as the Safe Drinking Water Act and the Clean Water Act. These laws set standards for water purity.

Laws are important. However, it takes people—like you—to help save water and keep it clean.

People waste fresh water more than they realize. Often water can be safely reused. At times when the rainfall is low, water supplies may be very low. You may live in a part of the country where water supplies are low much of the time. No matter where you live, saving and recycling water should be part of your daily routine.

Think and Write

1. How do you depend on the oceans, even if you don't live near one?

2. How can freshwater supplies be cleaned up?

3. How do wastes get into ocean water? Fresh water?

4. **Hypothesize** How does the Sun help provide you with freshwater supplies?

5. **Critical Thinking** How can you tell the amount of water wasted in a day by a leaky faucet? Find a way to tell without wasting any.

L·I·N·K·S

ART LINK

Make a collage. Cut out pictures from magazines showing the various ways people use water—swimming, doing laundry, washing a car or pet, or drinking.

MATH LINK

Make a graph. People use water every day. Show in a graph how much water is used in different tasks.

DAILY USES OF WATER	
Activity	**Amount of Water Used**
Flushing a toilet	16–24 liters
Washing dishes	32–80 liters
Taking a shower	80–120 liters
Taking a bath	120–160 liters

LITERATURE LINK

Read *Our Riverkeeper* to learn about cleaning up polluted waters. Try the activities at the end of the book.

TECHNOLOGY LINK

At the Computer Visit **www.mhscience02.com** for more links.

C 79

3 Lesson Review

Answers to Think and Write

1. Oceans are Earth's largest reservoir of water in the water cycle. Seafood, minerals, and fossil fuels also come from the oceans. (p. C72)

2. by allowing them to move through the water cycle or by treating them with chemicals and filtering them (p. C78)

3. Wastes may enter the ocean or fresh water through precipitation, seepage, runoff, industrial use, or by direct dumping. (p. C76)

4. **Hypothesize** The Sun's heat evaporates water, leaving salts and other solids behind. The evaporated water eventually condenses as fresh water. (p. C74)

5. **Critical Thinking** Possible answer: Collect the leaking water in a large container for 2 hours. Measure the amount of water collected. Multiply by 12 to find out how much is wasted in 24 hours. (p. C79)

Summarize
Check students' understanding by having them write a brief summary of the lesson in their own words.

ART LINK
Student's collages should include a variety of water uses. Encourage students to look for water being used from different types of sources.

MATH LINK
Students should write the type of activity along one axis and the amount of water used along the other. Students may want to make the graph using a scale ranging from 0 to 170 liters in increments of 10 or 15 liters.

LITERATURE LINK
Have students read the Grade-Level Science Book, *Our Riverkeeper*. For additional books to read, see page C1·b

Science, Technology, and Society

Build on Prior Knowledge

Ask students what kind of water is used to grow plants. (fresh water) Then ask them what farmers do in areas where there is little water. (irrigation) Ask:

■ **Where does the water come from to irrigate fields in dry areas?** (possible answers: rivers, lakes, reservoirs)

To Dam or Not to Dam

Developing the Main Idea

Discuss the purposes of dams. Ask:

■ **Why are dams built?** (possible answers: to generate clean, renewable energy; to help control flooding; to provide water for irrigation)

■ **What recreational uses do dams serve?** (They form reservoirs that are used for fishing and boating.)

Thinking Further: *Making Generalizations*

Ask:

■ **Some dams have "ladders" that allow salmon to swim upstream past the dam. How might these be helpful?** (Possible answers: This could allow the salmon to reach their nesting area and lay eggs to reproduce.)

■ **Some dams are used to provide water for irrigation. How is this beneficial?** (Possible answers: It allows dry land to be farmed, providing food for people in those areas.)

To Dam or Not to Dam

Many salmon live their adult lives in the ocean. Then they return to the river where they were born to lay their eggs. If a dam blocks the salmons' path, they may die before producing the next generation.

C 80

Have you ever stepped in a stream of water trickling down the driveway? If so, you built a dam. The small stream of water stopped flowing, and a small puddle formed behind your foot.

Dams block the flow of water in a river in the same way that your foot blocks the trickling stream. Dams are often built to generate clean, renewable energy. Some dams also help control flooding.

Dams in the United States provide about 10 percent of our electricity and about 50 percent of our renewable energy. The reservoirs that form behind dams are popular with fishers and boaters.

However, there's a downside to dams—they change rivers. In a river free of dams, water flows according to the seasons. The river may be high in the spring after the winter snows melt and low during a dry summer. After a river is dammed, the water flows only when the dam's gates are raised. These unnatural changes in water level can harm species that have adapted to the seasonal changes.

A dam also changes the water temperature. When a dam is built, a reservoir of water forms. Warmed by the Sun, the water at the top of a reservoir becomes warmer than normal. However, deep below, at the reservoir's bottom, the water becomes colder. These changes in temperature make dammed rivers less livable for some species and better for others.

Inclusion

Making a Dam

Use a flat square pan filled with sand, tilted slightly at one end. Have students slowly pour a thin stream of water from the high end. As they observe the water's course, have a student place a long piece of plastic foam with a small hole poked at the top across the stream. Have students observe the flow above and below the block. Ask them to compare their observations with what occurs with a dam on a river. **Kinesthetic; Linguistic**

Advanced Learners

Debating a Dam's Value

In some areas, dams and irrigation projects have drawn so much water off a river that it is severely reduced downstream. Have students work in two teams. Ask them to imagine they are a member of either the upstream or downstream community and choose whether or not to keep the dam in place. They can then have a "town meeting" to reach a final decision. **Social; Linguistic**

The first dam on the Elwha River was finished in 1914. In 2000 the dam was bought by the United States government. It may soon be removed to restore the Elwha River.

Dams harm fish by blocking their path up and down the river. For example, consider the Elwha River in the Pacific Northwest. Before any dam was built on the river, about 380,000 adult salmon and trout returned each year to the Elwha to lay eggs. Today that number has fallen below 3,000.

What should we do? Should we keep the dams or get rid of them? The answer depends on which dam you're talking about.

On some rivers researchers are studying the advantages and disadvantages of the dams. Does the dam generate a large amount of clean energy? Does it cause great harm to the local ecosystem? Then the researchers weigh the good against the bad. If a dam does not provide much energy, or it harms the environment, it might be removed. The rest are left to control flooding and to make clean, renewable energy.

What Did I Learn?

1. Which fraction represents the renewable energy generated by dams in the United States?

A $\frac{1}{4}$

B $\frac{1}{3}$

C $\frac{1}{2}$

D $\frac{3}{4}$

2. Which of the following is a way that a dam benefits the environment?

F A dam blocks fish from swimming up and down the river.

G A dam generates clean, renewable energy.

H A dam increases the chance of flooding.

J A dam changes the temperature of the river's water.

 **AT THE COMPUTER** Visit www.mhscience02.com to learn more about dams.

C 81

Cultural Perspective

Controversial Dams

There are a number of dams or planned dams throughout the world that are controversial. Have students research one of these dams to find out the benefits and disadvantages. Then conduct a debate as to whether the dam should be built—or if already built, should it be kept or torn down. Examples can be found in China, the southwestern United States, southern Africa, and the Amazon region. **Logical; Social; Linguistic**

Thinking Further: *Inferring*

Ask students to recall the definition of erosion (the transportation of sediments). Ask:

◼ **How does a dam affect the erosion of sediments?** (Sediments get stuck behind the dam and less sediment is carried downstream.)

◼ **What kind of effect might this have on the river banks downstream?** (Less sediment will be available to replace other sediment carried farther downstream. The riverbanks may erode.)

Exploring the Main Idea

Have students make a list of the effects building a dam has on a community. Remind them to include the effects on plants and animals. Write Pros on one side of the board, and Cons on the other side of the board. Have students share their lists with the class and determine which effects are pros and which are cons. Challenge students to determine pros and cons that may not have been mentioned in the text.

Test Prep:  What Did I Learn?

1. C

2. G

Summarize

Check students' understanding by having them write a brief summary of the magazine in their own words.

LESSON 7 — Earth's Oceans

Objectives

- Explore the difference between ocean water and fresh water.
- Understand that oceans have many valuable resources.
- Understand what causes currents, waves, and tides.
- Describe the topography of the ocean floor.

Resources

- Activity Resources, pp. 110–114
- Reading in Science Resources, pp. 171–176
- Vocabulary Cards
- Reading Aid Transparency C7
- Visual Aid Transparency 20

Build on Prior Knowledge
Have students discuss what they know about the oceans. Ask:

- **How would you describe what you know about the way ocean water moves?** (Students may describe how water moves higher and lower on the shore each day and the up-and-down movements of waves.)

Then have students create a list of words that describe the ocean. (Possible answers: salty, huge, wavy)

1 Get Ready

Developing the Main Idea
Ask students to list ways in which the ocean serves a useful purpose. (Possible answers: It provides fish and other seafood; it contains minerals; it provides a habitat for many organisms; it provides recreation for people.) Explain that for the reasons they have just listed, the ocean is a natural resource.

LESSON 7 — Earth's Oceans

Vocabulary

basin, C84

current, C86

continental shelf, C90

continental slope, C90

continental rise, C90

abyssal plain, C90

seamount, C90

trench, C91

mid-ocean ridge, C91

Get Ready

Nearly three-fourths (71 percent) of Earth's surface is covered by water. In fact, you could call Earth a "water planet." Most of Earth's water is contained in the oceans that encircle our planet.

Process Skill
You experiment when you perform a test to support or disprove a hypothesis.

C 82

Science Background

Salinity

The ocean's salinity, or dissolved salt content, is measured as the amount of dissolved salts in 1 kg of ocean water, expressed in parts per thousand of water (ppt). Ten ppt is 1 percent by weight. Ocean salinities range from 33 ppt to 38 ppt, and average about 35 ppt. Chlorine, sodium, magnesium, potassium, sulfur, and calcium make up over 90 percent of salts dissolved in the oceans.

Inclusion — SCIENCE FOR ALL

Watch the Wave

Tie a jump rope to a doorknob. Shake the rope so that students can see the movement of a wave through the rope. Ask them how the wave moving through the rope is similar to a water wave. (Only the wave moves along the rope; it returns to the same position after the wave passes.) **Spatial**

Explore Activity

How Do Ocean and Fresh Water Compare?

Procedure

1 Spread wax paper on your desk before you begin to work.

2 **Predict** What happens when you mix fresh and ocean water?

3 **Experiment** From the bottom of the straw, make a mark every 4 cm. Gently place the bottom of the straw 4 cm under the surface of the "ocean water." Seal the top of the straw with your finger. With your finger still sealing the straw, lift it out of the water. Keeping your finger on top of the straw, place the bottom of the straw 8 cm down in the "fresh water." Lift your finger off the straw, and then put it back again and lift the straw out of the water.

4 **Observe** What happened? Record the results. Now try it again, starting with "fresh water" first. Observe and record what happens.

Drawing Conclusions

1 **Communicate** Which liquid combinations mixed in the straw and which made layers?

2 **Going Further: Experiment** Make a third liquid by mixing equal parts of ocean water and fresh water. Experiment with the three liquids to see how many layers you can make.

Materials

3 small plastic cups

"ocean water"

"fresh water"

clear-plastic straw

waterproof marking pen

wax paper

ruler

C 83

Alternative Explore Activity

Materials water, salt, food coloring, teaspoon, cup, deep glass bowl

Salt Water Density Fill a cup with water. Add several teaspoons of salt and three drops of food coloring. Fill a deep glass bowl with water. Pour the salt water carefully into fresh water. Observe. (Salt water sinks beneath fresh water.) Repeat activity reversing salt and fresh water. (Fresh water mixes near the top of salt water.) Explain which is denser and why.

Spatial

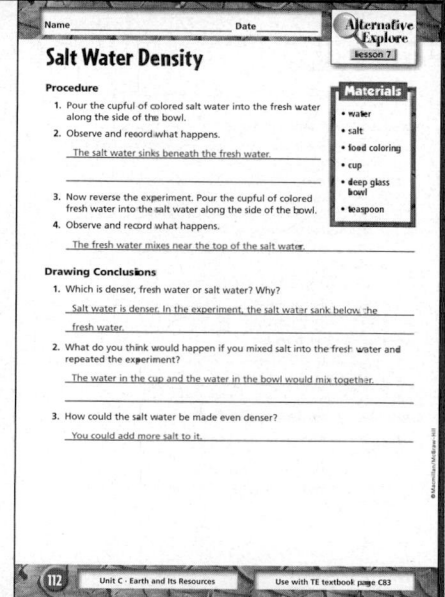

Activity Resources, p. 112

Explore Activity

How Do Ocean and Fresh Water Compare?

Science Process Skills *predict, experiment, observe, communicate*

Resources Activity Resources, pp. 110–111

Pacing 20–30 minutes

Grouping small groups

Plan Ahead Make ocean water by placing several drops of food coloring and 3 teaspoons of salt in a cup of water. Stir until salt is dissolved. Fill another cup with fresh water and add several drops of a different color food coloring.

Procedure

2 Predictions may include that the salt and fresh water won't mix or that salt water will float on fresh water or the reverse.

3 Students may need to practice sealing the water in the straw with their finger.

4 In both trials, water is drawn into the straw.

Answers to Drawing Conclusions

1 When salt water is placed on top, it sinks and mixes with the freshwater drawn into the straw. When fresh water is on top, it forms a separate layer floating on the salt water drawn in.

2 Students should be able to make three layers with fresh water on top, mixed next, and salt water at the bottom.

 Inquiry Students can ask their own questions to explore. They might ask: What would happen if we substituted warm and cold water for the fresh and salt water? (Cold water is denser than warm water so it will sink and form a layer beneath the warm water.)

 ## Technology

■ When time is short, preview the activity with the **Explore Activity Video.**

What Are Oceans, Seas, and Basins?

Before Reading
Have students try to answer the red question at the top of the page.

Developing the Main Idea
Show students a globe from different aspects. Point out that some people do not consider the Antarctic a separate ocean, while others mark its boundary at 40°S latitude. Ask:

- **Why do you think there is disagreement about whether the Antarctic is a separate ocean?** (The Antarctic does not have any visible boundaries to separate it from the other oceans. The Pacific and Atlantic are mainly separated by large landmasses.)

Thinking Further: *Inferring*
Ask:

- **How do you think water in lakes such as the Great Salt Lake turned from fresh to salt water?** (Fresh water lakes are turned to salt water in the same way that some salt gets into the ocean. Minerals from weathered rocks flow into streams that empty into lakes. If there is no outlet, the salt stays in the lake.)

Developing Vocabulary

basin Show students a picture of an old-fashioned wash basin and explain that a *basin* is a bowl with sloping sides used to contain water. Have students compare and contrast the wash basin with an ocean basin. (Both containers hold water and are sloped at the edges. The ocean basin contains mountains and valleys while a wash basin is smooth.)

Read to Learn

Main Idea Ninety-seven percent of Earth's water comes from oceans. Oceans are an important natural resource.

What Are Oceans, Seas, and Basins?

Most of Earth's water is contained in large bodies of salt water called oceans. Examples include the Atlantic and Pacific Oceans.

If all the water evaporated from the oceans, a layer of salt about 60 m (200 ft) thick would be left on the ocean floor. Not all of the salt is table salt. There are many other forms of salt, too. Where does all this salt come from?

One source is the rocks on Earth's surface. Rocks break down through weathering. Their minerals flow into streams. Eventually, the minerals end up in the ocean—more than 2,500 million tons each year.

The other source is from deep inside Earth. When volcanoes erupt, they let out water vapor and other gases. The water vapor is the major source of Earth's water. The other gases include some of the salts that are found in the ocean.

Why doesn't the ocean get saltier and saltier? Because the salts are removed as fast as they are added. Plants and animals use them as they build shells and skeletons. Other minerals fall out of the water to become part of the ocean floor.

Although you may have heard the ocean called the "sea," a sea is actually a body of water much smaller than an ocean. Some seas are part of an ocean. The North Sea, for example, is connected to the Atlantic Ocean and the Arctic Ocean, just north of Europe.

The ocean floor, or **basin**, is as varied as Earth's continents. It contains mountains, valleys, and plains.

Resources from the Ocean

As you saw in Lesson 6, the oceans are rich in natural resources. Seawater is an important source of minerals. To obtain these minerals, people use the heat of the Sun to evaporate water. The minerals left behind are then harvested.

Some resources, such as oil, natural gas, and coal, lie beneath the ocean floor. Drilling rigs such as the one shown are used to extract oil and natural gas from beneath the sea.

The ocean's living creatures are also a valuable resource. People use fish, crabs, and squid for food. They eat

C 84

BLACKLINE | Lesson Outline

Name _____ Date _____

Lesson Outline Lesson 7

Earth's Oceans

Fill in the blanks. Reading Skill: Draw Conclusions - questions 1, 3, 4, 6, 10, 12, 16

What Are Oceans, Seas, and Basins?

1. Most of Earth's water is contained in large bodies of salt water called ___oceans___

2. The ocean floor, or ___basin___, contains mountains, valleys, and plains.

3. If all the water evaporated from the oceans, a layer of ___salt___ about 60 meters (200 feet) thick would be left on the ocean floor.

4. When volcanoes erupt, they let out water ___vapor___ and other gases.

5. Seawater is an important source of ___minerals___

6. Drilling rigs are used to extract ___oil___ and ___natural gas___ from the land beneath the sea.

What Causes Ocean Currents?

7. A stream of water that flows through the ocean like a river is a ___current___.

8. ___Surface___ currents are driven by the wind.

How Does the Water in a Wave Move?

9. As a wave passes through the ocean, water ___particles___ move in circles.

10. Each ___breaking wave___ may hurl thousands of tons of water against the shore, breaking rocks apart and smoothing the fragments into pebbles and sand.

Unit C · Earth and Its Resources | Use with textbook pages C82–C95 | **171**

Reading in Science Resources, p. 171

SCIENCE | Reading Strategy

Organize Information

Developing Reading Skills
Have students reread the first section of p. C84 to find two questions within the text; the last sentence of paragraph 2 and the first sentence of paragraph 5. Have them write out each question and an answer to each based on the text.

From space it is easy to see that 71 percent of Earth's surface is covered by water. Oceans contain valuable resources such as fish and oil.

some kinds of seaweed. A product made from seaweed—called carrageenan—is used as an ingredient in everything from toothpaste to ice cream.

Other resources are too difficult for us to take from the ocean at this time. For example, certain parts of the ocean floor are covered with lumps called nodules. These nodules contain manganese, iron, and other useful minerals. Gold is an example of a mineral that is dissolved in ocean water. However, we do not yet know how to mine these minerals economically.

▷ **What are oceans like?**
Oceans are bodies of salt water that contain resources such as oil, seafood, and minerals.

FOR SCHOOL OR HOME

Salt Water and Fresh Water

1. Fill a jar with fresh water to about 1 cm from the top. Carefully push a thumbtack into the center of the eraser of a pencil.

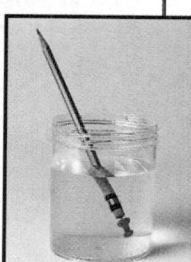

2. **Observe** Place the pencil, eraser side down, in the water. Let go. What happens?

3. **Measure** Using a waterproof marker, mark the pencil to show where the water line is. Use a ruler to measure the length of the pencil above the water mark. Record this measurement.

4. Fill the jar with salt water. Repeat steps 2–3.

5. How do your results for fresh water compare with your results for salt water?

6. **Predict** What do you think will happen if you add a tablespoon of salt to your salt water? Test your prediction.

C 85

Developing the Main Idea

Discuss that seawater is also an important source of minerals. To obtain the minerals, people use the Sun's heat to evaporate seawater. The minerals are left behind and harvested. Ask:

■ **What are some ocean resources that you use?**
(Possible answers: seafood, oil, sea salt, fresh water, carrageenan)

▶ **After Reading**
Have students answer the red question in the student book as **ongoing assessment**.

FOR SCHOOL OR HOME

Materials jar, fresh water, salt water, thumbtack, pencil with eraser, waterproof marker, paper towel, metric ruler

Science Process Skills *observe, measure, predict*

Resources Activity Resources, pp. 113–114

Step 2 Students should observe that the pencil floats upward.

Step 3 Measurements will vary.

Step 5 Students should observe that the pencil floated higher in salt water.

Step 6 Students should predict that the more salt added, the higher the pencil should float (until the water can dissolve no more salt).

Reading Strategy

Compare and Contrast
Developing Reading Skills
Encourage students to compare a sea with an ocean using context clues on page C84. (Examples: "smaller than," "part of," "connected to") Have them continue this strategy as they read about surface and deep-water currents (pp. C86–C87) and parts of the ocean floor (pp. C90–C91). **Linguistic**

Inclusion

Densities
Use various liquids of different densities such as water, cooking oil, vinegar, as well as an ice cube and a heavy coin. Pour the liquids gently into a glass so that they form layers. Drop the coin into the glass as students watch. Float the ice cube on top. Ask:

■ **Which is the densest? least dense?** (coin; ice)

■ **Why don't the liquids mix?** (They are of different densities.) **Spatial**

What Causes Ocean Currents?

Before Reading

Have students try to answer the red question at the top of the page.

Exploring the Main Idea

Show students a map of the global winds. Have them compare the wind direction to the major ocean currents shown on the map. Ask:

- **What direction do the wind and ocean currents flow from the equator northward?** (clockwise)

- **What direction do the wind and ocean currents flow from the equator southward?** (counterclockwise)

Use this comparison to emphasize how the winds drive the surface currents. Point out that both surface currents and winds are affected by Earth's rotation.

Using the Illustrations

Draw students' attention to the satellite photo of the Gulf Stream. Ask:

- **Why does the Gulf Stream appear a different color than the surrounding waters?** (The waters of the Gulf Stream are warmer.)

Have students describe the location of the other warm water currents. (moving from the equator either north or south)

READING
Maps

It might follow the California current, get picked up by the Equatorial current, and move toward Australia or Southeast Asia.

Technology

- Visual Aid Transparency 20: *Ocean Currents*

Developing Vocabulary

current Have students look up the word *current* in the dictionary to find out how many meanings the word has. Have them write a sentence for each meaning of the word.

What Causes Ocean Currents?

Ocean waters are constantly pushed around the planet by currents. A **current** is a stream of water that flows through the ocean like a river. Some currents are on the surface. Others move deep beneath the surface.

Surface currents are driven by the wind. As the winds blow steadily across the ocean, they cause the top layer of water to move in huge circular patterns. A current may move water hundreds of kilometers through the ocean.

Earth's rotation also affects surface currents. As Earth rotates, it pulls great masses of water on the surface along with it. This causes currents to bend to the right in the Northern Hemisphere and to the left in the Southern Hemisphere. The currents start flowing in huge circles.

Surface currents move at a speed of about 220 km (137 mi) a day. Some of these currents are huge. A surface current may move water hundreds of kilometers through the ocean and may carry more water than the Amazon River.

READING
Maps

What if you enclosed a message in a bottle and dropped it in the ocean off the California coast? Where might the bottle be found?

The Gulf Stream is a surface current that begins near the equator and flows north past the United States, bringing warm waters to the eastern coast. What causes surface currents like the Gulf Stream?

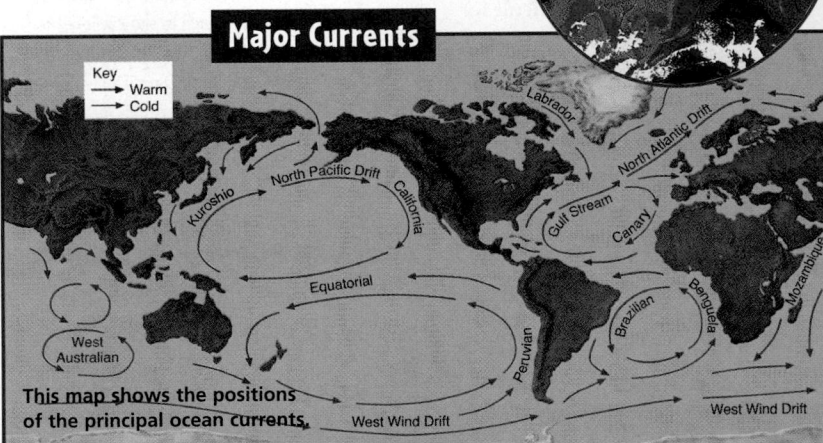

Major Currents

Key
→ Warm
→ Cold

Labrador
North Pacific Drift
North Atlantic Drift
Kuroshio
California
Gulf Stream
Canary
Equatorial
West Australian
Brazilian
Peruvian
Benguela
Mozambique
West Wind Drift
West Wind Drift

This map shows the positions of the principal ocean currents.

C 86

BLACKLINE
Interpret Illustrations

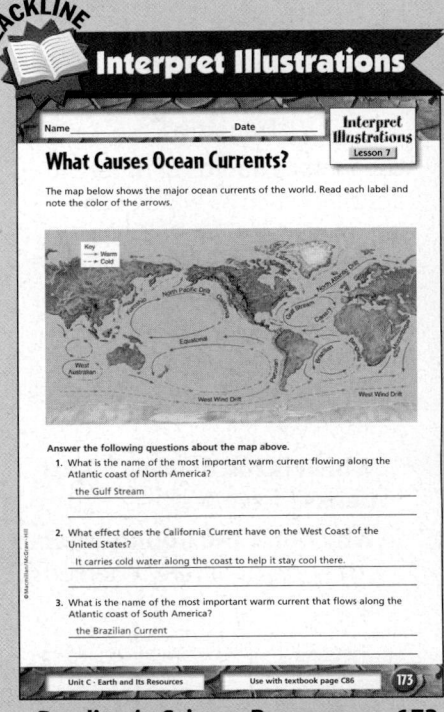

Name_____ Date_____

Interpret Illustrations
Lesson 7

What Causes Ocean Currents?

The map below shows the major ocean currents of the world. Read each label and note the color of the arrows.

Answer the following questions about the map above.

1. What is the name of the most important warm current flowing along the Atlantic coast of North America?

   the Gulf Stream

2. What effect does the California Current have on the West Coast of the United States?

   It carries cold water along the coast to help it stay cool there.

3. What is the name of the most important warm current that flows along the Atlantic coast of South America?

   the Brazilian Current

Unit C - Earth and Its Resources   Use with textbook page C86   173

Reading in Science Resources, p. 173

SCIENCE
Reading Strategy

Cause and Effect

Developing Reading Skills
Ask students to find examples of cause and effect on these two pages. Have them list them with arrows leading from the cause to the effect. (Example: Earth's rotation → currents bend to the right in the Northern Hemisphere and to the left in the Southern Hemisphere)

As ocean water freezes, the salts do not become part of the ice. The remaining water becomes saltier, causing it to become more dense. It begins to flow to the bottom of the ocean.

As ocean currents flow along the edges of continents, they affect the land's climate. The California current carries cold water along the West Coast of our country, helping it to stay cool there. On the East Coast, the Gulf Stream keeps the climate warm.

Deep-water currents move far beneath the ocean. They are set in motion by differences in the temperature and saltiness of water.

Near Earth's poles, water at the surface of the ocean loses heat to the atmosphere. It may also become saltier as water is removed by evaporation or freezing. This colder, saltier water is *denser* than the water below it. It slowly sinks toward the ocean bottom.

The less dense water below flows in to replace it closer to the surface.

In this way, a deep-water current is set up. The water in a deep-water current moves much slower than the water in a surface current—just a few meters a day.

Dense water forms mainly in Antarctica and in the North Atlantic Ocean. From there the water sinks and spreads slowly outward toward the equator. The water may not resurface for another 500 years.

 **What are three ways an ocean current may form?**

Currents are caused by wind, by Earth's rotation, and by changes in water density.

C 87

Developing the Main Idea

As students read this page, focus on the cause of deep currents. Have students recall the Explore Activity, then ask:

- **Which is denser—salt water or fresh water? How does increasing the saltiness of water affect its density?** (Salt water; the saltier the water, the denser it is.)

- **How does denser water behave when added to less dense water?** (It sinks.)

Thinking Further: *Drawing Conclusions*
Ask:

- **What are the causes and effects related to the fact that most deep-water currents originate in Antarctica and the North Atlantic?** (Cause: The water is cooled by polar temperatures and becomes saltier as much of it freezes. Effect: The increased saltiness and cooling make the water denser and it sinks. A current is formed when it sinks and less dense water flows in.)

▶ After Reading
Have students answer the red question in the student book as **ongoing assessment**.

SCIENCE FOR ALL **Advanced Learners**

Thermohaline Circulation
The downward movement of water as it becomes denser is called thermohaline circulation. Have students research roots of this word. (*Thermo* is from Greek *therme,* meaning "heat". *Haline* is from *halite,* or salt.) Ask how this word is related to the factors that increase water's density. (The lower the temperature and more salt contained in a mass of water, the denser the water.) **Linguistic**

SCIENCE **Reading Strategy**

Compare and Contrast
Developing Reading Skills
Have students continue the strategy from p. C85 —this time, to compare and contrast surface currents and deep-water currents. (Both are streams of water that flow through the ocean. Surface currents flow at the surface while deep-water currents flow at great depths. Global winds and Earth's rotation cause surface winds. Differences in density cause deep currents.)

How Does the Water in a Wave Move?

Before Reading
Have students try to answer the red question at the top of the page.

Using the Illustrations
Have students trace in the air the movement of a water particle as a wave passes through it. Have students focus on the diagram of wave motion. Then ask:

- **What does the arrow indicate?** (the direction in which the wave is traveling)

Reemphasize that energy is passed forward from particle to particle. Also point out that the energy moves downward from one particle to another. Point out that the illustration shows only one circle near the surface. Have them visualize that energy is also transferred in circular motion to water below the surface. Ask:

- **How are the water particles affected below the surface?** (They all move in circles, but water particles below the surface move in smaller circles than those nearer the surface.)

- **Why does the circular motion become smaller moving downward from the surface?** (Energy is lost as it is passed from particle to particle. At a certain point there is no more movement.)

▶After Reading
Have students answer the red question in the student book as **ongoing assessment**.

Technology

- **Science Experiences Videotapes**
  Staying Alive: Adaptations for Survival (Package 4)

How Does the Water in a Wave Move?

Have you ever watched a toy boat bobbing on the surface of a lake or ocean? As the waves go by, the boat moves up, around, down, and then back. It returns to almost the same position where it started. This is exactly what happens to the water particles in waves—they move in circles.

All waves carry energy from place to place. In the ocean the winds blow across the surface, passing energy to the water. The energy of a wave moves forward across the water, but not the water particles themselves. As a wave passes through the ocean, each water particle moves in a circle, returning to almost its original position.

As the winds blow across the ocean, they also drag the water forward slightly, causing the surface currents you read about on page C86. However,

How Water Moves in a Wave

most of the energy passes through the water as waves, as shown in the illustration above.

When a wave approaches the shore, it begins to slow down. At the same time, it gets higher. The tall wave reaches a point where it collapses, or breaks, against the shore.

The force of breaking waves can be very powerful. Each wave may hurl thousands of tons of water against the shore, breaking rocks apart and smoothing the fragments into pebbles and sand.

▶ **What is the motion of water particles as a wave passes through water?**
Water particles move in a circular motion.

C 88

Interpret Illustrations

Reading in Science Resources, p. 174

Advanced Learners

Water Particle Motion
Challenge students to imitate a water particle as a wave passes. (Tape an *x* on the floor. Begin by standing straight up on the *x*. Take a step forward while crouching halfway down, then take a step backward back onto the *x* while crouching all the way down. Next, take a step back while crouching halfway back up. Finally, return to the *x* standing straight up.)
Kinesthetic

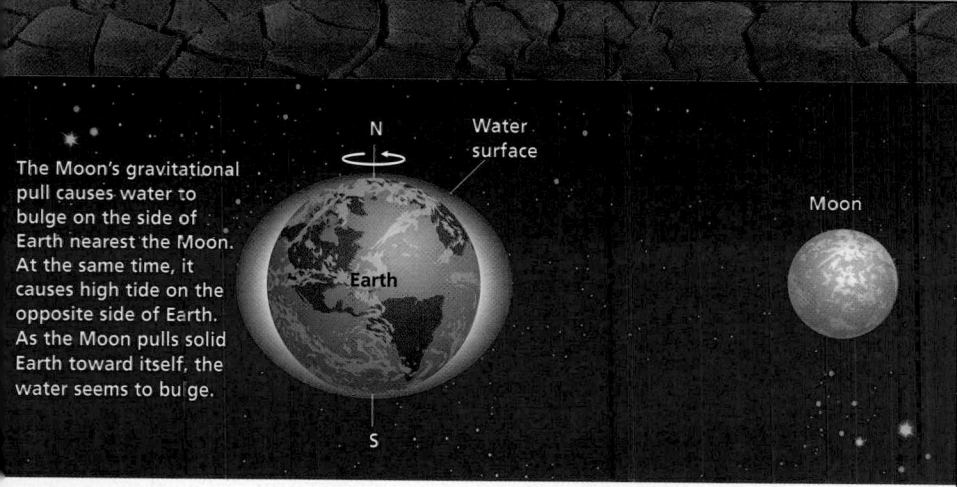

The Moon's gravitational pull causes water to bulge on the side of Earth nearest the Moon. At the same time, it causes high tide on the opposite side of Earth. As the Moon pulls solid Earth toward itself, the water seems to bulge.

N

Water surface

Earth

Moon

S

What Causes the Tides?

People living along the coasts are familiar with the rise and fall of the ocean's surface, called the tide. Tides result from the pull of the Moon's and the Sun's gravity on Earth. Although the Moon is much smaller than the Sun, it is also much closer to Earth. It is the Moon that has the greatest effect on the tides.

The Sun also influences the tides. However, it is so far away that it has less than half the pull of the Moon. About twice a month, near the times of new and full Moons, the Sun and the Moon line up. Their combined pull causes the highest high tides and lowest low tides, called *spring tides*.

The tides with the smallest range, called *neap tides*, occur between spring tides. During a neap tide, the Moon and the Sun are at right angles to Earth, and their pulls partly cancel each other.

Spring Tides

Full Moon

Earth

New Moon

Sun

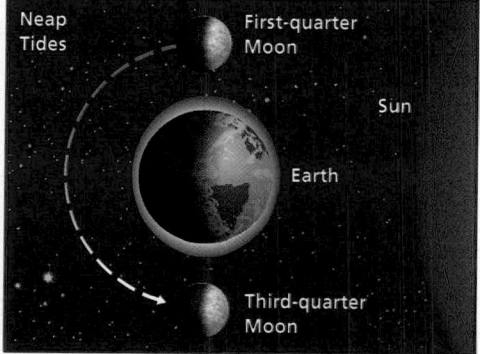

Neap Tides

First-quarter Moon

Earth

Sun

Third-quarter Moon

READING Drawing Conclusions
What are tides the result of?

C 89

What Causes the Tides?

Before Reading
Have students try to answer the red question at the top of the text column.

Developing the Main Idea
As students read this page, focus on the positions of the Sun, the Moon, and Earth. Ask:

- **What areas of Earth experience high tides?** (the areas within the bulges of water)
- **What is occurring in the areas outside those bulges at the same time?** (low tides)
- **Where do the bulges occur?** (on the side of Earth nearest the Moon and on the side opposite)
- **Why do low tides occur?** (The high tide bulges draw the water away from the other areas of Earth [cause], resulting in low tide at that location [effect].)

Thinking Further: *Making Generalizations*
Ask:

- **Why do many places experience two high and two low tides each day?** (Students should be aware that the Earth rotates each day. Thus, an area of earth would pass from a bulge into a "nonbulge" and then back into a bulge and then into a "nonbulge.")

▶After Reading
Have students answer the red question in the student book as **ongoing assessment**.

SCIENCE

Reading MiniLesson

Draw Conclusions

Develop Tell students that we draw conclusions every day based on the facts that we receive. For example, you could draw conclusions about attending an after-school activity based on the time or day of the activity, who else will participate, your ability or aptitude, and your interest.

Practice Ask students to list three facts from this page to draw a conclusion about why the lowest low tides occur when they do. (Answers should include: High tides occur on two sides of Earth where the water bulges. The lowest low tides occur at the same time as the highest high tides. The spring tide drawing shows water pulled away from the area of Earth between the bulges. The conclusion is that the bulges are largest during spring tide resulting in the most water.)

What Is the Ocean Floor Like?

Before Reading

Have students try to answer the red question at the top of the page.

Using the Illustrations

Explain that the continents do not end at the shore. The continental shelf and slope are also part of the continents. The continental crust merges with ocean crust along the continental rise. The shelf, slope, and rise together are called the continental margin. Ask:

- **Where does the sediment come from that forms the continental rise?** (from the continents and continental shelf)

- **Which is deeper, the continental shelf or abyssal plain?** (abyssal plain)

- **What feature on land does a seamount most resemble?** (a volcano)

- **Can you name some seamount ranges that broke the ocean surface to become chains of islands.** (the Hawaiian Islands, the Aleutian Islands, the Florida Keys, and some island groups in the Caribbean such as the Greater and Lesser Antilles)

Developing Vocabulary

continental shelf Ask students to reread the paragraph with *continental shelf* to determine clues to its meaning.

continental slope Have students define *slope* (a slant). Underline the suffix *-al* (relating to). Define *continental*.

continental rise Discuss *rise* as a science term. Compare to common usage (a spot higher than its surroundings).

abyssal plain Explain that *abyss* means "something very deep." This is a plane that lies very deep under the ocean surface.

seamount Have students break this word into two pieces to paraphrase a definition, *a mount in the sea*.

Technology

- **Science Experiences Videotapes**
  Researching the Ocean Depths
  (Package 7)

What Is the Ocean Floor Like?

If you could ride in a submarine from the shore of the Atlantic Ocean out to its deepest part, you would see a varied landscape of mountains, valleys, and plains. As you left the shore, your trip would start above the **continental shelf**, the underwater edge of a continent. It extends from the shore to a depth of about 200 m (600 ft) and has a gentle slope.

About 80 km (50 mi) out from the shore, the land would slope steeply down. You would now be above the **continental slope**. The continental slope leads from the continental shelf toward the sea floor. It is steeper, deeper, and narrower than the shelf.

After traveling another 20 km (12.4 mi) out into the ocean, you would find yourself above the **continental rise**. The continental rise is a buildup of sediment on the sea floor at the bottom of the continental slope. It is a zone of sand and mud that stretches from the slope down to the deep-sea floor.

At the end of the continental rise, you would reach one of the flattest places on Earth—the **abyssal** (uh·BIS·uhl) **plain**. Most of the hills and valleys at the bottom of the ocean were buried under a layer of sand and mud long ago. This created the level abyssal plains. These vast, flat lands cover almost half of the deep ocean floor.

As your trip continued across the abyssal plain, you might come to a huge underwater mountain called a **seamount**. The peak of a seamount rises hundreds of kilometers above the ocean floor. A seamount is a volcano. It is formed in the same way as a volcano on land—hot molten rock from inside Earth rises to the surface and cools to a solid.

A seamount may never cross the surface of the ocean. However, if it

Ocean Floor

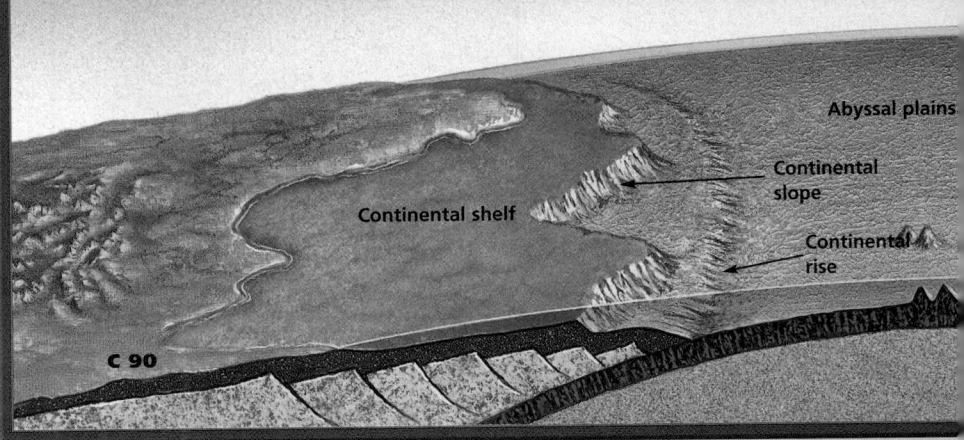

Abyssal plains

Continental slope

Continental shelf

Continental rise

C 90

Advanced Learners

Deep Sea Explorers

Ask interested students to find information on famous divers or ocean explorers and then pick one to research and tell the class about. Two well-known examples would be Charles William Beebe and Jacques Cousteau of television fame. **Linguistic**

Inclusion

Model the Ocean Floor

Ask students to make a papier mâché diorama showing details of the ocean floor. Have them show examples of the vocabulary words on this page. They can insert a toothpick beside each site and attach a stickie note banner to it giving the name of the ocean floor feature of the site. **Spatial; Kinesthetic; Linguistic**

grows large enough, it may emerge as an island. The Hawaiian Islands are an example of a chain of seamounts.

As your travels continued, your submarine might come to a long, narrow V-shaped valley known as a `trench`. Deep-sea trenches are the deepest points on Earth. They plunge as far down as 8,000–10,000 m (5–6 mi) below sea level. One is more than 11,000 m (7 mi) deep. If you could put the tallest mountain on Earth—Mount Everest—in the trench, its tip would still be about 2,000 m (1.25 mi) below the ocean surface.

The trenches are too deep beneath the ocean to ever see the sunlight. They are pitch black and freezing cold. Your submarine couldn't dive to the bottom of a trench—the pressure of the water above is so great that it would crush a normal submarine.

As you reached the middle of the Atlantic Ocean, you would see a mountain range rising above the ocean floor. This is known as the mid-Atlantic ridge. It is part of the chain of mountains, called `mid-ocean ridges`, that winds its way through all the world's major oceans. The mid-Atlantic ridge runs the entire length of the Atlantic Ocean. Like seamounts, these mountain ranges were formed by molten rock that cooled and hardened.

▷ **What are some of the features of the ocean floor?**

Some of the features are the continental shelf, slope, and rise; the flat abyssal plains; seamounts; trenches; and the mid-ocean ridge.

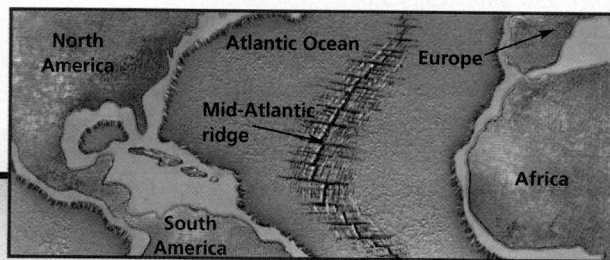

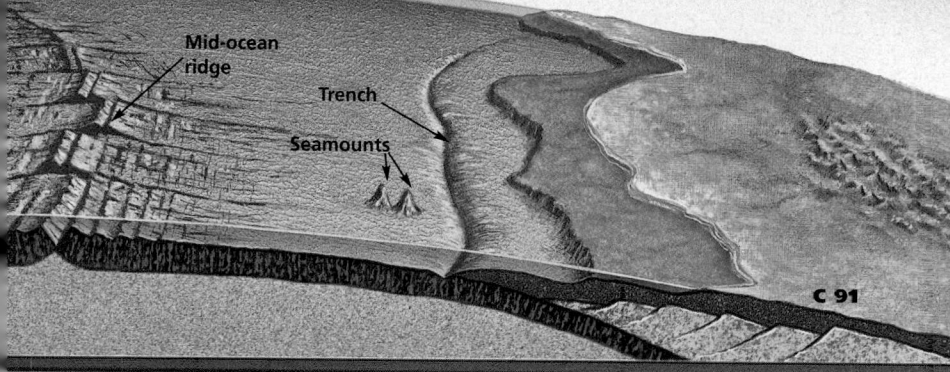

Mid-ocean ridge

Trench

Seamounts

C 91

Inclusion

The Recovery of the *Titanic*
Have students find out some details about the recovery of the *Titanic* from the ocean floor. They might compare and contrast the mini-sub that reached the stranded vessel with earlier inventions for deep-sea exploration, such as the bathysphere and the bathyscaphe. Have students draw pictures of these vessels. Then ask them to report what they have learned and show their art work to the class.
Linguistic; Spatial; Kinesthetic

SCIENCE

Reading Strategy

Interpret Graphic Sources of Information
Developing Reading Skills
Have pairs of students draw pictures of each vocabulary word in this lesson and then explain their drawings to other pairs of students.

Compare and Contrast
Have students continue the strategy (from p. C85) of finding words to compare and contrast parts of the ocean floor.

Exploring the Main Idea
On the board, draw to scale the depth of an ocean trench, Mount Everest, and the Grand Canyon (1 mile or 1.6 km deep). Use the diagram to emphasize the enormous depth of these ocean floor trenches. Then ask:

■ **Why is it so difficult to explore these trenches?** (The water pressure is too high for most submarine vessels.)

Explain that not all continental shelves drop off smoothly into slopes with rises at their edge. Some continental shelves drop off abruptly and are edged by trenches.

Thinking Further: *Compare and Contrast*
Ask:

■ **How are mid-ocean ridges and seamounts similar? How are they different?** (They are both formed by volcanic activity. Seamounts are isolated volcanic mountains. Mid-ocean ridges are long chains of interconnected volcanoes that extend through all the world's oceans.)

▶**After Reading**
Have students answer the red question in the student book as **ongoing assessment**.

Developing Vocabulary

`trench` Discuss *trench* as a science term, then compare to more common usage, *a long cut in the ground or ditch.*
`mid-ocean ridge` Ask students to look up the prefix *mid-*, "middle part of," and to define *ridge*, "an elevated strip."

How Do We Explore the Oceans?

Before Reading
Have students try to answer the red question at the top of the page.

Developing the Main Idea
Have student make a list of the different techniques for ocean exploration. Ask:

- **What part of the ocean can be explored from scuba diving?** (the surface waters, shallow continental shelf, underwater seamounts)

- **What type of sea exploration equipment is needed to explore trenches?** (submersibles)

- **How can viewing layers of ocean sediment help scientists understand how oceans have changed over time?** (Possible answers: They can compare changes in sediment type, organisms found in each layer, gases trapped there, and so on.)

Thinking Further: *Drawing Conclusions*
Ask:

- **What equipment or features would a submersible need for people to explore the deep-ocean floor?** (Possible answers: bright underwater lights, cameras, "grabber" arms to collect samples, pressurizing system, oxygen system)

How Do We Explore the Oceans?

Today ocean scientists explore the oceans using a variety of techniques. One of the first breakthroughs in technology came in the 1920s, when sonar equipment was invented. Sonar helps scientists map the ocean floor. Sonar instruments give out sound waves that hit the ocean floor and send back echoes. The echoes are recorded. Their pattern is traced on paper to make a "sound map" of features like underwater mountains and trenches.

The ability of people to move about underwater was aided by the invention in the 1940s of scuba (self-contained underwater breathing apparatus). Scuba was invented by Jacques Cousteau and Emile Gagnan. For the first time, divers had their own air supply.

A diver wearing scuba gear can explore the ocean to about 50 m. After that, the water pressures are too great for the human body to handle safely.

Starting in the 1960s, scientists began using deep-diving research vessels called submersibles to explore the ocean. They can go much deeper than a diver can go. Using submersibles like *Alvin*, scientists have found a new world deep beneath the sea. They have studied new

The *Titanic*

C 92

SCIENCE Reading Strategy

Organize Information
Developing Reading Skills
Ask students to organize the information on pp. C92–C93 into an outline. They can start by listing two main headings — *Techniques of Exploration* and *Sea-floor Vents* and follow each heading with details.

animals like tube worms. Submersibles also helped locate and explore the ocean liner *Titanic*. The cruise ship lies on the Atlantic floor almost 4,000 m (2.5 mi) below the surface.

Satellites are yet another way to study the ocean. Satellites can measure surface temperature, wave height and direction, sea level, currents, sea ice, and levels of marine plant life. This information can be used in different ways. For example, patterns in ocean temperatures and currents can be used to predict the weather. Satellites can also monitor ocean pollution.

Deep-sea drilling is also used to study the ocean. Research vessels collect samples from beneath the sea floor. The sediment gathered allows scientists to understand how the oceans have changed over time.

Sea-Floor Vents

In 1977 scientists in a submersible traveled deep below the ocean to one of the mid-ocean ridges. They were there to study hot springs called *sea-floor vents*. These vents are formed when seawater trickles down into the hot, newly formed oceanic crust. The water becomes saturated with minerals. Eventually, it boils out of a vent in the crust.

To the scientists' amazement, large wormlike animals were waving in the water near some of the vents. They named the animals *tube worms*. Tube worms get nourishment from bacteria living inside them. The bacteria, in

Tube worms are found deep beneath the ocean near vents in the ocean floor. How can tube worms get nutrients in these deep, dark waters?

turn, use the hydrogen sulfide and oxygen taken in by the worms to create nutrients through a process called *chemosynthesis* (kee·moh·SIN·thuh·sis).

Recall that photosynthesis is the food-making process in green plants that uses sunlight. Never before had scientists seen a food chain that did not rely on photosynthesis for energy and food. Instead, the bacteria–tube worm food chain gets its food and energy from the mineral-rich waters and the heat energy from the hot vents.

Since that first discovery, more than 400 species new to science have been found living in and around sea-floor vents.

 **What are some of the ways that today's scientists explore the oceans?**
Scientists today use scuba gear or submersibles to dive beneath the water. They also use sonar, satellites, and deep-sea drills.

C 93

Developing the Main Idea
Ask students to recall what they have learned about plate tectonics. Remind them that areas of newly formed crust occur where the sea-floor is spreading apart and molten rock from deep in the mantle is rising. This is where sea-floor, or *hydrothermal*, vents are found. Ask:

■ **Sea-floor vents may also be found where seamounts are forming. Why would this occur?** (Magma is rising through the ocean floor in those places as well.)

■ **What kind of adaptations would an organism need to survive near sea-floor vents?** (Possible answers: the ability to withstand great heat and pressure, the ability to survive by chemosynthesis)

■ **What was so unusual about the discovery of the way tube worms get energy and food?** (Their food chain, unlike all others on Earth, does not rely on photosynthesis, but on chemosynthesis instead.)

Tell students that the discovery of chemosynthesis has major importance for astronomers seeking other forms of life in our solar system. On the volcanic moons of Jupiter, for example, there may not be enough sunlight to support photosynthesis, but another process such as chemosynthesis might be possible in such circumstances.

▶ **After Reading**
Have students answer the red question in the student book as **ongoing assessment**.

How Do People Affect the Oceans?

Before Reading
Have students try to answer the red question at the top of the page.

Developing the Main Idea
Emphasize the ways in which people pollute the ocean and use its resources. Ask:

- **How are the ways that people affect the oceans similar to the ways rivers might be affected?** (the dumping of sewage, factory waste, and fertilizers)

- **Besides deep-sea drilling, what is another way that the ocean can be polluted because of the oil industry?** (when ships carrying oil break open in the ocean and there's an oil spill)

- **How might people be able to reduce the effect we have on the oceans?** (possible answers: reduce the use of phosphates and nitrogen fertilizers; rely less on offshore sources of oil and natural gas; don't eat endangered fish species)

Thinking Further: *Making Generalizations*
Ask:

- **What are some recreational uses of the ocean?** (possible answers: swimming, fishing, scuba diving, boating, water skiing, jet skiing)

- **How might these uses negatively affect the ocean?** (possible answers: dumping of more human wastes or fuel into the ocean, disturbing the marine life, taking endangered fish)

- **Could there be any positive effects?** (more awareness of and attention to conservation)

▶ After Reading
Have students answer the red question in the student book as **ongoing assessment**.

Technology

- **Science Experiences Videotapes**
  Life in a Coral Reef (Package 2)

People can help clean up polluted waters.

How Do People Affect the Oceans?

The oceans have a tremendous ability to absorb human waste. Unfortunately, at some point the pollution becomes too much for the water to handle. Marine pollution has become a serious problem for the world's oceans.

Each year sewage, waste from factories, and fertilizer and waste from farms are dumped into rivers that flow into the sea or into the ocean itself. Ships may spill oil or dump sewage overboard. Offshore drilling for oil and natural gas also harms the environment.

Ocean pollution can harm or kill marine animals and plants. It is also dangerous to people who eat seafood from the polluted waters.

Overfishing is another threat to marine animals. People around the world depend on fish and marine animals, such as crabs and lobsters, for food. According to the United Nations Food and Agriculture Organization, 70 percent of the fish species caught to be sold are being overfished. If this continues, entire species may die out. People pollute the ocean by dumping and spilling waste and by drilling. They also overfish certain species of fish and marine animals.

▶ **What are some of the ways that people affect the ocean environment?**

A factory fishing boat is a huge boat where thousands of fish at a time can be caught, cleaned, and quick frozen. How might such a boat contribute to overfishing?

C 94

 English Language Learners

Harvesting Seafood
Ask students to choose a type of ocean seafood they enjoy eating. Challenge them to research how that type of seafood is harvested. Have them present an oral report on the effect that harvesting this type of seafood has on the ocean. **Linguistic**

 **Advanced Learners**

Seafood Shopping
Plan a field trip to a large fish market or the seafood section of a supermarket. Have students record the types of fish and shellfish for sale in the market. Have them research the kinds of seafood found in the market to see how many of them are listed as being overfished. **Social; Linguistic**

Lesson Review

Why It Matters

Oceans provide many valuable resources. Most of the world's nations are now aware of the need to protect their coasts and water from pollution. They have begun to enforce laws to keep sewage, chemicals, and other waste out of the water.

Many countries have also agreed to prevent overfishing. They limit the number of fish that can be caught in their waters.

Many governments have also set aside protected areas in their waters where marine animals can live undisturbed. By the mid-1990s, 1,200 marine protected areas existed throughout the world.

Think and Write

1. What resources are found in oceans?

2. Where do the oceans' salts come from?

3. How does the water in waves move? In currents?

4. What does the ocean floor look like?

5. **Critical Thinking** In the Indian Ocean, there are seasonal wind shifts known as the summer and winter monsoons. What do you think happens to the surface currents when the winds change direction? Explain.

ART LINK

Make a diorama. Make a model of the ocean floor. Show the continental shelf, slope, and rise, and the abyssal plain. You may want to show a trench, a seamount, or sea-floor vents, too.

WRITING LINK

Write a paragraph. What are some of the ocean resources you use? Which ones do you use the most? Tell about them in a paragraph.

TECHNOLOGY LINK

Science Newsroom CD-ROM Choose *Sea to Shining Sea* to learn more about Earth's water and how it moves through the water cycle.

At the Computer Visit **www.mhscience02.com** for more links.

C 95

Informal Assessment

Easy/Average Have students make a picture for each of the three major ways in which the ocean's water move. For example, for tides, they can draw the tidal bulges on Earth or show a seashore where the water's edge has moved down the beach.

Challenge Have students draw on a graph the height of tidal ranges they would see from one new moon to the next. (Graphs should begin with the highest tidal range, decrease until the first-quarter moon, increase again until the full moon, about the same range as the new moon. The tidal range will decrease again until the third-quarter moon and increase once more until it reaches the highest range again at the next new moon.)

3 Lesson Review

Answers to Think and Write

1. The oceans provide fish and other seafood; they contain minerals; they provide a habitat for many organisms; they provide recreation for people.) (pp. C84–C85)

2. Salts from weathered rocks are washed into the ocean. Salts from deep inside Earth are released during volcanic eruptions. (p. C85)

3. Water in waves moves in a circle as the wave's energy passes through. Water in currents moves in a stream. (pp. C86–C88)

4. From the coast, the ocean floor slopes down along the continental shelf, dropping off at the continental slope. It rises slightly along the continental rise and stretches into the flat expanse of the abyssal plain. The plain, possibly dotted by seamounts, may end at the mid-ocean ridge or at a trench. (pp. C90–C91)

5. **Critical Thinking** Possible answers: The winds drive surface ocean currents. If the wind shifts direction, the current will shift as well. (p. C86)

Summarize

Check students' understanding by having them write a brief summary of the lesson in their own words.

ART LINK

Encourage students to make models that accurately portray features of each portion of the ocean basin. Features need not be to scale.

WRITING LINK

Students may mention salt and other minerals; oil and natural gas; fish and seafood; seaweed-containing products, such as ice cream and toothpaste; and the ocean itself.

Science Magazine

Build on Prior Knowledge

Ask students whether they have ever swum under water: Ask:

■ **How long were you able to stay under?** (no more than a few minutes)

■ **What are some ways that people use to stay under water for longer periods?** (Possible answers: snorkeling and scuba-diving equipment, submarines, submersibles)

Voyager to the Bottom of the Ocean

Developing the Main Idea
Focus on the job of a submersible pilot. Ask:

■ **Why did Professor Van Dover become a submersible pilot?** (As a child she liked the weird animals at the beach, and as an adult she wanted to study deep-ocean vents and the creatures that live around them.)

■ **What were her three responsibilities as a submersible pilot?** (the safety of her passengers, the safety of the sub, to help her passengers conduct scientific tests and gather data on the vent creatures)

Science Magazine

Voyager to the Bottom of the Ocean

When Cindy Lee Van Dover was growing up, she thought that sea creatures were the most interesting animals. She liked finding weird animals on the beach.

Van Dover never imagined that in 1989 she would become the first female pilot of the submersible, *Alvin.* At the bottom of the ocean, she found lots of weird animals.

Van Dover was a submersible pilot until 1991. During this time she took *Alvin* as deep as 3,584 meters. That's more than 2 miles below the surface!

On a typical dive, *Alvin* might take $1\frac{1}{2}$ hours to reach the bottom of the ocean. Then the pilot uses the sub's manipulators to gather samples of sea-floor creatures for the scientists. She also takes readings of the water pressures and temperatures outside the submersible. After about five hours on the bottom, the pilot releases weights from the sub, and it floats back to the surface.

During one of Van Dover's trips, *Alvin* got stuck in the mud deep below the ocean. How did this happen? *Alvin* is taken completely apart and then rebuilt every three years. During the rebuilding process, some metal flaps were accidentally left off *Alvin*'s "belly." The openings allowed mud to fill the bottom.

When Van Dover tried to move the submersible off the ocean bottom, it was stuck. After discussing the problem with engineers on the ship at the surface, Van Dover dropped *Alvin*'s weights and waited. Luckily, *Alvin* was now light enough to slowly float back to the surface.

Today Van Dover is an oceanographer who studies the ecology of sea-floor vents. She still dives to the ocean floor about three times a year, but these days she goes as a scientist, not a pilot. Van Dover studies the communities of mussels that live near the vents. When she's not out on a dive gathering samples to study in her laboratory, Professor Van Dover teaches at a university in Virginia.

C 96

Inclusion

Submersibles

Encourage students to learn more about the submersibles used to conduct research on the ocean bottom. Have students collect pictures or make drawings of different submersibles such as *Alvin, Aluminaut, Archimede,* and *Trieste.* Have them write a short paragraph describing the submersible. **Linguistic**

Advanced Learners

Deep Sea Creatures

Challenge students to learn more about the deep-sea vent organisms that are studied by scientists like Professor Van Dover. Have them prepare a report on one type of creature such as tube worms, bristle worms, albino crabs, yellow mussels, and pink sea urchins. They should describe any unusual adaptations and provide a drawing or photo of the creature. **Linguistic**

NATIONAL GEOGRAPHIC

What Did I Learn?

1. As pilot of the submersible *Alvin*, Cindy Lee Van Dover might

   A take readings of water pressure

   B measure water temperature

   C gather samples of sea creatures

   D all of the above

2. How does *Alvin* get back to the surface?

   F It drops weights and floats back to the surface.

   G It uses its engines.

   H A surface ship pulls it to the surface.

   J Metal flaps on its belly are closed.

Like tube worms, these mussels depend on chemosynthesis for food. Each mussel may be 20–25 centimeters across. Professor Van Dover studies the ecology of deep-ocean mussel beds. There may be 30–70 species found at each vent—including shellfish, worms, and snails. Van Dover studies how the different species interact with each other.

AT THE COMPUTER Visit www.mhscience02.com to learn more about oceans.

C 97

Science Background

Jacques Cousteau

One of the most well known and respected oceanographers was Jacques Cousteau, a French scientist. In 1943, he helped invent scuba equipment. He also helped develop the bathyscaphe, a submersible. Every year, beginning in 1951, he went on expeditions to study the ocean and its many creatures. He wrote many books and made many documentaries about his trips and research.

Exploring the Main Idea

Demonstrate to students how far Professor Van Dover has traveled beneath the ocean surface by making a diagram on the board. Use a scale of 1 meter = 1 millimeter. Show the highest mountain, Mount Everest, at 8,850 m; the highest building, the Petronas Towers, Kuala Lumpur, Malaysia, at 1483 m. The depth of the professor's deepest dive would fall between the two. Then ask:

■ **How long does it take the sub to reach so deep below the surface?** ($1\frac{1}{2}$ hours)

■ **How does the pilot help collect data?** (She uses the manipulators to gather samples of sea floor creatures and takes readings of the water pressures and temperatures.)

Thinking Further: *Inferring*

Ask:

■ **How does the sub get back to the surface? How might this help conserve fuel?** (The pilot releases weights and it floats back up. By floating to the surface, they do not need to use as much fuel as they do getting to the bottom.)

Encourage students to think about how Professor Van Dover's interest in sea creatures led to her job as a submersible pilot and how that led to her becoming an oceanographer and university teacher.

Test Prep:  What Did I Learn?

1. D

2. F

Summarize

Check students' understanding by having them write a brief summary of the magazine in their own words.

LESSON 8 Energy Resources

LESSON 8 Energy Resources

Vocabulary

alternative energy source, C104

geothermal energy, C104

biomass, C106

Objectives

- Explore ways that people use energy each day.
- Compare and contrast fossil fuel use with world reserves.
- Identify alternative energy sources.
- Identify ways to use energy more wisely.

Resources

- Activity Resources, pp. 115–119
- Reading in Science Resources, pp. 177–182
- Vocabulary Cards
- Reading Aid Transparency C8
- Visual Aid Transparency 21
- School To Home Activities, pp. 20–22

Build on Prior Knowledge

Ask:

- **What kind of energy are we using right now?**
  (Possible answers: electricity if lights are on in classroom; gas or fossil fuels if heat or air conditioning is being used)

1 Get Ready

Developing the Main Idea

Help students estimate the number of hours a day they use energy and how they might use less. Students may not realize that they use energy 24 hours a day. Ask them to include their use of electricity for lights and other appliances, and fuels for cooking, heating, and cooling.

Get Ready

How many hours a day do you use energy? What kinds do you use, and what do you use them for? You use energy all the time. How is that possible? How many different ways is energy being used in this picture?

Process Skill

You hypothesize when you make a statement that can be tested to answer a question.

C 98

Science Background

Energy and Pollution

When fossil fuels are burned, they produce energy, carbon dioxide, other gases, and ash. Coal produces large amounts of carbon dioxide, nitrogen oxides, sulfur dioxide, ash, and sulfate solids. Coal produces more carbon dioxide than oil or natural gas for the same amount of energy. Natural gas burns most cleanly, leaving no ash behind and much less carbon dioxide than the other fossil fuels.

Reading Strategy

Organize Information

Developing Reading Skills

Ask students to organize the information in this lesson into an outline. Have them decide on one main concept word as a heading for the content on each page and under that word list details that support that word.

Explore Activity

How Do People Use Energy?

Procedure

1 **Communicate** Make a list of all the different ways you use energy.

2 Make a table listing all the kinds of energy you use in a day, how you use that energy, and how many hours you use each kind.

Drawing Conclusions

1 How many different ways do you use electricity each day? How many hours a day do you use electricity? What other sources of energy do you use? How many hours a day do you use each?

2 **Infer** Make a log to keep track of your energy use at home and at school. How can you use that information to help you make a plan to save energy?

3 **Use Numbers** If it costs you an average of ten cents an hour for the energy you use, how much would the energy you use cost each week? About how much would it cost each month?

4 **Going Further: Hypothesize** How can you use less electricity? How much money do you think you could save on energy use in a month? How would you go about testing your hypothesis?

C 99

Alternative Explore Activity

Materials data collected on use of energy (as in the Explore Activity), file cards, chart paper, marking pens

Pool the Data Have students share collected data about how they use energy and construct a large chart that shows the different uses of energy and the amounts of time involved for each type of use. Suggest that students arrange the information on the chart from greatest use to lowest use. **Spatial; Social**

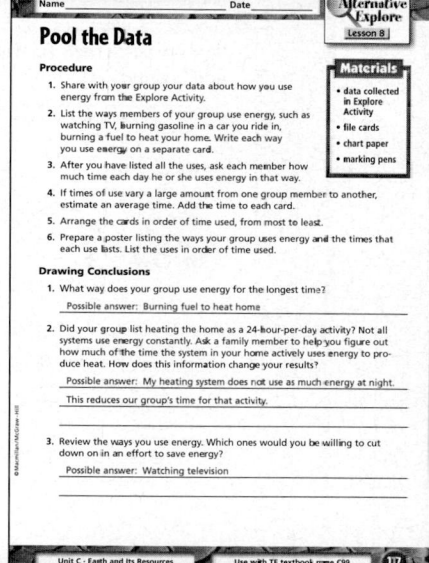

Activity Resources, p. 117

Explore Activity

How Do People Use Energy?

Science Process Skills *communicate, infer, use numbers, hypothesize*

Resources Activity Resources, pp. 115–116

Pacing 30–40 minutes 🕐

Grouping individual

Procedure

1 Advise students to keep adding to their lists throughout the day as they use energy in different ways. Suggest they record the amount of time they use each kind of energy source or the amount of time they do an activity. (Uses include: cooking, heating or air conditioning, transportation, lighting, TV, computers, and so on.)

2 Students may wish to identify the source of the energy if they are having difficulty identifying the kind of energy being used. (Other sources include: gasoline, natural gas, oil, wood, and solar energy.)

Answers to Drawing Conclusions

1 Request that students summarize the data from the table they made in step 2.

2 By keeping careful logs, students can find specific energy uses that could be decreased.

3 Students should multiply the total number of hours of energy use per day by $0.10, then multiply the result by 7 to find their weekly cost or by 30 to find an estimate for the monthly cost.

4 Students might suggest reducing their electricity use by curtailing some of their activities. The amount of money saved could be determined by multiplying the number of energy hours saved by $0.10. Students might suggest testing their hypotheses by trying their idea for one day.

Technology

■ When time is short, preview the activity with the **Explore Activity Video.**

2 Read to Learn

How Are Fossil Fuels Turned into Energy?

Before Reading
Have students try to answer the red question at the top of the page.

Developing the Main Idea
Have students list which appliances and devices in their homes are run by electricity, batteries, or by burning of fuel such as natural gas. Guide them to include major items such as water heaters, furnaces, and air conditioners.

Thinking Further: *Inferring*
Ask students to discuss how people solved their energy problems in the past. (In the past, people used wood, coal, peat, or other fuels to heat their homes and to cook food. Before cars and planes were invented, they used the energy of animals such as horses to help them transport things and people. They also used water and wind power to run machines.)

Using the Illustrations
Have students trace the path the electricity takes from the power plant to the home. Explain to students that they receive their electricity in much the same fashion as shown in the diagram.

2 Read to Learn

Main Idea Some energy sources will last forever, while others will run out eventually.

How Are Fossil Fuels Turned into Energy?

You use a number of different energy sources each day. Where does the energy you use come from? Try tracing it back to its source. Many homes, schools, and businesses get heat by burning oil or natural gas. Some older buildings still burn coal for heat. Some homes burn wood for heat.

The heat in many other homes and businesses comes from electricity. So does the energy to run many common devices, such as lights, computers, radios, TVs, and washers. Some small devices such as flashlights and portable CD players get their electricity from batteries. Most of the other devices use electricity from a wall outlet. That electricity comes from a power plant. Electricity from that plant reaches your home through wires. However, the power plant makes electricity by using energy from burning fuels such as coal, oil, and natural gas.

It takes a lot of energy to move a car, bus, or train. Public and private transportation is one of the greatest uses of energy in today's world. Most vehicles get their energy from burning fuels such as gasoline or diesel oil. Others run on electricity, propane, or liquefied natural gas.

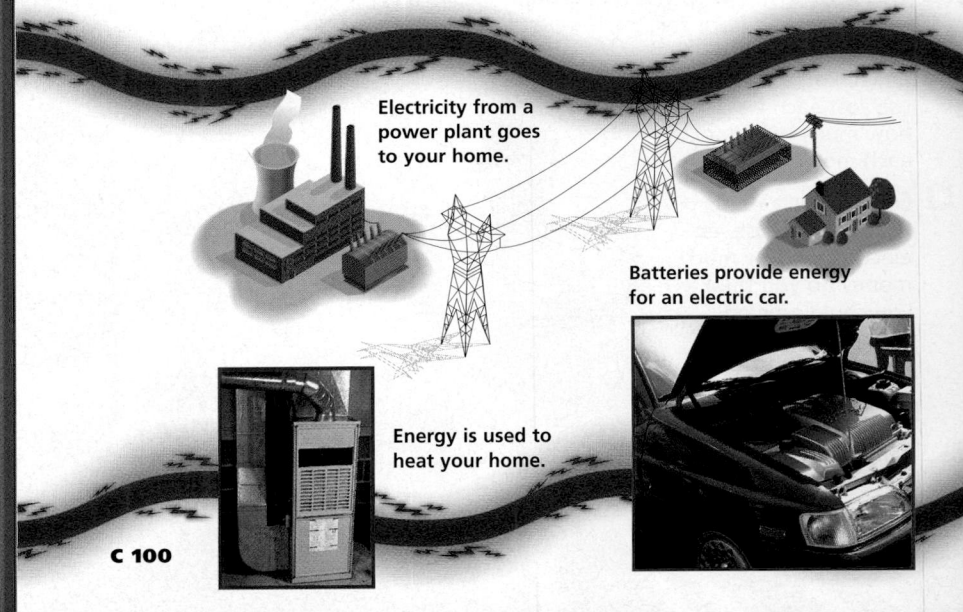

Electricity from a power plant goes to your home.

Batteries provide energy for an electric car.

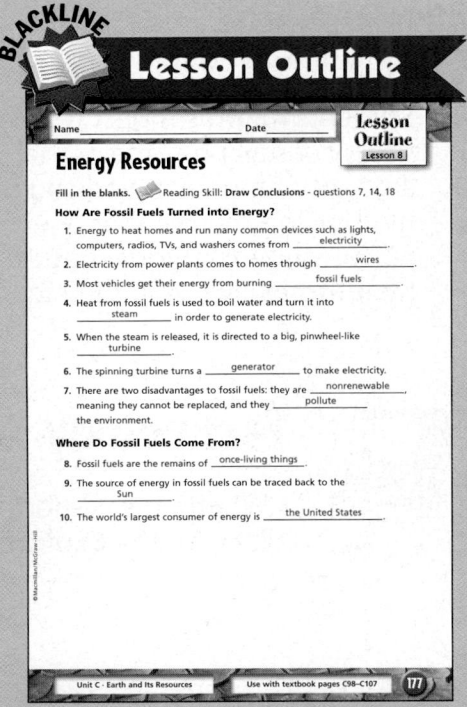

Energy is used to heat your home.

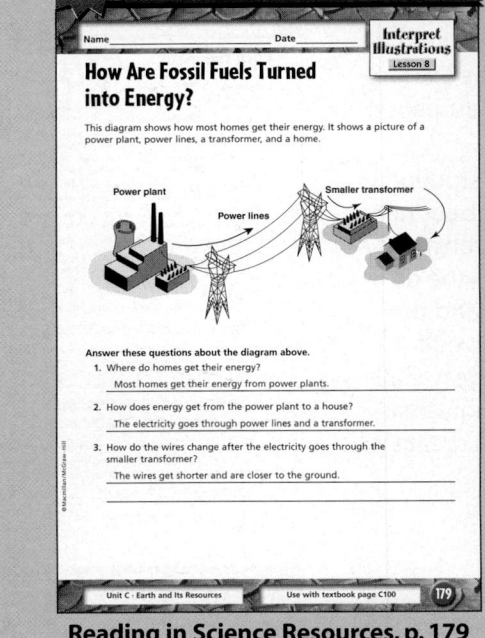

C 100

Smog is air pollution that is a mixture of smoke and fog. Smog also occurs when sunlight reacts with exhaust fumes from cars and factories. Smog can make people ill.

As you can see, most of the energy you use can be traced back to fossil fuels—coal, oil, or natural gas. The energy in fossil fuels, in turn, can be traced back to the Sun.

Heat from burning fossil fuels can be used directly to heat homes, schools, businesses, and factories.

The heat can also be used to generate electricity. The heat is used to boil water and turn it into steam. The steam is trapped, and pressure builds up. Then the steam is released. The steam is directed at a big, pinwheel-like turbine. When the steam hits the turbine, it causes it to spin. The spinning turbine turns a generator to make electricity.

All fuels have advantages and disadvantages. The advantage of using fossil fuels is that they contain a lot of energy. However, fossil fuels take millions of years to form. Once used they cannot be replaced fast enough for future use. Therefore, they are nonrenewable.

Burning a fossil fuel also gives off smoke, gases, and other by-products. These pollute the environment. That is why the search is on for other, cleaner fuels.

 **What are some energy sources that come from fossil fuels?**

Answers may include: oil, gas, and electricity.

C 101

Developing the Main Idea
Have students classify their energy uses and sources from the Explore Activity into those that use fossil fuels directly or indirectly. Ask:

■ **What are some direct uses of fossil fuels you listed?** (Burning them to produce heat, cook, and run motor vehicles.)

■ **How do you use fossil fuels indirectly?** (By using electricity.)

■ **Why is being nonrenewable a disadvantage to using fossile fuels?** (because they took millions of years to form and can't be replaced fast enough for future use)

Differentiate between renewable and nonrenewable resources. Make a list of natural resources on the board. (minerals, fossil fuels, land and soil, forests, water—and as they will learn in this lesson, wind, tides, Earth's heat, and sunlight). Ask:

■ **Which of these resources cannot be replaced in their lifetime?** (mineral deposits, fossil fuels)

▶**After Reading**
Have students answer the red question in the student book as **ongoing assessment**.

Where Do Fossil Fuels Come From?

Before Reading
Have students try to answer the red question at the top of the page.

Developing the Main Idea
Remind students that fossil fuels contain a lot of energy. Ask:

- **Is the energy in fossil fuels potential energy or kinetic energy? Why?** (Potential, since the energy is stored in the fuel and released when it's burned.)

Explain to students that the energy in the fuels came from energy stored in plants and animals that lived millions of years ago.

Thinking Further: *Inferring*
Ask:

- **Where did the plants and animals get that energy?** (From food; the plants made their own food and the animals ate the plants or other animals that ate plants.)

Exploring the Main Idea
Show students a sample of fossil coal with a fern imprint (or a picture of such a piece of coal). Ask:

- **What can you tell about where this coal was formed?** (The print shows that the coal was formed in a place where ferns were buried.)

Using the Illustrations
Explain to students that the process of forming fossil fuels took place over a long period of time. Organisms accumulated and deposits of fossil fuels were formed.

Developing the Main Idea
Ask:

- **To whom do Earth's energy resources "belong"?** (Student responses may indicate that the Earth's energy resources belong to all the people.)

- **How could these resources be conserved?** (Possible suggestions for conserving energy resources include finding alternatives, such as solar energy, and cutting down on usage.)

Help students understand that it is everyone's responsibility to use energy wisely.

Where Do Fossil Fuels Come From?

Fossil fuels are the remains of once-living things. Coal formed from the remains of dead plants buried in ancient swamps and forests. Natural gas and oil formed from the remains of tiny ocean plants and animals. These sea creatures died and fell to the bottom of the ocean. There their bodies were buried by layers of sand and mud. As more and more layers covered these remains, pressure on them built up. Eventually, the layers of sediments turned into sedimentary rock. Over millions of years, the plant and animal remains changed into oil and natural gas. Plants and animals get their energy from the Sun. Therefore, the source of energy in fossil fuels can be traced back to the Sun.

Our supplies of fossil fuels are limited, and fossil fuels are not a renewable energy source.

With the growth of industry, the demand for and use of energy also grows. The United States is the world's largest consumer of energy. The energy we use makes our lives easier.

How Fossil Fuels Are Formed

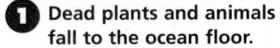
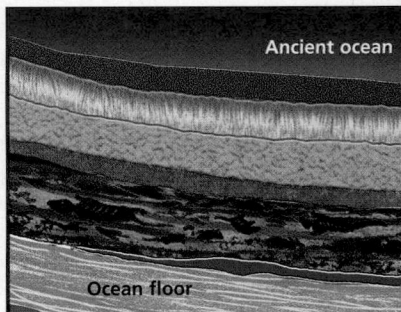

1 Dead plants and animals fall to the ocean floor.

2 Dead plants and animals are covered with layers of sand and mud.

C 102

Interpret Illustrations

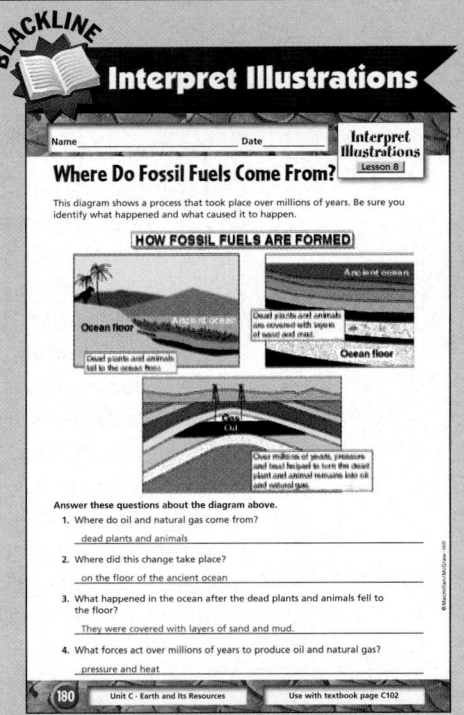

Reading in Science Resources, p. 180

Science Background

Coal Varieties
Coal is a solid fuel composed mainly of carbon. Sulfur impurities are often present in some coal deposits. Anthracite, or hard coal, has the greatest amount of carbon and therefore the greatest heat content per unit weight. Bituminous coal, or soft coal, has less carbon and less heat content than anthracite. Lignite has the lowest heat content of the grades of coal.

However, energy use pollutes the environment. It also speeds up the rate at which Earth's energy resources are used up.

If we continue to use fossil fuels at our present rate, we will run out of them. There are two possible solutions to this problem. One is to conserve our energy resources so that they will last longer. Another is to search for other sources of energy.

▷ **How do fossil fuels form?**
Fossil fuels form over long periods of time as heat and pressure turn once-living things into oil and gas.

3 Over millions of years, pressure and heat help to turn the dead plant and animal remains into oil and natural gas.

FOR SCHOOL OR HOME

Fuel Supply

This table shows how fast we are using up oil and natural gas.

World Supply of Oil and Natural Gas (as of January 1, 1996)	
Oil	1,007 billion barrels (1,007,000,000,000)
Natural gas	4,900 trillion cubic feet
World Use of Oil and Natural Gas for 1995	
Oil	about 70 million barrels a day (70,000,000)
Natural gas	about 78 trillion cubic feet

1. **Observe** Examine the data in the table.

2. **Communicate** Draw a graph showing how long the fossil fuels we know about will last, based on the data in the table.

3. **Infer** How long will it be until we run out of each type of fossil fuel? Assume that the rate of use remains the same.

C 103

Advanced Learners

Storage
Among the responsibilities of the Department of Energy (DOE) is the management of the Strategic Petroleum Reserve, a program to store oil in the event of a national emergency. Have interested students find out more about this program and other national energy concerns and report to the class. **Linguistic**

Inclusion

Convert Quantities
A barrel of crude oil contains 42 gallons. When refined, it produces 21 gallons of gasoline, 9 gallons of fuel oils, 5 gallons of jet fuel, 4 gallons of lubricants, and 3 gallons of asphalt. Ask students to draw a bar graph to show the products obtained from a barrel of crude oil. **Logical; Spatial**

Using the Illustrations
Have students focus on the three panels of the diagram. Ask:

■ **In your own words, describe the process of fossil fuel formation.** (First, dead microscopic plants and animals fall to the ocean floor. Then, they are covered with layers of sand and mud. Over millions of years, pressure and heat help to turn the remains into oil and natural gas.)

▶ **After Reading**
Have students answer the red question in the student book as **ongoing assessment**.

FOR SCHOOL OR HOME

Science Process Skills *observe, communicate, infer*

Resources Activity Resources, pp. 118–119

Step 2 A line graph for each type of fossil fuel may be most suitable.

Step 3 Explain to students that they need to extend the line at the same slope to predict the year in which Earth will run out of each type of fossil fuel. (Years of oil = 1,007 billion barrels ÷ 70 million barrels/day ÷ 365 days/year = 39 years; 1996 + 36 = 2035. Years of gas = 4,900 trillion cubic feet ÷ 78 trillion cubic feet /year = 63 years; 1996 + 63 = 2059)

Technology

■ Visual Aid Transparency 21: *How Fossil Fuels Form*

What Other Sources of Energy Are There?

Before Reading
Have students try to answer the red question at the top of the page.

Exploring the Main Idea
Waterwheels were used by ancient Greek and Roman cultures. Early waterwheels were used mainly for milling grain. Many early American communities were situated along streams where the energy of the moving water could be harnessed to mill grain and saw lumber. Water from the streams was directed toward the wheel. The moving wheel turned a shaft, which in turn propelled the machinery of the factory or mill. In New England, the textile industry flourished because of the availability of waterpower.

Many garden decorations are wind-powered machines. Some are pinwheels, others depict characters moving or performing simple tasks like chopping wood. Show one of these items to the class. Direct a stream of air from a fan or hair dryer toward the device to illustrate how the wind has energy.

Developing Vocabulary

alternative energy source *Alternative* means "other". Students may be familiar with other energy sources, such as solar collectors.

geothermal energy Tell students this word is derived from the Greek *geo-* "of the Earth" and *-thermal* "heat". Have students name other words that include either of these two words.

Technology

- **Science Experiences Videotapes**
Environmentally Friendly Transportation
(Package 8)

What Other Sources of Energy Are There?

Sources of energy other than the burning of fossil fuels are called **alternative energy sources**. Here are some alternative energy sources.

Water
Any whitewater rafter can tell you that running water has a lot of energy. That energy can be harnessed to do work using waterwheels. Running or falling water turns the wheel. The turning wheel spins an axle, which is attached to various machines to do work.

In a mill the axle turns a big stone that grinds up grain. In a sawmill it spins a blade to cut wood. In a *hydroelectric* (high·droh·i·LEK·trik) *plant*, running or falling water spins a generator to make electricity.

Wind
Wind, or moving air, can also spin a wheel. Windmills generate electricity in the same way waterwheels do.

Hydroelectric Plant

C 104

Internal Heat
The Earth's interior is very hot. The most common evidence of that heat is simply hot water or steam coming out of the ground. The water is heated below the surface in places where magma collects. Earth's internal heat is called **geothermal** (jee·oh·THUR·muhl) **energy**. Geothermal energy can be used to heat homes and produce electricity.

- Homes in Boise, Idaho, have been heated by hot springs since the 1890s.
- At The Geysers in California, steam drives turbines that generate electricity. The steam comes from underground water heated by geothermal energy.

Geothermal energy helps keep the country of Iceland warm.

Science Background

Is Coal Still Being Formed?
Addressing Misconceptions
Students might think that no more coal will ever be formed. Explain that coal formation begins when plant materials accumulate in a bog-type ecosystem. The material forms into peat. With time and pressure, the peat is transformed to lignite, then bituminous coal, and finally anthracite. The process is taking place today but the transformation is a very slow process taking millions of years.

Solar houses use solar cells for electric energy and solar collectors for heat.

The Sun

Every day the Sun bathes Earth in energy. We usually think of that solar energy simply as sunlight. Plants harness the Sun's energy through photosynthesis to make chemical compounds rich in energy. When you burn wood, you are releasing energy that a tree absorbed from the Sun.

Sunlight also gives water the energy to evaporate and rise into the atmosphere. In this way the energy of running water can also be traced back to sunlight.

Today people are using new ways to harness the power of sunlight. One way is to trap or concentrate sunlight with the use of solar panels, or collectors. The trapped sunlight can be used to heat water or entire homes. Another way to use it is with solar cells. Solar cells are devices that convert sunlight into electric energy.

Tides

Every day the tide causes the water level to rise and drop along the world's coastlines. Now imagine a big tank built just below the high-water level. The tide rises, and water fills the tank. When the tide drops, the water flows out of the tank. Add a waterwheel so the water flowing out of the tank spins the wheel. Now you have a spinning axle that can be used to do work. That's the idea behind tidal power plants.

>  **What are five alternative energy sources?**
> Five sources of energy are water, wind, internal heat, the Sun, and tides.

The windmills in this array spin generators to make electricity.

Tidal power plant in Holland

 C 105

Developing the Main Idea

Discuss that geothermal energy is transferred to Earth's surface by the movement of magma (molten rock) and deep water, which can be accessed with wells and pumps. Geothermal energy has a low impact on the environment, but it can only be easily extracted at a few places.

Emphasize that we indirectly use solar energy every time we eat, burn fossil fuels, and feel the wind. We use solar energy directly whenever we use solar-powered calculators, toys, or other devices.

Using the Illustrations

Point out that we are using solar energy in many places to supplement and/or replace the energy normally provided by fossil fuels. Ask:

- **How will using solar or tidal energy affect our fossil fuel reserves?** (The reserves will last longer.)

▶ After Reading

Have students answer the red question in the student book as **ongoing assessment**.

How Can We Conserve Energy?

Before Reading
Have students try to answer the red question at the top of the first text column.

Developing the Main Idea
Point out that students use biomass for fuel whenever they burn wood.

Using the Illustration
Explain to students that a mixture of up to 10 percent alcohol and 90 percent gasoline may be used as a fuel for automobiles. The mixture is called *gasohol*. Ask:

■ **What might be an advantage of using gasohol?** (The alcohol component of gasohol is a renewable energy source. The use of gasohol reduces the consumption of gasoline, which is obtained from crude oil—a nonrenewable form of energy.)

▶**After Reading**
Have students answer the red question in the student book as **ongoing assessment**.

Developing Vocabulary

biomass This word is a combination of *bio-* ("life") and *mass* ("amount of matter"). In addition to the meaning of this word in an energy context, it can also mean "the amount of living matter in a unit area or volume."

Cars can be powered by a special mixture that combines alcohol from biomass with gasoline.

How Can We Conserve Energy?

Unfortunately, alternative energy sources are not fully replacing fossil fuels. Therefore, we need to conserve these nonrenewable resources.

What does it mean to conserve our resources? It means we don't waste what we have and we use as little of what we have as possible. Take a typical house as an example. Better insulation of homes has cut United States' consumption of fuel oil almost in half. Newly designed bodies and engines have doubled the gasoline

C 106

mileage of most cars. If we could cut our present consumption in half, our oil reserves would last twice as long! How can we do that?

One way is to use alternative energy sources such as water, wind, and solar energy. Every watt of electricity we get from a solar cell is one less watt we have to get by burning oil or coal.

You have learned that fossil fuels are the stored energy that came from once-living plants and animals. Fossil fuels are nonrenewable. However, plant matter and animal wastes or other remains—called **biomass**—can be used as a renewable energy source. Plant material and animal wastes that might wind up as garbage can be processed to form fuel. This is done in waste-treatment plants. The treated wastes can then be burned. Special devices called scrubbers help prevent pollutants from entering the air when these wastes are burned. Solid wastes can also be digested by bacteria. The bacteria produce methane gas in the process. Methane gas can be used as fuel.

Corn and other grains, and even sugarcane, can also be turned into fuel. This fuel can be used to heat foods. It can also be mixed with gasoline to help run cars while saving gasoline supplies.

READING Draw Conclusions
How can biomass help conserve energy?

Biomass can be processed to form fuel. Bacteria that digest solid waste produce methane gas, which can also be used as fuel.

Reading MiniLesson

Draw Conclusions

Develop Discuss the question about turning biomass into fuel on page C106 with students and help them draw the conclusion that as an alternate form of energy, biomass helps us conserve our nonrenewable resources. Also help students conclude that biomass is a kind of fossil fuel because it's made from animal remains. Biomass, however, is renewable whereas it would take millions of years for new fossil fuels to form.

Practice Ask students what evidence they find in the second paragraph on page C106 to help them draw the conclusion that businesses are developing ways to help conserve energy. (Answers should include that better insulation has cut use of fuel oil in homes and better designed car engines and bodies have cut use of gasoline.)

Science Background

Alcohols
There are many kinds of alcohol. Methanol is very toxic and is used as a solvent, for antifreeze, and to make other compounds. Propanol is another type of alcohol. It can be used as a disinfectant and its common name is rubbing alcohol.

Why It Matters

You probably look forward to driving a car someday. Won't it be great to get around on your own? Well, think about this: Cars run on gasoline, and gasoline comes from oil. Remember the graph you did comparing known oil reserves with our current rate of use? If we don't conserve, will there be enough gas for your children's cars? Will there be enough gas for their children?

Think and Write

1. How do you use energy each day?

2. Why are coal, oil, and natural gas called "fossil" fuels?

3. How does the burning of fossil fuels pollute the environment?

4. List five ways people can help to conserve fossil fuels. Which of these suggestions do you think would conserve the most fuel? Which of these suggestions do you think more people would be willing to try?

5. **Critical Thinking** What alternatives do we have to using fossil fuels for energy? What are some of the advantages and disadvantages to using these energy sources?

L·I·N·K·S

ART LINK

Design an advertisement. There are many alternative energy sources. Develop an ad trying to convince people to use an alternative energy source.

MATH LINK

Calculate percents. A barrel of crude oil contains 42 gallons. When refined, it produces 21 gallons of gasoline, 9 gallons of fuel oils, 5 gallons of jet fuel, 4 gallons of lubricants, and 3 gallons of asphalt. Convert these numbers to percents and make a circle graph with your results.

TECHNOLOGY LINK

Science Newsroom CD-ROM Choose *Fuels Rush In* to learn how fossil fuels are formed and used.

At the Computer Visit **www.mhscience02.com** for more links.

C 107

3 Lesson Review

Answers to Think and Write

1. Answers should parallel those activities listed during the Explore Activity, such as cooking, heating, and transportation. (p. C99)

2. because they formed from organisms that lived million of years ago (p. C102)

3. Burning fossil fuels releases smoke, gases, and other by-products into the air. (p. C101)

4. Possible answers: insulate homes, car pool, recycle, use alternative energy sources, use fuel efficiently. Students might choose alternative energy sources to conserve the most fuel, and mention ways their families use alternative energy sources as easy choices. (pp. C103–C106)

5. **Critical Thinking** Possible answers: power from water, wind, geothermal energy, solar energy, and tides. Advantage: less reliance on fossil fuels, cleaner environment. Disadvantages: unsuitable locations, expense. (pp. C104–C105)

Summarize

Check students' understanding by having them write a brief summary of the lesson in their own words.

ART LINK

Students' ads may include the benefits of alternative energy sources, efficient ways to conserve energy, or the disadvantages of fossil fuels. Encourage the use of drawings or photos.

MATH LINK

To find percentages, have students divide the amount of each fuel by the total amount of crude oil (42 gallons), then multiply by 100 for the percent. Answers: gasoline, 50%; fuel oils, 21.4%; jet fuel, 11.9%; lubricants, 9.5%; asphalt, 7.1%.

Chapter Review and Test Preparation

Resources

- Reading in Science Resources, pp. 183–184
- Assessment Book, pp. 35–38

Answers to Vocabulary

1. ozone layer
2. water table
3. smog
4. reservoir
5. acid rain
6. continental slope
7. continental shelf
8. Biomass
9. geothermal energy
10. fossil fuel

Answers to Test Prep

11. B
12. H
13. D
14. H
15. B

Chapter 7 Review

Vocabulary

Fill each blank with the best word or words from the list.

acid rain, C65
biomass, C106
continental shelf, C90
continental slope, C90
fossil fuel, C64
geothermal energy, C104
ozone layer, C63
reservoir, C75
smog, C64
water table, C75

1. The _____ screens out much of the Sun's UV rays.

2. The top of the water-filled spaces in the ground is the _____.

3. Dangerous air pollution is called _____.

4. A(n) _____ is a storage area for fresh water.

5. A type of precipitation caused by air pollution is _____.

The **6.** _____ of the ocean floor is steeper and deeper than the **7.** _____.

8. _____ and **9.** _____ are alternative energy sources to **10.** _____.

Test Prep

11. Most of Earth's oxygen supply is produced by _____.
    - **A** bacteria in the soil
    - **B** one-celled algae of the ocean
    - **C** green plants
    - **D** the ozone layer

12. All of the following are examples of nonrenewable resources EXCEPT _____.
    - **F** oil
    - **G** coal
    - **H** oxygen
    - **J** natural gas

13. Geothermal energy comes from _____.
    - **A** the Sun
    - **B** falling water
    - **C** fossil fuels
    - **D** Earth's internal heat

14. Fossil fuels are stored energy that came from _____.
    - **F** sedimentary rocks
    - **G** wind and water
    - **H** once-living plants and animals
    - **J** waste-treatment plants

C 108

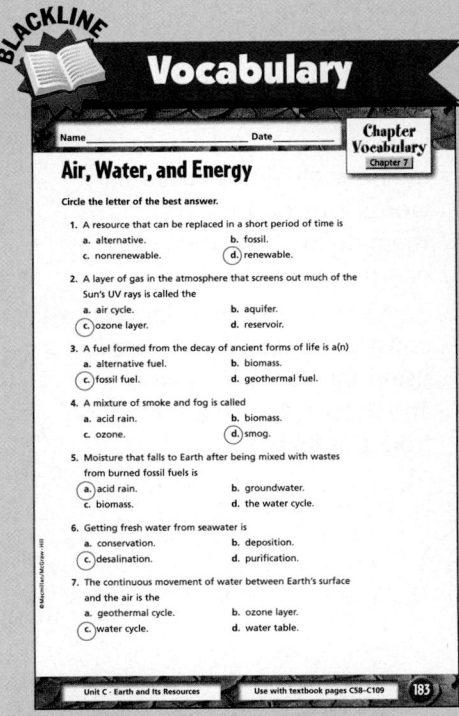

Reading in Science Resources, p. 183

15. An underground layer of rock or soil that is filled with water is _____.

  A a reservoir

  B an aquifer

  C a lake

  D groundwater

Concepts and Skills

16. Process Skills: Hypothesize Does rain remove pollutant particles from the air? Form a hypothesis. What could you do to test your hypothesis?

17. Reading in Science All electricity is made by burning fossil fuels. Is this true or false? Explain your answer.

18. Making Decisions Solar energy is considered "too expensive" to use in the Northeast. However, sunlight is a renewable resource. Is it better to use solar energy or depend on fossil fuels? What are the benefits and disadvantages to both?

19. Scientific Methods How can salt water be turned into drinkable water?

20. Critical Thinking Does filtering water remove all impurities? Explain your answer. How would you prove your answer?

Boost your test scores!

Be Smart!

Visit www.mhscience02.com

C 109

16. Process Skills: Hypothesize Students have learned that rain can pick up pollutants in the air. Accept all logical hypotheses.

17. Reading in Science Much electricity is produced by burning fossil fuels. However, because fossil fuels are nonrenewable resources, efforts have recently been made to create alternative energy sources, such as the wind, heat energy inside Earth, tidal power, and solar energy.

18. Making Decisions Accept all reasonable responses, keeping in mind that fossil fuels are nonrenewable.

19. Scientific Methods Through the use of a process called desalination, through which salt water is evaporated, leaving dissolved materials behind. The liquid water that collects at the end of the process is free of dissolved materials, including salt.

20. Critical Thinking Filtering water removes the larger impurities. However, bacteria may still be present in the filtered water. Chlorine is added to the water to kill the bacteria. Accept all reasonable student responses for proving their answers.

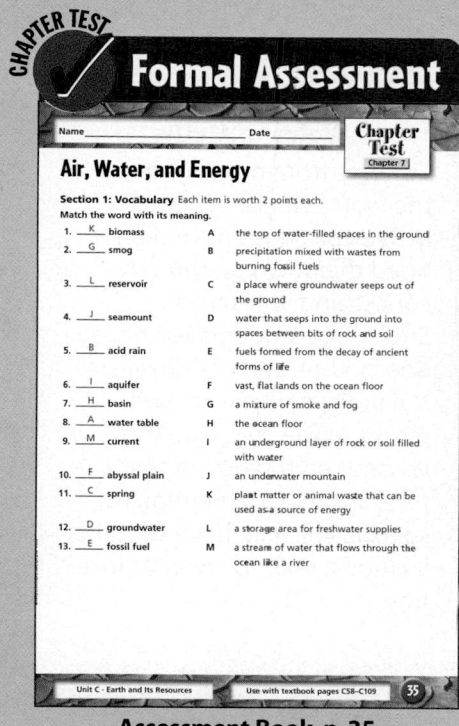

Assessment Book, p. 35

People in Science

People in Science

Objective

- Describe what a volcanologist does and how to become one.

Build on Prior Knowledge

Ask students whether any of them have ever seen a volcano erupt on TV. Ask them to describe what they saw. (They might describe flowing, glowing hot lava shooting or pouring from a mountain top [lava eruption] or plumes of gray smoke or ash pouring from the mountain [ash eruption].)

Volcanologist
Randy White

Developing the Main Idea

Focus on the career of volcanologist by asking students to recall the definitions of *magma* and *lava* (hot molten rock below Earth's surface; magma that reaches the surface). Have students define *geologist* (a scientist who studies Earth). Ask:

- **Why are volcanologists a type of geologist?** (because they study volcanoes and their rocks, which are part of Earth)

- **What kinds of rocks would a volcanologist study? Why?** (Possible answer: igneous, because they form from lava or magma that has cooled)

Volcanologist
Randy White

U.S. Geological Survey

When a volcano starts to rumble, most people in the area think about leaving. However, some scientists, called volcanologists, head right for the action! It is their job to predict what a volcano is going to do. Randy White is a volcanologist and a member of the Volcano Disaster Assistance Program, a division of the United States Geological Survey (USGS).

White's interest in volcanoes started in high school, when he was a foreign exchange student in Japan. He lived near an erupting volcano called Mount Sakurajima. He was so fascinated by the eruption that he decided to become a volcanologist. After receiving his graduate degree in geophysics from Stanford University in 1974, he went to work for the USGS.

Speed is vital when a volcano is showing signs of waking. White and his team must always be ready to reach a site within 24 hours. When they reach the volcano, they have to answer three important questions. Is the volcano going to erupt? How big an eruption will it be? When will it erupt?

White uses many special instruments in his work. One of the most important is a seismometer. A seismometer measures ground movement and is used to predict earthquake activity. Earthquakes often signal volcanic eruptions. White also takes samples of the atmosphere to check the levels of carbon dioxide and sulfur dioxide. If levels of these gases are high, the volcano might be ready to blow!

In 1991, White and his team were sent to Mount Pinatubo in the Philippines. Using their equipment, they

C 110

 Cultural Perspective

Volcano Myths

Cultures from many parts of the world where there are active volcanoes have developed their own mythology concerning volcanoes. Encourage students to choose one culture, such as Hawaiian, Icelandic, or Mexican, and report to the class about the volcano mythology of that culture. If the myth mentions a specific volcano, have students include a map to show its location.

Careers IN SCIENCE

A seismologist checks seismometer readings.

Career Track

Here are some different types of careers related to the study of volcanology. You can use the Internet or library resources to find out more about these careers.

- seismologist
- geologist
- geochemist
- meteorologist
- physicist

were able to predict the time and size of the eruption. Pinatubo turned out to be the largest volcanic eruption in the world in 80 years. Thanks to the team's predictions, the area was evacuated before the eruption. About 20,000 lives were saved!

Write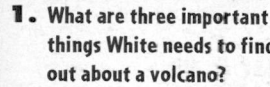
ABOUT IT

1. What are three important things White needs to find out about a volcano?

2. What two measurements help predict a volcanic eruption?

AT THE COMPUTER Visit www.mhscience02.com to learn more about careers.

C 111

Developing the Main Idea

Point out that a volcano may give little sign of eruption even a week or two before erupting. Usually scientists can make these predictions only within hours to a few days of an actual eruption. Then ask:

- **Why must Dr. White and his team reach a site quickly when a volcano shows signs of waking?** (so that they can test if an eruption is coming, in case there is little warning)

- **What might be some hazards of working near a volcano?** (Possible answers: getting caught in an eruption, being hit by rocks flying from the volcano, getting caught in a mudslide that the eruption caused)

- **Why is the prediction of volcanic eruption so important?** (Possible answer: to give people time to evacuate)

Thinking Further: *Inferring*
Ask:

- **What might happen if you wrongly predict that an eruption will occur? What might happen if you predict that one will not occur and one does?** (Possible answer: If you predict an eruption that doesn't occur and people evacuate, the same people might not believe you the next time and be harmed when the volcano does erupt. If you predict no eruption and one occurs, no one will have evacuated.)

Encourage students to discuss the difficulties in making the most accurate prediction possible.

Answers to **Write**  ABOUT IT

1. whether an eruption will occur; if so, how large an eruption; when the eruption will likely occur
2. measurements from seismometer; samples of the air to check carbon dioxide and sulfur dioxide levels

---

 SCIENCE FOR ALL

Inclusion

Eruptions and Climate

Encourage students to learn more about how the ash from volcanic eruptions can make its way into the atmosphere and affect climates halfway around the world. (Unlike most human-made pollutants, ash and gases from volcanoes reach the stratosphere.) Suggested eruptions to investigate are Laki (Iceland) in 934, Eldgja (Iceland) in 1783, Tambora in 1815, Krakatoa in 1883, Agung (Bali) 1963, and Mount Pinatubo in 1991. **Linguistic**

 SCIENCE FOR ALL

Advanced Learners

Interplanetary Volcanoes

Challenge students to find out about volcanoes and other eruptions of lava on other planets and moons. They can research either Mars, Venus, Io (a moon of Jupiter) or the Moon. Have them report to the class what they have learned about the planet or moon's volcanoes or igneous rock deposits. **Linguistic**

Unit C Performance Assessment

Name That Mineral (Chapter 6)

Materials: labeled mineral samples, copper penny or wire, iron nail, glass plate, steel file, streak plate, porcelain tile, hand lens, nail, mineral property table (page C35 in text)

Teaching Tips: Use ten minerals for the testing samples. Choose from the following: gypsum, quartz, pyrite, calcite, galena, feldspar, mica, hornblend, bauxite, chalcopyrite, hematite. Use tape and a marker to label each sample with a number. Caution students to lay the porcelain tile flat on a desk or table when testing for hardness.

Spot the Source (Chapter 7)

Materials: drawing paper, colored pencils, scissors, glue, magazines

Teaching Tips: Include photos of air pollution sources such as automobiles, smoke stacks, volcanic eruptions, lawn mowers, and so on. Also include photos of things that don't pollute air, such as a forest, animals grazing, people walking, people riding bikes. Show students how to fold a piece of paper for a brochure.

Answers to Analyze Your Results

1. Several examples of pollution from energy use: heating, transportation, manufacturing.

2. Both water and air pollution can be injurious to the health or life of living organisms. They can do damage to nonliving things.

Performance Assessment

Name That MINERAL

Your goal is to test properties of minerals to determine their identity.

What to Do

1. Make a table with the column headings shown below.

2. Do the following tests to determine properties. Record data in your table for each sample.

   Color(s): What color is its surface?

   Luster: How shiny is the sample?

   Porcelain plate test: What color is the powder when the mineral streaks?

   Cleavage: How many directions does it break into?

   Hardness: How well does the mineral resist scratching?

   Density: How heavy does the sample feel compared with a sample of water with the same volume?

Analyze Your Results

Complete the table. Use the results of your tests and the chart Properties of Minerals (page C35) to name each mineral.

SPOT the SOURCE

Your goal is to make a brochure to educate people about air pollution.

What to Do

1. Look at pictures in a newspaper or magazine. Which of the pictures show things that cause air pollution?

2. Create a brochure about air pollution. Your brochure should do three things:

   a. explain what air pollution is

   b. name the sources of air pollution in the pictures

   c. describe how those sources pollute

Analyze Your Results

1. Name one way that people use energy that causes air pollution.

2. How are air pollution and water pollution alike?

C 112

Rubrics

Name That Mineral (5-point rubric)

5 points = Student identifies 9 or 10 minerals correctly.

4 points = Student identifies 7 or 8 minerals correctly.

3 points = Student identifies 5 or 6 minerals correctly.

2 points = Student identifies 3 or 4 minerals correctly.

1 point = Student identifies 1 or 2 minerals correctly.

0 points = Student identifies 0 minerals correctly.

Spot the Source (5-point rubric)

5 points = Five student responses are correct. (Responses are the a, b, and c parts of the brochure and the two questions in Analyze Your Results.)

4 points = Four student responses are correct.

3 points = Three student responses are correct.

2 points = Two student responses are correct.

1 point = One student response is correct.

0 points = No student responses are correct.

Formal Assessment

Name_____ Date_____

Unit Performance Assessment
Chapter 6

Nature's Art

Model

Using the resources provided by your teacher, choose a natural formation found in the United States. Research your formation. Make notes in the space below. Then use the information you have and the materials given to you to create a model of the natural formation.

Analyze the Results

1. Describe the process you used to create a model of the natural formation. How did you decide which materials to use?

2. What forces do you think helped to shape this formation? Be specific.

3. What might the formation look like several thousand years from now? Consider the forces that shaped this formation as you write your response.

Unit C · Earth and Its Resources | Use with textbook pages C2–C57 | 41

Assessment Book, pp. 39–42

Earth Science

UNIT D

Weather and Climate

NATIONAL GEOGRAPHIC

Weather and Climate

Main Idea: Many atmospheric factors affect weather and climate. Weather changes on a daily basis depending on conditions. Climate is defined by the weather pattern over a period of time.

Unit Organizer

CHAPTER 8 Weather,
pp. D2–D49
Main Idea: Weather varies depending on the insolation, humidity, and air pressure. These factors are closely interrelated. A change in any one can bring about a change in the others.

LESSON 1 Atmosphere and Air Temperature,
pp. D4–D13
Main Idea: The Sun warms Earth's surface, which transmits heat to the air above it.

LESSON 2 Water Vapor and Humidity, *pp. D14–D21*
Main Idea: Water on Earth's surface and in the atmosphere changes form and affects the weather.

LESSON 3 Clouds and Precipitation, *pp. D22–D31*
Main Idea: Water vapor and ice form clouds that can produce precipitation.

LESSON 4 Air Pressure and Wind, *pp. D34–D45*
Main Idea: Differences in air pressure on Earth's surface cause wind.

CHAPTER 9 Weather Patterns and Climate, *pp. D50–D93*
Main Idea: Air masses meet and produce weather fronts and, at times, severe storms. The pattern of overall weather changes is the climate of a region, a pattern affected by many factors.

LESSON 5 Air Masses and Fronts, *pp. D52–D61*
Main Idea: Weather changes often occur at fronts, where different air masses meet.

LESSON 6 Severe Storms, *pp. D64–D77*
Main Idea: Thunderstorms, tornadoes, and hurricanes are severe storms that can cause great damage.

LESSON 7 Climate, *pp. D80–D91*
Main Idea: Long-term weather patterns determine climates, which can change over time.

Grade-Level Science Books

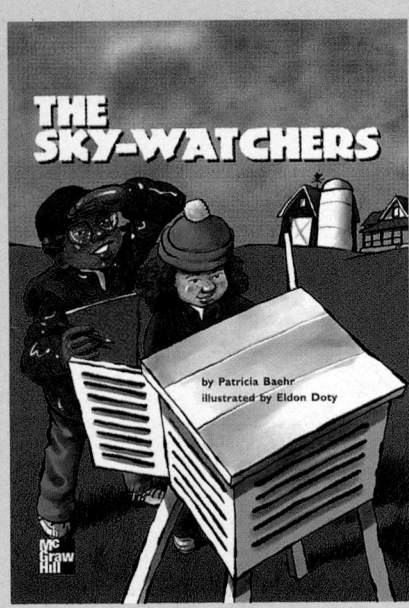

EASY

EASY

CHALLENGE

THE SKY-WATCHERS When the radio forecasts snow, Luke makes a prediction on his school bus that there will not be school the next day. Stacy challenges him. When she proves to be right, she invites him home and introduces him to her family's weather station.

TROUBLE AT FOREST PARK Trina is going on her first camping trip—to Forest Park. Her brothers don't think she is old enough for the trip, but a storm gives Trina the chance to prove them wrong.

THE GREAT JOHNSTOWN FLOOD The author explains the causes and effects of the great flood of 1889 in Johnstown, Pennsylvania.

To order from Macmillan/McGraw-Hill, call 800-442-9685.

Cross Curricular Books from Macmillan/McGraw-Hill

James, Laura. **Animals Sense the Weather.**

James, Laura. **The Great Galveston Hurricane.**

To order, call 800-442-9685.

Student Bibliography

Burleigh, Robert. **Black Whiteness: Admiral Byrd Alone in the Antarctic.** New York: Atheneum Books for Young Readers, 1998.

Elsom, Derek. **Weather Explained.** New York: Henry Holt, 1997.

Hooper, Meredith. **The Drop in My Drink: The Story of Water on Our Planet.** New York: Viking, 1998.

Howarth, Lesley. **Weather Eye.** Cambridge, MA: Candlewick Press, 1995.

Lauber, Patricia. **Hurricanes: Earth's Mightiest Storms.** New York: Scholastic, 1996.

Simon, Seymour. **Lightning.** New York: Morrow Junior Books, 1997.

Simon, Seymour. **Tornadoes.** New York: Morrow/HarperCollins, 1999.

Reading in Science

McGraw-Hill Science

Teacher Editions provide point-of-use strategies and resource support for students to practice reading skills as they read their science texts.

- **Reading MiniLessons**
- **Reduced Blackline Masters** from *Reading in Science Resources*
- **Additional Reading Strategies**

Reading in Science Resources

Boxes beneath the reduced Pupil Edition pages identify specific places in a lesson where students can complete worksheets from the *Reading in Science Resources* blackline masters. Reduced worksheets for this unit are found on the following pages of this Teacher Edition.

Lesson Outlines: pp. D6, D16, D24, D36, D54, D66, D82

Interpret Illustrations: pp. D6, D10, D18, D20, D26, D29, D36, D39, D55, D56, D67, D70, D82, D87

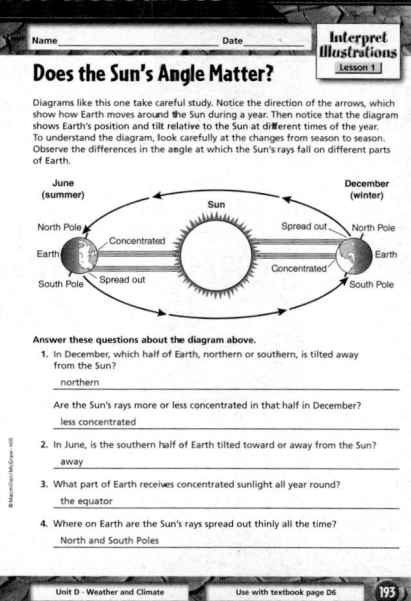

Reading in Science Resources, p. 193

Reading MiniLesson

Reading MiniLessons provide a brief tutorial and activity for students to practice a specific reading skill for each chapter. In this unit, the chapter reading skills are:

Find the Main Idea and Supporting Details: pp. D12, D19, D27, D42

Sequence of Events: pp. D55, D71, D89

Reading Strategy

Additional opportunities for students to develop and apply reading skills are provided in this unit as follows:

- ◉ **Cause and effect:** p. D8, D30
- ◉ **Compare and contrast:** pp. D16, D24, D58, D78
- ○ **Draw conclusions**
- ○ **Find the main idea**
- ◉ **Sequence of events:** pp. D32, D74
- ◉ **Summarize:** pp. D13, D21, D33, D41, D47, D61, D77, D79, D91
- ◉ **Ask questions:** p. D60
- ◉ **Reread:** p. D19
- ◉ **Retell (paraphrase):** p. D28

- ◉ **Interpret graphic sources of information:** pp. D7, D8, D9, D10, D11, D16, D18, D20, D25, D26, D28, D36-D39, D41, D54-D55, D57, D59, D66, D67, D69, D70, D86, D87
- ◉ **Build on prior knowledge:** pp. D4, D14, D22, D32, D34, D46, D52, D62, D64, D78, D80, D94
- ◉ **Organize information:** pp. D40, D62, D79, D90

CROSS CURRICULUM IDEAS for integrating science

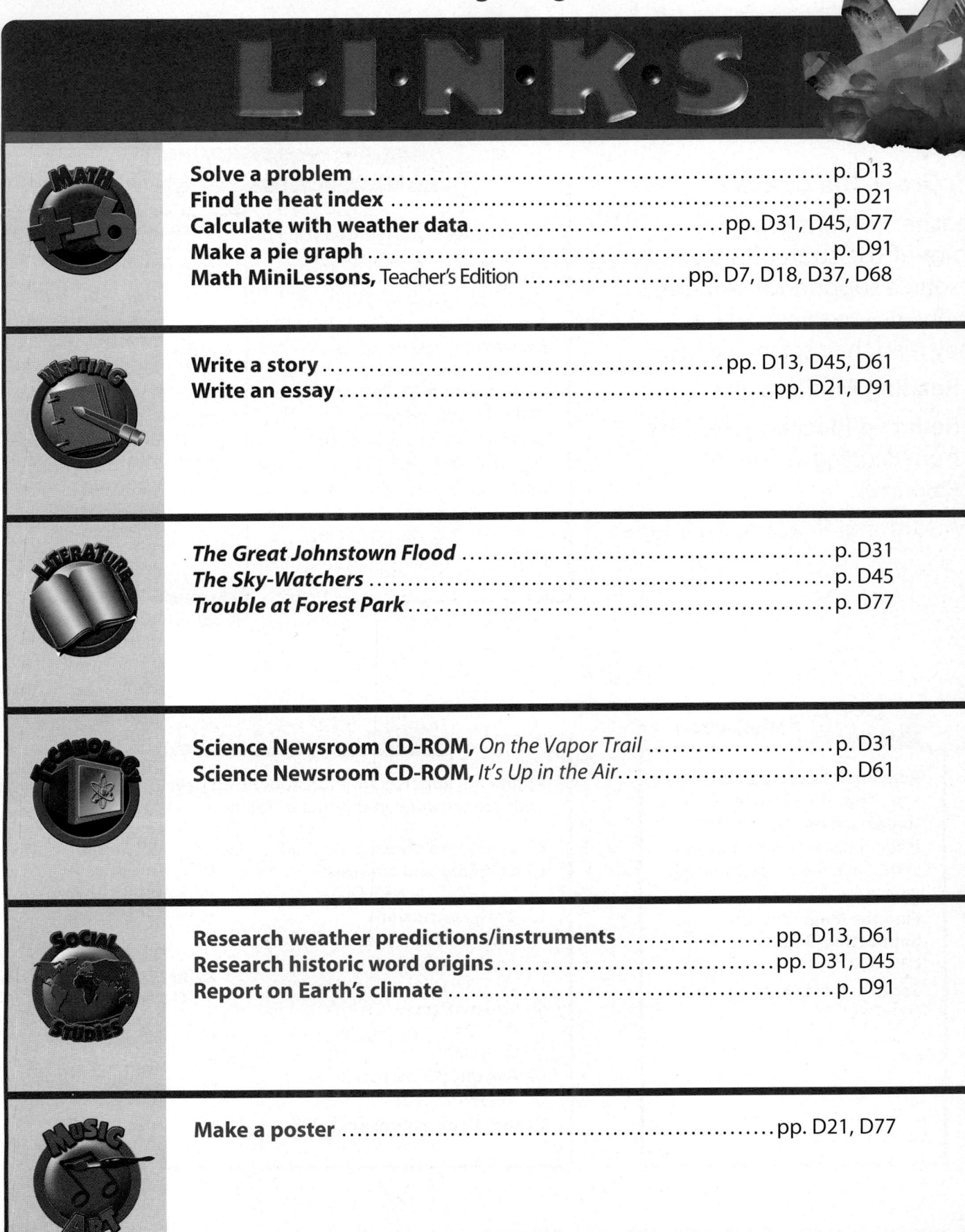

L·I·N·K·S

Meeting Individual Needs

McGraw-Hill Science includes all students in the learning process by providing a variety of strategies in this unit.

English Language Learners

Hurricane Names
Point out that in the Atlantic Ocean hurricanes are named each year starting at the beginning of the alphabet. Suggest that students do a similar activity, using the letters of the alphabet, in order, as the first letter in words describing hurricanes. Allow time for students to share their lists with the class. **Linguistic; Social**

Advanced Learners

Hurricane Prediction
Have students research parameters used to predict a more or less active hurricane season. Include the Stratospheric Quasi-Biennial Oscillation, the El Niño-Southern Oscillation, and the amount of African rainfall. Have them present a chart of their findings to the class. **Logical**

Inclusion

Inclusion
Public Service Announcements
Have groups of students write public service announcements designed to educate people about storm safety. Allow time for each group to perform its announcement for the class. **Social; Linguistic**

For additional support, see pp. D9, D41, D47, D57, D59, D62, D63, D64, D69, D71, D73, D75, D76, D79, D83–D85, D87, D88, D94

Learning Styles

Students acquire knowledge in a variety of ways that reflect different, often distinct, learning styles. The seven learning styles are:

- **Kinesthetic** pp. D68, D94
- **Social** pp. D57, D64, D73, D75, D79, D87, D89
- **Intrapersonal**
- **Linguistic** pp. D8, D28, D32, D40, D41, D59, D71, D73, D76, D78, D79, D81, D83, D85, D88, D94
- **Logical** pp. D9, D41, D47, D57, D62, D63, D65, D75, D85
- **Auditory/Musical**
- **Visual/Spatial** pp. D5, D15, D23, D35, D47, D53, D54, D63, D76

Technology for McGRAW-HILL SCIENCE

CD-ROMs

Science Newsroom CD-ROM

Student-directed computer activities

Chapter 8: On the Vapor Trail

Explore the relationship between humidity, temperature, and conder

Chapter 9: It's Up in the Air

Explore how fronts affect weather.

Join me in the Science Newsroom

Videotapes

Explore Activity Videos

All Explore Activities are available on videotape. Introduce lessons with Explore Activity

MindJogger Videos

Stage a quiz show in your classroom!

Science Experiences Videotapes

Chapter 9:

Lesson 6 Severe Storms
Sky Watch: Tracking a Winter Storm (Package 6)

Transparencies

Visual Aid Transparencies

- **9–12** Building a Water Cycle
- **22** Types of Clouds
- **23** Types of Precipitation
- **24** A Weather Front
- **25** How a Thunderstorm Forms
- **26** Hurricanes

Reading Aid Transparencies

- D1–D7

Internet Resources

McGRAW-HILL SCIENCE is online at *www.mhscience02.com* with projects and activities for students, teachers, and parents.
Internet Research Projects pp. D13, D77
Links pp. D13, D21, D31, D45, D61, D77, D91
Science Magazines and Features pp. D33, D47, D49, D62, D79, D93, D95

AMERICAN MUSEUM Ö NATURAL HISTORY

Visit
www.amnh.org/resources/mhscience
for a behind-the-scenes look at the exhibitions, collections, and research of the Museum. You'll find resources for teachers and students, such as online expeditions, profiles of scientists, interactives, links to professional development courses and more.

AVIATION WEEK'S
THE NEXT CENTURY OF FLIGHT™

LIFTOFF! with *AVIATION WEEK*.
Visit *www.AviationNow.com/LIFTOFF* for lessons, activities, and videos on Weather and Climate.

NATIONAL GEOGRAPHIC

* To order National Geographic Products, visit us online at *www.nationalgeographic.com/education* or call 1-800-368-2728. To order NGS Picture Show and NGS Picture Pack, call Macmillan/McGraw-Hill at 1-800-442-9685.

National Geographic Society Videos

- **Where Storms Begin**
- **Weather**
- **Telling the Weather**

NGS Picture Show CD-ROMs

- **Introduction to Weather**

NGS Picture Pack Transparencies

- **Introduction to Weather**

Curriculum Kit

- **GeoKit:** Weather

Process Skills

Science Process Skills	Explore Activities (Pupil Edition)	Quick Labs (Pupil Edition)	Process Skill Builders
Observe	pp. D5, D23, D35	pp. D17, D30, D68	Pupil Edition p. D83
Infer	pp. D5, D15, D23, D35, D53, D65	pp. D7, D30, D60, D68	
Classify			
Measure		p. D7	Pupil Edition p. D83 Teacher Edition (MiniLesson) p. D83 Activity Resources pp. 156–157
Use Numbers	pp. D65, D81		Pupil Edition p. D83
Communicate	pp. D5, D15, D23, D65, D81	p. D17	Pupil Edition pp. D43, D83
Predict	pp. D5, D53	p. D17	
Interpret Data	pp. D53, D65, D81		Pupil Edition p. D43 Teacher Edition (MiniLesson) p. D43 Activity Resources pp. 138–139
Form a Hypothesis	p. D15		
Use Variables	pp. D5, D15, D35	p. D7	
Experiment	pp. D5, D15, D35		
Make a Model	pp. D23, D35	p. D68	Pupil Edition p. D83
Define Based on Observations			

Materials

Consumable materials (based on six groups)

Materials	Quantity Needed per group	Kit Quantity	Lesson
Bag, plastic sandwich	14	80	4
Bag, specimen	1	12	2
Batteries, D-cell	2	24	1
Bulb, 100-W	1	6	1, 7
Clay, modeling (cream)		2 lb	1
Crayons			5
Cup, clear plastic, 9 oz		150	2, 3
Food coloring, dark red, 30 mL		2 bottles	2, 3
Ice			2, 3
Marker, blue	1		6
Marker, red	1		6
Notepaper, stick-on			7
Paper, black	1 sheet		1
Paper towels			2, 6
Paper, white	1 sheet		1
Paper, graph	1 sheet		1
Pencil or pen, marking	1		7
Plant, potted house	1		2
Rubber band, medium	1	100	3, 4
Soil, clay		10 kg	7
Tape			1
Tape, masking			4
Toothpick	3	3 boxes	1

Non-consumable materials (based on six groups)

Materials	Quantity Needed per group	Kit Quantity	Lesson
Blocks, triangular 30°, 60°, 90°	1 of each angle	6 of each angle	1
Bottle, 2-L plastic	2		6
Bottle, spray	1	6	7
Bowl, foam, 12 oz	1	25	1
Cloth, cotton	1	1	3
Container, clear, w/drilled hole	1	6	4
Flashlight	1	6	1
Goggles	5		2
Light socket, porcelain	2	6	1, 7
Map, newspaper weather (optional)	1		5
Map of U.S., including Alaska and Hawaii	1		6
Meterstick	1		3
Mug	1		3
Pan, aluminum foil, 8" × 8" × $\frac{1}{4}$"	2	12	7
Refrigerator or freezer			3
Ruler	1		1
Ruler, centimeter	1		1
Scissors	1		1
Stopwatch	1	6	1
Thermometer	6	18	1, 2, 3, 7
Tornado Tube	1	6	6

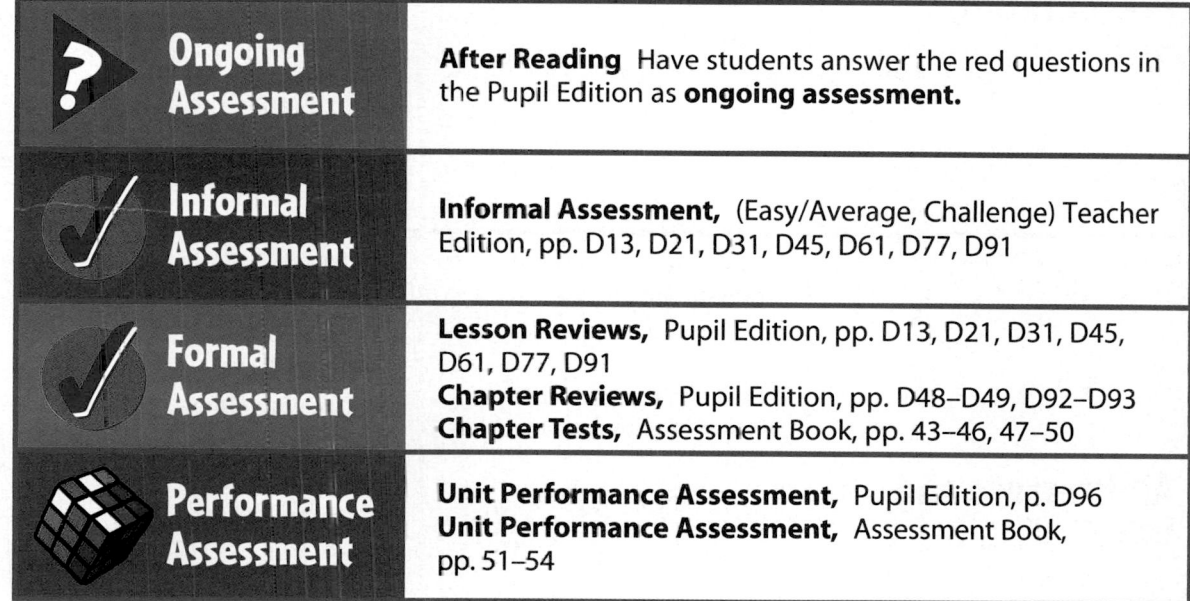

NATIONAL GEOGRAPHIC

UNIT D   Earth Science

Weather and Climate

LOOK!

A powerful hurricane swirls over the Atlantic Ocean. What causes such severe storms?

D 1

Resources

- Reading in Science Resources, Unit Vocabulary, pp. 241–243
- School to Home Activities, pp. 23–27
- Cross Curricular Projects, pp. 25–32

Answers to

Most hurricanes form over tropical oceans. A hurricane is a kind of "heat engine" that is fueled by the heat released when water vapor over the oceans condenses. This heat warms the air and reduces the pressure, which causes an inward rush of warm, moist surface air.

Assessment Strand

McGraw-Hill Science provides a variety of strategies for assessing students' learning and progress, including ongoing assessment, informal assessment, formal assessment, and performance assessment.

? **Ongoing Assessment**	**After Reading** Have students answer the red questions in the Pupil Edition as **ongoing assessment.**
✓ **Informal Assessment**	**Informal Assessment,** (Easy/Average, Challenge) Teacher Edition, pp. D13, D21, D31, D45, D61, D77, D91
✓ **Formal Assessment**	**Lesson Reviews,** Pupil Edition, pp. D13, D21, D31, D45, D61, D77, D91 **Chapter Reviews,** Pupil Edition, pp. D48–D49, D92–D93 **Chapter Tests,** Assessment Book, pp. 43–46, 47–50
Performance Assessment	**Unit Performance Assessment,** Pupil Edition, p. D96 **Unit Performance Assessment,** Assessment Book, pp. 51–54

Lesson Planner

Lesson	Objectives	Vocabulary	Pacing	Resources and Technology
LESSON 1 **Atmosphere and Air Temperature,** pp. D4–D13	■ Explore how the angle of light affects temperature. ■ Identify factors that affect temperatures on Earth. ■ Explain how the atmosphere changes with elevation. ■ Identify conditions that make up the weather.	**insolation** **atmosphere** **troposphere** **air pressure** **weather** **barometer**	3 days	■ Activity Resources, pp. 120–124 ■ Reading in Science Resources, pp. 191–196 ■ Vocabulary Cards ■ School to Home Activities, pp. 24–25 ■ Reading Aid Transparency D1 ■ **Explore Activity Video**
LESSON 2 **Water Vapor and Humidity,** pp. D14–D21	■ Explore how water changes as a result of heating and cooling. ■ Relate humidity to the processes of evaporation. ■ Explain what happens to water vapor with cooling. ■ Describe a series of changes that water goes through.	**water vapor** **humidity** **evaporation** **condensation** **relative humidity**	3 days	■ Activity Resources, pp. 125–129 ■ Reading in Science Resources, pp. 197–202 ■ Vocabulary Cards ■ Reading Aid Transparency D2 ■ **Explore Activity Video**
LESSON 3 **Clouds and Precipitation,** pp. D22–D31	■ Explore how clouds form. ■ Identify causes and types of clouds and precipitation. ■ Put in sequence the processes of the water cycle. ■ Describe how to compare amounts of rainfall and cloud cover.	**stratus cloud** **cumulus cloud** **cirrus cloud** **fog** **precipitation** **water cycle**	3 days	■ Activity Resources, pp. 130–134 ■ Reading in Science Resources, pp. 203–208 ■ Vocabulary Cards ■ School to Home Activities, p. 26 ■ Grade-Level Science Book, *The Great Johnstown Flood* ■ Reading Aid Transparency D3 ■ Visual Aid Transparencies 9, 10, 11, 12, 22, 23 ■ **Explore Activity Video** ■ **Science Newsroom CD-ROM** *On the Vapor Trail*
LESSON 4 **Air Pressure and Wind,** pp. D34–D45	■ Explore what causes air pressure to change. ■ Explain how air pressure is related to winds. ■ Describe the paths of winds in global wind zones. ■ Identify how wind is measured and recorded at weather stations.	**wind** **convection cell** **sea breeze** **land breeze** **Coriolis effect** **isobar** **weather vane** **anemometer**	4 days	■ Activity Resources, pp. 135–139 ■ Reading in Science Resources, pp. 209–214 ■ Vocabulary Cards ■ School to Home Activities, p. 28 ■ Grade-Level Science Book, *The Sky-Watchers* ■ Reading Aid Transparency D4 ■ **Explore Activity Video**

Activity Planner

Activity	Process Skills	Materials	Plan Ahead
LESSON 1 **Explore Activity** **Does the Sun's Angle Matter?** p. D5	observe, predict, communicate, use variables, infer, experiment	3 thermometers, triangular blocks, black paper, white paper, centimeter ruler, scissors, tape, 150-W clear-bulb lamp, stopwatch, foam bowl, clay	No advance planning is needed.
QUICK LAB **FOR SCHOOL OR HOME** **Investigating Angles** p. D7	use variables, measure, infer	flashlight, graph paper, 3 small lumps of clay, 3 toothpicks	No advance planning is needed.
LESSON 2 **Explore Activity** **Where Does the Puddle Come From?** p. D15	form a hypothesis, experiment, communicate, infer, use variables	plastic cups, ice, paper towels, food coloring, thermometer, goggles	No advance planning is needed.
LESSON 3 **Explore Activity** **How Do Clouds Form?** p. D23	make a model, observe, communicate, infer	hot tap water, 2 identical clear containers, mug, 3 ice cubes, food coloring	No advance planning is needed.
LESSON 4 **Explore Activity** **What Can Change Air Pressure?** p. D35	make a model, experiment, observe, infer, use variables	plastic jar with hole in bottom, plastic sandwich bag, rubber band, masking tape	No advance planning is needed.
Process Skill **BUILDER** **A Weather Station Model** p. D43	interpret data, use numbers, communicate	none	No advance planning is needed.

Additional Quick Labs are found on pp. D17, D30. No advance planning is needed.

Reading in Science Resources

McGraw-Hill Science **Reading in Science Resources** provides the following **Blackline Master** worksheets for this chapter.

Chapter Graphic Organizer

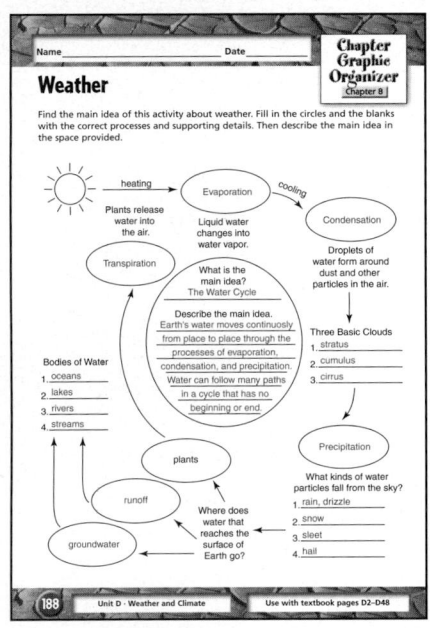

Reading in Science Resources,
p. 188

Chapter Reading Skill

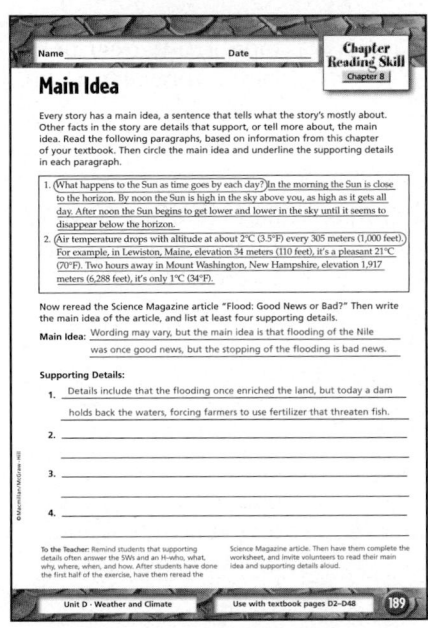

Reading in Science Resources,
pp. 189–190

Chapter Vocabulary

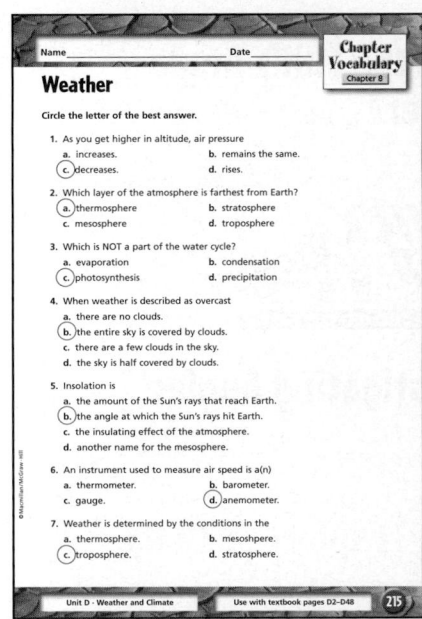

Reading in Science Resources,
pp. 215–216

McGraw-Hill Science **Reading in Science Resources** provides the following **Blackline Master** worksheets for every lesson in this chapter.

Lesson Outline

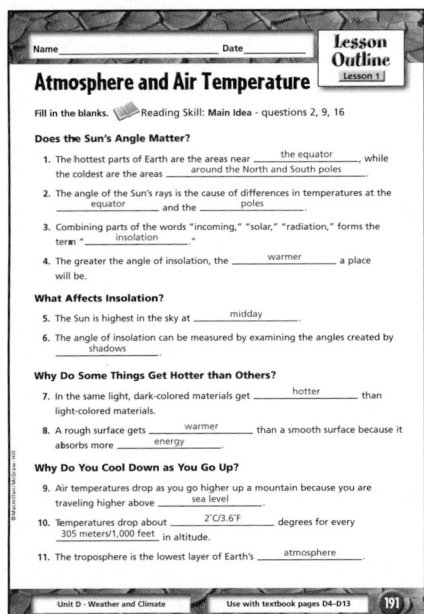

Reading in Science Resources,
pp. 191–192, 197–198, 203–204,
209–210

Interpret Illustrations

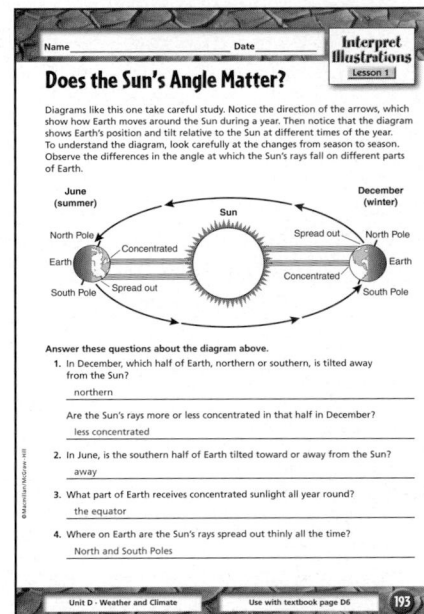

Reading in Science Resources,
pp. 193–194, 199–200, 205–206,
211–212

Lesson Vocabulary and Cloze Test

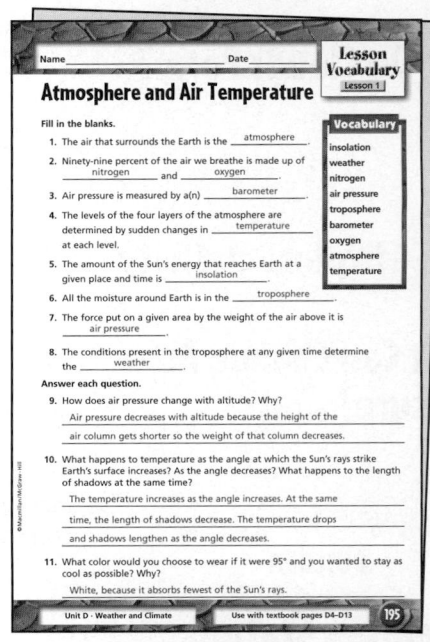

Reading in Science Resources,
pp. 195–196, 201–202, 207–208,
213–214

Activities and Assessment

McGraw-Hill Science **Activity Resources** provides the following **Blackline Master** worksheets for every lesson in this chapter.

Explore Activity and Alternative Explore Activity

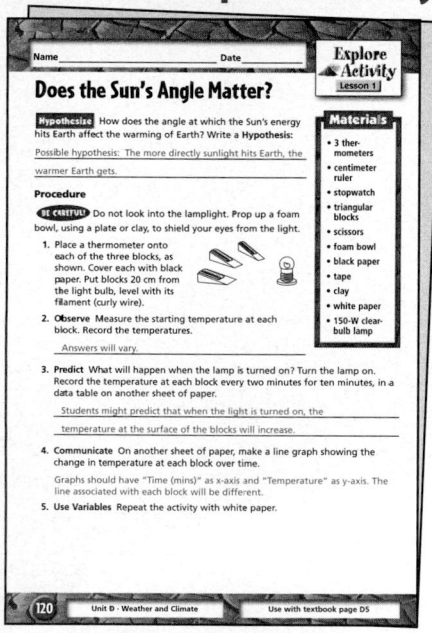

Activity Resources, *pp. 120–122, 125–127, 130–132, 135–137*

Quick Lab for School or Home

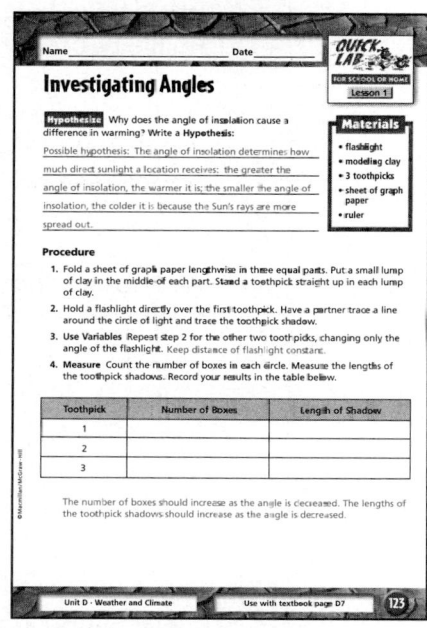

Activity Resources, *pp. 123–124, 128–129, 133–134*

Process Skill Builder

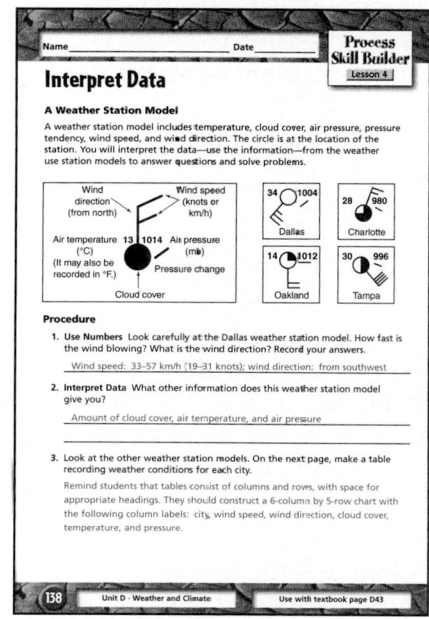

Activity Resources, *pp. 138–139*

McGraw-Hill Science **Assessment Book** provides the following **Blackline Master** worksheets for this chapter.

Chapter Test

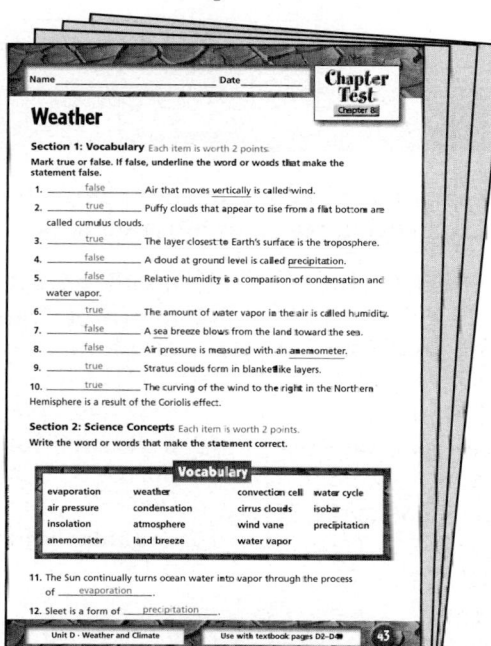

Assessment Book, *pp. 43–46*

CHAPTER
8 Weather

Resources
- Reading in Science Resources, pp. 188–217
- Assessment Book, pp. 43–46

Did You Ever Wonder?

Answers will vary depending on climate, but students should note that there are certain differences from day to day and season to season.

CHAPTER
8 Weather

LESSON 1
Atmosphere and Air Temperature, D4

LESSON 2
Water Vapor and Humidity, D14

LESSON 3
Clouds and Precipitation, D22

LESSON 4
Air Pressure and Wind, D34

Did You Ever Wonder?

What is frost? What causes frost to form? Frost forms when the air is cold enough that water vapor in the air changes from gas to ice crystals on trees, grass, and other objects. In warmer weather dew would form instead of frost. Is the weather always the same where you live, or does it change from day to day and season to season?

D 2

Reading Strategy

This chapter provides MiniLessons and other opportunities for developing and practicing the following reading skills:

- ◉ **Cause and Effect:** pp. D8, D30
- ◉ **Compare and Contrast:** pp. D16, D24
- ○ **Draw Conclusions**
- ◉ **Find the Main Idea:** pp. D12, D19, D27, D42
- ◉ **Sequence of Events:** pp. D32
- ◉ **Summarize:** pp. D13, D21, D31, D33, D41, D45, D47
- ○ **Ask Questions**
- ◉ **Reread:** p. D19

- ◉ **Retell (paraphrase):** p. D28
- ◉ **Interpret Graphic Sources of Information:** pp. D7, D8, D9, D10, D11, D16, D18, D20, D25, D26, D28, D36–D39, D41
- ◉ **Build on Prior Knowledge:** pp. D4, D14, D22, D32, D34, D46
- ◉ **Organize Information:** p. D40

Encourage students to keep a Science Dictionary. Remind them to add the Vocabulary words for each lesson in this chapter to their Dictionary as they complete each lesson.

insolation, D7

atmosphere, D10

troposphere, D10

air pressure, D11

weather, D12

barometer, D12

water vapor, D16

humidity, D16

evaporation, D16

condensation, D17

relative humidity, D18

stratus cloud, D24

cumulus cloud, D24

cirrus cloud, D24

fog, D24

precipitation, D26

water cycle, D29

wind, D38

convection cell, D38

sea breeze, D39

land breeze, D39

Coriolis effect, D40

isobar, D42

weather vane, D44

anemometer, D44

AMERICAN MUSEUM OF NATURAL HISTORY

Visit www.amnh.org/resources/mhscience to discover more about what causes changes in weather and how scientists track and monitor storms.

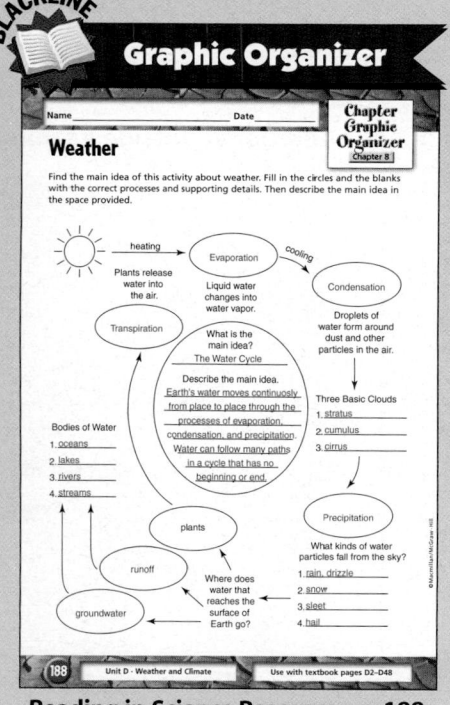

Reading in Science Resources, p. 188

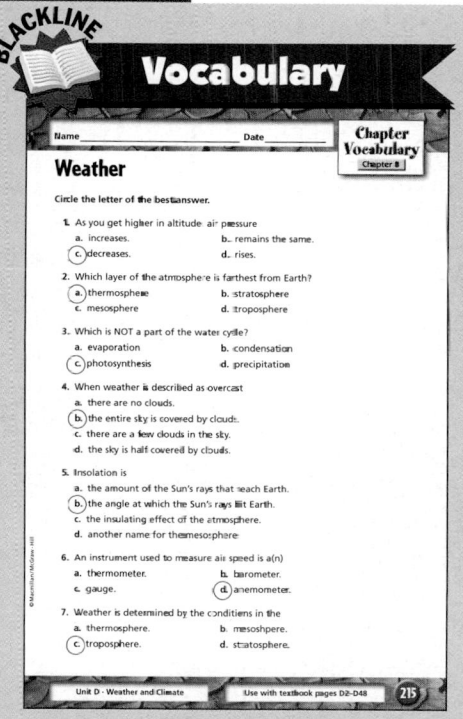

Reading in Science Resources, pp. 215–216

LESSON 1
Atmosphere and Air Temperature

Objectives

- Explore how the angle of light affects temperature.
- Identify factors that affect temperatures on Earth.
- Explain how the atmosphere changes with elevation.
- Identify conditions that make up the weather.

Resources

- Activity Resources, pp. 120–124
- Reading in Science Resources, pp.191–196
- Vocabulary Cards
- Reading Aid Transparency D1
- School to Home Activities, pp. 24–25

Build on Prior Knowledge

Have students discuss temperature changes that occur with different seasons. Have them determine the current temperature. Then ask:

- **What are temperatures usually like three months from now? Six months?** (Answers will vary depending on area's elevation and latitude.)

1 Get Ready

Developing the Main Idea

Have students discuss how two places on Earth can have such different temperatures on the same day. (Places closer to the equator have higher temperatures than those closer to the poles; places are at higher elevations; seasons are reversed north and south of the equator. The higher the angle at which the Sun's energy hits Earth, the more concentrated the energy.)

LESSON 1
Atmosphere and Air Temperature

Vocabulary

insolation, D6
atmosphere, D10
troposphere, D10
air pressure, D11
weather, D12
barometer, D12

Get Ready

If it's summer, is it always hot? These animals may find it warmer in summer than in winter. However, it isn't exactly hot here on this beautiful summer day. How can summer be hot in some places and so cold in others?

How does the angle at which the Sun's energy hits Earth affect the warming of Earth?

Process Skill

You experiment when you perform a test to support or disprove a hypothesis.

D 4

Science Background

Our Sun

The Sun is Earth's source of energy and light. The Sun's heat comes from continually occurring nuclear reactions. As matter is converted to energy, the Sun's mass decreases by about four million tons per second. However, scientists predict that the Sun will still warm Earth for another 6 billion years.

Cross Curricular Books

Additional Outside Reading

Animals Sense the Weather

written by Laura James
illustrated by Brian Killeen

To order, see page D1•b.

Explore Activity

Does the Sun's Angle Matter?

Procedure

BE CAREFUL! Do not look into the lamplight.

1. Place a thermometer onto each of the three blocks, as shown. Cover each with black paper. Put the blocks 20 cm from the light bulb, level with its filament (curly wire).

2. **Observe** Measure the starting temperature at each block. Record the temperatures.

3. **Predict** What will happen when the lamp is turned on? Turn the lamp on. Record the temperature at each block every two minutes for ten minutes.

4. **Communicate** Make a line graph showing the change in temperature at each block over time.

5. **Use Variables** Repeat the activity with white paper.

Drawing Conclusions

1. **Communicate** Which block's surface was warmed most by the lamplight? Which block's surface was warmed the least?

2. **Infer** How does the angle at which light hits a surface affect how much the surface is heated? How does the surface color affect how much it is heated?

3. **Going Further: Experiment** What other factors might affect how much a surface is warmed by sunlight? How would you test your ideas?

Materials

3 thermometers
triangular blocks
black paper
white paper
centimeter ruler
scissors
tape
150-W clear-bulb lamp
stopwatch
foam bowl
clay

D 5

Alternative Explore Activity

Materials globe, flashlight

Cold at the Poles Demonstrate for students how the angle of sunlight affects temperature. Darken the classroom, then shine a flashlight onto the globe from the side, so that the beam is directly striking the equator. Encourage students to describe the way in which the light strikes the poles. (The rays strike the poles at an angle, and are spread out and less intense.)

Spatial

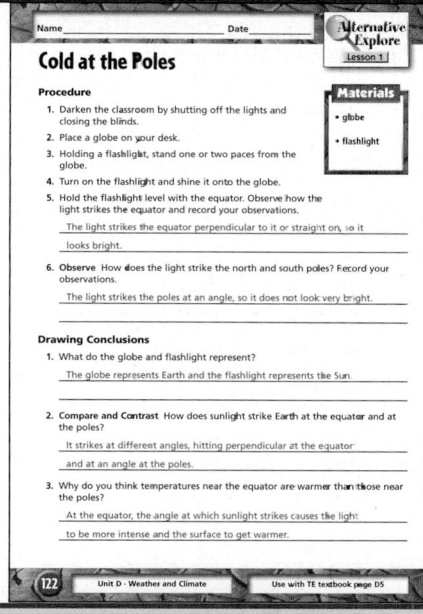

Activity Resources, p. 122

Explore Activity

Does the Sun's Angle Matter?

Science Process Skills *observe, predict, communicate, use variables, infer, experiment*

Resources Activity Resources, pp. 120–121

Pacing 30–40 minutes ⏰

Grouping small groups

Procedure

Be Careful! Warn students not to look into the lamplight. Have them use a foam bowl to shield their eyes from the light.

3. Students might predict that when the light is turned on, the temperature on the surface of the blocks will increase; they may recognize that the angle that the light hits will be a factor in determining how warm each block gets.

Answers to Drawing Conclusions

1. The block whose surface was most vertical was warmed the most. The block with the lowest angle was least affected.

2. The more vertically the light hits the surface, the more it is warmed. Students should infer that darker colors absorb more light, warming the surface more.

3. Possible answers might include how rough or smooth a surface is, how shiny or dull it is, or what the material is made of. They can set up a controlled experiment for each.

Inquiry Students can ask their own questions to explore, such as: Does the time of year affect temperature on different parts of Earth?

Technology

■ When time is short, preview the activity with the **Explore Activity Video.**

Does the Sun's Angle Matter?

Before Reading
Have students try to answer the red question at the top of the page.

Exploring the Main Idea
Demonstrate why the equator is always hotter than the North Pole by shining a flashlight straight down onto a tabletop in front of the class, directing them to observe the circle of light formed. Tilt the flashlight so that the beam hits the tabletop at an angle; again encourage students to observe the shape that the light forms. Ask:

- **What does the flashlight represent?** (the Sun)

Point out that the first demonstration represented the manner in which the Sun reaches Earth at the equator, while the second demonstration represented the way in which the Sun reaches Earth at the poles.

- **How was the sunlight different at the poles?** (The light was spread over a larger area; there was a larger, dimmer oval.)

- **How do you think the sunlight the poles received compared to what the equator received? How were they different?** (The angle of incoming sunlight is low and it was spread over a larger area at the poles.)

- **If the poles receive the same amount of light as the equator, why is it so much colder there?** (The energy from slanted rays of the Sun is spread out and less intense than the energy from direct sunlight.)

▶After Reading
Have students answer the red question in the student book as **ongoing assessment**.

Developing Vocabulary

insolation The word *insolation* is a combination of three words—*in*coming *sol*ar radi*ation*. *Sol* is Latin for Sun. Ask students to list some other words that contain *sol*.

Read to Learn

Main Idea The Sun warms Earth's surface, which transmits heat to the air above it.

Does the Sun's Angle Matter?

Where do you think you might find warm temperatures all year long? Where would you find very cold weather? That depends a lot on the angle at which sunlight hits a region. Angles make a difference in how much the Sun warms an area. The areas around the equator are hottest. That's because the Sun's path is high overhead at midday. In those areas the Sun's rays hit Earth at their strongest.

The areas around the North and South Poles are coldest. In those areas the Sun is much lower at midday.

The Sun's rays hit Earth's surface at a low angle. The strength of the rays is much weaker at this angle.

The angle at which sunlight strikes Earth's surface is called the angle of **insolation**. *Insolation* is short for *incoming solar radiation*. It means the amount of the Sun's energy that reaches Earth at a given place and time.

The diagram shows how sunlight warms Earth in summer and winter. The amount of warming depends on the angle of insolation. The greater the angle, the warmer it gets. The angle of insolation is always smaller near the poles than near the equator. That means while it's freezing cold in one part of the world, it's hot in another.

▷ **How do differing angles of insolation cause differences in warming?**
Areas with a higher angle of insolation receive more direct sunlight.

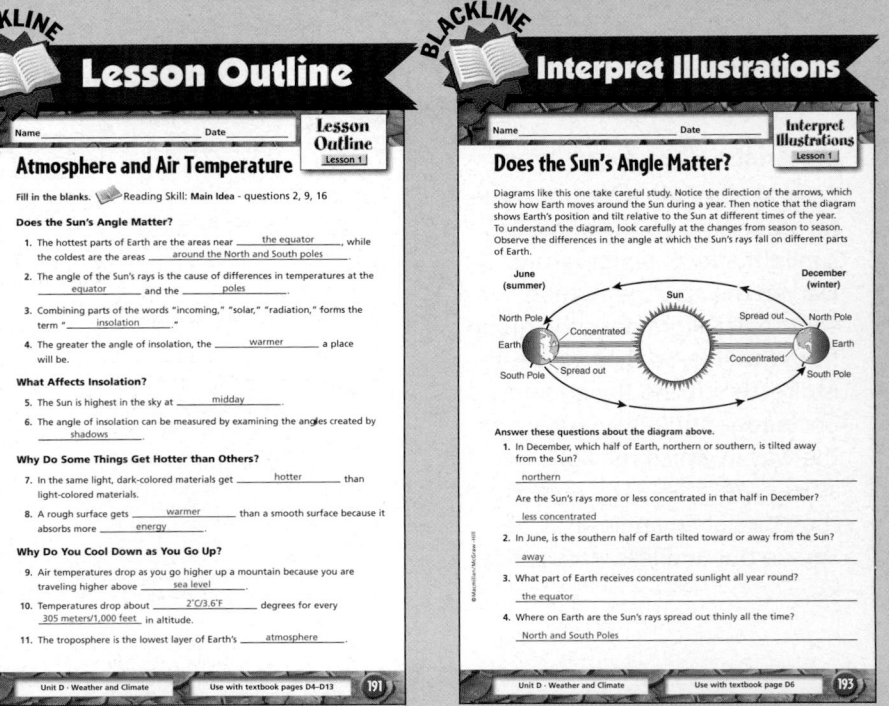

How Sunlight Warms Earth

The Sun's rays strike the surface at different angles as Earth travels around the Sun.

June (summer in Northern Hemisphere)
North Pole
Earth
Concentrated
South Pole
Spread out
Sun
December (winter in Northern Hemisphere)
Spread out
North Pole
Earth
Concentrated
South Pole

D 6

Lesson Outline

Name _____ Date _____
Lesson Outline Lesson 1

Atmosphere and Air Temperature

Fill in the blanks. 📖 Reading Skill: Main Idea - questions 2, 9, 16

Does the Sun's Angle Matter?

1. The hottest parts of Earth are the areas near ___the equator___, while the coldest are the areas ___around the North and South poles___

2. The angle of the Sun's rays is the cause of differences in temperatures at the ___equator___ and the ___poles___.

3. Combining parts of the words "incoming," "solar," "radiation," forms the term "___insolation___."

4. The greater the angle of insolation, the ___warmer___ a place will be.

What Affects Insolation?

5. The Sun is highest in the sky at ___midday___

6. The angle of insolation can be measured by examining the angles created by ___shadows___

Why Do Some Things Get Hotter than Others?

7. In the same light, dark-colored materials get ___hotter___ than light-colored materials.

8. A rough surface gets ___warmer___ than a smooth surface because it absorbs more ___energy___

Why Do You Cool Down as You Go Up?

9. Air temperatures drop as you go higher up a mountain because you are traveling higher above ___sea level___

10. Temperatures drop about ___2°C/3.6°F___ degrees for every ___305 meters/1,000 feet___ in altitude.

11. The troposphere is the lowest layer of Earth's ___atmosphere___

Unit D · Weather and Climate | Use with textbook pages D4–D13 | 191

Reading in Science Resources, p. 191

Interpret Illustrations

Name _____ Date _____
Interpret Illustrations Lesson 1

Does the Sun's Angle Matter?

Diagrams like this one take careful study. Notice the direction of the arrows, which show how Earth moves around the Sun during a year. Then notice that the diagram shows Earth's position and tilt relative to the Sun at different times of the year. To understand the diagram, look carefully at the changes from season to season. Observe the differences in the angle at which the Sun's rays fall on different parts of Earth.

June (summer)
North Pole
Earth
Concentrated
South Pole
Spread out
Sun
December (winter)
Spread out
North Pole
Earth
Concentrated
South Pole

Answer these questions about the diagram above.

1. In December, which half of Earth, northern or southern, is tilted away from the Sun?
___northern___

Are the Sun's rays more or less concentrated in that half in December?
___less concentrated___

2. In June, is the southern half of Earth tilted toward or away from the Sun?
___away___

3. What part of Earth receives concentrated sunlight all year round?
___the equator___

4. Where on Earth are the Sun's rays spread out thinly all the time?
___North and South Poles___

Unit D · Weather and Climate | Use with textbook page D6 | 193

Reading in Science Resources, p. 193

1. Which location on the graph has the biggest change between winter and summer? Which has the smallest change?

2. How can you describe the pattern of temperatures using what you know about the Sun's rays?

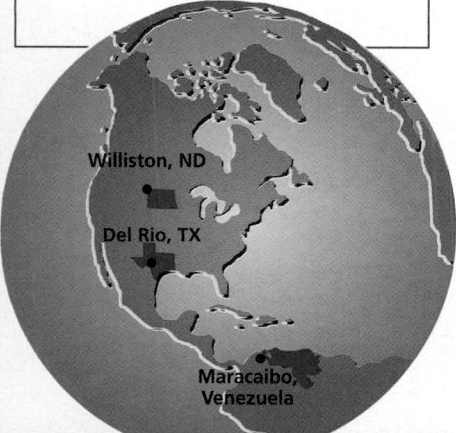

Williston, ND

Del Rio, TX

Maracaibo, Venezuela

Monthly Mean Temperature

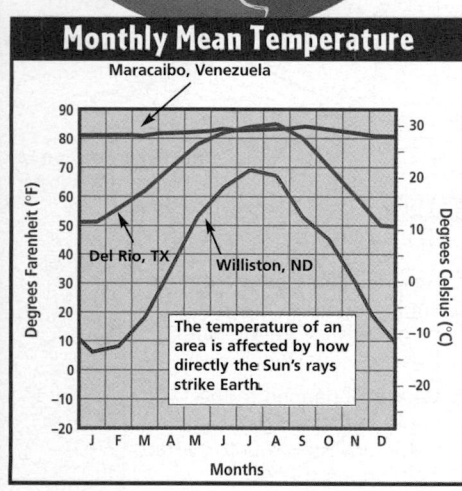

Maracaibo, Venezuela

Del Rio, TX   Williston, ND

The temperature of an area is affected by how directly the Sun's rays strike Earth.

Degrees Farenheit (°F)

Degrees Celsius (°C)

J F M A M J J A S O N D
Months

QUICK LAB

FOR SCHOOL OR HOME

Investigating Angles

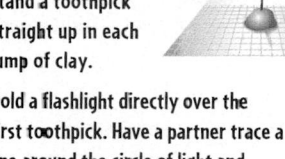

1. Fold a sheet of graph paper lengthwise in three equal parts. Put a small lump of clay in the middle of each part. Stand a toothpick straight up in each lump of clay.

2. Hold a flashlight directly over the first toothpick. Have a partner trace a line around the circle of light and trace the toothpick shadow.

3. **Use Variables** Repeat step 2 for the other two toothpicks, changing only the angle of the flashlight.

4. **Measure** Count the number of boxes in each circle. Measure the lengths of the toothpick shadows. Record your results.

5. **Infer** How is the length of the shadows related to the angle?

6. **Infer** How is the number of boxes in the circle related to the angle?

D 7

1. Williston, ND; Maracaibo, Venezuela.

2. The greatest change in temperature occurs nearest the poles; the least occurs nearest the equator.

QUICK LAB

FOR SCHOOL OR HOME

Materials graph paper, 3 small lumps of modeling clay, 3 toothpicks, flashlight, ruler

Science Process Skills *use variables, measure, infer*

Resources Activity Resources, pp. 123–124

Step 3 Encourage students to compare and contrast the circles of light and shadows cast for each of the three toothpicks.

Step 5 When the Sun is directly overhead (at a 90° angle), its shadow is shortest. As the angle decreases, the shadow lengthens.

Step 6 When the light is overhead, the fewest squares are covered with light, but it is direct. When the angle decreases, light is spread out over more boxes.

Math MiniLesson

Temperatures

Develop Temperatures can be measured in degrees Fahrenheit (°F) or degrees Celsius (°C).

You can use these formulas to convert temperatures between the two scales.

$C = \frac{5}{9} \times (F - 32)$

Complete.   68°F = ☐°C

$\frac{5}{9} \times (68 - 32) = \frac{5}{9} \times 36 = 20$

So, 68°F is about 20°C.

$F = (1.8 \times C) + 32$

Complete. 8°C = ☐°F

 1.8 ☒ 8 M⁺ ⊞ 32 ⊟ 46.4

So, 8°C is about 46.4°F.

Practice Complete.

1. 77°F = ☐°C   (34.7)
2. 15°C = ☐°F   (25)

Activity Have students estimate the temperatures for the four seasons in both degrees Celsius and degrees Fahrenheit.

Science Background

More About the Sun

The Sun is a huge mass of swirling gases located about 150 million kilometers (93 million miles) from Earth. Its tremendous heat is caused by nuclear reactions. As matter is converted into energy, the mass of the Sun dwindles; some estimate that it loses about 4 million tons per second! Even though its mass is shrinking, scientists aren't too concerned; they predict that the Sun will be able to warm Earth for another 6 billion years.

What Affects Insolation?

Before Reading
Have students try to answer the red question at the top of the page.

Exploring the Main Idea
With the class, locate a flagpole or lamppost on the school grounds. Point out that the length of shadows change as the angle of insolation changes during the day. Have a student volunteer measure the length of the shadow cast by the flagpole or lamppost, recording the time and date. Ask another student to record the temperature. Return to the site at different times to repeat the measurements. Ask:

- **What do the shadows tell you about the Sun?** (They tell you the position of the Sun in the sky; the higher the Sun is in the sky, the shorter the shadows.)

- **When does the Sun feel the hottest?** (The heat from the Sun is most intense when the Sun is high overhead.)

- **Why do you think the temperature of the air is higher at a time when the Sun is not directly overhead?** (Encourage speculation, and guide students to infer that the heat we feel in the afternoon is the result of Earth absorbing heat during the intense midday Sun, then transferring it to the air even when the Sun feels less intense.)

Using the Illustrations
Ask:

- **How is the angle of insolation determined?** (It is equal to the angle between the tip of a shadow and the top of the object that cast it.)

READING Diagrams

> 1. You can measure the angle of insolation by measuring the angles created by shadows on objects.
>
> 2. The angle will increase. The temperature will rise.

▶ After Reading
Have students answer the red question in the student book as **ongoing assessment.**

What Affects Insolation?

In the morning the Sun is close to the horizon. What happens as time goes by? At midday the Sun is high up in the sky, as high as it gets during the day. After midday the Sun is lower and lower in the sky.

How does this affect the angle of insolation? How do we measure it? In an earlier illustration, you saw that both location and time of year affect this angle. This illustration shows how the time of day affects the angle of insolation.

Measuring the angle of insolation is a challenge. It is not easy to see individual light rays. How can you find the angle at which they hit the surface?

Look at the shadows cast by objects they strike! The lower the angle of the light rays, the longer the shadows. As you can see in the diagram, the angle of insolation is the same as the angle between the ground and the line from the tip of the shadow to the top of the wall.

▷ How does the time of day affect the angle of insolation?

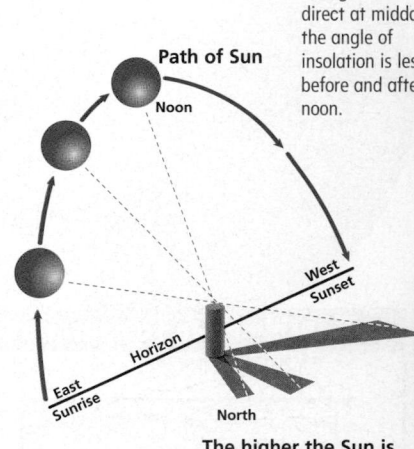

Sunlight is most direct at midday the angle of insolation is less before and after noon.

Path of Sun

Noon

West / Sunset

Horizon

East / Sunrise

North

The higher the Sun is in the sky, the shorter the shadow.

Angle of Insolation

The angle of insolation can be measured by examining the angles created by shadows.

Sun's ray

Wall

Tip of shadow — 30°

Angle of insolation

Ground — 30°

|← Shadow of wall →|

D 8

READING Diagrams

1. How can you measure the angle of insolation without being able to see the Sun's rays individually?

2. What will happen to the angle as the Sun gets higher in the sky? How will this affect the temperature?

SCIENCE Reading Strategy

Cause and Effect

Developing Reading Skills
Focus students' attention on the four factors (details) that cause substances to heat up differently given the same amount of sunlight (main idea). Construct a chart titled, "Factors that Affect How Substances Heat Up," with numbers 1–4 listed on the left side. Have students read the text to fill in the blanks. (color, texture, types of substance, plants) **Linguistic**

Why Do Some Things Get Hotter than Others?

As you may know, dark colors get hotter than light colors in the same light. This is why black asphalt roads get so hot in the sunlight. Dark soils and rocks also get very hot. White sand and light-colored soils do not get as hot in sunlight. Plants can also help keep an area cooler in sunlight than surrounding rocks and soil, or black asphalt.

Texture is how smooth or rough a surface is. Rough textures cause light to bounce around at many angles. Each time a little more energy is absorbed by the surface. Rough surfaces tend to get hotter in sunlight than smooth surfaces.

Why do you go swimming when it is hot and you want to cool off? You go

Rough texture
More impacts = more heat energy absorbed

Smooth texture
Fewer impacts = less heat energy absorbed

swimming because the water is cooler than the air. The air above the land is warmed by the land. Although the water and the land next to it are both being warmed by the Sun, the water is cooler. Why? The same amount of light energy will heat land to a higher temperature than it will heat water.

▷ **How do color and texture affect the amount of heat absorbed?**

READING
Charts

1. Which material is warmer after being placed near the light?

2. How can you use the graph to tell which substance heats faster?

Darker colors absorb more heat than light colors. Rough textures cause light to bounce around, allowing more heat to be absorbed.

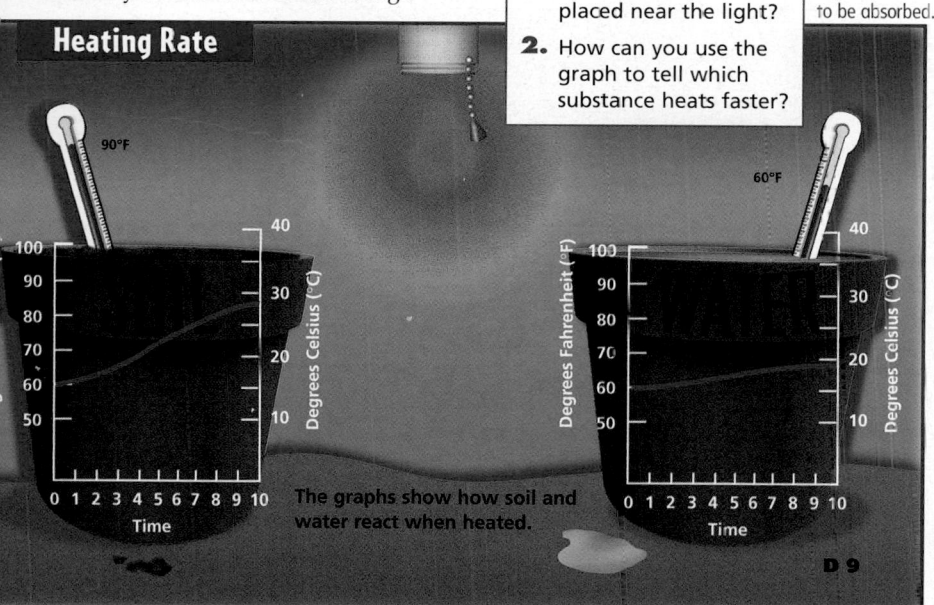

Heating Rate

90°F   60°F

The graphs show how soil and water react when heated.

D 9

Why Do Some Things Get Hotter than Others?

Before Reading
Have students try to answer the red question at the top of the page.

Developing the Main Idea
Ask:

- **Why do you think that large bodies of water stay cool during the hot summer?** (It takes more heat to raise the temperature of water than it takes to raise the temperature of land.)

- **How do you think bodies of water affect air temperature over and near them?** (In winter, the relatively warm water warms the air, and in summer, the cooler water cools the air. Water, in general, moderates the air temperature, so that areas near water have less extreme temperatures than inland areas.)

READING
Charts

1. the soil

2. by comparing the slope of the lines

▶ **After Reading**
Have students answer the red question in the student book as **ongoing assessment.**

SCIENCE FOR ALL

Inclusion

Color and Heat Absorption
Encourage students to design an experiment by which they can investigate how color affects the absorption of heat. Direct them to write their procedure and note their results. (Students might use several containers, identical except for color, filled with water and placed in a sunny location for an hour so that temperature differences can be noted.)
Logical

Why Do You Cool Down as You Go Up?

Before Reading
Have students try to answer the red question at the top of the page.

Developing the Main Idea
Ask students:

- **What happens to air as it warms?** (Remind students of what they have learned about the behavior of molecules, and guide them to answer that the molecules move faster, moving apart so that the air expands and rises.)

- **If air rises when it's warmed, why does it get cooler as you climb a mountain?** (Encourage students to speculate, and tell them that they will learn more about how altitude affects temperature.)

- **How does air temperature change with altitude?** (Air temperature decreases about 3.5°F for every 1,000 feet in altitude.)

READING
Diagrams

Students should describe a pattern of decreasing and increasing temperatures that alternates with each layer of the atmosphere.

▶After Reading
Have students answer the red question in the student book as **ongoing assessment.**

Developing Vocabulary

atmosphere Students may know from math that a *sphere* is a geometric shape used to describe a ball or globe. *Atmos-* is from Greek for "gas" or "vapor." So the word literally means a ball or sphere of gases — surrounding Earth.

troposphere *Tropos-* means "turning" This prefix attached to *sphere* may indicate the ancient belief that the sky turned around Earth while Earth remained stationary.

Why Do You Cool Down As You Go Up?

Did you ever climb a high mountain? As you go higher and higher above sea level, air temperatures drop. The natural drop in air temperature with altitude is about 2°C (3.6°F) for every 305 meters (1,000 ft).

Climbing up a mountain is really a journey up into the **atmosphere**, the air that surrounds Earth. The atmosphere reaches from Earth's surface to the edge of space. What if you could travel to the top part of the atmosphere? The diagram of the atmosphere shows what you would find.

In the troposphere, as altitude increases, temperature decreases.

READING
Diagrams

Describe how the temperature changes in each layer of the atmosphere.

You would find that the temperature does not fall steadily with altitude. It changes abruptly several times. These changes mark the boundaries of four main layers. These layers surround Earth like huge shells.

The layer closest to Earth's surface is the **troposphere** (TROP·uh·sfeer). It's the narrowest layer—between 8 and 18 kilometers (5–11 miles) thick—but it contains most of the air in the atmosphere. All life on Earth exists here. In this layer all moisture is found and all clouds, rain, snow, and thunderstorms form. Above this layer the air gradually thins out to the near-emptiness of space, with no exact upper boundary.

▷ **What is the relationship between altitude and temperature?**

Layers of the Atmosphere

Thermosphere

Ionized gas

80 km — Mesosphere

Radio waves

50 km — Ozone

Stratosphere

8–18 km — Troposphere

0 km — Mt. Everest

−100°C −50°C 0°C 50°C
Low Temperature High

Most weather occurs in the troposphere. The ozone layer in the stratosphere helps shield us from the Sun's ultraviolet light. *Auroras* (the northern and southern lights) may form in the *ionized* (electrically charged) gas in the thermosphere.

D 10

SCIENCE
Reading Strategy

Interpret Graphic Sources of Information

Developing Reading Skills
Have students interpret the diagram on page D10, summarizing the layers of the atmosphere. They can also interpret the chart on p. D11 to summarize the composition of the air.

BLACKLINE
Interpret Illustrations

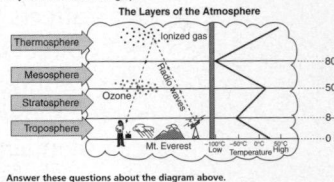

Reading in Science Resources, p. 194

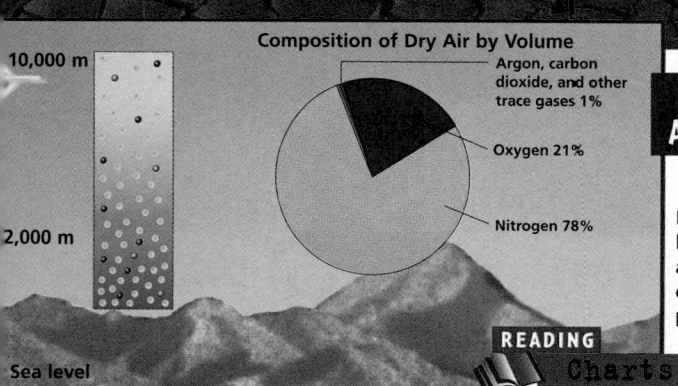

Composition of Dry Air by Volume

Argon, carbon dioxide, and other trace gases 1%

Oxygen 21%

Nitrogen 78%

10,000 m

2,000 m

Sea level

Air in the Atmosphere

Lower altitudes have a larger air column above them, which creates greater air pressure.

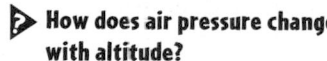

READING Charts

1. What is meant by *trace*?
2. Which gas is the most abundant in the atmosphere?

What Happens to the Air Pressure?

As you go higher in altitude, **air pressure** decreases steadily. Air pressure is the force put on a given area by the weight of the air above it. Air is a mixture of gases. It is made up mostly of *molecules* of nitrogen and oxygen. Molecules are the smallest pieces that a substance can be broken into without changing what the substance is.

The molecules have mass. They are attracted to Earth by gravity, so they have weight.

Normal air pressure is greatest at sea level. There the column of air extending above the surface to the top of the atmosphere is tallest. Sea level air pressure is about 1.04 kilograms per square centimeter (14.7 pounds per square inch). As you go higher in altitude, the height of the air column above you becomes shorter. Therefore the weight of that column—or air pressure—becomes less.

In the lower atmosphere, the composition of air varies very little. Up to an altitude of about 100 km (62 mi), air consists of a mixture of gases, water vapor, and dust particles. Nitrogen and oxygen make up 99 percent of the gases in dry air.

Water vapor is a gas. It should not be confused with clouds or fog, which are made of liquid or solid water. The amount of water vapor in air varies from $\frac{1}{10,000}$ of air in dry arctic regions to $\frac{1}{25}$ of air in moist equatorial regions.

The dust in air is made of particles so tiny that 100,000 lined up would only form a row 1 cm (0.4 in.) long. Some of it comes from Earth's surface, from fires and volcanic eruptions, or from tiny crystals of salt.

 How does air pressure change with altitude?

As altitude increases, air pressure decreases.

D 11

What Happens to the Air Pressure?

Before Reading
Have students try to answer the red question at the top of the page.

Exploring the Main Idea
As students observe, place an index card over the top of a drinking glass filled to the brim with water, making sure that the opening is completely covered. Hold the card in place as you turn the glass over, then remove your hand from the card. Ask:

- **Why didn't the water spill out of the glass?** (The air pressure pushing upward against the card was greater than the gravity pulling down.)

- **What do you think will happen when water soaks into the card?** (Encourage speculation; students might suggest that as the card becomes heavier with water, the force of gravity will become stronger than the air pressure, causing the card to fall and the water to spill.)

Discussing the Main Idea
Ask:

- **How does altitude affect air pressure?** (As altitude increases, air pressure decreases.)

READING Charts

1. A trace is a very small amount of something.
2. Nitrogen is most abundant.

▶ After Reading
Have students answer the red question in the student book as **ongoing assessment**.

Developing Vocabulary

air pressure Remind students that air is a mixture of gases and the weight of the gases exerts a force on the area below the gases.

What Is Weather?

Before Reading
Have students try to answer the red question at the top of the page.

Developing the Main Idea
Ask students to define weather based on what they already know. Encourage discussion; students may list weather conditions such as rain, snow, and so on.

Ask students to brainstorm, listing as many conditions that make up weather as they can. Write the responses on the chalkboard, and guide students to infer that the term weather describes a number of conditions that, together, describe the lower atmosphere. Ask:

- **Do any of these conditions exist alone?** (No; weather includes a number of conditions at any one time.)

Encourage students to identify conditions that commonly occur together, such as cold and snow, warm and humid, and so on.

▶ After Reading
Have students answer the red question in the student book as **ongoing assessment.**

Developing Vocabulary

weather To help students understand that weather is the total of conditions in the atmosphere, ask them to list words that they would use to describe what it is like outside at any given time.

barometer The suffix "-meter" is used to describe an instrument that measures something. Ask students if they can list other words that end in "-meter".

What Is Weather?

When you say, "It sure is hot today!" the *it* is the air. You really mean that the air around you is hot. The same is true if you say, "It is windy, " or "It is cloudy," or give any other similar description of the **weather**. The weather is simply what the lower atmosphere, or troposphere, is like at any given place and time.

The conditions that make up weather are the characteristics that change. They are air temperature, air pressure, amount of moisture in the air, wind, clouds, and rain or snow.

Measuring Temperature
You can measure temperature with a thermometer. Thermometers can use two different temperature scales. The Celsius scale is marked with the letter C. The Fahrenheit scale is shown by the letter F.

Measuring Air Pressure
Air pressure is measured with a **barometer** (buh·ROM·i·tuhr). Two common types of barometers are the mercury barometer and the aneroid barometer.

Mercury barometers use a mercury-filled glass tube with one closed end. The open end is submerged in liquid mercury. Air pressure on the mercury pushes it up into the tube. When the weight of the mercury column equals the air pressure, the mercury stops rising.

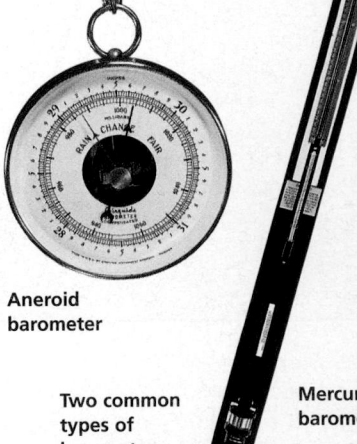

Aneroid barometer

Two common types of barometers

Mercury barometer

An *aneroid* (AN·uh·royd) barometer is an accordion-like metal can with most of the air removed. Inside, a spring balances the outside air pressure. When outside air pressure increases, the can squeezes the spring. When air pressure decreases, the spring pushes outward. A needle inside indicates changes in pressure.

You can monitor and record weather conditions for your own weather station. Measure and record air temperature several times a day. Record daily air pressure by using a barometer or by getting air pressure readings from the weather reports.

READING Main Idea
What conditions make up weather?

air temperature, air pressure, wind, amount of moisture in the air, clouds, and rain or snow

---

Reading MiniLesson

Main Idea and Supporting Details

Develop Discuss with students how every story, poem, play, article, and even a paragraph has a main idea—what the written material is mostly about. Other facts in the document are details that support, or tell more about, the main idea. Point out that in paragraph 3, the main idea is stated in the first sentence. Discuss how the other sentences in that paragraph support the main idea that thermometers measure temperature.

Practice Ask students to suggest supporting facts that would back up the main idea of the fifth paragraph—that a tube of liquid mercury can be used to measure air pressure. (Answers should include statements of how air pressure pushes mercury up the column of a tube that's submerged in it and stops rising when the pressure and weight of the mercury are equal.)

L·I·N·K·S

Why It Matters

Have you ever heard a day called a "scorcher"? That means a really hot day. On really hot days, your body can lose a lot of moisture. Your body gives off sweat gradually most of the time. On a hot day, your body tends to give off more and more. That's why it's important to have plenty of drinking water handy on a hot day.

On really cold days, many people have other problems—such as frostbite. You have to cover your face, ears, and hands to avoid contact with air at extremely low temperatures.

Visit **www.mhscience02.com** to do a research project on the atmosphere.

Think and Write

1. How do temperatures on Earth depend on angles?
2. List factors that affect temperatures of places on Earth.
3. What is air pressure? How does it change in the atmosphere?
4. What is the troposphere? What happens there?
5. **Critical Thinking** Is the weather one or more than just one thing? Defend your answer.

MATH LINK

Solve this problem. The sunniest place on Earth is in the eastern Sahara Desert, where sunlight shines an average of 4,300 hours per year. Calculate the percentage of possible sunlight hours a year this number represents. (Assume 12 hours of daylight per day.)

WRITING LINK

Write a story. How do you depend on the weather? Write a story explaining how the weather affects your life.

SOCIAL STUDIES LINK

Research the history of the thermometer. The maximum-and-minimum thermometer was invented in 1780 by Cambridge scientist James Six. A column of mercury moves up and down a U-shaped tube. An index moves with it, recording the highest and lowest temperatures. Research the history of the thermometer, and write a report for the class.

TECHNOLOGY LINK

At the Computer Visit **www.mhscience02.com** for more links.

D 13

Informal Assessment

Easy/Average Have small groups create posters showing Earth, its atmosphere, and how rays of the Sun reach Earth. Have them add labels describing how angle of insolation, altitude, water, air, pressure, and temperature affect weather. Display the posters in the classroom.

Challenge Have students explore Ben Franklin's forays into meteorology. Urge students to consider whether modern technology is essential to further our knowledge, or if Franklin possessed the necessary tools for weather exploration. Have students write reports to defend their positions.

3 | Lesson Review

Answers to Think and Write

1. The angle at which rays of the Sun strike a surface affects how much heat it will receive. The more vertical the rays the greater the heat. (pp. D5–D8)

2. angle of insolation, water, plants, altitude (pp. D7–D10)

3. Air pressure is the force on an area caused by the weight of air above it. It is greatest at sea level and decreases with increasing altitude. (pp. D10–D11)

4. The troposphere is the lowest part of the atmosphere. Most air is found and most weather occurs in the troposphere. (p. D10)

5. **Critical Thinking** Weather is made up of many conditions that describe what the lower atmosphere is like at any given time. (p. D12)

Summarize

Check students' understanding by having them write a brief summary of the lesson in their own words.

MATH LINK

Students first calculate the number of *possible* sunlight hours in a year: 365 days/year × 12 hours/day = 4,380 hours/year. Then calculate the percent of time the Sun is actually shining: $\frac{4,300}{4,380}$ = 0.981, or 98 percent.

WRITING LINK

Stories may include activities possible only during certain types of weather, information about types of clothing, homes people live in, and/or how their weather makes them feel, should also be included.

SOCIAL STUDIES LINK

Students' research should focus on information about Six's thermometer, as well as Galileo and Gabriel Fahrenheit's.

Technology

Internet Research Project Have students visit **www.mhscience02.com** to do a research project on the atmosphere. They will find a suggested outline for the project, questions to research, and links to Internet reference sites.

LESSON 2 Water Vapor and Humidity

Objectives

- Explore how water changes as a result of heating and cooling.
- Relate humidity to the processes of evaporation.
- Explain what happens to water vapor with cooling.
- Describe a series of changes that water goes through.

Resources

- Activity Resources, pp. 125–129
- Reading in Science Resources, pp. 197–202
- Vocabulary Cards
- Reading Aid Transparency D2

Build on Prior Knowledge

Have students discuss what they know about water in the air. Ask:

- **Where does rain come from?** (clouds)
- **Where does the moisture that forms clouds come from?** (air)
- **How does water get into the air?** (It evaporates from oceans, lakes, and other water sources.)

1 Get Ready

Using the Illustrations

Have students discuss how they might feel if they were walking across the bridge in the photograph. (They might feel the moisture from the fog on their skin.) Fog is water vapor in the air. Water on the outside of a cold lemonade glass does not come from inside the glass but from water vapor that condenses outside the glass.

Have students describe how they feel on a humid day. (Students may answer that they feel sticky or damp and hot.) Point out that the stickiness they feel on a humid day is from moisture in the air.

LESSON 2 Water Vapor and Humidity

Vocabulary

water vapor, D16
humidity, D16
evaporation, D16
condensation, D17
relative humidity, D18

Get Ready

What if you were walking on this bridge? What would you see and feel all around you? It's fog. What is fog made of? Here's a hint. What if you put a cold glass of lemonade outside on a table on a hot, humid day? What would you see and feel on the outside of the glass?

What is a humid day like? Where is the moisture on a humid day?

Process Skill

You use variables when you identify and separate things in an experiment that can be changed or controlled.

D 14

Science Background

Hygrometer

John Frederic Daniell (1790-1845), a British chemist, invented the dew-point hygrometer. Dew point is the temperature at which water vapor of a certain percentage in air condenses. A hygrometer cools air to its dew point, then compares that temperature with the actual temperature to show relative humidity.

Explore Activity

Where Does the Puddle Come From?

Materials
plastic cups
ice
paper towels
food coloring
thermometer
goggles

Procedure: Design Your Own

BE CAREFUL! Wear goggles.

1 Form a Hypothesis Write down your idea about why a puddle forms around a frosty drink. Where do you think the puddle came from?

2 Experiment Describe what you would do to test your idea. How would your test support or reject your idea?

3 Communicate Draw a diagram showing how you would use the materials. Keep a record of your observations.

Drawing Conclusions

1 Communicate Describe the results of your investigation.

2 Communicate What evidence did you gather? Explain what happened.

3 Infer How does this evidence support or reject your explanation?

4 Going Further: Use Variables Do you get the same results on a cool day as on a warm day? Do you get the same results on a humid day as on a dry day? How might you test your ideas?

D 15

Alternative Explore Activity

Materials two jars, one with a lid, wax pencil, and water

Where'd It Go? Have students pour an equal amount of water into the jars, tightly screwing the lid onto one. Have them mark the water level with a wax pencil. Leave the jars undisturbed overnight. Direct students to check the water level in each. Challenge them to explain what occurred. (There is less water in the open jar because water moved into the air by evaporation; the closed jar may have condensation on its sides.) **Spatial**

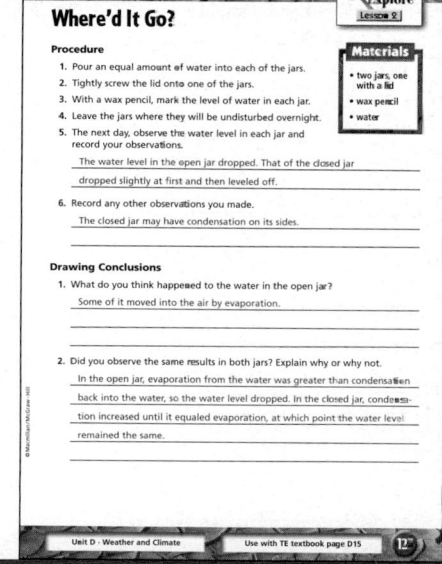

Name _____ Date _____

Where'd It Go?

Procedure

1. Pour an equal amount of water into each of the jars.
2. Tightly screw the lid onto one of the jars.
3. With a wax pencil, mark the level of water in each jar.
4. Leave the jars where they will be undisturbed overnight.
5. The next day, observe the water level in each jar and record your observations.
   The water level in the open jar dropped. That of the closed jar dropped slightly at first and then leveled off.
6. Record any other observations you made.
   The closed jar may have condensation on its sides.

Materials
• two jars, one with a lid
• wax pencil
• water

Drawing Conclusions

1. What do you think happened to the water in the open jar?
   Some of it moved into the air by evaporation.

2. Did you observe the same results in both jars? Explain why or why not.
   In the open jar, evaporation from the water was greater than condensation back into the water, so the water level dropped. In the closed jar, condensation increased until it equaled evaporation, at which point the water level remained the same.

Unit D • Weather and Climate   Use with TE textbook page D15

Activity Resources, p. 127

Explore Activity

Where Does the Puddle Come From?

Science Process Skills *form a hypothesis, experiment, communicate, infer, use variables*

Resources Activity Resources, pp. 125–126

Pacing 30–40 minutes

Grouping individual

Procedure

Be Careful! Have students wear goggles to prevent getting food coloring in their eyes.

2 Students might describe placing ice and tinted water into a cup, adding a straw, marking the water level on the straw, measuring and recording the temperature of the water and the air at intervals, and comparing the conditions when water droplets form with those at the beginning of the experiment.

Answers to Drawing Conclusions

1 The water level does not go down, and the water droplets are not tinted.

2 Answers will vary, but might include that the temperature of the water increased, that the temperature of the air decreased, untinted water droplets formed, and the water level in the cup did not change.

3 The untinted water droplets that formed support the hypothesis that the water comes from the air.

4 On a cool day, less water will form on the glass. Students might suggest testing this by using the apparatus they used in the Explore activity, and cooling the area with a fan or placing the setup in the refrigerator.

 Inquiry Students can ask their own questions to explore, such as whether anything happens when a container holding a hot liquid is placed in cool surroundings.

Technology

■ When time is short, preview the activity with the **Explore Activity Video.**

Where Does Water Vapor Come From?

Before Reading
Have students try to answer the red question at the top of the page.

Exploring the Main Idea
With students, make a hygrometer to measure the water in the air. Punch a hole in an index card, about halfway down the short side and an inch from the edge. Then cut a thin lengthwise strip from the second card, cutting one end diagonally to form a point. Attach the unpointed end of the strip to the index card (through the hole) with a brass brad-type fastener. To the pointed end of the strip, tape a strand of hair that is at least 4 inches long. Tape the other end of the hair to the top of the card so that the pointed strip hangs in the middle of the card. Draw a line on the card indicating where the pointed arrow reaches. Tell students that certain materials, including hair, soak up water on humid days.

READING
Diagrams

by looking at a map or a globe and comparing the amount of Earth's land with the amount of Earth's waters

Developing Vocabulary

water vapor Have students look up the science meaning of *vapor* in the dictionary to come up with a definition of *water vapor*. (a gaseous state of a substance that is usually a liquid or a solid; water in the gaseous state)

humidity Students may be able to see *humid* in this word. They can describe the uncomfortable feeling they may have on humid days.

evaporation Students may find *vapor* in this word. See *water vapor* above. The prefix *e-* means "to become" or "to leave" — that is, "to become a gas" or "to leave the ground as a gas."

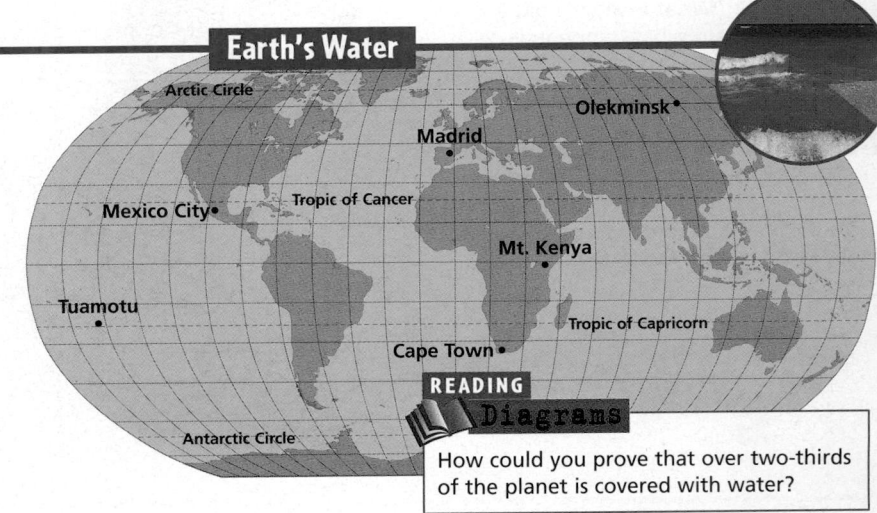

Read to Learn

Main Idea Water on Earth's surface and in the atmosphere changes form and affects the weather.

Where Does Water Vapor Come From?

Put a frosty glass of lemonade on a table on a hot day. What happens? A puddle forms on the table. Where does the puddle come from? The water level in the glass does not drop as the puddle forms. The water in the puddle isn't lemonade.

The water in the puddle comes from the air around the glass. When the warm air touches the cold glass, the air cools. Droplets of water form, run down the side of the glass, and make a puddle on the table.

The water in the air is **water vapor**. Water vapor is water in the form of a gas. Water vapor is invisible, colorless, odorless, and tasteless. The amount of water vapor in the air is called **humidity**. Do not confuse humidity with droplets of liquid water you see in rain, fog, or clouds.

How does water vapor get into the air in the first place? More than two-thirds of planet Earth is covered with liquid water—oceans, rivers, and lakes. There is also water in the ground and in plants. To get into the air, this liquid water must be changed into water vapor.

The changing of a liquid into a gas is called **evaporation**. This takes lots of energy. The main energy source for Earth is the Sun. Each day the Sun turns trillions of tons of ocean water into water vapor.

Water molecules absorb the Sun's energy and speed up. "Speedy" water

Earth's Water

Arctic Circle
Olekminsk•
Madrid•
Tropic of Cancer
Mexico City•
Mt. Kenya•
Tuamotu•
Tropic of Capricorn
Cape Town•
Antarctic Circle

READING
Diagrams

How could you prove that over two-thirds of the planet is covered with water?

D 16

BLACKLINE
Lesson Outline

Name_____ Date_____

Lesson Outline
Lesson 2

Water Vapor and Humidity

Fill in the blanks. 📖 Reading Skill: Main Idea - questions 2, 11, 19

Where Does Water Vapor Come From?

1. When water drops form on a cold glass, the water comes from the ___air around the glass___

2. Water vapor is water in the form of a(n) ___gas___.

3. The amount of water in the air is ___humidity___.

4. Water covers more than ___two-thirds___ of Earth's surface.

5. Liquid water becomes a gas called water vapor through the process of ___evaporation___.

6. The Sun's energy enables ___water molecules___ from the water's surface to escape into the atmosphere.

7. The change from a gas to a liquid is called ___condensation___.

8. The second-largest source of water vapor is ___transpiration___ from plant leaves.

What Is Relative Humidity?

9. Humidity is measured in grams per ___cubic meter___

10. If water is available, warm air will take on ___more___ water vapor than cold air.

11. Relative humidity is a comparison between how much ___water vapor___ is in the air and how much the air could hold.

12. Fifty-percent relative humidity means that air is holding ___half___ of what it could if it were full.

13. The relative humidity of your air depends upon changes in your ___weather___

Unit D · Weather and Climate   Use with textbook pages D14–D21   197

Reading in Science Resources, p. 197

SCIENCE
Reading Strategy

Compare and Contrast
Developing Reading Skills
Have students compare and contrast the movement of water into the air as a vapor with the formation of water droplets by condensation.

molecules near the surface of the liquid "escape" or evaporate into the atmosphere as water vapor. Some hit other molecules and return to the liquid. When air is cooled, molecules in the air slow down. The molecules of water vapor in the air also slow down. If they slow enough, water vapor molecules that collide stick together and change to liquid droplets on cool surfaces. Condensation is the changing of a gas into a liquid. You see condensation on shower doors, on cold drink glasses, and as dew on grass in the early morning.

Plants' roots absorb water that has seeped into the ground. Plants transport the liquid water through their roots and stems to their leaves.

The leaves then give off water in the process called transpiration. This is the second-largest source of water vapor in the atmosphere. The water in the air comes from the evaporation of water from oceans, lakes, rivers; from water in the ground; and from plants giving off water vapor.

▷ **How does water get into the air?**

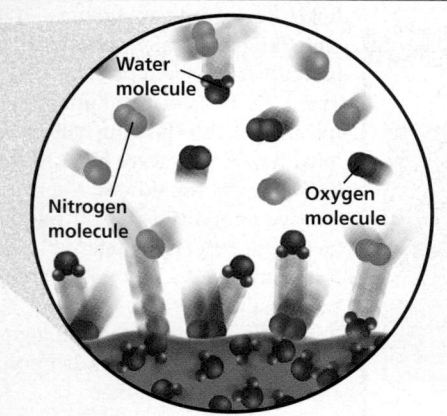

Some water molecules "escape" into the air. Some water molecules are knocked back into the liquid.

Water molecule

Nitrogen molecule

Oxygen molecule

QUICK LAB

FOR SCHOOL OR HOME

Transpiration

1. Place a clear-plastic bag completely over a houseplant. Tie the bag tightly around the base of the stem. Do not put the soil-filled pot in the bag.

2. **Observe** Place the plant in a sunny location. Observe it several times a day. When you are done, remove the plastic bag from the plant.

3. **Communicate** Describe what you see on the inside of the bag. How can you explain what happened?

4. **Draw Conclusions** *Transpiration* sounds like *perspiration*–sweating. How might the two processes be alike?

5. **Predict** How would your results vary if you put the plant in the shade?

D 17

Exploring the Main Idea
Reinforce the concept that evaporation requires heat, and point out that places where evaporation takes place become cooler as a result. As students observe, dampen a cotton ball with water and wrap it around the bulb of a thermometer. Place a second thermometer, without damp cotton, next to the first. Direct the breeze from a fan onto the two thermometers. Leave them undisturbed for 10 minutes. Have a student volunteer read both. Ask:

■ **What happened? Why?** (The wet thermometer registers a lower temperature because, as the water from the cotton ball evaporated, heat energy was removed from the thermometer.)

▶ **After Reading**
Have students answer the red question in the student book as **ongoing assessment.**

FOR SCHOOL OR HOME

Materials potted houseplant (such as geranium), clear plastic bag, string

Science Process Skills *observe, communicate, draw conclusions, predict*

Resources Activity Resources, pp. 128–129

Step 2 Students will observe moisture forming in the bag.

Step 3 Water droplets form on the inside of the bag as a result of transpiration. The plant absorbs water through its roots, then gives off water through its leaves.

Step 4 Both transpiration and perspiration are processes where water is given off by a plant or an animal, respectively.

Step 5 The transpiration process would be slower.

Developing Vocabulary

condensation Students may see the word *dense,* "thick, packed together," in *condensation* and infer the word means "the act or process of making something dense." The molecules of gas are compacted into a smaller volume when the gas becomes liquid.

What Is Relative Humidity?

Before Reading
Have students try to answer the red question at the top of the page.

Developing the Main Idea
Remind students that humidity is a measure of water vapor in the air, then ask:

- **How are humidity and relative humidity related?** (They are both measures of water in the air; relative humidity compares the amount of water in the air at a certain temperature with the amount of water the air can hold at that temperature.)

READING
Graphs

Because the warmer the temperature, the faster water evaporates, there would be more water vapor per cubic centimeter at 40°C than at 25°C. At 25°C, there are 25 grams per cm³. At 40°C, there are 50 grams per cm³.

Developing Vocabulary

relative humidity Remind students of the definition of *humidity*. Use the graph in the text to explain relative humidity. Explain that *relative* means that this term is "a comparison."

What Is Relative Humidity?

Humidity and relative humidity both describe the amount of water vapor in the air. Do they mean the same thing, or are they different? Think of a "box" of air that is one cubic meter in volume. Humidity is the actual amount or mass of water vapor in that "box." Humidity is measured in grams per cubic meter.

Two factors determine the amount of humidity in the air. First, there has to be water available to evaporate. Second, the warmer the temperature, the faster the water evaporates. This means that if water is available, warm air will take on more water vapor than cold air.

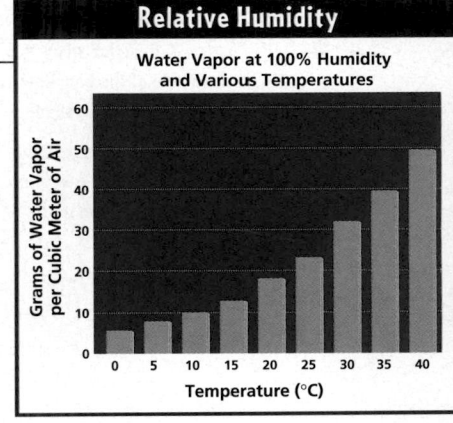

Weather forecasters often use temperature readings from a wet bulb/dry bulb thermometer—or *hygrometer*—along with a chart to find the relative humidity.

READING
Graphs

How does the amount of water vapor per cubic centimeter compare at 25°C and 40°C?

Relative Humidity

Water Vapor at 100% Humidity and Various Temperatures

(graph: Grams of Water Vapor per Cubic Meter of Air vs. Temperature (°C))

Is there a limit to how much water vapor air can hold? Yes. Air at any temperature has a water vapor capacity or limit. When it becomes full, we say it is saturated. If there is very little water vapor in the air, we say the air is dry.

Relative humidity is a comparison between how much water vapor is in the air and how much the air could hold—at a given temperature—if it were full or saturated. Relative humidity is given in percents (%). Therefore, 50% relative humidity means that air is holding half of what it could if it were full.

On a very humid day, the relative humidity of the air might be 70% or 80%. If the relative humidity is just 25% or 30%, we say the air is dry. The relative humidity of your air may change from day to day. It depends upon changes in your weather.

D 18

Math   MiniLesson

Fractions, Decimals, and Percents

Develop Percents, fractions, and decimals are related.

Write 20% as a fraction.

Think: percent means per one hundred

$20\% = \frac{20}{100} = \frac{10}{50} = \frac{1}{5}$

So, $20\% = \frac{1}{5}$

Write 80% as a decimal.

$80\% = \frac{80}{100} = 0.80$

So, $80\% = 0.80$ or 0.8

Write $\frac{3}{5}$ as a percent.

Use the **F↔D** key on a fraction calculator to convert a fraction to a decimal.

Press the following:

3 b/c 5 F↔D 0.6

$0.6 = 0.60 = \frac{60}{100} = 60\%$

So, $\frac{3}{5} = 60\%$

Practice Write each percent as a fraction and as a decimal.

1. 75% ($\frac{3}{4}$, 0.75)

2. 90% ($\frac{9}{10}$, 0.9)

Activity Have students find percents in food labels. Have them rewrite the percents as fractions and as decimals.

BLACKLINE
Interpret Illustrations

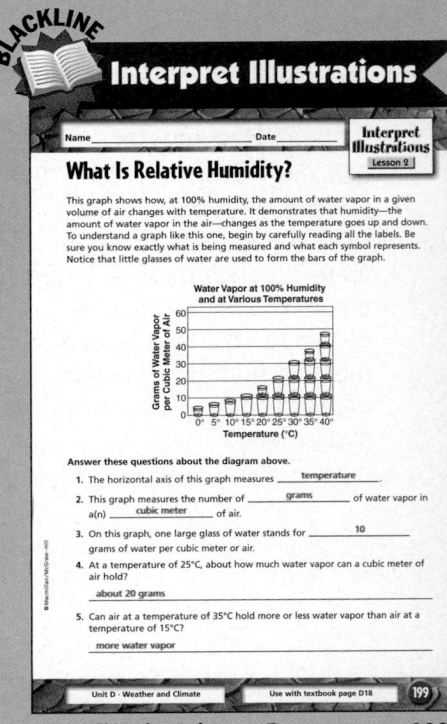

Interpret Illustrations
Lesson 2

Name_____ Date_____

What Is Relative Humidity?

This graph shows how, at 100% humidity, the amount of water vapor in a given volume of air changes with temperature. It demonstrates that humidity—the amount of water vapor in the air—changes as the temperature goes up and down. To understand a graph like this one, begin by carefully reading all the labels. Be sure you know exactly what is being measured and what each symbol represents. Notice that little glasses of water are used to form the bars of the graph.

Water Vapor at 100% Humidity and at Various Temperatures

(graph)

Answer these questions about the diagram above.

1. The horizontal axis of this graph measures ____temperature____
2. This graph measures the number of ____grams____ of water vapor in a(n) ____cubic meter____ of air.
3. On this graph, one large glass of water stands for ____10____ grams of water per cubic meter or air.
4. At a temperature of 25°C, about how much water vapor can a cubic meter of air hold?
____about 20 grams____
5. Can air at a temperature of 35°C hold more or less water vapor than air at a temperature of 15°C?
____more water vapor____

Unit D - Weather and Climate | Use with textbook page D18 | **199**

Reading in Science Resources, p. 199

D18 UNIT D *Weather and Climate*

Relative humidity can be used to predict how the air will feel to a person. The higher the relative humidity, the less water can evaporate into the air. The less water, such as sweat, can evaporate from our skin, the wetter and "stickier" the air feels.

Relative humidity can also be used to predict when condensation will occur. Remember that condensation, like the drops of water on the lemonade glass, is the changing of a gas into a liquid. In the atmosphere condensation is usually the result of warm air being cooled. That is, when warm air is cooled, water vapor in it condenses.

Condensation explains what happened to the glass of lemonade. The cold glass cooled the air that touched it. Water vapor condensed, forming liquid droplets on the outside of the glass.

Can you see condensation happening? Have you ever seen frozen food held over hot water? What do you notice? You see a mist forming. When this happens in the air, a cloud forms. The greater the relative humidity, the more likely condensation will occur, and the greater the chance of clouds—and rain.

You may have heard people complain on a hot day, "It's not the heat, it's the humidity." Why do you think humidity is so important, especially when the weather is hot? Why doesn't a cold day with 70% relative humidity feel as uncomfortable as a hot day with 70% relative humidity?

READING Main Idea
How does temperature affect relative humidity?

Relative humidity is a comparison between how much water is in the air and how much the air could hold if it were saturated. Evaporation increases with temperature. The warmer it is, the more water vapor the air can take on.

Do you think these runners would feel more comfortable on a hot, damp day; a hot, dry day; a cool, damp day; or a cool, dry day? Explain.

D 19

Developing the Main Idea
Ask students to recall the Explore activity. Ask:

■ **What do you think would happen if the ice melted and the drink warmed? If the air temperature increased as well?** (Eventually, the air surrounding the cup would warm again, and evaporation would take place. If the air temperature increased, evaporation would occur more rapidly.)

Exploring the Main Idea
Encourage students to investigate how surface area affects evaporation. Have them place two containers, one deep and one shallow, containing equal volumes of water, in a sunny location. The next day, have them measure the volume of water in each container. Ask:

■ **What happened? Why?** (The shallow dish contains less water than the deep dish. This is because water molecules can only escape to the air from the surface of a liquid; water evaporates more quickly from the container with a larger surface area.)

■ **What role does heat play in evaporation?** (Molecules in warm water move more rapidly and escape more easily into the air than do molecules of cold water. Heat causes water to change to water vapor, and also lets the air hold more water vapor.)

▶ **After Reading**
Have students answer the red question in the student book as **ongoing assessment.**

Reading MiniLesson

Main Idea and Supporting Details

Develop Discuss with students how supporting details often answer the **5 Ws** and an **H**—who, what, when, where, why and how—about the main idea. Reread paragraph 1 of page D19 and point out that in this case the first sentence is the main idea and the other sentences explain how and why relative humidity can tell us how the air will feel today.

Practice Help students remember what relative humidity is by constructing word-web graphic organizers. Have students write "relative humidity" in a center circle, then surround it with other circles in which they write details from pages D18 and D19 to support that main idea. (Possible details: compares how much water is in the air with how much the air could hold if it were saturated; used to predict how air will feel; used to predict rain; helps scientists predict weather.)

Reading Strategy

Reread
Developing Reading Skills
Have students reread the Explore Activity, supplementing their answers to Drawing Conclusions with what they learn on page D19.

What Happens When Warm, Moist Air Cools?

Before Reading
Have students try to answer the red question at the top of the page.

Developing the Main Idea
Ask:

- **How can warm air become cool?** (It can be pushed upward by winds, it can be pushed up by cool air, and it can cool by rising and expanding.)

- **What part of the water cycle did the Explore Activity illustrate?** (condensation)

- **How did the condensation that occurred rely on evaporation?** (For condensation to occur, there must have been water, formed by evaporation, in the air.)

READING Diagrams

1. Air can rise by being pushed over mountains, by being displaced by cooler air, or by being heated by the Sun.

2. As air rises, it expands and cools.

▶ **After Reading**
Have students answer the red question in the student book as **ongoing assessment.**

What Happens When Warm, Moist Air Cools?

How can warm, moist air cool off? In the lower atmosphere, the air gets colder with increasing altitude.

- Air can cool by being pushed upward over mountains by winds.

- Heating the air also causes it to rise. When the Sun heats the ground, air above the ground warms and rises. As it rises, it expands and cools.

- Air can also be pushed upward when cooler air and warmer air meet. When the two meet, they don't mix. The lighter, warm air is pushed up over the heavier, cold air. The result is the warm air, pushed higher into the atmosphere, cools.

In each case the end result is the same. As the air rises and cools, the water vapor in it condenses into tiny water droplets, forming clouds.

If the temperature is below the freezing point of water, its water vapor will form a cloud of tiny ice crystals.

In order for water vapor to condense, it must have a surface on which the liquid droplet or ice crystal will form. This surface is provided by tiny dust particles in the air. You will learn more about clouds in the next lesson.

▷ **How can warm air rise and cool?**

Warm air can be pushed upward over mountains by winds or pushed upward when warm and cool air meet, and can rise when heated by the Sun.

D 20

How Clouds Form

1 Cloud forms / Warm air

2 Cloud forms / Warm air

3 Cloud forms / Warm air / Cool air

READING Diagrams

1. What can cause air to rise?

2. What happens to the air temperature as air rises?

Science Background

Erasmus Darwin

Erasmus Darwin, an eighteenth century British physician, was the first scientist to hypothesize that the rising of air is an important method of cooling. To test his hypothesis, he charged an unloaded pellet gun and allowed it to reach room temperature before discharging it, releasing air under pressure onto the bulb of the thermometer.

When the thermometer registered a drop in temperature, Darwin concluded that the cooling mechanism was the abrupt expansion of air as it was released from the gun. Ask students to describe how Darwin's experiment produced cool air. (release of pressured air expands it, causing cooling)

BLACKLINE Interpret Illustrations

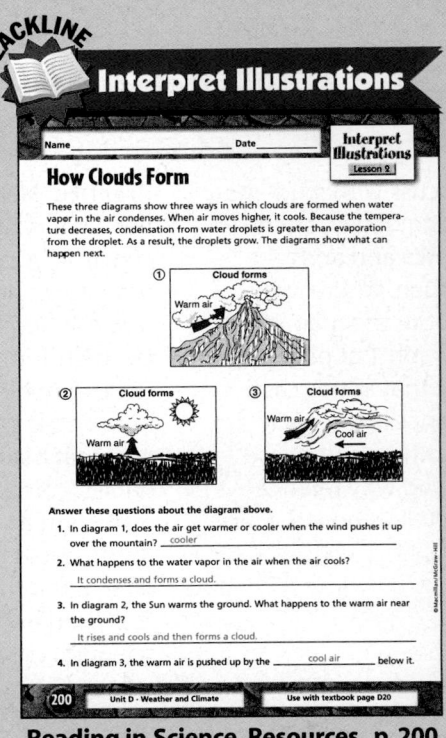

Reading in Science Resources, p. 200

Why It Matters

Have you ever had sweat trickle down your face on a hot day? People sweat every day. Sweating is a way our bodies release wastes. We don't always feel the sweat because we sweat gradually, and it evaporates.

As sweat evaporates, the water droplets absorb heat from the skin's surface, cooling it. It is a way your body controls surface temperature.

On very hot days and when you are physically active, you may sweat a lot. The sweat builds up, does not evaporate fast, and collects. On a high-humidity day, you feel even "stickier." On a low-humidity day, the sweat evaporates more quickly. You might think you're not sweating—but you are.

Think and Write

1. Where does water vapor in the air come from? What process produces it?

2. How is relative humidity different from humidity? How are the two terms alike?

3. What causes water vapor to change into droplets of liquid water?

4. How does water vapor get cooled in the atmosphere?

5. **Critical Thinking** Would you say that the Sun is a cause of clouds? Defend your answer.

L·I·N·K·S

WRITING LINK

Write an essay. Why are you more comfortable in lower relative humidity? Write an essay explaining how relative humidity can affect you.

MATH LINK

Find the heat index. Use an almanac to find a heat index prepared by the weather service. This chart tells how warm a person feels at a particular temperature and humidity level. Using the chart, find the heat index for each of the days in the table below. Then use newspaper weather reports for one week last summer. Find the heat index for each of those days.

	Mon	Tues	Wed	Thurs	Fri
High temp.	25°C	35°C	30°C	35°C	25°C
Relative humidity	90%	97%	89%	48%	45%

ART LINK

Make a poster. Very hot, humid weather can be dangerous. Make a poster warning about the dangers of very hot, humid weather. Include a list of safety tips.

TECHNOLOGY LINK

At the Computer Visit www.mhscience02.com for more links.

D 21

3 Lesson Review

Answers to Think and Write

1. water vapor from the water that covers the surface of Earth; evaporation (pp. D14–15)

2. Both describe water in the air. Humidity is a measure of the amount of water in the air. Relative humidity compares the amount of water in the air with the amount of water that the air could hold at a given temperature. (pp. D16, D18)

3. Water vapor must be cooled and have something on which to condense. (pp. D19–D20)

4. by being pushed upward and expanding (p. D20)

5. **Critical Thinking** The Sun heats air, causing it to rise. As air rises, it expands and cools. Condensation then occurs, forming clouds. (p. D20)

Summarize
Check students' understanding by having them write a brief summary of the lesson in their own words.

WRITING LINK
When relative humidity is high, more moisture is held in the air. There is less room in the air for more moisture. Thus, the sweat on your skin does not evaporate as quickly as on a day with low relative humidity. On a humid day, your skin feels damp and sticky, and you are less comfortable.

MATH LINK
The heat index is the combined effect of temperature and relative humidity. The heat index temperature tells you how warm the weather feels to you regardless of the actual temperature. The heat index for the following days is: Mon—87; Tues—140; Wed—105; Thurs—90; and Fri—79.

ART LINK
Make a wall display of students' posters.

✓ Informal Assessment

Easy/Average Have students explore methods elephants use to cool off and explain why these methods are effective. (Elephants spray themselves with water. They also use their ears as fans to cause the water to evaporate and cool themselves.)

Challenge Have small groups create posters illustrating the water cycle. Have them find out more about evaporation and condensation. Challenge students to tell how evaporation and condensation move water from the surface of Earth to the atmosphere and back. Display the posters in the classroom.

LESSON 3 — Clouds and Precipitation

Objectives

- Explore how clouds form.
- Identify causes and types of clouds and precipitation.
- Put in sequence the processes of the water cycle.
- Describe how to compare amounts of rainfall and cloud cover.

Resources

- Activity Resources, pp. 130–134
- Reading in Science Resources, pp. 203–208
- Vocabulary Cards
- Reading Aid Transparency D3
- Visual Aid Transparencies, 9–12, 22, 23
- Grade-Level Science Book, *The Great Johnstown Flood*
- School to Home Activities, p. 26

Build on Prior Knowledge

Have students discuss what they know about clouds and precipitation. Have students look at the clouds outside the classroom. Ask them if they think there is a good chance of rain or snow and then have them explain their ideas. (Possible answers: Gray clouds may produce rain or snow depending on the day's temperature; a nearly cloudless sky may mean a rainless day.)

1 Get Ready

Developing the Main Idea

Review cloud formation from the previous lesson: when rising warm air cools, water vapor in the air condenses into tiny water droplets or ice crystals. The formation of clouds depends on air temperature and the amount of water vapor in the air.

LESSON 3 — Clouds and Precipitation

Vocabulary

- **stratus cloud,** D24
- **cumulus cloud,** D24
- **cirrus cloud,** D24
- **fog,** D24
- **precipitation,** D26
- **water cycle,** D29

Get Ready

How can you predict the weather without using the instruments weather forecasters use? Look at the sky. There are clues up there. They're called clouds. Different kinds of clouds bring different kinds of weather. What is a cloud? What makes a cloud form? What do evaporation and condensation have to do with it?

Process Skill

You infer when you form an idea from facts or observations.

D 22

Science Background

Cloud Classification

The English chemist Luke Howard (1722–1864) created the basic system of cloud classification. Though he didn't understand how the different kinds of clouds formed, he assigned them Latin names based on their appearance. Cirrus clouds, for example, resemble curls of hair, while cumulus clouds look like heaps and stratus clouds lie flat. Still in use today, these categories now have further subdivisions.

Explore Activity

How Do Clouds Form?

Materials
hot tap water
2 identical clear containers
mug
3 ice cubes
food coloring

Procedure

BE CAREFUL! Be careful handling the hot water.

1. Chill container 1 by putting it in a refrigerator or on ice for about ten minutes.

2. Fill a mug with hot water.

3. **Make a Model** Fill container 2 with hot water. Place empty cold container 1 upside down on top of container 2 with the water. Fit the mouths together carefully. Place the ice cubes on top of container 1.

4. **Observe** Record your observations.

Drawing Conclusions

1. **Communicate** What did you observe?

2. **Communicate** Where did this take place?

3. **Infer** Where did the water come from? Explain what made it happen.

4. **Going Further: Infer** Where would you expect to find more clouds—over the ocean or over a desert? Why?

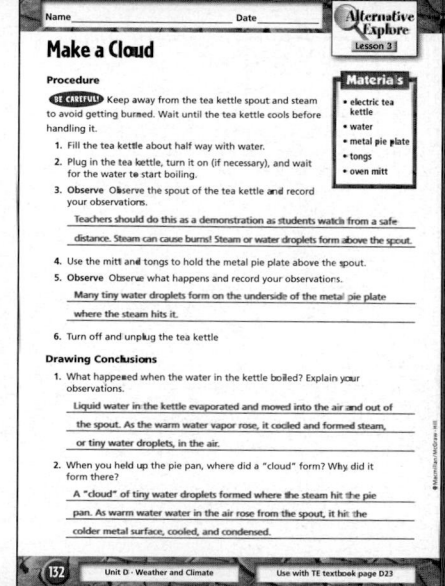

D 23

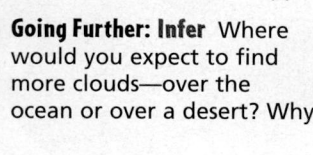

Alternative Explore Activity

Materials electric tea kettle, water, metal pie plate, tongs, oven mitt

Make a Cloud Boil water in the kettle. As students observe, hold a metal pie plate in the cloud above the spout. (Hold your hand away from the steam to prevent burns.) Have students explain how the result confirms that clouds are formed by condensation. (Heated air holding water vapor cools as it rises, and condenses forming a cloud of visible water droplets on the pie plate.) **Spatial**

Name_____ Date_____

Make a Cloud

Alternative Explore Lesson 3

Procedure

BE CAREFUL! Keep away from the tea kettle spout and steam to avoid getting burned. Wait until the tea kettle cools before handling it.

Materials
• electric tea kettle
• water
• metal pie plate
• tongs
• oven mitt

1. Fill the tea kettle about half way with water.
2. Plug in the tea kettle, turn it on (if necessary), and wait for the water to start boiling.
3. **Observe** Observe the spout of the tea kettle and record your observations.

   Teachers should do this as a demonstration as students watch from a safe distance. Steam can cause burns! Steam or water droplets form above the spout.

4. Use the mitt and tongs to hold the metal pie plate above the spout.
5. **Observe** Observe what happens and record your observations.

   Many tiny water droplets form on the underside of the metal pie plate where the steam hits it.

6. Turn off and unplug the tea kettle

Drawing Conclusions

1. What happened when the water in the kettle boiled? Explain your observations.

   Liquid water in the kettle evaporated and moved into the air and out of the spout. As the warm water vapor rose, it cooled and formed steam, or tiny water droplets, in the air.

2. When you held up the pie pan, where did a "cloud" form? Why did it form there?

   A "cloud" of tiny water droplets formed where the steam hit the pie pan. As warm water vapor in the air rose from the spout, it hit the colder metal surface, cooled, and condensed.

132   Unit D · Weather and Climate   Use with TE textbook page D23

Activity Resources, p.132

Explore Activity

How Do Clouds Form?

Science Process Skills *make a model, observe, communicate, infer*

Resources Activity Resources, pp. 130–131

Pacing 30–40 minutes

Grouping pairs

Procedure

Be Careful! Be sure the tap water is not so hot that it could cause scalding.

3. Ask students to predict what will happen to the hot water. (Some of the water will evaporate into the air and the warm, moist air will rise into the cold container.)

Answers to Drawing Conclusions

1. Droplets of water collected on the inside bottom of the container holding the ice.

2. Invisible water vapor moved upward from the hot water, cooling as it rose; droplets formed on the bottom inside of the container holding ice.

3. The water evaporated from the hot water into the air. Then as the air was cooled, some of the water vapor in the air condensed. Students might infer that the upper container cooled the air containing water vapor rising from below. As it cooled, the air couldn't hold as much water as it had before, so the water condensed, forming droplets on the underside of the cool container.

4. Clouds form from condensing water vapor. You could expect more clouds over an ocean, where water would evaporate into the air, than over a desert, where there is little water to evaporate into the air.

 Inquiry Students can ask their own questions to explore, such as whether the water in clouds evaporates.

Technology

■ When time is short, preview the activity with the **Explore Activity Video.**

How Do Clouds Form?

Before Reading
Have students try to answer the red question at the top of the page.

Developing the Main Idea
Point out that historically, sophisticated weather instruments are very new, but that people have predicted weather since ancient times by noting the shapes, sizes, colors, and movements of clouds.

▶ **After Reading**
Have students answer the red question in the student book as **ongoing assessment**.

Developing Vocabulary

stratus cloud Stratus comes from a Latin word meaning "to spread out." A stratus cloud looks spread out in a layer, covering most of the sky overhead. Students may also think of a similar word, a rock layer, a rock *stratum*.

cumulus cloud An everyday meaning of this word is "heap, pile, accumulation." This cloud looks like many fluffy mounds or heaps one over the other.

cirrus cloud In biology, cirrus means "a threadlike, flexible appendage of an animal, such as a feeler or tentacle." Students can see wispy curls in the picture of cirrus clouds.

fog The word *fog* comes from a Danish word meaning "driving snow" Thick ground fog may resemble piles of snow on the ground.

Read to Learn

Main Idea Water vapor and ice form clouds that produce precipitation.

How Do Clouds Form?

What has to happen for a cloud to form? Clouds are made up of tiny water droplets or ice crystals. The air is filled with water vapor. When the air is cooled, the water vapor condenses. That is, the water molecules clump together around dust and other particles in the air. They form droplets of water.

Clouds look different depending on what they are made of. Water-droplet clouds tend to have sharp, well-defined edges. If the cloud is very thick, it may look gray, or even black. That's because sunlight is unable to pass through. Ice-crystal clouds tend to have fuzzy, less distinct edges. They also look whiter.

All clouds form in the troposphere. There are three basic cloud forms. Stratus clouds form in blanketlike layers. Cumulus clouds are puffy clouds that appear to rise up from a flat bottom. Cirrus clouds form at very high altitudes out of ice crystals and have a wispy, featherlike shape. If rain or snow falls from a cloud, the term *nimbo* or *nimbus*—for "rain"—is added to the cloud's name.

Clouds are further grouped into families by height and form. They are low clouds, middle clouds, high clouds, and clouds that develop upward—clouds of vertical development. Cumulonimbus clouds develop upward. These clouds bring thunderstorms.

D 24

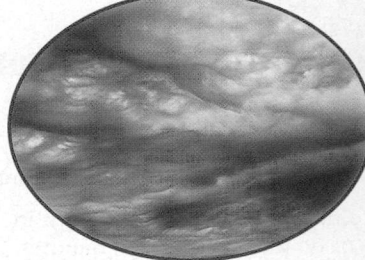
Stratus clouds

Cumulus clouds

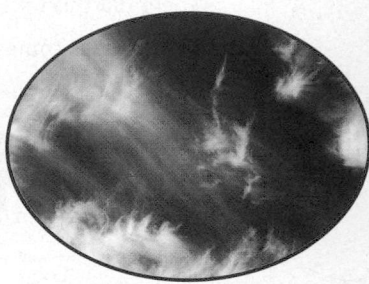
Cirrus clouds

They can start as low clouds and reach up to the highest clouds. If moist air at ground level cools, a cloud can form right there. A cloud at ground level is called fog.

▷ **What are three basic cloud forms?**
stratus—blanketlike clouds; cumulus—puffy clouds; cirrus—featherlike clouds

---

Lesson Outline

Name _____ Date _____

Lesson Outline lesson 3

Clouds and Precipitation

Fill in the blanks. 📖 Reading Skill: Main Idea - questions 2, 5

How Do Clouds Form?

1. Clouds are made up of __water droplets__ or __ice crystals__

2. All clouds form when the air cools and water vapor __condenses__ around dust and other particles.

3. A thick, sharp-edged gray cloud is probably made of __water droplets__ not __ice crystals__

4. All clouds form in the lower atmosphere, or __troposphere__

5. The three basic cloud forms are:
   a. blanketlike layers, or __stratus__
   b. puffy, flat-based __cumulus__, and
   c. high-altitude, feathery __cirrus__

6. The prefix "nimbo-," or nimbus, as in nimbostratus, refers to a cloud that brings __rain__ or __snow__

7. A cloud at ground level is called __fog__

What Is Precipitation?

8. Any form of water particles that falls to the ground from the atmosphere is __precipitation__

9. Precipitation occurs when water droplets or ice crystals join together and become __too heavy__

10. A dust particle is the __nucleus__ around which water molecules condense.

11. The type of precipitation formed from ice crystals that occurs when the ground temperature is cold is __snow__

12. When cloud droplets collect and freeze around an ice crystal, and the process repeats over and over, __hail__ is formed.

Unit D - Weather and Climate   Use with textbook pages D22–D31   **203**

Reading in Science Resources, p. 203

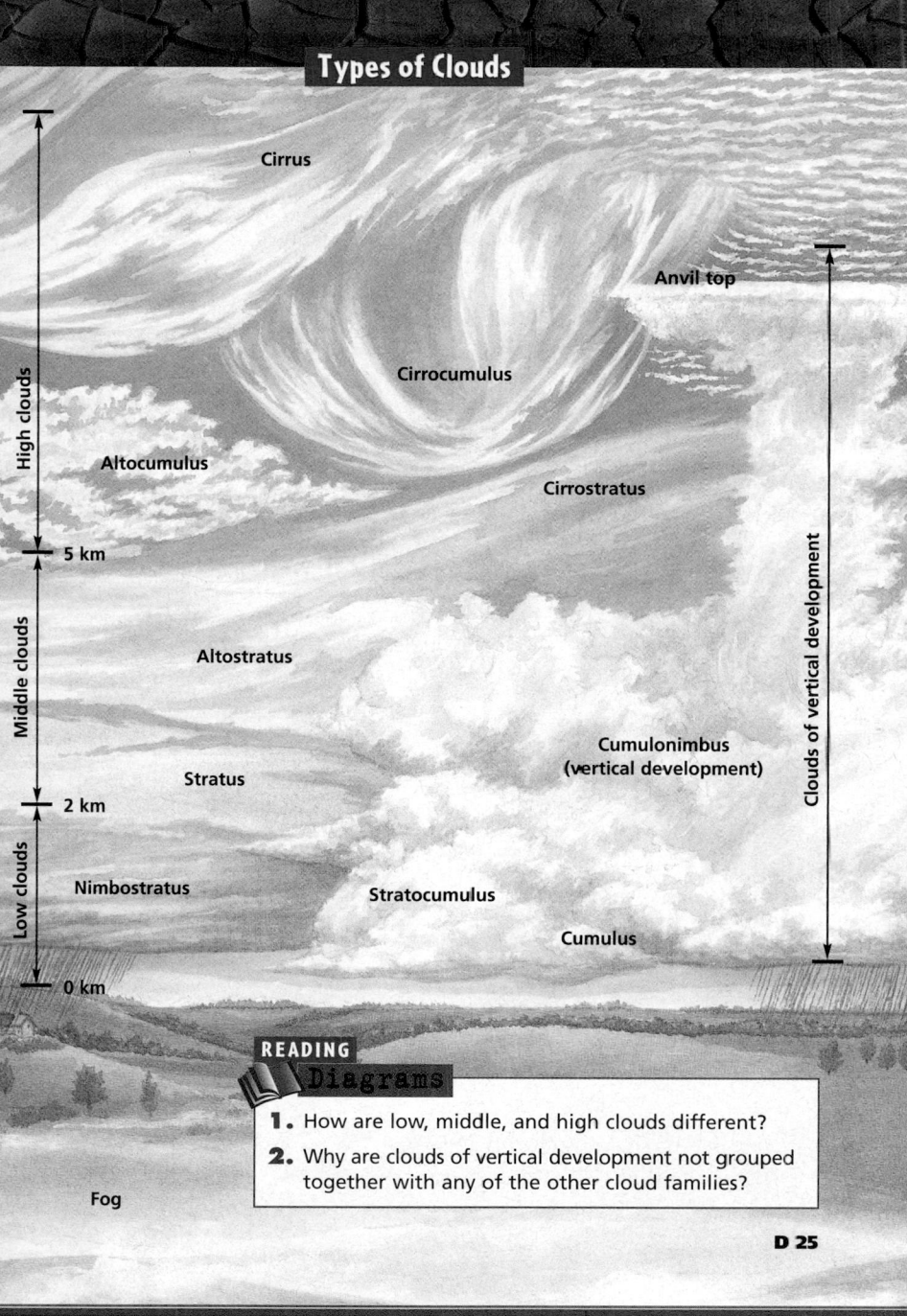

Types of Clouds

High clouds

Cirrus

Anvil top

Cirrocumulus

Altocumulus

Cirrostratus

— 5 km

Middle clouds

Altostratus

Clouds of vertical development

Cumulonimbus
(vertical development)

Stratus

— 2 km

Low clouds

Nimbostratus

Stratocumulus

Cumulus

— 0 km

Fog

D 25

Using the Illustrations
Encourage students to compare and contrast the different kinds of clouds. Ask:

■ **How are cumulus, cirrus, and stratus clouds alike? How are they different?** (They are all formed from water in one of its forms. Stratus clouds form in blanket-like layers, cumulus are flat-bottomed and globular, and cirrus clouds are wispy and feather-like.)

READING
Diagrams

1. Low clouds have bases that are lower than 2 km above Earth; middle clouds have bases that are between 2 and 6 km above Earth; high clouds have bases that are higher than 6 km above Earth.

2. because their bases are usually only about 1 km above Earth, but their tops can extend beyond 20 km in altitude.

Technology

■ Visual Aid Transparency 22:
Types of Clouds

Science Background

Cloud Classification
The English chemist Luke Howard (1722–1864) created the basic system of cloud classification. Though he didn't understand how the different kinds of clouds formed, he assigned them Latin names based on their appearance. Cirrus clouds, for example, resemble curls of hair, while cumulus clouds look like heaps and stratus clouds lie flat. Still in use today, these categories now have further subdivisions.

What Is Precipitation?

Before Reading
Have students try to answer the red question at the top of the page.

Using the Illustrations
Ask:

- **Which two types of precipitation are the most similar? Why?** (Rain and drizzle are the most similar because they are both made up of water droplets that form when cloud droplets collide and combine.)

- **How are sleet, snow, and hail alike? How do they differ?** (They are all made of ice. Sleet is made of clear pellets of ice, snow is made up of ice crystals, and hail is layered balls of ice.)

READING
Diagrams

1. Rain falls as liquid; snow, sleet, and hail are solids, because they fall as ice.

2. Rain forms when cloud droplets collide and combine; sleet and hail both form from cloud droplets that freeze (though hail is thrust upward so that more layers form).

▶ After Reading
Have students answer the red question in the student book as **ongoing assessment**.

Developing Vocabulary

precipitation To reinforce the meaning of the word, have students list or describe any form of water particles that fall from the atmosphere, that is, hail, rain, snow.

Technology

- Visual Aid Transparency 23:
  Types of Precipitation

What Is Precipitation?

How do rain and snow form and fall? **Precipitation** is any form of water particles that falls from the atmosphere and reaches the ground. Precipitation can be liquid (rain) or solid (such as snow).

Clouds are made up of tiny water droplets or ice crystals—only about $\frac{1}{50}$ of a millimeter across. These tiny particles are so light that they remain "hanging" in the air. This is why many clouds do not form precipitation.

Precipitation occurs when cloud droplets or ice crystals join together and become heavy enough to fall. They clump around particles of dust in the air. Each particle is like a *nucleus* that the water molecules condense around. The chart shows the different types of precipitation and how they form.

▶ **When does precipitation occur?**
when cloud droplets become heavy enough to fall

READING
Diagrams

1. Classify the types of precipitation into two groups—solids and liquids.

2. Which types of precipitation form in similar ways?

Types of Precipitation

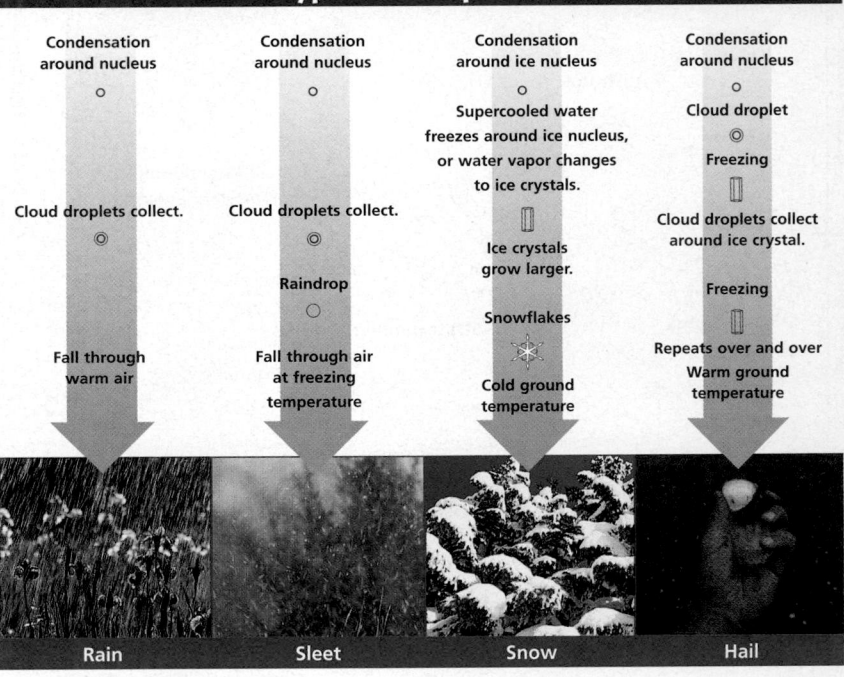

| Rain | Sleet | Snow | Hail |

Rain: Condensation around nucleus · Cloud droplets collect. · Fall through warm air

Sleet: Condensation around nucleus · Cloud droplets collect. · Raindrop · Fall through air at freezing temperature

Snow: Condensation around ice nucleus · Supercooled water freezes around ice nucleus, or water vapor changes to ice crystals. · Ice crystals grow larger. · Snowflakes · Cold ground temperature

Hail: Condensation around nucleus · Cloud droplet · Freezing · Cloud droplets collect around ice crystal. · Freezing · Repeats over and over · Warm ground temperature

D 26

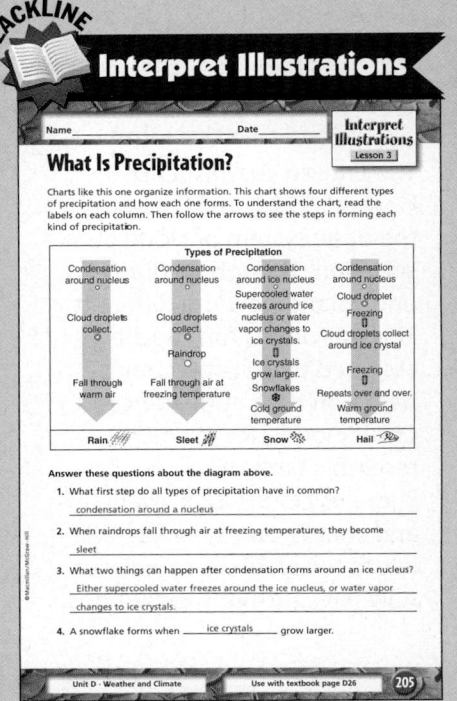

BLACKLINE
Interpret Illustrations

Name_____ Date_____

Interpret Illustrations Lesson 3

What Is Precipitation?

Charts like this one organize information. This chart shows four different types of precipitation and how each one forms. To understand the chart, read the labels on each column. Then follow the arrows to see the steps in forming each kind of precipitation.

Answer these questions about the diagram above.

1. What first step do all types of precipitation have in common?
   condensation around a nucleus

2. When raindrops fall through air at freezing temperatures, they become
   sleet

3. What two things can happen after condensation forms around an ice nucleus?
   Either supercooled water freezes around the ice nucleus, or water vapor changes to ice crystals.

4. A snowflake forms when ___ice crystals___ grow larger.

Unit D · Weather and Climate   Use with textbook page D26   **205**

Reading in Science Resources, p. 205

Are Cloud Type and Precipitation Related?

Do certain kinds of clouds give certain kinds of precipitation? Yes.

- In tall clouds there is more chance for droplets to run into one another and combine, making larger raindrops.

- Precipitation from large cumulus clouds is often heavy rain or snow showers that don't last too long.

- Precipitation from stratus clouds is usually long lasting, with smaller drops of rain or snowflakes.

- Clouds with great vertical development hold a lot of water. These clouds are very *turbulent*, or violent. Their tops often reach heights where it is below freezing. They often produce great downpours. They also sometimes produce *hail*. Hail is pellets or lumps of ice.

  These clouds have updrafts—strong winds that move up inside. Hail forms when updrafts in these huge clouds hurl ice pellets upward again and again. As the pellets fall, they become coated with water. As they rise, the water freezes into an icy outer shell. This process usually happens over and over, adding more and more layers to the hailstones. The more violent the updrafts, the bigger the hailstone can get before it falls to the ground.

READING Main Idea
What kind of cloud can produce hail? Why?
Clouds of vertical development; they have updrafts— winds that can hurl ice crystals upward again and again, creating hailstones.

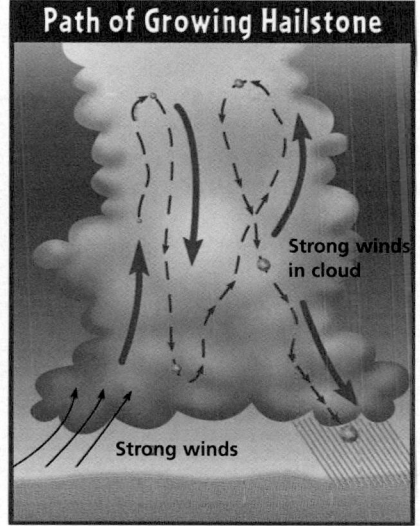
Path of Growing Hailstone
Strong winds in cloud
Strong winds

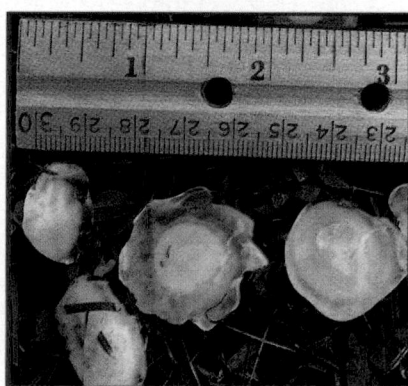

Hailstones form in layers and can sometimes grow very large. Hailstorms can be very dangerous.

D 27

Are Cloud Type and Precipitation Related?

Before Reading
Have students try to answer the red question at the top of the page.

Developing the Main Idea
Ask:

- **How does the size of a cloud affect the amount of precipitation that it can form?** (Encourage speculation; students might respond that larger clouds can hold more water, so they can produce more precipitation.)

- **What type of precipitation do stratus clouds usually produce?** (Longer-lasting steady rain with small drops. The cloud shape does not cause the type of precipitation. Other factors cause the cloud shape and precipitation.)

- **What type of clouds tend to produce hail? Why?** (Hail tends to form in clouds with great vertical development. These clouds are very tall, with the tops often reaching above the point where water freezes. Their turbulence can force pellets of ice up again and again, forming hail.)

▶**After Reading**
Have students answer the red question in the student book as **ongoing assessment**.

Reading MiniLesson

Main Idea and Supporting Details

Develop Discuss with students how a diagram title usually states the main idea and supporting details are illustrated in the diagram. Review the diagram on page D27 and note how the diagram labels and arrows explain how, where, and when a hailstone grows.

Practice Have students illustrate the main idea of the relationship between "cloud type and precipitation" by writing those words in one large circle, then drawing a tall cloud, a large cumulus cloud, stratus cloud, and a cumulonimbus cloud around it. Inside the cloud shapes, students should describe the precipitation from that type of cloud.

Science Background

Hail Damage
Hailstones are usually small, with a diameter below 0.4 inches (10 mm). Sometimes, however, they are much larger, and very destructive. On May 8, 1926, baseball-sized hailstones caused $2 million worth of damage in Dallas, Texas in just 15 minutes. During a 1979 football game in Fort Collins, Colorado, grapefruit-sized hail pounded the field. Luckily, the players were wearing helmets, but a spectator died from a skull fracture.

What Is the Water Cycle?

Before Reading
Have students try to answer the red question at the top of the page.

Using the Illustrations
Direct students' attention to the diagram of the water cycle. Ask:

- **What are the processes involved in the water cycle?** (evaporation, condensation, and precipitation)

Remind students that plants give off water by transpiration. Ask:

- **How is water released into the air by transpiration?** (Water is released to the air as a gas; water vapor is added to the air.)

READING

Diagrams

Some of the water evaporates back into the atmosphere, some of it runs off the surface into rivers and streams, and much of it seeps into the ground.

What Is the Water Cycle?

When precipitation reaches Earth's surface, it doesn't just disappear. Some of it evaporates right back into the atmosphere. Some of it runs off the surface into rivers and streams. We call this water *runoff*.

Much of it seeps into the ground. We call this water *groundwater*. Groundwater collects in tiny holes, or pores, in soil and rocks. Groundwater can often seep down through soil and rocks when the pores are interconnected. It can fill up all the pores in a layer of rock below the surface. Much of this water eventually moves back to the rivers and then to lakes or oceans.

Earth's water moves from place to place through the processes of evaporation, condensation, and precipitation. Condensation and precipitation take water out of Earth's atmosphere.

READING
Diagrams

What happens to precipitation once it reaches Earth's surface?

The Water Cycle

Condensation the process in which a gas is changed to a liquid

Transpiration the process by which plant leaves release water into the air

Evaporation the process in which a liquid changes directly to a gas

D 28

Evaporation puts water back into the atmosphere. This complex web of changes is called the water cycle.

The water cycle is the continuous movement of water between Earth's surface and the air, changing from liquid to gas to liquid. The diagram shows the many different paths water can take into and out of the atmosphere in the water cycle.

▷ **What are the main processes of the water cycle?**

evaporation, condensation, precipitation

Precipitation any form of water particles that falls to Earth's surface

Groundwater water that seeps into pores in soil and rocks

Runoff water that runs off Earth's solid surface

D 29

Interpret Illustrations

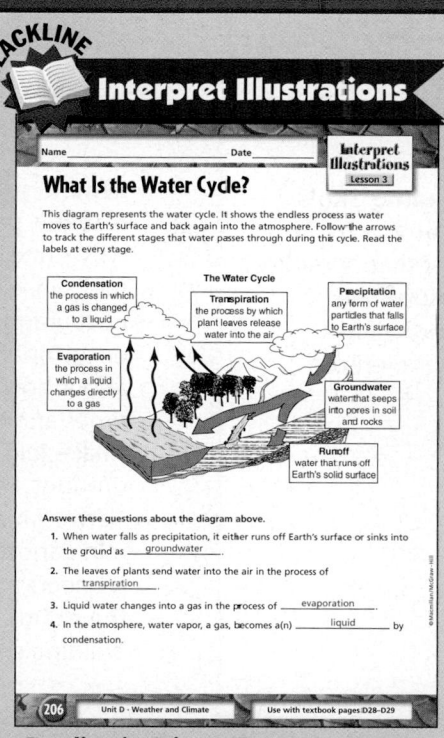

Reading in Science Resources, p. 206

Developing the Main Idea
Ask:

■ **What happens to water in rivers, lakes, and oceans?** (Heat from the sun evaporates some of it, adding water vapor to the air.)

■ **What is the next step in the water cycle?** (As the warm air holding water rises, it cools; water condenses.)

■ **What happens when water is returned to Earth's surface as precipitation?** (Some runs off into rivers and streams, some seeps into the ground.)

■ **What eventually happens to groundwater?** (It eventually moves back to rivers, lakes, or oceans. It can cycle again, entering the air by evaporation, falling to Earth as precipitation, and so on.)

Developing Vocabulary

water cycle A *cycle* is something that is continuous; that repeats itself. In this cycle, water changes state from liquid to gas to liquid and back again. Have students keep this in mind as they apply the terms *evaporation*, *condensation*, and *precipitation* to the water cycle.

▶ **After Reading**
Have students answer the red question in the student book as **ongoing assessment**.

Technology

■ Visual Aid Transparencies 9–12: *Building a Water Cycle*

How Do You Record How Cloudy It Is?

Before Reading
Have students try to answer the red question at the top right of the page.

Developing the Main Idea
On the chalkboard, draw the circular symbols for sunny, partly cloudy, mostly cloudy, and overcast. Ask students to describe the amount of cloud cover for each. Ask:

Why do you think scientists use symbols like these to describe weather? (Symbols are a sort of universal language that can be understood by all scientists, no matter where they're from.)

▶After Reading
Have students answer the red question in the student book as **ongoing assessment**.

Materials thermometer, $\frac{1}{2}$ cup cold water in a foam cup, 1 cup warm water, 5-cm-square piece of cotton cloth, rubber band

Science Process Skills *observe, infer*

Resources Activity Resources pp. 133–134

Be Careful! Tell students to be careful when handling hot water.

Step 1 Remind students to handle thermometers with care to prevent breakage and to avoid touching them should breakage occur.

Step 5 The temperature of the wet cloth drops. When the cloth is touched, it feels cool.

Step 6 Because water evaporates more slowly when the air is moist and more rapidly on a dry day, the difference between the two temperatures would be greater on a dry day than on a humid day.

FOR SCHOOL OR HOME

Feel the Humidity

1. **Observe** Use a thermometer to record the air temperature.

2. Put the thermometer in cold water. Slowly add warm water until the water temperature matches the air temperature.

3. Wrap a 5-cm-square piece of old cotton cloth around the bulb of the thermometer. Gently hold it with a rubber band. Dampen the cloth in the water.

4. **Observe** Gently wave the thermometer in the air. Record temperatures every 30 seconds for 3 minutes.

5. **Infer** What happened to the temperature of the wet cloth? How does the cloth feel? Explain.

6. **Infer** If you try this experiment on a day that is humid and on a day that is dry will you get the same results? Explain.

D 30

How Do You Record How Cloudy It Is?

As you observe the weather each day, you might wish to record the types of clouds you see in the sky. You can use the charts in this lesson to indicate the cloud family and the types of clouds.

Try to estimate the cloud cover—that is, the amount of the sky covered by clouds. Use the terms *clear, scattered clouds, partly cloudy, mostly cloudy,* or *overcast* to describe cloud cover.

One way to record cloud cover is to make a weather station model. Start by drawing a circle for each day. An empty circle means "clear skies." A fully shaded circle means "completely overcast." Portions of a circle are shaded to show different amounts of cloud cover.

Precipitation is measured with a rain gauge. You can make a simple rain gauge from an empty coffee can. Place it outside, open end up, away from buildings or trees. When the precipitation stops, measure its depth in the can. Keep track of the type of precipitation and how much falls.

▷ **What are the terms used to record cloud cover?** clear, scattered clouds, partly cloudy, mostly cloudy and overcast

◯	Clear
●	Overcast
◔	Scattered clouds
◑	Partly cloudy
◕	Mostly cloudy

Symbols are used to show cloud cover on a weather station model.

SCIENCE Reading Strategy

Cause and Effect

Developing Reading Skills
Have students summarize in writing the effect that humidity has on evaporation. (The greater the humidity, the slower the evaporation can occur.) **Summarize**

Cultural Perspective

Making Rain
Remind students that until recently, people did not know why some clouds produced rain, while others did not. Encourage students to use encyclopedias to learn more about how people in different times and cultures have tried to "make rain" during times of drought. For example, many Native American groups held rain dances, while American pioneers attempted to induce the clouds to release rain by building smoky fires.

Why It Matters

If you ever had a baseball game rained out, you know how rain can ruin your day.

Rain may ruin your plans for a day, and flooding can sometimes cause disasters. However, rain is vital for life on Earth. Rain helps crops grow. That means food for you and others. Rain helps build the amount of water in wells and water-collecting areas, such as reservoirs. If you ever had a drought in your area, a time when there is little or no precipitation, you know how scarce water can be.

Hail, on the other hand, can ruin entire crops. It can also damage cars and buildings.

Think and Write

1. How do clouds form?

2. What are some different types of precipitation? Why are there different types?

3. What are the main processes that show how liquid water changes in the water cycle? List them in order.

4. How can you measure and describe the amount of precipitation and cloud cover on a given day?

5. **Critical Thinking** "Sun showers" are sudden rainfalls on a sunny day. How can a sun shower happen?

L·I·N·K·S

LITERATURE LINK

Read *The Great Johnstown Flood*, the story of the storm that destroyed a town. When you finish reading, think about how you would prepare for a flood. Try the activities at the end of the book.

MATH LINK

Calculate your accuracy. Observe the clouds in your area each day for a week. Predict the weather based on the precipitation those clouds are likely to produce. Keep a record of how accurate your predictions are. At the end of the week, calculate—in percent—your accuracy.

SOCIAL STUDIES LINK

Research Inuit words. The Inuit have more than 20 different words for snow. Research and write a report on why you think they use so many.

TECHNOLOGY LINK

Science Newsroom CD-ROM Choose *On the Vapor Trail* to learn more about how warm, moist air reacts when it cools.

At the Computer Visit **www.mhscience02.com** for more links.

D 31

Informal Assessment

Easy/Average Have small groups create word search puzzles using lesson vocabulary words. Have students write clues describing the words hidden in a grid of letters. Allow time for groups to exchange and solve the puzzles.

Challenge Provide students with jars, soil, water, stones, and plants to create models of the water cycle by building terrariums. Have them describe, in writing, the components of their models, as well as the events that occur.

Answers to Think and Write

1. Clouds form by water vapor in the air condensing into droplets. (p. D24)

2. Different types of precipitation form in different conditions. Cold air forms sleet and snow; cold turbulent clouds form hail; and rain and drizzle fall as liquids. (pp. D26–D27)

3. Water changes in the water cycle through evaporation, condensation, and precipitation. (pp. D28–D29)

4. Precipitation is measured with a rain gauge; cloud cover is described by the amount of sky that is covered by clouds. (p. D30)

5. **Critical Thinking** Sun showers can happen if cloud cover is so low that the Sun shines between the rain clouds. (pp. D24–D26, D30)

Summarize

Check students' understanding by having them write a brief summary of the lesson in their own words.

LITERATURE LINK

Have students read the Grade-Level Science Book, *The Great Johnstown Flood*. Additional books to read can be found on TE p. D1·b.

MATH LINK

Students should record their predictions in the same notebook each day. A description of actual weather should follow each prediction. Percent correct is calculated using this formula: Days Correct/Total Number of Days Predicted $\times$ 100% = Percent Correct. For example, $\frac{5}{7} \times 100\% = 71.4\%$ correct predictions.

SOCIAL STUDIES LINK

Students' research should focus on snow as a constant and integral part of Inuit life. The areas in which the Inuit dwell are covered in snow for much of the year. Different types of snow present various kinds of conditions and are the result of different weather conditions. Some examples of Inuit words for snow are: "snow" (in general): *aput;* "snow" (like salt): *pukak;* "soft deep snow": *mauja;* "soft snow": *massak;* "watery snow": *mangokpok*

Science, Technology, and Society

Objective

■ Describe causes and effects of floods.

Build on Prior Knowledge
Ask:

■ **What are the advantages of flood prevention? The disadvantages?** (Restraining water protects buildings and other structures from damage, but prevents the distribution of rich, fertile soil that is caused by flooding.)

Flood: Good News or Bad?

Developing the Main Idea
When students have read the article, ask:

■ **What did ancient Egyptians think caused the annual flooding of the Nile? How did their beliefs differ from what actually occurs?** (Ancient Egyptians believed that great rains near the source of the Nile caused flooding. Actually, the rains originate in Ethiopia, where rain-filled streams join to form a river that carries water to the Nile, causing flooding in Egypt.)

■ **How has the annual flood been controlled?** (A high dam holds back the water, forming a large lake.)

■ **What are the benefits of the high dam at Aswan? The drawbacks?** (The dam prevents flooding, so that structures stay in place, and farmers can plant two crops each year rather than one. On the other hand, farmers must now use fertilizer, fish that were once common are now gone, and snails that thrive in the now-slow water cause the spread of a serious disease.)

Science, Technology,

Flood: Good News or Bad?

Can you imagine a flood being good news? It was to many ancient Egyptians living near the Nile River. They looked forward to its annual summer flood. Land that was flooded was better for crops!

No one knew for sure why the flood came. Some people believed that great rains fell near the source of the Nile to start the flood. Much of the water actually comes from rains that fall in the mountains of Ethiopia.

Ethiopia has many mountains over 4,000 meters (13,000 feet) tall. In June the monsoons blow from the South Atlantic over the rain forests of Africa. When the winds reach the mountains of Ethiopia, giant rain clouds let loose their water in great thunderstorms. Rain-filled mountain streams join to form a great river. The river carries the water to the Nile. By July the water reaches Egypt and produces the flood.

Summer winds

MEDITERRANEAN SEA

EGYPT

SAUDI ARABIA

NILE RIVER

RED SEA

SUDAN

ETHIOPIA

D 32

Reading Strategy

Sequence of Events
Draw students' attention to the map on this page. Encourage them to list the sequence of events in the movement of the June–July winds that result in flooding rains. Have them reread the last paragraph on p. D32 to be sure they have the details correct. **Linguistic**

Cultural Perspective

Mississippi Delta
Point out to students that despite the problems caused by flooding, people have historically tended to settle in areas where flooding is common in order to satisfy their need for fertile land for their crops. One such region is the Mississippi Delta in the United States. Encourage interested students to use encyclopedias to learn about the crops produced, and the flooding that occurs, in the Mississippi Delta, comparing this region with the Nile delta.

and Society — NATIONAL GEOGRAPHIC

Aswan Dam, Egypt

Today the flood waters are stopped soon after they reach Egypt. A high dam holds back the water to form a great lake. The good news is that buildings on the shore are no longer swept away. Farmers no longer depend on floods to plant one crop each year. Now they have water to plant during summer and winter.

Stopping the flood has changed the environment, and that's bad news. The flood kept the fields fertile; but now farmers must use fertilizer. The Mediterranean Sea was nourished by mud from the Nile. Now fish that were common are gone, and a serious disease is spread by snails thriving in the Nile's slow waters.

What Did I Learn?

1. Where did the Nile flooding start?

   A in the Red Sea
   B in the Mediterranean Sea
   C in the mountains of Ethiopia
   D in Saudi Arabia

2. Stopping the Nile flooding

   F kept the fields fertile
   G increased the fish population
   H killed off the snails
   J changed the environment

AT THE COMPUTER Visit www.mhscience02.com to learn more about floods

D 33

■ **Was it important to gain an understanding of the source of the flooding before trying to prevent it? Explain.** (Knowing the source of flooding can help people decide where to build a dam. While it wasn't really necessary to know that the rains originate in Ethiopia, it was necessary to build the dam at a location far enough upriver to prevent the flooding.)

■ **Why might the people regret that the dam was built? Why might they be grateful for it?** (Flooding enriched the soil, making the use of fertilizers unnecessary. On the other hand, property is no longer destroyed by floodwaters.)

Test Prep: What Did I Learn?

1. C

2. J

Summarize

Check students' understanding by having them write a brief summary of the magazine in their own words.

Science Background

Very Early Dams

One of the earliest dams designed to prevent one kind of flooding was a predecessor of the Suez Canal. Built by Ptolemy II, the dam prevented water from the Red Sea from overflowing into the Mediterranean Sea. The earliest dam for pure flood control, however, was built by Chryses of Alexandria in A.D. 550.

Near the eastern border of the Roman Empire, this dam consisted of an arch pointing upstream in a small river. In contrast, the regular, extensive flooding of the Nile River was not controlled until the high dam at Aswan was built in the 1960s.

LESSON 4 — Air Pressure and Wind

Objectives

- Explore what causes air pressure to change.
- Explain how air pressure is related to winds.
- Describe the paths of winds in global wind zones.
- Identify how wind is measured and recorded at weather stations.

Resources

- Activity Resources, pp. 135–139
- Reading in Science Resources, pp. 209–214
- Vocabulary Cards
- Reading Aid Transparency D4
- Grade-Level Science Book, *The Sky-Watchers*
- School to Home Activities, p. 28

Build on Prior Knowledge

Have students discuss what they know about how wind affects things. Turn on a fan. Then ask:

- **What effect does the movement of air have?** (Possible answers: cools the air; moves light things such as paper)
- **What effect might the air movement have if it were ten times stronger?** (Possible answers: could knock things over, blow them away, or cause other damage)

1 Get Ready

Developing the Main Idea

Have students discuss how different places have different air pressure. These differences in air pressure are the result of variations in altitude or elevation above Earth's surface, air temperature, and the amount of water vapor.

LESSON 4 — Air Pressure and Wind

Vocabulary

wind, D38
convection cell, D38
sea breeze, D39
land breeze, D39
Coriolis effect, D40
isobar, D42
weather vane, D44
anemometer, D44

Get Ready

What makes the air move? What causes wind? Winds make these kites fly. Some winds move so fast and powerfully, they can knock down trees or even lift trucks into the air. Some winds can be so gentle, they hardly ruffle your hair. Air moves from one place to another because of differences in air pressure. What causes these differences?

Process Skill

You use variables when you identify and separate things in an experiment that can be changed or controlled.

D 34

Science Background

Human Bodies and Air Pressure

Air pressure is the weight of all the air above a certain place pressing down. The average column of air above Earth exerts 106 dynes of pressure per sq cm. Our bodies contain air that exerts pressure outward equal to the atmospheric air pressure exerted on our bodies.

Explore Activity

What Can Change Air Pressure?

Materials

plastic jar with hole in bottom

plastic sandwich bag

rubber band

masking tape

Procedure

1 **Make a Model** Set up a jar-and-bag system as shown. Make sure the masking tape covers the hole in the jar. Have a partner place both hands on the jar and hold it firmly. Reach in and slowly pull up on the bottom of the bag. Describe what happens.

2 **Experiment** Pull the small piece of tape off the hole in the bottom of the jar. Repeat step 1. Push in on the bag. Record your results.

3 **Observe** Place some small bits of paper on the table. Hold the jar close to the table. Point the hole toward the bits of paper. Pull up on the bag, and observe and record what happens.

4 **Experiment** Do just the opposite. Push the bag back into the jar. What happened?

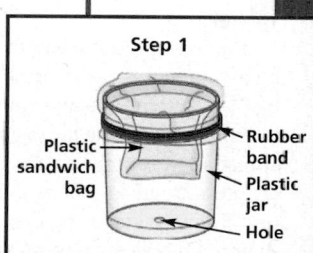

Step 1

Plastic sandwich bag — Rubber band — Plastic jar — Hole

Drawing Conclusions

1 **Observe** What differences did you observe with the hole taped and with the tape removed?

2 **Infer** Explain what happened each time you pushed the bag back into the jar. How does this model show air pressure changes?

3 **Going Further: Use Variables** Will the model work the same with paper clips? Bits of cotton? Make a prediction, and test it.

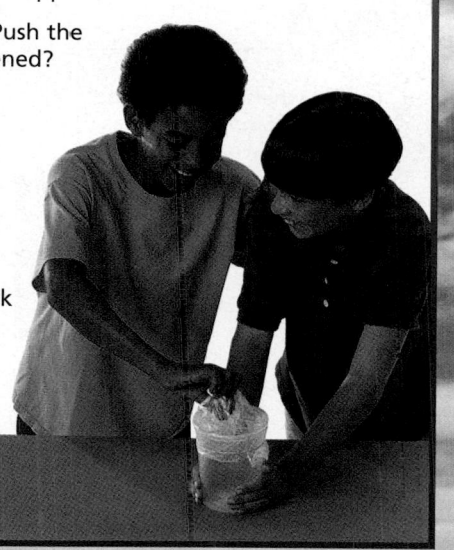

D 35

Alternative Explore Activity

Materials large suction cup

Pushing Air Demonstrate differences in air pressure by pressing a large suction cup or "plumber's helper" against the board. Point out to students that pushing in on the suction cup forces air out of the cup. When the rubber (or plastic) springs back, it causes a low pressure under the cup. The higher air pressure on the outside of the cup makes it stick to the board. **Spatial**

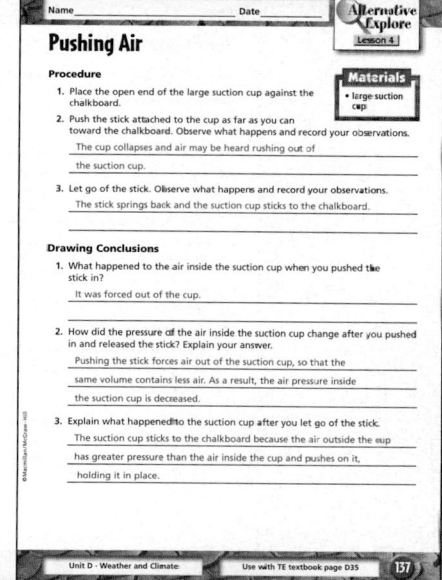

Name_____ Date_____

Alternative Explore Lesson 4

Pushing Air

Procedure

Materials
• large suction cup

1. Place the open end of the large suction cup against the chalkboard.

2. Push the stick attached to the cup as far as you can toward the chalkboard. Observe what happens and record your observations.
   The cup collapses and air may be heard rushing out of the suction cup.

3. Let go of the stick. Observe what happens and record your observations.
   The stick springs back and the suction cup sticks to the chalkboard.

Drawing Conclusions

1. What happened to the air inside the suction cup when you pushed the stick in?
   It was forced out of the cup.

2. How did the pressure of the air inside the suction cup change after you pushed in and released the stick? Explain your answer.
   Pushing the stick forces air out of the suction cup, so that the same volume contains less air. As a result, the air pressure inside the suction cup is decreased.

3. Explain what happened to the suction cup after you let go of the stick.
   The suction cup sticks to the chalkboard because the air outside the cup has greater pressure than the air inside the cup and pushes on it, holding it in place.

Unit D · Weather and Climate   Use with TE textbook page D35   **137**

Activity Resources, p. 137

Explore Activity

What Can Change Air Pressure?

Science Process Skills *make a model, experiment, observe, infer, use variables*

Resources Activity Resources, pp. 135–136

Pacing 30–40 minutes

Grouping pairs

Procedure

1 When an attempt is made to pull up the bag, it cannot be done successfully.

2 The bag can be pulled up. When the bag is pushed in, air moves out of the hole in the jar.

3 The bits of paper are drawn to the hole.

4 The paper bits are blown away by the air leaving the jar.

Answers to Drawing Conclusions

1 When the hole was taped, air pressure inside the bag kept it from being pulled out of the jar. When the hole was opened, air was able to move into the jar.

2 When the bag was pushed into the jar, air was pushed out of the bottom of the jar. The air was being squeezed into a smaller space so it escaped out the hole. The model shows that volume affects air pressure; when more space is available, pressure is lower, but when air is confined in a smaller volume, air pressure increases.

3 Students might predict that some materials will be blown by the air leaving the jar.

Inquiry Students can ask their own questions to explore, such as whether air temperature affects air pressure. (Warm air has lower pressure than cold air.)

Technology

■ When time is short, preview the activity with the **Explore Activity Video.**

How Can Air Pressure Change?

Before Reading
Have students try to answer the red question at the top of the page.

Developing the Main Idea
Ask:

- **How do you increase the volume inside the bag? How does increasing the volume in the bag-jar system affect air pressure?** (Pulling up on the bag increases the volume. The amount of air inside stays the same. It spreads out into a larger volume, so pressure inside becomes less.)

- **How does height above sea level affect air pressure?** (At sea level, molecules are more densely packed than higher above sea level. Thus, air pressure is greater at sea level than above.)

- **How does temperature affect molecules of air? How does this affect air pressure?** (Warming causes the molecules to speed up and spread out. It lowers air pressure.)

READING
Diagrams

As you push in on the bag, the volume decreases and air pressure increases.

Read to Learn

Main Idea Differences in air pressure on Earth's surface cause wind.

How Can Air Pressure Change?

Many factors can affect the air pressure of a region. Here are some of those factors.

Volume

Pulling up on the bag in the diagram below increases the volume inside the bag-jar system. The amount of air inside stays the same. The air inside the jar spreads out into the larger volume. The air pressure inside the bag-jar becomes less. The outside air pushes in harder than the inside air pushes out. That extra force pushing in is what you pull against as you pull up on the bag.

Height Above Earth's Surface

Air pressure depends on the weight of its molecules pressing down on a given area. Molecules are closer together, or more dense, at sea level than high in the atmosphere. Denser air weighs more than an equal volume of less dense air and pushes down harder. That is why air pressure is higher at sea level than high in the atmosphere.

Temperature

Air pressure also depends on temperature. When air is heated, its molecules speed up. The faster-moving molecules move around more. They

An Air Pressure Model

READING
Diagrams

Explain what happens to the air pressure inside the jar as you push down on the bag.

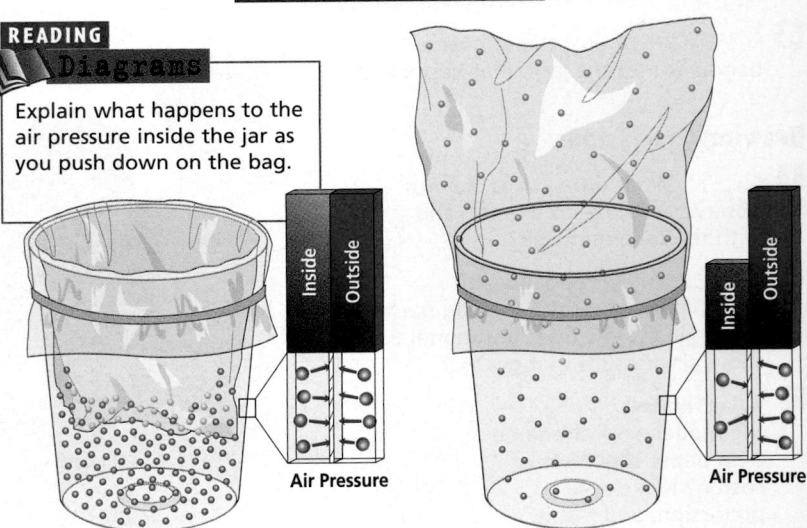

Air Pressure   Air Pressure

D 36

Interpret Illustrations

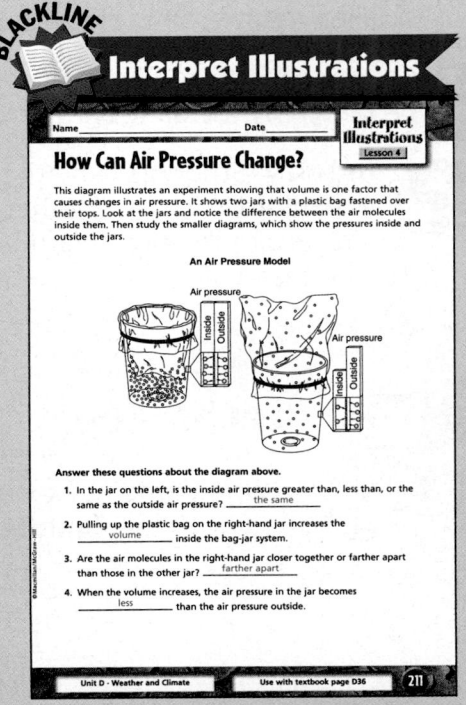

How Can Air Pressure Change?

Reading in Science Resources, p. 211

Lesson Outline

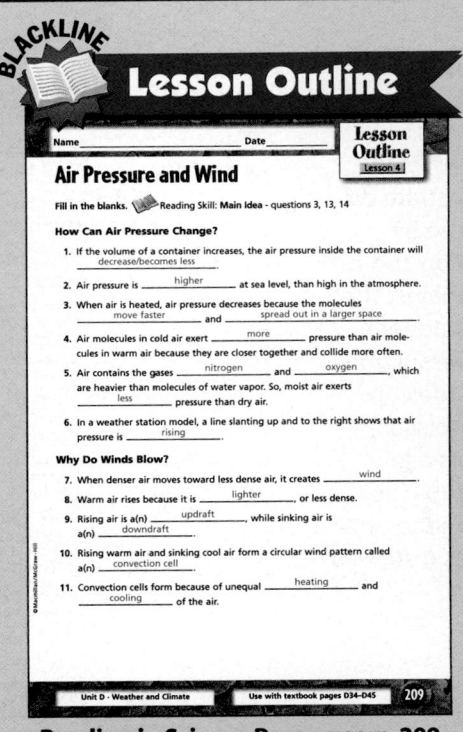

Air Pressure and Wind

Reading in Science Resources, p. 209

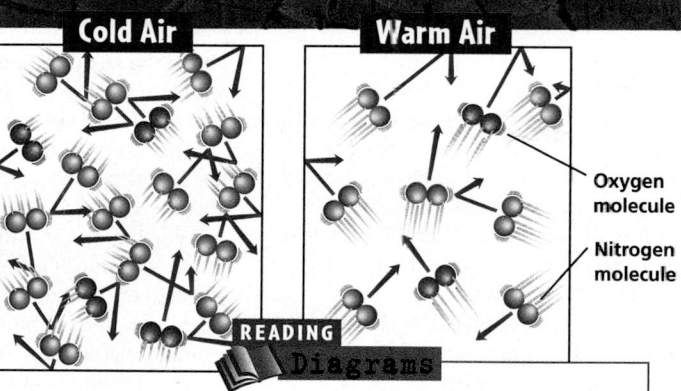

Cold Air	Warm Air

Even though the molecules are moving slower and collide with less force, the cold air on the left exerts more pressure because its closely spaced molecules collide much more frequently.

Oxygen molecule

Nitrogen molecule

READING
Diagrams

What differences do you see between the pictures for cold air and warm air?

spread out into a larger space. The same volume of air weighs less, and the pressure decreases. What do you think happens when air is cooled?

Amount of Water Vapor

Air is a mixture of nitrogen, oxygen, and other gases. Adding water vapor to air also affects air pressure. Molecules of oxygen or nitrogen are heavier than molecules of water vapor. Light molecules exert less pressure because they weigh less. In moist air lighter water vapor molecules take the place of heavier oxygen and nitrogen molecules. Moist air exerts less pressure than dry air.

You can now enter two more bits of information on your weather station model. To the upper right, place the air pressure reading in millibars. Right below this number, you may wish to put a short line. This line tells how air pressure is changing at that station.

- A line slanting to the upper right indicates the air pressure is rising (a rising barometer). A rising barometer may indicate fair weather approaching.

- A line slanting to the lower right indicates the air pressure is falling (a falling barometer). A falling barometer may be a sign that a storm is on its way.

- A horizontal line indicates the air pressure is not changing. In the station model, the air pressure is 980 millibars and is rising.

▷ **How would an increase in temperature affect air pressure?**
Air pressure would decrease.

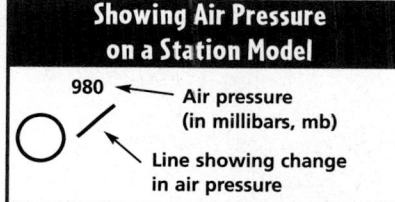

Showing Air Pressure on a Station Model

980 ← Air pressure (in millibars, mb)

← Line showing change in air pressure

D 37

Developing the Main Idea
Remind students that air is composed of many different gases. Ask:

■ **Why does moist air exert less pressure than dry air?** (Molecules of water vapor weigh less than oxygen and nitrogen in the air, and thus exert less pressure.)

Ask students if they've ever heard a weather forecaster mention the barometric pressure and then add whether the pressure is rising or falling. Ask:

■ **Why is it important to observe which direction the pressure is changing?** (The direction a barometer is changing can be a clue to future weather. A falling barometer may be a sign that a storm is on its way; a rising barometer may be a sign that fair weather is approaching.)

READING
Diagrams

The gas molecules in the cold air are spaced more closely together. They collide more frequently than do the gas molecules in the warm air.

▶**After Reading**
Have students answer the red question in the student book as **ongoing assessment.**

Math MiniLesson

Volume of Cylinders

Develop A cylinder has 2 congruent circular bases. You can find the volume of a cylinder the same way you find the volume of a prism, $V = b \times h$, where V is the volume, b is the area of the base, and h is height.

Find the volume of a cylinder with a radius of 2 inches and a height of 5 inches.

Think: The area of a circle is πr^2, where r is the radius.

$$V = b \times h$$
$$= \pi r^2 \times h$$

$$\approx 3.14 \times 2^2 \times 5$$
$$\approx 62.8$$

So the volume of the cylinder is about 62.8 cubic inches.

 Use the $\boxed{\pi}$ key or press 3.14 for approximate value of π.
$\boxed{\pi}\boxed{\times}2\boxed{\times}2\boxed{\times}5\boxed{=}$ **62.831853**

Practice Find the volume of each cylinder.

1. height: 10 cm
radius: 3 cm
($\approx$282.6 cm³)

2. height: 6 in.
radius: 5 in.
($\approx$471 in.³)

Why Do Winds Blow?

Before Reading
Have students try to answer the red question at the top of the page.

Exploring the Main Idea
Demonstrate for students how temperature affects the movement of air. Remove the shade from a lamp, and sprinkle some talcum powder above the bulb. Then light the lamp and allow it to get warm. Again sprinkle talcum powder from above. Ask students to describe what they observe. (When the lamp is unlit, the powder slowly drifts down; when it is lit, the powder rises.) Ask:

■ **What happens? Why?** (Warming the air causes the air to move. As the warm air rises, it carries the powder with it.)

■ **What is this kind of air movement called?** (an updraft)

■ **What is a downdraft? What causes it?** (A downdraft is air that sinks. A downdraft occurs when air pressure above is higher, and the air moves downward to an area of lower pressure.)

READING
Diagrams

When direct sunlight heats city A, the air above it warms, expands, and exerts less air pressure. The air rises, creating an updraft. The warm air cools as it rises and sinks over city B, increasing the air pressure over that city. Surface winds blow from city B (higher pressure) to city A (lower pressure).

▶ After Reading
Have students answer the red question in the student book as **ongoing assessment**.

Developing Vocabulary

wind Have students describe situations when they have experienced wind or used wind to their advantage e.g., flying a kite.

convection cell Remind students from lessons on heat in previous grades that *convection* is the transfer of heat from one place to another. This transfer can occur in a circular pattern. When this occurs in the atmosphere, winds are formed.

Why Do Winds Blow?

Think of what happens if you put a blob of soft clay on a table and push down on it, using a flat hand. The clay squishes out from under your fingers, where the pressure is high. It moves to the spaces between your fingers, where the pressure is lower.

Air acts in a similar way. Denser air exerts a higher pressure than less dense air. Like the clay, denser air flows toward less dense air. This flow of air is wind. Air that moves horizontally is called **wind**. Air that rises or sinks is an *updraft* or a *downdraft*.

Convection Cells

How can air become more or less dense? As the Sun's rays hit an area, they transfer energy to the air. The air heats up. Because it is warmer, the heated air is less dense. Then, just like a cork in water, the warm air rises above the surrounding cooler, denser air. On the other hand, if a region of air is cooled, it becomes denser and sinks.

This unequal heating and cooling of the air often makes a pattern of rising air, sinking air, and winds, called a **convection** (kuhn·VEK·shuhn) **cell**. A convection cell is a part of the atmosphere where air moves in a circular pattern because of unequal heating and cooling.

The drawing shows how a convection cell forms. Cities A and B have the same air pressure. Then direct sunlight heats city A. The air above it warms and expands. It becomes less dense and rises, forming an updraft. The air pressure goes down. The unheated air on either side has a higher pressure. This air moves in toward the low-pressure area, making a surface wind.

▷ How are winds produced?
Air flows from areas of higher pressure to areas of lower pressure

READING
Diagrams

Use the diagram to explain what happens to city B during the formation of the convection cell.

Updraft

Warm air rising

Cool air sinking

Downdraft

Wind

CITY A

CITY B

🦉 Science Background

Saharan Winds
The Sahara Desert is located in one of the high-pressure belts that circle Earth, flanking the equator at about 30° north and south. The Saharan air is ordinarily still, but when a low pressure system forms over the Mediterranean Sea, nearly a thousand miles to the north, the dry desert air is drawn toward the area of low pressure so rapidly that fierce sirocco winds are created.

D 3

Sea breeze

Valley breeze

What Are Sea and Land Breezes?

An example of convection is a breeze that occurs along a coastline.

In Lesson 1 you learned that land warms faster than water. On sunny days air over land warms faster than air next to it over the sea. The warm air expands and rises. Cooler air from over the ocean replaces the rising warm air. A wind blows onto the land. A wind that blows from the sea toward the land is called a **sea breeze**.

At night the reverse happens. The air over the land cools more rapidly than the air over the water. A **land breeze** blows from land toward the water.

Convection cells also occur along mountains. As the Sun shines on a mountain during the day, the slope heats up faster than the valley below.

READING
Diagrams

These pictures show what happens during the day. How would you show what happens at night?

Air over the slope warms and rises. Cooler air over the valley replaces the rising warm air, creating a *valley breeze* that blows up the slope. At night the mountain slope cools rapidly. This causes a *mountain breeze* to blow down the slope.

▶ **How are sea and land breezes produced?**

Temperature differences between two areas cause air to move from a higher pressure, cooler area to a lower pressure, warmer area. **D 39**

BLACKLINE
Interpret Illustrations

Name _____ Date _____ **Interpret Illustrations** Lesson 4

What Are Sea and Land Breezes?

Land temperatures change faster than water temperatures do. This diagram shows how those temperature changes can affect winds and wind directions along a coastline. This diagram shows how a sea breeze—a breeze that blows from the ocean—is created during the day.

Warm air

Cold air

Sea breeze

Answer these questions about the diagram above.

1. On a sunny day, does the air over land get warmer or cooler than the air over the water? ___warmer___

2. In what direction does the warmer air move? ___It rises.___

3. When a sea breeze blows, it brings ___cooler___ air to the land.

4. This diagram shows why a sea breeze blows inland during the day. Now figure out what will happen to these wind patterns at night. Remember that land temperatures change faster than water temperatures. Explain what you think will happen.

The land cools off faster. Then the cooler air moves out from the

land to the water, causing a land breeze.

212 Unit D · Weather and Climate   Use with textbook page D39

Reading in Science Resources, p. 212

What Are Sea and Land Breezes?

Before Reading
Have students try to answer the red question at the top of the text column.

Developing the Main Idea
Ask:

■ **What causes a sea breeze to form?** (When the air over the land gets hotter than the air over water, it expands, becomes less dense and it rises. The cooler air from above the water moves toward land, causing a sea breeze.)

■ **What air pressure differences cause the air to move from one place to another?** (Air moves from an area with higher pressure to an area of lower pressure.)

■ **In conditions that give rise to a sea breeze, how does air pressure over the water compare with air pressure over land?** (The air pressure over the sea is higher than the air pressure over the land.)

READING
Diagrams

At night air over land cools more rapidly than air over water. A land breeze forms. Mountain breezes blow down the mountain slope during the night, with cool air and high pressure over the mountain slope and low pressure over the valley. In short, the arrows would be reversed.

▶**After Reading**
Have students answer the red question in the student book as **ongoing assessment**.

Developing Vocabulary

sea breeze The name of the breeze indicates the direction the wind is coming from: the wind blows *from the sea*.

land breeze The wind blows *from the land*.

Have students describe situations when they have experienced breezes from the land or sea.

What Is the Coriolis Effect?

Before Reading
Have students try to answer the red question at the top of the page.

Developing the Main Idea
The rotation of Earth affects the winds blowing across its surface. Because Earth rotates, winds follow a curved path over its surface. No matter which way the wind blows, it curves to the right in the Northern Hemisphere, and to the left in the Southern Hemisphere. This is known as the Coriolis Effect. Winds and pressure belts (zones) around the globe are caused by huge convection cells.

Ask:

- **The Coriolis effect causes winds in the Northern Hemisphere to curve to the right. Does it also cause changes in ocean currents? How?** (Yes, the Coriolis effect also causes ocean currents in the Northern Hemisphere to curve to the right; it causes ocean currents in the Southern Hemisphere to curve to the left.)

▶ After Reading
Have students answer the red question in the student book as **ongoing assessment**.

Developing Vocabulary

Coriolis effect Use a globe to demonstrate to students how the rotation of the Earth causes winds to curve in different directions in each hemisphere. The effect is named after Gustave Gaspard Coriolis, the French engineer/mathematician who described it in 1835.

What Is the Coriolis Effect?

Earth's rotation affects winds blowing across its surface. As Earth rotates, every spot on its surface moves with it. However, in the same 24-hour period, places near the poles travel a shorter distance than places near the equator. This means that places near the poles are moving slower!

Now what if you are in an airplane flying in a straight line from the North Pole to Chicago? While you are in the air, Earth is *rotating*, or spinning, underneath you. Earth rotates counterclockwise as seen from the North Pole. As Earth rotates, Chicago is moving west to east. To someone in Chicago, though, the plane's flight path seems to curve to the southwest.

The same thing happens with winds blowing from the North Pole. Because Earth rotates, the winds seem to curve to the right as they head southward.

No matter which way the wind blows, it will curve to the right in the Northern Hemisphere. This curving is called the Coriolis effect. In the Southern Hemisphere, the Coriolis effect causes winds to curve to the left. This is because, as viewed from the South Pole, Earth rotates clockwise. The effect works on other moving objects as well, such as missiles and rockets.

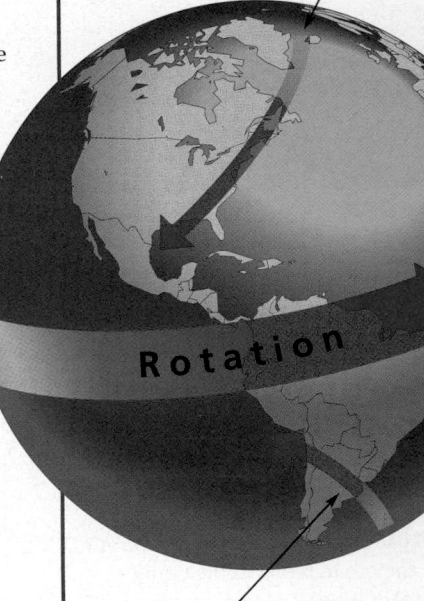

Coriolis Effect

If you were standing at the North Pole looking south, this arrow would appear to curve to the right.

R o t a t i o n

If you were standing at the South Pole looking north, this arrow would appear to curve to the left.

▶ What causes the Coriolis effect?
Earth's rotation causes winds to curve to the right in the Northern Hemisphere and to the left in the Southern Hemisphere.

D 40

Reading Strategy

Organize Information
Developing Reading Skills
Students can organize information about global wind zones into a table. **Linguistic**

Science Background

Ballot's Law
In 1857, Buys Ballot was the first scientist to note that when wind blows onto an observer's back, low pressure lies to the left in the Northern Hemisphere, concluding that in the Northern Hemisphere wind always blows counterclockwise around the center of a low pressure system, and clockwise around the center of a high pressure system. Ballot's Law builds upon the work of French mathematician Coriolis.

How Are Global Wind Patterns Produced?

Year round the equator is heated strongly by sunlight. The air becomes very warm. Heat also causes evaporation, so the air becomes moist. Warm, moist air over the equator creates a zone of low pressure around the globe.

As the air at the equator warms, it becomes less dense and rises. It rises to the top of the troposphere and spreads out, moving north and south. As the air moves away from the equator, it cools and becomes denser. At about 30° north and south latitudes, the cold air begins to sink toward the surface. This sinking air creates a high-pressure zone on both sides of the equator at these latitudes. A belt of winds is set in motion around Earth by air moving from these high-pressure zones toward the low pressure

at the equator. These are the *trade winds*. The Coriolis effect curves these winds, as you see in the diagram.

The poles get very low-angle sunlight, and the air there is very cold. Cold, dense air can hold very little water vapor. Cold, dry air over the poles has high pressure. Air at the poles moves toward 60° latitude, forming winds. Because of the Coriolis effect, the winds curve. These are the polar *easterly winds*. *Easterly* means the wind blows "from the east."

Other winds occur between 60° latitude and the poles as well as between 30° and 60° latitudes. Between 30° and 60° latitudes is the zone of *westerly winds*. The continental United States is in the zone of westerly winds.

▷ What causes the global trade winds?

a belt of winds set in motion around Earth by air moving toward the equator

Global Wind Zones

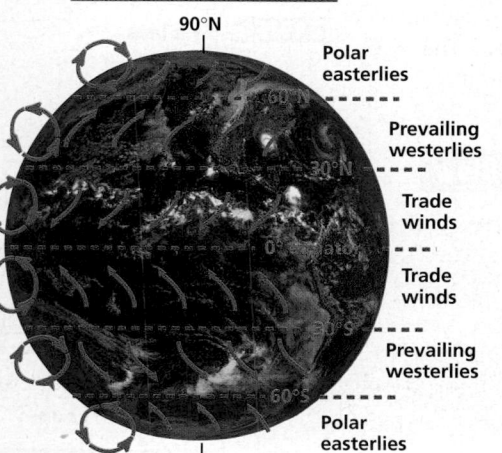

90°N

Polar easterlies

Prevailing westerlies

Trade winds

Trade winds

Prevailing westerlies

Polar easterlies

90°S

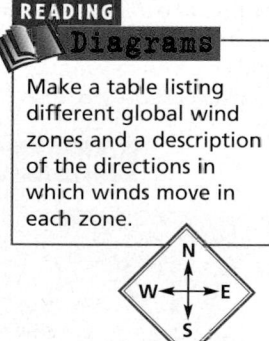

D 41

Before Reading
Have students try to answer the red question at the top of the page.

Developing the Main Idea
Ask:

- **How do convection cells near the equator cause the trade winds to form?** (The air at the equator is warm and moist. It rises, spreading out and cooling. As it cools, the air becomes more dense, and at about 25° to 30° north and south of the equator, it starts to sink. High pressure zones are thus formed. The trade winds blow from these high pressure zones to the lower pressure zones near the equator.)

Exploring the Main Idea
Ask:

- **How would winds behave if Earth did not rotate on its axis?** (Air would rise and travel away from the equator, toward the poles, cooling along the way. At the poles, the air would sink, and move back toward the equator.)

A simple model can illustrate how winds would behave in the absence of rotation. Form loops of tape, sticky-side-out, and affix them to a globe between the poles and the equator.

READING

Diagrams

Tables should include information such as: polar easterly winds move from the east, curving to the right in the Northern Hemisphere and to the left in the Southern Hemisphere; westerly winds move from the west, between 30° latitude and 60° latitude.

▶ After Reading
Have students answer the red question in the student book as **ongoing assessment**.

READING Diagrams

Make a table listing different global wind zones and a description of the directions in which winds move in each zone.

What Are Isobars?

Before Reading
Have students try to answer the red question at the top of the page.

Using the Illustrations
Draw students attention to the map showing isobars. Remind students that when plotting air pressure, scientists begin by marking the air pressure at many different places on the map. Ask:

- **Why do you think they go a step further and draw isobars, when they already have recorded the data?** (Isobars show patterns that are not as easily seen when numbers are plotted.)

▶ **After Reading**
Have students answer the red question in the student book as **ongoing assessment**.

What Are Isobars?

Why is it important to know about air pressure? Knowing where the air pressure is high or low allows you to predict which way air will move. This is why weather scientists make maps showing air pressure. They start by plotting the air pressure at many different locations on a map. Then they connect all places with the same air pressure with a line. A line on a map connecting places with equal air pressure is called an isobar. Isobars make pressure patterns easier to see.

Find the series of circular isobars in the west, surrounding a region of high pressure (H). This pattern is called a *high-pressure system*. Since the center has higher pressure than its surroundings, winds blow outward from the center in a clockwise pattern.

A similar set of isobars in the east marks a *low-pressure system* (L). In a low-pressure system, the central region is surrounded by higher pressure. The winds blow in toward the center in a counterclockwise pattern.

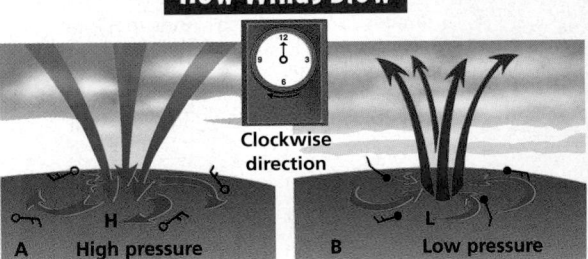

The pressure on each isobar is in millibars (mb).

Isobars also help scientists predict how fast air will move. Big differences in air pressure over short distances cause strong winds. This is shown on a map by drawing closely spaced isobars. Small differences in air pressure cause gentle winds. This is shown by widely spaced isobars.

You show wind on a station model by a straight line touching the circle. The line tells where the wind is blowing from. "Feathers" are used to show speed.

READING Main Idea
How do isobars help scientists predict how air will move?
They make it easier to see patterns of high- and low-pressure areas.

How Winds Blow

Clockwise direction

A High pressure

B Low pressure

Showing Wind on a Station Model
NE = Northeast wind
Full feather = 14–22 km/h (8–12 knots)
Half feather = 5–13 km/h (3–7 knots)

D 42

Process Skill BUILDER

SKILL Interpret Data

A Weather Station Model

A weather station model includes temperature, cloud cover, air pressure, pressure tendency, wind speed, and wind direction. The circle is at the location of the station. You will interpret the data—use the information—from the weather station models to answer questions and solve problems.

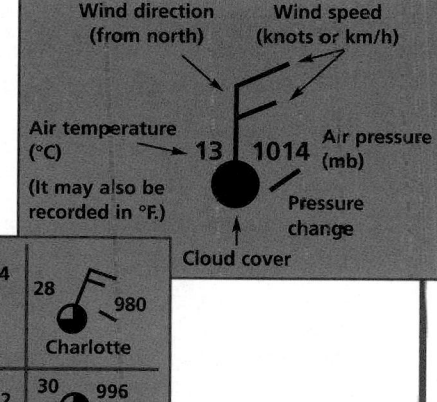

Procedure

1. **Use Numbers** Look carefully at the Dallas weather station model. How fast is the wind blowing? What is the wind direction? Record your answers.

2. **Interpret Data** What other information does this weather station model give you?

3. Look at the other weather station models. Make a table recording weather conditions for each city.

Drawing Conclusions

1. Compare the information in the table you made with these station models. Which way is the information easier to interpret?

2. **Interpret Data** Where was wind fastest? Slowest? Which tells you this information more quickly, the table or the models?

3. **Communicate** Compare and contrast other weather conditions in the cities.

D 43

Process Skills

MiniLesson

Interpret Data

Develop This skill involves studying information in a table, chart, graph, paragraph, or picture and looking for relationships, comparisons, or cause and effect to solve a problem.

Practice Have students look at the graph on page D18. Ask students to tell about how many more grams of water vapor per cubic centimeter there are at 30°C than there are at 0°C.

Students answer the question by first finding how many grams are represented by the bar at 30° (about 32) and at 0° (about 5). They subtract the two numbers to determine the final answer (27).

A complete list of Science Process Skills appears on p. S7.

Process Skill
BUILDER

A Weather Station Model

Science Process Skills *interpret data,* use numbers, communicate

Resources Activity Resources, pp. 138–139

Pacing 30–40 minutes

Grouping individuals

Procedure

1. The wind is blowing at 19–31 knots (33–57 km/h). The wind direction is from the southwest.

2. amount of cloud cover, air temperature, and air pressure and pressure change

3. Remind students that tables consist of columns and rows, with space for appropriate headings. They should construct a 6 column by 4 row chart with the following column labels: city, air pressure, wind speed, wind direction, cloud cover, and temperature. Dallas: 34°C, 1004 mb, clear skies, southwest winds at 19–31 knots; Charlotte: 28°C, 980 mb, mostly cloudy skies, northeast winds at 11–19 knots; Tampa: 30°C, 996 mb, partly cloudy, southeast winds at 24–48 knots; Oakland: 14°C, 1012 mb, scattered clouds, south winds at 16–24 knots.

Answers to Drawing Conclusions

1. Tables are easier to interpret.

2. It was the fastest in Tampa, and the slowest in Charlotte. A chart gives this information more quickly.

3. Charlotte, North Carolina, had the most cloud cover, while Dallas had the clearest skies. Oakland had the lowest temperature, while Dallas had the highest. Air pressure was highest in Oakland and lowest in Charlotte.

How Do We Study the Wind?

Before Reading
Have students try to answer the red question at the top of the page.

Using the Illustrations
Draw students' attention to the photograph of the weather vane. Ask:

- **What information do weather vanes tell us? How do they do this?** (They tell us which direction the wind is blowing. Their tails have a wider surface area than their pointers, so when wind blows, the tip points in the direction the wind is blowing from.)

- **Does the weather vane give us any other information? How does it do this?** (Because it is marked with compass markings, we can tell which direction the wind is blowing from.)

▶**After Reading**
Have students answer the red question in the student book as **ongoing assessment**.

Developing Vocabulary

weather vane A vane is a flat piece of metal that is fixed on a object and is capable of moving. Ask students to describe what a weather vane would be used for.

anemometer The word *anemometer* is derived from two Greek words meaning "wind" and "measure". Ask students to describe a use for this instrument.

Anemometer   weather vane

How Do We Study the Wind?

What is that curious-looking device on the roof? It is a **weather vane**. It is used to tell wind direction. A weather vane has a pointer that blows around in the wind. The pointer is mounted so it can point to the different compass markings.

The tail of the pointer has a larger surface area than the tip. When a wind blows, it exerts more pressure on the tail than the tip. This causes the tail to swing around so that the tip points in the direction the wind is blowing from.

Wind speed is measured with a device called an **anemometer** (an·uh·MAHM·i·tuhr). An anemometer is a series of cups mounted on a shaft that can spin freely. When the wind blows against the cups, they spin like a pinwheel. The faster the wind blows, the faster the cups spin the shaft. A speedometer is attached to the shaft to measure wind speed.

The Beaufort Scale
Strong winds create high waves. That is why sailors have always been concerned about wind speed. In 1805, Sir Francis Beaufort of the British Navy devised a system for measuring wind speed by observing its effect on the surface of the sea. He assigned a number from 0 to 12 to each effect. This is the Beaufort scale.

Scientists use anemometers and weather vanes to measure wind speed and direction.

▶ **What devices are used to find wind speed and direction?**

Type of Wind	Kilometers per Hour	Miles per Hour	Observations
Beaufort Wind Scale			
0 Calm	less than 1	less than 0.6	Calm; smoke rises straight up
1 Light air	1–5	0.6–3	Weather vanes don't move
2 Light breeze	6–11	4–7	Weather vanes move slightly
3 Gentle breeze	12–19	8–12	Leaves move; flags stretch out
4 Moderate breeze	20–29	13–18	Small branches sway
5 Fresh breeze	30–38	19–24	Trees sway; white caps on ponds
6 Strong breeze	39–50	25–31	Large branches sway
7 Moderate gale	51–61	32–38	Hard to walk into the wind
8 Fresh gale	62–74	39–46	Branches break off trees
9 Strong gale	75–87	47–54	Shingles blow off roofs
10 Whole gale	88–101	55–63	Trees are uprooted
11 Storm	102–117	64–73	Extensive damage
12 Hurricane	118+	74+	Violent destruction

D 44

 Science Background

Knots and Wind Speed
Using knots to measure wind speed has a seafaring origin. Sailors measured their speed by throwing a log with a rope attached to it over the side of their ship. Once in water, the log floated. As the boat sailed on, the sailors would reel out rope for one minute. Every knot that reeled out in one minute was roughly equal to 1 nautical mile (6076 feet) per hour. To determine the ship's speed, the sailor simply counted the number of knots reeled out in a minute.

 Science Background

Wind Vane Readings
Address Misconceptions
Many people believe that weather vanes indicate the direction in which wind is blowing. Point out that the structure of the vane causes it to spin so that it points in the direction from which the wind comes (into the wind), but that the wind blows in the opposite direction.

L·I·N·K·S

Why It Matters

Wind can be very useful. It is often used as a source of power. Winds turn special machinery— windmills— that produce electricity. They run the machinery that grinds grain. Windmills are still used today to pump water.

Wind also carries pollen to flowers. Seeds form as a result. Many kinds of seeds, in turn, are carried by wind to new places.

Think and Write

1. What makes air pressure change?

2. What causes wind to blow in a particular direction?

3. Why are there zones of winds around the world?

4. **Interpret Data** On a weather map, how can you compare the speed and direction of winds in different locations?

5. **Critical Thinking** How might you make a simple device to tell wind direction?

LITERATURE LINK

Read *The Sky-Watchers,* the story of how two students maintained a weather station. When you finish reading, think about how you would build a weather station. Try the activities at the end of the book.

WRITING LINK

Write a story. List all the ways you can think of that people can make use of the wind. Write a story about them.

MATH LINK

Calculate weather factors. Collect a week's worth of national weather maps from a newspaper. Select a region of the country, such as the Midwest or Southeast. Calculate its average temperature, wind speed, and air pressure.

SOCIAL STUDIES LINK

Write a report. Research the origin of the term "trade winds," and write a report on your findings.

TECHNOLOGY LINK

At the Computer Visit www.mhscience02.com for more links.

D 45

Informal Assessment

Easy/Average Have students draw diagrams showing air circulation in a convection cell. Have them indicate rising and sinking air, horizontal movement between areas of higher and lower pressure, and labels for updraft and downdraft.

Challenge Make a model of wind currents. Fill a small jar with warm water and food coloring. Cover the top tightly with plastic wrap. Place the small jar inside a large jar of cold water. Poke two small holes in the plastic wrap. Challenge students to explain. (Warm water rises, then sinks as it cools.)

3 | Lesson Review

Answers to Think and Write

1. A change in altitude, temperature, and humidity causes a change in air pressure. (pp. D36–D37)

2. Winds blow in a particular direction because air moves from an area of high pressure to an area of lower pressure. (pp. D38–D39)

3. Huge convection cells cause winds and pressure belts around the world. (p. D41)

4. **Interpret Data** Organize the map's information into a table so that it is easier to make comparisons. (p. D43)

5. **Critical Thinking** Students might describe making a weather vane from everyday materials. Their plans will vary, but the tail of the pointer must have a larger surface area than the tip. (p. D32)

Summarize
Check students' understanding by having them write a brief summary of the lesson in their own words.

LITERATURE LINK

Have students read the Grade Level Science Book, *The Sky-Watchers.* Additional books to read can be found on TE p. D1·b.

WRITING LINK

Wind is one of Earth's greatest natural resources. People have been using wind power and energy for centuries. Wind is a reliable and nonconsumable resource.

MATH LINK

To calculate the average wind speed, temperature, and air pressure, students should add the week's readings of each measurement, then divide the total of each by seven.

SOCIAL STUDIES LINK

Students' reports should mention that trade winds are the main east-west wind in two belts from the equator to 30° north and 30° south latitude. Trade winds are so named because merchant sailors could count on them to blow reliably, carrying ships loaded with goods to their destinations on schedule.

Amazing Stories

Objective

- Describe how hurricane hunters help predict a hurricane's course.

Build on Prior Knowledge

Ask students if any of them have ever been in an airplane during bad weather or when a flight was bumpy. Then ask:

- **What might be some dangers of flying through a storm?** (Possible answers: being struck by lightning, hitting high winds, low visibility)

Hurricane Hunters

Developing the Main Idea

Discuss with students what it might feel like to be on the plane with the hurricane hunters as they go through a hurricane. Then focus on the necessity of hurricane prediction. Ask:

- **What information do the hurricane hunters gather?** (They find out what direction the storm is heading.)

- **How do they gather this information?** (They fly into the eye of the storm and drop dropsondes that send measurements back to the hunters.)

- **Why is this information important?** (People in the path of the storm can be warned so that they have time to prepare or evacuate.)

Amazing Stories

Hurricane Hunters

Winds are blowing at 200 kilometers per hour (125 miles per hour). There's so much rain, city streets look like rivers. Huge waves pound the shores, flooding coastal areas. This is not your average storm. It's a hurricane. It's time to stay indoors and protect yourself, right? Not if you're a hurricane hunter. For hurricane hunters, it's time to get in an airplane and fly into the middle of the storm.

Hurricanes are powerful storms. They form over warm oceans and sometimes move onto land. It's important to know where a hurricane will hit land. Meteorologists measure air pressure, temperature, and wind speeds to try to predict a hurricane's path. They track the storm with satellites and radar, but these efforts are often not enough. The most helpful measurements are taken inside the storm.

People who fly specially equipped airplanes into hurricanes are called hurricane hunters. Their planes can withstand wind speeds up to 483 km/h (300 mph). As the plane enters the hurricane, it passes through bands of howling winds, blinding rain, and thunderstorms. The ride gets very bumpy. Often the crew cannot read instruments because the plane is shaking so much. The rain is so loud, they cannot hear each other speak, and the plane is often hit by lightning!

Hurricane winds swirl around the "eye"—a calm area in the center of the storm. As the airplane flies through the eye, a crew member drops a device called a dropsonde from the plane. A dropsonde is a small tube with an attached parachute. The tube contains measuring instruments and a radio transmitter. As the dropsonde falls toward the sea, it

D 46

Science Background

Hurricane Hunters' Missions

The hurricane hunters are based at Keesler Air Force Base near Biloxi, Mississippi. From 1984 to 1994, they each averaged 86 missions and 1,100 hours. They flew 157 missions between January 1995 and November 1, 1995.

What Did I Learn?

1. Hurricane hunters

  A track storms from their offices in Florida

  B parachute through hurricanes

  C watch for hurricanes from the seashore

  D fly special planes into hurricanes

2. A dropsonde is

  F what the hurricane hunters call their airplanes

  G a parachute carried into a hurricane

  H a small tube with special instruments that is dropped from a plane

  J the radio hurricane hunters use to call the National Weather Service

transmits weather data up to the airplane. Crew members send these data to the National Hurricane Center in Miami, Florida. There, scientists use the weather data to determine the strength of the hurricane, and predict the direction it is heading. Sometimes they alert people to move from their homes near the coast to safer buildings inland.

Hurricane hunters brave some of Earth's roughest weather. To get all the information needed, a crew may make several passes through a storm. Flights may last 11 hours or more, but hurricane hunters know their efforts may save many lives.

AT THE COMPUTER Visit www.mhscience02.com for more amazing stories and facts about storms.

D 47

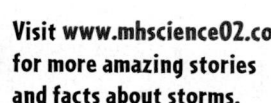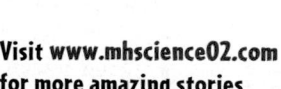
SCIENCE FOR ALL Advanced Learners

Hurricane Prediction

Have students research parameters used to predict a more or less active hurricane season. Include the Stratospheric Quasi-Biennial Oscillation, the El Niño-Southern Oscillation, and the amount of African rainfall. Have them present a chart of their findings to the class.
Spatial; Logical

Using the illustrations

Direct students' attention to the satellite photograph. Ask:

- **What information can you get from viewing the photograph?** (Possible answers: size of the storm, the location of the eye, the islands or land directly beneath the storm, areas that may be in the hurricane's path)

Then direct students' attention to the picture of the hurricane's effects on land. Ask:

- **What is happening in this photograph?** (The hurricane is causing high waves to come up on shore, and high winds are blowing trees and other objects.)

- **How do hurricanes harm people?** (Possible answers: People can be caught in floods, homes can be blown apart, and objects can blow through the air.)

Thinking Further: *Inferring*
Ask:

- **Why do you think the hurricane hunters pass through the hurricane so many times?** (Hurricanes are constantly moving. By going back and forth through the storm, hurricane hunters can get a clear idea of the actual direction of the storm for many hours, making the prediction more accurate.)

Test Prep: What Did I Learn?

1. D

2. H

Summarize

Check students' understanding by having them write a brief summary of the amazing story in their own words.

Chapter Review and Test Preparation

Answers to Vocabulary

1. precipitation
2. Coriolis effect
3. stratus cloud
4. evaporation
5. humidity
6. sea breeze
7. land breeze
8. condensation
9. cirrus cloud
10. barometer

Answers to Test Prep

11. C
12. H
13. B
14. H
15. A

Chapter 8 Review

Vocabulary

Fill each blank with the best word or words from the list.

> barometer, D12
> cirrus cloud, D24
> condensation, D17
> Coriolis effect, D40
> evaporation, D16
> humidity, D16
> land breeze, D39
> precipitation, D26
> sea breeze, D39
> stratus cloud, D24

1. Rain, snow, and sleet are kinds of _____.

2. The _____ causes winds to follow a curved path over Earth's surface.

3. A(n) _____ forms in blanketlike layers.

4. Liquid changes directly to a gas by the process called _____.

5. The amount of water vapor in the air is called _____.

6. Wind blowing from the ocean toward the land is called a(n) _____.

7. Wind blowing from the land toward the ocean is called a(n) _____.

8. The process that turns water vapor into raindrops is called _____.

9. A high, wispy cloud made of ice crystals is a(n) _____.

10. A(n) _____ measures air pressure.

Test Prep

11. The water cycle describes how water _____.
    - **A** flows upstream
    - **B** spins in a tornado
    - **C** changes form
    - **D** heats up the atmosphere

12. Weather takes place in the _____.
    - **F** thermosphere
    - **G** mesosphere
    - **H** troposphere
    - **J** stratosphere

13. Water drops that collect on a cold glass of lemonade come from _____.
    - **A** the lemonade
    - **B** the air
    - **C** a puddle
    - **D** the glass itself

14. Isobars indicate _____.
    - **F** humidity
    - **G** temperature
    - **H** air pressure
    - **J** cloud cover

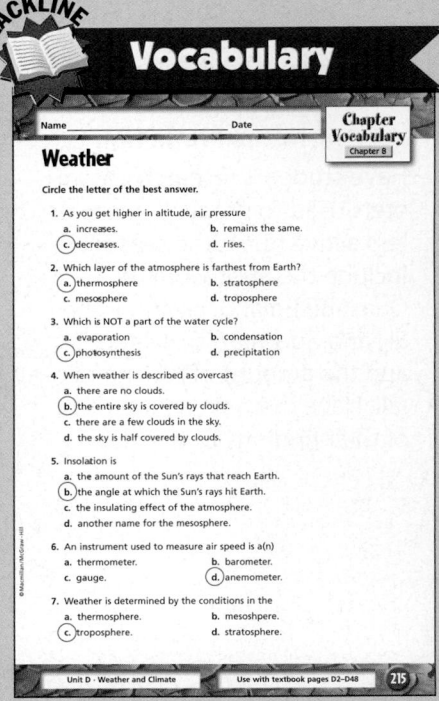

Reading in Science Resources, p. 215

15. On a hot day, a lake is likely to be _____.

  A cooler than nearby land

  B hotter than nearby land

  C the same temperature as the land

  D the cause of the heat

Concepts and Skills

16. Reading in Science Write a paragraph explaining why north winds blow to the southwest.

17. Safety Why do you need to be careful on hot days when the relative humidity is high? Write a paragraph explaining your answer.

18. Scientific Methods How much does humidity change over a day? Write up a design for an experiment that would test this.

19. Process Skills: Interpret Data You are given this information on a weather map: What kind of weather is city A having? What kind of weather is city B having? Write a paragraph explaining your answer.

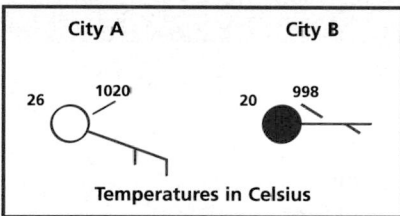

Temperatures in Celsius

20. Critical Thinking What if there were no plants? Do you think Earth would still get as much rain as it does now? Write your ideas. Describe how you might test them.

Boost your test scores!

Be Smart!

Visit www.mhscience02.com

D 49

Answers to Concepts and Skills

16. Reading in Science The Coriolis effect causes wind to curve to the right, so winds blowing from the north will travel to the south and west.

17. Safety When the relative humidity is high, less water can evaporate into the air. It is harder to cool off on a hot, humid day because less sweat evaporates.

18. Scientific Methods Students might use a glass of cold water, a thermometer, and a timer and might carry out an experiment similar to the Explore Activity in Lesson 2.

19. Process Skills: Interpret Data A: clear, SE winds, 26 degrees Centigrade, air pressure 1020 mb; B: overcast, E winds, 20 degrees Centigrade, air pressure 998 mb.

20. Critical Thinking Because plants add water vapor to the atmosphere, a lack of plants would result in less humidity. Students might suggest testing by placing a plant and an empty pot into separate plastic bags, to observe differences in the amount of water.

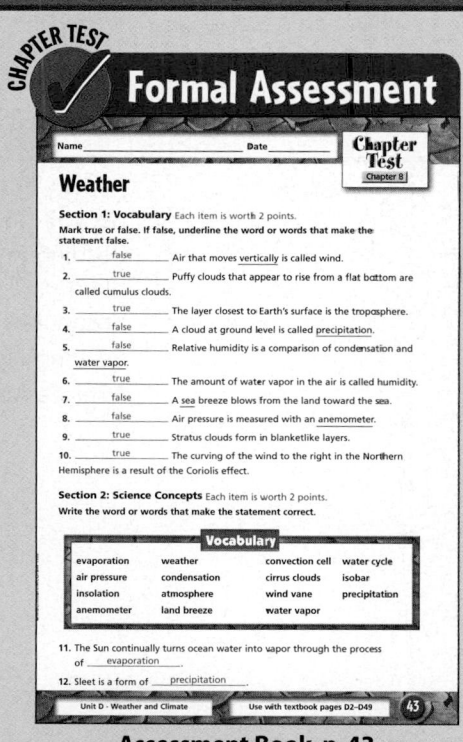

Assessment Book, p. 43

Lesson Planner

Lesson	Objectives	Vocabulary	Pacing	Resources and Technology
LESSON 5 **Air Masses and Fronts,** pp. D52–D61	■ Explore how weather can differ in different parts of the country. ■ Explain how air masses produce different kinds of weather along fronts. ■ Describe how satellites can be used to help predict the weather. ■ Identify different methods for making weather predictions.	**air mass** **front** **cold front** **warm front** **occluded front** **stationary front**	3 days	■ Activity Resources, pp. 140–146 ■ Reading in Science Resources, pp. 221–226 ■ Vocabulary Cards ■ Reading Aid Transparency D5 ■ Visual Aid Transparency 24 ■ **Explore Activity Video** ■ **Science Newsroom CD-ROM** *It's Up in the Air*
LESSON 6 **Severe Storms,** pp. D64–D77	■ Explore where tornadoes are most likely to happen. ■ Explain how thunderstorms and tornadoes are related. ■ Describe what hurricanes are and how they can cause damage. ■ Identify safety procedures and methods for predicting storms.	**thunderstorm** **tornado** **hurricane** **storm surge**	4 days	■ Activity Resources, pp. 147–152 ■ Reading in Science Resources, pp. 227–232 ■ Vocabulary Cards ■ Grade-Level Science Book, *Trouble at Forest Park* ■ Reading Aid Transparency D6 ■ Visual Aid Transparencies 25, 26 ■ **Explore Activity Video** ■ **Science Experiences Videotapes** *Sky Watch: Tracking a Winter Storm* (Package 6)
LESSON 7 **Climate,** pp. D80–D91	■ Explore how temperatures and precipitation differ from place to place. ■ Identify factors that make up and determine climate. ■ Distinguish among the ways climates may change. ■ Identify how climate affects health and food production.	**climate** **radiative balance** **greenhouse effect**	4 days	■ Activity Resources, pp. 153–157 ■ Reading in Science Resources, pp. 233–238 ■ Vocabulary Cards ■ Reading Aid Transparency D7 ■ **Explore Activity Video**

Activity Planner

Activity	Process Skills	Materials	Plan Ahead
5 Explore Activity **How Can You Compare Weather?** p. D53	communicate, infer, predict, interpret data	station model key, newspaper weather map (optional), pencil, crayons	No advance planning needed.
QUICK LAB FOR SCHOOL OR HOME **Weather Prediction** p. D60	analyze, infer	none	No advance planning needed.
6 Explore Activity **Where Do Tornadoes Occur?** p. D65	infer, use numbers, interpret data, communicate	map of the U.S., including Alaska and Hawaii, blue marker, red marker	No advance planning is needed.
QUICK LAB FOR SCHOOL OR HOME **Tornado in a Bottle** p. D68	make a model, observe, infer	two 2-L plastic bottles, duct tape, water, paper towel, pencil	No advance planning is needed.
7 Explore Activity **What Do Weather Patterns Tell You?** p. D81	use numbers, interpret data, communicate	none	No advance planning is needed.
Process Skill BUILDER **Modeling Climates** p. D83	measure, make a model, use numbers, observe, communicate	stick-on notepaper, marking pencil or pen, 2 trays of dry soil, spray bottle of water, lamp, thermometer	No advance planning is needed.

CHAPTER 9 Teaching Resources

Reading in Science Resources

McGraw-Hill Science **Reading in Science Resources** provides the following **Blackline Master** worksheets for this chapter.

Chapter Graphic Organizer

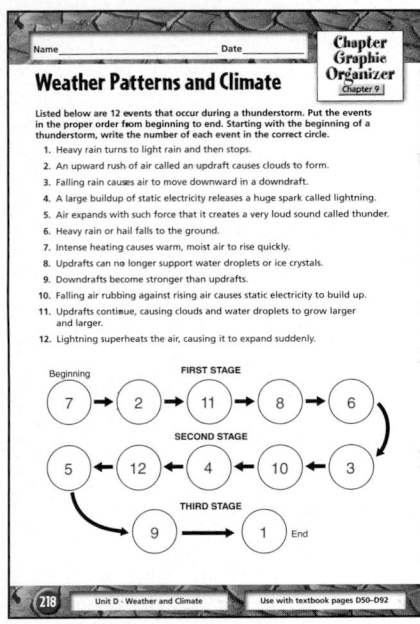

Reading in Science Resources, p. 218

Chapter Reading Skill

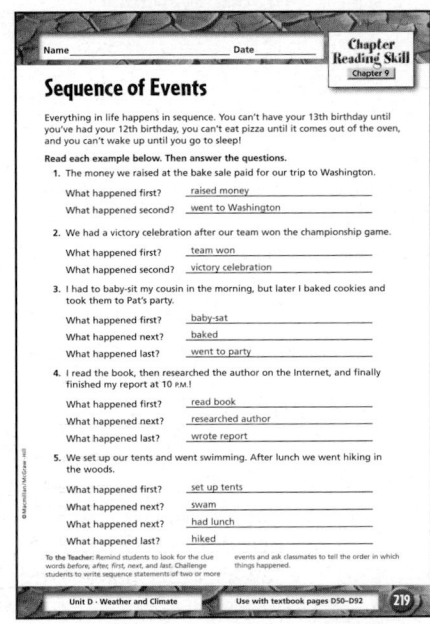

Reading in Science Resources, pp. 219–220

Chapter Vocabulary

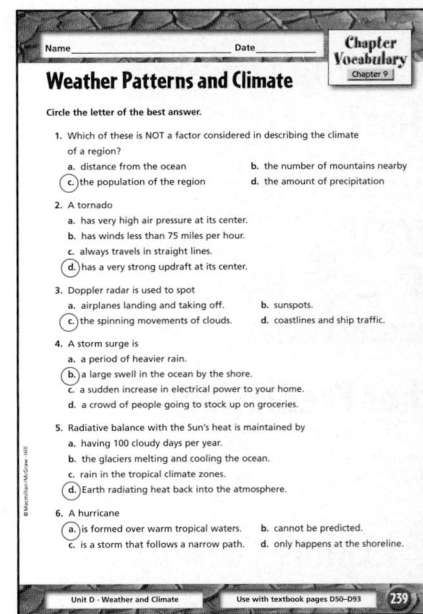

Reading in Science Resources, pp. 239–240

McGraw-Hill Science **Reading in Science Resources** provides the following **Blackline Master** worksheets for every lesson in this chapter.

Lesson Outline

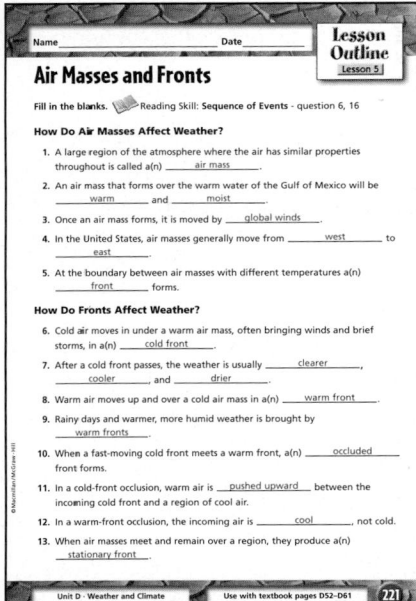

Reading in Science Resources, pp. 221–222, 227–228, 233–234

Interpret Illustrations

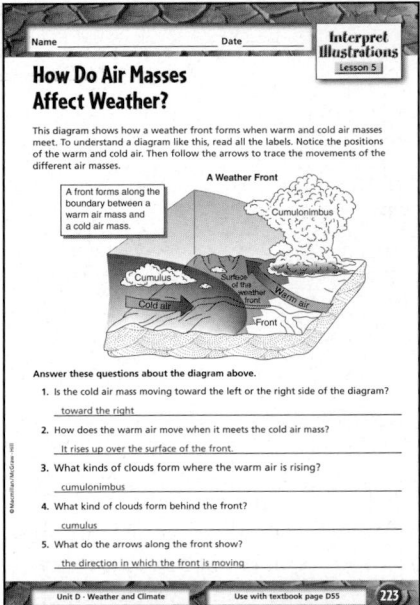

Reading in Science Resources, pp. 223–224, 229–230, 235–236

Lesson Vocabulary and Cloze Test

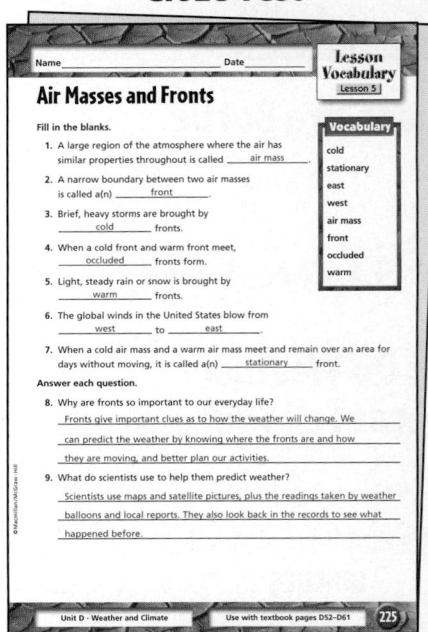

Reading in Science Resources, pp. 225–226, 231–232, 237–238

Activities and Assessment

McGraw-Hill Science **Activity Resources** provides the following **Blackline Master** worksheets for every lesson in this chapter.

Explore Activity and Alternative Explore Activity

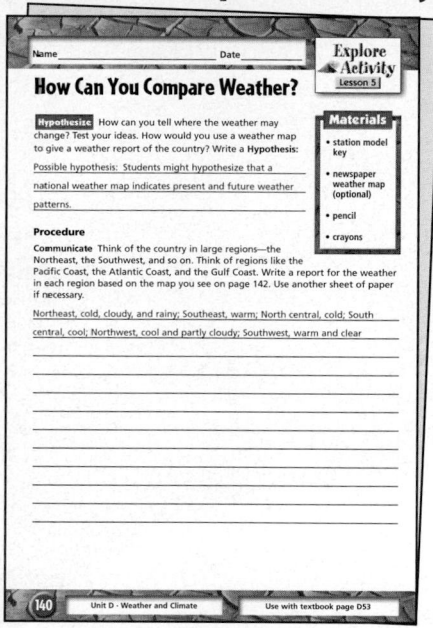

Activity Resources, pp. 140–143, 147–150, 153–155

Quick Lab for School or Home

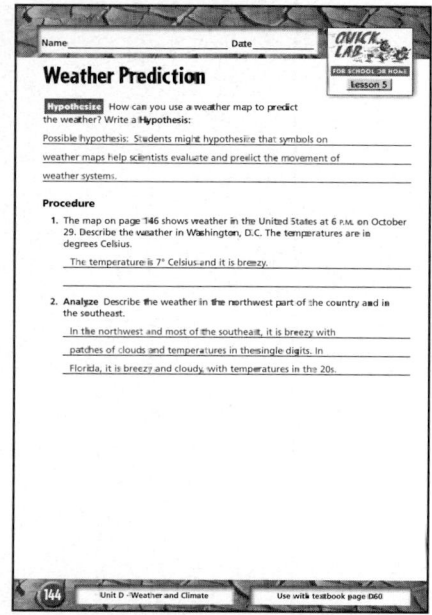

Activity Resources, pp. 144–146, 151–152

Process Skill Builder

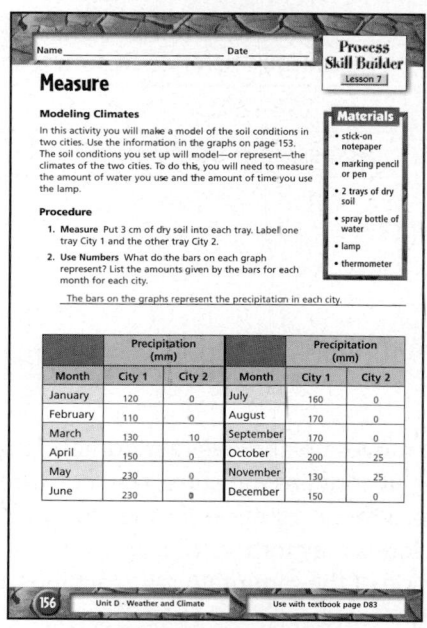

Activity Resources, pp. 156–157

McGraw-Hill Science **Assessment Book** provides the following **Blackline Master** worksheets for this chapter.

Chapter Test

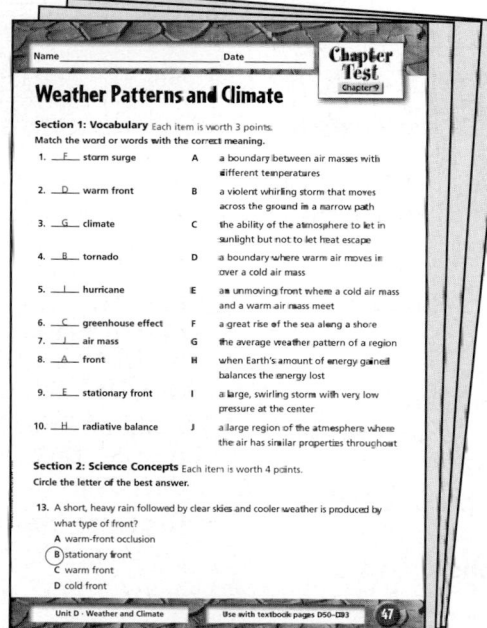

Assessment Book, pp. 47–50

CHAPTER

9 Weather Patterns and Climate

Resources

- Reading in Science Resources, pp. 218–240
- Assessment Book, pp. 47–50

Did You Ever Wonder?

As air moves up and over a mountain, the air cools. If that air contains moisture, the moisture will condense. If there is sufficient moisture condensing, rain clouds may form and drop their moisture on that side of the mountain. Air reaching the other side is often dry.

CHAPTER

9 Weather Patterns and Climate

Did You Ever Wonder?

Why is a desert hot and dry? Conditions in the Mojave Desert in California are partly caused by the mountains you see in the background. Rain falls on the other side of the mountains before it can reach the Mojave. Why does one side of a mountain get a lot of rain while the other side gets very little?

D 50

 SCIENCE

Reading Strategy

This chapter provides MiniLessons and other opportunities for developing and practicing the following reading skills:

- ○ Cause and Effect
- ◉ Compare and Contrast: pp. D58, D78
- ○ Draw Conclusions
- ○ Find the Main Idea
- ◉ Sequence of Events: pp. D55, D71, D74, D89
- ◉ Summarize: pp. D61, D77, D79, D91
- ◉ Ask Questions: p. D60
- ○ Reread

- ○ Retell (paraphrase)
- ◉ Interpret Graphic Sources of Information: pp. D54, D55, D57, D59, D66, D67, D69, D70, D86, D87
- ◉ Build on Prior Knowledge: pp. D52, D62, D64, D78, D80, D94
- ◉ Organize Information: pp. D62, D79, D90

D 51

Vocabulary Preview

Encourage students to keep a Science Dictionary. Remind them to add the Vocabulary words for each lesson in this chapter to their Dictionary as they complete each lesson.

air mass, D54

front, D55

cold front, D56

warm front, D56

occluded front, D56

stationary front, D57

thunderstorm, D66

tornado, D68

hurricane, D70

storm surge, D72

climate, D82

radiative balance, D86

greenhouse effect, D87

AMERICAN MUSEUM OF NATURAL HISTORY

Visit www.amnh.org/resources/mhscience to discover more about weather patterns and climate.

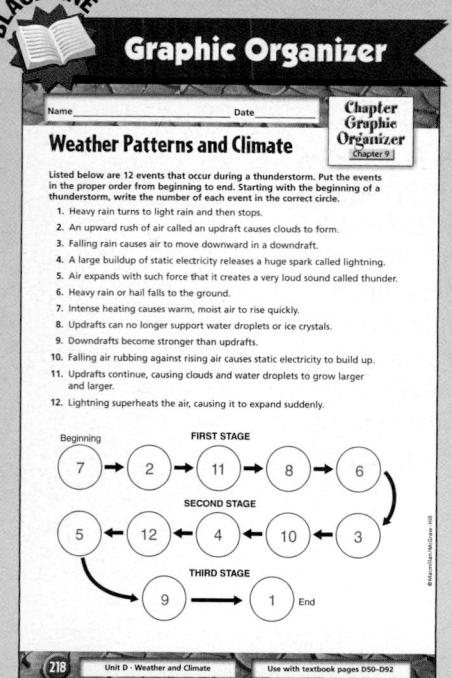

Reading in Science Resources, p. 218

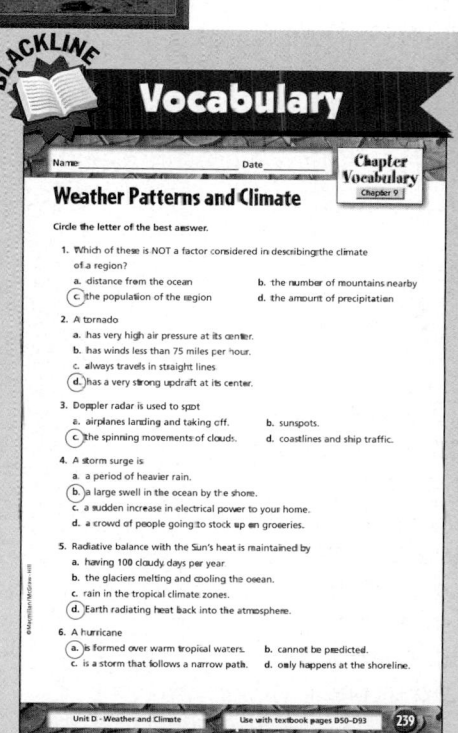

Reading in Science Resources, pp. 239–240

LESSON 5 — Air Masses and Fronts

Objectives

- Explore how weather can differ in different parts of the country.
- Explain how air masses produce different kinds of weather along fronts.
- Describe how satellites can be used to help predict the weather.
- Identify different methods for making weather predictions.

Resources

- Activity Resources, pp. 140–146
- Reading in Science Resources, pp. 221–226
- Vocabulary Cards
- Reading Aid Transparency D5
- Visual Aid Transparency 24

Build on Prior Knowledge

Have students discuss what they know about forecasting weather. Review what they learned about the information given by weather station models. Draw a weather map similar to the one on page D53. Then ask students to label the part of the map that shows: wind direction, wind speed, air pressure, pressure change, cloud cover, and air temperature.

1 Get Ready

Using the Illustrations

Direct student's attention to the picture of the thunderstorm. Have students describe weather conditions portrayed in the photograph. Then have them describe other conditions present in a thunderstorm not visible in the picture. (Possible answers: strong winds, lightning, flooding, the sound of thunder) Discuss movement of air masses and fronts that might lead to this type of storm. Discuss changes in air movement and fronts that might lead to clear sunny skies.

LESSON 5 — Air Masses and Fronts

Vocabulary

air mass, D54

front, D55

cold front, D56

warm front, D56

occluded front, D56

stationary front, D57

Get Ready

Have you ever watched a "wall" of clouds heading toward you? Did the clouds bring gentle, steady rain or heavy downpours? Knowing what kind of weather is on the way can help you make plans.

Part of what weather forecasters need to watch for is approaching air masses and fronts. Why might your weather today depend on what someone else's weather was like yesterday?

Process Skill

You **interpret data** when you use the information that has been gathered to answer questions or solve a problem.

D 52

🦉 Science Background

Frontal Theory

Norwegian physicist Vilhellm Bjerknes (1862–1951) and his son Jakob set up a network of weather stations in Norway. Their observations helped develop the frontal theory that states that large air masses with different properties do not mix right away; instead, they form boundaries called fronts.

Explore Activity

How Can You Compare Weather?

Materials

station model key

newspaper weather map (optional)

pencil

crayons

Procedure

Communicate Think of the country in large regions—the Northeast, the Southwest, and so on. Think of regions like the Pacific Coast, the Atlantic Coast, and the Gulf Coast. Write a report for the weather in each region based on the map you see here.

Drawing Conclusions

1 **Infer** Which areas are having warm, rainy weather?

2 **Infer** Where is the weather cool and dry?

3 **Predict** How do you think weather in any part of the country may change, based on the data in this map? Give reasons for your answer. How would you check your predictions?

4 **Going Further: Interpret Data** Using weather maps in a newspaper, or the one on this page, describe the weather.

W   E

San Francisco

Lines are drawn to show wind direction, not speed. This is a wind coming from the east, going west—an east wind.

Temperatures here are given in Fahrenheit degrees.

® = rain

Explore Activity

How Can You Compare Weather?

Science Process Skills *communicate, infer, predict, interpret data*

Resources Activity Resources, pp. 140–142

Pacing 30–40 minutes

Grouping pairs

Answers to Drawing Conclusions

1 New Orleans, Galveston, Cincinnati

2 The Northwest, including Seattle and the Midwest including Denver and Kansas City

3 Answers will vary but should be based on the wind direction indicators on the map showing a general tendency to move from west to east.

4 Answers will vary.

Inquiry Students can ask their own questions to explore, such as why nearby cities can have different weather, or distant cities can have similar weather.

Technology

- When time is short, preview the activity with the **Explore Activity Video.**

Alternative Explore Activity

Materials same as Explore Activity above

On the Table Have students organize the data in the weather station models into a table. Encourage them to group the cities by region, so that regional patterns can be easily seen. **Spatial**

Activity Resources, p. 143

2 Read to Learn

How Do Air Masses Affect Weather?

Before Reading
Have students try to answer the red question at the top of the page.

Using the Illustrations
Draw students' attention to "Air Masses." Ask:

- **Why are air masses formed over the Gulf of Mexico warm and moist?** (because they share the properties of their source region, the Gulf of Mexico, which is warm water)

- **Which source region differs the most from the Gulf of Mexico? Why?** (the polar region, because it is very cold and dry)

Developing the Main Idea
Remind students of what they have learned about the properties of air. Ask:

- **What is a front? How does it form?** (A front is the boundary between two air masses. It forms when air masses with different conditions meet.)

- **What happens when cold air meets warm air? Why?** (The cold air sinks, and the warm air rises. This is because cold air is denser, while warm air is less dense.)

Developing Vocabulary

air mass Discuss how the meaning of *mass,* an amount or body of matter sticking together, such as a mass of clay, can apply to the gases in air. Namely, the gases in an air mass are defined by their density; they are more or less dense than gases in the surrounding air.

front Remind students that *front* means "leading edge." Ask students how this would apply to weather conditions.

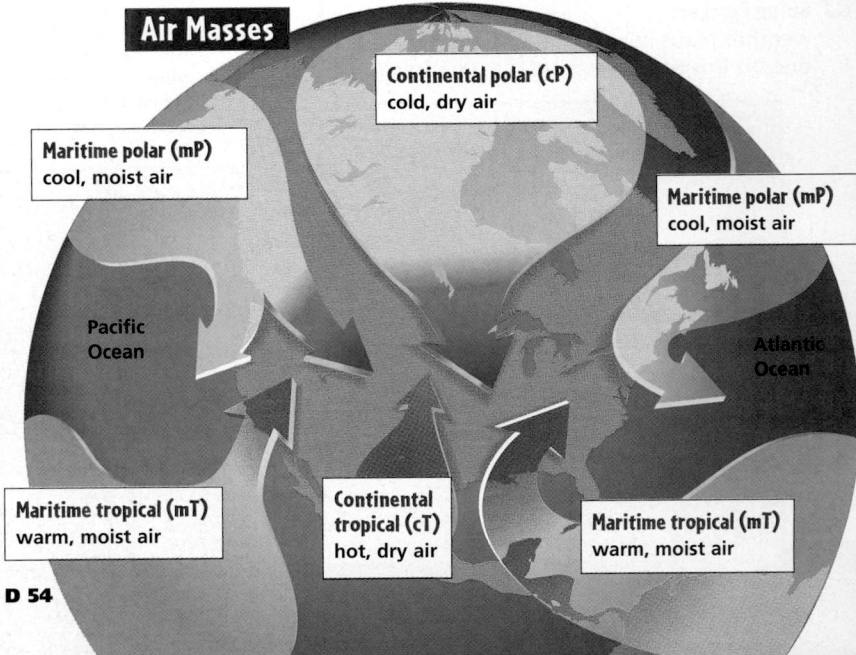

Read to Learn

Main Idea Weather changes often occur at fronts, where different air masses meet.

How Do Air Masses Affect Weather?

Weather maps show that cities across a large region can share the same weather. They also show how the weather in different areas can differ.

Why are weather conditions in one part of a country different from those in another part? Look back at the map on page D53. Some of the cities are having clear, cool weather. The air throughout this region is cool and dry. Other cities are having warmer, cloudy weather. The air throughout this region is warm and moist. A large region of the atmosphere where the air has similar properties throughout is called an air mass.

An air mass gets its properties from the region where it forms. Air over the Gulf of Mexico is above very warm water. The water warms the air, and evaporation from the Gulf adds water vapor. The air becomes warm and moist. Air masses are named for the region they come from.

As air masses move, they bring these conditions with them. What happens if a cool, moist air mass moves over an area that has warm, dry weather? The warm, dry weather will change.

Air Masses

Continental polar (cP)
cold, dry air

Maritime polar (mP)
cool, moist air

Maritime polar (mP)
cool, moist air

Pacific Ocean

Atlantic Ocean

Maritime tropical (mT)
warm, moist air

Continental tropical (cT)
hot, dry air

Maritime tropical (mT)
warm, moist air

D 54

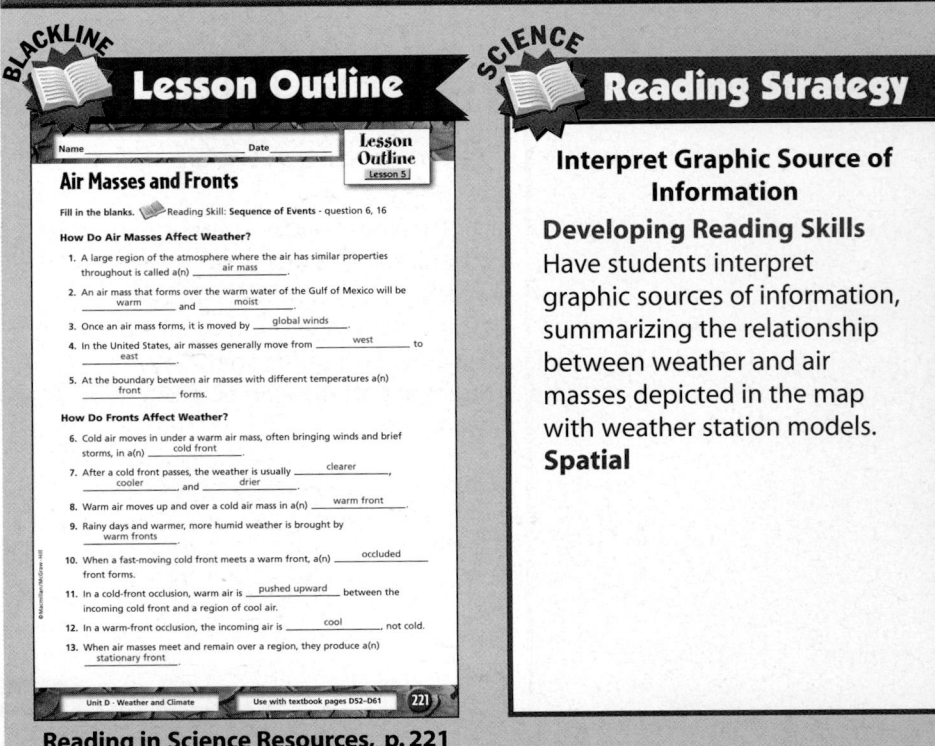

Reading in Science Resources, p. 221

Reading Strategy

Interpret Graphic Source of Information

Developing Reading Skills
Have students interpret graphic sources of information, summarizing the relationship between weather and air masses depicted in the map with weather station models.
Spatial

A Weather Front

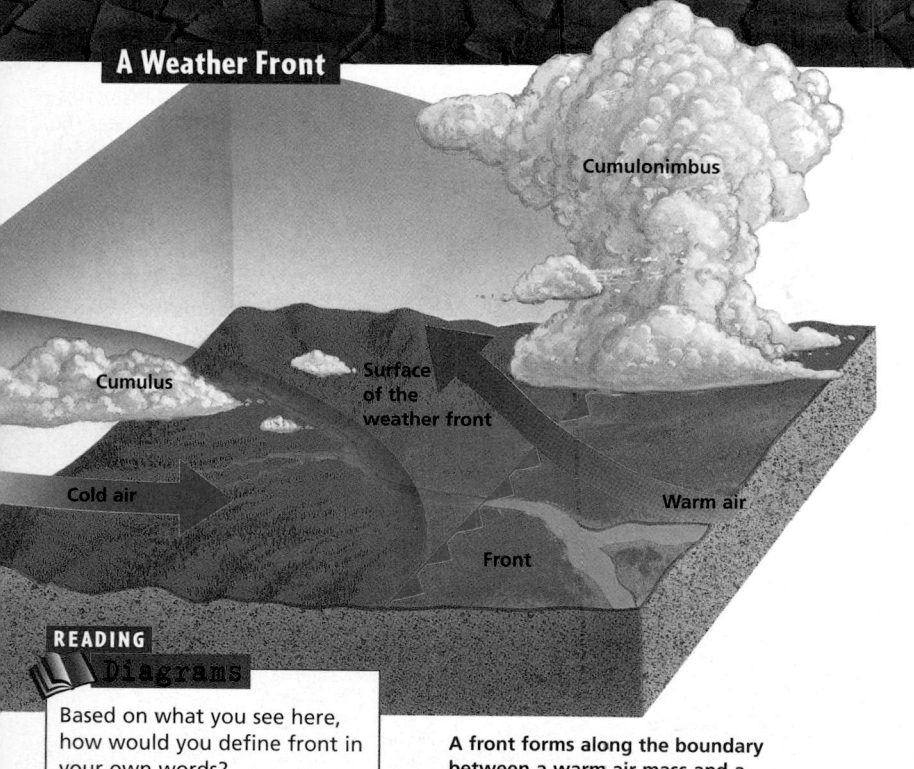

Cumulonimbus

Cumulus

Surface of the weather front

Cold air

Warm air

Front

A front forms along the boundary between a warm air mass and a cold air mass.

Once an air mass is formed, it is moved by global winds. In the United States, global winds tend to move air masses from west to east.

Air masses with different conditions can "meet." That is, one runs into another. What happens when air masses with different temperatures meet? They don't mix together. Instead, a narrow boundary forms between them. This boundary is called a front. It marks the leading edge, or front, of

an air mass that is moving into an area where another air mass is moving out. Weather changes rapidly at fronts. That's because you pass from one kind of air mass into another. Fronts often cause rainy, unsettled weather. There are several types of fronts that can form.

READING Sequence of Events
What happens when a cold air mass meets with a warm air mass?

They form a boundary called a front.

D 55

Thinking Further: *Inferring*
Ask:

■ **What kind of weather would you expect, then, if a cold air mass moved into a warm air mass, and the cold air moved under the warm air?** (Students should infer that the weather would be cooler.)

■ **What weather would you expect if warm air moved in above cold air? Why?** (The weather would be warmer, because warm air was moving in on cold air that was already there, warming the region.)

READING
Diagrams

Students' answers will vary, but should note that a front is formed along the boundary between the two air masses.

▶ **After Reading**
Have students answer the red question in the student book as **ongoing assessment**.

Technology

■ Visual Aid Transparency 24: *A Weather Front*

Reading in Science Resources, p. 223

How Do Fronts Affect Weather?

Before Reading
Have students try to answer the red question at the top of the page.

Developing the Main Idea
Ask:

- **What kind of weather would you expect a cold front to produce?** (short, heavy rains, often thunderstorms with heavy winds, followed by clear skies and cooler, drier weather)

- **What kind of weather does a warm front produce?** (steady rain or snow that may last for days and light winds, followed by warmer and more humid weather)

Using the Illustrations
Draw students' attention to "Weather Produced by Fronts." Point out that in chemistry, the term *occlude* means "to take up and hold." Ask:

- **How does a cold-front occlusion differ from a warm-front occlusion?** (In a cold-front occlusion, the air behind the advancing cold front is cold. Cold air moves in on cool air, and warm air is pushed up between them, producing weather like that of a cold front. In a warm-front occlusion, the air behind the incoming cold front is simply cool, while the air in front of the warm front is cold. The weather produced is more like that of a warm front.)

Developing Vocabulary

The first word in the name of each kind of front gives a clue to help students distinguish one front from another.

cold front In a cold front, the *cold* air mass moves in under the warm air mass.

warm front In a warm front, the *warm* air mass moves in over a cold air mass.

occluded front The verb *occlude* means "to stop" or "to block." In this kind of front, two fronts meet and the regular movement of the fronts is blocked, although they do move.

stationary front The word *stationary* means "nonmoving, staying in place." This front remains in place.

How Do Fronts Affect Weather?

- In a **cold front**, cold air moves in under a warm air mass. Cold fronts often bring brief, heavy storms. There may be thunderstorms and strong winds. After the storm the skies are usually clearer, and the weather is usually cooler and drier.

- In a **warm front**, warm air moves in over a cold air mass. Warm fronts often bring light, steady rain or snow. The precipitation may last for days. Winds are usually light.

Warm fronts may also bring fog—stratus clouds that form near the ground. Afterward the weather is usually warmer and more humid.

- An **occluded** (uh-KLEWD-uhd) **front** occurs when a cold front and a warm front meet. A fast-moving cold front moves in on a warm front. There are two ways this can happen:

    In a cold-front occlusion, the air behind the front is cold. The air ahead of the warm front is cool. What is happening is that cold air is

Weather Produced by Fronts

COLD FRONT

Warm air

Cold air

Warm air

Colder, denser air moves in under a region of warm air.

COLD-FRONT OCCLUSION

Warm air

Cold air

Cool air

A cold front catches up with a warm front, pushing the warm air up and away.

Different fronts produce different kinds of weather. The weather along a front depends upon how the air masses interact.

D 56

Cultural Perspective

Andean Farmers
Point out to students that while weather satellites and weather stations are relatively new, there is nothing at all new about weather prediction. Modern Andean farmers, the descendants of ancient Incas, observe the weather to help them make decisions about planting and harvesting. Like both their ancient ancestors and modern-day meteorologists, Andean farmers make observations that are based on patterns in the environment.

Interpret Illustrations

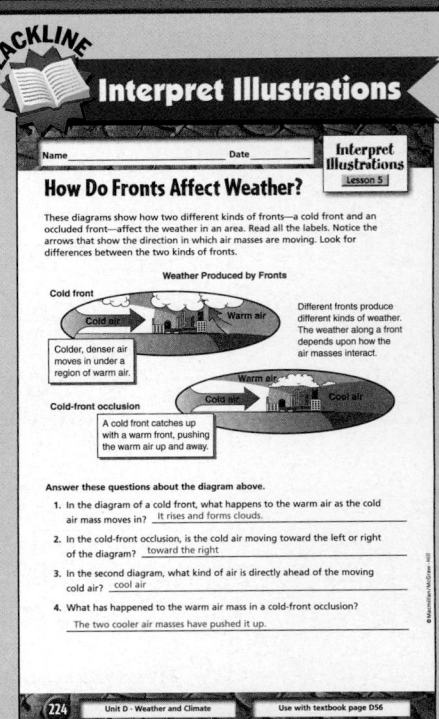

Name _____ Date _____

Interpret Illustrations
Lesson 5

How Do Fronts Affect Weather?

These diagrams show how two different kinds of fronts—a cold front and an occluded front—affect the weather in an area. Read all the labels. Notice the arrows that show the direction in which air masses are moving. Look for differences between the two kinds of fronts.

Weather Produced by Fronts

Cold front

Cold air — Warm air

Colder, denser air moves in under a region of warm air.

Different fronts produce different kinds of weather. The weather along a front depends upon how the air masses interact.

Cold-front occlusion

Cold air — Cool air

A cold front catches up with a warm front, pushing the warm air up and away.

Answer these questions about the diagram above.

1. In the diagram of a cold front, what happens to the warm air as the cold air mass moves in? *It rises and forms clouds.*

2. In the cold-front occlusion, is the cold air moving toward the left or right of the diagram? *toward the right*

3. In the second diagram, what kind of air is directly ahead of the moving cold air? *cool air*

4. What has happened to the warm air mass in a cold-front occlusion? *The two cooler air masses have pushed it up.*

224 | Unit D • Weather and Climate | Use with textbook page D56

Reading in Science Resources, p. 224

---

moving in on cool air and warm air is pushed up between them. The weather along this front will be like that produced by a cold front.

In a warm-front occlusion, the air behind the incoming cold front is just cool, not cold. The air in front of the warm front, however, might be cold. Then the weather will be more like that produced by a warm front.

- A cold air mass and a warm air mass may meet and remain over an area for

days without moving. This is called a **stationary front**. Stationary fronts usually have calm weather.

▶ **What kind of weather does a cold front usually produce?**

brief, heavy precipitation followed by cooler, drier weather

READING
Diagrams

1. Write a paragraph comparing a warm front with a cold front.

2. Write an explanation of what an occluded front is.

WARM FRONT

Warm air

Cold air

Warm air moves into a region, rising up and over the colder air mass already there.

WARM-FRONT OCCLUSION

Warm air

Cool air

Cold air

A cold front catches up with a warm front, pushing the warm air up and away.

D 57

1. Students' paragraphs should note that in both fronts, a cold air mass and warm air mass meet. In a cold front, however, cold air advances on and moves under a mass of warm air, producing brief storms followed by cooler, drier weather; in a warm front, warm air advances on and moves above a mass of cold air, producing steady precipitation followed by warmer, more humid weather.

2. An occluded front occurs when a cold-front catches up to a warm front, pushing the warm air up and away.

▶**After Reading**
Have students answer the red question in the student book as **ongoing assessment**.

SCIENCE FOR ALL — Advanced Learners

Buys Ballot's Law
Point out that fronts are usually located along a low-pressure trough. This means that air pressure drops as a front moves in, and rises after it has passed. Using Buys Ballot's Law (have them use encyclopedias), challenge students to predict the behavior of winds in the Northern Hemisphere as a front passes. (Buys Ballot's Law states that when wind is at one's back, low pressure is always on the left in the Northern Hemisphere, so the winds would blow to the left.) **Logical**

SCIENCE FOR ALL — English Language Learners

Create Word Search Puzzles
Divide the class into small groups to create word search puzzles using lesson vocabulary. Direct them to write clues and construct puzzles hiding the terms horizontally, diagonally, or vertically in a grid of letters. Photocopy each puzzle, and distribute them to each student. **Social**

Why Are Weather Satellites Important?

Before Reading
Have students try to answer the red question at the top of the page.

Developing the Main Idea
Discuss with students that some satellites that orbit Earth are equipped to take pictures of weather patterns. They orbit in a way that allows them to follow a weather pattern as it moves across Earth's surface. Fronts are an important clue to how weather will change. In areas just ahead of a front, weather changes are imminent. When fronts collide, scientists can locate places where the weather may change quickly. Ask:

- **What information do satellites give weather scientists?** (They show large weather patterns, such as fronts and storms.)

Why Are Weather Satellites Important?

Pictures taken from space are great tools for seeing large weather patterns, such as fronts and storms. Scientists send up satellites in orbit around Earth. Some of these satellites are equipped to take pictures of weather patterns. These satellites move in orbit in a way that allows them to follow a weather pattern as it moves slowly across Earth's surface.

To find fronts on a satellite map, look for swirling lines of clouds. The curved lines often mark the movement of fronts.

Fronts are an important clue to how weather will change. As a front moves, areas just ahead of the front are about to have a change in weather.

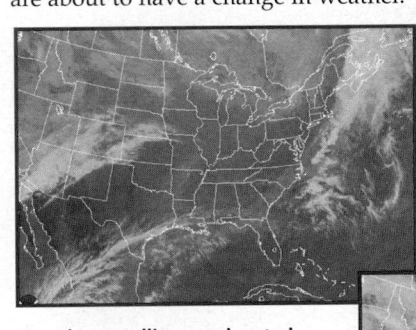

Weather satellites are located above the equator. They are more than 36,000 km (22,000 mi) above Earth's surface. Several of these satellites work together to produce a nearly complete picture of the globe every half-hour.

Reading Strategy

Compare and Contrast
Developing Reading Skills
Encourage students to compare and contrast the satellite image with the weather map of the United States.

Science Background

Weather Satellites
The U.S. satellite Explorer VII, launched in 1959, was the first satellite to provide weather data. The Explorer was not dedicated solely to weather, however. The first specialized weather satellite, TIROS I, was launched the following year. Currently, the U.S. makes use of two sun-synchronous satellites. Cruising at a height of about 500 miles, the two satellites orbit above each pole every 2 hours, taking pictures of most parts of Earth every 6 hours.

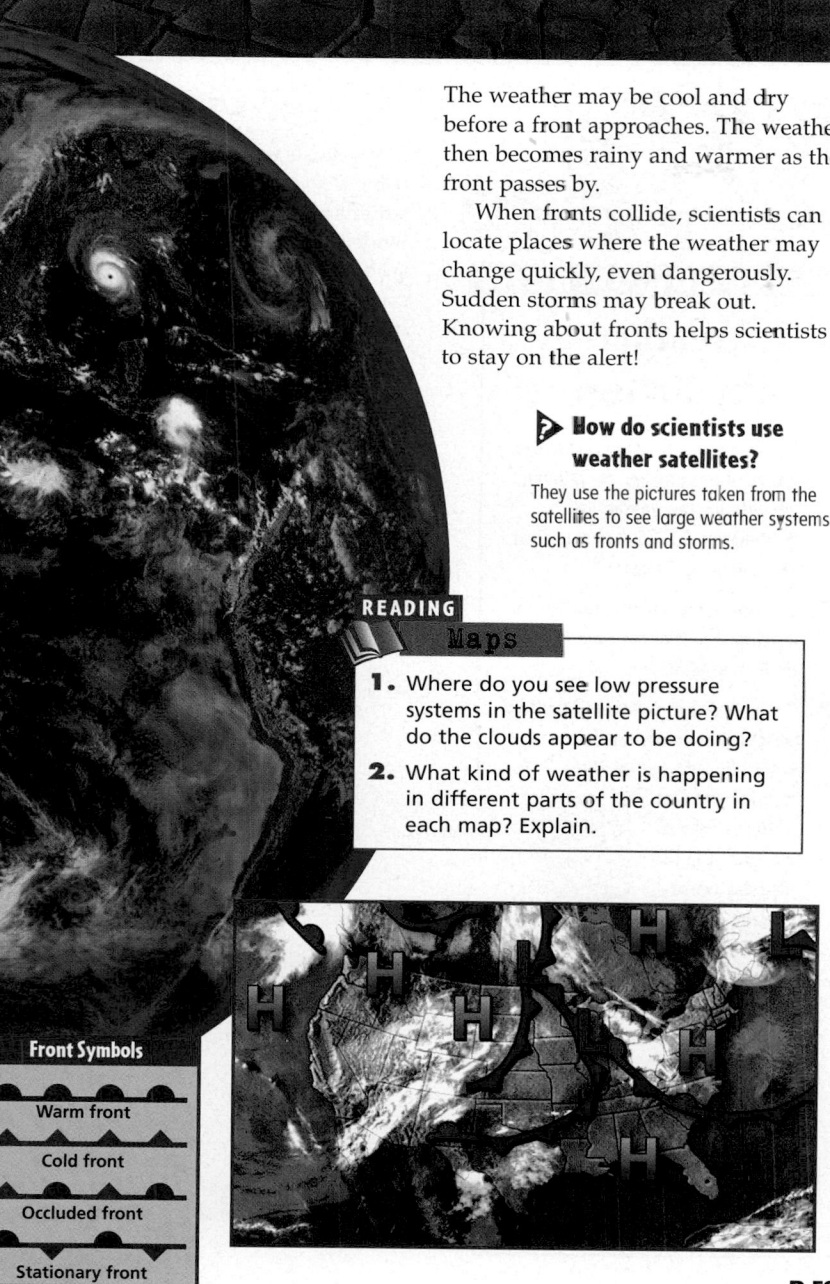

The weather may be cool and dry before a front approaches. The weather then becomes rainy and warmer as the front passes by.

When fronts collide, scientists can locate places where the weather may change quickly, even dangerously. Sudden storms may break out. Knowing about fronts helps scientists to stay on the alert!

▶ **How do scientists use weather satellites?**

They use the pictures taken from the satellites to see large weather systems such as fronts and storms.

READING

Maps

1. Where do you see low pressure systems in the satellite picture? What do the clouds appear to be doing?

2. What kind of weather is happening in different parts of the country in each map? Explain.

Front Symbols

Warm front

Cold front

Occluded front

Stationary front

D 59

Developing the Main Idea
Ask:

■ **What can watching the movement of weather fronts for a period of days help you do?** (It can help you predict when warmer or cooler weather might arrive.)

■ **If the weather before a front is cool and dry, what might happen as the front passes?** (It might become rainy and hot.)

■ **If fronts collide, what might happen?** (The weather may change quickly, producing sudden, dangerous storms.)

Encourage interested students to further investigate how fronts affect the weather.

Thinking Further: *Inferring*
Ask:

■ **If you wanted to know how fronts were likely to affect the weather in your area over the next few days, how would you use a weather map?** (Students should recall that fronts generally move from west to east in the United States. They should infer that, to find out what kind of weather to expect, they should study the areas on the map to the west of their area.)

READING

Maps

1. The white areas are clouds reflecting the Sun's light. These are areas of low pressure. The dark areas indicate clear skies and high pressure.

2. Accept all accurate student explanations.

▶**After Reading**
Have students answer the red question in the student book as **ongoing assessment**.

SCIENCE FOR ALL

Advanced Learners

Proverbs
Point out to students that there are a number of proverbs that give tidbits of useful information about storms and fronts. For example, "Dark clouds in the west, best stay indoors and rest." Encourage students to apply lesson concepts to write proverbs of their own. Allow time for them to share their proverbs with the class.
Linguistic

Why Use Weather Records?

Before Reading
Have students try to answer the red question at the top right of the page.

Developing the Main Idea
Point out to students that while watching fronts and analyzing other conditions give forecasters a good basis for predicting the kind of weather that will move in over an area, other atmospheric events may arise that unexpectedly change the outlook.

Discuss an answer to the question that makes up the last sentence of the text column. Students could predict that the weather would become clearer and colder.

▶ After Reading
Have students answer the red question in the student book as ongoing assessment.

Science Process Skills *infer*

Resources Activity Resources, pp. 144–146

Grouping pairs

Step 1 7 degrees Celsius, clear, wind from the south and the pressure is 1027 mb

Step 2 in both the southeast and northwest, high pressure, partly to mostly cloudy, low temperatures

Step 3 The weather will become cooler in the area just east of the cold front as the cold front passes over it. There will be a period of thunderstorms, although the area east of the cold front is already having rain. As the front approaches Washington, D.C. that area will have milder temperatures with increasing clouds, but will get cold as the front passes over the area.

FOR SCHOOL OR HOME

Weather Prediction

1. The map shows weather across the United States at 6 P.M. on October 29. Describe the weather in Washington, D.C. The temperatures are in degrees Celsius.

2. Describe the weather in the northwest part of the country and in the southeast.

3. Infer Weather patterns move from west to east across the United States. How do you think the weather just east of the cold front will change in the next day or so? Explain.

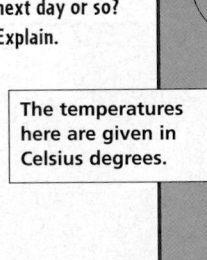

The temperatures here are given in Celsius degrees.

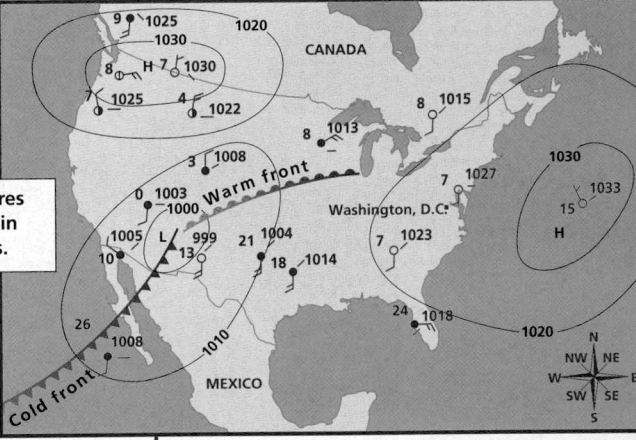

D 60

Why Use Weather Records?

Scientists usually forecast the weather using a *synoptic weather map*. It shows a summary of the weather using station models. By comparing maps made every six hours, scientists can tell how weather systems are moving and use this information to predict the weather.

If you look at weather records to see what happened in the past, you can find patterns. *Statistical forecasting* is based on finding patterns.

What if the wind has just started blowing from the west? Past records show that 75 out of the last 100 times the wind blew from the west, your weather became clearer and colder. What weather prediction would you make?

> By studying past weather records, scientists can find patterns. This is called statistical forecasting.

▶ **How do scientists use weather records to forecast weather?**

SCIENCE
Reading Strategy

Ask Questions

Developing Reading Skills
Encourage students to raise unanswered questions about how scientists predict weather. They can use their questions as a basis for class discussion or research.

Why It Matters

Weather forecasting is hard. Knowing how the atmosphere is moving lets you predict the weather. The problem is that the atmosphere is huge and complex. A weather forecaster might predict clear weather for tomorrow. However, another air mass might move in. Everything can change.

Computers do high-speed calculations to predict the atmosphere's motion. Predictions are compared with forecasts to account for any differences. Two-day forecasts are calculated every 12 hours. A five-day forecast is calculated daily.

Think and Write

1. What are four different kinds of air masses? How are they different?

2. What kind of weather is produced by a cold front? A warm front?

3. How can satellites help predict the weather?

4. How can you use weather maps to predict weather?

5. **Critical Thinking** How can you tell what kind of front is passing by just by observing the weather?

L·I·N·K·S

WRITING LINK

Write a story. Explain how changes in the weather affected the way three different people spent their day.

SOCIAL STUDIES LINK

Research the history of weather prediction. Use encyclopedias or other reference books to learn about the *Book of Signs*. The *Book of Signs* is a book of 200 weather indicators. It was written in 300 B.C. by Theophrastus. Pick one of the signs dealing with weather fronts. Do you think that sign might be helpful in predicting the weather? Write a paragraph explaining why or why not.

TECHNOLOGY LINK

Science Newsroom CD-ROM Choose *It's Up in the Air* to learn more about how air masses affect weather conditions.

At the Computer Visit **www.mhscience02.com** for more links.

D 61

3 | Lesson Review

Answers to Think and Write

1. Arctic air masses form over very cold arctic regions; polar air masses form over cold polar regions; tropical air masses form over warm southern regions; and maritime air masses form over water. (p. D54)

2. Cold fronts bring brief, heavy storms, followed by clear skies and cooler, drier weather; warm fronts often bring light, steady precipitation followed by warmer, more humid weather. (pp. D56–D57)

3. They provide pictures of fronts that help scientists predict how weather may change. (pp. D58–D59)

4. They show where fronts are located. This helps predict likely weather because areas ahead of fronts are likely to experience weather changes. (p. D60)

5. **Critical Thinking** Brief, heavy storms can indicate a cold front or occluded front; fog or light, steady rain or snow indicate a warm front or occluded front; calm weather may indicate a stationary front. (pp. D56–D57)

Summarize

Check students' understanding by having them write a brief summary of the lesson in their own words.

WRITING LINK

Students' stories should mention specific weather conditions and their impact on normal daily activities.

SOCIAL STUDIES LINK

Encourage students to choose a sign that they can relate to frontal activity. Arguments for and against should be well supported.

✓ Informal Assessment

Easy/Average Have groups create crossword puzzles using lesson vocabulary and concepts. Have them write clues and construct the puzzles, then exchange with partners and complete.

Challenge Provide copies of daily newspaper maps for one week and a U.S. map showing the states. Have small groups draw the most westerly cold front on the map and plot the front's movement. Use data from the maps to record temperature, air pressure, wind direction and speed, and cloud cover. Have students write a caption on the map that tells how fronts affect weather across the country.

History of Science

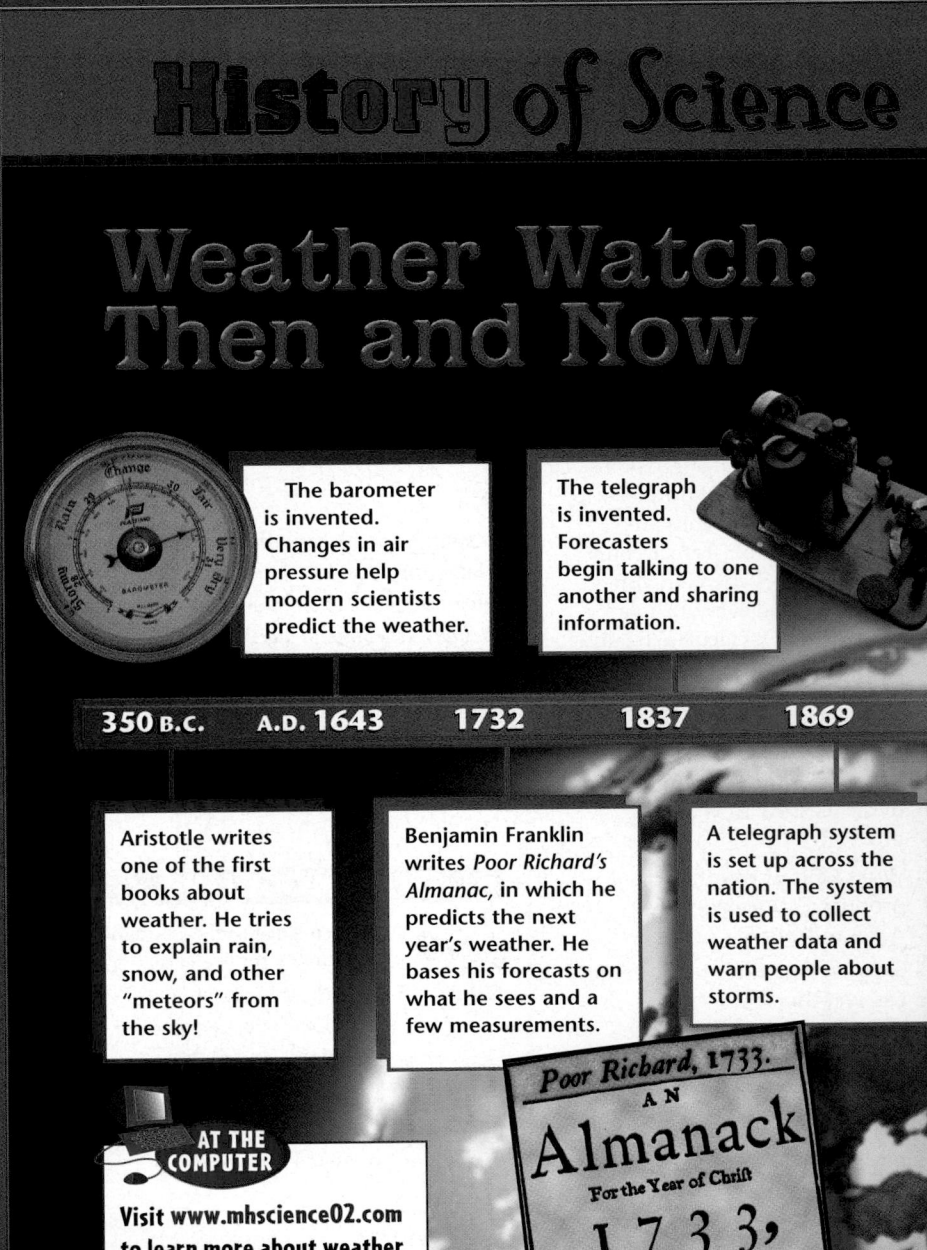

Weather Watch: Then and Now

The barometer is invented. Changes in air pressure help modern scientists predict the weather.

The telegraph is invented. Forecasters begin talking to one another and sharing information.

| 350 B.C. | A.D. 1643 | 1732 | 1837 | 1869 |

Aristotle writes one of the first books about weather. He tries to explain rain, snow, and other "meteors" from the sky!

Benjamin Franklin writes *Poor Richard's Almanac*, in which he predicts the next year's weather. He bases his forecasts on what he sees and a few measurements.

A telegraph system is set up across the nation. The system is used to collect weather data and warn people about storms.

 **AT THE COMPUTER**

Visit www.mhscience02.com to learn more about weather.

Poor Richard, 1733.

AN
Almanack
For the Year of Christ
1 7 3 3,
Being the First after LEAP YEAR.

	Years
And makes since the Creation	7241
By the Account of the Eastern Greeks	6932
By the Latin Church, when ☉ ent ♈	5742
By the Computation of W.W.	5689
By the Roman Chronology	5494

D 62

Objective

- Describe methods of weather prediction from the past.

Build on Prior Knowledge

Have students suggest ways that people predicted the weather before we had television and newspapers to tell us what to expect. (Possible answer: they used their common sense, observations, and experience.)

Weather Watch: Then and Now

Developing the Main Idea
Ask:

- **Why was it helpful for forecasters to be able to communicate with each other using the telegraph?** (If they knew about a storm or snowfall in another area, they could measure wind speed and direction and have a good idea whether it would affect their own area.)

- **Why would people be concerned about the weather during wartime?** (Being able to predict storms or even cloudy weather could help them plan troop movements and attacks.)

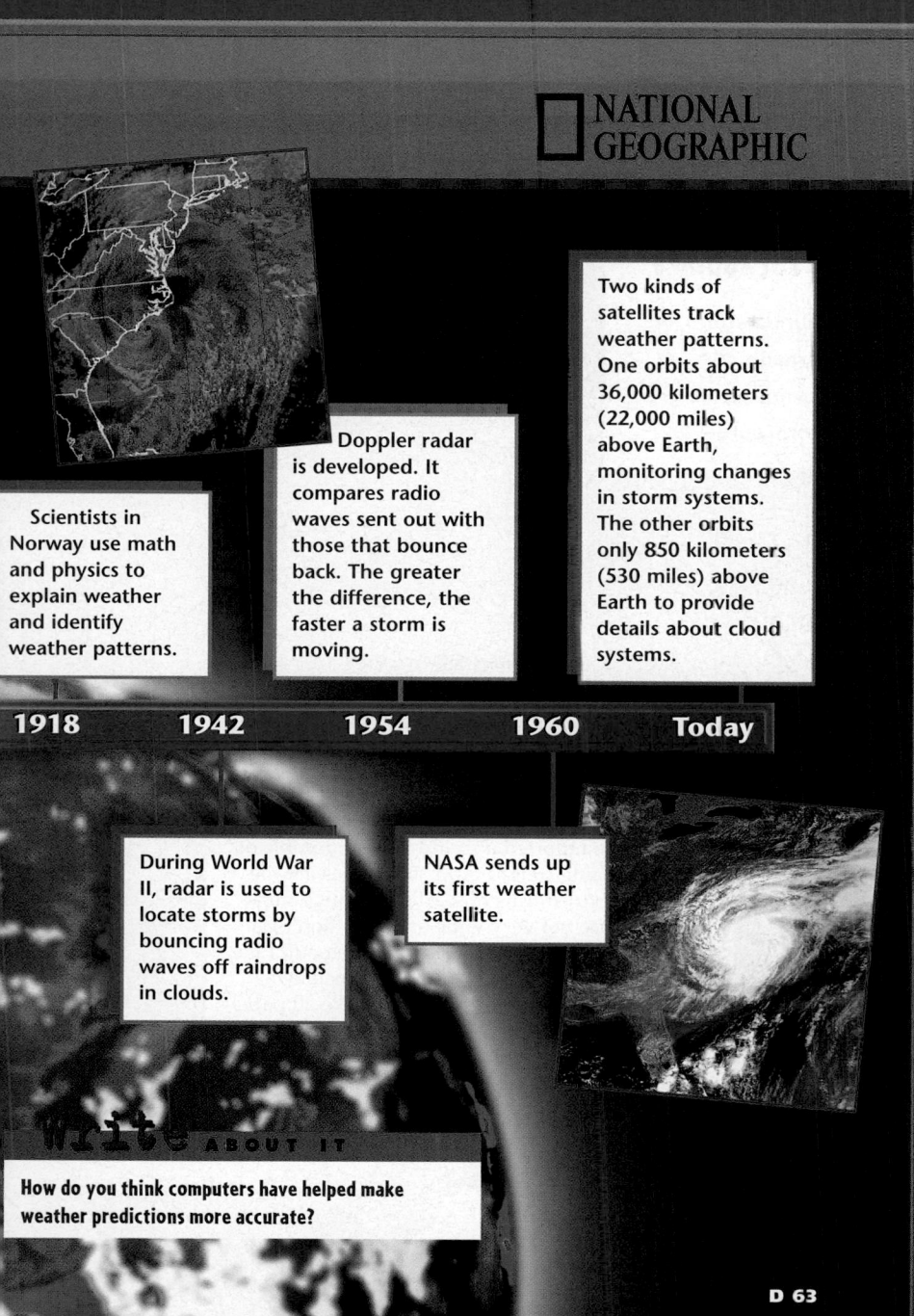

NATIONAL GEOGRAPHIC

Scientists in Norway use math and physics to explain weather and identify weather patterns.

Doppler radar is developed. It compares radio waves sent out with those that bounce back. The greater the difference, the faster a storm is moving.

Two kinds of satellites track weather patterns. One orbits about 36,000 kilometers (22,000 miles) above Earth, monitoring changes in storm systems. The other orbits only 850 kilometers (530 miles) above Earth to provide details about cloud systems.

| 1918 | 1942 | 1954 | 1960 | Today |

During World War II, radar is used to locate storms by bouncing radio waves off raindrops in clouds.

NASA sends up its first weather satellite.

Write ABOUT IT

How do you think computers have helped make weather predictions more accurate?

D 63

Developing the Main Idea
Ask:

■ **How have worldwide communication systems contributed to weather prediction?** (Weather takes place globally, with fronts and pressure systems affecting each other. The more forecasters know about weather in other areas, the better they can predict what will happen locally.)

■ **Why do you think today's weather forecasters are still wrong part of the time?** (Weather changes depend on complex interactions that aren't always predictable.)

■ **Everyone profits from knowing what weather is ahead. Why might some nations not want weather satellites stationed above them?** (They might think the satellites are spying on secret activities in their nations.)

Answers to Write ABOUT IT

Computers allow for quick and accurate integration and organization of immense amounts of data from many sources.

Science Background

Figuring Out Forecasts

The first national forecasting agency was the United States Weather Bureau, which began in 1870 as a branch of the military. In 1891, it came under civilian control and is now known as the National Weather Service.

Today, computers at the National Meteorological Center, a branch of the National

Weather Service, create maps of weather conditions from gathered data, which are sent to National Weather Service offices, the media, and weather organizations in other nations. Meteorologists there study this information and create their own forecasts.

Inclusion

Designing Weather Maps

Have pairs of students create their own symbols to show the weather on a map of the United States. They must decide how to show high and low pressure areas and warm, cold, and stationary fronts. Have each pair mark the weather they predict on a map of the United States. Then combine pairs into groups of three. Each pair will explain to other group members what its symbols represent. As a class, discuss which symbols were clearest and why. **Spatial; Logical**

LESSON 6 Severe Storms

Objectives

- Explore where tornadoes are most likely to happen.
- Explain how thunderstorms and tornadoes are related.
- Describe what hurricanes are and how they can cause damage.
- Identify safety procedures and methods for predicting storms.

Resources

- Activity Resources, pp. 147–152
- Reading in Science Resources, pp. 227–232
- Vocabulary Cards
- Reading Aid Transparency D6
- Visual Aid Transparencies 25, 26
- Grade-Level Science Book, *Trouble at Forest Park*

Build on Prior Knowledge

Have students discuss severe storms. Ask students who have experienced a tornado or thunderstorm if they would like to share their experiences.

1 Get Ready

Developing the Main Idea
Ask:

- **How do you think scientists predict tornadoes?** (They watch for certain weather conditions that cause tornadoes to form.)

- **Where in the United States is "tornado country?"** (the Central Plains area)

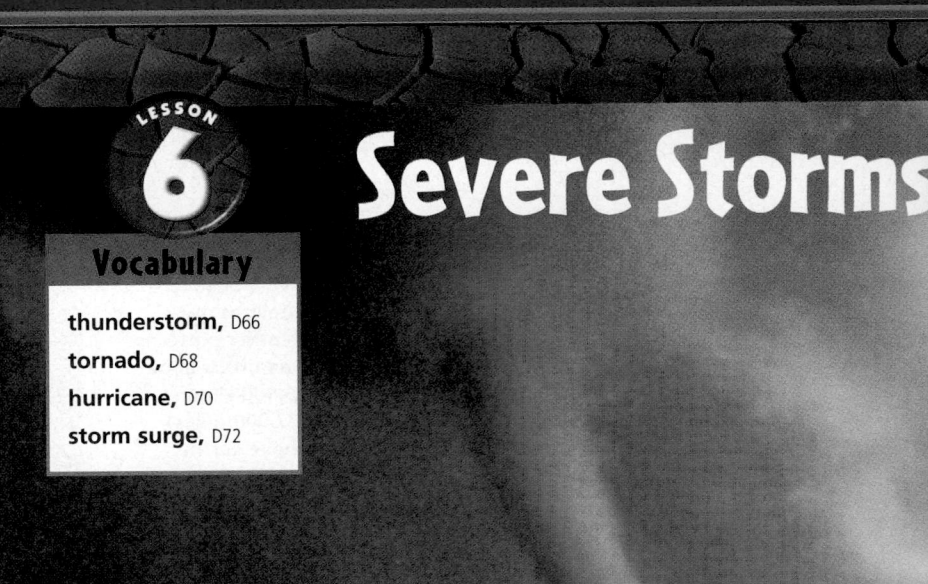

LESSON 6 Severe Storms

Vocabulary

thunderstorm, D66
tornado, D68
hurricane, D70
storm surge, D72

Get Ready

What's it like to be in the path of a tornado? People have reported a sound like the rumble of an approaching freight train. Tornadoes are the most powerful storms on Earth. Although most tornadoes are not very wide and they don't last too long, when they touch down watch out! Like deadly whirling brooms, they can sweep away anything in their path. Tornadoes strike all parts of the United States, but they are more frequent in some regions than in others. Where in the U.S. is "tornado country"?

Process Skill

You use numbers when you use ordering, counting, adding, subtracting, multiplying, and dividing to explain data.

D 64

Cross Curricular Books

Additional Outside Reading

The Great Galveston Hurricane

To order, see page D1·b.

Inclusion

Wind in a Jug

Students can simulate tornado-like air rings. Divide the class into pairs, providing each with a one-gallon plastic milk jug. Have one student aim the jug at the other, and slap the bottom with his or her hand. The other student's hair will be blown by the air ring that forms. Remind students that air moves from an area of high pressure to an area of low pressure, which creates winds.
Social

Explore Activity

Where Do Tornadoes Occur?

Procedure

1 **Infer** The table shown here lists how many tornadoes occurred in each state over a 30-year period. It also shows about how many tornadoes occur in each state each year. Look at the data in the table for two minutes. Now write what part of the country you think gets the most tornadoes.

2 Use the red marker to record on the map the number of tornadoes that occurred in each state over the 30-year period. Use the blue marker to record the average number of tornadoes that occurred in a year in each state.

Drawing Conclusions

1 **Use Numbers** Which states had fewer than 10 tornadoes a year? Which states had more than 20 tornadoes a year?

2 **Interpret Data** Which six states had the most tornadoes during the 30-year period?

3 **Interpret Data** Which part of the country had the most tornadoes?

4 **Going Further: Communicate** Many people refer to a certain part of the country as "Tornado Alley." Which part of the country do you think that is? Why do you think people call it that? What else might these states have in common? Describe how you would go about finding the answer to that question.

Materials

map of U.S., including Alaska and Hawaii

blue marker

red marker

State	Total	Average per year
AL	668	22
AK	0	0
AZ	106	4
AR	596	20
CA	148	5
CO	781	26
CT	37	1
DE	31	1
FL	1,590	53
GA	615	21
HI	25	1
ID	80	3
IL	798	27
IN	604	20
IA	1,079	36
KS	1,198	40
KY	296	10
LA	831	28
ME	50	2
MD	86	3
MA	89	3
MI	567	19
MN	607	20
MS	775	26
MO	781	26
MT	175	6
NE	1,118	37
NV	41	1
NH	56	2
NJ	78	3
NM	276	9
NY	169	6
NC	435	15
ND	621	21
OH	463	15
OK	1,412	47
OR	34	1
PA	310	10
RI	7	0
SC	307	10
SD	864	29
TN	360	12
TX	4,174	139
UT	58	2
VT	21	1
VA	188	6
WA	45	2
WV	69	2
WI	625	21
WY	356	12

D 65

Alternative Explore Activity

Materials encyclopedias and other research materials

In the Alley Remind students that more tornadoes occur in the Central Plains of the United States than anyplace else on Earth. Encourage them to use encyclopedias to investigate the weather conditions that contribute to tornado formation, and challenge them to identify the relationship between these conditions and the Central Plains region. **Logical**

In the Alley

Procedure

1. Find out about the weather conditions that cause tornadoes to form. Use encyclopedias and any other research materials that may be helpful. Write down what you learned.

   Tornadoes form where dry, cold air masses mix with warm, moist air masses.

2. Research the climate in the Central Plains region. What are conditions like there during the spring and early summer?

   During the spring and early summer, warm, moist air from the south or southwest meets cool, dry air from the west or northwest in the Central Plains region.

Materials
• encyclopedias and other research materials

Drawing Conclusions

1. Why do you think tornadoes are common in the Central Plains region?

   During the spring and early summer, the mixing of warm, moist air with cool, dry air in the Central Plains region causes tornadoes to form.

2. Compare the climate where you live to the climate in the Central Plains region. Are tornadoes common where you live? Why or why not?

   Answers will vary depending on the local climate.

150   Unit D · Weather and Climate   Use with TE textbook page D65

Activity Resources, p. 150

Explore Activity

Where Do Tornadoes Occur?

Science Process Skills *infer, use numbers, interpret data, communicate*

Resources Activity Resources, pp. 147–149

Pacing 30–40 minutes

Grouping pairs

Procedure

1 Tornadoes occur most frequently through the midsection of the country, from the Gulf Coast through the Great Plains.

Answers to Drawing Conclusions

1 AK, AZ, CA, CT, DE, HI, ID, ME, MD, MA, MT, NV, NH, NJ, NM, NY, OR, RI, UT, VT, VA, WA, and WV experienced fewer than 10 tornadoes per year; AL, CO, FL, GA, IL, IA, KS, LA, MS, MO, NE, ND, OK, SD, TX, and WI had more than 20 tornadoes per year. AR had an average of 20 per year.

2 FL, IA, KS, NE, OK, and TX had the most tornadoes in a 30-year period.

3 the midsection of the country

4 Students might suggest that "Tornado Alley" runs, like an alley, through the middle of the United States, from the Gulf Coast up through the Great Plains. They might suggest that these areas share certain weather conditions that contribute to the formation of tornadoes, and that they could use encyclopedias to investigate these conditions.

Inquiry Students can ask their own questions to explore, such as what causes the increased incidence of tornadoes in the "Tornado Alley."

Technology

■ When time is short, preview the activity with the **Explore Activity Video.**

2 Read to Learn

What Are Thunderstorms?

Before Reading
Have students try to answer the red question at the top of the page.

Developing the Main Idea
Ask:

- **What causes lightning?** (Air from updrafts rubs against air from downdrafts, creating static electricity. The static electricity builds up, until lightning sparks.)

Developing Vocabulary

thunderstorm Have students recall the last time they experienced a thunderstorm. Invite them to discuss the components of the storm. (Thunder, lightning, heavy downpours tapering off to lighter rain)

Read to Learn

Main Idea Thunderstorms, tornadoes, and hurricanes are severe storms that can cause great damage.

What Are Thunderstorms?

A tornado is a violent kind of storm that forms under special conditions. Often such storms grow out of another, more common kind of storm—a **thunderstorm**.

Thunderstorms are the most common kind of severe storm. They form in clouds called *thunderheads*—cumulonimbus clouds. The storms cause huge electric sparks called *lightning*. The lightning heats the air and causes the noise called *thunder*. Thunderstorms usually have heavy rains and strong winds. Some thunderstorms also produce hail.

First Stage
A thunderstorm starts when intense heating causes air to rise very quickly. A cloud forms where there is an upward rush of heated air, an *updraft*. As more and more warm, moist air is carried upward, the cloud grows larger and larger. Strong updrafts keep droplets of water and ice crystals in the cloud, so they grow in size, too. When the updrafts can't support them anymore, they fall as heavy rain or even hail.

Second Stage
Once the rain falls, it causes downdrafts in the cloud. That is, air moves downward. When the air going up rubs against air going down, static electricity builds up. When enough builds up, there's a huge spark—lightning.

How a Thunderstorm Forms

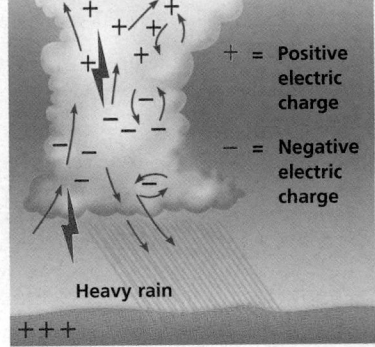

+ = Positive electric charge

− = Negative electric charge

Warm air rises.

Heavy rain

1 Strong updrafts form inside the cloud.

2 Electric charges build up inside the cloud.

D 66

Reading Strategy

Interpret Graphic Sources of Information

Developing Reading Skills
Encourage students to interpret the graphic sources of information on p. D66 to explain how a thunderstorm forms.

Lesson Outline

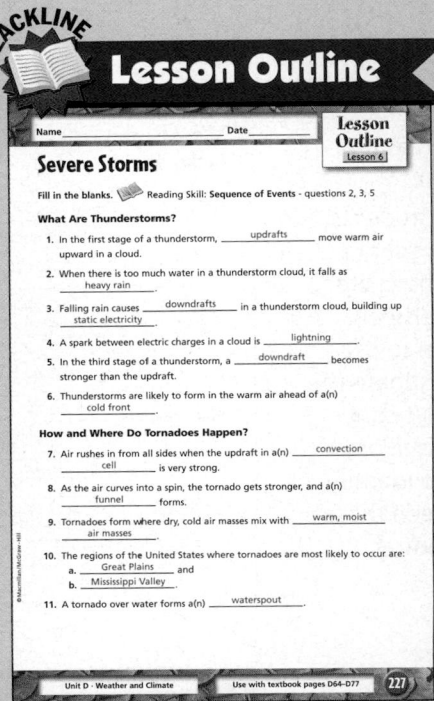

Reading in Science Resources, p. 227

Thunderstorms form in cumulonimbus clouds. Thunderstorms often produce strong winds and heavy downpours along with the lightning and thunder.

Lightning is unpredictable. It may jump from the cloud to the ground or from the ground to the cloud. It may jump between two thunderclouds. It may also jump from one spot to another within the cloud. Lightning superheats the air so the air suddenly expands. It slams into the air around it with such force that it makes a mighty sound—thunder.

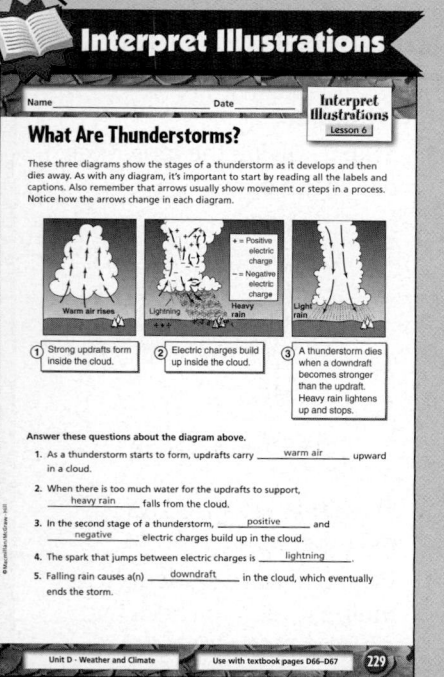

Light rain

A thunderstorm dies when a downdraft becomes stronger than the updraft.

Third Stage

The storm dies when a downdraft becomes stronger than the updraft. Heavy rain lightens up and stops.

Thunderstorms usually form in the warm air just ahead of a cold front. The cold, dense air wedges under the warm, moist air and causes the warm air to rise rapidly. Be on the lookout for thunderstorms. They are likely when the weather is hot and humid and a cold front is approaching.

▶ **Where do thunderstorms usually form?** in the warm air just ahead of a cold front

READING
Diagrams

Write a description of how a thunderstorm forms. Identify what happens during each stage of formation.

D 67

Exploring the Main Idea

Darken the classroom. Rub an inflated balloon with a piece of fur, nylon, or wool. Tell students to watch closely as you bring your finger near the balloon. Ask:

■ **Why do you think the spark forms?** (Students will probably know that the sparks are caused by electricity. Explain that rubbing the balloon caused an electric charge to build up on the balloon. When your finger came close to the balloon, electricity jumped from the balloon to your finger.)

■ **How is this like lightning?** (In lightning, the rubbing of downdraft air against updraft air causes molecules to split into pieces with opposite charges. This static electricity builds up, and is released as lightning.)

READING
Diagrams

First, strong updrafts form inside a cloud. Warm air rises, and water droplets and ice crystals form in the cloud. When they get too heavy for the updrafts to support, they fall as rain or hail. Downdrafts form, and electric charges build up as a result of updraft air rubbing against downdraft air. Lightning occurs. Thunder occurs because lightning heats, expands, and slams the air into surrounding air. Heavy rain then tapers off to light rain.

▶ **After Reading**

Have students answer the red question in the student book as **ongoing assessment**.

Technology

■ Visual Aid Transparency 25: *How a Thunderstorm Forms*

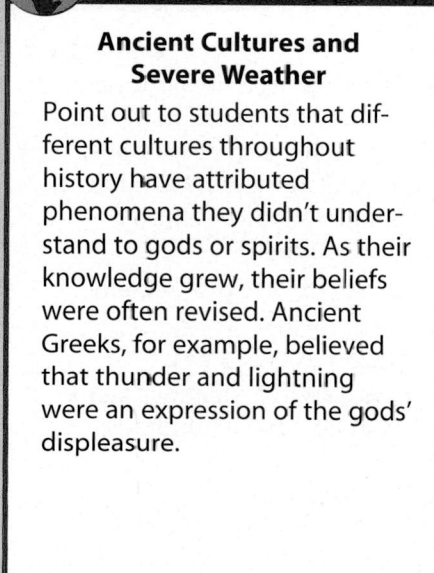
Reading in Science Resources, p. 229

Cultural Perspective

Ancient Cultures and Severe Weather

Point out to students that different cultures throughout history have attributed phenomena they didn't understand to gods or spirits. As their knowledge grew, their beliefs were often revised. Ancient Greeks, for example, believed that thunder and lightning were an expression of the gods' displeasure.

How and Where Do Tornadoes Happen?

Before Reading
Have students try to answer the red question at the top right of the page.

Developing the Main Idea
Ask:

- **What do thunderstorms and tornadoes have in common?** (They are both kinds of severe storms, they both begin as convection cells, and they both are more likely to occur when a cold front meets warm, moist air.)

- **When warm air is drawn up into a convection cell, what happens to the air pressure?** (It drops.)

- **If the convection cell is very strong, how would air move?** (It would rush in at high speed.)

- **How would the pressure be affected?** (It would continue to drop.)

Materials two 2-L plastic bottles, duct tape, water, paper towel, pencil

Science Process Skills *make a model, observe, infer*

Resources Activity Resources, pp. 151–152

Grouping pairs

Step 3 Students should describe that the water in the top bottle spins in a counterclockwise direction as it flows into the bottom bottle.

Step 4 The model is like a real tornado because the water, like a tornado, formed a funnel shape.

Developing Vocabulary

tornado Students may not be able to differentiate between types of storms. Have them describe a tornado as seen from television, news, or weather reports. *Tornado* may relate back to a Latin word, *tonare,* for "to thunder."

FOR SCHOOL OR HOME

Tornado in a Bottle

1. **Make a Model** Fill a 2-L plastic bottle one-third full of water. Dry the neck of the bottle, and tape over the top with duct tape. Use a pencil to poke a hole in the tape.

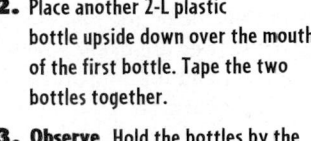

2. Place another 2-L plastic bottle upside down over the mouth of the first bottle. Tape the two bottles together.

3. **Observe** Hold the bottles by the necks so the one with the water is on top. Swirl them around while your partner gently squeezes on the empty bottle. Then place the bottles on a desk with the water bottle on top. Describe what you see.

4. **Infer** How is this like what happens when a tornado forms? Explain.

D 68

How and Where Do Tornadoes Happen?

The most violent thunderstorms often spin off even more dangerous storms—tornadoes. A tornado is a violent whirling wind that moves across the ground in a narrow path.

How They Happen
Late in the day, when Earth's surface is very warm, convection can get very strong. This can lead to a tornado. A tornado is a sort of runaway convection cell.

- When the updraft in a convection cell is really strong, the air rushes in from all sides at high speeds.

- The air curves into a spin. This lowers the pressure even more. Air rushes in even faster, and the pressure gets even lower, and so on. Like a spinning skater who pulls her arms in close to her sides, the spinning tornado gets faster and faster.

- As the tornado gets stronger, a funnel forms that eventually touches the ground. In the center of a tornado, winds can reach speeds of 500 km per hour (about 300 mi per hour) or more. At such high speeds, winds can destroy anything in their path.

The speed of the wind in the tornado is not the speed with which the tornado moves across the ground. It moves across the ground very fast but can change its direction continually.

Math MiniLesson

Divide by a 1-Digit Number

Develop Weather airplanes fly into the center of a hurricane to watch the storm. Suppose an airplane flew 1,950 miles in 3 hours. What was the airplane's speed?
Divide to solve the problem.
Find: $1,950 \div 3$
Step 1 Think: $3 > 1$
Write the first digit of the quotient above the hundreds.

$$\begin{array}{r} 6 \\ 3\overline{)1950} \\ \underline{18} \quad \leftarrow 3 \times 6 = 18 \\ 1 \quad \leftarrow 9 - 8 = 1 \end{array}$$

Step 2 Divide the tens. Then divide the ones.

$$\begin{array}{r} 650 \\ 3\overline{)1950} \\ \underline{18} \\ 15 \\ \underline{15} \quad \leftarrow 3 \times 5 = 15 \\ 0 \end{array}$$

 1950 ÷ 3 = 650

The airplane's speed was 650 miles per hour.

Practice Have students use multiplication to check the answers for the exercise.

Where They Happen

Most tornadoes in the United States seem to occur in the Midwest and in the South.

Tornadoes form where dry, cold air masses mix with warm, moist air masses. In the United States, this is most likely to happen in the Great Plains region and the Mississippi Valley. Florida also gets lots of tornadoes.

Tornadoes are most likely to occur when there are big differences in the air masses. This happens most often in early spring and summer. Tornadoes can also form over water. Such tornadoes are called *waterspouts*.

Tornadoes form when dry, cold air masses mix with warm, moist air masses. They are more likely to occur if there are big differences between the air masses.

READING
Maps

What states are in Tornado Alley?

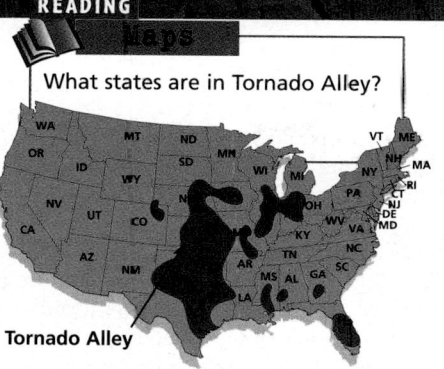

Tornado Alley

More tornadoes occur in the United States than in any other country, especially in the area known as Tornado Alley.

▷ **When are tornadoes likely to form?**

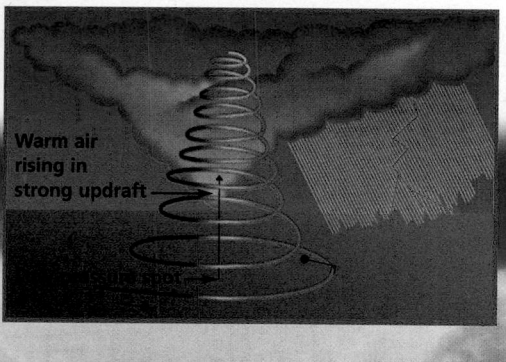

Warm air rising in strong updraft

READING
Diagrams

1. Where is the pressure lowest in the tornado?

2. In what direction is the wind spinning—clockwise (like the hands of a clock) or counterclockwise (the opposite direction)?

Tornadoes that form over water are called waterspouts.

D 69

Using the Illustrations

Draw students' attention to the diagram showing how a tornado forms from a thunderstorm. Ask them to summarize the information depicted by the diagram. (Warm air rises into a thundercloud, causing the air pressure to drop. The decrease in pressure causes air to rush in, decreasing pressure further. The Coriolis effect causes the air to spin, which even further drops the air pressure. Finally, the spinning clouds may turn into a tornado and form a funnel.)

READING
Maps

TX, OK, MO, KS, NE, IA, IL, IN; FL, MS, GA, and AL also get a large number of tornadoes.

READING
Diagrams

1. The pressure in a tornado is the lowest at its center.

2. The wind spins counterclockwise.

▶ **After Reading**
Have students answer the red question in the student book as **ongoing assessment**.

Inclusion

Spinning Tornado
Encourage students to use their bodies to investigate how a spinning tornado accelerates. In a wide open space, direct them to spin, noting how they move faster as momentum picks up. As they gain speed, suggest that they pull their arms into their sides to see how their movement is affected.
Kinesthetic

Science Background

Tornado Detection
Tornadoes are cyclonic in nature. That is, they are characterized by the rapid, inward circulation of air around a low-pressure center. Though certain weather conditions give rise to tornadoes, they are unpredictable. Scientists, however, are making strides in the early detection of tornadoes. Doppler radar detects the rapidly rising air, as well as the descending funnels, allowing time to warn people likely to be affected.

How Do Hurricanes Form?

Before Reading
Have students try to answer the red question at the top of the page.

Using the Illustrations
Ask:

- **How does the air move in a hurricane?** (Hot air enters at the bottom and spirals upward. At the top, the hot air cools, and goes back down through the center, or eye, of the storm.)

Developing Vocabulary

hurricane Ask students if they or anyone they know have experienced the force of a hurricane. Have them share their experiences. See *English Language Learners* on page D71.

Technology

- Visual Aid Transparency 26: *Hurricanes*

How Do Hurricanes Form?

If you live near an ocean or the Gulf Coast, you may have experienced a **hurricane**. Hurricanes are very large, swirling storms with very low pressure at their center. They form over tropical oceans—near the equator.

Air masses near the equator tend to be very much alike. They don't form the fronts that you learned about in Lesson 5. Instead, they form lots of thunderstorms.

- Strong heating and lots of evaporation over the ocean can cause a large low-pressure center to form. If this happens, winds begin to blow in toward the low. As this rushing air nears the center, it moves upward and forms a ring of tall thunderstorms.

- The Coriolis effect causes winds to spiral counterclockwise in the Northern Hemisphere. Clusters of thunderstorms are pulled into the spiral. The thunderstorms merge, forming a single large storm.

- As water vapor in the storms condenses, heat is released. The air

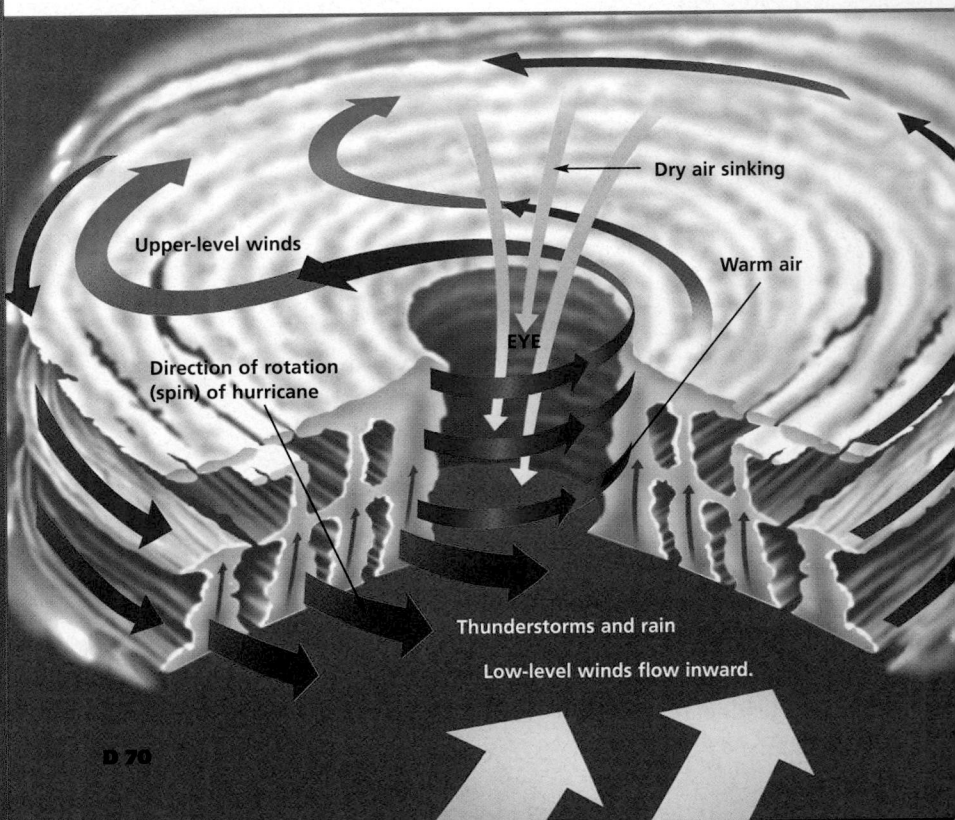

Dry air sinking

Upper-level winds

Warm air

EYE

Direction of rotation (spin) of hurricane

Thunderstorms and rain

Low-level winds flow inward.

D 70

Reading Strategy

Interpret Graphic Sources of Information

Developing Reading Skills
Have students interpret the graphic illustration on p. D70 to explain how a hurricane develops.

Interpret Illustrations

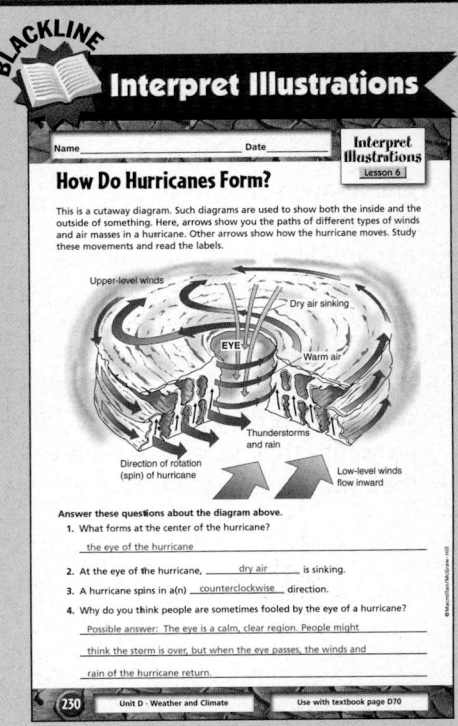

Reading in Science Resources, p. 230

is warmed. This decreases the air's density and pressure. Moisture evaporating into the air decreases the air's density and pressure even more. Low air pressure favors more evaporation. This lowers the pressure even more.

- The lower the air pressure, the faster are the winds that blow in toward the center of the storm. When the winds reach speeds of 120 km per hour (about 75 mi per hour) or higher, the storm is a hurricane.

- As the moist air in the storm rises and cools, condensation takes place. The clouds thicken. Heavy rains fall through the high winds. When fully formed, a hurricane has an eye at its center. The eye is an area of light winds and skies that are nearly clear.

Hurricanes can easily grow to more than 700 km (about 400 mi) in diameter. For example, Hurricane Fran was almost as large as the entire state of Florida!

READING Sequence of Events
How does lower and lower air pressure lead to the formation of a hurricane?

The lower the air pressure, the faster the winds blow in toward the center of the storm. When the winds reach a speed of 120 km per hour (about 75 mi per hour), the storm is a hurricane.

This satellite photograph shows a hurricane and its eye. Hurricanes can pick up about 20 billion tons of water a day from the oceans. Much of this water falls as rain over land areas.

Direction of wind

D 71

Developing the Main Idea
Ask:

- **How is the formation of a hurricane like that of a tornado?** (They both can arise from thunderstorms.)

- **How does their formation differ?** (Tornadoes form when cold, dry air masses move into warm, moist air masses. Hurricanes form when clusters of thunderstorms are pulled into a spiral formed by a large low pressure area.)

- **What are the things that the two kinds of storms have in common?** (They both arise from thunderstorms; they both are destructive; the air spins counterclockwise in both; and they both are dependent on the formation of a low-pressure center.)

- **In what ways do tornadoes and hurricanes differ?** (Tornadoes form over land, while hurricanes form over water; the formation of tornadoes involves fronts; tornadoes are much smaller than hurricanes; the wind in a tornado may be much stronger than that of a hurricane; tornadoes last a much shorter period of time than hurricanes; hurricanes can be more easily predicted than tornadoes.)

▶**After Reading**
Have students answer the red question in the student book as **ongoing assessment**.

Reading MiniLesson

Sequence of Events

Develop Discuss in order to understand hurricane formation, students must be aware of why and how events happen. List the main events in order on the board, using bullets to focus students' attention on the sequence: thunderstorms line up, large low pressure center, winds spiral, air heats and lowers air pressure, faster winds, clouds and heavy rain.

Practice Have students reread the information about the Coriolis effect on page D70 and make flowcharts to follow the sequence. Interested students may wish to illustrate their flowcharts.

English Language Learners

The Word *Hurricane*
Point out to students that the word *hurricane* probably came from a Taino word used in the Caribbean meaning "big wind." The 15th-century explorers who first reached the Caribbean had never experienced winds so strong, and did not have a word in their vocabulary to describe them. They therefore incorporated the native term into Spanish, and its use has persisted. **Linguistic**

How Do Hurricanes Affect Ocean Waves?

Before Reading

Have students try to answer the red question at the top of the page.

Developing the Main Idea

Ask:

- **How do air pressure changes cause the storm surge to form?** (A drop in air pressure releases some of the pressure on the surface of the ocean, allowing it to rise.)
- **What happens as the hurricane moves over the coast?** (The water level can rise, or surge, several feet.)
- **How else is water forced ashore?** (Hurricane winds push water ahead of the storm, forcing it ashore.)
- **How do storm surges cause damage?** (They cause flooding, which destroys property; they also can cause drownings.)

Developing Vocabulary

storm surge Students will be familiar with the definition of *storm*. *Surge* means to "rise and fall." Have students try to define the term from the two words.

How Do Hurricanes Affect Ocean Waves?

Just north of the equator, gentle global winds move hurricanes west to northwest at 10 to 20 km per hour (6 to 12 mi per hour). As they move north, away from the equator, their speed tends to increase.

Hurricane winds whip up large waves in the ocean. These waves move outward from the storm and pound against a shore for days before the storm arrives. However, it is the **storm surge** that causes the most destruction. Storm surge is a great rise of the sea along a shore. Its main cause is low air pressure.

Air pressure normally presses down on the surface of the sea like a giant hand. When the pressure drops in a hurricane, it is like lifting the hand slightly. The surface of the sea rises, forming a bulge beneath a hurricane.

When the hurricane moves over a coast, the bulge can cause water levels to suddenly rise several feet, or surge.

Hurricane winds also push water ahead of the storm, forcing water onshore and adding to the storm surge. If the storm surge comes at high tide, it is even worse. Great storms have surges that raise the water level by 7 meters (about 20 feet) or more.

During a great storm, the surge, large waves, high winds, and torrential rain of the storm all happen at the same time. Low-lying coastal areas are flooded. Beachfront homes are destroyed. Beaches can get worn away.

A Real Hurricane—Fran

On August 22, 1996, a storm formed off the coast of Africa and began moving west-northwest at about 16 km per hour (10 mi per hour). By August 29 it had become more concentrated. Winds reached hurricane strength. Hurricane Fran was born. Fran continued moving

Scientists from the National Hurricane Center in Florida keep an eye on dangerous hurricanes.

D 72

Science Background

The Galveston Hurricane

In 1900, Galveston, Texas, experienced the disastrous effects of a fierce hurricane. Even before the storm hit the island, huge waves had completely inundated it. The wind speed approached 120 miles per hour, and 6,000 people were drowned or killed by flying debris. Thousands were injured, and nearly 4,000 homes were destroyed. When the city was rebuilt, it was done behind massive sea walls designed to protect against similar storms in the future.

Science Background

Real Damage

Addressing Misconceptions

Students may believe that hurricanes, like tornadoes, wreak most of their havoc with dangerous winds. In fact, the storm surge causes more destruction than the winds; coastal flooding destroys property, erodes the coast, and can cause drowning.

A hurricane's storm surges and heavy rains can cause flooding. Strong winds can damage homes, trees, and power lines.

Developing the Main Idea
Ask:

- **What conditions are necessary in order for a hurricane to form?** (water and heat)
- **Why do hurricanes begin to die out when they move over land?** (Cut off from the warm ocean, there is no water to replace what falls as rain.)
- **Why does wind speed decrease?** (because of the friction between the winds and the land)

▶ **After Reading**
Have students answer the red question in the student book as **ongoing assessment**.

west and was even stronger by the time it skirted the Bahamas. By September 5, 1996, Fran had 105-knot winds and was 400 km (250 mi) off the Florida coast.

A large low-pressure system over Tennessee steered it westward, and it struck North Carolina and Virginia on September 6. Winds of 120 knots were clocked off Cape Fear as Fran came ashore. Sea level surged to 3.6 m (12 ft) above normal. As much as 40 cm (16 in.) of rain fell in parts of North Carolina. Thirty-four people died. Flash flooding caused most deaths. A storm surge on the North Carolina coast destroyed many beachfront houses.

High winds damaged trees and roofs. They also downed power lines, leaving 4.5 million people without power. Nearly half a million people were ordered to evacuate the coast. Altogether it is estimated that Fran caused 3.2 billion dollars of damage.

Hurricanes begin to die out when they move over land. Cut off from the warm ocean, the hurricane has no water to replace what falls as rain. Friction between the winds and the land decreases wind speed. When it has been over land long enough, it will completely die out.

Once Hurricane Fran moved ashore, it steadily weakened. By the time it reached central North Carolina, it was no longer a hurricane. By the time it reached the Great Lakes on September 9, it was no longer even a storm. The remains of Fran disappeared on September 10.

 **What do hurricanes do to ocean waves?**

Winds create big waves, lower air pressure causes storm surges, rain adds to rising sea level.

D 73

 Science Background

Franklin's Observations
Have students use encyclopedias or history references to learn about Benjamin Franklin's accidental observations that led to his conclusion that hurricanes are cyclonic storms that travel counterclockwise from south to north. Encourage students to consider the importance of this discovery in terms of our understanding of weather and storms. (Until Franklin's time, people believed that storms materialized overhead, then simply disappeared.)

English Language Learners

Hurricane Names
Point out that, in the Atlantic Ocean, hurricanes are named each year starting at the beginning of the alphabet. Suggest that students do a similar activity, using the letters of the alphabet, in order, as the first letter in words describing hurricanes. Allow time for students to share their lists with the class. **Linguistic; Social**

What Can You Do to Be Safe in a Storm?

Before Reading
Have students try to answer the red question at the top of the page.

Developing the Main Idea
Ask:

- **What is the difference between a storm watch and a storm warning? What should you do for either?** (A storm watch means that conditions are right for a storm, and a storm warning means that one has been spotted. For either, you should follow the instructions that are broadcast.)

▶ **After Reading**
Have students answer the red question in the student book as **ongoing assessment**.

Technology

- **Science Experiences Videotape**
  Tracking a Winter Storm (Package 6)

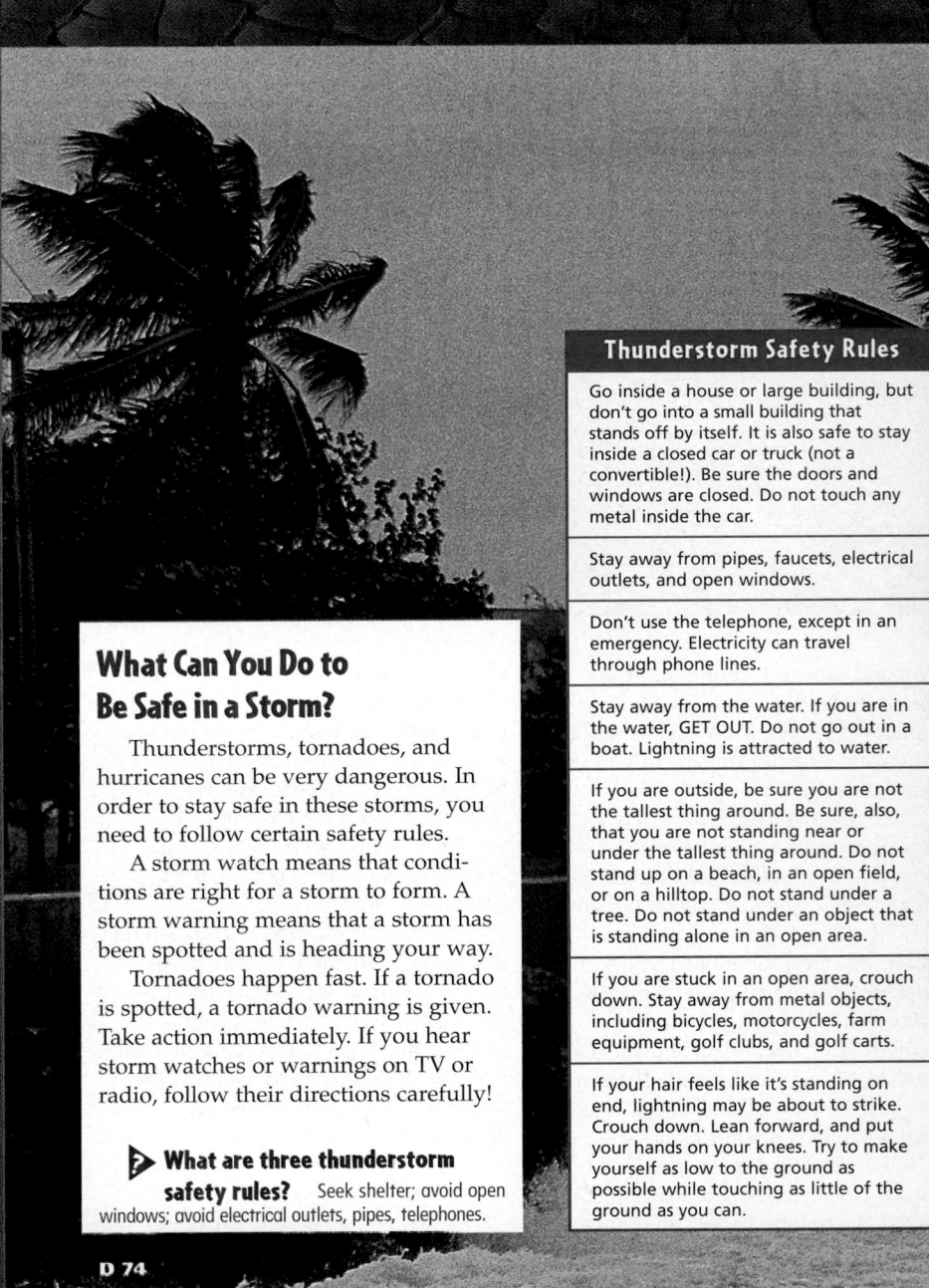

Thunderstorm Safety Rules

Go inside a house or large building, but don't go into a small building that stands off by itself. It is also safe to stay inside a closed car or truck (not a convertible!). Be sure the doors and windows are closed. Do not touch any metal inside the car.

Stay away from pipes, faucets, electrical outlets, and open windows.

Don't use the telephone, except in an emergency. Electricity can travel through phone lines.

Stay away from the water. If you are in the water, GET OUT. Do not go out in a boat. Lightning is attracted to water.

If you are outside, be sure you are not the tallest thing around. Be sure, also, that you are not standing near or under the tallest thing around. Do not stand up on a beach, in an open field, or on a hilltop. Do not stand under a tree. Do not stand under an object that is standing alone in an open area.

If you are stuck in an open area, crouch down. Stay away from metal objects, including bicycles, motorcycles, farm equipment, golf clubs, and golf carts.

If your hair feels like it's standing on end, lightning may be about to strike. Crouch down. Lean forward, and put your hands on your knees. Try to make yourself as low to the ground as possible while touching as little of the ground as you can.

What Can You Do to Be Safe in a Storm?

Thunderstorms, tornadoes, and hurricanes can be very dangerous. In order to stay safe in these storms, you need to follow certain safety rules.

A storm watch means that conditions are right for a storm to form. A storm warning means that a storm has been spotted and is heading your way.

Tornadoes happen fast. If a tornado is spotted, a tornado warning is given. Take action immediately. If you hear storm watches or warnings on TV or radio, follow their directions carefully!

▷ **What are three thunderstorm safety rules?** Seek shelter; avoid open windows; avoid electrical outlets, pipes, telephones.

D 74

 **Reading Strategy**

Sequence of Events
Developing Reading Skills
Have students act out the sequence of events to practice storm safety procedures.

 Science Background

Tornado Trackers
These trackers throw caution to the wind in their quest to get a close look at the storms, providing meteorologists with a great deal of information. And now, both can rely on TOTO — Totable Tornado Observatory, a new, portable weather station that can record wind speed, air pressure, and other data as a tornado moves over it. Scientists hope that TOTO will provide valuable information that has been, until now, elusive due to the damaging nature of tornado winds.

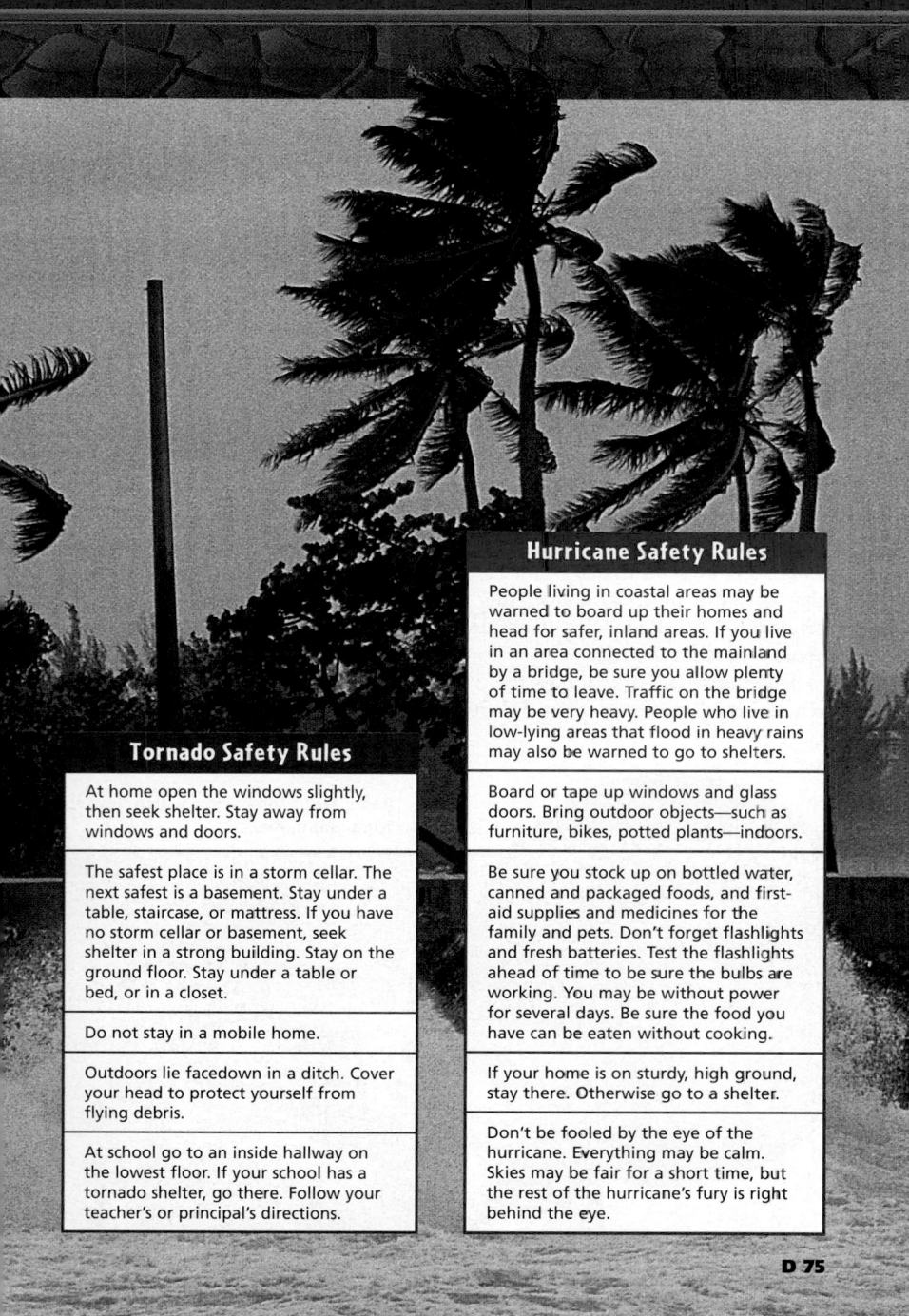

Tornado Safety Rules

At home open the windows slightly, then seek shelter. Stay away from windows and doors.

The safest place is in a storm cellar. The next safest is a basement. Stay under a table, staircase, or mattress. If you have no storm cellar or basement, seek shelter in a strong building. Stay on the ground floor. Stay under a table or bed, or in a closet.

Do not stay in a mobile home.

Outdoors lie facedown in a ditch. Cover your head to protect yourself from flying debris.

At school go to an inside hallway on the lowest floor. If your school has a tornado shelter, go there. Follow your teacher's or principal's directions.

Hurricane Safety Rules

People living in coastal areas may be warned to board up their homes and head for safer, inland areas. If you live in an area connected to the mainland by a bridge, be sure you allow plenty of time to leave. Traffic on the bridge may be very heavy. People who live in low-lying areas that flood in heavy rains may also be warned to go to shelters.

Board or tape up windows and glass doors. Bring outdoor objects—such as furniture, bikes, potted plants—indoors.

Be sure you stock up on bottled water, canned and packaged foods, and first-aid supplies and medicines for the family and pets. Don't forget flashlights and fresh batteries. Test the flashlights ahead of time to be sure the bulbs are working. You may be without power for several days. Be sure the food you have can be eaten without cooking.

If your home is on sturdy, high ground, stay there. Otherwise go to a shelter.

Don't be fooled by the eye of the hurricane. Everything may be calm. Skies may be fair for a short time, but the rest of the hurricane's fury is right behind the eye.

D 75

Developing the Main Idea
Ask:

- **What precautions would you take if you heard a thunderstorm watch? Would you do anything different if there were a warning?** (Students might respond that for a watch, they would seek shelter. For a warning, they might take the extra precautions of staying away from pipes, faucets, electrical outlets, and windows; avoiding the use of a telephone; staying out of water; and, if stuck outdoors, crouching close to the ground.)

- **Are there additional precautions that need to be taken for tornado watches and warnings?** (Yes. If there is a tornado watch or warning, windows should be opened slightly, and people should move away from windows and doors. They should move to a basement, storm cellar, or an inside hallway on the lowest floor.)

- **What is the most important safety precaution for a hurricane?** (Evacuating coastal areas and moving to higher ground.)

- **Why should people stock up on bottled water, batteries, flashlights, and canned food before a hurricane?** (They might find themselves confined to their homes, without power or drinkable water, for several days.)

- **When the skies clear during a hurricane, what is the greatest risk?** (that people will believe that the storm is over, when it really is a calm due to being in the eye of the hurricane)

 **Inclusion**

Public Service Announcement

Have groups of students write public service announcements designed to educate people about storm safety. Allow time for each group to perform its announcement for the class.
Social

 **Advanced Learners**

Storm Safety

Encourage interested students to use science texts to investigate the rationale behind the safety precaution of crouching close to the ground when outside during a storm. Have them write paragraphs explaining how the nature of electricity makes it important to remain low, and allow them to share their findings with the class.
Logical

How Can Radar Track Storms?

Before Reading
Have students try to answer the red question at the top of the page.

Developing the Main Idea
Ask:

- **How does Doppler radar work?** (It bounces sound waves off the storm clouds. The waves reflect back and are recorded. The difference between the original waves and the echo gives clues about the movement of the storm.)

- **What kind of information does Doppler radar give? How is this useful?** (It can tell if raindrops are moving toward or away from observers, and it can spot spinning movements in clouds. This information can help scientists predict which way storms will travel.)

Thinking Further: *Inferring*
Ask:

- **How do you think storms were tracked in the early days of America?** (Students might suggest that storm-tracking consisted mainly of observing conditions in one place, and reconstructing events in other places using newspaper reports, word-of-mouth reports, and so on.)

▶After Reading
Have students answer the red question in the student book as **ongoing assessment**.

How Can Radar Track Storms?

Storms are hard to predict because they form so quickly. Scientists use the best methods possible to try to identify conditions long before a storm occurs. They look for clues, like the movement of fronts and the formation of very low pressure areas. Once these conditions are located, scientists keep a "weather eye" on them to see how they develop.

Special methods are used to find storms as they form. One such method is Doppler radar. The word *radar* stands for *ra*dio *d*etection *a*nd *r*anging. Radar works by sending out radio waves and recording their echo. The change in the radio signal from the original to the echo tells us something about where it reflected.

Doppler radar looks at how the echoes have changed in frequency from the original signals. This information gives clues about the movement of the reflective surface. Doppler radar is a very good tool for scientists to track storms. The radio waves reflect off storm clouds and are picked back up again at the radar stations.

With Doppler radar scientists can tell if rain is moving toward or away from them. Doppler radar can also spot spinning motions of clouds. These motions help warn scientists that tornadoes or hurricanes may be forming. Scientists use Doppler radar to find and track thunderstorms, tornadoes, and hurricanes. Doppler radar helps forecasters predict which way the storms will travel.

▷ **How can Doppler radar help in predicting severe storms?**

It can show if rain is moving toward or away from an area and if there is spinning motion in the clouds.

Radar helps forecasters watch how storms form and move.

D 76

Advanced Learners

Doppler Radar
Encourage interested students to use encyclopedias or physical science references to learn more about how Doppler radar works. Have them prepare diagrams illustrating the process, and display them in the classroom. **Spatial; Linguistic**

 ## Science Background

The Doppler Effect
Doppler radar relies on the Doppler effect, named for Christian Johann Doppler (1803–1853). The Doppler effect is a change in the frequency of waves when the source and the observer are either approaching each other or moving apart. When Doppler radar is used to track a storm, the wavelength of a signal is compared with the echo that bounces back. The change in wavelength indicates whether the storm is approaching or moving away.

Lesson Review

Why It Matters

Scientists have used radar systems to track storms since the 1950s. NEXRAD—"NEXt generation of weather RADar"—is a newer form of Doppler radar that is replacing older radar systems. NEXRAD can spot small particles such as blowing dust, very light snow, and even drizzle. NEXRAD is more accurate than conventional radar at predicting floods and flash floods. It can show the exact locations of different fronts. It also shows changes in wind speed and direction. This helps scientists make more accurate weather predictions.

Visit **www.mhscience02.com** to do a research project on storms.

Think and Write

1. How does a thunderstorm form?
2. How is a tornado related to a thunderstorm?
3. What causes a hurricane to form? What moves it in a certain direction?
4. Why can hurricanes cause so much damage?
5. **Critical Thinking** Why do you think predicting a severe storm is so difficult?

L·I·N·K·S

LITERATURE LINK

Read *Trouble at Forest Park*, the story of a family surviving getting lost in the woods. When you finish reading, think about how you would stay safe in the woods. Try the activities at the end of the book.

ART LINK

Make a poster. Let others know what to do in a storm. Make a poster illustrating important storm safety rules.

MATH LINK

Find the number of tornadoes. Research how many tornadoes hit your state in the past year. Compare that number with the average number listed for your state in the chart on page D65. Were the number of tornadoes in your state last year higher, lower, or the same as the listed average?

TECHNOLOGY LINK

At the Computer Visit **www.mhscience02.com** for more links.

D 77

Informal Assessment

Easy/Average Ask students to make flowcharts describing the formation of a thunderstorm. Have them include conditions favorable to the storm's formation and the resulting movement of air, precipitation, thunder, and lightning.

Challenge Have students create a storm safety board game. Observe that in challenging board games, players must overcome obstacles (storm conditions) to reach the end unharmed. Have them design a board, write rules, and make game pieces. Play the games in class.

---

3 Lesson Review

Answers to Think and Write

1. Thunderstorms start as convection cells. Heating causes air to rise, so the cloud grows. Strong updrafts keep droplets of water and ice in the cloud until they fall as rain. As rain falls, downdrafts form. Friction between updraft and downdraft air forms static electricity, released as lightning. Lightning rapidly heats and expands air, causing it to slam into the surrounding air, creating thunder. (pp. D66–D67)

2. Tornadoes can come from thunderstorms. Both are likely to occur when the weather is hot and humid and a cold front approaches. (p. D68)

3. Heating and evaporation over the ocean cause hurricanes. The Coriolis effect directs the movement of the air. (pp. D70–D71)

4. They can cause flooding and storm surges; wind can damage houses, down power lines and trees, and cause debris to fly. (pp. D72–D73)

5. **Critical Thinking** Predicting severe storms is difficult because they form so quickly that meteorologists do not have much warning before they occur. (p. D74)

Summarize

Check students' understanding by having them write a brief summary of the lesson in their own words.

LITERATURE LINK

Have students read the Grade Level Science Book, *Trouble at Forest Park*. Additional books to read can be found on TE p. D1·b.

ART LINK

Students' posters should include ideas from the safety rules provided on pages D74–D75. Illustrations should be an integral part of the posters.

MATH LINK

The local weather service or news station will have information on the number of tornadoes in your area.

Technology

■ **Internet Research Project** Have students visit **www.mhscience02.com** to conduct a research project on storms. They will find a suggested outline for the project, questions to research, and links to Internet reference sites.

Science, Technology, and Society

Build on Prior Knowledge

Ask:

■ **How was weather predicted before computers and radar were invented?** (Students might respond that people relied upon their observations and folklore. For example, a red sky at night was supposed to bring fair weather the following day, while a red sky in the morning predicted bad weather.)

Storm Tracking

Developing the Main Idea

Ask:

■ **What information does computer projection give us? How?** (It tells us the path that a storm is likely to follow. Computers analyze data about a storm's location, wind direction, air pressure, and rainfall to predict the likely path of the storm.)

Thinking Further: *Inferring*

Ask:

■ **If we can't do anything to *prevent* storms such as hurricanes, how can knowing what to expect from the weather protect us?** (Though we can't control the weather, we can prepare for it.)

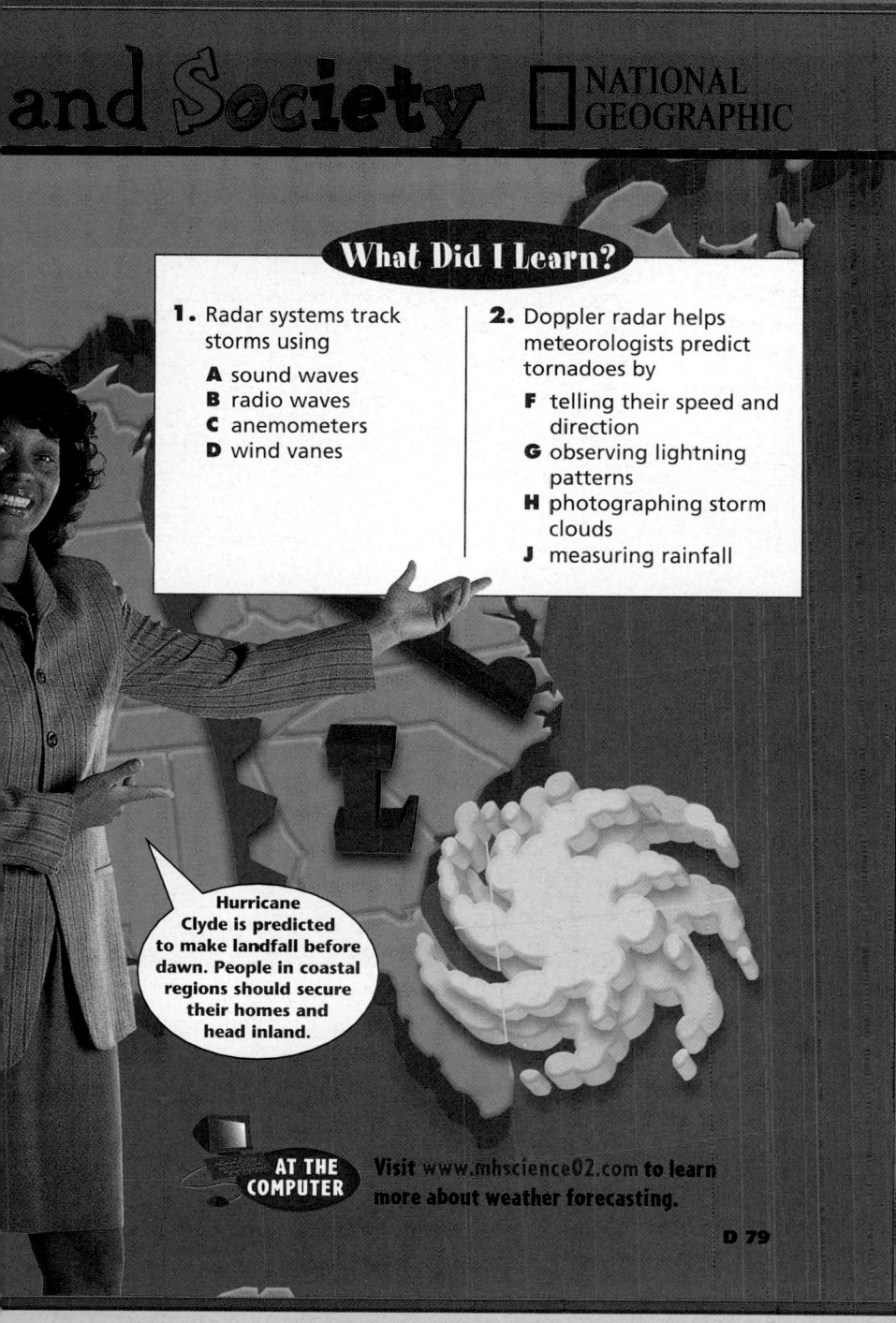

and Society

What Did I Learn?

1. Radar systems track storms using

A sound waves
B radio waves
C anemometers
D wind vanes

2. Doppler radar helps meteorologists predict tornadoes by

F telling their speed and direction
G observing lightning patterns
H photographing storm clouds
J measuring rainfall

Hurricane Clyde is predicted to make landfall before dawn. People in coastal regions should secure their homes and head inland.

 **AT THE COMPUTER** Visit www.mhscience02.com to learn more about weather forecasting.

D 79

- **Before computers and radar, was it possible to predict the weather? How?** (People relied on their observations, such as the appearance of clouds, wind speed and direction, animal behavior, and so on to predict the weather.)

- **What advantages do modern methods of storm tracking offer?** (They allow more accurate predictions, and earlier warning, than traditional methods.)

- **How do the advanced methods of tracking storms and warning people help prevent damage and injury?** (It allows people to secure their buildings and evacuate areas likely to be hit by a serious storm.)

Test Prep: *What Did I Learn?*

1. B

2. F

Summarize
Check students' understanding by having them write a brief summary of the magazine in their own words.

Reading Strategy

Organize Information
Developing Reading Skills
Have interested students use encyclopedias or physical science books to learn more about radar. Encourage them to investigate both its mechanics and its applications. Allow time for them to share their findings with the class.
Linguistic; Social

English Language Learners

Acronyms
Divide the class into small groups. Tell students that *radar* is an acronym, and encourage them to use dictionaries to learn its meaning. Challenge each group to list as many other acronyms as they can within a specified time period. Allow time for each group to share its list with the class.
Linguistic

Climate

Objectives

- Explore how temperatures and precipitation differ from place to place.
- Identify factors that make up and determine climate.
- Distinguish among the ways climates may change.
- Identify how climate affects health and food production.

Resources

- Activity Resources, pp. 153–157
- Reading in Science Resources, pp. 233–238
- Vocabulary Cards
- Reading Aid Transparency D7

Build on Prior Knowledge

Have students discuss what they know about climate. Have them describe their climate. (Students may mention temperature, amount of rain, and how these conditions change throughout the year.)

1 Get Ready

Using the Illustrations

Discuss the hot, dry climate shown in the photograph. Students may note that summer in the desert might be very hot, while winter would not be very cold. Students may note the presence, absence, and/or type of plant cover, the presence of sand, and their personal experiences.

Have students compare their climate to the desert climate. Point out that the average weather pattern of a region is based on factors such as temperature, humidity, and type and amount of precipitation. A graph showing temperature and precipitation differences for one year would indicate a location's average or seasonal weather.

Climate

Vocabulary

climate, D82

radiative balance, D86

greenhouse effect, D87

Get Ready

What if you lived here, in this desert? What would summers be like? What would winters be like?

Think about what factors are used to describe the average weather pattern of a region. How might you use graphs of year-round weather in different places to test your ideas?

Process Skill

You communicate when you share information.

D 80

Science Background

Global Circulation

Encourage students to think of Earth as a single system, working to maintain balance. Earth is heated unevenly. One way to maintain balance is to move heat from the equator to the poles. Global circulation, air moving Earth's heat, helps account for climate and relies on the fact that warm air rises and cold air sinks.

Explore Activity

What Do Weather Patterns Tell You?

Procedure

1 Use Numbers Look at the graph for city 1. The bottom is labeled with the months of the year. The left side is labeled with the temperature in degrees Celsius. Use this scale to read the temperature line. What is the average temperature in city 1 during July?

2 Use Numbers The right side of the graph is labeled with millimeters of precipitation. Use this scale when reading the precipitation bars. What is the average precipitation in city 1 during July?

3 Repeat steps 1 and 2 for city 2.

Drawing Conclusions

1 Use Numbers How do the annual amounts of precipitation compare for the two cities? Record your answer.

2 Interpret Data When is the average temperature highest for each city? Lowest? When does each city receive the greatest amount of precipitation?

3 Interpret Data Describe the average weather pattern for each city. Be sure to include temperature and precipitation, and their relationship to the seasons.

4 Going Further: Communicate How would you go about making a graph of the weather patterns for your town?

City 1

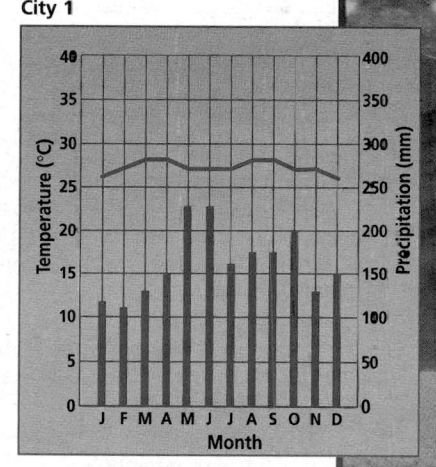

City 2

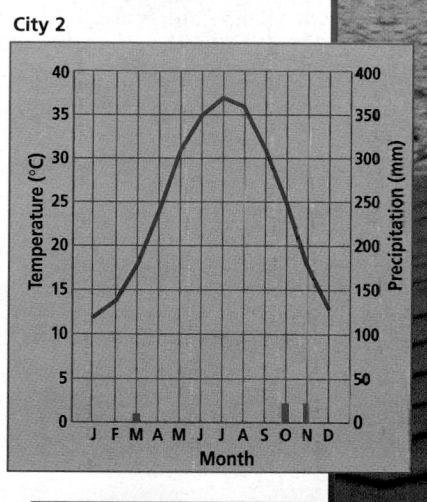

— Temperature (in Celsius)
■ Precipitation (in millimeters)

D 81

Alternative Explore Activity

Adapting to Climate Changes
Point out to students that they have come, over time, to expect certain weather at certain times of the year. Challenge them to write creative stories about what might happen if they were to wake up one morning, and find that the climate had drastically changed. Encourage students to use humor as they describe the adaptations they would have to make. Allow time for students to share their stories with the class. **Linguistic**

Adapting to Climate Changes

Procedure

1. Think about what might happen if you woke up one morning and found that the climate had drastically changed.
2. Write a story about it on a separate sheet of paper. Include how the climate changed and the adaptations you made in response to the climate changes. Students should use humor as they describe the adaptations they would have to make.

Drawing Conclusions

1. What adaptations did you make to the climate changes?
   Answers will vary.

2. How was the climate different from before?
   Answers will vary.

3. What are adaptations you make to regular climate changes during the year?
   Answers will vary. Students might respond that during the summer they wear less clothing and drink more water; during the winter they wear more clothing and stay indoors.

Unit D · Weather and Climate   Use with TE textbook page D81   155

Activity Resources, p. 155

Explore Activity

What Do Weather Patterns Tell You?

Science Process Skills *use numbers, interpret data, communicate*

Resources Activity Resources, pp. 153–154

Pacing 30–40 minutes

Grouping pairs

Procedure

1 27°C.

2 160 mm.

3 For city 2: the average July temperature is 37°C; the average July precipitation is 0 mm.

Answers to Drawing Conclusions

1 City 1 much higher than city 2.

2 City 1: highest temperatures—March, April, August, and September; lowest temperatures—January and December. City 2: highest temperature—July; lowest temperature—January. City 1 receives the greatest amount of precipitation in May and June; city 2 in October and November.

3 City 1 has fairly constant, warm temperatures throughout the year, and receives a good amount of rain each month, with May and June as its rainiest months. City 2 is a very dry climate with precipitation occurring only in March, October, and November. Its temperatures change seasonally, with June, July, and August its hottest months, and December, January, and February its coldest.

4 Students might suggest either finding historical data or recording daily temperatures and precipitation, calculating monthly averages for temperature and total monthly precipitation, and plotting these on a graph similar to the one in the activity.

 Inquiry Students can explore what causes the difference in weather conditions from place to place.

Technology

■ When time is short, preview the activity with the **Explore Activity Video.**

What Is Climate?

Before Reading
Have students try to answer the red question at the top of the page.

Developing the Main Idea
Point out that the kinds of plants that grow in a particular region can describe its climate. Ask:

- **What clues about climate do plants give us?** (Because different kinds of plants have different needs, we can make inferences about the weather conditions of a place based on the kinds of plants that grow there.)

▶After Reading
Have students answer the red question in the student book as **ongoing assessment**.

Developing Vocabulary

climate Remind students that the average of all types of weather makes up the climate of an area. Encourage students to draw on their prior knowledge to give meaning to the term *climate*.

Read to Learn

Main Idea Long-term weather patterns determine climates, which can change over time.

What Is Climate?

Weather changes from day to day. However, the weather in any area tends to follow a pattern throughout the year. For example, Fairbanks, Alaska, tends to have long, cold winters and short, cool summers. Miami, Florida, tends to have long, hot summers and short, cool winters.

When you make descriptions such as these, you are describing the **climate** (KLIGH·mit) of a region. Climate is the average weather pattern of a region. One way to describe a region's climate is with a temperature-precipitation graph.

The climate of a region can also be described by some other factors, such as winds, distance from a coast,

temperature, precipitation, winds, distance from the coast, mountain ranges, ocean currents, proximity to water, and altitude

mountain ranges, and ocean currents. The *climate zones* shown here take all these factors into account.

Another way to describe the climate of a region is by the plants that grow there, such as grasslands or coniferous forests. Each kind of plant requires its own conditions for growth, such as amount of sunlight, precipitation, and temperature.

▶ **What factors describe climate?**

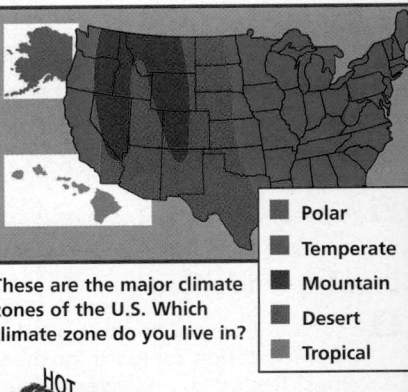

These are the major climate zones of the U.S. Which climate zone do you live in?

- Polar
- Temperate
- Mountain
- Desert
- Tropical

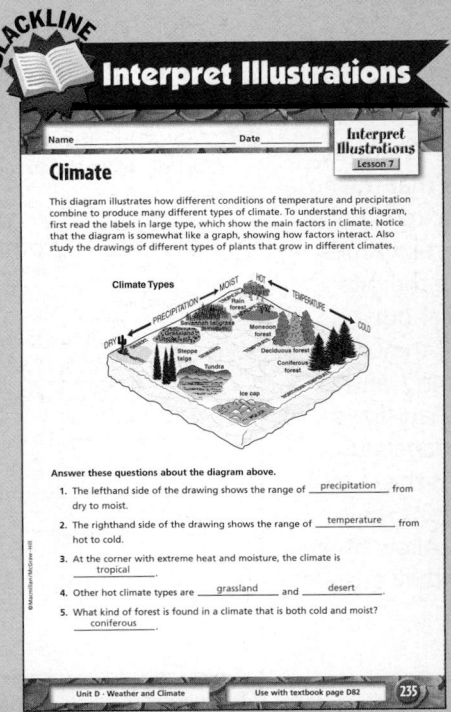

D 82

Reading in Science Resources, p. 233

Reading in Science Resources, p. 235

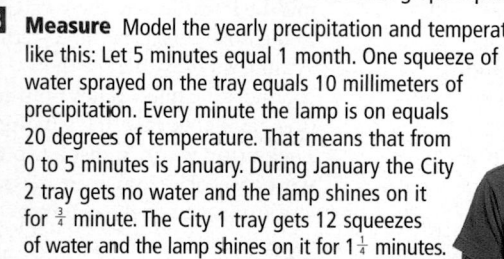

Process Skill BUILDER

SKILL Measure

Modeling Climates

In this activity you will make a model of the soil conditions in two cities. Use the information in the graphs on page D81. The soil conditions you set up will model—or represent—the climates of the two cities. To do this, you will need to measure the amount of water you use and the amount of time you use the lamp.

Procedure

1 **Measure** Put 3 cm of dry soil into each tray. Label one tray City 1 and the other tray City 2.

2 **Use Numbers** What do the bars on each graph represent?

3 **Measure** Model the yearly precipitation and temperature like this: Let 5 minutes equal 1 month. One squeeze of water sprayed on the tray equals 10 millimeters of precipitation. Every minute the lamp is on equals 20 degrees of temperature. That means that from 0 to 5 minutes is January. During January the City 2 tray gets no water and the lamp shines on it for $\frac{3}{4}$ minute. The City 1 tray gets 12 squeezes of water and the lamp shines on it for $1\frac{1}{4}$ minutes.

4 **Make a Model** Model the two cities for all 12 months. Record your observations.

Drawing Conclusions

1 **Observe** Examine the soil in the trays. Compare them for the same months. How do they differ?

2 **Communicate** How did measuring help you model climates?

> **Materials**
> stick-on notepaper
> marking pencil or pen
> 2 trays of dry soil
> spray bottle of water
> lamp
> thermometer

D 83

Process Skill BUILDER

Modeling Climates

Science Process Skills *measure,* use numbers, make a model, observe, communicate

Resources Activity Resources, pp. 156–157

Pacing 30–40 minutes

Grouping pairs

Procedure

2 The bars on the graphs represent the precipitation in each city. City 1 (in mm): J–120; F–110; M–130; A–150; M–230; J–230; J–160; A–170; S–170; O–200; N–130; D–150. City 2 (in mm): J–0; F–0; M–10; A–0; M–0; J–0; J–0; A–0; S–0; O–25; N–25; D-0.

4 Students will probably note that the soil for City 1 remains considerably drier than that of City 2.

Answers to Drawing Conclusions

1 The model representing City 2 remains much drier than the model representing City 1.

2 Measuring the water and the amount of time under the lamp made it possible to simulate two different sets of conditions in a way that allowed useful comparisons.

Process Skills

MiniLesson

Measure

Develop This skill involves finding the size, volume, area, mass, weight, or temperature of an object, or how long an event occurs. Measuring often involves quantifying observations. Measurement tools, such as rulers, measuring cups, graduated cylinders, thermometers, balance scales, clocks, make observations more precise because they are based on some standard of measure.

Practice Make available to students a clock or watch with a second hand. Have students time each other doing various activities using the clock or watch. Have them find an activity that takes:

- about 15 seconds to do
- about 2 minutes to do
- about 45 seconds to do
- about 1 minute, 30 seconds to do

A complete list of Science Process Skills appears on p. S7.

 Inclusion

Climate Changes Over Time

Tell students that climates can change over time. The bones of desert animals such as camels have been found in the Arctic, indicating that, despite the harsh conditions today, it once had conditions suitable for animals to find food and survive. Encourage interested students to use encyclopedias or other references to investigate how climates have changed over time. Suggest that they research the Ice Ages, as well as the warm periods that occurred in between them.
Linguistic

What Affects Climate?

Before Reading
Have students try to answer the red question at the top of the page.

Developing the Main Idea
Ask:

- **What factors affect temperature?** (distance from the equator, air pressure and winds, altitude, distribution of water)

- **How do you think scientists can tell that climates have changed?** (Guide students to infer that they examine fossil evidence. Because plants and animals require certain conditions to grow, scientists can make inferences about the weather conditions in an area.)

- **What is latitude?** (distance from the equator)

Thinking Further: *Drawing Conclusions*
Ask:

- **How does latitude affect climate?** (At different latitudes, the angle of insolation differs. Therefore, temperatures are different at different latitudes.)

Using the Illustrations
Draw students' attention to the diagram showing how latitude affects climate. Ask:

- **Which zone has the most precipitation?** (tropical) **Which zones have the least precipitation?** (polar) **In which zone do you live?**

Developing the Main Idea
Ask:

- **How does water affect temperature?** (Land and water heat and cool at different rates, so air temperatures over land are warmer in summer and cooler in winter than they are over water at the same latitude.)

What Affects Climate?

Several things affect temperature and precipitation over a long period of time.

Latitude

One way to describe location is to tell the latitude of a place. Latitude is a measure of how far north or south a place is from the equator. The angle of insolation is different at different latitudes. As a result, the temperatures are different at different latitudes.

- **Tropical Zone** Near the equator temperatures are high all year. Rainfall is plentiful. At about 30° latitude in each hemisphere are deserts, areas of high temperatures and low precipitation.

- **Temperate Zones** In the middle latitudes, summers are warm and winters are cool or cold. Precipitation may be plentiful.

- **Polar Zones** At high latitudes winters are long and cold. Summers are short and warm. Precipitation all year is low.

Bodies of Water

A glance at any globe shows that land and water are not evenly distributed. Most of the globe is covered with water. However, some places on a continent can be more than 1,600 km (1,000 mi) from any large body of water. Land

and water heat and cool at different rates. Land heats up faster in the sunlight than water does. Land also cools off faster than water. As a result, air temperatures over land are warmer in summer and cooler in winter than they are over oceans at the same latitude.

Winds and Ocean Currents

In Lesson 4 you learned that wind patterns circle the globe. These patterns are not the day-to-day winds. Instead they are winds that blow continually above Earth's surface.

- **Wind Patterns** For example, just above and below the equator, the trade winds blow continually. In the middle latitudes are the westerlies. In the polar areas are the easterlies. Westerlies blow across the continental United States from west (the Pacific) to east (the Atlantic). They bring warm, moist air to the west coast. They push air masses and fronts across the country.

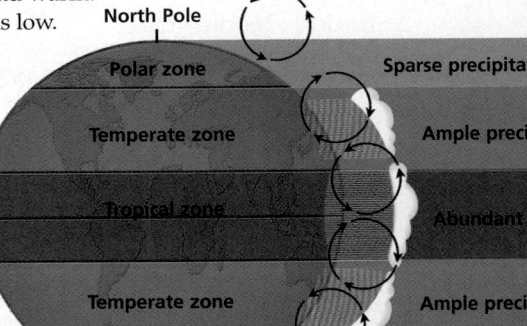

North Pole

Polar zone — Sparse precipitation

Temperate zone — Ample precipitation

Tropical zone — Abundant rainfall

Temperate zone — Ample precipitation

Polar zone — Sparse precipitation

South Pole

D 84

Science Background

Isotherms

Isotherms are another tool scientists use to study climate. Isotherms are lines on a weather map connecting places that have the same temperature at the same time. Mean July isotherms for each hemisphere are prepared each year. These isotherms allow scientists to determine the quality of summers throughout the world, identifying areas of temperature excess. Recently, as concern about global warming has increased, this has been of particular interest to scientists.

SCIENCE FOR ALL English Language Learners

Understanding Isotherms

Point out to students that the term *isotherm* is derived from the Greek *iso-*, meaning "same" and *therme-*, meaning "heat." Encourage them to use word origins to define the term *isobar*. (*Baros-* means "pressure," so *isobar* means "equal pressure.")

- **Currents** These winds also move water across the surface of the ocean. As ocean water moves, it moves warm or cool air with it. A warm current, the Gulf Stream, flows up along the east coast. The California Current, a cool current, moves down along the west coast.

Altitude

Altitude is a measure of how high above sea level a place is. The higher a place is above sea level, the cooler its climate is.

- **Mountains** Along the base of a high mountain, you may find tropical plants growing. Halfway up you may find pine forests. At the mountain peaks, you will find permanent ice and snow. Mountain ranges affect climate, too. The Alps protect the Mediterranean coast from cold polar air. The Himalayas protect the lowlands of India from cold Siberian air. Mountain ranges also affect rain patterns. Often one side of the mountain gets lots of rain while the other side gets very little.

Air passing over a mountain cools. Rain clouds may form and drop their moisture on that side of the mountain. Air reaching the other side is often dry.

- **Rain Shadow** Global wind patterns can force air up along the side of a mountain. For example, warm, moist air from the Pacific Ocean is blown up the side of the Sierra Nevada and the Cascades. As the air moves up, there is precipitation on the windward side. Having lost the moisture, dry air descends down the leeward side of the mountain. This side is said to be in a *rain shadow*.

▷ **How does latitude affect climate?**

Distance from the equator affects the angle of insolation, and therefore the temperature, of a region. Equatorial regions are hotter; polar regions, colder.

Ocean currents move surface water in huge circular patterns. As ocean currents flow past land areas, they affect the land's climate.

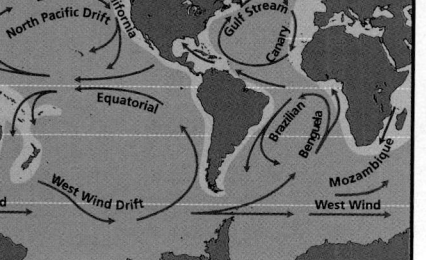

Using the Illustrations

Draw students' attention to the world map with global currents. Ask:

- **How do wind and ocean currents affect climates?** (They bring along cold or warm air or water with them.)

Developing the Main Idea

Ask:

- **How do mountains affect climate?** (Air moving up the side of a mountain will cool, causing condensation and precipitation. The air that passes to the other side of the mountain will then be drier. Climate is also cooler as altitude increases.)

▶ After Reading

Have students answer the red question in the student book as **ongoing assessment**.

SCIENCE FOR ALL — Advanced Learners

Diffusion

Encourage students to use physical science references to learn about diffusion. Have them write paragraphs comparing diffusion to the movement of air from areas of high pressure to areas of low pressure. (They are both passive, high-to-low movements designed to create balance.)
Logical

SCIENCE FOR ALL — English Language Learners

Local professional

Invite a local landscape architect to visit the classroom to discuss the plants that are indigenous to your area. Ask him or her to explain how the plants describe the area's climate. Students should have a list of questions ready to ask the person. You can have students work in pairs to write questions and have pairs share questions to avoid duplication and to make sure questions are clear. **Linguistic; Logical**

How Does Earth Gain and Lose Energy?

Before Reading
Have students try to answer the red question at the top of the page.

Developing the Main Idea
Ask:

- **Why doesn't the temperature of Earth continually increase?** (because Earth is constantly radiating energy.)

READING
Diagrams

The Sun's energy is absorbed by the atmosphere and Earth; heat energy is lost to space at night.

Developing Vocabulary

radiative balance Have students define *radiate* and *balance* to help find a possible meaning for the compound term. (*radiate:* to spread out in all directions from a source; *balance:* equality between opposing forces)

How Does Earth Gain and Lose Energy?

Earth's climates depend a great deal on the Sun's energy. Earth absorbs heat from sunlight. It also gives off, or *radiates*, heat into space. Earth gains and loses energy.

If the amount of energy gained balances the energy lost, Earth is in **radiative** (RAY·dee·uh·tiv) **balance**. Then Earth's average temperature remains about the same. Earth's average temperature is about 14°C (59°F). A tip of the balance will cause Earth's average temperature to rise or fall.

The atmosphere plays an important role in Earth's radiative balance. If Earth had no atmosphere, it would be a lot like the Moon, which has no atmosphere. Daytime temperatures on the Moon soar to more than 100°C (212°F). Nighttime temperatures drop to 115°C (240°F) below zero.

Earth's atmosphere acts as a protective blanket. Clouds and dust in the atmosphere reflect about 30 percent of incoming sunlight back out into space. The atmosphere absorbs another 15–20 percent. Only about half of incoming sunlight reaches Earth's surface. This keeps surface temperatures from rising much higher during the day.

At night Earth's surface radiates heat. If there are lots of clouds in the atmosphere, they absorb most of this

Earth's Energy Budget

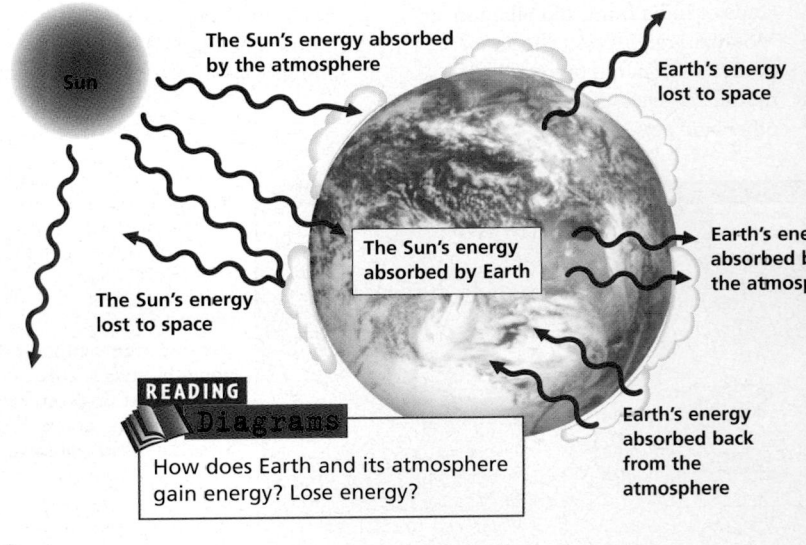

The Sun's energy absorbed by the atmosphere

Earth's energy lost to space

Sun

The Sun's energy lost to space

The Sun's energy absorbed by Earth

Earth's ene[rgy] absorbed b[y] the atmosp[here]

Earth's energy absorbed back from the atmosphere

READING
Diagrams

How does Earth and its atmosphere gain energy? Lose energy?

D 86

SCIENCE
Reading Strategy

Interpret Graphic Sources of Information
Developing Reading Skills
Have students interpret graphic sources of information, using the diagram to define radiative balance.

Science Background

Greenhouse Effect
Scientists fear that adding greenhouse gases, such as chlorofluorocarbons, to the atmosphere in the form of aerosol will cause the retention of excess heat, irreparably altering Earth's climates.

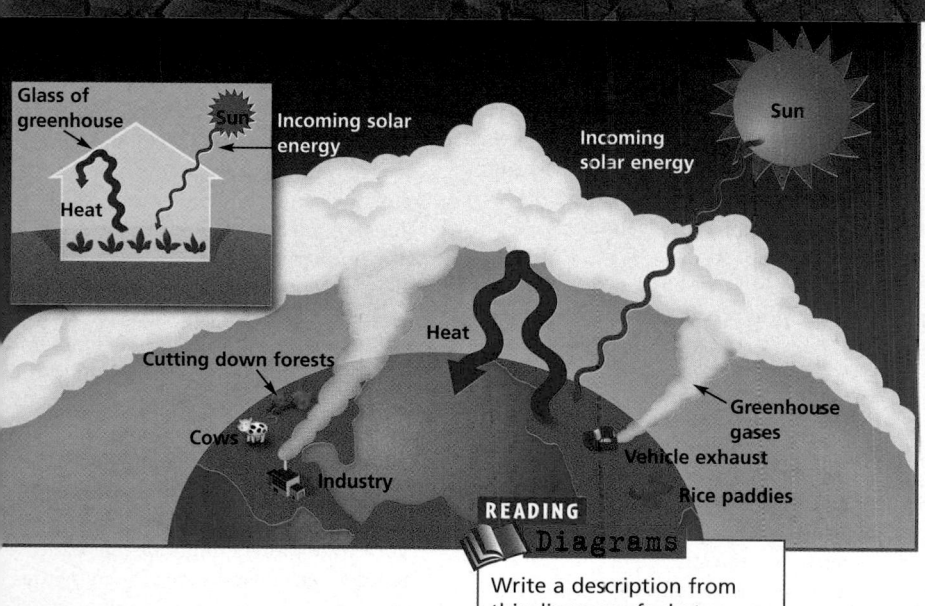

Glass of greenhouse
Sun
Incoming solar energy
Heat

Incoming solar energy
Sun

Heat
Cutting down forests
Cows
Industry
Greenhouse gases
Vehicle exhaust
Rice paddies

READING
Diagrams

Write a description from this diagram of what causes the greenhouse effect.

heat. This keeps the night from getting too cold. If there are few clouds, less heat is absorbed, and the night is cooler.

The Greenhouse Effect

Why doesn't all of Earth's heat just go out into space? The atmosphere keeps Earth warmer than it would otherwise be. This is called the greenhouse effect. Earth's atmosphere acts somewhat like the glass in a greenhouse. In a greenhouse the glass lets sunlight in but does not let heat escape. This helps create a warm environment in which plants can flourish.

Earth's greenhouse effect is caused by just a few gases. These greenhouse gases make up only a tiny part of the air. The main greenhouse gases are water vapor and carbon dioxide. Other gases also have less of an effect. These

gases are methane, nitrous oxide, and chlorofluorocarbons (CFCs).

Human activities are putting more and more greenhouse gases into the atmosphere. Many scientists are worried that these gases may change Earth's climate. Even a small increase in these gases adds to the greenhouse effect, making our planet warmer.

Scientists are still examining and interpreting data in order to understand the greenhouse effect better.

▶ **How does the greenhouse effect keep Earth from losing energy?**

Earth's atmosphere acts like the glass in a greenhouse—letting in sunlight but not letting heat escape.

D 87

Inclusion

Public Service Announcement

Divide the class into small groups, and challenge each to write a public service announcement designed to increase the public's awareness of how their activities can contribute to the greenhouse effect. Allow time for each group to perform its announcement for the class. **Social**

Using the Illustrations

Draw students' attention to the drawings that illustrate the greenhouse effect. Ask:

■ **How is the atmosphere like a greenhouse?** (Its gases hold in more heat than they allow to escape.)

■ **What is the result?** (Earth is warmer than it would be otherwise.)

■ **When scientists compare the warming of Earth to what occurs in a greenhouse, what represents the glass?** (the greenhouse gases in the atmosphere)

READING
Diagrams

Answers should reflect an understanding that greenhouse gases prevent heat from radiating back into space. Like the glass in a greenhouse, the gases hold heat close to Earth. Students should also note that human activities can contribute more greenhouse gases, which has the potential for changing Earth's temperature.

▶**After Reading**

Have students answer the red question in the student book as **ongoing assessment**.

Developing Vocabulary

greenhouse effect To help understand this term ask students if they are familiar with the temperature inside a greenhouse on a sunny day.

What Causes Climate Change?

Before Reading
Have students try to answer the red question at the top of the page.

Developing the Main Idea
Ask:

- **In general, what causes climate changes?** (changes in temperature)

- **Then what factor, more than any other, affects the temperature on Earth?** (the Sun)

- **Does the amount of energy released by the Sun stay the same all the time? What causes it to change?** (No; sunspots cause it to change every 11 years.)

Using the Illustrations
Draw students' attention to "The Sun's Surface." Ask:

- **How does sunspot activity affect Earth?** (Every 11 years, it reaches a maximum, and causes increased solar activity. Records on temperatures are not definitive. Radio and TV broadcasts are affected.)

What Causes Climate Change?

There is much evidence that over long periods of time, Earth goes through warming and cooling trends. Warming and cooling are signs that Earth's radiative balance has shifted. What causes such shifts?

The shifts are caused by changes in sunlight. They are also caused by changes in the movements of air, water, landmasses, and Earth itself.

The Sun's Output
The amount of energy the Sun sends out changes. One clue to how the Sun's output may be changing comes from sunspots. Sunspots are dark areas that appear on the surface of the Sun. They appear dark because they are cooler than the surrounding regions. They appear to be "storms" on the Sun.

Sunspots have been observed for centuries. However, they are not permanent. They appear and disappear over several days or several months.

At times there are many large sunspots. Such a high count is called a sunspot maximum. The last sunspot maximum was in 2000.

A sunspot maximum appears to happen about every 11 years. Scientists also record changes in Earth's temperatures about the same times. Around the time of a sunspot maximum, Earth's average temperature has gone up. The pattern is not exact or complete. However, it has led some scientists to suggest that droughts, rainfall, and very cold winters might be related to times when sunspots are very numerous or very few.

The Sun's Surface

Sunspot

This false-color image of the Sun shows temperature differences on the sun's surface. Why do sunspots appear dark?

D 88

Inclusion

Maria Mitchell's Contributions

Encourage students to research, and write brief reports describing, the contributions that Maria Mitchell, the first woman to be elected to the American Academy of Arts and Sciences, made to our understanding of sunspots and other astronomical phenomena. **Linguistic**

Science Background

Changes in the Air
The air in Earth's atmosphere has changed over time. Variations in the amounts of greenhouse gases are only one example of change in the air's composition. A billion years ago, for example, the atmosphere contained almost no oxygen. Most of the oxygen has come from plants, which release the gas as a byproduct of photosynthesis. Over the course of millions of years, the oxygen level of the atmosphere has increased to its current level.

Currents and Landmasses

How do the oceans help move Earth's heat around? Ocean currents act like huge conveyor belts, carrying heat from the equator to the poles. Changes in the speed and direction of these currents could explain sudden and long-term climate changes.

The continents have changed their positions over time. In fact, the continents are still moving very gradually. Their climates are likely to change with their locations.

Volcanoes

When volcanoes erupt, they send dust and gases into the atmosphere. Atmospheric dust can block sunlight, causing cooling. In the past eruptions were more frequent. The dust from all of those eruptions may have caused enough cooling to trigger ice ages. Volcanic eruptions are not as common today as they were in the past. While eruptions still cause cooling, they probably don't affect long-term climate as much as in the past.

READING Sequence of Events
How might frequent volcanic eruptions change the climate?

Volcanoes that send huge amounts of dust and gases into the atmosphere could block out sunlight, causing cooling.

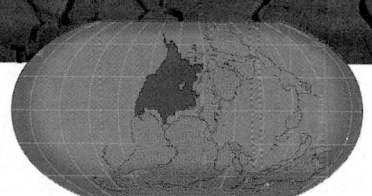

300 Million Years Ago

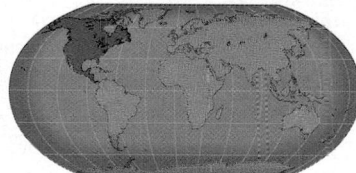

Present

Do you think the ocean currents were the same 300 million years ago as they are today? Changes in ocean currents would profoundly affect climates.

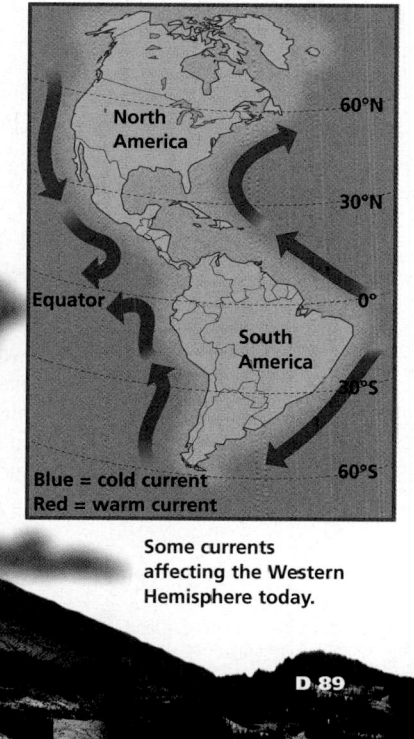

Blue = cold current
Red = warm current

Some currents affecting the Western Hemisphere today.

D 89

Using the Illustrations

Draw students' attention to the maps showing continental drift. Ask:

■ **Are ocean currents the same as they were 300 million years ago? How do you know?** (No; because the land masses have changed position, the currents can't follow the same routes.)

■ **Is the climate the same as it was? How do you know?** (It is different because changes in ocean currents cause profound changes in climate.)

▶ **After Reading**
Have students answer the red question in the student book as **ongoing assessment**.

Reading MiniLesson

Sequence of Events

Develop As you discuss how frequent volcanic eruptions might change the climate, point out that human activity such as burning vast areas of trees in rain forests can also send up huge amounts of smoke and gases that could cause the blocking of sunlight. Help students understand that by breaking one part of the chain of events—burning trees or exploding volcanoes—the outcome becomes different.

Practice Have students use information from paragraph six on page D88 to make flowcharts illustrating the sequence of events suspected around the time of the sunspot maximum. (Answers should include: 1. sunspot maximum, 2. Earth's average temperature rises, 3. cold winters, droughts, rainfalls.)

Cultural Perspective

Adapting to Climate

Point out to students that many cultural traditions stem from the fact that people must adapt to their environments. For example, the people of the jungle of Borneo are nomadic, moving frequently to make use of the jungle's resources. Divide the class into small groups, directing each to select a country to research, paying particular attention to how its cultural traditions are related to the climate. **Social**

How Can Climate Affect You?

Before Reading
Have students try to answer the red question at the top of the page.

Developing the Main Idea
Ask:

- **Are you as likely to suffer ill consequences in hot, damp weather as in hot, dry weather? Why or why not?** (Yes; in hot, damp weather, bacteria grow quickly and disease-carrying insects thrive; in hot, dry weather hyperthermia can result.)

▶After Reading
Have students answer the red question in the student book as **ongoing assessment**.

How Can Climate Affect You?

How do you deal with cold weather? Cold weather cools the surface of the body. The body responds by circulating warm blood faster to counteract the cooling. The heart pumps faster. Blood pressure increases and puts a strain on the heart.

Cold Climates

How can you stay warm in cold weather? Use proper clothing and shelter. Clothing traps body heat to warm the air close to your body. Cold-weather clothes are often made with materials that trap air between loose fibers. Your body heats the trapped air, and soon a thin, warm layer of air surrounds you.

Hot Climates

In hot, dry climates, the main health problem is water loss. Heating the body triggers sweating. When sweat evaporates, it cools the skin. However, if you don't drink enough water, your body eventually stops sweating. No sweat, no cooling. Body temperature rises. This can cause *hyperthermia* (overheating), which can be fatal.

Clothing can help you deal with the heat. Light-colored fabric protects the skin and reflects a lot of the sunlight. Loose clothing lets air circulate so sweat can evaporate and cool the body.

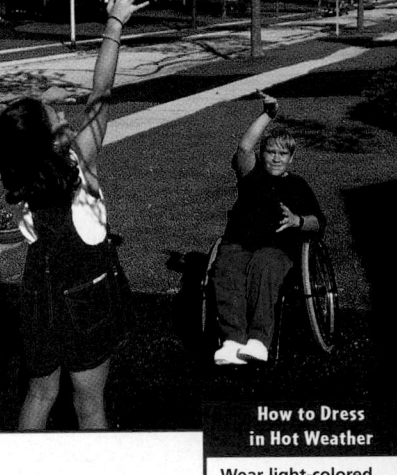

How to Dress in Hot Weather

Wear light-colored, loose clothing that protects you from the Sun and lets your skin breathe.
Wear a sun hat.
Use sunscreen.

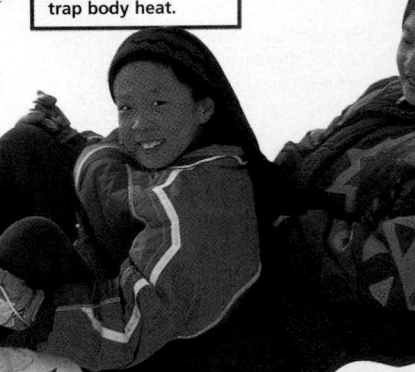

How to Dress in Cold Weather

Protect nose and ears on blustery, cold days.
Keep hands, head, and feet warm.
Dress in layers to trap body heat.

▷ What is the main health problem in hot, dry climates?
water loss—which can lead to hyperthermia

D 90

Reading Strategy

Organize Information
Developing Reading Skills
Have students organize information about extreme temperatures, their effects on the body, health consequences, and safety measures into a table.

Science Background

Human Thermostat
The human body has an amazing ability to maintain a constant temperature in the face of external temperature changes. The hypothalamus acts as a biological thermostat; it senses the temperature of the blood, then stimulates a response in the blood vessels. As the environment gets hotter, for example, the hypothalamus senses warming of the body, and triggers the blood vessels to dilate, which permits the heat to travel to the surface of the body and dissipate.

Why It Matters

Since 1900, Earth's average temperature has increased by about 0.5°C (1°F). Most of the warming has come in two periods—from 1920 to 1940 and since the mid-1970s. A drought during the 1920s–1940s led to the Dust Bowl days. Millions of acres of United States farmland dried out. Crops failed. Farmers went broke trying to pay their bills. Many families lost their homes and farms.

Today the warming trend continues. Cutting down on the use of greenhouse gases and preserving forests may help slow the trend.

Think and Write

1. What is climate? What are the main factors that are used to describe the climate of an area?

2. What is the greenhouse effect?

3. Why are climates different at different places on Earth?

4. **Measure** What variables do you have to measure to describe the average weather pattern, or climate, of a region?

5. **Critical Thinking** Do you think people can live in all climates? Explain your answer.

L·I·N·K·S

WRITING LINK

Write an essay. Choose a climate different from your own. Write an essay on how the climate affects the lives of the people who live there.

SOCIAL STUDIES LINK

Write a report about changing climates. The illustration shows a winter fair held on the Thames River in England during the Little Ice Age. Research how Earth's climate has changed since farming began. Write a report for the class.

MATH LINK

Make a pie graph. Find out what proportions of greenhouse gases exist in the atmosphere. Make a pie graph.

TECHNOLOGY LINK

At the Computer Visit www.mhscience02.com for more links.

Informal Assessment

Easy/Average The average temperature on Mars is 0°C, ranging from 20°C at noon, to −140°C at night. Have students write science fiction stories about adaptations needed for survival on Mars. Then have them share their stories with the class.

Challenge Scientists are not sure if human activities that add greenhouse gases to the atmosphere are contributing to Earth's warming trend. Have the class debate: Are people responsible for the warming of Earth? Have each team research its position beforehand.

---

3 | Lesson Review

Answers to Think and Write

1. Climate is the average weather pattern of a region. Temperature and precipitation describe it. (pp. D82–D83)

2. Gases in the atmosphere allow more energy from the Sun to reach Earth than can radiate back into space, thus warming Earth's atmosphere. (p. D87)

3. Latitude affects the angle of insolation. (p. D84)

4. **Measure** The seasonal amount of precipitation and the seasonal temperatures (pp. D82–D83)

5. **Critical Thinking** Students might respond that people could live in all climates because, unlike plants or other animals, they protect themselves from extremes of temperature. (p. D90)

Summarize

Check students' understanding by having them write a brief summary of the lesson in their own words.

WRITING LINK

Essays should reflect students' understanding that people adapt to their climate. They should also reflect an understanding of the climate in which students currently live.

SOCIAL STUDIES LINK

Students' research should focus on the continuous changes, occurring every 100 to 300 years, in climates of various areas. Research should specifically refer to the impact of those changes on crops and farming. Farming began about 6,000 years ago when average temperatures were about 2°C (4°F) warmer than today. There was more rainfall. About A.D. 200, the climate started to cool, but warmed up by A.D. 900–1100. It cooled again by 1300. Between 1450 and 1850, there was a cold period called the Little Ice Age, with harsh winters.

MATH LINK

The "greenhouse gases," or those responsible for retaining Earth's radiated heat, are water vapor, carbon dioxide, chlorofluoro-carbons, methane, nitrous oxide, and ozone. They are calculated according to their relative volumes: carbon dioxide is 0.13% while the amount of water vapor varies from 0 to 100 percent.

Chapter Review and Test Preparation

Resources

- Reading in Science Resources, pp. 239–240
- Assessment Book, pp. 47–50

Answers to Vocabulary

1. front
2. tornado
3. warm front
4. thunderstorm
5. storm surge
6. greenhouse effect
7. air mass
8. hurricane
9. cold front
10. climate

Answers to Test Prep

11. C
12. J
13. C
14. J
15. B

Chapter 9 Review

Vocabulary

Fill each blank with the best word or words from the list.

air mass, D54
climate, D82
cold front, D56
front, D55
greenhouse effect, D87
hurricane, D70
storm surge, D72
thunderstorm, D66
tornado, D68
warm front, D56

1. A boundary between air masses of different temperatures is called a(n) _____.

2. A storm often created in thunderstorms is a(n) _____.

3. A(n) _____ may bring fog.

4. A storm that produces lightning is a(n) _____.

5. A great rise of sea level at a shore due to a hurricane is a(n) _____.

6. The _____ may be making Earth warmer.

7. A large region of the atmosphere in which the air has similar properties is a(n) _____.

8. A dangerous storm that forms over warm ocean waters is a(n) _____.

9. A(n) _____ forms when cold air moves in under a warm air mass.

10. The average weather pattern of a region is its _____.

Test Prep

11. Statistical weather forecasts are based on _____.
   A the kinds of fronts moving out of an area
   B severe storms
   C the chance of a weather pattern repeating itself
   D weather station symbols

12. Earth gets its heat from _____.
   F trees
   G convection
   H greenhouses
   J the Sun

13. When a cool air mass and a warm air mass meet and stay over an area for days without moving, this is called a(n) _____.
   A warm front
   B occluded front
   C stationary front
   D cold front

D 92

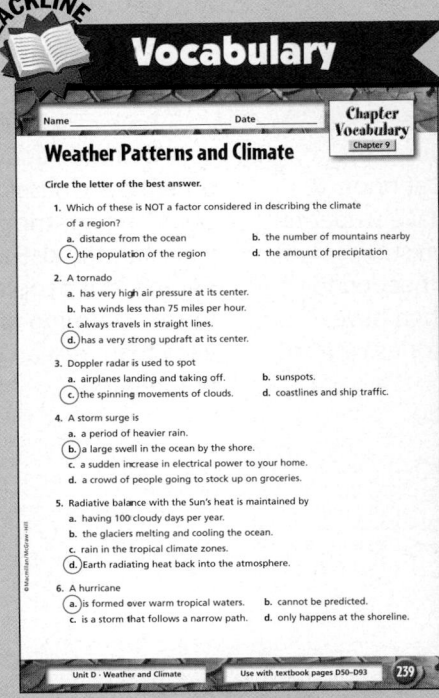

Reading in Science Resources, p. 239

14. A balance between energy lost and energy gained is called _____.

  F the greenhouse effect
  G climate
  H solar energy
  J radiative balance

15. A hurricane can cause sea level to rise because the air pressure under the hurricane _____.

  A is higher than normal
  B is lower than normal
  C is the same as usual
  D does not affect why a hurricane makes the sea level rise

Concepts and Skills

16. Reading in Science Write a paragraph explaining how a thunderstorm forms.

17. Safety Write a paragraph explaining safety rules to follow in a thunderstorm.

18. Product Ads What products are advertised to protect you from the weather in the winter? In the summer? What is each product supposed to do? Are the products as good as the ads say? Write a paragraph explaining your answer.

19. Process Skills: Measure What if your area were to get twice as much rain as usual for the next ten years? Write a paragraph explaining how you would make a model of your climate as it is now. How would you adjust it to study the effect of extra rainfall?

20. Critical Thinking Do you think that Earth is getting warmer? Write a paragraph explaining your hypothesis. Describe what you might do to test your ideas.

Boost your test scores!
Be Smart!
Visit www.mhscience02.com

D 93

Answers to Concepts and Skills

16. Reading in Science Thunderstorms form in clouds called thunderheads. Intense heating causes air to rise quickly. A cloud forms where there is an upward rush of heated air, an updraft. As more and more warm, moist air is carried upward, the cloud grows larger and larger. Strong updrafts keep droplets of water and ice crystals in the cloud, so they grow in size, too. When the updrafts cannot support them anymore, they fall as heavy rain or hail. Lightning superheats the air, causing thunder.

17. Safety It's possible for lightning to strike someone who is outside, near a tree, near the water. People should go into a building, get into a closed car, and shut the doors and windows, and stay away from the water. Stay away from metal pipes, electrical appliances, and open windows. Do not use the phone except in an emergency.

18. Product Ads Accept all reasonable examples and answers. (Possible answers might include insulated gloves, boots, waterproof gear, sunscreens, etc.)

19. Process Skills: Measure Possible answer: Make a model using a tray and sand, adding water to observe the changes caused by extra rainfall.

20. Critical Thinking Students could use data collected at weather stations throughout the world, noting temperature changes over time.

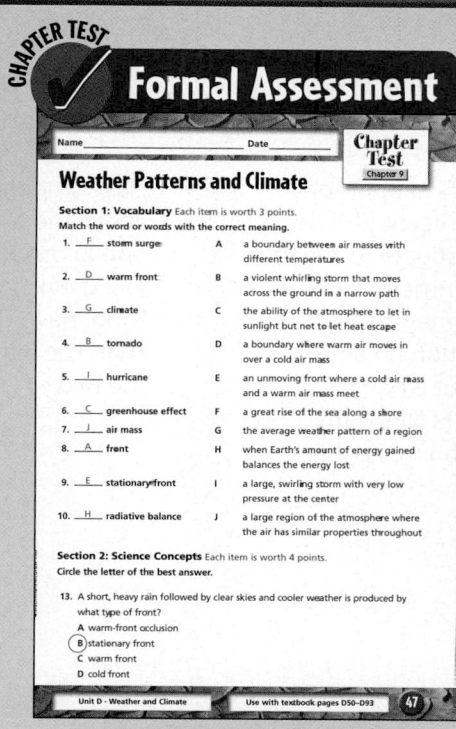

Assessment Book, p. 47

People in Science

People in Science

Objective

■ Describe the work and interests of a climatologist.

Build on Prior Knowledge

Ask:

■ **How often do you watch the weather report on the news? For what reasons?** (Possible answers: finding out how to dress for the day, to plan activities, or to plan for major storm)

■ **What kinds of information do you get from a weather report?** (Possible answers: temperature, how much precipitation and what kind, humidity, impending storms, and so on)

Climatologist
Dr. Henry Diaz

Developing the Main Idea

Focus students on the job of a climatologist by asking:

■ **What kind of interests and training does a climatologist need?** (an interest in weather and climate, a special interest in a climate area such as water resources or El Niño, and a doctorate degree)

■ **What is the "Hurricane Belt"?** (an area of the Caribbean where hurricanes most likely hit)

■ **What events in Dr. Diaz's life first interested him in climatology?** (growing up in two hurricane-prone areas)

■ **What is El Niño?** (the largest single weather influence that causes huge climate changes around the world resulting in floods, droughts, cyclones, and fire damage)

Climatologist

Dr. Henry Diaz

National Oceanic and Atmospheric Administration

Is it going to rain tomorrow? Will it be warm enough to go swimming? Sometimes it's important to know what the weather is going to be. The weather reporter on TV is usually good at forecasting the weather. Some meteorologists, however, do more than just predict tomorrow's weather.

These meteorologists conduct research. They use tools like radar, satellites, computers, and special aircraft. They might study the chemical properties of the atmosphere. They might study how energy is transferred. Some meteorologists are climatologists. A climatologist studies past records of weather. These records may help to predict future changes that could affect human life.

Dr. Henry Diaz is a climatologist. He works for the National Oceanic and Atmospheric Administration (NOAA). Dr. Diaz was born and raised in Cuba, an island in the Caribbean Sea. Cuba is part of the "Hurricane Belt." As a teenager living in Florida, he experienced some violent hurricanes. These storms fueled his interest in weather. He decided to become a meteorologist.

This radar image of the western Pacific Ocean shows temperature differences that might help explain El Niño.

D 94

Advanced Learners

El Niño

Ask students to find out more about the most recent El Niño. Have them investigate its effect on different countries around the world. They may also include information on any predictions about when to expect the next El Niño and how scientists can make this prediction. **Linguistic**

Inclusion

La Niña

Have students find out more about the climate phenomenon known as La Niña—generally speaking, the opposite of El Niño. Have them describe or chart the differences between the two. **Linguistic; Kinesthetic**

Dr. Diaz received his doctorate in climatology from the University of Colorado in 1985. He was hired by the NOAA and conducted research projects. One project was on how climate affects the water resources of the western United States.

Dr. Diaz has also become an expert on El Niño. El Niño is the largest single weather influence on Earth. El Niño occurs every few years when areas of high-pressure and low-pressure air suddenly switch places along the equator in the South Pacific. The shift causes huge climate changes around the world. The result is floods, droughts, cyclones, and even fire damage.

Dr. Diaz is working with other scientists to try to predict when future El Niños will occur. This will give people around the world a chance to prepare for the El Niños. If their research is successful, many lives will be saved!

Careers IN SCIENCE

Physicist

If you're interested in meteorology, you may want to be a physicist. A physicist studies the laws of nature. He or she applies these laws to everyday life. Physicists study matter and energy. Some physicists study atoms. Some study the stars.

Most physicists work for colleges and universities. Some work for the government. Wherever a physicist works, his or her office is the laboratory. Physicists need to be familiar with tools like computers, telescopes, and lasers.

A career in physics starts with four years of college. Almost all physicists study to get doctorates in physics. Many teach college physics while still doing their research.

Write ABOUT IT

1. What is the difference between a TV weather reporter and a climatologist?

2. Where does El Niño begin? How does it begin?

AT THE COMPUTER Visit www.mhscience02.com to learn more about careers.

Part of Highway 1 near Half Moon Bay was washed out by **El Niño.**

D 95

Science Background

Causes of El Niño

Switching of high- and low-pressure air over the Pacific equatorial zone (the Southern Oscillation) is linked with extensive warming of ocean waters in that area. The switch in air pressure results in weakened westward-blowing trade winds over the equatorial Pacific, which are linked to Pacific Ocean circulation changes.

Developing the Main Idea

Encourage students to find out more about climatologists. They may be interested in some subfields of climatology such as paleoclimatology, which is the study of ancient climates as evidenced in fossils, plate tectonics, and preserved gas samples in ice among other things. They may also research bioclimatology, which studies the effect of the physical environment on living organisms.

Thinking Further: *Inferring*

Ask:

■ **Why is predicting future El Niños so important?** (Because of the devastating effects of the flooding and droughts that El Niño brings, knowing when the next will occur can help save lives and help people and countries prepare for them.)

Encourage students to think about what they have learned about the climate of your region or another area from their own experiences.

Answers to Write ABOUT IT

1. While both predict future weather, a climatologist also studies past records of weather to help predict future change in climate that may affect human life. The TV reporter is trying to help people be prepared for daily weather.

2. Along the equator in the Pacific Ocean; it begins when areas of high- and low-pressure air suddenly switch places.

Unit D Performance Assessment

Where's the Water? *(Chapter 8)*

Materials: ice, food coloring, ceramic or metal bowl, hot tap water in a mug, 2 identical clear containers (one cold), mug, 8 ice cubes, food coloring, bucket containing 10-15 ice cubes

Teaching Tips: Be Careful! Be sure the hot water is not hot enough to scald the students.

Answers to Analyze Your Results

1. The outside of the container started dry and became wet as it cooled the air around it, causing water droplets to form.

2. The water formed on the underside of the cooled container. The water came from the warmed air above the hot water. Once the air touched the cooled surface water vapor condensed.

3. Compare the hot water in the container to the ocean. The Sun heats the ocean water, causing it to evaporate. The water vapor rises until it cools and condenses. A cloud forms.

Climate on a Chart *(Chapter 9)*

Materials: graph paper, markers, precipitation and temperature data, writing paper, ruler

Teaching Tips: Obtain monthly averages of temperature and precipitation from a local weather station. Organize the data into a data table and write it on the board in advance.

Where's the WATER?

Your goal is to determine why water droplets form from the air.

What to Do

1. Place five ice cubes in a clear bowl. Add a drop of food coloring. Stir. Wait three minutes. Observe the outside of the bowl. Record your observations.

2. Carefully pour hot water into an identical bowl. Empty the first bowl and place it on top to form a sphere. Put three ice cubes on top. Record your observations.

Analyze Your Results

1. In Step 1, where did the water on the outside of the bowl come from? Explain.

2. Where did water droplets form in Step 2? Where did the water come from? Explain.

3. How is what you observed in Step 2 similar to how a cloud forms over the ocean?

CLIMATE on a CHART

Your goal is to make a climate chart of your local area.

What to Do

A climate chart shows average values for temperature (°C) and precipitation (mm). Use local data to make a climate chart for your area.

Analyze Your Results

1. What is the rainiest month where you live? The least rainy month?

2. What is the hottest month where you live? The coldest?

3. Describe your local climate in words based on your climate chart.

D 96

Rubrics

Where's the Water? *(5-point rubric)*

5 points = All student responses are correct (observations and all answers to Analyze Your Results questions).

4 points = Four student responses are correct.

3 points = Three student responses are correct.

2 points = Two student responses are correct.

1 point = One student response is correct.

0 points = No student responses are correct.

Climate on a Chart *(5-point rubric)*

5 points = Chart is completely correct and answers to Analyze Your Results questions are correct.

4 points = Chart is mostly correct and answers to Analyze Your Results questions are correct.

3 points = Three answers are correct.

2 points = Two answers are correct.

1 point = One answer is correct.

0 points = No student responses are correct.

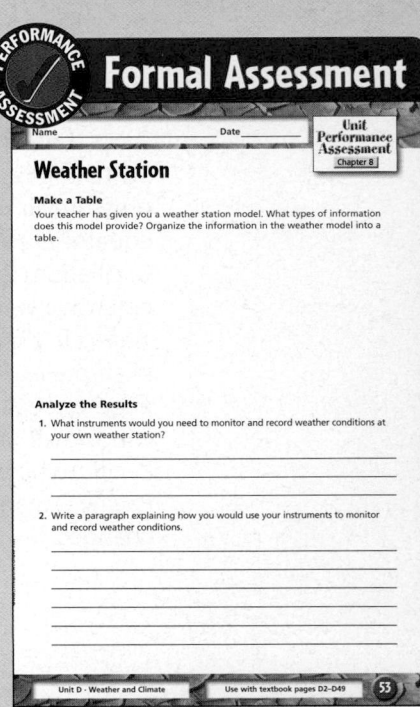

Formal Assessment

Weather Station

Make a Table

Your teacher has given you a weather station model. What types of information does this model provide? Organize the information in the weather model into a table.

Analyze the Results

1. What instruments would you need to monitor and record weather conditions at your own weather station?

2. Write a paragraph explaining how you would use your instruments to monitor and record weather conditions.

Unit D · Weather and Climate   Use with textbook pages D2–D49   53

Assessment Book, pp. 51–54

For Your Reference

Science Handbook

Health Handbook

Glossary

Index

Units of Measurement

Build on Prior Knowledge

Write the word "ruler" on the board and then have students add other measuring tools to the list. For each tool, ask:

- **What does this tool measure? What units of measurement are used with this tool?** (inch, foot, centimeter, and so on)

Developing the Main Idea

Explain that in this lesson students will review some common measuring instruments and two systems of units used to record measurements.

Using the Illustrations

Discuss each of the pictures on pages R2 and R3. For each picture ask:

- **What is being measured? What measuring tool is being used? What units of measure could be used to record the data?**
  (Temperature: thermometer; degrees Celsius or degrees Fahrenheit. Length and distance: metric stick or ruler; meters, centimeters. Mass: balance; grams, kilograms. Volume: graduated cylinder or measuring cup; liters, milliliters, quarts, ounces, pints, gallons. Weight: scale; pounds, ounces. Time: stopwatch or clock; minutes, seconds, hours.)

Science Background

Systems of Measurement

There are two systems of measurement commonly used in the United States—the English or customary system and the metric system. Scientists throughout the world use the metric system so that information can be easily shared. The metric system is based on units of length (meter) and mass (kilogram). Temperature is not actually part of the system. It is included here for convenience of comparing the more familiar units (English system and Fahrenheit scale) and less familiar units (metric system and Celsius scale). The abbreviation SI stands for Système Internationale, in French.

Units of Measurement

This bottle of juice has a volume of 1 liter.

That is a little more than 1 quart.

She can walk 20 meters in 5 seconds.

That means her speed is 4 meters per second.

Table of Measurements

International System of Units (SI)	English System of Units
Temperature Water freezes at 0°C and boils at 100°C.	**Temperature** Water freezes at 32°F and boils at 212°F.
Length and Distance 1,000 meters (m) = 1 kilometer (km) 100 centimeters (cm) = 1 meter 10 millimeters (mm) = 1 centimeter	**Length and Distance** 5,280 feet = 1 mile 3 feet = 1 yard 12 inches = 1 foot
Volume 1,000 milliliters (mL) = 1 liter (L) 1 cubic centimeter (cm³) = 1 milliliter	**Volume of Fluids** 4 quarts = 1 gallon 2 pints = 1 quart 2 cups = 1 pint 8 fluid ounces = 1 cup
Mass 1,000 grams (g) = 1 kilogram (kg)	**Weight** 2,000 pounds = 1 ton 16 ounces = 1 pound

R 3

Using the Illustrations

Have students study the table of measurements. Ask:

- **What are two systems used to report measurements?** (the SI or metric system; the English or customary system)

- **What kind of information can you find in a table of measurement?** (different units of measure; ways of converting between different units)

- **Where can you find tables of measurement?** (Possible answers: in the back of a math or science textbook; in a large dictionary; in an encyclopedia)

WRITING LINK

Students may write about their experiences using at least two different kinds of measuring instruments.

Informal Assessment

Write these words on the board: *distance, mass, temperature,* and *capacity.* Ask:

- **For each word, name a tool used to measure each quantity. Then name at least two units of measure.** (Distance: ruler, tape measure, meterstick; meter, centimeter, inch, foot. Mass: balance; kilograms, grams. Temperature: thermometer; degrees Celsius, degrees Fahrenheit. Capacity: calibrated beaker, graduated cylinder; liters, milliliters, cubic centimeters.)

- **What units can you use to report the speed of a moving object? Give both metric and English system examples.** (Metric: kilometers per hour, meters per second, kilometers per minute. English: miles per hour, feet per second, miles per minute.)

Math | MiniLesson

Metric Conversions

Develop An aquarium is 132 millimeters (mm) wide. Will this width fit on a table that is 15 centimeters (cm) wide?

To solve this problem, change 132 millimeters to centimeters. To change between metric units, you multiply or divide by powers of ten.

132 mm = ■ cm
Think: 10 mm = 1 cm
Divide to change from smaller to larger units.
132 ÷ 10 = 13.2

132 mm = 13.2 cm
13.2 < 15
The aquarium will fit.

2.51 km = ■ meters
Think: 1 km = 1,000 m
To change from larger to smaller units, multiply.
2.51 × 1,000 = 2,150 meters

Practice Complete.
1. 35 cm = ■ m   (0.35 m)
2. 6.25 L = ■ mL   (6,250 mL)
3. 1.75 kg = ■ g   (1,750 g)
4. 58 mm = ■ cm (5.8 cm)

Use a Hand Lens and a Microscope

Objective

- Practice collecting data using hand lenses and microscopes.

Build on Prior Knowledge

Display a hand lens and a microscope. Have students share past experiences using these tools. Ask:

- **How are these tools like a pair of eyeglasses?** (Both use lenses to help a person see better.)

- **How are these tools alike? How are they different?** (They both magnify objects. Differences include: the microscope is more powerful, more expensive, and more difficult to learn to use.)

Exploring the Main Idea

For the two activities on page R4, provide each group with the needed materials. Have groups read all the directions before they begin working. After students have drawn their pictures of the cereal, allow time for them to examine other objects with the lenses. When they are finished, ask:

- **How do you know how close the hand lens should be to the object?** (You don't; you must experiment until the object looks clear and not blurred.)

Have students complete the activity with the radish seeds. (Sprouting times will vary.)

Collect Data

Use a Hand Lens

You use a hand lens to magnify an object, or make the object look larger. With a hand lens, you can see details that would be hard to see without the hand lens.

Magnify a Piece of Cereal

1. Place a piece of your favorite cereal on a flat surface. Look at the cereal carefully. Draw a picture of it.
2. Look at the cereal through the large lens of a hand lens. Move the lens toward or away from the cereal until it looks larger and in focus. Draw a picture of the cereal as you see it through the hand lens. Fill in details that you did not see before.
3. Look at the cereal through the smaller lens, which will magnify the cereal even more. If you notice more details, add them to your drawing.
4. Repeat this activity using objects you are studying in science. It might be a rock, some soil, or a seed.

Observe Seeds in a Petri Dish

Can you observe a seed as it sprouts? You can if it's in a petri dish. A petri dish is a shallow, clear, round dish with a cover.

1. Line the sides and bottom of a petri dish with a double layer of filter paper or paper towel. You may have to cut the paper to make it fit.
2. Sprinkle water on the paper to wet it.
3. Place three or four radish seeds on the wet paper in different areas of the dish. Put the lid on the dish, and keep it in a warm place.
4. Observe the seeds every day for a week. Use a hand lens to look for a tiny root pushing through the seed. Record how long it takes each seed to sprout.

R 4

Science Background

Hand Lenses and Microscopes

A hand lens consists of a convergent lens of short focal length. Most hand lenses have a magnifying power of about 5 times actual size. To examine objects too small for a hand lens, a microscope can be used. Like a telescope, a microscope is based on two lenses in a tube that can be focused by changing the length of the tube.

Collect Data

Use a Microscope

Hand lenses make objects look several times larger. A microscope, however, can magnify an object to look hundreds of times larger.

Examine Salt Grains

1. Look at the photograph to learn the different parts of your microscope.
2. Place the microscope on a flat surface. Always carry a microscope with both hands. Hold the arm with one hand, and put your other hand beneath the base.
3. Move the mirror so that it reflects light up toward the stage. Never point the mirror directly at the Sun or a bright light. Bright light can cause permanent eye damage.
4. Place a few grains of salt on the slide. Put the slide under the stage clips. Be sure that the salt grains you are going to examine are over the hole in the stage.
5. Look through the eyepiece. Turn the focusing knob slowly until the salt grains come into focus.
6. Draw what the grains look like through the microscope.
7. Look at other objects through the microscope. Try a piece of leaf, a human hair, or a pencil mark.

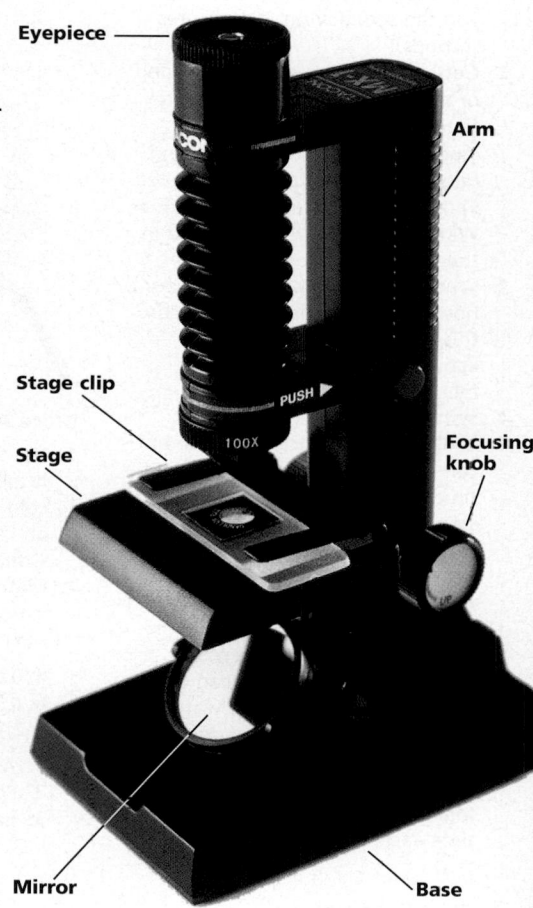

Eyepiece

Arm

Stage clip

Stage

Focusing knob

Mirror

Base

R 5

Using the Illustrations

Ask students to study the diagram on page R5 showing the parts of a microscope. Have them use the diagram to find corresponding parts of a real microscope.

Exploring the Main Idea

Many students will need help when first using a microscope. Try to group students so that they can help each other learn. You may need to first teach a small group of students how to use the microscope and then have those students work with others until everyone has learned the skill.

Have students work through the steps. Demonstrate how to hold and carry a microscope. Stress the need for never pointing the mirror directly at the Sun or another bright light.

WRITING LINK

Students may write about objects they would like to examine with a hand lens or a microscope.

Informal Assessment

Have students choose a flower or the skin of a fruit. Have them draw what they see without using a hand lens. Then have them look at the object through the hand lens and add more detail to their drawings. Ask:

■ **Why are lenses and microscopes important in scientific work?** (Possible answer: Scientists can learn more about objects by finding out what they look like when highly magnified.)

Inclusion

One Eye, Two Eyes

As students begin to use a microscope, they may tend to close the eye that is not looking into the eyepiece. Have them practice viewing specimens with both eyes open and explain if there is any difference. (No. They are still seeing a 1-dimensional view of the specimen.) Having both eyes open allows them to keep a specimen under view while they attempt to draw their observations. **Kinesthetic; Spatial**

Measure Time

Build on Prior Knowledge

Ask students to describe different kinds of clocks and watches. Ask:

- **What are some units we use to measure time?** (days, hours, minutes, seconds)

Using the Illustrations

Have students look at the picture of the stopwatch. Ask:

- **How many seconds are shown on the stopwatch?** (25.75 seconds)

Exploring the Main Idea

Tell students that the first part of the page will give them practice in measuring time. When students have finished activities 1–6, ask:

- **Did you get exactly the same time in both experiments?** (No. There is some measurement error in any measurement activity.)

WRITING LINK

Students may write about measuring time.

Informal Assessment

Ask:

- **What are some advantages in using a stopwatch?** (With the stopwatch, you don't have to subtract one time from another; a stopwatch is probably more precise.)

Make Measurements

Measure Time

You use timing devices to measure how long something takes to happen. Some timing devices you use in science are a clock with a second hand and a stopwatch. Which one is more accurate?

Comparing a Clock and Stopwatch

1. Look at a clock with a second hand. The second hand is the hand that you can see moving. It measures seconds.
2. Get an egg timer with falling sand or some device like a wind-up toy that runs down after a certain length of time. When the second hand of the clock points to 12, tell your partner to start the egg timer. Watch the clock while the sand in the egg timer is falling.
3. When the sand stops falling, count how many seconds it took. Record this measurement. Repeat the activity, and compare the two measurements.
4. Switch roles with your partner.
5. Look at a stopwatch. Click the button on the top right. This starts the time. Click the button again. This stops the time. Click the button on the top left. This sets the stopwatch back to zero. Notice that the stopwatch tells time in minutes, seconds, and hundredths of a second.
6. Repeat the activity in steps 1–3, using the stopwatch instead of a clock. Make sure the stopwatch is set to zero. Click the top right button to start timing the reading. Click it again when the sand stops falling. Make sure you and your partner time each other twice.

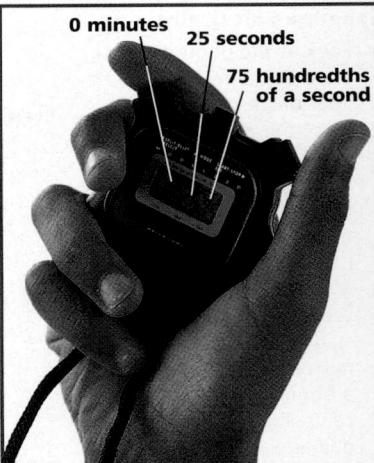

0 minutes 25 seconds 75 hundredths of a second

More About Time

1. Use the stopwatch to time how long it takes an ice cube to melt under cold running water. How long does an ice cube take to melt under warm running water?
2. Match each of these times with the action you think took that amount of time.

   a. 0:00:14:55
   b. 0:24:39:45
   c. 2:10:23:00

   1. A Little League baseball game
   2. Saying the Pledge of Allegiance
   3. Recess

R 6

Inclusion

Clocks

A standard, or analog, clock shows the time by the movement of hands. A digital clock displays time in numbers. A stopwatch can measure time to the nearest hundredth of a second. Have students discuss another kind of clock, the sundial. Have them explain how it tells time and give its limitations. (not useful at night or on very cloudy days) **Linguistic**

Make Measurements

Measure Length

SCIENCE • HANDBOOK

Find Length with a Ruler

1. Look at this section of a ruler. Each centimeter is divided into 10 millimeters. How long is the paper clip?
2. The length of the paper clip is 3 centimeters plus 2 millimeters. You can write this length as 3.2 centimeters.
3. Place the ruler on your desk. Lay a pencil against the ruler so that one end of the pencil lines up with the left edge of the ruler. Record the length of the pencil.
4. Trade your pencil with a classmate. Measure and record the length of each other's pencil. Compare your answers.

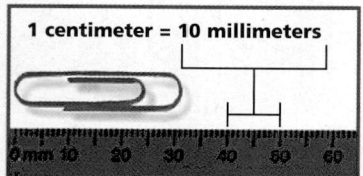

1 centimeter = 10 millimeters

Measuring Area

Area is the amount of surface something covers. To find the area of a rectangle, multiply the rectangle's length by its width. For example, the rectangle here is 3 centimeters long and 2 centimeters wide. Its area is 3 cm x 2 cm = 6 square centimeters. You write the area as 6 cm².

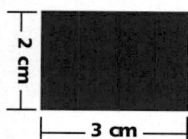

2 cm
3 cm

1. Find the area of your science book. Measure the book's length to the nearest centimeter. Measure its width.
2. Multiply the book's length by its width. Remember to put the answer in cm².

Find Length with a Meterstick

1. Line up the meterstick with the left edge of the chalkboard. Make a chalk mark on the board at the right end of the meterstick.
2. Move the meterstick so that the left edge lines up with the chalk mark. Keep the stick level. Make another mark on the board at the right end of the meterstick.
3. Continue to move the meterstick and make chalk marks until the meterstick meets or overlaps the right edge of the board.
4. Record the length of the chalkboard in centimeters by adding all the measurements you've made. Remember, a meterstick has 100 centimeters.

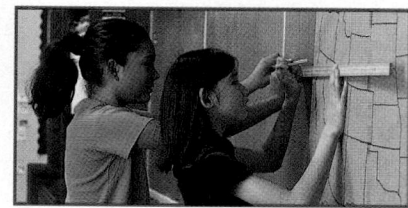

Estimating Length

Try estimating the length of objects in the room. Then measure the length, and compare the estimation with the measurement.

Inclusion

Rulers

Rulers measure length and distance. In contrast to length, area is usually calculated rather than measured. However as an activity, students can use centimeter graph paper to draw the outline of small objects that have a flat side—such as blocks or small books. They can count the number of boxes on the graph paper to find the area.
Spatial

Measure Length

Objective

- Use centimeter rulers to measure length and multiply to calculate area.

Build on Prior Knowledge

Hold up a ruler or a pencil that is about 10 centimeters long. Ask:

- **This object is 10 centimeters long. Find some objects that are more and some that are less than 10 centimeters long.** (More: desk, table, door, book. Less: crayon, scissors.)

- **One meter equals 100 centimeters. Find things that are about 1 meter long.** (height of a door knob, width of a desk)

Using the Illustrations
Ask:

- **How long is the paper clip in the diagram?** (32 millimeters or 3.2 centimeters)

- **What are two ways to represent the same length?** (32 mm; 3.2 cm)

Developing the Main Idea

Draw a rectangle on the board and label its sides 8 cm and 3 cm. Ask:

- **How can you find the area of a rectangle?** (Multiply the length times the width.)

- **What is the area of this rectangle?** (24 square centimeters, or 24 cm²)

Check that students have labeled their areas using the symbol cm².

WRITING LINK

Students may write about giving examples of lengths and areas they might use in a science experiment.

Informal Assessment

Have students draw a rectangle. Have them measure the length and width to the nearest tenth of a centimeter, then find the area.

Measure Mass

Measure Mass

Objective

- Use a pan balance to compare masses.

Build on Prior Knowledge
Ask students if they have ever used a scale to find their weight. Then show them a pan balance. Ask:

- **How is this balance like a scale? Different?**
  (They both are instruments used to measure. The scale gives a number for a weight; the balance compares two different masses.)

Developing the Main Idea
Explain to students that grams are used for small masses and kilograms for more massive objects. The prefix *kilo-* means thousand. So 1 kilogram equals 1,000 grams.

Using the Illustrations
Ask:

- **How can you tell when the pans hold equal masses?** (The pointer must point exactly to the middle mark on the scale.)

WRITING LINK

Students may write about using a pan balance, including directions on how to use this tool.

Informal Assessment
Have students choose three light objects and find the mass of each in grams. Have them estimate how many crayons equal a mass of 1 kilogram. Then have them use a balance to check their estimate.

Answers
1. 1.97 kilograms (1,970 grams)
2. Have students name combinations of the mass that exceed 1 kilogram: such as 2 of the 500 g mass plus any of the smaller masses.

Mass is the amount of matter an object has. You use a balance to measure mass. To find the mass of an object, you balance it with objects whose masses you know. Let's find the mass of a box of crayons.

Measure the Mass of a Box of Crayons
1. Place the balance on a flat, level surface. Check that the two pans are empty and clean.
2. Make sure the empty pans are balanced with each other. The pointer should point to the middle mark. If it does not, move the slider a little to the right or left to balance the pans.
3. Gently place a box of crayons on the left pan. This pan will drop lower.
4. Add masses to the right pan until the pans are balanced.
5. Add the numbers on the masses that are in the right pan. The total is the mass of the box of crayons, in grams. Record this number. After the number write a *g* for "grams."

Estimating Mass
Once you become familiar with the mass of objects, you can try estimating the masses of objects. Then you can compare the estimation with the actual mass.

More About Mass
The mass of your crayons was probably less than 100 grams. You may not have enough masses to balance a pineapple. It has a mass of about 1,000 grams. That's the same as 1 kilogram, because *kilo* means "1,000."

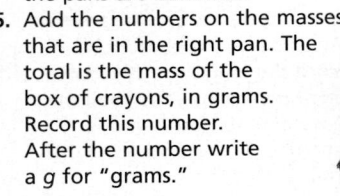
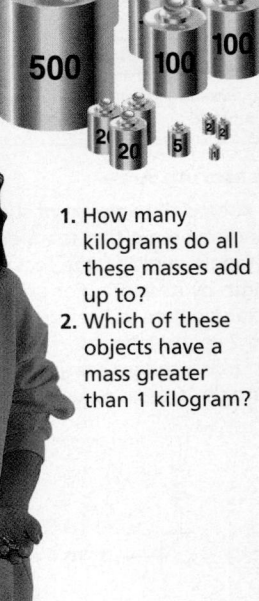

1. How many kilograms do all these masses add up to?
2. Which of these objects have a mass greater than 1 kilogram?

R 8

Science Background

Mass
Mass is the amount of material in an object. In the metric system, mass is measured in units such as grams, kilograms, and milligrams. A pan balance is used to compare masses. A scale measures weight, the pull of gravity on an object.

Make Measurements

Measure Volume

Volume is the amount of space something takes up. In science you usually measure the volume of liquids by using beakers and graduated cylinders. These containers are marked in milliliters (mL).

Measure the Volume of a Liquid

1. Look at the beaker and at the graduated cylinder. The beaker has marks for each 25 mL up to 200 mL. The graduated cylinder has marks for each 1 mL up to 100 mL.
2. The surface of the water in the graduated cylinder curves up at the sides. You measure the volume by reading the height of the water at the flat part. What is the volume of water in the graduated cylinder? How much water is in the beaker? They both contain 75 mL of water.
3. Pour 50 mL of water from a pitcher into a beaker.
4. Now pour the 50 mL of water into a graduated cylinder.

Find the Volume of a Solid

Here's a way to find the volume of a solid, such as a rock.

1. Start with 50 mL of water in a graduated cylinder.
2. Place a small rock in the water. The water level rises.
3. Measure the new water level. Subtract 50 mL from the new reading. The difference is the volume of the rock. Record the volume in cm³.

Estimating Volume

Once you become familiar with the volumes of liquids and solids, you can estimate volumes. Estimate the amount of liquid in a glass or can. Estimate the volume of an eraser.

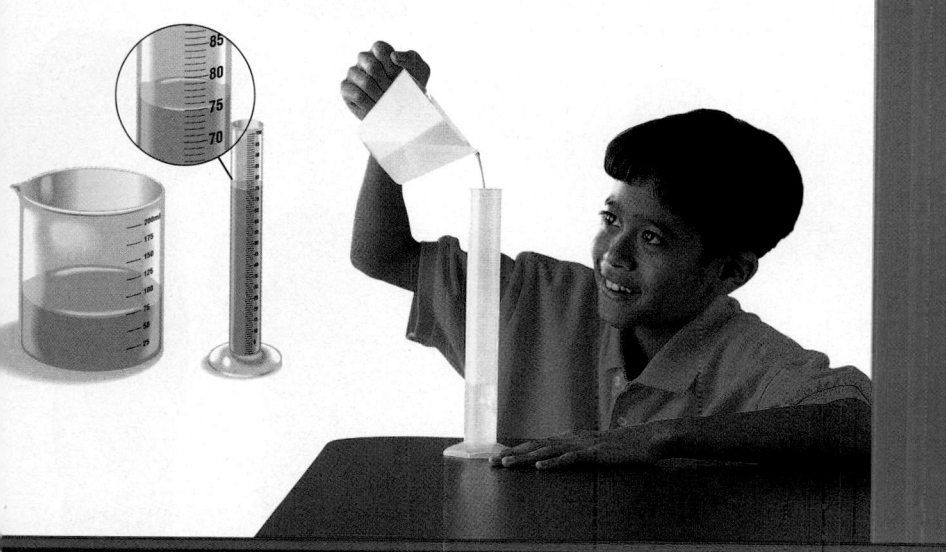

Inclusion

Units of Volume

The basic unit for measuring the volume of a liquid in the metric system is the liter. (Students will use milliliters more frequently.) There are 1,000 milliliters in 1 liter. The volume of a solid can be measured in cubic centimeters. One cubic centimeter equals 1 milliliter. Have students practice converting from milliliters to liters by dividing by 1,000; and from liters to milliliters by multiplying by 1,000. **Logical**

Measure Volume

Objective

- Use beakers and graduated cylinders to measure volume.

Build on Prior Knowledge

Hold up a graduated cylinder marked in milliliters. Ask:

- **What do the marks mean on this tool?** (Each mark shows one milliliter.)
- **What is the symbol for liter?** (L)
- **What is the symbol for milliliter?** (mL)

Using the Illustrations

Ask the following about the illustration:

- **How is using a beaker different from using a graduated cylinder?** (With the beaker, the liquid is flatter. With the graduated cylinder, it curves up at the sides.)

Exploring the Main Idea

Have students practice steps 3 and 4 of "Measure the Volume of a Liquid," using other equal volumes, to visualize the same volume in two different containers.

Have students "Find the Volume of a Solid" by the displacement of water. Ask:

- **How can you measure the volume of a marble?** (Measure an amount of water in a graduated cylinder. Place the marble in the cylinder. Measure the new water level. Subtract the water level with the marble from the water level without the marble to find the marble's volume.)

WRITING LINK

Students may write about what they have learned about measuring volume.

Informal Assessment

Tell students to pour about 200 mL of water into an unmarked cup without measuring. Then have them measure to find out how close their estimate was. (Students should measure volumes to the nearest milliliter.)

Measure Weight/Force

- Use spring scales to measure weight.

Build on Prior Knowledge

Ask students if they have ever used a bathroom scale.

- **What unit of measure is used on a bathroom scale?** (pounds or kilograms)

Developing the Main Idea

Explain that a spring scale measures weight in newtons (N). There are about 4.5 N in 1 pound.

Exploring the Main Idea

Ask students if they could find their weight with a spring scale like this one? (No, the scale can only be used for objects up to 20 newtons, or about 5 pounds.)

WRITING LINK

Students may write about weighing objects using a spring scale.

Informal Assessment

Ask:

- **How is a spring scale like a pan balance? How are they different?** (They are both measurement tools; the pan balance compares two masses; the spring scale gives weight as a number.)

Make Measurements

Measure Weight/Force

You use a spring scale to measure weight. An object has weight because the force of gravity pulls down on the object. Therefore, weight is a force. Weight is measured in newtons (N) like all forces.

Measure the Weight of an Object

1. Look at your spring scale to see how many newtons it measures. See how the measurements are divided. The spring scale shown here measures up to 5 N. It has a mark for every 0.1 N.
2. Hold the spring scale by the top loop. Put the object to be measured on the bottom hook. If the object will not stay on the hook, place it in a net bag. Then hang the bag from the hook.
3. Let go of the object slowly. It will pull down on a spring inside the scale. The spring is connected to a pointer. The pointer on the spring scale shown here is a small bar.
4. Wait for the pointer to stop moving. Read the number of newtons next to the pointer. This is the object's weight. The mug in the picture weighs 4 N.

More About Spring Scales

You probably weigh yourself by standing on a bathroom scale. This is a spring scale. The force of your body stretches a spring inside the scale. The dial on the scale is probably marked in pounds—the English unit of weight. One pound is equal to about 4.5 newtons.

A bathroom scale, a grocery scale, and a kitchen scale are some other spring scales you may have seen.

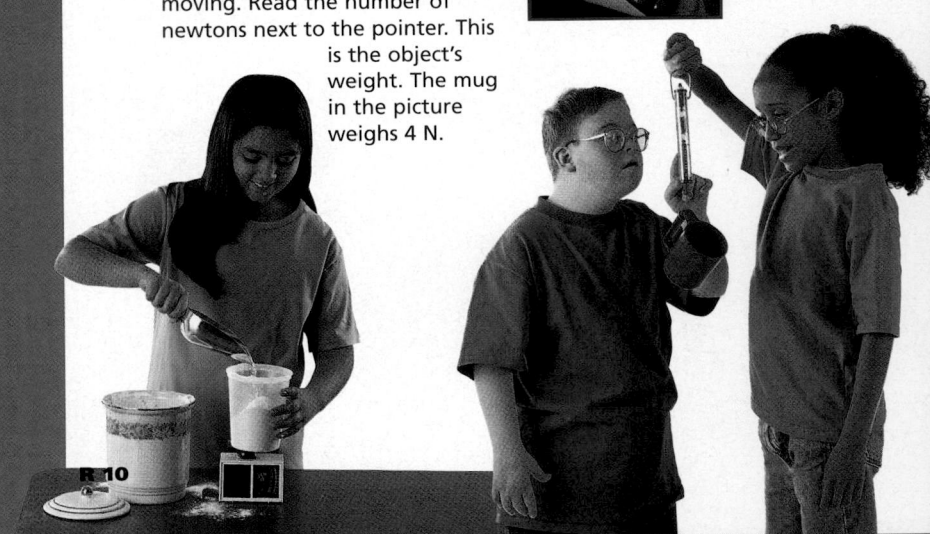

R10

🦉 **Science Background**

Weight

Weight is the pull of gravity on an object. Mass and weight are connected, in that we can measure weight to find mass. The newton is a derived unit in the metric system: one newton equals the force required to give one kilogram an acceleration of one meter per second. Students might practice converting familiar pound measures to newtons by multiplying by 4.5.

Measure Temperature

You use a thermometer to measure temperature—how hot or cold something is. A thermometer is made of a thin tube with colored liquid inside. When the liquid gets warmer, it expands and moves up the tube. When the liquid gets cooler, it contracts and moves down the tube. You may have seen most temperatures measured in degrees Fahrenheit (°F). Scientists measure temperature in degrees Celsius (°C).

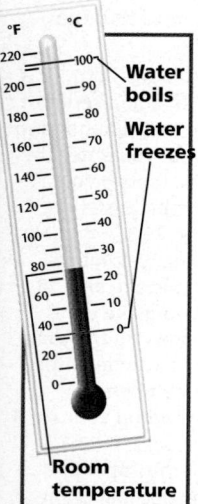

°F **°C**

Water boils

Water freezes

Room temperature

Read a Thermometer

1. Look at the thermometer shown here. It has two scales—a Fahrenheit scale and a Celsius scale.
2. What is the temperature shown on the thermometer? At what temperature does water freeze?

What Is Convection?

1. Fill a large beaker about two-thirds full of cool water. Find the temperature of the water by holding a thermometer in the water. Do not let the bulb at the bottom of the thermometer touch the sides or bottom of the beaker.
2. Keep the thermometer in the water until the liquid in the tube stops moving—about 1 minute. Read and record the temperature in °C.
3. Sprinkle a little fish food on the surface of the water in the beaker. Do not knock the beaker, and most of the food will stay on top.
4. Carefully place the beaker on a hot plate. A hot plate is a small electric stove. Plug in the hot plate, and turn the control knob to a middle setting.
5. After 1 minute measure the temperature of water near the bottom of the beaker. At the same time, a classmate should measure the temperature of water near the top of the beaker. Record these temperatures. Is water near the bottom of the beaker heating up faster than near the top?
6. As the water heats up, notice what happens to the fish food. How do you know that warmer water at the bottom of the beaker rises and cooler water at the top sinks?

Science Background

Temperature Scales

Two common scales for measuring temperature are the Fahrenheit and Celsius scales. In the Celsius scale, each degree is $\frac{1}{100}$ of the difference between the temperature of melting ice and boiling water. In the Fahrenheit scale, each degree is $\frac{1}{180}$ of this difference.

Measure Temperature

Objective

- Use thermometers to measure temperature.

Build on Prior Knowledge

Ask students what the outside temperature is. What tool is used to measure temperature? (a thermometer)

Developing the Main Idea

Point out that there are two scales on the thermometer, one for Fahrenheit and one for Celsius.

Using the Illustrations

Have students look at the diagram of the thermometer. Ask:

- **At what temperature does water boil?** (212°F, 100°C)

- **At what temperature does water freeze?** (32°F, 0°C)

Exploring the Main Idea

As students do the convection activity, they will find that at first, in step 5, the water is heated faster at the bottom. In minutes, however, that is, in step 6, they will see the fish food spread out and move down to the bottom and then rise in a continuous current. The heated water rises, cools at the surface and sinks, bring the fish food along.

WRITING LINK

Students may write about measuring temperature.

Informal Assessment

Ask:

- **A student measured a temperature and reported it was 35 degrees. Why is this not a complete measurement?** (The student must record whether the temperature was in Fahrenheit or Celsius.)

Use Calculators

Objective

■ Use calculators to analyze collected data.

Build on Prior Knowledge

Have students share experiences using calculators. Ask:

■ **Why do you sometimes get the wrong answer when using a calculator?** (The numbers are not entered correctly; the wrong operation was chosen.)

Developing the Main Idea

Explain that students will practice using a calculator, first, to add a list of numbers, and second, to find the average or mean.

Ask students to read the left column on page R12. Ask:

■ **How can you find the total amount of rain that fell over the 11 weeks?** (Add the numbers in the second column.)

Exploring the Main Idea

Have students work in pairs to complete the steps of the "Find the Mean" activity. One student can read off the numbers while the other enters them. Before they do step 4, the division, they might estimate what the average rainfall per week might be (by scanning through the numbers in the Rain column of the table).

Ask students to generalize a method that they could use to find the mean of any set of numbers. (Find the total of a set of numbers. Divide the total by the number of members of the set.)

Use Calculators

Sometimes after you make measurements, you have to analyze your data to see what it means. This might involve doing calculations with your data. A calculator helps you do time-consuming calculations.

Find an Average

After you collect a set of measurements, you may want to get an idea of a typical measurement in that set. What if, for example, you are doing a weather project? As part of the project, you are studying rainfall data of a nearby town. The table shows how much rain fell in that town each week during the summer.

Week	Rain (cm)
1	2.0
2	1.4
3	0.0
4	0.5
5	1.2
6	2.5
7	1.8
8	1.4
9	2.4
10	8.6
11	7.5

What if you want to get an idea of how much rain fell during a typical week in the summer? In other words, you want to find the average for the set of data. There are three kinds of averages—mean, median, and mode. Does it matter which one you use?

Find the Mean

The mean is what most people think of when they hear the word *average*. You can use a calculator to find the mean.

1. Make sure the calculator is on.
2. Add the numbers. To add a series of numbers, enter the first number and press ⊞. Repeat until you enter the last number. See the hints below. After your last number, press ⊟. Your total should be 29.3.
3. While entering so many numbers, it's easy to make a mistake and hit the wrong key. If you make a mistake, correct it by pressing the clear entry key, CE. Then continue entering the rest of the numbers.
4. Find the mean by dividing your total by the number of weeks. If 29.3 is displayed, press ÷ 1 1 =. Rounded up to one decimal point, your mean should be 2.7.

Hints:
- If the only number to the right of the decimal point is 0, you don't have to enter it into the calculator. To enter 2.0, just press 2.
- If the only number to the left of the decimal point is 0, you don't have to enter it into the calculator. To enter 0.5, just press . 5.

Inclusion

Calculators

Calculators are used in scientific work to perform basic computation. They are particularly useful with long lists of quantitative data. They can help analyze data to find averages (means) and percents of totals. Means that students might look for as they study science include mean number of corn kernels of different colors; mean number of students with attached or unattached earlobes; mean lengths of leaves of a given tree when studying variation; mean magnitude of earthquakes in a given area; mean time it takes water to seep through a soil sample; mean distance or time measured when studying speed or acceleration. Have students measure and tabulate student heights and find the mean, medium, and mode. **Logical**

Use Technology

Find the Median

The median is the middle number when the numbers are arranged in order of size. When the rainfall measurements are arranged in order of size, they look like this.

0.0
0.5
1.2
1.4   The median is 1.8.
1.4   This number is in
1.8 ──── the middle; there
2.0   are five numbers
2.4   above it and five
2.5   numbers below it.
7.5
8.6

Find the Mode

The mode is the number that occurs most frequently. From the ranked set of data above, you can see that the most frequent number is 1.4. It occurs twice. Here are your three different averages from the same set of data.

Average Weekly Rainfall (cm)

Mean	2.7
Median	1.8
Mode	1.4

Why is the mean so much higher than the median or mode? The mean is affected greatly by the last two weeks when it rained a lot. A typical week for that summer was much drier than either of those last two weeks. The median or mode gives a better idea of rainfall for a typical week.

Find the Mean, Median, and Mode

The table shows the length of 15 peanuts. Find the mean, median, and mode for this set of data. Which do you think best represents a typical peanut?

Peanut	Length (mm)
1	32
2	29
3	30
4	31
5	33
6	26
7	28
8	27
9	29
10	29
11	32
12	31
13	23
14	36
15	31

Find the Percent

Sometimes numbers are given as percents (%). *Percent* literally means "per hundred." For example, 28% means 28 out of 100. What if there are about 14,000 trees in the forest and 28% are over 50 years old? How many of them are over 50 years old? Use your calculator. You want to find 28% of 14,000. Press 1 4 0 0 0 × 2 8 %. The answer should be 3,920.

R 13

Developing the Main Idea

Have students read "Find the Median". Explain that this is not a calculator activity, but is another way of finding the "center" of the data. Ask:

- **How is this list of numbers like or unlike the rainfall numbers listed on page R12?** (They are the same numbers, but listed in order from least to greatest, top to bottom.)

Exploring the Main Idea

Have students generalize a method for finding the median. (List a set of numbers in order. If there is an odd number of numbers, the middle number is the median. If there is an even number of numbers, the median is the average (mean) of the two middle numbers.)

Developing the Main Idea

Have students read "Find the Mode". Point out again that this is not a calculator activity.

- **Does every set of numbers have a mode?** (No; for example, if every number appears once in a set, there is no mode.)

Have students read "Find the Mean, Median, and Mode" and discuss how to find each number and note which can be found by using a calculator. (finding the mean) Have them read "Find the Percent". Point out that another way to do the calculation is to express 28% as a decimal (0.28) and multiply 14,000 × 0.28 with the calculator.

WRITING LINK

Students may write about their experiences using a calculator.

Informal Assessment

Have students do "Find the Mean, Median, and Mode" on page R13. (mean = 29.8, median = 30, mode = 29)

Inclusion

Range

Another way to analyze data is to find the range, the difference between the greatest and least numbers in a set. Students can use calculators to find the range of the rainfall data on page R12 and the peanut lengths on page R13. Point out that ordering the numbers helps to find the greatest and least numbers. (rainfall = 8.6 − 0.0 = 8.6; peanut length = 36 − 23 = 13)

Logical

Use Computers

It is recommended that students of this age access the Internet with adult supervision.

Build on Prior Knowledge
Have students share computer experiences such as using various application programs and writing or getting e-mail. Ask:

■ **How is using a computer like going to the library?** (Both are ways to find information.)

Developing the Main Idea
Explain that in this lesson students will learn about some different ways they can use computers to learn science.

Using the Illustrations
Have students read the top of page R14 and study the two photographs. Explain that a table on a computer can be created with a spreadsheet program. Ask:

■ **What kinds of information are these students putting into the computer?** (measurements they have made about the weather)

Use Computers

A computer has many uses. The Internet connects your computer to many other computers around the world, so you can collect all kinds of information. You can use a computer to show this information and write reports. Best of all you can use a computer to explore, discover, and learn.

You can also get information from CD-ROMs. They are computer disks that can hold large amounts of information. You can fit a whole encyclopedia on one CD-ROM.

R 14

Use Computers for a Project
Here is how one group of students uses computers as they work on a weather project.

1. The students use instruments to measure temperature, wind speed, wind direction, and other parts of the weather. They input this information, or data, into the computer. The students keep the data in a table. This helps them compare the data from one day to the next.

Use Technology

2. The teacher finds out that another group of students in a town 200 kilometers to the west is also doing a weather project. The two groups use the Internet to talk to each other and share data. When a storm happens in the town to the west, that group tells the other group that it's coming their way.

3. The students want to find out more. They decide to stay on the Internet and send questions to a local TV weather forecaster. She has a Web site and answers questions from students every day.

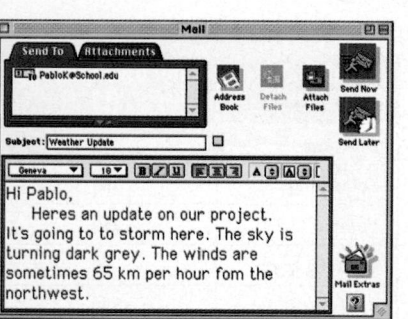

4. Meanwhile some students go to the library to gather more information from a CD-ROM. The CD-ROM has an encyclopedia that includes movie clips. The clips give examples of different kinds of storms.

5. The students have kept all their information in a folder called Weather Project. Now they use that information to write a report about the weather. On the computer they can move around paragraphs, add words, take out words, put in diagrams, and draw weather maps. Then they print the report in color.

Inclusion

Birthdate Weather

Work with students to use the Internet to research weather patterns from the year and month they were born. Demonstrate to students how to perform keyword searches. They may want to narrow their searches as they research sites.
Linguistic

Using the Illustrations

Have students read page R15 and look at the illustration about e-mail. Ask:

- **What is e-mail?** (a message you write or read that is sent from one computer to another computer)

- **Why does a computer need to be hooked up to a telephone line for someone to get e-mail?** (The e-mail messages travel over the telephone lines from one place to another. Many newer e-mail systems do not require the use of telephone lines.)

Developing the Main Idea

Explain that using an on-line encyclopedia or looking for information on the Internet requires the use of key words. Ask:

- **What key words would you use for a project about last year's weather in Virginia?** (Virginia and weather and the specific date)

WRITING LINK

Students may write about their experiences receiving and sending e-mail or using a computer for a school project.

Informal Assessment

Ask students to describe how a computer can be used to organize facts or to gather information for a project. (The computer can be used to make tables and graphs; a word processor can be used to write a report; an on-line encyclopedia or a Web-page search can provide facts and pictures.)

Make Graphs to Organize Data

Objective

- Compare graphs and choose one type to represent a set of data.

Build on Prior Knowledge
Take a class tally on favorite pizza toppings—students can vote only once—mushrooms, peppers, olives, or onions. Discuss different ways to collect and display the data, including graphs, posters, tables.

Using the Illustrations
Have students read page R16 and study the bar graph. Ask:

- **What are the parts of a bar graph?** (the bars, the two scales, the title, the labels on the two scales)

- **What do you do if a bar doesn't exactly meet one of the lines on a bar graph?** (Estimate the number the bar shows.)

Developing the Main Idea
Have students read the section about pictographs. Ask:

- **How is a pictograph different from a bar graph?** (A pictograph uses symbols; a bar graph uses bars.)

- **Why is the key important on a pictograph?** (It tells what each symbol on the graph stands for.)

Have students answer the questions in the text. (Bar graphs: 3 clips with 20 coils, 9 clips with 50 coils Pictographs: 1. Washing clothes; 2. Drinking)

Represent Data

Make Graphs to Organize Data

When you do an experiment in science, you collect information. To find out what your information means, you can organize it into graphs. There are many kinds of graphs.

Bar Graphs
A bar graph uses bars to show information. For example, what if you do an experiment by wrapping wire around a nail and connecting the ends of the wire to a battery? The nail then becomes a magnet that can pick up paper clips. The graph shows that the more you wrap the wire around the nail, the more paper clips it picks up. How many paper clips did the nail with 20 coils pick up? With 50 coils?

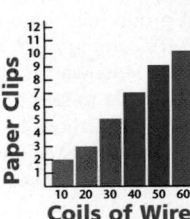

Pictographs
A pictograph uses symbols, or pictures, to show information. What if you collect information about how much water your family uses each day? The table shows what you find.

You can organize this information into the pictograph shown here. The pictograph has to explain what the symbol on the graph means. In this case each bottle means 20 liters of water. A half bottle means half of 20, or 10 liters of water.

1. Which activity uses the most water?
2. Which activity uses the least water?

Activity	Water Used Each Day (L)
Drinking	10
Showering	180
Bathing	240
Brushing teeth	80
Washing dishes	140
Washing hands	30
Washing clothes	280
Flushing toilet	90

A Family's Daily Use of Water

Drinking	
Showering	
Bathing	
Brushing teeth	
Washing dishes	
Washing hands	
Washing clothes	
Flushing toilet	

= 20 liters of water

R 16

Science Background

Graphs
Graphs are visual ways of representing quantitative data. Students can use graphs to identify relationships, make comparisons, and predict future occurrences. Often, more than one kind of graph can be used to display the same set of data. Different kinds of graphs can be used for different kinds of emphasis—such as to compare amounts or to show change over time.

Represent Data

Circle Graphs

A circle graph is helpful to show how a complete set of data is divided into parts. The circle graph here shows how water is used in the United States. What is the single largest use of water?

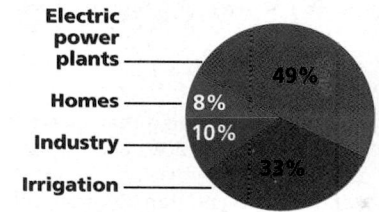

Electric power plants —— 49%
Homes —— 8%
Industry —— 10%
Irrigation —— 33%

Line Graphs

A line graph shows information by connecting dots plotted on the graph. It shows change over time. For example, what if you measure the temperature out of doors every hour starting at 6 A.M.? The table shows what you find.

You can organize this information into a line graph. Follow these steps.

1. Make a scale along the bottom and side of the graph. The scales should include all the numbers in the chart. Label the scales.
2. Plot points on the graph. For example, place your finger at the "6 A.M." on the bottom line. Place a finger from your other hand on the "10" on the left line. Move your "6 A.M." finger up and your "10" finger to the right until they meet, and make a pencil point. Plot the other points in this way.
3. Connect the points with a line.

The line graph to the right organizes measurements you collected so that you can easily compare them.

1. Between which two weeks did the plant grow most?
2. When did plant growth begin to level off?

Time	Temperature (°C)
6 A.M.	10
7 A.M.	12
8 A.M.	14
9 A.M.	16
10 A.M.	18
11 A.M.	20

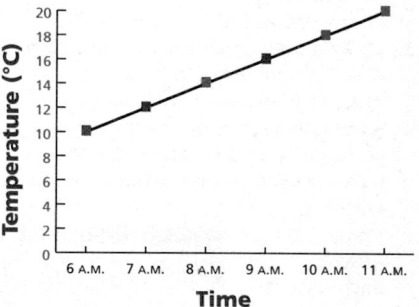

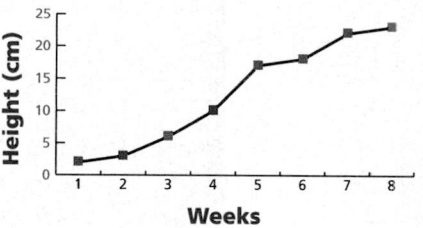

R 17

Developing the Main Idea

Read the circle graph information together. Point out that all the values can be represented as either fractions, decimals, or percents—that is, the individual pieces of data are converted to "parts of a whole", which are gotten by dividing one piece of data by the sum of all the data. The parts of the graph total 100% (or 1) The single largest use of water is electric power plants, 49%.

Exploring the Main Idea

Read the first line graph data together. Students may conclude that this kind of graph shows how one kind of data changes over time, such as weeks. Have students answer the questions. (1. Growth was greatest where the line is steepest, between weeks 4 and 5. 2. Growth levels off after week 7.)

WRITING LINK

Students may write about graphs they may have seen in newspapers or magazines.

Informal Assessment

Have students use the data from the pictograph section, "Water Used Each Day, " to make another kind of graph — circle, bar, or line. (Converting these data to percents is difficult since there is a wide range from small to large numbers and the total is 1,050. A bar graph can show the data as they are without converting them. Since there is no change over time involved, a line graph is inappropriate.)

SCIENCE FOR ALL

Inclusion

Graph It

This table sums up some of the medal winning countries at the 25th Summer Olympic Games:

Country	Number of Medals
Cuba	31
Hungary	30
South Korea	29
France	29
Australia	27
Spain	22

Have students choose a type of graph and make a graph of this information. **Logical; Spatial**

Make Maps to Show Information

Objective

- Read and make geographical maps and idea maps.

Build on Prior Knowledge

Have students share experiences about using road maps, then ask:

- **How is a road map like the area it represents? Different?** (Both show key features such as streets and important buildings. The map is smaller and not as detailed.)

Developing the Main Idea

Explain that students will use two kinds of maps. The first is like a road map. The second type of map is a way to show how ideas are related.

Using the Illustrations

Ask:

- **How can you indicate the location of the red building?** (Put your finger on the red building. Then move the finger *up* or *down* to the closest side of the map. Record the number. Then put your finger on the building again. Move the finger *across* to the closest side of the map. Record the letter.)

Exploring the Main Idea

Have students work in small groups to complete the first three exercises. (**1.** red; **2.** D1; **3.** Answers will vary.) Then have them look at the idea map about rocks. Explain that this kind of diagram can also be called a "map."

WRITING LINK

Students may write about how coordinates are used to locate places on road maps.

Informal Assessment

Have students make a map showing how to get to school from home. (Maps should include written instructions as well as sketches of major streets and buildings.)

Represent Data

Make Maps to Show Information

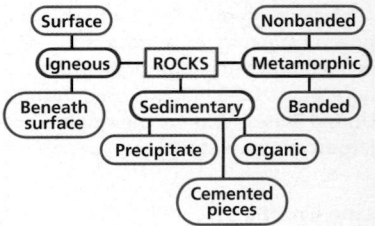

Locate Places

A map is a drawing that shows an area from above. Most maps have coordinates—numbers and letters along the top and side. Coordinates help you find places easily. For example, what if you wanted to find the library on the map? It is located at B4. Place a finger on the letter B along the side of the map, and another finger on the number 4 at the top. Then move your fingers straight across and down the map until they meet. The library is located where the coordinates B and 4 meet, or very nearby.

1. What color building is located at F6?
2. The hospital is located three blocks north and two blocks east of the library. What are its coordinates?
3. Make a map of an area in your community. It might be a park or the area between your home and school. Include coordinates. Use a compass to find north, and mark north on your map. Exchange maps with classmates, and answer each other's questions.

Idea Maps

The map below shows how places are connected to each other. Idea maps, on the other hand, show how ideas are connected to each other. Idea maps help you organize information about a topic.

The idea map above connects ideas about rocks. This map shows that there are three major types of rock—igneous, sedimentary, and metamorphic. Connections to each rock type provide further information. For example, this map reminds you that igneous rocks are classified into those that form at Earth's surface and far beneath it.

Make an idea map about a topic you are learning in science. Your map can include words, phrases, or even sentences. Arrange your map in a way that makes sense to you and helps you understand the ideas.

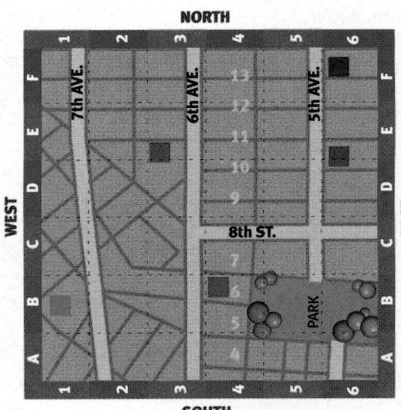

Make Maps to Show Information

SCIENCE FOR ALL — Advanced Learners

Maps

Explain that geographical maps are used to show key features of geographical areas. They can present other information, such as elevation. Have students locate countries on a world map and give coordinates of cities, using longitude in degrees East and West of the prime meridian and latitude in degrees North and South of the equator. **Spatial**

Make Tables and Charts to Organize Information

Tables help you organize data during experiments. Most tables have columns that run up and down, and rows that run across. The columns and rows have headings that tell you what kind of data goes in each part of the table.

A Sample Table

What if you are going to do an experiment to find out how long different kinds of seeds take to sprout? Before you begin the experiment, you should set up your table. Follow these steps.

1. In this experiment you will plant 20 radish seeds, 20 bean seeds, and 20 corn seeds. Your table must show how many radish seeds, bean seeds, and corn seeds sprouted on days 1, 2, 3, 4, and 5.

2. Make your table with columns, rows, and headings. You might use a computer to make a table. Some computer programs let you build a table with just the click of a mouse. You can delete or add columns and rows if you need to.
3. Give your table a title. Your table could look like the one here.

Make a Table

Now what if you are going to do an experiment to find out how temperature affects the sprouting of seeds? You will plant 20 bean seeds in each of two trays. You will keep each tray at a different temperature, as shown below, and observe the trays for seven days. Make a table you can use for this experiment.

Make a Chart

A chart is simply a table with pictures as well as words to label the rows or columns.

R19

Make Tables and Charts to Organize Information

Objective

- Read and make tables and charts.

Build on Prior Knowledge

Write *cat, dog, fish, other* vertically on the board. Ask for three volunteers who have at least two pets. Write the students' names horizontally and use the data to make a simple table. Ask:

- **How can you find how many dogs a particular student has?** (Find the number listed under the word dog next to the student's name in the table.)

Using the Illustrations

Have students read the first column on page R19 and study the sample table on the computer screen. Ask:

- **What do the columns of this table show?** (number of seeds that sprout; Day 1, Day 2, Day 3, Day 4, Day 5)
- **What do the rows show?** (radish seeds, bean seeds, corn seeds)
- **How can you show that 12 corn seeds sprouted on the third day?** (Enter the number 12 in the corn seeds row under Day 3.)

Exploring the Main Idea

Have students carry out the "Make a Table" activity, the experiment with the 20 bean seeds. Ask:

- **What will the columns in your table show?** (Answers will vary.)
- **What will the rows show?** (Answers will vary.)

WRITING LINK

Students can write a description of information given in a table they find.

Informal Assessment

Ask:

- **A student recorded the temperature for 5 days. Can the student make a table with these data?** (Yes, but the table will have only one row or column. Most tables have more.)

The Skeletal System - Joints

Objectives

- Explore the structure, function, and care of the skeleton and bones.
- Distinguish among three kinds of joints.

Build on Prior Knowledge

Have students discuss what they know about the parts of the body that support it and help it move. Ask:

- **What supports or holds up a building?** (steel or wood frame, concrete walls)
- **What supports your body?** (bones)
- **What happens if a bone is broken?** (It can't support the weight of the body around it.)
- **What do we call the place where bones meet, like at your elbow or knee?** (joint)

Developing the Main Idea

Invite students to suggest how their lives would be different if their bodies had no bones. (They wouldn't be able to sit, stand, or move and they'd have nothing to protect their hearts, lungs, or other organs inside their bodies.)

Using the Illustrations

Ask:

- **What is the name of the long bone at the top of the arm?** (humerus)
- **What is the long bone at the top of the leg?** (femur)
- **What is the name of the shoulder bone?** (clavicle)
- **What is the large bone that covers the head?** (skull)
- **What is the set of bones that goes up the back of the body?** (vertebrae)

HEALTH Handbook — The Skeletal System

The body has a supporting frame, called a skeleton, which is made up of bones. The skeleton has several jobs.
- It gives the body its shape.
- It protects organs in the body.
- It works with muscles to move the body.

Each of the 206 bones of the skeleton is the size and shape best fitted to do its job. For example, long and strong leg bones support the body's weight.

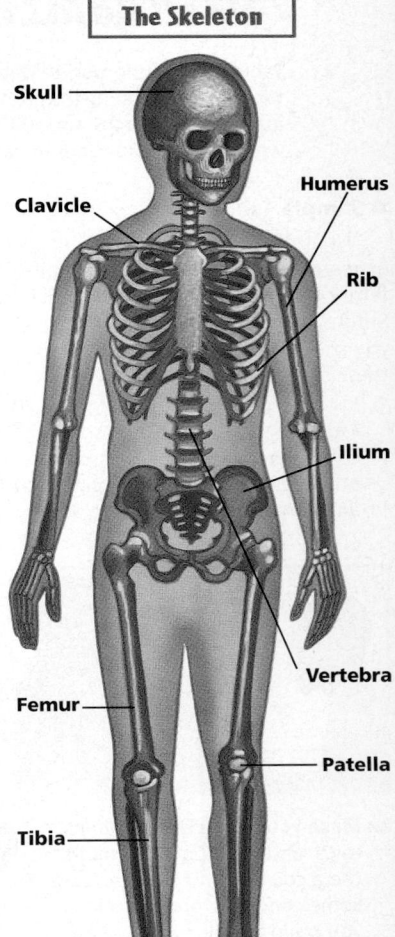

The Skeleton

Skull
Clavicle
Humerus
Rib
Ilium
Vertebra
Femur
Patella
Tibia

CARE!

- **Exercise to keep your skeletal system in good shape.**
- **Don't overextend your joints.**
- **Eat foods rich in vitamins and minerals. Your bones need the minerals calcium and phosphorus to grow strong.**

R 20

Science Background

Internal Skeletons

A skeleton gives a body shape, allows it to move, and protects its internal organs. Animals with internal skeletons and a backbone are called *vertebrates*. The group consists of mammals, birds, reptiles, amphibians, and fish. *Invertebrates* are animals without backbones. Some invertebrates, such as crustaceans and insects, have *exoskeletons*, or outer skeletons. Hard plates support the animals' bodies and protect the organs inside.

Joints

The skeleton has different types of joints. A joint is a place where two or more bones meet. Joints can be classified into three major groups—immovable joints, partly movable joints, and movable joints.

Types of Joints

Immovable Joints

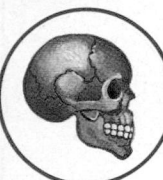

Head

Immovable joints are places where bones fit together too tightly to move. Nearly all the 29 bones in the skull meet at immovable joints. Only the lower jaw can move.

Partly Movable Joints

Partly movable joints are places where bones can move only a little. Ribs are connected to the breastbone with these joints.

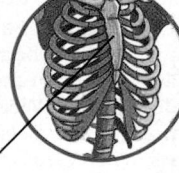

Breastbone

Ribs

Movable Joints

Movable joints are places where bones can move easily.

Gliding joint

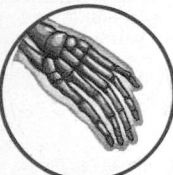

Hand and wrist

Small bones in the wrists and ankles meet at gliding joints. The bones can slide against one another. These joints allow some movement in all directions.

Ball-and-socket joint

The hips are examples of ball-and-socket joints. The ball of one bone fits into the socket, or cup, of another bone. These joints allow bones to move back and forth, in a circle, and side to side.

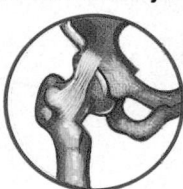

Hip

Hinge joint

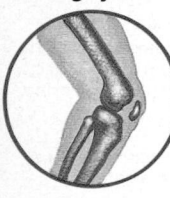

Knee

The knees are hinge joints. A hinge joint is similar to a door hinge. It allows bones to move back and forth in one direction.

Pivot joint

The joint between the skull and neck is a pivot joint. It allows the head to move up and down, and side to side.

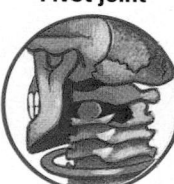

Neck

R 21

Using the Illustrations
Ask:

- **What are the three kinds of joints?** (immovable, partly movable, movable)

- **Why are some joints immovable?** (bones fit together too tightly)

- **What kind of joints connect the ribs to the breastbone?** (partly movable)

- **What are the four different kinds of movable joints?** (gliding, ball-and-socket, hinge, pivot)

- **Which kind of movable joint do you think your elbow is?** (hinge) **your shoulder?** (ball-and-socket)

WRITING LINK
Have students write a description of how their bones and joints help them as they go to lunch, sit down, and eat.

Informal Assessment
Ask students to draw a skeleton showing a body in motion, then label as many bones and joints as possible without looking back at the illustrations on pages R20 and R21. Then, if necessary, allow students to complete their labeling using information from the diagrams.

Math MiniLesson

Measure the Angle

Develop Make a large circle-protractor to measure the motion of a joint. Tie a pencil to one end of a 20-cm length of string. Press the free end of the string with your thumb onto the center of a large piece of posterboard and draw a circle with the pencil by holding the string taut. Draw a straight line through the center of your circle. Use a small protractor to divide the large circle into 12 equal "pie pieces." Each piece = 30°.

To measure motion of the shoulder, one student ("the measurer") holds the large circle protractor with the center at a partner's shoulder. The partner moves the arm as far back as possible without straining or stretching. The measurer lines up a radius line on the protractor with the arm. Then the partner moves the arm forward and back as much as possible, without straining. The measurer notes how many pie pieces on the protractor are covered by the motion.

Inclusion

Angle Practice
Multiply the number of pie pieces by 30° and add any estimated portion of a pie piece, if the arm moved into part of a pie piece.

Find ways to measure the motion of each movable joint using the large circle protractor. Compare the amounts. (shoulder: 360°; hip: 50°-100°; elbow bending: 180°; elbow twisting: 250°-270°; head: 160°-180°; knee: 160°) **Spatial**

The Muscular System

Objective

- Explore the three kinds of muscles in the body: skeletal, cardiac, and smooth.

Build on Prior Knowledge

Discuss with students what they know about their muscles and how to take care of them. Ask:

- **How do muscles help you move?** (pull on bones in the skeleton)

- **Why are warm-up and cool-down exercises important?** (protect muscles from being overstretched or being strained)

Developing the Main Idea

Invite students to discuss activities that their muscles help them perform and how they think muscles work to move bones. Ask a volunteer to use muscles that move body parts other than bones. (blinking eye, smiling mouth, wrinkling nose, and so on) Then ask:

- **What important muscle keeps blood pumping through your body?** (heart)

Using the Illustrations
Ask:

- **What are the names of the muscles in the upper arm?** (biceps and triceps)

- **What happens when a muscle contracts?** (It becomes shorter and thicker; it pulls on the bone it's attached to.)

WRITING LINK

Have students write detailed plans indicating how they'll care for their muscles, including kinds of exercise, food choices, and sleep and rest times.

Informal Assessment

Ask students to hold a book in one hand and hold that arm straight out in front of them. Have them put their other hands on the muscle of that upper arm (biceps). Discuss how the muscle feels, then have students lift their books up toward their shoulders. Ask:

- **What did you feel?** (Muscles shorten and bunch up.)

The Muscular System

Three types of muscles make up the body—skeletal muscle, cardiac muscle, and smooth muscle.

The muscles that are attached to and move bones are called skeletal muscles. These muscles are attached to bones by a tough cord called a tendon. Skeletal muscles pull bones to move them. Muscles do not push bones.

Cardiac muscles are found in only one place in the body—the heart. The walls of the heart are made of strong cardiac muscles. When cardiac muscles contract, they squeeze blood out of the heart. When cardiac muscles relax, the heart fills with more blood.

Smooth muscles make up internal organs and blood vessels. Smooth muscles in the lungs help a person breathe. Those in the blood vessels help control blood flow around the body.

CARE!

- Exercise to strengthen your muscles.
- Eat the right foods.
- Get plenty of rest.
- Never take steroids unless your doctor tells you to.

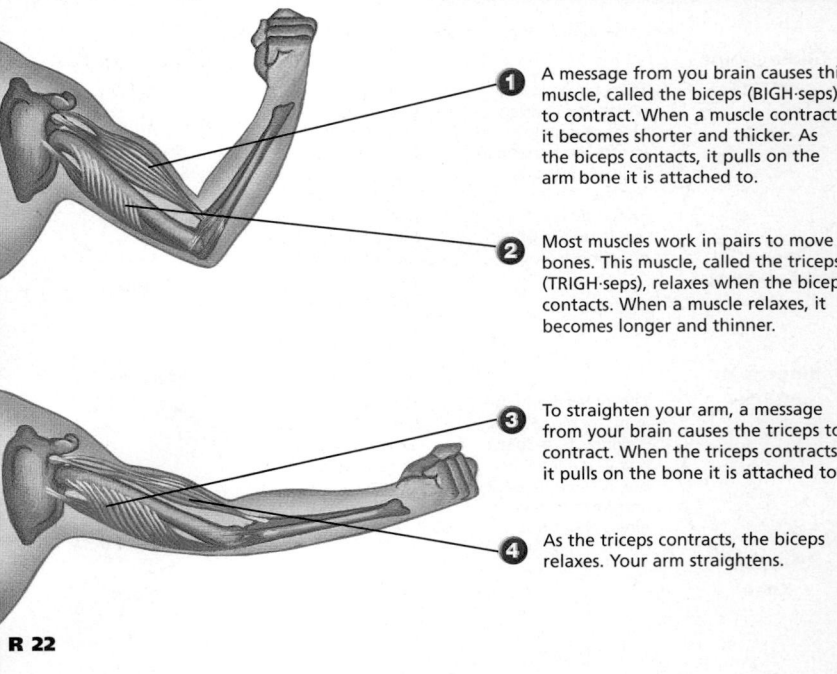

1. A message from you brain causes this muscle, called the biceps (BIGH·seps), to contract. When a muscle contracts, it becomes shorter and thicker. As the biceps contacts, it pulls on the arm bone it is attached to.

2. Most muscles work in pairs to move bones. This muscle, called the triceps (TRIGH·seps), relaxes when the biceps contacts. When a muscle relaxes, it becomes longer and thinner.

3. To straighten your arm, a message from your brain causes the triceps to contract. When the triceps contracts, it pulls on the bone it is attached to.

4. As the triceps contracts, the biceps relaxes. Your arm straightens.

R 22

 Science Background

Muscles

Most skeletal muscles move in pairs. As one muscle in a pair contracts, the other relaxes. The contracting muscle pulls on the bone to which it's attached by a tendon. Cardiac muscles pump blood, and smooth muscles make up our internal organs. We sit on the largest muscle in the body, the *gluteus maximus*, which also helps us run, jump, and climb. The smallest muscle, the *stapedius,* is inside the ear. It protects our ears from loud sounds.

The Circulatory System

The circulatory system consists of the heart, blood vessels, and blood. Circulation is the flow of blood through the body. Blood is a liquid that contains red blood cells, white blood cells, and platelets. Red blood cells carry oxygen and nutrients to cells. White blood cells work to fight germs that enter the body. Platelets are cell fragments that make the blood clot.

The heart is a muscular organ about the size of a fist. It beats about 70 to 90 times a minute, pumping blood through the blood vessels. Arteries carry blood away from the heart. Some arteries carry blood to the lungs, where the cells pick up oxygen. Other arteries carry oxygen-rich blood from the lungs to all other parts of the body. Veins carry blood from other parts of the body back to the heart. Blood in most veins carries the wastes released by cells and has little oxygen. Blood flows from arteries to veins through narrow vessels called capillaries.

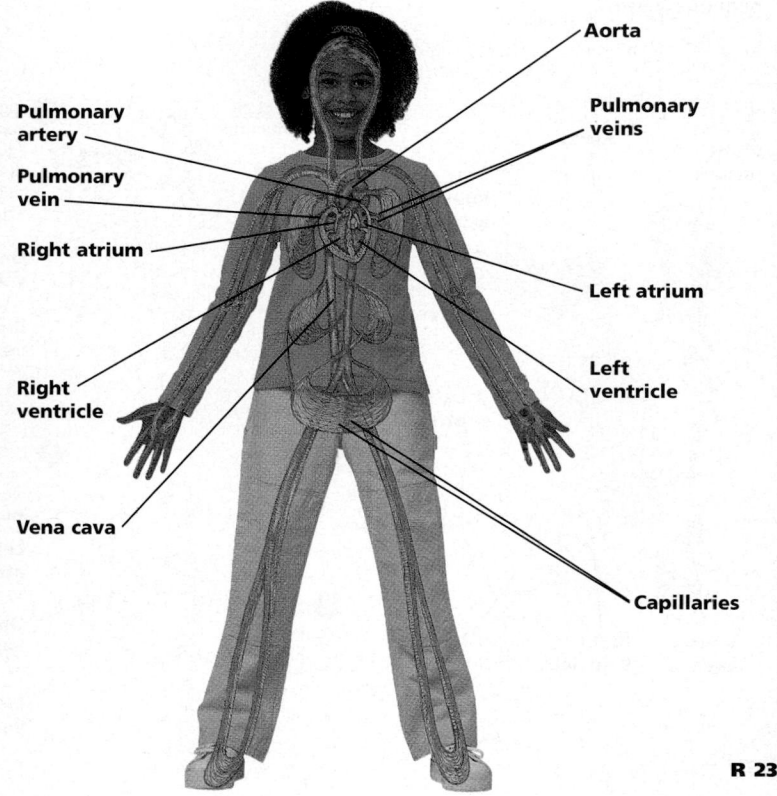

- Aorta
- Pulmonary artery
- Pulmonary veins
- Pulmonary vein
- Right atrium
- Left atrium
- Left ventricle
- Right ventricle
- Vena cava
- Capillaries

R 23

Science Background

The Circulatory System

The circulatory system includes the heart, blood, and blood vessels. Blood is made of red and white blood cells and platelets, or cell fragments. These platelets collect at a point where there is a wound and form a clot. White blood cells that fight germs also come to the wound site to fight infection. Blood flows from and back to the heart through arteries, veins, and capillaries. Red blood cells follow the flow, bringing oxygen and nutrients to cells in the body.

The Circulatory System

Objective

- Explore the circulatory system, including the heart and the parts of and functions of blood.

Build on Prior Knowledge
Have students discuss what they know about how blood moves throughout their bodies. Ask:

- **What is the muscle that pumps blood through your body?** (heart) **How big do you think the heart is?** (about the size of a fist)

Have students examine the veins in the backs of their hands. Point out that these blood vessels are returning blood *to* the heart. Then have students locate the blood vessel on the wrist that's used to check the pulse. Stress that this blood vessel carries blood *from* the heart.

Developing the Main Idea
Ask:

- **What's in blood?** (red and white blood cells, platelets)
- **How often does the heart beat?** (about 70-90 times per minute)
- **Which blood vessels carry blood away from the heart?** (arteries)
- **What are capillaries?** (narrow vessels that connect arteries and veins)

Using the Illustrations
Discuss with students the various parts of the diagram. Ask:

- **What does the diagram show?** (part of the circulatory system)
- **What are the tubelike parts in the circulatory system?** (blood vessels)

Continue the lesson on p. R24.

The Heart

Developing the Main Idea
This discussion of the heart continues the lesson on the circulatory system from p. R23. Ask:

- **What separates the two sides of the heart?** (wall of thick muscle)
- **Where does the pulmonary artery carry blood?** (to the lungs)
- **How does the nicotine in tobacco affect the heart?** (makes the heart beat faster and work harder to pump blood)

Using the Illustrations
When students read the labels, they have to place the book onto their chests so that "right" will be on their right side and "left" will be on their left side. Ask:

- **What is the upper right chamber called?** (right atrium)
- **What is the lower left chamber called?** (left ventricle)
- **What are the two veins near the top of the heart called?** (pulmonary veins)
- **Where do they lead?** (from the lungs to the heart)

WRITING LINK
Invite students to imagine they are a drop of blood and describe their trip through the heart, out an artery, and back again through a vein.

Informal Assessment
Ask students to describe in their own words, or draw and label a sketch to show, how blood circulates through the body.

Technology

- **Science Newsroom CD-ROM** Have students use *We Got the Beat* to learn more about the heart and the circulatory system.

The Heart

The heart has two sides, right and left, separated by a thick muscular wall. Each side has two chambers for blood. The upper chamber is the atrium. The lower chamber is the ventricle. Blood enters the heart through the vena cava. It leaves the heart through the aorta.

The pulmonary artery carries blood from the body into the lungs. Here carbon dioxide leaves the blood to be exhaled by the lungs. Fresh oxygen enters the blood to be carried to every cell in the body. Blood returns from the lungs to the heart through the pulmonary veins.

CARE!

- Don't smoke. The nicotine in tobacco makes the heart beat faster and work harder to pump blood.
- Never take illegal drugs, such as cocaine or heroin. They can damage the heart and cause heart failure.

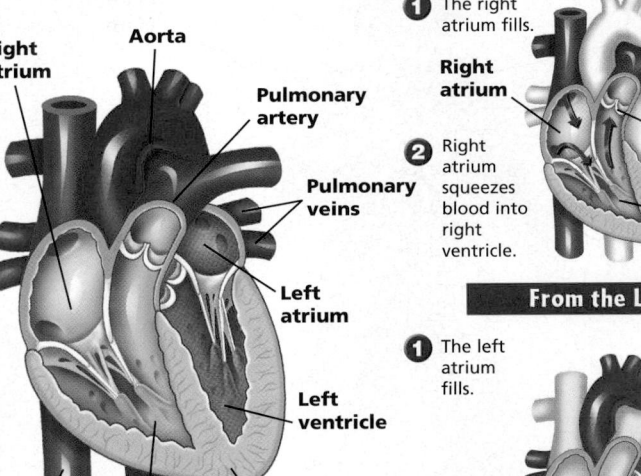

How the Heart Works

Right atrium · Aorta · Pulmonary artery · Pulmonary veins · Left atrium · Left ventricle · Vena cava · Right ventricle · Muscle wall

To the Lungs

1. The right atrium fills.
2. Right atrium squeezes blood into right ventricle.
3. Right ventricle squeezes blood into pulmonary artery.

Right atrium · One-way valve · Right ventricle

From the Lungs

1. The left atrium fills.
2. Left atrium squeezes blood into left ventricle.
3. Left ventricle squeezes blood into aorta.

Left atrium · One-way valve · Left ventricle

R 24

Science Background

The Heart

The human heart is a four-chambered double pump that circulates blood. The top two chambers, the atria, receive blood. The bottom two chambers, or ventricles, pump blood out of the heart. Blood loaded with carbon dioxide arrives in the right atrium from all parts of the body. From there it flows to the right ventricle and is pumped to the lungs, where the carbon dioxide is exchanged for oxygen. Then the oxygen-rich blood returns to the left atrium of the heart, flows to the left ventricle, and is pumped to all parts of the body. The "thump-thump" we hear when our hearts beat is the sound of closing valves. The first noise is made when valves close between the atria and the ventricles; the second is the sound of valves closing between the ventricles and the great vessels.

The Respiratory System

The process of getting and using oxygen in the body is called respiration. When a person inhales, air is pulled into the nose or mouth. The air travels down into the trachea. In the chest the trachea divides into two bronchial tubes. One bronchial tube enters each lung. Each bronchial tube branches into smaller tubes called bronchioles.

At the end of each bronchiole are tiny air sacs called alveoli. The alveoli exchange carbon dioxide for oxygen.

Oxygen comes from the air a person breathes. Two main muscles control breathing. One is located between the ribs. The other is a dome-shaped sheet of muscle called the diaphragm.

To inhale, the diaphragm contracts and pulls down. Other muscles pull the ribs up and out. This makes more room in the chest. Air rushes into the lungs and fills the space.

To exhale, the diaphragm relaxes and returns to its dome shape. The lungs get smaller and force the air out.

CARE!

- Don't smoke. Smoking damages your respiratory system.
- Exercise to strengthen your breathing muscles.
- If you ever have trouble breathing, tell an adult at once.

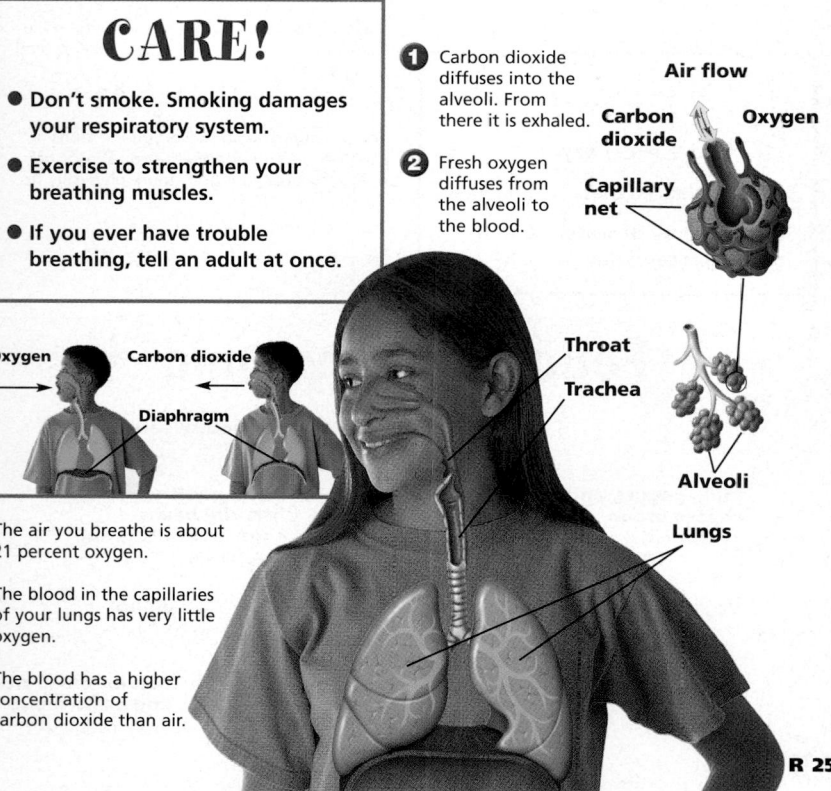

1 Carbon dioxide diffuses into the alveoli. From there it is exhaled.

2 Fresh oxygen diffuses from the alveoli to the blood.

Air flow

Carbon dioxide

Oxygen

Capillary net

Oxygen — Carbon dioxide

Diaphragm

Throat

Trachea

Alveoli

Lungs

The air you breathe is about 21 percent oxygen.

The blood in the capillaries of your lungs has very little oxygen.

The blood has a higher concentration of carbon dioxide than air.

R 25

Science Background

Breathing

The respiratory system includes the nose, mouth, trachea, bronchial tubes, alveoli, lungs, and the diaphragm, a sheet of muscle that's below the chest cavity, under the lungs, and above the abdomen. It's in the alveoli that carbon dioxide is exchanged for oxygen. Each lung has about 300 million alveoli that, if flattened out, would cover about 600 to 1,000 square feet (56 to 93 square meters). The lungs' total surface area is about 25 times that of the skin covering the body.

The Respiratory System

Objective

- Explore the parts of the respiratory system and what happens when we breathe.

Build on Prior Knowledge
Have students discuss what they know about breathing and why humans need to breathe.

Developing the Main Idea
Ask students to hold their breaths as long as possible, then ask:

- **Why did you finally have to take a breath?** (need oxygen)
- **How did the oxygen from the air get into your body?** (through nose or mouth)
- **What is the diaphragm?** (sheet of muscle)
- **What happens when the diaphragm relaxes?** (lungs get smaller; air forced out)

Using the Illustrations
Ask:

- **What parts of the respiratory system are shown in the diagrams?** (throat, trachea, lungs, alveoli, diaphragm)
- **Where's the diaphragm located?** (under the lungs)
- **What kind of gas comes out when you exhale?** (carbon dioxide)

WRITING LINK

Have students write public service announcements that would convince people not to smoke because it's harmful to their respiratory systems.

Informal Assessment
Ask students to use the diagrams on page R25 to describe in their own words how humans breathe.

Technology

- **Science Newsroom CD-ROM** Have students use *A Breath of Fresh Air* to learn more about the lungs.

Activity Pyramid
Food Guide Pyramid

Objective

- Understand that physical fitness involves activity and proper nutrition.

Build on Prior Knowledge
Have students discuss what they know about how physical activities and food affect their health.

Developing the Main Idea
Have students list exercises and activities that build physical fitness. Invite them to jump in place, to discover how it affects their heart rates. Ask:

- **How does this help the body?** (Heart and lungs bring oxygen to the muscles and get rid of carbon dioxide.)

- **What kind of food might you eat to get energy to exercise?** (food high in vitamins; fruit; nuts)

Using the Illustrations
Ask:

- **What kind of activities should you only do occasionally?** (inactive ones)

- **What kind should you do 3-5 times a week?** (aerobic activities)

- **What kinds of foods should you eat most?** (bread, cereal, rice, and pasta) **least?** (fats, oils, and sweets)

- **In which group does carrots belong?** (Vegetable) **Where does candy belong?** (fats, oils, and sweets)

WRITING LINK

Ask students to plan a physically-fit day that includes different exercises and healthful foods. Suggest they prepare their plans as daily schedules and menus.

Informal Assessment
Ask each student what activities and foods he or she did or ate yesterday and how each contributes to physical fitness.

Activity Pyramid

Physical fitness is the condition in which the body is healthy and works the best it can. It involves working the skeletal muscles, bones, joints, heart, and respiratory system.

Occasionally Inactive pastimes such as watching TV, playing board games, talking on the phone

2–3 times a week Leisure activities such as gardening, golf, softball

3–5 times a week Aerobic activities such as swimming, biking, climbing; sports activities such as basketball, handball

Daily Substitute activity for inactivity—take the stairs, walk instead of riding, bike instead of taking the bus

The activity pyramid shows you the kinds of exercises and other activities you should be doing to make your body more physically fit.

CARE!

- Stay active every day.
- Eat a balanced diet.
- Drink plenty of water—6 to 8 large glasses a day.

Food Guide Pyramid

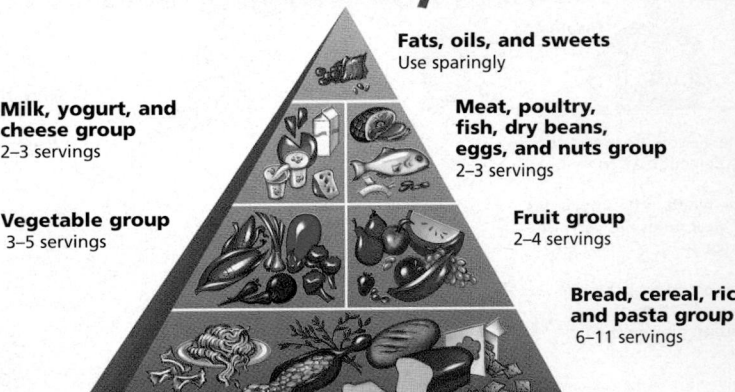

Fats, oils, and sweets Use sparingly

Milk, yogurt, and cheese group 2–3 servings

Meat, poultry, fish, dry beans, eggs, and nuts group 2–3 servings

Vegetable group 3–5 servings

Fruit group 2–4 servings

Bread, cereal, rice, and pasta group 6–11 servings

R 26

Science Background

Physical Fitness

In order to function optimally, a person needs a balance of exercise, rest, and a steady supply of food and water. Regular exercise and proper diet can delay the loss of muscle strength and the thinning of bones that come with age. The USDA Food Pyramid illustrates the amounts of different kinds of foods that we should eat daily. The higher an edible is on the food pyramid, the less of it we should eat. The higher a pastime is on the activity pyramid, the less we should do it!

The Digestive System

Digestion is the process of breaking down food into simple substances the body can use. Digestion begins when a person chews food. Chewing breaks the food down into smaller pieces and moistens it with saliva. Saliva is produced by the salivary glands.

Digested food is absorbed in the small intestine. The walls of the small intestine are lined with villi. Villi are tiny fingerlike projections that absorb digested food. From the villi the blood transports nutrients to every part of the body.

The shape of the small intestine's villi increases the amount of nutrients that can be absorbed from the food.

CARE!

- Chew your food well.
- Drink plenty of water to help move food through your digestive system.

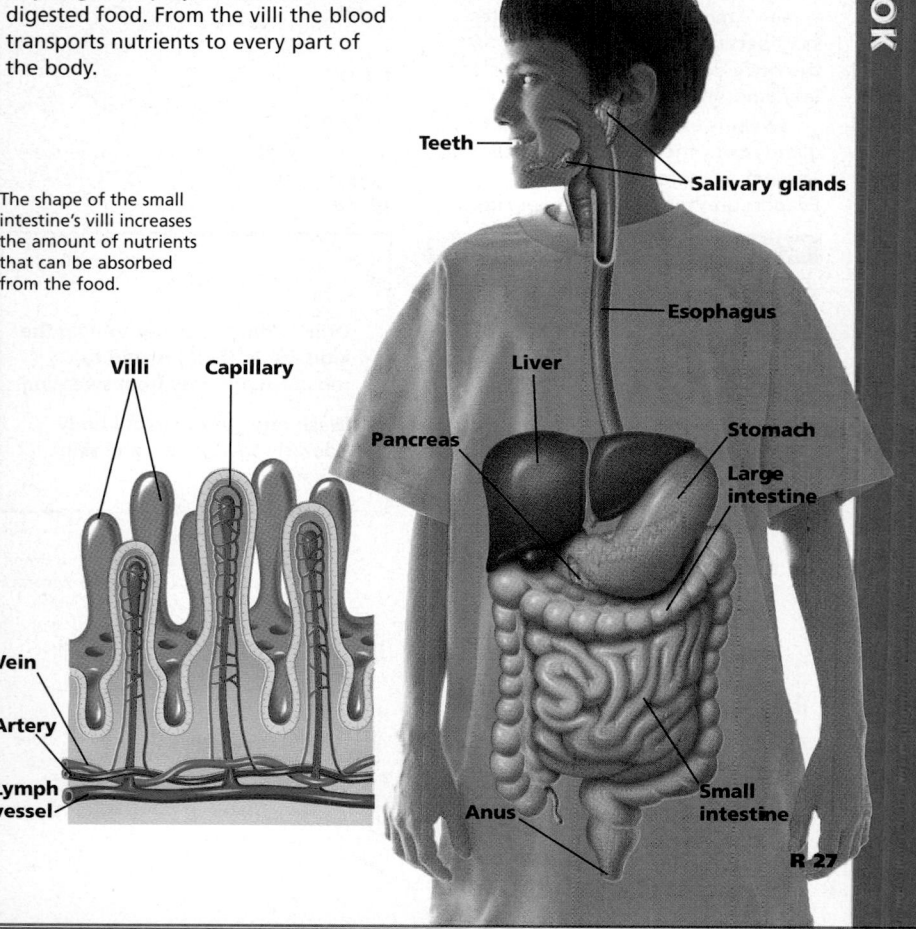

Teeth
Salivary glands
Esophagus
Liver
Pancreas
Stomach
Large intestine
Villi
Capillary
Vein
Artery
Lymph vessel
Anus
Small intestine

R 27

Science Background

Saliva and Digestion

Digestion, the process of breaking down food, begins in the mouth, where food is bitten, chewed, and softened by saliva. The saliva flows through tiny tubes into the mouth from glands under the tongue, in the lower jaw, and in the mouth below the ears. Sour, dry, and hard foods stimulate the flow of saliva and bitter foods make it thicker. Enzymes in saliva begin to break complex carbohydrates, such as those in a cracker, into simple sugars, thus changing the taste of the cracker.

The Digestive System

Objective

- Explore how the digestive system breaks down food so that our bodies can use it.

Build on Prior Knowledge
Ask:

- **What gives your body energy?** (food)
- **Does food give you energy as soon as you put it into your mouth?** (No, it must be broken down so the body can use it.)
- **How do your teeth help break down food?** (cut or mash large pieces into smaller bits)

Developing the Main Idea
Have students feel their teeth, then ask:

- **Which teeth are shaped for biting or tearing off food? Which are shaped for mashing food?** (front, incisors; molars)

Using the Illustrations
Ask:

- **What two things in the mouth start the digestive process?** (teeth and saliva)
- **What is the tube that leads from the mouth to the stomach?** (esophagus)
- **How does the absorbed digested food get from the villi to the rest of the body?** (through blood vessels)

WRITING LINK
Have students describe how life would change if they had no teeth or gums with which to chew or mash food to start the digestive process.

Informal Assessment
Ask students to explain in their own words what happens to food once it enters the mouth.

The Excretory System

Objective

- Explore how the body gets rid of wastes.

Build on Prior Knowledge
Ask:

- **What would happen if we never threw anything away?** (trash would pile up; have no room to live)

- **What kind of gas do we breathe out?** (carbon dioxide)

- **Is this one way our bodies get rid of waste?** (Yes.)

- **How else might our bodies get rid of wastes?** (through sweat, through the kidneys, through the intestine)

Developing the Main Idea
Remind students that during the digestive process the body takes what it needs from food and sends what it doesn't need to the intestines.

Using the Illustrations
Ask:

- **How does blood enter the kidneys?** (through an artery)

- **What do nephrons do?** (sort out wastes from useful nutrients)

- **What happens to the useful nutrients?** (flow back through veins)

- **Where is urine stored?** (in the bladder)

- **What are the small holes in skin called?** (pores)

WRITING LINK

Have students write about a very hot day that causes people to sweat a lot. Remind students to tell how people replace the lost moisture.

Informal Assessment
Ask students to explain in their own words what people should do to care for their excretory systems. (Drink plenty of water; keep the body clean.)

The Excretory System

Excretion is the process of removing waste products from the body. The liver filters wastes from the blood and converts them into urea. Urea is then carried to the kidneys for excretion. Each kidney contains more than a million nephrons. Nephrons are structures in the kidneys that filter blood.

The skin takes part in excretion when a person sweats. Glands in the inner layer of the skin produce sweat. Sweat is mostly water. Sweat tastes salty because it contains mineral salts the body doesn't need. There is also a tiny amount of urea in sweat.

Sweat is excreted by the sweat glands onto the outer layer of the skin. There it evaporates into the air. Evaporation takes place in part because of body heat. When sweat evaporates, a person feels cooler. On hot days or when exercising, a person sweats more to keep the body from overheating.

How You Sweat

Glands under your skin push sweat up to the surface, where it collects.

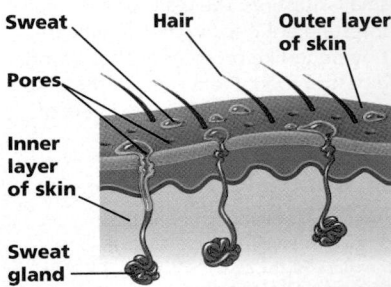

Labels: Sweat, Hair, Outer layer of skin, Pores, Inner layer of skin, Sweat gland

How Your Kidneys Work

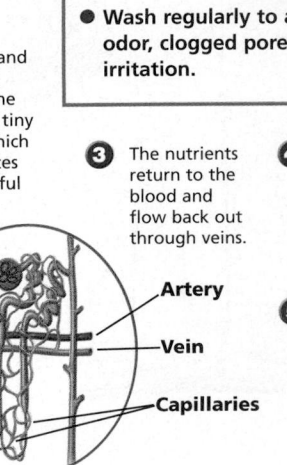

Labels: Kidneys, Ureters, Bladder, Urethra, R 28

Labels (nephron detail): Artery, Vein, Capillaries

1. Blood enters the kidney through an artery and flows into capillaries.

2. Sugars, salts, water, urea, and other wastes move from the capillaries to tiny nephrons, which sort out wastes from the useful nutrients.

3. The nutrients return to the blood and flow back out through veins.

4. Urea and other wastes become urine, which flows down the ureters.

5. Urine is stored in the bladder and excreted through the urethra.

CARE!

- Drink plenty of water to help the kidneys do their job and to replace water loss from sweating.

- Wash regularly to avoid body odor, clogged pores, and skin irritation.

Science Background

Water and the Body
The human body is mostly water that can be lost to sweat, respiration, and urine. The kidneys filter blood and separate out materials, recycling some back to the blood and turning others into urine. We must constantly replace the water to help our kidneys keep wastes moving out of our bodies. Our skin excretes wastes in the form of sweat. Sweat glands are found all over the body, but are concentrated in the armpits, palms of the hands, and soles of the feet.

The Nervous System

The nervous system has two parts. The brain and the spinal cord are the central nervous system. All other nerves are the outer, or peripheral, nervous system.

The largest part of the brain is the cerebrum. A deep groove separates the right half, or hemisphere, of the cerebrum from the left half. Both the right and left hemispheres of the cerebrum contain control centers for the senses.

The cerebellum lies below the cerebrum. It coordinates the skeletal muscles so they work smoothly together. It also helps in keeping balance.

The brain stem connects to the spinal cord. The lowest part of the brain stem is the medulla. It controls heartbeat, breathing, blood pressure, and the muscles in the digestive system.

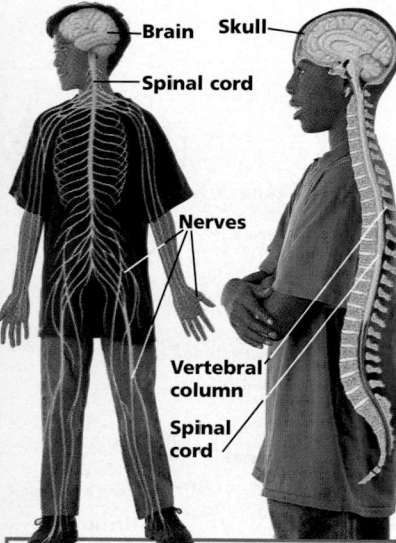

Brain — Skull — Spinal cord — Nerves — Vertebral column — Spinal cord

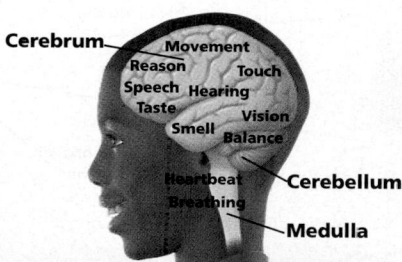

Cerebrum — Movement — Reason — Touch — Speech — Hearing — Taste — Vision — Smell — Balance — Heartbeat — Breathing — Cerebellum — Medulla

CARE!

- Wear protective headgear when you play sports or exercise.
- Stay away from drugs, such as stimulants, which can speed up the nervous system.
- Stay away from alcohol, which is a depressant and slows down the nervous system.

Parts of a Neuron

The nerves in the nervous system are made up of nerve cells called neurons. Each neuron has three main parts—a cell body, dendrites, and an axon. Dendrites are branching nerve fibers that carry impulses, or electrical signals, toward the cell body. An axon is a nerve fiber that carries impulses away from the cell body.

When an impulse reaches the tip of an axon, it must cross a tiny gap to reach the next neuron. This gap between neurons is called a synapse.

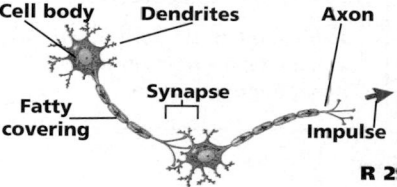

Cell body — Dendrites — Axon — Fatty covering — Synapse — Impulse

R 29

Science Background

Nerves

Electrical signals (impulses) travel between the body and the brain along neurons, each having a cell body, dendrites, and an axon. The three types of neurons are sensory, associative, and motor. For example if you stub your toe, sensory neurons immediately send a message to associative neurons in your spinal cord and brain, where the message is interpreted and conveyed to motor neurons that make you hop on one foot and say "Ow!"

The Nervous System

Objective

- Explore the nature and care of the body's nervous system.

Build on Prior Knowledge
Ask:

- **What part of your body helps you know and understand things?** (brain)
- **How could your brain make your leg move?** (by sending a message along nerves to the leg muscles)

Developing the Main Idea
Explain to students that in this section they'll discover that their bodies actually produce electricity—electrical signals that relay messages between the brain and other body parts. Then ask:

- **What are the parts of the central nervous system?** (brain, spinal cord)
- **What are neurons?** (nerve cells)
- **What is the gap between neurons?** (synapse)

Using the Illustrations
Ask:

- **What protects the spinal cord?** (vertebral column)
- **Which part of the brain controls the five senses—taste, smell, touch, hearing, vision?** (cerebrum)
- **What are the long fibers between nerve cells?** (axons)

WRITING LINK
Have students make a flowchart showing how the nervous system gets a message to the brain. (Receptor cells send signals to the brain where they are interpreted and an action taken.)

Informal Assessment
Ask students to name the parts of the central nervous system.

The Senses

The Senses

Objective

■ Explore the workings and care of the five senses.

Build on Prior Knowledge

You may wish to review the nervous system on p. R29. Ask:

■ **What are the five senses?** (see, hear, touch, taste, smell)

■ **How does your body let you know if something is hot to the touch?** (Nerve endings in your fingers send a message to your brain.)

Developing the Main Idea

Explain to students that in this section they'll discover just how their five senses work to give them information. Add that the senses involve nerves that relay messages to the brain.

Read page R30 with students, then ask:

■ **Where are the receptor cells in the eye?** (on the retina)

■ **How do signals from the receptor cells get to the brain?** (along the optic nerve)

■ **What is the nerve in the ear that carries impulses to the brain?** (auditory nerve)

■ **How can you protect your eyes and ears?** (Avoid eye strain from watching too much TV, sitting too close to the TV or computer screen, or reading in an area that's not well lighted. Avoid loud noises, protect ears with headphones and listen to music with volume turned down.)

Using the Illustrations

Ask:

■ **What are the six parts of the eye?** (cornea, pupil, lens, iris, retina, optic nerve)

■ **Why does your eye bend light?** (so it will hit the retina)

■ **Where does the optic nerve take the impulses?** (the seeing center of the brain)

■ **What are the three tiny ear bones that vibrate?** (hammer, anvil, stirrup)

■ **To which part of the ear is the auditory nerve connected?** (cochlea)

■ **Where does the auditory nerve send the impulses?** (the hearing center of the brain)

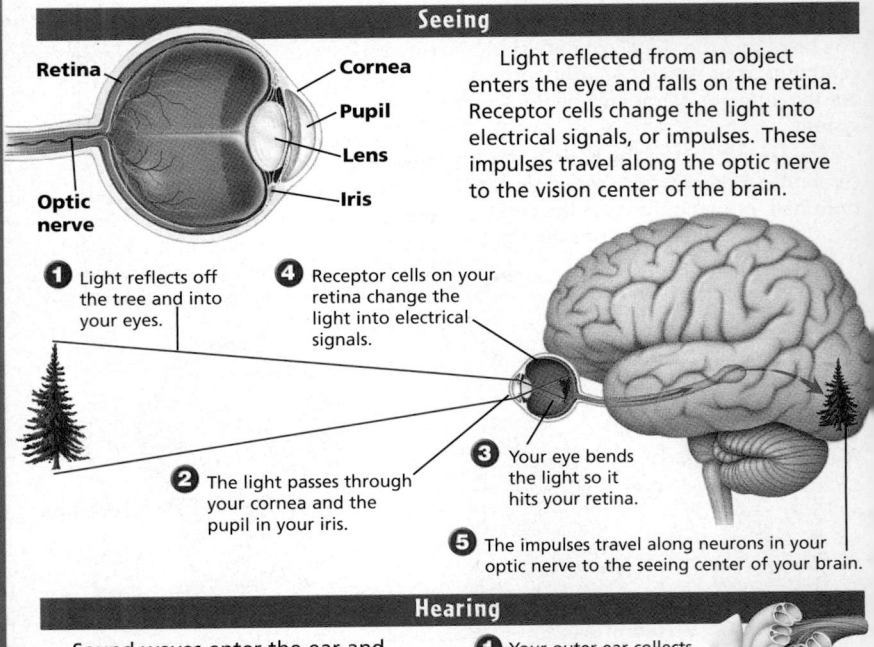

The Senses

Seeing

Retina • Cornea • Pupil • Lens • Optic nerve • Iris

Light reflected from an object enters the eye and falls on the retina. Receptor cells change the light into electrical signals, or impulses. These impulses travel along the optic nerve to the vision center of the brain.

❶ Light reflects off the tree and into your eyes.

❷ The light passes through your cornea and the pupil in your iris.

❸ Your eye bends the light so it hits your retina.

❹ Receptor cells on your retina change the light into electrical signals.

❺ The impulses travel along neurons in your optic nerve to the seeing center of your brain.

Hearing

Sound waves enter the ear and cause the eardrum to vibrate. Receptor cells in the ear change the sound waves into impulses that travel along the auditory nerve to the hearing center of the brain.

Hammer • Anvil • Stirrup • Cochlea • Auditory nerve • Semicircular canals • Hearing center

❶ Your outer ear collects sound waves.

❷ They are funneled down your ear canal.

❸ The eardrum vibrates.

❹ Three tiny ear bones vibrate.

❺ The cochlea vibrates.

❻ Receptor cells inside your cochlea change.

❼ The impulses travel along your auditory nerve to the brain's hearing center.

CARE!

● To avoid straining your eye muscles, don't sit too close to the TV screen or computer monitor.

● Avoid loud music. Turn down the volume when wearing headphones.

R 30

Science Background

Seeing and Hearing

Each sensory organ contains receptors that convert stimuli from the environment into electrical impulses that are carried to specific regions of the brain, where they are interpreted. The visual cortex, or sight center, of the brain interprets shapes and colors to help us identify things we see. The auditory cortex, or hearing center, of the brain receives sounds and identifies them by comparing them with sound patterns in our memory banks.

The Senses

Smelling

The sense of smell is really the ability to detect chemicals in the air. When a person breathes, chemicals dissolve in mucus in the upper part of the nose. When the chemicals come in contact with receptor cells, the cells send impulses along the olfactory nerve to the smelling center of the brain.

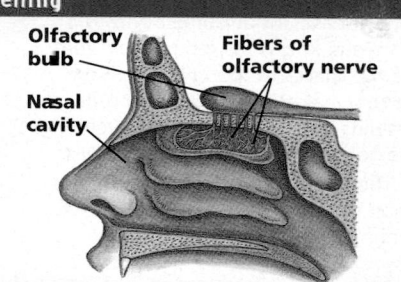

Olfactory bulb

Fibers of olfactory nerve

Nasal cavity

Tasting

When a person eats, chemicals in food dissolve in saliva. Saliva carries the chemicals to taste buds on the tongue. Inside each taste bud are receptors that can sense the four main tastes—sweet, sour, salty, and bitter. The receptors send impulses along a nerve to the taste center of the brain. The brain identifies the taste of the food, which is usually a combination of the four main tastes.

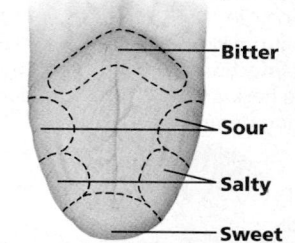

- Bitter
- Sour
- Salty
- Sweet

Touching

Receptor cells in the skin help a person tell hot from cold, wet from dry, and the light touch of a feather from the pressure of stepping on a stone. Each receptor cell sends impulses along sensory nerves to the spinal cord. The spinal cord then sends the impulses to the touch center of the brain.

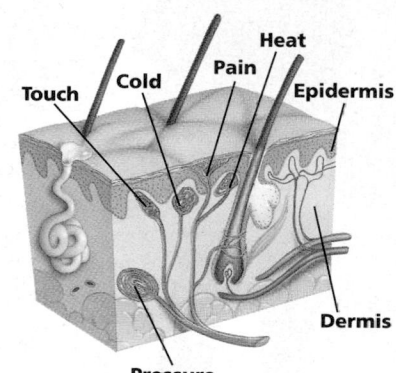

Touch   Cold   Pain   Heat   Epidermis

Dermis

Pressure

R 31

CARE!

- To prevent the spread of germs, always cover your mouth and nose when you cough or sneeze.

Science Background

Smell, Taste, and Touch

Our bodies are constantly collecting information from external stimuli. When we smell something, chemicals dissolved in mucus contact the nose's receptor cells that send a message to the brain's smelling center for interpretation. When we eat, food chemicals stimulate receptors in taste buds that contact the taste center of the brain. When we feel something, receptors in the skin send impulses to the spinal cord, which relays the message to the brain's touch center.

Developing the Main Idea
Ask:

- **What does the sense of smell help you detect in the air?** (chemicals)
- **What sends messages to the brain's smelling center?** (olfactory nerve)
- **What are the receptors on the tongue?** (taste buds)
- **What helps you know if something is cold?** (receptor cells in the skin)

Using the Illustrations
Ask:

- **What is the name of sensory nerve in the nose?** (olfactory nerve)
- **What are the four main tastes the tongue can identify?** (sweet, salty, sour, bitter)
- **Where is the bitter taste bud located?** (at the back of the tongue)
- **What four things do the skin's receptor cells help you feel?** (touch, cold, pain, heat)

WRITING LINK

Have students describe a cookout or picnic using sensory words so that a reader would see, hear, smell, feel, and taste what the writer saw, heard, smelled, felt, and tasted.

Informal Assessment

Ask students to make a flowchart to show how a message is transmitted to either the vision, hearing, smell, touch, or taste center of the brain.

Technology

- **Science Newsroom CD-ROM** Have students use *You Have Some Nerve* to learn more about nerves and the nervous system.

The Immune System

Objective

■ Explore the structure, function, and care of the immune system.

Build on Prior Knowledge
Ask:

■ **What does an immunization shot do?** (Helps the body fight off that disease.)

Developing the Main Idea
Explain to students that they'll learn how the immune system helps the body fight off diseases. Add that if the immune system is not working properly, the body is defenseless against many diseases.

Read page R32 with students, then ask:

■ **What is the soft tissue inside some bones?** (red marrow) **How does it help the body?** (makes new red blood cells, platelets, and germ-fighting white cells)

■ **What is lymph?** (straw-colored fluid around cells) **How do lymph nodes help fight disease?** (filter out harmful materials; produce white blood cells)

Using the Illustrations
Ask:

■ **Where is red marrow located?** (in spaces of spongy bone)

■ **What covers the outside of a bone?** (thin, tough membrane)

■ **What do lymph vessels do?** (collect fluid and return it to bloodstream)

■ **How are lymph vessels like blood vessels?** (both carry fluid through body)

WRITING LINK

Have students write a PSA (public service announcement) stressing the importance of immunizations against diseases such as polio, measles, or the flu.

Informal Assessment
Ask students to explain in their own words how the immune system helps when a person is cut.

The Immune System

The immune system helps the body fight disease. Inside some bones is a soft tissue known as red marrow that fills the spaces in spongy bone. Red marrow makes new red blood cells, platelets that stop a cut from bleeding, and germ-fighting white blood cells.

There are white blood cells in the blood vessels and in the lymph vessels. Lymph vessels are similar to blood vessels. Instead of blood, they carry lymph. Lymph is a straw-colored fluid surrounding body cells.

Lymph nodes filter out harmful materials in lymph. Like red marrow, they also produce white blood cells to fight infections. Swollen lymph nodes in the neck are a clue that the body is fighting germs.

CARE!

● Be sure to get immunized against common diseases.

● Keep cuts clean to prevent infection.

1 A bone is covered with a tough but thin membrane that has many small blood vessels. The blood vessels bring nutrients and oxygen to the living parts of the bone and remove wastes.

2 Inside some bones is a soft tissue known as marrow. Yellow marrow is made mostly of fat cells and is one of the body's energy reserves. It is usually found in the long, hollow spaces of long bones.

3 Part of the bone is compact, or solid. It is made up of living bone cells and nonliving materials. The nonliving part is made up of layers of hardened minerals such as calcium and phosphorus. In between the mineral layers are living bone cells.

4 Red marrow fills the spaces in spongy bone. Red marrow makes new red blood cells, germ-fighting white blood cells, and cell fragments that stop a cut from bleeding.

5 Part of the bone is made of bone tissue that looks like a dry sponge. It is made of strong, hard tubes. It is also found in the middle of short, flat bones.

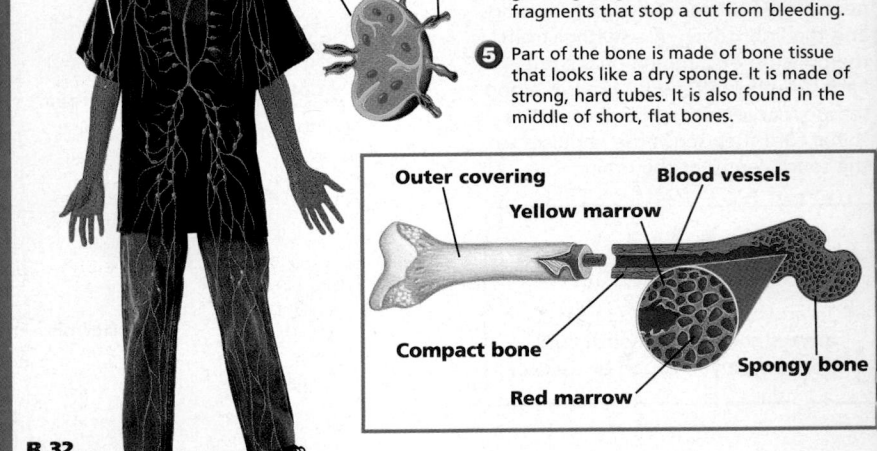

Lymph vessels
Lymph nodes
Lymph node
Lymph vessels

Outer covering   Blood vessels
Yellow marrow
Compact bone
Red marrow   Spongy bone

R 32

Science Background

The Immune System
Organs in the immune system are called lymphoid organs. Lymphoid organs include the bone marrow, lymph nodes, spleen, tonsils, adenoids, and appendix. Common allergic reactions occur when a person's immune system responds to a substance. For example, when a susceptible person is around house dust or grass pollen, the immune system attacks the substance believed to be a threat to the body.

The Endocrine System

Hormones are chemicals that control body functions. A gland that produces hormones is called an endocrine gland. Sweat from sweat glands flows out of tubes called ducts. Endocrine glands have no ducts.

The endocrine glands are scattered around the body. Each gland makes one or more hormones. Every hormone seeks out a target organ, the place in the body where the hormone acts.

CARE!

- Doctors can treat many diseases, such as diabetes, caused by endocrine glands that produce too little or too much of a hormone.

Some Glands in the Endocrine System

- Hypothalamus
- Pituitary gland
- Parathyroid gland
- Thyroid gland
- Adrenal glands
- Pancreas
- Ovaries
- Testes

Science Background

Jobs of the Endocrine Glands

Hypothalamus: produces hormones that tell the pituitary gland which of its hormones to start or stop producing

Pituitary gland: produces many hormones that control day-to-day body functions and long-term growth

Parathyroid glands: produce a hormone that controls the amount of calcium in the blood

Thyroid gland: produces hormones that affect the rate at which cells use oxygen to release energy from foods

Adrenal glands: produces hormones that control how much salt is in the blood, how much water is in the body, how well a person fights disease, and how quickly person can handle emergencies

Pancreas controls the amount of sugar in the bloodstream

Ovaries/Testes produce sex hormones that result in physical changes between the ages of 9 and 14

The Endocrine System

Objective

- Explore the glands of the endocrine system.

Build on Prior Knowledge

Have students discuss changes in their sleep patterns, energy level, or weight. Ask:

- **How do you think the body "knows" when it's time to grow or sleep or get more energy?** (Something in the body tells it; chemicals signal changes to start.)

Developing the Main Idea

Explain to students that the prefix *endo-* comes from the Latin for "inside." Add that in this lesson, they'll learn about the endocrine system in their bodies that helps to control body functions. Explain that chemicals made in one part of the body and carried in the bloodstream to a target site can change the way the body functions. Such chemicals, or hormones, can affect growth, sleep, energy, and weight.

Using the Illustrations

Ask:

- **What are the names of some glands in the endocrine system?** (hypothalamus, pituitary, parathyroid, thyroid, adrenal, pancreas, ovaries, testes)

- **Which endocrine glands are in the throat?** (parathyroid, thyroid)

WRITING LINK

Invite students to write about a time when they were very frightened or had a sudden burst of energy. Explain that these effects are due to hormones produced by the endocrine system.

Informal Assessment

Ask students to explain what a hormone is and where it is produced. (chemical; in an endocrine gland)

The Reproductive System

Objective

- Describe the male and female reproductive systems.

Build on Prior Knowledge

Ask:

- **What is puberty?** (teen years when a boy or girl matures into a man or woman) **What are some changes that take place?** (growth of body hair, change of body shape and size, and so on)

Developing the Main Idea

Explain to students that the reproductive system allows the human species to continue.

Read page R34 with students, then ask:

- **What are testes?** (male reproductive organs)

- **What do the female reproductive organs contain?** (eggs)

- **What is the only way to avoid sexually-transmitted diseases?** (abstinence)

- **What does abstinence mean?** (avoiding, not taking part in)

WRITING LINK

Encourage students to write about their feelings as they look forward to or are entering puberty. Help them build self-esteem by reminding them to feel proud about all the things they do that makes them special.

Informal Assessment

Ask students to compare and contrast the female and male reproductive systems. (both produce hormones and sex cells, but differ in location and structure)

The Reproductive System

The testes are the male reproductive organs. At puberty the testes begin to produce sperm. Sperm move through sperm ducts, where they mix with fluid from endocrine glands.

The ovaries are the female reproductive organs, which contain eggs. After puberty one mature egg is released about once every 28 days. The egg moves to the oviduct, a narrow tube leading from the ovary.

The Male Reproductive System

Sperm move from the testes through sperm ducts, where they mix with fluid from the glands. The sperm and fluid move through the urethra, a tube that leads out through the penis.

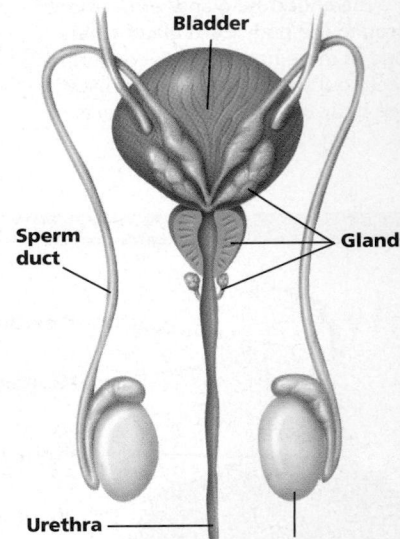

Bladder

Sperm duct

Glands

Urethra

Testis

CARE!

- Abstinence is the only sure way to avoid sexually transmitted diseases.

The Female Reproductive System

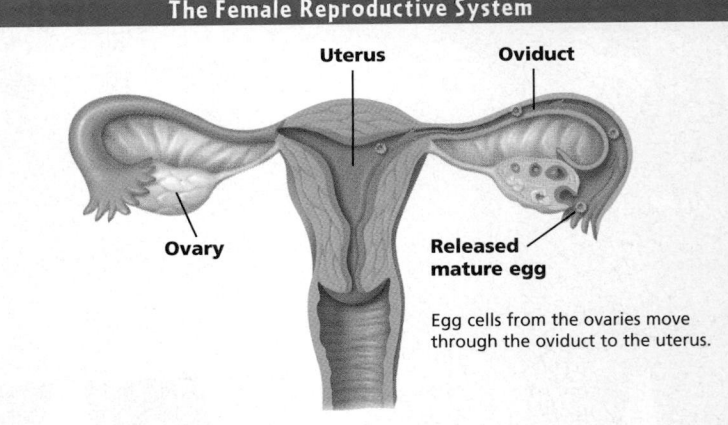

Uterus

Oviduct

Ovary

Released mature egg

Egg cells from the ovaries move through the oviduct to the uterus.

R 34

Science Background

Puberty

During the natural transition from childhood to adulthood, puberty, youngsters go through many physical, mental, and social changes. Girls usually enter puberty at a younger age than boys. Once this was at about age 11, but today girls as young as 9 may begin the transition. The first sign of physical change for girls is usually developing breasts; for boys, it's a growth spurt. Changes are essentially due to hormones in the reproductive organs that are suddenly released into the young person's body.

Glossary

This Glossary will help you to pronounce and understand the meanings of the Science Words introduced in this book. The page number at the end of the definition tells where the word appears.

A

abiotic factor (ā′bī ot′ik fak′tər) A nonliving part of an ecosystem. (p. B6)

absorption (əb sôrp′shən) The disappearance of a sound wave into a surface. (p. F66)

abyssal plain (ə bis′əl plān) The vast flat lands beyond the continental shelf that cover almost half of the deep ocean floor. (p. C90)

acceleration (ak sel′ə rā′shən) Change in velocity with respect to time. (pp. F13, F22)

acid (as′id) A substance that tastes sour and turns blue litmus paper red. (p. E82)

acid rain (as′id rān) Moisture that falls to Earth after being mixed with wastes from burned fossil fuels. (p. C65)

acidity (ə sid′ə tē) The strength of an acid. (p. E86)

action (ak′shən) The force one object applies to a second, as in Newton's third law of motion, which states, "For every action, there is an equal but opposite reaction." *See* **reaction**. (p. F24)

adaptation (ad′əp tā′shən) A characteristic that enables a living thing to survive in its environment. (pp. A82, A106, B52)

aerial root (âr′ē əl rūt) A root that never touches the ground but can take in moisture from the air. (p. A21)

aerosol (âr′ə sōl′) A type of colloid in which liquid drops or solid particles are spread throughout a gas. (p. E60)

air mass (âr mas) A large region of the atmosphere where the air has similar properties throughout. (p. D54)

air pressure (âr presh′ər) The force put on a given area by the weight of the air above it. (p. D11)

alkalinity (al′kə lin′i tē) The strength of a base. (p. E86)

alternation of generations (ôl′tər nā′shən uv jen′ə rā′shənz) The process in which offspring are reproduced sexually, their offspring are reproduced asexually, and so on. (p. A53)

alternative energy source (ōl tûr′nə tiv en′ər jē sôrs) A source of energy other than the burning of a fossil fuel. (p. C104)

PRONUNCIATION KEY

The following symbols are used throughout the McGraw-Hill Science 2002 Glossaries.

a	at	e	end	o	hot	u	up	hw	white	ə about
ā	ape	ē	me	ō	old	ū	use	ng	song	taken
ä	far	i	it	ôr	fork	ü	rule	th	thin	pencil
âr	care	ī	ice	oi	oil	ù	pull	<u>th</u>	this	lemon
ô	law	îr	pierce	ou	out	ûr	turn	zh	measure	circus

′ = primary accent; shows which syllable takes the main stress, such as **kil** in **kilogram** (kil′ə gram′).
′ = secondary accent; shows which syllables take lighter stresses, such as **gram** in **kilogram**.

R 35

ammonia (ə mōn′yə) A compound that contains the element nitrogen and is used as a fertilizer. (p. B34)

anemometer (an′ə mom′i tər) A device that measures wind speed. (p. D44)

aneroid barometer (an′ə roid bə rom′i tər) A spring enclosed in a pleated metal can that expands or contracts to indicate changes in air pressure. (p. D12)

angiosperm (an′jē ə spûrm′) A seed plant that produces flowers. *See* **gymnosperm.** (p. A58)

aquifer (ak′wə fər) An underground layer of rock or soil filled with water. (p. C75)

asexual reproduction (a sek′shü əl rē′prō duk′shən) The production of a new organism from only one cell. (p. A52)

atmosphere (at′məs fîr′) The blanket of gases that surrounds Earth. (pp. C12, D10)

atom (at′əm) The smallest unit of an element that retains the properties of that element. *See* **molecule.** (p. E26)

aurora (ə rôr′ə) The northern or southern lights that appear in the night sky, especially in polar regions. (p. D10)

aurum (ôr′əm) The Latin word for *gold*. (p. E23)

B

bacterium (bak tîr′ē əm) *sing., n. pl.* **bacteria** (-ē ə) A member of either of two kingdoms of one-celled living things that have no nucleus, or center, in their cell body. (p. A15)

balanced forces (bal′ənst fôrs′əz) Forces that cancel each other out when acting together on a single object. (p. F21)

barometer (bə rom′i tər) A device for measuring air pressure. (p. D12)

base (bās) A substance that tastes bitter and turns red litmus paper blue. (p. E82)

basin (bās′in) The floor of an ocean, containing mountains, valleys, and plains. (p. C84)

Beaufort scale (bō′fərt skāl) A system for measuring wind speed by observing its effect on the surface of the sea, using a scale of 0 (low) to 12 (high) for each effect. (p. D44)

bench mark (bench′märk′) A plaque left by surveyors to tell the exact location and elevation of a place. (p. C18)

benthos (ben′thos) Organisms that live on the bottom in aquatic ecosystems. (p. B72)

biomass (bī′ō mas′) Energy from plant matter or animal waste. (p. C106)

biome (bī′ōm) One of Earth's large ecosystems, with its own kind of climate, soil, plants, and animals. (p. B64)

biotic factor (bī ot′ik fak′tər) A living part of an ecosystem. (p. B7)

boiling point (boil′ing point) The particular temperature for each substance at which it changes state from a liquid to a gas. (p. E37)

buoyancy (boi′ən sē) The upward push of a liquid on an object placed in it. (p. E12)

C

cambium (kam′bē əm) The layer in plants that separates the xylem from the phloem. (p. A21)

camouflage (kam′ə fläzh′) An adaptation in which an animal protects itself against predators by blending in with the environment. (p. A108)

carbon cycle (kär′bən sī′kəl) The continuous exchange of carbon dioxide and oxygen among living things. (p. B37)

carnivore (kär′nə vôr′) An animal that eats another animal. (p. B20)

chemical change (kem′i kəl chānj) A change of matter that occurs when atoms link together in a new way, creating a new substance different from the original substances. (p. E71)

chemical formula (kəm'i kəl fôr'myə lə) A way to write a compound's name using symbols. The letters tell what elements are in the compound, and the subscripts tell the number of particles in the compound. (p. E25)

chemical reaction (kem'i kəl rē ak'shən) Another name for chemical change. (p. E71)

chemosynthesis (kē'mō sin'thə sis) In tube worms the process by which bacteria create nutrients from hydrogen sulfide and oxygen, using chemical reactions rather than light. (p. C93)

chlorophyll (klôr'ə fil') A green chemical in plant cells that allows plants to use the Sun's energy for making food. (pp. A6, A32)

chloroplast (klôr'ə plast') The part of a plant cell containing chlorophyll, the green substance that enables the plant to produce food. (p. A24)

cirrus cloud (sir'əs kloud) A high-altitude cloud with a featherlike shape, made of ice crystals. (p. D24)

classification (klas'ə fi kā'shən) The science of finding patterns among living things. (p. A8)

classification key (klas'ə fi kā'shən kē) A series of paired choices describing organisms that is arranged in a way that leads to the identity of a given organism. (p. A100)

classify (klas'ə fi) To place things that share properties together in groups. (p. S7)

cleavage (klē'vij) The tendency of a mineral to break along flat surfaces. (p. C34)

climate (klī'mit) The average weather pattern of a region. (p. D82)

climate zone (klī mat' zōn) A region that has similar weather patterns based on temperature, precipitation, wind, distance from a coast, mountain ranges, ocean currents, and vegetation. (p. D82)

climax community (klī'maks kə mū'ni tē) The final stage of succession in an area, unless a major change happens. (p. B84)

cold front (kōld frunt) A front where cold air moves in under a warm air mass. (p. D56)

colloid (kol'oid) A special type of mixture in which the particles of one material are scattered through another and block the passage of light without settling out. (pp. E54, E60)

commensalism (kə men'sə liz'əm) A relationship between two kinds of organisms that benefits one without harming the other. (p. B57)

communicate (kə mū'ni kāt') To share information. (p. S7)

community (kə mū'ni tē) All the living things in an ecosystem. (p. B10)

complete flower (kəm plēt' flou'ər) A flower that has sepals, petals, stamens, and pistils. (p. A70)

compound (kom'pound) Any substance that is formed by the chemical combination of two or more elements and acts like a single substance. (p. E24)

compression (kəm presh'ən) **1.** The part of a sound wave where molecules are crowded together. (p. F51) **2.** A movement of plates that presses together or squeezes Earth's crust. (p. C20)

concave lens (kon kāv' lenz) A lens that is thicker at the edges than at the middle. As it curves inward, it spreads light rays apart, making images appear smaller. (p. F100)

PRONUNCIATION KEY

a **at**; ā **ape**; ä **far**; âr **care**; ô **law**; e **end**; ē **me**; i **it**; ī **ice**; îr **pierce**; o **hot**; ō **old**; ôr **fork**; oi **oil**; ou **out**; u **up**; ū **use**;
ü **rule**; u̇ **pull**; ûr **turn**; hw **white**; ng **song**; th **thin**; <u>th</u> **this**; zh **measure**; ə **about, taken, pencil, lemon, circus**

concave mirror (kon kāv′ mir′ər) A mirror that curves in on the shiny side. (p. F88)

condensation (kon′den sā′shən) *n.* The changing of a gas into a liquid. (pp. B32, D17) —**condense** (kən dens′) *v.* (p. E37)

conduction (kən duk′shən) *n.* The passing of heat through a material while the material itself stays in place. (p. E97) —**conduct** (kən dukt′) *v.* (p. E14)

conifer (kon′ə fər) Any of a group of gymnosperms that produce seeds in cones and have needlelike leaves. (p. A59)

conserve (kən′sûrv′) To save, protect, or use resources wisely. (p. C39)

constellation (kon′stə lā′shən) Any of the patterns formed by groups of stars in the night sky. To people in the past, these patterns looked like pictures of animals or people. (p. C14)

consumer (kən sü′mər) Any animal that eats plants or eats other plant-eating animals. (pp. B7, B20)

continental rise (kon′tə nen′təl rīz) A buildup of sediment on the sea floor at the bottom of the continental slope. It is a zone of sand and mud that stretches from the slope down to the deep-sea floor. (p. C90)

continental shelf (kon′tə nen′təl shelf) The underwater edge of a continent. (p. C90)

continental slope (kon′tə nen′təl slōp) The steep slope leading down from the continental shelf toward the sea floor. (p. C90)

contour plowing (kon′tür plou′ing) Preventing erosion by plowing across rather than up and down a slope. (p. C51)

contract (*v.*, kən trakt′) To shrink, as when a material gets colder. (p. E41)

convection (kən vek′shən) The flow of heat through a liquid or a gas, causing hot parts to rise and cooler parts to sink. (p. E97)

convection cell (kən vek′shən sel) A circular pattern of air rising, air sinking, and wind. (p. D38)

convex lens (kon veks′ lenz) A lens that is thicker at the middle than at the edges. As it curves outward, it brings light together, making images appear larger. (p. F100)

convex mirror (kon veks′ mir′ər) A mirror that curves out on the shiny side. (p. F88)

coquina (kō kē′nə) A sedimentary rock formed from seashell fragments. (p. C44)

Coriolis effect (kôr′ē ō′lis i fekt′) The curving of the path of a moving object caused by Earth's rotation. (p. D40)

cortex (kôr′teks) The layer of tissue just inside the epidermis of a plant's roots and stems. (p. A20)

cotyledon (ko′tə lē′dən) A tiny leaflike structure, also called a seedleaf, inside the seed of an angiosperm. (p. A62)

crop rotation (krop rō tā′shən) Growing different crops each year so that the soil does not use up the same kinds of minerals year after year. (p. C51)

crossbreeding (krôs′brēd′ing) Producing offspring by mating individuals from two distinct breeds or varieties of the same species. (p. A112)

cross-pollination (krôs′pol′ə nā′shən) The transfer of pollen from one flower to another. (p. A72)

crust (krust) The rocky surface that makes up the top of the lithosphere and includes the continents and the ocean floor. (p. C12)

crystal (kris′təl) The geometric shape a mineral forms when its atoms and molecules get into fixed patterns. (p. C32)

cumulus cloud (kū′myə ləs kloud) A puffy cloud that appears to rise up from a flat bottom. (p. D24)

current (kûr′ənt) An ocean movement; a large stream of water that flows in the ocean. (p. C86)

cycad (sī′kad) One of the evergreen gymnosperms that resemble palms and have seed-bearing cones. (p. A59)

D

decibel (dB) (des'ə bel') A unit that measures loudness. (p. F58)

deciduous (di sij'ü əs) Said of a plant that loses its leaves each fall. *See* **evergreen**. (pp. A59, B70)

deciduous forest (di si'jə wəs fôr'ist) A forest biome with many kinds of trees that lose their leaves each autumn. (p. B70)

decomposer (dē'kəm pōz'ər) Any of the fungi or bacteria that break down dead plants and animals into useful things like minerals and rich soil. (pp. B7, B21, B34)

define based on observations (di fīn' bāst ôn ob'zər vā'shənz) To put together a description that relies on examination and experience. (p. S7)

density (den'si tē) A measure of how tightly packed the matter in an object is. (pp. C35, E8)

deposition (dep'ə zish'ən) The dropping off of bits of eroded rock. (p. C25)

desalination (dē sal'ə nā'shən) Getting fresh water from seawater. (p. C73)

desert (dez'ərt) A sandy or rocky biome, with little precipitation and little plant life. (p. B69)

dicot (dī'kot') An angiosperm with two cotyledons in each seed. *See* **monocot**. (p. A62)

dinoflagellate (din'ə flaj'ə lāt') A protist containing chlorophyll that has two flagella for motion. When they overreproduce, they can cause "red tides." (p. A14)

distillation (dis'tə lā'shən) The process of separating the parts of a mixture by evaporation and condensation. (p. E64)

diversity (di vûr'si tē) A wide variety of traits in individuals from the same population. (p. A114)

Doppler effect (dop'lər i fekt') The change in frequency (and pitch) as a source of sound moves toward or away from you. (p. F71)

downdraft (doun'draft') A downward rush of air caused by the falling of rain during a thunderstorm. (pp. D38, D67)

E

echo (e'kō) A reflected sound wave. (p. F68)

echolocation (ek'ō lō kā'shən) Finding an object by using reflected sound. (p. F70)

ecological succession (ek'ə loj'i kəl sək sesh'ən) The gradual replacement of one community by another. (p. B82)

ecology (ē kol'ə jē) The study of how living and nonliving things interact. (p. B6)

ecosystem (ek'ō sis'təm) All the living and non-living things in an environment, including their interactions with each other. (p. B6)

electromagnetic spectrum (i lek'trō mag net'ik spek'trəm) All the wavelengths of visible and invisible light in order, from short (gamma rays) to long (radio). (p. F119)

electromagnetism (i lek'trō mag'ni tiz'əm) The production of magnetism by electricity (and the production of electricity by magnets). (p. F118)

electron (i lek'tron) A particle in the space outside the nucleus of an atom that carries one unit of negative electric charge. (p. E27)

element (el'ə mənt) A pure substance that cannot be broken down into any simpler substances. (p. E22)

PRONUNCIATION KEY

a at; ā ape; ä far; âr care; ô law; e end; ē me; i it; ī ice; îr pierce; o hot; ō old; ôr fork; oi oil; ou out; u up; ū use; ü rule; u̇ pull; ûr turn; hw white; ng song; th thin; <u>th</u> this; zh measure; ə about, taken, pencil, lemon, circus

R 39

elevation (el'ə vā'shən) The height of a place above sea level. (p. C18)

embryo (em'brē ō') The immature plant inside a seed. (p. A74)

emulsion (i mul'shən) A type of colloid in which one liquid is spread throughout another. (p. E60)

epidermis (ep'i dûr'mis) An outermost layer of such plant parts as roots and leaves. (p. A20)

erosion (i rō'zhən) The picking up and carrying away of pieces of rocks. (p. C22)

evaporation (i vap'ə rā'shən) The slow changing of a liquid into a gas. (pp. B32, D16, E38)

evergreen (ev'ər grēn') Said of a gymnosperm that keeps its leaves for at least a few years. *See* **deciduous**. (p. A59)

expand (ek spand') To spread out, as when a material gets hotter. (p. E41)

experiment (ek sper'ə ment') To perform a test to support or disprove a hypothesis. (p. S7)

F

fault (fôlt) A crack in Earth's crust whose sides show evidence of motion. (p. C18)

fault-block mountain (fôlt blok moun'tən) A mountain formed by blocks of Earth's crust moving along a fault. (p. C21)

fertilization (fûr'tə lə zā'shən) The joining of a sperm cell with an egg cell to make one new cell, a fertilized egg. (pp. A52, A73)

fertilizer (fûr'tə li'zər) A substance used to add minerals to the soil. (p. B34)

fibrous root (fi'brəs rüt) One of the many hairy branching roots that some plants have. (p. A21)

filament (fil'ə mənt) The wire in a light bulb that gives off light and heat. (p. E92)

foam (fōm) A type of colloid in which a gas is spread throughout a liquid. (p. E60)

fog (fôg) A cloud that forms at ground level. (p. D24)

fold mountain (fōld moun'tən) A mountain made up mostly of rock layers folded by being squeezed together. (p. C20)

food chain (füd chān) The path of the energy in food from one organism to another. (p. B18)

food web (füd web) The overlapping food chains in an ecosystem. (p. B20)

force (fôrs) A push or pull exerted by one object on another, causing a change in motion. (p. F6)

form a hypothesis (fôrm ə hī poth'ə sis) To make a statement that can be tested to answer a question. (p. S7)

fossil (fos'əl) Any remains or imprint of living things of the past. (p. C45)

fossil fuel (fos'əl fü'əl) A fuel formed from the decay of ancient forms of life. (p. C64)

fracture (frak'chər) The characteristic way some minerals break in uneven patterns. (p. C35)

freezing point (frēz'ing point) Another name for *melting point,* that temperature at which a substance changes state, either from a liquid to a solid or from solid to liquid. (p. E37)

frequency (frē'kwən sē) The number of times an object vibrates per second. (p. F57)

friction (frik' shen') A force that opposes the motion of one object moving past another. (p. F8)

frond (frond) The leaf of a fern. (p. A51)

front (frunt) A boundary between air masses with different temperatures. (p. D55)

fruit (früt) The ripened ovary of a flowering seed plant. (p. A75)

fundamental frequency (fun'də men'təl frē'kwən sē) The lowest frequency at which an object vibrates. (p. F72)

fungus (fung'gəs) *n.,* **fungi** (fun'jī) *pl.* Members of a kingdom that contains one-celled and many-celled living things that absorb food from their environment. (p. A13)

G

gas (gas) A form of matter that does not take up a definite amount of space and has no definite shape. (p. E36)

gel (jel) A type of colloid in which a solid is spread throughout a liquid. (p. E60)

gem (jem) A mineral valued for being rare and beautiful. (p. C38)

geologist (jē ol'ə jist) A scientist who studies rocks to tell how they formed and to predict when an earthquake may occur. (p. C18)

geothermal energy (jē'ō thûr'məl en'ər jē) Earth's internal energy. (p. C104)

germination (jûr'mə nā'shən) The sprouting of a seed into a new plant. (p. A75)

ginkgo (ging'kō) *n., pl.* **ginkgoes** A large gymnosperm with fan-shaped leaves. (p. A59)

gnetophyte (ne'tō fīt') One of the gymnosperms that are closely related to flowering plants and live in both deserts and the tropics. (p. A59)

grassland (gras'land') A biome where grasses, not trees, are the main plant life. Prairies are one kind of grassland region. (p. B66)

gravitropism (grav'ī trō'pi'zəm) The response of a plant to gravity. (p. A80)

gravity (grav'i tē) A force of attraction, or pull, between any object and any other objects around it. Gravity is a property of all matter. (pp. C8, F35)

greenhouse effect (grēn'hous' i fekt') The ability of the atmosphere to let in sunlight but not to let heat escape. (p. D87)

groundwater (ground wô'tər) Precipitation that seeps into the ground and is stored in tiny holes, or pores, in soil and rocks. (pp. B33, C74, D28)

gymnosperm (jim'nə spûrm') A seed plant that does not produce flowers. *See* **angiosperm**. (p. A58)

H

habitat (hab'i tat) The place where a plant or animal naturally lives and grows. (p. B11)

hail (hāl) Pellets made of ice and snow. (p. D27)

hardness (härd'nis) How well a mineral resists scratching. (p. C34)

herbivore (hûr'bə vôr') An animal that eats plants, algae, and other producers. (p. B20)

heredity (hə red'i tē) The passing down of inherited traits from parents to offspring. (p. A110)

hertz (Hz) (hûrts) A unit for measuring frequency. One hertz equals a frequency of one vibration per second. (p. F57)

heterogeneous (het'ər ə jē'nē əs) Differing in kind or nature; dissimilar; not homogeneous. (p. E54)

high-pressure system (hī'presh'ər sis'təm) A pattern surrounding a high pressure center, from which winds blow outward. In the Northern Hemisphere these winds curve to the right in a clockwise pattern. (p. D42)

host (hōst) The organism a parasite lives in or on and is harmed by. (p. B56)

humidity (hū mid'i tē) The amount of water vapor in the air. (p. D16)

humus (hū'məs) Decayed plant or animal material in soil. (pp. B14, C49)

hurricane (hûr'i kān') A very large, swirling storm with very low pressure at the center. (p. D70)

PRONUNCIATION KEY

a at; ā ape; ä far; âr care; ô law; e end; ē me; i it; ī ice; îr pierce; o hot; ō old; ôr fork; oi oil; ou out; u up; ū use; ü rule; u̇ pull; ûr turn; hw white; ng song; th thin; th this; zh measure; ə about, taken, pencil, lemon, circus

R 41

hybrid (hī′brid) An organism produced by the crossing of parents that have different forms of the same trait. (p. A112)

hydrocarbon (hī′drə kär′bən) Any of the large group of compounds made solely from hydrogen and carbon atoms. (p. E32)

hydroelectric plant (hī′drō i lek′trik plant) A factory where running or falling water spins a generator to make electricity. (p. C104)

hydrosphere (hī′drə sfîr′) Earth's water, found in continents and oceans, including the fresh water in ice, lakes, rivers, and underground water. (p. C12)

hydrotropism (hī drot′rə piz′əm) The response of a plant to a nearby source of water. (p. A81)

hyperthermia (hī′pər thûr′mē ə) The overheating of the body that can be caused by overexposure in a hot, dry climate. (p. D90)

hypothesis (hī poth′ə sis) A guess or *if . . . then* statement that can be answered clearly in an experiment. (p. A35)

I

ice age (īs āj) Any period when glaciers and ice sheets covered much of Earth's surface. (p. B58)

igneous rock (ig′nē əs rok) A rock formed when melted rock material cools and hardens (p. C43)

image (im′ij) A "picture" of the light source that light rays make in bouncing off a polished, shiny surface. (p. F89)

imperfect flower (im pûr′fikt flou′ər) A flower with either a stamen or a pistil, but not both. (p. A70)

incomplete flower (in′kəm plēt′ flou′ər) A flower that lacks sepals, petals, stamens or pistils. (p. A70)

indicator (in′di kā′tər) A substance such as litmus paper whose color changes when it is mixed with an acid or a base. (p. E84)

inertia (i nûr′shə) The tendency of a moving object to keep moving in a straight line or of any object to resist a change in motion. (pp. C9, F7)

inexhaustible resource (in′eg zôs′tə bəl rē′sôrs′) A resource that cannot be depleted or used up easily. (p. B40)

infer (in fûr′) To form an idea from facts or observations. (p. S7)

inherited trait (in her′i təd trāt) A characteristic that is passed from parents to offspring. (p. A110)

insolation (in′sə lā′shən) The amount of the Sun's energy that reaches Earth at a given time and place. *Insolation* is short for *in*coming *sol*ar radi*ation*. (p. D6)

instinct (in′stingkt′) An inherited behavior, one that is not learned but is done automatically. (p. A110)

insulate (in′sə lāt′) To prevent heat from passing through. (p. E14)

interpret data (in tûr′prit dā′tə) To use the information that has been gathered to answer questions or solve a problem. (p. S7)

intertidal zone (in′tər tī′dəl zōn) The shallowest section of the marine, or ocean, ecosystem, where the ocean floor is covered and uncovered as the tide goes in and out. (p. B73)

invertebrate (in vûr′tə brit) An animal that does not have a backbone. (p. A95)

ionized (ī′ə nīzd′) Electrically charged by radiation, as gas particles of auroras in the night sky. (p. D10)

isobar (ī′sə bär′) A line on a weather map connecting places with equal air pressure. (p. D42)

K

kinetic energy (ki net′ik en′ər jē) The energy of any moving object. (p. E95)

L

land breeze (land brēz) Wind that blows from land to sea. (p. D39)

laser (lā'zər) A device that produces a thin stream of light of just a few close wavelengths. (p. F122)

lava (lä'və) Magma that reaches Earth's surface. (pp. C21, C43)

law of reflection (lô uv ri flek'shən) The angle between an incoming light ray and a surface equals the angle between the reflected light ray and the surface. (p. F87)

light ray (līt rā) A straight-line beam of light as it travels outward from its source. (p. F85)

lightning (līt'ning) One of the huge electric sparks that leap from clouds to the ground in thunderstorms. (p. D66)

limiting factor (lim'ə ting fak'tər) Anything that controls the growth or survival of a population. (p. B50)

liquid (lik'wid) A form of matter that takes up a definite amount of space and has no definite shape. (p. E36)

lithosphere (lith'ə sfîr') The hard outer layer of Earth, about 100 km thick. (p. C12)

long-day plant (lông'dā plant) A plant that blooms when there is much more daylight than darkness. (p. A82)

low-pressure system (lō'presh'ər sis'təm) A pattern surrounding a low-pressure center, in which winds blow in toward the center. In the Northern Hemisphere, these winds blow to the right in a counterclockwise pattern. (p. D42)

luster (lus'tər) The way light bounces off a mineral's surface. (p. C33)

M

magma (mag'mə) Hot, molten rock deep below Earth's surface. (p. C21)

magnetic (mag net'ik) The property of a material like iron in which the particles line up pole to pole, causing it to be attracted or repelled by a magnet. (p. E15)

make a model (māk ə mod'əl) To make something to represent an object or event. (p. S7)

mare (mär'ā) *n., pl.* **maria** (mär'ē ə) Dark-colored land on the Moon that is dry and flat and is surrounded by mountains and ridges. (p. C13)

mass (mas) A measure of the amount of matter in an object. (p. E6)

matter (ma'tər) Anything that has mass and takes up space. (pp. E6, F51)

measure (mezh'ər) To find the size, volume, area, mass, weight, or temperature of an object, or how long an event occurs. (p. S7)

melting point (melt'ing point) The particular temperature for each substance at which it changes state from a solid to a liquid. (p. E37)

membrane (mem'brān) A thin envelope surrounding the nucleus of a cell. (p. A14)

metal (met'əl) Any of a group of elements found in the ground that conducts heat and electricity. (p. C38)

metamorphic rock (met'ə môr'fik rok) A rock formed under heat and pressure from another kind of rock. (p. C46)

meteorite (mē'tē ə rīt') A chunk of rock from space that strikes the surface of Earth or the Moon. (p. C26)

mid-ocean ridge (mid ō'shun rij) Chain of mountains that wind along all the world's major oceans. (p. C91)

PRONUNCIATION KEY

a **at**; ā **ape**; ä **far**; âr **care**; ô **law**; e **end**; ē **me**; i **it**; ī **ice**; îr **pierce**; o **hot**; ō **old**; ôr **fork**; oi **oil**; ou **out**; u **up**; ū **use**; ü **rule**; u̇ **pull**; ûr **turn**; hw **white**; ng **song**; th **thin**; <u>th</u> **this**; zh measure; ə **about, taken, pencil, lemon, circus**

R 43

mimicry (mim′i krē) An adaptation in which an animal is protected against predators by its resemblance to another, unpleasant animal. (p. A106)

mineral (min′ə rəl) A solid material of Earth's crust with a definite composition. (p. C32)

mixture (miks′chər) A physical combination of two or more substances that are blended together without forming new substances. (p. E52)

molecule (mol′ə kūl′) A particle that contains more than one atom joined together. (p. E30) *See* **atom**. (p. E26)

monocot (mon′ə kot′) An angiosperm with one cotyledon in each seed. *See* **dicot**. (p. A62)

mountain breeze (moun′tən brēz) A cool night wind that blows down a mountain slope to replace the warmer air in the valley. (p. D39)

mutualism (mū′chü ə liz′əm) A relationship between two kinds of organisms that benefits both. (p. B54)

N

neap tide (nēp tīd) The slightest changes from high to low tide that occur when the Sun, the Moon, and Earth form a right angle or are perpendicular to each other. (p. C89)

nekton (nek′tən) Organisms that swim through the water in aquatic ecosystems. (p. B72)

neutral (nü′trəl) Neither acid nor base. (p. E82)

neutron (nü′tron) A particle in the nucleus of an atom that has no net electric charge. (p. E27)

newton (nü′tən) A basic unit measuring the amount of pull or push a force such as gravity produces between two masses. (pp. E7, F20)

NEXRAD (neks′rad′) A new form of Doppler radar that is used to track storms. The word stands for *NEXt generation of weather RADar*. (p. D77)

niche (nich) The role of an organism in a community. (p. B11)

nitrogen cycle (nī′trə jən sī′kəl) The continuous trapping of nitrogen gas into compounds in the soil and its return to the air. (p. B38)

nonrenewable resource (non′ri nü′ə bəl rē′sôrs′) A resource that cannot be replaced within a short period of time or at all. (pp. B40, C64)

nonvascular (non vas′kyə lər) Containing no plant tissue through which water and food move. (p. A9)

nucleus (nü′klē əs) **1.** A dense structure inside the cell. (p. A14) **2.** One of the airborne dust particles around which water condenses as droplets or ice crystals before falling as precipitation. (p. D26) **3.** An atom's dense center, where most of its mass is. (p. E27)

O

observe (əb sûrv′) To use one or more of the senses to identify or learn about an object or event. (p. S7)

occluded front (ə klüd′id frunt) A front formed where a warm front and a cold front meet. (p. D56)

omnivore (om′nə vôr′) An animal that eats both plants and animals. (p. B21)

opaque (ō pāk′) Completely blocking light from passing through it. (p. F96)

orbit (ôr′bit) The path of a planet traveling around a star. (p. C6)

ore (ôr) A mineral containing a useful substance. (p. C38)

organ (ôr′gən) A group of tissues that work together to do a certain job. (p. A94)

organism (ôr′gə niz′əm) Any living thing that can carry out its life on its own. (p. B6)

ovary (ō′və rē) A structure containing egg cells; the base of a pistil in a flower. (p. A70)

overtone (ō′vər tōn′) One of a series of pitches that blend to give a sound its quality. (p. F72)

ozone layer (ō′zōn lā′ər) A layer of ozone gas in the atmosphere that screens out much of the Sun's UV (ultraviolet) rays. (p. C63)

P

parasitism (par′ə sī tiz′əm) A relationship in which one organism lives in or on another organism and benefits from that relationship while the other organism may be harmed by it. (p. B56) **—parasite** (par′ə sīt′) (p. A61)

perfect flower (pûr′fikt flou′ər) A flower with both male and female parts, that is, both a stamen and a pistil. (p. A70)

permafrost (pûr′mə frôst′) A layer of permanently frozen soil found in arctic and antarctic regions. (p. B68)

pH (pē′aitch′) The scale that tells how acidic or basic a solution is. (p. E86)

phloem (flō′em) The tissue through which food from the leaves moves down through the rest of a plant. (p. A21)

photon (fō′ton) The tiny bundles of energy by means of which light travels. (p. F119)

photoperiodism (fō′tō pîr′ē ə diz′əm) The flowering response of a plant to changing periods of daylight and darkness. (p. A82)

photosynthesis (fō′tə sin′thə sis) The food-making process in green plants that uses sunlight. (p. A32)

phototropism (fō tot′rə piz′əm) The response of a plant to changes in light. (p. A80)

phylum (fī′ləm) *n., pl.* **phyla** (-lə) One of the large groups in the animal kingdom. (p. A12)

physical change (fiz′i kəl chānj) A change of matter in size, shape, or state without any change in identity. (p. E70)

pioneer community (pī′ə nîr′ kə mū′ni tē) The first community thriving in a once lifeless area. (p. B83)

pioneer species (pī′ə nîr′ spē′shēz) The first species living in an otherwise lifeless area. (p. B83)

pitch (pich) How high or low a sound is. (p. F56)

planet (plan′it) Any of the nine objects that travel around the Sun and shine by reflecting its light. (p. C6)

plankton (plangk′tən) Organisms that float on the water in aquatic ecosystems. (p. B72)

plate (plāt) One of the moving pieces of Earth's crust that has been broken by upward pressure from the mantle. (p. C19)

plate tectonics (plāt tek ton′iks) A scientific theory that Earth's crust is made of moving plates. (p. C19)

polarization (pō′lər ə zā′shən) Allowing light vibrations to pass through in only one direction. (p. F97)

pollen (pol′ən) Dustlike grains in the flower of a plant that contain its male sex cells. (p. A64)

pollination (pol′ə nā′shən) The transfer of a pollen grain to the egg-producing part of a plant. (p. A72)

pollute (pə lūt′) *v.* To add unnatural substances to Earth's land, water, or air. (p. C50) **—pollutant** (pə lü′tənt) *n.* Something that pollutes. (p. C50) **—pollution** (pə lü′shən) *n.* A polluted condition. (p. C50)

PRONUNCIATION KEY

a at; ā ape; ä far; âr care; ô law; e end; ē me; i it; ī ice; îr pierce; o hot; ō old; ôr fork; oi oil; ou out; u up; ū use; ü rule; ú pull; ûr turn; hw white; ng song; th thin; <u>th</u> this; zh measure; ə about, taken, pencil, lemon, circus

population – reflection

population (pop′yə lā′shən) All the members of one species in an area. (p. B10)

potential energy (pə ten′shəl en′ər jē) Stored energy. (p. E95)

precipitation (pri sip′i tā′shən) Any form of water particles that falls from the atmosphere and reaches the ground. (pp. B33, D26)

predator (pred′ə tər) An animal that hunts other anmals for food. (pp. A106, B21)

predict (pri dikt′) To state possible results of an event or experiment. (p. S7)

prey (prā) A living thing that is hunted for food. (p. B21)

primary color (prī′mer′ē kul′ər) Red, green, or blue. Mixing these colors can produce all the colors of the spectrum. (p. F110)

primary pigment (prī′mer′ē pig′mənt) Magenta, cyan, or yellow. Materials with any of these colors absorb one primary color of light and reflect the other two. (p. F112)

primary succession (prī′mer′ē sək sesh′ən) The beginning of a community where few, if any, living things exist, or where earlier communities were wiped out. (p. B82)

prism (priz′əm) A cut piece of clear glass (or plastic) with two opposite sides in the shape of a triangle or other geometric shape. (p. F108)

producer (prə dü′sər) Any of the plants and algae that produce oxygen and food that animals need. (p. B7)

product (prod′ukt) A new substance produced by a chemical change. (p. E71)

prop root (prop rüt) One of the roots that grow out of a plant's stemlike main roots and help prop up the plant. (p. A21)

property (prop′ər tē) A characteristic of matter that can be observed, such as mass, volume, weight, or density. (pp. E6, E24)

protective coloration (prə tek′tiv kul′ə rā′shən) A type of camouflage in which the color of an animal blends in with its background, protecting it against predators. (p. A109)

protein (prō′tēn) A substance rich in nitrogen that the body uses for growth and the repair of cells. (p. B38)

protist (prō′tist) A member of a kingdom that contains one-celled and many-celled living things, some that make food and some that hunt for food. (p. A14)

proton (prō′ton) A particle in the nucleus of an atom that carries one unit of positive electric charge. (p. E27)

Q

quality (kwol′i tē) The difference you hear between two sounds of the same loudness and pitch. (p. F72)

R

radar (rā′där) A device for tracking the position and path of a distant moving object. It works by sending out radio waves and recording their echoes. The word stands for *RAdio Detecting And Ranging.* (p. D76)

radiation (rā′dē a′shən) The transfer of heat through electromagnetic rays. (p. E97)

radiative balance (rā′dē a′tiv bal′əns) A balance between energy lost and energy gained. (p. D86)

rarefaction (râr′ə fak′shən) The part of a sound wave where molecules are spread apart. (p. F51)

raw material (râ mə tîr′ē əl) Material not yet refined, manufactured, or processed. (p. B40)

reactant (rē ak′tənt) An original substance at the beginning of a chemical reaction. (p. E71)

reaction (rē ak′shən) The force with which an object responds to an action, as in Newton's third law of motion, which states, "For every action, there is an equal but opposite reaction." *See* **action.** (p. F24)

reflection (ri flek′shən) The bouncing of a sound wave off a surface. (p. F66)

refraction (ri frak'shən) The bending of light rays as they pass from one substance into another. (p. F98)

relative humidity (rel'ə tiv hū mid'i tē) A comparison between how much water vapor is in the air and how much the air could hold at a given temperature if it were full, or saturated. (p. D18)

renewable resource (ri nü'ə bəl rē'sôrs') A resource that can be replaced in a short period of time. (pp. B40, C62)

reservoir (rez'ər vwär') A storage area for fresh water supplies. (p. C75)

resonance (rez'ə nəns) In an instrument or object, a unique blend of the fundamental frequency and its overtones. When an external force vibrates at the same frequency, a buildup of that resonance can occur. (p. F72)

resource (rē'sôrs') Any material that helps support life on Earth. (p. C12)

respiration (res'pə rā'shən) The release of energy in plants and animals from food (sugar). (p. A33)

response (ri spons') What a living thing does as a result of a stimulus. (p. A80)

rhizoid (rī'zoid) One of the hairlike fibers that anchor a moss to the soil and take in water from the soil. (p. A48)

rhizome (rī'zōm) The underground stem of a fern. (p. A51)

rock (rok) A naturally formed solid in the crust made up of one or more minerals. (p. C42)

rock cycle (rok sī'kəl) Rocks changing from one into another in a never-ending series of processes. (p. C52)

root cap (rüt kap) A thin covering made up of cells that protect the root tip of a plant as it grows into the soil. (p. A20)

root hair (rüt hâr) Any of the threadlike projections from a plant root that absorb water and dissolved minerals from the soil. (p. A20)

rotate (rō'tāt) To make a complete spin on an axis, causing one day on a planet. A day differs in length from planet to planet. (p. C10)

runoff (run'ôf) Precipitation that flows across the land's surface or falls into rivers and streams. (pp. B33, D28)

S

savanna (sə van'ə) A tropical grassland with some trees and shrubs. (p. B66)

scanning tunneling microscope (scan'ing tun'əl ing mī'krə skōp') A device that uses electric current flowing through a needle to trace the contours of atoms and magnify them as much as 30 million times. (p. E26)

scavenger (skav'ən jər) A meat-eating animal that feeds on the remains of dead animals. (p. B21)

sea breeze (sē brēz) Wind that blows from sea to land. (p. D39)

sea-floor vent (sē'flôr' vent) An opening in a mid-ocean ridge where mineral-saturated water boils up from the seafloor crust. (p. C93)

seamount (sē'mount') A huge underwater volcanic mountain that may emerge from the ocean surface as an island. (p. C90)

secondary succession (sek'ən der'ē sək sesh'ən) The beginning of a new community where an earlier community already exists. (p. B82)

sedimentary rock (sed'ə men'tə rē rok) A rock made of bits of matter joined together. (p. C44)

PRONUNCIATION KEY

a at; ā ape; ä far; âr care; ô law; e end; ē me; i it; ī ice; îr pierce; o hot; ō old; ôr fork; oi oil; ou out; u up; ū use; ü rule; ù pull; ûr turn; hw white; ng song; th thin; <u>th</u> this; zh measure; ə about, taken, pencil, lemon, circus

R 47

seed – subscript

seed (sēd) An undeveloped plant with stored food sealed in a protective covering. (p. A58)

seed coat (sēd kōt) The outer covering of a seed. (p. A74)

seed dispersal (sēd di spûr'səl) The movement of a seed from the flower to a place where it can sprout. (p. A75)

self-pollination (self'pol'ə nā'shən) The transfer of pollen from an anther to a stigma in the same plant. (p. A72)

sexual reproduction (sek'shü əl rē'prō duk'shən) The production of a new organism from a female sex cell and a male sex cell. (p. A52)

shear (shîr) A movement of plates that twists, tears, or pushes one part of Earth's crust past another. (p. C20)

short-day plant (shôrt'dā plant) A plant that blooms when there is more darkness and less daylight. (p. A82)

smog (smog) A mixture of smoke and fog. (p. C64)

solar system (sō'lər sis'təm) The Sun and the objects that are traveling around it. (p. C6)

solid (sol'id) A form of matter that has a definite shape and takes up a definite amount of space. (p. E36)

solubility (sol'yə bil'i tē) The ability of a substance to be dissolved by another substance. (p. E58)

solute (sol'ūt) A substance that is dissolved by another substance to form a solution. (p. E57)

solution (sə lü'shən) A mixture of substances that are blended so completely that the mixture looks the same everywhere. (p. E54)

solvent (sol'vənt) A substance that dissolves one or more other substances to form a solution. (p. E57)

sound wave (sound wāv) A vibration that spreads away from a vibrating object. (p. F51)

spectrum (spek'trəm) A band of colors produced when light goes through a prism. (p. F108)

speed (spēd) How fast an object's position changes with time at any given moment. (p. F11)

spore (spôr) Cells in seedless plants that grow into new organisms. (p. A48)

spring (spring) A place where groundwater seeps out of the ground. (p. C75)

spring tide (spring tīd) The greatest changes from high to low tide that occur when the Sun, the Moon, and Earth are lined up. (p. C89)

state of matter (stāt uv mat'ər) One of the three forms that matter can take—solid, liquid, or gas. (p. E36)

stationary front (stā'shə ner ē frunt) An unmoving front where a cold air mass and a warm air mass meet. (p. D57)

statistical forecasting (stə tis'ti kəl fôr'kas'ting) Predicting weather by using past weather records, based on the chances of a pattern repeating itself. (p. D60)

stimulus (stim'yə ləs), *n., pl.* **stimuli** (-lī) Something in the environment that causes a living thing to react. (p. A80)

stomata (stō'mə tə) *pl. n., sing.* **stoma** Pores in the bottom of leaves that open and close to let in air or give off water vapor. (p. A24)

storm surge (stôrm sûrj) A great rise of the sea along a shore caused by low pressure clouds. (p. D72)

stratus cloud (strā'təs kloud) A cloud that forms in a blanketlike layer. (p. D24)

streak (strēk) The color of the powder left when a mineral is rubbed against a hard, rough surface. (p. C34)

strip farming (strip fär'ming) Trapping runoff by alternating tightly growing grasses with more widely spaced plants. (p. C51)

subscript (sub'skript') A number in a chemical formula that tells the number of atoms in the compound. (p. E25)

surveyor (sər vā′ər) A specialist who makes accurate measurements of Earth's crust. (p. C18)

suspension (sə spen′shən) A mixture in which suspended particles can easily be seen. (p. E59)

symbiosis (sim′bē ō′sis) A relationship between two kinds of organisms that lasts over time. (p. B54)

synoptic weather map (si nop′tik we͟th′ər map) A type of map showing a summary of the weather using station models. (p. D60)

system (sis′təm) A group of organs that work together to carry on life functions. (p. A94)

T

taiga (tī′gə) A cool forest biome of conifers in the upper Northern Hemisphere. (p. B67)

taproot (tap′rüt′) A root that has few hairy branches and grows deep into the ground. (p. A21)

temperate (tem′pər it) Free from extremes of temperature. (p. B66)

tension (ten′shən) A movement of plates that stretches or pulls apart Earth's crust. (p. C20)

terracing (ter′is ing) Shaping hillsides into steps so that runoff and eroded soil get trapped on the steps. (p. C51)

texture (teks′chər) An identifying quality of a rock based on how coarse, fine, or glassy it is and on how angular or rounded it is. (p. C42)

thunder (thun′dər) The noise caused by lightning-heated air during a thunderstorm. (p. D66)

thunderhead (thun′dər hed′) A cumulonimbus cloud in which a thunderstorm forms. (p. D66)

thunderstorm (thun′dər stôrm′) The most common severe storm, formed in cumulonimbus clouds. (p. D66)

tissue (tish′ü) A group of similar cells that work together at the same job. (pp. A7, A94)

topsoil (top′soil′) The dark, top layer of soil, rich in humus and minerals, in which many tiny organisms live and most plants grow. (p. B14)

tornado (tôr nā′dō) A violent whirling wind that moves across the ground in a narrow path. (p. D68)

trade wind (trād wind) A belt of winds around Earth moving from high pressure zones toward the low pressure at the equator. (p. D41)

translucent (trans lü′sənt) Letting only some light through, so that objects on the other side appear blurry. (p. F96)

transparent (trans pâr′ənt) Letting all light through, so that objects on the other side can be seen clearly. (p. F96)

transpiration (tran′spə rā′shən) The loss of water through a plant's leaves, which draws water up through the plant to replace it. (pp. A25, D17)

trench (trench) A deep valley in the sea floor. (p. C91)

tropical rain forest (trop′i kəl rān fôr′ist) A hot, humid biome near the equator, with much rainfall and a wide variety of life. (p. B71)

tropism (trō′piz′əm) A growth response of a plant toward or away from a stimulus. (p. A80)

troposphere (trop′ə sfîr′) The layer of the atmosphere closest to Earth's surface. (p. D10)

PRONUNCIATION KEY

a at; ā ape; ä far; âr care; ô law; e end; ē me; i it; ī ice; îr pierce; o hot; ō old; ôr fork; oi oil; ou out; u up; ū use; ü rule; u̇ pull; ûr turn; hw white; ng song; th thin; t͟h this; zh measure; ə about, taken, pencil, lemon, circus

R 49

tube worm (tüb wûrm) Large wormlike animals that live near sea floor vents and obtain their food through bacterial chemosynthesis. (p. C93)

tundra (tun'dra) Large, treeless plain in the arctic regions, where the ground is frozen all year. (p. B68)

ultrasonic (ul'trə son'ik) Said of a sound with a frequency too high to be heard by humans. (p. F57)

unbalanced forces (un bal'ənst fôrs'əz) Forces that do not cancel each other out when acting together on a single object. (p. F21)

updraft (up'draft') An upward rush of heated air during a thunderstorm. (pp. D38, D66)

use numbers (ūz num'bərz) To order, count, add, subtract, multiply, and divide to explain data. (p. S7)

use variables (ūz vâr'ē ə bəlz) To identify and separate things in an experiment that can be changed or controlled. (p. S7)

vacuum (vak'ū əm) A space through which sound waves cannot travel because it contains no matter. (p. F116)

valley breeze (val'ē brēz) A cool wind that blows up a mountain slope and replaces the slope's rising Sun-warmed air. (p. D39)

variable (vâr'ē ə bəl) One of the changes in a situation that may affect the outcome of an experiment. (p. A35)

vascular (vas'kyə lər) Containing plant tissue through which water moves up and food moves down. (p. A9)

velocity (və los'i tē) The speed and direction of a moving object. (p. F12)

vertebrate (vûr'tə brit) An animal that has a backbone. (p. A95)

vibration (vī brā'shən) A back-and-forth motion. (p. F50)

volume (vol'ūm) **1.** A measure of how much space an object takes up. (p. E6) **2.** The loudness or softness of a sound. (p. F58)

warm front (wôrm frunt) A front where warm air moves in over a cold air mass. (p. D56)

water cycle (wô'tər sī'kəl) The continuous movement of water between Earth's surface and the air, changing from liquid to gas to liquid. (pp. B33, C74, D29)

water table (wô'tər tā'bəl) The top of the water-filled spaces in the ground. (p. C75)

water vapor (wô'tər vā'pər) Water in the form of a gas. (pp. B32, D16)

waterspout (wô'tər spout') A tornado that forms over water. (p. D69)

weather (weth'ər) What the lower atmosphere is like at any given place and time. (p. D12)

weather vane (weth'ər vān) A device that indicates wind direction. (p. D44)

weathering (weth'ər ing) Breaking down rocks into smaller pieces. (p. C22)

weight (wāt) The force of gravity between Earth and an object. (pp. E7, F36)

well (wel) A hole dug below the water table that water seeps into. (p. C75)

wind (wind) Air that moves horizontally. (p. D38)

X

xylem (zī'ləm) The tissue through which water and minerals move up through a plant. (p. A20)

Y

year (yîr) The time it takes a planet to orbit the Sun. A *year* is different from planet to planet. (p. C7)

Index

A

Abiotic factors, B6–7
Absorption, of sound, F66–67
Abyssal plain, C90
Acceleration, F13, F18, F26–27
  calculation of, F20
  force and, F18
  mass and, F19, F20
  of falling objects, F36
  of the Moon, F37
Acidity, E86
Acid rain, C23, C65
Acids, C65*
  identifying, E81*–82, E84–85
  reactivity of, E83
  strength of, E86–87
  uses of, E88
Action, F24
Adaptation, A78–89, A104–109
  camouflage as, A108–109
  chemical, A84
  competition as, A83*, B23
  in sow bugs, A105*
  in taste, A107
  mimicry as, A106
  root growth as, A79*
  thorns as, A107
  to harsh environments, B52–53
  tropisms, A80–81
Aerial roots, A21
Aerogels, E16
Aerosol, E60
Agnatha, A98
Air, C62–63
  as solution, E56
  cleaning up, C66
  composition of, D11
  cooling of, D20
  dirty, C61*
  dust in, D11
  nitrogen in, B38
  pollution of, C64, C67
Air masses, D54–55
Air pressure
  altitude and, D11

changes in, D35*–37
convection cells and, D38
isobars, D42
measuring, D12
storm surges and, D72
Air resistance, F34
Air sac (swim bladder), A98
Air temperature
  altitude and, D10
  mean, D6
  measuring, D12
  relative humidity and, D19
  Sun's angle and, D5*–7*
Algae, B24, B73
  as producers, B7
  blooms, B26
  green, A14, A54
Alkalinity, E86
Alloys, E56
Alternation of generations, A53
Alternative energy sources,
  C104–105, C106
Altitude
  air pressure and, D11, D36
  air temperature and, D10
  climate and, D85
Aluminum, C38, E23
Alvin (submersible), C92, C96–97
AM, F120
Amazon rain forest, B76–77
Ammeter, E93
Ammonia, B34, B38, B39, E83
Amphibia, A98
Amphibians, A12
Amplifier, F60
"Ancient" bacteria kingdom, A15
Anemometer, D44
Anemones, A12, A96, B57
Aneroid barometer, D12
Angiosperms, A11, A54, A58,
  A59, A60–61, A60–65
  aromatic flowers, A64
  cotyledons, A62–63*, A74
Animals, A12, A92–120. *See also*
  Populations.
  adaptation of, A104–109
    camouflage, A108–109

  mimicry, A106
  sow bugs, A105*
  taste, A107
  thorns, A107
as consumers, B7
carbon cycle and, B37
classification of, A93*–101
  invertebrates, A95–97
  traits used for, A94–95
  vertebrates, A95, A98–99
crossbreeds, A112–113
diversity among, A114–15
habitat change and, B12
hoofed, B66
hybrids, A112, A113*
in deciduous forests, B70
inherited vs. learned traits in,
  A110–111
in nitrogen cycle, B39
in prairie ecosystem, B8–9
in tropical rain forests, B71
plants vs., A12
water cycle and, B33
Annelida (segmented worms),
  A97
Antacids, E88
Anther, A70, A72
Anthracite (hard coal), C47
Aquifer, C75
Arica, Chile, B69
Aristotle, D62, E22, F35
Armadillo, B9
Arthropoda, A12, A97
Asexual reproduction, A52
Atacama Desert, B69
Atmosphere, C12, C60–67, D10
  acid rain and, C65
  greenhouse effect and, D87
  living things' need for,
    C62–63
  of other planets, C68–69
  radiative balance and, D86
  weather and, D12
Atoms, E26–27
Auroras, D10
Auxin, A81
Aves (birds), A12, A99

* Indicates an activity related to this topic.

R 51

*Indicates an activity related to this topic.

D

*Indicates an activity related to this topic.

I

Ice, E18–19
   erosion by, C24–25
   melting, E35*
Ice ages, B58
Ice crystals, D24
Igneous rocks, C42–43, C52
Image, F89
Imperfect flowers, A70–71
Incomplete flowers, A70
Incomplete metamorphosis, A103
Independent variable, B13*
Indicators, E84–85
Industry, fresh water pollution by,
   C76
Inertia, C9, F7, F9
Inexhaustible resource, B40
Inferring skills, A68, B30, B87, C40,
   D22, E68
Infrared light, F120
Inherited vs. learned traits
   A110–111
Insolation, D6–8
Instinct, A110
Insulators, E14
International Whaling Commission
   (IWC), B74
Interpreting data, skill at, B87,
   D43*, D52, E80, E90
Intertidal zone, B73
Invertebrates, A95, A95–97
Ionized gas, D10
Irish potato famine, A66
Iron, C38
Iron disulfide, E52
Iron filings, E52
Iron oxide (rust), A13, C23, E74, E75
Isobars, D42

J

Jack–in–the–pulpit, A64
Jackson, Dr. Shirley, F126–127
Jellyfish, A96
Joshua tree (yucca plant), B54–55
Jupiter, C68, C69, E20
   moons of, C27

K

Kaleidoscopes, F96
Kaolinite, C33
Kinetic energy, E95
Kudzu, A16

L

Lakes, B67, C75, C77*
Lamprey, A98
Land breeze, D39
Land food chain, energy pyramid
   for, B24
Land food web, B20
Land masses, climate change and,
   D89
Langmuir, Irving, F93
Larva, A103
Lasers, F122, F126–127
Latimer, Lewis Howard, F93
Latitude, climate and, D84, D85
Lava, C21, C43
Law of reflection, F87
Leaf butterflies, A108
Leaves, A24–25*, A34, A38
Lenses, F100*–102, F103
Life cycles, B30–41
   carbon cycle, B36–37
   nitrogen cycle, B38–39
   of animals, A102–103
   of conifer, A76
   of ferns, A52–53
   of moss, A52–53
   tree recycling, B34–35
   water cycle, B31*–33, C74, C78,
      D28–29
Light, F79–123
   as energy, F82
   controlling, F97
   formed from chemical reaction,
      E73
   infrared, F120
   invisible, F119–121
   material passed through by,
      F96*
   plants and, A31*–33
   production of, F83

reflection of, F86*–90
refraction of, F98–99, F100
seeing without, F81*–82
travel by, F84–85
ultraviolet, C63, D10, F121
wavelengths of, F119
white, F108–109
Light bulbs, F92–93
Light ray, F85
Light waves, F85, F97, F118–119
Lightning, C69, D66–67
Limestone, C44, C45
Limiting factor, B50
Lions, B66
Liquids, E36–37
   density of, E10–11
   properties of, E40–41
   sound through, F52
Lithosphere, C12
Litmus, E84
Liverworts, A10, A48–49
Living things, C62–63. *See also*
   Animals; Classification; Plants;
   Populations.
Lobsters, A97
London Music Hall, F67
Long–day plants, A82
Loudness (volume), F58
Low–pressure system, D42
Lumber, B67
Luster of minerals, C33, C35

M

Magenta, F112
"Magic lantern," F104, F105
Magma, C21, C36, C43
Magnesium, B14
Magnetism, E15
Mammals (*Mammalia*), A12, A99
Manta ray, A98
Mantle of Earth, C19
Marble, C46, C47
Margerie Glacier, C24
Maria, C13
Marine food chain, energy pyramid
   for, B25
Marine food web, B21

*Indicates an activity related to this topic.

*Indicates an activity related to this topic.

*Indicates an activity related to this topic.

*Indicates an activity related to this topic.

Teacher's Notes

Credits

Cover Design and Illustration: Robert Brook Allen

Cover Photos: ©Tim Flach/Stone; (bg) ©Darrell Gulin/Natural Selection; (i) ©PhotoSpin 2000.

Illustrations: Kenneth Batelman: pp. C9, C89, F24, F35, F37, F39; Denny Bond: pp. A32, B38; Ka Botzis: pp. B20, B21; Drew-Brook-Cormack: pp. D20, D25; Susan Carlson: p. A12; Karen Carr: p. S1; Andrea Champlin: p. F31; Barbara Cousins: pp. B28 R24, R26, R27, R28; Marie Dauenheimer: pp. A6, A7; John Edwards: pp. C6, E7, E10, E12, F70, F84, F85, F89, F90, F100; Peter Fasolino: pp. E43, E61; Robert Frank: p. B36; Function Thru Form: pp. A32, A62, A117, B18, B20, B21, B24, B25, B27, B40, B51, C7, C8, C31, C33, C37, C39, C46, C50, C65, C72, C76, C103, D6, D7, D8, D10, D11, D16, D17, D25, D26, D30, D35, D38, D39, D41, D43, D51, D53, D69, D81, D85, D86, D89, D93, E15, E26, E27, E29, E30, E31, E32, E36, E37, E39, E46, E69, E82, E86, E92, E97, F6, F7, F10, F11, F12, F18, F19, F20, F21, F22, F23, F36, F38, F51, F55, F57, F59, F60, F61, F66, F69, F71, F76, F108, F110, F112, F117, F119, F124, F125; Thomas Gagliano: pp. D36, D37, D39; Greg Harris: pp. B73, D55; Carlyn Iverson: pp. B32, B80, B81; Sidney Jablonski: p. C86; John Karapelou: pp. R29, R30, R31; Virge Kask: pp. A12, A70, A72, A73, A74, A76, B18, B24, B25; George Kelvin: pp. A24, A35, A52, A53, A54, A79, A81, A82, C12, C14, C19, C20, C25, C47, C49, C62, C63, C74, C75, C88, C90, C91, C102, C103, F27, F85, F101, F118; Katie Lee: pp. A102, B6, B7, B84; Tom Leonard: pp. F102, R20, R21, R22, R32; Rebecca Merrilees: pp. A20, A21, A22, A37, A38, A51; Dave Merrill: pp. B9, B52, B54, C21, D85; Mowry Graphics: pp. D28, D54, D89; Steve Oh: pp. A94, F3, F14, F22, F25, F26, F27, F34, R25, R27, R28, R29, R32, R33, R34; Chris Porter: pp. B7, C14; Saul Rosenbaum: pp. D8, D9, D27, D38, D56, D57, D66, D67, D87, F99, F116, F117; Wendy Smith: pp. A8, A10, A11, A60, A62, F112; Steve Stankiewicz: pp. B64, B77, B89, C32, C52, C73, C78, C100, D18, D40, D53, D60, D69, D89, E38, E42, E92, E94, F74, F86, F93, F101, F104, F105, F110, F122, R8, R9, R12, R13; Art Thompson: pp. C10, C11, D7, D42, D70, D82, D84, E12, E62, E63, E64; Patricia Wynne: pp. R23, R31.

Photography Credits: All photographs are by the Macmillan/McGraw-Hill School Division (MMSD) and Dan Howell for MMSD except as noted below.

Contents: iv: ©Norbert Wu. v: ©Tim Flach/Stone. vi: l ©Jules Cowan/Index Stock Imagery; b ©Joyce Photographics/Photo Researchers, Inc; r ©A.J. Copley/VU. vii: l ©NOAA, colored by John Wells/Science Photo Library/Photo Researchers, Inc; r ©Runk/Schoenberger/Grant Heilman. viii: l ©Roger Ressmeyer/Corbis; b ©Science/VU; ix: ©Duomo/Corbis.

National Geographic Invitation to Science: S1: ©Gianni Tortoli/ Photo Researchers, Inc. S2: ©Tom Bean/Tom & Susan Bean Photography Inc. S3: ©Chris Hondros/Liaison Agency Inc. S4: ©Carlos Munoz-Yague/ Eurelios/Science Photo Library/Photo Researchers, Inc. S5: ©Mark Pilkington/Geological Survey of Canada/Science Photo Library/Photo Researchers, Inc. S7: ©Richard Hutchings.

National Geographic Unit Opener A: A0 ©Kelvin Aitken/Peter Arnold,Inc;A1 ©Norbert Wu; A1 ©Kelvin Aitken/Peter Arnold,Inc. **Unit A:** A2: ©William Waterfall/The Stock Market. A4: ©Ted Levin/Animals Animals/Earth Scenes. A5: ©Richard Hutchings. A6: ©Peter Miller/Photo Researchers, Inc. A7: ©Dick Thomas/VU. A9: ©Rob Hadlow/Bruce Coleman, Inc. A13: (bc) ©Doug Sokell/VU; (br) ©R.M. Meadows/Peter Arnold, Inc.; (bl) ©Veronika Burmeister/VU. A14: (tr) ©Cabisco/VU; (bl) ©Gilbert S. Grant/Photo Researchers, Inc.; (tl) ©Patrick W. Grace/Science Source/Photo Researchers, Inc.; (br) ©R. Kessel-G. Shih/VU; (tc) ©Veronika Burmeister/VU. A15: (br) Blair Seitz/Photo Researchers, Inc.; (bmr) ©A. & F. Michler/Peter Arnold, Inc.; (bml) ©Telegraph Colour Library/FPG; (bl) R. Robinson/VU. A16: (b) ©Adam Jones/Dembinsky Photo Associates; (br) ©Arthur R. Hill/VU. A17: ©Manfred Kage/Peter Arnold, Inc. A18: ©Dominique Braud/Dembinsky Photo Associates. A19: ©Richard Hutchings. A23: (tl) ©George Bernard/Animals Animals/Earth Scenes; (tr) ©Robert Maier/Animals Animals/Earth Scenes; (br) ©Willard Clay/Dembinsky Photo Associates. A25: ©G.Buttner/OKAPIA/Photo Researchers, Inc. A26: (m) ©David S. Addison/VU; (tr) ©Tim Hauf/VU. A27: ©James R. Holland/National Geographic Society. A 28: (inset) Tom & Pat Leeson/Photo Researchers, Inc.; (bl) ©Michael J. Balick/Peter Arnold, Inc.; (br) ©Ray Pfortner/Peter Arnold, Inc. A29: ©J.C. Teyssier/ Publiphoto/Photo Researchers, Inc. A30: ©Robert Maier/Animals Animals/Earth Scenes. A31: ©Richard Hutchings. A32: ©PHOTODISC/ Gettyone. A34: ©Willard Clay/Dembinsky Photo Associates. A36: (t)

©Gerry Ellis/ENP Images; (bl, br) ©Jack M. Bostrack/VU. A37: ©Phil Degginger/Color-Pic. A40: ©Jim Olive/Pictor/Uniphoto. A41: (tl) ©courtesy of Katherine Banks/Prof. K. Banks; (tr) ©Hans Reinhard/ Bruce Coleman, Inc.; (r) ©WHM Bildarchiv/Peter Arnold, Inc. A43: ©Hans Reinhard/Bruce Coleman, Inc. A44: ©Bob Krist/Corbis. A46: ©Michael Fogden/Bruce Coleman, Inc. A47: ©Richard Hutchings. A48: (br) ©David Sieren/VU; (bml) ©Doug Sokell/VU; (bl) ©John Trager/VU. A49: (br) ©E.F.Anderson/ VU; (bl) ©Ed Reschke/Peter Arnold, Inc.; (bc) ©Mike Perry/Pictor/ Uniphoto. A50: (tl) ©Dan Suzio/Photo Researchers, Inc.; (br, tr) ©Richard Hutchings. A51: ©David Dennis/ Animals Animals/Earth Scenes. A54: ©Dick Keen/VU. A55: ©Ed Degginger/Color-Pic, Inc. A56: ©Michael Gadomski/Animals Animals/Earth Scenes. A57: ©Richard Hutchings. A58: (bl) ©Jim Hughes/VU; (br) ©V.P. Weinland/Photo Researchers, Inc.; (bc) ©W. Ormerod/VU. A59: (tr) ©Ed Degginger/ Bruce Coleman, Inc.; (br) ©E. Webber/VU; (bc) ©Gerald & Buff Corsi/VU;(ml) ©Jan Taylor/Bruce Coleman, Inc.; (l) ©John N. Trager/VU. A60: (b) ©Dick Keen/VU; (tr) ©V. McMillan/ VU. A61: (br) ©Bud Nielsen/VU; (t) ©E.F. Anderson/VU. A63: (br) ©Arthur R. Hill/VU; (r) ©Mark S. Skalny/VU. A64: (tr) ©Jerome Wexler/Photo Researchers, Inc.; (tl) ©John Gerlach/VU. A66: (br) ©Jeff Greenberg/ VU; (tr) ©Larry Lefever/Grant Heilman Photography, Inc. A67: ©Jim Sugar Photography/Bettmann/CORBIS. A68: ©Robert P. Carr/Bruce Coleman, Inc. A69: ©Richard Hutchings. A71: (b) ©Adam Jones/Photo Researchers, Inc.; (tl) ©Derrick Ditchburn/VU; (i) ©Doug Sokell/VU. A74: ©Henry T. Kaiser/ Pictor/Uniphoto. A75: (tl) ©Inga Spence/VU; (tr) ©Ken Wagner/VU; (br) ©Stephen J. Lang/VU. A76: ©Scott T. Smith. A78: ©Joel Harrington/VU. A80: ©David Newman/VU. A81: ©R. Calentine/VU. A83: (tr) ©Dick Keen/VU; (br) ©Richard Hutchings. A84: (b) ©Bill Beatty/VU; (tr) ©Parke H. John, Jr./VU. A85: ©Runk/ Schoenberger/ Grant Heilman Photography, Inc. A86: (bg) ©Brock May/Photo Researchers, Inc.; (tr) ©Joel Sartore/Grant Heilman Photography, Inc. A87: ©Catherine Karnow/CORBIS. A89: (b) ©Hans Reinhard/ Bruce Coleman, Inc.; (t) ©John McAnulty/CORBIS. A90: ©R&V Taylor/Bruce Coleman, Inc. A92: ©Frank Krahmer/Bruce Coleman, Inc. A95: (bl) ©BIOS Klein/Hubert/Peter Arnold, Inc.; (m) ©Joe McDonald/Bruce Coleman, Inc.; (tr) ©John Hyde/Bruce Coleman, Inc. A96: (mr, br) ©Ed Degginger/Color-Pic; (tr) ©Jeff Mondragon/ Mondragon Photography; (ml) ©Scott Johnson/Animals Animals/ Earth Scenes; (tl) ©Susan Blanchet/Dembinsky Photo Associates; (bl) ©Tom E. Adams/Peter Arnold, Inc. A97: (bl) © Breck P. Kent/ Animals Animals/Earth Scenes; (tr, br) ©Fred Bavendam/Peter Arnold, Inc.; (tl) ©Hans Pfletschinger/Peter Arnold, Inc.; (ml) ©Jeff J. Daly/Stock Boston; (mr) ©Pictor/Uniphoto; (m) ©Robert Lubeck/Animals Animals/ Earth Scenes. A98: (br) ©Gary Meszaros/ Bruce Coleman, Inc.; (mr) ©Marilyn Kazmers/Dembinsky Photo Associates; (ml) ©Norbert Wu/Peter Arnold, Inc.; (bl) ©Skip Moody/Dembinsky Photo Associates; (tr) ©Pictor/Uniphoto; (tl) ©Zig Leszczynski/Animals Animals/Earth Scenes. A99: (mr) ©Bob Cranston/Animals Animals/ Earth Scenes; (tl) ©Darrell Gulin/CORBIS; (m) ©Des & Jen Bartlett/ Bruce Coleman, Inc.; (ml) ©Ed Degginger/ Color-Pic; (tm) ©Michael Newman/PhotoEdit; (br) ©Rob Simpson/ Pictor/Uniphoto; (tr) ©Pictor/Uniphoto. A100: (tr) Mark Downey/Lucid Images/ Picturequest; (bm) ©Jim Roetzel/Dembinsky Photo Associates; (tl) ©John Cancalosi/Peter Arnold, Inc.; (br) ©John Shaw/Bruce Coleman, Inc.; (m) ©Skip Moody/Dembinsky Photo Associates. A101: ©Graham Pizzey/Bruce Coleman, Inc. A104: (bg) ©John Gerlach/Dembinsky Photo Associates; (m) ©Rolf Kopfle/ Bruce Coleman, Inc. A106: (tr) ©Stan W. Elems/VU; (bl) ©L. West/ Bruce Coleman, Inc.; (br) ©Stan W. Elems/VU. A107: (bl) ©Ed Degginger/Color-Pic; (br) ©Rod Planck/Dembinsky Photo Associates; (tl) ©Stan W. Elems/VU. A108: ©Steve Kaufman/Peter Arnold, Inc. A109: ©Kim Taylor/Bruce Coleman, Inc. A110: ©Ed Degginger/ Color-Pic. A111: (bl) ©D. Robert Franz/Bruce Coleman, Inc.; (br) ©Erwin & Peggy Bauer/Bruce Coleman, Inc.; (tc) ©John Shaw/Bruce Coleman, Inc.; (tl) ©John Snyder/Bruce Coleman, Inc.; (tr) ©Skip Moody/Dembinsky Photo Associates. A112: (ml, tr) ©Ed Degginger/Color-Pic; (tl) ©Randa Bishop/Pictor/Uniphoto. A113: (br) ©Fritz Prenzel/Animals Animals/Earth Scenes; (bm, bl) ©Hans Reinhard/Bruce Coleman, Inc. A114: ©Stan Osolinski/Dembinsky Photo Associates. A115: ©Gerard Lacz/Animals Animals/Earth Scenes. A118: ©Courtesy of HSWRI. A119: ©Courtesy of HSWRI.

National Geographic Unit Opener B: B0 ©Tim Flach/Stone; B1 ©Art Wolfe/Stone; B1 ©Tim Flach/Stone. **Unit B:** B2: ©Lee Rentz/Bruce Coleman, Inc. B4: ©Zig Leszczynski/Animals Animals/Earth Scenes. B5: ©Richard Hutchings. B8: (t) ©John Shaw/Bruce Coleman, Inc.; (br) ©John Shaw/Bruce Coleman, Inc. B9: (tc) ©David J. Sams/ Stock, Boston; (br) ©Joe McDonald/CORBIS; (bl) ©John Giustina/ Bruce Coleman, Inc. B10: ©Lee Rentz/Bruce Coleman, Inc. B11: (tr) ©Laura Riley/Bruce Coleman, Inc.; (br) ©Robert M. Balou/Animals Animals/ Earth Scenes. B12: (b) ©Bruce Coleman, Inc.; (tr) ©N.E. Swedberg/ Bruce Coleman, Inc. B13: ©Joe McDonald/Animals Animals/Earth Scenes. B14: ©John Shaw/Bruce Coleman, Inc. B16: ©Beverly Joubert/National Geographic Collection/GettyOne Images. B19:

R 66

©Richard Hutchings. D88: (bl) ©Science/VU (br) ©VU. D89: ©Jim Sugar Photography/CORBIS. D90: (tr) ©Don Smetzer/Stone; (br) ©Jeff Greenberg/PhotoEdit D91: ©Frost Fair on the Thames, Abraham Hondius, Museum of London, UK/The Bridgeman Art Library International Ltd. D93: ©Mark A. Schneider/Dembinsky Photo Associates. D94: (r) ©CORBIS; (tl) ©courtesy of Dr. Henry Diaz/Climate Diagnostics Ctr, NOAA. D95: ©Jim Sugar/CORBIS.

National Geographic Unit Opener E: E0, E1 ©Roger Ressmeyer/ CORBIS. **Unit E:** E2: ©Christine Osborne/CORBIS. E4: ©Michael T. Sedam/CORBIS. E5: ©Richard Hutchings. E6: ©Ken Karp/McGraw-Hill School Division. E8: (m,bl,br) ©Ken Karp/McGraw-Hill School Division. E9: ©Richard Hutchings. E11: (tl) Klaus Guldbransen/Photo researchers, Inc.; (tr) George Bernard/Photo researchers, Inc.; (bl) ©Buddy Mays/Bettmann /CORBIS; (ml) ©The Purcell Team/ Bettmann/CORBIS; (mr) ©Vaughan Fleming/ Science Photo Library/ Photo Researchers, Inc.; (br) ©Wolfgang Kaehler/ Bettmann/ CORBIS. E13: ©Walter Meayers Edwards. E14: (bl) ©Kim Sayer/ CORBIS; (tr) ©Phil Degginger/Color-Pic; (br) ©Phil Degginger/Color-Pic. E16: (m) ©IBM Research/Peter Arnold, Inc.; (tr) ©Lawrence Livermore National Laboratory/Science Photo Library/Photo Researchers, Inc.; (b) ©National Railway of Japan/PhotoTake. E18: ©Rod Plack/Photo Researchers, Inc. E20: ©NASA/Science Photo Library/Photo Researchers, Inc. E21: ©Richard Hutchings. E22: (m) ©Lowell Georgia /Photo Researchers, Inc.; (b) ©Rich Treptow/Photo Researchers, Inc. E23: (bl, mr, tr, br) ©Charles D. Winters/Photo Researchers, Inc.; (ml) ©Russ Lappa/ Science Source/Photo Researchers, Inc.; (tl) ©Science/ VU. E24: (i) ©Bill Beatty/VU/ Visuals Unlimited.; (m) ©Charles D. Winters/Photo Researchers, Inc.; (br) ©1998 PhotoDisc, Inc.; (bl) ©Yoav Levy/PhotoTake. E25: (tl) ©David Taylor/Photo Researchers, Inc.; (tc) ©David Taylor/Photo Researchers, Inc.; (tr) ©David Taylor/Photo Researchers, Inc. E28: (bl) ©Charles D. Winters/Photo Researchers, Inc.; (tr, tl, bmr) ©Dr. E. R. Degginger/Color-Pic; (ml) ©George Bernard/Photo Researchers, Inc.; (m, mr) ©Klaus Guldbrandsen/ Science Photo Library/Photo Researchers, Inc.; (br) ©Russ Lappa/Photo Researchers, Inc. E32: (bl, ml) ©Christine Coscioni/CO2, Inc.; (tr) ©Leonard Lessin/Peter Arnold, Inc. E33: (r) ©The Image Bank/ GETTYONE. E34: ©W.Wisniewski/Okapia/Photo Researchers, Inc. E35: ©Richard Hutchings. E36: (bc) ©Clyde H. Smith/Peter Arnold, Inc.; (bl) ©Gordon Wiltsie/Peter Arnold, Inc.; (br) ©Jeff & Alexa Henry/Peter Arnold, Inc. E37: ©Cesar Llacuna. E40: (umr) ©Carolina Biological Supply/PhotoTake.; (tr) ©Cesar Llacuna; (br, bmr) ©Charles D. Winters/Photo Researchers, Inc. (m) ©Christine L. Coscioni/CO2, Inc. E41: ©Richard Hutchings. E42: (bl) ©Jack Plekan/Fundamental Photographs; (tr) ©Richard Choy/Peter Arnold, Inc.; (br) ©Chris Rogers/The Stock Market. E44: (tr) ©Vic Bider/ PhotoEdit. E45: (m) ©Charles Pefley/Stock Boston; (b) ©Deborah Davis/PhotoEdit; (tr) ©Hal Charms/PhotoEdit. E48: ©Paul A. Souders/ CORBIS. E50: ©Nathan Benn/CORBIS. E51: ©Richard Hutchings. E52: (bl) ©Charles D. Winters/Photo Researchers, Inc.; (br) ©Jacana/Photo Researchers, Inc. E53: (m) ©Becky Luigart-Stayner/CORBIS; (bl,tr) ©Dr. Ed Degginger/Color-Pic; (tl,br) ©Phil Degginger/Color-Pic. E54: (bl, br) ©Phil Degginger/Color-Pic; (tr) ©Richard Hutchings. E55: (bmr) ©Adam Jones/Photo Researchers, Inc.; (m) ©Artville; (b) ©EyeWire/ GETTYONE; (br, tr, umr) ©Phil Degginger/Color-Pic. E56: (tr) ©Charles D. Winters/Photo Researchers, Inc.; (b) ©Phil Degginger/Color-Pic. E57: (tc, tr) ©Richard Hutchings; (tl) ©Richard Megna/ Fundamental Photographs. E59: (tr) ©Joyce Photographics/Photo Researchers, Inc.; (bl, br) ©Richard Hutchings. E60: ©S. Strickland/ Naturescapes/VU. E61: (l) ©M.I. Walker/Photo Researchers, Inc.; (br) ©Richard Hutchings. E62: (bl) ©Richard Hutchings. E64: ©Mark E. Gibson/VU. E65: ©PhotoDisc. E66: ©Larry Lefever/Grant Heilman Photography, Inc. E67: (l) ©David R. Frazier/ Photo Researchers, Inc.; (r) ©David S. Addison/VU. E68: ©Nik Wheeler/CORBIS. E70: ©Richard Hutchings. E71: ©Richard Hutchings. E72: (bl) ©Ed Degginger/Color-Pic; (br) ©Richard Hutchings. E73: (br) ©Lee Snyder/Photo Researchers, Inc.; (tr, tl) ©Richard Hutchings; (bl) ©Richard Megna/Fundamental Photographs. E74: (l inset) ©Science/ VU; (tl) ©Christine L. Coscioni/ CO2, Inc.; (tr, r inset) ©Leonard Lessin/Peter Arnold, Inc.; (br) ©NASA. E75: ©Richard Hutchings. E76: (tr) ©Cesar Llacuna; (bl) ©Christine Coscioni/CO2, Inc. E78: (br) ©Henry Horenstein/Stock Boston; . E79: (bg) ©LSF OSF/ Animals Animals/Earth Scenes; (tl) ©Michael Newman/ PhotoEdit. E80: ©Michael P. Gadomski/Photo Researchers, Inc. E82: (bmr) ©PhotoDisc; (br) ©Ed Degginger/Color-Pic; (bml) ©Ken Karp; (bl) ©Richard Megna/Fundamental Photographs. E83: ©Kristen Brochmann/ Fundamental Photographs. E84: (tl) ©John Cunningham/ VU; (bl) ©Geoff Bryant/Photo Researchers, Inc. E85: ©Ken Karp. E86: ©Renee Lynn/Photo Researchers, Inc. E87: (b,m) ©Dan Howell; (tl) ©Ed Degginger/Color-Pic. E88: ©Paul Silverman/Fundamental

Photographs. E89: ©Tony Freeman/ PhotoEdit. E90: ©Denise Mattia/Denise Mattia Underwater Photography. E91: ©Richard Hutchings. E96: (bl) ©Andrew McClenaghan/Photo Researchers, Inc.; (r) ©Science/VU. E97: ©Michael Dalton/Fundamental Photographs. E98: ©Richard Hutchings. E99: ©Sheila Terry/Photo Researcher, Inc. E101: ©Craig Lovell/ Bettmann/ CORBIS. E102: (tr) ©Courtesy of Dr Mario Molina/MIT; (m) ©NASA/Science Photo Library/Photo Researchers, Inc. E103: (m) ©NASA/Photo Researchers, Inc.

National Geographic Unit Opener F: F0 ©Comstock; F1 ©Duomo/ CORBIS. **Unit F:** F2: ©Photri/Tom Sanders/The Stock Market. F4: ©Annie Griffiths Belt/CORBIS. F7: ©Paul Silverman/Fundamental Photographs. F8: (m) ©NASA/Ed Degginger/Color-Pic; (b) ©Neil Rabinowitz/CORBIS. F9: (br) ©Duomo/Chris Trotman/Duomo Photography Inc.; (bl) ©Joe McDonald/CORBIS; (tl) 'Museum of Flight'/CORBIS. F10: ©Bill Aron/Photo Researchers, Inc. F11: ©Jerry Wachter/Photo Researchers, Inc. F12: ©Peter Turnley/CORBIS. F13: (b) ©George Lepp/CORBIS; (tr) ©Robert Mathena/Fundamental Photographs. F15: ©TSM/Photri/The Stock Market. F16: ©Ed Kashi/ CORBIS. F20: (tr,lmr) ©Ed Degginger/Color-Pic; (umr,br) ©Tony Freeman/PhotoEdit. F21: (br) ©Ed Degginger/Color-Pic; (tr) ©Phil Degginger/Color-Pic. F22: ©LBJ Space Center/Nasa NASA. F28: (b) ©Kevin R. Morris/CORBIS; (tr) ©Paul A. Souders/CORBIS; (mr) ©Peter Turnley/CORBIS; (ml) ©Russ Schleipman/CORBIS. F30: (t) ©Barney McGrath/Science Photo Library/Photo Researchers, Inc.; (m) ©JPL/NASA; (b) ©MSSS/JPL/NASA/ Science Photo Library/ Photo Researchers, Inc. F32: ©Bettmann/CORBIS. F35: ©G.Sauvage/ Vandystadt/Photo Researchers, Inc. F36: ©J-L Charmet/Science/ Photo Library/Photo Researchers, Inc. F40: (tr) ©Davis Barber/ PhotoEdit; (bl) ©Kevin R. Morris/CORBIS; (tl) ©The Image Bank/ Gettyone. F41: ©NASA/Media Dallas. F42: (bg) ©JSC/NASA; (bl) ©Zero/JSC/NASA. F45: ©NASA. F46: ©Miro/Vintoniv/Stock Boston F48: ©NASA/Galaxy Contact/Oxford Scientific Film and Photo Library. F49: ©Richard Hutchings. F50: (bl,bml,bmr) ©Artville; (br) ©Cartesia Software. F52: (tl) ©PhotoDisc; (b) ©Ken Fisher/Stone. F54: ©Ulrike Welsch. F55: ©Richard Hutchings. F56: ©Artville LLC 1997. F57: ©Tim Davis/Photo Researchers, Inc. F58: (bl) ©Courtesy Alexander Graham Bell/National Historic Park; (tr) ©William James Warren/CORBIS. F59: ©George Hall/CORBIS. F60: ©1998 PhotoDisc, Inc. F61: ©Dr. Jeremy Burgess/ Photo Researchers, Inc. F62: ©Brenda Tharp/Photo Researchers, Inc. F64: ©Kevin Fleming/CORBIS. F65: ©Richard Hutchings. F66: (br) Allsport/Brian Bahr; (bl) ©Duomo/ CORBIS. F67: (tr) ©Marty Loken/ Stone; (br) ©Museum der Stadt, Vienna/Austria Superstock. F68: (br) ©TSM/John M. Roberts/The Stock Market. F69: ©Wolfgang Kaehler/ CORBIS. F72: (tr) ©Artville; (b) ©Joseph Schuyler/Stock Boston. F73: ©Luc Novovitch/Gamma Liaison Agency. F77: ©Artville. F78: ©VCG/FPG. F80: ©Richard Cummins/CORBIS. F81: ©Richard Hutchings. F82: (tr) ©Arthur Morris/VU; (b) ©Robert Holmgren/Peter Arnold, Inc. F83: (t) ©Barb Gerlach/VU; (mr) ©C.P. George/VU; (m) ©Rich Treptow/ VU. F84: ©Richard Hutchings. F85: ©Image courtesy of Barry Luokkala, Department of Physics/Carnegie Mellon University. F86: (br) ©Richard Hutchings; (tl) ©PhotoDisc. F87: (tr) ©Paul Silverman/ Fundamental Photographs; (bl, m) ©Richard Hutchings. F88: (mr,tr) ©Richard Hutchings; (bc, bl) ©Roger Ressmeyer/CORBIS. F90: ©Cesar Llacuna. F91: ©Dr. Ed Degginger/ Color-Pic. F92: (bc) ©North Wind Picture Archive/North Wind Pictures; (bl) ©Science Photo Library/ Photo Researchers, Inc.; (r) ©Wolfgang Kaehler/ CORBIS. F93: (bl) ©The Queens Borough Public Library, Long Island Division, Latimer Family Papers/The Queens Borough Library; (bc) ©The Schenectady Museum. F94: ©Jack Plekan/Fundamental Photographs. F95: ©Richard Hutchings. F96: (m) ©Alfred Pasieka/ Science Photo Library/ Photo Researchers, Inc.; (b) ©Richard Hutchings; (tr) ©Science/VU. F97: (tr) ©Jeff Greenberg/VU; (bl, br) ©Richard Hutchings. F98: (tr) ©Bill Beatty/VU; (bl, ml) ©Richard Hutchings. F99: ©Richard Hutchings. F100: (tl) ©PhotoDisc, 2000; (r,bc) ©Richard Hutchings. F103: ©James Webb/PhotoTake. F106: ©Jeremy Walker/Stone Gettyone. F107: ©Richard Hutchings. F109: ©Richard Hutchings. F113: ©Ed Degginger/Color-Pic. F114: ©NASA/ Media Dallas. F116: ©Richard Hutchings. F118: ©Bettmann/CORBIS. F119: ©Hewlitt Packard Fundamental Photographs. F120: (br) ©1998 PhotoDisc, Inc.; (i) ©Science/VU. F121: ©Carolyn A. McKeone/Photo Researchers, Inc. F122: ©Science/VU. F126: (t) ©Gary Gold/Rennsslaer Polytechnical Institute; (b) ©courtesy of Dr. Shirley Jackson/Rennsslaer Polytechnical Institute.

Science and Health Handbook: All photos ©Richard Hutchings with the following exceptions: R10: (m) ©Jim Harrison/Stock Boston/PNI. R14: (m) ©G.R. Roberts/Photo Researchers, Inc.

Teacher's Notes

Contents

Correlated to
National Science Education Content Standards
(Grades 5–8)

National Science Education Content Standards	Units of *McGraw-Hill Science*: Grade 5					
	UNIT A Structures of Plants/Animals	**UNIT B** Interactions of Living Things	**UNIT C** Earth and Its Resources	**UNIT D** Weather and Climate	**UNIT E** Properties of Matter/Energy	**UNIT F** Motion and Energy
Science as Inquiry						
Abilities necessary to do scientific inquiry	✔	✔	✔	✔	✔	✔
Understanding about scientific inquiry	✔	✔	✔	✔	✔	✔
Physical Science						
Properties and changes of properties in matter	✔	✔	✔	✔	✔	
Motion and forces			✔	✔		✔
Transfer of energy	✔	✔	✔	✔	✔	✔
Life Science						
Structure and function in living things	✔					
Reproduction and heredity	✔					
Regulation and behavior	✔	✔				
Populations and ecosystems	✔	✔				
Diversity and adaptations of organisms	✔	✔			✔	
Earth and Space Science						
Structure of the Earth system	✔	✔	✔	✔		✔
Earth's history	✔	✔	✔	✔		
Earth in the solar system			✔	✔		✔
Science and Technology						
Abilities of technological design	✔	✔	✔	✔	✔	✔
Understanding about science and technology	✔	✔	✔	✔	✔	✔
Science in Personal and Social Perspectives						
Personal health	✔	✔	✔	✔	✔	
Populations, resources, and environments	✔	✔				✔
Natural hazards	✔	✔	✔	✔		
Risks and benefits	✔	✔	✔	✔	✔	
Science and Technology in Society	✔	✔	✔	✔	✔	✔
Nature and History of Science						
Science as a human endeavor; Nature of science	✔	✔	✔	✔	✔	✔
History of science	✔			✔	✔	✔
Unifying Concepts and Processes						
Systems, order, and organization	✔	✔	✔	✔	✔	
Evidence, models, and explanation	✔	✔	✔	✔	✔	✔
Change, constancy, measurement	✔	✔	✔	✔	✔	✔
Evolution and equilibrium		✔	✔			
Form and function	✔					

Correlated to
Benchmarks for Science Literacy
(Grades 3–5)

	Units of *McGraw-Hill Science:* Grade 5					
	UNIT A Structures of Plants and Animals	**UNIT B** Interactions of Living Things	**UNIT C** Earth and Its Resources	**UNIT D** Weather and Climate	**UNIT E** Properties of Matter and Energy	**UNIT F** Motion and Energy
The Nature of Science						
Scientific view of the world	✔	✔	✔	✔	✔	✔
Scientific inquiry	✔	✔	✔	✔	✔	✔
The scientific enterprise	✔	✔	✔	✔	✔	✔
The Nature of Technology						
Technology and science	✔		✔		✔	✔
Design and systems			✔	✔	✔	✔
Issues in technology	✔	✔	✔			✔
The Physical Setting						
The universe			✔	✔		✔
The Earth	✔		✔	✔		✔
Processes that shape Earth			✔			✔
Structure of Matter			✔	✔		
Energy transformations			✔	✔		
Motion			✔	✔		✔
Forces of nature	✔	✔	✔			✔
The Living Environment						
Diversity of life	✔	✔	✔		✔	✔
Heredity	✔	✔				
Cells	✔					
Interdependence of life	✔	✔				
Flow of matter and energy	✔	✔	✔			
Evolution of life	✔	✔				
The Human Organism						
Human identity	✔	✔		✔	✔	✔
Basic functions	✔	✔			✔	
Physical health	✔	✔			✔	✔
Common Themes						
Systems	✔	✔	✔	✔	✔	✔
Models		✔	✔	✔	✔	✔
Constancy and change	✔	✔	✔	✔	✔	✔
Scale	✔	✔			✔	✔

McGraw-Hill Curriculum Integration: Science and Reading

Correlation of *McGraw-Hill Science* with:
- *Spotlight on Literacy* • *McGraw-Hill Reading*

McGraw-Hill Science correlates with these reading programs by means of its content as well as of the Reading Skills highlighted in each unit.

McGraw-Hill Science Grade 5	Spotlight on Literacy selections with corresponding content or skills	McGraw-Hill Reading selections with corresponding content or skills
UNIT A STRUCTURES OF PLANTS AND ANIMALS **Topic Focus** • diversity of life • using sunlight to make food • survival, response • reproduction, life cycles **Process Skill Builders** • Experiment • Classify • Observe **Chapter Reading Skills** • Draw conclusions • Summarize • Compare and contrast	**Content** • The Gold Coin (farming, crops) • The Best Bad Thing (harvesting, crops) **Skills** *Draw conclusions* • The Voyage of the *Dawn Treader* • The Gold Coin *Compare and contrast* • Dive to the Coral Reefs • New Providence: A Changing Cityscape *Summarize* • Dive to the Coral Reefs • The News About Dinosaurs	**Content** • The Gold Coin (farming, crops) • Carlos and the Skunk • Tonweya and the Eagles **Skills** *Draw conclusions* • The Voyage of the *Dawn Treader* * • Hot on Lewis & Clark's Trail *Compare and contrast* • The Riddle * • Breaker's Bridge *Summarize* • The Marble Champ * • The Paper Dragon
UNIT B INTERACTIONS OF LIVING THINGS **Topic Focus** • ecosystems, roles of living things • cycles • biomes, oceans & land • change in ecosystems • environmental concerns **Process Skill Builders** • Use variables • Infer **Chapter Reading Skills** • Sequence of Events • Summarize	**Content** • Dive to the Coral Reefs (ocean ecosystems) • Human-Made Reef Relief • Grandma Essie's Covered Wagon (prairie) • The News About Dinosaurs (ancient ecosystems) **Skills** *Sequence of events* • It's Our World, Too! • Breaker's Bridge *Summarize* • Dive to the Coral Reefs • A Wave in Her Pocket	**Content** • Amazon Alert (rain forests) • An Island Scrapbook **Skills** *Sequence of events* • The Paper Dragon * • Amazon Alert! *Summarize* • The Marble Champ * • The Paper Dragon
UNIT C EARTH AND ITS RESOURCES **Topic Focus** • Earth in space • changes on Earth, landforms • minerals, rocks, soil • Earth's air, water, energy • environmental concerns **Process Skill Builders** • Define • Form a hypothesis **Chapter Reading Skills** • Sequence of events • Draw conclusions	**Content** • New Providence: A Changing Cityscape (human impact on land) • Identified Flying Objects (solar system) • It's Our World, Too! **Skills** *Sequence of events* • It's Our World, Too! • Breaker's Bridge *Draw conclusions* • The Voyage of the *Dawn Treader* • Einstein Anderson	**Content** • It's Our World, Too! • Cleaning Up America's Air **Skills** *Sequence of events* • The Paper Dragon * • Amazon Alert! *Draw conclusions* • The Voyage of the *Dawn Treader* * • Hot on Lewis & Clark's Trail

*Skill is introduced in McGraw-Hill Reading with a two-page lesson that accompanies the selection.

McGraw-Hill Science Grade 5	**Spotlight on Literacy** selections with corresponding content or skills	**McGraw-Hill Reading** selections with corresponding content or skills
UNIT D WEATHER AND CLIMATE **Topic Focus** • the Sun as energy source • water cycle, making clouds • weather conditions, storms • climate, past and present **Process Skill Builder:** • Interpret data • Measure **Chapter Reading Skills** • Find the main idea & supporting details • Sequence of events	**Content** • The Big Storm ***Main idea & supporting details*** • Dive to the Coral Reefs • The News About Dinosaurs ***Sequence of events*** • It's Our World, Too! • The Big Storm • Breaker's Bridge • Tonweya and the Eagles • Klondike Fever	**Content** • Tornado Watch: Tracking Storms • The Big Storm **Skills** ***Main idea & supporting details*** • It's Our World, Too! * • Rediscovering Jamestown ***Sequence of events*** • The Paper Dragon * • Grandma Essie's Covered Wagon
UNIT E PROPERTIES OF MATTER AND ENERGY **Topic Focus** • properties, atomic structure • solids, liquids, gases • mixtures, acids, bases • chemical changes, energy **Process Skill Builder** • Make a model • Experiment **Chapter Reading Skills** • Find the main idea & supporting details • Cause and effect	**Content** • Money, Money, Money (metals as money) • Klondike Fever (gold) **Skills:** ***Main idea & supporting details*** • Dive to the Coral Reefs • The News About Dinosaurs ***Cause and effect*** • Klondike Fever • The Wreck of the *Zephyr*	**Content** ***Main idea & supporting details*** • It's Our World, Too! * • Rediscovering Jamestown ***Cause and effect*** • Wilma Unlimited * • Sea Maidens of Japan
UNIT F MOTION AND ENERGY **Topic Focus** • Newton's Laws • nature of sound, properties of sound • visible light, mirrors, lenses, color • uses of invisible light • how scientists found out what light is **Process Skill Builder** • Use numbers • Communicate • Predict **Chapter Reading Skills** • Draw conclusions • Cause and effect • Compare and contrast	**Content** • How to Think Like a Scientist **Skills** ***Predict*** • The Talking Eggs • The Voyage of the *Dawn Treader* ***Draw conclusions*** • The Voyage of the *Dawn Treader* • Einstein Anderson ***Cause and effect*** • The Silent Lobby • The Wreck of the *Zephyr* ***Compare and contrast*** • Dive to the Coral Reefs • New Providence: A Changing Cityscape	**Content** • How to Think Like a Scientist • The Marble Champ **Skills** ***Predict*** • The Gold Coin * • Dear Mr. Henshaw ***Draw conclusions*** • The Voyage of the *Dawn Treader* * • Hot on Lewis & Clark's Trail ***Cause and effect*** • Wilma Unlimited * • Amazon Alert ***Compare and contrast*** • The Riddle * • Breaker's Bridge

Inch Graph Paper

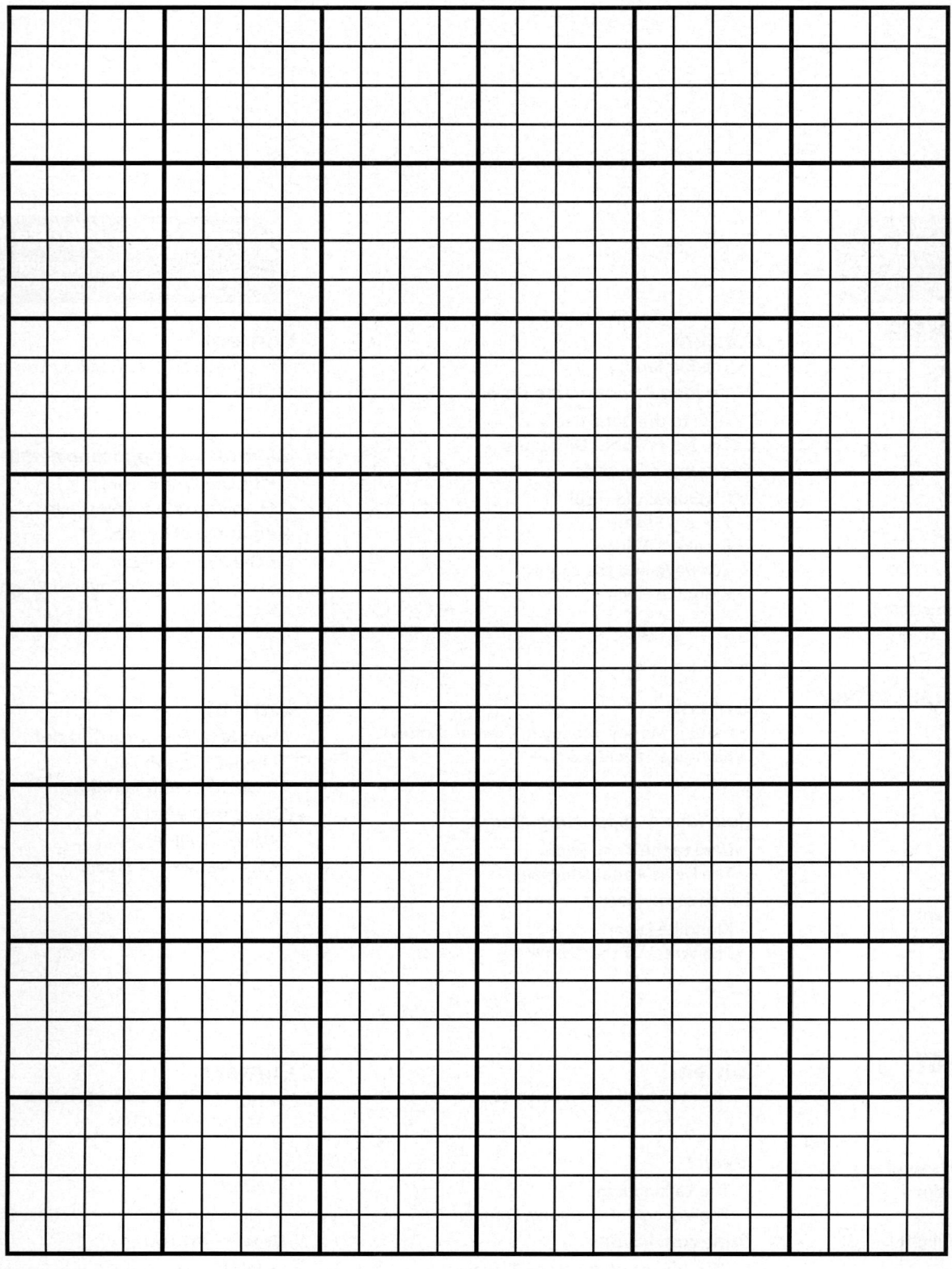

Macmillan/McGraw-Hill

Rulers: Inch, Centimeter

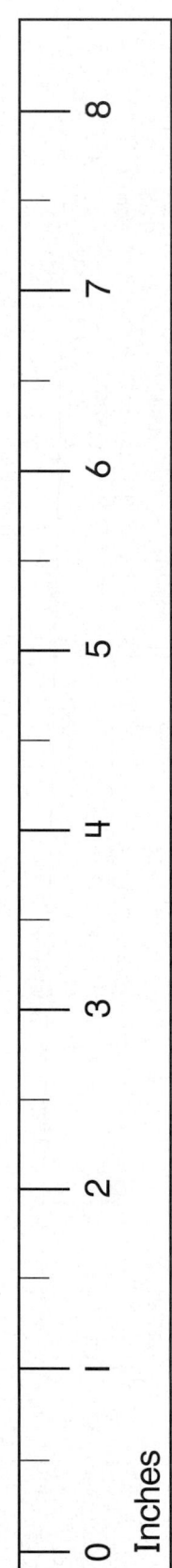

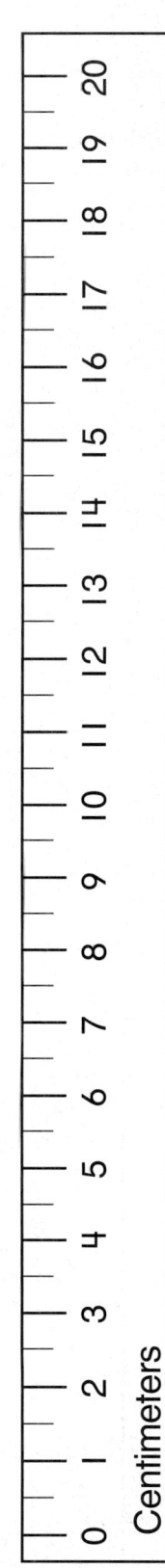

Map of United States

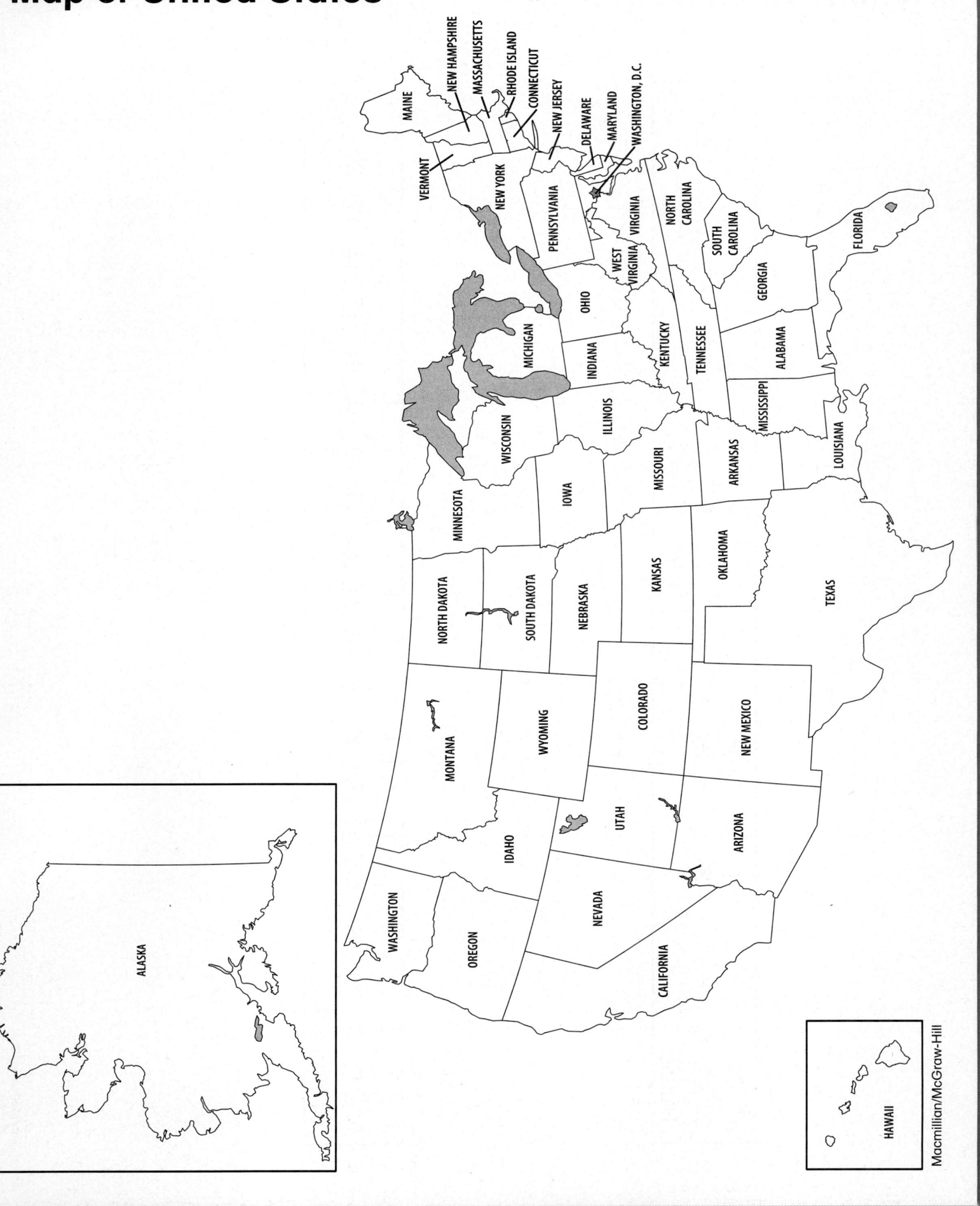

Macmillian/McGraw-Hill

World Map

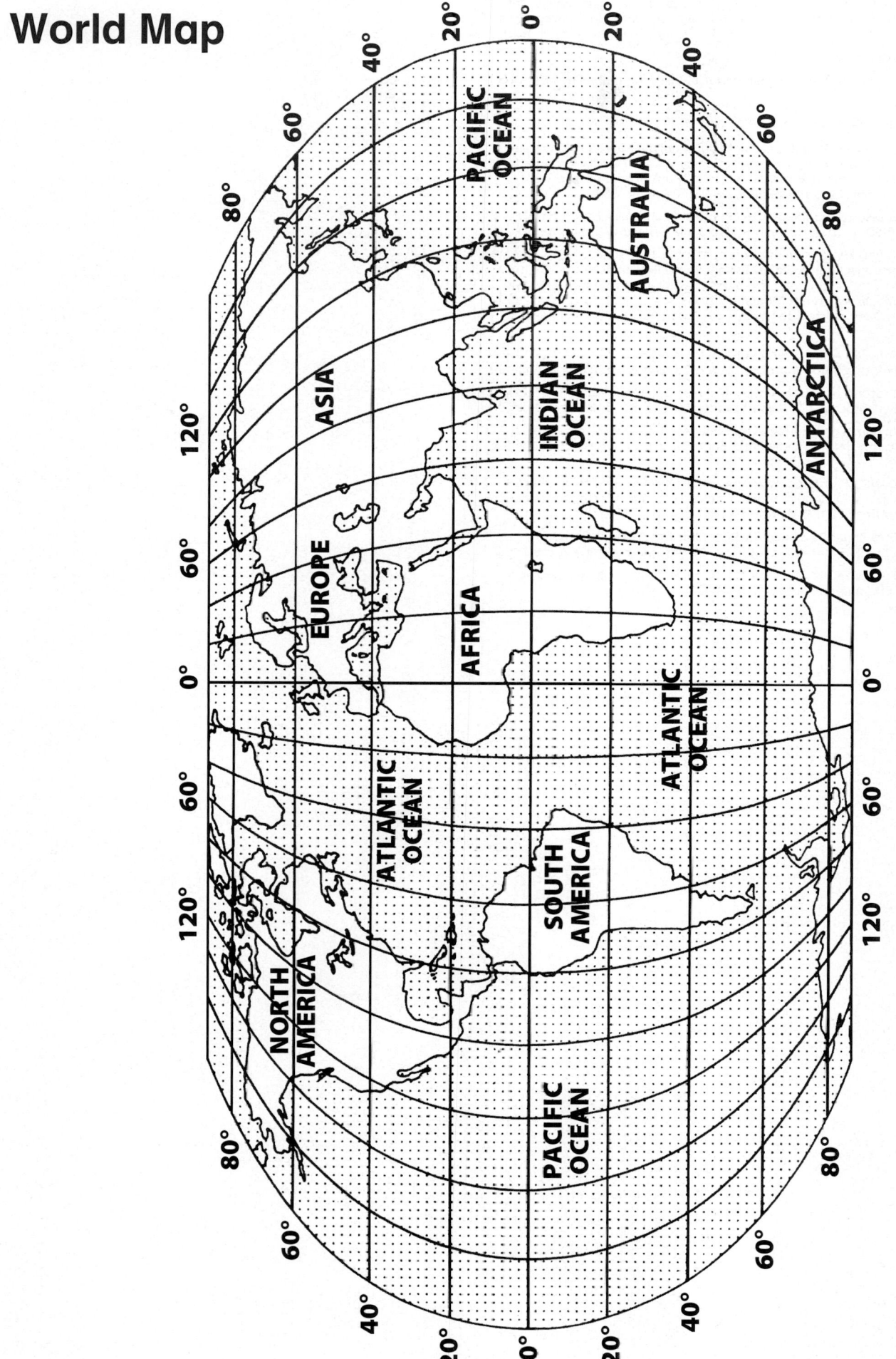

Credits for Teacher's Edition

Teacher's Notes

Teacher's Notes

Teacher's Notes

Teacher's Notes

Teacher's Notes

PERIODIC TABLE OF THE ELEMENTS

Key

6 — Atomic number
C — Element symbol
Carbon — Element name

Phase at 20° C

C	Solid
Br	Liquid
H	Gas

Metallic Properties

Li	Metal
B	Metalloid
C	Nonmetal

1	2	3	4	5	6	7	8	9	10	11	12	13	14	15	16	17	18
1 **H** Hydrogen																	2 **He** Helium
3 **Li** Lithium	4 **Be** Beryllium											5 **B** Boron	6 **C** Carbon	7 **N** Nitrogen	8 **O** Oxygen	9 **F** Fluorine	10 **Ne** Neon
11 **Na** Sodium	12 **Mg** Magnesium											13 **Al** Aluminum	14 **Si** Silicon	15 **P** Phosphorus	16 **S** Sulfur	17 **Cl** Chlorine	18 **Ar** Argon
19 **K** Potassium	20 **Ca** Calcium	21 **Sc** Scandium	22 **Ti** Titanium	23 **V** Vanadium	24 **Cr** Chromium	25 **Mn** Manganese	26 **Fe** Iron	27 **Co** Cobalt	28 **Ni** Nickel	29 **Cu** Copper	30 **Zn** Zinc	31 **Ga** Gallium	32 **Ge** Germanium	33 **As** Arsenic	34 **Se** Selenium	35 **Br** Bromine	36 **Kr** Krypton
37 **Rb** Rubidium	38 **Sr** Strontium	39 **Y** Yttrium	40 **Zr** Zirconium	41 **Nb** Niobium	42 **Mo** Molybdenum	43 **Tc** Technetium	44 **Ru** Ruthenium	45 **Rh** Rhodium	46 **Pd** Palladium	47 **Ag** Silver	48 **Cd** Cadmium	49 **In** Indium	50 **Sn** Tin	51 **Sb** Antimony	52 **Te** Tellurium	53 **I** Iodine	54 **Xe** Xenon
55 **Cs** Cesium	56 **Ba** Barium	71 **Lu** Lutetium	72 **Hf** Hafnium	73 **Ta** Tantalum	74 **W** Tungsten	75 **Re** Rhenium	76 **Os** Osmium	77 **Ir** Iridium	78 **Pt** Platinum	79 **Au** Gold	80 **Hg** Mercury	81 **Ti** Thallium	82 **Pb** Lead	83 **Bi** Bismuth	84 **Po** Polonium	85 **At** Astatine	86 **Rn** Radon
87 **Fr** Francium	88 **Ra** Radium	103 **Lr** Lawrencium	104 **Rf** Rutherfordium	105 **Db** Dubnium	106 **Sg** Seaborgium	107 **Bh** Bohrium	108 **Hs** Hassium	109 **Mt** Meitnerium	110	111	112		114		116		118

Lanthanide Series

| 57 **La** Lanthanum | 58 **Ce** Cerium | 59 **Pr** Praseodymium | 60 **Nd** Neodymium | 61 **Pm** Promethium | 62 **Sm** Samarium | 63 **Eu** Europium | 64 **Gd** Gadolinium | 65 **Tb** Terbium | 66 **Dy** Dysprosium | 67 **Ho** Holmium | 68 **Er** Erbium | 69 **Tm** Thulium | 70 **Yb** Ytterbium |

Actinide Series

| 89 **Ac** Actinium | 90 **Th** Thorium | 91 **Pa** Protactinium | 92 **U** Uranium | 93 **Np** Neptunium | 94 **Pu** Plutonium | 95 **Am** Americium | 96 **Cm** Curium | 97 **Bk** Berkelium | 98 **Cf** Californium | 99 **Es** Einsteinium | 100 **Fm** Fermium | 101 **Md** Mendelevium | 102 **No** Nobelium |

Structures of Plants and Animals

Main Idea: All living things can be classified based on similarities and differences. Plants use photosynthesis to produce their own food. Animals must get food by eating plants or other animals. Sexual and asexual reproduction is found in plants and animals.

Unit Organizer

CHAPTER 1 Plants and Their Parts, *pp. A2–A43*

Main Idea: Plants have great diversity in both nonvascular and vascular groups. However, all plants have chlorophyll, enabling them to make food. Vascular plants have special tissue for transporting materials.

LESSON 1 Classifying Living Things, *pp. A4–A17*

Main Idea: All plants have common characteristics, such as the same parts and the ability to make food.

LESSON 2 Roots, Stems, and Leaves, *pp. A18–A27*

Main Idea: All plants have certain parts with the same function.

LESSON 3 The Importance of Plants, *pp. A30–A39*

Main Idea: Plants make food and produce oxygen through photosynthesis.

CHAPTER 2 Plant Diversity, *pp. A44–A89*

Main Idea: The presence or absence of seeds is a major grouping criterion for plants. Plants with seeds reproduce sexually, with some mechanisms of vegetative propagation as well. Plants without seeds reproduce asexually.

LESSON 4 Plants Without Seeds, *pp. A46–A55*

Main Idea: Seedless nonvascular plants and seedless vascular plants have different structures but similar life cycles.

LESSON 5 Plants with Seeds, *pp. A56–A65*

Main Idea: One group of seed plants produces seeds on cones, the other group produces seeds inside fruits.

LESSON 6 Flowers and Seeds, *pp. A68–A77*

Main Idea: Fertilized flowers produce seeds that become new plants.

LESSON 7 Plant Responses and Adaptations, *pp. A78–A85*

Main Idea: Plants have certain behaviors and adaptations that help them survive.

CHAPTER 3 Animal Diversity, *pp. A90–A117*

Main Idea: Animals have adapted to their environment in a variety of ways. The diversity of animals has been enhanced through genetics.

LESSON 8 Animal Structure and Function, *pp. A92–A101*

Main Idea: Animals can be classified using various characteristics.

LESSON 9 Animal Adaptations, *pp. A104–A115*

Main Idea: Animals have certain characteristics, behaviors, and adaptations that help them survive.

Grade-Level Science Books

EASY

EASY

CHALLENGE

THE POWER OF GREEN Students are introduced to the process of photosynthesis, which creates oxygen for us to breathe as well as food for plants, animals, and ourselves. They visit various sites around the globe and see that the process takes place constantly.

JONATHAN CHAPMAN: THE APPLESEED MAN Jonathan Chapman loved apples so much that he planted them all over the West. Legends grew up around him, and he became known as Johnny Appleseed.

DINO FLIGHT This account of the ancestry of birds describes how scientists have traced three separate and independent origins of flight among vertebrates.

To order from Macmillan/McGraw-Hill, call 800-442-9685.

Cross Curricular Books from Macmillan/McGraw-Hill

Apple, Gary. **The Galapagos Islands.**

Brightfield, Richard. **The Breadfruit Mutiny.**

DeMauro, Lisa. **The Mills Green Team.**

To order, call 800-442-9685.

Student Bibliography

Anderson, Peter. **John Muir: Wilderness Prophet.** New York: Franklin Watts, 1996.

Cassie, Brian. **National Audubon Society First Field Guide.** New York: Scholastic Reference, 1999.

Dobson, David. **Can We Save Them? Endangered Species of North America.** Watertown, MA: Charlesbridge Publishing, 1997.

Fleischman, Paul. **Seedfolks.** New York: Joanna Cotler Books/HarperCollins, 1997.

Grupper, Jonathan. **Destination Rain Forest.** Washington, D.C.: National Geographic Society, 1997.

Henderson, Douglas. **Dinosaur Tree.** New York: Bradbury Press, 1994.

Lasky, Kathryn. **The Most Beautiful Roof in the World: Exploring the Rainforest Canopy.** San Diego: Gulliver Green/Harcourt Brace, 1997.

Markle, Sandra and William. **Gone Forever! An Alphabet of Extinct Animals.** New York: Atheneum Books for Young Readers, 1998.

Winner, Cherie. **The Sunflower Family.** Minneapolis: Carolrhoda Books, 1996.

Reading in Science

McGraw-Hill Science

Teacher Editions provide point-of-use strategies and resource support for students to practice reading skills as they read their science texts.

- **Reading MiniLessons**
- **Reduced Blackline Masters** from *Reading in Science Resources*
- **Additional Reading Strategies**

 **Reading in Science Resources**

Boxes beneath the reduced Pupil Edition pages identify specific places in a lesson where students can complete worksheets from the *Reading in Science Resources* blackline masters. Reduced worksheets for this unit are found on the following pages of this Teacher Edition.

Lesson Outlines: pp. A6, A20, A32, A48, A58, A70, A80, A94, A106

Interpret Illustrations: pp. A7, A8, A21, A24, A32, A33, A52, A53, A62, A64, A72, A73, A81, A82, A94, A99, A106, A109

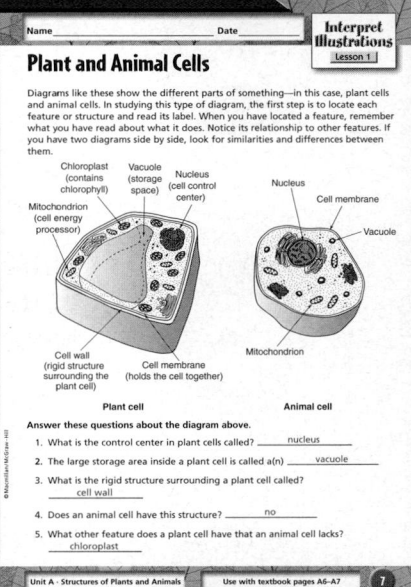

Reading in Science Resources, p. 7

 **Reading MiniLesson**

Reading MiniLessons provide a brief tutorial and activity for students to practice a specific reading skill for each chapter. In this unit, the chapter reading skills are:

Draw Conclusions: pp. A7, A21, A34

Compare and Contrast: pp. A49, A59, A71, A84

Summarize: pp. A95, A114

 **Reading Strategy**

Additional opportunities for students to develop and apply reading skills are provided in this unit as follows:

- ◉ **Cause and effect:** pp. A16, A40
- ◉ **Compare and contrast:** pp. A99, A113
- ◉ **Draw conclusions:** p. A38
- ○ **Find the main idea**
- ○ **Sequence of events**
- ◉ **Summarize:** pp. A10, A17, A26, A27, A29, A39, A41, A55, A65, A67, A70, A77, A85, A87, A101, A103, A115
- ◉ **Ask questions:** pp. A30, A56, A68, A80, A104

- ◉ **Reread:** pp. A24, A118
- ◉ **Retell (paraphrase):** pp. A92, A96
- ◉ **Interpret graphic sources of information:** pp. A7, A8, A10, A12, A13, A22, A24, A33, A37, A38, A50, A53, A62, A70, A72, A76, A82, A99
- ◉ **Build on prior knowledge:** pp. A4, A18, A28, A30, A40, A46, A56, A66, A68, A78, A86, A92, A102, A104, A107, A118
- ◉ **Organize information:** pp. A28, A55, A58, A83

CROSS CURRICULUM IDEAS for integrating science

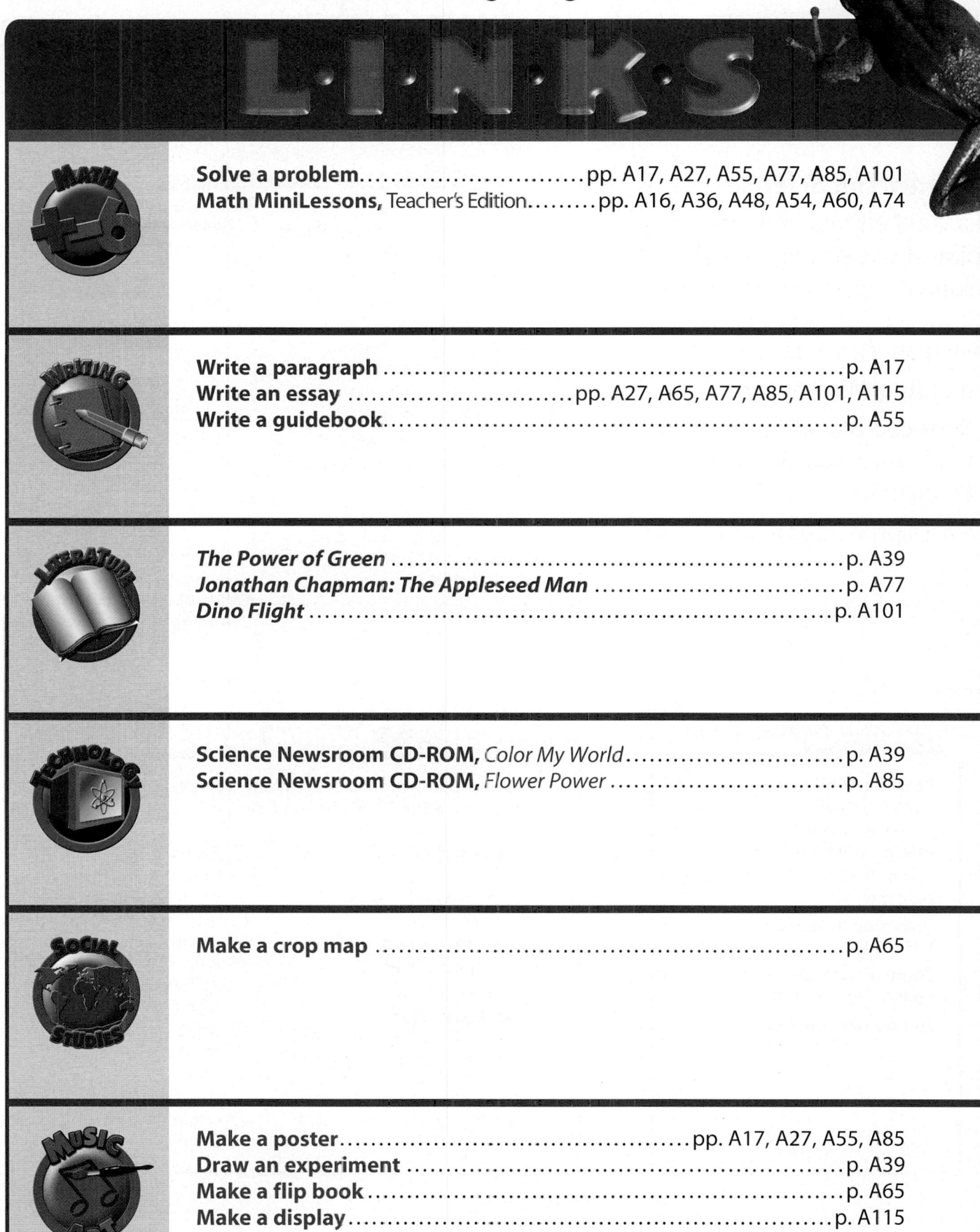

L·I·N·K·S

Meeting Individual Needs

McGraw-Hill Science includes all students in the learning process by providing a variety of strategies in this unit.

 **English Language Learners**

Life Cycles

Invite students to use construction paper, leaves and twigs, markers, cellophane, and so on to make 3-D displays showing the life cycles of mosses and ferns. Pepper can be used for spores. Remind students to label their displays and provide explanations of what is being illustrated. **Spatial; Linguistic**

 **Advanced Learners**

Flower Names

Tell students that the oak tree is part of the "witch hazel" group of trees. One explanation of the name is that *witch* comes from the Old English word meaning "to yield" because witch hazel branches have been used as divining rods. Challenge students to find out the stories behind the names of flowers, such as skunk cabbage, black-eyed Susan, sunflower, buttercup, tumbleweed, morning glory, and day lily, then write or tell the story to the class. **Linguistic**

 **Inclusion**

Preventing Transpiration

Direct students to completely coat a leaf from top to bottom with petroleum jelly. Have them tie plastic bags around the coated leaf and an uncoated leaf and close them with twist ties. Suggest they observe what happens in each bag throughout the day and the next morning. Discuss how the two bags are different. (The one with the uncoated leaf is dry; the other contains water droplets.) **Kinesthetic; Spatial**

For additional support, see pp. A9–A11, A12–A15, A17, A22, A23, A25, A28, A33, A34, A36–A39, A41, A51, A53, A54, A59, A60, A61, A71, A73, A75, A76, A81, A83, A85, A86, A96–A98, A102, A108, A110, A111, A119

Learning Styles

Students acquire knowledge in a variety of ways that reflect different, often distinct, learning styles. The seven learning styles are:

- ◉ **Kinesthetic** pp. A5, A13, A17, A19, A37, A47, A51, A52, A54, A57, A70, A75, A102
- ◉ **Social** pp. A15, A25, A26, A33, A38, A69, A75, A79, A85, A100, A108
- ○ **Intrapersonal**
- ◉ **Linguistic** pp. A9, A10, A11, A12, A14, A22, A28, A38, A39, A41, A49, A50, A51, A53, A60, A61, A63, A71, A73, A76, A77, A81, A82, A83, A84, A86, A96,

A97, A98, A99, A105, A107, A111, A113, A114, A119
- ◉ **Logical** pp. A9, A11, A13, A17, A22, A25, A26, A33, A36, A52, A63, A69, A72, A77, A79, A97, A100, A108, A111
- ◉ **Auditory/Musical** p. A119
- ◉ **Visual/Spatial** pp. A5, A8, A9, A15, A23, A25, A31, A34, A36, A37, A39, A41, A47, A50, A52, A53, A57, A59, A61, A75, A76, A97, A105, A110, A111

Technology for McGRAW-HILL SCIENCE

CD-ROMs

Science Newsroom CD-ROM

Student-directed computer activities

Chapter 1: Color My World

Explore why leaves change color.

Chapter 2: Flower Power

Explore how flowers attract pollinators with color, scent, and shape.

Join me in the Science Newsroom

Videotapes

Explore Activity Videos

All Explore Activities are available on videotape. Introduce lessons with Explore Activity Videos.

MindJogger Videos

Stage a quiz show in your classroom!

Science Experiences Videotapes

Chapter 3:

Lesson 8 Animal Structure and Function
Camels, Cacti, & You: What All Living Things Share (Package 3)

Lesson 9 Animal Adaptations
Staying Alive: Adaptations for Survival (Package 4)

Transparencies

Visual Aid Transparencies

- **1** Parts of a Root
- **2** Photosynthesis
- **3** Life Cycle of a Moss
- **4** Life Cycle of a Fern
- **5** Parts of a Flower
- **6** Pollination
- **7** Fertilization

Reading Aid Transparencies

- A1–A9

Internet Resources

McGRAW-HILL SCIENCE is online at *www.mhscience02.com* with projects and activities for students, teachers, and parents.
Internet Research Projects pp. A39, A55, A115

Links pp. A17, A27, A39, A55, A65, A77, A85, A101, A115

Science Magazines and Features pp. A29, A41, A43, A67, A87, A89, A103, A117, A119

AMERICAN MUSEUM OF NATURAL HISTORY

Visit
www.amnh.org/resources/mhscience for a behind-the-scenes look at the exhibitions, collections, and research of the Museum. You'll find resources for teachers and students, such as online expeditions, profiles of scientists, interactives, links to professional development courses and more.

NATIONAL GEOGRAPHIC

* To order National Geographic Products, visit us online at *www.nationalgeographic.com/education* or call 1-800-368-2728. To order NGS Picture Show and NGS Picture Pack, call Macmillan/McGraw-Hill at 1-800-442-9685.

National Geographic Society Videos
- **What Is a Plant**
- **Great Cover-Up**
- **Wild Survivors**

NGS Picture Show CD-ROMs
- **Plants:** What It Means to Be Green

NGS Picture Pack Transparencies
- **Plants:** What It Means to Be Green
- **Classifying Plants and Animals**

Curriculum Kit
- **GeoKit:** Plants

Process Skills

Science Process Skills	Explore Activities (Pupil Edition)	Quick Labs (Pupil Edition)	Process Skill Builders
Observe	pp. A5, A19, A31, A47, A57, A69, A79, A105	pp. A9, A25, A50, A74, A83, A113	Pupil Edition pp. A35, A63, A100 Teacher Edition (MiniLesson) p. A63 Activity Resources, pp. 24–25
Infer	pp. A19, A31, A57 A69, A93, A105	pp. A50, A74, A113	Pupil Edition p. A35
Classify	p. A93	p. A74	Pupil Edition pp. A63, A100 Teacher Edition (MiniLesson) p. A100 Activity Resources, pp. 39–40
Measure	p. A47		
Use Numbers			
Communicate	pp. A5, A19, A57, A69, A79, A93	p. A74	
Predict	pp. A19, A47, A79		
Interpret Data	pp. A19, A31, A47, A57, A79	p. A9	Pupil Edition pp. A63, A100
Form a Hypothesis	p. A5	pp. A9, A83	
Use Variables	p. A31		
Experiment	pp. A31, A57, A105	p. A50	Pupil Edition p. A35 Teacher Edition (MiniLesson) p. A35 Activity Resources, pp. 14–15
Make a Model			
Define Based on Observations	p. A5		

Materials

Consumable materials (based on six groups)

Materials	Quantity Needed per group	Kit Quantity	Lesson
Animal; pill bugs or sow bugs	8	coupon for 50	9
Cardboard sheet	6		5
Conifer, small pine seedling, or other	1		5
Cup, paper, 360 mL	1	25	7
Fingernail polish, clear			5
Foil, aluminum, 12" × 25'		1 roll	3
Food, celery stalk, piece of moss, or leaf			1
Food coloring, dark red		30 mL (2 bottles)	1
Knives, plastic	3	24	1
Leaves, edible			2
Leaves, from various flowers and angiosperms			5
Magazines, old			8
Paper, black	1 sheet		6
Paper towels			7, 9
Pen, marking	1		7
Pencil, wax marking	1	3	7
Plant, cactus	1		2
Plant, *Elodea*	2	coupon for 12 sprigs	1, 2
Plant, fern	2		1
Plant, fern leaf w/ spore cases	1	coupon for 1 plant	4
Plant, flowering, such as geranium	1		2
Plants, flowers, several large, from different plants	1		6
Plant, garden or house, such as geranium	1		5
Plant, geranium (or other flowering plant)	1		1
Plant, grass	1		5
Plant, ivy	1		7
Plant, moss	2		1, 4
Plants, various house			7
Plant, window or aquarium	1		3
Seeds, corn		30 g	6
Seeds, grass		2 pkgs	7
Seeds, lima bean		2 oz	6
Seeds, pinto bean	4	1 lb	7

Materials	Quantity Needed per group	Kit Quantity	Lesson
Soil, potting		24 lb	7
String		200 ft	throughout
Tape			7, 8
Toothpicks		3 boxes (2,250)	4, 6

Non-consumable materials (based on six groups)

Materials	Quantity Needed per group	Kit Quantity	Lesson
Bottle, 1 qt	1	*	1
Camera (optional)	1		7
Dropper	3	18	1, 4, 6
Forceps	2	6	4, 6
Hand lens	6	6	1, 2, 4, 5, 6
Microscope	1	3	1, 4, 5
Microscope coverslip	2	100	1, 4, 5
Microscope slide	6	72	1, 4, 5
Pan, aluminum, 32 × 22 × 3 cm	1	6	9
Petri dish (plastic)	1	6	7
Scissors	1		8

* Kit provides 6 containers.

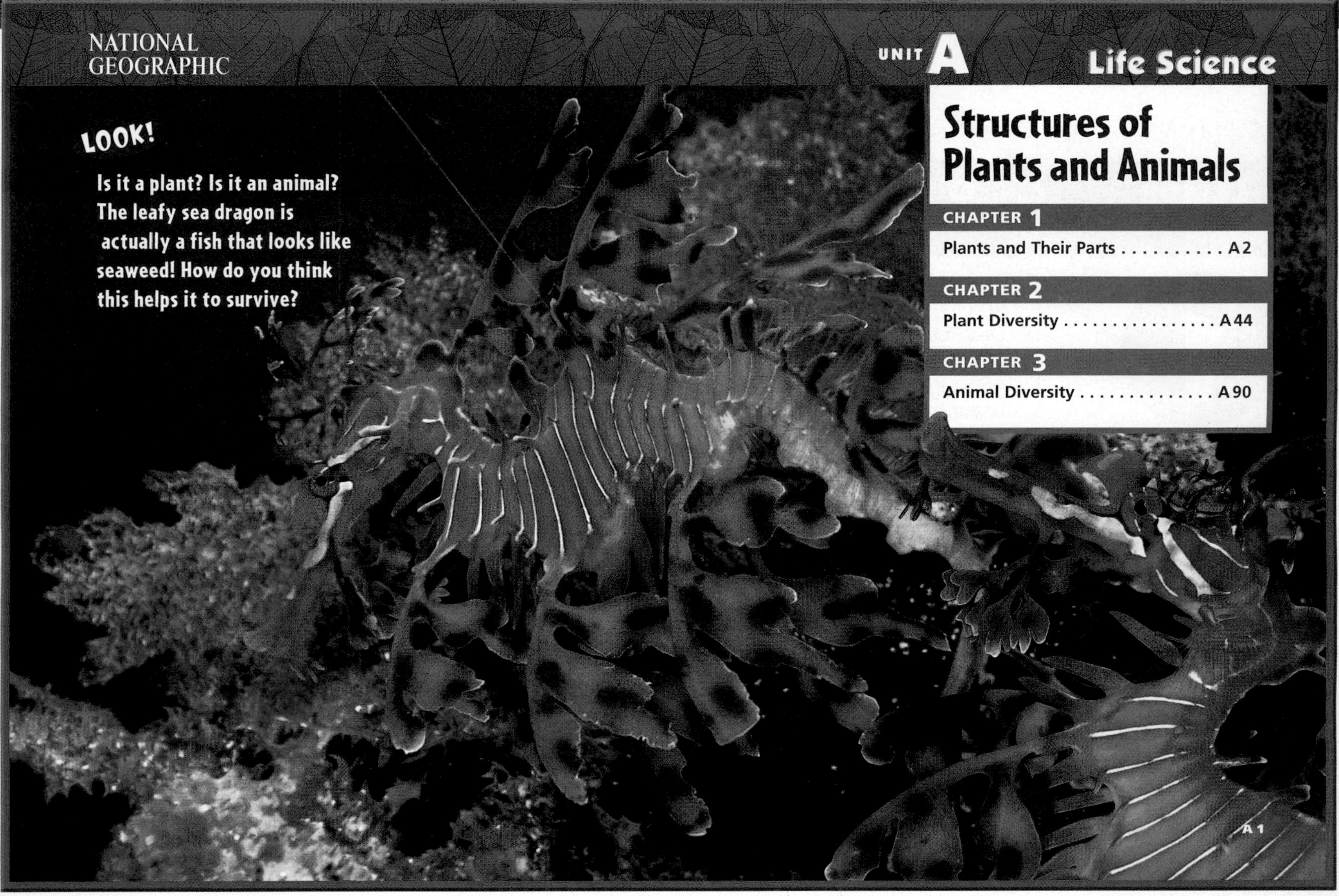

NATIONAL GEOGRAPHIC

LOOK!

Is it a plant? Is it an animal? The leafy sea dragon is actually a fish that looks like seaweed! How do you think this helps it to survive?

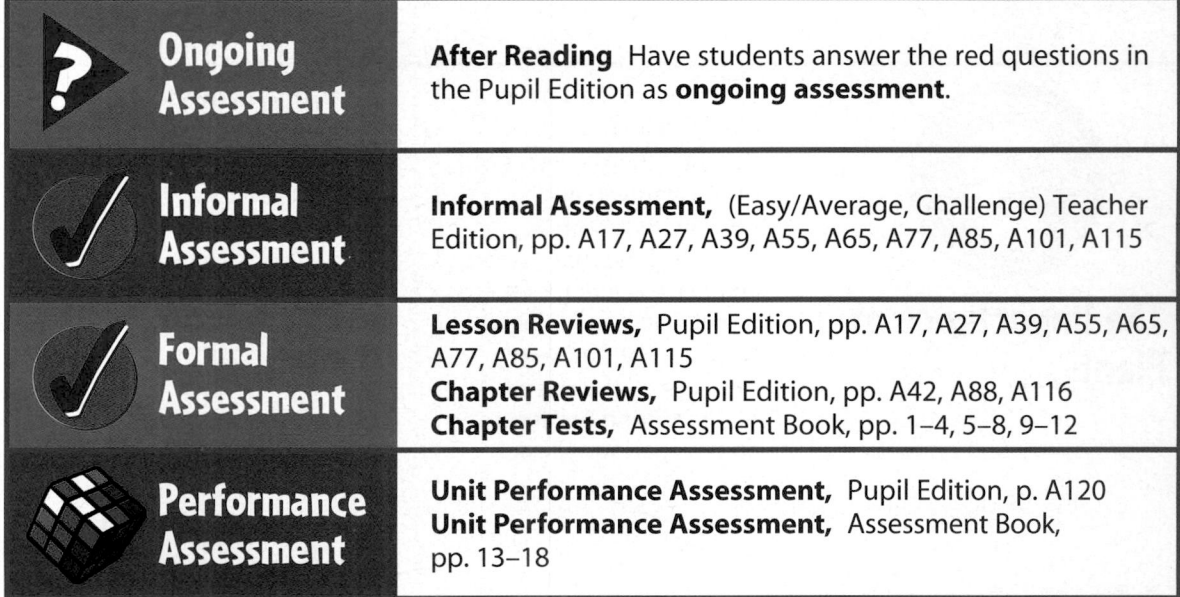

Structures of Plants and Animals

Resources

- Reading in Science Resources, Unit Vocabulary, pp. 73–75
- School to Home Activities, pp. 1–8
- Cross Curricular Projects, pp. 1–10

Answers to

The leafy sea dragon—a fish— is an animal. Looking like sea- weed helps hide it from its enemies.

Assessment Strand

McGraw-Hill Science provides a variety of strategies for assessing students' learning and progress, including ongoing assessment, informal assessment, formal assessment, and performance assessment.

?	**Ongoing Assessment**	**After Reading** Have students answer the red questions in the Pupil Edition as **ongoing assessment**.
✓	**Informal Assessment**	**Informal Assessment,** (Easy/Average, Challenge) Teacher Edition, pp. A17, A27, A39, A55, A65, A77, A85, A101, A115
✓	**Formal Assessment**	**Lesson Reviews,** Pupil Edition, pp. A17, A27, A39, A55, A65, A77, A85, A101, A115 **Chapter Reviews,** Pupil Edition, pp. A42, A88, A116 **Chapter Tests,** Assessment Book, pp. 1–4, 5–8, 9–12
🎲	**Performance Assessment**	**Unit Performance Assessment,** Pupil Edition, p. A120 **Unit Performance Assessment,** Assessment Book, pp. 13–18

Lesson Planner

Lesson	Objectives	Vocabulary	Pacing	Resources and Technology
LESSON 1 **Classifying Living Things,** pp. A4–A17	■ Explore traits plants have in common. ■ Describe the characteristics of plants. ■ Compare plants to other organisms. ■ Understand the environmental problems caused by imported plants.	**chlorophyll vascular nonvascular fungus protist bacterium**	4 days	■ Activity Resources, pp. 1–5 ■ Reading in Science Resources, pp. 5–10 ■ Vocabulary Cards ■ School to Home Activities, p. 2 ■ Reading Aid Transparency A1 ■ **Explore Activity Video**
LESSON 2 **Roots, Stems, and Leaves,** pp. A18–A27	■ Explore how a plant's parts help it survive. ■ Understand the functions of roots and stems. ■ Understand the functions of leaves.	**root cap root hair epidermis cortex xylem phloem cambium chloroplast transpiration**	3 days	■ Activity Resources, pp. 6–10 ■ Reading in Science Resources, pp. 11–16 ■ Vocabulary Cards ■ School to Home Activities, pp. 3–4 ■ Reading Aid Transparency A2 ■ Visual Aid Transparency 1 ■ **Explore Activity Video**
LESSON 3 **The Importance of Plants,** pp. A30–A39	■ Explore how light affects a plant's leaves. ■ Describe the processes of photosynthesis and respiration in plants. ■ Describe how roots, stems, and leaves work together to get water and minerals to all parts of the plant. ■ Understand the role of plants as food producers and oxygen suppliers.	**photosynthesis respiration**	4 days	■ Activity Resources, pp. 11–15 ■ Reading in Science Resources, pp. 17–22 ■ Vocabulary Cards ■ Grade-Level Science Book, *The Power of Green* ■ Reading Aid Transparency A3 ■ Visual Aid Transparency 2 ■ **Explore Activity Video** ■ **Science Newsroom CD-ROM** *Color My World*

Activity Planner

Activity	Process Skills	Materials	Plan Ahead
LESSON 1 **Explore Activity** **What Do Plants Have in Common?** p. A5	observe, communicate, define, hypothesize	*Elodea* plant, moss plant, fern plant, geranium (or other flowering plant), microscope, microscope slide, coverslip, dropper, water	Flowering plants can be bought locally or students can bring in plants from home. The *Elodea* and flowering plants will be used again in Lesson 2.
QUICK LAB **FOR SCHOOL OR HOME** **Tubelike Plant Parts** p. A9	observe, hypothesize, interpret data	celery stalk, bit of moss, lettuce leaf, oak or maple leaf, water, food coloring, narrow-mouthed bottle, hand lens, knife	Use fresh celery and other plants.
LESSON 2 **Explore Activity** **How Do a Plant's Parts Help It Survive?** p. A19	observe, communicate, interpret data, infer, predict	cactus, water plant, such as an Elodea or a duckweed, flowering plant, such as a geranium	In addition to the plants from Lesson 1, common houseplants, wildflowers, and duckweed from ponds can be used. Try to obtain cactus plants with roots that the students can see.
QUICK LAB **FOR SCHOOL OR HOME** **Leaves** p. A25	observe	various plant leaves that you eat, hand lens	No advance planning is needed.
LESSON 3 **Explore Activity** **What Does Light Do for a Plant?** p. A31	use variables, experiment, observe, interpret data, infer	growing plant (window plants from home or plants from an aquarium), opaque paper or aluminum foil	The plants from Lessons 1 and 2 may also be used for this activity.
Process Skill **BUILDER** **Why Leaves Change Color** p. A35	experiment, observe, infer	none	No advance planning is needed.

Reading in Science Resources

McGraw-Hill Science **Reading in Science Resources** provides the following **Blackline Master** worksheets for this chapter.

Chapter Graphic Organizer

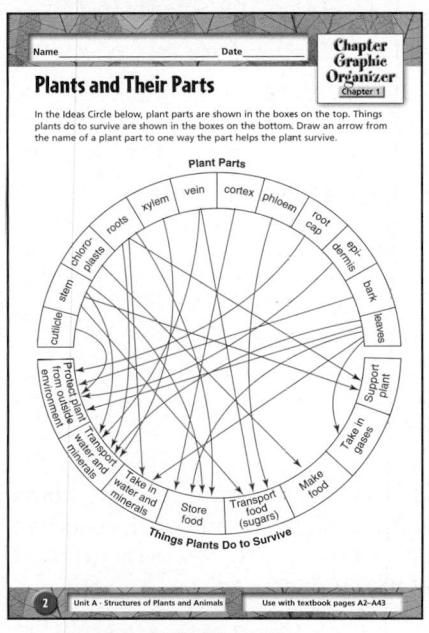

*Reading in Science Resources,
p. 2*

Chapter Reading Skill

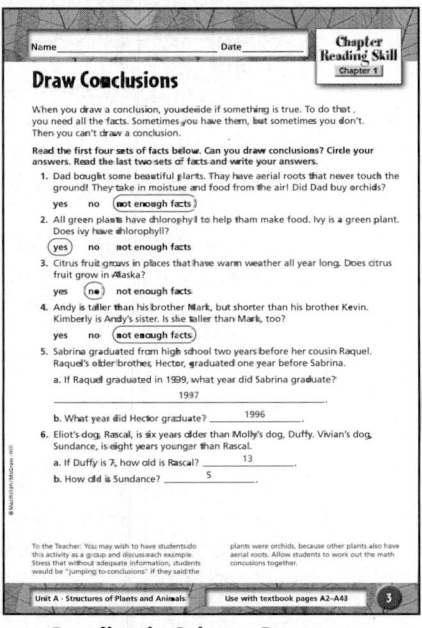

*Reading in Science Resources,
pp. 3–4*

Chapter Vocabulary

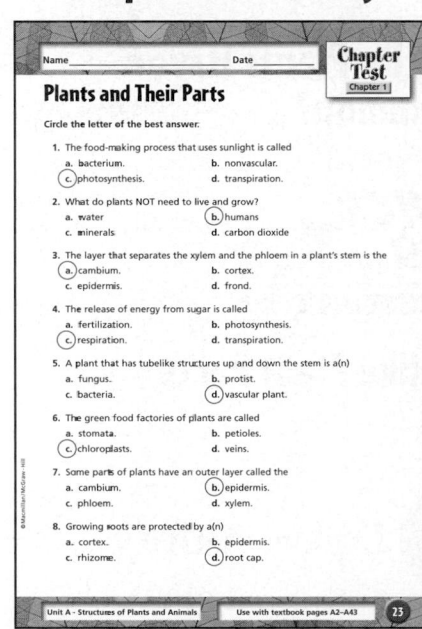

*Reading in Science Resources,
pp. 23–24*

McGraw-Hill Science **Reading in Science Resources** provides the following **Blackline Master** worksheets for every lesson in this chapter.

Lesson Outline

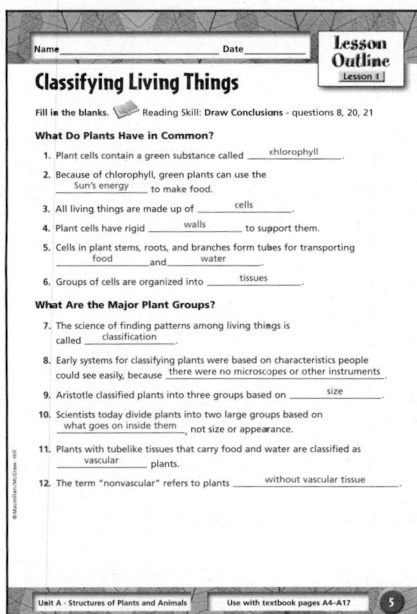

*Reading in Science Resources,
pp. 5–6, 11–12, 17–18*

Interpret Illustrations

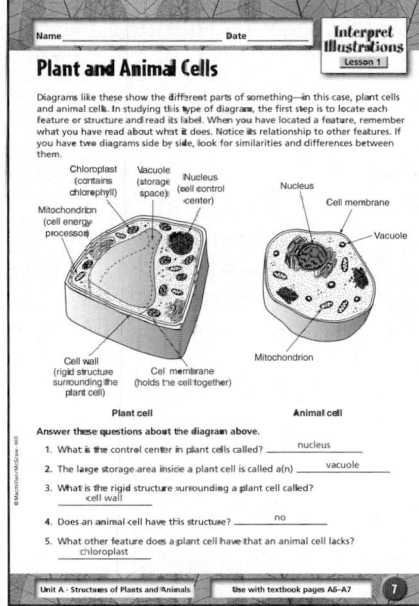

*Reading in Science Resources,
pp. 7–8, 13–14, 19–20*

Lesson Vocabulary and Cloze Test

*Reading in Science Resources,
pp. 9–10, 15–16, 21–22*

Activities and Assessment

McGraw-Hill Science **Activity Resources** provides the following **Blackline Master** worksheets for every lesson in this chapter.

Explore Activity and Alternative Explore Activity

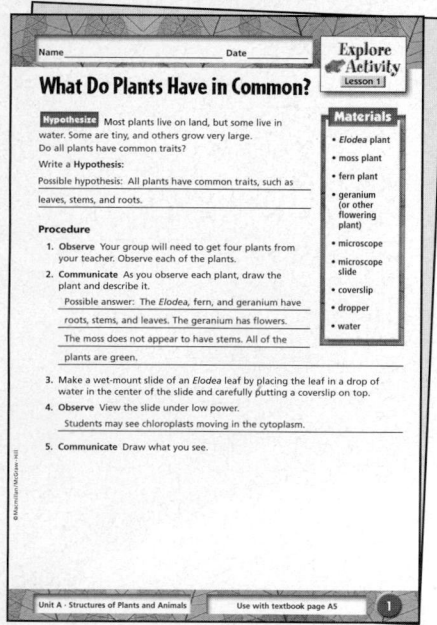

Activity Resources, pp. 1–3, 6–8, 11–13

Quick Lab for School or Home

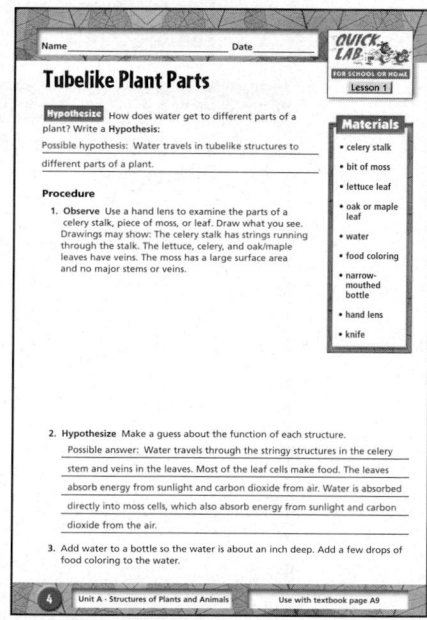

Activity Resources, pp. 4–5, 9–10

Process Skill Builder

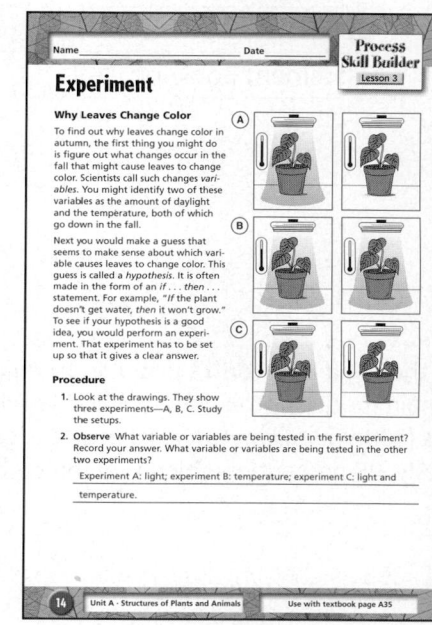

Activity Resources, pp. 14–15

McGraw-Hill Science **Assessment Book** provides the following **Blackline Master** worksheets for this chapter.

Chapter Test

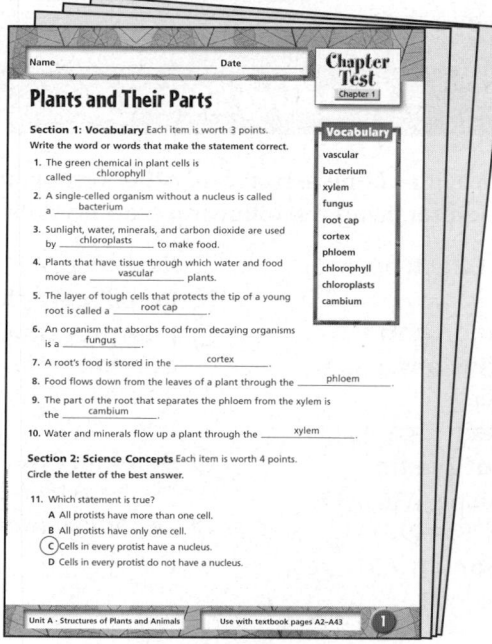

Assessment Book, pp. 1–4

CHAPTER
1 Plants and Their Parts

Resources

- Reading in Science Resources, pp. 2–25
- Assessment Book, pp. 1–4

Did You Ever Wonder?

More than half the world's population relies on rice as a main food. Approximately 364-432 billion kilograms (800-950 billion pounds) of rice is grown annually, 95 percent of which is eaten by humans.

CHAPTER
1 Plants and Their Parts

Did You Ever Wonder?

Where does rice come from? Most of the world's rice is grown in Asia, often in flooded fields called paddies. It takes 5,000 liters (1,320 gallons) of water to grow 1 kilogram (2.2 pounds) of rice. These rice paddies are growing on terraces—step-like fields cut into a hillside. Why is rice an important food crop?

A 2

Reading Strategy

This chapter provides MiniLessons and other opportunities for developing and practicing the following reading skills:

- ● **Cause and Effect:** pp. A16, A40
- ○ **Compare and Contrast**
- ● **Draw Conclusions:** pp. A7, A21, A34, A38
- ○ **Find the Main Idea**
- ○ **Sequence of Events**
- ● **Summarize:** pp. A10, A17, A26, A27, A29, A39, A41
- ● **Ask Questions:** p. A30

- ● **Reread:** p. A24
- ○ **Retell (paraphrase)**
- ● **Interpret Graphic Sources of Information:** pp. A8, A10, A12, A13, A22, A24, A33, A37, A38
- ● **Build on Prior Knowledge:** pp. A4, A18, A28, A30, A40
- ● **Organize Information:** p. A28

Vocabulary Preview

Encourage students to keep a Science Dictionary. Remind them to add the Vocabulary words for each lesson in this chapter to their Dictionary as they complete each lesson.

chlorophyll, A6

vascular, A9

nonvascular, A9

fungus, A13

protist, A14

bacterium, A15

root cap, A20

root hair, A20

epidermis, A20

cortex, A20

xylem, A20

phloem, A21

cambium, A21

chloroplast, A24

transpiration, A25

photosynthesis, A32

respiration, A33

AMERICAN MUSEUM OF NATURAL HISTORY

Visit www.amnh.org/resources/mhscience to discover more about plants and how to identify their different parts.

A 3

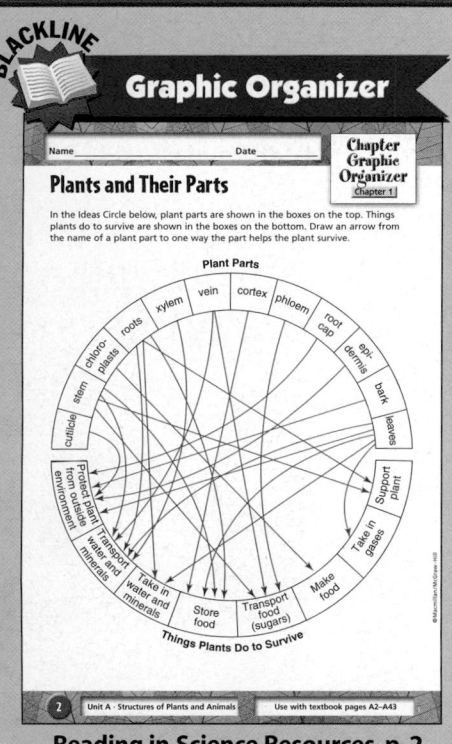

Reading in Science Resources, p. 2

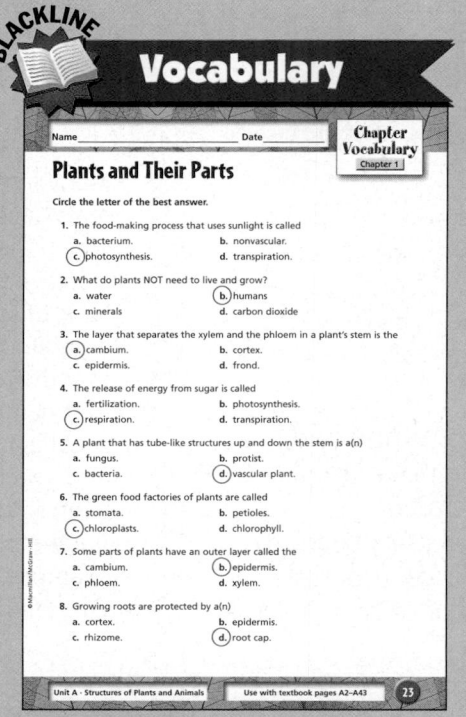

Reading in Science Resources, pp. 23–24

Classifying Living Things

Objectives

- Explore traits plants have in common.
- Describe the characteristics of plants.
- Compare plants to other organisms.
- Understand the environmental problems caused by imported plants.

Resources

- Activity Resources, pp. 1–5
- Reading in Science Resources, pp. 5–10
- Vocabulary Cards
- Reading Aid Transparency A1
- School to Home Activities, p. 2

Build on Prior Knowledge

Have students discuss what they know about plants and how they are used. Ask:

- **What are some examples of plants you have seen today.** (Examples: trees, flowers, grass)
- **Have you eaten any plants today?** (Examples: fruits, vegetables, cereal, nuts)
- **Are you wearing clothes made from plants?** (Examples: cotton, linen, hemp)

1 Get Ready

Developing the Main Idea

Point out to students that mushrooms (fungi) and seaweed (a kind of algae, a protist) are not plants. Explain that all plants have common traits. (For example, they all have chlorophyll.) Ask them to list traits they would use to classify plants. (Possible answers: color, flowers, leaf shape, kind of stem, edibility)

Classifying Living Things

Vocabulary

chlorophyll, A6

vascular, A9

nonvascular, A9

fungus, A13

protist, A14

bacterium, A15

Get Ready

What are plants? Trees, shrubs, grasses, fruits, flowers and vegetables are familiar and easy to identify as plants. Others may not be so familiar. Are mushrooms plants? Is seaweed a plant? Some plants are tiny. Others grow very large. Do all plants have common traits? What traits would you use to classify plants?

Process Skill

You define based on observation when you put together a description that is based on observations and experience.

A 4

Science Background

Classification

Many familiar plants and animals have common names by which they are known. However, to help classify millions of species of plants and animals, biologists also use binomial nomenclature, a two-part naming system. Each organism is named by genus and species. The names are in Latin so that they can be understood worldwide. For example, the domestic dog is *Canis familiaris.*

Cross Curricular Books

Additional Outside Reading

The Breadfruit Mutiny

written by Richard Brightfield
illustrated by Stephen Marchesi

To order, see page A1·b.

Explore Activity

What Do Plants Have in Common?

Materials
Elodea plant
moss plant
fern plant
geranium (or other flowering plant)
microscope
microscope slide
coverslip
dropper
water

Procedure

1 **Observe** Your group will need to get four plants from your teacher. Observe each of the plants.

2 **Communicate** As you observe each plant, draw the plant and describe it.

3 Make a wet-mount slide of an *Elodea* leaf by placing the leaf in a drop of water in the center of the slide and carefully putting a coverslip on top.

4 **Observe** View the slide under low power.

5 **Communicate** Draw what you see.

Drawing Conclusions

1 **Communicate** What plant traits can you observe without using the microscope?

2 **Communicate** What other plant traits can you observe with the microscope?

3 **Define** From what you observed, come up with your own definition of a plant.

4 **Going Further: Hypothesize** Examine some other kinds of plants with the microscope. Do all the plants seem to have the same traits, or do some plants look quite different from the others? Do plants that look similar under the microscope have the same traits? How would you set up an experiment to find out?

A 5

Alternative Explore Activity

Materials prepared slides of plant cells, various colors of clay, toothpicks, colored paper

A Look at Plant Cells Invite students to look at prepared slides of cells from various plants and compare their characteristics. Have them draw and describe their observations in their journals, then make a clay model of what they see under the microscope. Make sure they show the cell walls and green pigment (chloroplasts). **Spatial; Kinesthetic**

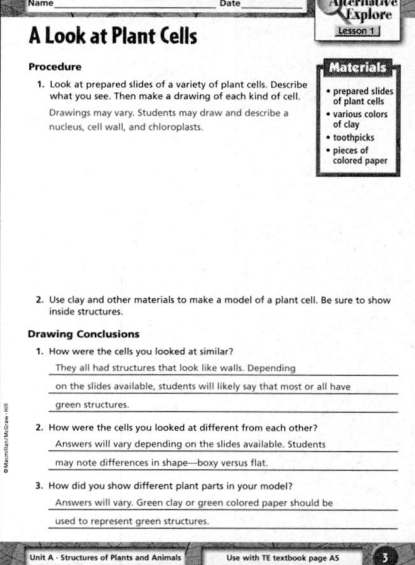

Name_____ Date_____

A Look at Plant Cells

Procedure

1. Look at prepared slides of a variety of plant cells. Describe what you see. Then make a drawing of each kind of cell.
   Drawings may vary. Students may draw and describe a nucleus, cell wall, and chloroplasts.

2. Use clay and other materials to make a model of a plant cell. Be sure to show inside structures.

Drawing Conclusions

1. How were the cells you looked at similar?
   They all had structures that look like walls. Depending on the slides available, students will likely say that most or all have green structures.

2. How were the cells you looked at different from each other?
   Answers will vary depending on the slides available. Students may note differences in shape—boxy versus flat.

3. How did you show different plant parts in your model?
   Answers will vary. Green clay or green colored paper should be used to represent green structures.

Unit A · Structures of Plants and Animals   Use with TE textbook page A5   3

Activity Resources, p. 3

Explore Activity

What Do Plants Have in Common?

Science Process Skills *observe, communicate, define, hypothesize*

Resources Activity Resources, pp. 1–2

Pacing 30–40 minutes

Grouping small groups

Plan Ahead Flowering plants can be bought locally or students can bring in plants from home. The *Elodea* and flowering plants will be used again in Lesson 2.

Procedure

3 Take the *Elodea* sample from the tip of the plant, where the leaves are thinner. You might wish to demonstrate how to make a wet-mount slide.

4 Ask students if they see anything moving on the slide. (They may see chloroplasts moving in the cytoplasm.)

Answers to Drawing Conclusions

1 The plants have differently shaped green leaves and roots. Some have stems. One plant has flowers.

2 Plants are made of many boxlike cells that have walls and green pigment that seems to move.

3 Possible answer: A plant is an organism that has green leaves, roots, and boxlike cells with walls.

4 Under the microscope, plant cells look similar even though the plants may look very different. Plants with similar-looking cells could be examined to see if they have share any other traits.

Inquiry Students can ask their own questions to explore, such as: What is inside plant cells? (nucleus, cytoplasm, and chloroplasts)

Technology

- When time is short, preview the activity with the **Explore Activity Video**

2 Read to Learn

What Do Plants Have in Common?

Before Reading
Have students try to answer the red question at the top of the page.

Developing the Main Idea
Mention that all plants that make their own food have chlorophyll even if you can't see the green color, which can be masked by other plant pigments.

Using the Illustrations
Explain that cell walls often thicken with age, as can be seen when a twig grows into a rigid branch. Ask:

■ **What is in a plant cell that makes a plant green?** (chlorophyll)

Developing Vocabulary

chlorophyll Tell students that the Greek words *chloros* means "pale green" and *phyllon* translates as "leaf."

Read to Learn

Main Idea All plants have common characteristics, such as the same parts and the ability to make food.

What Do Plants Have in Common?

You don't need a microscope to discover that plants are green. That's because their cells contain a green chemical called **chlorophyll** (KLAWR·uh·fil). It allows plants to use the Sun's energy to make their own food. The other things plants need to make food are water and minerals from the soil and carbon dioxide from the air.

If you look at an *Elodea* leaf under a microscope, you will see what looks like little boxes. These are the cells, or basic building blocks, of the *Elodea*. All living things are made up of cells. Plants are made up of many different kinds of cells. All plant cells have certain things in common that help plants live and grow.

Let's look at a tree to find out how its cells help it survive. A tree rises up from the ground. Its rigid trunk supports all its weight. Its roots anchor it into the soil. It doesn't walk, run, or swim. In order to live and grow, the

Plant Cell

Plant cells have rigid walls and contain chlorophyll.

Mitochondrion (cell energy processor—helps supply energy for the cell)

Vacuole (storage space—stores food, water, and wastes)

Chloroplast (contains chlorop▮

Nucleus (cell control center—directs everything the cell does)

Cell wall (rigid structure surrounding the plant cell)

Cell membran◀ (holds the ce▮ together)

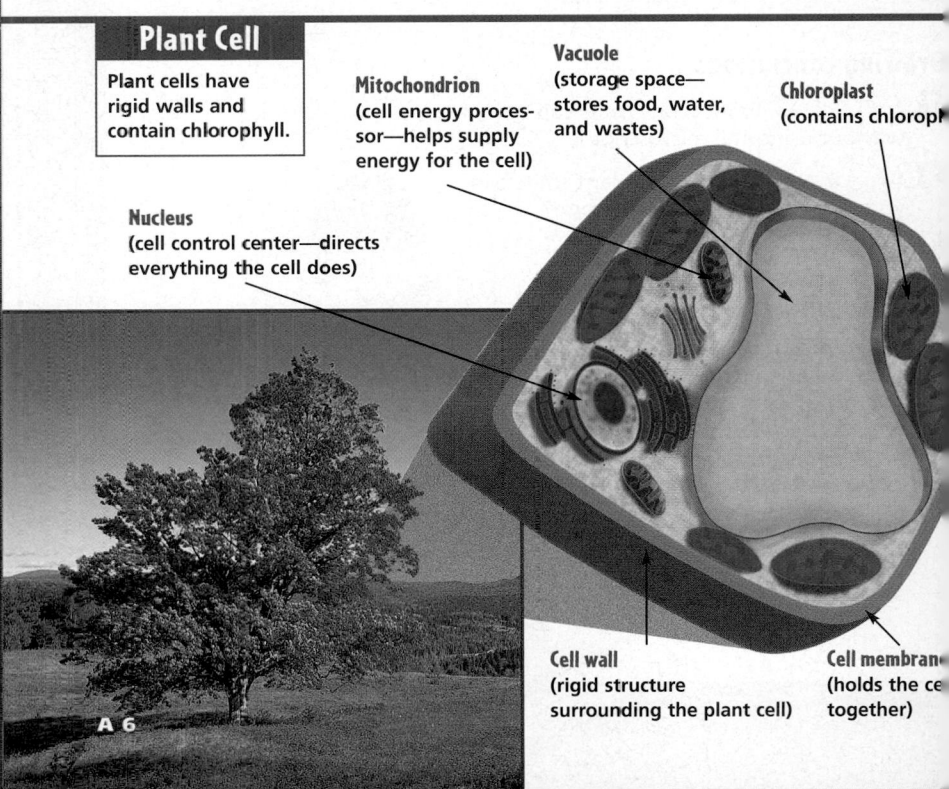

A 6

BLACKLINE Lesson Outline

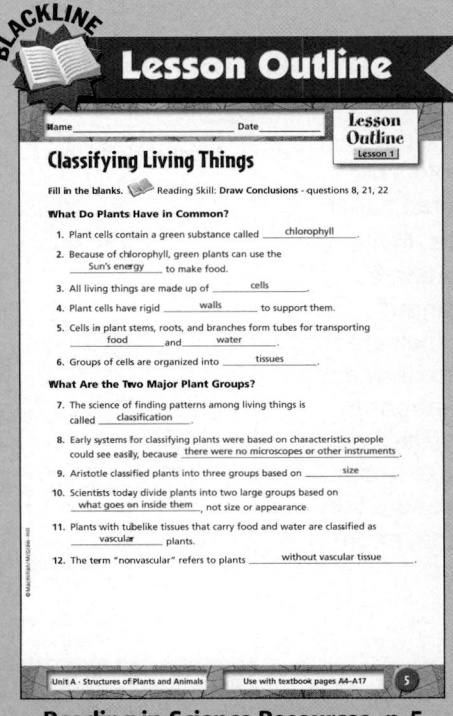

Name_____ Date_____

Lesson Outline Lesson 1

Classifying Living Things

Fill in the blanks. Reading Skill: Draw Conclusions - questions 8, 21, 22

What Do Plants Have in Common?

1. Plant cells contain a green substance called ___chlorophyll___
2. Because of chlorophyll, green plants can use the ___Sun's energy___ to make food.
3. All living things are made up of ___cells___
4. Plant cells have rigid ___walls___ to support them.
5. Cells in plant stems, roots, and branches form tubes for transporting ___food___ and ___water___
6. Groups of cells are organized into ___tissues___

What Are the Two Major Plant Groups?

7. The science of finding patterns among living things is called ___classification___
8. Early systems for classifying plants were based on characteristics people could see easily, because ___there were no microscopes or other instruments___
9. Aristotle classified plants into three groups based on ___size___
10. Scientists today divide plants into two large groups based on ___what goes on inside them___ not size or appearance.
11. Plants with tubelike tissues that carry food and water are classified as ___vascular___ plants.
12. The term "nonvascular" refers to plants ___without vascular tissue___

Unit A · Structures of Plants and Animals   Use with textbook pages A4–A17   5

Reading in Science Resources, p. 5

tree must be made of rigid building blocks—rigid cells that support it.

Under the microscope, *Elodea* cells look like boxes. What is one characteristic of boxes? They have walls, which keep them from collapsing into a heap. All plant cells have walls. That's why an oak tree can stand tall and strong.

The cells of all plants work together to keep the plants alive. Different kinds of cells do different kinds of jobs. Each job contributes to the health and survival of the plant. For example, in a tree, cells in leaves make the plant's food. Cells in stems, branches, roots, and the trunk form tubes through which the food or water is moved, or *transported* (trans·PAWRT·uhd). Other cells may form flowers, fruits, and seeds that allow the tree to reproduce.

Cells are organized into *tissues* (TISH·ewz). The "strings" in celery stalks and the flesh of fruits are examples of plant tissues. The tissues that carry water and minerals support the plant.

READING Draw Conclusions
What is one of the things plants have in common that helps an oak tree stand tall and strong?

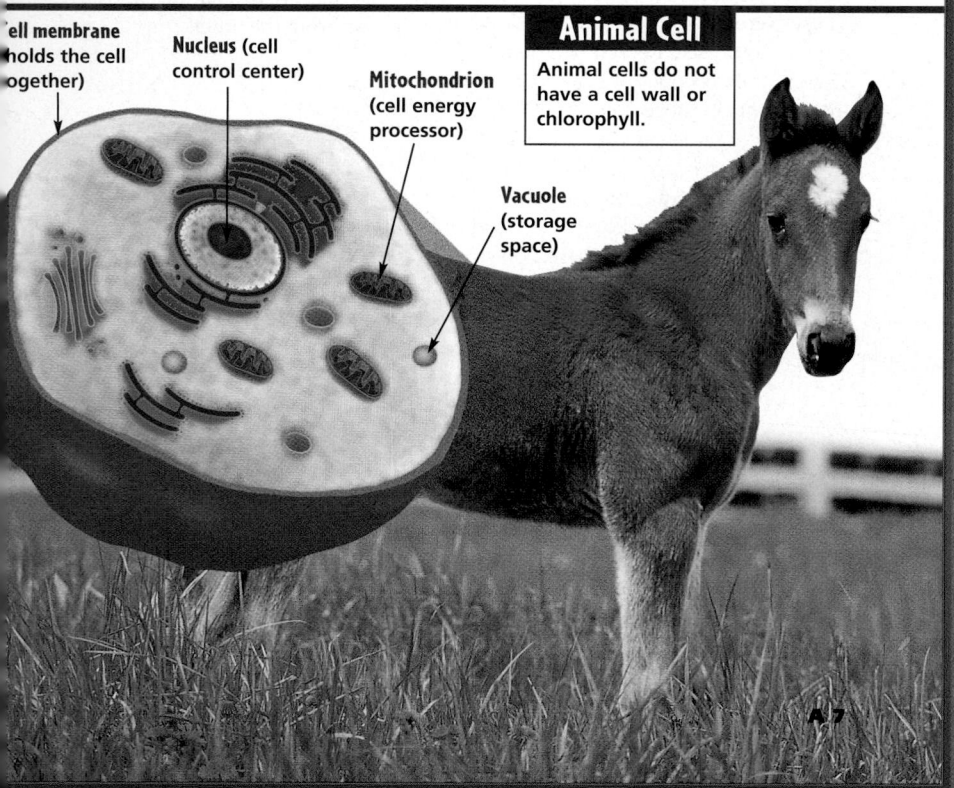

Cell membrane (holds the cell together)

Nucleus (cell control center)

Mitochondrion (cell energy processor)

Vacuole (storage space)

Animal Cell
Animal cells do not have a cell wall or chlorophyll.

A7

Developing the Main Idea
Let volunteers come to the board and draw the parts of a plant. Ask:

- **What do you think should be in a "typical plant"?** (leaves, branches, stem or trunk, roots)

- **Give an example of how cells in your body work together in ways similar to those in a plant.** (Examples: Bone tissue helps support the body. Blood tissue carries oxygen and nutrients to various part of the body.)

Thinking Further: *Compare and Contrast*
Ask:

- **How is the class plant like a "real" plant? How is it different?** (The plant may have all the parts but not resemble any plant students have seen; stems, roots, leaves, and flowers, and other tissues may or may not be present in real plants.)

▶ **After Reading**
Have students answer the red question in the student book as **ongoing assessment**.

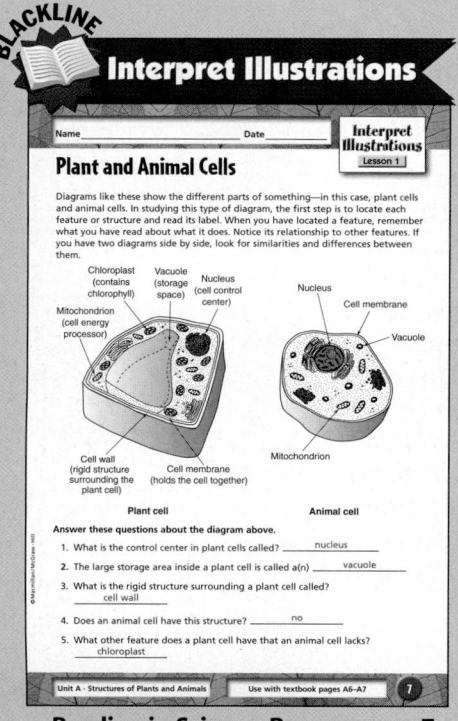

Reading in Science Resources, p. 7

Interpret Illustrations

Plant and Animal Cells

Diagrams like these show the different parts of something—in this case, plant cells and animal cells. In studying this type of diagram, the first step is to locate each feature or structure and read its label. When you have located a feature, remember what you have read about what it does. Notice its relationship to other features. If you have two diagrams side by side, look for similarities and differences between them.

Answer these questions about the diagram above.

1. What is the control center in plant cells called? nucleus
2. The large storage area inside a plant cell is called a(n) vacuole
3. What is the rigid structure surrounding a plant cell called? cell wall
4. Does an animal cell have this structure? no
5. What other feature does a plant cell have that an animal cell lacks? chloroplast

Reading MiniLesson
SCIENCE

Draw Conclusions

Develop As students answer the question on page A7, discuss the importance of using common sense as well as all the facts to draw a conclusion. Point out that common sense tells us an oak tree's thick trunk and deep roots hold it tall and strong. That, together with facts about plant cells in the text, help us conclude that it's the rigid cell walls of the oak tree's trunk and roots that hold the tree up.

Practice Ask students to find evidence in paragraph 2 on page A7 to support the conclusion that each cell in a plant has an important job. (Answers should include that cells have to work together to keep the plant alive, some cells make food and others transport water or food, and some cells allow the plant to reproduce its own kind.)

What Are the Major Plant Groups?

Before Reading
Have students try to answer the red question at the top of the page.

Developing the Main Idea
Focus on the difficulties of classifying living things. Ask:

- **How are plants classified?** (vascular and non-vascular plants)

- **On what is the system based?** (vascular plants have tissues, like tubes, that carry water. Nonvascular plants do not have these tubes.)

- **Is it always easy to classify animals?** (No; sometimes animals have to be closely examined to decide how they are classified.)

Using the Illustrations
Call students' attention to the pictures of the tree and fern. Ask:

- **What do ferns and trees have in common that a piece of moss does not?** (long stems)

READING
Charts

Student paragraphs should include the idea that in vascular plants food and water are transported to all parts of the plant through tubes, whereas in nonvascular plants, water passes directly into cells. Possible examples: vascular—tree, fern; nonvascular—moss, liverwort.

What Are the Major Plant Groups?

People have always tried to make sense of their surroundings. One way to do this is to look for patterns. Finding such patterns among plants can help answer very important questions, such as: What plants are good to eat? What plants are poisonous? What plants contain valuable medicines? What plants produce wood that is strong and hard?

The science of finding patterns among living things is called *classification* (klas·uh·fi·KAY·shuhn). Ancient scientists came up with very simple classification systems for plants. These were based on characteristics that anyone could see. Remember, there were no microscopes or other complex instruments in those days. In 350 B.C. the Greek scientist Aristotle classified plants into three large groups—herbs (little plants), shrubs (bigger plants), and trees (the biggest plants). Aristotle's classification system was based on size.

This made sense at the time. However, as scientists learned more about plants, they realized that size was not a sensible way to classify them.

For example, today we know that a tiny blade of grass is more like a bamboo that is as tall as a ten-story building than it is like a moss that grows close to the ground.

Vascular and Nonvascular Plants

By getting a look at what goes on inside plants—not what they look like on the outside—scientists have been able to divide them into two large groups. Let's take a close look inside plants to see what scientists found; something that separates one large group from the other.

READING
Charts

Write a paragraph describing the differences between vascular and nonvascular plants. Give two examples of each.

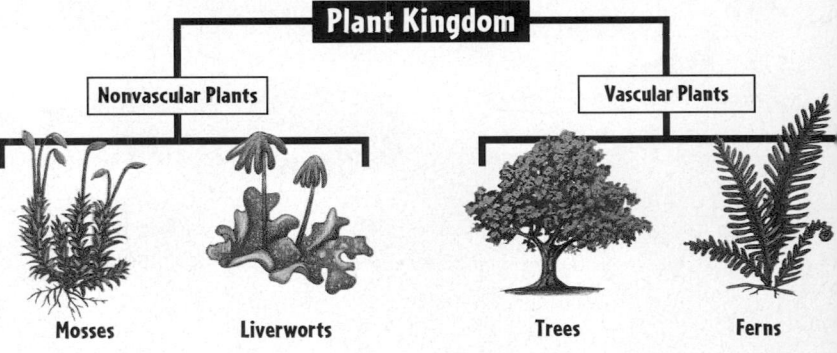

Plant Kingdom

Nonvascular Plants | **Vascular Plants**

Mosses   Liverworts   Trees   Ferns

A 8

Science Background

Vascular Plants
Plant tubes or veins are either xylem (carry water and minerals from roots to leaves) or phloem (carry sugars to cells). In stemmed plants, these tubes are either scattered or patterned, which provides another means for classification (monocot, dicot). As plants evolved, the presence of tubes in plants meant that plants could grow much larger. Have students find out about tube patterns in vascular plants. **Spatial**

Interpret Illustrations

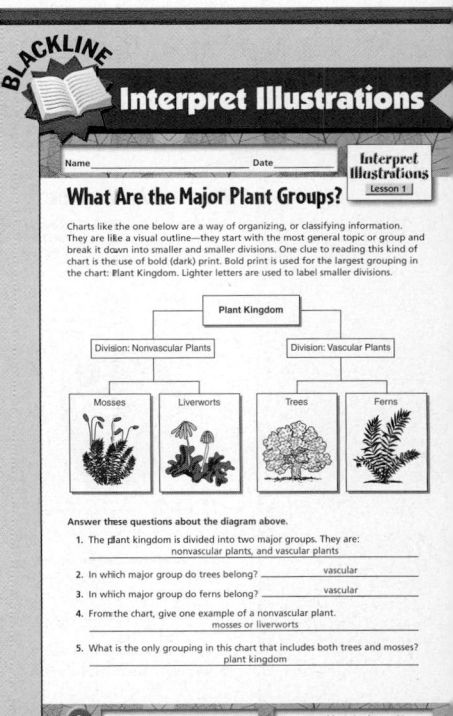

First, look inside the stem of a moss. What do you see? You see lots of cells packed together like pieces in a jigsaw puzzle. The cells look very much like one another. Water from outside is passing directly into the cells.

Now, do the same thing with the stem of a corn plant. You see something very different here. Lengths of tubelike cells tunnel up and down the stem. Water taken in by the plant's roots is moving up one set of tubes toward the plant's leaves, flowers, and other parts. At the same time, foods made in the leaves are moving down the other set of tubes, which lead to all of the plant's parts. These tubes are called *vascular tissue*.

Scientists call plants that have this kind of tissue—such as trees and flowering plants—vascular (VAS·kyuh·luhr) plants. *Vascular* means "composed of or containing vessels," like the veins and arteries in your body. Scientists call plants that don't have this kind of tissue—such as mosses and other simple plants— nonvascular plants. All plants fall into one of these two groups.

▷ **What is the difference between vascular and nonvascular plants?**

Vascular plants have tubes that run between the roots and leaves; nonvascular plants do not.

QUICK LAB

FOR SCHOOL OR HOME

Tubelike Plant Parts

1. **Observe** Use a hand lens to examine the parts of a celery stalk, piece of moss, or leaf. Draw what you see.

2. **Hypothesize** Make a guess about the function of each structure.

3. Add water to a bottle so the water is about an inch deep. Add a few drops of food coloring to the water.

4. Try putting different plant pieces in the colored water. Observe them after a few minutes. Record what you see.

5. **Interpret Data** Write an explanation for what you see. Explain why your observations support or don't support your guess.

A 9

Inclusion

Support from Water
Ask students what a fire hose looks like when water is not running through it. (It is flat.) Then ask what a plant would look like without water. (It would be limp.) Demonstrate what happens when a limp piece of celery is placed in water. (As water rises up the tubes, it gives the plant strength.) **Spatial; Logical**

Cultural Perspective

State Plants
Provide students with the name of the official state flower and tree for your state. Challenge students to explain why they think these were chosen. Ask them if they often see examples of the state flower and tree. Encourage them to find out what flowers and trees neighboring states have chosen. **Linguistic**

Exploring the Main Idea
Show students a piece of moss from the Quick Lab. Challenge students to define the word *vascular* by looking at the picture of the celery plant and comparing the celery to the moss.

▶ **After Reading**
Have students answer the red question in the student book as **ongoing assessment**.

FOR SCHOOL OR HOME

Materials celery stalk, bit of moss, lettuce leaf, oak or maple leaf, water, food coloring, narrow-mouthed bottle, hand lens, knife

Science Process Skills *observe, hypothesize, interpret data*

Resources Activity Resources, pp. 4–5

Plan Ahead Use fresh celery and other plants.

Step 1 The celery stalk has strings through the stalk. The leaves have veins. Moss has no stems or veins.

Step 2 Students might suggest that water gets to different plant parts through the roots or stems, and that the stringy structures in celery carry something from the roots to the leaves.

Step 4 It may take 10 or 15 minutes before results will be obvious.

Step 5 Student explanations should include the idea that in some plants, water directly enters the cells of different plant parts, while in other plants, water is transported through tubelike structures in the stem.

Developing Vocabulary

vascular Stemming from the Latin word *vascularis*, meaning "small vessel," you may have students relate this term to their own bodies and compare the vascular systems of animals and plants.

nonvascular Explain to students that the prefix *non-* can usually be interpreted as "the opposite of" the base word.

What Are the Divisions of the Plant Kingdom?

Before Reading
Have students try to answer the red question at the top of the page.

Developing the Main Idea
Help students focus on the similarities and differences between the plant divisions shown. For example: Which reproduce by seeds? Which by spores?

Exploring the Main Idea
Ask students how plants differ from organisms such as animals or bacteria. Have students list on the chalkboard as many plants as they can in three minutes. Ask them to divide the list into three or more groups and to explain the basis for the groupings. (Examples: size, habitat, type)

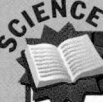

READING Charts

1. Possible answer: roses and maple tree—vascular plants.
2. Possible answer: Alike: Nonvascular plants and vascular plants are green, both divisions have some short plants; different: vascular plants have both seed plants and seedless plants, whereas nonvascular are all seedless; vascular plants may be tall while nonvascular plants are all short.

What Are the Divisions of the Plant Kingdom?

As you've discovered, all plants have certain characteristics in common. Every living thing that has these characteristics belongs to the plant kingdom. A kingdom is the largest subdivision of living things.

While all plants have certain characteristics in common, they have their differences, too. As you have seen, plants may be vascular or nonvascular. However, the plants within each of these two groups are far from identical. This observation prompted scientists to divide nonvascular plants into smaller and smaller

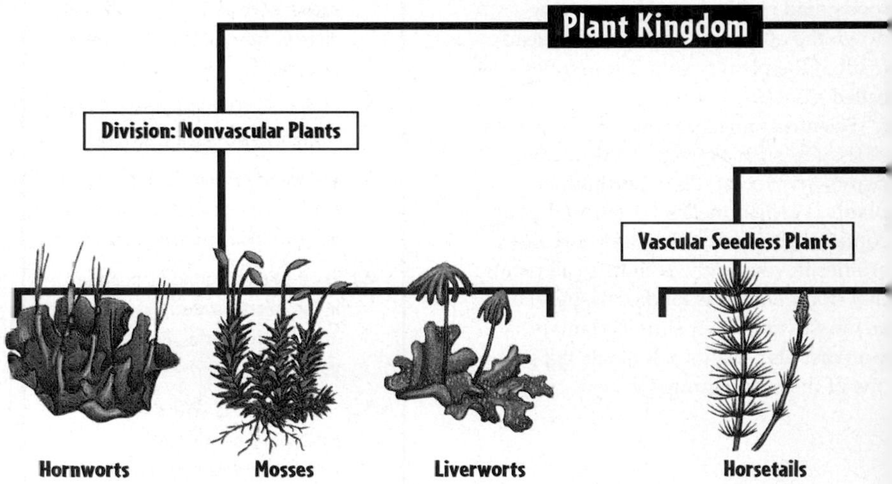
Plant Kingdom
Division: Nonvascular Plants
Vascular Seedless Plants
Hornworts
Mosses
Liverworts
Horsetails

READING Charts

1. Name two plants you are familiar with and the division you think each belongs to.
2. Pick two plant divisions from the chart. List two ways they are alike. List two ways they are different.

SCIENCE Reading Strategy

Summarize

Developing Reading Skills
Ask students to summarize the characteristics of the organisms described in this lesson. Then ask them to group the organisms according to divisions of the plant kingdom.

SCIENCE FOR ALL Advanced Learners

Earth Science
Water hyacinths are floating plants that were originally imported from South America. Invite interested students to research and report to the class how water hyacinths are used in purifying water, what problems these plants have caused, and efforts made to control some of these problems. (The plants are good absorbers of certain pollutants; but, they grow so abundantly they make waterways difficult for ships to pass through.) **Linguistic**

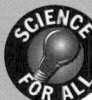

groups. The scientists did the same for vascular plants. They divided vascular plants into seedless plants and plants with seeds. Then they divided seed plants into flowering and nonflowering plants.

The smallest groups would have plants most like one another. The larger groups would have plants least like one another. This meant that the smaller the group, the more closely related were its members.

The chart on these two pages shows the plants divided into groups called *divisions*. These divisions make up the plant kingdom. You will discover the other kingdoms of living things on the following four pages.

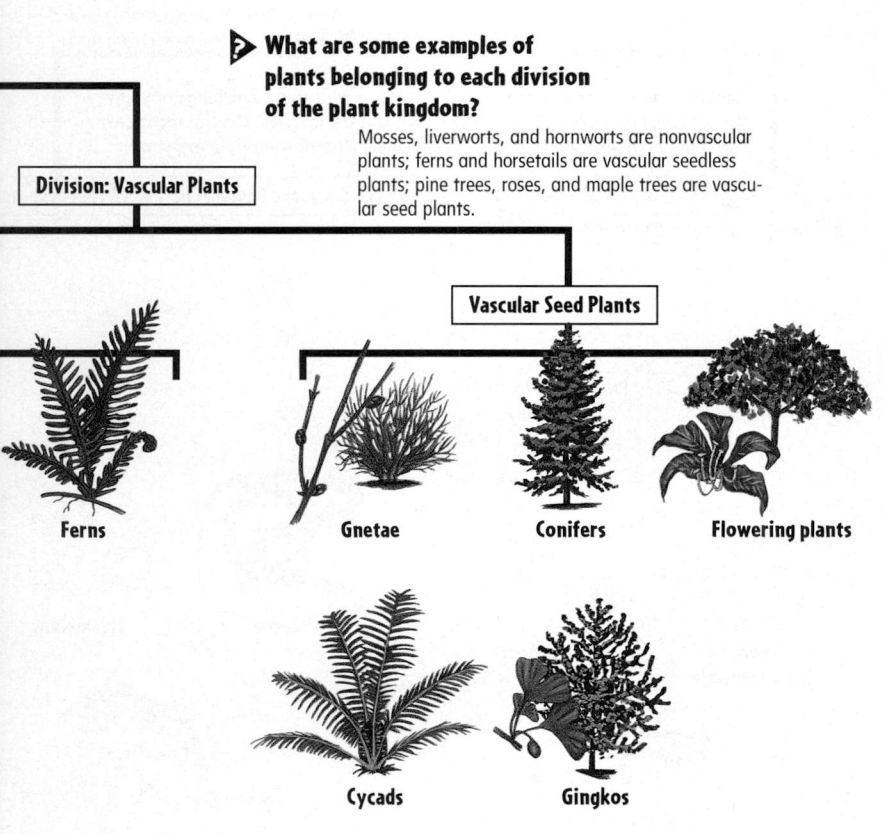

▷ **What are some examples of plants belonging to each division of the plant kingdom?**

Mosses, liverworts, and hornworts are nonvascular plants; ferns and horsetails are vascular seedless plants; pine trees, roses, and maple trees are vascular seed plants.

Division: Vascular Plants

Vascular Seed Plants

Ferns

Gnetae

Conifers

Flowering plants

Cycads

Gingkos

A 11

Using the Illustrations

Invite students to bring in pictures or drawings of plants from each division. Suggest they arrange the pictures according to the divisions on the diagram. Encourage them to comment on whether they think the samples look similar.

Developing the Main Idea

"Three let it be" and "red never dread" are used to remind people to stay away from poison ivy. Though the plant takes on many forms, it always has three leaves and its berries are never red. One way to relieve a poison ivy rash is to use jewel weed—a plant often found conveniently near poison ivy. If possible, display pictures of both plants and discuss the characteristics of each that can be used for identification.

Exploring the Main Idea

Challenge students to find out what plants are common to the area in which they live. Have them describe how these plants are different from those found in other areas with different kinds of plant life. Then have interested students make dioramas or collages showing the different kinds of plants found in two different kinds of environments.

▶ After Reading

Have students answer the red question in the student book as **ongoing assessment**.

Science Background

Classification

To keep track of the millions of species of plants and animals, biologists use a two-part naming system (binomial nomenclature)—*genus* and *species*. The parts are in Latin so the name will be understood around the world. Many familiar plants and animals also have a common name. Have students make a chart showing the Latin and common names for some plants. **Linguistic**

English Language Learners

Plant Adjectives

Challenge students to list all the adjectives they can think of to describe characteristics of plants. (Examples: prickly, smooth, spongy, hard, fluffy, flaky, furry) Have them use these characteristics to develop their own classification system. Then challenge them to use their system to classify several plants. **Linguistic; Logical**

What Makes Animals Different from Plants?

Before Reading
Have students try to answer the red question at the top of the page.

Developing the Main Idea
Help students contrast the basic characteristics of plants and animals. Ask:

- **How do animals get food? How do plants get food?** (Animals get food from plants or other animals that eat plants; plants make their own food.)

- **What structures do plants have that animals don't?** (roots, stems, leaves)

- **What structure do some animals have that plants don't?** (nerve cord)

- **Name five animals you are familiar with and the phylum or class you think each belongs to.** (Possible answers: dog, cat, rabbit—mammals; parakeet, parrot, cockatiel—birds; insects, spiders, lobsters, crabs—arthropods.)

- **Pick two classes. Tell how the members are alike and different.** (Possible answer: Birds and fish both have nerve cords and skeletons (backbones). Fish breathe underwater; birds that swim underwater must come up for air. Most birds are built for flying; fish are built for swimming.)

READING
Charts

> *Porifera, Platyhelminthes, Cnidaria, Arthropoda, Chordata*

▶ After Reading
Have students answer the red question in the student book as **ongoing assessment**.

What Makes Animals Different from Plants?

Unlike plants, animals cannot make their own food. Animals also differ from plants because animals can move from one place to another during some parts of their lives.

All animals are grouped into one kingdom, known as the animal kingdom. The animal kingdom is divided into smaller and smaller groups. The chart on this page shows two of these groups. The first level contains groups called *phyla* (FIGH·luh) (singular, *phylum*). Some are shown on the left. The next level contains groups called *classes*. Some examples of animals in these groups are shown on the right.

▷ **How are animals different from plants?**
Animals move from place to place and cannot make their own food.

Animal Kingdom

Phyla in the animal kingdom are like divisions in the plant kingdom. On the left are members of four phyla without backbones. On the right are five classes of the phylum with backbones. Not all the phyla are shown.

Phyla Without Backbone

Classes of the Phylum *Chordata* with Backbone

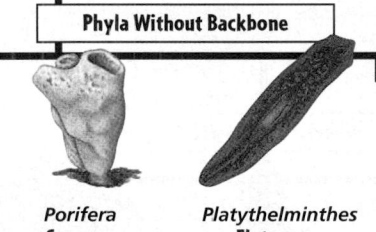

Porifera
Sponges

Platythelminthes
Flatworms

Fish

Birds

Cnidaria
Sea Anemones

Arthropoda
Crustaceans

Reptiles

Amphibians

READING
Charts

List the five phyla shown.

Mammals

SCIENCE FOR ALL   Advanced Learners

Animals with Nerve Cords
Chordates all had a "notochord" (nerve cord) at some time during their life cycle. In vertebrates this notochord is surrounded or replaced by the vertebral column. Have students find out the roots in the word *notochord* and use the information to make captions for photographs or hand-drawn pictures of such notochords as those of the lancelet or the lamprey.
Linguistic

What Is a Fungus?

It may be one celled or many celled. It doesn't make its own food as plants do or eat food as animals do. Instead it simply absorbs (takes in) food from decaying dead organisms and wastes in its environment. What is it? It's a **fungus** (FUNG·guhs).

Fungi (FUN·jigh)—the plural of *fungus*—can be very useful living things. Some of them have great flavors. Others contain chemicals that fight diseases. Still others help your bread to rise or turn cheeses sharp and tangy. Fungi in soil break down decaying plants and animals so that their chemicals can be used by living things. You might say that such fungi clean up our environment.

Unfortunately, the fungus kingdom also contains organisms that cause

problems for people. Some fungi are poisonous. Some fungi give people itchy diseases, like athlete's foot. Some fungi can spoil food and make you sick. Some fungi coat bathroom tiles and basement walls with smelly black or white fuzz. In the autumn of 1997, one kind of fungus was even responsible for the closing of a library in Staten Island, a part of New York City. The fungus, which grows in damp places like the library's basement, caused people to cough and sneeze as if they had the flu.

The chart on this page shows the groups of the fungus kingdom.

▷ **How are members of the fungus kingdom different from plants?**
Fungi don't make their own food but absorb it from decaying organisms

Fungus Kingdom

Yeasts, morels, mildews | **Molds** | **Mushrooms, smuts, rusts**

READING Diagrams

1. What are the three main groups of fungi?
2. Make a chart listing things useful fungi can do.

A 13

 **Science Background**

Edible Fungi

Edible fungi are found in most local grocery stores. Have students look for edible fungi: different kinds of mushrooms, yeast, the mold in blue cheese, and anything with truffles. Roquefort and Camembert cheeses get their flavor from the mold *Penicillium*, which is why someone allergic to penicillin may also be allergic to these cheeses.

SCIENCE FOR ALL **Inclusion**

Grow Bread Mold

Have students moisten a piece of bread and place it in a dish. Expose it to air for about 24 hours. Then place it in a self-sealing plastic bag and place it in a warm, dark place. Students should observe the bread every day to check for mold. Caution all students, especially those with mold allergies, not to remove the moldy bread from the plastic bag. (Students should observe black mold spores on the bread.) **Kinesthetic; Logical**

What Is a Fungus?

Before Reading
Have students try to answer the red question at the top of the page.

Developing the Main Idea
Ask:

■ **Describe the main differences between fungi and green plants.** (Plants make their own food; fungi absorb food from other organisms.)

Explain to students that a simple mold changed medical history when it was found that an antibiotic, penicillin, could be made from it. Point out that students may have seen this mold growing on spoiled citrus fruits. Another important medicine, the antibiotic Aureomycin™, is also made from a fungus. Yeastlike fungi are also used to produce vitamin D and other vitamins.

READING Diagrams

1. yeasts, morels, and mildews; molds; mushrooms, smuts, and rusts

2. Student charts might include fungi used to make antibiotics (*Penicillium* mold), cheeses (molds), edible mushrooms, breads, beer and wine (yeasts).

▶ **After Reading**
Have students answer the red question in the student book as **ongoing assessment**.

Developing Vocabulary

fungus The word *fungus* comes from the Greek word *spongos*, or sponge. Relate this to the fact that fungi absorb their food from decaying dead organisms and environmental wastes, similar to the way a sponge absorbs water.

What Is a Protist?

Before Reading
Have students try to answer the red question at the top of the page.

Developing the Main Idea
Compare and contrast protists and plants. Ask:

- **Which protists are most similar to green plants? Why?** (green algae; because they contain chlorophyll and can make their own food)

- **How do you think protists got their name?** (*Pro-* means "before" and protists are the first or most primal organisms.)

Challenge students to use this information to define the words *prologue* and *prototype*. (*Prologue* is an introduction, *prototype* is a model made before something begins to be manufactured.)

Compare protists and animals. Ask:

- **How are some protists like animals?** (They can move from place to place, they eat other organisms for food, they are made up of cells, and they have nuclei.)

▶ **After Reading**
Have students answer the red question in the student book as **ongoing assessment**.

Developing Vocabulary

protist Remind students that the prefix *pro-* means "before" and relate to them that the word *protist* is derived from the Greek *protistos*, or first. The word *protist* can be loosely translated as "first organism."

What Is a Protist?

What do you see when you look into a lake, pond, river, or ocean? Sometimes it looks like clear water. However, that "clear" water is home to millions of microscopic living things that belong to the **protist** (PROH·tist) kingdom. This kingdom isn't made up of just microscopic living things. It also includes living things you can see without a microscope, such as seaweed and green pond scum. Although most protists live in water, some inhabit the land.

Some protists are single cells that swim in the water in search of smaller living things to eat. Others, like seaweeds, are made up of groups of the same cells that are linked together. Called algae, these protists don't have to hunt for food. They contain chlorophyll. All they have to do is float on water in the sunlight, soak up the Sun's rays, and make their own food. Still other kinds of protists are one celled, swim around, and contain chlorophyll.

Members of the protist kingdom certainly seem very different. However, if scientists put them in the same kingdom, they must have something in common. You would discover that "something" if you peered at the cells of protists under a microscope. You'd notice a dense, dark structure, called a *nucleus* (NEW·klee·uhs) inside each cell. If you looked very carefully, you'd see that the nucleus was surrounded by a thin envelope. Scientists call this envelope a *membrane* (MEM·brayn). The chart shows some of the groups of the protist kingdom.

▷ **How are some protists like plants?**
Many make their own food; all have cells with nuclei.

Protist Kingdom

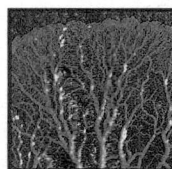
Slime molds

Diatoms

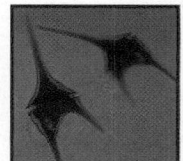
Dinoflagellates

Green algae

Euglenas

A 14

Inclusion

Protists
The category "protista" was suggested in 1866, but scientists are still discussing what goes into this classification. A good example is a eukaryote (has a nucleus) that is not a fungus, plant, or animal. Some scientists have included fungi, but others include only single-celled organisms with a nucleus. Protists have a cell membrane, usually are unicellular, and live in colonies. Have students find out more about protists and report their findings to the class. **Linguistic**

What Are Bacteria?

Bacteria (bak·TEER·ee·uh) are the tiniest living things. They are also very simple. Some can cause a great deal of trouble, like infections. Others are necessary for animals and plants to survive.

Some kinds of bacteria group together in clusters or chains. Other kinds don't. You can only see bacteria under a microscope. Each *bacterium* (bak·TEER·ee·uhm) is a single cell without a nucleus.

The "ancient" bacteria kingdom includes some fascinating organisms. One type lives in the digestive system of cows. It helps the cow by digesting cellulose, the main substance in grass, which the cow eats but can't digest. Still another kind of "ancient" bacterium lives deep in the ocean, where lava seeps through cracks in

the ocean floor. The red-hot lava heats the water up to 105°C. That's hotter than the temperature of boiling water!

The true bacteria kingdom also contains some unusual members. Have you ever seen a blue-green spot in a polar bear's white fur? If so, you detected *cyanobacteria* (sigh·uh·noh·bak·TEER·ee·uh). The prefix *cyano-* means "blue."

Some true bacteria cause diseases in plants and animals. A "strep" throat is caused by a true bacterium. If your stomach aches after eating spoiled food, the culprit is likely to be another true bacterium. More serious diseases like tuberculosis and certain kinds of pneumonia are also caused by true bacteria.

▷ **How are bacteria different from plants and other organisms?**

They are single-celled organisms that do not have nuclei.

Bacteria Kingdoms

"Ancient" Bacteria	True Bacteria

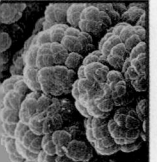 

These bacteria are methanogens. They use carbon dioxide and produce methane (natural gas).

 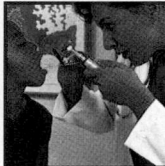

These bacteria are streptococci—the ones that can give you a strep throat.

A 15

Science Background

Clean Water

Water purification, particularly the removal of harmful bacteria, is the responsibility of local water utility services or treatment facilities. Most communities screen out debris, then remove small particles with chemicals, then finish by using a disinfectant (either chlorine or ozone) to kill the remaining bacteria. Still, most communities have an acceptable level of different types of bacteria.

Inclusion

SCIENCE FOR ALL

Pond Water

Place pond water and a piece of a pond plant in a jar. Put the jar in a safe spot that gets lots of Sun but not in direct sunlight. Have students work in groups and take turns observing and drawing pictures of what they see. Allow volunteers to report significant observations to the class. Continue observations for about 2 weeks. **Social; Spatial**

What Are Bacteria?

Before Reading
Have students try to answer the red question at the top of the page.

Developing the Main Idea
Compare and contrast bacteria with plants and the other organisms studied in this lesson.

- **What do bacteria have in common with protists?** (They are single-celled like many protists.)
- **How are bacteria different from all plants, animals, and fungi?** (Bacteria do not have nuclei in their cells.)
- **What are two kinds of ancient bacteria?** (Possible answer: cellulose-digesting bacteria and bacteria that live deep in the ocean in undersea hot springs.)
- **Describe two kinds of true bacteria.** (Possible answer: cyanobacteria and strep-throat bacteria; both are microscopic, single-celled organisms without nuclei. Cyanobacteria appear blue-green in color and strep-throat bacteria cause disease.)

▶ **After Reading**
Have students answer the red question in the student book as **ongoing assessment**.

Developing Vocabulary

bacterium (sing.), **bacteria** (plural)
Derived from the diminutive form of the Greek word *baktron*, meaning "a staff," the word *bacteria* was probably first used to describe the rod-shaped bacillus (which translates from the Latin *bacillum*, meaning "little rod").

What Was "The Vine That Ate the South?"

Before Reading
Have students try to answer the red question at the top of the page.

Developing the Main Idea
Ask students to name or describe weeds they are familiar with. Discuss problems weeds cause by asking them why people want to get rid of weeds. Ask students to describe their favorite flowers or plants and explain why they favor them.

Using the Illustrations
Ask students how the photographs illustrate one of the reasons kudzu became so popular in the United States. (The purple flowers are beautiful.) Point out that kudzu dies out in the winter and returns the next spring. It is still being used to feed cows.

▶After Reading
Have students answer the red question in the student book as **ongoing assessment**.

What Was "The Vine That Ate the South"?

The Philadelphia Centennial Exposition in 1876 was part of the United States' 100th birthday celebration. Many countries had exhibits. The Japanese, known for their fine gardens, exhibited many unusual plants.

One of those plants was a woody vine. It had hairy green leaves and tiny purple flowers that hung in long clusters. It was called "kudzu" (KOOD·zew).

Today people in America's southern states call it other things: "Mile-a-Minute Vine," "Foot-a-Night Vine," and, more frighteningly, "The Vine That Ate the South."

"The Vine That Ate the South," and "Mile-a-Minute Vine" are exaggerations, but "Foot-a-Night Vine" is not. The plant can grow that much each day. It can spread out over 18 meters (60 feet) in a single summer and choke the life out of other, weaker plants. Fortunately, it dies back in the winter.

How did kudzu escape from Philadelphia? Why does it now cover seven million acres of America's southland? It was pretty. In the late 1800s, homeowners used it to decorate gardens and homes. It was tasty to animals. In the 1920s farmers grew it to feed cows, sheep, and other farm animals. Its huge 2-meter-long (6-foot-long) roots grew to be 18 centimeters (7 inches) in diameter and weighed up to 182 kilograms (400 pounds). Those roots hung on to soil in a tight grip. In the 1940s

A 16

conservation workers planted it all over the South to keep soil from being washed away by heavy rains.

What nobody counted on was the hardiness of the plant. It grew best in hot, rainy areas. It found an ideal home in the South. There was something else that promoted its rapid growth—its lack of natural enemies. They kept it in check in Japan but not in America. These were insect pests that lived in Japan but not in the American South.

Today kudzu is labeled a weed by the United States Department of Agriculture. Kudzu can be controlled with weed killers.

▷ Why did kudzu become such a problem in the South?
Weather conditions help it grow fast; it chokes out other plants; it has no natural insect enemies there.

The purple flowers of the kudzu are very beautiful. They smell good, too. Lots of people bought the plants to decorate their properties.

Kudzu is a very fast growing plant. It can spread 18 meters (60 feet) in a single summer.

SCIENCE Reading Strategy

Cause and Effect
Developing Reading Skills
Have students give examples of cause-and-effect relationships described on this and the facing page. They can list a cause followed by an arrow and an effect. For example: It can spread out over 18 meters (60 feet) in a single summer.
→ It chokes weaker plants.

Math | MiniLesson

Change Units Between Metric and Customary Length

Develop As students read about lengths of kudzu plants, they can use this table to estimate equivalents between metric and customary units of lengths.

Length	
1 in. ≈ 2.5 cm	1 cm ≈ 0.4 in.
1 yd. ≈ 0.9 m	1 m ≈ 1.1 yd.
1 mi. ≈ 1.6 km	1 km ≈ 0.6 mi.

Note: ≈ means "is approximately equal to"

Complete: 8 in. ≈ ▢ cm

Think: 1 in. ≈ 2.5 cm

$8 \times 2.5 = 20$

So, 8 in. is about 20 cm.

Practice Have pairs of students measure the length of their table using a centimeter ruler. Then have them measure the length again using an inch ruler.

Activity Complete.
1. 5 mi. ≈ ▢ km (8)
2. 86 cm ≈ ▢ in. (34.4)

Why It Matters

There are many different kinds of plants, but they are all very important. Without plants, life would be impossible on Earth. Almost everything you eat comes from plants, or from animals that eat plants.

Think and Write

- What do plants have in common?

- How are plants similar to animals, protists, fungi, and bacteria? How are plants different?

- How are vascular plants different from nonvascular plants?

- Describe three characteristics of plants.

- **Critical Thinking** How can plants that are imported from other parts of the world become pests here?

L·I·N·K·S

WRITING LINK

Write a paragraph. Tell what plants are important in your life, and explain why.

MATH LINK

Solve this problem. Under ideal conditions a bacterium can divide into two bacteria every 20 minutes. Then each of those bacteria can divide into two new ones after another 20 minutes. If you start with one bacterium, how many will you have after one hour? After two hours? After three hours? Five hours? Eight hours?

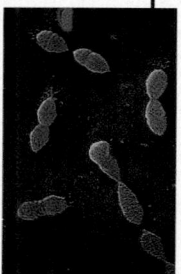

ART LINK

Make a poster. Design a poster using spore prints. Take a ripe mushroom, and remove the stalk. Examine the mushroom cap with a hand lens. Then put the cap, with the underside facing down, on a piece of poster paper. Cover it with a bowl. After three hours, remove the bowl. Experiment with making various designs.

TECHNOLOGY LINK

At the Computer Visit www.mhscience02.com for more links.

A 17

---

3 Lesson Review

Answers to Think and Write

1. All plants have cell walls and contain chlorophyll, and most have stems, leaves and roots. (pp. A5–A7)

2. All are made up of cells. All perform functions necessary for life. Almost all plants make their own food. Animals and fungi cannot make their own food. Plants cannot move from place to place as animals can. Bacteria do not have nuclei; plant cells do. Only plant cells have cell walls. (pp. A12–A15)

3. Vascular plants have tubes that carry water, food, and minerals throughout the plant. Nonvascular plants do not have tubes. (p. A9)

4. Almost all plants are green because they contain chlorophyll; they make their own food; they have roots, stems, and leaves; they have cells with cell walls. (pp. A5–A9)

5. **Critical Thinking** Possible answer: An imported plant may not have natural enemies, which means its growth would go unchecked. (p. A16)

Summarize
Check students' understanding by having them write a brief summary of the lesson in their own words.

WRITING LINK
Students might write about the trees they see everyday on their way to school or describe some other aspect of their lives affected by plants.

MATH LINK
Students can calculate the number of bacteria using the formula: $B = 2^t$ where $t = 3 \times$ the number of hours. 1 hour (8); 2 hours (64); 3 hours (512); 5 hours (32,768); 8 hours (16,777,216)

ART LINK
Students' posters can be an exercise in pattern making, using the spore prints to create patterns. Students might also experiment with other kinds of transfer art, such as stamp pad prints.

Inclusion

Kudzu Growth
Have students measure the perimeter of the classroom or the length of the hallway outside the room. Then have them calculate how long it would take a single kudzu vine to grow that distance if the vine grows at the rate of one foot per day. **Logical; Kinesthetic**

✓ Informal Assessment

Easy/Average Ask students to make a diagram classifying plants, animals, fungi, and protists. Challenge them to put in as much detail as possible and review the diagrams as a class.

Challenge Have students name examples for each of the major categories shown in the diagrams (pp. A10–A14) in the lesson.

LESSON 2 · Roots, Stems, and Leaves

Objectives

- Explore how a plant's parts help it survive.
- Understand the functions of roots and stems.
- Understand the functions of leaves.

Resources

- Activity Resources, pp. 6–10
- Reading in Science Resources, pp. 11–16
- Vocabulary Cards
- Reading Aid Transparency A2
- Visual Aid Transparency 1
- School to Home Activities, pp. 3–4

Build on Prior Knowledge

Have students discuss what they know about plant parts and how they help a plant to survive. Ask them to describe ways that people survive in different environments, such as the Arctic, desert regions, or rain forests. (Possible answers: ways to stay warm, cool, and dry; different kinds of clothing; different kinds of shelters)

1 Get Ready

Developing the Main Idea

Ask students to list needs they have in common with plants. (Possible answers: food, water, favorable temperatures) Ask students to describe how plants from different environments might be different. (Leaves might be shiny or dull, be of different sizes or shapes, or have different roots and stems.) Explain that these differences are adaptations that help plants survive by aiding in the absorption of water, sunlight, and nutrients, or that act to protect the plant from environmental factors or predators.

LESSON 2 · Roots, Stems, and Leaves

Vocabulary

xylem, A20
cortex, A20
epidermis, A20
root cap, A20
root hairs, A20
phloem, A21
cambium, A21
chloroplast, A24
transpiration, A25

Get Ready

What do you have in common with a plant? Would you believe that you and a plant have similar needs? Still, there is a big difference. You can move around to get things. You can change things around you—like your room temperature. Plants stay in one place, yet different kinds of plants can survive in very different places. How? What helps plants survive in their surroundings?

Process Skill

You predict when you state possible results of an event or experiment.

A 18

Science Background

Succulents

Succulents are fleshy plants such as cactus, aloe, and yucca. Their roots, stems, and leaves are adapted to survive extreme heat and dryness. Some have tiny leaves with a hard covering. Others have thick, fleshy leaves with a waxy covering. Both types reduce evaporation. Their stems contain juicy tissue to retain and store water. Their roots are deep or broad to reach nearby water.

Explore Activity

How Do a Plant's Parts Help It Survive?

Materials
cactus

water plant, such as an *Elodea* or a duckweed

flowering plant, such as a geranium

Procedure

1. **Observe** Look at the physical properties of the leaves of each plant. Note the color, size, and shape of the leaves.

2. **Communicate** List any other plant parts that you see.

3. **Communicate** Observe the physical properties of these parts. Record your observations.

Drawing Conclusions

1. **Interpret Data** How do the parts of a cactus help it survive in a hot, dry desert?

2. **Infer** Would the geranium be able to survive in the desert? Why or why not?

3. **Infer** Could the water plant survive out of water? Why or why not?

4. **Going Further: Predict** Could these plants survive outside where you live? Why or why not? For each plant, what conditions would you have to change so that the plant could survive outside where you live?

A 19

Alternative Explore Activity

Materials stems, roots, and leaves from a variety of plants, such as leaves of different sizes and shapes (like pine needles), stems of different lengths, taproots and fibrous roots. (Make sure nothing can hurt when touched.)

Plant Parts Have students feel the various stems and describe how they are different. Ask students to predict where a plant with this part might live and how the part helps the plant survive. Have them do the same for the various stems and leaves. **Kinesthetic**

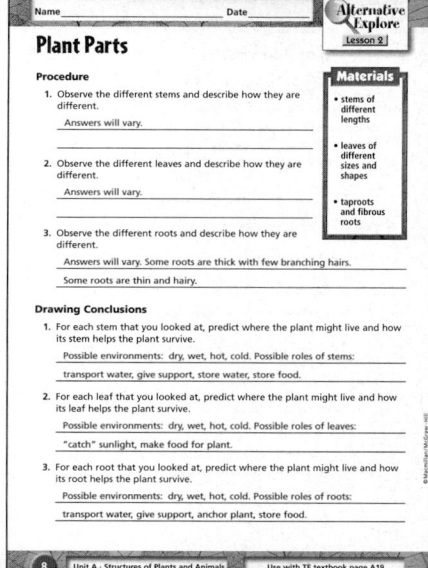

Activity Resources, p. 8

Explore Activity

How Do a Plant's Parts Help It Survive?

Science Process Skills *observe, communicate, interpret data, infer, predict*

Resources Activity Resources, pp. 6–7

Pacing 30–40 minutes

Grouping individual

Plan Ahead In addition to the plants from Lesson 1, common houseplants, wildflowers, and duckweed from ponds can be used. Try to obtain cactus plants with roots that the students can see.

Procedure

1. As an option, you may wish to provide students with a hand lens to use when making their observations.

Answers to Drawing Conclusions

1. The spines minimize water loss and protect the plant from animals. The stem is green and can make food; it can also store water. Cactus roots spread out a long way close to the surface.

2. Probably not; too much water would be lost through the large surface area of the leaves and the thin stem couldn't store water.

3. No; water plants lack the roots needed to live in soil.

4. Answers depend on the precipitation and temperature conditions of your area. By providing proper temperature and water conditions, the cactus and flowering plant might survive, but the water plant probably would not.

 Inquiry Students can ask their own questions to explore, such as, How do plants adapt to the change of seasons? (Possible answer: In some climates, leaves fall off trees in winter and grow back in spring.)

Technology

- When time is short, preview the activity with the **Explore Activity Video**.

How Do a Plant's Parts Help It Survive?

Before Reading
Have students try to answer the red question at the top of the page.

Developing the Main Idea
Help students focus on the important work of roots by asking them to make a list of the verbs used on this page. Ask:

■ **What do these verbs tell you about roots?** (They anchor plants, draw up water and minerals, are always growing.)

■ **What roots and stems do you eat?** (Possible answers: roots: carrots, sweet potatoes, turnips; stems: celery, asparagus.)

Developing Vocabulary

xylem To help students remember that this is the tissue through which water rises, tell them that the syllable *xy-* rhymes with "sky."

cortex Tell students that *cor-*, the first syllable of this word, echoes the word "core," a helpful reminder that it is the tissue that surrounds the core of the root.

epidermis Tell students that the Latin root *derm*, meaning "skin," is also found in *dermatologist*, meaning "skin doctor."

root cap To help students understand the term *root cap*, tell them to think of a cap they wear on their heads. Then compare it to the tough layer of cells that cap the tip of a root.

root hair Tell or show students that root hairs resemble the hairs on their own heads.

Read to Learn

Main Idea All plants have certain parts with the same functions.

How Do a Plant's Parts Help It Survive?

Some plant roots help you survive. That's because they are foods. Beets, carrots, sweet potatoes, radishes, and turnips are the roots of different plants. How do roots help a plant survive?

Most plants have roots that hold them in the ground. Some plants, like mosses, don't have true roots. Still, mosses have rootlike structures that anchor them. Roots help keep plants from getting swept away by wind and running water. Roots draw up water and minerals from the soil. Plants mus[t] have water and minerals to make their own food. Roots also store food for th[e] plant. That's especially true of sweet potato, sugar beet, and carrot plants.

A root gets its start early in the life of a plant. If you were to look at a lim[a] bean as it sprouted, you would see a tiny piece of the young plant growing straight downward. This is the plant's first root.

This root bores deeper and deeper into the soil. Why don't the rough particles of soil rub away and harm the young root? The tip of the root is protected by a layer of tough cells called the root cap.

Parts of a Root

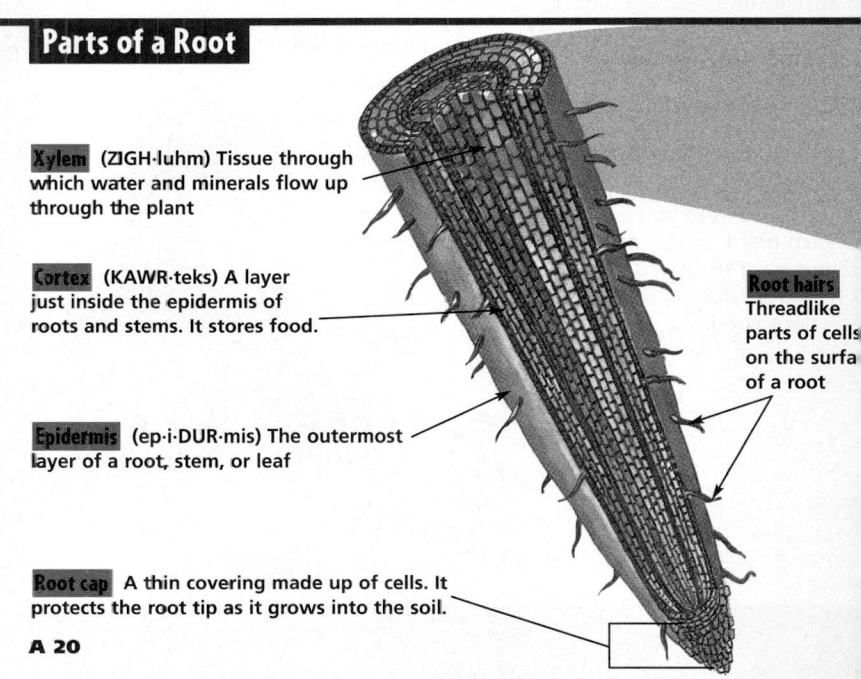

Xylem (ZIGH-luhm) Tissue through which water and minerals flow up through the plant

Cortex (KAWR-teks) A layer just inside the epidermis of roots and stems. It stores food.

Epidermis (ep-i-DUR-mis) The outermost layer of a root, stem, or leaf

Root cap A thin covering made up of cells. It protects the root tip as it grows into the soil.

Root hairs Threadlike parts of cells on the surfa[ce] of a root

A 20

Lesson Outline

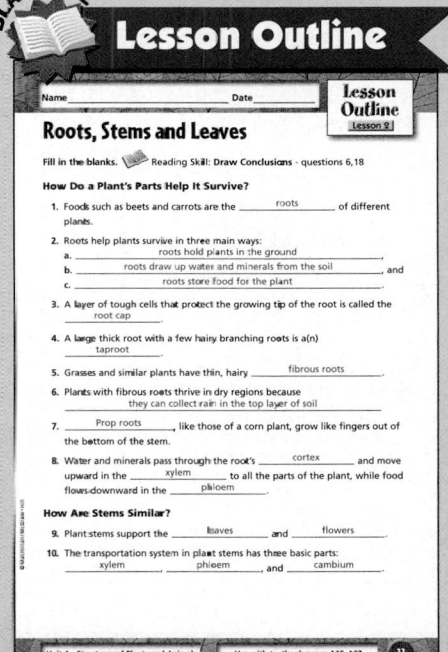

Reading in Science Resources, p. 11

Science Background

Roots
Only one root is present in each seed. This primary root is the first part of the plant to break out of the sprouting seed. Roots tend to grow downward (influenced by gravity and the presence of water) no matter which way a seed is planted. Dicots have taproots and monocots have fibrous roots. Prop roots and aerial roots are "adventitious roots"—coming from the side of a plant or from a stem or leaf. Root hairs greatly increase the surface area of the root.

Soon more roots branch out from the sides of the original root. *Taproots* have one large root with a few hairy branching roots. They look like a carrot or a beet. Other roots, like those of grass or rye plants, are made up of only thin hairy branching roots called *fibrous roots*.

Taproots tend to grow deep into the ground and reach water deep down. Fibrous roots spread out near the soil's surface. They collect water where there is little rain that only soaks into the very top layer of soil.

Fibrous roots can make huge networks. The total surface area of the root system of a single rye plant was 639 square meters (6,879 square feet)!

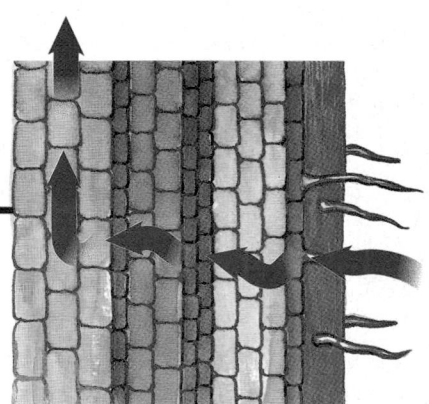

Phloem (FLOH·em) Tissue through which food from the leaves moves down through a plant

Cambium (KAM·bee·uhm) A layer that separates the xylem from the phloem. The cambium is where new xylem and phloem grow.

Some plants like orchids, that grow high in the branches of rain forest trees, have *aerial roots*. These roots never touch the ground. They take in moisture from the air. *Prop roots*, like those of a corn plant, grow like fingers out of the bottom of the stem. These roots help prop up the plant.

The structure of a root helps it absorb water and minerals and send them to other parts of the plant. The diagram shows how this happens.

Water and minerals enter the root hairs. They pass through the root's cortex to the xylem. They then move up the xylem, into the plant's stem, and to all parts of the plant.

READING Draw Conclusions
How do you think fibrous roots would help a plant grow in a dry or desert area?

A 21

Developing the Main Idea

Ask students to write a paragraph from the viewpoint of a drop of water in the soil. Have them describe how the root absorbs water and minerals and sends them to other parts of the plant.

Students may have seen tree roots that have cracked or broken up sidewalks. Explain that millions of plant cells all working together can create a tremendous amount of force.

▶After Reading
Have students answer the red question in the student book as **ongoing assessment**.

Technology

- ■Visual Aid Transparency 1: *Parts of a Root*

Developing Vocabulary

phloem To help students remember that food flows down through this tissue, tell them to think of its echo in the word "flows."

cambium This word comes from a Latin word that means "exchange," because its cells change into both xylem and phloem cells.

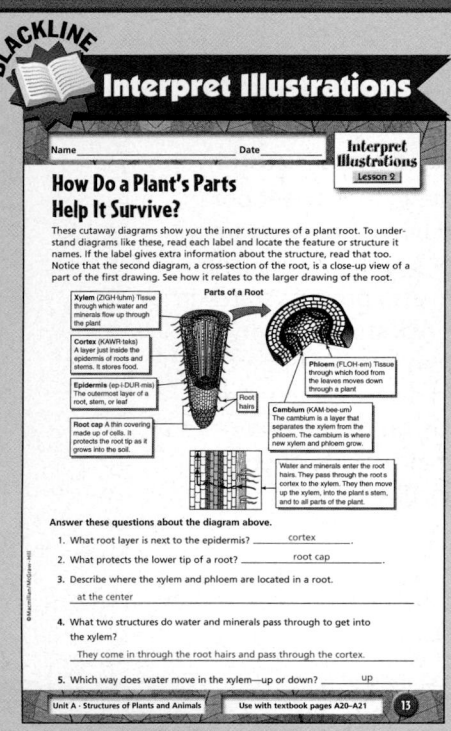
SCIENCE **Reading MiniLesson**

Draw Conclusions

Develop Discuss with students the meaning of the word *aerial* (in the air or up above). Point out that knowing the meaning helps us draw a conclusion about where to find aerial roots (up in trees, not on the ground). Adding facts from the text, students should be able to conclude that aerial roots never touch the ground and take moisture from the air.

Practice Ask students what evidence they find in the text on page A20 to support these conclusions: 1. The structures on mosses are rootlike. (Answer: They anchor moss like a plant's roots do.) 2. We eat roots. (Carrots, potatoes, radishes, and turnips are roots of plants.)

How Are Stems Similar?

Before Reading
Have students try to answer the red question at the top of the page.

Developing the Main Idea
Explain that during growing season, cambium cells in a woody stem divide rapidly producing xylem toward the center of the tree and phloem toward the outer edge or bark.

Provide students with a picture of a cross-section of a tree showing the annual rings. Tell them that each ring represents a year's growth. Point out examples of where the rings are thicker and thinner. Ask:

- **What can these rings tell you about the growing conditions during the years the tree grew?** (Thick rings mean good growing conditions, such as plenty of light, moisture, and proper temperatures; thin rings indicate poor conditions, such as drought.)

READING Diagrams

The woody stem has many concentric circles and consists mostly of xylem with the phloem concentrated near the outside. In the soft stem, there are about equal amounts of xylem and phloem arranged in a circle. Point out that cambium is the region of growth in both kinds of stems.

How Are Stems Similar?

Some stems are soft and delicate, like those of a young corn plant. Others are hard and tough, like those of a giant redwood tree. No matter what they look like, all stems have certain things in common.

All stems support leaves. Some also support flowers. Stems help leaves reach open places, where the leaves can be bathed in sunlight.

Stems also hold the transportation system for plants. This system lets water and minerals move from the roots to all parts of the plant, especially its leaves. It moves foods made in leaves to all other parts of the plant.

The *xylem* makes up the part of the transportation system that moves water and minerals up from the roots. The *phloem* moves food from the plant's leaves to its other parts. Many stems also have a *cambium*—a layer of cells—that separates the two. In addition, woody stems are protected by a tough outer layer of tissue, called bark.

READING Diagrams

How are the xylem, phloem, and cambium arranged differently in a woody stem and in a soft stem?

A 22

Parts of a Stem

Soft and woody stems have the same basic parts for transporting water, minerals, and food to all parts of a plant.

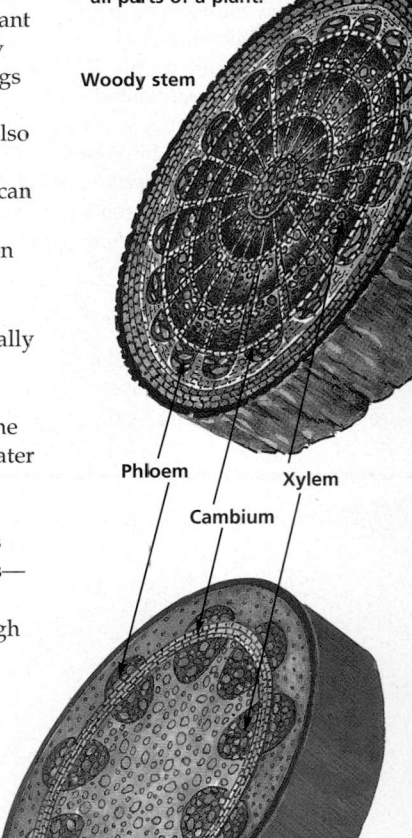

Woody stem

Phloem

Cambium

Xylem

Soft stem

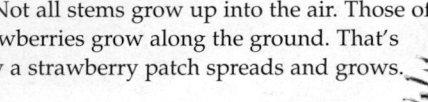

Strawberry stems, called runners, grow along the ground.

A potato is an underground stem.

Some stems do more than support a plant and give it a transportation system. For example, the stems of plants like potatoes and sugarcane store food for the plants to use later. The potatoes and sugarcane you eat actually are stems. The stems of cactus plants store water, which the plants use during long dry periods in the desert. Still other stems, like those of asparagus, help make the plant's food.

Not all stems grow up into the air. Those of strawberries grow along the ground. That's how a strawberry patch spreads and grows.

The stem of the cactus stores water.

 What are two ways in which all stems are similar?
They support leaves and hold the transportation system of the plant.

Using the Illustrations
Have students focus on the picture of a potato plant. Explain that although they grow underground, white potatoes are not roots like sweet potatoes. They are modified stems called tubers—short, thick, fleshy parts of underground stems.

Developing the Main Idea
Ask students to brainstorm ways in which stems are useful in our daily lives. (Maple trees are tapped for maple sugar; some medicines such as quinine and salicylic acid are made from certain tree barks; bamboo stems are used for building houses, many household items, and tools.)

▶ **After Reading**
Have students answer the red question in the student book as **ongoing assessment**.

Cultural Perspective

Potatoes
People of the Andes were the first to grow potatoes more than 6,000 years ago. They used such scientific methods as terracing and freeze-drying to improve their crops, hydrological techniques that are still in use today.

When the potato was first introduced in Europe in the 16th century people did not want to eat it because it grew in the ground. Wars and pillaging armies had devoured all the food in sight, which forced people to dig in the ground for the only food left.

Inclusion

Stem Collage
Invite students to make a collage or display of examples of different kinds of stems. Have them label each with the name of the plant and the kind of stem. They can also add adjectives, such as *soft* or *hard*, *thick* or *thin*. **Spatial**

What Are Leaves?

Before Reading
Have students try to answer the red question at the top of the first text column.

Developing the Main Idea
Remind students that leaves can be classified as simple (single) or compound (in clusters). A typical leaf has an epidermis, cells with chloroplasts, and stomata, or pores. We eat many different kinds of leaves as part of our diet. Ask students what kinds of leaves they eat. (Lettuce and salad greens)

Exploring the Main Idea
Show students a prepared microscope slide of a leaf section. Help students locate the structures mentioned in the text.

Help students locate an open stoma on the diagram and the guard cells on either side of the stoma. Ask:

- **Why are the epidermis and cuticle important to a plant?** (They keep leaves from drying out.)

READING Diagrams

1. the petiole
2. Student paragraphs should include the idea that a leaf needs sunlight, water, minerals, and air to make food.

Developing Vocabulary

chloroplast Tell students that the prefix *chloro-* is from the Greek word *chloros*, meaning "pale green." The suffix *-plast* is a derivative of the Greek word *plassein*, meaning "to form." Chloroplasts are the green "factories" where food is formed.

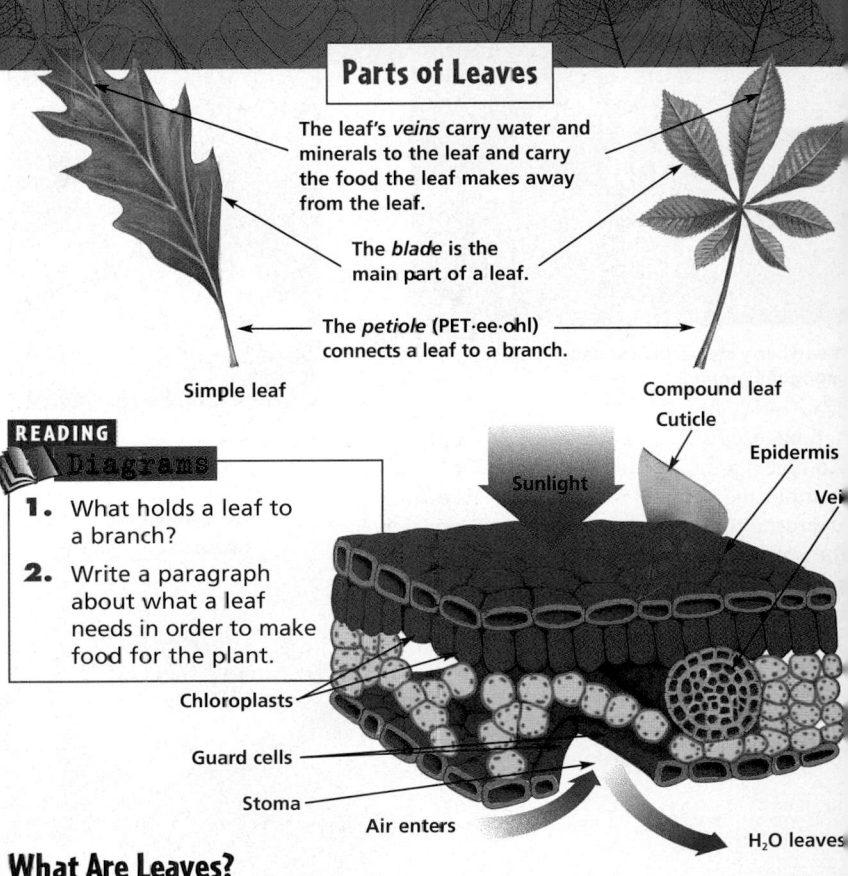

Parts of Leaves

The leaf's *veins* carry water and minerals to the leaf and carry the food the leaf makes away from the leaf.

The *blade* is the main part of a leaf.

The *petiole* (PET·ee·ohl) connects a leaf to a branch.

Simple leaf

Compound leaf

Cuticle

Epidermis

Ve[in]

Sunlight

Chloroplasts

Guard cells

Stoma

Air enters

H_2O leaves

READING Diagrams

1. What holds a leaf to a branch?
2. Write a paragraph about what a leaf needs in order to make food for the plant.

What Are Leaves?

Leaves come in all shapes and sizes. Most of the leaves you see hang from their plants as single leaves or in groups. Maple and oak trees have single leaves. They're called *simple* leaves.

Horse chestnut and locust leaves come in clusters. These are called *compound* leaves.

The parts of a leaf work together to help keep the plant alive.

The outermost layer of a leaf is its *epidermis*. Cells of the epidermis secrete a waxy coating, called a *cuticle* (KYEW·ti·kuhl). The cuticle helps keep water from leaving the leaf.

The leaf makes food in cells between the layers of the epidermis. These cells contain chloroplasts (KLAWR·uh·plasts), the green food factories of plants. In addition to sunlight, these factories need water, minerals, and the carbon dioxide in air to make food.

The air comes through tiny pores in the bottom of the leaves called *stomata* (STOH·muh·tuh) (singular, *stoma*).

A 24

Reading Strategy

Reread
Developing Reading Skills
Ask students to reread the text on these two pages and identify the different parts of leaves and the different words used to describe leaves.

Interpret Illustrations

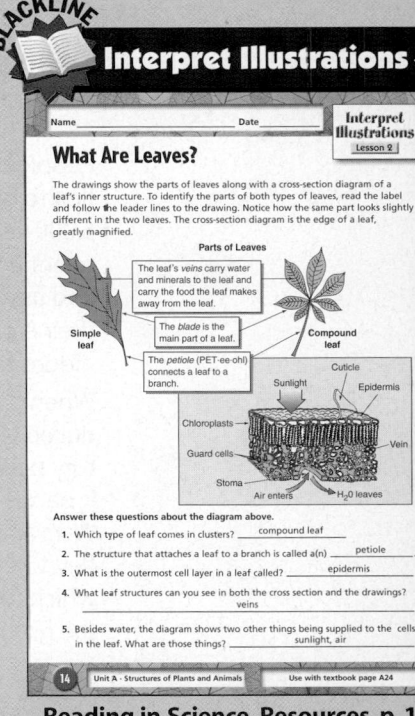

Name _____ Date _____
Interpret Illustrations
Lesson 2

What Are Leaves?

The drawings show the parts of leaves along with a cross-section diagram of a leaf's inner structure. To identify the parts of both types of leaves, read the label and follow the leader lines to the drawing. Notice how the same part looks slightly different in the two leaves. The cross-section diagram is the edge of a leaf, greatly magnified.

Answer these questions about the diagram above.

1. Which type of leaf comes in clusters? _____ compound leaf
2. The structure that attaches a leaf to a branch is called a(n) _____ petiole
3. What is the outermost cell layer in a leaf called? _____ epidermis
4. What leaf structures can you see in both the cross section and the drawings? _____ veins
5. Besides water, the diagram shows two other things being supplied to the cells in the leaf. What are those things? _____ sunlight, air

Unit A · Structures of Plants and Animals   Use with textbook page A24

Reading in Science Resources, p. 1

When the stomata are open to let in air, water can also evaporate from the leaf. The job of opening and closing each stoma is performed by two *guard cells* that surround it.

When the plant has plenty of water, the guard cells swell and pull open the stoma. When the plant has too little water, the guard cells shrink and close the stoma.

Importance of Leaves

Many leaves have green, broad, flat surfaces that help "capture" the sunlight the plant needs to make its food. Other leaves have different shapes for different purposes. The spines on a cactus protect the plant. The needles of a pine tree are covered with a wax that keeps the tree from losing too much water. The crunchy layers of an onion store food. The leaves of the garden pea plant wind around objects to give the plant added support.

The leaves of the Venus's-flytrap are colorful insect traps. They snap shut when an insect flies inside.

Leaves are often far from roots, yet they help roots take in water from soil. When water evaporates from the leaves, more water moves up through the plant to replace the lost water. This process is called transpiration (tran·spuh·RAY·shuhn).

People eat all parts of plants, including leaves such as lettuce, cabbage, parsley, and spinach. Why are leaves important to you?

▶ **What do leaves do for a plant?**
Possible answers: make food, store food, regulate water loss, help support the plant

QUICK LAB

FOR SCHOOL OR HOME

Leaves

1. Collect a variety of different leaves that you eat as food.

2. **Observe** Examine them with a hand lens. Draw what you see.

3. In what ways are the leaves you observed alike? In what ways are they different?

4. Compare the leaves you examined with the leaves your classmates looked at. In what ways are your leaves similar to theirs? In what ways are they different? Record your observations.

A 25

Developing the Main Idea
Help students understand the leaf adaptations described on this page. Ask:

- **How are pine needles and cactus spines alike?** (Both are shaped to minimize water loss.)

- **How can leaves support a plant?** (They may wind around objects.)

- **What would happen if water wasn't lost from leaves?** (Important minerals dissolved in soil water would not be taken in through the roots.)

▶ **After Reading**
Have students answer the red question in the student book as **ongoing assessment**.

QUICK LAB

FOR SCHOOL OR HOME

Materials various plant leaves that you eat, hand lens

Science Process Skills *observe*

Resources Activity Resources, pp. 9–10

Step 1 Students should bring in fresh leaves.

Step 2 Drawing may show that all the leaves have veins and petioles. Most are a shade of green. Size, shape, and texture vary.

Step 3 Most of the leaves are green and have veins. Leaves may differ in size, texture, and shade of green.

Step 4 The leaves may differ in size, texture, and color, but all have the same basic parts.

Developing Vocabulary

transpiration Taken from the verb *transpire*, which means to "give off vapor or moisture through the pores of skin or leaf surfaces," *transpiration* relates to animals as well as plants. Ask students what it is called when transpiration occurs in humans. (sweating)

Cultural Perspective

Vegetarianism
Whether observed for reasons of religion, ethics, or health, the idea of avoiding some or all animal foods is not new. Certain Eastern religions hold that all life is sacred and that people may be reincarnated as animals. Some vegetarians believe that killing animals is cruel and unethical. Organize a class debate presenting different viewpoints on these issues and beliefs. **Social**

Inclusion

Transpiration
Gather a variety of plants. Have students place a small plastic bag around a leaf (or a few leaves) of each plant and close with a twist tie. Leave the plants where they will get sunlight. Encourage students to observe the plants over the course of the day and the next morning. Students should see droplets of water collecting on the inside of the bag, given off as the plants transpire. **Spatial; Logical**

How Do Orchids Grow?

Before Reading
Have students try to answer the red question at the top of the page.

Developing the Main Idea
Ask students to describe the function of roots and the different types of roots they learned about earlier in this lesson. Show students a sample or picture of lichens. Explain that a lichen is made up of a plant and a fungus, but no roots.

Using the Illustrations
Ask:

- **How does the plant get water?** (It absorbs it from the air.)

- **How do the adaptations of these orchids help them survive in the rain forest?** (Possible answers: They grow up high so they can get sunlight, they mimic female bees to attract pollinators, the exposed roots can take in water running down a tree's bark, the green roots can make food.)

▶After Reading
Have students answer the red question in the student book as **ongoing assessment**.

How Do Orchids Grow?

Many kinds of orchids are rooted in the ground. However, in tropical rain forests, certain orchids grow high up in the trees, dangling their roots in the air. The orchids' colors "paint" the trees with flashes of red, purple, pink, and orange.

One kind of orchid looks and smells a lot like a certain kind of female bee. The orchid attracts male bees. As the bees go from flower to flower, they help the orchids reproduce.

A sudden shower drenches the tree where the orchid lives. Tiny streams of water trickle down the tree's bark. The orchid's exposed roots soak up some of the water that washes off the tree trunk and branches above. Along with the water come minerals the orchid needs.

The roots of a nearby orchid are very strange. They are flat, as long as you are tall, and wrapped around the branches of a tree like a huge flat worm. In fact, the scientific name of the orchid means "tapeworm leaf."

You might think that this is a strange name for a root. However, in a way, it makes sense. The roots of this plant are green, like leaves! Scientists have discovered that these roots do two jobs for the orchid. They absorb

Dangling their roots in the air, these orchids cling to trees high in the canopy of a tropical rain forest. Their aerial roots soak up water that trickles along tree trunks and branches.

water and minerals that pass by, and like leaves, they make food for the orchid. This orchid needs no leaves, although it has some very little ones covering its stem.

 What makes the roots of some tropical rain forest orchids unusual?

A 26

Some dangle in the air; some wrap around tree branches; some are green and make food as well as absorb water and minerals.

 **Reading Strategy**

Summarize
Developing Reading Skills
Ask students to write summaries of the information about special orchids. Then have them share their summaries with other class members. **Social; Logical**

Science Background

Orchids
There are over 15,000 species of orchids. They have three petals: two are alike and the third one varies from species to species. The stigma, style, and stamens form a single column, which is unique to orchids. One genus of orchids bears pods that give us the vanilla flavoring we use in cooking. Have students discuss why orchids are so often used as corsages and why they are so costly. **Social**

L·I·N·K·S

Why It Matters

We depend on plants for many things. Among them are food, clothing, and shelter. Since plants are needed by all living things, it is important to know how they survive. Part of a plant's ability to survive depends on how well its parts work together to move water and minerals in one direction and food in the other direction. The parts that do this are roots, stems, and leaves.

Think and Write

1. List three things plants need in order to live and grow.

2. Compare and contrast two or more different kinds of roots. Do the same for stems and leaves.

3. How do roots, stems, and leaves help a plant survive?

4. How can rain forest orchids live high up in the trees?

5. **Critical Thinking** How does having flowers that look like bees help a plant survive?

ART LINK

Make a poster. Find out the names of different orchids and where they come from. Make a poster using photographs or drawings of at least two orchids. Under each illustration, write what you know about the orchid.

WRITING LINK

Write an essay. The giant leaves of the royal lily pad are strong enough to hold up the weight of a small child. Research this Amazon plant, and write an essay about it.

MATH LINK

Solve this problem. Find the total surface area of the leaves of a single tree. Use graph paper to estimate the surface area of a single leaf. Then estimate the number of leaves on a single branch. (Find the average of several branches.) Estimate the number of branches on the tree. Find the total number of leaves, then find their total surface area.

TECHNOLOGY LINK

At the Computer Visit **www.mhscience02.com** for more links.

A 27

---

3 Lesson Review

Answers to Think and Write

1. Plants need air, water, and sunlight. (pp. A20–A25)

2. Possible answers: Taproots with few branches grow deep in the ground; fibrous roots with many branches grow close to the surface. Delicate soft stems bend easily; stiff woody stems have bark. Simple leaves grow alone; compound leaves grow in clusters. (pp. A20–A25)

3. Roots anchor the plant and take in needed water and minerals; stems take water and minerals to the rest of the plant and support the plant; leaves manufacture food and get rid of excess water. (pp. A20–A25)

4. Rain forest orchids have exposed roots, which take in water and minerals. Some roots act as leaves, making food for the orchid. (p. A26)

5. **Critical Thinking** If bees are attracted to a plant, they will take the pollen from that plant to another, thus helping the plant reproduce. (p. A26)

Summarize

Check students' understanding by having them write a brief summary of the lesson in their own words.

ART LINK

Posters should display different types of orchids, tell how to tell one type from another, and mention common traits.

WRITING LINK

Students' essays may include the size of the plant's leaves (2.5 m wide), double flowers that bloom at night, and the fact that they grow in sluggish streams of the Amazon Basin.

MATH LINK

Students can calculate total surface area of all leaves on a tree with this formula: average surface area of one leaf × number of leaves on a branch × number of branches on the tree = total surface area of all leaves on a tree.

Science Background

Root Pressure

Plants need water to carry out chemical reactions and to stay firm and erect. The plant moves water from its roots to all its parts through the process of transpiration. Pressure known as root pressure is the driving force behind water movement in plants, pushing it upward from roots to leaves.

Informal Assessment

Easy/Average Ask students to draw a typical root, stem, and leaf. Encourage them to include as much detail as possible, and review the drawings as a class.

Challenge Have students name as many parts of roots, stems, and leaves as they can. Ask them to list and describe the function of each part. Challenge them to draw a plant that includes each part.

Science, Technology, and Society

Objective

- Describe how plant parts benefit humans.

Build on Prior Knowledge
Ask:

- **What do we get from plants?** (Answers may include food, textiles, medicines, and building materials.)

- **Have you ever used a plant to get well?** (Students may have taken herbs for health, gotten vitamin C from rose hips, or drunk herbal tea.)

Plant Power: Medicines

Developing the Main Idea
Focus on the benefits of plants by asking such questions as:

- **What benefit do we get from the cinchona tree?** (We get quinine, a cure for malaria.)

- **What benefit do we get from the Pacific yew?** (This tree yields a chemical that kills cancer cells.)

Science, Technology,

Plant Power:
MEDICINES

What good are plant parts? Bitter or poisonous chemicals in some plant parts protect them from predators. The chemicals have powerful effects on animals that eat them. They might also be useful in medicines for humans!

Fever Powder of Peru

Missionaries to Peru in the 1600s found natives making a bitter powder. It was ground-up bark from the cinchona, a rare jungle tree. The powder cured the fever of malaria!

Suddenly there was a demand for cinchona bark, and the quinine in it.

Doctors now use artificial quinine and other drugs to treat malaria. However, the parasite that causes malaria is becoming resistant to the drugs. Cinchona bark still works when modern medicine fails!

Poison to Kill Cancer?

Humans have used yews for thousands of years. Spears and bows were made from the wood. The bark yielded a poison.

In the 1960s the National Cancer Institute began looking for plant chemicals that might kill cancer cells.

Pacific yews weren't valued for their wood, so many were cut down and thrown away!

Cinchona

A 28

Quinine is a bitter chemical found in the bark of the cinchona tree.

Reading Strategy

Organize Information
Developing Reading Skills
Encourage students to use a dictionary to find the meanings of the medicines and the conditions they are used to treat (leukemia, for example) in the table.

Advanced Learners

Plant Cures
Ask students to find out more about how plants are used to cure diseases. They can investigate the plants in the chart or others they may have seen in a pharmacy or health food store.
Linguistic

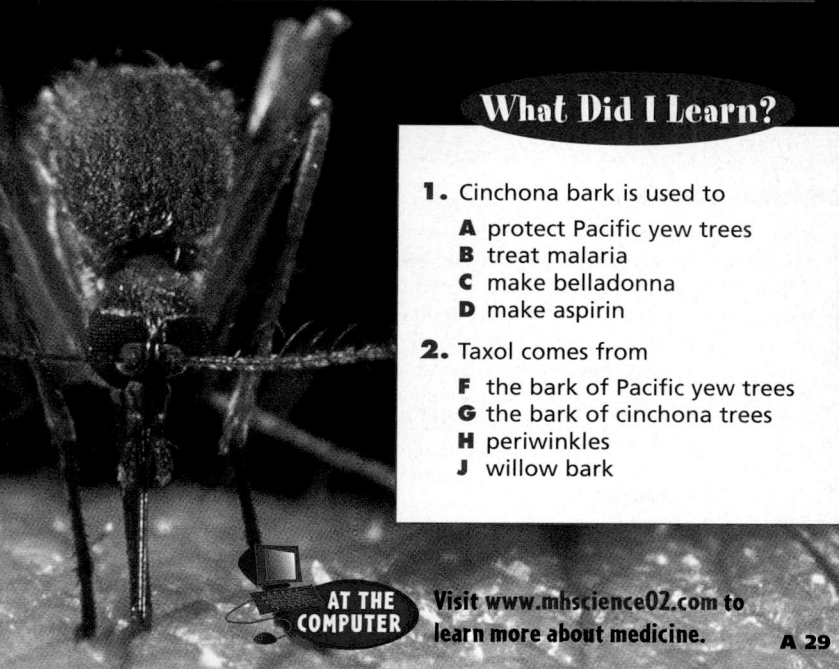

and Society   ■ NATIONAL GEOGRAPHIC

In 1963 they found such a chemical, taxol, in the bark of the Pacific yew.

By the time cancer scientists proved that taxol works against cancer, the Pacific yew was thought to be rapidly disappearing. It was even protected by the federal government for a while. Today scientists make taxol from needles and twigs of all kinds of yews, not just the bark of the Pacific yew.

Many plants may be in danger of extinction. People are destroying Earth's rain forests. If plants die off before they're found, we'll never know if their chemicals could have cured diseases.

MEDICINES FROM PLANTS
Here are a few medicines made from plant parts.

PLANT	PARTS	MEDICINE	USED FOR
Belladonna	leaves/roots	atropine	eye disorders
Foxglove	leaves	digitalis	heart problems
Periwinkle	leaves	vinblastine	leukemia
Rauwolfia	roots	reserpine	high blood pressure
Willow	bark	aspirin	reducing pain and fever
Wild Mexican yam	tuberous roots	cortisone	curbing inflammation

What Did I Learn?

1. Cinchona bark is used to

  A protect Pacific yew trees
  B treat malaria
  C make belladonna
  D make aspirin

2. Taxol comes from

  F the bark of Pacific yew trees
  G the bark of cinchona trees
  H periwinkles
  J willow bark

AT THE COMPUTER   Visit www.mhscience02.com to learn more about medicine.   A 29

👀 Science Background

Malaria

Malaria claims 1 or 2 million people every year. It is caused by a parasite that is transmitted by mosquitoes in tropical and subtropical areas. The main symptoms are alternating chills and fever. One synthetic drug, chloroquine, can both treat and prevent malaria. Travelers should take it before going to areas where malaria exists.

Thinking Further: *Drawing Conclusions*
Ask:

■ **Why do you think people like the natives in Peru have taught us so much about medicine?** (Through generations, they learned about local plants as medicines through trial and error.)

Encourage students to think about how they have learned about foods through trial and error.

Test Prep:    What Did I Learn?

1. B
2. F

Summarize
Check students' understanding by having them write a brief summary of this article on medicines and plants in their own words.

LESSON 3
The Importance of Plants

LESSON 3
The Importance of Plants

Get Ready

Why are plants important? Plants give us food. They also give us oxygen we need to breathe. What do plants need in order to do this? Did you ever wonder why crops are planted in open fields, not in the shade? What happens to plants that are kept in a dark corner of the room? Do they do as well as plants that get more light? How will a plant change if it does not get sunlight for several days?

Process Skill

You use variables when you identify and separate things in an experiment that can be changed or controlled.

A 30

Objectives

- Explore how light affects a plant's leaves.
- Describe the processes of photosynthesis and respiration in plants.
- Describe how roots, stems, and leaves work together to get water and minerals to all parts of the plant.
- Understand the role of plants as food producers and oxygen suppliers.

Resources

- Activity Resources, pp. 11–15
- Reading in Science Resources, pp. 17–22
- Reading Aid Transparency A3
- Vocabulary Cards
- Visual Aid Transparency 2
- Grade-Level Science Book, *The Power of Green*

Build on Prior Knowledge

Have students discuss what they know about what plants need to survive. Ask them where they keep their plants at home and why. (Most plants need to be kept in a warm sunny place to get enough light and the proper temperatures.)

1 Get Ready

Using the Illustrations

Draw students' attention to the picture of the orchard and identify factors that would favor a good crop. Help them recall that plants need water, light, minerals, and proper temperatures to function.

 **Reading Strategy**

Ask Questions
Developing Reading Skills
Have students ask questions as they read this page and the steps of the Explore Activity. For example, why do plants need light? What is the reason for this step?

 Science Background

Variegated Plants
Variegation is the presence of two or more colors in a plant. Variegation is most commonly caused by mutations resulting in faulty or absent chloroplasts, and thus a lack of green pigment. Variegation interferes with a plant's ability to photosynthesize food. As a result, variegated plants are not as hardy as all-green plants. They are rarely seen in the wild but are desirable to gardeners for their beauty.

Explore Activity

What Does Light Do for a Plant?

Materials

growing plant (window plants from home or plants from an aquarium)

opaque paper or aluminum foil

Procedure

1 Cover part of a leaf of a growing plant. Be sure to wash your hands after handling plants.

2 **Use Variables** Cover at least four different leaves of the plant in the same way.

3 Place the whole plant in a window that gets lots of light.

4 **Experiment** Remove the foil from one leaf after one class period. How is that leaf different from the uncovered leaves? Record your observations. Then cover the leaf again.

5 **Experiment** Continue your observations. Remove the foil from another leaf after one day, another after two days, and another after a week. Record your observations. Replace the foil each time.

Drawing Conclusions

1 **Observe** After one class period, how was the leaf you had just uncovered different from the uncovered leaves?

2 **Interpret Data** How did the difference you noticed change after a day, two days, and a week?

3 **Infer** How do light and darkness affect the growth of leaves?

4 **Going Further: Use Variables** Remove the coverings from the four leaves, and observe them for another week. How do these leaves respond to being uncovered?

A 31

Alternative Explore Activity

Materials two similar plants per group

In the Dark Have students put one plant in a dark area, such as a closet, and another one in a sunny area. Have them observe their plants each day over the course of two weeks and record daily observations. Ask them to explain any differences they observe. **Spatial**

Name_____ Date_____

Alternative Explore Lesson 3

In the Dark

Procedure

Materials
• two similar plants

1. Obtain two similar plants.
2. Place one plant in a dark area, such as a closet. Place the other plant in a sunny area.
3. Observe the plants each day over the course of two weeks and record your observations. Remember to give both plants the same amount of water.

Day	Plant in a Sunny Place	Plant in a Dark Place

Drawing Conclusions

1. After two weeks, how did the plants look?
   The plant from the sunny area looked healthy. The plant in the dark was a paler shade of green. Its stem grew long and thin.

2. What do you think will happen to the plant that was in the dark if you put it in the light?
   Answers will vary, but students will likely predict that the plant will become a deeper shade of green.

Unit A · Structures of Plants and Animals | Use with TE textbook page A31 | 13

Activity Resources, p. 13

Explore Activity

What Does Light Do for a Plant?

Science Process Skills *use variables, experiment, observe, interpret data, infer*

Resources Activity Resources, pp. 11–12

Pacing 30–40 minutes

Grouping small groups

Plan Ahead The plants from Lessons 1 and 2 may also be used for this activity.

Procedure

1 Caution students not to harm the plant leaf when they attach the cover.

3 If a sunny window is not available, a grow light (available at nurseries) can be used.

4 There is no noticeable change.

5 The leaves lose their green color. Students may need to continue observing the plant for several weeks to see a marked difference.

Answers to Drawing Conclusions

1 After one class period little or no difference in the leaves should be observed.

2 Students should see the leaves lose more of their green color the longer they are covered.

3 Leaves in the light stay green and grow; leaves kept in the dark lose their green color and start to die.

4 The leaves should begin to regain their green color. Eventually, the differences will disappear.

? **Inquiry** Students can ask their own questions to explore, such as what are the optimal levels of light for a given plant. (Students should find that some types of plants grow best with many hours of direct sunlight, some need indirect light for only a few hours of light a day, while others do well in shady conditions.)

Technology

■ When time is short, preview the activity with the **Explore Activity Video**.

2 Read to Learn

What Is Photosynthesis?

Before Reading
Have students try to answer the red question at the top of the page.

Developing the Main Idea
Remind students that during photosynthesis, green plants use carbon dioxide and water to make sugars and release oxygen. During respiration, plants use oxygen to break down sugars and release energy.

Relate what students know about plant structure to photosynthesis. Ask:

- **How does water get into the leaf?** (It travels from the roots, up through the xylem in the stem and leaf veins.)
- **How does carbon dioxide get into the leaf?** (through the stomata)
- **Where is chlorophyll found?** (in the chloroplasts)
- **How does oxygen leave the leaf?** (through the stomata)

Thinking Further: *Inferring*
Ask:

- **How do the sugars get to all parts of the plant?** (They travel through the phloem in the veins and stem.)

Developing Vocabulary

photosynthesis Write *photosynthesis* on the board, circling each part as you say, "I know *photo* means "light," *syn* means "with," and *thesis* means "to put, do, or make." So *photosynthesis* must mean "to make with light."

Technology

- Visual Aid Transparency 2: *Photosynthesis*

Read to Learn

Main Idea Plants make food and produce oxygen through photosynthesis.

What Is Photosynthesis?

When you walk to a grocery store to buy food, you are really doing two things. You are using energy to get to the store, and you are buying energy at the store. Walking uses energy. Food provides you with energy.

All living things need energy to survive. Where do they get energy? Animals eat food to get energy. Plants make their own food. However, the very process of making food uses up energy. Where does the plant get this energy? It comes from light, especially sunlight.

Light is a form of energy that plants use to make their food. Plants capture the energy of light and trap it in the foods they make. Later, when they need this energy, they get it back from the food. The food-making process is called **photosynthesis** (foh·tuh·SIN·thuh·sis). This term comes from Greek words that mean "putting together by light." The process is very complex, but basically here's how it happens.

First, sunlight strikes a green part of a plant, such as a leaf. The leaf is green because it has a green chemical called chlorophyll. Chlorophyll helps the plant make its food. The chlorophyll is found in plant parts called chloroplasts. The chloroplasts act like tiny chemical factories. Inside them water and carbon

A 32

Photosynthesis

Carbon dioxide	Light	Sugar
+	→	+
Water	Chlorophyll	Oxygen

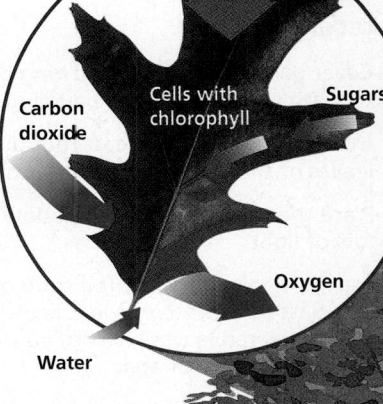

Photosynthesis Hydrogen (from water) and carbon dioxide join in the presence of sunlight and chlorophyll to form sugars and oxygen.

The water and carbon dioxide that form are released into the air.

BLACKLINE
Lesson Outline

Name_____ Date_____

Lesson Outline Lesson 3

The Importance of Plants

Fill in the blanks. Reading Skill: Draw Conclusions - questions 6,10, 14

What Is Photosynthesis?

1. All living things need ___energy___ to survive.
2. The energy that plants use in making food comes from ___light/sunlight___.
3. The food-making process in plants is called ___photosynthesis___.
4. Parts of plants are green because of a chemical called ___chlorophyll___, located in the ___chloroplasts___.
5. Inside the chloroplasts, ___water___ and ___carbon dioxide___ react chemically, helped by light energy.
6. Photosynthesis cannot occur without energy from ___light/the sun___.
7. Photosynthesis produces both ___sugar___ and ___oxygen___.
8. Photosynthesis sets up a relationship between plants and animals:
   a. Plants give off ___oxygen___, which animals breathe, into the air.
   b. Animals breathe out ___carbon dioxide___, which plants use in photosynthesis.
9. Plants and animals break up sugar, releasing energy, in the process of ___respiration___.

How Do Leaves Change Color?

10. The yellow and orange colors in leaves aren't visible during the summer because leaves have too much ___green chlorophyll___.
11. When temperatures get colder, the green chlorophyll ___breaks down___ and ___disappears___.

Unit A - Structures of Plants and Animals   Use with textbook pages A30-A39   **17**

Reading in Science Resources, p. 17

BLACKLINE
Interpret Illustrations

Name_____ Date_____

Interpret Illustrations Lesson 3

What Is Photosynthesis?

The leaf in this diagram is like a small factory where the process of photosynthesis takes place. The arrows in the diagram show the substances that enter and leave the leaves of green plants during this process. Notice the formula on top of the diagram that sums up the process. The arrow in the formula shows the results of the chemical processes that take place in the leaf.

Photosynthesis

Carbon dioxide	Light	Sugar
+		+
Water	Chlorophyll	Oxygen

Answer these questions about the diagram above.

1. What is the source of the light used in photosynthesis? ___sunlight___
2. What chemical enters the leaf from the air? ___carbon dioxide___
3. The chemical in the leaf cells is ___chlorophyll___.
4. The leaf makes food in the form of ___sugar___.
5. What substance does the leaf give off into the air? ___oxygen___

Unit A - Structures of Plants and Animals   Use with textbook page A32   **19**

Reading in Science Resources, p. 19

dioxide from the air combine to make sugar and oxygen. However, this reaction could not happen without the help of light energy.

The sugars that the Sun's energy helps the leaf to make then go into the leaf's veins and off to all parts of the plant.

The oxygen the plant makes goes into the air. All animals must breathe in oxygen to stay alive. At the same time, they breathe out carbon dioxide, which the plants need.

Now that the Sun's energy is trapped in the sugars that the plant made, how does the plant get the energy back out? Its cells use oxygen to break apart the sugar. When the sugar breaks apart, it releases energy that the plant uses. This process is called **respiration** (res·puh·RAY·shuhn). This is the same process that releases energy in animals.

▶ **How is photosynthesis different from respiration?**

During photosynthesis, plants change carbon dioxide and water into sugars and oxygen. During respiration, plants and animals use oxygen to break down sugar to produce energy, water, and carbon dioxide.

READING
Diagrams

In what process is carbon dioxide released?

The oxygen is released into the air.

The sugars that form are stored in green plants.

Respiration In respiration, which occurs in plants and animals, sugars and oxygen join to produce water, carbon dioxide, and energy.

A 33

Developing the Main Idea

Point out that photosynthesis is not simple or even a single chemical reaction. Explain that scientists at first thought that carbon dioxide was broken down to give off oxygen. Using radioactive tracers, they found that the oxygen comes from the water. The leftover hydrogen joins the carbon dioxide to make sugar.

Stress the interdependence between plants and animals. Ask:

- **How do animals depend on plants?** (to get food, energy, and oxygen)
- **How do plants depend on animals?** (for carbon dioxide)

Point out the cyclical nature of photosynthesis and respiration. Ask:

- **How is respiration related to photosynthesis?** (Respiration uses the products of photosynthesis to produce what is needed for photosynthesis.)
- **How is photosynthesis related to respiration?** (Photosynthesis uses the products of respiration to produce what is needed for respiration.)

READING
Diagrams

respiration

▶**After Reading**
Have students answer the red question in the student book as **ongoing assessment**.

Developing Vocabulary

respiration This term comes from the verb form *respire*, which can be traced to the Latin word *respirare*. The prefix *re-* means "back" and *spirare* translates to "to breathe."

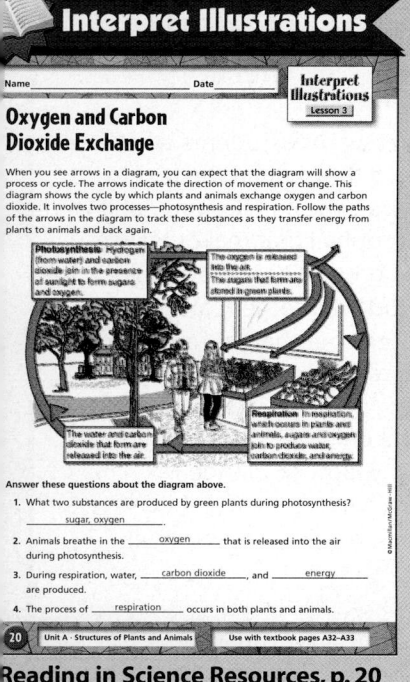
SCIENCE FOR ALL
Inclusion

Light and Plant Growth
Have students work in groups to design an experiment over several weeks to observe how light affects a plant's growth. Using two plants per group, their plans should include how they will set up the experiment, what variables they will control, what data they will collect, how they will measure differences in plant growth, and how long they will continue the experiment. **Social; Logical**

How Do Leaves Change Color?

Before Reading
Have students try to answer the red question at the top of the first text column.

Developing the Main Idea
Help students understand what happens when trees stop making chlorophyll. Ask:

- **Can a leaf make food when there is no chlorophyll?** (No.)

Thinking Further: *Inferring*
Ask:

- **How does a tree stay alive if the leaves are not making food?** (The tree lives off food stored during the growing season. Also, many of its life processes slow down or stop during fall and winter, so it needs less energy.)

▶ After Reading
Have students answer the red question in the student book as **ongoing assessment**.

In autumn cooling temperatures signal trees to stop making green chlorophyll. The chlorophyll disappears, uncovering other colors.

How Do Leaves Change Color?

Do you live in an area where the leaves change color in the autumn? If so, you may have noticed that the leaves of all plants, except evergreens, change color in the fall. You wake up one morning in September or October, and the trees near where you live are speckled with flashes of yellow, orange, and maybe red.

All the yellows and oranges were inside the leaves ever since summer. However, you couldn't see them because there was too much green chlorophyll there.

It's as if you put some yellow and orange objects in the bottom of a bucket of green paint. The yellow and orange objects would be in there, yet all you would see is green.

However, if you could take out all the green paint, what would you see? The answer is what you see in the fall.

How is the greenness taken out of leaves in the fall?

As temperatures begin to drop, the leaves of trees other than evergreens stop making chlorophyll. Slowly the chlorophyll that remains begins to break down and vanishes. Now you can see the yellow and orange colors. If the weather is especially cool and the sky is clear most of the time, you may see another color—red. This color wasn't in the leaves to begin with. It's made by them in places where the fall climate is cool and clear. Where the climate is warmer and the sky is cloudy a lot of the time, the colors will be mostly yellows and oranges.

READING Draw Conclusions
Where would you expect to see a greater variety of autumn colors—in Vermont or South Carolina?
Vermont—red is seen only when the weather is especially cool.

A 34

English Language Learners

Plant Pigments
The same pigments that give yellow leaves their color also give yellow color to bananas, carrots, sweet potatoes, and pumpkins. They are called carotenes and xanthophylls. Pigments responsible for reds and purples develop only in the presence of sunlight. One, anthocyanin, is also found in radishes and beets. Have students make a chart listing plant pigments and the plant containing them. **Visual**

Reading MiniLesson

Draw Conclusions

Develop Review with students how common sense can play a part in helping us draw conclusions. Ask a volunteer to read aloud paragraph 1 on page A34, then ask, "Which plants do not change color in autumn? (evergreens) How could your common sense help you draw that conclusion without reading the text? (The name means "always green.")

Practice Ask students what evidence they find in the text to support the conclusion that it is chlorophyll that makes leaves look green. (Answers should include that other colors are present but there is much more chlorophyll than any other color, and that when there is no more chlorophyll, the leaves look yellow or orange.)

Process Skill
BUILDER

SKILL Experiment

Why Leaves Change Color

To find out why leaves change color in autumn, the first thing you might do is figure out what changes occur in the fall that might cause leaves to change color. Scientists call such changes *variables*. You might identify two of these variables as the amount of daylight and the temperature, both of which go down in the fall.

Next you would make a guess that seems to make sense about which variable causes leaves to change color. This guess is called a *hypothesis*. It is often made in the form of an "*if . . . then . . .*" statement. For example, "*If* the plant doesn't get water, *then* it won't grow." To see if your hypothesis is a good idea, you would perform an experiment. That experiment has to be set up so that it gives a clear answer.

Procedure

1 Look at the drawings. They show three experiments—A, B, C. Study the setups.

2 **Observe** What variable or variables are being tested in the first experiment? Record your answer. What variable or variables are being tested in the other two experiments?

Drawing Conclusions

1 **Infer** Which experiment is testing to see whether light causes leaves to change color? Explain.

2 **Infer** Which experiment is testing to see whether temperature causes leaves to change color? Explain why.

3 **Infer** Which experiment will not give a clear answer? Explain why not.

A 35

Process Skill
BUILDER

Why Leaves Change Color

Science Process Skills **experiment,** *observe, infer*

Resources Activity Resources, pp. 14–15

Pacing 20 minutes

Grouping individual

Procedure

2 Ask students what the variable was in the Explore Activity (light), then ask whether light is a variable in any of the experiments shown here (A and C). Stress that for an experiment to be valid, there must be only one variable tested at a time. (Temperature is a variable in B and C.)

Answers to Drawing Conclusions

1 A; because both temperatures are kept the same and light is the only factor that varies.

2 B; because both plants get light and temperature is the only factor that varies.

3 C; because both light and temperature are being varied.

Process Skills

MiniLesson

Experiment

Develop This process skill involves performing a test that either supports or disproves a hypothesis. Factors that change and that can have an affect on an experiment are called *variables*. For a scientific experiment to be valid, only one variable can change. The other variables must stay the same.

Practice Present this hypothesis: If I roll a penny across a smooth surface, it will move farther than if I roll it across a rough surface. Ask: What are the variables? (the penny, the surface, the force which the penny is rolled) Which variables must be kept the same? (the same penny must be used in each trial, the force should be the same) Which variable would change? (the surface) A complete list of Science Process Skills appears on p. S7.

Science Background

The Needs of Plants

Plants need water, air, and light in order to survive. If the leaves do not get enough light the plant will die. Some plants, such as impatiens, are more tolerant of strong sunlight and some, such as pachysandra, are shade-loving; however, all plants require some degree of light in order to thrive. When planning a garden, it is important to note the amount of sunlight needed by different plants.

How Does Water Get from Roots to Leaves?

Before Reading

Have students try to answer the red question at the top of the page.

Developing the Main Idea

Ask:

- **How does a leaf lose water?** (through transpiration, the evaporation of water from the leaves)

- **What happens to the guard cells when a plant has too little water?** (They shrink and close the stomata.)

Exploring the Main Idea

Ask students to share their experiences about what happens if they forget to water house plants for too long a time. (The plant wilts and may die.) Show students a fresh lettuce leaf and a wilted lettuce leaf. Then put the leaves on a pan balance. Ask:

- **What is the difference between these leaves?** (Answers should include that one leaf looks wilted and shriveled up.)

- **Which weighs less?** (The wilted leaf should weigh less.)

- **What do you think makes the difference?** (The wilted leaf has lost water.)

▶After Reading

Have students answer the red question in the student book as **ongoing assessment**.

How Does Water Get from Roots to Leaves?

If you were to dry 1,000 g (2.2 lb) of leaves, you would end up with between 50 and 300 g (1.8–11 oz) of crumbly matter. That's because plants are made up of 70–95 percent water.

Cells in all parts of a plant need water to live and grow. They need water to carry out many vital chemical reactions, including photosynthesis. They also need water to stay firm and not wilt.

Plants constantly lose water through *transpiration*. Over its lifetime an average plant in a mild climate area will lose more than 100 times its weight in water!

It is very important for a plant to efficiently move water from its roots to all its other parts. The diagram on page A37 shows how this is done.

Tropical rain forests pump great amounts of water into the air.

▷ **Why is it important to move water from a plant's roots?**
to carry out chemical reactions and to keep from wilting

If a normal plant (left) gets too little water, it will lose firmness and wilt (right).

A 36

Math MiniLesson

Solve a Multistep Problem

Develop What would 1,000 grams of leaves weigh without water if the leaves are 90% water? You can solve this problem step by step.

First, find how many grams of water make up the leaves.

$90\% \times 1,000 = \frac{90}{100} \times 1,000 = 900$

So, 900 grams of water make up the leaves.

Second, find how many grams the leaves would weigh without water.

$1,000 - 900 = 100$

The leaves would weigh 100 g without water.

Practice Solve.
Susan had $200. She gave 20% of her money to her brother. How much money does Susan have left? ($160)

Activity Have students try this multistep number puzzle: Pick a number less than 10, add 5, multiply by 2, subtract 10, divide by 2.

(The result is always the original number.)

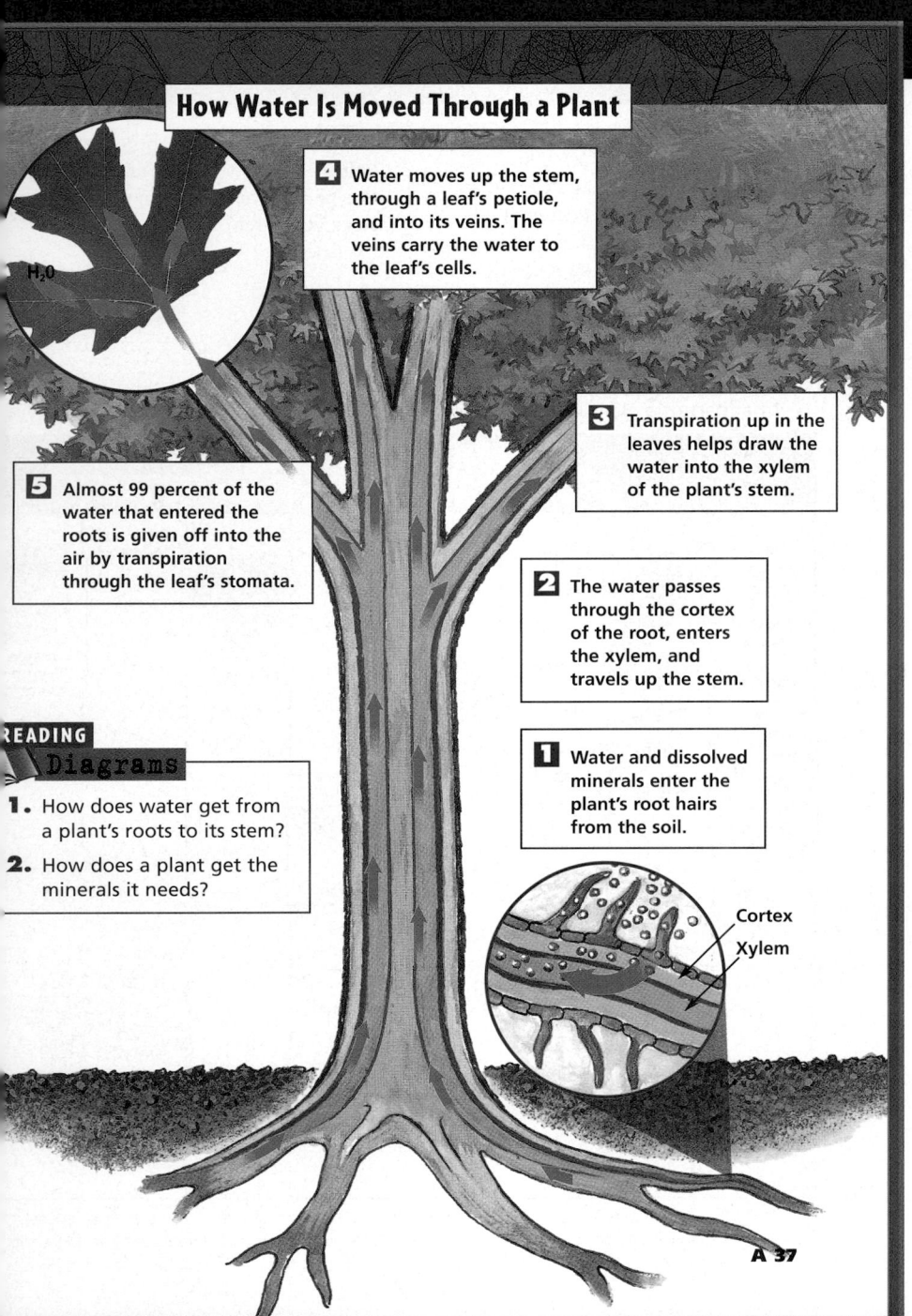

How Water Is Moved Through a Plant

4 Water moves up the stem, through a leaf's petiole, and into its veins. The veins carry the water to the leaf's cells.

H₂O

3 Transpiration up in the leaves helps draw the water into the xylem of the plant's stem.

5 Almost 99 percent of the water that entered the roots is given off into the air by transpiration through the leaf's stomata.

2 The water passes through the cortex of the root, enters the xylem, and travels up the stem.

1 Water and dissolved minerals enter the plant's root hairs from the soil.

Cortex
Xylem

READING Diagrams

1. How does water get from a plant's roots to its stem?

2. How does a plant get the minerals it needs?

A 37

Exploring the Main Idea
Using two 6-inch pieces of cotton clothesline and two beakers with equal amounts of colored water you can demonstrate the relationships between absorption and surface area. Unravel the end of one piece of clothesline and place in a test tube. Place the end of the other piece in the second beaker. Ask:

- **Which piece absorbs more water? Why?** (the unraveled one, because it has more surface area)

- **What does that tell you about roots that spread out?** (They can absorb more water.)

Using the Illustrations
Ask students to write down the names of familiar structures in the illustration. Then invite them to work in pairs to quiz each other on how each structure helps the plant move water from the soil to all parts. Challenge them to pick structures at random rather than going in sequence.

READING Diagrams

1. Transpiration in leaves draws water from the roots up through the xylem in the stem.

2. The minerals are dissolved in the water that enters the root hairs from the soil.

 Science Background

At the Same Time?
Addressing Misconceptions
Some students may think that only photosynthesis or respiration can occur at any one time. Stress that both occur at the same time during the day, as the plant continuously needs and uses energy to grow, take in water, and perform other life functions.

 **Inclusion**

Preventing Transpiration
Direct students to completely coat a leaf from top to bottom with petroleum jelly. Have them tie plastic bags around the coated leaf and an uncoated leaf still on the plant. Close the bags with twist ties. Suggest they observe what happens in each bag throughout the day and the next morning. Discuss how the two bags are different. (The one with the uncoated leaf is dry; the other contains water droplets.)
Kinesthetic; Spatial

What Parts of Plants Do You Eat?

Before Reading
Have students try to answer the red question at the top of the page.

Developing the Main Idea
Point out that seeds such as peanuts and beans are sources of protein. Help students understand why plant parts can be used for food. Ask:

- **What nutrients can we get from some plant roots? Why?** (Starches and sugars, because some plants store excess food in their roots.)
- **Why are some plant leaves nutritious?** (Plant leaves are the sites of food production.)
- **Why is maple syrup sweet?** (Sap contains sugars that the plant uses for food.)

READING
Diagrams

fruit; seed

▶After Reading
Have students answer the red question in the student book as **ongoing assessment**.

What Parts of Plants Do You Eat?

There probably isn't a part of a plant that you haven't eaten at one time or another. Whether you know it or not, you've eaten roots, stems, leaves, seeds, fruits, flowers, and even the bark and sap of plants. If you don't believe this is true, look at the chart on this page. Which of these plant parts have you eaten?

READING
Diagrams

What part of a plant is a tomato? A peanut?

▶ **What are five examples of plant parts that people use for food?**

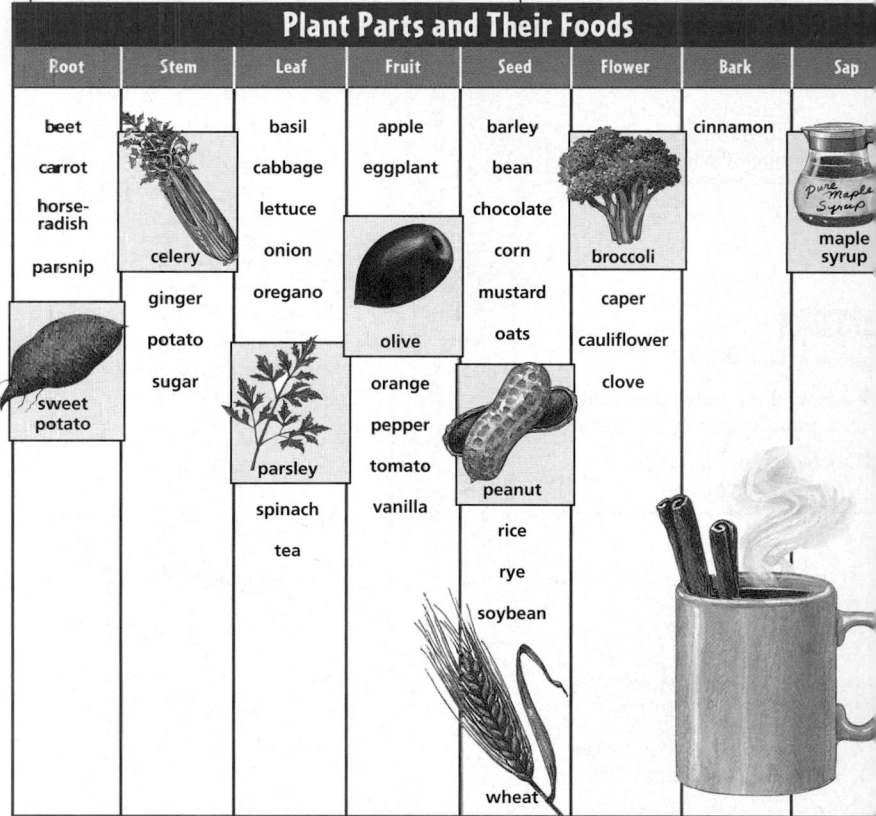

Plant Parts and Their Foods

Root	Stem	Leaf	Fruit	Seed	Flower	Bark	Sap
beet		basil	apple	barley		cinnamon	
carrot		cabbage	eggplant	bean			
horse-radish		lettuce		chocolate			maple syrup
parsnip	celery	onion		corn	broccoli		
	ginger	oregano		mustard	caper		
	potato		olive	oats	cauliflower		
sweet potato	sugar		orange		clove		
		parsley	pepper	peanut			
		spinach	tomato	rice			
		tea	vanilla	rye			
				soybean			
				wheat			

A 38

Possible answers include: roots, such as carrots; stems, such as potatoes; leaves, such as lettuce; fruits, such as apples; seeds, such as barley; flowers, such as broccoli; bark, such as cinnamon; sap, such as maple syrup.

Reading Strategy

Draw Conclusions
Developing Reading Skills
Ask students to draw conclusions about their eating habits based on the text on this page and the "Why It Matters" on p. A39 about the relationship between plants and animals.

Inclusion

Taking Care of Earth
Help students become aware of the "green revolution" and what that means to them. Suggest they look for recycling signs and posters with a green theme, and see if they can find products with the word *green* on the label. Ask:

- **What do you think the word *green* indicates?** (Products are "environmentally friendly.")

- **Why is green the color used to promote caring for the environment?** (A healthy environment has healthy plants with green leaves.) **Social; Linguistic**

Lesson Review

Why It Matters

About 21 percent of the air you breathe is oxygen. You use this oxygen to release energy from the foods you eat.

Most of the oxygen in air comes from plants and other green living things, like algae, that carry on photosynthesis.

Plants and animals need each other in order to survive. Animals need the food and oxygen plants make during photosynthesis. Plants need the carbon dioxide animals give off when they breathe out. Visit **www.mhscience02.com** to do a research project on photosynthesis.

Think and Write

1. Describe photosynthesis.

2. Describe the process of respiration in plants.

3. Trace the path of water from the soil, through a plant, and into the air.

4. **Experiment** How would you design an experiment to see if the changing temperature or the changing amount of daylight plays a bigger part in why leaves change color in autumn?

5. **Critical Thinking** If there were no plants, would animals be able to survive? Explain.

L·I·N·K·S

LITERATURE LINK

Read *The Power of Green*, the story of some of the plants and protists that live in different areas of the world. When you finish reading, think about the plants and protists that live in your area. Try the activities at the end of the book.

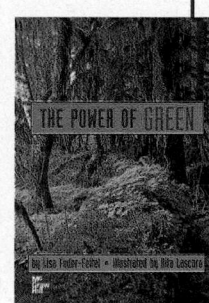

THE POWER OF GREEN

ART LINK

Draw an experimental setup. Let's say you thought the amount of rainfall was the reason leaves changed color. Make a set of drawings showing an experiment that would test this hypothesis.

TECHNOLOGY LINK

Science Newsroom CD-ROM Choose *Color My World* to learn more about how leaves change color.

At the Computer Visit **www.mhscience02.com** for more links.

A 39

---

3 Lesson Review

Answers to Think and Write

1. In photosynthesis, a plant converts water and carbon dioxide into sugars and oxygen in the presence of light and chlorophyll. (pp. A32–A33)

2. During respiration, plant cells use oxygen to break apart sugars and release energy. (p. A33)

3. Water goes from soil into roots through root hairs, through root's cortex into the xylem, up the stem, through the petiole into leaf's veins, and to cells. Stomata pass water into the air. (p. A37)

4. **Experiment** Design a separate experiment for each variable. If changing temperature is critical, give all plants equal daylight but different temperatures. If changing daylight is critical, keep all plants at same temperature but give different amounts of light. (pp. A34–A35)

5. **Critical Thinking** No, animals need oxygen and food produced by plants. (p. A39)

Summarize
Check students' understanding by having them write a brief summary of the lesson in their own words.

LITERATURE LINK

Have students read the Grade-Level Science Book, *The Power of Green*. Additional books to read can be found on TE p. A1•b.

ART LINK

Diagrams should show all materials and indicate each variable being tested.

Technology

Internet Research Project Have students visit **www.mhscience02.com** to conduct a research project on photosynthesis. They will find a suggested outline for the project, questions to research, and links to Internet reference sites.

✓ Informal Assessment

Easy/Average Ask students to refer to the diagrams in the lesson and write a paragraph that explains how photosynthesis, respiration, and transpiration are related

Challenge Invite students to use everyday objects to make a display relating respiration and photosynthesis. Challenge them to include the details of how water moves throughout a plant. Ask them to include captions and label all the important structures.

SCIENCE FOR ALL — Advanced Learners

Plants in the News
Challenge students to find articles in recent newspapers and magazines about plants as producers of food and oxygen. (Examples include the effects of weather on crops, food shortages in various parts of the world, what is happening to the rain forests, the genetics of food production, new farming methods, and dealing with air pollution.) Have students summarize the articles and make a bulletin board display about plants in the news. **Linguistic; Spatial**

Amazing Stories

Objective

- Describe the use of plants as tools in the cleanup of a variety of soil pollution.

Build on Prior Knowledge

Ask students to discuss the things that we depend on plants for. (building material, food) Then ask:

- **What is the energy source for plants?** (the Sun)

- **How do plants draw water and minerals from the soil?** (through their roots or root hairs)

- **How do oxygen and nutrients get from the plants into the soil?** (through the roots)

Cleaning Pollution with Plants

Developing the Main Idea

When students have read the article, have them recall the different types of roots. (Possible answers: tap-roots, fibrous roots, prop roots, aerial roots.) Focus on fibrous roots by showing a photo or living example of the roots of a plant such as grass. Ask:

- **What kind of roots are these?** (fibrous)

- **What are the characteristics of fibrous roots?** (They are thin and branch into wide networks.)

Point out that this is the type of root system that clovers and alfalfa have. Ask:

- **How do plants help the microbes that clean up oil spills?** (They speed up the microbes' activity by getting more oxygen into the soil and by supplying nutrients to the microbes.)

- **How is the fibrous root structure helpful?** (The wide network gets the roots in contact with as much soil as possible.)

Amazing Stories

Cleaning Pollution with Plants

Plants help us in many different ways. They produce oxygen for us to breathe. They provide food for us to eat. We build homes with wood from trees. Lifesaving medicines are made from some plants. Now research shows plants have another amazing use—they help us clean up pollution!

Every year millions of gallons of oil leak into the soil from pipelines, storage tanks, and industrial sites. The usual method of cleanup is to dig up the polluted soil and dispose of it elsewhere. This method is very expensive and disturbs the soil structure.

Researchers Katherine Banks and Paul Schwab have discovered that certain plants—along with tiny soil microbes—will clean up the soil pollutants. The microbes in the soil break down the oil and use it for food. The plants speed up the microbes' activity by getting more oxygen into the soil.

Banks and Schwab have found that certain grasses clean pollution well.

Clover and alfalfa plants also are effective because they increase microbe growth. Finding the right plant, however, can be tricky. Since oil spills occur in different parts of the world, scientists need to use plants that will survive in different climates.

Plants can be used to clean up other kinds of soil pollution, too. Some plants can absorb heavy metals and radioactive material from soil. The plants store the substances in their tissues. Then the plants become toxic and must be destroyed. Mustard plants, for example, can soak up metals, such as lead. In Ukraine, mustard plants were used to remove radiation pollution from the soil around a nuclear plant that exploded.

There are many reasons why using plants may one day be the best way to clean up soil pollution. The method is cheaper, prettier, and powered by an unlimited source of energy—the Sun!

A 40

Reading Strategy

Cause and Effect

Developing Reading Skills

Ask students to point out examples of cause and effect on pages A40–A41. For example: Plants get more oxygen and nutrients into the soil (cause), thereby speeding up the microbes' activity (effect).

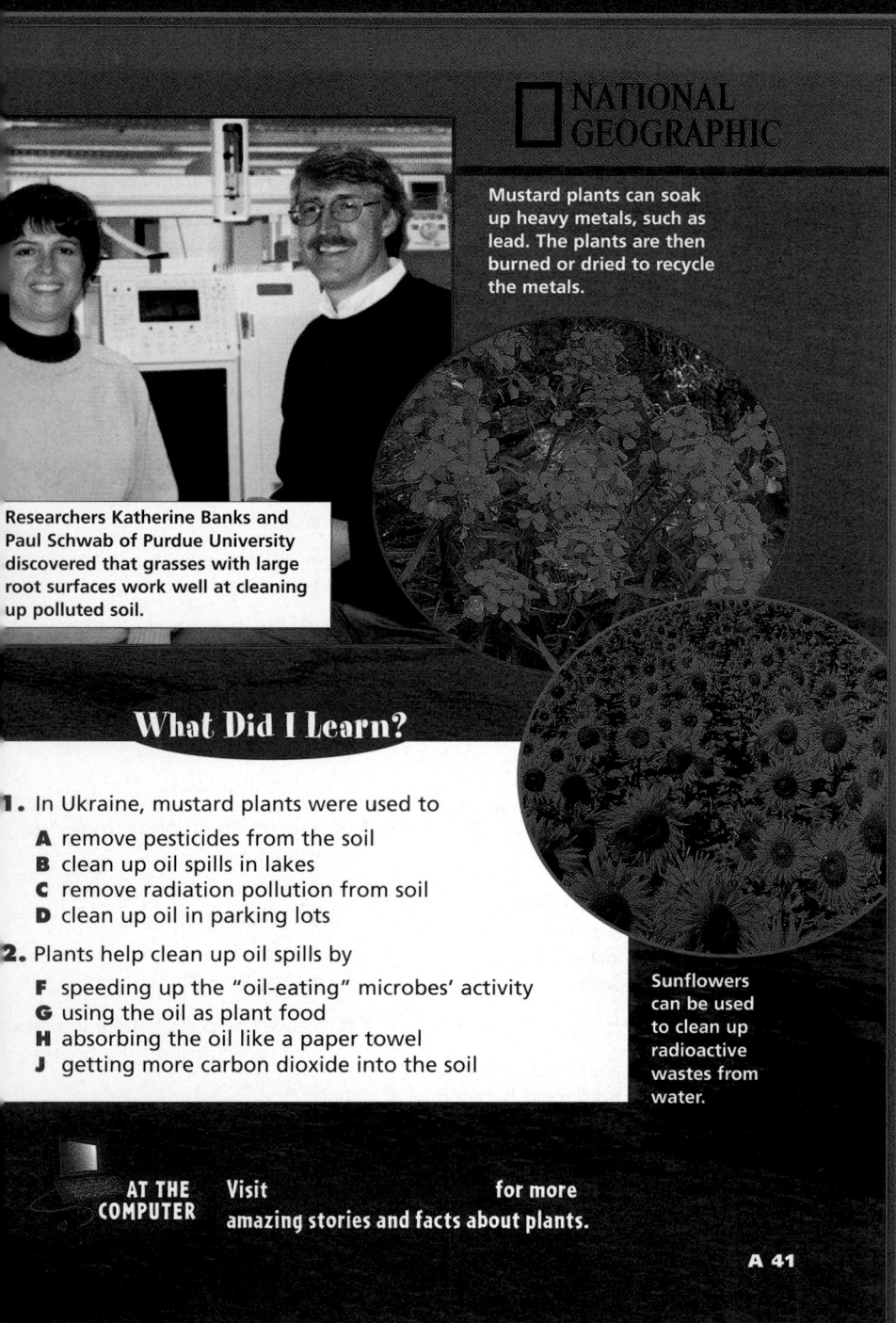

Mustard plants can soak up heavy metals, such as lead. The plants are then burned or dried to recycle the metals.

Researchers Katherine Banks and Paul Schwab of Purdue University discovered that grasses with large root surfaces work well at cleaning up polluted soil.

What Did I Learn?

1. In Ukraine, mustard plants were used to

   A remove pesticides from the soil
   B clean up oil spills in lakes
   C remove radiation pollution from soil
   D clean up oil in parking lots

2. Plants help clean up oil spills by

   F speeding up the "oil-eating" microbes' activity
   G using the oil as plant food
   H absorbing the oil like a paper towel
   J getting more carbon dioxide into the soil

Sunflowers can be used to clean up radioactive wastes from water.

 AT THE COMPUTER Visit _____ for more amazing stories and facts about plants.

A 41

 **Inclusion**

Expanded Plant Uses

Sunflowers, alfalfa, mustard, and clover have other uses besides their role in cleaning pollution. Have students research one of these plants and make a collage or poster demonstrating these uses. They can use their artwork to present a report to the rest of the class. **Spatial**

Advanced Learners

Phytoremediation

The use of plants to clean different types of pollution from soil or water is called *phytoremediation.* Have students research more thoroughly the ways in which one of the plants mentioned or any other plant is being used as a solution to the cleaning of oil, radioactive materials, heavy metals, pesticides, or other chemicals. **Linguistic**

Exploring the Main Idea

Expand the discussion of the research of Banks and Schwab. Inform students that, even with the use of the grasses, it still take several years to clean up a moderately contaminated area. Ask:

- **Why do you think this is so?** (because it is a natural process and the microbes can only work at their normal rate of eating)

Point out that while other methods may be faster, this technology is less expensive and leaves the soil in place. Other methods require the soil to be dug up and treated somewhere else. Then ask:

- **What are some of the problems involved with the use of plants for clean up?** (Possible answers: finding plants that work in different types of soil in different climates, finding plants that won't die from contact with the pollutant)

Developing the Main Idea

Inform students that poplar trees can grow 15 feet in one year. The trees also can take up 25 gallons of water in a day. Ask:

- **How can these characteristics help clean up a chemical polluted area?** (Possible answers: The larger the trees are, the more chemicals or polluted water in the soil they can absorb; since the trees grow quickly, they can be planted on a site after a spill and grow large enough in a short time to be useful quickly.)

Thinking Further: *Inferring*

Ask:

- **Why are plants useful in cleaning up only the uppermost six feet of soil?** (because the plants' roots do not reach further into the soil)

Test Prep:  **What Did I Learn?**

1. C

2. F

Summarize

Check students' understanding by having them write a brief summary of the amazing story in their own words.

Chapter Review and Test Preparation

Resources

- Reading in Science Resources, pp. 23–24
- Assessment Book, pp. 1–4

Answers to Vocabulary

1. epidermis
2. xylem
3. phloem
4. cortex
5. chlorophyll
6. fungus
7. photosynthesis
8. root cap
9. transpiration
10. cambium

Answers to Test Prep

11. A
12. H
13. A
14. G
15. C

Chapter 1 Review

Vocabulary

Fill each blank with the best word or words from the list.

> **cambium,** A21
> **chlorophyll,** A6
> **cortex,** A20
> **epidermis,** A20
> **fungus,** A13
> **phloem,** A21
> **photosynthesis,** A32
> **root cap,** A20
> **transpiration,** A25
> **xylem,** A20

1. The outer layer of a root is the _____.

2. Water and minerals flow up through the _____.

3. Foods flow down from the leaves through the _____.

4. Water and minerals then pass through the root's _____ to the xylem.

5. A green chemical called _____ allows plants to use the Sun's energy to make their own foods.

6. A mushroom is a _____.

7. The process by which plants make their own food is called _____.

8. The layer of tough cells that protects the root is called the _____.

9. The process by which water goes out of leaves is known as _____.

10. The _____ separates xylem from phloem.

Test Prep

11. Which of the following is a fungus?
    - **A** mold
    - **B** moss
    - **C** fern
    - **D** conifer

12. In the process of making food, plants give off _____.
    - **F** sugar
    - **G** carbon dioxide
    - **H** oxygen
    - **J** chloroplasts

13. The green "food factories" of plants are _____.
    - **A** chloroplasts
    - **B** phloem
    - **C** stoma
    - **D** epidermis

14. Leaves help roots take in water from soil through the process called _____.
    - **F** photosynthesis
    - **G** transpiration
    - **H** respiration
    - **J** perspiration

A 42

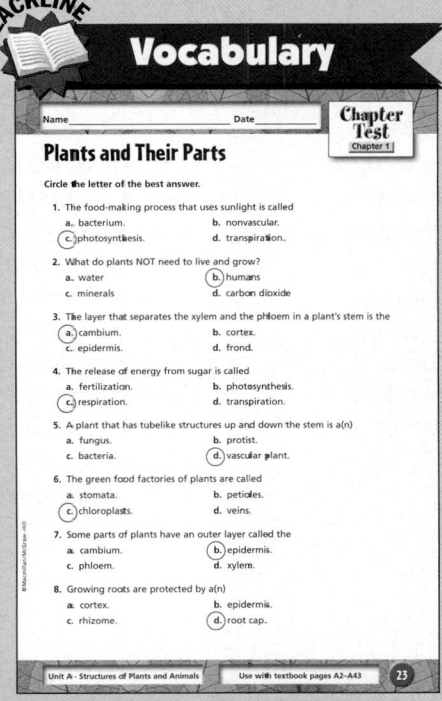

Reading in Science Resources, p. 23

15. When plants use stored sugar for energy, they go through a process called _____.

  A photosynthesis

  B transpiration

  C respiration

  D perspiration

Concepts and Skills

16. Reading in Science Write a paragraph explaining why ferns can grow taller than mosses.

17. Scientific Methods How would you determine how much light a geranium plant needs in order to survive? Write up a design for an experiment that would test this.

18. Decision Making Is there a single correct way to classify an organism? Write a paragraph explaining your answer.

19. Process Skills: Experiment Design an experiment to determine how much mosses, ferns, and grasses depend on water for survival. Write how you would set up the experiment. Write down your hypothesis. Tell what variables you would test.

20. Critical Thinking You dig in the ground and find a fossil of a fern. You then dig deeper and find a fossil of a club moss. What reasoning might let you conclude that club mosses evolved earlier than ferns? Write a paragraph explaining your reasoning.

Boost your test scores!

Be Smart!
Visit www.mhscience02.com

A 43

Answers to Concepts and Skills

16. Reading in Science Ferns have vascular tissue, mosses do not.

17. Scientific Methods Accept all reasonable student proposals for experiments, including the use of a geranium that receives little light over a period of a week and a geranium that receives adequate light.

18. Decision Making There is no single correct way to classify an organism. But classification can be closely approximated via kingdoms and divisions.

19. Process Skills: Experiment Use several fern, moss, and grass plants. Give measured amounts of water to each. Record observations and analyze results.

20. Critical Thinking The deeper you dig, the further back in time you go; or deeper layers of rock are older than shallower layers.

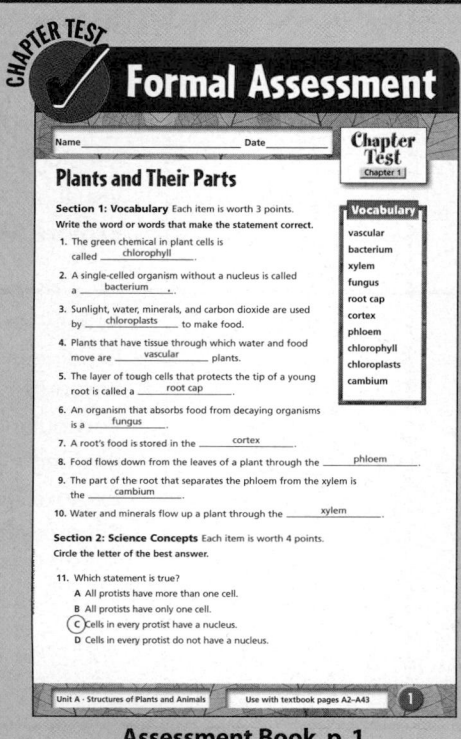

Assessment Book, p. 1

Lesson Planner

Lesson	Objectives	Vocabulary	Pacing	Resources and Technology
LESSON 4 **Plants Without Seeds,** pp. A46–A55	■ Explore parts mosses have for living in a moist environment. ■ Compare and contrast seedless nonvascular plants with seedless vascular plants. ■ Describe the life cycles of mosses and ferns. ■ Describe the adaptations of plants for living on land.	**rhizoid** **spore** **frond** **rhizome** **asexual reproduction** **fertilization** **sexual reproduction**	3 days	■ Activity Resources, pp. 16–20 ■ Reading in Science Resources, pp. 29–34 ■ Vocabulary Cards ■ Reading Aid Transparency A4 ■ Visual Aid Transparency 3, 4 ■ **Explore Activity Video**
LESSON 5 **Plants with Seeds,** pp. A56-A65	■ Explore how seed plants are alike and different. ■ Compare gymnosperms with angiosperms. ■ Compare and contrast monocots and dicots. ■ Identify why plants have aromas.	**seed** **angiosperm** **gymnosperm** **conifer** **cotyledon** **monocot** **dicot**	4 days	■ Activity Resources, pp. 21–25 ■ Reading in Science Resources, pp. 35–40 ■ Vocabulary Cards ■ Reading Aid Transparency A5 ■ **Explore Activity Video**
LESSON 6 **Flowers and Seeds,** pp. A68–A77	■ Explore the relationship between the parts of a flower and how the flower reproduces. ■ Identify the different parts of a flower and infer the function of each. ■ Explain the processes of seed dispersal, germination, and growth.	**ovary** **pollination** **embryo** **seed coat** **fruit**	3 days	■ Activity Resources, pp. 26–30 ■ Reading in Science Resources, pp. 41–46 ■ Vocabulary Cards ■ School to Home Activities, p. 5 ■ Grade-Level Science Book, *Jonathan Chapman: The Appleseed Man* ■ Reading Aid Transparency A6 ■ Visual Aid Transparency 5, 6, 7 ■ **Explore Activity Video**
LESSON 7 **Plant Responses and Adaptations,** pp. A78–A85	■ Explore how seed roots grow. ■ Identify tropisms. ■ Identify various adaptations plants have for survival.	**response** **stimulus** **tropism** **adaptation**	3 days	■ Activity Resources, pp. 31–35 ■ Reading in Science Resources, pp. 47–52 ■ Vocabulary Cards ■ Reading Aid Transparency A7 ■ **Explore Activity Video** ■ **Science Newsroom CD ROM** *Flower Power*

Activity Planner

Activity	Process Skills	Materials	Plan Ahead
LESSON 4 Explore Activity **How Do Mosses Get Water?** p. A47	observe, measure, interpret data, predict	hand lens, forceps, dropper, microscope, 3 microscope slides, coverslip, microscope, moss plant	Obtain moss plants with mature spores. Review how to make a wet-mount slide.
QUICK LAB FOR SCHOOL OR HOME **Ferns** p. A50	observe, experiment, infer	fern plant, fern leaf with spore cases, microscope, microscope slide, toothpick, water	Obtain fresh fern plants for the activity.
LESSON 5 Explore Activity **How Do Seed Plants Differ?** p. A57	observe, communicate, interpret data, infer, experiment	small pine seedling or other conifer, grass plant, garden plant or houseplant, such as a geranium, hand lens, microscope, microscope slide, coverslip	Obtain the plants needed for the activity. Any plant with parallel veins can be used in place of the grass plant. Label each plant. Review how to make a wet-mount slide.
Process Skill BUILDER **Flowering Plants** p. A63	observe, interpret data, classify	sample leaves and flowers from various angiosperms	Review poisonous plants with the students before they go out. If it is not possible for students to collect samples from the environment, provide samples for them or work from clear pictures of leaves and flowers from magazines and books.
LESSON 6 Explore Activity **How Do Flowers Differ?** p. A69	observe, communicate, infer	several large flowers from different plants, hand lens, forceps, dropper, toothpick	Any flower could be used, including wildflowers. A lily is a good choice because the stamen and pistil are easily visible. Florists may be willing to donate flowers that they can no longer use.
LESSON 7 Explore Activity **How Do Roots Grow?** p. A79	predict, communicate, observe, interpret data	petri dish (plastic), 2 paper towels, marking pen, tape, 4 bean seeds that have been soaked in water overnight	Soak the bean seeds in water overnight.

CHAPTER 2 Teaching Resources

Reading in Science Resources

McGraw-Hill Science **Reading in Science Resources** provides the following **Blackline Master** worksheets for this chapter.

Chapter Graphic Organizer

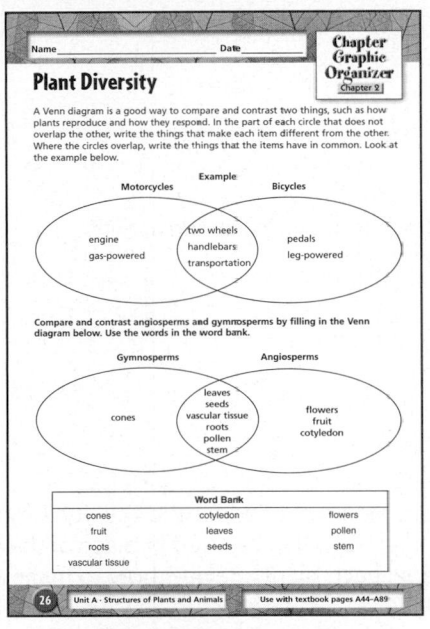

Reading in Science Resources, p. 26

Chapter Reading Skill

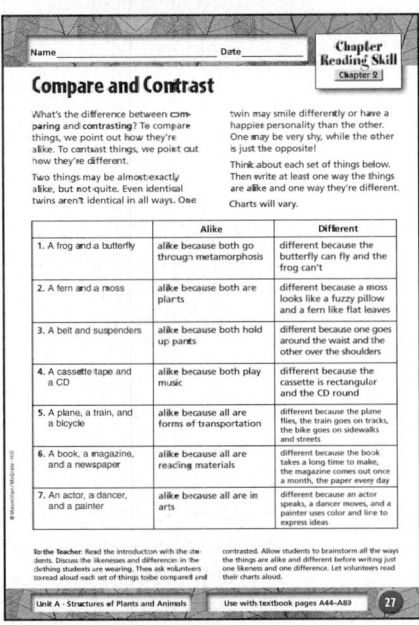

Reading in Science Resources, pp. 27–28

Chapter Vocabulary

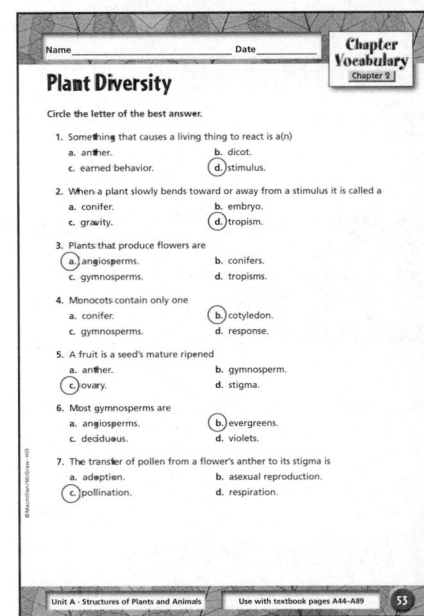

Reading in Science Resources, pp. 53–54

McGraw-Hill Science **Reading in Science Resources** provides the following **Blackline Master** worksheets for every lesson in this chapter.

Lesson Outline

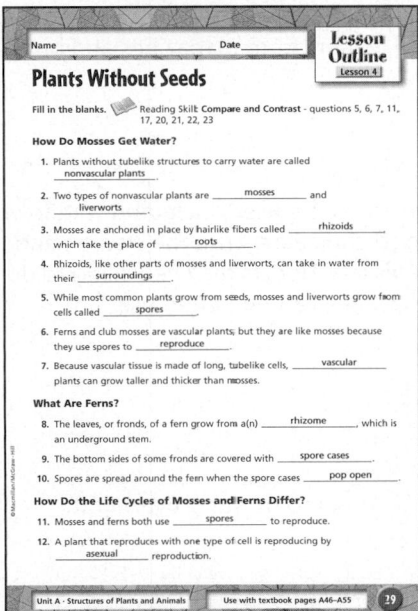

Reading in Science Resources, pp. 29–30, 35–36, 41–42, 47–48

Interpret Illustrations

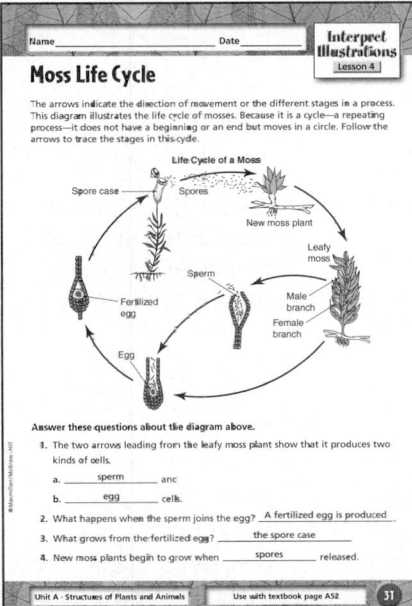

Reading in Science Resources, pp. 31–32, 37–38, 43–44, 49–50

Lesson Vocabulary and Cloze Test

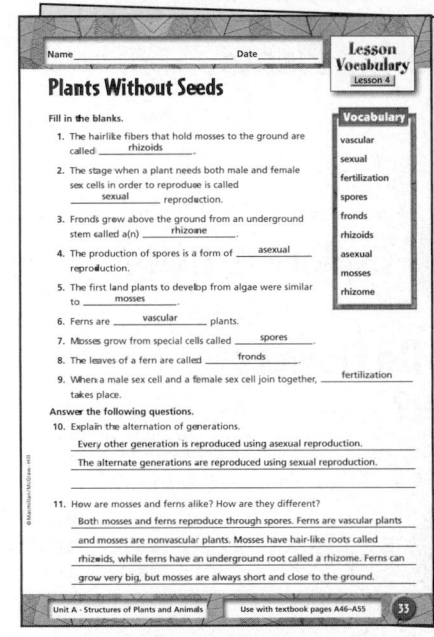

Reading in Science Resources, pp. 33–34, 39–40, 45–46, 51–52

Activities and Assessment

McGraw-Hill Science **Activity Resources** provides the following **Blackline Master** worksheets for every lesson in this chapter.

Explore Activity and Alternative Explore Activity

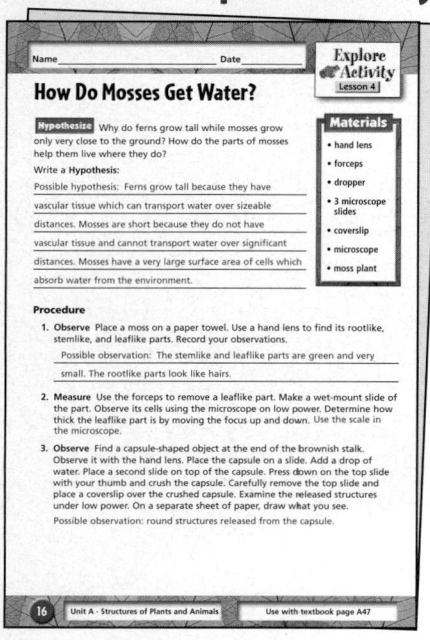

Activity Resources, *pp. 16–18, 21–23, 26–28, 31–33*

Quick Lab for School or Home

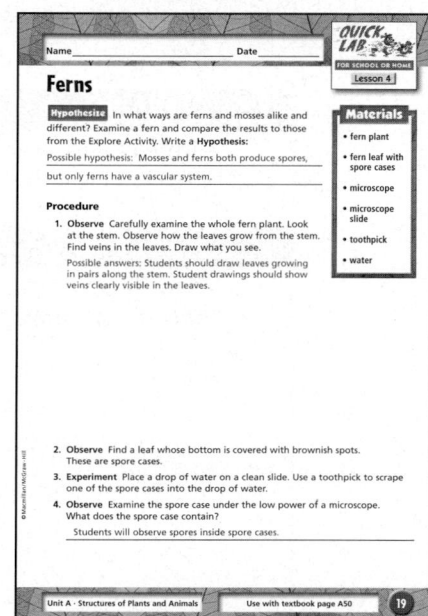

Activity Resources, *pp. 19–20, 29–30, 34–35*

Process Skill Builder

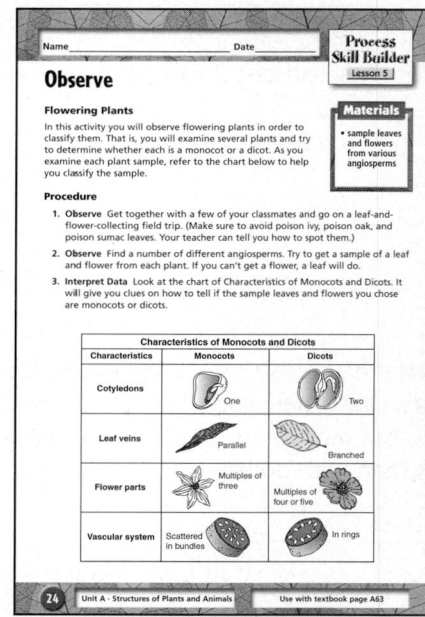

Activity Resources, *pp. 24–25*

McGraw-Hill Science **Assessment Book** provides the following **Blackline Master** worksheets for this chapter.

Chapter Test

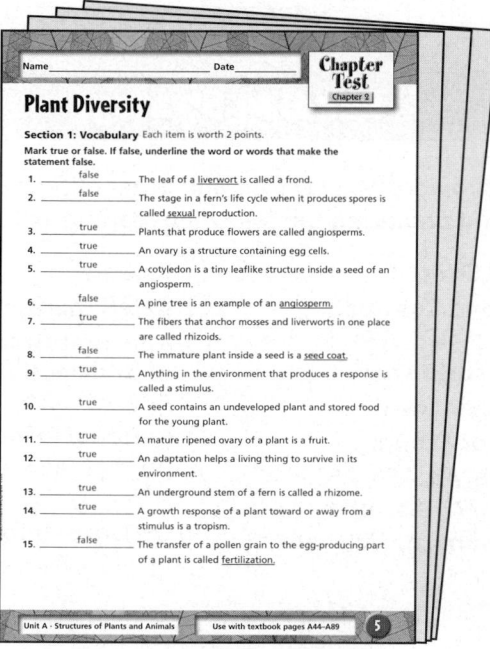

Assessment Book, *pp. 5–8*

CHAPTER
2 Plant Diversity

Resources

- Reading in Science Resources, pp. 26–55
- Assessment Book, pp. 5–8

Did You Ever Wonder?

Orchids are angiosperms. They produce seeds and flowers. Like other seed plants, orchids attract pollinators, but most orchids attract them with nectar rather than with pollen.

CHAPTER
2 Plant Diversity

LESSON 4
Plants without Seeds, A46

LESSON 5
Plants with Seeds, A56

LESSON 6
Flowers and Seeds, A68

LESSON 7
Plant Responses and Adaptations, A78

Did You Ever Wonder?

Where do orchids grow? Of the thousands of different kinds of orchids, many grow in tropical rain forests. However, about 100 kinds of orchids grow in Europe, Asia, and North America. What do orchids have in common with other flowering plants?

A 44

Reading Strategy

This chapter provides MiniLessons and other opportunities for developing and practicing the following reading skills:

- ○ Cause and Effect
- ◉ Compare and Contrast: pp. A49, A59, A71, A84
- ○ Draw Conclusions
- ○ Find the Main Idea
- ○ Sequence of Events
- ◉ Summarize: pp. A55, A65, A67, A70, A77, A85, A87
- ◉ Ask Questions: pp. A56, A68, A80

- ○ Reread
- ○ Retell (paraphrase)
- ◉ Interpret Graphic Sources of Information: pp. A50, A53, A62, A70, A72, A76, A82
- ◉ Build on Prior Knowledge: pp. A46, A56, A66, A68, A78, A86
- ◉ Organize Information: pp. A55, A58, A83

A 45

Vocabulary Preview

Encourage students to keep a Science Dictionary. Remind them to add the Vocabulary words for each lesson in this chapter to their Dictionary as they complete each lesson.

rhizoid, A48

spore, A48

frond, A51

rhizome, A51

asexual reproduction, A52

fertilization, A52

sexual reproduction, A52

seed, A58

angiosperm, A58

gymnosperm, A58

conifer, A59

cotyledon, A62

monocot, A62

dicot, A62

ovary, A70

pollination, A72

embryo, A74

seed coat, A74

fruit, A75

response, A80

stimulus, A80

tropism, A80

adaptation, A82

AMERICAN MUSEUM OF NATURAL HISTORY

Visit www.amnh.org/resources/mhscience to discover more about how new techniques and technology affect farming and the environment.

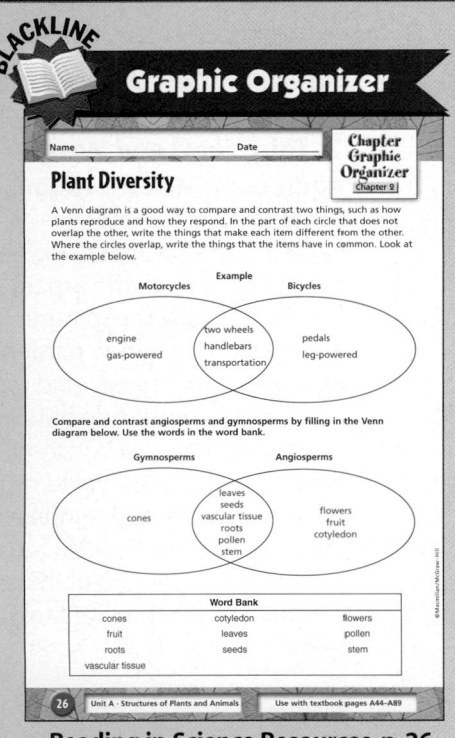

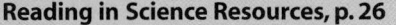

Reading in Science Resources, p. 26

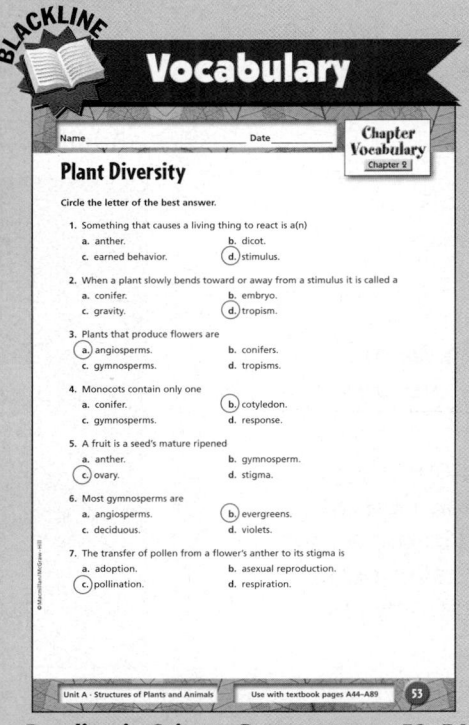

Reading in Science Resources, pp. 53–54

LESSON 4 Plants Without Seeds

Objectives

- Explore parts mosses have for living in a moist environment.
- Compare and contrast seedless nonvascular plants with seedless vascular plants.
- Describe the life cycles of mosses and ferns.
- Describe the adaptations of plants for living on land.

Resources

- Activity Resources, pp. 16–20
- Reading in Science Resources, pp. 29–34
- Vocabulary Cards
- Reading Aid Transparency A4
- Visual Aid Transparencies 3, 4

Build on Prior Knowledge

Have students discuss what they know about mosses and ferns. Show some samples of mosses. Then ask students to compare these samples with a leafy plant. Encourage them to note differences and similarities. (Mosses have no leaves, roots, or stems; both are green.)

1 Get Ready

Developing the Main Idea
Ask:

- **Why do mosses and ferns do best in warm, wet places?** (They need a lot of moisture and cannot withstand cold temperatures.)

Explain why mosses and ferns grow differently. Ferns are vascular and mosses are nonvascular. Vascular plants have tubelike structures needed to grow tall. Nonvascular plants lack these. Mosses have rootlike structures to take in water and leaflike structures to get rid of excess water.

LESSON 4 Plants Without Seeds

Vocabulary

rhizoid, A48
spore, A48
frond, A51
rhizome, A51
asexual reproduction, A52
fertilization, A52
sexual reproduction, A52

Get Ready

Have you ever seen plants like these? If so, there were probably none as tall as these. You are looking at ferns in Costa Rica's Monteverde rain forest, one of Earth's dampest places. These ferns grow taller than a six-story building. Their leaves are more than three times longer than you are tall.

Ferns do best in warm, wet places. So do mosses, but mosses grow low to the ground. Why do ferns grow tall while mosses don't? How do the parts of mosses help them live where they do?

Process Skill

You predict when you state possible results of an event or experiment.

A 46

Cross Curricular Books

Additional Outside Reading

The Mills Green Team

written by Lisa deMauro
illustrated by Patty Fleckenstein

To order, see page A1·b.

Science Background

False Ferns and Mosses
Addressing Misconceptions
Some species commonly named "fern" or "moss" are neither. For example, the asparagus fern is really the mature leaves of the common garden asparagus. The "moss" said to grow on the north side of trees is really an algae, as is Irish moss. Beard moss, Iceland moss, oak moss, and reindeer moss are lichens. Spanish moss is a flowering plant. Club moss is actually a plant related to ferns.

Explore Activity

How Do Mosses Get Water?

Materials
hand lens
forceps
dropper
3 microscope slides
coverslip
microscope
moss plant

Procedure

1 **Observe** Place a moss on a paper towel. Use a hand lens to find its rootlike, stemlike, and leaflike parts. Record your observations.

2 **Measure** Use the forceps to remove a leaflike part. Make a wet-mount slide of the part. Observe its cells using the microscope on low power. Determine how thick the leaflike part is by moving the focus up and down.

3 **Observe** Find a capsule-shaped object at the end of the brownish stalk. Observe it with the hand lens. Place the capsule on a slide. Add a drop of water. Place a second slide on top of the capsule. Press down on the top slide with your thumb, and crush the capsule. Carefully remove the top slide and place a coverslip over the crushed capsule. Examine the released structures under low power. Draw what you see.

Drawing Conclusions

1 **Observe** Which parts of the moss are green? Explain why they are green.

2 **Observe** How many cell layers make up the leaflike structure?

3 **Interpret Data** What structures anchor the moss plant? What was the capsule?

4 **Going Further: Predict** What do you think the objects inside the capsule do? How would you test your prediction?

A 47

Alternative Explore Activity

Materials pictures of different mosses and parts of mosses

Parts of Mosses Have students work in groups to examine the illustrations. Challenge them to identify the rootlike hairs, the stemlike part, and leaflike part, and record their observations about the color, shape, and size. Then ask them to look at illustrations of moss cells and the inside of a spore capsule. Have them draw what they see.

Spatial; Kinesthetic

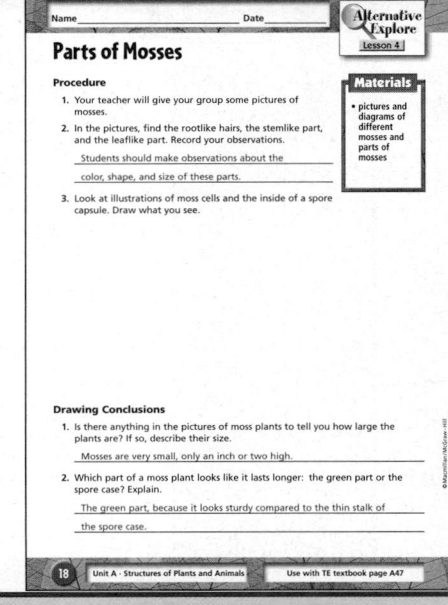

Activity Resources, p. 18

Explore Activity

How Do Mosses Get Water?

Science Process Skills *observe, measure, interpret data, predict*

Resources Activity Resources pp. 16–17

Pacing 30–40 minutes

Grouping individual

Plan Ahead Obtain moss plants with mature spores. Review how to make a wet-mount slide. (See Explore Activity, p. A5, step 3.)

Procedure

1 The stemlike and leaflike parts are green and very small. The rootlike parts look like hairs.

2 Ask students how moving the focus up and down tells them how thick the leaf is. (It shows how many layers of cells there are.)

3 The spore capsules may need to be cut with a knife before students can crush them with fingers. (Round structures are released from the capsule.)

Answers to Drawing Conclusions

1 The leaflike structures of the moss contain chlorophyll, making them green.

2 Students should see one or two layers of cells.

3 the rootlike cells; spore capsule containing tiny particles (spores)

4 Students may suggest the particles have something to do with making new plants. They could plant some to find out what happens.

Inquiry Students can ask their own questions to explore, such as how cells of mosses compare with other plant cells.

Technology

■ When time is short, preview the activity with the **Explore Activity Video**.

How Do Mosses Get Water?

Before Reading
Have students try to answer the red question at the top of the page.

Developing the Main Idea
Help students focus on the characteristics of mosses by comparing and contrasting their characteristics with those of the plants they studied in the last lesson. Ask:

- **What structure do mosses share with other plants?** (a rootlike structure)
- **What is different about how water travels in mosses with how it travels in other plants?** (In mosses, water travels directly from one cell to the next instead of through tubes.)

Developing Vocabulary

rhizoid The term *rhizoid* stems from the Greek word *rhiza*, which means "root." The suffix *-oid* forms nouns or adjectives meaning "like or resembling something."

spore To help students remember the meaning of the term *spore,* relate the word to its Greek origin, *speirein*, meaning "to sow."

Read to Learn

Main Idea Seedless nonvascular plants and seedless vascular plants have different structures but similar life cycles.

How Do Mosses Get Water?

Mosses and their close relatives the liverworts are nonvascular plants. They don't have the long tubelike structures vascular plants have. They cling to damp soil, sheltered rocks, and the shady side of trees. Mosses and liverworts are tiny plants, only 2 to 5 centimeters (about 1 to 2 inches) tall. Mosses' leaves are only one or two cells thick.

Mosses and liverworts don't have roots. However, they stay anchored in one place. That's because they have hairlike fibers that do a job much like roots. The fibers are called **rhizoids** (RIGH·zoydz). Rhizoids, like other parts of mosses and liverworts, can take in water from their surroundings. The water then travels directly from one cell to the next.

Most of the plants you see every day grow from seeds. However, mosses and liverworts are seedless plants. They grow from **spores**. Spores are cells that can develop into new organisms.

Nonvascular

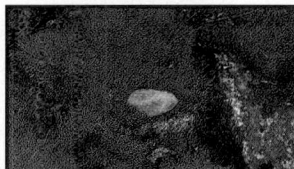

Mosses

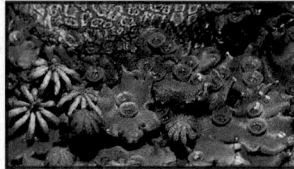

Liverworts

Mosses and liverworts grow in damp places. Most are tiny plants, growing only 2 to 5 centimeters (about 1 to 2 inches) tall.

Club mosses

Club mosses produce spores at the ends of stems in structures that look like tiny pine cones.

A 48

Math MiniLesson

Add and Subtract Decimals

Develop Jessica bought a plant that was 15.8 cm tall. A month later, the plant was 23.5 cm tall. How many centimeters did the plant grow?

You can subtract to solve the problem.

Find: 23.5 − 15.8
Line up the decimal points.
Subtract. Regroup if needed.

$$\begin{array}{r} 12 \\ 1\ \cancel{2}\ 15 \\ \cancel{2\ 3}.\cancel{5} \\ -\ 1\ 5.8 \\ \hline 7.7 \end{array}$$

The plant grew 7.7 cm

 23.5 − 15.8 = 7.7

Practice Add or subtract.

1. 84.3 − 57.5
   (26.8)
2. 46.87 + 8.6
   (55.47)

Activity Have students find two decimal money amounts in supermarket ads. Have them find the sum and the difference of the two decimals.

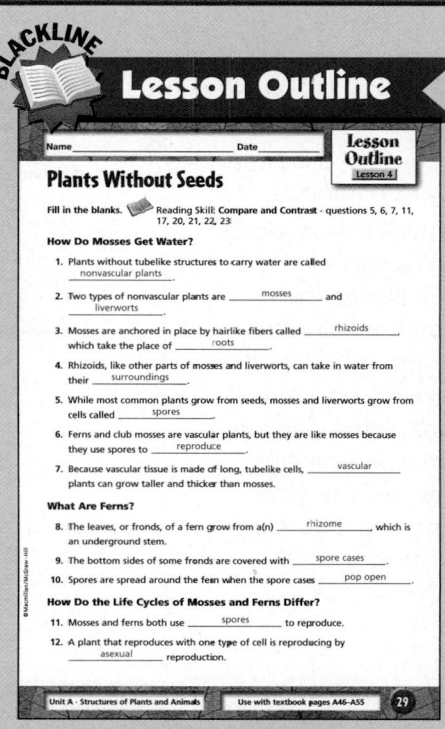

Lesson Outline

Name_____ Date_____

Lesson Outline Lesson 4

Plants Without Seeds

Fill in the blanks. Reading Skill: Compare and Contrast - questions 5, 6, 7, 11, 17, 20, 21, 22, 23

How Do Mosses Get Water?

1. Plants without tubelike structures to carry water are called ___nonvascular plants___
2. Two types of nonvascular plants are ___mosses___ and ___liverworts___
3. Mosses are anchored in place by hairlike fibers called ___rhizoids___ which take the place of ___roots___
4. Rhizoids, like other parts of mosses and liverworts, can take in water from their ___surroundings___
5. While most common plants grow from seeds, mosses and liverworts grow from cells called ___spores___
6. Ferns and club mosses are vascular plants, but they are like mosses because they use spores to ___reproduce___
7. Because vascular tissue is made of long, tubelike cells, ___vascular___ plants can grow taller and thicker than mosses.

What Are Ferns?

8. The leaves, or fronds, of a fern grow from a(n) ___rhizome___ which is an underground stem.
9. The bottom sides of some fronds are covered with ___spore cases___
10. Spores are spread around the fern when the spore cases ___pop open___

How Do the Life Cycles of Mosses and Ferns Differ?

11. Mosses and ferns both use ___spores___ to reproduce.
12. A plant that reproduces with one type of cell is reproducing by ___asexual___ reproduction.

Unit A · Structures of Plants and Animals | Use with textbook pages A46–A55 | **29**

Reading in Science Resources, p. 29

Spores are tiny structures found inside a capsule called a *spore capsule*.

Many mosses look like green, fuzzy pillows. Many liverworts look more like flat leaves. Ancient people thought that the shape of these plants resembled a liver. That's how they got their name.

Seedless Vascular Plants

True mosses and liverworts are seedless plants. So are their more distant relatives club mosses, spike mosses, horsetails, and ferns. All of them use spores to reproduce. However, mosses and liverworts are different from the other four in a very important way.

Mosses and liverworts don't have a vascular system. Club mosses, spike mosses, horsetails, and ferns do.

The vascular tissue in these plants is made up of long tubelike cells. These cells let water and food move easily over long distances. That is why vascular plants can grow very tall and thick. That is also why nonvascular plants like true mosses and liverworts are so short and delicate. The trunks of the largest ferns can be as thick as your body.

READING Compare and Contrast
How do mosses and ferns get water?

Mosses are nonvascular plants—they can't move water long distances; ferns are vascular plants—they have long tubes to move water.

Vascular

Spike mosses

Spike mosses, such as this "resurrection plant," live in the desert. Resurrection plants can dry out when there is no rain, but they do not die. They revive when water becomes available again.

Horsetails

The stems of horsetails are hollow, have a ring of vascular tissue and joints, and contain a gritty, sandy substance called silica.

Ferns

Ferns come in all sizes and shapes and live in different kinds of climates.

A 49

Using the Illustrations

Point out the spore-producing structures visible in the photographs of club mosses and horsetails. Horsetails may send up green or flesh-colored leafless stalks with spore cones at their ends. Spore cases on ferns are explored on p. A50.

Exploring the Main Idea

Resurrection plants can be used as rain meters. When conditions are dry, the fronds close up to limit water loss. When wet, special cells take in water and the fronds open. Students can demonstrate this by putting water on the fronds. These plants can become part of the classroom's weather station.

▶ After Reading

Have students answer the red question in the student book as **ongoing assessment**.

Reading MiniLesson

Compare and Contrast

Develop Discuss the use of the phrase *All of them* (page A49, paragraph 2, line 4) as a reading clue that things are being compared, and the word *However* (paragraph 2, line 5) as a clue that things will be contrasted. Follow up by discussing the compared characteristics (use spores to reproduce) **and the contrasted one** (vascular system in some, not all).

Practice Have students use information from page A49 to construct charts that compare and contrast a vascular and nonvascular plant. Categories to list on the charts might include: habitat, size, structure, reproduction, and appearance.

Cultural Perspective

The Many Uses of Moss

Invite students to find out how other cultures use mosses. For example, in Hawaii people use mosses to stuff cushions and mattresses. In northern countries like Scotland, peat moss is used for fuel. People in China use dried sphagnum to cure eye diseases, people in England use it to treat wounds, and Native Americans in Alaska use it to treat cuts. Have students brainstorm other uses for peat moss. **Social; Linguistic**

What Are Ferns?

Before Reading
Have students try to answer the red question at the top of the page.

Developing the Main Idea
Ask students how they think mosses reproduce from the spores they saw in the Explore Activity. Have students share their knowledge about the life cycles of different organisms. They may include protists and animals, as well as plants.

Prehistoric Earth had dense forests of tree-sized ferns and giant club mosses. The mosses and ferns fell to the ground and were buried, which led to the formation of coal.

Materials fern plant, fern leaf with spore cases, microscope, microscope slide, toothpick, water

Science Process Skills *observe, experiment, infer*

Resources Activity Resources. pp. 19–20

Step 1 Leaves grow in pairs along the stem.

Step 4 spores

Step 5 They both have spore cases containing spores.

Ferns

1. **Observe** Carefully examine a fern plant. Look at the stem. Observe how the leaves grow from the stem. Find the veins in the leaves. Draw what you see.

2. **Observe** Find a leaf whose bottom is covered with brownish spots. These are spore cases.

3. **Experiment** Place a drop of water on a clean slide. Use a toothpick to scrape one of the spore cases into the drop of water.

4. **Observe** Examine the spore case under the low power of a microscope. What does the spore case contain?

5. **Infer** What do ferns and mosses have in common?

A 50

What Are Ferns?
Ferns once formed huge forests on Earth. You can still find them today in many wooded areas. Many people also grow ferns at home. What are ferns like?

Finding spore cases on the bottom of a fern leaf

Preparing a slide for viewing one spore case

Ferns have leaves that are called **fronds** (FRAHNDZ). They grow above the ground from an underground stem called a **rhizome** (RIGH·zohm). Roots, which anchor the plant to the soil or to a tree, branch out from the rhizome.

The bottom sides of some fronds are covered with rows of brownish or rust-colored spore cases that contain spores. Under the right conditions, the spore cases pop open and spray spores as far away as a few meters. If the spores land in a place where conditions are right for fern growth, the spores will develop into the first stage in a new fern's life cycle.

Spore cases arranged on the bottom of a fern frond will pop open, spraying spores all around. If conditions are right where the spores fall, the spores will produce new fern plants.

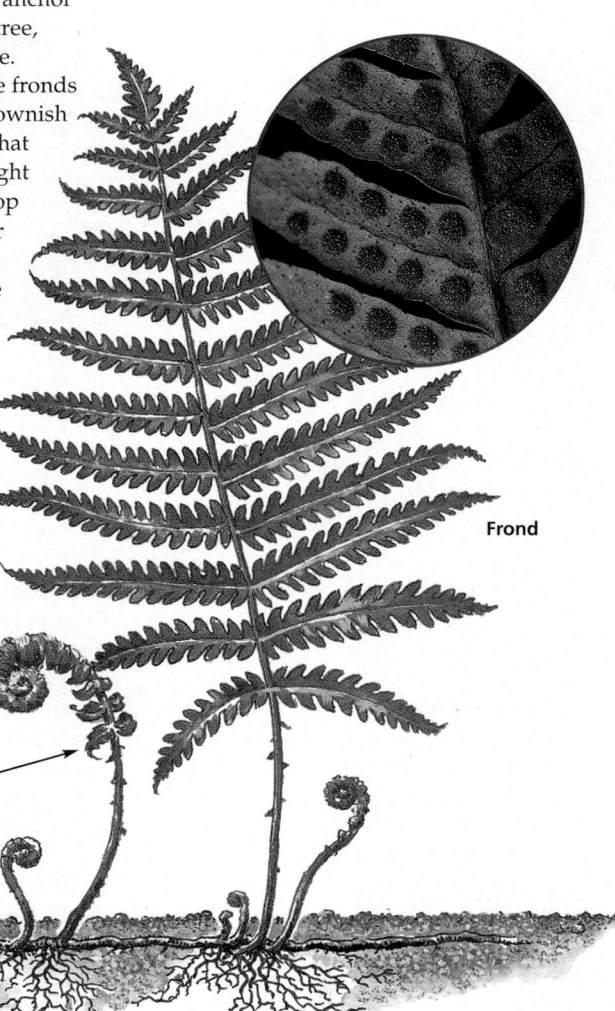

Frond

▷ **What are ferns like?**

Possible answer: Ferns have fronds for leaves, rhizomes that are underground stems that support the leaves, roots that branch out from rhizomes to anchor the plants, and spore cases that contain spores that produce new plants.

Young ferns (fiddleheads)

Rhizome

Roots

A 51

Developing the Main Idea

Call students' attention to the rows of spore cases on the fern in the photo. Point out that fronds hold many, many spore cases each containing a very large number of spores. Help students understand why by placing a few sticky notes, sticky side up, on flat surfaces in the front of the classroom. Put some pepper on a sheet of paper and blow on the paper. Ask:

■ **How many specks of pepper landed on the sticky notes?** (probably not many)

Thinking Further: *Inferring*
Ask:

■ **Why does a fern produce so many spores?** (Only a few will land in places where they can grow.)

▶ **After Reading**
Have students answer the red question in the student book as **ongoing assessment.**

Developing Vocabulary

frond This word is from Latin for "leafy branch, foliage."

rhizome The prefix *rhiz-* is from Greek for "root." It is used for *rhizoid* and *rhizome,* which are both rootlike structures, but not true roots. The "m" in *rhizome* can help students realize that a rhizome is an underground ste*m*, not a root at all.

Inclusion

Ferns, Anyone?
Young ferns are often referred to as fiddleheads. This is because the tightly curled fronds look like the top of violins—or fiddles. But did you know that many people consider them to be delicacies? Have students research the types of fiddlehead ferns that are used in cooking—such as ostrich ferns—and create some recipes for side dishes and salads. **Linguistic; Kinesthetic**

Science Background

Tree Moss
Addressing Misconceptions
An old legend says you can find your way in the forest by looking for moss on the sides of trees—the moss will always be on the side that faces north. The organism referred to, however, is an alga rather than a moss. Ask:

■ **Why do these organisms appear only on one side of the tree?** (In the northern hemisphere, the north side of the tree is shaded because of the positions of the Sun and Earth.)

How Do the Life Cycles of Mosses and Ferns Differ?

Before Reading
Have students try to answer the red question at the top of the text column.

Developing the Main Idea
Encourage students to find on the diagrams the descriptions given in the text, noting similarities and differences. Ask:

- **What do both the moss plant and fern plant need in their environment in order for the sperm to get to the egg?** (water)

Technology

- Visual Aid Transparency 3:
  Life Cycle of a Moss

Life Cycle of a Moss

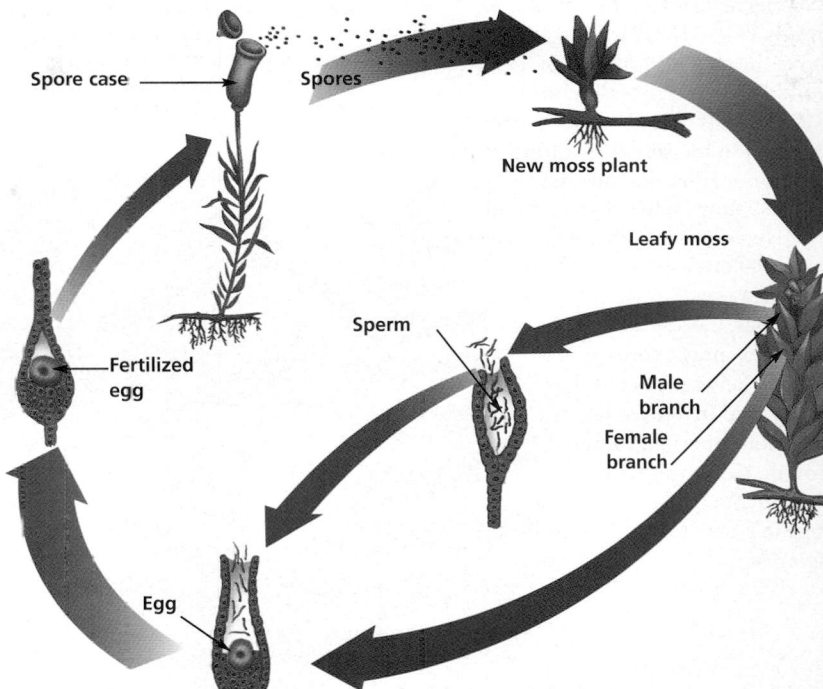

Spore case · Spores · New moss plant · Leafy moss · Sperm · Fertilized egg · Male branch · Female branch · Egg

How Do the Life Cycles of Mosses and Ferns Differ?

Since mosses and ferns use spores to *reproduce* (ree·pruh·DEWS)—make new plants—you might guess that their life cycles are similar. That guess would be correct, but there are differences, too.

The diagrams on these two pages will help you compare and contrast the life cycles of mosses and ferns.

Both mosses and ferns have two separate stages to their life cycles. One stage is when they produce spores.

This stage in the life cycle is called

A 52

asexual reproduction (ay·SEK·shew·uhl ree·pruh·DUK·shuhn). That's because the plant needs only one type of cell—the spore—in order to reproduce.

Moss spores grow into leafy moss plants that have male branches and female branches. The male branches produce *sperm*—male sex cells. The female branches produce eggs—female sex cells. When a male sex cell meets a female sex cell, the two may join together. This is called **fertilization** (fur·tuh·luh·ZAY·shuhn).

This stage in the cycle is called **sexual reproduction** (SEK·shew·uhl ree·pruh·DUK·shuhn). That's because

BLACKLINE   Interpret Illustrations

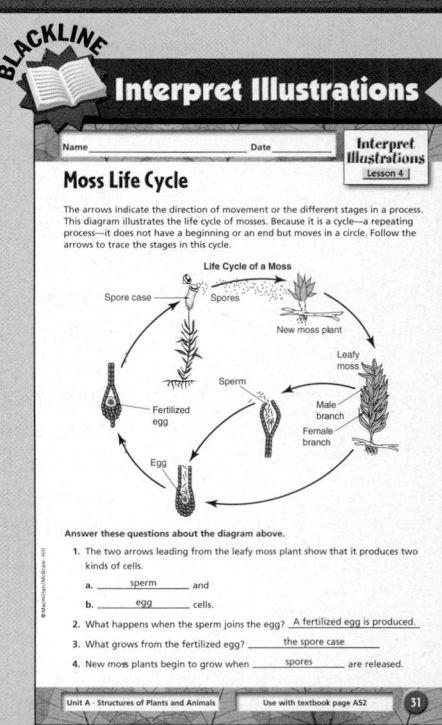

Moss Life Cycle

The arrows indicate the direction of movement or the different stages in a process. This diagram illustrates the life cycle of mosses. Because it is a cycle—a repeating process—it does not have a beginning or an end but moves in a circle. Follow the arrows to trace the stages in this cycle.

Life Cycle of a Moss

Answer these questions about the diagram above.

1. The two arrows leading from the leafy moss plant show that it produces two kinds of cells.
   a. _____sperm_____ and
   b. _____egg_____ cells.
2. What happens when the sperm joins the egg? _A fertilized egg is produced._
3. What grows from the fertilized egg? _____the spore case_____
4. New moss plants begin to grow when _____spores_____ are released.

Unit A · Structures of Plants and Animals   Use with textbook page A52   **31**

Reading in Science Resources, p. 31

Life Cycle of a Fern

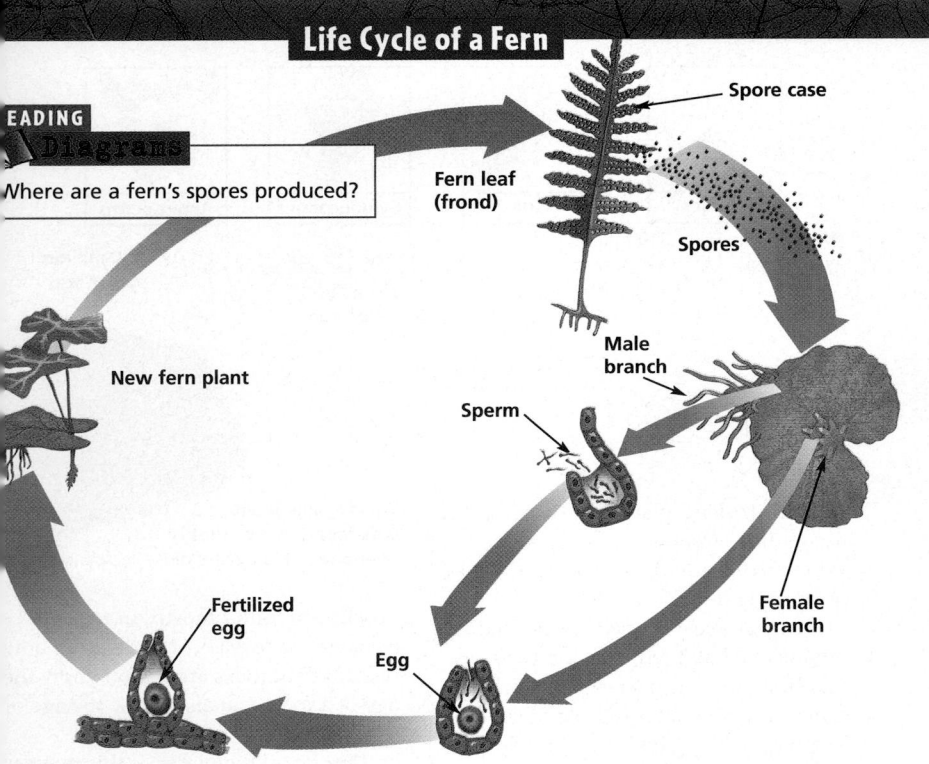

Spore case

Fern leaf (frond)

Spores

Male branch

Sperm

New fern plant

Fertilized egg

Egg

Female branch

The plant needs both male sex cells and female sex cells in order to reproduce.

The fertilized egg eventually becomes a thin stalk with a spore case on top. When the spore case opens, the spores are released. Spores that land on damp ground may grow into new moss plants, and the cycle begins again.

This process of going from sexual reproduction to asexual reproduction to sexual reproduction again is called *alternation of generations.*

Ferns also reproduce by alternation of generations. Leafy fern plants produce spores on the undersides of their fronds.

Spores landing in shady, moist soil are most likely to grow. The spores grow into small, heart-shaped plants. These plants produce male and female sex cells.

If a male sex cell fertilizes a female sex cell, the fertilized egg starts to form a new plant. The new plant develops into a leafy fern plant. Spore cases on the fern's fronds produce spores, and the cycle begins again.

▶ **In what ways are the life cycles of mosses and ferns alike?**
Both reproduce by alternation of generations, producing spores in one stage and sex cells in the other.

A 53

Developing the Main Idea
Clarify the difference between the spore-producing stage and the sex-cell-producing stages in both plants by drawing students' attention to the location in the cycle of (a) the spores, (b) the sperm and egg cells, and (c) the new leafy plants. Ask:

■ **What is meant by alternation of generations?** (Alternation of generations means that the plant reproduces in two stages, each following the other. In the asexual stage, spores produce a plant with sex cells. During the sexual stage, these sex cells unite to produce a plant that will form spores.)

READING
Diagrams

in the spore cases on the bottom sides of some fronds

▶**After Reading**
Have students answer the red question in the student book as **ongoing assessment.**

Technology

■ Visual Aid Transparency 4: *Life Cycle of a Fern*

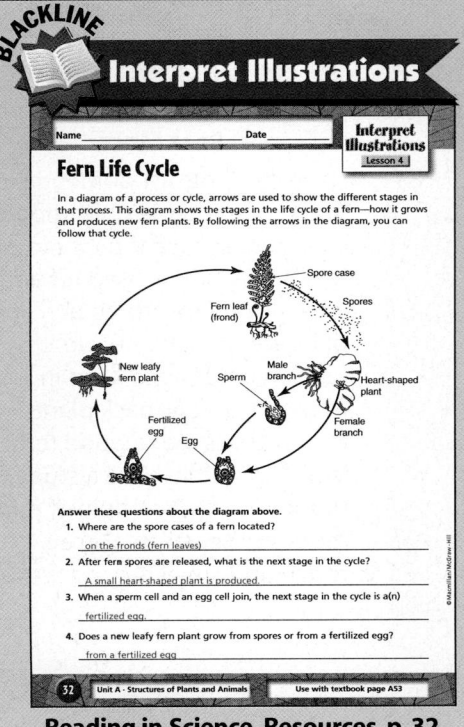

Name_____ Date_____

Interpret Illustrations
Lesson 4

Fern Life Cycle

In a diagram of a process or cycle, arrows are used to show the different stages in that process. This diagram shows the stages in the life cycle of a fern—how it grows and produces new fern plants. By following the arrows in the diagram, you can follow that cycle.

Spore case
Fern leaf (frond)
Spores
New leafy fern plant
Sperm
Male branch
Heart-shaped plant
Fertilized egg
Egg
Female branch

Answer these questions about the diagram above.
1. Where are the spore cases of a fern located?
   on the fronds (fern leaves)
2. After fern spores are released, what is the next stage in the cycle?
   A small heart-shaped plant is produced.
3. When a sperm cell and an egg cell join, the next stage in the cycle is a(n)
   fertilized egg.
4. Does a new leafy fern plant grow from spores or from a fertilized egg?
   from a fertilized egg

32 Unit A · Structures of Plants and Animals   Use with textbook page A53

Reading in Science Resources, p. 32

SCIENCE FOR ALL   English Language Learners

Life Cycles
Invite students to use construction paper, leaves and twigs, markers, cellophane, and so on to make 3-D displays showing the life cycles of mosses and ferns. Pepper can be used for spores. Remind students to label their displays and provide explanations of what is being illustrated. **Spatial; Linguistic**

What Were the Ancestors of Plants?

Before Reading
Have students try to answer the red question at the top of the text column.

Developing the Main Idea
As students read this page ask what structures plants needed to survive on land. (Answers may include a way to make food from the sun, a way to stand tall, and a way to conserve water.)

Thinking Further: *Drawing Conclusions*
Ask:

- **Were these structures present in the very first land plants? Why?** (No; the first plants didn't need to stand tall and conserve water; plants with these structures developed in response to changes in the environment.)

▶ After Reading
Have students answer the red question in the student book as **ongoing assessment**.

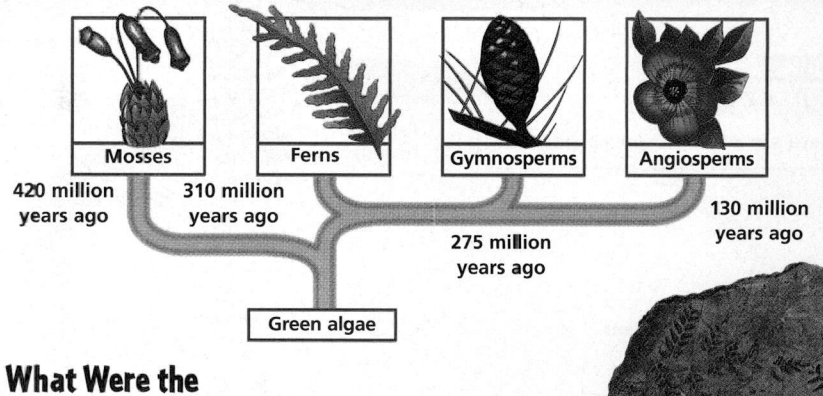

420 million years ago — Mosses

310 million years ago — Ferns

275 million years ago — Gymnosperms

130 million years ago — Angiosperms

Green algae

What Were the Ancestors of Plants?

The first land plants developed from living things that lived in the water. Which living things were the ancestors of land plants?

Scientists searched for clues linking organisms that lived in water to those that first grew on land. A good place to start was with photosynthetic organisms. These were living things that made their own food.

To narrow the search, the scientific detectives compared the chlorophyll of various simple organisms living today with that of plants. They found the closest match was with green algae.

Scientists found other clues. The cell walls of both green algae and plants contain cellulose. Cellulose can help plants survive on land, since a strong cell wall helps plants stay upright.

There was another clue. Both green algae and plants store food as starch.

Next, scientists hunted for fossils— the preserved remains of living things.

This fernlike plant was found in rock that is over 340 million years old.

Fossils are found mostly in rocks. Scientists have ways of finding out how old different rocks are. If you know the age of a rock, you also know the age of the fossil in it.

Putting all the pieces of this puzzle together, scientists concluded that the first land plants to evolve, or develop, from algae were probably nonvascular plants similar to mosses. These early land plants first appeared about 420 million years ago. Vascular plants appeared more recently. The earliest vascular plants, the ferns, were seedless. The first plants with seeds were gymnosperms, followed by angiosperms, or flowering plants.

▷ **How did scientists find the ancestors of plants?**

They found that green algae and plants have certain things in common: chlorophyll, cellulose, similar food storage methods. Then they looked for fossil evidence of the earliest plants.

A 54

Math   MiniLesson

Place Value

Develop As you discuss the millions of years in the art, review place value.

You can express a number in different forms.

Standard form: 837,650,000

Word form: eight hundred thirty-seven million, sixty-five thousand

Expanded form: 800,000,000 + 30,000,000 + 7,000,000 + 600,000 + 50,000

The *place* of the digit 8 is hundred millions.

The *value* of the digit 8 is 800,000,000.

Practice Write the standard form for each number.

1. 28 million
(28,000,000)

2. 4.65 million
(4,650,000)

Activity Have students write the expanded form for the numbers in exercises 1 and 2. Have them use a calculator to verify their answers.

SCIENCE FOR ALL   English Language Learners

Peat Moss

Have students ask someone at home or in the neighborhood who gardens what peat moss (or sphagnum) is used for and why. (It can absorb 20 percent of its weight in water, so it is used in gardens to keep in moisture and to pack plants. Peat moss is also a good fertilizer.) If possible have a student bring in a small sample of peat moss so that students can touch and smell it. **Kinesthetic**

L·I·N·K·S

Why It Matters

Mosses and ferns were among the first plants to live on land. Today mosses are often the first plants to return to an area where plant life has been destroyed. Mosses help break down rocks into soil. Mosses also help hold on to the soil, making it easier for other plants to survive in the area. Without mosses, perhaps your favorite plants would never have had a chance to grow where they do.

Visit **www.mhscience02.com** to do a research project on seedless plants.

Think and Write

1. Why do mosses grow close to the ground?

2. Why do people sometimes add moss to a garden?

3. How do mosses change rocky areas so other plants can grow?

4. List two differences between mosses and ferns.

5. **Critical Thinking** How do cell walls help plants survive on land?

ART LINK

Make a poster. Find pictures of different kinds of ferns, and make a chart. Label each fern, and write a brief description of where each one can be found. Try to include at least one of the following: interrupted fern, leather fern, strap fern, vine fern, shoestring fern, ostrich fern. How do you think these ferns got their names?

WRITING LINK

Write a guidebook. Put together a guidebook of the kinds of ferns found in your area. Each page should have a photo or drawing of one of the ferns. Include a description of the fern and information on where it can be found in your area.

MATH LINK

Solve this problem. Study the time line on page A54. About how long after early land plants first appeared did gymnosperms appear? About how long after gymnosperms did angiosperms appear?

TECHNOLOGY LINK

At the Computer Visit **www.mhscience02.com** for more links.

A 55

---

3 Lesson Review

Answers to Think and Write

1. Mosses pass water from cell to cell because they have no vascular system. All the cells must stay near the ground and close to each other. (p. A48)

2. People add moss to a garden to keep the soil moist and in place. (p. A55)

3. Mosses help break down rock into soil and also hold the soil in place, making it easier for other plants to survive. (p. A55)

4. Possible answers: Ferns have a vascular system to move food and water through the plant; mosses do not. Mosses grow close to the ground; ferns can grow tall. (pp. A48–A53)

5. **Critical Thinking** Possible answer: Cell walls help the plant to stay upright, hold in water, and take in needed sunlight. (pp. A49, A52)

Summarize

Check students' understanding by having them write a brief summary of the lesson in their own words.

ART LINK

Students can use the posters to compare and contrast different types of ferns. Many ferns are named for their appearance.

WRITING LINK

Students may be able to obtain information on local ferns from a nature center in your area. If you live in an arid region, students may need to research ferns from other areas.

MATH LINK

Gymnosperms appeared 145 million years after first land plants: 420 mya − 275 mya = 145 mya. Angiosperms appeared 145 million years after gymnosperms: 275 mya − 130 mya = 145 mya.

Technology

Internet Research Project Have students visit **www.mhscience02.com** to conduct a research project on seedless plants. They will find a suggested outline for the project, questions to research, and links to Internet reference sites.

✓ Informal Assessment

Easy/Average Ask students to make a table comparing seedless nonvascular and seedless vascular plants. The table should include structures and how the plants reproduce.

Challenge Have students write a paragraph explaining the evolutionary advantages of vascular plants. Then ask them to write a paragraph explaining the alternation of generations and how that reproductive process helps the plants survive.

SCIENCE Reading Strategy

Organize Information
Developing Reading Skills
Ask students to organize any piece of information from the lesson into a chart, such as the passage on pp. A48–A49 that discusses the similarities and differences between vascular and nonvascular plants.

LESSON 5 Plants with Seeds

Objectives

- Explore how seed plants are alike and different.
- Compare gymnosperms with angiosperms.
- Compare and contrast monocots and dicots.
- Identify why plants have aromas.

Resources

- Activity Resources, pp. 21–25
- Reading in Science Resources, pp. 35–40
- Vocabulary Cards
- Reading Aid Transparency A5

Build on Prior Knowledge

Have students discuss what they know about the many types and uses of seed plants. Ask students to list different foods they eat with seeds in them. Emphasize that all these foods with seeds are fruits and that fruits don't grow on all types of trees.

1 Get Ready

Using the Illustrations

Direct students' attention to the picture of the trees. Have them share observations about the differences among the leaves. (Students may note that some are broad, while others look like needles. They may also note differences in shape and size.) Review how water is lost through the stomata on the leaves. Lead students toward concluding that differences among leaves are related to the water regulation needs of different plants.

LESSON 5 Plants with Seeds

Vocabulary

seed, A58

angiosperm, A58

gymnosperm, A58

conifer, A59

cotyledon, A62

monocot, A62

dicot, A62

Get Ready

What do flowering plants and evergreens have in common? One way they are alike is they produce seeds. They are seed plants.

How are these plants different? One way they are different is that they have different kinds of leaves. How do these differences help the plants survive?

Process Skill

You experiment when you perform a test to support or disprove a hypothesis.

A 56

Science Background

Ginkgo

The ginkgo, or maidenhair tree, is the only remaining species of the family (Ginkgoaceae) and order (Ginkgoales) of gymnosperms. The male and female parts grow on separate trees. A terrible-smelling pulp surrounds its seed. Though often mistakenly referred to as a fruit, these seeds do not produce a flower. The roasted seeds of the tree are widely consumed in East Asia.

Reading Strategy

Ask Questions

Developing Reading Skills
Have students ask questions as they read p. A56 and the steps of the Explore Activity on p. A57. For example, how do seed plants produce seeds? How are the leaves alike? They can use these questions as a guide for reading the lesson.

Explore Activity

How Do Seed Plants Differ?

Procedure

1 Observe Examine each plant. Use the hand lens to examine a leaf from each one. Draw each leaf, and label it with the name of the plant it came from.

2 Observe Remove a part of the lower epidermis from the grass leaf. Make a wet-mount slide. Examine the slide under low power.

3 Communicate Draw what you observe.

4 Observe Repeat step 2 with a pine needle and a houseplant leaf (such as a geranium). Draw what you observe.

Drawing Conclusions

1 Interpret Data How are the leaves of the three plants alike? How are the leaves of the three plants different from one another?

2 Infer Which one of the plants do you think is least like the other two? Explain your reasoning.

3 Going Further: Experiment Predict which of the plants you examined could survive best in a dry environment. How do you think the plant's leaves would help it do this? Design an experiment that would test your prediction.

Materials

small pine seedling or other conifer

grass plant

garden plant or houseplant, such as a geranium

hand lens

microscope slide

coverslip

microscope

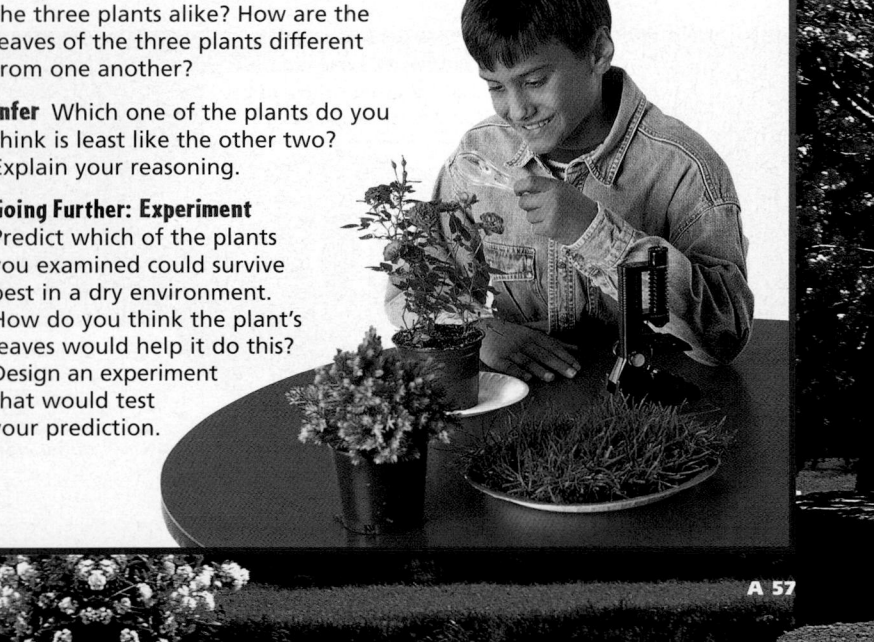

A 57

Alternative Explore Activity

Materials leaves of three different seed plants, crayons, paper

Compare Leaves of Seed Plants Have students make crayon rubbings of the different leaves and label each. Ask them to compare sizes, vein patterns, and the amount of chlorophyll in each leaf. **Kinesthetic; Spatial**

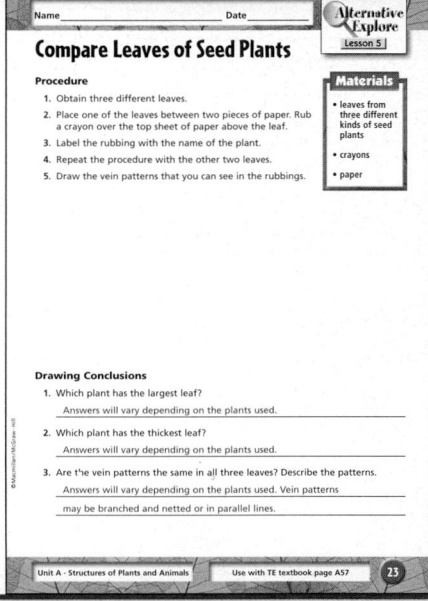

Name _____ Date _____   Alternative Explore Lesson 5

Compare Leaves of Seed Plants

Procedure

1. Obtain three different leaves.
2. Place one of the leaves between two pieces of paper. Rub a crayon over the top sheet of paper above the leaf.
3. Label the rubbing with the name of the plant.
4. Repeat the procedure with the other two leaves.
5. Draw the vein patterns that you can see in the rubbings.

Materials
• leaves from three different kinds of seed plants
• crayons
• paper

Drawing Conclusions

1. Which plant has the largest leaf?
   Answers will vary depending on the plants used.

2. Which plant has the thickest leaf?
   Answers will vary depending on the plants used.

3. Are the vein patterns the same in all three leaves? Describe the patterns.
   Answers will vary depending on the plants used. Vein patterns may be branched and netted or in parallel lines.

Unit A · Structures of Plants and Animals   Use with TE textbook page A57   23

Activity Resources, p. 23

Explore Activity

How Do Seed Plants Differ?

Science Process Skills *observe, communicate, interpret data, infer, experiment*

Resources Activity Resources, pp. 21–22

Pacing 30–40 minutes

Grouping small groups

Plan Ahead Obtain the plants needed for the activity. Any plant with parallel veins can be used in place of the grass plant. Label each plant. Review how to make a wet-mount slide. (See p. A5, step 3.)

Procedure

1 The grass (parallel venation) is a monocot; the geranium (netted venation) is a dicot.

2 To remove the lower epidermis, have students place a drop of clear fingernail polish on the underside of a freshly cut leaf. After the polish dries, they can carefully peel it from the leaf and place the peeling on the slide.

3 Drawings should show boxed structures.

4 Ask how the epidermis of a pine leaf is different from the other leaves. (The stomata in pine needles are sunken.)

Answers to Drawing Conclusions

1 The leaves are green, have stomata, and have a vascular system. The grass blade is thin; the pine leaves are like needles. The vascular tissues have different patterns.

2 Possible answer: The pine; its leaves are like needles and its veins are not parallel or netted.

3 Possible answer: The pine; the small, needlelike leaves would help conserve water. Tie plastic bags around samples of each plant, water each the same, and then compare the amount of water given off inside each bag due to transpiration.

 Inquiry Students can ask their own questions to explore, such as how the stomata are related to water loss in the leaf.

 **Technology**

■ When time is short, preview the activity with the **Explore Activity Video.**

2 Read to Learn

How Do Seed Plants Differ?

Before Reading
Have students try to answer the red question at the top of the page.

Developing the Main Idea
As students read this page help them focus on the differences between angiosperms and gymnosperms. Ask:

- **What environmental advantages do pine needles have when compared to the leaves of apple trees?** (Possible answers: Because needles are tougher and retain water better than leaves, pine trees are better adapted to cold, dry climates.)

Thinking Further: *Inferring*
Ask:

- **Why do you think gymnosperms developed before angiosperms?** (The simpler gymnosperms, without flowers and fruits, were suited to the climate and other conditions of early Earth.)

Developing Vocabulary

seed To help students remember the definition of a seed, have them draw a seed and label the embryo, the seed coat, and the stored food.

angiosperm Explain to students that if you break the word *angiosperm* down into two parts, *angio-* means "seedcase" and *-sperm* is a combining form meaning "seed." The seeds of angiosperms are surrounded by fruit, which protect them.

gymnosperm Interestingly the word *gymnosperm* is derived from the Greek word *gymnos,* meaning "naked" and *-sperm* which means "seed." Have students relate this to the fact that gymnosperm seeds are not surrounded by a fruit, but rather are protected within the woody scales of cones.

conifer Write the word *conifer* on the board and cover the second half of the word with your hand. Ask students what they can infer about this word based on the "con-" that they see. Breaking the word down, it means "cone-bearing."

Read to Learn

Main Idea One group of seed plants produces seeds on cones, the other group produces seeds inside fruits.

How Do Seed Plants Differ?

How are the leaves of a grass plant, a pine tree, and a geranium different? Two of these plants come from one major group of seed plants, while the other comes from a different group.

Both groups are vascular plants. Both groups reproduce from seeds. A seed contains an undeveloped plant and stored food for the young plant.

Most of the plants that you see every day are seed plants. They include grasses, trees, shrubs, and bushes. They all have roots, stems, and leaves. Some, called angiosperms (AN·jee·uh·spurmz), produce flowers. The others, called gymnosperms (JIM·nuh·spurmz), do not produce flowers. These are the two major groups of seed plants.

The gymnosperms are the oldest seed plants. They include such evergreen trees as pine, fir, cedar, juniper, yew, larch, and spruce.

Gymnosperms first appeared on Earth about 250 million years ago. One hundred million years would pass before the first angiosperms appeared.

The fruits, vegetables, grains, and almost all of the nuts you eat are produced by angiosperms. However, one tasty nut—the pine nut, or pignoli—is a gymnosperm seed. It is the seed of certain pine trees.

Gymnosperms

Gymnosperms include some of the largest and oldest living things.

The seed for this bristlecone pine sprouted about 5,000 years ago.

The giant redwood (left) can grow as tall as a 30-story building.

Conifers are found mostly in the northern parts of the world.

A 58

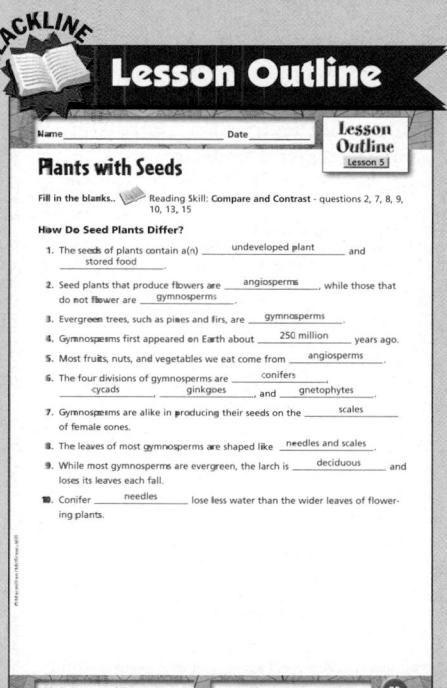

BLACKLINE
Lesson Outline

Name _____ Date _____

Lesson Outline
Lesson 5

Plants with Seeds

Fill in the blanks.. Reading Skill: **Compare and Contrast** - questions 2, 7, 8, 9, 10, 13, 15

How Do Seed Plants Differ?

1. The seeds of plants contain a(n) ___undeveloped plant___ and stored food

2. Seed plants that produce flowers are ___angiosperms___, while those that do not flower are ___gymnosperms___

3. Evergreen trees, such as pines and firs, are ___gymnosperms___

4. Gymnosperms first appeared on Earth about ___250 million___ years ago.

5. Most fruits, nuts, and vegetables we eat come from ___angiosperms___

6. The four divisions of gymnosperms are ___conifers___ ___cycads___ ___ginkgoes___ and ___gnetophytes___

7. Gymnosperms are alike in producing their seeds on the ___scales___ of female cones.

8. The leaves of most gymnosperms are shaped like ___needles and scales___

9. While most gymnosperms are evergreen, the larch is ___deciduous___ and loses its leaves each fall.

10. Conifer ___needles___ lose less water than the wider leaves of flowering plants.

Unit A - Structures of Plants and Animals | Use with textbook pages A56–A65 | 35

SCIENCE
Reading Strategy

Organize Information Developing Reading Skills
As students read pp. A58–A61, ask them to organize the information on angiosperms and gymnosperms into a table. When they are finished, have individual students share their tables with the class.

Reading in Science Resources, p. 35

The gymnosperms are divided into four divisions. They are the conifers (KAHN·uh·furz), *cycads* (SIGH·kadz), *ginkgoes* (GING·kohz), and *gnetophytes* (NE·toh·fights). Look at the photographs on these pages. You'll notice that these plants look different. However, they all have certain things in common.

Their seeds are produced on the scales of female cones. The seeds are not surrounded by a fruit. The leaves of most gymnosperms look like needles or scales. Most gymnosperms are *evergreens*. Evergreens lose only a few leaves at a time and constantly replace the leaves they have lost.

Some conifers, such as the larch, dawn redwood, and bald cypress, lose their leaves each fall. Plants that do this are called *deciduous* (di·SIJ·ew·uhs).

When gymnosperms evolved, most of Earth was cold and dry. These plants are well adapted to cold, dry climates. For example, the needles of conifers have a very small surface area and are covered with a thick cuticle. They lose less water than the wider leaves of flowering plants.

READING Compare and Contrast
How are angiosperms and gymnosperms different?

Angiosperms produce flowers; gymnosperms do not.

Cycads (left) live in warm climates. The red strawberry-shaped structures are not fruits but female cones.

The maidenhair tree (right) is the only member of the ginkgo division. It has fan-shaped leaves and round green fruit.

Gnetophytes (right) are more closely related to flowering plants than any other gymnosperm.

A 59

Developing the Main Idea
To help students understand how gymnosperms are adapted to dry climates, show them two wet paper towels: one crumpled and one spread out flat. Ask:

- **Which towel will dry more quickly? Why?** (The one that is spread out, because more of the surface area is exposed to the air.)

- **How is surface area related to the loss of water?** (The more surface area, the greater water loss.)

- **What traits would be helpful to a plant living in a dry climate?** (little surface area, waxy surface)

Exploring the Main Idea
Encourage students to select one of the trees mentioned and do further research to write a report about interesting gymnosperm facts. For example, the ginkgo tree is prized in Asia and its nut is regarded as a delicacy. The tree thrives in city air pollution and low sunlight, but female trees are not planted in cities because of the odor of the tissue that surrounds the seeds.

▶After Reading
Have students answer the red question in the student book as **ongoing assessment**.

What Are Angiosperms?

Before Reading
Have students try to answer the red question at the top of the page.

Developing the Main Idea
Invite students to read about angiosperms found in one of the environments discussed in the text on pages A60–A61. For example, they might want to look in a book about cacti to learn about different kinds found in the desert.

Exploring the Main Idea
Help students visualize how tall 100 meters is. Have them measure, or tell them, how tall their classroom is (probably about 2 to 3 meters). Ask them to calculate how many classrooms could be stacked next to the giant eucalyptus tree. Also review the concept of circumference (πd). Challenge students to join hands and form a circle 20 meters in circumference.

What Are Angiosperms?

Angiosperms are the most recently evolved and best-adapted division of seed plants. There are about 235,000 different kinds of angiosperms, which makes them the largest division in the plant kingdom.

Some, like duckweed, float on water and are about the size of a large bee's eye. Duckweed is the smallest flowering plant. The largest flowering plant is the giant eucalyptus tree, which can be 100 m (330 ft) tall and 20 m (66 ft) in circumference.

Flowering trees produce the fruits you eat.

Wheat seed

Wheat, an angiosperm, is a grass that produce one of the world's most important food crops.

A 60

Advanced Learners

Angiosperms
The development of flowering plants on Earth corresponded with the development of mammals. The plants were a major food source for mammals and the mammals could help with pollination and seed dispersal. Mammals could not have thrived in a world of gymnosperms. Have students write brief descriptions of an imaginary world without angiosperms and mammals.
Linguistic

 ## Math MiniLesson

Circumference
Develop When students read about the circumference of the giant eucalyptus tree, you might discuss circumference. The *circumference* (*C*) of a circle is the distance around it. You can use the formula $C = \pi \times$ diameter (*d*) or $C = \pi \times 2 \times$ radius (*r*) to find the circumference of a circle. The diameter of a circle is 12 cm. What is the circumference of the circle?

$C \approx 3.14 \times 12 \approx 37.68$

The circumference is about 37.68 cm.

You can use the $\boxed{\pi}$ key or press 3.14 for the approximate value of π.

$\pi \boxed{\times} \, 12 \boxed{=} \, \mathbf{37.699112}$

Practice Find the circumference.
1. $d = 8$ in. (about 25.12 in.)
2. $r = 6$ m (about 18.84 m)

Activity Have students fold a paper plate in half. Have them measure the diameter and then find the circumference of the plate.

The world's largest flower belongs to this parasitic plant, "the stinking corpse lily," which lives in Southeast Asia.

Angiosperms live in all climates and in all parts of the world. The saguaro cactus lives in the hot, dry desert. Duckweed and water lilies grow only in the water. Some orchids live high in the air attached to trees in hot, damp rain forests. Other angiosperms flower near the Arctic Circle. Still others grow on the sides of tall mountains. Oddly, a few angiosperms cannot live on their own. They have little or no chlorophyll and are *parasites*. That is, they live off other plants. The plant with the largest flower is this kind of parasitic angiosperm. The flower can be a meter across, as thick as your thumb, and weigh as much as a small dog.

This saguaro cactus lives in the desert of the southwest United States.

How can you tell an angiosperm from a gymnosperm? Angiosperms produce flowers; gymnosperms do not. The seeds of angiosperms are inside a fruit. Gymnosperms do not produce fruits.

What are two locations where angiosperms live?

Possible answers: duckweed—water; cactus—desert; orchid—rain forests

A 61

Using the Illustrations

Focus students' attention on the different photographs depicting the variety of angiosperms. Lead them to discuss the similarities and differences they observe. Suggest they compare size, structure, leaves, and how they are suited for their environments. Encourage students to give other examples of angiosperms they are familiar with or have studied in the student book.

▶After Reading

Have students answer the red question in the student book as **ongoing assessment**.

Inclusion

Angiosperms and Economics

Angiosperms have been largely responsible for the development of civilizations throughout history and continue to drive the economy in many areas of the world. From the rich agricultural regions of Mesopotamia to the heartlands of the United States, angiosperms have been crucial to economic development. Have students investigate the relationship between food crops and a nation's economy and write a brief description of their understandings.
Linguistic

Science Background

Fruit or Vegetable?
Addressing Misconceptions

Students are often surprised to learn that some common foods are actually fruits. A fruit is defined as the fleshy structure that surrounds seeds. If a food has a seed in it, it is a fruit. This includes tomatoes, cucumbers, squash, and eggplants. A vegetable is any vegetative part of a plant that is used for food. Have students find out more about fruits and vegetables and make a table of their findings. **Spatial**

What Are Cotyledons?

Before Reading
Have students try to answer the red question at the top of the page.

Developing the Main Idea
As students read this page, ask them to describe any experiences they've had with planting seeds. Have them think of different examples of seeds. Write these examples on the chalkboard with descriptions about size, shape, and possible uses by animals, including humans.

Exploring the Main Idea
Pass around some fresh corn kernels split in half, some lima beans split in half, and some hand lenses. Point out the cotyledons. Ask:

- **What else is inside the seed?** (an undeveloped plant)

- **What do you think the cotyledons are for?** (They supply the developing plant with food.)

▶After Reading
Have students answer the red question in the student book as **ongoing assessment**.

Developing Vocabulary

cotyledon To help students remember the meaning of *cotyledon,* show them a young plant (or illustration) with the cotyledons still attached. Make up a sentence such as "Cotyledons lead the plant on."

monocot Have students think of words starting with the prefix *mono-,* such as *monorail, monochrome, monologue,* or *monophonic.* Ask them what each of the words have in common. (They all relate to *one.*) Based on this discussion ask them what they think *monocot* means. If they have trouble, tell them that *-cot* is short for *cotyledon.*

dicot The prefix *di-* comes from the Greek word for "two." Have students develop the definition of *dicot* based on this information.

What Are Cotyledons?

Scientists divide the angiosperms into two classes. As you might guess, scientists are able to do this because of some particular characteristic that sets the two classes apart. That characteristic turns out to be the number of an angiosperm's **cotyledons** (kaht·uh·LEE·duhnz). A cotyledon, also called a seed leaf, is a tiny leaflike structure inside a seed.

Some angiosperm seeds contain only one cotyledon. Plants whose seeds contain only one cotyledon are called *monocotyledons,* or **monocots** (MAHN·uh·kahts) for short. (The prefix *mono-* comes from a Greek word meaning "one.") There are over 60,000 different kinds of monocots. Corn, rice, wheat, grasses, orchids, and coconut palms are examples of monocots.

Angiosperms whose seeds contain two cotyledons are called *dicotyledons,* or **dicots** (DIGH·kahts) for short. (The prefix *di-* comes from a Greek word meaning "two.") There are over 170,000 kinds of dicots. Bean plants, maple trees, rose plants, and cactuses are some of the dicots.

> **What are three differences between monocots and dicots?**

Characteristics of Monocots and Dicots

Characteristics	Monocots	Dicots
Cotyledons	One	Two
Leaf veins	Parallel	Branched
Flower parts	Multiples of three	Multiples of four or five
Vascular system	Scattered in bundles	In rings

Monocots have one seed leaf, parallel leaf veins, flower parts in multiples of three, vascular systems in bundles; dicots have two seed leaves, branched leaf veins, flower parts in multiples of four or five, vascular systems in rings.

A 62

Reading Strategy

Interpret Graphic Sources of Information
Developing Reading Skills
Encourage students to use the chart on p. A62 to understand what they read. For example, the chart illustrates what is meant by "parallel" and "branched."

Interpret Illustrations

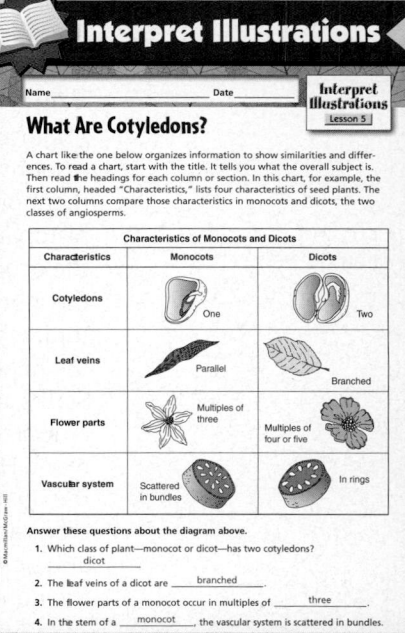

Name_____ Date_____

Interpret Illustrations Lesson 5

What Are Cotyledons?

A chart like the one below organizes information to show similarities and differences. To read a chart, start with the title. It tells you what the overall subject is. Then read the headings for each column or section. In this chart, for example, the first column, headed "Characteristics," lists four characteristics of seed plants. The next two columns compare those characteristics in monocots and dicots, the two classes of angiosperms.

Characteristics of Monocots and Dicots

Characteristics	Monocots	Dicots
Cotyledons	One	Two
Leaf veins	Parallel	Branched
Flower parts	Multiples of three	Multiples of four or five
Vascular system	Scattered in bundles	In rings

Answer these questions about the diagram above.

1. Which class of plant—monocot or dicot—has two cotyledons? dicot

2. The leaf veins of a dicot are ____branched____

3. The flower parts of a monocot occur in multiples of ____three____

4. In the stem of a ____monocot____, the vascular system is scattered in bundles.

Unit A · Structures of Plants and Animals   Use with textbook page A62   **37**

Reading in Science Resources, p. 37

Process Skill
BUILDER

SKILL Observe

Flowering Plants

In this activity you will observe flowering plants in order to try to classify them. That is, you will examine several plants and try to determine whether each is a monocot or a dicot. As you examine each plant sample, refer to the chart on page A62 to help you classify the sample.

Materials
sample leaves and flowers from various angiosperms

Procedure

1 **Observe** Get together with a few of your classmates and go on a leaf- and flower-collecting field trip. (Make sure to avoid poison ivy, poison oak, and poison sumac leaves. Your teacher can tell you how to spot them.)

2 **Observe** Find a number of different angiosperms. Try to get a sample of a leaf and flower from each plant. If you can't get a flower, a leaf will do.

3 **Interpret Data** Look at the chart of Characteristics of Monocots and Dicots. It will give you clues on how to tell if the sample leaves and flowers you chose are monocots or dicots.

Drawing Conclusions

1 **Observe** Examine the plant parts you have chosen. For each sample leaf, describe how the leaf veins look. For each sample flower, tell how many parts the flower has. Record your answers.

2 **Classify** Mount the leaves and flowers on a heavy sheet of cardboard, and indicate whether each came from a monocot or a dicot.

A 63

Process Skill
BUILDER

Flowering Plants

Science Process Skills *observe,* interpret data, classify

Resources Activity Resources, pp. 24–25

Pacing 40–50 minutes

Grouping small groups

Plan Ahead Review poisonous plants with the students before they go out. If it is not possible for students to collect samples from the environment, provide samples for them or work from clear pictures of leaves and flowers from magazines and books.

Procedure

2 Be sure students don't take more than they need from the plants they collect.

Answers to Drawing Conclusions

1 Students should describe the leaf veins as parallel or branched. The flower parts should be in multiples of 3, 4, or 5.

2 Answers will vary according to the samples, but should be consistent with the chart on page A62.

Process Skills
MiniLesson

Observe

Develop This is the most basic science skill. All other skills are built upon this skill. Observing involves using one or more senses to identify or learn about an object or event. Typically, people think that *observing* is synonymous with *seeing.* Although sight is the sense most often used when observing, hearing, tasting, smelling, and touching are also used when making observations.

Practice Give students small samples of cooking ingredients to identify, such as sugar, salt, baking soda, and corn starch. See if students can correctly identify the samples. Afterward have them discuss the observations that helped them to identify the samples.

A complete list of Science Process Skills appears on p. S7.

Cultural Perspective

Living Off the Land
For people who live on islands, the coconut palm is the "staff of life." Coconut oil is made into soaps and used for cooking. The sap is made into a fermented drink. The shells are used as vessels, cups, and spoons. The fibers are used to stuff cushions and make mats. The roots are used for medicine. Have students list advantages and disadvantages of using one plant for so many things. **Linguistic; Logical**

Why Do Flowers Have Aromas?

Before Reading
Have students try to answer the red question above the student text.

Developing the Main Idea
Ask:

- **Why is it necessary for insects to take pollen from one part of a flower to another?**
(Different parts of the flower hold the male and female sex cells. The cells must unite to start a new plant.)

Tell students that scientists have discovered ways to imitate the perfumes found in plants. Sometimes they decode the plant's molecules and copy them in the lab, as with vanillin. At other times, the odor is imitated by making new substances that are not like the substances found in plants. Ask:

- **Which branch of science works to decode the molecules of a plant's aroma?** (Students may answer chemistry or organic chemistry.)

▶After Reading
Have students answer the red question in the student book as **ongoing assessment**.

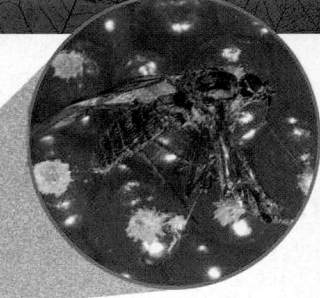

The awful-smelling jack-in-the-pulpit flower attracts insects that help the plant reproduce.

Why Do Flowers Have Aromas?

The characteristics of living things help them survive in their environment. It would make sense to expect that the aromas of flowers do the same for their plants.

To your nose, some of these aromas are very pleasing. That's why flowers such as roses and jasmines are used in perfumes. However, some flowers, like those of the jack-in-the-pulpit plant, smell awful. Surprisingly, both beautiful and awful aromas attract insects! What is the advantage of this?

When an insect enters the flower, it brushes against a part of the flower that holds tiny grains of dust, called *pollen*. These grains contain the plant's male sex cells.

The pollen sticks to the insect. As the insect moves around the flower—

A 64

or moves to another flower on the plant—some of the pollen rubs off on parts of the flower that hold female sex cells. The two sex cells join, and the reproduction of a new plant begins.

Many plants attract one particular kind of insect. The jack-in-the-pulpit attracts dung beetles and flies. These insects generally feed on dead or decaying animals or animal wastes, which smell awful. The insects mistake the aroma of the plant for that of a good meal.

Once inside the flower, the insects discover that its sides are so smooth, they can't climb out. As they rush around inside the flower, they keep transferring pollen to the part of the flower that holds female sex cells.

After about 24 hours, something strange happens. The inside of the flower changes from smooth to wrinkled. Their job done, the insects can now get a foothold, escape, and move on to another flower.

▷ **How does a flower's aroma help it survive?**

The aroma attracts insects that help pollinate the flower.

Science Background

Plant Odors
Flowers have aromas to attract insects that carry pollen from flower to flower or from part to part, helping plants reproduce. Odors from plants may be found in leaves (sage, thyme, mint), bark (cedar, sandalwood), seeds (anise, caraway), roots (orris), and fruit rinds (oranges), as well as in the flower petals (roses, violets). Some species of orchids produce an odor that mimics the smell of a food substance, such as nectar, to lure pollinators.

BLACKLINE Interpret Illustrations

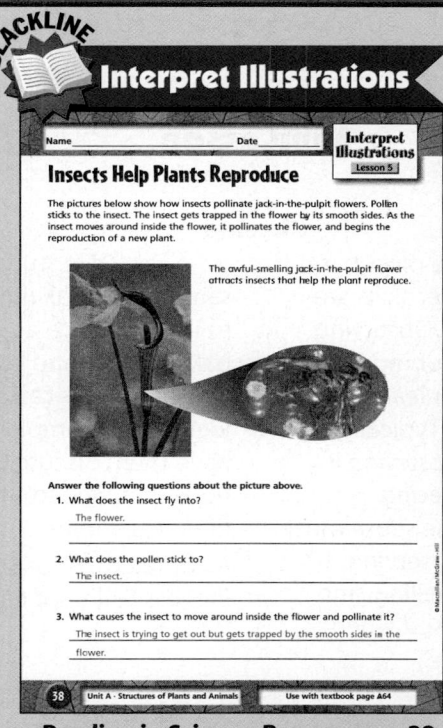

Insects Help Plants Reproduce

The pictures below show how insects pollinate jack-in-the-pulpit flowers. Pollen sticks to the insect. The insect gets trapped in the flower by its smooth sides. As the insect moves around inside the flower, it pollinates the flower, and begins the reproduction of a new plant.

The awful-smelling jack-in-the-pulpit flower attracts insects that help the plant reproduce.

Answer the following questions about the picture above.

1. What does the insect fly into?
   The flower.

2. What does the pollen stick to?
   The insect.

3. What causes the insect to move around inside the flower and pollinate it?
   The insect is trying to get out but gets trapped by the smooth sides in the flower.

Reading in Science Resources, p. 38

Lesson Review

Why It Matters

Almost all of the food you eat that comes from plants is produced by flowering plants. Flowering plants also decorate the landscape and homes with beautiful colors. Some produce chemicals that are used in perfumes and other cosmetics. Others, such as plants used as spices, flavor the foods you eat. Like all plants, flowering plants help keep the balance of gases in the air by using up carbon dioxide and producing oxygen.

Think and Write

1. How are gymnosperms and angiosperms alike? How are they different?

2. How are flowers important to a plant?

3. What are the differences between monocots and dicots?

4. Observe List five plants that are angiosperms and five plants that are gymnosperms. Explain what characteristics helped you determine which was which.

5. Critical Thinking How have seed plants become adapted to the environment?

L·I·N·K·S

WRITING LINK

Write an essay. Write about a day in your life and all the plants that are important to you. Classify the plants as angiosperms or gymnosperms and as monocots or dicots.

ART LINK

Make your own flip books. Illustrate a "year in the life of an angiosperm" by making a flip book. Do the same for a gymnosperm.

SOCIAL STUDIES LINK

Make a crop map. Look at the table showing food crops that come from monocots and dicots. Research where in the world these crops are grown. Then, using a different color for each crop, make a map showing where each of the crops is produced.

Monocots	Dicots
Corn	Apples
Onions	Beans
Rice	Cabbage
Wheat	Tomatoes

TECHNOLOGY LINK

At the Computer Visit **www.mhscience02.com** for more links.

A 65

3 Lesson Review

Answers to Think and Write

1. Both are vascular seed plants. Angiosperms produce fruit and flowers; gymnosperms do not. (pp. A58–A61)

2. Flowers from the plant are needed to reproduce. (p. A64)

3. Monocots have one cotyledon, parallel leaf veins, flower parts in multiples of three, and a vascular system in bundles scattered throughout the stem. Dicots have two cotyledons, branched leaf veins, flower parts in multiples of four or five, and a vascular system in rings. (p. A62)

4. Observe Possible answers: Angiosperms include duckweed, cacti, wheat, apple trees, and orchids; gymnosperms include pine, fir, cedar, yew, and spruce trees. Angiosperms produce fruits and flowers and gymnosperms produce cones. (pp. A58–A60)

5. Critical Thinking Possible answer: Gymnosperms have leaves that conserve water. Angiosperms are greatly varied and adapt to many environments. For example, orchids live high in rain forest trees to obtain sunlight. (pp. A58–A61)

Summarize

Check students' understanding by having them write a brief summary of the lesson in their own words.

WRITING LINK

Students may write about plants at home, plants in the neighborhood, at school, and plants they eat. Flowering plants are classified as angiosperms, and as monocots or dicots.

ART LINK

Angiosperm flip books might show a bare tree in winter change to one with green leaves, flowers, fruit, and then leaves that turn brown and fall. Most gymnosperms are not deciduous. They change little through the year except for the appearance of cones.

SOCIAL STUDIES LINK

Some of the different crops are produced in the same area. Students can use a striping of each representative color.

Informal Assessment

Easy/Average Have students create a chart comparing traits of angiosperms and gymnosperms. The chart should include examples of each and classify the angiosperms as monocots or dicots.

Challenge Have students write a paragraph explaining the differences between gymnosperms and angiosperms and the evolutionary advantages of angiosperms. Then ask them to write a paragraph explaining the role flowers play in reproduction.

Science Background

Flower Aroma

The aroma of flowers is derived from the essential oils found in their petals. These oils are formed in the chlorophyll-bearing parts of the plant and are transported to other tissues as the plant matures. The volatile nature of these oils accounts for the aromas that reach our noses.

Science, Technology, and Society

Objective
■ Understand the importance of seed banks.

Build on Prior Knowledge
Ask:

- **What does a corn seed contain?** (a tiny corn plant surrounded by the food it needs to sprout)

- **Where do a corn plant's traits come from?** (the parent plants)

- **What is a hybrid?** (a plant produced when two plants of different varieties are crossed)

Banking on Seeds

Developing the Main Idea
When students have read the article, focus on how hybrids have changed agricultural farming and led to the need for seed banks by asking such questions as:

- **Why did farmers once plant so many different kinds of corn?** (They did not know about plant heredity and used the seeds produced by corn they had previously grown.)

- **What are some advantages of growing hybrid corn plants?** (Possible answers: They grow faster and produce more food; the ears ripen at the same time and are the same size.)

Science, Technology,

BANKING ON SEED

Where do farmers get the corn seeds they plant each year? Before farmers knew about plant heredity, they just planted leftover seeds from the last year's crop. There were thousands of varieties of corn. Then farmers learned about hybrids.

Ears of corn from a hybrid all become ripe at the same time. They're the same size, so harvesting is easier.

Farmers can breed corn that thrives despite chemical pesticides and fertilizers. Many crops grow faster, produce more food, and store better.

That's the good news about farming. There's bad news, too. If farmers grow just one kind of plant, a disease or pest invasion can wipe out a whole crop.

In 1970, for example, the corn grown in the United States was too similar. Much of it caught the same disease at the same time. Fifteen percent of that year's corn crop was lost. The situation was even worse in Ireland in the 1840s. Almost every Irish farmer grew the same kind of potato. When a potato disease hit, it killed almost the entire Irish potato crop. There was a serious shortage of food, and many Irish people moved to the U.S.

If farmers grow only a few kinds of plants, other plants become extinct. Then animals that depend on a specific kind of plant die out as well.

As hybrids became more common, people became alarmed by the number of plant types dying out. Consequently seeds were collected from existing plants and placed in seed banks. The banks preserve the seeds from plants that otherwise might become extinct. Farmers have also been encouraged to grow more varied crops.

In a field of hybrids, all the corn looks the same

A 66

Science Background

The Last Curly-Coated Pig
Anyone who has seen a nursery rhyme book knows the pig with a curly coat. That pig, the Lincolnshire, is now extinct. It was the victim of a farming trend in the middle of the twentieth century that favored pork that was juicy and fatty. The lean Lincolnshire died out in 1967. Today, were it alive, the lean Lincolnshire might be a perfect fit for fat-conscious consumers.

What Did I Learn?

1. What can growing hybrid corn do?

A It can make harvesting easier.
B It can produce plants that are more pest-resistant.
C both A and B
D neither A nor B

2. Seed banks were started

F as a place farmers could buy seeds to feed animals
G to preserve seeds from plants that might otherwise become extinct
H to protect seeds from fertilizers
J to let farmers save seeds for the following year

AT THE COMPUTER

Visit www.mhscience02.com
to learn more about seed banks.

A 67

■ **How did growing the same kind of potato cause many people to migrate to the United States?** (A blight killed almost all the potatoes, and Irish people left Ireland for the United States.)

■ **What could happen if farmers continue to grow only a few kinds of plants?** (A disease or pest invasion could wipe out a crop; other kinds of plants could die out; animals dependent on those plants could also die out.)

Thinking Further: *Inferring*
Ask:

■ **Why might farmers of the future be glad seed banks were started?** (If they need crops with different characteristics, or their crops all die, they will have seeds from which they can grow new kinds of plants.)

Test Prep:  What Did I Learn?

1. C

2. G

Summarize
Check students' understanding by having them write a brief summary of the magazine in their own words.

Science Background

The Trouble with Seed Banks
Seed banks are not an all-purpose answer to the problems of diminishing plant diversity. A recent book, *The Genetic Gamble That Threatens to Destroy American Agriculture,* makes the case that seed bank technology and resources have not been fail-safe: The USDA's Agricultural Research Service reports that as many as 90 percent of the seeds deposited in seed banks before 1950 are no longer viable.

LESSON 6 Flowers and Seeds

Objectives

- Explore the relationship between the parts of a flower and how the flower reproduces.
- Identify the different parts of a flower and infer the function of each.
- Explain the processes of seed dispersal, germination, and growth.

Resources

- Activity Resources, pp. 26–30
- Reading in Science Resources, pp. 41–46
- Vocabulary Cards
- Reading Aid Transparency A6
- Visual Aid Transparencies 5, 6, 7
- Grade-Level Science Book, *Jonathan Chapman: The Appleseed Man*
- School-to-Home Activities, p. 5

Build on Prior Knowledge

Have students discuss what they know about flowers and how they grow. Show them several different types of flowers. Have students discuss what all the flowers have in common and also how they differ.

1 Get Ready

Developing the Main Idea

Some students may know that flowers are reproductive structures. Ask:

- **What are different ways flowers are used by people?** (as gifts, for food, as medicine)

- **What other animals are dependent on flowers?** (Bees, hummingbirds, and butterflies eat nectar.)

LESSON 6 Flowers and Seeds

Vocabulary

ovary, A70
pollination, A72
embryo, A74
seed coat, A74
fruit, A75

Get Ready

Have you ever seen bees buzzing around flowers? Don't disturb them. From a distance you might watch as a bee goes from flower to flower. What do you think it is doing? Not just bees, but other insects, such as butterflies, and other animals, such as hummingbirds, hover around flowers as well. What do you think they do for the plants? What do plants use their flowers for?

Process Skill

You infer when you form an idea from facts or observations.

A 68

Science Background

Fruit and Seeds

After fertilization, the ovules of a flower develop into seeds. The ovary develops into a fruit that protects and covers the seeds. Some fruits, such as plums, become soft, while others, such as acorns, are protected by a hard shell. Poppy seeds are surrounded by a seed box. Peas develop within a protective pod. Some fruits, such as peaches, have only one seed while others, such as apples, have many.

Reading Strategy

Ask Questions
Developing Reading Skills
Have students ask questions as they read p. A68 and the steps of the Explore Activity on p. A69. For example: What is the flower for? What is the reason for this step?

They can use the questions as the basis of a pre-Activity class discussion and as a guide for reading the lesson.

Explore Activity

How Do Flowers Differ?

Procedure: Design Your Own

1 Decide how you will compare the flowers you look at. You may choose to look for parts that they seem to have in common. Describe what the parts are and how they differ from plant to plant.

2 Begin by removing the outer leaflike parts. Examine them. Draw what they look like.

3 Remove the petals. Examine them. Draw what they look like.

4 **Observe** Examine the rest of the flower as you decide.

5 **Communicate** Draw the parts you examined.

Materials

several large flowers from different plants

hand lens

forceps

dropper

toothpick

Drawing Conclusions

1 **Communicate** What color is each flower? What do you think the job of the petals is? How would you design an experiment to find out?

2 **Infer** What do you think the various parts of each flower are for? Do you think the same parts of different flowers do the same kinds of jobs for their plants?

3 **Going Further: Infer** Why do you think a plant has flowers? Make a hypothesis. Design an experiment to test your ideas.

A 69

Alternative Explore Activity

Materials samples and pictures of different flowers

Design a Flower Have students work in teams to examine the flower samples and pictures and discuss what each part might do. Ask them to design their own flower. Invite them to share their flowers with the class and describe why they included each part. **Logical; Social**

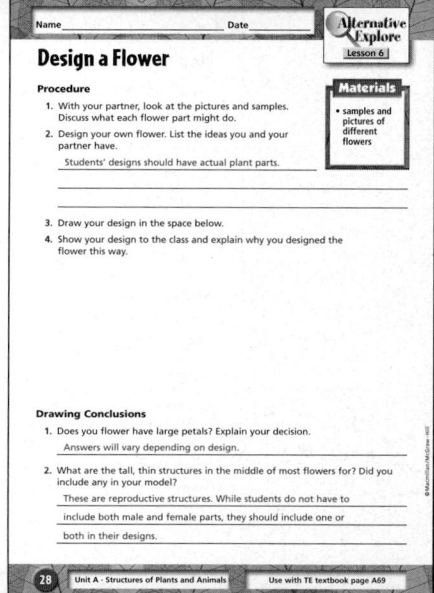

Activity Resources, p. 28

Explore Activity

How Do Flowers Differ?

Science Process Skills *observe, communicate, infer*

Resources Activity Resources, pp. 26–27

Pacing 30–40 minutes

Grouping individual

Plan Ahead Any flower could be used, including wildflowers. A lily is a good choice because the stamen and pistil are easily visible. Florists may be willing to donate flowers that they can no longer use.

Procedure: Design Your Own

2 In some flowers, these leaflike parts (sepals) are not green, but are colored to look like the petals.

4 As an option, you might have some students work with black paper underneath to catch pollen grains. They might try brushing the flower structures on the paper to see what happens. **Caution:** Students who are allergic to pollen should not do this activity.

Answers to Drawing Conclusions

1 Colors depend on flower samples. The petals attract insects and surround and protect the inner parts of the flower. Students may suggest taking the petals off one flower and not another and monitoring both to see which one attracts more insects.

2 Students may suggest that the outer leaflike parts protect the petals and that the inner parts produce the cells needed for reproduction. The same parts of different flowers do the same job in every plant.

3 A plant has flowers to attract insects and produce male and female sex cells. Students might suggest taking the inner parts out of one flower but not another and monitoring how many insects are attracted to each and how the insects behave.

 Inquiry Students can ask their own questions to explore, such as how the inner parts of the flower help a plant reproduce.

Technology

- When time is short, preview the activity with the **Explore Activity Video.**

How Do Flowers Differ?

Before Reading
Have students try to answer the red question at the top of the page.

Using the Illustrations
As students read the text, suggest they find each of the parts on the diagram. Ask:

■ **How could a flower be perfect and incomplete?** (It could be missing sepals or petals, but still have both a stamen and a pistil.)

READING
Diagrams

Charts should include the name of each part, its location, and function.

> male: stamen (includes filament, anther)
> female: pistil (includes ovary, style, stigma)

Developing Vocabulary

ovary Derived from the Latin word *ovum*, meaning "egg," an *ovary* is a structure that contains egg cells.

Read to Learn

Main Idea Fertilized flowers produce seeds that become new plants.

How Do Flowers Differ?

Not all flowers are alike. Some flowers are *complete flowers*. Complete flowers have sepals, petals, stamens, and pistils. *Incomplete flowers* are missing one of these parts. Some flowers are called perfect. *Perfect flowers* have both female and male parts, that is, both pistils (female parts) and stamens (male parts).

Imperfect flowers have either pistils or stamens, but not both. You might think of these flowers as "female" or "male." Some plants, like corn and oak trees, have separate male and female flowers on the same plant. Other plants,

Parts of a Flower

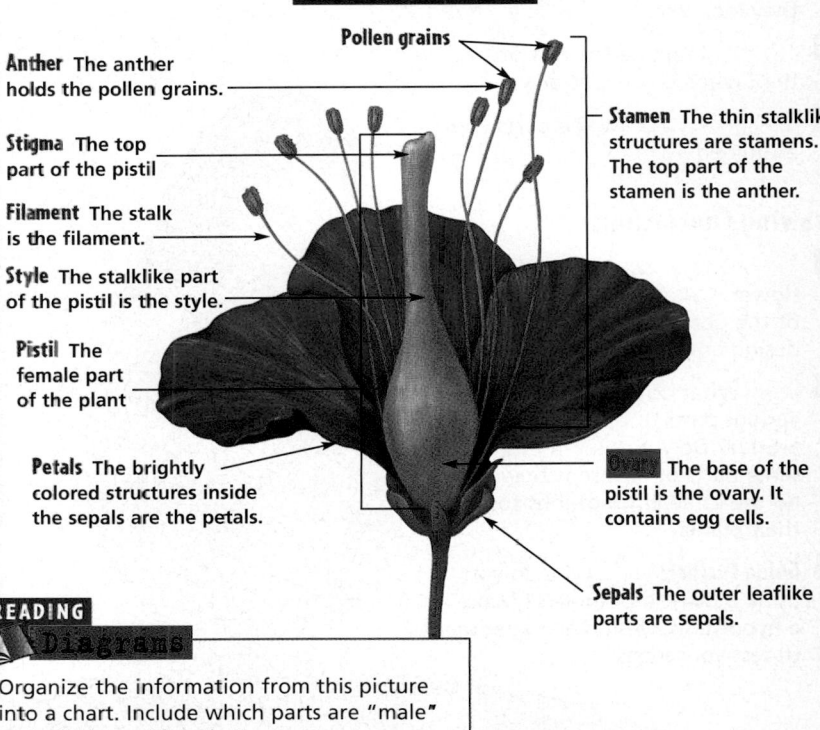

Anther The anther holds the pollen grains.

Stigma The top part of the pistil

Filament The stalk is the filament.

Style The stalklike part of the pistil is the style.

Pistil The female part of the plant

Petals The brightly colored structures inside the sepals are the petals.

Pollen grains

Stamen The thin stalklike structures are stamens. The top part of the stamen is the anther.

Ovary The base of the pistil is the ovary. It contains egg cells.

Sepals The outer leaflike parts are sepals.

READING
Diagrams

Organize the information from this picture into a chart. Include which parts are "male" and which are "female."

A 70

BLACKLINE Lesson Outline

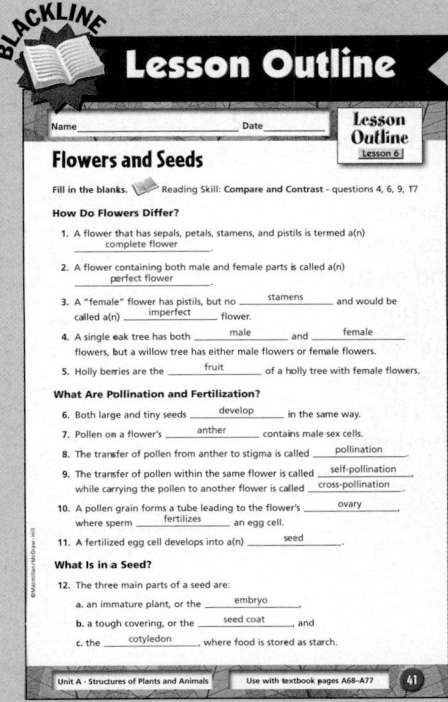

Reading in Science Resources, p. 41

like willow trees and holly trees, have only male flowers or female flowers.

The red holly berries that you see on holly trees in the late fall appear only on holly trees with female flowers. In order to produce the berries (the holly's fruit), the tree with female flowers needs to be fertilized by pollen from a holly tree with male flowers. An oak tree has both male and female flowers on the same tree.

Did this holly tree have male flowers or female flowers? How can you tell?

READING Compare and Contrast
How do complete and incomplete flowers differ?

Complete flowers have sepals, petals, stamens, and pistils; incomplete flowers are missing one of these parts.

An oak tree has tiny green flowers.

A 71

Using the Illustrations

Focus students' attention on the pictures of the oak and holly. Ask:

- **Do holly trees have perfect or imperfect flowers? Why?** (imperfect; because the flowers on one tree are either male or female)

- **Are oak tree flowers complete flowers? How do you know?** (No; since there are separate male and female flowers, some must be missing pistils and some must be missing stamens.)

Developing the Main Idea

Ask what fruit an oak tree produces (acorns) and where the male and female sex cells come from (the male and female flowers on the tree). Then ask:

- **Suppose you planted a single female holly tree with no other holly trees nearby. Would your tree have berries? Why?** (No; because there would be no male sex cells nearby to join with the female sex cells on the tree.)

▶ **After Reading**
Have students answer the red question in the student book as **ongoing assessment**.

Technology

■ Visual Aid Transparency 5: *Parts of a Flower*

Reading MiniLesson

Compare and Contrast

Develop Focus students' attention on the prefixes *in-*, as in *in*complete flower, and *im-*, as in *im*perfect flower, that mean "no". Discuss how the prefixes help students understand what structures make up a complete flower and a perfect flower. The prefixes signal that an incomplete flower does *not* have some of those structures.

Practice Have students make charts comparing and contrasting corn, holly, an oak, and the flower shown on page A70. Categories to compare and contrast might include: male part only, female part only, male and female parts on the same flower, male and female flowers on the same plant.

Advanced Learners

Flower Names

Tell students that the oak tree is part of the "witch hazel" group of trees. One explanation of the name is that *witch* comes from the Old English word meaning "to yield" because witch hazel branches have been used as divining rods. Challenge students to find out the stories behind the names of flowers, such as skunk cabbage, black-eyed Susan, sunflower, buttercup, tumbleweed, morning glory, and day lily, then write or tell the story to the class. **Linguistic**

What Are Pollination and Fertilization?

Exploring the Main Idea
Help students focus on the sequence of events involved in pollination and fertilization by having the class make a flow chart of the steps.

Using the Illustrations
Challenge students to work in pairs to use the illustration to explain the processes of pollination and fertilization to each other.

READING
Diagrams

Both involve the transfer of pollen grains from an anther to a stigma. In self-pollination the transfer occurs on the same flower; in cross-pollination the transfer is from one flower to another.

Developing Vocabulary

pollination Explain to students that the prefix *-ation* mean "the act of _____." Therefore, *pollination* means "the act of pollinating." *Pollen* is derived from Greek and Latin terms meaning "dust."

What Are Pollination and Fertilization?

Some seeds are very tiny, whereas others are really large. The largest is produced by the double-coconut tree, whose seeds can be about half your weight. Some of the smallest seeds belong to orchid plants. You could put thousands of them in a teaspoon.

No matter how large or small, all seeds develop the same way. Look at the diagram on this page. It will help you follow what you are reading.

First, a pollen grain must be transferred from a flower's anther to its stigma, or to another flower's stigma. Pollen grains contain sperm, which are male sex cells. This transfer is called **pollination** (pahl·uh·NAY·shuhn).

If the pollen is transferred from an anther to a stigma in the same flower, the process is called *self-pollination*. If the transfer is from one flower to the

Pollination

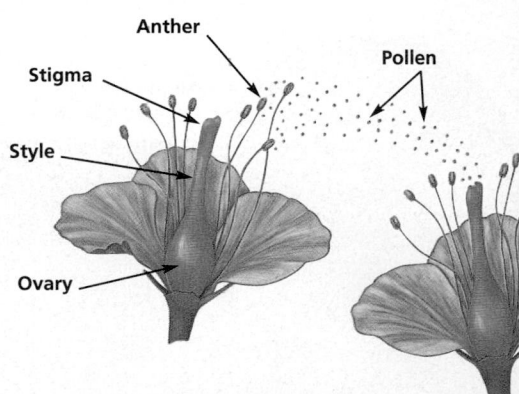

Anther
Pollen
Stigma
Style
Ovary

Self-Pollination
Pollination occurs when a pollen grain from an anther reaches the stigma. This flower is pollinating itself because its own pollen is reaching its own stigma.

READING
Diagrams

How are self-pollination and cross-pollination alike? How are they different?

Cross-Pollination
Pollination can occur between two or more flowers on separate plants. Here the pollen of one flower reaches the stigma of another.

A 72

BLACKLINE
Interpret Illustrations

Name _____ Date _____

Interpret Illustrations
Lesson 6

Ways Plants: Are Pollinated

These diagrams show two ways in which plants are pollinated. To compare the two methods, first read the explanations under the drawings. Then read the labels on the drawings and follow the leader lines to identify each part of a flower. Notice that the flowers have similar parts.

Pollination

Anther
Pollen
Stigma
Style
Ovary

Self-pollination
Pollination occurs when a pollen grain from an anther reaches the stigma. This flower is pollinating itself because its own pollen is reaching its own stigma.

Cross-pollination
Pollination can occur between two or more flowers on separate plants. Here the pollen of one flower reaches the stigma of another.

Answer these questions about the diagram above.

1. Grains of pollen come from the ___anther___ of a flower.

2. The top of the flower's style is called the ___stigma___.

3. Which method of pollination requires at least two flowers?
   ___cross-pollination___

4. In both types of pollination, pollen is transferred to the ___stigma___ of a flower.

Unit A · Structures of Plants and Animals   Use with textbook page A72   **43**

Reading in Science Resources, p. 43

flower of another plant, the process is called *cross-pollination*.

On the stigma a tube forms from the pollen grain. The tube grows down the style and into the flower's ovary. Sperm travel down the tube, through the style, and into the ovary. There a sperm cell combines with, or fertilizes, an egg cell. This combining is called *fertilization* (fur·tuh·luh·ZAY·shuhn).

A seed develops from a fertilized egg cell. Under the right conditions,

a new plant will develop from the seed. The process of making a new plant from the joining of a sperm and an egg cell is called *sexual reproduction*.

▶ What are the steps involved in cross-pollination and fertilization?

Pollen grain is transferred from the anther of one flower to the stigma of another; a tube grows from the pollen grain into the flower. Sperm travel down the tube to the ovary, where they combine with egg cells.

Fertilization

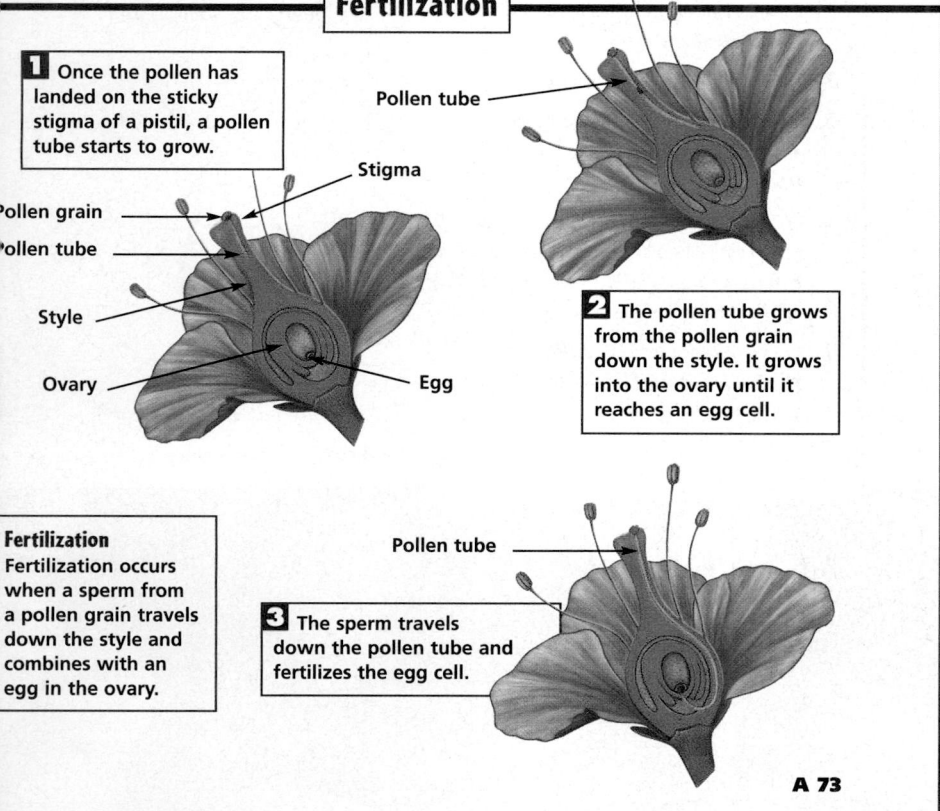

1 Once the pollen has landed on the sticky stigma of a pistil, a pollen tube starts to grow.

Pollen tube

Stigma

Pollen grain

Pollen tube

Style

Ovary

Egg

2 The pollen tube grows from the pollen grain down the style. It grows into the ovary until it reaches an egg cell.

Fertilization
Fertilization occurs when a sperm from a pollen grain travels down the style and combines with an egg in the ovary.

Pollen tube

3 The sperm travels down the pollen tube and fertilizes the egg cell.

A 73

Developing the Main Idea
Have students write a paragraph describing the steps in fertilization. Paragraphs should include the transfer of pollen to the stigma, the growth of the pollen tube down the style into the ovary, the travel of sperm through the tube to the ovary, and the sperm combining with the egg cell.

Exploring the Main Idea
Ask students to write their own definitions for each of the science terms used in the text. Then have them work in pairs to share their definitions and see if their partners can identify the term.

▶ After Reading
Have students answer the red question in the student book as **ongoing assessment**.

Technology

■ Visual Aid Transparencies 6, 7:
Pollination
Fertilization

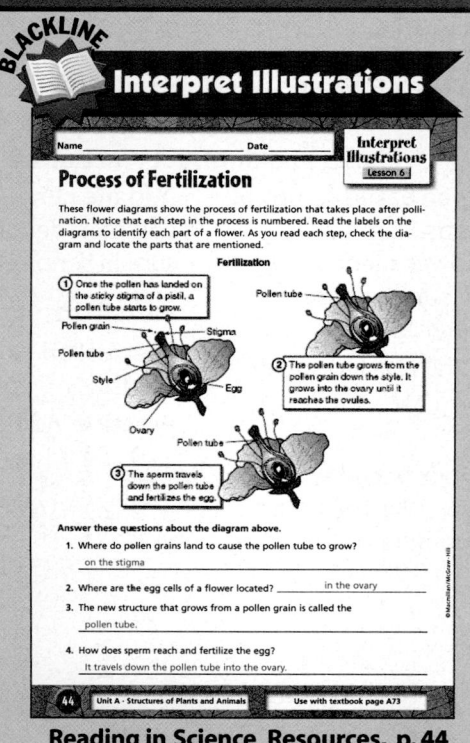
SCIENCE FOR ALL   **Advanced Learners**

Seed Banks
Invite students to learn about seed banks, especially the National Plant Germ Plasm System in the United States, the largest plant gene bank in the world. Suggest they find out why the bank is needed, how it stores seeds, what research is conducted, and how the bank benefits the whole world. **Linguistic**

What Is in a Seed?

Before Reading
Have students try to answer the red question at the top of the page.

Developing the Main Idea
Remind students that, unlike animals that are mobile, a plant must be able to disperse its seeds to places where they can germinate in order for the species to survive. Display different seeds for students to observe. Have them speculate how each seed travels from its parent plant.

Draw a diagram of a seed on the board. Ask students to identify each part.

FOR SCHOOL OR HOME

Materials bean seed (such as a lima bean), corn seed, water, hand lens

Science Process Skills *observe, infer, communicate, classify*

Resources Activity Resources, pp. 29–30

Step 3 The tiny plantlike structure is the embryo.

Step 4 Check students' drawings.

Step 5 Both have a plantlike structure (embryo) and store food. The corn seed has one cotyledon, the bean two.

Step 6 The corn is a monocot because it has one cotyledon; the bean a dicot because it has two.

Developing Vocabulary

embryo From the Greek word *embryon*, meaning "fetus" or "thing newly born," we get the word *embryo*. Explain to students that any plant or animal in the earliest stages of development may be referred to as an embryo.

seed coat Tell students that, just as they wear coats to protect themselves from the elements, seeds have their own coats to protect them. You may visualize this by drawing a cartoon of a seed wearing a "coat" to help students remember.

FOR SCHOOL OR HOME

Inside a Seed

1. Soak a lima bean in water overnight.

2. **Observe** Carefully pull apart the two halves of the lima bean. Examine the halves with a hand lens. Draw what you see.

3. **Infer** Which part is the embryo?

4. On your drawing label the seed coat and the cotyledon where food is stored.

5. **Communicate** Compare a corn kernel with a lima bean. Describe how its parts are similar to or different from the lima bean.

6. **Classify** Which seed is a dicot? Which is a monocot? Explain how you know which is which.

What Is in a Seed?
A seed is made up of three main parts. One part is an **embryo** (EM·bree·oh). An embryo is an immature plant. Another part is the cotyledon where food is stored in the form of starch. The third part is the **seed coat**. The seed coat encases the whole seed in a tough, protective covering.

Parts of a Seed

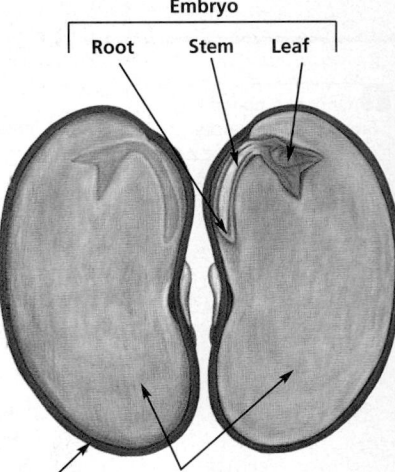

Embryo — Root · Stem · Leaf

Seed coat · Cotyledons

A 74

Math MiniLesson

Add and Subtract Fractions

Develop Renee baked $\frac{1}{4}$ cups of sunflower seeds. Tom baked $\frac{2}{3}$ cups of sunflower seeds. How many cups of sunflower seeds did they bake in all?

You can add fractions to solve the problem.

Find: $\frac{1}{4} + \frac{2}{3}$

Write equivalent fractions using the LCD. Think: 12 is the least common denominator (LCD)

$\frac{1}{4} = \frac{1 \times 3}{4 \times 3} = \frac{3}{12}$

$\frac{2}{3} = \frac{2 \times 4}{3 \times 4} = \frac{8}{12}$

Add the numerators. Use the common denominator. Write the sum in simplest form.

$\frac{1}{4} + \frac{2}{3} = \frac{3}{12} + \frac{8}{12} = \frac{11}{12}$

They baked $\frac{11}{12}$ cups of sunflower seeds.

Practice Add or subtract.

1. $\frac{7}{8} - \frac{5}{6}$ $\left(\frac{1}{24}\right)$

2. $\frac{3}{5} + \frac{1}{4}$ $\left(\frac{17}{20}\right)$

From Seed to Plant

Two things must happen for a seed to produce a new plant. First, the seed must move from the flower to a place where it can sprout. This is called *seed dispersal* (SEED di·SPUR·suhl). Second, the place must provide everything that is needed for sprouting, which is called *germination* (jur·muh·NAY·shuhn). A warm temperature and water are the two most important needs for germination. Food is not needed because the seed has its own supply of stored food.

Usually the seed must move a relatively long distance from its parent plant. Why? Competition from its parent, and plants like it, may make the development of a new plant difficult. For example, nearby plants may block sunlight from reaching the young plant. They may soak up the water or minerals from the soil that the new plant needs.

Seeds have evolved all sorts of adaptations for dispersal. For example, dandelion fruits and cottonwood seeds have feathery "parachutes." These parachutes can be blown great distances by the wind. Animals also help move plant seeds.

Animals eat `fruits`. A fruit is a mature ripened ovary of a plant. The animals digest the soft parts of the fruits but not the hard seeds inside. As the animals move from place to place, they deposit the seeds in their wastes.

Coconut seeds rely on ocean currents and sea breezes to move them.

The seeds of a cocklebur have tiny hooks that cling to the fur of animals or the clothing of people.

Animals eat fruits and the seeds inside.

How Gymnosperms Spread Seeds

Gymnosperms don't produce fruits. They disperse their seeds in other ways. For example, the cones of the balsam fir tree shatter. When they do this, they release winglike seeds that ride on the wind. Animals move cones from place to place. Heavy rains, floods, and streams can disperse them also.

▷ **What do the three main parts of a seed do?**

embryo becomes new plant; cotyledon stores starch for developing seed; seed coat protects embryo inside **A 75**

Using the Illustrations

Have students study the photographs and discuss characteristics of seeds that are dispersed by wind, water, and animals. For example, ask:

■ **What must be true about seeds that are carried by the wind?** (Possible answer: They must be very lightweight and have "wings" or "feathers.")

Exploring the Main Idea

Have students look closely at some cranberries. Point out the tight, thin skin and the spongy flesh. Demonstrate how these characteristics make cranberries good floaters and good bouncers.

Thinking Further: *Inferring*

Ask:

■ **What can you tell about the environment of the cranberry and any other seed that floats well?** (There must be water nearby in order to move the seed.)

Invite students to draw a poster showing how a seed gets from a plant to a new home, and how it starts to grow.

▶ After Reading

Have students answer the red question in the student book as **ongoing assessment**.

Developing Vocabulary

`fruit` Have students name some of the fruits they eat regularly and then compare and contrast them with fruits other animals eat. Point out that one of the word derivations of *fruit* (the Latin *fructus*) means "to enjoy."

Inclusion

Collecting Seeds

Late spring, summer, and autumn are good times to gather seeds. Take students on a field trip to a nearby park or open field. Have them wear tall socks over their shoes. Ask them to gather different fruits and seeds, including the ones that stick to their socks. Then challenge them to identify how the seeds are dispersed. They can also mount the seeds on posterboard or oaktag for a bulletin board display. **Kinesthetic; Social**

English Language Learners

Technology

Invite students to compare a piece of Velcro with a burdock seed or cocklebur. Many seeds have hooks that latch on to passing animals. These hooks inspired the invention of Velcro. Ask students to examine both the Velcro and the seeds with a hand lens and draw a picture of how each works. **Spatial**

What Is the Life Cycle of a Conifer?

Before Reading
Have students try to answer the red question at the top of the text column.

Developing the Main Idea
Before students begin their lists of the similarities and differences of gymnosperms and angiosperms, review with them the life cycle of angiosperms. Ask:

- **What is one way the life cycle of a conifer is different from that of a flowering plant?** (Possible answer: Conifers have a stage that produces spores containing the sex cells.)

- **What is one way the life cycles are similar?** (In both, fertilized egg cells eventually become seeds.)

READING Diagrams

A conifer, for instance, a pine tree, produces male and female cones in a mature tree. The scales that produce the cones have spore cases that produce the sperm and egg cells. Male cones produce pollen grains, which contain sperm cells. When the pollen grains fall away from a male cone, the wind carries them through the air. If a grain happens to fall on a female cone, a sperm cell from the pollen may fertilize an egg cell in the female cone. That fertilized cell eventually becomes a seed. As fall and winter come, female pine cones fall from the trees. Their seeds scatter on the ground. If wind or water carry the seeds far from the tree, and the seeds end up in a place where conditions are right for germination, the seeds will sprout, and a new pine tree will grow.

▶ After Reading
Have students answer the red question in the student book as **ongoing assessment**.

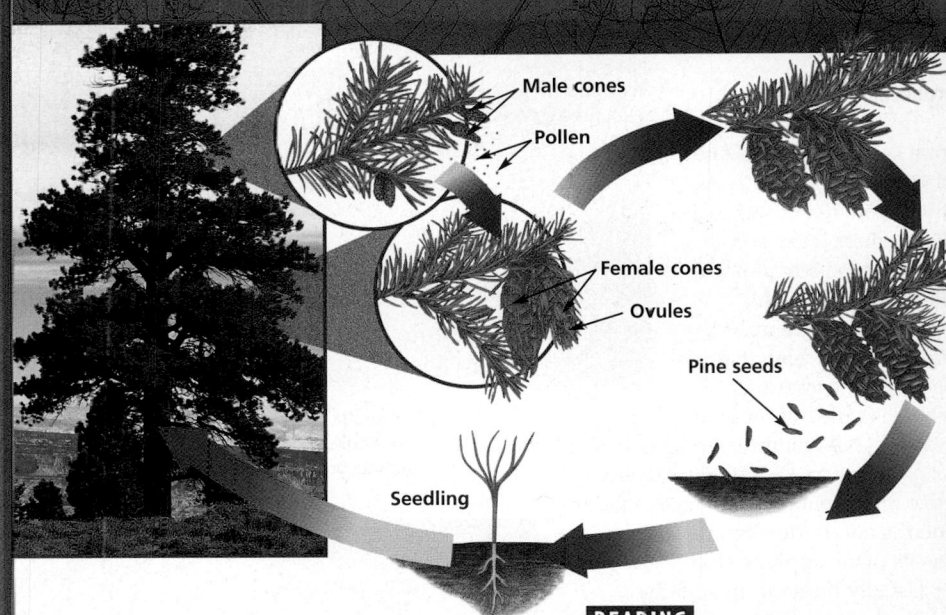

Male cones
Pollen
Female cones
Ovules
Pine seeds
Seedling

What Is the Life Cycle of a Conifer?

Since gymnosperms don't produce flowers or fruits, their life cycle is not the same as angiosperms. However, there are similarities. As you read on and look at the diagram on this page, make a list of the similarities and differences.

Let's examine the life cycle of a pine tree. A pine tree belongs to a group of gymnosperms called conifers. Pines produce male and female cones on a mature tree. The scales that form the cones carry spore cases that produce the plant's sperm and egg cells. Male cones produce pollen grains, which contain sperm cells.

When pollen grains fall away from a male cone, the wind carries them through the air. If a pollen grain

A 76

READING Diagrams

What are the steps in the life cycle of a conifer?

happens to land on a female cone, a sperm cell from the pollen may fertilize an egg cell in the female cone.

The fertilized cell eventually becomes a seed. As autumn and winter come, the female pine cones fall from the trees. Their seeds scatter on the ground. Sometimes wind or water will carry the seeds far from the tree. If they end up in a place where conditions are right for germination, the seeds will sprout, and a new pine tree will start growing.

▷ **Where are conifer seeds found?**
in female pine cones

 **English Language Learners**

Physical Science
Show students samples of the "whirly bird" or "helicopter," the pine seed. Using a fan on low power, demonstrate how these seeds are carried by the wind. Compare their action to that of a helicopter propeller. Take off one blade and then the other to see how that affects the distance traveled. Challenge students to design seeds for traveling great distances in the wind. **Spatial**

 Cultural Perspective

Christmas Trees
Challenge students to find out how the use of conifers as Christmas trees started. Some questions students might answer include: Why were conifers selected? What kinds of conifers are used? What are the advantages and disadvantages of each? **Linguistic**

Lesson Review

Why It Matters

Some plants can be grown from pieces of the plant—such as stems, leaves, and roots—rather than from seeds. This is called *vegetative propagation*. It is also called *asexual reproduction* because it happens without sperm and egg cells joining. For example, strawberry plants send shoots into the soil from stems that grow along the ground. Each shoot will make a new strawberry plant.

Flowering plants produce almost all of the plants you eat. People eat flowers, fruits, seeds, leaves, stems, and roots. Flowering plants are also eaten by animals that we eat.

Think and Write

1. Identify the different parts of a flower, and tell what each part does.

2. Explain how seeds are produced.

3. Give at least three examples of how seeds are dispersed.

4. Describe the difference between fertilization and germination.

5. **Critical Thinking** How do you think trees that produce seedless oranges are grown? Write down your prediction. Then do library research to see if your prediction was correct.

LITERATURE LINK

Read *Jonathan Chapman: The Appleseed Man*, the story of the man who brought apple trees to the Old West. When you finish reading, think about the advantages and disadvantages of bringing new plants into a region. Try the activities at the end of the book.

by Molly Bridger
Illustrated by Frederick Porter

WRITING LINK

Write an essay. Research at least two plants—besides strawberries—that can be grown by vegetative propagation. Write an essay discussing what the benefits are of growing plants in this manner.

MATH LINK

Solve this problem. The countries of the world produce about 1.8 billion metric tons of rice, wheat, and corn. A metric ton equals 1,000 kilograms, or 2,205 pounds. How many kilograms of these grains are produced? How many pounds?

TECHNOLOGY LINK

At the Computer Visit **www.mhscience02.com** for more links.

A 77

---

3 Lesson Review

Answers to Think and Write

1. Petals attract insects; sepals protect the petals; the stamen and pistil are the male and female parts of the flower; the anther holds the pollen; the ovary holds the egg; the stigma receives the pollen. (pp. A70, A72–A73)

2. A pollen grain is transferred from the anther to the stigma. On the stigma, a tube forms from the pollen grain to the ovary. A sperm travels down the tube and fertilizes the egg cell. A seed develops from the fertilized egg cell. (pp. A72–A73)

3. Seeds can be dispersed by animals, wind, and water. (pp. A72, A75–A76)

4. In fertilization, a sperm cell combines with an egg cell. In germination, a fertilized seed sprouts. (pp. A73, A75)

5. **Critical Thinking** Possible answers: A piece of one orange tree is grafted onto another orange tree; a piece of stem or leaf of an orange tree is planted in the soil. (p. A77)

Summarize

Check students' understanding by having them write a brief summary of the lesson in their own words.

LITERATURE LINK

Have students read the Grade-Level Science Book, *Jonathan Chapman: The Appleseed Man*. Additional books to read can be found on TE p. A1·b.

WRITING LINK

Students' essays should relate that the benefit of vegetative propagation is that the plants produced are genetically identical to the parent plant, thus traits are consistent for every plant. Examples of plants grown by vegetative propagation are navel orange trees and other fruit trees (grafting), potatoes, grapevines, African violets, and blackberry bushes.

MATH LINK

Calculations: 1.8 billion metric tons $\times$ 1,000 kg/1 metric ton = 1,800 billion kg; 1.8 billion metric tons $\times$ 2,205 lb/1 metric ton = 3,969 billion pounds.

✓ Informal Assessment

Easy/Average Give students a blank diagram of a flower and ask them to label it and explain the function of each part.

Challenge Have students draw a diagram to describe the steps in seed development. Have them label and define each structure and write a caption for each step.

Science Background

Vegetative Propagation

Plants produced asexually are identical in genetic makeup to the parent plant. In addition to stems and leaves, asexual structures in plants include spores, tubers, bulbs, stolons (runners), and rootstocks. In grafting, another form of vegetative propagation, a portion of the plant to be propagated (scion) is cut and joined to a seedling, or stock, of the same species. Have students make an outline of kinds of asexual propagation. **Linguistic; Logical**

LESSON 7

Plant Responses and Adaptations

LESSON 7

Plant Responses and Adaptations

Vocabulary

response, A80
stimulus, A80
tropism, A80
adaptation, A82

Get Ready

What happens when you jump up? Why don't you just fly up and away from Earth's surface?

There is a pull between Earth and everything on it. This pull is called gravity.

Does gravity affect how a plant grows? Do a plant's roots, stems, and leaves grow downward? What is happening to this tree as it grows on the side of the hill? Do roots always grow "down" no matter how you plant a seed?

Process Skill

You predict when you state possible results of an event or experiment.

A 78

Objectives

- Explore how seed roots grow.
- Identify tropisms.
- Identify various adaptations plants have for survival.

Resources

- Activity Resources, pp. 31–35
- Reading in Science Resources, pp. 47–52
- Vocabulary Cards
- Reading Aid Transparency A7

Build on Prior Knowledge

Have students discuss what they know about plant adaptations. Ask them to discuss ways they've seen plants respond to their environments. (Possible answers: leaves or needles adapted to water and sunlight conditions; orchids adapted to growth high in trees; plants that produce specialized flowers.)

1 Get Ready

Developing the Main Idea

Encourage students to speculate that roots will respond to gravity and grow downward. Explain that the other parts of plants—stems and leaves— respond to other factors, such as warmth or light, more than to gravity.

Science Background

Tropisms

Plants have adaptations that allow them to respond to stimuli. Stimuli can include light, heat, moisture, electricity, and chemicals. Different plant parts may respond differently to the same stimuli. For example, plant stems are positively phototropic while roots are negatively phototropic.

Science Background

Plant Behavior

Plant behavior is the response of the plant to changes in its environment. Factors affecting plant behavior include light, temperature, water, nutrients, and gravity. Some plant behavior is in response to the daily cycle of light and dark while some is strongly influenced by seasonal changes, particularly changes in night length.

Explore Activity

How Do Roots Grow?

Materials

petri dish (plastic)

2 paper towels

marking pen

tape

4 bean seeds that have been soaked in water overnight

Procedure

1 Soak two paper towels. Wrinkle the paper towels, and place them in the bottom half of the petri dish.

2 Place the four seeds on top of the wet paper towels as shown in diagram 1. Place the seeds so that the curved part is turned toward the center of the dish.

3 Place the top on the petri dish. The top will hold the seeds in the wet paper towels. Seal the top with transparent tape. Draw an arrow on the petri dish with the marking pen as shown in diagram 2. This will show which direction is down. Write the number or name of your group on the petri dish.

4 In a place your teacher provides, stand the petri dish on its edge so the arrow is pointing downward. Tape the petri dish so that it will remain standing. Do not lay the dish down flat.

5 **Predict** Make and record a prediction about the direction you think the roots will grow.

6 **Communicate** Examine the seeds for the next four days. Record the direction of root growth.

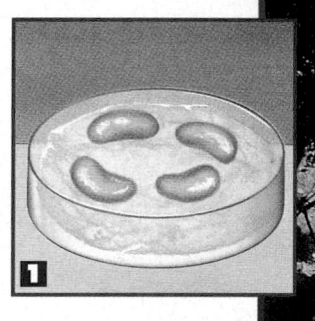
1

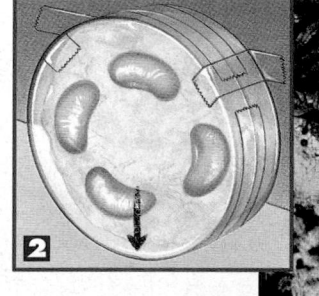
2

A 79

Drawing Conclusions

1 **Observe** In what direction were the roots growing on day 1? On day 4?

2 **Interpret Data** Is your prediction supported by your data?

3 **Going Further: Predict** What would happen if a seedling were not able to grow its roots down into the soil? Design an experiment to test your prediction.

Alternative Explore Activity

Materials presoaked corn seeds; marking pen; clear, tall plastic cups; paper towels

Which Way Do Corn Plant Roots Grow? Have students line the cups with wet paper towels. Then have them place corn seeds in different directions, between the paper towels, halfway from the top of the cup. Add an inch of water to the cup to keep the paper wet. Encourage students to observe the direction of root growth over the next few days. **Logical; Social**

Name_____ Date_____

Which Way Do Corn Plant Roots Grow?

Alternative Explore Lesson 7

Materials
- presoaked corn seeds
- marking pen
- clear, tall plastic cups
- paper towels

Procedure
1. Line a clear plastic cup with damp paper towels.
2. Place 5 soaked corn seeds between the paper towel and the side of the cup.
3. The seeds should be halfway between the bottom and the rim of the cup. Turn the seeds so that the pointed end of each one points in a different direction.
4. Use the marking pen to number the seeds.
5. Observe the growth of roots over the next few days. In the table, make drawings of each seed each day. Note the direction of the roots.

Day	Seed 1	Seed 2	Seed 3	Seed 4	Seed 5

Drawing Conclusions
1. At the beginning, in what direction did the roots grow?
   Straight out from the top of the seed.
2. After a few days in what direction did the roots grow?
   downward
3. What can you conclude about how roots grow?
   No matter how they start out, the roots grow downward.

Unit A · Structures of Plants and Animals | Use with TE textbook page A79 | 33

Activity Resources, p. 33

Explore Activity

How Do Roots Grow?

Science Process Skills *predict, communicate, observe, interpret data*

Resources Activity Resources, pp. 31–32

Pacing 30–40 minutes

Grouping small groups

Plan Ahead Soak the bean seeds in water overnight.

Procedure

1 Make sure the paper towels are kept very wet, especially if the heat is on in the school.

2 Make sure students place the seeds properly.

4 Provide a place where the dishes will not be disturbed and that does not get too hot or cold.

5 Students will probably predict "downward."

6 Day 1: minimal root growth; Days 2 and 3: root growth in any direction; Day 4: downward root growth.

Answers to Drawing Conclusions

1 On day 1, the roots may not be growing yet or may be growing in any direction. By day 4, the roots should be growing down.

2 Predictions that the roots will grow downward should be supported.

3 The seedling would not get the nutrients, water, and stability it needs. Students could design an experiment in which roots are allowed to grow but not in soil and note how long the seedlings survive.

 Inquiry Students can ask their own questions to explore, such as what happens if the dish is turned upside down after the roots begin to grow. (The root twists so it will again grow downward.)

 **Technology**

■ When time is short, preview the activity with the **Explore Activity Video**.

What Are Tropisms?

Before Reading
Have students try to answer the red question at the top of the page.

Developing the Main Idea
Help students distinguish between positive and negative tropisms. Ask:

- **Do roots display a positive or negative phototropism?** (negative)

Thinking Further: *Inferring*
Ask:

- **Do you think leaves would have a positive or negative phototropism? Why?** (Possible answer: Positive because they need light so would most likely turn toward it.)

Developing Vocabulary

response Explain to students that when you ask them a question they can give a response. They are reacting (response) to your question (stimulus). Ask them to apply this to plant behaviors; that is, plants react to (response) light (stimulus).

stimulus Associate this term with the more familiar word *stimulate*, which means "to excite to activity." A *stimulus* would be anything that acts to excite activity—such as light, heat, and gravity.

tropism Direct students' attention to the suffix *-ism*. Explain that this suffix means "the act, practice, or result of; a condition of being." *Trop-* is from a Greek word meaning "turning." Ask students to put these two concepts together to form their own definition of *tropism*.

Read to Learn

Main Idea Plants have certain behaviors and adaptations that help them survive.

What Are Tropisms?

If the flash of a camera goes off near your eyes, you are likely to respond to the bright light by blinking. The flash of light stimulated your blinking. Anything in the environment—light, heat, gravity, and more—that produces such a **response** is called a **stimulus** (STIM·yuh·luhs).

Plants also respond to a stimulus, but they tend to respond more slowly than animals do. Plants slowly bend or curve toward or away from a stimulus. Scientists call this kind of response a **tropism** (TROH·piz·uhm). Tropisms help a plant survive in its environment. For example, as seeds sprout, their roots grow downward. Why do you think the seeds' roots grow downward?

There are several major kinds of tropisms. One of these is *gravitropism*. A plant's roots respond to the stimulus of gravity and grow downward.

The roots of a plant show positive gravitropism. No matter how the plant is tilted, its roots will always grow downward into the soil. The roots grow in the direction Earth's gravity is pulling them. Stems show negative gravitropism. They grow away from the force of gravity. They grow into the air, where their leaves can get the most sunlight.

Light, of course, is very important to plants' survival. Plants respond to changes in light. These responses are called *phototropisms*. (*Photo* comes from a Greek word meaning "light.") If a plant is exposed to light coming from only one direction, its stem will bend in that direction. That is positive phototropism.

If a plant bends toward a stimulus, its change is called a positive tropism. If it bends away, the change is called a negative tropism.

A 80

Reading Strategy

Ask Questions
Developing Reading Skills
Ask students to raise unanswered questions about tropisms as they read pp. A80–A81. They can use these questions as the basis for a class discussion or individual or group research.

Lesson Outline

Name_____ Date_____

Lesson Outline Lesson 7

Plant Responses and Adaptations

Fill in the blanks. Reading Skill: **Compare and Contrast** - questions 3, 8, 17

What Are Tropisms?

1. Light, heat, and other things that produce a response are examples of a(n) __stimulus__.

2. A plant's movement toward or away from a stimulus is called __tropism__.

3. Plant roots grow downward in response to __gravity__.

4. The response of a plant to changes in light is called __phototropism__.

5. The roots of a willow tree show __positive hydrotropism__ as they grow toward a water source.

6. In Darwin's experiment, the plant shoots with __tips__ turned toward light, while the plants without tips did not.

7. Scientist Fritz Went believed that a(n) __chemical__ allowed the plant shoots to bend toward light.

8. Chemicals that stimulate plant growth are called __auxins__.

9. Plant shoots bend toward light because auxins cause cell growth on the __dark side__ of the stem, making it longer.

How Do Plants Survive?

10. Adaptations help plants survive in many kinds of __environments__.

11. A desert plant such as a cactus has adaptations for __collecting__, __storing__, and __saving water__.

12. "Long-day" plants such as spinach bloom at a time of year when there is more __daylight__ than __darkness__.

Unit A · Structures of Plants and Animals | Use with textbook pages A78–A85 | 47

Reading in Science Resources, p. 47

If you examine the roots of a willow tree growing near a stream, you will discover *hydrotropism*. *Hydro* means "water." The willow's roots show positive hydrotropism. They grow toward a source of water.

Some plants, like squash and grape plants, show a response to touch. Grape vines grow around posts farmers stick in the ground. The vines send out threadlike tendrils that coil toward whatever they touch.

People long knew about plant tropisms. However, they didn't always know the process inside a plant that made a plant's parts move. The first clue was discovered by Charles Darwin and his son Francis in the 1870s. Charles Darwin cut off the tips of some very young plant shoots. He left other plants alone. The plants with tips bent toward light. The plants without tips did not. Darwin

The tendrils of this plant respond to touch as they coil around other objects.

concluded that something in the tips was causing the bending, but what?

The second clue was found in the 1920s by Dutch scientist Frits Went. Went guessed that a chemical made only in the shoot's tip was responsible for the bending. He separated many chemicals from shoot tips. One by one he placed them on the cutoff tops of plant shoots. Finally, he found the chemical that let the cut shoots bend toward light.

The chemical is called an *auxin*. Auxins are chemicals that stimulate plant growth. Auxins work on all parts of the plant and cause tropisms of all kinds. How do auxins cause plant parts to bend? When one side of a stem is exposed to light, for example, auxins move to the other side and down. Auxins cause more cells to grow—and some to grow more in length—on the dark side, but not on the side facing the light. This unequal growth causes the stem to bend toward the light.

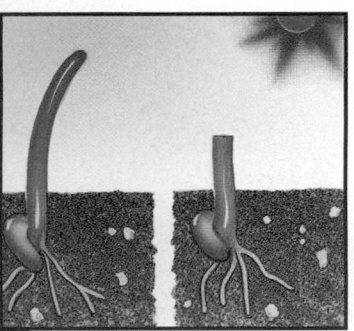

Charles Darwin showed that when the tip of a plant shoot is cut off, the plant will not bend toward light.

▶ **What are examples of a positive tropism and a negative tropism?**

Plants bending toward the light is a positive phototropism; plant stems growing upward is a negative gravitropism. **A 81**

Developing the Main Idea

Encourage students to focus on the sequence of events as they read the text. Ask them to state the questions each scientist must have asked. Challenge them to come up with their own questions for further research. Ask:

- **What is an example of a positive tropism and a negative tropism?** (Possible answer: Willow roots growing toward water is a positive hydrotropism; stems growing up is a negative gravitropism.)

- **Explain how auxins cause a positive phototropism in stems.** (The auxins in the stem move away from the light source causing more cells to grow on the dark side. The unequal growth causes the stem to bend toward the light.)

▶ **After Reading**
Have students answer the red question in the student book as **ongoing assessment**.

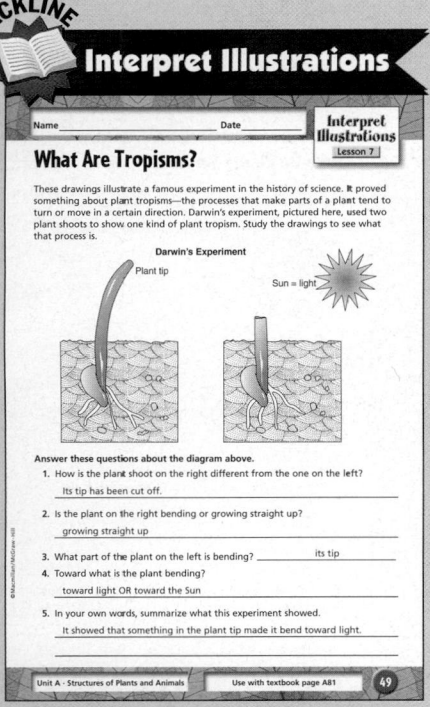
Advanced Learners

Hormones

Auxins were the first plant hormones discovered. Challenge students to find out how hormones are important to the human body and how they are similar to auxins. Have them report their findings to the class. **Linguistic**

Science Background

Tropisms

Thigmotropism is a plant's response to touch. Another kind of tropism is chemotropism (response to chemicals).

Plants can sometimes move in response to any stimulus. Nastic movements always occur in the same way, regardless of the stimulus—for example, the movement of a Venus's flytrap when an insect brushes against it. Have students list as many tropisms as they can think of. **Linguistic**

How Do Plants Survive?

Before Reading
Have students try to answer the red question at the top of the page.

Developing the Main Idea
Ask students in what kind of environments plants might have to cope with a lack of water (desert, arctic) and/or changes in the amount of light they receive (temperate climates, polar climates).

Ask students to give examples of plants that grow under various conditions and describe the characteristics of those plants. To introduce the concept of adaptation, encourage students to think of examples of characteristics organisms have to enable them to survive in their environments. Use the word *adapt* when explaining the examples.

READING Diagrams

1. B: long-day plant; A: short-day plant.
2. Plant A would bloom in early spring or fall.

▶ After Reading
Have students answer the red question in the student book as **ongoing assessment**.

Developing Vocabulary

adaptation Ask students for examples of how they have adapted to different situations. They may have moved to new homes or simply adapted to changes in the seasons. Relate this discussion to the concept of plant adaptations and how they help plants survive.

How Do Plants Survive?

Plants survive in deserts, rain forests, and the Arctic. They survive in all these places because they have adapted to their environment. An **adaptation** (ad·uhp·TAY·shuhn) helps an organism survive in its environment.

Desert plants have adaptations for collecting, storing, and saving water. Cactus plants have roots that absorb water very quickly. The water is stored in the center of the plant. A thick, waterproof, waxy coating helps stop water loss. Finally, the plant's stomata only open at night, when temperatures are cooler. Less water is lost through transpiration.

Carnivorous (meat-eating) plants can't get enough nutrients from the soil. These plants trap and digest insects to get some of the nutrients they need.

Plants like spinach, lettuce, and wheat bloom in late spring and early summer. They are called *long-day* plants. That's because when they bloom, there is much more daylight than darkness. By contrast, *short-day* plants, like strawberries, soybeans, and ragweed, bloom in early spring or in the fall. Short-day plants bloom when there is more darkness and less daylight. This flowering response is called *photoperiodism*.

▷ **What adaptations help plants survive water shortages?**

Possible answer: storing water in stem, waxy coating, roots that absorb water quickly

Short-Day, Long-Day Plants

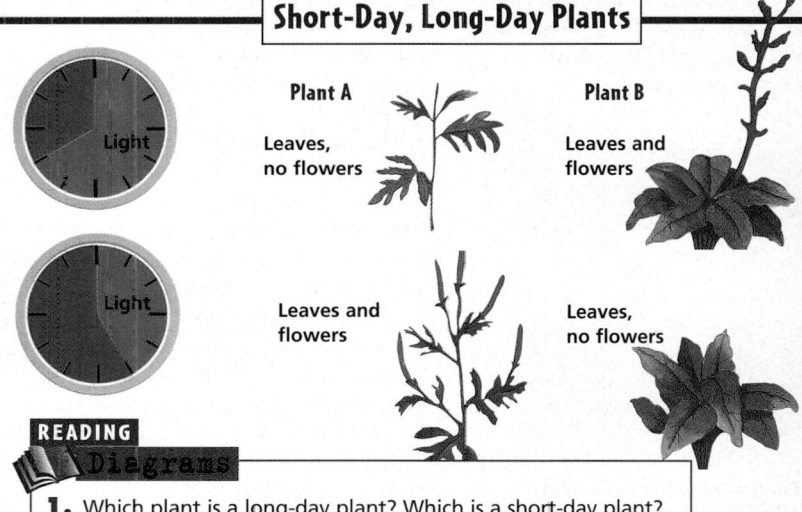

Plant A — Leaves, no flowers
Plant B — Leaves and flowers

Leaves and flowers
Leaves, no flowers

READING Diagrams

1. Which plant is a long-day plant? Which is a short-day plant?
2. In what season would plant A bloom?

A 82

Science Background

Photoperiodism
Detecting changes in day length is one way plants can tell when the seasons change. Reproductive cycles are often linked to the seasons because offspring survive best at certain times of the year. For example, wildflowers bloom during late spring and early summer when their pollinators (bees and butterflies) are most active and numerous. Have students find out the names of some long-day plants and some short-day plants. **Linguistic**

Interpret Illustrations

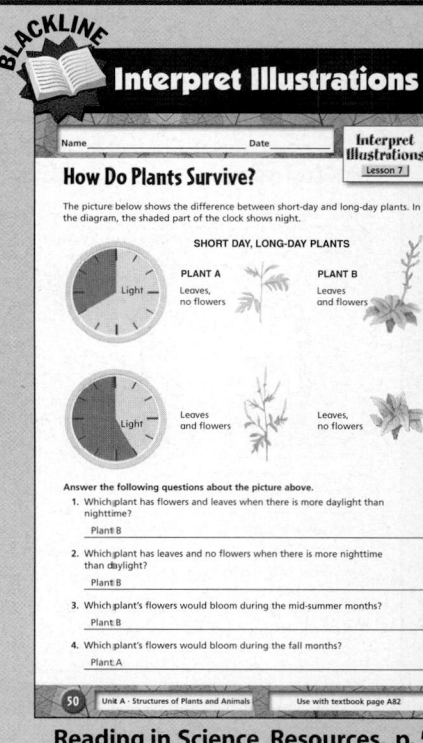

Name_____ Date_____
Interpret Illustrations
Lesson 7

How Do Plants Survive?

The picture below shows the difference between short-day and long-day plants. In the diagram, the shaded part of the clock shows night.

SHORT DAY, LONG-DAY PLANTS

PLANT A — Leaves, no flowers
PLANT B — Leaves and flowers

Leaves and flowers
Leaves, no flowers

Answer the following questions about the picture above.
1. Which plant has flowers and leaves when there is more daylight than nighttime?
   Plant B
2. Which plant has leaves and no flowers when there is more nighttime than daylight?
   Plant B
3. Which plant's flowers would bloom during the mid-summer months?
   Plant B
4. Which plant's flowers would bloom during the fall months?
   Plant A

50 Unit A · Structures of Plants and Animals   Use with textbook page A82

Reading in Science Resources, p. 5

Why Do Plants Compete?

Like all organisms, plants compete with one another for what they need to survive and grow—sunlight, water, and nutrients.

Each plant has its own strategy for winning its battle with other plants. Vines, like ivy and honeysuckle, climb the trunks of trees to get a greater share of sunlight. The trees themselves rise to great heights. They spread their branches to form leafy canopies above the forest. That's why in a forest, trees like oaks and maples have more leaves at their tops.

Have you ever been in a forest full of giant redwoods or other conifers? If so, you probably felt as if you were in a huge building filled with soaring columns. Only when you look high up do you see branches covered with green needles. Trees like these also preserve the nutrients and water in the soil for themselves. They do this by blocking sunlight from reaching the ground. Without sunlight few plants can grow in the soil and soak up nutrients and water near great trees.

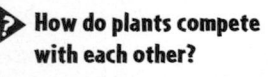 **How do plants compete with each other?**

Possible answer: Plants that need more light grow tall and block sunlight from reaching other plants on the ground.

QUICK LAB

FOR SCHOOL OR HOME

Plants Compete for Light

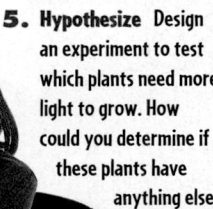

1. Collect samples of various houseplants that grow to different widths and heights.

2. Plant them, with some grass seed, in soil in a paper cup. Record the types of plants you used.

3. **Observe** Examine your plants over the next few days. Draw or photograph their progress.

4. **Observe** Which plants are being shaded by others? Are the plants in the shade doing as well as the plants that are getting more light?

5. **Hypothesize** Design an experiment to test which plants need more light to grow. How could you determine if these plants have anything else in common?

A 83

Why Do Plants Compete?

Before Reading
Have students try to answer the red question at the top of the page.

Developing the Main Idea
Help students understand how competition affects the types of plants that grow at various levels in a forest. Ask:

■ **What adaptations would plants have to have to survive on the floor of a forest?** (Possible answers: grow well in shade, not need a lot of water, grow low to the ground, get nutrients from decaying plant matter. A deciduous forest floor holds moisture well.)

Thinking Further: *Drawing Conclusions*
Ask:

■ **Where in a forest are you likely to find flowering plants? Why?** (Possible answer: In clearings or growing on limbs and trunks of the taller trees where they would get enough light and water.)

▶After Reading
Have students answer the red question in the student book as **ongoing assessment**.

FOR SCHOOL OR HOME

Materials grass seed, ivy plant, various houseplants, paper cup, soil, camera (optional)

Science Process Skills *observe, hypothesize*

Resources Activity Resources, pp. 34–35

Plan Ahead Students will need various plants of different sizes. Some plants must be able to shade others.

Step 4 Depending on the plants used, students may observe that the plants shaded by other plants do not do as well.

Step 5 Students might suggest growing duplicates of various types of plants under strong light, medium light, and shade to see which plants thrive in each condition. To determine if the plants have anything else in common, students could dissect the plants or run other experiments testing a particular variable, such as response to temperature change.

How Do Plants Use Chemicals to Survive?

Before Reading
Have students try to answer the red question at the top of the page.

Developing the Main Idea
Encourage students to ask questions while they read the text. For example, what is the advantage of keeping other plants at a distance? Why do creosote bushes release poison from their roots and not their leaves? Is it an advantage to discourage all insects from coming near?

Exploring the Main Idea
Ask students to share observations about different plants they are familiar with and any adaptations that may help the plant fight for survival (thorns on roses, needles on cacti, oils on poison ivy, poisons in holly berries and mistletoe).

▶After Reading
Have students answer the red question in the student book as **ongoing assessment**.

How Do Plants Use Chemicals to Survive?

Some plants use another strategy for keeping other plants at a distance. They produce chemicals that are poisons to other plants. Creosote bushes, which live in dry areas, release such a poison from their roots. The poison keeps the seeds of other plants from germinating. It may even kill other plants that are already growing.

Plants also make chemicals that discourage insects and animals from feeding on or infecting them. The most powerful insect-fighting plant chemical is made by the neem tree of Africa and Asia. This chemical is so strong that if you dissolved a teaspoon of it in a medium-sized swimming pool and sprayed the water on a plant, insects would not feed on it. Some plants, like the hemlock, even make poisons that can kill a person.

Unlike the plant below, which is being eaten by an insect, other plants such as the poison ivy above, produce chemicals that keep insects away or make them sick.

READING Compare and Contrast
What are two ways that plants use chemicals to survive?

produce chemicals poisonous to other plants; produce chemicals poisonous to animals and/or insects

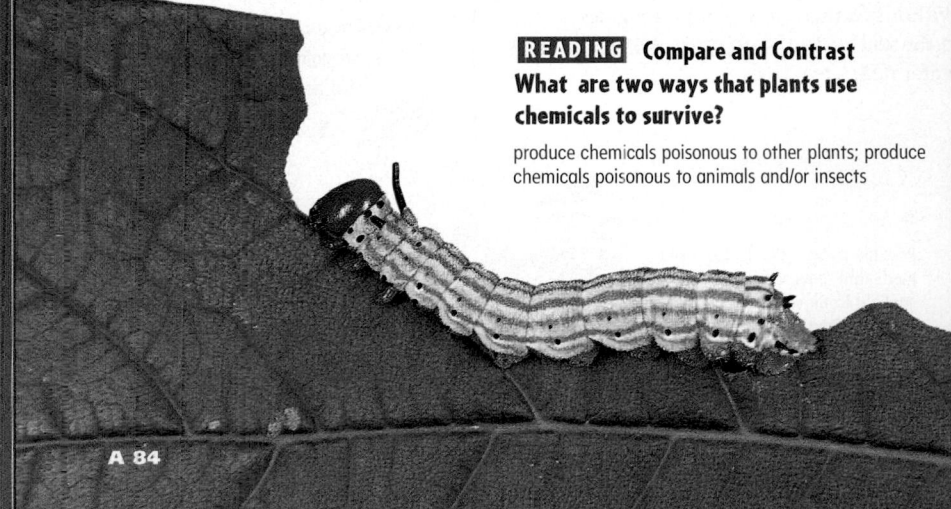

A 84

Science Background

Plant Poisons
The nightshade family of plants has many members that are poisonous. This led people in Europe to resist trying tomatoes because they belong to that family. Tobacco and belladonna are both members of the nightshade family. Have students research the Italian roots of this word. (*bella*, "beautiful"; *donna*, "lady") Ask them to find the origins of *tomato* and *tobacco*. **Linguistic**

Reading MiniLesson

Compare and Contrast

Develop As students answer the question on page A84 about the two ways plants use chemicals to survive, discuss how the two practices compare as well as contrast. Point out that both are forms of defense, both involve the use of chemicals, and both involve poisons produced by plants. They differ in which chemicals are used to poison. Stress that to compare and contrast objects, they need have only one thing alike or one thing different.

Practice Ask students to find evidence on page A84 to prove that different kinds of chemical-producing plants are alike in some ways and different in others. (Answers should include that the plants are alike because they produce chemicals, and that they differ in that creosote's poison keeps seeds from germinating, the neem tree's poison keeps plant-eating insects away, and hemlock's poison can kill people.)

L·I·N·K·S

Why It Matters

How can you tell a tree's age? You can do it by counting its rings. A tree forms a layer of wood each year. This process continues for as long as the tree lives. The size of a tree ring, however, can change depending on whether the weather has been warm and rainy or cold and dry.

Plants respond to changes in their environment. They have to be able to adapt to changes in light, water, and temperature. They need these adaptations in order to survive. Other equally important adaptations help plants reproduce successfully and fight off enemies such as insect pests.

Think and Write

1. What are tropisms? Give an example of one.

2. Where does a cactus store water?

3. How do auxins help plants grow toward the light?

4. Compare the way vines and trees compete for sunlight.

5. **Critical Thinking** What do you think might happen if all plants bloomed at the same time?

MATH LINK

Solve this problem. How big does a giant *sequoia* (si·KWOY·uh) grow? Research giant sequoias to find how tall they grow, how big around they get, and how much they weigh. Which weighs more—a giant sequoia or a blue whale?

WRITING LINK

Write an essay. Research how a tree's rings can tell scientists about weather conditions in an area, and write an essay on your findings. What can studying a tree's rings tell about how the tree adapted to its environment?

ART LINK

Make a poster. Find pictures illustrating several plant tropisms, and use them to help you design a poster. Include a description of each tropism you illustrate.

TECHNOLOGY LINK

Science Newsroom CD-ROM Choose *Flower Power* to learn more about how flowers attract pollinators.

At the Computer Visit **www.mhscience02.com** for more links.

A 85

Informal Assessment

Easy/Average Ask students to pick out the key terms in this lesson and to define each in their own words. Encourage them to share their definitions with a partner and see if the partner can identify the term.

Challenge Have students prepare an outline for a magazine article describing how plants adapt and behave.

---

3 Lesson Review

Answers to Think and Write

1. Tropisms are plant responses to stimuli. One example is gravitropism. (pp. A80, A82, A84)

2. A cactus stores water in its stem. (p. A82)

3. Auxins move to the side of the plant opposite the light, which causes the plant to bend in the direction of the light. (p. A81)

4. Vines climb the trunks of trees to get their share of sunlight. Trees grow tall and spread their branches, forming leafy canopies above the forest. (p. A83)

5. **Critical Thinking** Possible answer: All the plants would have to compete for nutrients, water, sunlight, and pollinators at the same time. (pp. A78–A85)

Summarize

Check students' understanding by having them write a brief summary of the lesson in their own words.

MATH LINK

The largest sequoia is 275 feet tall, 83 feet in diameter near the ground, and weighs about 2,500 metric tons, heavier than a blue whale, which can weigh up to 90 metric tons.

WRITING LINK

A thick ring indicates a year with warm temperatures and lots of rain; a thin rings indicates a year with cold temperatures and little rain

ART LINK

Posters can show basic tropisms—roots growing down, sunflowers facing the sun, trees bending toward sunlight along city streets.

Science, Technology, and Society

How Can Cutting Trees Save Forests?

I n Ancient Greece people told of an earlier "Golden Age" when the hills were covered with trees. Their forests were gone by then, and the Greeks discovered that when trees go, soil washes away. Greece has never recovered from the loss of its trees.

About a thousand years later, rich landowners in England saved some forests for hunting and fishing. Some villages had forests that they cut partway down. Trees were cut about 6 feet from the ground every few years. The tall stumps grew new shoots, which could be used for firewood.

Today some of the greatest forests left are in the western part of North America. Lots of rainfall west of the Rocky Mountains helps trees grow larger there than most places in the world. These are the giant redwoods and sequoia trees. Some of these giant trees are more than 2,000 years old!

In the 1850s it took four men 22 days to chop down one of these sequoia trees with hand axes. The trunk was 10 meters (33 feet) across!

A 86

Objective

■ Discuss how cutting down trees affects a forest.

Build on Prior Knowledge
Ask:

■ **Where do we get the lumber we use for making buildings, paper, and furniture?** (We get lumber from the forests.)

■ **How do some logging companies replace the trees they cut?** (They replace felled trees with saplings.)

How Can Cutting Trees Save Forests?

Developing the Main Idea
Ask:

■ **How does clear-cutting affect a forest?** (Clear-cutting removes all the trees; the soil, which was held by the trees, then washes away. Animals lose their homes and fishes' environments change.)

Ask students if they have ever been in a forest or a wooded place. Discuss what they saw there and what kinds of plants and animals live in the forests. Ask:

■ **Are forests valuable? Why or why not?** (Possible answers: Yes, because they provide essential products from paper to lumber for houses and they are a critical part of many ecosystems.)

Inclusion

Logging Today
Challenge students to find out how forests are logged today. What machines are used? How are the trees transported? How is the lumber processed? Have students summarize their research in a written report.
Linguistic

Lumber companies eventually built roads into the forests. They hauled in power-driven saws and giant cranes. Whole sections of the forest were cut down at once. That's called clear-cutting. It leaves large bare patches. Forest animals lose their homes. Soil washes into streams, and the fish's environment is changed!

Today there are other ways to use modern tools to cut trees but save the forests. Helicopters can fly in workers and tools. A tree can be cut and lifted away. The other trees, the animals, and the soil all remain in the forest.

What Did I Learn?

1. The giant trees found in the western part of North America are the

   A red oaks and red maples
   B red maples and sequoias
   C redwoods and red maples
   D redwoods and sequoias

2. Clear-cutting

   F leaves large bare patches in the forest
   G prevents soil from being washed away
   H means cutting down only a few trees at a time
   J is done by helicopter

AT THE COMPUTER

Visit www.mhscience02.com to learn more about forests.

A 87

Thinking Further: *Inferring*

Ask:

■ **Where does soil go if it washes away?** (Most soil that washes away goes into streams, and then into the ocean.)

■ **How might the views of a person who catches fish for a living and a person who builds homes for a living differ?** (The fishers may say that clear cutting must be stopped because it causes rivers to silt up and destroys the fishes' habitat. The builder may argue that clear cutting is the only way to keep lumber prices down.)

Test Prep:  **What Did I Learn?**

1. D

2. F

Summarize

Check students' understanding by having them write a brief summary of the magazine in their own words.

Science Background

Reforestation

The process of replanting trees that have been cut down is called reforestation. This is vital to the health of our biosphere as deforestation creates changes in the soil, runoff patterns, nearby streams and lakes, and types of plants that can grow. Lumber companies sometimes replant with only one species of tree.

However, this is not a wise practice since diversity is fundamental to the survival of organisms. The United States Forestry Service protects and manages our forest resources. However, people can help by planting native trees in their yards and communities.

Chapter Review and Test Preparation

Resources

- Reading in Science Resources, pp. 53–54
- Assessment Book, pp. 5–8

Answers to Vocabulary

1. angiosperm
2. adaptation
3. pollination
4. tropism
5. fruit
6. gymnosperm
7. spore
8. frond
9. cotyledon
10. stimulus

Answers to Test Prep

11. B
12. H
13. D
14. F
15. C

Chapter 2 Review

Vocabulary

Fill each blank with the best word from the list.

> **adaptation,** A82
> **angiosperm,** A58
> **cotyledon,** A62
> **frond,** A51
> **fruit,** A75
> **gymnosperm,** A58
> **pollination,** A72
> **spore,** A48
> **stimulus,** A80
> **tropism,** A80

1. A plant that has flowers is called a(n) _____.

2. A characteristic that helps an organism survive in its environment is a(n) _____.

3. Transferring a pollen grain from an anther to a stigma is known as _____.

4. Bending toward or away from a stimulus is a(n) _____.

5. A mature ripened ovary is called a(n) _____.

6. A seed plant that does not produce fruits is a(n) _____.

7. A new moss plant is produced by a(n) _____.

8. The leaflike structure of a fern is a(n) _____.

9. A tiny leaflike structure inside a seed is a(n) _____.

10. Something in the environment that produces a response in an organism is a(n) _____.

Test Prep

11. What kinds of plants do very well in hot, damp climates?
    - **A** apple trees
    - **B** ferns
    - **C** fir trees
    - **D** grains

12. Which of the following are gymnosperms?
    - **F** apple trees
    - **G** ferns
    - **H** fir trees
    - **J** grains

13. Bees help flowers reproduce through a process called _____.
    - **A** fertilization
    - **B** phototropism
    - **C** transpiration
    - **D** pollination

14. Tropism is the process of _____.
    - **F** movement of a plant toward or away from a stimulus
    - **G** making sugar from sunlight
    - **H** transporting water along a stem
    - **J** adaptation to a hot climate

A 88

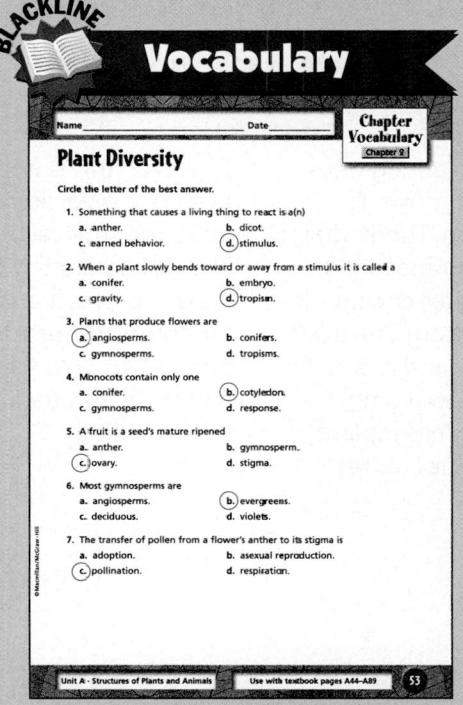

Reading in Science Resources, p. 53

15. What causes sunflowers to bend toward the sunlight?
A pollination
B transpiration
C positive phototropism
D negative phototropism

Concepts and Skills

16. Reading in Science Write a paragraph explaining the difference between a monocot and a dicot.

Rose

Lily

17. Product Ads Look at the ingredients listed on boxes of breakfast foods. What kinds of plants are most commonly used to make breakfast foods? Write a paragraph explaining why.

18. Scientific Methods Describe two ways that adaptations can help plants survive. Write up a design for an experiment that would test this.

19. Process Skills: Observe Tell which of these plants are angiosperms and which are gymnosperms—bristlecone pine, rose, wheat, oat, fir, cedar, lily, juniper, yew, larch, violet, tomato, spruce, giant redwood tree. Write a paragraph explaining your answer.

20. Critical Thinking If you were lost in the woods in the United States, had no compass, and could not see the sky, how might plants help you infer direction? Write a paragraph explaining your answer.

Boost your test scores!

Be Smart!
Visit www.mhscience02.com

A 89

Answers to Concepts and Skills

16. Reading in Science A monocot is a plant whose seeds contain only one cotyledon, a tiny leaflike structure. A dicot is a plant whose seeds contain two cotyledons. Students might also add that monocots have parallel leaf veins, while dicots have branched leaf veins; monocots have flower parts in multiples of three, while dicots' are in multiples of four or five; moncots' vascular systems are scattered in bundles while dicots' are in rings.

17. Product Ads Seeds of grains such as rye, barley, rice, oat, corn, and wheat are found in breakfast cereals. They are very nutritious for humans. Breads are made from flour, which is made mostly from ground up seeds of wheat plants.

18. Scientific Methods Plants that live in the desert have adaptations for collecting, storing, and saving water. Cactus plants have roots that absorb water very quickly. Carnivorous plants can't get enough nutrients from the soil, so they trap and digest insects to get some of the nutrients that they need. Accept all logical ideas for experiments that would test both these adaptations.

19. Process Skills: Observe angiosperms: rose, wheat, oat, lily, violet, tomato; gymnosperms: bristlecone pine, fir, cedar, juniper, yew, larch, spruce, giant redwood tree

20. Critical Thinking The phototropism of plants might help since sunlight comes from the south, and plants that show phototropism would bend in that direction.

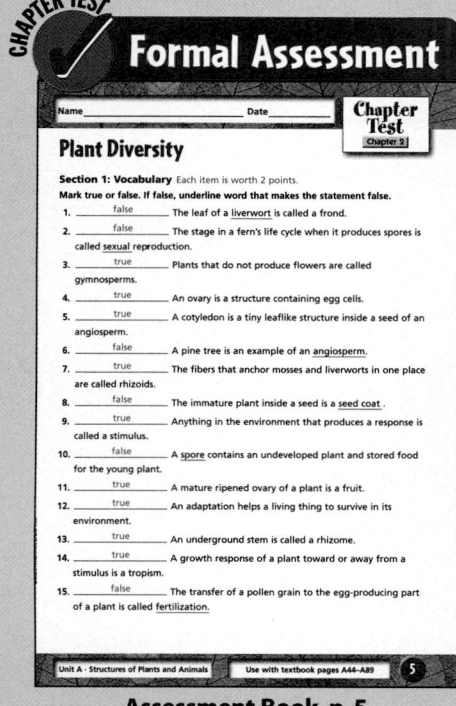

Assessment Book, p. 5

Lesson Planner

Lesson	Objectives	Vocabulary	Pacing	Resources and Technology
LESSON 8 **Animal Structure and Function,** pp. A92–A101	■ Explore how to classify animals. ■ Understand that animal cells are organized into tissues, organs, and systems. ■ Describe observable characteristics of vertebrates and invertebrates. ■ Classify animals by using a key.	**tissue** **organ** **system** **vertebrate** **invertebrate**	4 days	■ Activity Resources, pp. 36–40 ■ Reading in Science Resources, pp. 59–64 ■ Vocabulary Cards ■ School to Home Activities, p. 6 ■ Grade-Level Science Book, *Dino Flight* ■ Reading Aid Transparency A8 ■ **Explore Activity Video** ■ **Science Experiences Videotapes** *Camels, Cacti, and You: What All Living Things Share* (Package 3)
LESSON 9 **Animal Adaptations,** pp. A104–A115	■ Explore how sow bugs adapt to their environment. ■ Compare and contrast various forms of animal adaptations. ■ Understand that certain characteristics are inherited. ■ Describe the impact of hybridization and cross breeding on animal diversity.	**mimicry** **camouflage** **protective coloration** **heredity** **hybrid** **crossbreeding** **diversity**	4 days	■ Activity Resources, pp. 41–45 ■ Reading in Science Resources, pp. 65–70 ■ Vocabulary Cards ■ School to Home Activities, p. 7 ■ Reading Aid Transparency A9 ■ **Explore Activity Video** ■ **Science Experiences Videotapes** *Staying Alive: Adaptations for Survival* (Package 4)

Activity Planner

Activity	Process Skills	Materials	Plan Ahead
LESSON 8 Explore Activity **How Are Animals Classified?** p. A93	classify, communicate, infer	25 pictures of animals, 5 sheets of paper, tape, scissors	Collect old nature or science magazines with many drawings or photos of animals.
Process Skill BUILDER **Using a Key** p. A100	classify, observe, interpret data	none	No advance planning is needed.
LESSON 9 Explore Activity **How Do Sowbugs Adapt to Their Environment?** p. A105	observe, experiment, infer	10 sow bugs, tray, paper towels, water	Keep sow bugs in a moist, dark place at room temperature. Sow bugs are not insects; they are crustaceans and have gills.
QUICK LAB FOR SCHOOL OR HOME **Find the Hybrid Cat** p. A113	observe, infer	none	No advance planning is needed.

Reading in Science Resources

McGraw-Hill Science **Reading in Science Resources** provides the following **Blackline Master** worksheets for this chapter.

Chapter Graphic Organizer

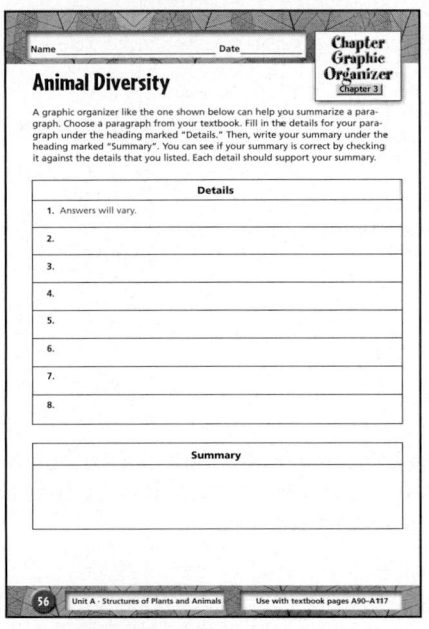

Reading in Science Resources,
p. 56

Chapter Reading Skill

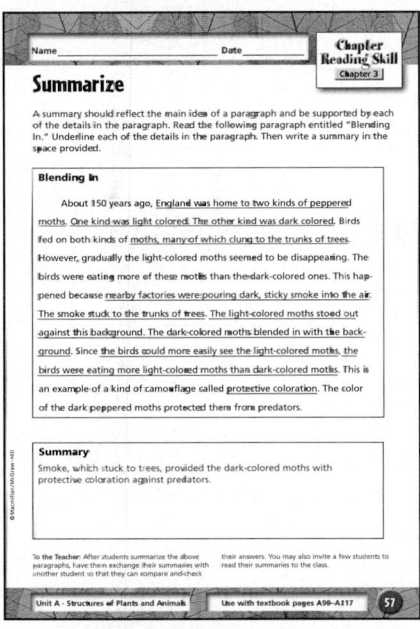

Reading in Science Resources,
pp. 57–58

Chapter Vocabulary

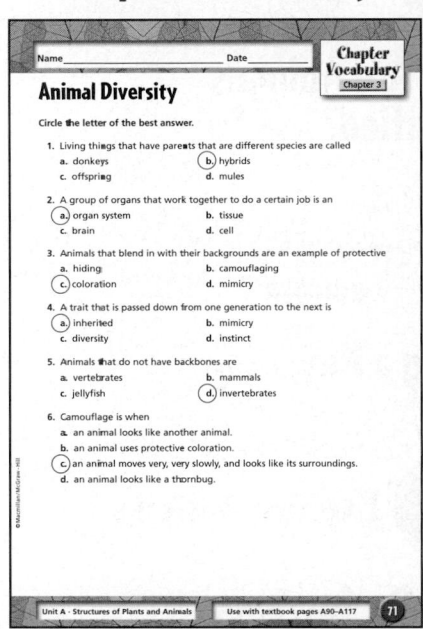

Reading in Science Resources,
pp. 71–72

McGraw-Hill Science **Reading in Science Resources** provides the following **Blackline Master** worksheets for every lesson in this chapter.

Lesson Outline

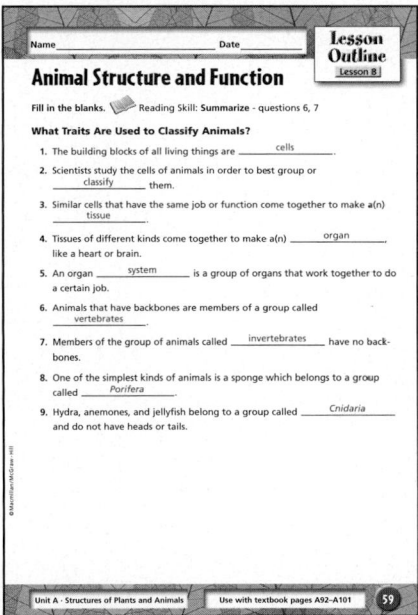

Reading in Science Resources,
pp. 59–60, 65–66

Interpret Illustrations

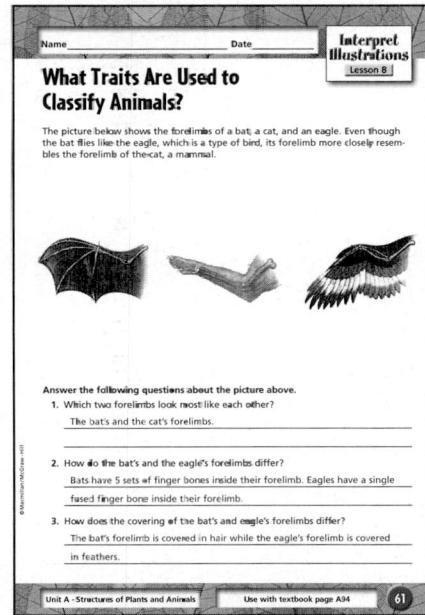

Reading in Science Resources,
pp. 61–62, 67–68

Lesson Vocabulary and Cloze Test

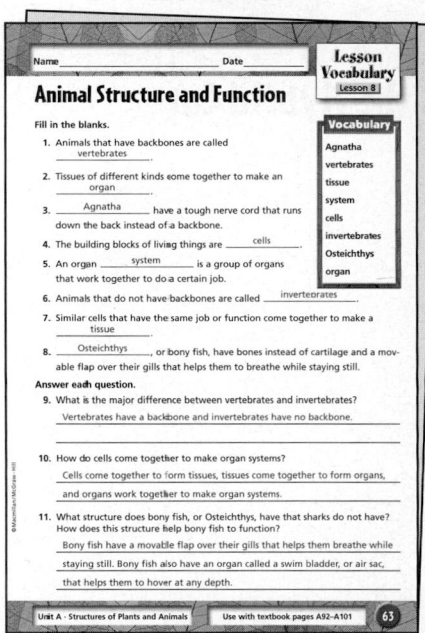

Reading in Science Resources,
pp. 63–64, 69–70

Activities and Assessment

McGraw-Hill Science **Activity Resources** provides the following **Blackline Master** worksheets for every lesson in this chapter.

Explore Activity and Alternative Explore Activity

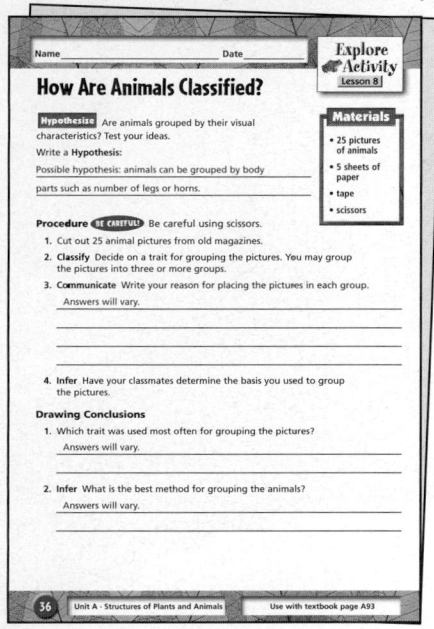

Activity Resources, pp. 36–37, 42–43

Quick Lab for School or Home

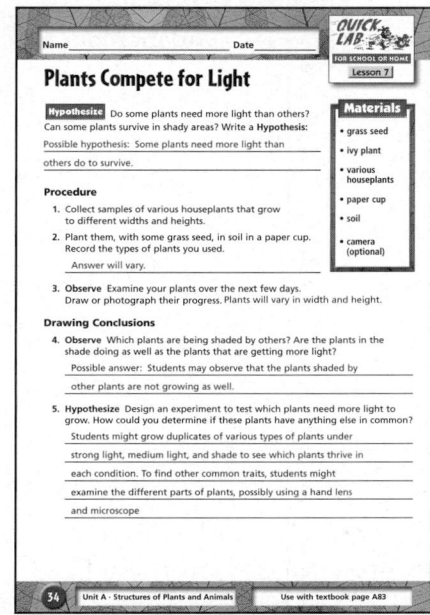

Activity Resources, pp. 34–35, 44–45

Process Skill Builder

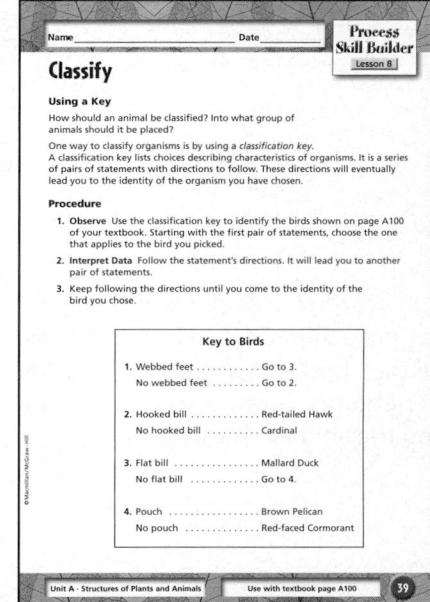

Activity Resources, pp. 39–40

McGraw-Hill Science **Assessment Book** provides the following **Blackline Master** worksheets for this chapter.

Chapter Test

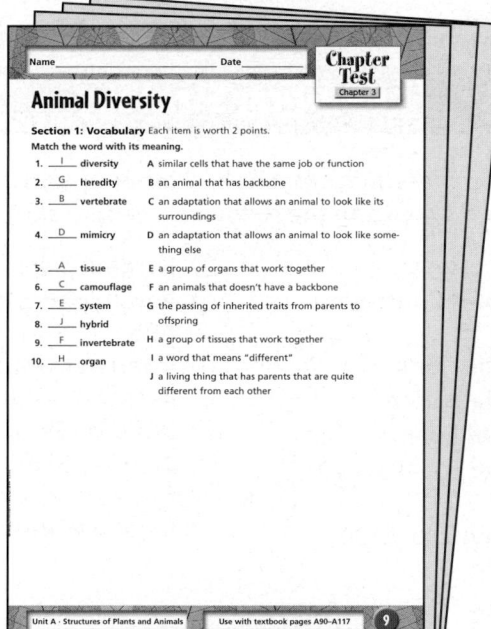

Assessment Book, pp. 9–12

CHAPTER

3 Animal Diversity

Resources

- Reading in Science Resources, pp. 56–72
- Assessment Book, pp. 9–12

Starfish belong to the phylum *Echinodermata,* that is, they are echinoderms. Starfish have a skeleton inside their bodies, but they are invertebrates. Fish are vertebrates. Sponges and sea anemones are among the animals in this picture.

CHAPTER

3 Animal Diversity

Did You Ever Wonder?

Where do starfish live? Although starfish live in every ocean on Earth, there are more kinds of starfish in the northern Pacific than anywhere else. Are starfish really fish? What other kinds of animals can you see in this photo?

A 90

Reading Strategy

This chapter provides MiniLessons and other opportunities for developing and practicing the following reading skills:

- ○ **Cause and Effect**
- ◉ **Compare and Contrast:** pp. A99, A113
- ○ **Draw Conclusions**
- ○ **Find the Main Idea**
- ○ **Sequence of Events**
- ◉ **Summarize:** pp. A95, A101, A103, A114, A115
- ◉ **Ask Questions:** p. A104

- ◉ **Reread:** p. A118
- ◉ **Retell (paraphrase):** pp. A92, A96
- ○ **Interpret Graphic Sources of Information**
- ◉ **Build on Prior Knowledge:** pp. A92, A102, A104, A107, A118
- ○ **Organize Information**

A 91

Vocabulary Preview

Encourage students to keep a Science Dictionary. Remind them to add the Vocabulary words for each lesson in this chapter to their Dictionary as they complete each lesson.

tissue, A94

organ, A94

system, A94

vertebrate, A95

invertebrate, A95

mimicry, A106

camouflage, A108

protective coloration, A109

heredity, A110

hybrid, A112

crossbreeding, A112

diversity, A114

AMERICAN
MUSEUM OF
NATURAL
HISTORY

Visit www.amnh.org/resources/mhscience to discover more about how scientists classify animals and explore various forms of animal adaptations.

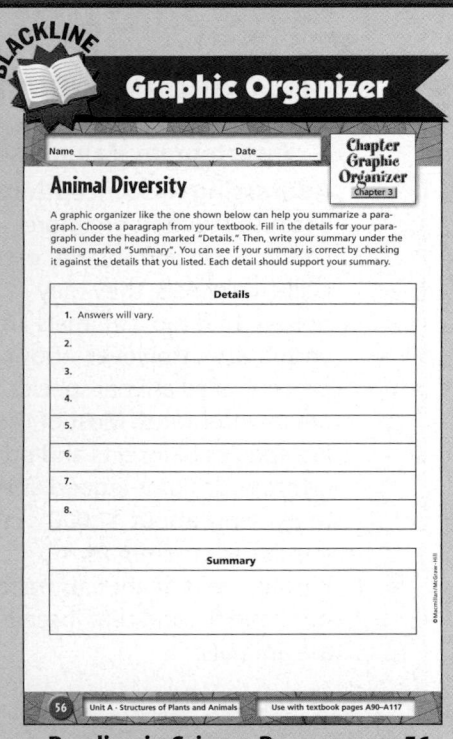

Reading in Science Resources, p. 56

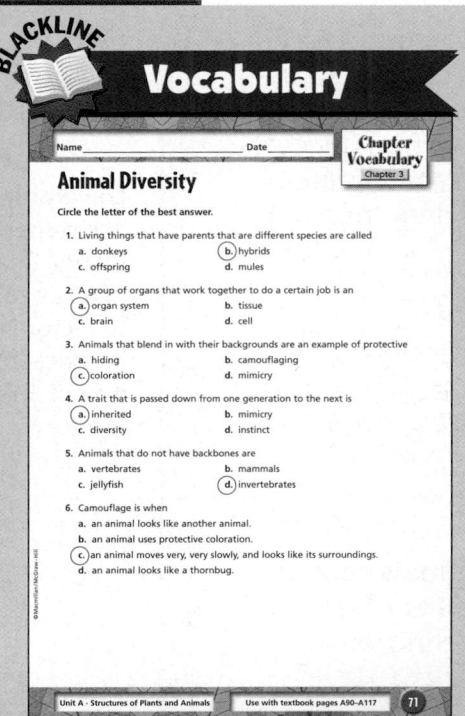

Reading in Science Resources, p. 71–72

LESSON 8 Animal Structure and Function

Objectives

- Explore how to classify animals.
- Understand that animal cells are organized into tissues, organs, and systems.
- Describe observable characteristics of vertebrates and invertebrates.
- Classify animals by using a key.

Resources

- Activity Resources, pp. 36–40
- Reading in Science Resources, pp. 59–64
- Vocabulary Cards
- Reading Aid Transparency A8
- Grade-Level Science Book, *Dino Flight*
- School to Home Activities, p. 6

Build on Prior Knowledge

Have students discuss what they know about classifying animals. Have them give examples of traits all animals have in common. (Possible answers: have many cells, cannot make their own food, move from place to place.) Have them list ways in which animals are different. (Possible answers: body coverings, number of legs, type of birth.)

1 Get Ready

Developing the Main Idea

Ask:

- **What are some of the ways that animals can be grouped?** (Possible answers: number of legs, with backbone or without, body covering, environment in which they live.)

LESSON 8 Animal Structure and Function

Vocabulary

tissue, A94
organ, A94
system, A94
vertebrate, A95
invertebrate, A95

Get Ready

Animals have different traits. These traits include shape, size, body parts, and color. Scientists use such traits to put similar animals into groups. This is not always as easy as it seems. What traits would you use to group animals? Many different kinds of animals visit a watering hole in Africa. How might these animals be grouped?

Process Skill

You classify when you place things that share properties together in groups.

A 92

 **Reading Strategy**

Paraphrase

Developing Reading Skills
Ask students to describe the mental images that the text on p. A92 evokes. Challenge them to picture how a watering hole in Africa looks and what groupings of animals might appear there.

 Science Background

Invertebrate Mammals
Addressing Misconceptions
Because students are more familiar with vertebrates, especially mammals, they may believe that most animals are vertebrates. However, about 95 percent of all animal species are invertebrates. Most of these are species of insects and other arthropods (joint-legged animals). Only about 41,000 species are mammals. Emphasize that animals need not have fur and that insects are animals.

Explore Activity

How Are Animals Classified?

Materials

25 pictures of animals

5 sheets of paper

tape

scissors

Procedure

BE CAREFUL! Be careful using scissors.

1 Cut out 25 animal pictures from old magazines.

2 **Classify** Decide on a trait for grouping the pictures. You may group the pictures into three or more groups.

3 **Communicate** Write your reason for placing the pictures in each group.

4 **Infer** Have your classmates determine the basis you used to group the pictures.

Drawing Conclusions

1 Which trait was used most often for grouping the pictures?

2 **Infer** What is the best method for grouping the animals?

3 **Going Further: Infer** Why do you think scientists all over the world use a single system for grouping organisms?

A 93

Alternative Explore Activity

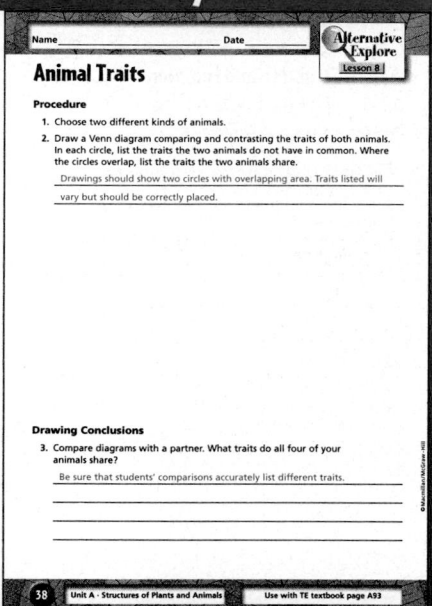

Materials (optional) pictures of two different animals, research materials

Animal Traits Have students compare and contrast the traits of two different kinds of animals, such as a parrot and a horse. (Possible answers: Both have two eyes and a mouth. Both live on land. Parrots have wings and two legs, horses have four legs; parrots have feathers, horses have hair; parrots lay eggs, horses bear live young.)

Activity Resources, p. 38

Explore Activity

How Are Animals Classified?

Science Process Skills *classify, communicate, infer*

Resources Activity Resources, pp. 36–37

Pacing 20–30 minutes

Grouping small groups

Plan Ahead Collect old nature or science magazines with many drawings or photos of animals.

Procedure

Be Careful! Remind students to be careful when using scissors and to put them out of reach when finished.

3 Encourage students to first compare traits that some of the animals have in common with those that are unique to each animal. Accept any supportable grouping.

4 Groups can exchange their animal groupings.

Answers to Drawing Conclusions

1 Possible answers: skin covering, mammal or not, number of legs, warm-blooded or cold-blooded

2 Possible answer: using more than several traits held in common by a number of animals.

3 They use a single system so that all scientists worldwide have a common system to communicate the groups to which an animal belongs.

 Inquiry Students can ask their own questions to explore, such as, How can the animals within each group be further classified? (Students can look for similarities and differences among animals in each group to make further classifications.)

 ## Technology

■ When time is short, preview the activity with the **Explore Activity Video.**

2 Read to Learn

What Traits Are Used to Classify Animals?

Before Reading
Have students try to answer the red questions at the top of the page.

Developing the Main Idea
Point out that while all animals' cells have similar basic structure, the specific structure and functions of these cells are very diverse. Human bodies, for example, have about 200 different types of cells. Ask:

- **Why would a wide variety of cell types be beneficial to an animal?** (Because tissue is composed of cells, tissues with many specialized functions are possible.)

- **How does comparing the type of tissue or organ systems animals have help group them?** (Animals with similar tissue, organs, and systems have more traits in common than animals with different kinds of tissue.)

Emphasize that the more cells, tissues, organs, and systems that organisms have in common or that are similar, the more closely related they are.

Developing Vocabulary

tissue The word *tissue* can also mean a thin fabric. Discuss how this meaning is helpful in understanding the word as a biological term.

organ Ask students to write a sentence showing how the words *cell* and *organ* are related.

system Have students name nonbiological systems, such as transportation or video game systems. Compare the common meaning of *system* with its biological meaning.

Read to Learn

Main Idea Animals can be classified using various characteristics.

What Traits Are Used to Classify Animals?

The building blocks of living things are cells. Whether an animal grows hair or feathers depends on the kinds of cells it has. Scientists often study the cells of animals in order to best group or classify them.

Similar cells that have the same job or function come together to make a **tissue**. Tissues of different kinds come together to make an **organ**, like a heart or brain.

Finally, a group of organs that work together to do a certain job makes up an organ **system**. For example, a bat's digestive system includes its mouth, stomach, and intestines. Birds have similar organs, but those of bats and cats are more like each other than like those of eagles.

Cells, tissues, organs, and systems—compare them carefully. By doing so, you can make groups that contain animals that are really closely related. They may be closely related even though at first glance they may look very different.

If you were to take a really close look, you would find that the wing of a bat is built more like the front leg of a cat than like the wing of an eagle. Bats have five sets of finger bones inside each wing. Eagles have a single fused finger bone inside each wing.

A 94

Eagle

Bat

Cat

The bones in the diagram above have been color-coded to show similar bones in each animal.

Lesson Outline

Name_____ Date_____

Lesson Outline Lesson 8

Animal Structure and Function

Fill in the blanks. Reading Skill: Summarize - questions 6, 7

What Traits Are Used to Classify Animals?

1. The building blocks of all living things are ____cells____

2. Scientists study the cells of animals in order to best group or ___classify___ them.

3. Similar cells that have the same job or function come together to make a(n) ___tissue___

4. Tissues of different kinds come together to make a(n) ___organ___ like a heart or brain.

5. An organ ___system___ is a group of organs that work together to do a certain job.

6. Animals that have backbones are members of a group called ___vertebrates___

7. Members of the group of animals called ___invertebrates___ have no backbones.

8. One of the simplest kinds of animals is a sponge which belongs to a group called ___Porifera___

9. Hydra, anemones, and jellyfish belong to a group called ___Cnidaria___ and do not have heads or tails.

Unit A · Structures of Plants and Animals | Use with textbook pages A92–A101 | 59

Reading in Science Resources, p. 59

Interpret Illustrations

Name_____ Date_____

Interpret Illustrations Lesson 8

What Traits Are Used to Classify Animals?

The picture below shows the forelimbs of a bat, a cat, and an eagle. Even though the bat flies like the eagle, which is a type of bird, its forelimb more closely resembles the forelimb of the cat, a mammal.

Answer the following questions about the picture above.

1. Which two forelimbs look most like each other?
   The bat's and the cat's forelimbs.

2. How do the bat's and the eagle's forelimbs differ?
   Bats have 5 sets of finger bones inside their forelimb. Eagles have a single fused finger bone inside their forelimb.

3. How does the covering of the bat's and eagle's forelimbs differ?
   The bat's forelimb is covered in hair while the eagle's forelimb is covered in feathers.

Unit A · Structures of Plants and Animals | Use with textbook page A94 | 61

Reading in Science Resources, p. 61

Vertebrates and Invertebrates

Scientists could use one similar trait to make a grouping. However, such groups might not make scientific sense. Why not? For example, this might lead to putting birds and bats in the same group because they both have wings and fly. However, these animals are very different. A bat is more like a cat than an eagle. That is, bats and cats have more similar characteristics than bats and birds do. Why?

For one thing, bats and cats have hair. For another thing, bats and cats feed their young milk. Eagles, like all birds, have feathers, not hair, and they don't feed their young milk. Then how do scientists put animals into different groups?

First, animals are divided into two large groups. One group is made up of animals that have backbones. The members of this group are called **vertebrates**. The members of the other group do not have backbones. They are called **invertebrates**.

As you might expect, vertebrates and invertebrates can be divided into smaller groups. What animals go into which group? Animals with similar traits go into the same groups. On the following pages are some of the groups of invertebrates and vertebrates. They are listed from the simplest to the most complex.

READING Summarize
What trait do scientists use to divide all animals into two main groups?

the presence or absence of a backbone

Even though bats and eagles have wings and fly, bats go in the same animal group as cats. Why is this true?

A 95

Reading | MiniLesson

Summarize

Develop Tell students that a summary briefly restates the meaning of a passage in the reader's own words. Summarizing helps you organize information.

Practice Have students summarize this page by writing a two- or three-sentence paragraph in response to the following questions: How are animal bodies organized? What can be learned from comparing the components of animals' bodies?

Developing the Main Idea

Give students other examples of animals that have a superficial trait in common but are classified differently. Ask:

- **What traits do a dolphin and a marlin have in common?** (Common traits are that both live in water, swim, and have fins and vertebra.)

- **What are differences between the two?** (Fish have vertical tail fins, dolphins have horizontal tail fins; fish have gills, dolphins have lungs; marlin lay eggs, dolphins bear live young; dolphins nurse their young, fish do not; dolphins have smooth skin; fish have scales;. dolphins are warm-blooded, fish are cold-blooded.)

- **What traits do a dolphin and a dog have in common?** (Common traits: Both give birth to live young, which they nurse; both have lungs.)

Point out that dolphins have hair in their fetal stage. Lead students toward the conclusion that dolphins have more significant traits in common with dogs than with fish.

▶ After Reading

Have students answer the red question in the student book as **ongoing assessment.**

Developing Vocabulary

vertebrate Have students place their hands on their spines and instruct them to feel an individual vertebra. While seated, have them turn their bodies side to side. Ask students why they think the root for *vertebra* means "to turn." (The backbone helps an animal turn its body.)

invertebrate Inform students that the prefix *in-* can mean *not.* Have students use this to recall the difference between invertebrates and vertebrates.

Invertebrates

Exploring the Main Idea

Emphasize the difference between vertebrates and invertebrates. Show students a mix of photos of both animal types. Include three of each of the following, as well as others: insects, mollusks, mammals, and fish. Have students classify them according to whether they have a backbone. Then have them try to arrange the animals into smaller groups based on common traits. Have them compare their groupings to those shown on this page and the following three pages.

Developing the Main Idea

As students read this page, focus on the traits that are used to differentiate among the groups of invertebrates. Ask:

- **What traits do sponges have that no other animal has? What other traits do all sponges have in common?** (They have no organs; they are covered with pores and live in water.)

- **What traits do all *Cnidaria* share?** (They live in water, have no heads or tails, and have soft bodies and tentacles. The stinging cells that poison prey are on the tentacles.)

- **What do flatworms have in common?** (Their bodies are flat, they have heads and tails, and they have some organs.)

- **How are they different from cnidarians?** (They have organs that cnidarians do not, and they do not have poison cells or tentacles.)

Invertebrates

One of the simplest kinds of animals is a sponge. Sponges belong to a group called *Porifera* (pawr·IF·er·ah). A sponge's body is like a hollow tube with lots of holes in it, called pores. Sponges have different kinds of cells that do different jobs. They have some tissues but no organs. Sponges live in water.

Sponge

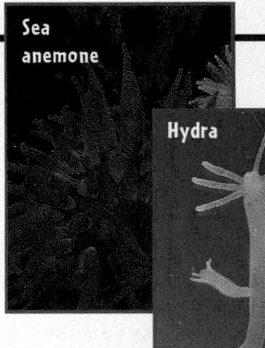

Sea anemone

Hydra

Hydras, sea anemones, and jellyfish are the *Cnidaria* (nigh·DAYR·ee·uh). They do not have heads or tails. They live in water. They have soft bodies and tentacles—long threadlike structures. At the end of each tentacle, they have cells that make poisons. They inject the poisons into small animals they kill to eat.

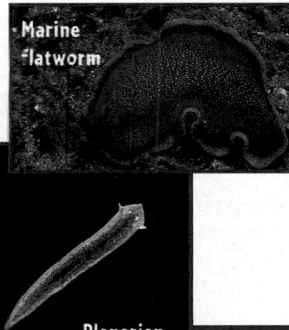

Marine flatworm

Flatworms are *Platyhelminthes* (pla·tee·hel·MIN·theez). Their bodies are flat. They have heads and tails. They also have organs cnidarians do not have. Most flatworms do not have true organ systems. Some flatworms live in water. Some live inside other animals.

Planarian

Roundworms, or *Nematoda* (nee·mah·TOHD·ah), have round bodies, a digestive system, and a simple nervous system. Roundworms live all over Earth, including inside plants and animals.

Hookworm

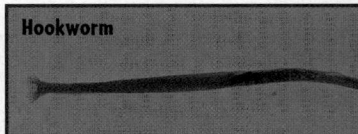

A 96

Reading Strategy

Paraphrase

Developing Reading Skills

Have students practice putting into their own words the identifying features of the animal life described on pp. A96–A99. Have them write down any paraphrases that they find helpful in understanding a particular life form. **Linguistic**

Inclusion

Objectivity

Point out that some of the life forms on p. A96, such as roundworms, can evoke unpleasant feelings in some people. Explain that our negative or positive feelings about an organism is of no use in classifying it, since classification is based on the objective description of actual traits and their similarities and differences.

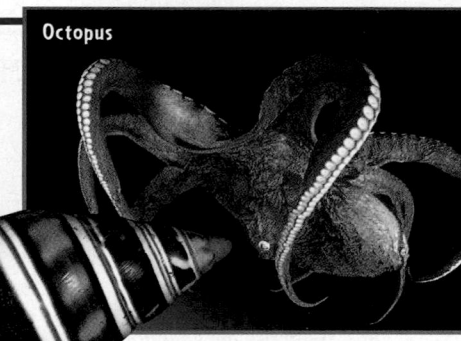

Earthworms belong to a group called segmented worms, or *Annelida* (AN·el·id·ah). Many segmented worms have eyes and other specialized organs, such as jaws or gills. Each of these animals also has a circulatory, digestive, and nervous system.

Earthworm

Octopus

Snails, clams, and octopuses belong to the *Mollusca* (MAHL·us·kah), the mollusks. Almost all mollusks have a shell. The shell may be either inside or outside the mollusk's body. Mollusks have three main body parts, a kind of foot, a tissue covering called a mantle, and a compartment holding internal organs. They have gills for breathing. They have jaws or other organs for capturing food. They each have a circulatory system for moving blood. More complex mollusks, like octopuses, have a well-developed brain.

Tree snail

Grasshopper

What has a tough outer skeleton, jointed legs, and a body made up of two, three, or more sections? It is an arthropod—a member of the group *Arthropoda* (AHR·thruh·pohd·ah). There are more arthropods on Earth than any other kind of animal. They include insects, spiders, centipedes, millipedes, lobsters, and crabs.

Spider

obster

Unlike arthropods, the *Echinodermata* (i·KIGH·noh·durm·ah·tah), or echinoderms, have a skeleton inside their bodies. Most also have a spiny skin and tubelike feet with suction cups.

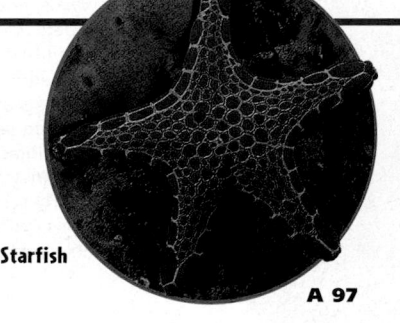

Starfish

A 97

Developing the Main Idea

Have students continue to make comparisons between specific animals to better understand the differences among the groups of invertebrates. Ask:

- **What do hydra and octopuses have in common? How are they different?** (They have soft bodies and tentacles and live in water. Octopuses do have a head, a foot, and organs, but do not have tentacles that have cells that make poison.)

- **How are the skeletons of arthropods and echinoderms different?** (Arthropods' skeletons are outside their bodies, and echinoderms' skeletons are inside their bodies.)

Thinking Further: *Making Generalizations*
Ask:

- **How do you know that octopuses have more traits in common with a snail than with a hydra?** (They are in the same group, *Mollusca*.)

Inclusion

Charting Invertebrate Traits

Have students make a chart on which to describe the similarities and differences among the kinds of invertebrates. They can use the following categories: *Backbone?, Body Type, Organs?, Water or Land, Skeleton?,* and *Special Traits.* Encourage students to add any other categories they think of. **Spatial; Logical**

Advanced Learners

Invertebrate Classes

Within each phylum (names given in italics in the lesson) there are subgroups called classes. Invite interested students to research and report to the class on the classes of one phylum and list the traits of the animals in that class. They should also give examples of animals in each class.
Linguistic

Vertebrates

Developing the Main Idea

After students have read about the three classes of fish, help them to compare and contrast the traits of each by asking:

- **Which two groups have cartilage, and which one group has bones?** (*Agnatha* and *Chondrichthyes,* cartilage; *Osteichthyes,* bones)

- **Which group doesn't have a backbone? What does it have to make it a vertebrate?** (*Agnatha;* has a tough nerve cord down its back)

- **Which group has a backbone made of cartilage?** (*Chondrichthyes*)

Point out that *Agnatha* and *Chondrichthyes* do not have scales. Ask:

- **How does this make them different from bony fish?** (Bony fish have scales.)

- **How does the adaptation of a gill flap help the bony fish survive?** (It allows them to breathe while staying still.)

- **What other adaptation of the bony fish makes it different from a shark? How does it help the bony fish survive?** (Bony fish have a swim bladder that allows them to hover at any depth.)

Vertebrates

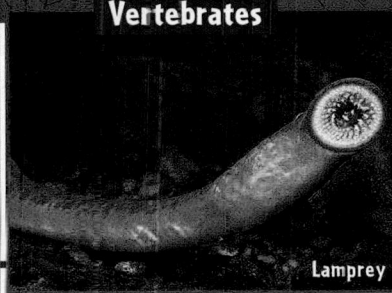
Lamprey

The simplest fish, the *Agnatha* (AG·nah·thuh), do not have jaws or bones. Their skeletons are made of tissue called cartilage. These fish do not have backbones, but each does have a tough nerve cord that runs down its back. They look more like big worms than like fish.

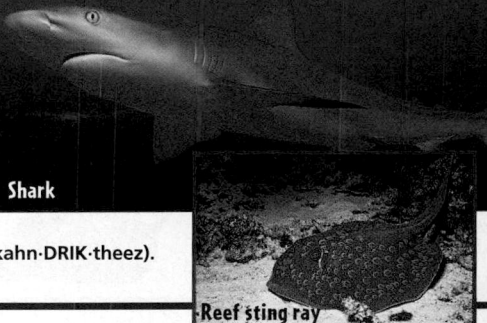
Shark

Reef sting ray

Like those of lampreys and hagfish, the skeletons of sharks and rays are made of cartilage, not bone. However, the cartilage running down their backs is made of a chain of smaller parts called vertebrae. Unlike lampreys and hagfish, sharks and rays have jaws. They also have paired fins. These fish are *Chondrichthyes* (kahn·DRIK·theez).

Tropical fish

Bony fish, or *Osteichthys* (AHS·tee·ik·theez), have bones instead of cartilage. Many have fins that look like fans with spokes in them. These fish have a movable flap over their gills. The movement of this flap lets bony fish breathe while staying still. Unlike sharks, most bony fish have an organ called a swim bladder, or air sac, that allows them to hover at any depth.

Frog

A 98

Salamander

Frogs, toads, and salamanders are *Amphibia* (am·FIB·ee·uh), the amphibians. Most adult amphibians have four legs and skin that is not covered with scales. Adult amphibians breathe with lungs instead of gills. In their early stages of life, amphibians live in water. As adults, most live on land.

English Language Learners

Adjectives for Vertebrates

Challenge students to list all the adjectives they can think of to describe the different characteristics of vertebrates. (Possible answers: scaly, dry, feathery, light, slimy, finned, smooth, slithery, furry, hairy, slippery) Then have them list the kinds of vertebrates to which each adjective refers.

Linguistic

Science Background

Lampreys

Several types of lampreys are common to North American waters. Most species of lamprey are not parasites. All lampreys spend their first four years as larvae, living as filter feeders buried in the mud at the mouth of small streams and rivers. Eventually, they change into their adult form through metamorphosis.

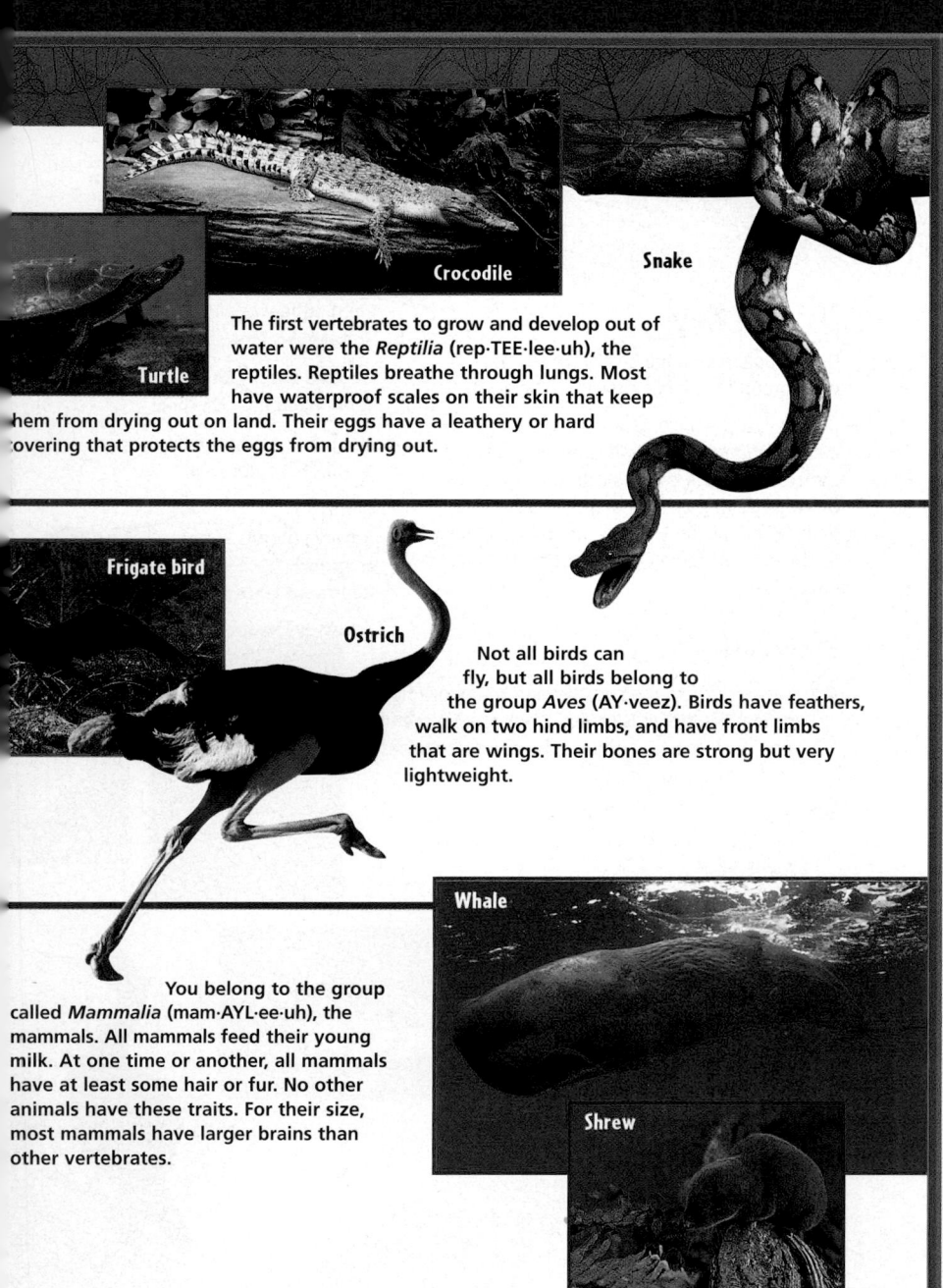

Crocodile

Snake

Turtle

The first vertebrates to grow and develop out of water were the *Reptilia* (rep·TEE·lee·uh), the reptiles. Reptiles breathe through lungs. Most have waterproof scales on their skin that keep them from drying out on land. Their eggs have a leathery or hard covering that protects the eggs from drying out.

Frigate bird

Ostrich

Not all birds can fly, but all birds belong to the group *Aves* (AY·veez). Birds have feathers, walk on two hind limbs, and have front limbs that are wings. Their bones are strong but very lightweight.

Whale

You belong to the group called *Mammalia* (mam·AYL·ee·uh), the mammals. All mammals feed their young milk. At one time or another, all mammals have at least some hair or fur. No other animals have these traits. For their size, most mammals have larger brains than other vertebrates.

Shrew

A 99

Developing the Main Idea

As students read this page, have them focus on the traits that make each group of vertebrates unique. Then ask:

- **Why must reptiles have waterproof scales and a leathery or hard egg covering?** (Because they spend their lives on land, they must be able to protect themselves and their eggs from drying out.)

- **Birds' bones are nearly hollow. They are strengthend by internal struts. How does this adaptation help them?** (It makes them weigh less so they are more able to fly.)

- **What other adaptations allow flight?** (wings, two hind legs, feathers)

- **What traits are unique to mammals?** (Fur; producing milk to feed their young; most have larger brains than other vertebrates.)

Thinking Further: *Inferring*
Ask:

- **What if you found an unusual vertebrate swimming in a pond? The animal laid eggs, had four legs, lungs, and smooth, moist skin. What group of organisms would it belong to?** (amphibians)

Technology

- **Science Experiences Videotapes**
  Camels, Cacti, and You: What All Living Things Share (Package 3)

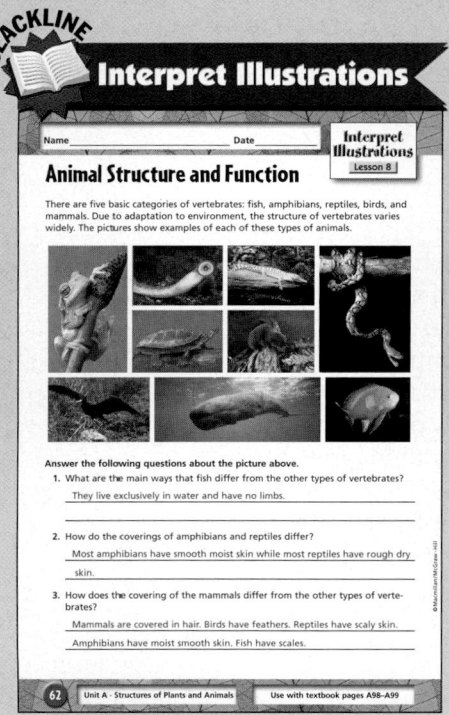

Name _____ Date _____

Interpret Illustrations Lesson 8

Animal Structure and Function

There are five basic categories of vertebrates: fish, amphibians, reptiles, birds, and mammals. Due to adaptation to environment, the structure of vertebrates varies widely. The pictures show examples of each of these types of animals.

Answer the following questions about the picture above.

1. What are the main ways that fish differ from the other types of vertebrates?
   They live exclusively in water and have no limbs.

2. How do the coverings of amphibians and reptiles differ?
   Most amphibians have smooth moist skin while most reptiles have rough dry skin.

3. How does the covering of the mammals differ from the other types of vertebrates?
   Mammals are covered in hair. Birds have feathers. Reptiles have scaly skin. Amphibians have moist smooth skin. Fish have scales.

62   Unit A · Structures of Plants and Animals   Use with textbook pages A98–A99

Reading in Science Resources, p. 62

SCIENCE
Reading Strategy

Compare and Contrast
Developing Reading Skills
Use examples of two different groups of vertebrates described on pages A98–A99. For example, have students compare similar characteristics of reptiles and birds. Some dinosaurs (reptiles) are thought to have been related to birds. Have students look for information that might support this theory and report their findings to the class. **Linguistic**

Process Skill
BUILDER

Using a Key

Science Process Skills *classify,* observe, interpret data

Resources Activity Resources, pp. 39–40

Pacing 20–30 minutes

Grouping individuals

Procedure

3 Have students write down the name of the bird they picked.

Answers to Drawing Conclusions

No; it's only useful if you are comparing the five kinds of birds shown. Other birds may have similar traits of each of the five listed.

Process Skill
BUILDER

SKILL Classify

Using a Key

How should an animal be classified? Into what group of animals should it be placed?

One way to classify organisms is by using a *classification key.* A classification key lists choices describing characteristics of organisms. It is a series of pairs of statements with directions to follow. These directions will eventually lead you to the identity of the organism you have chosen.

Key to Birds

1. Webbed feet........Go to 3.
   No webbed feet...Go to 2.

2. Hooked bill......Red-tailed hawk
   No hooked bill...Cardinal

3. Flat bill.....Mallard duck
   No flat bill....Go to 4.

4. Pouch...
   Brown pelican
   No pouch...
   Red-faced cormorant

Procedure

1 **Observe** Use the classification key, above right, to identify the birds shown. Starting with the first pair of statements, choose the one that applies to the bird you picked.

2 **Interpret Data** Follow the statement's directions. It will lead you to another pair of statements.

3 Keep following the directions until you come to the identity of the bird you chose.

Drawing Conclusions

Do you think this key would be helpful in identifying birds in your neighborhood? Explain.

A 100

Process Skills
MiniLesson

Classify

Develop Students use the skill *classify* in the Skill Builder. This skill involves grouping materials that share properties. The properties can be used to group many materials or objects into smaller and smaller groups.

Practice Have groups of six or eight students classify their shirts. Ask them to think of a characteristic that will divide the six shirts into two groups (example: short sleeve/long sleeve).

Then for each of the two groups, divide using another characteristic (example: striped/not striped). Continue to divide groups by characteristics until there is only one shirt in each group. Have them draw a diagram of their classification system. A complete list of Science Process Skills appears on page S7. **Social; Logical**

Lesson Review

Why It Matters

Nature holds many secrets and presents many mysteries. It is the job of scientists to discover the secrets and solve the mysteries. Classifying animals helps do this. Among other things, it shows which animals are most closely related to one another. It also can show the order in which they appeared on Earth. Classification can be thought of as a kind of calendar of life on Earth.

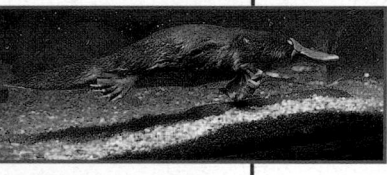

Think and Write

1. Name three traits you might use to classify an animal.

2. What are the building blocks of living things?

3. What is the main difference between an invertebrate and a vertebrate?

4. **Classify** Name a trait you would use to classify a fish as belonging to either the lamprey and hagfish group or the shark and ray group.

5. **Critical Thinking** Which do you think are more closely related—whales and goldfish or whales and mice? Explain.

A 101

Informal Assessment

Easy/Average Ask students to collect and bring to school pictures from magazines and newspapers showing vertebrates and invertebrates. Assemble the pictures on two sides of a bulletin board—one side for vertebrates, the other for invertebrates. The animals can also be further grouped within each side.

Challenge Invite students to make up an animal that belongs to a specific group of invertebrates or vertebrates. Have them describe the animal's characteristics to a classmate, who must then determine the group to which it belongs.

---

3 Lesson Review

Answers to Think and Write

1. Possible answers: shape, size, color, and specific characteristics such as scales, feathers, and hair. (pp. A94–A95)

2. Cells are the building blocks of living things. (p. A94)

3. Vertebrates have backbones; invertebrates do not. (p. A96)

4. **Classify** Jaws; the lamprey and hagfish group lack them, while the shark and ray group have them. (pp. A96-A99)

5. **Critical Thinking** Whales and mice; they both have hair, and females of both species nurse their young; fish have neither of these characteristcs. (pp. A96–A99)

Summarize

Check students' understanding by having them write a brief summary of the lesson in their own words.

LITERATURE LINK

Have students read the Grade-Level Science Book, *Dino Flight*. Additional books to read can be found on TE p. A1•b.

WRITING LINK

You may want to point out that the platypus is covered in fur and nurses its young. While the platypus is a mammal, students may perceive it to be a bird or reptile.

MATH LINK

The blue whale is 825 times (3,300 cm ÷ 4 cm = 825) or 3,296 cm (3,300 cm − 4 cm = 3,296 cm) longer than the bat.

Objective

■ Identify that certain animals also go through changes in their life cycles where the young do not look like their parents.

Build on Prior Knowledge
Ask:

■ **Do you know what a tadpole or a caterpillar is?** (Some students will know that tadpoles grow to be frogs and caterpillars grow to be butterflies.)

■ **How are these young animals different from most other young animals?** (They look nothing like the adults or parents.)

Animal Life Cycles

Developing the Main Idea
When students have read the article, focus on the process of metamorphosis by asking such questions as:

■ **What is metamorphosis?** (A series of changes some animals go through as they develop, in which the young start out looking nothing like the adults.)

■ **What changes occur as a frog develops from an egg to an adult?** (First, the egg hatches into a tadpole. Gradually, the tadpole grows legs, loses its tail, and grows lungs that replace its gills. Then it climbs onto the ground to live, and is an adult.)

Science Magazine

ANIMAL LIFE CYCLES

What if you saw a tadpole but had never seen a frog? Would people have a hard time convincing you a frog was a grown-up tadpole?

When you see seedlings, you can predict that the fully grown plants will be on stems and have leaves. However, some baby animals look nothing like the adults. They change shape by going through metamorphosis.

Frogs lay eggs in ponds and lakes. The eggs hatch into tadpoles. They must live in water because they have gills, like fish, not lungs.

The tadpoles begin to change. They grow legs. Their tails disappear. They develop lungs and lose their gills. Now they can live on land and in the water!

Insects have two kinds of metamorphosis—complete and incomplete. During complete metamorphosis an egg hatches into a wormlike larva. It eats a lot and grows to become a pupa. This is a resting phase. Many body changes take place. Some larvae spin protective cocoons. Finally, the adult winged insect emerges.

During incomplete metamorphosis the insect changes shape gradually. An egg hatches into a nymph that looks like a small adult without wings. The nymph grows and slowly changes. Finally, it grows wings and becomes an adult.

Eggs   Tadpole with gills   Tadpole with limbs   Young frog

A 102

 **English Language**

Interpreting Diagrams
Ask students to explain metamorphosis using the diagrams in the text or by drawing their own. Invite students to make paper puppets and use them to act out the stages of metamorphosis in frogs or insects.
Kinesthetic

Egg Larva Pupa Adult Butterfly

What Did I Learn?

1. To go from egg to adult, a frog goes through a process called

A childhood
B adolescence
C the pupa stage
D metamorphosis

2. The stages of complete metamorphosis are

F egg larva pupa adult
G egg larva nymph pupa adult
H egg nymph pupa adult
J egg nymph adult

Egg Nymph Adult Grasshopper

AT THE COMPUTER Visit www.mhscience02.com to learn more about metamorphosis.

A 103

■ **What are the four stages of complete metamorphosis in insects?** (egg, larva, pupa, and adult)

■ **How does a larva compare to a nymph?** (A larva is the second stage of complete metamorphosis; it looks nothing like the adult insect. A nymph is the second stage of incomplete metamorphosis; it looks like a small, wingless adult.)

Thinking Further: *Drawing Conclusions*
Ask:

■ **Why would butterflies have evolved over time so that caterpillars have teeth and adult butterflies have a long hollow tongue?** (The caterpillars must have needed the food in leaves, so they evolved with teeth and jaws to eat leaves. Nectar from flowers must have been a better food for a butterfly than leaves, and so butterflies evolved with hollow tongues.)

Test Prep: **What Did I Learn?**

1. D

2. F

Summarize
Check students' understanding by having them write a brief summary of the magazine in their own words.

Science Background

Caterpillar Defenses

Fat caterpillars are a favorite food of animals such as birds and toads. To protect themselves, caterpillars have devised a number of clever strategies. Some caterpillars are covered with spiky hairs. Others are so well camouflaged they look like the branches on which they rest. Still others are brightly colored and have poison within them that will taste bad or even kill predators, who quickly learn to recognize the bright colors as dangerous.

LESSON 9 Animal Adaptations

Objectives

- Explore how sow bugs adapt to their environment.
- Compare and contrast various forms of animal adaptations.
- Understand that certain characteristics are inherited.
- Describe the impact of hybridization and crossbreeding on animal diversity.

Resources

- Activity Resources, pp. 41–45
- Reading in Science Resources, pp. 65–70
- Vocabulary Cards
- Reading Aid Transparency A9
- School to Home Activities, p. 7

Build on Prior Knowledge

Have students discuss what they know about adaptations and their influence on survival. Have them list ways humans adapt to changes in the their environment, such as shivering or putting on heavy clothing. Ask them to decide which adaptations are physical adaptations and which are learned behaviors.

1 Get Ready

Developing the Main Idea
Ask:

- **Why would an animal appear white in the winter and brown in the summer?** (Possible answers: as a way of hiding in the snow in winter and in the grass or on the ground in summer.)

LESSON 9 Animal Adaptations

Vocabulary

mimicry, A106

camouflage, A108

protective coloration, A109

heredity, A110

hybrid, A112

crossbreeding, A112

diversity, A114

Get Ready

Alaska is home to many animals, including the snowshoe hare. You might think this hare is a little strange. Its fur changes color from white in the winter to brown in the summer. How does this help the snowshoe hare survive in its environment?

Process Skill
You experiment when you perform a test to support or disprove a hypothesis.

A 104

Cross Curricular Books

Additional Outside Reading

The Galapagos Islands
A Strange and Beautiful Place

written by Gary Apple
Illustrated by Howard S. Friedman

To order, see page A1·b.

Reading Strategy

Ask Questions

Developing Reading Skills
Have students ask questions as they read p. A104 and the steps of the Explore Activity on p. A105. For example, why are sow bugs found in damp places? What is the reason for each step?

Explore Activity

How Do Sow Bugs Adapt to Their Environment?

Materials
10 sow bugs
tray
paper towels
water

Procedure

BE CAREFUL! Handle live animals with care. Wash your hands well when you finish this activity.

1. **Observe** Place a sow bug in the center of the tray, and observe it. What traits does it have that enable it to live in the soil and under decaying wood or leaves? Record your observations.

2. **Observe** Touch the sow bug. How does it react?

3. **Experiment** Place all the sow bugs in the center of the tray. Do the animals tend to stay together?

4. **Experiment** Move the sow bugs to one end of the tray. Dampen three or four paper towels, and place them in the opposite end of the tray. Observe for several minutes. Record your observations. When the animals move, do they tend to move faster in the dry section or wet section of the box?

Drawing Conclusions

1. **Infer** How do sow bugs protect themselves?

2. **Infer** Can the behavior of sow bugs when exposed to moisture be related to their survival? If so, how?

3. **Going Further: Experiment** Design an experiment to test the reactions of sow bugs to light. Record your results.

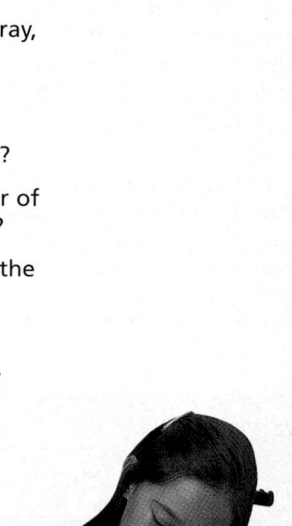

A 105

Alternative Explore Activity

Materials three earthworms, moist soil, plastic jar, foil, dark paper, cornmeal, tablespoon

Earthworms and Light Fill jar 3/4 full with soil. Place cornmeal on top. Add worms. Cover the top with foil. Observe the worms after one day. (Worms moved to the center of the dirt.) Replace the foil and cover the jar's side with the dark paper. Observe after one day. (Worms move toward the sides.) Describe how the worms respond to light and why.

Spatial; Linguistic

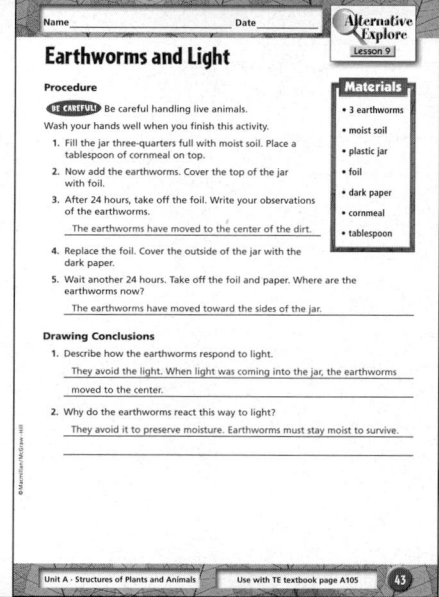

Activity Resources, p. 43

Explore Activity

How Do Sow Bugs Adapt to Their Environment?

Science Process Skills *observe, experiment, infer*

Resources, Activity Resources, pp. 41–42

Pacing 20–30 minutes

Grouping small groups

Plan Ahead Keep sow bugs in a moist, dark place at room temperature. Sow bugs are not insects; they are crustaceans and have gills.

Procedure

Be Careful! Tell students to handle live animals with care and to wash their hands when finished.

1. Traits include hard overlapping plates on their backs, a flattened body, brownish or slate gray color, and seven pairs of legs.

2. Sow bugs do not react to touch. Pillbugs will curl into a ball when touched.

3. Answers may vary. The bugs may scatter. They may also huddle.

4. They tend to move toward the wet end and move slower there. Note: This change may not occur on very humid days.

Answers to Drawing Conclusions

1. Possible answers: The plates protect their bodies; they huddle to conserve moisture; pillbugs roll into a ball.

2. Yes; sow bugs gravitate toward moisture. They must stay moist to survive.

3. Possible answer: Place sow bugs in a box that is half in light and half shaded. Then observe.

 Inquiry Students can ask their own questions to explore, such as: How do sow bugs react to temperature changes? (Because they are cold-blooded, they slow down in cold and move faster when heated. Prolonged exposure to temperatures over 40°C may kill the sow bugs.)

Technology

- When time is short, preview the activity with the **Explore Activity Video.**

2 Read to Learn

How Do Animals Adapt?

Before Reading
Have students try to answer the red question at the top of the page.

Developing the Main Idea
Ask students to think about how people learn from experience how to avoid certain plants and animals. For example, over time people have learned which kinds of mushrooms are poisonous and which are edible. Ask students to provide other examples of this learning. (Possible answers: Don't touch thorn bushes, avoid poison ivy or sumac, don't touch cacti, don't touch the young of a sharp-toothed animal or large bird.) Ask:

- **Do you think a bird, after getting sick from eating a monarch butterfly, will eat another one? Why or why not?** (No; because it learned from eating the first that they taste bad and make it sick.)

Developing Vocabulary

mimicry Ask students to write a paragraph explaining how mimicry works as a defense against predators. Paragraphs must include a paraphrasing of the definition of *mimicry*.

Read to Learn

Main Idea Animals have certain characteristics, behaviors, and adaptations that help them survive.

How Do Animals Adapt?

Certain traits animals have help them to survive in their environment. Such traits are called adaptations.

An animal has many adaptations. One important group of adaptations helps the animal keep from getting eaten by a *predator* (an animal that might eat it). How can an animal avoid being eaten?

Through experience, you have learned to avoid certain things. For example, if you see a buzzing black-and-yellow striped insect, you are not likely to try to touch it. Why? You have learned that insects that look like this can give you a painful sting. They are called yellow jackets. Animals that feed on insects have also learned to avoid yellow jackets.

They also avoid a harmless insect called a syrphid (SUHR·fuhd) fly. Why? It looks very much like a yellow jacket. In nature, looking like something else—especially something unpleasant—is called **mimicry**.

Mimicry

One of these insects stings. One does not. To be safe, insect-eating animals avoid both. This helps both the wasp (left) and the harmless syrphid fly (right) to survive. Animals avoid the harmless fly because it mimics a stinging wasp.

A 106

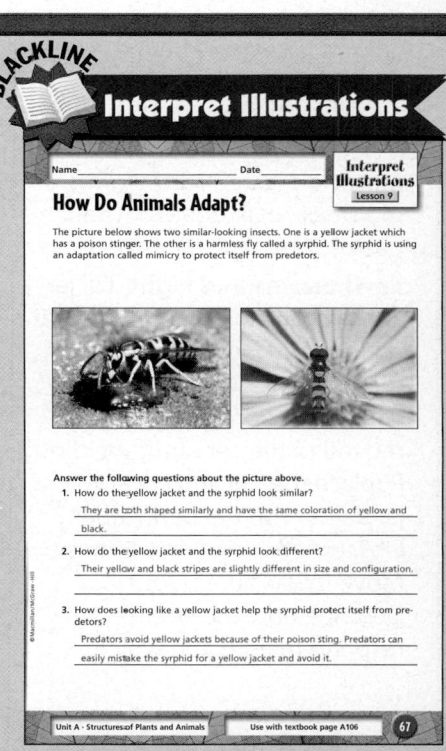

When food spoils, it tastes bad. If you don't want to get sick, you quickly dispose of spoiled food. Some birds might like to make a meal out of the good-tasting viceroy butterfly. However, birds often avoid gulping down a viceroy. Why? The viceroy looks like a monarch butterfly, which, birds have learned, tastes awful.

You are probably very careful when you meet a cat you don't know. You have learned that its sharp claws can give you a nasty scratch. Certain predators have learned the same thing about thorny plants. The predators stay away from such plants.

This gives thornbugs protection from being eaten. That's because thornbugs look like thorns. When the bugs cluster on the stem of a plant, a predator mistakes them for the thorns on a plant. The predator stays away, and the thornbugs live to see another day.

Viceroy

By mimicking something that predators avoid, an animal has a better chance of not being eaten.

Monarch

▷ **Why is mimicry a good adaptation for an animal to have?**

Birds avoid eating the good-tasting viceroy butterfly (top) because it looks like the awful-tasting monarch butterfly (bottom).

Monarch larvae (caterpillars) feed on milkweed. Milkweed contains a substance that can make animals ill. Birds that have eaten one monarch butterfly learn to avoid eating both monarchs and look-alike viceroys.

The dark "thorn" on the branch is a thornbug. Because thornbugs look like thorns that can scratch, predators stay away.

A 107

Using the Illustrations

Draw students' attention to the photos on pages A106 and A107. Have them describe how the three animals use mimicry for survival. (The syrphid fly looks like a stinging wasp; the viceroy butterfly looks like the foul-tasting monarch; the thornbug looks like a thorn on a plant.) Ask:

■ **What is the effect of mimicry for all three animals?** (It fools predators.)

Have students examine the syrphid fly and the viceroy butterfly. Ask:

■ **What do the coloring of the animals have in common?** (The colors are bright against a black background.)

■ **Do both the mimicked and mimicking animals benefit from this adaptation?** (The mimicked organism benefits because predators may have tasted others of its species and will therefore avoid it, and the mimicking animal benefits because it looks like the dangerous original.)

Point out that both the butterfly and fly imitate other animals with bright coloring. Explain that the bright colors are easily recognized by predators, especially those without keen eyesight, and that the colors are called warning coloration.

▶ **After Reading**

Have students answer the red question in the student book as **ongoing assessment.**

Science Background

Defense Mechanisms

Some animals have behavioral defenses against predators. Many amphibians pretend to be dead when threatened. Other animals put on elaborate displays. The Australian frilled lizard spreads its wide neck frill and displays a gaping mouth. Still other animals use group defenses. When threatened by wolves, adult musk oxen form a protective circle around their young, horns pointing outward.

Reading Strategy

Build on Prior Knowledge
Developing Reading Skills
Ask students to describe the mental images that the text on pp. A106–A107 evokes. Then, to prepare them for the discussion of camoflauge on p. A108, ask:

■ **What kind of clothing would make you harder to see in a forest? In a snowy landscape?** (a poncho or other outerwear with brown and green patterns; a parka or other snowsuit with white and gray patterns) **Linguistic**

What Is Camouflage?

Before Reading
Have students try to answer the red question at the top of the page.

Developing the Main Idea
Focus on how camouflage aids animals in survival. Show students pictures of soldiers or hunters wearing camouflage outfits. Ask students why they think these people are dressed this way. (to hide) Then ask why they don't wear bright clothing. (The people or animal they are hiding from would see them.) Direct their attention to the leaf butterfly. Ask:

- **What protects this animal from being eaten?** (It looks like a leaf.)

- **What behavior must the animal have to benefit from its appearance?** (It must hold very still when in danger.)

Developing Vocabulary

camouflage The word comes from *camoufler*, French for to "disguise." Ask students why they would wear a disguise (to sneak up on or follow someone unseen, for fun). Ask them how camouflage helps "disguise" an animal.

protective coloration Students may see familiar smaller words within the larger word: *protect, color.* Have them use the smaller words to write possible meanings for the larger word.

What Is Camouflage?

At one time or another, most people have dreamed about being invisible. For one thing, if people can't see you, they can't hurt you. You can't make yourself invisible. Neither can animals. Even so, you can make yourself look so much like your surroundings that you are almost invisible.

An animal that does not move, or moves very, very slowly, and looks like its surroundings is camouflaged. **Camouflage** is another important adaptation that helps animals avoid their predators.

There are two basic kinds of camouflage, or blending in with the environment. One has to do with an animal's shape. The other has to do with its color. Let's start off by exploring how shape can camouflage an animal.

What if you were a bird hunting for a butterfly? You would not be tempted to eat a leaf. That is what protects the leaf butterfly from being eaten. The wings of the leaf butterfly are shaped like the leaves of a plant. When this butterfly is perched on the stem of a plant, or resting on a forest floor littered with leaves, it is very hard to see. A bird passes it by as if it were not there.

Leaf butterflies look so much like leaves that a bird looking for a meal will fly right by.

A 108

 Math **MiniLesson**

Probability

Develop Three insects are sitting on a plant. A leaf butterfly and a thorn bug are sitting on a branch. A pale-colored butterfly is sitting on a green leaf. Predict what might happen if a hungry bird comes by. Which insect is the bird most likely to grab? Have students discuss the possible outcomes.

The bird is *most likely* to grab the pale-colored butterfly sitting on the green leaf. The bird is *least likely* to grab the leaf butterfly or the thorn bug sitting on the

branch. It is *equally likely* that the bird will eat either the leaf butterfly or the thorn bug.

Practice A bag contains 3 blue, 3 orange, and 6 red marbles. If one marble is drawn, which outcome is most likely? (that a red marble will be chosen)

Which outcomes are equally likely? (that a blue or orange marble will be chosen)

 **Inclusion**

Find It

Materials fifty toothpicks—25 toothpicks of one color and 25 of another, sheet of paper of one of the toothpick colors

Toss the toothpicks onto the paper. Have one student pick up, one at a time, as many toothpicks as possible in 15–20 seconds. Find the percentage of each color of "picked up" toothpick. Discuss which were harder to pick up, and why. (Ones the same color as the paper; they blended in.)
Logical; Social

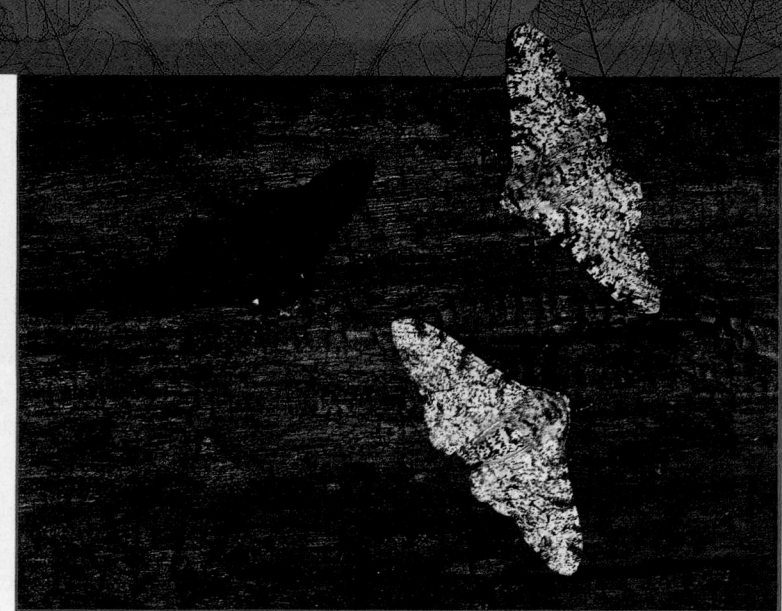

Birds can more easily spot a light-colored peppered moth (right) against a dark background than a dark-colored peppered moth (left) against a dark background.

About 150 years ago, England was home to two kinds of peppered moths. One kind was light colored. The other kind was dark colored. Birds fed on both kinds of moths, many of which clung to the trunks of trees.

However, gradually the light-colored moths seemed to be disappearing. The birds were eating more of these moths than the dark-colored ones. What was causing this?

Nearby factories were pouring dark, sticky smoke into the air. The smoke stuck to the trunks of trees. The light-colored moths stood out against this background. The dark-colored moths blended in with the background.

Since the birds could more easily see the light-colored moths, the birds were eating more light-colored moths than dark-colored moths. This is an example of a kind of camouflage called **protective coloration**. The color of the dark peppered moths protected them from predators.

▶ **How does camouflage help an animal survive?**
By blending into its surroundings—being camouflaged—an animal is difficult for a predator to see.

A 109

Using the Illustrations

Have students turn back to the first page of this lesson. Ask students what kind of adaptation the animal has to help it survive. (camouflage) Then ask what kind of camouflage the animal has. (protective coloration) Redirect students to the photo of the moths on page A109. Then ask:

- **What was causing the increase in the number of dark-colored moths?** (air pollution)
- **What do you think might have happened as the air pollution was reduced?** (The trees wouldn't be as dark, so more light-colored moths and fewer dark-colored moths would survive.)

Exploring the Main Idea

Expand the discussion of camouflage from prey to predators. Show students a picture of a lioness hiding in tall grass. Ask:

- **How does camouflage help this lioness survive?** (It helps her to hide from her prey, making it easier for her to sneak up and capture an animal.)

Then show students a picture of a herd of zebra, preferably one in which they are running. Explain that the zebras' stripes help camouflage them as they run. They make the zebras appear as a single mass rather than individuals, making it more difficult for a predator to pick one out for capture.

▶ **After Reading**

Have students answer the red question in the student book as **ongoing assessment.**

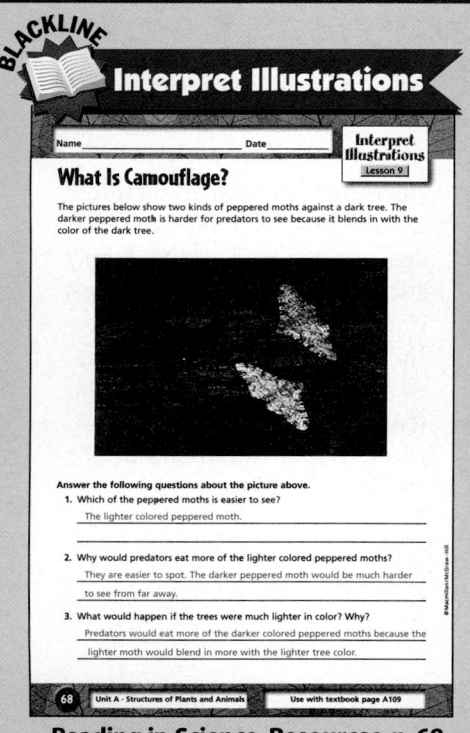

Reading in Science Resources, p. 68

What Is Inherited?

Before Reading
Have students try to answer the red question at the top of the first text column.

Developing the Main Idea
Before reading this page, draw students into a discussion of learned and inherited behaviors in humans. Ask:

- **What happens when you touch a hot stove?** (You quickly pull your hand back *automatically*.)

Explain that this is a reflex—a simple behavior. Ask:

- **Can you give some other examples of reflexes?** (blinking, knee jerks when hit)
- **Why wouldn't you touch the hot stove a second time?** (You've *learned* that this hurts.)
- **Can you give some other examples of learned reflexes?** (any conscious human action or acquired skill)

Explain that most human behavior is learned. Then focus on animal instincts and learned behavior. Ask:

- **What are some examples of instinctive behavior?** (Possible answers: fighting, nest building, migration, hibernation, mating, defense, escape.)
- **How do instincts help an animal?** (They help the animal survive.)
- **How are instincts different from reflexes?** (They are more complex, usually involving a series of actions.)
- **How are behaviors learned?** (by watching an adult animal)
- **How do learned behaviors help an animal?** (They help the animal survive.)
- **Can learned behavior be inherited?** (No; each generation must learn the behavior.)

Developing Vocabulary

heredity Explain that heredity is the passing of traits from parents to offspring. Add that traits can be either physical or behavioral. Ask students to use *heredity* in a sentence that conveys its meaning; for example, An animal's fur color is the result of heredity.

Nest building is an inherited trait. Robins (left) build their nests of twigs. Penguins (above) build their nests of pebbles.

What Is Inherited?

Animals behave in many different ways. They learn some kinds of behavior, like avoiding bad-tasting insects. You may have noticed learned behaviors in your pet. For example, if your cat cries for food every time it hears the electric can opener, your cat has learned that the sound of the can opener can mean mealtime. No wonder your cat acts disappointed when the canned food turns out to be something it doesn't like. However, not all behaviors are learned. Certain other kinds of behavior seem to be automatic.

Young birds will build the same kinds of nests their parents build. They do this even if the young birds have never seen their parents build a nest. In other words, birds do not learn how to build nests. They do it automatically.

Scientists would say that nest building is *inherited*, or passed down from one generation to the next. An inherited behavior is one that is not learned. It is done automatically. This inherited behavior is called *instinct*. The passing of inherited traits from parents to offspring is called **heredity**.

Many physical traits of an animal are also inherited. For example, the shape of a bird's feet and beak is inherited. The color of its feathers is inherited, too. This is easy to see, since young birds have the same-shaped feet and beaks as their parents.

A 110

Inclusion

Family Resemblances
Have students collect pictures of members of their own families—or of a well-known family, such as those of the Kennedy or Bush families. Then have them group together pictures of family members with similar features that show a family resemblance that might be the result of heredity. **Spatial**

Hawk

Duck

Woodpecker

The feet and beaks of birds are inherited physical traits. All woodpeckers have feet adapted for grasping the sides of tree trunks. All hawks have feet armed with claws adapted for grabbing smaller animals. All ducks have webbed feet adapted for swimming.

What physical traits are not inherited? Those that the environment can change. If there is not much food around, an animal's weight and size may be smaller than normal. Weight and size are physical traits, but they may not be inherited. Of course, certain animals—such as elephants—tend to be bigger and heavier than others—such as mice. Such tendencies are inherited.

The average weight and size of an elephant is greater than the average weight and size of a mouse. Even so, some elephants will be larger and heavier than others. Some mice will be larger and heavier than other mice. In other words, some traits are affected by both heredity and the environment.

 How are animal behaviors that are inherited different from those that are learned?

Behaviors that are done automatically, that are passed down from one generation to the next, such as nest building in birds, are inherited behaviors. They are not learned from experience.

Although gerbils are smaller than elephants, the environment can make some gerbils bigger than other gerbils and some elephants bigger than other elephants.

A 111

Developing the Main Idea

Discuss how physical traits are influenced by both heredity and by the environment. Ask:

■ **Is the general size of a duck inherited or controlled by the environment?** (inherited)

■ **What environmental factors can influence the duck's actual size?** (the amount of food available, amount of nurturing)

■ **How might an inherited behavior like nest building be influenced by the environment?** (Possible answer: A shortage of a certain material might cause a bird to use another nesting material or not build a nest at all.)

Thinking Further: *Making Generalizations*

Ask:

■ **Some people are naturally very strong and muscular. What if a person who is not naturally strong lifts weights and builds up large muscles? Can that person's children inherit the large muscles?** (No; that person's muscles were not an inherited physical trait; the environment, in this case, exercise, caused them.)

▶ After Reading

Have students answer the red question in the student book as **ongoing assessment**.

What Is a Hybrid?

Before Reading
Have students try to answer the red question at the top of the text column.

Developing the Main Idea
Have students think of familiar animals or plants that are of the same species. Have them think about how each might be changed for the better or improved by having certain traits of another organism. Discuss familiar fruits and vegetables that are new-and-improved hybrids or crossbreeds that come from parent plants that are quite different. Ask:

■ **Are horses and donkeys the same species?** (No.)

Explain that a hybrid can be a cross between two animals of different groups (species or subspecies) or the same species with different traits. Because animals of different species rarely mate, most animal hybrids are artificially bred by people. Ask:

■ **What physical traits does a mule have in common with a donkey? A horse?** (donkey: long ears, a tufted tail, slender legs, small hooves; horse: size, muscles)

■ **Can two mules mate to produce another mule?** (No; mules are sterile; they only result from the mating of a horse with a donkey.)

Technology

■ **Science Experiences Videotapes**
Staying Alive: Adaptations for Survival (Package 4)

Developing Vocabulary

hybrid *Hybrid* is a term used to describe any mixing of influences, cultures, or backgrounds. Some modern musical styles are called hybrids of earlier forms. Ask students to give examples.

crossbreeding Break larger words into smaller roots: *cross* and *breed*. *Cross* can mean to mix, and *breed* means a specific group of animals, such as poodles. Have students use these meanings as clues for *crossbreeding*.

Donkey

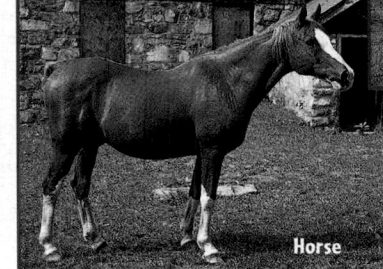

Mule

Horse

A mule is the hybrid offspring of the mating of a female horse and a male donkey. Many hybrids are sterile and cannot produce offspring of their own. This is true of mules.

What Is a Hybrid?

What looks a little like a horse and a little like a donkey, but isn't either? The answer to this riddle is . . . a mule! It looks the way it does because its male parent was a donkey and its female parent was a horse.

Living things that have parents that are quite different from each other, such as donkeys and horses, are called **hybrids**. People sometimes breed hybrids on purpose, since a hybrid may have more desirable traits than either of its parents.

A mule can do work that neither a donkey nor a horse can do. Mules are often used to carry heavy loads through rugged country. That's because mules do not slip as easily as horses. Mules also have more endurance than donkeys. Horses and donkeys do not normally mate. Even so, for thousands of years people have been breeding mules.

Crossbreeds

People often mate closely related living things on purpose. They may mate certain crop plants, flowers, dogs or cats. They do this to produce hearty crops or plants and animals with desirable traits. This process is sometimes called **crossbreeding**. A crossbreed is a product of the mating of individuals from two distinct breeds or varieties of the same *species* (kind of organism). Crossbreeding has produced new breeds of dogs and cats. Cross-breeding has also given us new kinds of corn that resist disease, produce more food on the same area of land, and are more nutritious.

A 112

 Science Background

Crossbreeding
When two organisms possessing different traits are cross-bred, the resulting organism inherits both desirable and undesirable traits. By repeatedly breeding individuals with more desirable than undesirable traits, desired characteristics are conserved and undesirable ones are suppressed more and more with each generation. Eventually, a group of individuals with the desired characteristics results.

Crossbreeds also occur naturally. If you have found a shady spot under the branches of a London plane tree, you have run across a hybrid. About 2,000 years ago, the oriental plane tree grew in the southern parts of Europe. It was so pretty that people living in northern Europe wanted to grow it there. Unfortunately, the oriental plane tree could not survive the cold northern winters. Then in about 1670, the oriental plane tree crossbred naturally with another kind of plane tree. The offspring, which came to be called the London plane tree, was a new kind of plant that could survive cold winters. Today these lovely trees are found on many streets in northern Europe and in the northern United States.

Cat Breeds

Cat breeds can be divided into two major groups—cats with short hair and cats with long hair. Different breeds of cats also vary in color, in length and texture of hair, and in temperament. Some are quiet and affectionate. Others tend to be vocal and demanding.

QUICK LAB
FOR SCHOOL OR HOME

Find the Hybrid Cat

1. **Observe** Look at the picture of the Siamese cat. What traits do you think it has been bred for?

2. **Observe** Look at the picture of the Persian cat. What traits do you think it has been bred for?

3. **Observe** Look at the picture of the Himalayan cat. What traits do you think it has been bred for?

4. **Infer** Which cat do you think is the hybrid? Explain your answer.

▷ **How is a mule an example of a hybrid?**
It is a cross between a horse and a donkey.

Persian cat

Siamese cat

Himalayan cat

A 113

Reading Strategy

Compare and Contrast
Developing Reading Skills
Have students examine the definitions of the terms *hybrid* and *crossbreeding.* Explain that *hybrid* is a broader term, while *crossbreeding* refers to breeding within the same species. Ask students to find similarities and differences between the terms.
Linguistic

Developing the Main Idea
Help students make the distinction between hybrids and crossbreeds. Ask:

- **What types of organisms are crossbred?** (organisms of the same species)

- **How is this different from a hybrid?** (Hybrids can be the result of breeding different species or organisms from the same species with different traits.)

- **How do the two crossbred organisms differ?** (They each have a different trait that is desired in the same organism.)

- **Why do people crossbreed organisms?** (to produce an organism with a desirable trait)

- **Does crossbreeding help an organism survive?** (Yes; if hardiness is the trait being bred for. At other times, no, if the trait is one for a specific appearance.)

Point out that in some cases, crossbreeding produces animals or plants that are less able to survive than either of its parents, but will result in a desired appearance.

▶ **After Reading**
Have students answer the red question in the student book as **ongoing assessment.**

QUICK LAB
FOR SCHOOL OR HOME

Materials cat pictures on p. A113

Science Process Skills *observe, infer*

Resources Activity Resources, pp. 44–45

Step 1 coloring: light body with darker points—face, ears, tail, lower legs, and paws; thin, muscular body; long, thin tail; long, tapered head; large ears; slanted blue eyes

Step 2 long, white fur; short, heavy legs; broad, short body, blue eyes; small, flattened face

Step 3 Persian-like body (thickset and low on the legs); Siamese coloring (light body with darker points); round, massive head set on a short, thick neck; short, broad nose; small, forward-tilted ears; long hair

Step 4 The Himalayan is the hybrid. It shares some traits with both the Persian and the Siamese.

Why Is Diversity Important?

Before Reading
Have students try to answer the red question at the top of the page.

Developing the Main Idea
Encourage students who own dogs to discuss whether they own purebreds or mixed breeds. Ask them to discuss their dog's physical and behavioral traits and any genetic disorders it may have. Ask students with mixed breeds to explain which traits of their dog were from each of its parents, if possible to tell.

Then direct students toward a more general discussion on diversity. Ask students to recall that traits are inherited from both parents. In cases where parents have traits in common, the offspring are more likely to have the same trait. When parents have different traits, the offspring can have either trait or show a mix of the two traits. For example, a child with a curly-haired parent and a straight-haired parent might have wavy hair. Then ask:

- **How does crossbreeding contribute to diversity?** (The offspring inherit different traits from both parents. This gives future generations more traits with which to adapt to changing environmental conditions.)

Thinking Further: *Inferring*
Ask:

- **What if ants from different family groups of the same species fight with each other when they meet? The fighting kills many ants. What could happen if the ants lost their diversity?** (They would all appear to be the same family and they might not fight with each other. The population could increase rather than continue to kill each other.)

▶ After Reading
Have students answer the red question in the student book as **ongoing assessment.**

Developing Vocabulary

diversity Show students examples or photographs of many different types of corn. Have students note similarities and differences among the ears. Use this example to impress the meaning of diversity in regard to plant and animal traits.

Why Is Diversity Important?

Would you rather have a mutt or a purebred dog? Purebred dogs—or other animals—look very much like their parents. They are bred to have certain traits. Mutts, on the other hand, may not look much like either parent. However, they do have a great mix of traits.

A group of dogs made up of mutts is a good example of animal **diversity**. *Diversity* means "different." Animal diversity refers to a group of the same kind of animal—like dogs—in which there are lots of animals with different traits. A group of mutts is made up of individual dogs with very different traits. Is there an advantage to being a mutt? The answer can be yes! Mutts may be healthier than certain purebred dogs. Some purebred dogs are known to have breathing problems. Some have hip problems. However, other purebred dogs come from very healthy breeds.

Threatened Cheetahs

Animal diversity is important. When an environment changes, only those animals that can adapt to the change will survive. If the population is made up of animals with the same traits—and those traits do not help the animals survive in a changing environment—the whole population may die out. This fate threatens the cheetahs of Africa. However, if the population holds animals with different traits, it is more likely that some will survive to keep the population going.

If the population lacks diverse traits and those traits do not help the animals survive in a changing environment, the whole population may die out. If the population has a lot of diversity, it is more likely some members will survive.

READING Summarize
Why is diversity important in an animal population?

Africa's cheetahs are in trouble. The traits of all cheetahs are so much alike, they have little diversity. This could threaten their survival against a new disease or other changes in their environment.

A 114

Reading MiniLesson

Summarize

Develop Tell students that a summary briefly restates the meaning of a passage in the reader's own words. Stopping to summarize partway through a lesson can help students to remember important points.

Practice Have students read page A114. Then, on the next page, point to the first two sentences in the first paragraph as a good summary of important facts. Have students explain why by locating the important facts in each paragraph on page A114. **Linguistic**

Why It Matters

Nature favors animal diversity. Hybridization, whether natural or artificial, produces animal diversity. Humans are no exception to this rule. Sometimes people carry traits that could be unhealthy for their children. Diversity among humans reduces the chances of inheriting such traits.

Visit **www.mhscience02.com** to do a research project on animal diversity.

Think and Write

1. What is one adaptation that helps an animal escape a predator?

2. What is an example of an inherited behavior?

3. What is an example of an inherited physical trait?

4. If two different kinds of animals mate and produce offspring, what might you infer about the traits of the offspring?

5. **Critical Thinking** Dark peppered moths cling to trees covered by black soot from factories. If the factories were not allowed to produce sooty smoke, what might happen to the dark peppered moths? Explain.

L·I·N·K·S

ART LINK

Make a display. Research two or three hybrid animals other than the ones discussed in this lesson. Find or make illustrations or models of the hybrid animals as well as their parents. Write descriptions of the hybrids, and add them to your display.

Tiglon

WRITING LINK

Write an essay. Write a paragraph about some of your favorite animal's behaviors. Which of its behaviors are automatic? Which of its behaviors are learned? Write another paragraph about some of your automatic responses. Compare them with some of the things you have learned to do.

TECHNOLOGY LINK

At the Computer Visit **www.mhscience02.com** for more links.

A 115

Informal Assessment

Easy/Average Provide several magazines with pictures of animals. Have students cut out and collect pictures of animals performing specific behaviors. Have them organize the pictures in a chart with two columns: *Automatic Behavior* and *Learned Behavior*.

Challenge Invite students to construct a crossword puzzle using vocabulary words and ten other terms from this lesson. Other terms may include *predator*, *adaptation*, *behavior*, *inherited*, *instinct*, and *species*.

3 | Lesson Review

Answers to Think and Write

1. Possible answers: mimicry, camouflage (pp. A106–A109)

2. Possible answer: nest-building by birds (p. A110)

3. Possible answers: feet and bills of birds, feather color (p. A110)

4. Possible answer: The offspring are likely to be healthier and heartier than either of their parents, but may be sterile. (pp. A112–A113)

5. **Critical Thinking** Possible answer: The trees would not be covered by soot. The dark moths would stand out against the lighter tree trunks. Predators would see the dark moths more easily and the dark moth population would decrease. (p. A109)

Summarize

Check students' understanding by having them write a brief summary of the lesson in their own words.

ART LINK

Displays should show the physical resemblance of the offspring to its parents and note both physical and behavioral inherited traits.

WRITING LINK

To organize their ideas, students may want to first make lists of the learned and automatic behaviors that they will write about.

Technology

Internet Research Project Have students visit **www.mhscience02.com** to conduct a research project on animal diversity. They will find a suggested outline for the project, questions to research, and links to Internet reference sites.

Chapter Review and Test Preparation

Resources

- Reading in Science Resources, pp. 71–72
- Assessment Book, pp. 9–12

Answers to Vocabulary

1. vertebrate
2. camouflage
3. mimicry
4. protective coloration
5. hybrid
6. organ
7. system
8. crossbreeding
9. heredity
10. invertebrate

Answers to Test Prep

11. C
12. J
13. B
14. J
15. B

Chapter 3 Review

Vocabulary

Fill each blank with the best word or words from the list.

camouflage, A108
crossbreeding, A113
heredity, A110
hybrid, A112
invertebrate, A96
mimicry, A106
organ, A95
protective coloration, A109
system, A95
vertebrate, A96

1. A(n) _____ is an animal that has a backbone.

2. An animal uses _____ to blend in with the background.

3. Looking like something a predator would not like to eat is an example of _____.

4. The changing color of an arctic hare's coat is an example of _____.

5. A mule is a(n) _____.

6. Tissues come together to form a(n) _____.

7. Organs come together to form a(n) _____.

8. Scientists use _____ to produce heartier crops.

9. The passing down of inherited traits is called _____.

10. A(n) _____ is an animal that does not have a backbone.

Test Prep

11. Insects, spiders, lobsters, and crabs are all _____.
    - A mammals
    - B amphibians
    - C arthropods
    - D syrphids

12. The skeletons of sharks are made of _____.
    - F scales
    - G bones
    - H fins
    - J cartilage

13. A bird's bones _____.
    - A are made of cartilage
    - B weigh very little for their size
    - C weigh a lot for their size
    - D are surprisingly thick

14. Animals with fur are _____.
    - F amphibians
    - G syrphids
    - H either arthropods or mollusks
    - J mammals

15. As adults, frogs breathe with _____.
    - A gills
    - B lungs
    - C cartilage
    - D mollusks

A 116

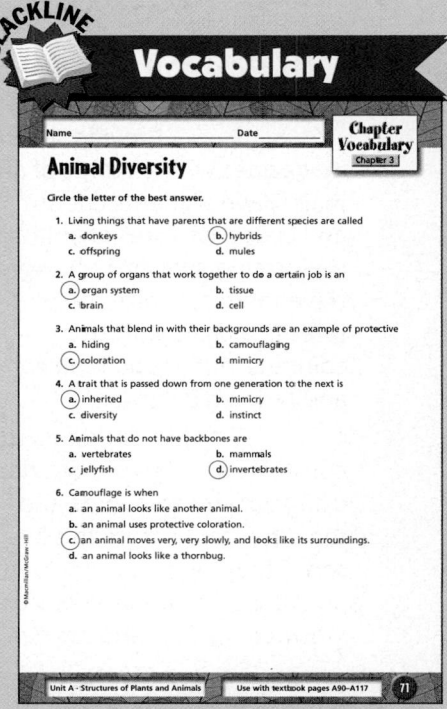

Reading in Science Resources, p. 71

Concepts and Skills

16. Reading in Science Write a paragraph explaining why a predator might avoid eating a syrphid fly.

17. Scientific Methods The two graphs below show changes in population size between a certain predator and its prey (the animals it eats). Identify which animal is the predator and which is the prey. Write a paragraph giving the reasons for your answer.

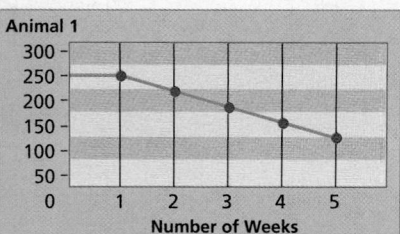

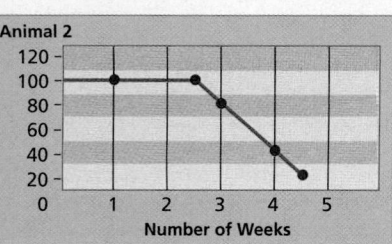

18. Decision Making A company is planning to build a factory near a river that is home to many different kinds of fish. The only thing the company is planning to dump in the river is clean water. However, the temperature of the water they are dumping is 18°C warmer than the warmest temperature the river usually reaches. You are on the planning committee that will decide whether or not to allow the factory to be built there. What factors do you need to consider when making your decision? Write a paragraph discussing these factors and explaining what your decision would be.

19. Process Skills: Classify Many members of different animal groups are found in water. Create a classification key to identify a whale among a hagfish, a shark, and a sea turtle. Write a paragraph explaining how your key works.

20. Critical Thinking You are a marine biologist, a scientist who studies living things in the ocean. You are exploring under the water and come upon a strange fish. You catch it in a net and take it back to your laboratory. What must you find out about the fish in order to classify it? Write your ideas.

Boost *your test scores!*
Be Smart!
Visit www.mhscience02.com

Answers to Concepts and Skills

16. Reading in Science A syrphid fly has adapted to look very much like a yellow jacket, a creature with a painful sting. A predator might mistake the syrphid fly for a yellow jacket, thereby avoiding it.

17. Scientific Methods The prey is represented by the Animal 1 graph that shows an initial decline in population. The predator is represented by the Animal 2 graph that shows a subsequent decline in population. Sample explanation: As the population of prey animals went down, the predators didn't have enough food to eat, so their population then began to go down as well.

18. Decision Making Accept all well-reasoned paragraphs. Some things to be taken into consideration might be whether the fish can survive in the water at higher temperatures, whether the fish can be diverted to another body of water, and the importance of the factory being built.

19. Process Skills: Classify Possible answer: lives in water (all four); has jaws (shark, turtle, whale); has lungs (turtle, whale); has hair and feeds its young mother's milk (whale).

20. Critical Thinking Possible answer: whether it has a backbone, jaws, a swim bladder, and whether its skeleton is made of cartilage or bones.

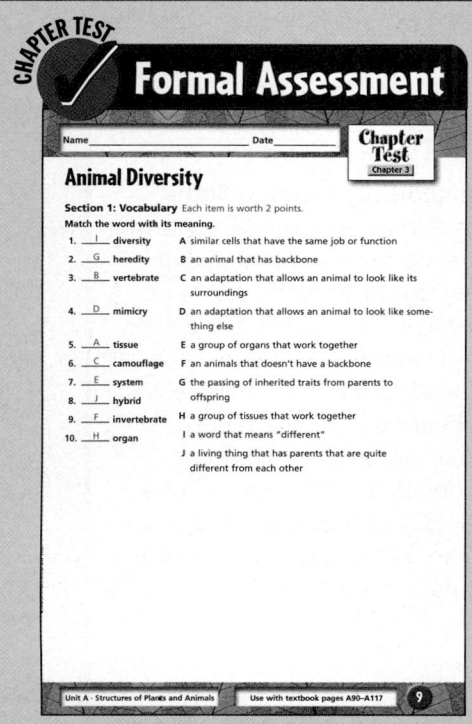

Assessment Book, p. 9

People in Science

People in Science

Dr. Ann Bowles
Hubbs-Sea World Research Institute

Objective

- Identify the work and research of a bioacoustician.

Build on Prior Knowledge

Ask any students who have seen a dolphin show at a marine center or on TV whether the animals make any noises. (squeaks, clicks, "laughs") Ask students why they think the animals make these noises. (Possible answers: to communicate with each other or humans, to get attention, to help orient themselves.)

Bioacoustician Dr. Ann Bowles

Developing the Main Idea

Focus on the career of a bioacoustician by asking students with pets to describe the kinds of sounds they make to communicate with people. (Possible answers: Dogs bark at the door to go out, cats meow in the kitchen to be fed.) Point out that animals can communicate with one another as well.

Then ask students to name animals they have heard of that communicate with one another. (Possible answers: dolphins, whales, dogs, birds) Ask:

- **What kind of adaptation does Dr. Bowles study?** (animal behaviors—communicating)

- **How does communication help the penguins' survival?** (By being able to find their way back to a mate, adults can help in food gathering and the rearing of the young. By not being mistaken for a predator, the penguins are less likely to be attacked by other penguins.)

- **What other adaptation do penguins have to help them survive?** (Possible answers: wings that are used for swimming, not flying; extra body fat and insulating feathers)

Dr. Doolittle talked with the animals. While his conversations were make-believe, there are scientists called bioacousticians who study how animals communicate, too. The only difference is they focus on understanding the animal instead of the other way around. They also study what animals can hear and the effects of human-made sounds.

Dr. Ann Bowles is a bioacoustician at Hubbs-Sea World Research Institute. She grew up in Peru where her father was helping to build a radio telescope in the desert outside Lima. Her love for animals started when she saw amazing animals like morpho butterflies, llama, and gigantic tadpoles during her family's travels throughout South America.

In college, Dr. Bowles earned a degree in linguistics—the study of human languages. However, she never lost her love of wildlife. In 1994 she completed a doctorate in marine biology from the Scripps Institute of Oceanography. Her expertise in language training and animal behavior has been the driving force of her career ever since.

Dr. Bowles' research has focused on the ways that adult emperor penguins recognize each other by voice. She is now trying to understand how killer whales develop their word-like calls. Information like this may help humans understand how their own language evolved.

Dr. Bowles has also studied the effect of human-made sounds on other

A 118

SCIENCE Reading Strategy

Reread

Developing Reading Skills

Have students reread People in Science. Then ask them what they think the prefix *bio-* means. ("life") Then have them guess at the meaning of *acoustic.* ("relating to the sense of hearing") Ask them how these word parts help them understand what a bioacoustician does. (Together, the parts mean "relating to the effects of sound on life.")

animals. Marine animals make life-and-death decisions based on what they hear. Unfortunately, human-made sounds can have a bad effect on marine animals. For example, noise made by shipping traffic can mask communications between whales and blasting can deafen them.

Sometimes, human-made sounds can be beneficial. For example, fishermen's nets now carry pingers, little devices that produce a peeping noise. Many marine mammals find the sound annoying, which keeps them out of nets and traps. Dr. Bowles is trying to understand why these tiny sounds are effective in a noisy ocean. With this information, better pingers can be designed. It's her way of respecting the needs of our animal neighbors.

AT THE COMPUTER

Visit www.mhscience02.com to learn more about careers.

Write ABOUT IT

1. How do adult emperor penguins communicate?

2. Why is it important to study the effect human sounds have on marine animals?

Careers IN SCIENCE

Career Track

Here are some different types of careers related to the study of bioacoustics. You can use the Internet or library resources to find out more about these careers.
- linguist
- naturalist
- marine biologist
- ecologist
- zoologist

A 119

Developing the Main Idea
Ask:

- **What kind of interests and training did Dr. Bowles have?** (Possible answers: a love of and interest in animals, an interest in languages and communication, a doctorate in marine biology and courses in linguistics.)

- **Dr. Bowles works mainly with marine animals. What land animals might a bioacoustician study?** (Possible answers: bats, elephants, insects.)

Inform students that bioacousticians do not work only with animals. They also deal with the way sound can be used for medical diagnosis and treatment in humans. For example, ultrasound can be used to look inside a patient without X-rays or surgery.

Thinking Further: *Inferring*
Ask:

- **Why might dolphins be attracted to the pinging nets?** (Possible answer: They may think the sounds come from other dolphins; they may think that food is near the nets/pingers; they become used to the noise and ignore it.)

Answers to Write ABOUT IT

1. They recognize each other by voice.
2. Possible answer: Human sound can interfere with the communicating and navigation of animals, thereby injuring or helping to kill them by confusing them regarding their whereabouts.

Advanced Learners

Pingers
Ask students to find out more about the way pingers have reduced the number of marine mammals killed in gill nets over the last few years. Ask them to find out where the pingers were first used, whether they are widely used, and how effective they've been. **Linguistic**

Inclusion

Whale Songs
Play an audiotape or CD of whale songs for students. Have them try to hear the differences among the sounds the whales are able to make and try to imitate them. Discuss how whales use the sounds to communicate, find prey, avoid obstacles, and locate one another. **Musical**

Unit A Performance Assessment

Plant Parts Do Their Part (Chapter 1)

Materials: hand lens, veined leaf, stem, root, colored pencils, drawing paper

Teaching Tips: Use fresh leaves. Leaves you collect locally are fine as long as they are green and veined.

Flowers for Lunch (Chapter 2)

Materials: beet, carrot, sweet potato, celery, sugar, cabbage, spinach, tea, bean, corn, chocolate, broccoli, cauliflower, cinnamon, maple syrup, rice, writing paper, colored pencils

Teaching Tips: A variety of foods can be used for this activity. Packaged foods such as multi-grain cereal can also be used as long as ingredients are listed. Caution students not to taste the foods. Students should wash their hands after their activity and be careful not to stain their clothes.

Cactus Creature (Chapter 3)

Materials: cactus, clay, hand lens, art materials such as glue, construction paper, fabric scraps, toothpicks, scissors

Teaching Tips: If you cannot obtain a real cactus, a photograph will work. **Be Careful!** Caution students to handle the cactus carefully. You may wish to supply a gardening glove for students to use while handling the cactus.

Performance Assessment

Plant Parts Do Their Part

Your goal is to identify plant parts and diagram water movement in a plant.

What to Do

1. Using a hand lens, identify veins and petioles in a leaf; root hairs, cortex, and xylem in a root; and xylem and phloem in a stem. Draw and label diagrams of each part.

2. Draw and label a tree. Show water movement from soil to leaf.

Analyze Your Results

Using the words *light*, *chlorophyll*, and *energy* describe how leaf cells use water.

Flowers for Lunch

Your goal is to identify common foods from plant parts.

What to Do

Examine each of several foods. What plant part is it? Create a table using the words below.

Root	Stem	Leaf	Fruit
Seed	Flower	Bark	Sap

Analyze Your Results

1. Fill in the table by classifying each of the foods you examined.

2. Make a menu with at least five foods made from plants and identify the source.

Cactus Creature

Your goal is to make a model animal adapted to life in the desert.

What to Do

BE CAREFUL! Handle sharp objects carefully! Examine a cactus with a hand lens. Think of how an animal that lives among cactus would look. Make a model of it.

Analyze Your Results

Describe the adaptations you gave your model animal. How would each of these adaptations help the animal survive in the desert? Compare it to a cactus.

A 120

Rubrics

Plant Parts Do Their Part
(3-point rubric)

3 points = Students' diagrams of leaf, stem, and root are correct; diagram of tree showing water use is correct; statement about how leaves use water is correct.

2 points = Two student responses are correct.

1 point = One student response is correct.

0 points = No student responses are correct.

Flowers for Lunch (2-point rubric)

2 points = Students' table and lunch menu are correct

1 point = Either table or lunch menu is correct.

0 points = Neither table nor menu is correct.

Cactus Creature (3-point rubric)

3 points = Students' model, description of animal adaptations, and description of cactus adaptations are correct.

2 points = Two student responses are correct

1 point = One student response is correct.

0 points = No student responses are correct.

Formal Assessment

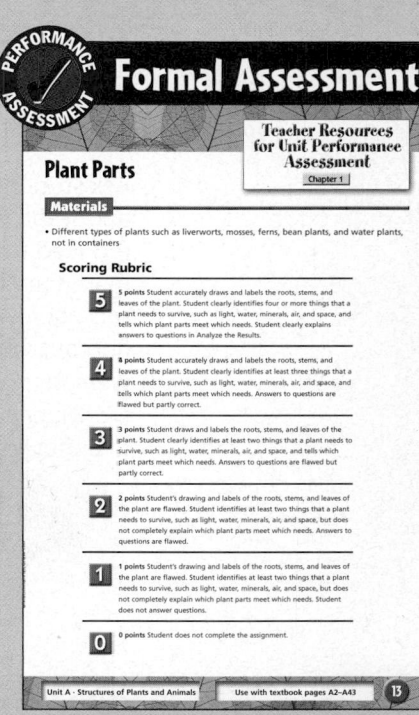

Teacher Resources for Unit Performance Assessment
Chapter 1

Plant Parts

Materials

• Different types of plants such as liverworts, mosses, ferns, bean plants, and water plants, not in containers

Scoring Rubric

5 5 points Student accurately draws and labels the roots, stems, and leaves of the plant. Student clearly identifies four or more things that a plant needs to survive, such as light, water, minerals, air, and space, and tells which plant parts meet which needs. Student clearly explains answers to questions in Analyze the Results.

4 4 points Student accurately draws and labels the roots, stems, and leaves of the plant. Student clearly identifies at least three things that a plant needs to survive, such as light, water, minerals, air, and space, and tells which plant parts meet which needs. Answers to questions are flawed but partly correct.

3 3 points Student draws and labels the roots, stems, and leaves of the plant. Student clearly identifies at least two things that a plant needs to survive, such as light, water, minerals, air, and space, and tells which plant parts meet which needs. Answers to questions are flawed but partly correct.

2 2 points Student's drawing and labels of the roots, stems, and leaves of the plant are flawed. Student identifies at least two things that a plant needs to survive, such as light, water, minerals, air, and space, but does not completely explain which plant parts meet which needs. Answers to questions are flawed.

1 1 points Student's drawing and labels of the roots, stems, and leaves of the plant are flawed. Student identifies at least two things that a plant needs to survive, such as light, water, minerals, air, and space, but does not completely explain which plant parts meet which needs. Student does not answer questions.

0 0 points Student does not complete the assignment.

Unit A · Structures of Plants and Animals   Use with textbook pages A2–A43   **13**

Interactions of Living Things

Main Idea: All organisms live in ecosystems where they depend on each other and the natural resources of the environment. Ecosystems change constantly, with some experiencing rapid modifications.

Unit Organizer

CHAPTER 4 Ecosystems, *pp. B2–B45*

Main Idea: All living and nonliving things interact in an ecosystem. Organisms interact by transferring energy in food to each other. Nonliving things interact by continuous recycling of their resources.

LESSON 1 Living Things and Their Environment, *pp. B4–B15*
Main Idea: Ecosystems have living and nonliving parts.

LESSON 2 Food Chains and Food Webs, *pp. B16–B27*
Main Idea: Food chains and food webs describe the feeding relationships in an ecosystem.

LESSON 3 Cycles of Life, *pp. B30–B41*
Main Idea: Earth's systems recycle materials such as water, carbon, and nitrogen.

CHAPTER 5 Populations and Ecosystems, *pp. B46–B93*

Main Idea: Different ecosystems around the world house a multitude of organisms constantly interacting with each other. All ecosystems change over time, with a few undergoing sudden transformations.

LESSON 4 How Populations Survive, *pp. B48–B61*
Main Idea: Living and nonliving things interact in an ecosystem. Survival is dependent on the adaptations and relationships organisms have.

LESSON 5 Biomes, *pp. B62–B75*
Main Idea: The world has a number of ecosystems and biomes that are the habitats of a great variety of organisms.

LESSON 6 How Ecosystems Change, *pp. B78–B91*
Main Idea: Ecosystems go through both slow and sudden changes.

Grade-Level Science Books

EASY	EASY	CHALLENGE
THE EAGLES ARE BACK! This book explains how the process of hacking enabled two eagles to be raised in a safe place and then be released to live in the wild.	**WILDFIRE: BATTLING THE WESTHAMPTON FIRE** This is the true story of a wildfire that consumed 5,000 acres of Westhampton, Long Island, New York, in August of 1995.	**ANTARCTICA** The book describes the special geographical features and plant and animal life found on the continent of Antarctica.

To order from Macmillan/McGraw-Hill, call 800-442-9685.

Cross Curricular Books from Macmillan/McGraw-Hill

Black, Shelia. **The Beekeeper's Story.**

Norby, Lisa. **Flight of the Trumpeters.**

To order, call 800-442-9685.

Student Bibliography

Bash, Barbara. **Ancient Ones: The World of the Old-Growth Douglas Fir**. San Francisco: Sierra Club Books for Children, 1994.

Cobb, Vicki. **This Place Is Wild: East Africa**. New York: Walker Publishing Company, 1998.

Galan, Mark. **There's Still Time: The Success of the Endangered Species Act**. Washington D.C.: National Geographic Society, 1997.

Kaner, Etta. **Animal Defenses: How Animals Protect Themselves**. Kids Can Press, 1999

Lasky, Kathryn. **The Most Beautiful Roof in the World: Exploring the Rainforest Canopy**. New York: Gulliver, 1998.

Markle, Sandra. **Super Cool Science: South Pole Stations Past, Present, and Future**. New York: Walker and Company, 1998.

Patent, Dorothy Hinshaw. **Back to the Wild**. San Diego: Gulliver/Harcourt Brace and Company, 1997.

Sauvain, Philip. **Geography Detective: Mountains**. Minneapolis, MN: Carolrhoda Books, Inc., 1996.

Sauvain, Philip. **Geography Detective: Rain Forests**. Minneapolis, MN: Carolrhoda Books, Inc., 1996.

Wright-Frierson, Virginia. **An Island Scrapbook**. New York: Simon & Schuster Books for Young Readers, 1998.

Reading in Science

McGraw-Hill Science

Teacher Editions provide point-of-use strategies and resource support for students to practice reading skills as they read their science texts.

- **Reading MiniLessons**
- **Reduced Blackline Masters** from *Reading in Science Resources*
- **Additional Reading Strategies**

 **Reading in Science Resources**

Boxes beneath the reduced Pupil Edition pages identify specific places in a lesson where students can complete worksheets from the ***Reading in Science Resources*** blackline masters. Reduced worksheets for this unit are found on the following pages of this Teacher Edition.

Lesson Outlines: pp. B6, B18, B32, B50, B64, B80

Interpret Illustrations: pp. B7, B9, B19, B20, B36, B39, B53, B58, B65, B73, B81, B84

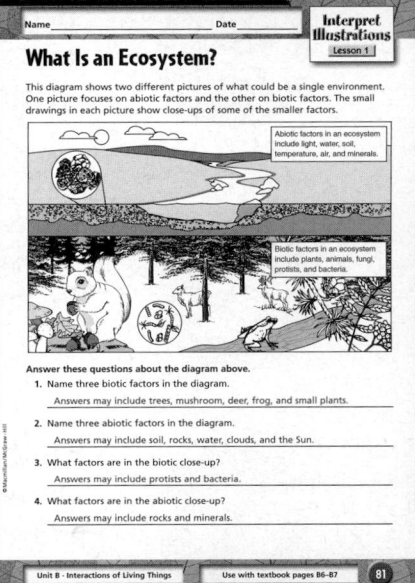

Reading in Science Resources, p. 81

 **Reading** **MiniLesson**

Reading MiniLessons provide a brief tutorial and activity for students to practice a specific reading skill for each chapter. In this unit, the chapter reading skills are:

Sequence of Events: pp. B8, B22, B33

Summarize: pp. B51, B67, B89

 **Reading Strategy**

Additional opportunities for students to develop and apply reading skills are provided in this unit as follows:

- ◉ **Cause and effect:** p. B12
- ◉ **Compare and contrast:** pp. B39, B64
- ○ **Draw conclusions**
- ◉ **Find the main idea:** p. B40, B80
- ○ **Sequence of events**
- ◉ **Summarize:** pp. B14, B15, B18, B27, B29, B41, B43, B60, B61, B74, B75, B90, B91
- ○ **Ask questions**
- ◉ **Reread:** pp. B64, B74, B88
- ◉ **Retell (paraphrase):** pp. B10, B26, B43

- ◉ **Interpret graphic sources of information:** pp. B7, B9, B19, B20, B37, B39, B40, B52, B54, B65, B81, B84
- ◉ **Build on prior knowledge:** pp. B4, B16, B28, B30, B42, B48, B62, B76, B78, B94
- ◉ **Organize information:** pp. B54, B66

CROSS CURRICULUM IDEAS for integrating science

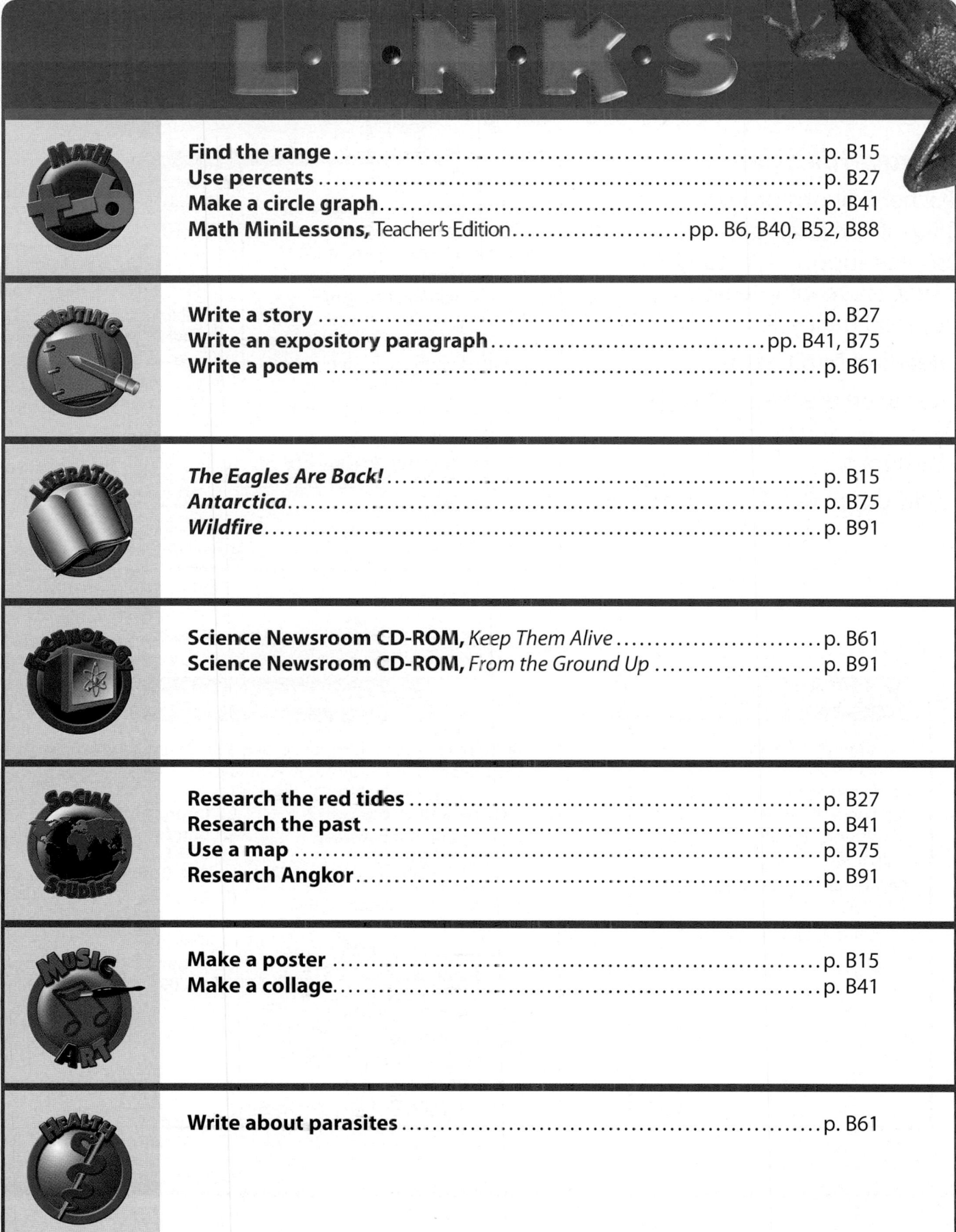

L·I·N·K·S

Meeting Individual Needs

McGraw-Hill Science includes all students in the learning process by providing a variety of strategies in this unit.

 **English Language Learners**

Opposites

Point out how *biotic* and *abiotic* are opposites. Compare the use of *a-* as a prefix with *non-* and *un-*. Ask students to use a dictionary to find examples of opposites using these prefixes, such as *typical* and *atypical*, *living* and *nonliving*, *developed* and *undeveloped*. Challenge students to find other words with these prefixes that they might see while studying ecosystems and to use each word in a sentence. **Linguistic**

 **Advanced Learners**

Journalism

Ask students to pretend they are journalists sent to cover the story of the Mount Saint Helens eruption. They should file their first story on May 20, 1980, two days after the eruption. Encourage them to describe for readers what they see, smell, hear, and feel. Invite them to add their personal comments about what they think the future holds for this area. **Kinesthetic; Linguistic**

 **Inclusion**

Biome Collage

Invite students to pick one of the biomes and make a collage showing the plants, animals, and other things they might see in that biome (such as land features). Challenge them to do research to find other organisms not mentioned in the text and to add pictures of these organisms and the people who live there. **Spatial**

For additional support, see pp. B7, B9, B10, B11, B21, B23–B25, B28, B32, B37, B38, B50, B51, B53, B55, B56, B57, B59, B60, B65, B67, B68, B69, B71–B73, B77, B83, B85, B89, B95

Learning Styles

Students acquire knowledge in a variety of ways that reflect different, often distinct, learning styles. The seven learning styles are:

- ◉ **Kinesthetic** pp. B17, B31, B32, B49, B53, B63, B69, B83
- ◉ **Social** pp. B5, B10, B11, B23, B37, B38, B72
- ◉ **Intrapersonal** pp. B28, B56, B60, B86
- ◉ **Linguistic** pp. B4, B7, B9, B11, B21, B23, B25, B32, B37, B38, B51, B55, B56, B57, B59, B67, B68, B70, B71–B73, B83, B85, B86, B89, B95
- ◉ **Logical** pp. B16, B24, B50, B52, B60, B71, B77, B79, B83
- ○ **Auditory/Musical**
- ◉ **Visual/Spatial** pp. B8, B10, B11, B17, B24, B28, B31, B50, B53, B59, B65, B69, B70, B79, B83, B85, B95

Technology for McGRAW-HILL SCIENCE

CD-ROMs

Science Newsroom CD-ROM
Student-directed computer activities

Chapter 5: Keep Them Alive
Explore how to help keep endangered species alive.

Chapter 5: From Ground Up
Explore the growth of an ecosystem.

Join me in the Science Newsroom

Videotapes

Explore Activity Videos
All Explore Activities are available on videotape. Introduce lessons with Explore Activity Videos.

MindJogger Videos
Stage a quiz show in your classroom!

Science Experiences Videotapes

Chapter 4:

Lesson 1 Living Things and Their Environment
Ponds: Freshwater Habitats (Package 1)
Life in a Coral Reef (Package 2)
Researching the Ocean Depths (Package 7)

Chapter 5:

Lesson 4 How Populations Survive
Staying Alive: Adaptations for Survival (Package 4)

Transparencies

Visual Aid Transparencies
- **8** Land Food Web
- **9–12** Building a Water Cycle
- **13** The Carbon Cycle
- **14** The Nitrogen Cycle
- **15** From Farm to Forest: Secondary Succession
- **16** A Pioneer Community

Reading Aid Transparencies
- B1–B6

Internet Resources

McGRAW-HILL SCIENCE is online at *www.mhscience02.com* with projects and activities for students, teachers, and parents.
Internet Research Projects pp. B41, B91
Links pp. B15, B27, B41, B61, B75, B91
Science Magazines and Features pp. B29, B43, B45, B77, B93, B95

Visit www.amnh.org/resources/mhscience for a behind-the-scenes look at the exhibitions, collections, and research of the Museum. You'll find resources for teachers and students, such as online expeditions, profiles of scientists, interactives, links to professional development courses and more.

NATIONAL GEOGRAPHIC

* To order National Geographic Products, visit us online at *www.nationalgeographic.com/education* or call 1-800-368-2728. To order NGS Picture Show and NGS Picture Pack, call Macmillan/McGraw-Hill at 1-800-442-9685.

National Geographic Society Videos
- **Web of Life**
- **Rain Forest**
- **Pollution:** World at Risk

NGS Picture Show CD-ROMs
- **Looking at Ecosystems**
- **Looking at Living Things**

NGS Picture Pack Transparencies
- **Looking at Living Things**

Process Skills

Science Process Skills	Explore Activities (Pupil Edition)	Quick Labs (Pupil Edition)	Process Skill Builders
Observe	pp. B5, B17, B31, B49, B63, B79	pp. B35, B72, B85	
Infer	pp. B5, B17, B31, B49, B63, B79	pp. B35, B51, B85	Pupil Edition pp. B13, B87 Teacher Edition (MiniLesson) p. B87 Activity Resources pp. 77–78
Classify		p. B19	
Measure		p. B51	
Use Numbers		p. B51	
Communicate	pp. B49, B63, B79	pp. B19, B72, B85	
Predict	pp. B17, B79	p. B85	
Interpret Data	p. B79	p. B72	
Form a Hypothesis			Pupil Edition p. B13
Use Variables	p. B49		Pupil Edition p. B13 Teacher Edition (MiniLesson) p. B13 Activity Resources pp. 49–50
Experiment	pp. B5, B17, B63		
Make a Model			
Define Based on Observations			

Materials

Consumable materials (based on six groups)

Materials	Quantity Needed per group	Kit Quantity	Lesson
Animal, sow bug	4	coupon for 12	1
Animal, earthworms	2	coupon for 12	1
Animal, snail, helix	2	coupon for 18	1
Animal, snail, pond	8	coupon for 12	1
Bulb, 100-W	1	6	3
Carton, small milk	4		4
Cup, clear plastic, 9 oz	2	150	5
Gravel/pebbles		3 kg	1
Hydrogen peroxide, 3%, 230 mL		1 bottle	5
Paper towel	1		3
Plant, duckweed, *Lemna minor*		coupon for 1 class package	1
Plant, *Elodea*		coupon for 12 sprigs	1
Plastic wrap, 50 sq ft		1 roll	1
Sand, fine		2.5 kg	5
Seed, grass		2 packages	1
Seeds, pinto bean	40	1 lb	4
Soil, clay		10 kg	3
Soil, potting		24 lb	1, 4, 5
Spoon, plastic	2	24	5
String		200 ft	2
Water (pond, lake, stream - at least 3 samples)			5
Water, pond, or aged tap			1

Non-consumable materials (based on six groups)

Materials	Quantity Needed per group	Kit Quantity	Lesson
Books, research			6
Calculator	1		4
Camera (optional)	1		2
Can, empty	1		3
Collecting net (optional)	1		2
Container, clear plastic, 2 qt	1	6	3
Container, plastic, with lid	3		5
Dropper	2	18	5
Fishbowl, 1 gal	2	2	1
Goggles	5		5
Internet			6
Light socket, porcelain	1	6	3
Meterstick	1		4
Microscope	1	3	5
Microscope cover slip	1	100	5
Microscope slide	1	72	5
Rocks, small			2
Ruler	1		1
Tape			2

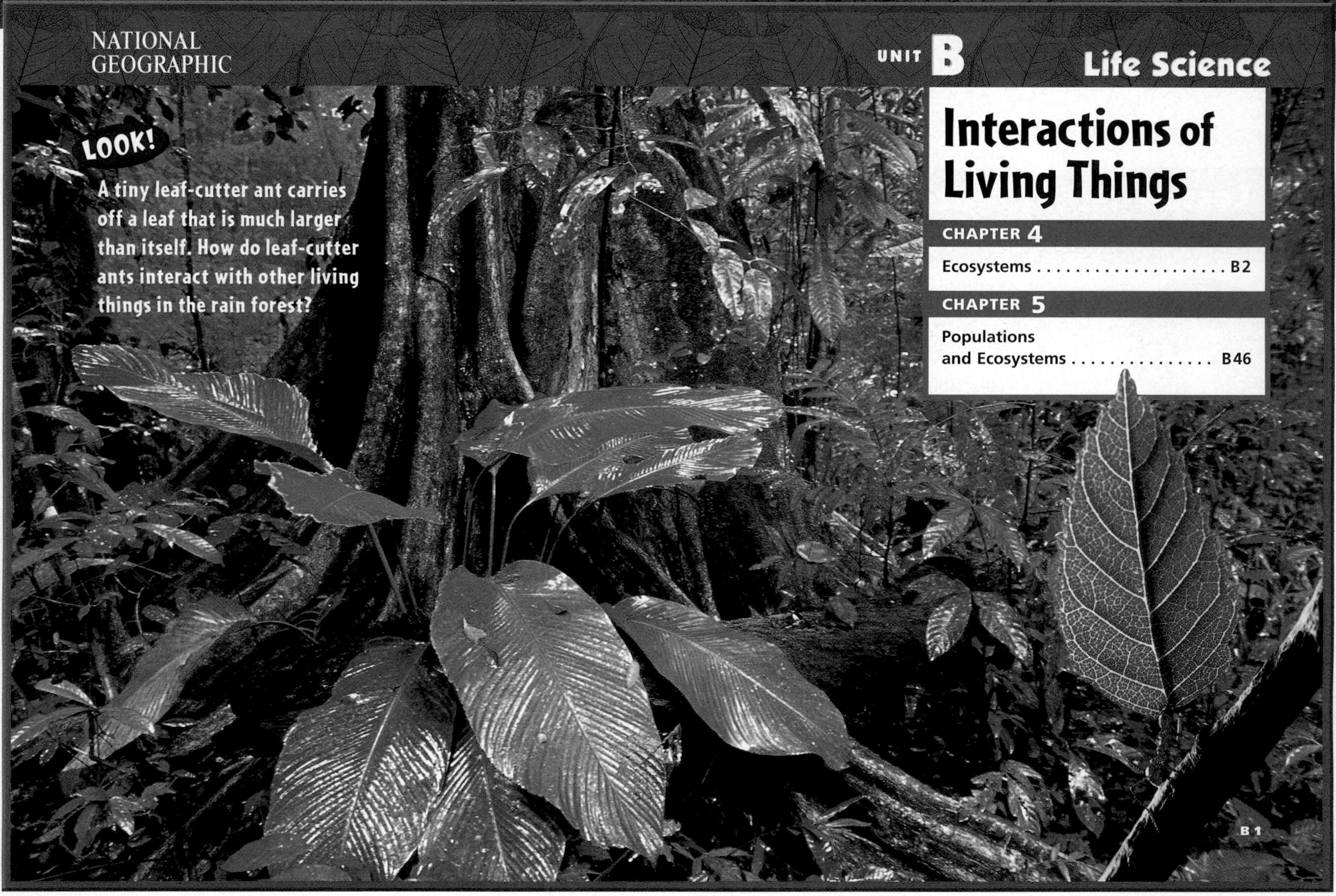

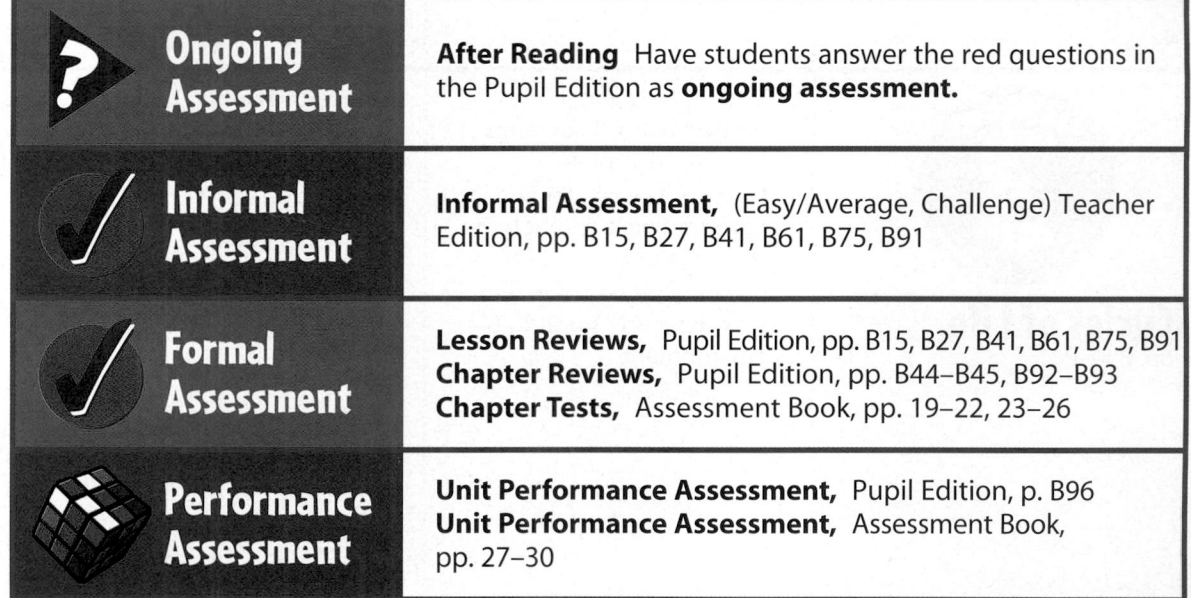

NATIONAL GEOGRAPHIC
UNIT B Life Science
Interactions of Living Things
CHAPTER 4
Ecosystems B2
CHAPTER 5
Populations and Ecosystems B46
LOOK!
A tiny leaf-cutter ant carries off a leaf that is much larger than itself. How do leaf-cutter ants interact with other living things in the rain forest?
B1

Resources

- Reading in Science Resources, Unit Vocabulary, pp. 123–125
- School to Home Activities, pp. 9–14
- Cross Curricular Projects, pp. 11–16

Answers to

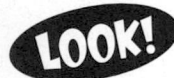

LOOK!

Leaf-cutter ants are fungus farmers. They cut off leaves or piece of leaves and carry them to their nests. There they use the leaf material to grow a fungus that the ants use for food.

Assessment Strand

McGraw-Hill Science provides a variety of strategies for assessing students' learning and progress, including ongoing assessment, informal assessment, formal assessment, and performance assessment.

Ongoing Assessment	**After Reading** Have students answer the red questions in the Pupil Edition as **ongoing assessment.**
Informal Assessment	**Informal Assessment,** (Easy/Average, Challenge) Teacher Edition, pp. B15, B27, B41, B61, B75, B91
Formal Assessment	**Lesson Reviews,** Pupil Edition, pp. B15, B27, B41, B61, B75, B91 **Chapter Reviews,** Pupil Edition, pp. B44–B45, B92–B93 **Chapter Tests,** Assessment Book, pp. 19–22, 23–26
Performance Assessment	**Unit Performance Assessment,** Pupil Edition, p. B96 **Unit Performance Assessment,** Assessment Book, pp. 27–30

Lesson Planner

Lesson	Objectives	Vocabulary	Pacing	Resources and Technology
LESSON 1 **Living Things and Their Environment,** pp. B4–B15	■ Explore a land or water environment to test what certain living things need to survive. ■ Describe various ecosystems and the biotic and abiotic factors involved in them. ■ Discuss variables that can affect population size and survival.	**ecosystem** **ecology** **abiotic factor** **biotic factor** **population** **community** **habitat** **niche**	4 days	■ Activity Resources, pp. 46–50 ■ Reading in Science Resources, pp. 79–84 ■ Vocabulary Cards ■ Grade-Level Science Book, *The Eagles Are Back* ■ Reading Aid Transparency B1 ■ **Explore Activity Video** ■ **Science Experiences Videotapes** *Ponds: Freshwater Habitats* (Package 1) *Life in a Coral Reef* (Package 2) *Researching the Ocean Depths* (Package 7)
LESSON 2 **Food Chains and Food Webs,** pp. B16–B27	■ Explore how a change in one population can affect an ecosystem. ■ Understand the relationship between food chains and food webs. ■ Describe a food pyramid and the roles various organisms play in them.	**food chain** **food web** **herbivore** **carnivore** **predator** **prey** **scavenger** **omnivore**	3 days	■ Activity Resources, pp. 51–56 ■ Reading in Science Resources, pp. 85–90 ■ Vocabulary Cards ■ Reading Aid Transparency B2 ■ School to Home Activities, pp. 10, 11 ■ Visual Aid Transparency 8 ■ **Explore Activity Video**
LESSON 3 **Cycles of Life,** pp. B30–B41	■ Explore how water evaporates and condenses in a closed system. ■ Describe how water and nutrients cycle through the environment. ■ Describe how carbon and nitrogen cycle through the environment.	**evaporation** **condensation** **precipitation** **water cycle** **carbon cycle** **nitrogen cycle**	3 days	■ Activity Resources, pp. 57–61 ■ Reading in Science Resources, pp. 91–96 ■ Vocabulary Cards ■ School to Home Activities, p. 12 ■ Reading Aid Transparency B3 ■ Visual Aid Transparencies 9, 10, 11, 12, 13, 14 ■ **Explore Activity Video**

Activity Planner

Activity	Process Skills	Materials	Plan Ahead
LESSON 1 Explore Activity **What Do Living Things Need to Survive?** p. B5	observe, infer, experiment	wide-mouthed, clear container with lid; washed gravel; pond water or aged tap water; water plants; water snails; soil; small rocks; grass seeds and small plants; earth-worms, land snails, sow bugs, or other small land animals that eat plants	No advance planning is needed.
Process Skill BUILDER **Vanishing Bald Eagles** p. B13	use variables, communicate, infer, hypothesize	ruler	No advance planning is needed.
LESSON 2 Explore Activity **How Do Populations Interact?** p. B17	observe, infer, experiment, predict	tape, string, population cards	No advance planning is needed.
QUICK LAB FOR SCHOOL OR HOME **Getting Food** p. B19	classify, communicate	camera (optional), collecting net (optional)	No advance planning is needed.
LESSON 3 Explore Activity **What Happens to Water?** p. B31	observe, infer	plastic food container with clear cover, small bowl or cup filled with water, small tray filled with dry soil, paper towel, 100-W lamp (if available)	Make sure the food containers are large enough to hold the water bowl and soil.
QUICK LAB FOR SCHOOL OR HOME **Soil Sample** p. B35	observe, infer	small can	Make sure students have permission to dig at the site.

Reading in Science Resources

McGraw-Hill Science **Reading in Science Resources** provides the following **Blackline Master** worksheets for this chapter.

Chapter Graphic Organizer

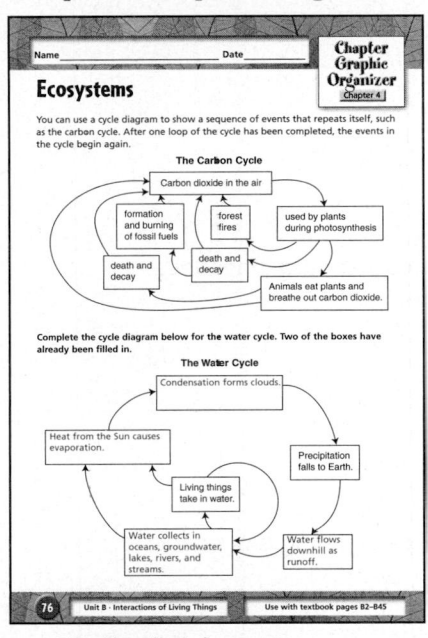

Reading in Science Resources,
p. 76

Chapter Reading Skill

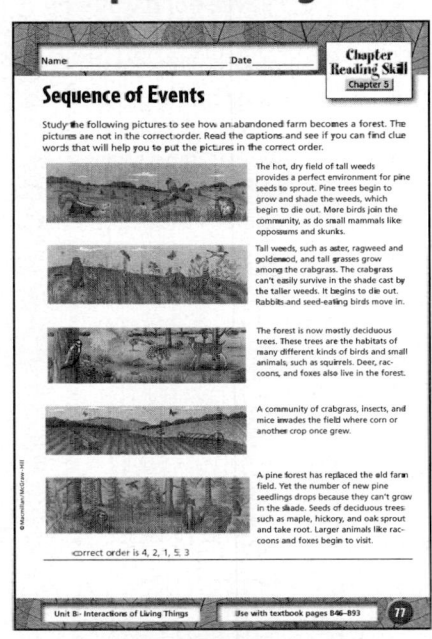

Reading in Science Resources,
pp. 77–78

Chapter Vocabulary

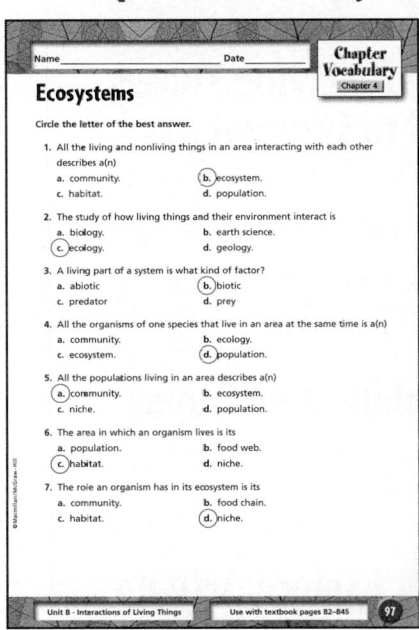

Reading in Science Resources,
pp. 97–98

McGraw-Hill Science **Reading in Science Resources** provides the following **Blackline Master** worksheets for every lesson in this chapter.

Lesson Outline

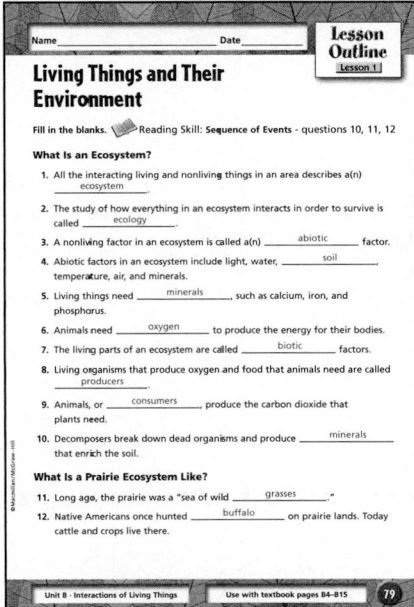

Reading in Science Resources,
pp. 79–80, 85–86, 91–92

Interpret Illustrations

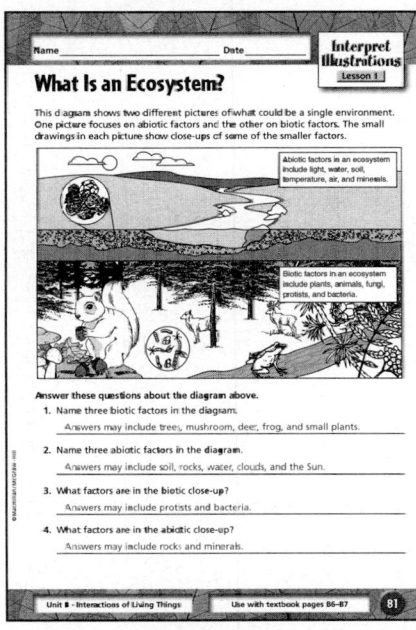

Reading in Science Resources,
pp. 81–82, 87–88, 93–94

Lesson Vocabulary and Cloze Test

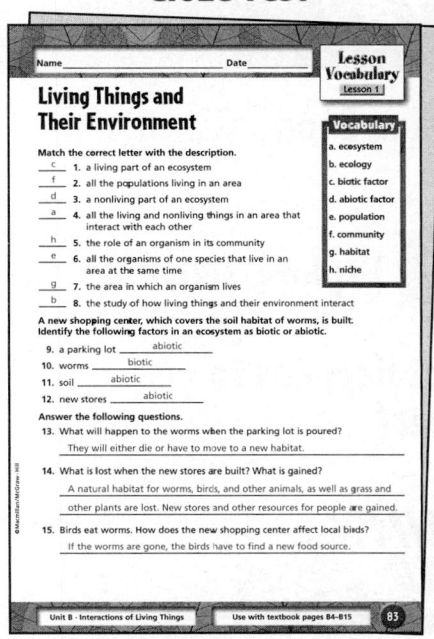

Reading in Science Resources,
pp. 83–84, 89–90, 95–96

Activities and Assessment

McGraw-Hill Science **Activity Resources** provides the following **Blackline Master** worksheets for every lesson in this chapter.

Explore Activity and Alternative Explore Activity

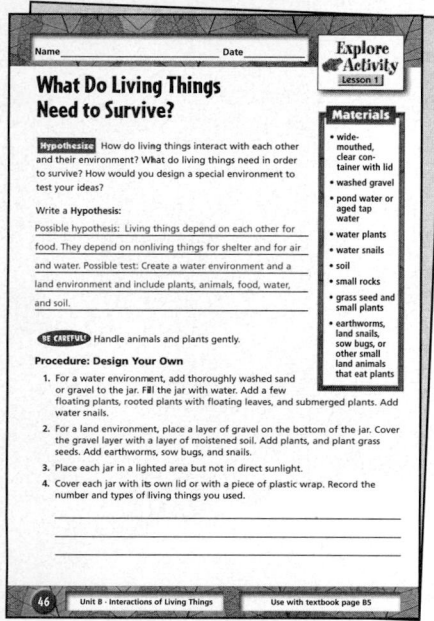

Activity Resources, pp. 46–48, 51–54, 57–59

Quick Lab for School or Home

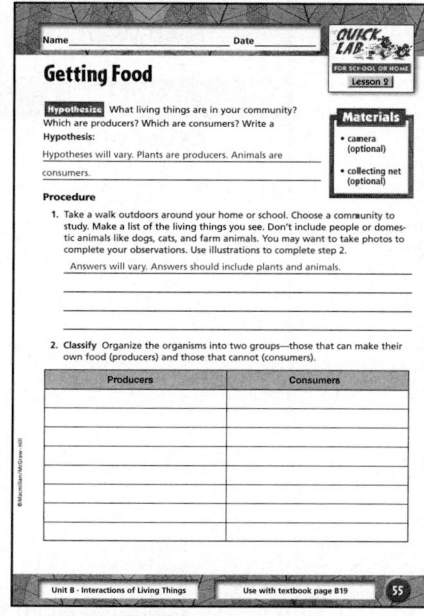

Activity Resources, pp. 55–56, 60–61

Process Skill Builder

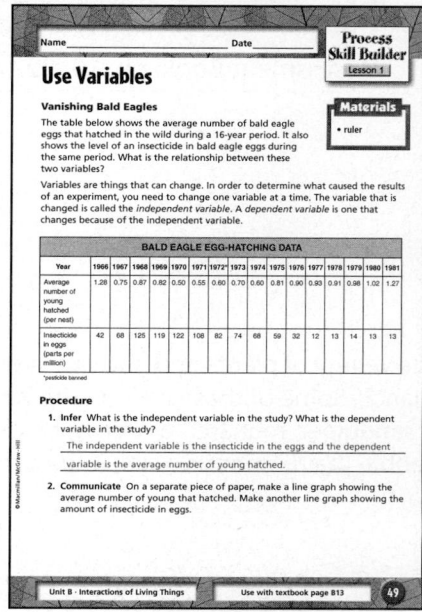

Activity Resources, pp. 49–50

McGraw-Hill Science **Assessment Book** provides the following **Blackline Master** worksheets for this chapter.

Chapter Test

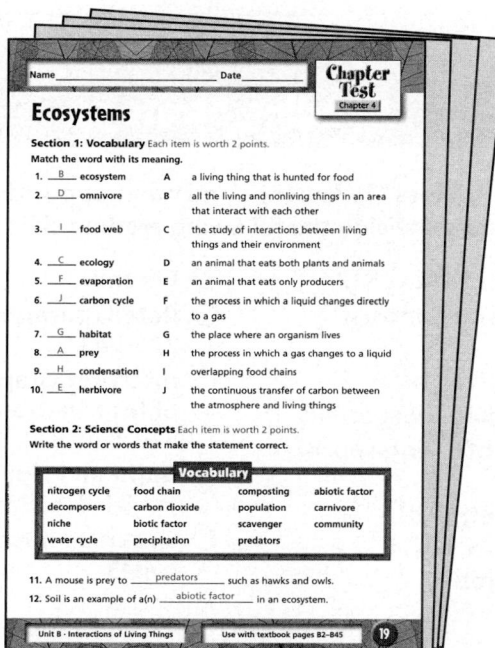

Assessment Book, pp. 19–22

CHAPTER

4 Ecosystems

Resources

- Reading in Science Resources, pp. 76–99
- Assessment Book, pp. 19–22

Did You Ever Wonder?

A large variety of plants and animals live in the grasslands. Some of these include the white-tailed deer, sandpiper, monarch butterfly, black-tailed jackrabbit, prairie shooting star, and pasque flower.

CHAPTER

4 Ecosystems

Did You Ever Wonder?

What happened to the buffalo? The huge herds of buffalo that once roamed the grasslands of the United States were hunted almost to extinction. Today, however, buffalo can once again be seen in places like Yellowstone National Park. What other kinds of animals live in the grasslands?

B 2

Reading Strategy

This chapter provides MiniLessons and other opportunities for developing and practicing the following reading skills:

B 3

Vocabulary Preview

Encourage students to keep a Science Dictionary. Remind them to add the Vocabulary words for each lesson in this chapter to their Dictionary as they complete each lesson.

ecosystem, B6

ecology, B6

abiotic factor, B6

biotic factor, B7

population, B10

community, B10

habitat, B11

niche, B11

food chain, B18

food web, B20

herbivore, B20

carnivore, B20

predator, B21

prey, B21

scavenger, B21

omnivore, B21

evaporation, B32

condensation, B32

precipitation, B33

water cycle, B33

carbon cycle, B37

nitrogen cycle, B38

AMERICAN
MUSEUM ᴼꜰ
NATURAL
HISTORY

Visit **www.amnh.org/resources/mhscience** to discover more about ecosystems, food chains and webs, and the cycles of life.

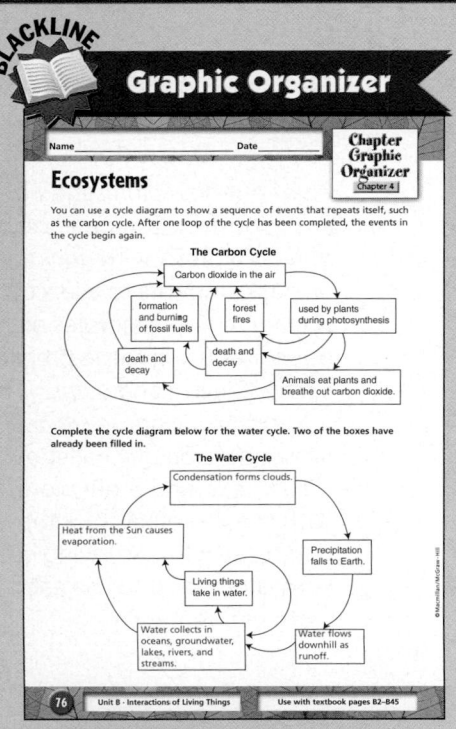

Reading in Science Resources, p. 76

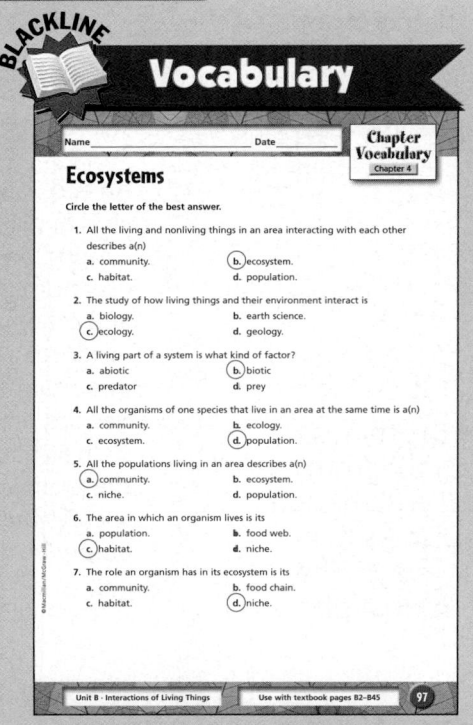

Reading in Science Resources, pp. 97–98

LESSON 1

Living Things and Their Environment

Objectives

- Explore a land or water environment to test what certain living things need to survive.
- Describe various ecosystems and the biotic and abiotic factors involved in them.
- Discuss variables that can affect population size and survival.

Resources

- Activity Resources, pp. 46–50
- Reading in Science Resources, pp. 79–84
- Vocabulary Cards
- Reading Aid Transparency B1
- Grade-Level Science Book, *The Eagles Are Back!*

Build on Prior Knowledge

Ask students who have terrariums or aquariums at home to discuss how they provide for the needs of the plants and animals in them. Have the class list the living and nonliving parts of the terrarium or aquarium. (Possible answers: living—fish, plants, lizards, snails; nonliving—rocks, water, gravel)

1 Get Ready

Developing the Main Idea

Ask students to explain where they get the things they need to survive. (Possible answers: food from stores, gardens, farms; heat from natural gas, the sun; shelter made from wood, brick, stone) Discuss that animals and plants have the same basic needs. They get them from their surroundings (except that plants make their own food).

LESSON 1

Living Things and Their Environment

Vocabulary

ecosystem, B6
ecology, B6
abiotic factor, B6
biotic factor, B7
population, B10
community, B10
habitat, B11
niche, B11

Get Ready

What do you need in order to survive? Food? Water? Comfortable temperatures? Shelter? What kinds of things does the animal shown here need to survive? What kinds of things do the plants need? Where do you think they get these things?

Process Skill

You experiment when you perform a test to support or disprove a hypothesis.

B 4

Science Background

Ecosystems

An ecosystem named for one kind of plant or animal may support a variety of other organisms through a food web and other relationships. For instance, a prairie-dog town is important to many species besides prairie dogs. Species such as badgers and hawks eat the prairie dogs. Other species, such as burrowing owls, use empty burrows.

English Language Learners

Opposites

Point out how *biotic* and *abiotic* are opposites. Compare the use of *a-* as a prefix with *non-* and *un-*. Ask students to use a dictionary to find examples of opposites using these prefixes, such as *typical* and *atypical*, *living* and *nonliving*, *developed* and *undeveloped*. Challenge students to find other words with these prefixes that they might see while studying ecosystems and to use each word in a sentence. **Linguistic**

Explore Activity

What Do Living Things Need to Survive?

Procedure: Design Your Own

BE CAREFUL! Handle animals and plants gently.

1 For a water environment, add thoroughly washed sand or gravel to the jar. Fill the jar with water. Add a few floating plants, rooted plants with floating leaves, and submerged plants. Add water snails.

2 For a land environment, place a layer of gravel on the bottom of the jar. Cover the gravel layer with a layer of moistened soil. Add plants, and plant grass seeds. Add earthworms, sow bugs, and snails.

3 Place each jar in a lighted area but not in direct sunlight.

4 Cover each jar with its own lid or with a piece of plastic wrap. Record the number and types of living things you used.

5 **Observe** Examine your jars every other day, and record your observations.

Drawing Conclusions

1 **Infer** What are the nonliving parts of your system? What are the living parts of your system?

2 **Infer** What do the living things need to survive? How do you know?

3 **Going Further: Experiment** How could you design an environment that contains both land and water areas?

Materials

- wide-mouthed, clear container with lid
- washed gravel
- pond water or aged tap water
- water plants
- water snails
- soil
- small rocks
- grass seed and small plants
- earthworms, land snails, sow bugs, or other small land animals that eat plants

B 5

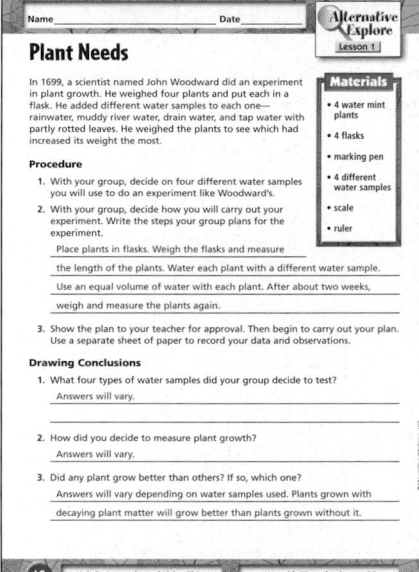

Alternative Explore Activity

Materials 4 water mint plants, 4 flasks, 4 different water samples, scale, ruler, marker

Plant Needs In 1699 John Woodward weighed four plants, put each in a flask, then added rainwater to one, muddy river water to the second, drain water to the third, and tap water with partly rotted leaves to the fourth. The fourth one increased its weight the most. He concluded that the growth was due to "terrestrial matter." Challenge teams to do a similar experiment and compare findings. **Social**

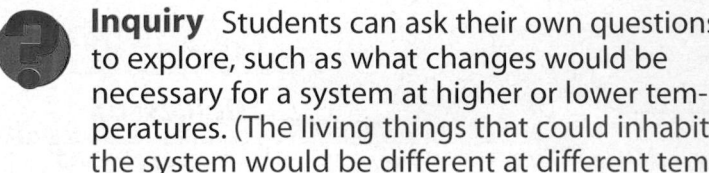

Activity Resources, p. 48

Explore Activity

What Do Living Things Need to Survive?

Science Process Skills *observe, infer, experiment*

Resources Activity Resources, pp. 46-47

Pacing 30-40 minutes 🕐

Grouping small groups

Procedure: Design Your Own

Be Careful! Stress the need to respect living things, plants and animals.

Suggest that some groups make land ecosystems and others make water ecosystems. Also suggest that students use reference materials to find out what resources their organisms need in their ecosystem

5 Students should record the growth and general health of the living things in their environment.

Answers to Drawing Conclusions

1 nonliving: water, sand, soil, gravel, rocks, sunlight, jar; living: plants, snails, earthworms, sow bugs

2 Air, water, food, light, shelter, warmth; both kinds of environments thrive when provided with these things.

3 Possible answer: Design a beach or a pond environment.

 **Inquiry** Students can ask their own questions to explore, such as what changes would be necessary for a system at higher or lower temperatures. (The living things that could inhabit the system would be different at different temperatures.)

Technology

- When time is short, preview the activity with the **Explore Activity Video**.

2 Read to Learn

What Is an Ecosystem?

Before Reading
Have students try to answer the red question at the top of the page.

Developing the Main Idea
Focus on the school as an ecosystem. Ask:

- **What living things do you see in your ecosystem?** (other students, teachers, staff; perhaps plants, trees, and small animals)

- **What nonliving things in this ecosystem help you survive?** (water fountains, food in the cafeteria, and the heating and cooling system)

Developing Vocabulary

ecosystem Derived from the Greek word *oikos*, for "house," *eco-* is the combining form meaning "environment or habitat." The word *system* means "a set of things so related or connected as to form a unity."

ecology The suffix *-logy* means "science, doctrine, or theory of." *Ecology* is the study of planet Earth.

abiotic factor *A-* means "not or without" and *bio-* translates to "of living things." Therefore, *abiotic factors* are the nonliving parts of an ecosystem.

Read to Learn

Main Idea Ecosystems have many parts.

What Is an Ecosystem?

What or whom do you interact with every day? Living things and nonliving things interact in an **ecosystem**. An ecosystem is all the living and nonliving things in an area. **Ecology** is the study of how all these things interact in order to survive.

An ecosystem may be very small, such as a backyard or pond. Some ecosystems, like the prairie ecosystem of North America, the deserts of Africa, and the rain forests of Brazil, cover large areas of a country or continent. Freshwater ecosystems cover less space than saltwater ecosystems. Saltwater ecosystems can cover entire oceans. It doesn't matter where they are or what they look like, all ecosystems have the same parts.

Abiotic Factors

The nonliving parts of an ecosystem are the **abiotic** (ay·bigh·AHT·ik) **factors**. All living things need certain nonliving things in order to survive. Abiotic factors include water, minerals, sunlight, air, climate, and soil.

All *organisms*, or living things, need water. Their bodies are 50 to 95 percent water. The processes that keep living things alive—like photosynthesis and respiration—can only take place in the presence of water. Living things also need minerals, such as calcium, iron, phosphorus, and nitrogen. Some living things, like plants and algae, need

sunlight to make food. Animals need oxygen to produce energy for their bodies. Plants and algae need carbon dioxide. The environment must also have the right temperature for organisms to survive.

B 6

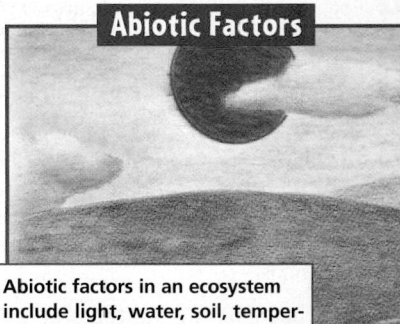

Abiotic Factors

Abiotic factors in an ecosystem include light, water, soil, temperature, air, and minerals.

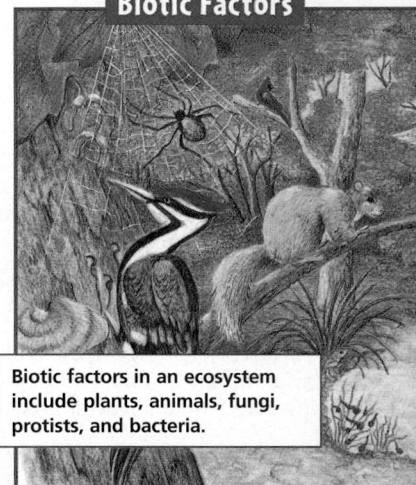

Biotic Factors

Biotic factors in an ecosystem include plants, animals, fungi, protists, and bacteria.

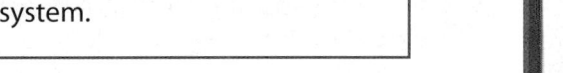

Math MiniLesson

Percent

Develop Percent is the ratio of a number to 100. *Percent* means "out of one hundred" or per 100.

The symbol for percent is %.

You can write a percent as a fraction with a denominator of 100.

$40\% = \frac{40}{100}$

To find the percent of a number, write the percent as a fraction and multiply.

Find 40% of 50 kg.

$40\% \times 50 = \frac{40}{100} \times 50 = 20$

So 40% of 50 kg is 20 kg.

 You can use the % key on a calculator to help find the percent of a number.

Find 40% of 50.
Enter the following:

5 0 ✕ 4 0 % ⬜ 20

Practice Find the percent of each number.

1. 72% of 100 (72)
2. 25% of 20 (5)
3. 8% of 50 (4)
4. 30% of 90 (27)

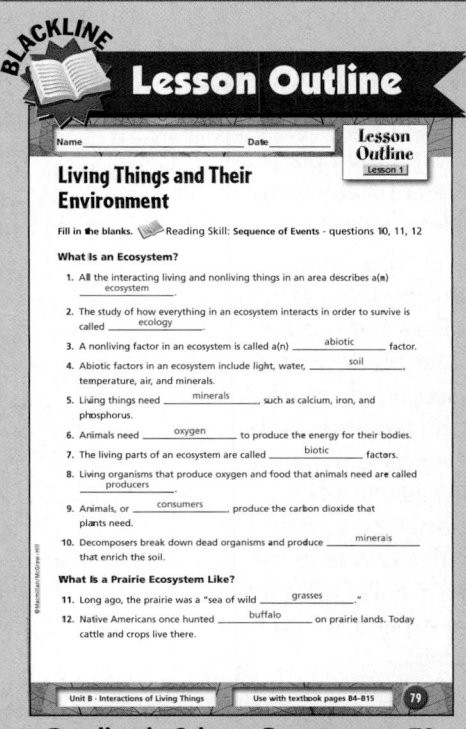

Lesson Outline

Reading in Science Resources, p. 79

1. How do these two diagrams differ? What does each diagram show?

2. Which of these two diagrams best shows the abiotic factors in the ecosystem? Explain your answer.

Biotic Factors

The right abiotic factors help make it possible for organisms in an ecosystem to survive. The living parts are animals, plants, fungi, protists, and bacteria. Mushrooms and molds are examples of fungi. Protists include one-celled organisms.

These organisms—animals, plants, fungi, protists, and bacteria—make up the **biotic** (bigh·AHT·ik) **factors**, or living parts, of an ecosystem.

Plants and algae are called *producers*. They produce oxygen and food that animals need. Animals are *consumers*. Animals consume, or eat, plants or animals. Animals also give off carbon dioxide that plants need to make food.

What do the fungi and bacteria contribute? They are a very important part of any ecosystem. Fungi and bacteria are *decomposers*. They *decompose*, or break down, dead plants and animals into useful things like minerals that enrich soil. Plants need these in order to grow.

Each of these kinds of organisms helps the others survive.

▶ **What are five abiotic and five biotic factors in an ecosystem?**

Water, sunlight, air, climate, minerals, and soil are abiotic factors. Animals, plants, fungi, protists, and bacteria are the biotic factors.

B 7

Developing the Main Idea

Ask students to think back to the Explore Activity and identify the producers (plants), consumers (animals), and decomposers (bacteria). Also ask them to identify the abiotic factors (the jar, sunlight, water).

1. The top diagram shows the nonliving parts of an ecosystem; the bottom diagram shows the living parts of an ecosystem.

2. the top diagram, since it shows Sun, water, soil, rocks and minerals, which are nonliving things

▶ After Reading

Have students answer the red question in the student book as **ongoing assessment**.

Developing Vocabulary

biotic factor Compare this term with *abiotic*, asking students to observe that the *a-* is no longer there. Students should infer that without that prefix, *biotic factors* must be the living parts of an ecosystem.

Interpret Illustrations

Name_____ Date_____

Interpret Illustrations
Lesson 1

What Is an Ecosystem?

This diagram shows two different pictures of what could be a single environment. One picture focuses on abiotic factors and the other on biotic factors. The small drawings in each picture show close-ups of some of the smaller factors.

Abiotic factors in an ecosystem include light, water, soil, temperature, air, and minerals.

Biotic factors in an ecosystem include plants, animals, fungi, protists, and bacteria.

Answer these questions about the diagram above.

1. Name three biotic factors in the diagram.
   Answers may include trees, mushroom, deer, frog, and small plants.

2. Name three abiotic factors in the diagram.
   Answers may include soil, rocks, water, clouds, and the Sun.

3. What factors are in the biotic close-up?
   Answers may include protists and bacteria.

4. What factors are in the abiotic close-up?
   Answers may include rocks and minerals.

Unit B · Interactions of Living Things   Use with textbook pages B6–B7   **81**

Reading in Science Resources, p. 81

Advanced Learners

Environmental Articles

Ask students to read about how changes in abiotic factors cause changes in the environment and affect living things. For example, they might look for newspaper, magazine, or Internet articles about the El Niño weather pattern or the eruption of a volcano, such as Mt. St. Helens. Encourage them to share what they learn in an oral report to the class.
Linguistic

What Is a Prairie Ecosystem Like?

Before Reading
Have students try to answer the red question at the top of the page.

Developing the Main Idea
Ask students to discuss the mental images the text evokes. Invite them to discuss what they would see if they had taken the first wagon train west in the nineteenth century. Ask them to include what they would take with them for survival and what they might find along the way.

Exploring the Main Idea
Invite students to use a map of the world to help them locate the various types of ecosystems as they learn about them. Distribute world outline maps for students to write on and color code the different ecosystems. For example, ask students to use reference materials to find out about grasslands all over the world. They are divided into two types—temperate and tropical. Grasslands have different names in different countries. Students may want to find out about steppes, savannas, and pampas; where they are found; and how they compare with prairies.

▶ After Reading
Have students answer the red question in the student book as **ongoing assessment**.

What Is a Prairie Ecosystem Like?

Long ago a "sea of wild grasses" covered North America from central Texas in the south to North Dakota in the north. These were America's prairie lands, the range of the famous song "Home on the Range."

The Blackland Prairie is the largest remaining prairie in America. It stretches 483 km (300 mi) across Texas, from Austin to Clarksville. The Blacklands got their name from the rich black soil the early settlers found there. The settlers found that the summers were hot and long, and that there was enough rain to grow profitable crops, like cotton.

Before the land became farms and ranches, huge herds of buffalo grazed on the prairie grasses. Native Americans once hunted the buffalo on this land for food and clothing as a means of survival.

Buffalo were not the prairie's only inhabitants. Plants and animals of all kinds lived there. At least 50 different kinds of tall and short grasses provided food for plant-eating animals. Many kinds of wildflowers painted the landscape with beautiful colors. These flowers included purple coneflowers, bluebells, yellow sunflowers, and golden daleas. Travelers might have come across oak, hickory, elm, or cedar trees along nearby streams.

The cattle and crops that provide much of our food live on the prairie today. Ranchers and farmers now graze cattle and plant crops such as corn and wheat on the Blacklands.

B 8

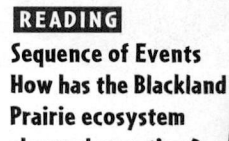
The Blackland Prairie covers almost 13 million acres. Many kinds of animals and plants live on a prairie. A prairie is a region of grasses. It may be flat or hilly grassland.

READING
Sequence of Events
How has the Blackland Prairie ecosystem changed over time?

At one time the Blackland Prairie was a grassland. Buffalo lived on the prairie and were hunted by Native Americans. Settlers moved onto the land and planted new crops. The buffalo left.

Reading MiniLesson

Sequence of Events

Develop Discuss the importance of putting events in sequence in order to make sense out of things. For example, knowing how the Blackland Prairie changed over time helps us better understand its ecosystem today.

Practice Have students point out words or phrases on page B8 that are clues to the sequence of events in the Blackland Prairie. (Answers should include: paragraph one begins with "Long ago"; paragraph three begins with "Before the land became farms and ranches"; details about the past have verbs in the past tense and details about today have verbs in the present tense.)

Science Background

Prairies
Prairies once covered one-fifth of North America, making them the largest grassland on the continent. Other types of grasslands include desert grasslands, California grasslands, and mountainous grasslands. There are three types of prairies—tall-grass in the east, short-grass in the west, and mixed-grass in between. Have students make a search for pictures of different kinds of grasslands and show them to the class. **Spatial**

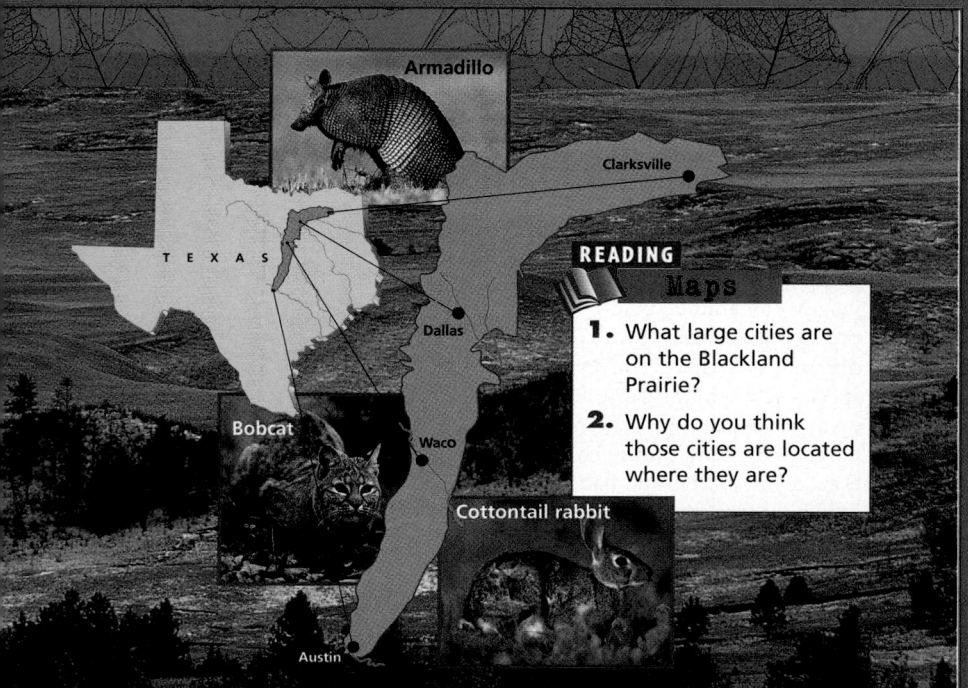

Armadillo

Clarksville

T E X A S

Dallas

Bobcat

Waco

Cottontail rabbit

Austin

READING

Maps

1. What large cities are on the Blackland Prairie?

2. Why do you think those cities are located where they are?

What Animals Live on the Blackland Prairie?

About 500 species, or different kinds, of animals still live on this prairie. The spotted chorus frog sings in the night near the streams and rivers. Rattlesnakes and lizards seek shelter under rocks.

Birds like pipits, longspurs, and horned larks, as well as 300 other kinds of birds, still live on the Blackland Prairie.

Raccoons, opossums, coyotes, white-tailed deer, and striped skunks live on the Blacklands. Cotton rats, white-footed mice, eastern cottontails, red bats, and bobcats live there, too.

Mountain lions, gray wolves, black bears, and jaguars used to come in search of prey. When people came and built towns, cities, and farms, the buffalo left. The animals that fed on the buffalo left, too. Some animals, however, came to the Blacklands from other places, and stayed. Armadillos arrived from Mexico as the Blacklands' climate warmed up over the past 150 years. Badgers invaded from northwestern Texas when their natural homes were cleared for development.

▷ **What are five animals that live on the prairie?**

Answer may include snakes, lizards, types of birds, raccoons, coyotes, deer, and bats.

Prairie dogs

B 9

Interpret Illustrations

Name_____ Date_____

Interpret Illustrations Lesson 1

The Blackland Prairie

The Blackland Prairie is the largest remaining prairie in the United States. About 500 species of animals live on this prairie.

Clarksville

T E X A S

Dallas

Waco

Austin

Answer the following questions about the map above.

1. Describe how the Blackland Prairie is situated within Texas.
   It curves from the northeast down into central Texas.

2. Name three cities or towns within the Blackland Prairie.
   Possible answers include Austin, Waco, Dallas, and Clarksville.

3. What do most of the cities have in common in terms of the geographical features of their location?
   Three of the four are located on rivers.

82   Unit B • Interactions of Living Things   Use with textbook page B9

Reading in Science Resources, p. 82

SCIENCE FOR ALL

Inclusion

American Buffalo

Encourage students to find out more about how important the American buffalo was to Native Americans and how they depended on the buffalo for food, clothing, and shelter. Challenge them to find out what happened to Native Americans once the buffalo were gone and how many buffalo are alive today in the United States and where they live. **Linguistic**

What Animals Live on the Blackland Prairie?

Before Reading
Have students try to answer the red question at the top of the text column.

Developing the Main Idea
Ask students to discuss other reasons why an animal might leave an environment. Help them explore changes in food availability, climate, and the amount of hunting. Ask:

■ **How do some animals survive such threats to their existence?** (They adapt by finding a new place to live or new food sources.)

Thinking Further: *Drawing Conclusions*
Ask:

■ **What happens to predators when their prey leave an environment?** (The predator has to find a new food source or a new environment.)

Using the Illustrations
Tell students that the Blackland Prairie of Texas actually consists of several Blackland Prairies: the Eagle Ford Prairie, the White Rock Prairie and the Taylor Black Prairie. The rock layers of the regions differ from each other.

READING

Maps

1. Austin, Waco, Dallas, Clarksville

2. The cities are located near lakes, streams, and rivers where the soil is fertile and rainfall is sufficient, making the land suitable for farming, grazing, and building.

▶ **After Reading**
Have students answer the red question in the student book as **ongoing assessment**.

How Are Living Things Organized?

Before Reading
Have students try to answer the red question at the top of the page.

Developing the Main Idea
Help students draw a pyramid that shows how organisms, species, populations, and communities are related.

Exploring the Main Idea
Have students observe different species that live in their area and keep track of them in a table. They should identify each species as prey, predators, producers, consumers, or decomposers.

▶After Reading
Have students answer the red question in the student book as **ongoing assessment**.

Developing Vocabulary

population *Population* is usually used in the context of the number of people in a given area. However, *population* does not apply only to people, but to any species in a given area.

community Ask students to describe their own communities—a group of people living in a particular city or town.

How Are Living Things Organized?

The Blackland Prairie, like all ecosystems, is home to many different organisms. Each kind of organism, whether an animal, plant, fungus, protist, or bacterium, is a member of a different species. All the organisms of a species living in the same area make up a **population**.

The Blackland Prairie has populations of armadillos and badgers. It has little bluestem grass and Indian grass. It has elm trees. It also has pond algae and soil bacteria.

Most people are satisfied with just identifying the populations around them. Scientists, however, want to know how populations interact. Scientists investigate the activities of animals, plants, fungi, protists, and bacteria in the ecosystem. They want to know which animals prey on others. Which animals eat plants? Which insects eat crops? They are interested in how bacteria and fungi make the soil fertile. All these questions need to be answered to understand how an ecosystem stays healthy.

Scientists have to do more than study individual organisms or even individual populations in the ecosystem. They have to study the interactions of all the populations in an area. All the populations living in an area make up a **community**.

▷ What are populations and communities?

A population consists of all organisms of the same species in the same area; a community consists of all the populations living in the same area.

Scientists study the interactions of different populations in an ecosystem's community. This helps them to understand what makes an ecosystem grow.

B 10

Reading Strategy

Paraphrase
Developing Reading Skills
Ask students to write a paragraph describing the prairie as an ecosystem, including all the factors that interact with each other (pp. B8–B9), as well as the organization of living things into populations and communities.

Science Background

Gause's Principle
C.F. Gause, a Russian biologist, said that no two species could share the same niche. Gause's principle has been accepted and scientists have found few exceptions. This specialization of niches allows many kinds of animals to live in the same area because they are not competing for the same resources.

Inclusion

Naturalists
Invite a naturalist from an area park or local conservation group to address the class about what kinds of populations live in your area, how those populations interact, and how different animals have different niches in the same area.
Spatial; Social

What Are Niches and Habitats?

The place where an organism lives is called its `habitat`. The chorus frog's habitat is in the scattered ponds of the Blacklands.

Each species in an ecosystem also has a role or place in the activities of its community. The role of an organism in the community is its `niche`.

A species' niche includes many factors. It includes what a species eats and what eats that species. It includes the kind of environment the species needs to live in. It even includes whether the species is active by day or night.

No two populations can have the same niche. Why is this true? To have the same niche, two populations would have to eat the same foods and be eaten by the same predators. They would have to live in the same space and reproduce in the same ways. They would have to grow under the same temperature, moisture, and light conditions, get the same diseases, and look and behave exactly alike. They would have to be identical! No two populations are identical though, so no two populations have the same niche.

Scientists study the habitats and niches of organisms in a community. They do this to see if the community is healthy or in trouble.

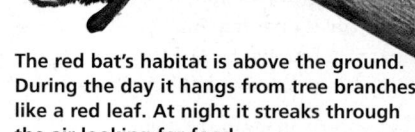

The red bat's habitat is above the ground. During the day it hangs from tree branches like a red leaf. At night it streaks through the air looking for food.

> **What is the difference between a niche and a habitat?**
> A habitat is the place where a population lives; a niche is an organism's role in the community.

The horned lark has its niche on the prairie.

B 11

What Are Niches and Habitats?

Before Reading
Have students try to answer the red question at the top of the page.

Developing the Main Idea
Ask students again to imagine their school as an ecosystem. Help them identify various niches. Ask them to discuss the roles various people have and how those roles affect other members of the community.

▶ After Reading
Have students answer the red question in the student book as **ongoing assessment**.

Developing Vocabulary

`habitat` Have students think about what kinds of habits they may have—they brush their teeth every morning, they eat breakfast, they get dressed. A habit is a tendency to behave in a certain way. A *habitat* is where organisms have a habit of living.

`niche` From the Latin word *nidus*, meaning "nest," *niche* is the specific space occupied by an organism. In ecological terms that "space" is defined as a particular role or activity in the community.

Technology

■ **Science Experiences Videotapes**
Ponds: Freshwater Habitats (Package 1)
Life in a Coral Reef (Package 2)
Researching the Ocean Depths (Package 7)

What Happens When Habitats Change?

Before Reading
Have students try to answer the red question at the top of the page.

Developing the Main Idea
Point out how the degree of specialization of a niche can determine if an animal thrives. Giant pandas, for example, have a narrow niche that depends on bamboo shoots. When the shoots are scarce, the pandas have a hard time surviving. The red fox is an opportunistic feeder and can thrive even in a developed city. Ask students to think about how an animal's niche affects its survival.

Exploring the Main Idea
Ask students to list factors that might cause changes in a habitat. (examples: weather changes such as floods and droughts; disasters such as fires, earthquakes, volcanic eruptions; human intervention) Ask students how their habitat may change and how they would adapt to such changes.

▶ After Reading
Have students answer the red question in the student book as **ongoing assessment**.

What Happens When Habitats Change?

The world is a place of changes. One day the weather may be dry and cold. The next day it may be wet and warm. Heavy rains may drench the land one spring and summer. The next year's spring and summer may have cloudless skies day after day. This makes habitats change. A good habitat for a certain organism at one time may be a threatening one at another time. How do populations survive difficult times?

Bald eagles were once common on the Blackland Prairie.

The Eastern Spadefoot Toad
The eastern spadefoot toad lives on the Blackland Prairie. This animal reproduces in water and needs water for its daily life. What happens if a drought strikes the Blacklands?

A close look at the toad's hind feet provided scientists with a clue to the answer. Its hind feet are shaped like little spades. They are adapted for digging. That's just what the spadefoot toad does when water is scarce. It digs into the ground and covers itself with soil. This toad can absorb water through its skin. There's a lot of clay in Blacklands soil, and clay holds water well. Usually there is some water in the soil, even though there may not be any water above it. The toad may be able to survive in the soil even during a drought.

B 12

American Bald Eagles
Many years ago there were bald eagles on the Blackland Prairie of Texas. Then they disappeared. A few have returned recently, especially around the lakes created by damming rivers. Why did the eagles disappear for a while?

Scientists carefully analyzed data to discover one reason why bald eagles may have vanished from the skies above the Blackland Prairie.

▷ **What happens to animals when habitats change?**

Animals find new habitats or find ways to adapt to their habitat in times of change.

The eastern spadefoot toad can survive in a dry, hot habitat by burrowing into the soil and absorbing water through its skin.

Reading Strategy

Cause and Effect
Developing Reading Skills
Ask students to write a paragraph to explain how changes in habitats can affect the eastern spadefoot toad and bald eagles. They should include their conclusions from the data on bald eagles given on p. B13.

Science Background

Eagles
Of the 60 species of eagles, only two are native to North America—the golden eagle and the bald eagle. The bald eagle has been protected by federal law for decades. Its numbers have dropped because of the loss of wilderness regions and increased pollution. The numbers have made a gradual comeback since the mid-1970s because of restrictions on pollutants, restocking of nesting areas, and the eagles' adaptation to living closer to humans.

SKILL Use Variables

Vanishing Bald Eagles

The table below shows the average number of bald eagle eggs that hatched in the wild during a 16-year period. It also shows the level of an insecticide in bald eagle eggs during the same period. What is the relationship between these two variables?

Variables are things that can change. In order to determine what caused the results of an experiment, you need to change one variable at a time. The variable that is changed is called the *independent variable*. A *dependent variable* is one that changes because of the independent variable.

Materials
ruler

Bald Eagle Egg-Hatching Data																
Year	1966	1967	1968	1969	1970	1971	1972*	1973	1974	1975	1976	1977	1978	1979	1980	1981
Average number of young hatched (per nest)	1.28	0.75	0.87	0.82	0.50	0.55	0.60	0.70	0.60	0.81	0.90	0.93	0.91	0.98	1.02	1.27
Insecticide in eggs (parts per million)	42	68	125	119	122	108	82	74	68	59	32	12	13	14	13	13

*pesticide banned

Procedure

1 **Infer** What is the independent variable in the study? What is the dependent variable in the study?

2 **Communicate** Make a line graph showing the average number of young that hatched. Make another line graph showing the amount of insecticide in eggs.

Drawing Conclusions

1 **Use Variables** Based on the graphs, what appears to be the relationship between the amount of insecticide in eggs and the number of young hatched?

2 **Hypothesize** Suggest a reason for the relationship.

B 13

Process Skill
B U I L D E R

Vanishing Bald Eagles

Science Process Skills *use variables*, *infer*, *communicate*, *hypothesize*

Resources Activity Resources, pp. 49–50

Pacing 30 minutes

Grouping individuals or pairs

Procedure

1 independent variable: amount of insecticide in the eggs; dependent variable: average number of young hatched

2 The first graph should show a general decrease until 1971 and then a general increase. The second graph should show a general increase until 1971 and then a general decrease.

Answers to Drawing Conclusions

1 As insecticide levels increased, the average number of young hatched decreased.

2 The insecticide interfered with the ability of the eggs to produce live young.

Process Skills
MiniLesson

Use Variables

Develop This skill involves identifying and separating things in an experiment that can be changed or controlled. When scientists conduct experiments, all factors that might influence the results should be kept the same except for the one that is being changed. The variable that is changed is called the *independent variable*. A variable that changes because of the independent variable is called the *dependent variable*.

Some variables that influence the rate at which seeds germinate, for example, include temperature, amount of water, type of soil, and type of seeds.

Practice Pose to students: You want to find the ideal growing conditions for a particular kind of forest plant. What would be some independent variables in your experiment? (light, moisture, soil type, temperature) A complete list of Science Process Skills appears on p. S7.

What Is the Treasure of the Blackland Prairie?

Before Reading
Have students try to answer the red question at the top of the text column.

Developing the Main Idea
Ask students what factors are important for plant growth. (water, sunlight, carbon dioxide, nutrients) Ask:

- **Where does a plant get water?** (Rain falls on the ground.)
- **What has to hold the water?** (the soil)
- **How does humus help soil hold water?** (It creates spaces where water can be trapped.)

Exploring the Main Idea
Ask students why good soil is important to plants. (It provides nutrients needed for plant growth.) Show students different soil samples. Have them observe the color, texture, and content of each one. Discuss which would be best for growing crops and why.

▶After Reading
Have students answer the red question in the student book as **ongoing assessment**.

What Is the Treasure of the Blackland Prairie?

Have you ever read about a buried treasure? Unlike those stories, the treasure of the Blackland Prairie is not buried underground. The treasure of the Blackland Prairie is the ground.

Prairie soils can often be identified by their dark brown to black *topsoil*. Topsoil is the top layer of soil. The dark color shows the presence of *humus*. Humus is partly decayed plant matter. The decay is produced by the bacteria and fungi.

The rich topsoil is full of minerals that prairie grasses and crops need. Two of the most important minerals are magnesium and calcium. Plants need magnesium in order to make chlorophyll. Calcium is an important element of cell walls in plants.

Today most of the natural grasses that used to sway in the wind like ocean waves are gone from the Blackland Prairie. They have been replaced by "seas" of cultivated grasses. Is this a good thing?

The nutrients in certain prairie soils tend to stay near the surface. That's true because of the low yearly rainfall on prairies. There isn't enough water to carry the nutrients deep into the ground. Farmers take advantage of this by growing crops that have shallow roots, such as corn, wheat, cotton, and sorghum. Sorghum is a grain that is used to feed livestock. What do these crops have in common with the plants that grow naturally on the prairie? They are all classified as grasses.

 How can you describe the soil of the Blackland Prairie?

The Blacklands soil is dark brown, is rich in humus, and contains many minerals or nutrients, which stay near the surface.

B 14

Why It Matters

In nature ecosystems tend to stay in balance. One population controls the number in another population. Communities help preserve and enrich the soil. Some organisms contribute to the health and well-being of others. This balance, however, can be upset by the actions of people. Cities are built on the land. Crops are cultivated. The land changes. Its natural inhabitants disappear. People gain certain things but lose others. It is important to make wise decisions when you think of changing an ecosystem. Otherwise you may lose more than you gain.

Think and Write

1. Describe the structure of an ecosystem.

2. What is the difference between a population and a community?

3. How does an animal's habitat relate to its niche?

4. **Use Variables** Give examples of how biotic and abiotic factors interact in an ecosystem.

5. **Critical Thinking** Identify changes caused by human activity in your ecosystem. Explain what was lost and what was gained. Evaluate the results.

L·I·N·K·S

ART LINK

Make a poster. Visit a local ecosystem like a park, pond, or even your backyard. Draw all the living and nonliving things you see. Label the biotic and the abiotic factors you included in your picture.

LITERATURE LINK

Read *The Eagles Are Back!* to learn about two eaglets named Ross and Betsey who were raised in a safe environment and then were returned to the wild. Try the activities at the end of the book.

MATH LINK

Find the range. Using the data on page B13, determine the range of young hatched and the range of insecticide in eggs from 1966 to 1981. Remember, the range is the difference between the largest number and the smallest number in a set of data.

TECHNOLOGY LINK

At the Computer Visit **www.mhscience02.com** for more links.

B 15

Informal Assessment

Easy/Average Ask students to define each of the science words to a partner. Also, ask them to define *producer*, *consumer*, and *decomposer*.

Challenge Invite students to design an illustrated brochure for visitors to the Blackland Prairie. Encourage them to include background information about prairies and ecosystems and the place of the prairie in U.S. history.

---

3 Lesson Review

Answers to Think and Write

1. An ecosystem consists of all the living and non-living things in an area interacting with one another. (p. B6)

2. A population is all the members of the same species in an area; a community is all the different populations living in an area. (p. B10)

3. A habitat is the place where it lives; its niche is its role in its community. (p. B11)

4. **Use Variables** Possible answer: The biotic factors (plants and animals) need oxygen and carbon dioxide from the air and water (abiotic factors) to breathe, carry on photosynthesis, and absorb food. (pp. B6, B7)

5. **Critical Thinking** Possible answer: The land was cleared for construction or farming. A building, or crop, was gained but natural habitat was lost. (pp. B8–B9, B12, B15)

Summarize

Check students' understanding by having them write a brief summary of the lesson in their own words.

ART LINK

Check that students have properly identified which factors are biotic and which are abiotic.

LITERATURE LINK

Have students read the Grade-Level Science Book, *The Eagles Are Back!* Additional books to read can be found on TE p. B1·b.

MATH LINK

Remind students to look for the lowest and highest numbers in each set. The range of young hatched is $1.28 - 0.50 = 0.78$. The range of the insecticide is $125 - 12 = 113$ ppm.

LESSON 2 Food Chains and Food Webs

Objectives

- Explore how a change in a population can affect an ecosystem.
- Understand the relationship between food chains and food webs.
- Describe a food pyramid and the roles various organisms play in them.

Resources

- Activity Resources, pp. 51–56
- Reading in Science Resources, pp. 85–90
- Vocabulary Cards
- Reading Aid Transparency B2
- Visual Aid Transparency 8
- School to Home Activities, pp. 10–11

Build on Prior Knowledge

Focus on interpedence. Ask:

- **Why do animals depend on plants?** (They need the plants for food and oxygen.)
- **How can some plants be helped by animals?** (Possible answers: Animals may help spread their seeds to new areas or may remove other plants that compete for space and resources.)

1 Get Ready

Developing the Main Idea

Ask students how a prairie community would be affected if a drought decreased the numbers of plants. (Possible answers: The insect population would decrease because there would be less food for them. Fewer insects would result in a decrease in insect-eating animals. Populations dependent on the insect-eaters would also decrease.)

LESSON 2 Food Chains and Food Webs

Vocabulary

food chain, B18
food web, B20
herbivore, B20
carnivore, B20
predator, B21
prey, B21
scavenger, B21
omnivore, B21

Get Ready

Populations provide energy-rich food for one another. Grasses and other green plants provide food for gazelles. Lions feed on gazelles. What do you think might happen if a drought reduced the number of grasses? How can changes in a population lead to changes in the ecosystem where it lives?

Process Skill

You predict when you state possible results of an event or experiment.

B 16

Cross Curricular Books

Additional Outside Reading

The Beekeepers' Story

To order, see page B1·b.

Science Background

Humans in Food Chains

Addressing Misconceptions
Some students may think that humans are always at the top of the food chain. That is not always the case. Humans can be in a food chain in which another organism is the top consumer, such as sharks or tigers. Decomposers are at the end of most food chains, for example. Humans are part of the great web of life, but they are not always on the top.
Logical

Explore Activity

How Do Populations Interact?

Procedure

1 Cut out the cards representing the plants and animals in the ecosystem.

2 Label the top of your paper *Sunlight*.

3 Place the plant cards on the paper, and link each to the sunlight with tape and string.

4 Link each plant-eating animal to a plant card. Link each meat-eating animal to its food source. Only two animals can be attached to a food source. Record the links you have made.

5 Fire destroys half the plants. Remove four plant cards. Rearrange the animal cards. Remove animal cards if more than two animals link to any one food source. Record the changes you have made.

Drawing Conclusions

1 **Observe** What has happened to the plant eaters as a result of the fire? To the animal eaters?

2 **Infer** Half of the plants that were lost in the fire grow back again. What happens to the animal populations?

3 **Experiment** Try adding or removing plant or animal cards. What happens to the rest of the populations?

4 **Going Further: Predict** If plants or prey become scarce, their predators may move to a new area. What will happen to the ecosystem the predators move into?

Materials
tape
string
population cards

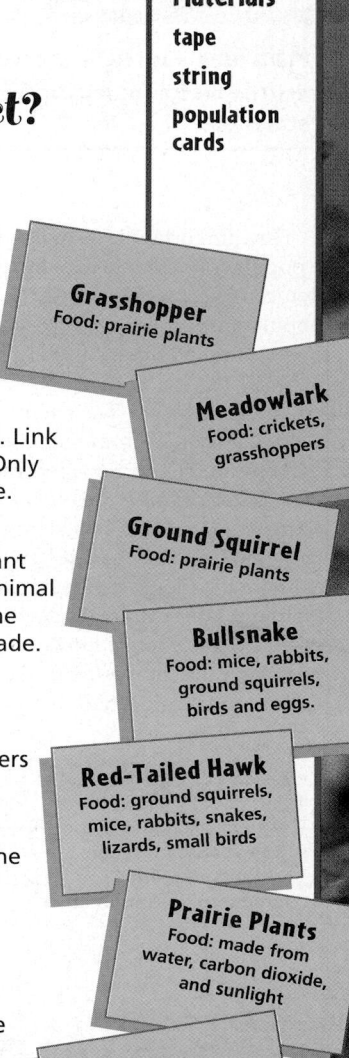

Grasshopper
Food: prairie plants

Meadowlark
Food: crickets, grasshoppers

Ground Squirrel
Food: prairie plants

Bullsnake
Food: mice, rabbits, ground squirrels, birds and eggs.

Red-Tailed Hawk
Food: ground squirrels, mice, rabbits, snakes, lizards, small birds

Prairie Plants
Food: made from water, carbon dioxide, and sunlight

Coyote
Food: rabbits, ground squirrels, meadow mice, other rodents

Alternative Explore Activity

Materials construction paper, scissors, tape, reference materials

Food Chain Model Ask students to construct a food chain starting with the Sun, then plants, organisms that eat plants, and meat eaters. Direct them to make and label a link for each member of the chain, and connect the links in the appropriate order. They can use reference books to identify individual species and add their names to the links. They can also connect more than one species to a link.
Spatial; Kinesthetic

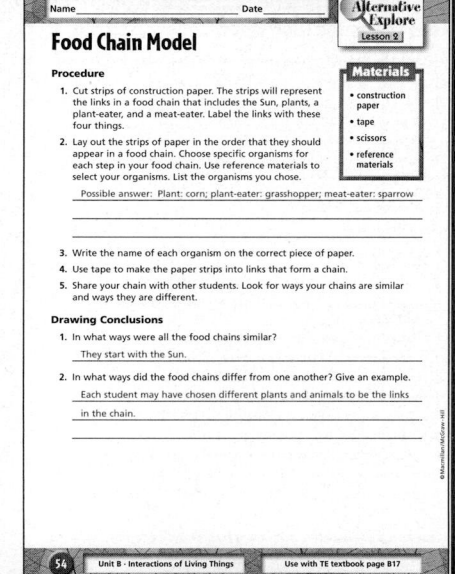

Explore Activity

How Do Populations Interact?

Science Process Skills *observe, infer, experiment, predict*

Resources Activity Resources, pp. 51–53

Pacing 30–40 minutes

Grouping individual

Procedure

1 Activity Resources, p. 53, contains 23 cards that can be used for this activity.

4 Possible answers: Prairie plants link to sunlight; grasshopper, squirrel link to prairie plants; meadowlark links to grasshopper; bullsnake to meadowlark; and red-tail hawk, coyote link to squirrel.

Answers to Drawing Conclusions

1 Since the number of plants decreased, the plants could no longer support the same number of plant eaters. The number of plant eaters decreased, as did the number of animal eaters.

2 The animal populations increase because more food is available.

3 Populations depend on each other for food and increase or decrease according to the amount of food available.

4 These predators will consume food that was previously consumed by other organisms. Competition for food in the new ecosystem will become greater and some organisms will have to move out or they will die.

Inquiry Students can ask their own questions to explore, such as what would happen if one of the animals were removed from the community. (Possible result: The plant population might increase, which would lead to an increase in the populations of plant-eating animals.)

Technology

■ When time is short, preview the activity with the **Explore Activity Video**.

What Is a Food Chain?

Before Reading
Have students try to answer the red question at the top of the page.

Developing the Main Idea
Point out that producers get energy from the Sun directly, while consumers get energy from the Sun indirectly.

Exploring the Main Idea
Help students build a food chain on the board. Ask:

- **What members of a prairie food chain are mentioned?** (plants, mouse, hawk, grasshopper, lizard)

- **Where does the food chain begin?** (with the Sun)

- **What are the first organisms in the food chain?** (plants)

- **Where does the food chain end?** (with decomposers)

Developing Vocabulary

food chain Remind students of the nursery rhyme *There Was an Old Lady Who Swallowed a Fly*. Ask them if this accurately depicts a food chain and what the primary producer is. (There is none.) Invite them to change the words or create their own rhyme describing a food chain found in nature.

Read to Learn

Main Idea Food chains and food webs describe the feeding relationship in an ecosystem.

What Is a Food Chain?

How important is a small change in a population? Changes in one population can affect several other populations in the same ecosystem. Every population needs energy in order to survive. Where does that energy come from? The energy in an ecosystem comes from the Sun.

You can feel the Sun's energy as it warms your skin. A meadow mouse scurrying through a Blacklands cornfield and a red-tailed hawk diving to snare the mouse can feel it, too. Neither of these animals can directly use the Sun's energy. However, they must have it to move, to breathe, to keep their hearts beating, and to stay alive.

The energy of the Sun is stored in food. The energy in food is passed from one organism to another in a **food chain**. A food chain is the path energy takes from producers to consumers to decomposers.

On the prairie the first organisms in a food chain are plants. Plants capture the Sun's energy during photosynthesis. This energy is stored in foods, or sugars, the plant makes for itself.

What happens when a plant eater such as a grasshopper eats the plant? It takes in the energy-rich sugars. Some of the energy is released for the grasshopper to use. Some of the energy is also stored in its tissues. Some is lost as heat. A Texas horned lizard may snap up the grasshopper, and a red-tailed hawk may eat the lizard. In the prairie community, the hawk is one of the organisms at the top of the food

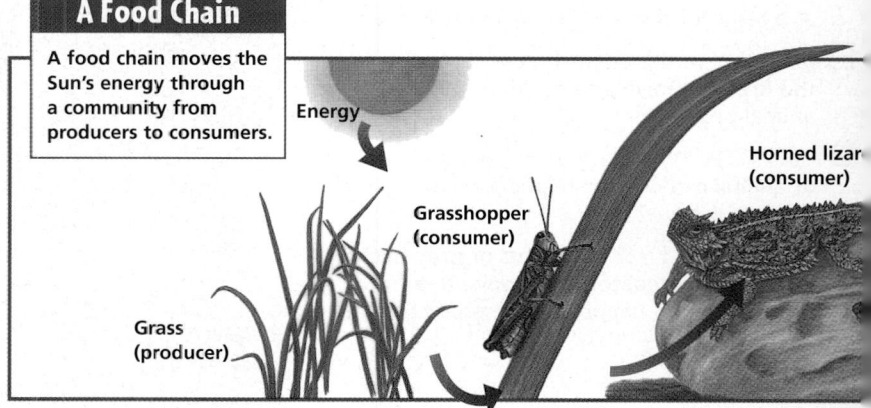

A Food Chain

A food chain moves the Sun's energy through a community from producers to consumers.

Energy

Grasshopper (consumer)

Horned lizard (consumer)

Grass (producer)

B 18

Lesson Outline

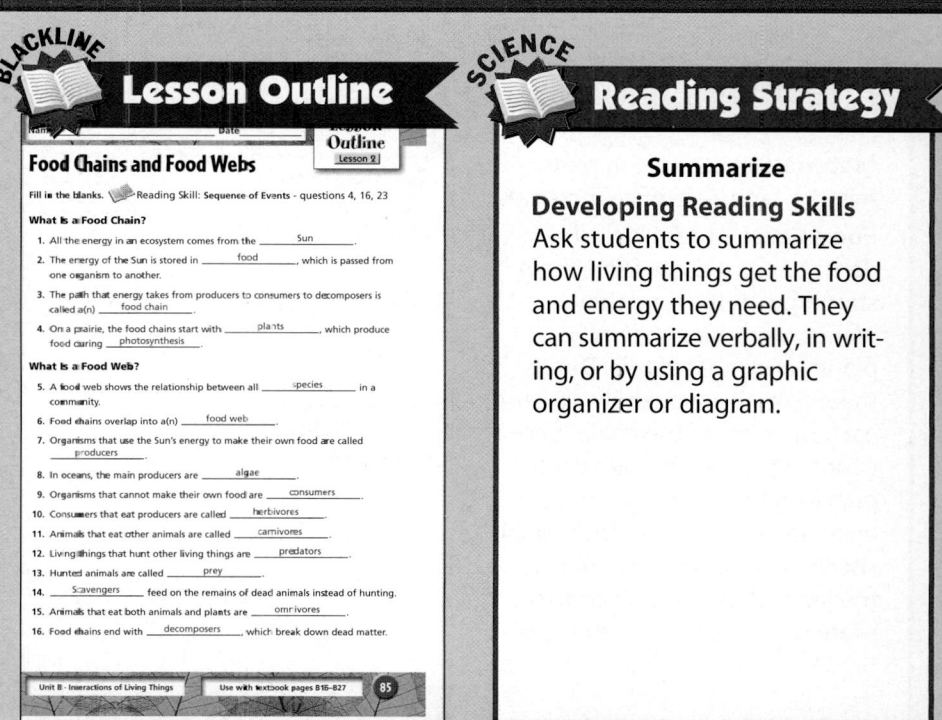

Name _____ Date _____

Reading and Writing Outline Lesson 2

Food Chains and Food Webs

Fill in the blanks. Reading Skill: Sequence of Events - questions 4, 16, 23

What Is a Food Chain?

1. All the energy in an ecosystem comes from the ___Sun___.

2. The energy of the Sun is stored in ___food___, which is passed from one organism to another.

3. The path that energy takes from producers to consumers to decomposers is called a(n) ___food chain___.

4. On a prairie, the food chains start with ___plants___, which produce food during ___photosynthesis___.

What Is a Food Web?

5. A food web shows the relationship between all ___species___ in a community.

6. Food chains overlap into a(n) ___food web___.

7. Organisms that use the Sun's energy to make their own food are called ___producers___.

8. In oceans, the main producers are ___algae___.

9. Organisms that cannot make their own food are ___consumers___.

10. Consumers that eat producers are called ___herbivores___.

11. Animals that eat other animals are called ___carnivores___.

12. Living things that hunt other living things are ___predators___.

13. Hunted animals are called ___prey___.

14. ___Scavengers___ feed on the remains of dead animals instead of hunting.

15. Animals that eat both animals and plants are ___omnivores___.

16. Food chains end with ___decomposers___, which break down dead matter.

Unit B - Interactions of Living Things   Use with textbook pages B15–B27   85

Reading in Science Resources, p. 85

Reading Strategy

Summarize

Developing Reading Skills
Ask students to summarize how living things get the food and energy they need. They can summarize verbally, in writing, or by using a graphic organizer or diagram.

chain. It eats snakes, mice, lizards, rabbits, and other birds.

The red-tailed hawk doesn't eat plants. However, because of the food chain, it gets some of the Sun's energy that was originally stored in plants.

What happens when plants and animals die? They become food for small organisms like crickets, worms, and ants. They are also a food source for microscopic organisms like bacteria.

▶ **What does a food chain show?**

A food chain shows the movement of energy from one organism to another.

READING
Diagrams

1. What are the members of this food chain?

2. Where does the food chain begin? End?

Red-tailed hawk (consumer)

Soil bacteria (decomposers)

QUICK LAB

FOR SCHOOL OR HOME

Getting Food

1. **Take a walk outdoors** around your home or school. Choose a community to study. Make a list of the living things you see. Don't include people or domestic animals like dogs, cats, and farm animals. You may want to take photos to complete your observations. Use illustrations to complete step 2.

2. **Classify** Organize the organisms into two groups—those that can make their own food (producers) and those that cannot (consumers).

3. **Classify** Which organisms did you list as producers?

4. **Classify** Which organisms did you list as consumers?

5. **Communicate** Draw two or more food chains to show how energy moves through this community.

B 19

BLACKLINE
Interpret Illustrations

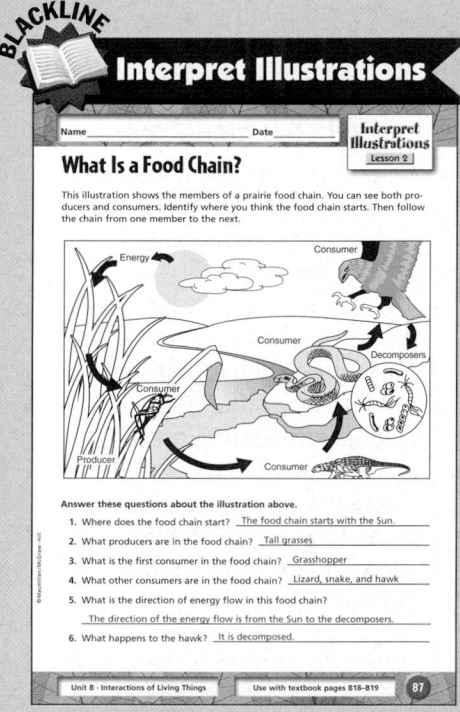

Reading in Science Resources, p. 87

Using the Illustrations

Ask students to think about why the term *food chain* is a good descriptor of the relationships shown in the illustration.

1. grass, grasshopper, horned lizard, red-tailed hawk, soil bacteria

2. The food chain begins with energy from the Sun being captured by the grass and ends with decomposers (soil bacteria).

▶**After Reading**

Have students answer the red question in the student book as **ongoing assessment**.

QUICK LAB

FOR SCHOOL OR HOME

Materials camera (optional), collecting net (optional)

Science Process Skills *classify, communicate*

Resources Activity Resources, p. 55–56

Step 1 Students might visit a park, a nearby pond, or even an empty lot.

Step 3 Answers may include any green plant.

Step 4 Answers may include animals such as insects, mice, and birds.

Step 5 Answers will depend on the organisms students see. Food chains should indicate that energy moves from producers to consumers.

What Is a Food Web?

Before Reading
Have students try to answer the red question at the top of the page.

Developing the Main Idea
Help students compare the role of plants in land and marine food webs. Ask:

■ **Why are algae called producers?** (They produce their own food.)

Exploring the Main Idea
Challenge students to find out more about herbivores, such as what they eat and how their bodies, especially teeth and beaks, are adapted for their diet.

READING Diagrams

> predators: hawks, mountain lions, snakes, insect-eating birds
> prey: rabbits, mice, beetles, deer, birds, snakes

Technology

■ Visual Aid Transparency 8: *Land Food Web*

Developing Vocabulary

food web Have students visualize a spider's web and imagine that each of the threads is a food chain. When the threads, or individual food chains, overlap they form a *food web*.

herbivore The prefix *herb-* means "grass" and *-vore* means "devour". A *herbivore* is an organism that "devours grass", or plants, which are primary producers.

carnivore The prefix *carni-* means "flesh". Combined with *-vore*, it means an organism that "devours flesh", or meat-eating organism.

What Is a Food Web?

Do all organisms eat only one food? Are all organisms eaten by only one type of animal? No. Animals often eat or are eaten by many different things. How can we study all of the things that an animal eats or is eaten by? A food chain only shows the path of energy as it moves from one organism to another. A **food web** shows the relationship between all of the species in a community. It shows how populations must compete for food. A food web is a map of overlapping food chains.

Producers
All food webs begin with *producers*. The producers on land include grasses, trees, and all other organisms that use the Sun's energy to make their own food. In oceans the main producers are algae.

Plant Eaters
Organisms that cannot make their own food are *consumers*. Consumers get energy from the food made by other organisms. Consumers can be grouped according to the type of food they eat. **Herbivores**

READING Diagrams
Which of these animals are predators? Which of these animals are prey?

B 20

(HUR·buh·vawrz) eat producers. Both Earth's land and waters are filled with herbivores—animals that eat plants, algae, and other producers.

Meat Eaters
Herbivores, in turn, are eaten by **carnivores** (KAHR·nuh·vawrz)—animals that eat other animals. All cats, big and small, are carnivores. So are dogs, wolves, foxes, coyotes, and other sharp-toothed animals. The sea also has carnivores. The most frightening of these is the great white shark.

Land Food Web

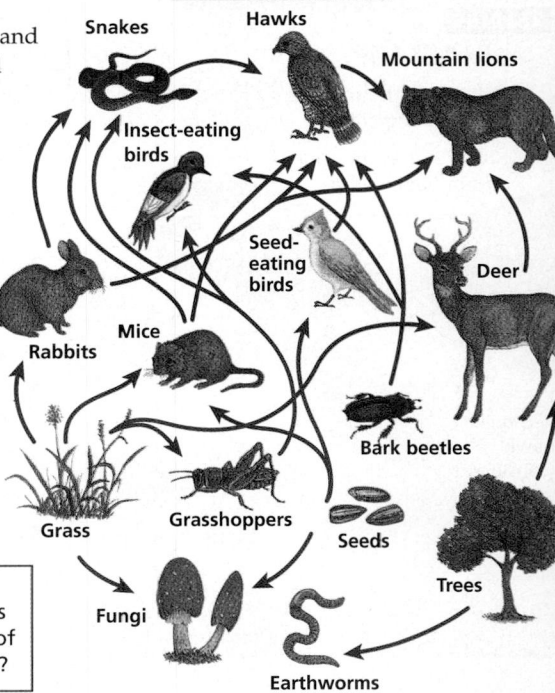

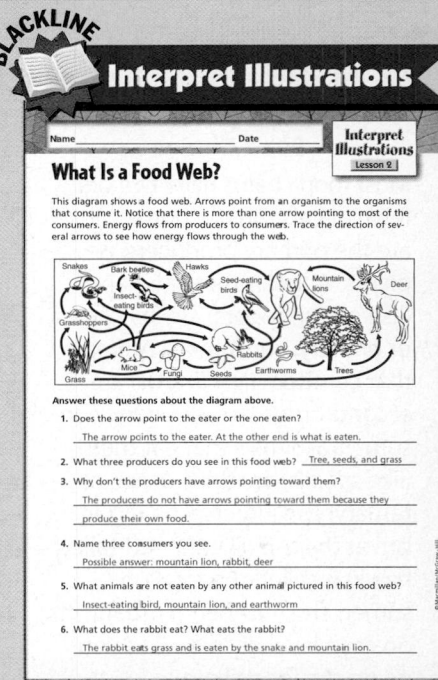

Science Background

Plant- and Animal-Eaters
Most mammals are herbivores. Their specialized teeth can withstand the wear and tear of eating plants. Some, like rodents and rabbits, have teeth that grow continuously. Some carnivores, such as pythons, can swallow other animals whole. Some omnivores change their diet according to the season. They eat plants when they are available in the summer and other animals during the winter.

Reading in Science Resources, p. 88

Marine Food Web

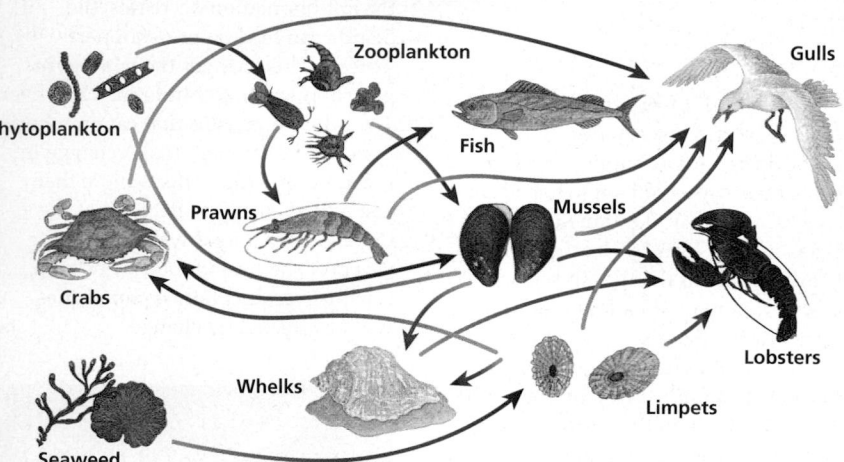

Phytoplankton

Zooplankton

Fish

Gulls

Prawns

Mussels

Crabs

Lobsters

Whelks

Limpets

Seaweed

Other sea dwellers also eat meat. Frolicking seals, playful dolphins, and gentle whales dine on fish, squid, and even penguins.

Living things that hunt other living things for food are **predators**. The hunted are called **prey**. The relationships between predators and prey are a key part of both food chains and food webs.

However, not all meat eaters are predators. Some animals eat meat but don't hunt it. Such meat eaters are called **scavengers**. They feed on the remains of dead animals. Have you ever seen vultures circling a spot of land? Then you have seen scavengers. Crows are also scavengers. You might see them on a road, pecking at the body of an animal.

The sea is home to many scavengers. One of these is the hagfish. It wanders

the ocean floor in search of dead or dying fish. Some tiny sea creatures also feed on the remains of dead sea animals.

When an animal eats both animals and plants, it is an **omnivore**. You are an omnivore. Bears are omnivores, too, eating things from berries to salmon.

Decomposers

Every food chain and food web ends with *decomposers* such as worms, insects, bacteria, and fungi. These organisms break down dead matter into substances that can be used by producers. Decomposers break down dead organisms and wastes into simpler substances. Some of these substances are absorbed by the decomposers. Some are returned to the soil.

> ### ▶ What are the parts of a food web?
>
> Food webs consist of producers, plant eaters, meat eaters, and decomposers.

B 21

Inclusion

Composting

Ask students to find out how people make compost in home gardens and for commercial use. They should research various containers and ways to speed up the decomposition. Challenge them to write a report about how decomposers work and what they contribute in making compost. Students should also explain how people use compost. **Linguistic**

Thinking Further: *Inferring*
Ask:

■ **Why do all food chains and webs start with producers at the bottom?** (Some organisms have to convert the energy of the Sun into food.)

■ **How do consumers in a food web get energy from the Sun?** (They get it indirectly by eating plants or eating other animals that have eaten plants.)

Developing the Main Idea
Help students keep track of the terms on these two pages by asking volunteers to write definitions on the board. Invite other volunteers to list examples under each definition.

Using the Illustrations
Ask students to think about why the term *food web* is a good descriptor of the relationships shown in the illustrations on pages B20 and B21.

▶ After Reading
Have students answer the red question in the student book as **ongoing assessment**.

Developing Vocabulary

predator To help students remember the concept of *predators,* present it to them in terms of a predator-prey relationship, with the predator being the hunter and the prey being the hunted.

prey As above, present the term *prey* as the member of a predator-prey relationship that is hunted by the other member. However, you may want to note that the prey in one food chain may also be a predator in a different food chain.

scavenger Ask students if they have ever been on a scavenger hunt, in which they are sent out to find different items without buying them. Similarly, a *scavenger* gets its meal without "buying", or killing it, but rather it feeds off the discarded remains of dead animals.

omnivore The prefix *omni-* translates to "all". When combined with *-vore* it loosely translates to "devours all". More accurately it means an organism, such as a human, that eats plants and animals.

How Are Populations Connected?

Before Reading
Have students try to answer the red question at the top of the page.

Developing the Main Idea
Remind students that food webs show the fundamental connectedness of Earth's living things. The example of the eradication of the ants demonstrates how a change in one part of a food chain brings about other, possibly more dramatic, changes in the entire food web. This is why it is so critical that we are knowledgeable and careful about the way we care for Earth's resources.

Exploring the Main Idea
Ask students what competition means to them, and to describe the different ways they compete with others. Have students use the classifieds to study the overlaps and differences in job descriptions that interest them. Ask them why some jobs have more competition than others.

▶ After Reading
Have students answer the red question in the student book as **ongoing assessment**.

How Are Populations Connected?

What would happen if farmers used powerful insecticides to kill pests? What might happen if these pesticides also killed some harmless ants? Ants live in the same habitat as Texas horned lizards. Because the lizards eat ants, changes in the ant population may tell a lot about the future of the lizards.

In the food chain, the relationship doesn't stop there. Birds of prey, such as hawks, feed on the lizards. What happens to the ants will also affect the lives of these birds. A change in one population affects all the other organisms in that food chain.

Animals may adapt to changes in their habitats. A varied diet can be useful. Texas horned lizards eat mainly ants. They also eat other insects such as grasshoppers. If the ant population decreases, the lizards can feed on grasshoppers instead. This changes the number of grasshoppers in a community, however. The other organisms that eat grasshoppers will be affected, too. A change in the ant population affects more than just a food chain. It affects all of the organisms in a food web.

Food chains and food webs help scientists predict how communities will be affected by change.

Lubber grasshoppers

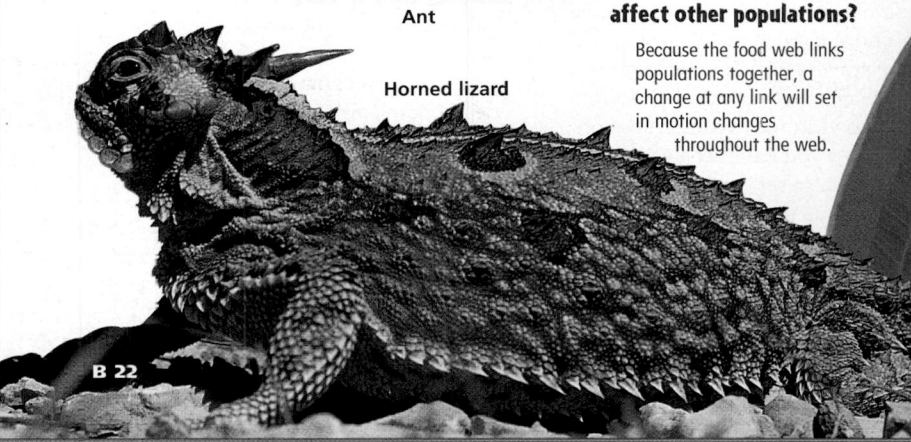
Ant

Horned lizard

READING Sequence of Events
How does a change in a food web affect other populations?

Because the food web links populations together, a change at any link will set in motion changes throughout the web.

B 22

Reading MiniLesson

Sequence of Events

Develop Discuss how the simple act of using pesticides can set off a chain, or sequence, of events that could wipe out a food web in an ecosystem.

Practice Have students make flowcharts spelling out a sequence of events for the food chain on page B18–B19 if lizards and hawks ate only one kind of food. (Flowcharts should follow this sequence: farmers use pesticides; pesticides kill ants; lizards have no ants to eat so lizards die; hawks have no lizards to eat so hawks die.) Discuss why a varied diet can help animals survive longer.

How Do Populations Adapt to Competition for Food?

Food webs show that animals compete for food. Fish and gulls must compete for a dinner of prawns, for example. In order to survive, an organism must adapt to competition. Sometimes this competition causes a population to change its habitat. This is what happened to Florida's green anole.

At one time green anoles could be spotted all over Florida, perched on the trunks of trees and the branches of bushes. Then a new and bigger species of anole arrived in Florida from the island of Cuba. Scientists don't know how it made the 144 km (90 mi) trip. Its size and, perhaps, other characteristics gave it a hunting edge over the small green anole, however.

Soon the smaller green anole seemed to disappear. Was it really gone? No. Scientists found the little green anole high in the trees. It had found a new habitat where it did not have to compete with the Cuban anole for food.

 **How did the green anole adapt to competition?**
The green anole found a new habitat.

The green anole (left), a native of the U.S. southeast, acquired a new habitat when Cuban anoles (above) were introduced.

B 23

How Do Populations Adapt to Competition for Food?

Before Reading
Have students try to answer the red question at the top of the page.

Developing the Main Idea
Make sure students know where Cuba is in relation to Florida. Ask them to hypothesize how the Cuban anole may have gotten to Florida.

Thinking Further: *Inferring*
Ask:

■ **Why is it important to make sure people do not carry native plants and animals from one country to another when they travel?**
(Introducing a new plant or animal to an environment can bring about changes in the community. Some of these changes can be serious and harmful.)

Using the Illustrations
Students may recognize anoles by the name *chameleon.* Point out that when anoles change their color to blend in with the environment, they are responding to temperature and moisture.

▶After Reading
Have students answer the red question in the student book as **ongoing assessment**.

 SCIENCE FOR ALL

Inclusion

Starlings
Invite students to find out about the introduction of the starling into the United States in 1890–1891, when 100 of the birds were brought to New York City. The story goes that someone wanted the United States to have every species of animal mentioned in Shakespeare's plays. Starlings have since become extremely common and are usually considered pests. Their competition with bluebirds almost eliminated those birds from America. **Linguistic**

SCIENCE FOR ALL

Advanced Learners

Saving Bluebirds
Suggest volunteers write to the North American Bluebird Society, P.O. Box 74, Darlington, WI 53530, for the history of bluebirds in the United States and present an oral report. (These insect-eaters became threatened when DDT killed many insects. They competed with house sparrows and starlings for nesting sites. People built nesting boxes to help.) **Linguistic; Social**

How Does Energy Move in a Community?

Before Reading
Have students try to answer the red question at the top of the text column.

Exploring the Main Idea
Model how energy is lost as it is moved by asking a volunteer to spread jam on a cracker. Point out how some jam sticks to the knife and how some cracker crumbs are also lost.

Developing the Main Idea
Point out how energy is lost as you go up the pyramid. Ask:

- **Decreasing the number of organisms in which level would disrupt the community the most? Why?** (The bottom level; all the other levels depend on it.)

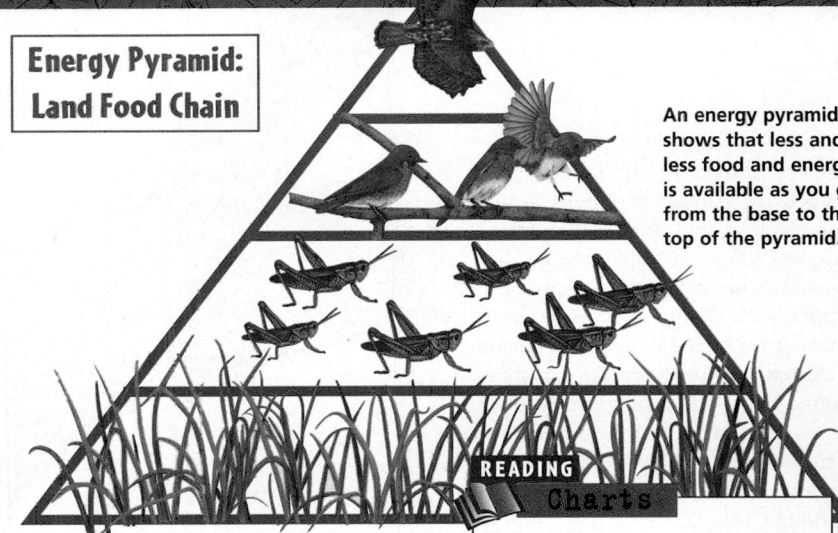

Energy Pyramid: Land Food Chain

An energy pyramid shows that less and less food and energy is available as you go from the base to the top of the pyramid.

How Does Energy Move in a Community?

Plants capture energy from sunlight. When you eat a plant, how much of that energy do you get? All organisms need energy to live. Producers get energy from the Sun. Consumers get it from the foods they eat. However, energy is lost as it passes from one organism to another in a food chain.

You can see the effect of this in the drawing of the energy pyramid on this page. An energy pyramid shows a number of things. It shows that there is less food at the top of the pyramid than at the base. It also shows that there are fewer organisms as you move from bottom to top.

Consumers get their energy from food. The less food there is, the less energy is available. Energy decreases from the base to the top of the pyramid.

In an ocean community in the Antarctic, algae form the base. Algae are producers that store energy from the Sun. Small fish that live in the icy waters eat some of these algae. The algae that are not eaten are lost to the community. Their energy is not passed up to the next level of the pyramid. Only some of the energy the fish get is passed up to the next level. The fish use some of the energy in swimming and other activities.

B 24

Science Background

Eltonian Pyramid
In the 1920s, ecologist Charles Elton developed this pyramid, sometimes called the Eltonian pyramid. He spent a summer watching foxes on an arctic island. He counted all the smaller animals eaten by one fox. Then he counted all the animals eaten by these animals. The result was a pyramid. He also found out that the weight, or biomass, at each level also formed a pyramid.

English Language Learners

Interpreting the Energy Pyramid
After reading about how energy is moved in a community, have students relate the conclusions to the pyramid. For example, the text states that there is less energy at the top of the pyramid, as well as fewer organisms. Ask them how the pyramid shows that. Also ask where in the pyramid we would find the least energy (top) and the most (bottom). Ask students if they can relate that to the numbers of organisms. **Spatial; Logical**

Energy Pyramid:
Ocean Food Chain

The penguins dive for the small fish and eat as many as they can catch. Many fish get away. Nevertheless, the penguins have snared some energy-rich fish as food. Some of the energy from the fish is stored in the penguins' tissues. Some of the energy is used to heat their bodies. A dip in the frigid water removes some of this heat from the penguins' bodies. Now they have less energy than they took in from the fish.

Rising from below, a leopard seal clamps its sharp teeth around a helpless penguin and eats it. Does this predator get all the energy that was originally in the algae the fish ate? No. Energy has been lost at each level in the pyramid.

Kilogram for kilogram there are fewer fish than algae. There are fewer

penguins than fish. There are fewer leopard seals than penguins. That's because there is less food and energy available at each higher level in the energy pyramid. The less food and energy there are, the fewer living things that can be supported.

How much energy is lost from one level of an energy pyramid to the next? Scientists have actually measured it. The startling figure is 90 percent! Of all the Sun's energy captured by the algae, the leopard seal gets only one-tenth of one percent.

▷ **What does an energy pyramid show?**

It shows that the amount of available energy decreases at each level of the food chain. The number of organisms and the food available decrease, too.

B 25

Developing the Main Idea
Emphasize that there are not only fewer organisms as you go up the pyramid, there is also less mass and less energy.

Ask students to think about what else they have learned from studying pyramids. (See *Health Handbook,* p. R26; see Science Magazine, p. B28; healthy eating habits from the Food Guide Pyramid; physical fitness exercises from the Activity Pyramid.)

Using the Illustrations
Have students compare and contrast the two energy pyramids, land and ocean. Both start out with producers at the bottom and show a progression of consumers in upper levels. Different organisms make up the bottom levels in the two pyramids, plants on land and algae in the ocean.

▶After Reading
Have students answer the red question in the student book as **ongoing assessment**.

 **SCIENCE FOR ALL** English Language Learners

Latin Plurals
The plural form of *alga* is *algae*. Tell students that the words come from Latin, a language many scientists use to communicate with each other. Many words in science are Latin, including genus and species names. Challenge students to identify other singular and plural Latin words used in science. (examples: *fungus* and *fungi; atrium* and *atria*) **Linguistic**

Science Background

Food Guide Pyramids
Have students draw a Food Guide Pyramid based on what they have learned about energy pyramids. Afterwards, encourage them to find an actual Food Guide Pyramid and compare their drawings to it. (A Food Guide Pyramid shows bread, cereal, rice, and pasta at the bottom; vegetables and fruits share the next level; dairy products and meats, eggs, fish, beans, and nuts share the third level; and fats, oils, and sweets top off the pyramid at the "use sparingly" level.)

How Do Food Webs Affect You?

Before Reading
Have students try to answer the red question at the top of the page.

Developing the Main Idea
Ask students how they feel when they first read the headline in the text. After they have read through the text, ask them how their feelings have changed. Ask if anyone has experienced a red tide or other environmental problem.

Exploring the Main Idea
Have students recall how insecticide use affected the bald eagle population. Then ask students to suggest ways people might be affected by changes in an ecosystem. Ask students why farmers and other plant growers use fertilizers. (to supply nutrients that help plants grow faster and stronger) Have students speculate about the effects of too much fertilizer on algae growing in a pond. (increase in number of algae) Ask:

■ **Besides humans and the organisms that eat algae, what organisms may a red tide harm?** (any organisms, such as seabirds and larger fish, that eat the small contaminated fish)

Thinking Further: *Inferring*
Ask:

■ **Why might shellfishing be halted in areas where there has been a red tide?** (If the shellfish have been contaminated, people can become ill from eating them.)

▶After Reading
Have students answer the red question in the student book as **ongoing assessment**.

How Do Food Webs Affect You?

"Red Tide Observed Off the Coast of Maine" might not seem like a scary headline. You might even ignore this important warning. However, it could mean trouble for the average person.

On page B24 you learned that single-celled organisms called algae are at the base of the marine food web. When the algae population increases very rapidly, or blooms, it can turn hundreds of square miles of ocean red. Scientists call this a red tide. Most red tides are not harmful. However, some algae produce poisons. Fire algae are an example. A bloom of these algae is very dangerous to all the species in a food web.

Small fish and mussels feed on the algae. The algae's poison may kill or infect the fish. The decline in the fish population reduces the energy available to the consumers that feed on fish.

How does this affect you? People who eat contaminated fish may become very sick. You are part of a food web, too. Humans are at the top of most food webs. Changes in any population may also affect you.

Deadly red tides, like this one, occur when the population of fire algae greatly increases.

▶ **How can changes in a food web affect you?**
Changes in a food web can affect you because humans are consumers in the food web.

B 26

SCIENCE ▶ Reading Strategy

Paraphrase
Developing Reading Skills
Ask students to paraphrase how an increase in fire algae can hurt humans. Students can work in small groups. One group is the "hearing" committee. Students present their paraphrases to the hearing committee. Committee members can make notes to help improve clarity of paraphrases.

Science Background

Other Red Tide Victims
Red tides are believed responsible for deaths in recent years within at least three species of endangered marine mammals: humpback whales, bottle-nosed dolphins, and manatees. In 1996, red tides may have killed almost 10 percent of the Florida manatee population and more than 100 dolphins in Mexico.

Lesson Review

Why It Matters

If a food chain, food web, or energy pyramid changes, the result might affect humans. On farms a decrease in predators like insect-eating birds might lead to a population explosion of insects. If the insects are plant pests, crops may suffer and food may become scarce. Humans may influence such changes. It is important to monitor how human actions affect the populations of an ecosystem.

Think and Write

1. What is the original source of energy in an ecosystem?

2. Is it possible to have a food chain that has only a producer and a decomposer?

3. What is the relationship between a food chain and a food web?

4. Choose a meat product you eat, and construct a food chain that includes yourself as the final consumer.

5. **Critical Thinking** Explain why there are fewer coyotes than mice in a prairie ecosystem.

L·I·N·K·S

MATH LINK

Use percents. An energy pyramid shows that 90 percent of the energy is lost from one level to the next. If you start with 100,000 units of energy, how much energy does the next level get? The fourth level?

100,000 × 0.10 = ?

100,000 units of energy

WRITING LINK

Write a story. The theme of your story is a changing ecosystem. Make sure the events in your story involve the lives or activities of people.

SOCIAL STUDIES LINK

Conduct research. Investigate what causes red tides. Where and when have they occurred? What can be done to stop them from occurring? Use the Internet or library resources for your research. Write a report to tell what you have learned.

TECHNOLOGY LINK

At the Computer Visit **www.mhscience02.com** for more links.

B 27

---

3 Lesson Review

Answers to Think and Write

1. The original source of energy in an ecosystem is the Sun. (pp. B18, B24)

2. It is possible because a producer that a consumer does not eat may be broken down by a decomposer after the producer dies. (pp. B18–B21)

3. A food web is made up of overlapping food chains. (pp. B20–B21)

4. Possible answers: grass, cattle, student; corn, hog, student; grain, chicken, student (pp. B18–B19)

5. **Critical Thinking** There is too little food and energy at the top of the energy pyramid to support large numbers of coyotes. (pp. B24–B25)

Summarize

Check students' understanding by having them write a brief summary of the lesson in their own words.

MATH LINK

If 90 percent of the energy is lost from one level to the next, then 10 percent remains. The calculations for the remaining energy should be as follows: level 1 to level 2: $100,000 \times 0.10 = 10,000$; level 2 to level 3: $10,000 \times 0.10 = 1,000$; level 3 to level 4: $1,000 \times 0.10 = 100$.

WRITING LINK

Stories may center on changes that humans cause. They might also tell how changes to other organisms in the ecosystem, such as a crop failure or forest fire, affect humans.

SOCIAL STUDIES LINK

Students' research should reveal that no one factor causes red tides. Red tides may result from a combination of conditions favorable to their growth. Nitrogen pollution has been identified as a factor but is no longer considered the major force. Though red tides occur throughout the world, in the United States they occur from the Gulf of Maine down to the Florida coast and throughout the Gulf of Mexico.

Science, Technology, and Society

Objectives

- Examine the choices people make to eat a balanced, healthful diet.

Build on Prior Knowledge
Ask students:

- **What kinds of food do you think are healthful? Do you eat any of these?** (Possible answers: fruit, vegetables, whole-grain breads)

- **What kinds of food do you think are unhealthful? Do you eat any of these?** (Possible answers: candy, chips, soda)

What Affects Your Food Choices?

Developing the Main Idea
Focus on what influences the food choices students make. Ask:

- **Have you ever bought a food product because you liked the ad? What kind of food was it?** (Answers will vary but because most food advertising is for mainly unhealthful foods, they will most likely fall into this category.)

- **What examples of advertising for healthful foods do you recall seeing?** (Possible answers: milk, cheese, raisins)

- **What else influences your food choices?** (Possible answers: person who does household shopping, news articles, other students)

What Affects Your Food Choices?

Hmmm, a shopper thinks. *Should I buy the oat or the wheat cereal?* In the next aisle, the shopper may decide between whole milk and skim milk, or between peaches and plums.

The shopper is part of a food web, and so are you. However, unless your family grows or hunts its own food, your food choices aren't limited by the food you can grow or catch. Your food choices are based on what's found in the supermarket. How do people decide what foods to buy?

First, we choose foods that look, taste, and smell good to us. However, many of our food choices are affected by advertising. Food advertising encourages people to choose one product over another. A shopper may pick the wheat cereal because of the colorful box. He may buy a certain brand of canned fruit because he has a coupon.

The food industry spends about $10 billion a year on advertising through television, magazines, and newspapers. It spends another $20 billion on coupons, games, and other gimmicks. In one recent year, a candy manufacturer

B 28

spent $67 million to advertise just one type of candy!

All this advertising encourages people to eat more. It also causes them to choose less healthful foods, like candy and chips, over more healthful foods, such as fruits and vegetables.

The advertising appears to be working. Americans today eat more food per person than they did 20 years ago. More people are overweight than ever before. More people have diseases related to being overweight, such as heart disease, diabetes, and certain cancers.

If you don't base your food choices on advertising, what can you use? Try using the U.S. Department of

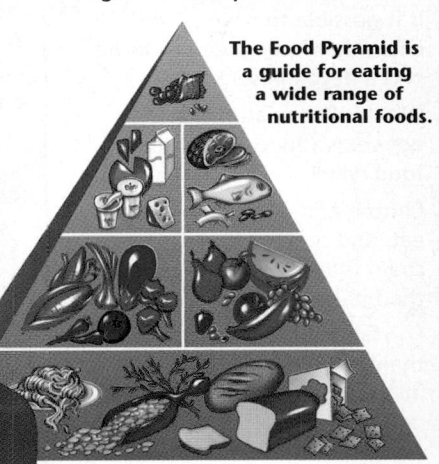

The Food Pyramid is a guide for eating a wide range of nutritional foods.

 English Language Learners

What We Eat
Encourage students to keep a record of all the food they eat each day for three days. Have them make a chart of all food items and list which food groups they fall under. For each day, have them determine whether they met the recommended servings of each food group and whether they exceeded any. Have students refer to the Food Guide Pyramid on p. R26. **Intrapersonal**

 Advanced Learners

Eating Healthier
Have students make their own food pyramids based on their diets. Have them compare their pyramids to the one on p. B28. Motivated students can use their food pyramids to evaluate the changes they can make in their diets to meet the food recommendations in the Food Guide Pyramid. **Intrapersonal; Spatial**

Agriculture's Food Guide Pyramid. It shows the amounts of food you should eat from each group. It's simple to use—just choose more foods from the bottom of the pyramid than from the top.

You should also eat a variety of foods from each food group. For example, look at the Vegetable Group. To eat three servings of vegetables, you might have a large salad at lunch (2 servings), and carrots at dinner (1 serving).

This doesn't mean you can never eat candy, chips, or other "favorite" foods. It just means that foods with fats, oils, and a lot of sugar should be used sparingly.

What Did I Learn?

1. Which of the following is NOT a result of food advertisements?

   A People buy more food.
   B People eat more food.
   C People grow their own vegetables.
   D People choose one brand of food over another.

2. According to the Food Guide Pyramid, from which food group should you eat the most servings per day?

   F Bread, Cereal, Rice, and Pasta Group
   G Vegetable Group
   H Fruit Group
   J Fats, Oils, and Sweets

 AT THE COMPUTER Visit www.mhscience02.com to learn more about food choices.

B 29

Cultural Perspective

Dietary Rules

Certain groups avoid some foods in some of the food groups. For example, some Jewish people and Muslims do not eat pork. Many Hindus do not eat beef. People who are vegetarians do not eat any meat. Vegans do not eat animal products, including milk products, meat, and eggs.
Vegetarian and vegan diets can be healthful when the proper amounts of protein, calcium, and iron are derived from other sources.

Using the Illustrations

Have students study the Food Guide Pyramid shown in the diagram. Ask:

- **Which type of food should you eat the most of each day?** (bread, cereal, rice, and pasta)

- **Which type of food should you eat the most sparingly? Why?** (fats, oils and sweets; because they do not provide very much nutrition or can be harmful to your health in large amounts)

- **Why do you need to eat each of the foods in the given amounts?** (This gives you a balanced diet—one that provides the proper amount of nutrition in the needed amounts.)

Thinking Further: *Inferring*

Ask:

- **Why are you encouraged to eat a variety of foods within the same group?** (They may have different kinds of vitamins and minerals you need.)

Encourage students to think about how they make their food choices and what they might want to change. Also encourage them to think about whether they eat mainly healthful or unhealthful food.

Test Prep: What Did I Learn?

1. C

2. F

Summarize

Check students' understanding by having them write a brief summary of this feature in their own words.

LESSON 3 Cycles of Life

Objectives

- Explore how water evaporates and condenses in a closed system.
- Describe how water and nutrients cycle through the environment.
- Describe how carbon and nitrogen cycle through the environment.

Resources

- Activity Resources, pp. 57–61
- Reading in Science Resources, pp. 91–96
- Vocabulary Cards
- Reading Aid Transparency B3
- Visual Aid Transparencies 9–14
- School to Home Activities, p. 12

Build on Prior Knowledge

Have students discuss what they know about the water and carbon cycles. Ask:

- **When you inhale, what is your body getting? Where do you get it from?** (oxygen; the air)

- **When you exhale, what does your body give off? Where does it go?** (carbon dioxide; the air)

1 Get Ready

Using the Illustrations
Ask:

- **Where might dew come from?** (Possible answers: from the air, soil, or grass) It forms when water vapor in the air condenses.

- **Where does dew go later, when it disappears?** (Possible answer: It evaporates or soaks into the grass or the ground.)

Vocabulary

evaporation, B32
condensation, B32
precipitation, B33
water cycle, B33
carbon cycle, B37
nitrogen cycle, B38

Cycles of Life

Get Ready

Have you ever walked in a grassy field early in the morning after a clear night? What did you observe about the grass? It was probably wet with dew. Where did all this water come from? It hadn't rained in the night. Dew comes from water in the air. How is water stored in the air? How does it change to dew?

Process Skill

You infer when you form an idea from facts or observations.

B 30

Science Background

Water Cycle

The water cycle affects entire ecosystems. During the rainy season in Serengeti National Park in Kenya, for example, thousands of gnus graze on its southeastern plains. When the dry season begins, the water holes dry up and the gnus migrate northwestward. The grazing and trampling of the grasses, plus the waste matter, stimulate grass growth.

Explore Activity

What Happens to Water?

Materials

plastic food container with clear cover

small bowl or cup filled with water

small tray filled with dry soil

paper towel

100-W lamp (if available)

Procedure

1. Place the dry paper towel, the dry soil, and the bowl of water in the plastic container. Close the container with the lid.

2. **Observe** Place the container under a lamp or in direct sunlight. Observe every ten minutes for a class period. Record your observations.

3. Observe the container on the second day. Record your observations.

Drawing Conclusions

1. What did you observe the first day? What did you observe the second day?

2. **Infer** What was the source of the water? What was the source of the energy that caused changes in the container?

3. What happened to the water?

4. **Going Further: Infer** How did the water move?

Alternative Explore Activity

Materials hot plate, teakettle, cookie sheet, ice cubes, water, oven mitts

Recycling Water Direct students to heat the water in the teakettle until they see "steam." Have them put the ice on the cookie sheet, and while wearing the oven mitts, hold the cookie sheet over the steam. Caution them to be careful with the hotplate and teakettle. (Droplets will form on the bottom of the cookie sheet.) Challenge them to explain what happened—in terms of how water is recycled in nature. **Spatial; Kinesthetic**

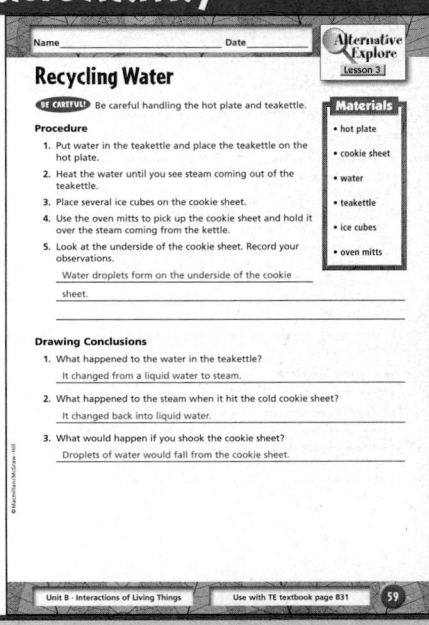

Activity Workbook, p. 59

Explore Activity

What Happens to Water?

Science Process Skills *observe, infer*

Resources Activity Resources pp. 57–58

Pacing 30–40 minutes

Grouping small groups

Plan Ahead Make sure the food containers are large enough to hold the water bowl and soil.

Procedure

2. Water drops condensed on the inside of the container.

3. Possible answer: Water drops condensed on the inside of the container and dropped onto the soil and paper towel.

Answers to Drawing Conclusions

1. Students should observe water droplets forming on the underside of the cover. They should see more water on the second day.

2. The water came from the bowl of water. The energy source was the heat from the lamp or sunlight.

3. The water in the bowl changed into a gas that went into the air inside the container. The water changed back to a liquid, forming drops on the lid.

4. Possible answer: The model demonstrated evaporation from a body of water, condensation in a cool environment, and water drops falling and wetting surfaces.

 Inquiry Students can ask their own questions to explore, such as: How can other resources be recycled?

Technology

- When time is short, preview the activity with the **Explore Activity Video**.

2 Read to Learn

What Is the Water Cycle?

Before Reading
Have students try to answer the red question at the top of the page.

Exploring the Main Idea
Fill a glass with ice cold water and add some food coloring. Set it in front of the students. They should soon see water form on the outside of the glass. Ask:

■ **What color is the water on the outside of the glass?** (colorless)

Thinking Further: *Inferring*
Ask:

■ **How do you know this water did not come from inside the glass?** (If it did, it would be colored.)

■ **Where did the water on the outside come from?** (the air)

■ **How did water get into the air?** (It evaporated from Earth's surface.)

■ **What process caused water to form on the outside of the glass?** (condensation)

Developing Vocabulary

evaporation The word *evaporation* comes from a Latin word meaning "to emit vapor from". Relate this to some familiar examples of evaporation, such as a puddle drying or sweat evaporating from skin.

condensation Ask students what they think the word *condense* means or if they have ever had to *condense* a piece of writing. They should understand that condense means "to reduce", such as in the reduction of a gas to a liquid.

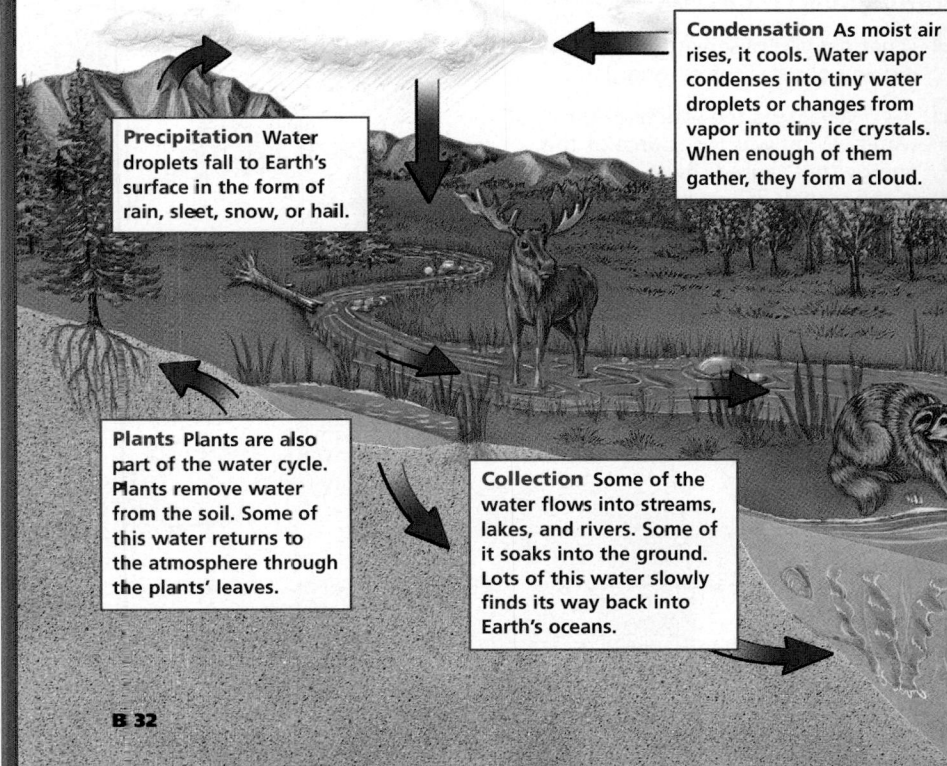

Read to Learn

Main Idea Earth's systems recycle materials such as water, carbon, and nitrogen.

What Is the Water Cycle?

What happens to rainwater after it falls? Does it simply vanish? Water moves from one part of the environment to another. It is not lost from an environment. In other words, water is recycled. How is this possible?

Here's how it happens. Heat from the Sun is absorbed by oceans, seas, lakes, streams, ponds, and even puddles. This heat makes the water evaporate and go into the air. **Evaporation** is the process in which a liquid changes into a gas.

As the *water vapor*, or water in its gas state, rises higher and higher into the atmosphere, it cools. When cooled enough, water vapor condenses into tiny water droplets. **Condensation** is

The Water Cycle

Condensation As moist air rises, it cools. Water vapor condenses into tiny water droplets or changes from vapor into tiny ice crystals. When enough of them gather, they form a cloud.

Precipitation Water droplets fall to Earth's surface in the form of rain, sleet, snow, or hail.

Plants Plants are also part of the water cycle. Plants remove water from the soil. Some of this water returns to the atmosphere through the plants' leaves.

Collection Some of the water flows into streams, lakes, and rivers. Some of it soaks into the ground. Lots of this water slowly finds its way back into Earth's oceans.

B 32

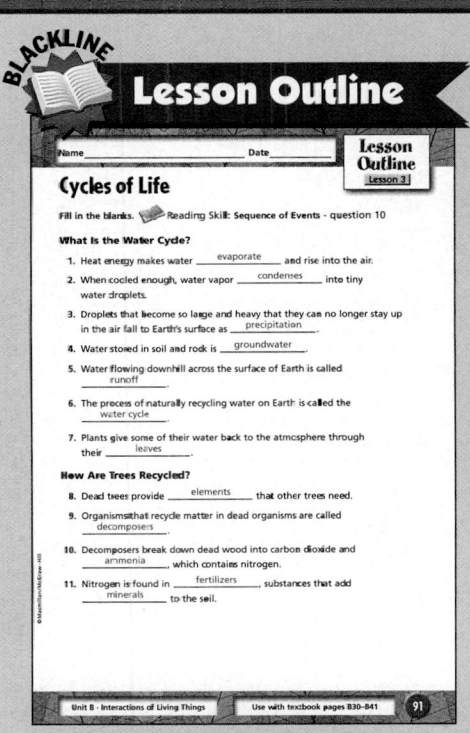

Reading in Science Workbook, p. 91

English Language Learners

The Water Cycle
Emphasize to students that the water cycle explains how the amount of water in our environment is always constant—it is recycled. Ask specific questions based on the diagram and have students give evidence to support their answers. For example, ask them to make a list of all the sources of water. (oceans, seas, lakes, streams, ponds, puddles, dew, plants)
Linguistic; Kinesthetic

the process in which a gas changes into a liquid.

When enough water droplets gather, a cloud is formed. As more and more droplets gather, they become too heavy to stay in the air. They fall to Earth's surface as **precipitation**. Precipitation is any form of water particles—rain, sleet, snow, or hail—that falls to Earth.

On land some of the precipitation seeps into the ground and is stored as *groundwater*. Some of the water, however, flows downhill across the surface. This water becomes *runoff*. It is collected in streams, lakes, or rivers. It slowly finds its way back to the ocean. Here it absorbs heat and evaporates into the atmosphere again. The **water cycle** is the continuous movement of water between Earth's surface and the air, changing from liquid to gas to liquid.

READING Sequence of Events
What are the stages of the water cycle?
Evaporation, condensation, precipitation, and collection make up the water cycle.

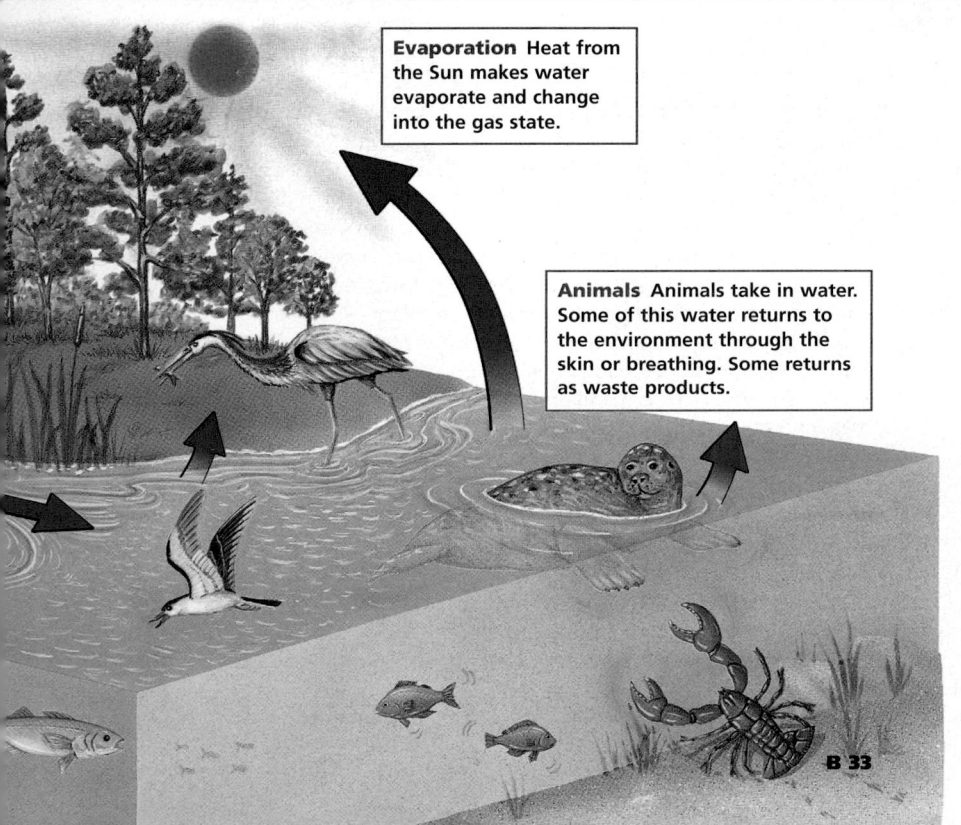

Evaporation Heat from the Sun makes water evaporate and change into the gas state.

Animals Animals take in water. Some of this water returns to the environment through the skin or breathing. Some returns as waste products.

B 33

Reading | MiniLesson

Sequence of Events

Develop Discuss with students the never-ending nature of the water cycle that's been going in sequence for millions of years. Point out that because of this sequence, the water we drink today may have filled lakes that existed at the time of the dinosaurs millions of years ago!

Practice To emphasize the never-ending water cycle, have students make circular flowcharts listing the sequence of events starting with the evaporation of water from a lake to the return of water, through precipitation and runoff, to the same lake. Allow interested students to make illustrations on their flowcharts as well.

Exploring the Main Idea
Challenge students to find news stories on flash floods. Ask them to investigate why such floods occur and what dangers they bring. Also ask students to suggest precautions people should take during flash floods. (For example, never drive, bicycle, or walk through standing water of unknown depth.)

Developing the Main Idea
Ask students to compare and contrast evaporation, condensation, and precipitation. (Evaporation happens when heat changes liquid water to a vapor; condensation happens when a gas cools and changes to a liquid; precipitation is water falling to Earth's surface in some form.)

Explain the difference between runoff and groundwater. (Runoff is water that flows across the surface because it cannot be absorbed. Groundwater is water that soaks into the ground and is stored there.)

▶After Reading
Have students answer the red question in the student book as **ongoing assessment**.

Developing Vocabulary

precipitation Ask students what they think it means when the weather forecaster says "Chance of precipitation 80%". Help them associate this term with any form of water particles falling to Earth's surface.

water cycle Have student think of words that end in *cycle*, such as *bicycle* or *lunar cycle*. Point out that the common theme is circular or repetitive things. Ask them to visualize a water wheel with the water constantly moving from the source, up and over the wheel, and back again, much like the movement of water between Earth's surface and the atmosphere.

Technology

■ Visual Aid Transparencies 9–12: *Building a Water Cycle*

How Are Trees Recycled?

Before Reading
Have students try to answer the red question at the top of the page.

Developing the Main Idea
Ask students to describe dead trees and other plants they have seen. (They may mention insects, decayed matter, and parts of the plant breaking into smaller pieces.) Invite students to put together a moving "flip" stack of pictures showing a tree falling and decaying.

Using the Illustrations
Ask:

- **How might a dead tree help living things?** (It can be decomposed so that it is a source of substances living things can use. It can also provide shelter for some animals and a place for plants to root.)

This dead tree is being decomposed by fungi, shown here, and microscopic bacteria.

How Are Trees Recycled?

How can a dead tree help living things? Even though the tree is dead, it is being turned into substances other organisms need to survive. Some of these organisms are other trees. The dead tree is providing elements for living trees. When these trees die, they will provide elements that other trees need. The cycling of matter is continuous. How does this happen?

An old, fallen tree is made of wood, bark, and other dead tree tissue. That tissue holds all sorts of complex chemical substances. Most of the chemicals are too complex to be used by other living things. They need to be broken down into simpler chemicals.

This is the job of the decomposers. They are organisms that recycle matter from dead organisms. Worms, crickets, cockroaches, bacteria, and fungi are decomposers. These organisms can break down dead wood and other dead plant parts into carbon dioxide and ammonia. All living plants need carbon dioxide in order to make sugars. Ammonia is a simple substance that contains the element nitrogen. Nitrogen is extremely important for plants. No plant can live or grow without nitrogen. All organisms need nitrogen in order to make proteins.

Nitrogen is a chemical found in plant *fertilizers*. Fertilizers are substances used to add minerals to the soil. Some fertilizers are natural. These are decaying plants and animals, and animal wastes. Other fertilizers are made in factories. Both natural and artificial fertilizers contain nitrogen. The next time you go to a store that sells fertilizers, read the labels. You're sure to find nitrogen as one of the ingredients.

B 34

 Science Background

Decomposers
Without decomposers, the world would be littered with dead plants and animals and all the nutrients in the world would be locked up in dead material. We would eventually drown in dead leaves, plants, and trees. Decomposers recycle the dead material back into the food chain.

Science Background

Recycling
Recycling is a very old process. Native Americans taught settlers how to use fish parts as fertilizer for corn plants. Recycling received increased awareness after the late 1960s. It is now part of the Space Age, as scientists experiment with ways to recycle wastes on long space voyages.

Composting

You can help nature recycle plant material by composting. Gardeners use compost to make soil more fertile. A good mixture for compost is three parts dry leaves and plant material, one part fresh grass clippings, and one part food scraps. Earthworms, insects, fungi, and bacteria break down the leaves, grass, and food scraps into compost. The compost contains nitrogen, phosphorous, and potassium, which enrich the soil.

As you'll soon discover, like water, nitrogen and carbon have their own cycles in nature. Earth is a closed system. With the exception of energy, almost nothing gets out or gets in. It is recycled.

How do decomposers recycle nutrients?

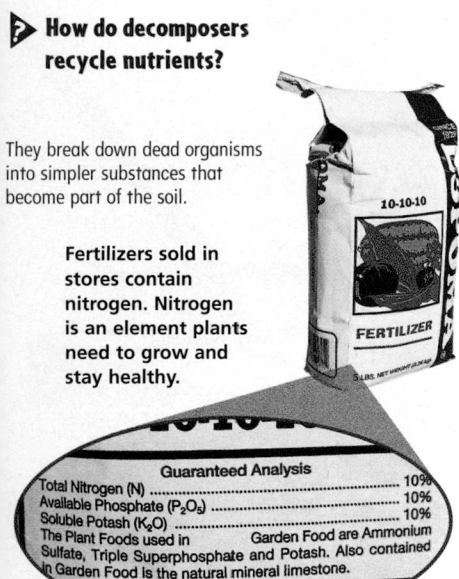

They break down dead organisms into simpler substances that become part of the soil.

Fertilizers sold in stores contain nitrogen. Nitrogen is an element plants need to grow and stay healthy.

Guaranteed Analysis

Total Nitrogen (N) 10%
Available Phosphate (P₂O₅) 10%
Soluble Potash (K₂O) 10%
The Plant Foods used in Garden Food are Ammonium Sulfate, Triple Superphosphate and Potash. Also contained in Garden Food is the natural mineral limestone.

Feed 10-10-10 is an agricultural

QUICK LAB

FOR SCHOOL OR HOME

Soil Sample

BE CAREFUL! Do not touch the sharp edges of the can.

1. Go to a wooded area in a park or other location near your school. Find a patch of soft, moist soil.

2. Press a can, open side down, into the soil to get a core sample. You might have to gently rotate the can so it cuts into the soil.

3. Observe Carefully remove the core so it stays in one piece. Describe and draw the core.

4. Infer From top to bottom, what kind of matter does the core hold? In what order did the layers form?

5. Infer Which layer holds the most available nutrients? Explain.

B 35

Developing the Main Idea

Make sure students understand the importance of composting. Ask:

- **What elements does compost contain?** (nitrogen, phosphorous, potassium)
- **Why are these elements important?** (They enrich the soil.)

▶ After Reading

Have students answer the red question in the student book as **ongoing assessment**.

QUICK LAB

FOR SCHOOL OR HOME

Materials small empty can

Science Process Skills *observe, infer*

Resources Activity Resources, pp. 60-61

Plan Ahead Make sure students have permission to dig at the site.

Be Careful! Stress that students may not touch the open end of the can because of the danger of cuts.

Step 3 You may want to model how to remove the core from the can so the core stays in one piece.

Step 4 The top layer may hold coarse, dead matter, such as leaves, twigs, and other plant parts. The next layer (top soil) should be dark, moist, and lumpy. The third layer may be lighter in color and finer. The bottom layer may be like clay. The most recent layers are at the top; the deeper you dig, the older the layer.

Step 5 The second layer, or top soil, holds the most available nutrients because it contains dead matter that has been broken down by decomposers. The top layer holds dead matter that has not been fully broken down by decomposers.

What Is the Carbon Cycle?

Before Reading

Have students try to answer the red question at the top of the page.

Developing the Main Idea

Ask students why carbon and nitrogen are important in their lives. (Carbon is part of carbohydrates that the body uses for energy; nitrogen is part of proteins needed to build muscle for proper growth.)

The greenhouse effect (excess carbon dioxide builds up in the atmosphere, preventing heat from escaping) and global warming (rise in Earth's overall temperature) are two effects of people upsetting the balance of carbon in the environment. Ask students where the increase in carbon dioxide may come from. (burning of fossil fuels)

Technology

■ Visual Aid Transparency 13:
   Carbon Cycle

What Is the Carbon Cycle?

Have you ever roasted marshmallows over a fire until the outsides turned black? Have you ever left bread in the toaster for so long that it burned? The "black" that you observe on burnt food is carbon.

Carbon is a very important element. It is one of the elements that make up all living things. It is found in the air as carbon dioxide and is used by plants in photosynthesis. It is found in many of the things we use every day, from fuel to chairs to nonstick pans.

The Carbon Cycle

Carbon enters the air when plants and animals decay. It enters the air when animals breathe out. It enters the air when fossil fuels such as coal, oil, gasoline, and natural gas are burned.

Plants During photosynthesis plants use the carbon from carbon dioxide to make sugars, starches, and proteins. They also give off oxygen, which is used by animals.

Car exhaust

Oil

B·36

BLACKLINE
Interpret Illustrations

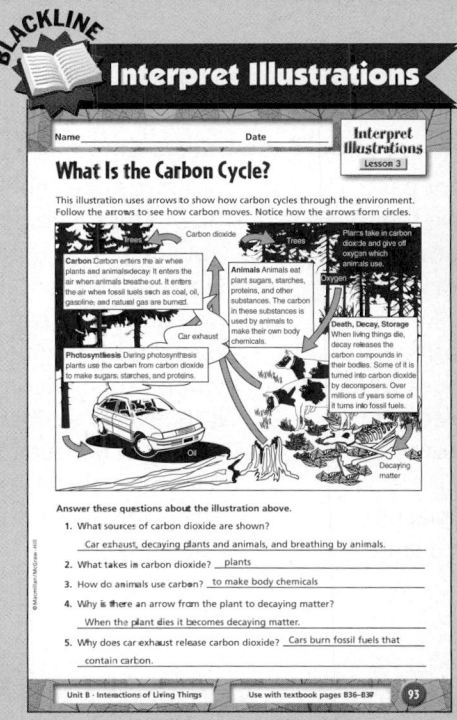

Reading in Science Resources, p. 93

Like water, carbon is recycled by nature. The process is called the carbon cycle. The carbon cycle shows the continuous transfer of carbon between the atmosphere and living things. Read the diagram to learn how nature does this.

▷ **What does the carbon cycle do?**
The carbon cycle is the process in which carbon is recycled in nature.

READING
Diagrams

1. When does carbon dioxide enter the air?

2. What happens to carbon when living things die?

Oxygen

Carbon

Death, Decay, Storage When living things die, the carbon in them goes into the air and ground. Some of it is turned into carbon dioxide by decomposers. Some is stored as fossil fuels. This is what happened to the carbon in certain organisms that died millions of years ago.

Animals Animals eat plant sugars, starches, proteins, and other substances. The animals use the carbon in these foods to make their own body chemicals.

Decaying matter

B 37

Exploring the Main Idea
Invite students to illustrate how organisms that lived long ago became the fuels we use today. Have them consult reference books to find out more details. Then have students draw their own cycle as they study the graphic in the text and explain the cycle in their own words to a partner.

READING
Diagrams

1. Carbon dioxide enters the air when animals breathe out, when plants and animals decay, when fossil fuels burn. Some students might also suggest it enters the air during forest fires.

2. Some of it is turned into carbon dioxide by decomposers and some is stored as fossil fuels.

▶**After Reading**
Have students answer the red question in the student book as **ongoing assessment**.

Developing Vocabulary

carbon cycle Remind students about what the term *cycle* means (a circular or repeating pattern). Ask them how this applies to the *carbon cycle*.

Inclusion

Coal Formation
Invite students to use an encyclopedia to find out what the Carboniferous period, which happened about 300 million years ago, has to do with coal formation. (During that time, plants died in shallow swamps and did not completely decompose. Earth's heat and the pressure of materials above them turned their carbon into coal.)
Linguistic

Advanced Learners

Write a Letter
Invite students to write a letter to the editor of the local newspaper or to an elected official. Ask them to share their thoughts about the increase of carbon dioxide in our atmosphere. Encourage students to back up their opinions with scientific facts about the carbon cycle. They may want to focus their letters on local concerns. Challenge them to find out about local policies that address air pollution and carbon dioxide emissions. **Social; Linguistic**

How Is Nitrogen Recycled?

Before Reading
Have students try to answer the red question at the top of the page.

Developing the Main Idea
Remind students that nitrogen is a key ingredient in fertilizers. The special group of bacteria discussed in the text, often found in fertilizers, converts nitrogen gas into compounds plants can use. Also discuss with students how important proteins, which contain nitrogen, are to life.

Tell students that nitrogen in the atmosphere is inert, meaning it does not easily react with other chemicals. That means that the nitrogen we exhale is the same as the nitrogen we inhale. To be useful for life, nitrogen has to be "fixed" in the soil by bacteria. These bacteria convert the nitrogen gas molecules to nitrates, which also contain oxygen. Today, factories can do the same thing as the bacteria to make fertilizer. Students may be interested to find out more about how factories use nitrogen gas to make fertilizers.

▶ After Reading
Have students answer the red question in the student book as **ongoing assessment.**

Developing Vocabulary

nitrogen cycle To help students remember the concept of the *nitrogen cycle*, have them look up the word *cycle* in the dictionary (circular or repeating pattern) and apply it to the behavior of nitrogen in nature.

How Is Nitrogen Recycled?

What do you need nitrogen for? When you eat meat, fish, cereal, or vegetables, you are taking in the nutrients that your body needs to make *proteins*. Proteins are a part of your muscles and many cell structures.

Among other things, proteins are rich in the element nitrogen. You need nitrogen to make parts of your body, such as muscles, nerves, skin, bones, blood, and digestive juices.

Since air is 78 percent nitrogen, you might think that you do not need to eat protein to get nitrogen. However, animals and plants cannot use the nitrogen that is in the air. Animals get nitrogen by eating proteins. Plants get nitrogen by absorbing it from the soil. Some plants even get nitrogen with the help of a special group of bacteria.

The way nitrogen moves between the air, soil, plants, and animals is called the **nitrogen cycle**.

▷ What organisms are involved in the nitrogen cycle?
Plants, animals, bacteria, and decomposers are all involved with recycling nitrogen.

Decomposers When plants die, decomposers in the soil break down the plant proteins. One product is the nitrogen-containing substance ammonia. Soil bacteria change ammonia into nitrites.

Ammonia

B 38

The Nitrogen Cycle

Air Air is made up of about 78 percent nitrogen gas.

Nitrogen-Fixing Bacteria Some bacteria that grow on pea and bean roots give those plants the nitrogen they need. The bacteria turn nitrogen gas in the air to nitrogen-containing substances the plants can use to make their proteins.

Science Background

Nitrogen Cycle
A rotting cow chip is a good place to witness the nitrogen cycle on a small scale. The chip contains large amounts of nitrogen that were locked up in proteins that the animal ate. Bacteria working around the chip break down the proteins into smaller compounds and eventually into nitrates. Plants that need these nitrates will sprout up around the chip, making this area very fertile. Raw animal waste is frequently used to fertilize plants.

Inclusion

Protein Consumption
Challenge students to keep a record for one week of how much nitrogen their families eat in the form of proteins. They should review what proteins are and what foods contain them. Ask them to research how much protein a healthy diet should have and how their diets compare.
Linguistic; Social

READING
Diagrams

1. Compare the different ways various kinds of bacteria help in the nitrogen cycle.

2. How do pea and bean plants get the nitrogen they need?

Denitrifying Bacteria Some soil bacteria turn nitrates back into nitrogen gas.

Animals Animals eat plant proteins, or they eat other animals that eat plant proteins. Animal wastes contain nitrogen compounds.

Plants Plants absorb nitrates dissolved in water through their roots. The nitrogen is then used by the plant to make proteins.

Nitrites   Nitrates

Nitrogen compounds

Nitrites and ammonia

Bacteria Certain bacteria can use nitrogen from the air to make nitrogen-containing substances called *nitrites*. Other bacteria can turn nitrites into *nitrates*—another group of nitrogen-containing substances.

B 39

Exploring the Main Idea

Write each heading from the diagram on a separate card or piece of paper. Ask seven volunteers to choose a card at random. Challenge students to decide, with books closed, how these students should line up to show the nitrogen cycle. Invite each volunteer to describe what happens during that step. Have students think about carbon and nitrogen as they relate to the ecosystem. (Both cycle from the biotic to the abiotic parts of the ecosystem.)

READING
Diagrams

1. Some bacteria turn nitrogen from the air into nitrites. Other bacteria turn those nitrites into nitrates. Soil bacteria change ammonia from dead plants into nitrites. Bacteria growing on plant roots turn nitrogen from the air into nitrogen-containing substances plants use to make proteins. Denitrifying bacteria in the soil turn nitrates back into nitrogen gas.

2. Bacteria growing on their roots turn nitrogen gas into nitrogen-containing substances the plants can use.

Technology

■ Visual Aid Transparency 14: *Nitrogen Cycle*

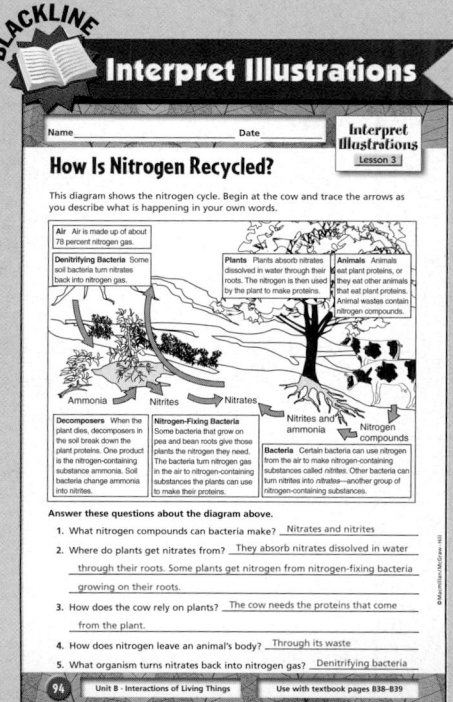

Reading in Science Resources, p. 94

BLACKLINE
Interpret Illustrations

SCIENCE
Reading Strategy

Compare and Contrast

Developing Reading Skills
Contrast the roles of organisms in the carbon and nitrogen cycles. Students can make a table to record their answers, for example:

	carbon cycle	nitrogen cycle
plants		
animals		
decomposers		

Why Recycle?

Before Reading
Have students try to answer the red question at the top of the page.

Developing the Main Idea
Ask students what resources they think are renewable and what resources are nonrenewable. Have them make a list of things at home that they reuse (such as plastic containers, jars), throw out, and recycle. Encourage them to think about how this helps the environment.

Exploring the Main Idea
Have students identify ways their community recycles, including locations where items are collected for recycling. Ask them if they know a place where something should be recycled but isn't. Encourage them to take action, perhaps by writing a letter to someone in authority.

READING
Graphs

504,000,000 kg

▶ **After Reading**
Have students answer the red question in the student book as **ongoing assessment**.

Why Recycle?

Have you ever seen a paper bag with a symbol that says "Printed on recycled paper"? Why is this important?

The environment provides the materials people use to make products. Sunlight is an *inexhaustible resource*. The Sun will last for millions, if not billions, of years. Other resources, however, are not inexhaustible. The paper to make books, magazines, newspapers, and containers comes from the wood in trees. Metals mined from the ground are used to make cars, ships, pots and pans, appliances, and many other things. Glass is made from sand. Plastics are made from chemicals in oil found deep underground.

Wood, metals, sand, and oil are called *raw materials*. Raw materials are the building blocks of products.

Many raw materials, such as oil and metals, are *nonrenewable resources*. Earth's oil was formed millions of years ago. There's a limited amount of it. When it's gone, it's gone forever.

Certain other resources, such as wood, are *renewable resources*. If trees are cut down for lumber and paper, more can be planted to replace them. Even so, trees take years to grow. Recycling paper and other wood products can help keep forests from being destroyed. This can also help keep the animals in them from losing their homes and, perhaps, from facing extinction.

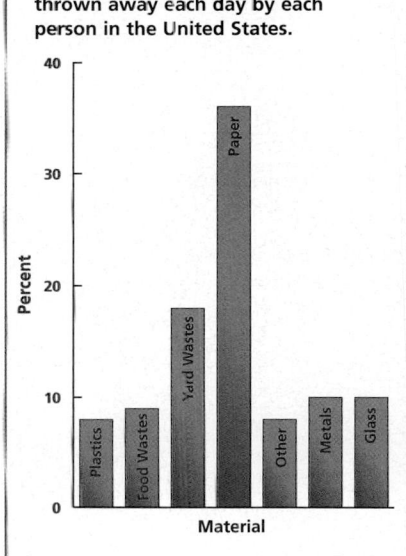

Garbage Thrown Away Daily in the United States

This graph shows the percent of different materials in garbage thrown away each day by each person in the United States.

▷ **Why is it important to recycle both renewable and nonrenewable resources?**
Nonrenewable resources can eventually be used up; renewable resources may take a long time to be replaced.

READING
Graphs

Let's say there are 280,000,000 people in the United States. Each person throws away 1.8 kg (4 lb) of garbage each day. How much garbage is thrown away by all the people each day?

B 40

Math MiniLesson

Multiply Whole Numbers by Decimals

Develop Multiply: 23×35.76

Step 1 Multiply as with whole numbers

```
    1
  12 +
  35.76
× 23
 107 28
 715 20
 822 48
```

Step 2 Count the decimal places in the factors. Write the same number of decimal places in the product.

```
      1
    12 +
    35.76   ← 2 decimal places
 ×    23
   107 28
   715 20
   822.48   ← 2 decimal places
```

  $23 \times 35.76 = 822.48$

Practice Multiply.
1. 35×56.07 (1,962.45)
2. 46×78.77 (3,623.42)

SCIENCE Reading Strategy

Find the Main Idea
Developing Reading Skills
Ask students to write a paragraph to explain why recycling is important. Ask them to include at least one of the terms in italicized print on this page. (*Nonrenewable resources* is the most applicable term to use.)

Why It Matters

Many people urge that we conserve raw materials by recycling them—just as nature recycles water, carbon, and nitrogen. Many communities have recycling programs. Glass products, metal, plastics and papers can all be recycled. Service stations can save oil that is drained from car engines.

The environment provides all the things we need. The environment will keep doing these things as long as we let it recycle the substances that make life possible and comfortable. People can either help or hinder the process.

Visit **www.mhscience02.com** to do a research project on recycling.

Think and Write

1. By what process does water move from oceans, lakes, rivers, and streams into the air?

2. What organisms turn a dead tree into substances that can be used by living trees?

3. Describe three ways that carbon dioxide gets into the air.

4. Name two substances that contain nitrogen.

5. **Critical Thinking** How can you and other people conserve trees?

L·I·N·K·S

MATH LINK

Make a circle graph. Use the data from page B40. Calculate (in kilograms) how much of each type of garbage Americans produce every day.

ART LINK

Make a collage. Weigh the amount of garbage you throw away each day. Estimate how much of it is paper, glass, plastic, and food scraps. Represent this in a collage.

WRITING LINK

Write a paragraph. Explain the importance of using recycled materials.

SOCIAL STUDIES LINK

Conduct research. The Carboniferous period happened about 300 million years ago. Research it by using the Internet or an encyclopedia.

TECHNOLOGY LINK

At the Computer Visit **www.mhscience02.com** for more links.

B 41

---

3 | Lesson Review

Answers to Think and Write

1. evaporation (pp. B31–B33)

2. Decomposers, such as bacteria and fungi, break it down. (p. B34)

3. Possible answers: when plants and animals decay, when animals breathe out, when fossil fuels burn (pp. B36–B37)

4. Possible answers: ammonia, fertilizers, compost, proteins, nitrates (pp. B34–B35, B38–B39)

5. **Critical Thinking** Possible answers: recycle paper, borrow books from the library, buy recycled products, and buy products not made from wood (pp. B40–B41)

Summarize

Check students' understanding by having them write a brief summary of the lesson in their own words.

MATH LINK

Multiply 504,000,000 kg by the percent for each bar: plastics (8%) 40,320,000; food wastes (9%) 45,360,000; yard wastes (18%) 90,720,000; paper (37%) 186,480,000; other (8%) 40,320,000; metals (10%) 50,400,000; glass (10%) 50,400,000

ART LINK

Provide students with a table categorizing the various kinds of garbage. Have them use this table in estimating their garbage on any given day.

WRITING LINK

Students' paragraphs may include such reasons for recycling as providing a market for recyclables, conserving resources, and preserving the environment.

SOCIAL STUDIES LINK

The Carboniferous Period occurred from 360 million years ago to 286 million years ago. It is named for the coal-bearing rocks (coal consists mainly of carbon) formed during this time period.

Technology

Internet Research Project Have students visit **www.mhscience02.com** to conduct a research project on recycling. They will find a suggested outline for the project, questions to research, and links to Internet reference sites.

Cultural Perspective

Direct Irrigation

Deserts can have rich soil but little water. For crops to grow, people must irrigate the land. Most commonly, that meant flooding the land or sprinkling, both of which waste water. People in Israel pioneered a more efficient way to irrigate called drip irrigation. This process reduces evaporation and waste by pumping water through holes in plastic pipes to each individual plant. The pipes can even be put underground so the water drips directly on the roots.

✓ Informal Assessment

Easy/Average Ask students to use the diagrams in the text to explain the water, carbon, and nitrogen cycles to a partner.

Challenge Ask students to describe each of the three cycles to a partner without referring to the text. They may draw their own diagrams to accompany their description.

Amazing Stories

Amazing Stories

Coral Reefs

Objective

- Describe the development and ecosystem of coral reefs.

Build on Prior Knowledge

Ask students to discuss what an ecosystem is. (all living and nonliving things in an area interacting with each other) Then ask:

- **For what do animals depend on plants? Why?** (for food, because animals cannot produce their own)

- **For what do animals depend on nonliving things?** (for shelter, air, water)

Coral Reefs
Rain Forests of the Sea

Developing the Main Idea

Point out that algae are not plants because they lack roots, leaves, and other plant structures. However, they do perform photosynthesis. Ask:

- **Why is the role of algae in water the same as plants on land?** (They perform photosynthesis, thus producing oxygen.)

- **Why can coral not survive in deep water?** (Coral polyps depend on algae, and sunlight does not reach the depths in great enough amounts to allow the algae to perform photosynthesis.)

Rain Forests of the Sea

They're sometimes called "rain forests of the sea." That's because they're home for an amazing variety and number of creatures—up to a quarter of all the oceans' animals. They can take thousands of years to form. They grow in shallow, warm waters. Creatures smaller than your thumbnail build them, and they can be over a thousand miles long. What are they? Coral reefs!

A coral reef is built by millions of tiny animals called coral polyps. They live together in colonies, or groups. Coral polyps secrete a substance that hardens into skeletons. The hard skeletons build up reefs over time. Special algae live inside coral polyps. The algae produce food for the polyps. Coral reefs form only in shallow waters because the algae need sunlight to produce food.

A coral reef often looks like a sea garden because of its beautiful shades of orange, yellow, purple, and green. The colors come from the different algae and sea animals that live among the corals. Coral reefs provide food and shelter for thousands of ocean plants and animals, including hundreds of kinds of fish.

Some of the more unusual inhabitants of coral reefs include small fish and shrimp known as cleaners. Cleaners eat parasites from larger fish, such as barracudas and eels.

B 42

Cultural Perspective

Reef Destruction

Worldwide, reef system death or partial destruction in recent decades has accelerated. Factors that may be involved vary in different regions and may include overfishing, sedimentation, blast fishing, cyanide fishing, tourism, and mangrove destruction. Have students choose a region and research the problems occurring in those reef systems and the measures being taken to prevent further damage.

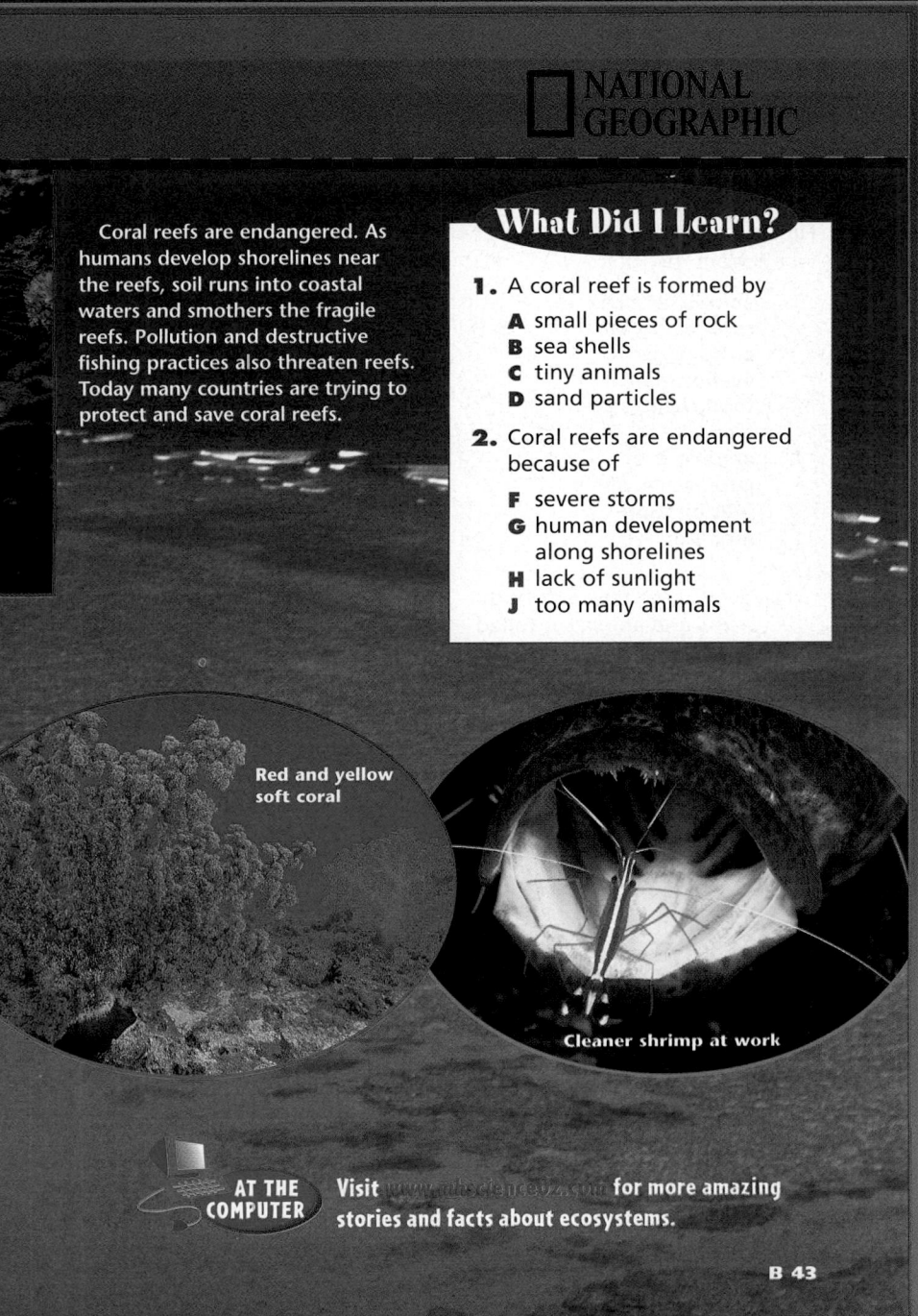

NATIONAL GEOGRAPHIC

Coral reefs are endangered. As humans develop shorelines near the reefs, soil runs into coastal waters and smothers the fragile reefs. Pollution and destructive fishing practices also threaten reefs. Today many countries are trying to protect and save coral reefs.

What Did I Learn?

1. A coral reef is formed by
  A small pieces of rock
  B sea shells
  C tiny animals
  D sand particles

2. Coral reefs are endangered because of
  F severe storms
  G human development along shorelines
  H lack of sunlight
  J too many animals

Red and yellow soft coral

Cleaner shrimp at work

AT THE COMPUTER Visit www.mhscience02.com for more amazing stories and facts about ecosystems.

B 43

SCIENCE Reading Strategy

Paraphrase
Developing Reading Skills
Ask students to use context clues to explain why the coral reefs are called the "rain forest of the sea." (possible answers: take thousands of years to form, look like sea gardens, provide habitats for more organisms than any other ecosystem)

Using the Illustrations
Direct students' attention to the photographs of the fish and coral reef ecosystem. Ask:

■ **What are some biotic factors in this picture? Abiotic?** (biotic: fish, coral polyps, aquatic plants; abiotic: coral skeleton, water)

■ **What is the relationship between the fish living in the reef and coral polyps?** (commensalism if the fish are protected and given shelter by the sharp coral skeleton, or mutualism if the fish also eat harmful algae or other organisms that could harm the reef)

Direct students' attention to the picture of the cleaner shrimp. Ask:

■ **What is the cleaner shrimp's niche in its community?** (cleaning parasites off the fish)

Thinking Further: *Inferring*
Ask:

■ **Why do some regions require an environmental study in the waters off the shore where someone wants to build a block of apartments?** (because construction close to a coral reef could cause erosion that might smother the reef)

■ **How might coral be affected by a drop in sea level? An increase?** (Because coral reefs grow so close to the surface, a drop in sea level would leave the reef above sea level and the polyps would die. An increase in sea level would also cause the polyps to die if the water became too deep for adequate sunlight to reach it.)

Test Prep: **What Did I Learn?**

1. C

2. G

Summarize
Check students' understanding by having them write a brief summary of this amazing story in their own words.

Chapter Review and Test Preparation

Resources

- Reading in Science Resources, pp. 97–98
- Assessment Book, pp. 19–22

Answers to Vocabulary

1. omnivore
2. abiotic factor
3. population
4. community
5. ecology
6. niche
7. Evaporation
8. predator
9. Precipitation
10. food chain

Answers to Test Prep

11. C
12. G
13. A
14. G
15. D

Chapter 4 Review

Vocabulary

Fill each blank with the best word or words from the list.

abiotic factor, B6
community, B10
ecology, B6
evaporation, B32
food chain, B18
niche, B11
omnivore, B21
population, B10
precipitation, B32
predator, B21

1. A consumer that eats both plants and animals is called a(n) _____.

2. Water is an example of a(n) _____.

3. A(n) _____ includes all the members of a single species in a certain place.

4. Corn, elms, and armadillos are part of the _____ of the prairie ecosystem.

5. The study of how living and nonliving things interact in the same place is called _____.

6. All populations have a unique _____ in their habitat.

7. _____ is the process in which a liquid becomes a gas.

8. A(n) _____ is a consumer that hunts for its food.

9. _____ may include sleet and snow.

10. You can trace how energy moves in a community with a(n) _____.

Test Prep

11. All of the following are abiotic factors in an ecosystem EXCEPT
    - **A** water
    - **B** minerals
    - **C** bacteria
    - **D** soil

12. A vulture is an example of a
    - **F** predator
    - **G** scavenger
    - **H** carnivore
    - **J** all of the above

13. Plants absorb nitrogen
    - **A** from the soil
    - **B** from the atmosphere
    - **C** from the Sun
    - **D** from insects

14. In the carbon cycle, carbon is transferred between _____ and living things.
    - **F** the ocean
    - **G** the atmosphere
    - **H** bacteria
    - **J** minerals

B 44

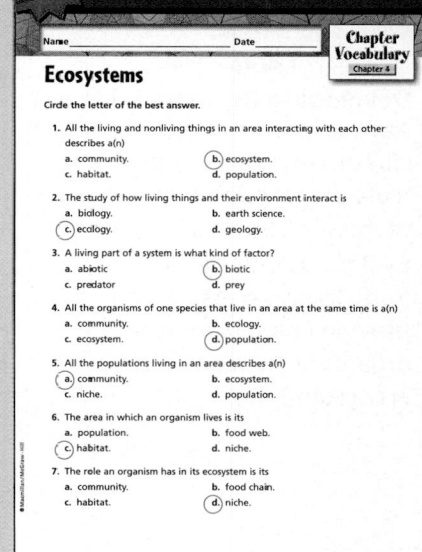

Reading in Science Resources, p. 97

15. As it absorbs heat energy from the Sun, water
  A soaks into the ground
  B flows into streams, lakes, and rivers
  C forms tiny ice crystals
  D evaporates into the air

Concepts and Skills

16. Process Skills: Use Variables
Study the table below. Suggest a reason for the change in the eagle population.

Population Size			
Year	Grasslands (mi²)	Rabbits	Eagles
1960	10,200	101,000	1,050
1970	9,100	89,000	864
1980	8,200	78,000	782
1990	5,300	42,000	386
2000	5,140	41,900	378

17. Reading in Science Describe the sequence by which the Sun's energy is moved through a community.

18. Scientific Methods Conclude how plants take in nitrogen based on the data in the nitrogen cycle.

19. Critical Thinking What is the relationship between herbivores and carnivores? Explain your answer in a paragraph.

20. Decision Making Is it important to recycle the waste you produce? Why or why not?

Boost *your test scores!*
Be Smart!
Visit www.mhscience02.com

B 45

Answers to Concepts and Skills

16. Process Skills: Use Variables The table suggests that as the grasslands got smaller, the rabbit population moved to an area with more grasslands to serve as food. Consequently the eagle population in the area dwindled as well, with fewer rabbits as prey.

17. Reading in Science The Sun's energy passes from one organism to another in a food chain; from the Sun to plants, which convert the energy to food. Animals eat the plants, absorbing some of the energy for the animals to use. Some energy is also stored in the animals' tissues. Some energy is lost as heat. Other animals eat the animals that ate the plants. When the plants and animals die, they become food for small organisms such as crickets, worms, and ants.

18. Scientific Methods Some bacteria that grow on pea and bean roots give plants the nitrogen they need. The bacteria turn nitrogen gas in the air to nitrogen-containing substances the plants can use to make their proteins. Plants also absorb nitrates dissolved in water through their roots. The nitrogen is then used by the plant to make proteins.

19. Critical Thinking Carnivores eat herbivores; carnivores are predators, herbivores are prey.

20. Decision Making Accept all reasonable answers from students both for and against the recycling of waste.

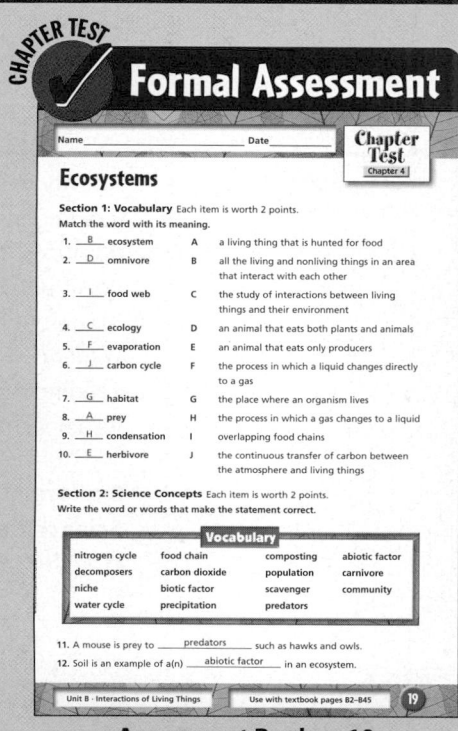

Assessment Book, p. 19

Lesson Planner

Lesson	Objectives	Vocabulary	Pacing	Resources and Technology
LESSON 4 **How Populations Survive,** pp. B48–B61	■ Explore the effects of light and water on the growth and survival of seeds. ■ Describe the role of limiting factors, including competition. ■ Understand the interactions of organisms in symbiosis, mutualism, parasitism, and commensalism. ■ Explain how environmental changes affect an organism's survival.	**limiting factor adaptation symbiosis mutualism parasitism commensalism**	3 days	■ Activity Resources, pp. 62–66 ■ Reading in Science Resources, pp. 103–108 ■ Vocabulary Cards ■ Reading Aid Transparency B4 ■ **Explore Activity Video** ■ **Science Newsroom CD-ROM** *Keep Them Alive* ■ **Science Experiences Videotapes** *Staying Alive: Adaptations for Survival* (Package 4)
LESSON 5 **Biomes,** pp. B62–B75	■ Explore the importance of soil. ■ Identify and locate Earth's six major land biomes. ■ Compare and contrast the various biomes and aquatic ecosystems. ■ Discuss how whales are threatened with extinction and how they are being protected.	**biome grassland taiga tundra desert deciduous forest tropical rain forest**	3 days	■ Activity Resources, pp. 67–71 ■ Reading in Science Resources, pp. 109–114 ■ Vocabulary Cards ■ School to Home Activities, pp. 13, 14 ■ Grade-Level Science Book, *Antarctica* ■ Reading Aid Transparency B5 ■ **Explore Activity Video**
LESSON 6 **How Ecosystems Change,** pp. B78–B91	■ Explore how ecosystems affect each other and change over time. ■ Describe the changes to an ecosystem that occur during primary and secondary succession. ■ Explain how catastrophic (sudden) changes can affect an ecosystem. ■ Explain how resource use affects the environment.	**ecological succession pioneer species pioneer community climax community**	4 days	■ Activity Resources, pp. 72–78 ■ Reading in Science Resources, pp. 115–120 ■ Vocabulary Cards ■ Grade-Level Science Book, *Wildfire* ■ Reading Aid Transparency B6 ■ Visual Aid Transparencies 15, 16 ■ **Explore Activity Video** ■ **Science Newsroom CD-ROM** *From the Ground Up*

Activity Planner

Activity	Process Skills	Materials	Plan Ahead
LESSON 4 **Explore Activity** **What Controls the Growth of Populations?** p. B49	use variables, observe, communicate, infer	4 small, clean milk cartons with the tops removed; 40 pinto bean seeds that have been soaked overnight; soil; water	No advance planning is needed.
QUICK LAB **FOR SCHOOL OR HOME** **Playground Space** p. B51	measure, use numbers, infer	meterstick, calculator	No advance planning is needed.
LESSON 5 **Explore Activity** **Why Is Soil Important?** p. B63	observe, communicate, experiment, infer	washed sand, soil, hydrogen peroxide, 2 plastic cups, 2 plastic spoons, dropper, goggles, apron	No advance planning is needed.
QUICK LAB **FOR SCHOOL OR HOME** **Freshwater Communities** p. B72	observe, communicate, interpret data	dropper; microscope slide; coverslip; microscope; at least 3 samples of pond, lake, or stream water; 3 or more plastic containers with lids	No advance planning is needed.
LESSON 6 **Explore Activity** **How Do Ecosystems Change?** p. B79	observe, communicate, infer, interpret data, predict	none	No advance planning is needed.
Process Skill **BUILDER** **Comparing Ecosystems in Volcanic Areas** p. B87	infer, communicate, interpret data	research books, Internet	No advance planning is needed.

An additional Quick Lab is provided on p. B85. No advance planning is needed.

CHAPTER 5 Teaching Resources

Reading in Science Resources

McGraw-Hill Science **Reading in Science Resources** provides the following **Blackline Master** worksheets for this chapter.

Chapter Graphic Organizer

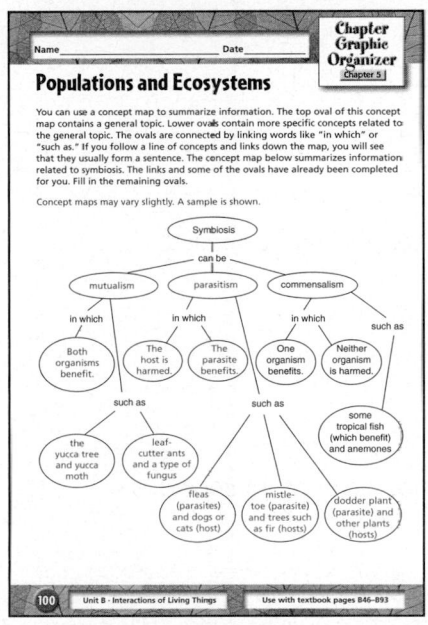

Reading in Science Resources,
p. 100

Chapter Reading Skill

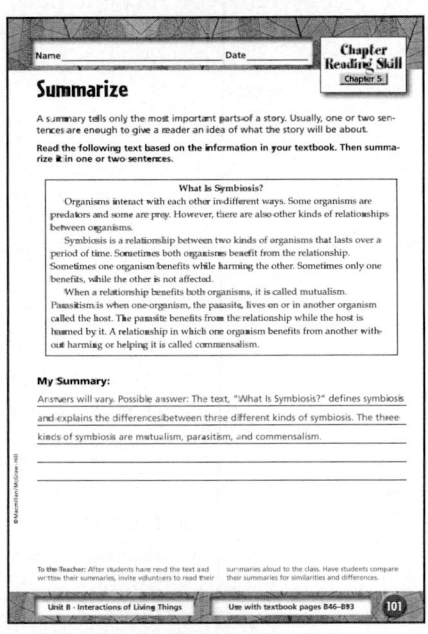

Reading in Science Resources,
pp. 101–102

Chapter Vocabulary

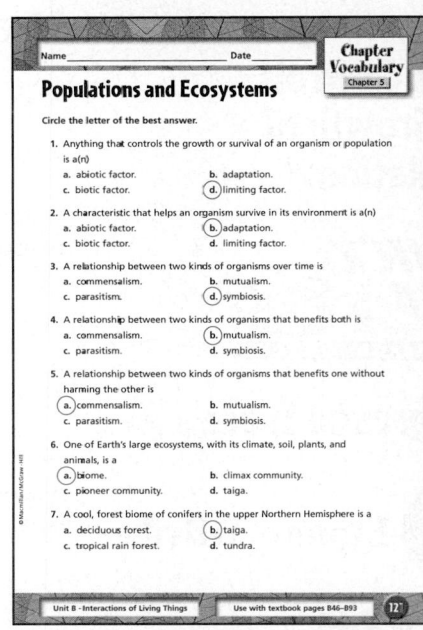

Reading in Science Resources,
pp. 121–122

McGraw-Hill Science **Reading in Science Resources** provides the following **Blackline Master** worksheets for every lesson in this chapter.

Lesson Outline

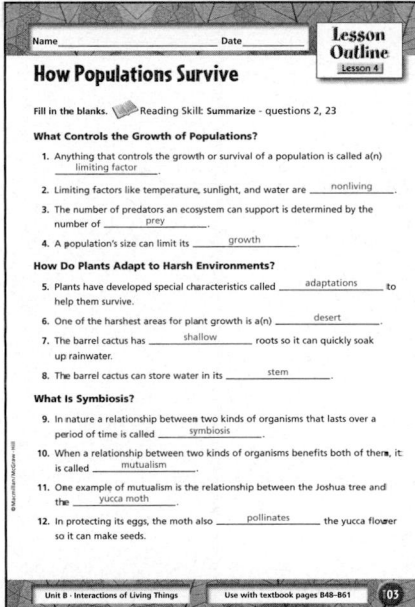

Reading in Science Resources,
pp. 103–104, 109–110, 115–116

Interpret Illustrations

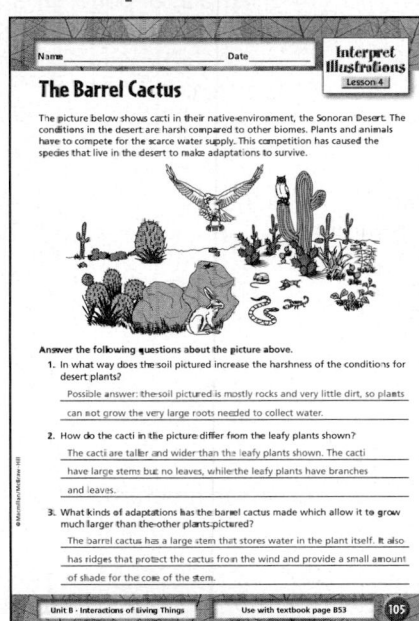

Reading in Science Resources,
pp. 105–106, 111–112, 117–118

Lesson Vocabulary and Cloze Test

Reading in Science Resources,
pp. 107–108, 113–114, 119–120

Activities and Assessment

McGraw-Hill Science **Activity Resources** provides the following **Blackline Master** worksheets for every lesson in this chapter.

Explore Activity and Alternative Explore Activity

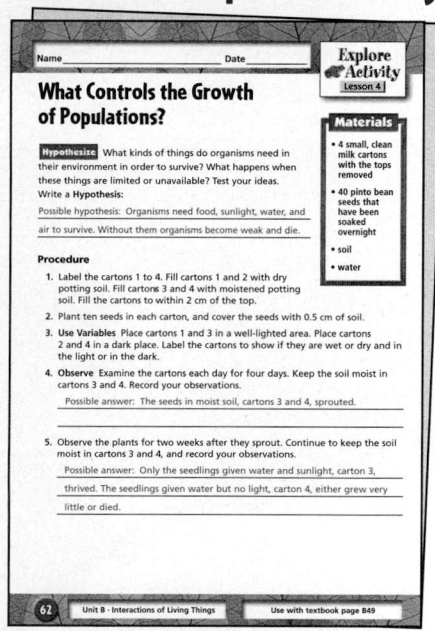

Activity Resources, pp. 62–64, 67–69, 72–74

Quick Lab for School or Home

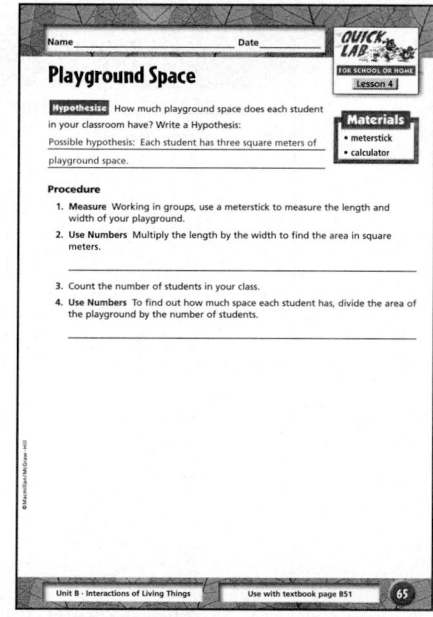

Activity Resources, pp. 65–66, 70–71, 75–76

Process Skill Builder

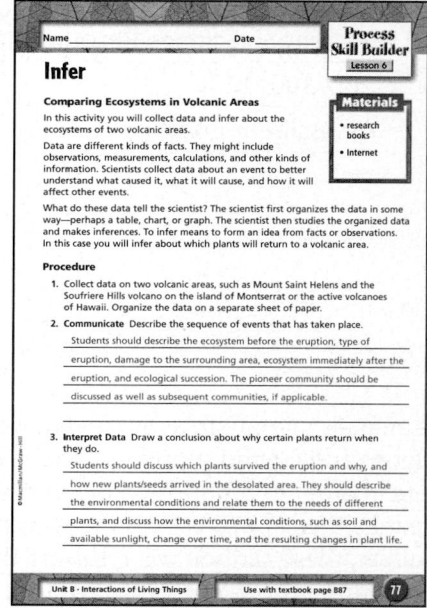

Activity Resources, pp. 77–78

McGraw-Hill Science **Assessment Book** provides the following **Blackline Master** worksheets for this chapter.

Chapter Test

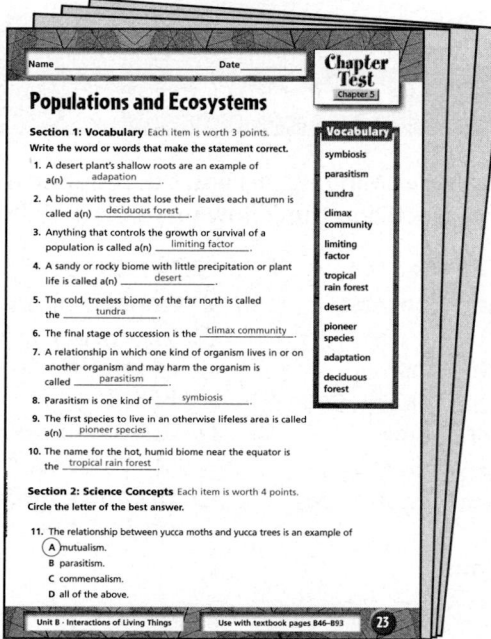

Assessment Book, pp. 23–26

CHAPTER

5 Populations and Ecosystems

Resources

- Reading in Science Resources, pp. 100–122
- Assessment Book, pp. 23–26

Did You Ever Wonder?

Some animals migrate to avoid severe weather conditions and limited supplies of food. Some migrate in order to produce young in the same area where they themselves were born. As winter turns to summer, these caribou will return to their home in the tundra.

CHAPTER

5 Populations and Ecosystems

LESSON 4

How Populations Survive, B48

LESSON 5

Biomes, B62

LESSON 6

How Ecosystems Change, B78

Did You Ever Wonder?

Why do some animals—such as mallard ducks, humpback whales, and salmon—migrate, whereas others do not? In winter, these caribou leave their home on the tundra and migrate south, where they can find food and give birth to their young. What do you think they will do when summer comes?

B 46

Reading Strategy

This chapter provides MiniLessons and other opportunities for developing and practicing the following reading skills:

- ○ **Cause and Effect**
- ◉ **Compare and Contrast:** p. B64
- ○ **Draw Conclusions**
- ◉ **Find the Main Idea:** p. B80
- ○ **Sequence of Events**
- ◉ **Summarize:** pp. B51, B60, B61, B67, B74, B75, B77, B89, B90, B91
- ○ **Ask Questions**

- ◉ **Reread:** pp. B64, B74
- ○ **Retell (paraphrase)**
- ◉ **Interpret Graphic Sources of Information:** pp. B52, B54, B65, B84
- ◉ **Build on Prior Knowledge:** pp. B48, B62, B76, B78, B94
- ◉ **Organize Information:** pp. B54, B66

B 47

Vocabulary Preview

Encourage students to keep a Science Dictionary. Remind them to add the Vocabulary words for each lesson in this chapter to their Dictionary as they complete each lesson.

limiting factor, B50

adaptation, B52

symbiosis, B54

mutualism, B54

parasitism, B56

commensalism, B57

biome, B64

grassland, B66

taiga, B67

tundra, B68

desert, B69

deciduous forest, B70

tropical rain forest, B71

ecological succession, B82

pioneer species, B83

pioneer community, B83

climax community, B84

AMERICAN MUSEUM OF NATURAL HISTORY

Visit **www.amnh.org/resources/mhscience** to discover more about populations, ecosystems, and how they change over time.

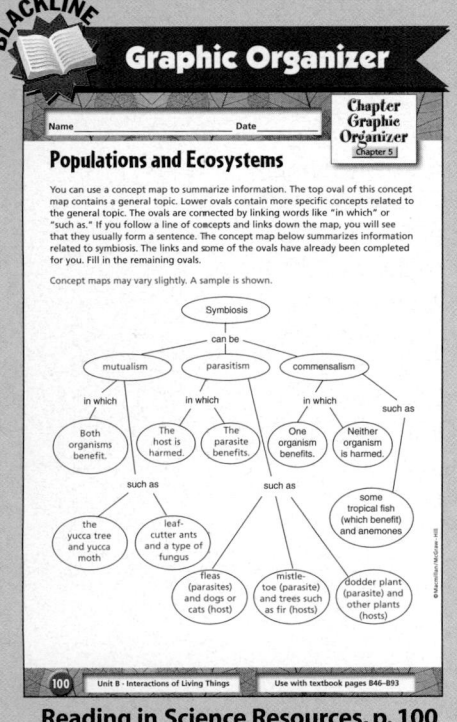

Reading in Science Resources, p. 100

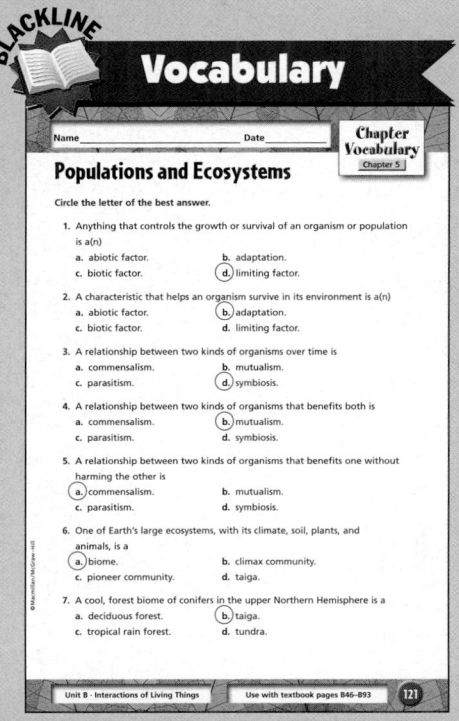

Reading in Science Resources, pp. 121–122

LESSON 4

How Populations Survive

Objectives

- Explore the effects of light and water on the growth and survival of seeds.
- Describe the role of limiting factors, including competition.
- Understand the interactions of organisms in symbiosis, mutualism, parasitism, and commensalism.
- Explain how environmental changes affect an organism's survival.

Resources

- Activity Resources, pp. 62–66
- Reading in Science Resources, pp. 103–108
- Vocabulary Cards
- Reading Aid Transparency B4

Build on Prior Knowledge
Have students discuss what they know about how organisms interact with various factors in their environment. Ask:

- **What kinds of things affect your growth, health, and overall well-being?** (possible answers: diet, exercise, amount of sleep, where you live, emotional factors)

1 Get Ready

Developing the Main Idea
Ask students to discuss what things determine the type of trees growing in a forest, and how well they grow. (Possible answers: nutrients in the soil, available sunlight, amount of water, temperature, interactions with other organisms)

LESSON 4

How Populations Survive

Vocabulary

limiting factor, B50
adaptation, B52
symbiosis, B54
mutualism, B54
parasitism, B56
commensalism, B57

Get Ready

What affects the size of a population? Some forests are so thick with trees and shrubs that you would have a tough time hiking through them. However, hiking through other forests would be as easy as walking down a country road or the street in front of your house. What makes some areas crowded and others empty? What do organisms need in an environment in order to survive?

Process Skill

You communicate when you share information.

B 48

Science Background

World's Forests
Many factors, especially human activities have shrunk forested areas. The former Soviet Union has 21 percent of the world's remaining forests; Africa has 20 percent, Latin America has 24 percent, and the United States and Canada share 16 percent. In the last 300 years, the total forested area of the United States has shrunk by about one half to one third.

Explore Activity

What Controls the Growth of Populations?

Materials

4 small, clean milk cartons with the tops removed

40 pinto bean seeds that have been soaked overnight

soil

water

Procedure

1. Label the cartons 1 to 4. Fill cartons 1 and 2 with dry potting soil. Fill cartons 3 and 4 with moistened potting soil. Fill the cartons to within 2 cm of the top.

2. Plant ten seeds in each carton, and cover the seeds with 0.5 cm of soil.

3. **Use Variables** Place cartons 1 and 3 in a well-lighted area. Place cartons 2 and 4 in a dark place. Label the cartons to show if they are wet or dry and in the light or in the dark.

4. **Observe** Examine the cartons each day for four days. Keep the soil moist in cartons 3 and 4. Record your observations.

5. Observe the plants for two weeks after they sprout. Continue to keep the soil moist in cartons 3 and 4, and record your observations.

Drawing Conclusions

1. **Communicate** How many seeds sprouted in each carton?

2. **Observe** After two weeks how many plants in each carton were still living?

3. What factor is needed for seeds to sprout? What is needed for bean plants to grow? What evidence do you have to support your answers?

4. **Going Further: Infer** Why did some seeds sprout and then die?

B 49

Alternative Explore Activity

Materials 4 similar plants, labels, water

Effect of Water and Light on Plants Have students label the plants 1, 2, 3, and 4. Tell them to put plants 1 and 2 in a sunny spot and water plant 1 each day, but not plant 2. Direct them to put plant 3 in a sunny spot and plant 4 in a dark spot and water both plants the same way. Have students record their observations for 2 weeks and draw conclusions about how light and water affect plant growth. **Kinesthetic**

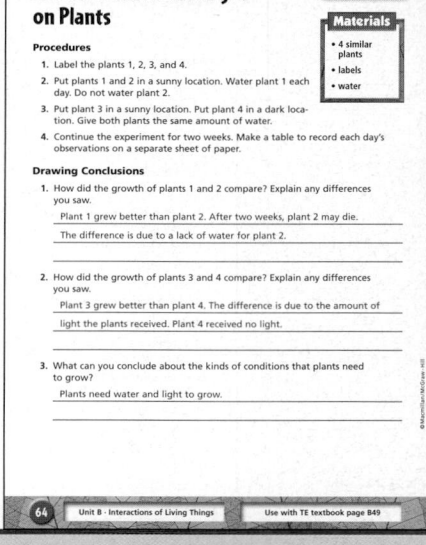

Activity Workbook, p. 64

Explore Activity

What Controls the Growth of Populations?

Science Process Skills *use variables, observe, communicate, infer*

Resources Activity Resources pp. 62–63

Pacing 30–40 minutes

Grouping small groups

Procedure

4. Suggest students give cartons 3 and 4 the same amount of water. Seeds should sprout in these cartons.

5. Seeds in carton 3 thrive. Seeds may have sprouted in carton 4, but grew little or died without light.

Answers to Drawing Conclusions

1. Answers will vary, but the greatest amount of seeds should sprout in cartons 3 and 4, the cartons that were watered.

2. Answers will vary, but carton 3 should have more living plants after 2 weeks.

3. Seeds need water to sprout. Bean plants need water and light to continue growing. The evidence is based on the number of seeds that sprouted and the number of plants that stayed alive after 2 weeks.

4. Once the seeds sprouted, they needed more than just water to stay alive.

Inquiry Students can ask their own questions to explore, such as what other factors affect plant growth. (air, soil type, amount of nutrients)

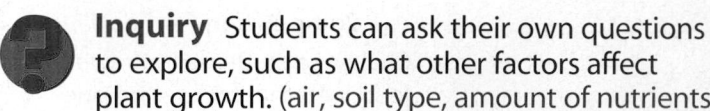

Technology

- When time is short, preview the activity with the **Explore Activity Video**.

What Controls the Growth of Populations?

Before Reading
Have students try to answer the red question at the top of the page.

Developing the Main Idea
Have students think about their classroom as an ecosystem. Ask:

■ **What populations are in this ecosystem?** (Answers should include students, at least one teacher, and perhaps plants and small animals such as turtles or mice.)

■ **What abiotic factors limit the size of the student population?** (Answers may include desks, books, or chairs.)

Developing Vocabulary

limiting factor Have students think about what the word *limit* means to them (the greatest number or amount allowed). A *limiting factor* sets the limit on the growth or survival of a population by controlling the amount of food or space available.

Read to Learn

Main Idea Living and nonliving things interact in ecosystems.

What Controls the Growth of Populations?

How much do living things depend on conditions in their environment in order to survive? Certain factors control the growth and survival of living things. What do these factors include?

A dry wind howls across the prairie. The hot Sun bakes the ground below. No rain has fallen in days. Grasses have withered. Plant-eating insects have gone hungry.

High in the bright, cloudless sky, a hawk flies one way and then another. Its sharp eyes sweep over the barren land below. An unsuspecting deer mouse scurries along the ground in search of an insect.

The mouse's tan fur blends in with the dusty soil, but its movement gives it away. The hawk tucks in its wings and dives like a falling rock. In a flash its talons grab the mouse.

Hidden in this story are clues to how the size of a population is limited. Anything that controls the growth or survival of a population is called a **limiting factor**.

Some limiting factors are nonliving. In the story the sunlight, wind, water, and temperature were nonliving limiting factors. They controlled the population of grasses on the prairie.

The grasses, insects, deer mice, and hawks were living limiting factors. The grasses had withered. There was less food for plant-eating insects, so the number of insects living on the prairie decreased. That meant there was less food for the insect-eating deer mice. The deer mouse population was also limited by the hawks, which are predators.

Competition
The number of predators in an ecosystem affects the number of prey. The number of prey in an ecosystem

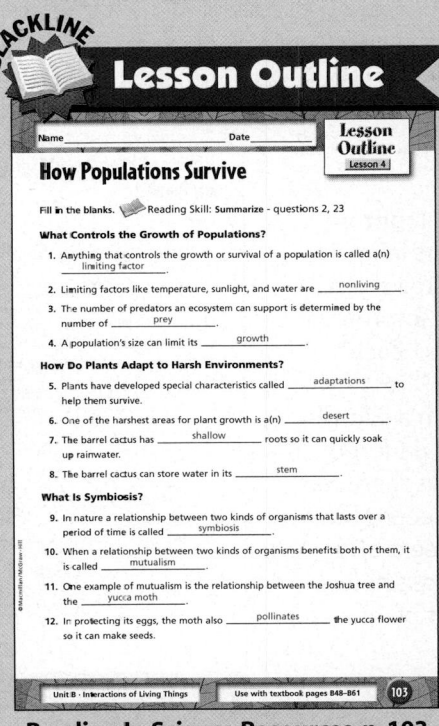

B 50

Organisms like coyotes (above) and raccoons (left) compete with each other for resources such as food, water, and territory.

English Language Learners

Competition for Food
Challenge students to draw a food web that focuses on one animal, such as the coyote or the raccoon. Ask them to include animals that are predators competing for the same prey. **Logical; Spatial**

BLACKLINE
Lesson Outline

Name_____ Date_____

Lesson Outline Lesson 4

How Populations Survive

Fill in the blanks. Reading Skill: Summarize - questions 2, 23

What Controls the Growth of Populations?

1. Anything that controls the growth or survival of a population is called a(n) ___limiting factor___

2. Limiting factors like temperature, sunlight, and water are ___nonliving___

3. The number of predators an ecosystem can support is determined by the number of ___prey___

4. A population's size can limit its ___growth___

How Do Plants Adapt to Harsh Environments?

5. Plants have developed special characteristics called ___adaptations___ to help them survive.

6. One of the harshest areas for plant growth is a(n) ___desert___

7. The barrel cactus has ___shallow___ roots so it can quickly soak up rainwater.

8. The barrel cactus can store water in its ___stem___

What Is Symbiosis?

9. In nature a relationship between two kinds of organisms that lasts over a period of time is called ___symbiosis___

10. When a relationship between two kinds of organisms benefits both of them, it is called ___mutualism___

11. One example of mutualism is the relationship between the Joshua tree and the ___yucca moth___

12. In protecting its eggs, the moth also ___pollinates___ the yucca flower so it can make seeds.

Unit B - Interactions of Living Things   Use with textbook pages B48-B61   103

Reading In Science Resources, p. 103

can also determine how many predators the ecosystem can support. If there were few hawks, the deer mouse population might stay steady or even rise. More hawks, however, mean fewer deer mice.

Hawks compete with other predators, like coyotes and raccoons. Coyotes and raccoons hunt many animals, including small rodents like deer mice.

Coyotes and raccoons also compete with each other for food, water, and places to live. The population that wins such competitions is likely to grow.

However, even a growing population faces problems. Its size will soon limit its own growth. The organisms in the population will become crowded. They will have to compete with one another for food, water, and shelter. Some will die. Eventually there will be enough for the number of organisms that remain.

READING Summarize **What are six limiting factors that control population growth?**
Possible answers: sunlight, wind, water, temperature, predators, prey, and overcrowding

Overcrowding, as in this group of walruses, limits the growth of any population.

QUICK LAB

FOR SCHOOL OR HOME

Playground Space

1. **Measure** Working in groups, use a meterstick to measure the length and width of your playground.

Schoolhouse

2. **Use Numbers** Multiply the length by the width to find the area in square meters.

3. **Count** the number of students in your class.

4. **Use Numbers** To find out how much space each student has, divide the area of the playground by the number of students.

5. **Infer** What would happen to the space each student had if the number of students doubled?

6. **Infer** Assume two other classes with the same number of students as yours used the playground at the same time as your class. What effect might this have on your class?

B 51

Developing the Main Idea
Ask students what foods coyotes and raccoons compete for. (They both eat small rodents like deer mice.) Discuss what would happen to coyotes and raccoons if the deer mice population suddenly decreases. (They would either have to find other food, move to a new habitat, or decrease their own population.)

▶ After Reading
Have students answer the red question in the student book as **ongoing assessment**.

QUICK LAB

FOR SCHOOL OR HOME

Materials meterstick, calculator

Science Process Skills *measure, use numbers, infer*

Resources Activity Resources, pp. 65-66

Steps 2–4 Work the students through each step of the math. Length × width = area; area ÷ number of students = area per student.

Step 5 The space would be halved.

Step 6 There would be less room for each student to play and move around. Students would have to compete more for playground resources, such as balls, bats, and so on.

Advanced Learners

Limiting Reagents
A limiting reagent determines how much product can be generated in a chemical reaction. For example, 61 grams of carbon dioxide gas will react with 27 grams of water to produce sugar molecules during photosynthesis. If there are only 13.5 grams of water, only 30.5 grams of carbon dioxide will react. Challenge students to compare limiting reagents with limiting factors in their own words. **Linguistic; Logical**

Reading MiniLesson

Summarize

Develop Discuss with students that a summary is a brief retelling of the most important facts in a story or article, and can't include all the little details. Review the assessment question and have volunteers express their answers as a one- or two-sentence summary of pages B50 and B51. (Possible answer: Weather conditions, food supply, overcrowding, and the ratio of predators and prey can limit the growth of a population in an ecosystem.)

Practice Remind students that a good poster summarizes to get across an important idea. Invite students to make posters that summarize a limiting factor that controls population. For example, a student might draw a plant-eating insect sitting on Sun-baked ground with the poster title, "Insects Need Food and Water to Survive."

How Do Plants Adapt to Harsh Environments?

Before Reading
Have students try to answer the red question at the top of the page.

Developing the Main Idea
Ask students how desert plants look different from other plants they're familiar with. (Students may mention their thick stems and needle-like spines.)

Exploring the Main Idea
Ask students to research the different deserts in the United States and to locate them on a map. They should identify the Great Basin, the Mojave Desert, Death Valley, and the Sonoran Desert.

READING
Maps

The Sonoran Desert lies primarily between southwestern Arizona and southeastern California.

Developing Vocabulary

adaptation Have students discuss ways in which they have adapted to their environment; that is, wearing warmer clothes in the winter or applying sunscreen in the Sun. Ask them why these behaviors are not considered to be *adaptations*. (They are not inherited traits.)

How Do Plants Adapt to Harsh Environments?

Plants live almost everywhere on Earth. They live in deserts, where rain seldom falls. They live in the icy northland, where there is little sunlight and winters are long and frigid. They live on the floor of rain forests, where the Sun rarely shines and the soil has few nutrients.

Plants can survive in these conditions because they have developed special characteristics. Characteristics that help an organism survive in its environment are called **adaptations**. Adaptations are inherited traits, not learned behaviors.

One of the harshest areas for plant growth is a desert. What adaptations do desert plants have that allow them to live where less than 5 cm (2 in.) of rain falls each year? Most people in the United States live where that much rain might fall in a few hours.

The Sonoran Desert stretches from southern California to western Arizona. If you were to visit there, you would see the barrel cactus. The barrel cactus is very well adapted to desert conditions.

Sonoran Desert

READING
Maps

Describe where in the United States the Sonoran Desert is.

The barrel cactus is adapted to the harsh conditions of the Sonoran Desert.

Math MiniLesson

Scale Drawings

Develop The *scale* in a scale drawing is the *ratio* of length in the drawing to an actual length.

Suppose the scale on a map is 1 inch = 8 feet. What is the actual distance for a scale distance of 6 inches?

Write a proportion to solve.

$$\frac{1}{8} = \frac{6}{n}$$
$$1 \times n = 6 \times 8$$
$$n = (6 \times 8) \div 1 = 48$$

 Use the $\boxed{M^+}$. Solve the proportion.

$6 \boxed{\times} 8 \boxed{M^+} \boxed{\div} 1 \boxed{=} 48$

Practice Use the scale 1 in. = 16 ft to find the actual distance for each scale distance.

1. 10 in. (160 ft) **2.** $5\frac{1}{2}$ in. (88 ft)

Activity Have students work in pairs to make a scale drawing of the school library.

The Barrel Cactus

The plant's roots are very shallow and grow only about 7.5 cm (3 in.) into the dry soil. There is an advantage to this. When rain does fall, the roots catch the rain and soak it up very quickly. However, during long dry spells, the fine ends of the roots fall off. What's the advantage? The lack of a fine network of root ends prevents water stored in the cactus from passing out into the soil.

The stem of the barrel cactus also helps it survive in the desert. It is folded and covered with needle-sharp spines. What are the advantages? The stem stores water. The folds, which are deepest during dry spells, protect moist parts of the stem from hot, dry desert winds. Otherwise these winds would draw away water from the stem's surface. The spines keep away birds and small animals that try to get water from the stems of plants. If you have a small spiny cactus plant at home, you've probably learned two things—you don't have to water it often, and it is better not to touch it.

 **What are three adaptations that help a barrel cactus to survive in a desert?**

It has shallow roots that quickly soak up water; its stem stores water; its spines keep away animals that might try to get water from its stem.

B 53

Exploring the Main Idea

Invite students to write a report on different kinds of cacti, where they are found, adaptations they have made, and products they give us. Students can illustrate their reports and share with the class.

Challenge students to write a report on farming in the desert. Crops include the date palm, cereals, and fruit. A new crop being studied is the jojoba, which does not need irrigation and produces oil. Students should include how the plants get water and how the crops adapt to their environment.

Developing the Main Idea

Have students summarize this page. Ask:

■ **How is a barrel cactus adapted to survive in a desert?** (Possible answer: It has shallow roots that quickly soak up water; its stem stores water; its spines keep away animals that might try to get water from its stem.)

 After Reading

Have students answer the red question in the student book as **ongoing assessment**.

Interpret Illustrations

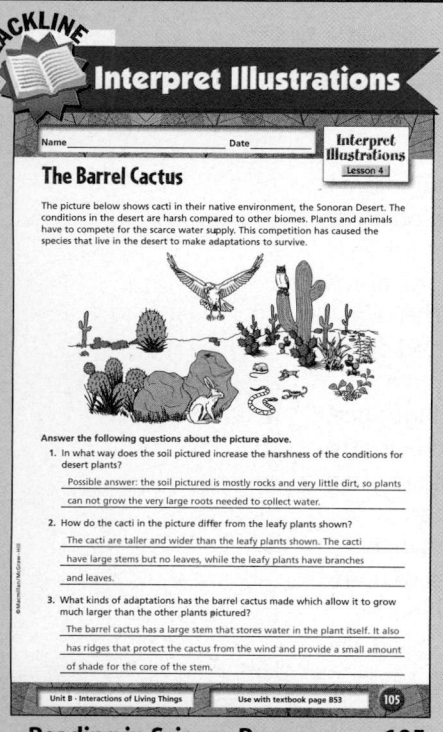

| Name | Date | Interpret Illustrations Lesson 4 |

The Barrel Cactus

The picture below shows cacti in their native environment, the Sonoran Desert. The conditions in the desert are harsh compared to other biomes. Plants and animals have to compete for the scarce water supply. This competition has caused the species that live in the desert to make adaptations to survive.

Answer the following questions about the picture above.

1. In what way does the soil pictured increase the harshness of the conditions for desert plants?

   Possible answer: the soil pictured is mostly rocks and very little dirt, so plants can not grow the very large roots needed to collect water.

2. How do the cacti in the picture differ from the leafy plants shown?

   The cacti are taller and wider than the leafy plants shown. The cacti have large stems but no leaves, while the leafy plants have branches and leaves.

3. What kinds of adaptations has the barrel cactus made which allow it to grow much larger than the other plants pictured?

   The barrel cactus has a large stem that stores water in the plant itself. It also has ridges that protect the cactus from the wind and provide a small amount of shade for the core of the stem.

Unit B - Interactions of Living Things | Use with textbook page B53 | **105**

Reading in Science Resources, p. 105

English Language Learners

Observing Cacti

Invite students to observe some adaptations of cactus plants. Slice off the spines and let the students handle them carefully. Then have them look at the plants' roots. Slice the stem open and let students examine it for water. (Be sure to remove any spines from the stem.) **Kinesthetic; Spatial**

Science Background

Arctic Plants
Addressing Misconceptions
Students may not think that plants grow in Arctic regions. Although trees do not grow there, plants abound during the brief summer. In the tundra, buttercups, poppies, sedges, grasses, and shrubs with berries provide food for the animals that live there as well as for summer visitors. During the winter, animals will dig for food under the snow. Some of the animals have feet adapted for digging through snow for the buried plants.

What Is Symbiosis?

Before Reading
Have students try to answer the red question at the top of the page.

Developing the Main Idea
Ask students what they know about ways organisms interact with each other. Ask students what relationships they've had that have lasted over a period of time. (examples: family, friends, team members) Have them give examples of human relationships that benefit or harm at least one person.

READING Maps

The Mojave Desert is located in southeastern California.

Developing Vocabulary

symbiosis Ask students what *sym-*, as in *sympathy* and *symphony*, means. (together) Discuss with them what *bio-* means. (life) Show how the word *symbiosis* means "life together".

mutualism Discuss what the word *mutual* means (students may look it up in the dictionary) and how this definition can help students understand the concept of *mutualism*.

What Is Symbiosis?

Organisms interact with each other in a number of different ways. You have already seen that some organisms hunt others. Some organisms are predators. Some organisms are prey. You have also seen that organisms may compete with each other for food or territory. Two different kinds of predators may hunt the same prey. However, there are also other kinds of relationships between different kinds of organisms. Some of these relationships are long lasting.

In nature a relationship between two kinds of organisms that lasts over a period of time is called **symbiosis**. There are different kinds of symbiosis. Sometimes both organisms benefit from the relationship. Sometimes one organism benefits while harming the other. Sometimes only one benefits, and the other is not affected. Let's take a closer look at each kind of symbiosis.

READING Maps

Describe where in the United States the Mojave Desert is.

B 54

Mutualism
When a relationship between two kinds of organisms benefits both of them, it is called **mutualism**.

A strange-looking plant grows in the Mojave Desert of southern California. It's called a Joshua tree, or yucca plant.

When this tree's creamy flowers are in bloom, small gray shadows seem to dart from flower to flower. A more careful look reveals that the "shadows" are actually moths. These are yucca moths.

Yucca trees and yucca moths depend on each other for survival. Each helps the other reproduce.

Mojave Desert

Reading Strategy

Organize Information
Developing Reading Skills
Ask students to organize the information in the text into a table.
Possible headings: *Kind of symbiosis, Explanation, Example*

Science Background

Lichens
Another example of mutualism is the lichens often found on rocks and the sides of trees. A lichen is a combination of two organisms, an alga and a fungus. This relationship may have started out as parasitic but evolved into a mutualistic one. The fungus gets food from the alga and helps the alga get water. Lichens are often the first life found on bare rock. They break the rock down to make soil. Lichens are also used as indicators of air pollution. A treelike form indicates good air quality.

The Yucca Moth and the Yucca Tree

Yucca moths cannot survive without yucca trees. The yucca trees would also quickly become extinct if the moths vanished. The yucca moths and the yucca trees benefit from each other and share a relationship of mutualism. How does this work?

At night a female yucca moth visits a yucca flower. Inside the flower the moth picks up pollen and rolls it up into a ball, which it holds gently in its mouth. Then the moth flutters over to another flower. There it makes a hole in the flower's ovary. The moth injects its eggs through the hole. Finally, it packs the sticky ball of pollen onto the flower's stigma. The stigma and ovary are female reproductive parts of a flower. Pollen holds male sex cells.

In protecting its eggs, the moth has also pollinated the yucca flower. The pollinated flower can then make seeds. Eventually some of the seeds will sprout into new yucca plants. This means yucca plants will continue to grow in the desert.

The moth's eggs and the tree's seeds develop at the same time. When the eggs hatch into larvae, the larvae will feed on some of the seeds. All this is happening inside the protective ovary wall. The larvae are not only getting needed food, they are also safe from predators.

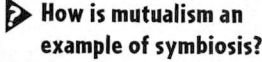

▷ How is mutualism an example of symbiosis?

In mutualism two kinds of organisms have a relationship that over time benefits both organisms.

Yucca moth

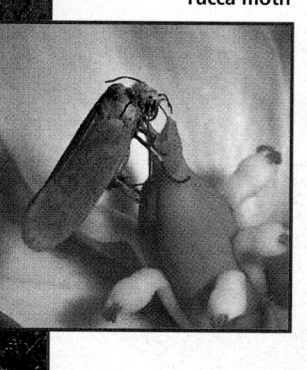

B 55

Developing the Main Idea

Draw two diagrams of yucca plants with flowers on the board. Ask volunteers to use these diagrams and their imaginations to act out what happens when a yucca moth visits a yucca flower.

Exploring the Main Idea

Invite students to write a story from the viewpoint of the yucca moth. Challenge them to go through a life cycle.

▶ After Reading

Have students answer the red question in the student book as **ongoing assessment**.

Technology

■ **Science Experiences Videotapes**
Staying Alive: Adaptations for Survival (Package 4)

What Is Parasitism?

Before Reading
Have students try to answer the red question at the top of the page.

Developing the Main Idea
Ask students what other parasites they know about. Responses may include ticks, viruses, and tapeworms. Lead them in a discussion of how parasites can harm humans.

Thinking Further: *Inferring*
Ask:

- **Why do you think parasites cause disease in humans?** (They use humans as hosts and the hosts are harmed.)

▶ After Reading
Have students answer the red question in the student book as **ongoing assessment**.

Developing Vocabulary

parasitism *Parasite* is derived from the Greek word *parasitos*, meaning "one who eats at the table of another." Ask students how they would relate *parasitism* to eating at a table. (A parasite eats off someone else's plate and that person then does not have enough food to eat.)

What Is Parasitism?

A relationship in which one kind of organism lives on or in another organism and may harm that organism is called **parasitism** (PAR·uh·sigh·tiz·uhm). The organisms that live on or in other organisms are called *parasites* (PAR·uh·sights). The organisms they feed on are called *hosts*. The parasites benefit from the relationship. The hosts are harmed by it.

Fleas are parasites of dogs and cats. The fleas live off the blood of these hosts and give nothing back but itching and irritation. Plants also have parasites, which often are other plants.

The bright orange dodder plant has little chlorophyll. This means that it can't make enough food to live on. Instead it winds around a plant that can make its own food. The dodder then sends tubes into the stem of the plant it is coiled around. Next, the dodder gets food from the plant through the tubes. Although the plant it lives on usually does not die, it is weakened, grows more slowly, and is not able to easily fight off diseases.

The coiling dodder plant, which can't make enough of its own food, draws food from other plants.

▷ How does parasitism differ from mutualism?

In mutualism both organisms benefit. In parasitism the parasite benefits and the host is harmed.

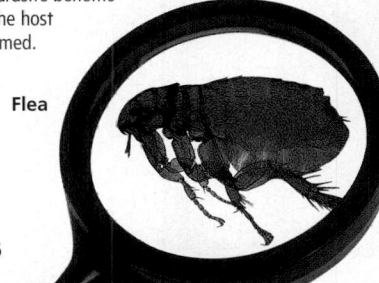

Flea

B 56

Mistletoe is another parasitic plant. It is an evergreen that grows on the trunk or branches of trees such as hawthorn, poplar, fir, or apple.

Science Background

Parasitic Relationships
Parasites are found among all major groups of living things. For example, the lamprey is a fish that sucks out the body fluids of other fish. The remora, on the other hand, has a commensalistic relationship with other fish. It hitches a ride on a large fish and eats the scraps scattered by its host. A parasite and host may develop a mutual tolerance because if the host dies, so does the parasite. But the host is always harmed in a parasitic relationship.

Advanced Learners

Parasitic Diseases
Human parasites include viruses, bacteria, fungi, protozoans, worms, and flukes. Although viruses are not living organisms, they need a host in order to replicate. Viral diseases include measles and chicken pox. Bacterial diseases include tuberculosis and tooth decay. Sleeping sickness is caused by a protozoan; a similar organism causes malaria. Invite students to find out how different parasitic diseases are transmitted and treated. **Intrapersonal; Linguistic**

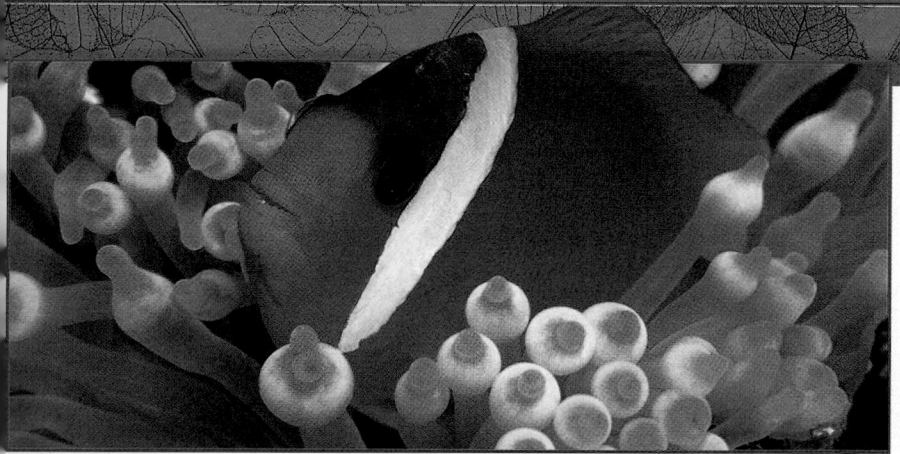

Some tropical fish are protected from predators by the poison in a sea anemone's tentacles.

Orchids benefit from their position on the trunks of trees.

What Is Commensalism?

Few plants can grow on the floor of a rain forest. One reason is that the thick canopy above keeps light from reaching the ground. Some plants, like orchids, attach themselves to the trunks of trees high above the rain forest floor. The orchids, which make their own food, don't take anything from the trees. They simply use the trees to get needed sunlight. This relationship, in which one organism benefits from another without harming or helping it, is called commensalism (kuh·MEN·suh·liz·uhm).

Many animals also have this kind of relationship. There are certain tropical fish that live unharmed among the poisonous tentacles of sea anemones. The anemones provide safety for the fish. However, the fish neither harm nor help the anemones.

 **What kind of relationship is commensalism?**

Commensalism is a form of symbiosis in which one organism benefits while the other is neither helped nor harmed.

B 57

What Is Commensalism?

Before Reading
Have students try to answer the red question at the top of the page.

Exploring the Main Idea
Ask students to think about their own symbiotic relationships. They may be more familiar with parasitic relationships, such as those with viruses, bacteria, and worms; however, you may want to explore mutualistic relationships such as the presence of *E. coli* in our intestines. If you have agar plates available you may want to take several rubbings from a volunteer's hands, face, or legs with a sterile swab. Smear each sample on an agar plate and leave them in a warm place for 24–48 hours. Discuss with students if these bacteria are harmful or if they are just looking for a warm place to live.

Thinking Further: *Making Generalizations*
Ask:

■ **How would you explain commensalism?** (One organism benefits from a host without helping or harming the host.)

▶**After Reading**
Have students answer the red question in the student book as **ongoing assessment**.

Developing Vocabulary

commensalism In relation to the analogy used to define *parasitism*, students may describe *commensalism* as eating at a table where each organism has its own plate of food.

How Do Populations Survive Earth's Changes?

Before Reading
Have students try to answer the red question at the top of the page.

Developing the Main Idea
Help students identify at least five changes described in the text. For example, ask:

- **How does a temperature change on Earth affect the amount of land exposed?** (As the temperature warms, ice melts, and more land is exposed.)

- **How does a temperature change affect sea level?** (As the temperature rises and ice melts, the liquid flows into the sea, causing the level to rise.)

Exploring the Main Idea
Show students a map of the world. Ask them what they see that may prove that continents have moved. They should see that South America and Africa look as though they were together at one time.

How Do Populations Survive Earth's Changes?

Earth is constantly changing. About 18,000 years ago, great sheets of ice moved deep into the heartland of what is now the United States. Vast ice sheets also covered much of Europe and parts of South America. Sea levels dropped as more and more water froze. New land was exposed. Earth was a cold place.

Slowly Earth began to warm up. The ice melted. Sea levels rose. Coastal land became flooded.

These kinds of changes have occurred no fewer than seven times during the past 700,000 years. Scientists call these cold periods *ice ages*.

Earth has also changed in other ways. Over millions of years, continents have moved north and south, east and west. Huge mountain-sized rocks have crashed into Earth. Volcanoes have poured gases and dust into the air.

Each of these events has had an effect on living things. Some organisms have survived these changes, while others have died out, or become extinct. Why have some of these organisms vanished while others survived?

To answer this, let's look at the age of the dinosaurs. Fossils from about 65 million years ago suggest that dinosaurs shared the land with many other animals. These animals included frogs, snails, insects, turtles, snakes, and some small furry mammals. Plants of all kinds grew everywhere. The seas were full of organisms like fish, sea urchins, clams, and algae.

B 58

Dinosaur footprints

Scientific evidence suggests that a meteorite up to 10 km (6 mi) in diameter struck Earth from outer space. One theory states that the impact created a huge explosion. It gouged out a crater 64 km (40 mi) across and threw huge amounts of

---

Science Background

Dinosaurs

Addressing Misconceptions
Dinosaurs were an incredibly diverse group of animals and had many adaptations to live in various climates. Scientists now think that dinosaurs were very maternal and some lived in colonies. Their brains were more developed than previously thought, and they could probably see colors. They would have developed bright colors to attract mates.

BLACKLINE · Interpret Illustrations

Name_____ Date_____

Interpret Illustrations
Lesson 4

How Do Populations Survive Earth's Changes?

This drawing shows an event that scientists think happened in Earth's history.

Scientific evidence suggests that about 65 million years ago, an asteroid (larger than shown) from outer space may have struck Earth, killing off many animals and plants.

Answer these questions about the drawing above.
1. How long ago did this event occur?
   65 million years ago
2. What is hurtling toward Earth? _____ A meteorite
3. What organisms are on the ground?
   Plants, trees, dinosaurs, insects, frogs, snails, turtles, and snakes
4. What happened to the meteorite? _____ It struck Earth.
5. What effect did the meteorite have on Earth?
   It killed many plants and animals.

106 Unit B · Interactions of Living Things   Use with textbook pages B58–B59

Reading in Science Resources, p. 106

dust into the sky. The dust may have hung in the sky for months, even years. Sunlight was probably blocked from reaching the ground.

Plants needing lots of sunlight may have died out. That means that the large plant-eating dinosaurs could not get enough food. They would have died out. The large dinosaurs preying on plant eaters would have also died out. It may have been that every animal weighing more than about 121 kg (55 lb) became extinct.

However, many of the smaller animals could have survived. They needed less food to live. They could have moved more easily from habitat to habitat. They would no longer have been in competition with the dinosaurs. They would have been free to grow in size and variety. Possibly this is how a world once ruled by dinosaurs became ruled by mammals.

 **How do changes on Earth affect organisms?**

Changes may cause some organisms to die out and may enable others to grow and evolve.

Dinosaurs became extinct about 65 million years ago. Scientists can study them today, however, by searching for fossils such as footprints and skeletons.

B 59

Exploring the Main Idea
Invite students to find out more about how Earth looked during the Mesozoic Age (age of reptiles) and the Cenozoic Age (age of mammals).

Developing the Main Idea
Have students summarize these two pages. Ask:

- **How might changes on Earth have affected organisms?** (Possible answers can include students' own suggestions: Changes such as floods, volcanic eruptions, continental movements, and meteorites hitting the surface, could have caused some organisms to die out, while others survived because of reduced competition for resources.)

▶**After Reading**
Have students answer the red question in the student book as **ongoing assessment**.

Science Background

Dinosaur Extinction

For a long time, scientists thought that the climate slowly cooled and the dinosaurs gradually died out from starvation. But in the 1970s, Luis and Walter Alvarez found traces of iridium and shocked quartz in soil layers deposited 65 million years ago around the world. Iridium is rare on Earth but is found in meteorites. Shocked quartz is produced only in gigantic explosions. After impact, great clouds of dust would have caused a period of darkness and a cooler climate.

SCIENCE FOR ALL English Language Learners

Storyboards

Challenge students to translate the theory in the text into pictures. They can do a storyboard that outlines what a movie would look like. Remind them that their pictures need to be scientifically accurate. **Spatial; Linguistic**

How Do People Change the Environment?

Before Reading
Have students try to answer the red question at the top of the page.

Developing the Main Idea
As students read this page ask them how they think they affect the environment. Have students recall how carbon is recycled in the environment. Discuss how a carbon atom from a tree in Brazil could end up in their bodies. Have them consider how the oxygen they breathe might have traveled from afar.

Exploring the Main Idea
Ask a volunteer to blow up a balloon, then release the air. Ask:

- **Where did the air breathed into the balloon go?** (all over the classroom)

- **Do you think it will stay in the classroom? Why?** (No; when the door or window opens, all the air in the classroom will circulate with the outside air.)

▶After Reading
Have students answer the red question in the student book as **ongoing assessment**.

How Do People Change the Environment?

How do you affect your environment? About fifteen times a minute, you change the environment. That's the number of times you probably breathe in and out every 60 seconds. Each time you exhale, you add carbon dioxide and water to the air. Each time you inhale, you remove oxygen.

The amount of these substances you breathe in and out is small. However, they change the environment around you and far away. That's because air circulates around Earth. The carbon dioxide you exhaled might find its way into a local tree or a plant miles away. Oxygen that the plant gives off might be inhaled by an animal even farther from your home.

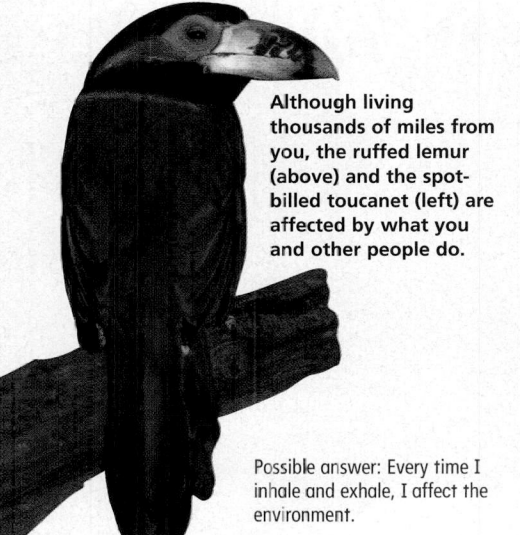

Although living thousands of miles from you, the ruffed lemur (above) and the spot-billed toucanet (left) are affected by what you and other people do.

Eventually some of the air you exhaled might go through several cycles. In the process that air might also travel around the world.

Some of that air might find its way into a *jaborandi* (zha·buh·ran·DEE) tree in northern Brazil. Some of it might wind up in a periwinkle shrub in Madagascar. Madagascar is an island in the Indian Ocean off the east coast of Africa.

The plants use the carbon to build their stems, leaves, roots, and other parts. Some of these parts will be eaten by animals. They might be Madagascar's big-eyed ruffed lemurs or Brazil's many-colored spot-billed toucanets. Each of these animals seeks food and shelter among the plants of its environment.

Possible answer: Every time I inhale and exhale, I affect the environment.

▷ **What is one way you affect the environment?**

B 60

Why It Matters

People interact with their environment. They can do good and bad things to the environment. They can interfere with an ecosystem by damming up rivers, using pesticides, and cutting down trees. They can also preserve an ecosystem by passing laws that protect its animals and plants.

The lives of all organisms are affected by other living things and by nonliving things. By understanding how living things interact with one another and with their environment, people can help preserve the treasures of nature.

Think and Write

1. Identify two biotic and two abiotic limiting factors.

2. How is mutualism like commensalism? How is it different?

3. Identify an organism and an adaptation that helps it survive in its environment.

4. Make a list of ways you and your community affect your environment.

5. **Critical Thinking** Several species of whales are threatened with extinction. Propose two hypotheses that might account for the threat.

L·I·N·K·S

HEALTH LINK

Investigate parasites. How do parasites affect humans? What do these organisms gain from their host? How do they harm it? Write a paragraph.

Human tapeworm

WRITING LINK

Write a poem. Write about a relationship in your life that is symbiotic. Explain what makes the relationship symbiotic. Who is helped? Who is the helper?

TECHNOLOGY LINK

Science Newsroom CD-ROM Choose *Keep Them Alive* to learn how sea turtles and other species get what they need to survive from their environment.

At the Computer Visit **www.mhscience02.com** for more links.

B 61

✔ Informal Assessment

Easy/Average Ask students to define *symbiosis* and give examples of the three kinds discussed in the lesson. Then have them define and discuss limiting factors and adaptations.

Challenge Invite teams of students to develop and give each other 10-question quizzes with answer keys. These should cover the main ideas of the lesson.

3 | Lesson Review

Answers to Think and Write

1. biotic: predators, food supply; abiotic: water, air, sunlight, minerals (pp. B50–B51)

2. Both are symbiotic relationships in which neither member is harmed. In mutualism, both organisms benefit; in commensalism, one organism benefits and the other is not harmed. (pp. B54, B57)

3. Possible answer: A barrel cactus can store water in its stem and ward off pests with its spines. (p. B52)

4. Possible answers: construction, land clearing, use of off-road vehicles, pollutants that factories release, pesticide use, over-hunting or over-fishing (pp. B60–B61)

5. **Critical Thinking** Human activity that increases water temperatures or causes pollution may threaten the whales; humans may have hunted too many of the whales; or the population of the whales' major food source may have decreased for some reason. (pp. B60–B61)

Summarize

Check students' understanding by having them write a brief summary of the lesson in their own words.

HEALTH LINK

Students' research should focus on certain species of parasites that affect humans, such as the protozoan *Plasmodium*, which causes malaria, and the flatworm *Schistosoma*, which causes schistosomiasis. They should describe the nutrients that parasites gain and the effects of different parasites on their hosts.

WRITING LINK

Students' poems should reflect an understanding of the term *symbiosis*. They may include any or all of the three types.

LESSON 5 Biomes

Objectives

- Explore the importance of soil.
- Identify and locate Earth's six major land biomes.
- Compare and contrast the various biomes and aquatic ecosystems.
- Discuss how whales are threatened with extinction and how they are being protected.

Resources

- Activity Resources, pp. 67–71
- Reading in Science Resources, pp. 109–114
- Vocabulary Cards
- Reading Aid Transparency B5
- Grade-Level Science Book, *Antarctica*
- School to Home Activities, pp. 13–14

Build on Prior Knowledge

Have students discuss what they know about different types of soil. Have them compare the type of soil they would find at a beach with the type they would use to pot a houseplant. (Beach soil tends to be rocky or sandy; potting soil is dark, moist, and coarse in texture.) Based on their experiences, have students list the kinds of things that might be found in soil. (possible answers: water, minerals, rock particles, plant matter, organisms)

1 Get Ready

Using the Illustrations

Ask students if the plants shown differ from those in your own biome. Ask what they know about the soil in the rain forest and in their own biome. (Soil in a rain forest is nutrient-poor; other soils are described on page B64 and page B65.)

LESSON 5 Biomes

Vocabulary

biome, B64

grasslands, B66

taiga, B67

tundra, B68

desert, B69

deciduous forest, B70

tropical rain forest, B71

Get Ready

What kinds of plants and animals live in the tropical rain forest? Are they the same as the ones that live in your community? Why do certain plants live in some areas and not others?

Soil varies greatly and is a distinctive factor in each ecosystem. Soil content can determine what plants and animals can live there.

Process Skill

You observe when you use your senses to learn about an object or event.

B 62

Science Background

Location of Biomes

If you drew the biomes on a globe you would be able to connect similar biomes within roughly horizontal bands, corresponding to bands of different climates. That is because climate has a tremendous influence on the type of biome formed. The biomes also depend on wind patterns, the extent of glaciers, and human activity.

Explore Activity

Why Is Soil Important?

Materials
washed sand

soil

hydrogen peroxide

2 plastic cups

2 plastic spoons

dropper

goggles

apron

Procedure

BE CAREFUL! Wear goggles and an apron.

1 Place 1 tsp. of washed sand in a plastic cup.

2 **Observe** Using the dropper, add hydrogen peroxide to the sand, drop by drop. Count each drop. Bubbles will form as the hydrogen peroxide breaks down any decayed matter.

3 **Communicate** Record the number of drops you add until the bubbles stop forming.

4 **Experiment** Repeat steps 1–3 using the soil.

Drawing Conclusions

1 Which sample—soil or sand—gave off more bubbles?

2 **Infer** Why was the sand used?

3 **Infer** Decayed materials in soil release their nutrients to form humus. The amount of humus in soil depends on the rate of decay and the rate at which plants absorb the nutrients. Which sample had more humus?

4 **Going Further: Infer** In which sample could you grow larger, healthier plants? Why?

B 63

Explore Activity

Why Is Soil Important?

Science Process Skills *observe, communicate, experiment, infer*

Resources Activity Resources, pp. 67–68

Pacing 30–40 minutes

Grouping individual

Procedure

Be Careful! Stress the need for protecting the eyes from chemicals, sand, and soil by wearing goggles. Explain how an apron will protect against spills.

3 Answers will vary. However, the sand should react with relatively few drops of hydrogen peroxide, compared to the soil.

Answers to Drawing Conclusions

1 Soil should give off more bubbles than sand.

2 Sand was used as the control. It contains mostly rock with very little decayed matter.

3 The soil had more humus.

4 Plants would grow better in the soil because it contains more nutrients.

 **Inquiry** Students can ask their own questions to explore, such as what else is found in soil that makes it important to an ecosystem. (air, water, organisms)

Technology

■ When time is short, preview the activity with the **Explore Activity Video**.

Alternative Explore Activity

Materials washed sand; compost, potting soil, or garden soil; distilled water; petri dishes; pH test paper; spoons

Testing Soil pH Have students mix a spoonful of sand with a little distilled water in a petri dish. Then have them test the mixture with pH paper. Explain that a pH less than 7 indicates the soil is acidic and not as nutrient-rich. Ask them to see if there is a relationship between pH value and the amount of decayed matter (humus) in soil.

Kinesthetic

Name _____ **Date** _____

Alternative Explore Lesson 5

Testing Soil pH

Procedure

1. Mix a spoonful of washed sand and a little distilled water in a petri dish.

2. Test the mixture with pH paper. What was the pH of the sand mixture?

   Answers will vary. Students may need assistance in using the pH paper and interpreting the results.

3. Test the other soil sample(s) in the same way. Record your results in the table.

Materials
• washed sand
• distilled water
• pH test paper
• compost, potting soil, or garden soil
• petri dishes
• spoons

Sample	pH

Drawing Conclusions

1. Which sample had the highest pH?

   Answers will vary.

2. Which sample had the lowest pH?

   Answers will vary.

3. A low pH means the sample is acidic and not as nutrient rich as soils with a higher pH. Which sample is the most nutrient-rich? Explain your answer.

   Answers will vary depending on the source of the soil. The most nutrient-rich sample is the one with the highest pH.

Unit B · Interactions of Living Things   Use with TE textbook page B63   69

Activity Resources, p. 69

2 Read to Learn

What Is a Biome?

Before Reading
Have students try to answer the red question at the top of the page.

Developing the Main Idea
Have students locate and identify the biome they live in. Then ask them to discuss the climate and how it compares with the description in the text. Also ask them what plants and animals they have seen in their biome and whether these plants and animals are listed under the descriptions of other biomes.

▶**After Reading**
Have students answer the red question in the student book as **ongoing assessment**.

Developing Vocabulary

biome Explain that *bi-* is a form of *bio-*, which means "life" and *-omes* is formed from the Greek word *oma*, meaning "group or mass". (This suffix is also used to describe masses of cells or tumors.) Ask students to develop a definition of *biome* based on this background.

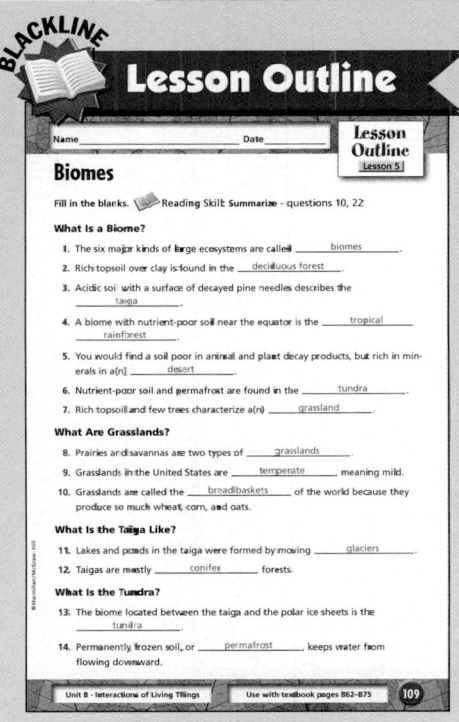

Read to Learn

Main Idea The world has a great number of ecosystems and biomes.

Taiga

What Is a Biome?

The land on Earth is divided into six major kinds of large eco-systems, called biomes (BIGH·ohmz). Each biome has its own kind of climate, soil, plants, and animals. Each biome can be found in different parts of the world. A desert biome is found in North America. Another is found in Africa. Still others are found in South America, Asia, and Australia. The map shows where Earth's six biomes are located around our planet.

Deciduous forest

Tropical rain forest

▷ **What are the six major biomes?**

desert, grassland, tundra, taiga, deciduous forest, and tropical rain forest

Taiga	Deciduous Forest	Tropical Rain Forest
Location: Mid- to high latitudes **Climate:** Very cold winters, cool summers; about 50 cm (20 in.) of precipitation a year **Soil:** Acidic, mineral-poor, decayed pine and spruce needles on surface **Plants:** Mostly spruce, fir, and other evergreens **Animals:** Rodents, snowshoe hares, lynx, sables, ermine, caribou, bears, wolves, birds in summer	**Location:** Midlatitudes **Climate:** Relatively mild summers and cold winters, 76–127 cm (30–50 in.) of precipitation a year **Soil:** Rich topsoil over clay **Plants:** Hardwoods such as oaks, beeches, hickories, maples **Animals:** Wolves, deer, bears, and a wide variety of small mammals, birds, amphibians, reptiles, and insects	**Location:** Near the equator **Climate:** Hot all year round, 200–460 cm (80–180 in.) of rain a year **Soil:** Nutrient-poor **Plants:** Greatest diversity of any biome; vines, orchids, ferns, and a wide variety of trees. **Animals:** More species of insects, reptiles, and amphibians than any place else; monkeys, other small and large mammals, including in some places elephants, all sorts of colorful birds

B 64

SCIENCE ▸ Reading Strategy

Reread Compare and Contrast

Developing Reading Skills
Have students compare and contrast biomes, detail by detail. They can reread as necessary. Working in pairs, one student can describe biomes by detail to the other and the partner must name the biome.

BLACKLINE ▸ Lesson Outline

Name _____ Date _____

Lesson Outline Lesson 5

Biomes

Fill in the blanks. 📖 Reading Skill: Summarize - questions 10, 22

What Is a Biome?

1. The six major kinds of large ecosystems are called ____biomes____.
2. Rich topsoil over clay is found in the ____deciduous forest____.
3. Acidic soil with a surface of decayed pine needles describes the ____taiga____.
4. A biome with nutrient-poor soil near the equator is the ____tropical rainforest____.
5. You would find a soil poor in animal and plant decay products, but rich in minerals in a(n) ____desert____.
6. Nutrient-poor soil and permafrost are found in the ____tundra____.
7. Rich topsoil and few trees characterize a(n) ____grassland____.

What Are Grasslands?

8. Prairies and savannas are two types of ____grasslands____.
9. Grasslands in the United States are ____temperate____ meaning mild.
10. Grasslands are called the ____breadbaskets____ of the world because they produce so much wheat, corn, and oats.

What Is the Taiga Like?

11. Lakes and ponds in the taiga were formed by moving ____glaciers____.
12. Taigas are mostly ____conifers____ forests.

What Is the Tundra?

13. The biome located between the taiga and the polar ice sheets is the ____tundra____.
14. Permanently frozen soil, or ____permafrost____, keeps water from flowing downward.

Unit B · Interactions of Living Things | Use with textbook pages B62-B75 | **109**

Reading in Science Resources, p. 109

🦉 Science Background

Location of Biomes
If you were to draw the biomes on a globe, you would see them basically stacked up in horizontal bands from pole to pole. This is because climate depends on the angle at which sunlight hits Earth. At the equator, sunlight hits straight on, giving that part of the globe more energy. The biomes also depend on how air circulates the globe, the extent of glaciers, and human activity.

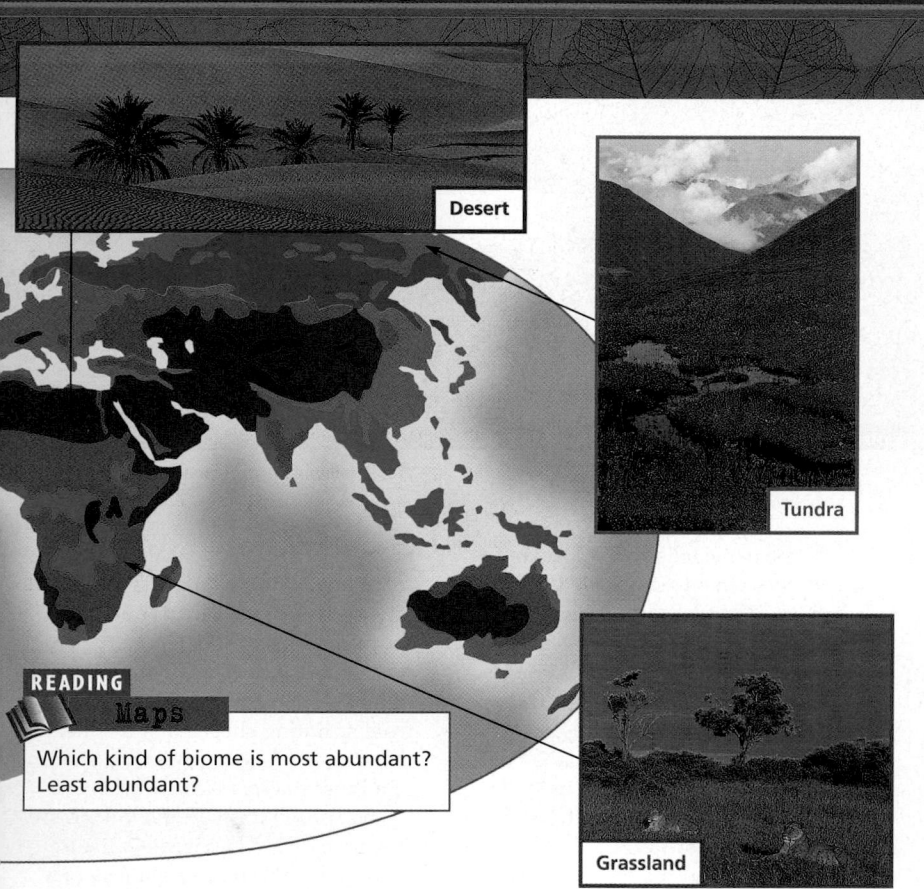

Desert

Tundra

Grassland

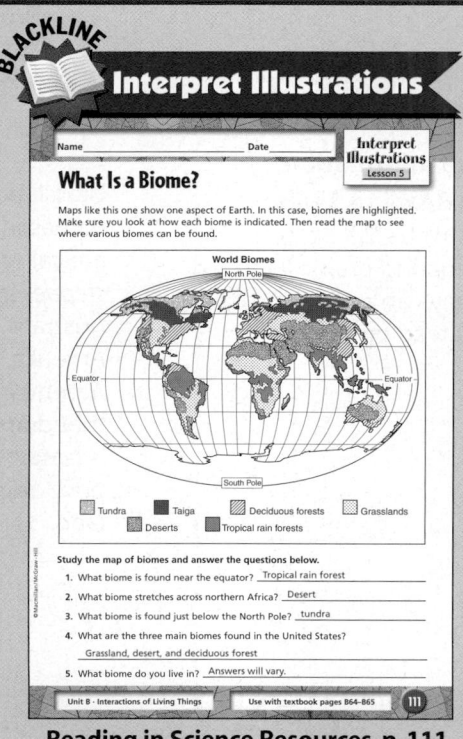 *(within Grassland region)*

READING
Maps

Which kind of biome is most abundant? Least abundant?

Desert

Location: Midlatitudes
Climate: Generally very hot days, cool nights; precipitation less than 4 cm (10 in.) a year
Soil: Poor in animal and plant decay products but often rich in minerals
Plants: None to cacti, yuccas, bunch grasses, shrubs, and a few trees
Animals: Rodents, snakes, lizards, tortoises, insects, and some birds. The Sahara in Africa is home to camels, gazelles, antelopes, small foxes, snakes, lizards, and gerbils.

Tundra

Location: High northern latitudes
Climate: Very cold, harsh, and long winters; short and cool summers; 10–25 cm (4–10 in.) of precipitation a year
Soil: Nutrient-poor, permafrost layer a few inches down
Plants: Grasses, wildflowers, mosses, small shrubs
Animals: Musk oxen, migrating caribou, arctic foxes, weasels, snowshoe hares, owls, hawks, various rodents, occasional polar bears

Grassland

Location: Midlatitudes, interiors of continents
Climate: Cool in winter, hot in summer; 25–75 cm (10–30 in.) of precipitation a year
Soil: Rich topsoil
Plants: Mostly grasses and small shrubs, some trees near sources of water
Animals: American grasslands include prairie dogs, foxes, small mammals, snakes, insects, various birds. African grasslands include elephants, lions, zebras, giraffes.

B 65

Exploring the Main Idea

Encourage students to find connections between all the aspects of the biomes. For example, in the desert biome, the lack of plants is consistent with the lack of plant decay products in the soil. Insects would be important in such a biome to provide food for the other animals since there are few plants. Plants that do grow in the desert have to be able to store water because of the low precipitation.

Developing the Main Idea

Ask students what they know about plants that grow in deserts and rain forests. Help them use world climate maps to locate areas with similar amounts of rainfall and temperature ranges across the world. Discuss whether students think these areas would have similar soils, plants, and animals.

READING
Maps

Grasslands are most abundant. Tundra are least abundant.

BLACKLINE
Interpret Illustrations

Name_____ Date_____

Interpret Illustrations Lesson 5

What Is a Biome?

Maps like this one show one aspect of Earth. In this case, biomes are highlighted. Make sure you look at how each biome is indicated. Then read the map to see where various biomes can be found.

World Biomes
North Pole

Equator — Equator

South Pole

☐ Tundra ■ Taiga ☐ Deciduous forests ☐ Grasslands
☐ Deserts ■ Tropical rain forests

Study the map of biomes and answer the questions below.

1. What biome is found near the equator? _Tropical rain forest_
2. What biome stretches across northern Africa? _Desert_
3. What biome is found just below the North Pole? _tundra_
4. What are the three main biomes found in the United States? _Grassland, desert, and deciduous forest_
5. What biome do you live in? _Answers will vary._

Unit B • Interactions of Living Things   Use with textbook pages B64–B65   111

Reading in Science Resources, p. 111

SCIENCE FOR ALL
Inclusion

Biome Collage

Invite students to pick one of the biomes and make a collage showing the plants, animals, and other things they might see in that biome (such as land features). Challenge them to do research to find other organisms not mentioned in the text and to add pictures of these organisms and the people who live there. **Spatial**

What Are Grasslands?

Before Reading
Have students try to answer the red question at the top of the text column.

Developing the Main Idea
Have students compare and contrast the different kinds of grasslands. Ask:

- **How do the animals of the savanna differ from the animals of the American grassland?** (The savanna has zebras, giraffes, and wildebeests.)

- **How are the animals of the savanna similar to animals found in the American grassland?** (They are hoofed.)

- **How is the savanna changing in the same way the American grassland changed?** (The land of the savanna is being taken over for grazing cattle.)

Exploring the Main Idea
Ask students to list ways their lives depend on grasslands and forests. (Examples: Cereals, grains, and meat come from grassland plants and animals; paper and wood come from forest trees.)

▶ After Reading
Have students answer the red question in the student book as **ongoing assessment**.

The lion lives on the savanna.

What Are Grasslands?

As the name tells you, **grasslands** are biomes where grasses are the main plant life. They are areas where rainfall is irregular and not usually plentiful.

Prairies, like the Blackland Prairie, are one kind of grassland. Called the "bread baskets" of the world, few temperate grasslands look as they did years ago. *Temperate* means "mild." It refers to grasslands such as those in the United States and Ukraine. Today many of these grasslands are covered with crops such as wheat, corn, and oats.

However, large parts of the world's tropical grasslands still look much as they have for hundreds of years. *Savannas* are grasslands that stay warm all year round. Their soil is not as fertile as that of temperate grasslands. However, they get more rain—about 86–152 cm (34–60 in.) a year.

The most famous savanna covers the middle third of Africa. Here the dust rises as countless hoofed animals thunder across the land. There are more hoofed animals in savannas than anywhere else on Earth. Graceful zebras and giraffes live here. Wildebeests travel in awesome herds of tens of thousands. Antelopes run from sprinting cheetahs. In the heat of the afternoon, lions rest in the shade of a thorny acacia tree. Nearby, hyenas prowl through the low grasses in search of dead or weak animals.

If you want to get a glimpse of a savanna while it still looks like this, you'd better do so soon. The land on savannas is being used more and more to graze domestic cattle. It won't be long until they replace the native animals, at least in unprotected parts of the savanna.

▷ What are two types of grasslands? How are they different?

Prairies and savannas are types of grasslands. Prairies are temperate and have fertile soil. Savannas are tropical grasslands that get more rain and have less-fertile soil.

B 66

What Is the Taiga Like?

Evidence indicates that about 15,000 years ago, huge fingers of ice, called glaciers, inched down from Earth's arctic regions. The ice was hundreds of feet thick. As it moved southward, it gouged great chunks of land out of northern Europe, Asia, and North America.

Some of the sediment carried by the glaciers dammed up streams, forming ponds and lakes. More lakes formed when the ice began to pull back. Holes dug by the glaciers filled with fresh water. These are the lakes and ponds of a cool, forested biome called the taiga (TIGH·guh).

Taigas are mostly conifer forests. They spread out over 11 percent of Earth's land. They are located in the upper latitudes of the Northern Hemisphere—in Alaska, Canada, Norway, Sweden, Finland, and Russia.

If you visit the taiga in the summer, you may hear the pleasant songs of birds. Many different kinds migrate to the taiga in summer. However, they head for warmer regions in the fall. You might also hear the whining sound of chain saws. That's because the taiga is a major source of lumber and pulpwood. Much of the lumber is used for making houses for the world's growing population. The pulpwood is turned into paper products of all kinds, such as the pages of this book.

READING Summarize
What are the main characteristics of the taiga?

cool to cold climate; evergreen conifer forests; ponds and lakes

Thousands of years ago, moving sheets of ice dug away the land of the taiga. The dug-out land would become some of its lakes and ponds. Today these bodies of water are guarded by great stands of evergreen trees.

B 67

What Is the Taiga Like?

Before Reading
Have students try to answer the red question at the top of the page.

Developing the Main Idea
Remind students that most conifers are evergreen plants with needlelike leaves and seed-bearing cones. Ask:

- **What are some examples of conifers?**
  (Conifers include pine, spruce, and fir trees.)

Exploring the Main Idea
Invite students to find out about threats to the taiga such as acid rain (especially in northern Europe), flooding from construction of hydroelectric dams (especially the James Bay Project in Quebec), timber harvesting (especially in Scandinavian countries), development, and ozone depletion. Encourage students to also research what is being done about these threats and to share what they find out with the class.

▶ After Reading
Have students answer the red question in the student book as **ongoing assessment**.

Developing Vocabulary

taiga Explain to students that this is a Russian term. Have them practice saying the word and draw pictures of what they imagine it to look like.

Reading MiniLesson

Summarize

Develop Have students give their answers to the assessment question in the form of one- or two-sentence summaries. For example, "A taiga is a biome that has a cool to cold climate, evergreen forests, and ponds and lakes dug out by glaciers thousands of years ago."

Practice Ask students to reread the last paragraph on page B67 and summarize what a taiga is like in summer. (Summaries should include reference to birds that have migrated to the taiga for the summer, and the people and machines cutting trees for lumber and paper products.)

Inclusion

Surviving Winter
Ask students to read about how animals survive the harsh taiga winters. All but 30 of the 300 species migrate. Some, like the arctic ground squirrel, hibernate. Bears do not actually hibernate, but they do rest. They do not eat, drink, or urinate during the winter months, but they can give birth and nurse their young, rouse easily, and may even take a walk outside. **Linguistic**

What Is the Tundra?

Before Reading
Have students try to answer the red question at the top of the page.

Developing the Main Idea
Use a globe or world map to make sure students know where the tundra is. Ask:

- **What feature is unique to the tundra?** (the permafrost)

Exploring the Main Idea
Invite students to find out about the great trek to find the North Pole by Robert Peary and Matthew Henson in 1909. Students should find out how they supplied the trip, what kind of transportation they used, the role of the Inuit people, what hardships they endured, and what happened to them when they returned to the United States.

▶ After Reading
Have students answer the red question in the student book as **ongoing assessment**.

Developing Vocabulary

tundra To help students remember this Russian term, have them identify the region on a world map or globe. Ask them to visualize what they think it looks like and either draw a picture or write a descriptive paragraph of this biome using the word *tundra*.

The caribou, a member of the deer family, is among the large animals of the tundra.

What Is the Tundra?

Where is the ground frozen even in summer? Only 10–25 cm (4–10 in.) of precipitation fall here each year. Winters are long and icy cold. Summers are short and cool. Just a few inches below the surface, the ground is frozen all the time.

You can't find many plants taller than about 30 cm (12 in.). However, you have no trouble spotting weasels, arctic foxes, snowshoe hares, hawks, musk oxen, and caribou. Near the coast you see a polar bear. When warmer weather comes, mosquitoes by the millions buzz through the air. Where are you?

You are in the far north. You're between the taiga and the polar ice sheets. It could be northern Alaska or northern Canada. It could be Greenland or frigid parts of Europe or Asia. No matter which of these places you are in, you are in the same biome. This cold biome of the far north is the **tundra**.

Why is it so cold? Even in summer the Sun's rays only strike the tundra at a low, glancing angle. The Sun melts ice in the top layer of the soil. However, this water is kept from flowing downward by a layer of *permafrost*, or permanently frozen soil, underneath. The top layer of soil acts like a vast sponge for the melted ice.

Many tundra plants are wildflowers and grasses. The permafrost keeps large plants from developing the deep root systems they need. The growing season is very short—as little as 50 days in some places. The tundra soil is poor in nutrients, so the tundra cannot support large plants.

▷ **What are conditions in the tundra like?**

cold climate; permanently frozen soil; little rainfall

B 68

Science Background

Alpine Tundra
As you go up a tall mountain, you reach an area that looks much like a tundra. Beyond the tree line is the alpine tundra, which has a lot in common with the Arctic tundra. In fact, you might see some Arctic tundra plants, especially in the southern Rocky Mountains and the northern Appalachians. High altitudes share many characteristics with the high latitudes.

Advanced Learners

Building
Challenge students to find out what adaptations are made for the environment when constructing buildings in the tundra and/or desert. For example, in the tundra, precautions have to be made to keep the building from sinking into the permafrost. Even with special foundations, buildings still slowly sink. In the desert, buildings and homes are often at least partly underground to help keep the interior cool.
Linguistic

What Is the Desert Biome Like?

Sahara, Gobi and Atacama stir up thoughts of adventures in strange, dangerous places. These are among the world's greatest deserts. A desert is a sandy or rocky biome, with little precipitation and little plant life.

Every continent has at least one desert. Africa has an enormous desert called the Sahara. Its sands dip down to the Atlantic Ocean in the west, the Mediterranean Sea to the north, and the Red Sea to the east. It is the largest desert on Earth, with an area of about 9,000,000 km² (3,500,000 mi²). It is so large that it could cover all of the United States south of Canada. Picture those 48 states covered with sand and you get an idea of the size of the Sahara.

The Gobi Desert in China and Mongolia is the world's second largest desert. It is about 1,300,000 km² (500,000 mi²). That's about twice the size of Texas.

In South America the Atacama Desert runs 968 km (600 mi) from the southern tip of Peru down through Chile. It lies between the Andes Mountains to the east and the Pacific Ocean in the west. The driest place on Earth is found in Arica, Chile. It averages only about 0.08 cm (0.03 in.) of rain a year. That's about the depth of six sheets of paper.

Few animals and plants live in deserts. Those that do are very hardy. They are well adapted to living in the desert.

 **How is the desert similar to and different from the tundra?**

Both have dry climates and little plant life. The desert is hot, and the tundra is cold.

To reach water, the roots of the mesquite plant (above) have been known to grow more than 79 m (260 ft) deep. That's the height of a 26-story building. Elf owls (left) build nests in cacti.

B 69

What Is the Desert Biome Like?

Before Reading
Have students try to answer the red question at the top of the page.

Developing the Main Idea
Use a globe or map of the world to identify each of the deserts mentioned in the text. Ask students to discuss the thoughts of adventure that come up when hearing the names of these deserts.

Exploring the Main Idea
Have students look in an encyclopedia to find the areas of deserts in North America, such as the Sonoran (120,000 square miles) and the Mojave (15,000 square miles). Challenge them to find ways to compare the areas, such as what percent of the total land area of North America is desert.

▶After Reading
Have students answer the red question in the student book as **ongoing assessment**.

 Developing Vocabulary

desert To help students remember the term *desert,* have them draw a picture of what they imagine a desert to look like. Encourage them to keep their drawings so they can assemble a biome vocabulary book at the end of this lesson.

English Language Learners

Painted Desert

Invite students to research the Painted Desert in Arizona and to draw a picture of a part of it. Challenge them to find out how the desert was formed and why it is so colorful.
Spatial; Kinesthetic

Cultural Perspective

Desertification

Desertification claims an estimated 15 million acres a year. People are responding by using better farming methods, planting trees, and conserving water. In oil-rich countries, oil residues are sprayed on sand to stabilize it, allowing grasses and other small plants to take root. In other places, small stones are used to build barriers to slow the runoff of water. Satellites also help to identify where water is so it can be accessed. Have students research where their nearest desert is located. **Spatial**

What Is a Deciduous Forest?

Before Reading
Have students try to answer the red question at the top of the page.

Developing the Main Idea
Make sure students understand the meaning of the word *deciduous.* Unlike evergreen trees, deciduous trees shed their leaves annually. Ask:

- **In which biome would you find evergreen trees?** (in the taiga)

Exploring the Main Idea
Challenge students to find out the chemistry behind the leaves changing color in the fall. They may want to concentrate on one color since there are different reactions for different colors.

Thinking Further: *Drawing Conclusions*
Ask:

- **What is the advantage of shedding leaves in preparation for winter?** (Possible answers: Sunlight decreases so the leaves are not needed for photosynthesis; water becomes more scarce so the tree can conserve water by losing the leaves that give off water during transpiration.)

▶ After Reading
Have students answer the red question in the student book as **ongoing assessment**.

Developing Vocabulary

deciduous forest The word *deciduous* comes from the Latin word meaning "to fall off," making a *deciduous forest* one in which many of the trees lose their leaves each year. Have students draw what a deciduous forest might look like in summer and winter.

What Is a Deciduous Forest?

Have you ever seen leaves on trees change color in the fall? If you have, you have seen the deciduous (di·SIJ·ew·uhs) forest biome. This is a forest biome with many trees that lose their leaves each year.

This is where broad-leaved trees grow. Each autumn the leaves turn shades of yellow, orange, and red, giving the land beautiful colors. Then the leaves fall to the ground—which is what *deciduous* means—and decay. The dead leaves help make the soil rich and fertile.

Deciduous forests once covered most of the United States east of the Mississippi River and almost all of western Europe. Much has been cut down to make room for towns, cities, farms, and factories.

Many animals that once lived in deciduous forests still live on the land that was cleared for suburbs, farms, and towns. Chipmunks dart around bushes. Squirrels leap from branch to branch. Raccoons turn over trash cans. Skunks meander through the underbrush.

Birds like cardinals, robins, crows, and hawks, and insects such as bees still live in deciduous forests. Turn over a rock and you might discover a salamander or garter snake.

Many deciduous forests in the United States and Europe are now part of national parks or are in places where few people live. As long as they stay that way, people will be able to see the changing seasons.

▷ **What are the main characteristics of the deciduous forest?**

temperate climate; broad-leaved trees that shed leaves in fall; fertile soil

The trees of a deciduous forest shed their leaves each autumn, painting the land yellow, orange, and red.

B 70

Although you'd probably not enjoy an encounter with this family, it's an important part of the deciduous forest biome.

Science Background

Forest Threats
The leaves that fall from deciduous trees enrich the soil so much that the trees become vulnerable to being cleared for farmland. Because of this, deciduous forests have been changed more than any other habitat.

Science Background

Jungles
Addressing Misconceptions
The rain forest is not the same as the jungle. Jungle usually describes an area of thick, tangled plant growth at ground level. In a jungle, the light that hits this area promotes dense growth of vines, small trees, and other plants. In a true rain forest, light hardly penetrates the thick canopy to reach the ground. Have students do research to find their closest rain forest. **Spatial; Linguistic**

What Are Tropical Rain Forests?

In areas along and near Earth's equator are tropical rain forests. These biomes are hot and humid, with much rainfall. They support a wide variety of life.

The canopy of a tropical rain forest spreads like a huge umbrella. It is so thick that little sunlight ever reaches the ground. With little light few plants can grow on the ground. Most of the life is up high in the branches, where howler monkeys and purple orchids cling.

There are no tropical rain forests in North America or Europe. They are too far from the tropics. However, Central America, South America, India, Africa, Southeast Asia, Australia, and many Pacific Islands have rain forests. Each has its own kinds of plants and animals.

Millions of species of animals live in the world's tropical rain forests. Many species have yet to be discovered.

In Africa you might see a silverback gorilla or a troop of playful chimpanzees.

On the island of Borneo, you might see a red-haired, long-armed orangutan (uh·RANG·oo·tan) swinging through the trees.

The anaconda is the largest snake on the planet.

The world's most colorful birds—such as toucans (TEW·kanz) and quetzals (ket·SAHLZ)—live in tropical rain forests. Giant snakes like the 9 m (30 ft), 136 kg (300 lb) South American anaconda also live in tropical rain forests.

The world's tropical rain forests have been victims of people's needs for lumber, farmland, and minerals. Fortunately, people are now replanting and restoring tropical rain forests. Still, some of their millions of undiscovered plant and animal species may become extinct before they are discovered.

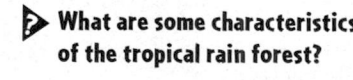 **What are some characteristics of the tropical rain forest?**

hot, humid climate; canopy of leaves; few plants on ground; great diversity of plant and animal life

Some of the most colorful birds on Earth, like this toucan, live in tropical rain forests like those of South America.

B 71

What Are Tropical Rain Forests?

Before Reading
Have students try to answer the red question at the top of the page.

Developing the Main Idea
Make sure students know that the canopy is the top layer of the rain forest. Beneath that is the understory, then the shrub layer, and then the forest floor. Some trees grow above the canopy layer and are called emergent trees. Most organisms in the rain forest live in the canopy or the understory.

Exploring the Main Idea
Invite students to use an outline map of the world to color in the areas that are covered by the different tropical rain forests. Then have them add pictures of animals and plants they would find in each one.

▶ ### After Reading
Have students answer the red question in the student book as **ongoing assessment**.

Developing Vocabulary

tropical rain forest Show students the area on a globe between the Tropic of Cancer and the Tropic of Capricorn. Remind students that areas close to the equator receive the direct rays of the Sun, which in combination with the ocean currents, result in a hot, humid climate. Have them draw a picture of what their image of a *tropical rain forest* is.

 **English Language Learners**

Hyphenated Adjectives
Ask students to look through the text and identify words that are hyphenated. Ask them what part of speech these hyphenated words are. (They are adjectives.) Point out how the first word modifies the second, as in "red-haired." Ask students to write a paragraph about their classroom and use at least three hyphenated adjectives. **Linguistic**

 **Advanced Learners**

Letter to the Editor
Challenge students to write a letter to the editor of a newspaper saying why it is important to protect the different species of the rain forests. Encourage them to include details about what the rain forest has already given us and the great potential for more benefits. **Logical; Linguistic**

What Are Water Ecosystems Like?

Before Reading
Have students try to answer the red question at the top of the page.

Developing the Main Idea
Write the names of the categories of aquatic organisms on the board. Then have volunteers write their definitions next to the terms. Ask other volunteers to write examples for each category. Ask:

■ **In what category would you classify an aquatic worm?** (benthos)

Materials dropper; microscope slide; coverslip; microscope; at least 3 samples of pond, lake, or stream water; 3 or more plastic containers with lids

Science Process Skills *observe, communicate, interpret data*

Resources Activity Resources pp. 70–71

Step 2 Students should describe the shape, features, and relative sizes of the organisms in each sample.

Step 4 Possible answer: One factor that affects the make-up of the population is water depth.

Freshwater Communities

1. Obtain from your teacher samples of pond, lake, or stream water taken at different locations. Use a different container for each sample. Record on the container the location each sample came from.

2. **Observe** Place a drop of water on a slide, and carefully place a coverslip over it. Examine the slide under a microscope.

3. **Communicate** Record the location of each sample and what you see. Use low and high power.

4. **Interpret Data** What does this tell you about aquatic ecosystems?

B 72

What Are Water Ecosystems Like?

Temperature and precipitation differ among ecosystems on land. For Earth's watery ecosystems, the main difference is saltiness.

Lakes, streams, rivers, ponds, and certain marshes, swamps, and bogs tend to have little salt in them. They're all freshwater ecosystems. Oceans and seas are saltwater ecosystems.

In fresh water or salt water, organisms can be divided into three main categories. *Plankton* (PLANGK·tuhn) are organisms that float on the water. *Nekton* (NEK·tahn) are organisms that swim through the water. *Benthos* (BEN·thahs) are bottom-dwelling organisms.

Freshwater Organisms
Many plants live in the shallow waters of lakes, ponds, and other bodies of fresh water. If you were to wade here, you might get your feet tangled in cattails, bur reeds, wild rice, and arrowheads. You might also spot a frog, a turtle, or maybe a crayfish.

Farther out, where the water gets deeper, are microscopic plankton like algae and protozoa.

Look beneath the surface, and nekton come into view. There might be large trout or other game fish. All the way to the bottom, an aquatic worm might be burrowing into the mud.

Saltwater Organisms
Like the freshwater ecosystem, the marine, or ocean, ecosystem is divided into several sections.

The shallowest is the *intertidal zone*. There the ocean floor is covered and uncovered as the tide goes in and out. Crabs burrow into the sand so they won't be washed away. Mussels and barnacles attach themselves to rocks.

The open ocean is divided into two regions. The first region is up to 200 m (656 ft) deep. In this upper region are many kinds of fish and whales. The world's largest animals—the 150-ton blue whales—live here.

The lower region goes from 200 m (656 ft) to the ocean bottom—perhaps 10.5 km (6.5 mi) down. At depths greater than about 1,000 m (3,281 ft), there is no sunlight. It is completely black!

Photosynthetic organisms, like algae, can only live where there is sunlight. They are found in the intertidal zone and in waters up to about 100 m (328 ft) deep. Many fantastic creatures live on the dark ocean bottom. Some of these fish "light up" like underwater fireflies. Other bottom-dwelling fish are blind. There are even bacteria that live in boiling water where fiery lava seeps out of the sea floor.

▷ **What are two water ecosystems? How do they differ?**

Two water ecosystems are freshwater and saltwater. They differ in the types of plants and animals they support.

The types of animals you see in the ocean change as you go deeper.

B 73

Exploring the Main Idea

Invite students to find out about the hydrothermal vents on the ocean floor and the amazing life forms found there.

Developing the Main Idea

Engage students in a discussion comparing the sea and the rain forest. Look for similarities such as the vertical stratification of plant and animal life due to the penetration of sunlight. In both biomes, most life is near the top because that is where the sunlight strikes. Have students compare the layers of the rain forest (canopy, understory, shrub layer, and forest floor) with the layers, or zones, of the sea (intertidal, neritic, oceanic, bathyal, and abyssal).

▶ After Reading

Have students answer the red question in the student book as **ongoing assessment**.

Reading in Science Resources, p. 112

Can Humans Change Ecosystems?

Before Reading
Have students try to answer the red question at the top of the text column.

Developing the Main Idea
Ask students what they know about endangered species. Have students share experiences about how their pets enrich their lives. Then ask them how they would be affected if all domesticated animals—such as dogs, cats, birds, aquarium fish—were extinct.

Exploring the Main Idea
Play a tape or CD for students that features whale songs. Tell them that scientists think this is how whales communicate with each other.

▶ After Reading
Have students answer the red question in the student book as **ongoing assessment**.

Will the remaining whale populations survive? Will the eerie song of the humpback no longer be heard?

Can Humans Change Ecosystems?

People started hunting whales for their meat and oil at least 4,000 years ago. However, back then oceans held so many whales that hunting didn't have much effect on their populations.

As the centuries passed, however, whale hunting increased. So did the technology of finding and killing these gentle mammals. By 1850 American whalers alone accounted for the killing of 10,000 a year.

Over the next 100 years, new technologies made whale hunting easier and more efficient. In 1962 alone 66,000 whales were killed. The whales could not reproduce fast enough to replace those that were being killed. Many species, like blue whales, humpbacks, bowheads, and right whales, became threatened with extinction.

The whales were being used for human and animal food, oil for lamps, and fertilizer. However, there were other sources of such products. Recognizing this and the danger to whale populations, the major whaling countries formed the International Whaling Commission (IWC) in 1946.

In 1971 the United States banned its citizens from whaling for profit or even buying products made from whales. By the 1990s the IWC had succeeded in getting whaling countries to reduce or stop hunting threatened whales.

▷ **How have humans affected the whale population?**

B 74

People hunted whales and brought many species close to extinction; they have also written laws to help protect the whales.

Reading Strategy

Reread
Summarize

Developing Reading Skills
Ask students to summarize how whales have become endangered. Students can reread as needed to help them decide upon a comprehensive summary statement. They can share their summaries with the class for comparisons and contrasts.

Science Background

Whales
The blue whale, almost exterminated in the early 1900s, is Earth's largest animal. It can be over 100 feet long and weigh 150 tons. A pilot whale is about one-fourth that size. Some whales are social animals and travel in schools. Whales are warm-blooded mammals and breathe with lungs. The familiar "Thar she blows!" refers to the cloud of condensed air exhaled by the whale when it surfaces. Whale blubber, which protects the whale from the cold waters, is a source of valuable oil.

Why It Matters

The world's biomes remain constant as long as their climates and populations do not change greatly. However, human and natural activities can change biomes. Changes in a biome can affect the kinds of plants and animals that can live there. It can also affect people's lifestyles. It is important to know if, how, and why these factors are changing.

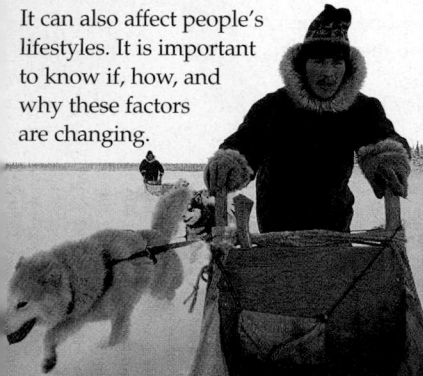

Think and Write

1. Describe the taiga biome in terms of its climate, soil, and inhabitants.

2. How do organisms found in desert and tundra biomes adapt to their environments?

3. Explain why few plants live on the floor of tropical rain forests.

4. Briefly describe the two types of aquatic ecosystems.

5. **Critical Thinking** Choose one biome, and explain how a change in its climate might affect its populations.

L·I·N·K·S

SOCIAL STUDIES LINK

Use a map. Choose a country, and identify its biomes. Find the major cities and other landmarks in each of the biomes. What plants and animals live in these areas? Construct a map. Draw each biome, and show which plants and animals live in it.

LITERATURE LINK

Read *Antarctica,* the story of the coldest continent on Earth. Try the activities at the end of the book.

Antarctica

Written by Carol Barkin

WRITING LINK

Write a paragraph. Explain how your lifestyle would change if the biome where you live got warmer. What might happen if it got colder or if the precipitation decreased or increased? How would you have to adapt?

TECHNOLOGY LINK

At the Computer Visit **www.mhscience02.com** for more links.

B 75

Informal Assessment

Easy/Average Ask students to work in teams to make a chart listing each of the ecosystems studied in this lesson. As a team, they should decide what other headings are needed and fill in the appropriate information.

Challenge Invite teams of students to design a museum exhibit displaying the various biomes. The exhibit should include an information card about each biome, to be hung near its display. Students may also want to design a brief guide booklet for the exhibit.

---

3 Lesson Review

Answers to Think and Write

1. The taiga has very cold winters, cool summers, and about 50 cm of precipitation in a year. The soil is acidic and mineral poor, with decayed pine and spruce needles on the surface. (p. B64)

2. In deserts, animals and plants have adaptations to conserve water and dissipate heat. In the tundra, animals and plants have adaptations, such as blubber and fur, to conserve heat and to insulate themselves from the cold. (pp. B68–B69)

3. Little sunlight is able to penetrate through the thick canopy. (p. B71)

4. Freshwater ecosystems include lakes, ponds, and rivers. Saltwater ecosystems include the oceans and saltwater seas. Both have a diversity of organisms. (pp. B72–B73)

5. **Critical Thinking** Possible answers: If it stops raining in the rain forest, some populations may die out and the area would be less diverse. If it rained more frequently in the desert, more types of plants could grow there. (pp. B64–B71)

Summarize

Check students' understanding by having them write a brief summary of the lesson in their own words.

SOCIAL STUDIES LINK

Use the map on pp. B64–B65 to identify the different biomes on each continent. Check that each city or landmark the students choose is located in the biome indicated.

LITERATURE LINK

Have students read the Grade-Level Science Book, *Antarctica.* For additional books to read, see page B1·b.

WRITING LINK

Students' paragraphs should address each of the four climate changes. For example, the change in lifestyle resulting from a warmer climate might include the need for lighter clothing and more or less time spent outdoors, depending on how warm the climate already is.

Science, Technology, and Society

Objectives

- Understand the dangers of rain-forest destruction.

Build on Prior Knowledge

Ask students:

- **What do you know about the rain forest?** (Answers may include that rain forests are in tropical regions and have many plants and animals. Students may also know that we are destroying the rain forest.)

- **Why do people clear forests?** (Answers may include that people clear forests for farms and places to live.)

Are Rain Forests Worth Saving?

Developing the Main Idea

Focus on the importance of rain forests by asking such questions as:

- **What do you think a rain forest looks like?** (It is probably lush, green, and damp, with many plants and animals.)

- **Why is oxygen from the rain forest important to us?** (We need that oxygen to breathe.)

- **What are minerals used for?** (Minerals are used in building materials, fertilizers, and manufactured products.)

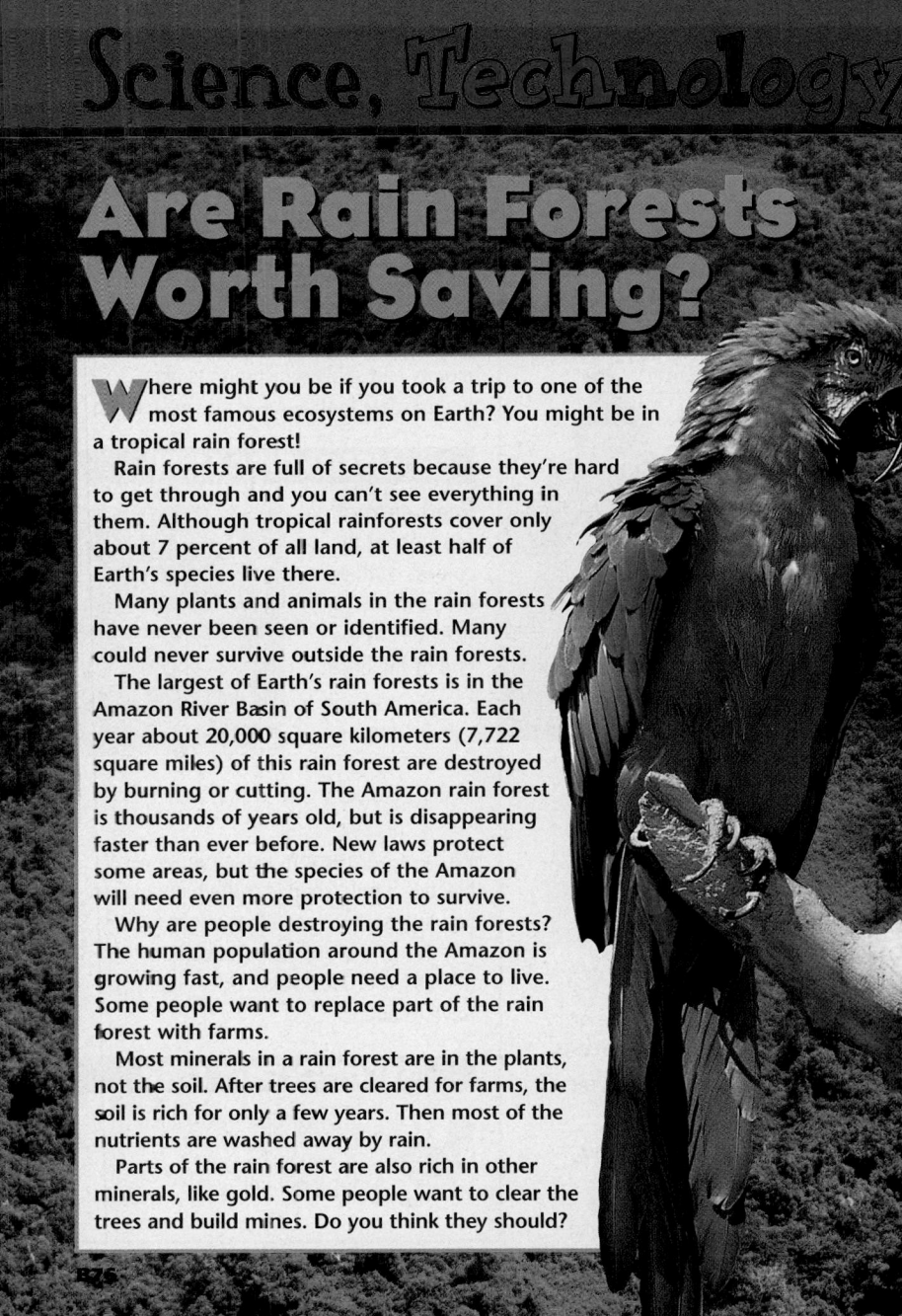

Science, Technology,

Are Rain Forests Worth Saving?

Where might you be if you took a trip to one of the most famous ecosystems on Earth? You might be in a tropical rain forest!

Rain forests are full of secrets because they're hard to get through and you can't see everything in them. Although tropical rainforests cover only about 7 percent of all land, at least half of Earth's species live there.

Many plants and animals in the rain forests have never been seen or identified. Many could never survive outside the rain forests.

The largest of Earth's rain forests is in the Amazon River Basin of South America. Each year about 20,000 square kilometers (7,722 square miles) of this rain forest are destroyed by burning or cutting. The Amazon rain forest is thousands of years old, but is disappearing faster than ever before. New laws protect some areas, but the species of the Amazon will need even more protection to survive.

Why are people destroying the rain forests? The human population around the Amazon is growing fast, and people need a place to live. Some people want to replace part of the rain forest with farms.

Most minerals in a rain forest are in the plants, not the soil. After trees are cleared for farms, the soil is rich for only a few years. Then most of the nutrients are washed away by rain.

Parts of the rain forest are also rich in other minerals, like gold. Some people want to clear the trees and build mines. Do you think they should?

B76

Science Background

Benefits of the Rain Forest Addressing Misconceptions
Students may not appreciate the benefits of the rain forest and the effect their actions have on it. Plants in the rain forest supply much of the oxygen they breathe. The temperature outside is moderated because rain forests take in excess carbon dioxide from the atmosphere. Some peoples' lives depend on medicines found in the rain forests. Some of the meat we eat comes from cattle that graze on what was once rain forest.

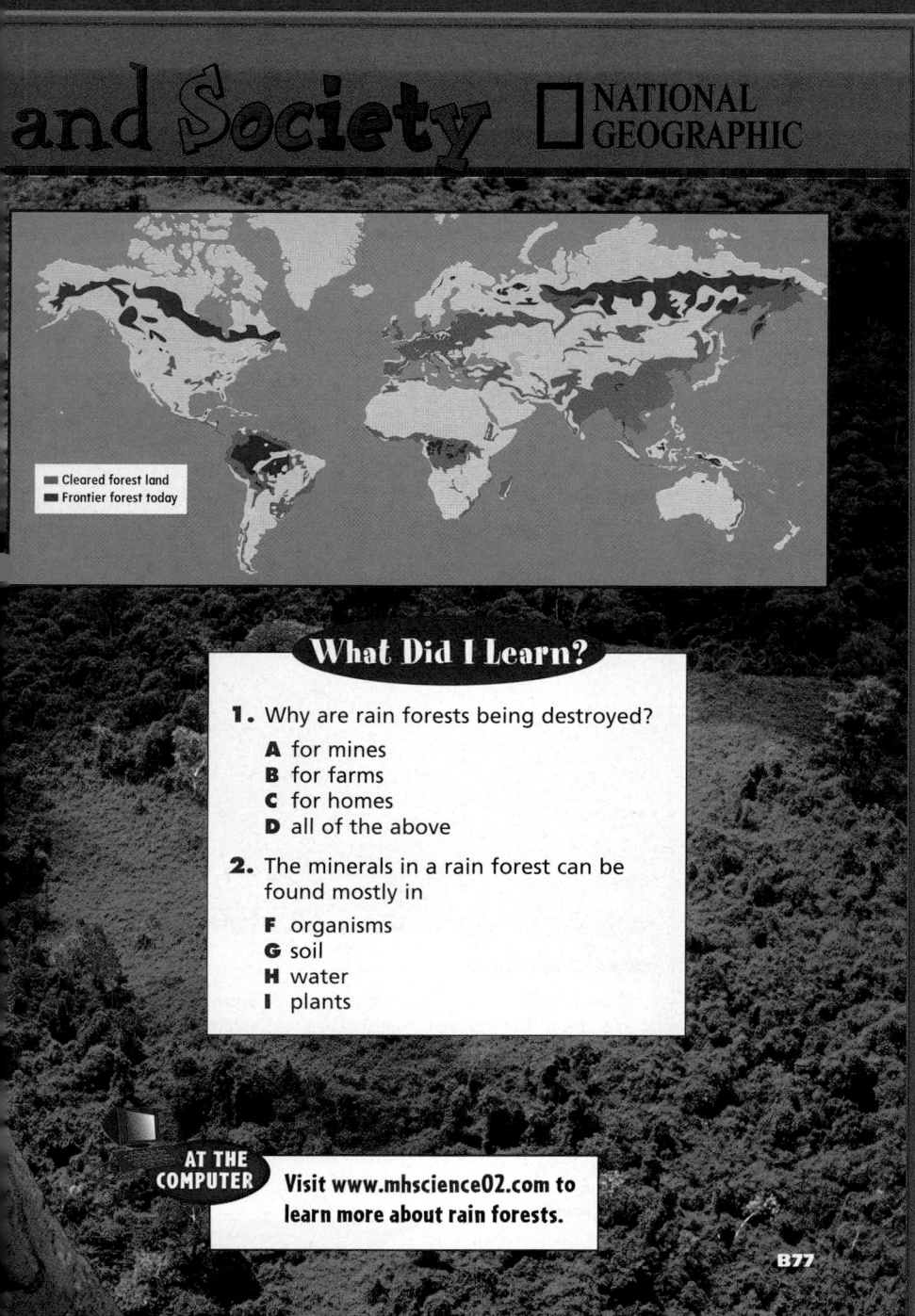

and Society ▢ NATIONAL GEOGRAPHIC

■ Cleared forest land
■ Frontier forest today

What Did I Learn?

1. Why are rain forests being destroyed?

A for mines
B for farms
C for homes
D all of the above

2. The minerals in a rain forest can be found mostly in

F organisms
G soil
H water
I plants

AT THE COMPUTER Visit www.mhscience02.com to learn more about rain forests.

B77

Exploring the Main Idea

Challenge students to find out the history of efforts to conserve the rain forest. They can search the Internet or contact such groups as the Environmental Defense Fund, the Rainforest Conservation Fund, and the Rainforest Action Network.

Thinking Further: *Drawing Conclusions*

Ask:

■ **Why is it important for people in North America to care about the rain forest in South America?** (The rain forest is important to our quality of life.)

Encourage students to think about ways they can help conserve the rain forest.

Test Prep: *What Did I Learn?*

1. D

2. I

Summarize

Check students' understanding by having them write a brief summary of this feature in their own words.

SCIENCE FOR ALL

Inclusion

Rain Forest Statistics

Challenge students to find statistics on the rain forest. For example, although rain forests cover only 2% of Earth's surface, they contain over 50% of all the plants and animals. Scientists estimate that we destroy 100 acres of rain forest per minute. **Logical**

LESSON 6 How Ecosystems Change

Objectives

- Explore how ecosystems affect each other and change over time.
- Describe the changes to an ecosystem that occur during primary and secondary succession.
- Explain how catastrophic (sudden) changes can affect an ecosystem.
- Explain how resource use affects the environment.

Resources

- Activity Resources, pp. 72–78
- Reading in Science Resources, pp. 115–120
- Vocabulary Cards
- Reading Aid Transparency B6
- Visual Aid Transparencies 15, 16
- Grade-Level Science Book, *Wildfire*

Build on Prior Knowledge

Have students discuss what natural occurrences can cause an ecosystem to change. (Possible answers: volcanic eruption, earthquakes, tornadoes, floods) Then ask students to brainstorm a list of human activities that can cause a change. (Possible answers: land clearing, logging, landfill, mining)

1 Get Ready

Developing the Main Idea

Ask students what the area around Mount Saint Helens might have looked like after the mountain erupted. (Possible answers: covered with ash, burnt plants, and knocked-over trees; no animals left)

LESSON 6 How Ecosystems Change

Vocabulary

ecological succession, B82

pioneer species, B83

pioneer community, B83

climax community, B84

Get Ready

Before May 18, 1980, the area around Mount Saint Helens in the state of Washington was decorated with, wildflowers and beautiful groves of Douglas fir and western hemlock trees. Animals of many kinds made their home here. Then the mountain exploded. What happened to the community? How did this ecosystem change?

Process Skill

You predict when you state possible results of an event or experiment.

B 78

Science Background

Fish Mystery

Natural changes on Earth can suddenly change ecosystems, such as those on Mount Saint Helens. When it erupted, the water in Spirit Lake was heated and not one lake fish survived. Recently, some fish have been found there. They may have survived in the ice-covered waters of Saint Helens Lake and washed downstream into Spirit Lake.

Cross Curricular Books

Additional Outside Reading

Flight of the Trumpeters

written by Lisa Norby
illustrated by Susan Kathleen Hartung

To order, see page B1·b.

Explore Activity

How Do Ecosystems Change?

Procedure

1 **Observe** Examine the photograph.

2 **Communicate** Describe what you see.

Drawing Conclusions

1 **Infer** What happened to this farm after the owner left and moved to the city?

2 **Infer** Think about how this farm might have looked ten years ago. What kinds of plants lived there then?

3 **Interpret Data** How can one ecosystem be changed into another?

4 Compare what you think will happen to the abandoned farm with what happened at Mount Saint Helens. In what ways would the changes in ecosystems be similar? In what ways would they be different?

5 **Going Further: Predict** Think of another ecosystem that might be changed by nature. Think of an ecosystem that might be changed by humans. Describe how such ecosystems might continue to change over time.

Explore Activity

How Do Ecosystems Change?

Science Process Skills *observe, communicate, infer, interpret data, predict*

Resources Activity Resources, pp. 72–73

Pacing 30–40 minutes

Grouping individuals

Answers to Drawing Conclusions

1 The land was untended. The farmhouse was worn down by weather. Wild grasses, shrubs, and weeds grew untended where crops had once grown.

2 Plants that the farmer grew lived there then.

3 Animals and wind move seeds. Plants from one ecosystem start to grow in the other and animals from one start to live in the other.

4 New plant and animal life would come to the abandoned farm as it came to Mount Saint Helens. The abandoned farm might not change as much since it wasn't completely destroyed by hot volcanic dust, gases, and ash.

5 Natural disasters (fires, floods, volcanic eruptions, earthquakes) destroy ecosystems. Humans cut forests, mine, plow fields, and pollute. Ecosystem recovery depends on the amount of ecosystem remaining, proximity to a fertile ecosystem, and the extent of continued human involvement.

 Inquiry Students can ask their own questions to explore, such as how other ecosystems affect each other.

Technology

■ When time is short, preview the activity with the **Explore Activity Video**.

Alternative Explore Activity

Materials reference materials

From Pond to Forest Ask students to draw a side view of a pond showing plants growing at the edges. Then, based on their research, challenge them to draw three more pictures showing how the pond could change into a new ecosystem. (They should draw the pond becoming a marsh, with plants growing into the center; the marsh becoming a field with shrubs and small trees, and the water gone; and, lastly, the same area becoming a mature woodland with tall trees.)

Spatial; Logical

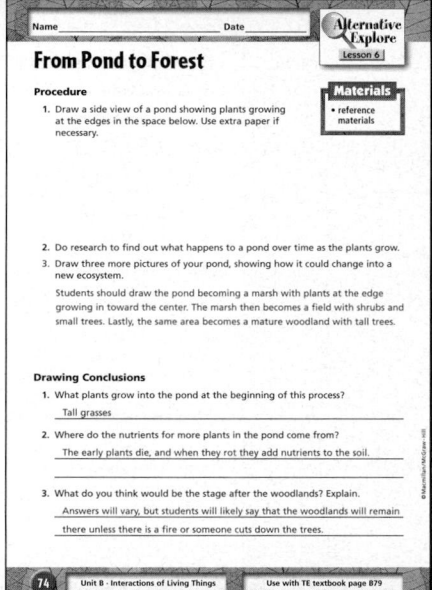

Activity Resources, p. 74

How Do Ecosystems Change?

Before Reading
Have students try to answer the red question at the top of the page.

Developing the Main Idea
As students read this page have them discuss why a city would be abandoned. Ask:

- **What activities would stop when people leave an area?** (There would be no more farming, clearing land, gardening, building, or making garbage.)

Exploring the Main Idea
Ask students what they know about how ecosystems and communities might change. Have students pretend they are living near a recently abandoned farm. Ask how they think it would look 1 year later, 5 years later, and 25 years later. Discuss what they might need to know before they can answer. (what the neighboring ecosystems are)

Read to Learn

Main Idea Ecosystems go through both slow and sudden changes.

How Do Ecosystems Change?

Changes happen everywhere on Earth. They can occur in your backyard. They can happen in an empty city lot or on one of its abandoned streets. If given a chance, nature has a way of changing an ecosystem or producing a new one. How does nature change an abandoned farm's field into a flourishing forest?

In the first year, a community of crabgrass, insects, and mice invades the field where corn or another crop once grew.

Abandoned cities of Angkor in Cambodia became covered by jungle.

Tall weeds, such as asters, ragweed, and goldenrod, and tall grasses grow among the crabgrass. The crabgrass can't easily survive in the shade cast by the taller weeds. It begins to die out in the second and third year. Rabbits and seed-eating birds move in.

The hot, dry field of tall weeds provides a perfect environment for

From Farmland to Forest

Abandoned Farm—First Year

Second and Third Years

B 80

Reading Strategy

Find the Main Idea
Developing Reading Skills
Ask students to write a paragraph to describe an ecosystem changing. They should include the main idea sentence at the beginning of the paragraph and use the other sentences to supply supporting details.

Lesson Outline

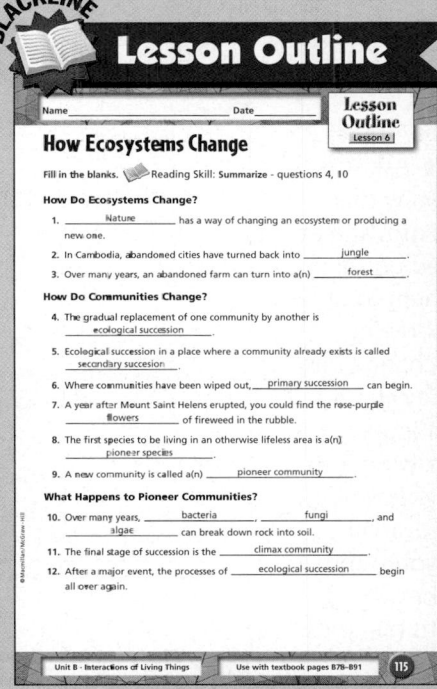

Reading in Science Resources, p. 115

pine seeds to sprout. By the fourth year, pine trees begin to grow and shade the weeds, which begin to die out. More birds join the community, as do small mammals like opossums and skunks.

A pine forest has replaced the old farm field within twenty-five years. The number of new pine seedlings drops, however, because they can't grow in the shade. Seeds of deciduous

Crabgrass, insects, and small animals come to live. As taller weeds grow, the crabgrass dies; birds and larger animals begin to move in. Tree seeds begin to sprout and grow, and more animals move in.

trees such as maple, hickory, and oak sprout and take root. Larger animals like raccoons and foxes begin to visit.

The forest is now mostly deciduous trees. These trees are the habitats of many different kinds of birds and small animals, such as squirrels. Deer, raccoons, and foxes also live in the forest.

How can an abandoned farm become a deciduous forest ecosystem?

Four to Six Years Later

Twenty-Five Years Later

One Hundred Years Later

B 81

Exploring the Main Idea
Challenge students to draw pictures of Angkor that are similar to the pictures showing how the farm changed. Ask them to show how a jungle taking over a city is different from a forest taking over a farm.

▶ **After Reading**
Have students answer the red question in the student book as **ongoing assessment**.

Technology

■ Visual Aid Transparency 15:
From Farmland to Forest: Secondary Succession

Interpret Illustrations

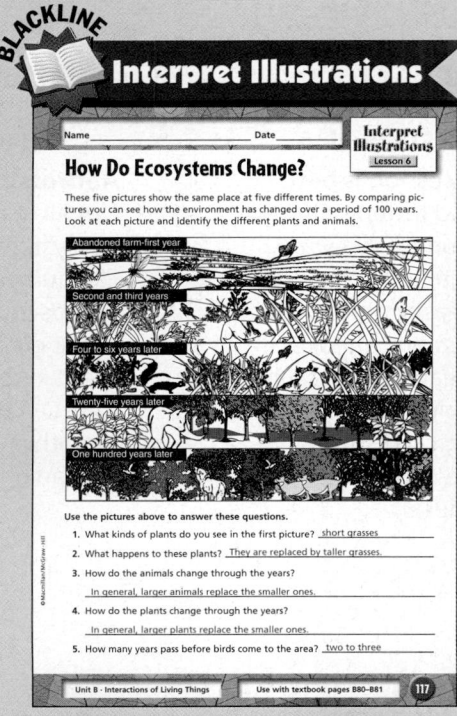

Reading in Science Resources, p. 117

Science Background

Battlefield Preservation
Civil War battlefields are an important part of U.S. history. Changing ecosystems, along with encroaching development, threaten the battlefields. Some groups are working to keep the areas looking the same as they did during the war or restore them to their original state after a century and a quarter of change. One example is Gettysburg, where orchards are now fields and meadows have become overgrown. Such changes make it hard to picture what happened there.

How Do Communities Change?

Before Reading
Have students try to answer the red question at the top of the page.

Developing the Main Idea
Have students explain in their own words the difference between primary succession and secondary succession. (primary: begins where communities were wiped out; secondary: occurs where a community already exists) Discuss with students the steps in succession on the abandoned farm on pp. B80–B81. Ask:

- **Why is an abandoned farm an example of secondary succession?** (A community existed there before it was abandoned.)

Exploring the Main Idea
Describe the line of succession to the U.S. presidency. Discuss why that word is used (One comes after another.), what the two kinds of succession have in common, and how they are different. (They are similar because both have one organism coming after another. They are different because in the line to the presidency all organisms are the same.)

Thinking Further: *Inferring*
Ask:

- **Why do you think crabgrass appeared first?** (Crabgrass can survive in a harsh environment.)

Developing Vocabulary

ecological succession Tell students that *succession* means to come after another in order or sequence. Since *ecology* relates to Earth's living things, then *ecological succession* is the sequence of plants and animals that appear in the development of a community.

How Do Communities Change?
The abandoned farm field you just read about gave way to short crabgrass, then tall grasses and shrubs. Later, pine trees and, finally, deciduous trees grew there. Scientists call the gradual replacement of one community by another **ecological succession**.

Ecological succession can begin in two different kinds of places. It can begin where a community already exists—such as in an abandoned farm field. Ecological succession in a place where a community already exists is called *secondary succession*.

Ecological succession can also happen where there are few, if any, living things. This is called *primary succession*. Primary succession can begin where communities were wiped out. Such places would include land swept clean by a volcanic eruption or forest fire. It can also begin where communities never existed before, such as on a new island that rises out of the sea.

Mount Saint Helens
Explore what happened to Mount Saint Helens in the state of Washington shortly after May 18, 1980.

Mount Saint Helens had just erupted. The blast from the volcano knocked down thousands of trees. The whole area was covered knee-deep with hot volcanic ash and finely smashed up rock.

The landscape was different shades of gray as far as you could see. No spot of green greeted your eyes, not even a blade of grass. If you didn't

Ecological Succession on Mount Saint Helens

1 year The rose-purple flowers of fireweed announced that life was returning to the destroyed land.

4 years Seedlings of Douglas fir trees began to take root in the rubble of the volcano.

B 82

Science Background

Ecological Succession
Ecological succession is both predictable and orderly. Once it starts, the sequence of events and which organisms come in when can be easily predicted. Primary succession can take hundreds of years. Secondary succession, which can heal the scars of ecological disturbances, can be completed in years or decades.

Science Background

Helpful Changes
Addressing Misconceptions
Not all major changes to an ecosystem are destructive. Just like humans, ecosystems age and become less productive. A major change, such as a forest fire, can rejuvenate an ecosystem. Old plants and undergrowth are destroyed and new life can grow and thrive.

know better, you might have thought you were on the Moon.

A year passes. You return to the slopes of Mount Saint Helens expecting to see unbroken stretches of rock and stumps of dead trees. However, something has happened in the year you were gone. Wind and rain have cleared some of the ash and dust, especially from steep slopes. The wind has also blown in some seeds and fruits from nearby forests. You see a scattering of rose-purple objects among the charred and fallen tree trunks. They are the flowers of a plant called fireweed. It gets its name from the fact that it is often the first plant to grow after a forest fire.

Scientists would call the fireweed a pioneer species. That's because it is the first species to be living in an otherwise lifeless area. You notice that the blooming of fireweed has attracted animals such as insects and an occasional insect-eating bird. A new community, called a pioneer community, is beginning to thrive around Mount Saint Helens.

You return in 1984 and almost step on a little green shoot. You bend down and take a closer look. The shoot has little needlelike leaves. It is the sprout of a Douglas fir tree. Its seed was probably blown here from a forest miles away.

Now picture the land around Mount Saint Helens 100 or 200 years in the future. It is covered with a dense forest of evergreens. The forest is much like the one that spread around it before that explosive day in 1980.

Ecological succession is the gradual replacement of one community by another community.

▷ **How does ecological succession change communities?**

11 years Fir trees grow tall 11 years after the blast.

B 83

Using the Illustrations

Have students summarize the development shown in the photographs and discussed in the captions. Have them use the terms *pioneer species* (fireweed) and *pioneer community* in their summaries. Ask:

- **Are the fir trees the end of succession? Explain.** (Not necessarily, another event could wipe out this community and succession might occur again.)

▶ After Reading

Have students answer the red question in the student book as **ongoing assessment**.

Developing Vocabulary

pioneer species Have students look up a definition of *pioneer* and relate that meaning to a species. (One of the first to settle in an area; the first species to live in an area) Encourage students to find other examples of pioneer species.

pioneer community Ask students to explain the difference between a pioneer species and a pioneer community. (A pioneer community would include many species. It is the first community to develop in an area.)

Advanced Learners

Journalism

Ask students to pretend they are journalists sent to cover the story of the Mount Saint Helens eruption. They should file their first story on May 20, 1980, two days after the eruption. Encourage them to describe for readers what they see, smell, hear, and feel. Invite them to add their personal comments about what they think the future holds for this area. **Kinesthetic; Linguistic**

English Language Learners

Paint a Picture

Invite students to paint a picture of the scene as described in the text. Ask them to view pictures of the lunar landscape for inspiration. Challenge them to show some sign of hope in their pictures. They may also want to paint a picture of the scene a year later. **Spatial; Logical**

What Happens to Pioneer Communities?

Before Reading
Have students try to answer the red question at the top of the page.

Developing the Main Idea
Help students list the steps needed to establish a pioneer community. Ask:

■ **What has to be done first?** (Rocks must be broken down into soil.)

■ **What are the first life forms you would see?** (plants or lichens)

Thinking Further: *Inferring*
Ask:

■ **Why are decomposers needed?** (Decomposers break down dead plants to make nutrients that enrich the soil for other plants.)

READING Diagrams

Flowcharts should include the breakdown of rock into soil; seeds sprouting; plants dying; new plants sprouting and growing; animals arriving.

Developing Vocabulary

climax community Review with students what the word *climax* means, perhaps relating it to the climax of a story. (It is the final, culminating element or event in a series.) In the context of ecology, it is the final stage of succession.

What Happens to Pioneer Communities?

Are the first organisms in a pioneer community always plants? In some places the answer is no. This is usually the case in newly formed, fiery volcanic islands that rise from the sea. Here the pioneer community is often made up of bacteria, fungi, and algae. Over many years these organisms slowly break down the volcanic rock into soil.

What happens when there is enough soil, and other conditions are right for plants to grow? A seed blown to the island by the wind or dropped by a passing bird will take root. The new plant, and others like it, will gradually spread over the land.

During their life cycles, plants will die and further enrich the soil.

Perhaps a coconut will drift ashore. When it germinates, its roots will find a good supply of nutrients. A coconut palm will spring up, and a new island paradise will be created.

Climax Communities

More years will pass—perhaps hundreds of them. The climate of the island will remain almost unchanged. Its community will grow. Its populations will become balanced and stable. Few new animals and plants will arrive. Few will leave. Ecological succession will slow down or stop altogether. This is a **climax community**, a final stage of succession. This community will stay largely unchanged unless some major event occurs.

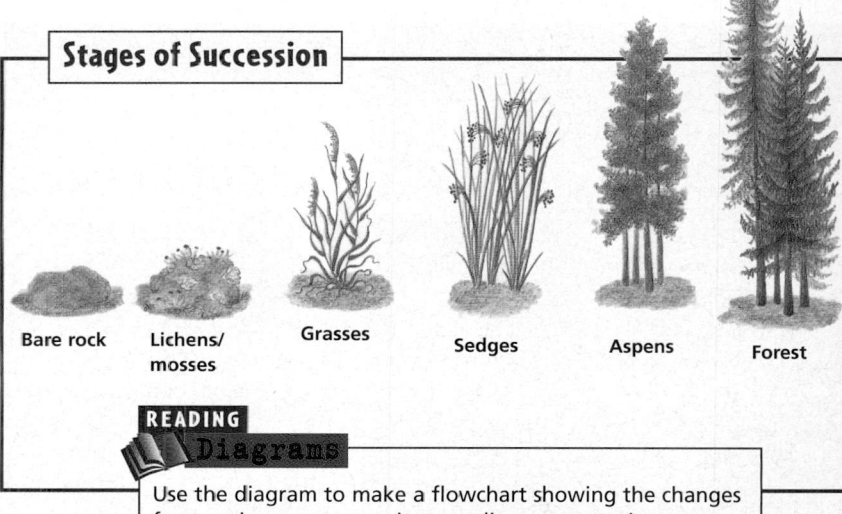

Stages of Succession

Bare rock | Lichens/mosses | Grasses | Sedges | Aspens | Forest

READING Diagrams
Use the diagram to make a flowchart showing the changes from a pioneer community to a climax community.

B 84

Science Background

Climax Communities
A climax community is in a state of equilibrium. Any kind of seed can be brought into the community but only certain types will grow. Animals also reach a climax in a particular ecosystem. For example, the type of bird living in an ecosystem will change along with the succession of plants, until the climax bird community is established. A continuous disturbance, such as logging, plowing, or overgrazing, at any point during succession can disturb the balance.

BLACKLINE Interpret Illustrations

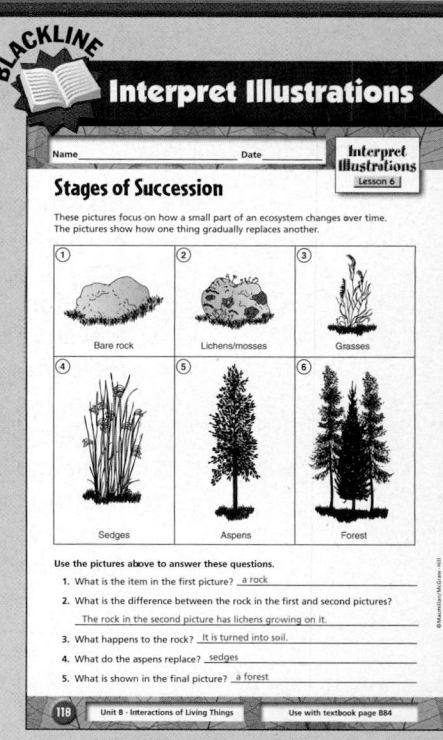

Name_____ Date_____

Interpret Illustrations
Lesson 6

Stages of Succession

These pictures focus on how a small part of an ecosystem changes over time. The pictures show how one thing gradually replaces another.

① Bare rock ② Lichens/mosses ③ Grasses
④ Sedges ⑤ Aspens ⑥ Forest

Use the pictures above to answer these questions.
1. What is the item in the first picture? _a rock_
2. What is the difference between the rock in the first and second pictures?
   The rock in the second picture has lichens growing on it.
3. What happens to the rock? _It is turned into soil._
4. What do the aspens replace? _sedges_
5. What is shown in the final picture? _a forest_

118   Unit B - Interactions of Living Things   Use with textbook page B84

Reading in Science Resources, p. 118

What kind of event could change an entire ecosystem? A hurricane may sweep across the island. The volcano that created it might erupt again. People might come and build hotels or introduce new plants or animals. The climate might change. Then the processes of ecological succession would begin all over again. Another climax community would eventually develop. It might—or might not—be the same as the earlier climax community.

▶ **What is the difference between a pioneer community and a climax community?**

A pioneer community is seen in the first stages of ecological succession while the land continues to change and develop. A climax community is in the final stage of succession.

The volcano Kilauea erupting on the island of Hawaii

QUICK LAB

FOR SCHOOL OR HOME

Predicting Succession

1. **Observe** Identify an area near you where you think ecological succession is taking place.

2. **Communicate** Describe the area. List the evidence you have that indicates ecological succession is taking place.

3. **Infer** Do you think the succession will be primary or secondary? Explain.

4. **Predict** In what order do you think new species will colonize the area? Explain the reasons for your predictions.

5. **Communicate** Describe the climax community that you think will eventually live in the area. Give reasons for your conclusion.

B 85

Inclusion

Story Climax

Ask students to compare the climax in a story with the climax in an ecosystem. A story's climax is the most forceful and most dramatic part of the story. It is the highest point of interest and the turning point. Changes can happen after the climax, but they are not significant. **Linguistic**

Cultural Perspective

Using Coconuts

People use the leaves of coconut trees for thatch roofs, hats, and baskets. The wood is used to build houses. Husks make mats, ropes, and brooms. The sap is made into drinks, vinegar, and sugar. The coconut itself gives tasty meat, flakes, and oil to make margarine and soap. Have students research the uses of coconuts and create posters to illustrate their findings. **Linguistic; Spatial**

Exploring the Main Idea

Invite students to review how hurricanes, volcanoes, earthquakes, tsunamis, and other catastrophic changes happen on Earth's surface. They may also want to research how one of these events has recently caused changes in an ecosystem.

▶ **After Reading**

Have students answer the red question in the student book as **ongoing assessment**.

QUICK LAB

FOR SCHOOL OR HOME

Science Process Skills *observe, communicate, infer, predict*

Resources Activity Resources, pp. 75-76

Step 1 Possible answers: abandoned property, a burnt field or forest, or a destroyed shoreline

Step 3 Primary succession would be supported by a catastrophic event, such as fire, that killed nearly all organisms in the original ecosystem. Secondary succession would be supported by describing the previous ecosystem and the major environmental change that has occurred.

Step 4 Simple plants will come first, because they can most easily survive in a harsh environment. Other plants will follow when the soil is richer with nutrients from the plants that die and decay. Animals that feed on plants will come later, when they have a food supply.

Step 5 Answers should include plants and animals found in an established local community.

Technology

■ Visual Aid Transparency 16: *A Pioneer Community*

What's Living on Surtsey?

Before Reading
Have students try to answer the red question at the top of the page.

Developing the Main Idea
Discuss with students how the location of an island can help determine what kind of ecosystem forms there. Show them on a map where Madagascar, Surtsey, and Hawaii are. Ask:

- **Why would you expect Madagascar to have an ecosystem similar to one found in Africa?** (Madagascar is close to Africa.)

- **What types of plants and animals do you think will live on Surtsey?** (plants and animals similar to those on Iceland)

- **Why do you think Hawaii has a unique ecosystem?** (It is so far from other land masses.)

▶ After Reading
Have students answer the red question in the student book as **ongoing assessment**.

What's Living on Surtsey?

In 1963 the island of Surtsey, near Iceland, was formed from a volcano. Between 1963 and 1996, at least 45 types of plants were seen growing there. Several kinds of birds, such as snow buntings, were also found raising their young on the island. Flying insects have also been found there. Scientists expect that more types of plants and birds will live on Surtsey in the future.

▷ **How is Surtsey an example of ecological succession?**

Surtsey is a newly formed island that is beginning to establish communities.

Surtsey, a volcanic island, rose from the sea near Iceland in 1963.

By 1996 many plants and birds lived on Surtsey.

B 86

Cultural Perspective

Life on Montserrat

The volcano on Montserrat is an ongoing threat. The people moved to the northern end of the island. Students may want to find out how the island and the inhabitants are recovering from this crisis. All four of their industries—agriculture, fishing, tourism, and light manufacturing—have been lost or severely depleted. Students may also want to find out about relief efforts being made for plants and animals, as well as for people. **Intrapersonal; Linguistic**

Process Skill BUILDER

 **SKILL** Infer

Comparing Ecosystems in Volcanic Areas

In this activity you will collect data and infer about the ecosystems of two volcanic areas.

Data are different kinds of facts. They might include observations, measurements, calculations, and other kinds of information. Scientists collect data about an event to better understand what caused it, what it will cause, and how it will affect other events.

What do these data tell the scientist? The scientist first organizes the data in some way—perhaps a table, chart, or graph. The scientist then studies the organized data and makes inferences. To infer means to form an idea from facts or observations. In this case you will infer about which plants will return to a volcanic area.

Materials
research books
Internet

Procedure

1 Collect data on two volcanic areas, such as Mount Saint Helens and the Soufriere Hills volcano on the island of Montserrat or the active volcanoes of Hawaii. Organize the data.

2 **Communicate** Describe the sequence of events that has taken place.

3 **Interpret Data** Draw a conclusion about why certain plants return when they do.

Drawing Conclusions

1 In what ways is succession in the two areas alike? In what ways is it different?

2 **Infer** Why is the succession in these two areas similar or different?

3 **Infer** What abiotic factors must you consider when drawing conclusions? What biotic factors must you consider?

B 87

Process Skills
MiniLesson

Infer

Develop This skill involves forming an idea from facts or observations. It's a conclusion based on facts gathered through direct observation or collected data. For example, someone infers from the smell of smoke that there is a fire nearby. Smelling smoke is the direct observation. That there is a fire nearby is inferred and based on observation.

Practice Have students use what they know about living things to make inferences about this situation.

■ **Several sow bugs are placed in a box that is partly lit by the Sun and partly shaded. Several minutes later, all of the sow bugs are observed in the shaded part of the box.** (Sow bugs prefer shade.)

A complete list of Science Process Skills appears on p. S7.

Process Skill
BUILDER

Comparing Ecosystems in Volcanic Areas

Science Process Skills *infer, communicate, interpret data*

Resources Activity Resources, pp. 77–78

Pacing 20–30 minutes

Grouping individual

Procedure

2 Students should describe the ecosystem before the eruption, type of eruption, damage to the surrounding area, ecosystem immediately after the eruption, and ecological succession. The pioneer community should be discussed as well as any subsequent communities.

3 Students should discuss which plants survived the eruption and why, and how new plants/seeds arrived in the desolated area. They should describe the environmental conditions and relate them to the needs of different plants, and discuss how the environmental conditions, such as soil and available sunlight, change over time, and the resulting changes in plant life.

Answers to Drawing Conclusions

1 In both places, succession starts with simple life forms and proceeds in a predictable way. Life forms that move in later will vary according to the environment.

2 The two areas are in different geographic regions so they will establish different climax communities.

3 Abiotic factors may include the type of eruption and resulting ground condition (lava flow vs. ash layers), wind direction, climate (temperature, precipitation), topology (slope and elevation of the land), geography (how near to or far from the sea), and latitude. Biotic factors may include the ecological community that existed before the eruption, location of nearby plants, characteristics of the plants and their parts (especially seeds), their means of reproduction, and their needs for water, light, nutrients, and temperature.

How Do Changes Affect Populations?

Before Reading
Have students try to answer the red question at the top of the page.

Developing the Main Idea
Encourage students to use a present-day map as they discuss the clues. Have them stick notes on the map to get a picture of what probably happened.

Ask students to reread, then discuss the material in the text as they try to put the clues together.

How Do Changes Affect Populations?

Our planet is changing all the time. Its continents move north and south, east and west. Climates change from hot to cold, cold to hot, wet to dry, or dry to wet. As these changes occur, populations and communities change with them.

Take, for example, the following mystery and its solution.

- Scientists gathering fossils in Italy make a discovery. About six million years ago, fish and other sea creatures disappeared from the Mediterranean Sea.

- Other fossils from a slightly later period reveal that horselike animals from Africa arrived in Europe.

- The fossil of an ancient African hippopotamus is found on an island in the middle of the Mediterranean.

- Fossil palm trees of the same age are dug up in Switzerland.

- Then there is another surprising discovery. Five-million-year-old fossils of fish turn up in the Mediterranean area.

What could have gone on back then to have these clues make sense? Scientists have developed hypotheses. One theory is called *plate tectonics*.

Scientists study fossils to discover how the Mediterranean area changed.

B 88

Math | MiniLesson

Patterns of Multiplication

Develop As you discuss millions of years above, introduce a lesson on using basic facts and patterns to find the products of a number and a multiple of 10, 100, and 1,000.

$6 \times 5 = 30$
$6 \times 50 = 300$
$6 \times 500 = 3,000$
$6 \times 5,000 = 30,000$

You can also use patterns to multiply decimals by powers of 10. Note: 10, 100, 1,000 and other multiples of ten are called powers of 10.

$3.8 \times 1 = 3.8$
$3.8 \times 10 = 38$
$3.8 \times 100 = 380$
$3.8 \times 1,000 = 3,800$

Practice Multiply.

1. $90 \times 10,000$ (900,000)
2. $0.4 \times 1,000$ (400)
3. $4.52 \times 10,000$ (45,200)
4. $500 \times 6,000$ (3,000,000)

Science Background

Moving Plates
The idea of continental drift was proposed by Alfred Wegener in 1912. However, scientists did not accept the idea until the 1960s. Now plate tectonics tells us that Earth's plates move a few inches each year. In 1985, astronomers made exact measurements of the arrival times of radiation from distant quasars to three observatories, two in Europe and one in North America. Calculations showed that the observatories had moved apart by more than a foot.

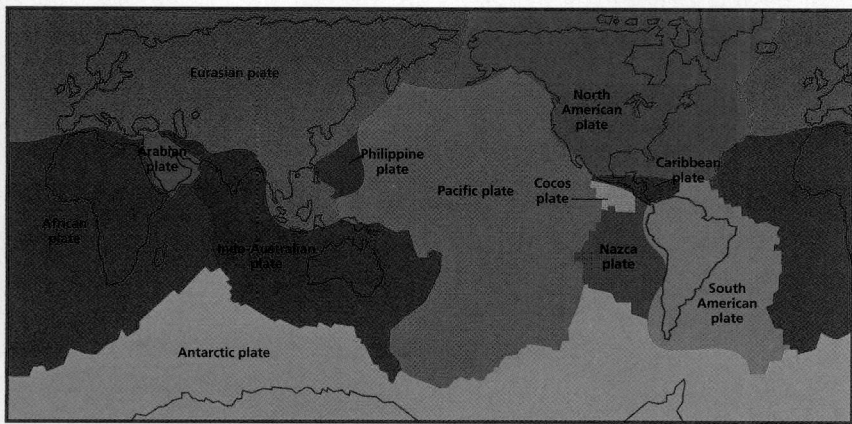

Earth's plates

Earth's crust is made up of moving plates—pieces of crust. About six million years ago, two plates—the African and the Eurasian—collided. The continents of Africa and Europe bumped into each other. This happened at what is now the Strait of Gibraltar. This collision created a natural dam between the Atlantic Ocean and the Mediterranean Sea.

Without a source of water from the ocean, the sea dried up in perhaps as little as 1,000 years. The Mediterranean Sea became a desert. The sea's fish and other marine life died out. Animals from Africa migrated across the desert to Europe. Palm trees sprouted in Switzerland.

Then about five million years ago, the dam began to crumble. A gigantic waterfall poured water into the desert. It carried many kinds of marine life from the Atlantic Ocean. The Mediterranean became a sea again.

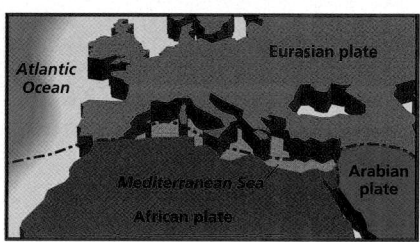

6 million years ago

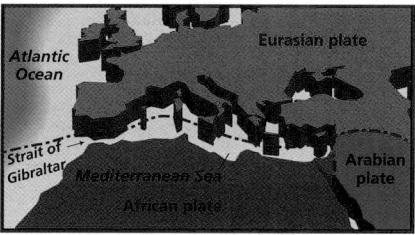

Present day

READING Summarize
How did changes in the Mediterranean affect populations?
New populations appeared in Europe, while others disappeared as a result of change.

B 89

Developing the Main Idea
Ask students to list ways Earth is constantly changing. (Examples: soil gets washed or blown away; new soil forms and rock layers get built up.) Ask students what changes might occur if a large lake or pond dried up. (The lake organisms would die. Animals could walk across the dried-up area to ecosystems on the other side.)

Using the Illustrations
Have students use the two small maps to describe in their own words the changes that occurred in the Mediterranean Sea area. They can start by finding this area on a world map and finding the Strait of Gibraltar.

▶**After Reading**
Have students answer the red question in the student book as **ongoing assessment**.

Reading MiniLesson

Summarize

Develop Have students reread the assessment question on page B89 and summarize what happened to the area of the Mediterranean Sea by listing the sequence of events. For example: "When two of Earth's plates collided and made a dam between the Atlantic Ocean and the Mediterranean Sea, the sea dried up and all the water animals and plants died. Over time the dam crumbled and water once again poured in from the ocean, forming the Mediterranean Sea."

Practice Ask students to use information from pages B88 and B89 to write a summary about this lesson about how changes affect populations. For example: "Earth's plates are constantly moving. When two plates bumped into one another millions of years ago, animals and plants from one land area moved onto the other land area to live. We know this because scientists have found fossils of palm trees that grow in warm countries in the colder climate of Switzerland."

English Language Learners

Word Usage

Point out to students the use of the words *sea* and *ocean* in the text. Ask students to find the definition of each word and to compare and contrast them. Challenge students to find more words that describe bodies of water and their precise definitions. Then have them locate examples of each on a map. **Linguistic**

Can Human Events Change Environments?

Before Reading
Have students try to answer the red question at the top of the text column.

Developing the Main Idea
Ask students where metals come from (on or beneath Earth's surface) and how mining might affect ecosystems. Ask students to list 10 ways they use metals every day. Have them discuss which metals are recycled in your community. (examples: iron, steel, and aluminum)

Using the Illustrations
Have students focus on the picture of a strip mine. Discuss with them where the ore is. Ask them what other types of mines they know about. They should mention underground mines.

▶After Reading
Have students answer the red question in the student book as **ongoing assessment**.

Can Human Events Change Environments?

The soil under your feet looks brown. The rocks are mostly gray. However, both hold a treasure chest of glittering colorful metals—gold, silver, aluminum, iron, copper, and many more.

People use these metals in many ways. Gold is made into jewelry and coins. Silver is, too. Silver is also used in photographic film and tableware.

Fly in an airplane. Ride in an automobile. Open a soft drink can. Squeeze a toothpaste tube. Marvel at fireworks. For all these things, you can thank aluminum. It's in each of these products.

Every large building, bridge, ship, train, and piece of machinery has iron in it—usually as part of steel.

Turn on your TV, your home's lights, a CD player. Electricity flowing through copper wires gets them going.

Clearly metals play an important part in our modern society. However, we pay a price for them—and not only

B 90

in money. Since metal-containing rocks are buried in the ground, we must change the ground to get at them. If the rocks are near the surface, we simply carve away huge areas of land. This is called surface mining, open-pit mining, or strip mining.

In the United States alone, about 2,331 km² (900 mi²) of land has been cleared for mining. That's about three-fourths of the area of the entire state of Rhode Island.

Surface-mined land is loaded with substances that are harmful to living things. Rainwater flows easily over this kind of land and carries pollutants into nearby streams, rivers, and lakes. The wind picks up dust, which pollutes the air. In both cases, living things are harmed.

The easiest way to mine metals that are near the surface is to scrape the surface away. However, this leaves the land barren and often covered with dangerous chemicals.

▷ How does mining affect the environment?

Mining may upset or destroy ecosystems and may increase water and air pollution.

Reading Strategy
Summarize
Developing Reading Skills
Ask students to summarize what happens to land that has been mined.

Science Background
Mining
The type of mining used to extract ores depends on the shape and location of the deposit. Coal, oil shale, and salt are often found in flat and continuous deposits and are surface mined. If the deposit is underground, a variety of methods can be used. U.S. laws now require that all surface mines be filled when exhausted, graded to about the original contour, and planted or made available for farming or recreational purposes.

Why It Matters

The activities and health of all living things on Earth are interconnected. What happens to one living thing and one ecosystem usually affects other living things and other ecosystems. Human activities like strip mining can harm soil and the environment. Human actions can also help the environment, however. Composting, for example, can help restore soil. We can also help the environment by using only the things we need, and by not wasting materials.

Visit **www.mhscience02.com** to do a research project on conserving metals.

Think and Write

1. Describe how an abandoned farm field becomes a deciduous forest.

2. Give an example of a pioneer community and a climax community.

3. List the evidence that supports the conclusion that the Mediterranean Sea once dried up.

4. **Infer** How might a volcanic eruption affect an ecosystem?

5. **Critical Thinking** What things do you do every day that can affect the ecosystem you live in?

L·I·N·K·S

LITERATURE LINK

Read *Wildfire* to learn about the true story of a wildfire that destroyed 5,000 acres of land in New York. Try the activities in the back of the book.

SOCIAL STUDIES LINK

Conduct research. What happened to Angkor? What was the culture like? Why did the people leave their city? Use the Internet or an encyclopedia for your research.

TECHNOLOGY LINK

Science Newsroom CD-ROM Choose *From the Ground Up* to learn how ecosystems change over time.

At the Computer Visit **www.mhscience02.com** for more links.

B 91

✓ Informal Assessment

Easy/Average Ask teams of students to choose an ecosystem and draw a comic book showing how it can change into another one. Ask them to use the vocabulary words as labels.

Challenge Invite teams to script a play about how one ecosystem can change into another. A narrator should explain what is happening.

---

3 Lesson Review

Answers to Think and Write

1. First, different plants and later, animals from the forest slowly become established on the farm field. (pp. B80–B81)

2. pioneer community: fireweed, insects, and insect-eating bird community; climax community: a deciduous forest (pp. B83–B84)

3. Fossils found in Italy indicate that sea animals disappeared from the Mediterranean Sea 6 million years ago. Other fossils show that horse-like animals from Africa arrived in Europe slightly later, African hippos lived on what is now an island in the sea, palm trees grew in what is now Switzerland, and fish lived in areas that are now dry land. (p. B88)

4. **Infer** The blast from a volcano can knock down trees; hot volcanic ash or lava might burn the land and kill all plants and animals. Eventually, new ecosystems may replace the old ones. (pp. B82–B83)

5. **Critical Thinking** Possible answers: eat, dispose of wastes, breathe, and walk on the ground (pp. B80, B90)

Summarize

Check students' understanding by having them write a brief summary of the lesson in their own words.

LITERATURE LINK

Have students read the Grade-Level Science Book, *Wildfire*. Additional books to read can be found on TE p. B1·b.

SOCIAL STUDIES LINK

Students' research should explain that Angkor was abandoned when the Thai army conquered and ransacked the city and temples.

Technology

Internet Research Project Have students visit **www.mhscience02.com** to conduct a research project on conserving metals. They will find a suggested outline for the project, questions to research, and links to Internet reference sites.

Chapter Review and Test Preparation

Resources

- Reading in Science Resources, pp. 121–122
- Assessment Book, pp. 23–26

Answers to Vocabulary

1. tundra
2. mutualism
3. Parasitism
4. taiga
5. pioneer community
6. adaptation
7. climax community
8. biome
9. Symbiosis
10. desert

Answers to Test Prep

11. A
12. J
13. C
14. H
15. D

Chapter 5 Review

Vocabulary

Fill each blank with the best word or words from the list.

> adaptation, B52
> biome, B64
> climax community, B84
> desert, B69
> mutualism, B54
> parasitism, B56
> pioneer community, B83
> symbiosis, B54
> taiga, B67
> tundra, B68

1. Part of the soil of the _____ is frozen all year round.

2. The relationship of _____ means that both populations benefit.

3. _____ is a relationship between two organisms in which one benefits while the other is harmed.

4. The _____ has many evergreen trees.

5. A(n) _____ is made up of the first organisms to colonize an area.

6. A characteristic that helps an organism survive is called a(n) _____.

7. When ecological succession slows down, a(n) _____ has formed.

8. A deciduous forest is an example of a(n) _____.

9. _____ describes relationships that last from one generation to the next.

10. The Gobi and Mojave are examples of the _____.

Test Prep

11. One example of a parasitic plant is _____.
    - A mistletoe
    - B an orchid
    - C a fir tree
    - D seaweed

12. Surface mining can harm the environment when _____.
    - F trees are cut down to clear the land
    - G dust from surface-mined land causes air pollution
    - H rainwater washes pollutants into nearby streams
    - J all of the above

13. A relationship in which one organism benefits from another without helping or harming it is called _____.
    - A parasitism
    - B mutualism
    - C commensalism
    - D symbiosis

B 92

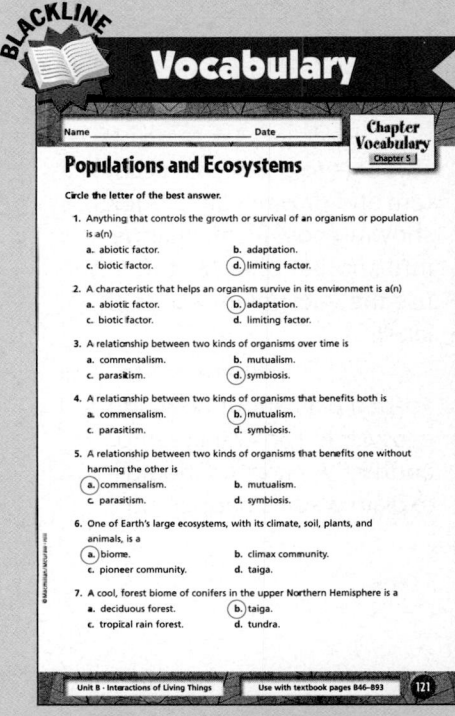

Reading in Science Resources, p. 121

14. _____ is an example of a biome.
- F A pond
- G Bacteria
- H A grassland
- J A mammal

15. The shallow roots of the barrel cactus help it survive in the desert by _____.
- A resisting flood damage
- B allowing the cactus to be blown to a wetter place
- C allowing the cactus to float
- D soaking up rain very quickly

Concepts and Skills

16. Process Skills: Infer
What can you infer from the data below?

Pond Populations and Acid Content

Acid	Yellow Perch	Brown Trout	Salamanders	Mayflies
High	23	6	2	0
Medium	28	11	7	2
Low	36	18	10	14

Boost your test scores! **Be Smart!** Visit www.mhscience02.com

17. Reading in Science Summarize how the structure of a cactus enables it to survive in the desert.

18. Critical Thinking How might a change in the biome you live in affect your way of life?

19. Scientific Methods You discover that there are no fossils of dinosaurs above a certain layer of rock, but there are below it. The rock in this layer has more in common with rocks from space than with Earth rocks. Hypothesize how these two discoveries may be linked.

20. Product Ads Advertisements for some products claim that the products are environmentally friendly. What does that mean? What are examples of products that are environmentally friendly and products that are not?

Answers to Concepts and Skills

16. Process Skills: Infer As the acidity of the pond increases, each of its populations decreases.

17. Reading in Science The roots of a cactus are shallow and grow only about 3 inches into the dry soil, enabling the roots to catch rain and soak it up quickly. During dry spells the fine ends of the roots fall off, preventing stored water from passing out onto the soil. The folds of the cactus stem are covered with sharp spines. The folds protect moist parts of the stem from hot, dry desert winds. The spines also keep away birds and small animals that try to get water from the cactus's stems.

18. Critical Thinking It would affect life in every way: how you live from day to day, how you eat, how you play, and how you sleep.

19. Scientific Methods Students may infer that rocks from space may have crashed into Earth, resulting in the extinction of the dinosaurs.

20. Product Ads Accept all reasonable answers from students.

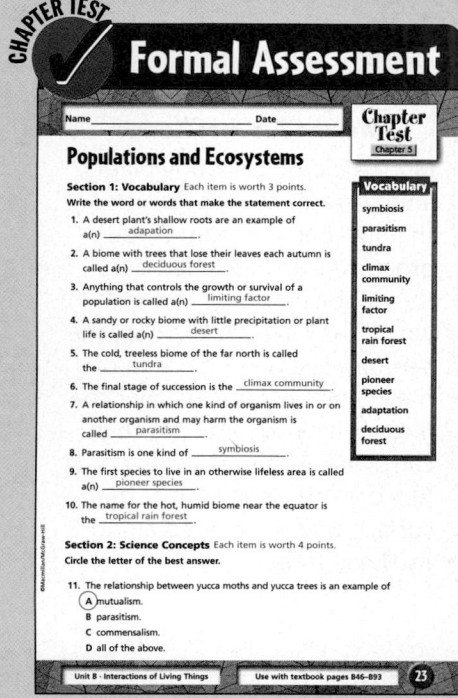

Assessment Book, p. 23

People in Science

People in Science

Objective

- Describe what a marine biologist does and how to become one.

Build on Prior Knowledge

Ask students whether they have ever been to the seashore. Ask what kinds of organisms they saw and how they were able to view them. (visible in shallow water, using a snorkel or diving equipment)

Marine Biologist
Dr. Lauren Mullineaux

Developing the Main Idea

Explain to students that, like land ecosystems, water ecosystems are part of a biome. Remind students that a land biome is a large ecosystem with its climate, soil, plants, and animals. Ask:

- **What factors would be used to describe a water biome?** (Possible answers: plants, animals and other organisms; water temperature; amount of sunlight; salinity and other chemical levels)

- **What animals live in the ecosystem that Dr. Mullineaux explores?** (tube worms, white crabs, and giant clams)

- **What special conditions must the organisms she studies adapt to?** (extremely hot water, great depth and pressure, darkness, volcanic chemicals)

MARINE BIOLOGIST
Dr. Lauren Mullineaux

Woods Hole Oceanographic Institution

Earth's oceans are home to many populations of strange and unusual organisms. What different kinds of habitats exist on the ocean floor? What kinds of organisms live there, and how do they survive? How can we use new discoveries to benefit society? These are some of the questions inspiring today's oceanographers.

Dr. Lauren Mullineaux is a marine biologist at Woods Hole Oceanographic Institution in Massachusetts. She studies ocean ecosystems. One of the unanswered questions she is studying is how the animals of the ocean floor survive. These animals include tube worms, white crabs, and giant clams. Many live in hydrothermal vents created by volcanoes under the sea floor. The vents might seem to be too harsh an environment for living things, but these animals cannot survive anywhere else.

Sometimes the research of a marine biologist is not easy. To study the unique organisms of the ocean floor, Dr. Mullineaux has to dive in a submersible. A submersible is a special kind of submarine that can dive very deep. The vents are located thousands of meters beneath the ocean surface! Dr. Mullineaux sets up her experiments on the ocean floor.

Dr. Mullineaux grew up in Colorado, far from the ocean, but she's always had a love for nature and animals. She became interested in science as a way to understand nature. In college she studied ecology but soon realized that she wanted to study the mysteries of the ocean. After receiving her doctorate degree in biological oceanography, she was able to start her research career and begin unlocking the mysteries of the deep.

B 94

Science Background

Marine Animal Zones

Marine biologists study plants, animals, and other organisms that live in the ocean. These organisms are classified by their habits and ocean depth in which they live. One group, the *benthos,* live on or depend on the ocean bottom. Another, the *nekton,* includes animals that can swim. A third is *plankton,* tiny organisms at or near the surface that are carried along by the currents.

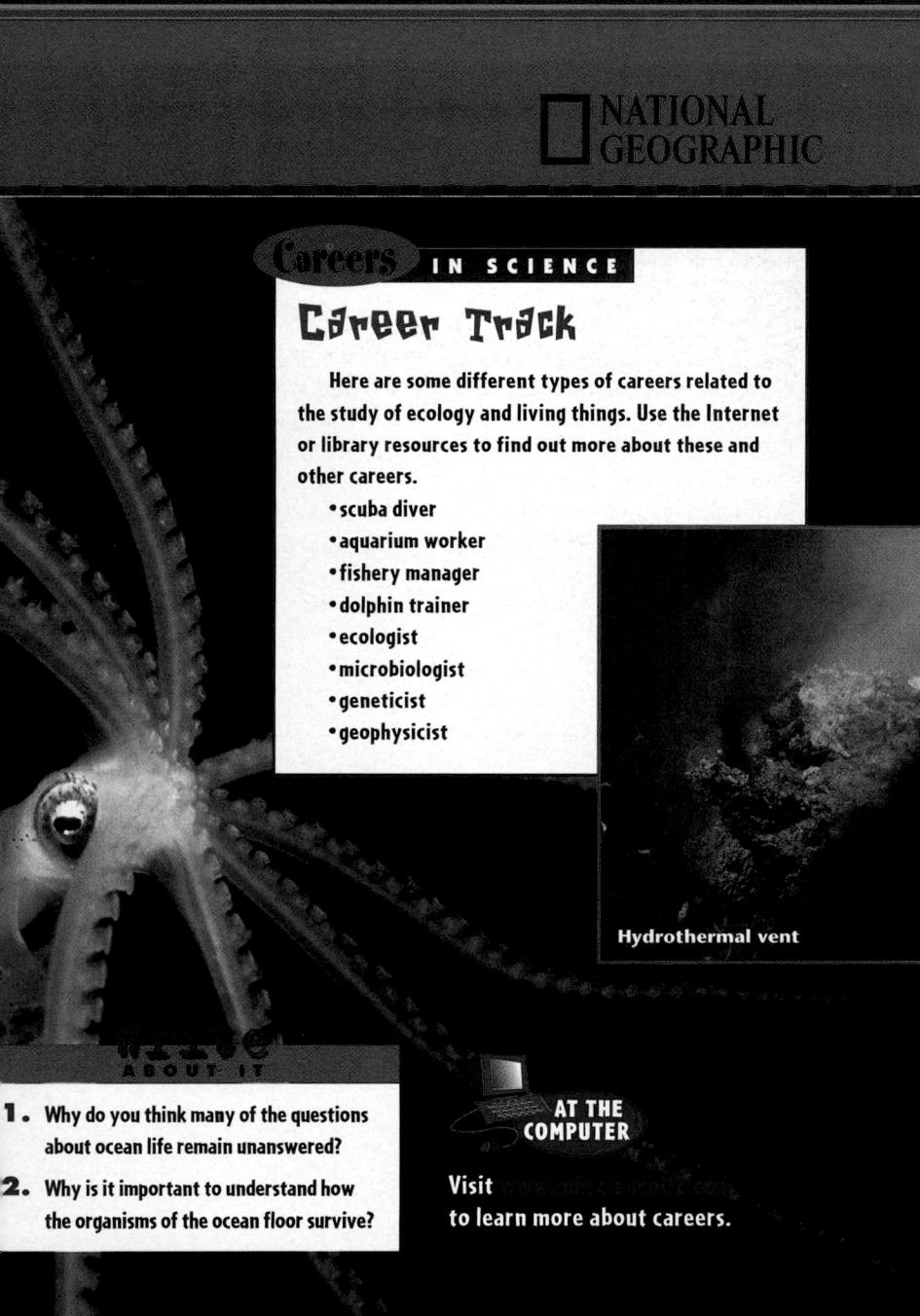

NATIONAL GEOGRAPHIC

Careers IN SCIENCE

Career Track

Here are some different types of careers related to the study of ecology and living things. Use the Internet or library resources to find out more about these and other careers.

- scuba diver
- aquarium worker
- fishery manager
- dolphin trainer
- ecologist
- microbiologist
- geneticist
- geophysicist

Hydrothermal vent

Write ABOUT IT

1. Why do you think many of the questions about ocean life remain unanswered?

2. Why is it important to understand how the organisms of the ocean floor survive?

AT THE COMPUTER

Visit
to learn more about careers.

B 95

Developing the Main Idea
Focus on the job of marine biologist. Ask:

- **What kind of interests and training does a marine biologist need?** (Possible answers: a love of nature and animals; an interest in understanding nature; a curiosity about ocean organisms; a desire to work on or in the ocean; a doctorate or advanced degree in marine biology)

- **Besides the deep ocean vents where Dr. Mullineaux does her research, where else might a marine biologist work?** (Possible answers: along the seashore, at the ocean's surface, along shallow ocean floor, along coral reefs, in a laboratory)

Thinking Further: *Compare and Contrast*
Ask:

- **What similarities does the hydrothermal vent ecosystem have with a desert ecosystem?** (Possible answer: Because both can be very hot, very few animals live there and those that do have special adaptations to help them survive the harsh conditions.)

Answers to  Write ABOUT IT

1. Much of the deep ocean is difficult to explore because of the special equipment needed to overcome the harsh conditions.

2. Possible answers: Knowledge of how the organisms survive can be helpful in conservation and protection efforts, in understanding how other organisms survive, to learn more about extinct organisms, or in discovering information that can benefit humans in our own survival.

Unit B Performance Assessment

Ecosystem Discovery (Chapter 4)

Materials: colored pencils, drawing paper, magazine photos, scissors, glue

Teaching Tips: Provide photos of a wide variety of plants and animals that live in different kinds of habitats. Be sure to include producers as well as consumers.

Answers to Analyze Your Results

1. Students should indicate: the plants are producers; how the animals obtain their food; what else do the organisms need.

2. interaction of nonliving and living things

3. Animals needing more energy are at the top.

Will Succession Succeed? (Chapter 5)

Materials: colored pencils, drawing paper

Teaching Tips: If possible, take students to an area on campus where there is evidence of succession.

Answers to What to Do

1. Student essays can be based on pp. B82 to B88.

2. Mount Saint Helens and Yellowstone National Park are examples of ecological succession.

Answers to Analyze Your Results

1. new types of trees and plants and animals

2. Simple species come to a community first.

3. fires or other catastrophes

Performance Assessment

Ecosystem Discovery

Your goal is to invent and describe a new ecosystem.

What to Do

1. Imagine you are an explorer. You have found the world's last unexplored ecosystem. Give your ecosystem a name.

2. Describe this new ecosystem. Write about the plants and animals there. Tell what each one needs to survive.

3. Draw a picture of your ecosystem.

Analyze Your Results

1. Tell how each plant and animal gets what it needs to survive in your ecosystem.

2. What nonliving things help plants and animals survive in your ecosystem?

3. Draw an energy pyramid to show how energy moves in your ecosystem. What belongs at the bottom of the pyramid? At the top?

Will Succession Succeed?

Your goal is to identify a place where ecological succession is taking place.

What to Do

1. Write a short paragraph describing what ecological succession is.

2. Think of an area you have visited where succession is taking place. If you can't think of an area near you, describe a place you have read about. Write down the name of the place or tell its location. Draw a picture.

Analyze Your Results

1. List evidence that succession is taking place in your area.

2. In what order will new species come to live in your area? Explain.

3. What could happen to prevent succession in your area?

Rubrics

Ecosystem Discovery (5-point rubric)

5 points = All student responses are correct. (Written description, ecosystem diagram, and answers to the three questions are correct.)

4 points = Four student responses are correct.

3 points = Three student responses are correct.

2 points = Two student responses are correct.

1 point = One student response is correct.

0 points = No student responses are correct.

Will Succession Succeed?
(5-point rubric)

5 points = All student responses are correct (paragraph, picture, answers to three Analyze Your Results questions).

4 points = Four student responses are correct.

3 points = Three student responses are correct.

2 points = Two student responses are correct.

1 point = One student response is correct.

0 points = No student responses are correct.

Formal Assessment

Name _____ **Date** _____

Unit Performance Assessment Chapter 4

Eco-Brochures

Communicate

Use the materials provided by your teacher to create a brochure that advertises a specific ecosystem. Design the brochure to appeal to a specific species that could live in that ecosystem. When making your brochure, highlight the biotic and abiotic factors of the ecosystem. Discuss the niche of the species you have chosen, including two food chains in which it could participate.

Analyze the Results

1. List the specific aspects of the ecosystem that you chose to advertise.

_____
_____

2. Explain why the aspects you chose would be of interest to the species you selected.

_____
_____
_____

3. Choose another species that lives in the ecosystem your brochure advertises. How would you change the brochure so that it appeals to the other species?

_____
_____
_____
_____

Unit B · Interactions of Living Things   Use with textbook pages B2–B45   29

Assessment Book, pp. 27-30

For Your Reference

Science Handbook

Health Handbook

Glossary

Index

Units of Measurement

SCIENCE Handbook

Units of Measurement

Objective

- Review and compare units in the metric and English systems of measurement.

Build on Prior Knowledge

Write the word "ruler" on the board and then have students add other measuring tools to the list. For each tool, ask:

- **What does this tool measure? What units of measurement are used with this tool?** (inch, foot, centimeter, and so on)

Developing the Main Idea

Explain that in this lesson students will review some common measuring instruments and two systems of units used to record measurements.

Using the Illustrations

Discuss each of the pictures on pages R2 and R3. For each picture ask:

- **What is being measured? What measuring tool is being used? What units of measure could be used to record the data?**
  (Temperature: thermometer; degrees Celsius or degrees Fahrenheit. Length and distance: metric stick or ruler; meters, centimeters. Mass: balance; grams, kilograms. Volume: graduated cylinder or measuring cup; liters, milliliters, quarts, ounces, pints, gallons. Weight: scale; pounds, ounces. Time: stopwatch or clock; minutes, seconds, hours.)

Science Background

Systems of Measurement

There are two systems of measurement commonly used in the United States—the English or customary system and the metric system. Scientists throughout the world use the metric system so that information can be easily shared. The metric system is based on units of length (meter) and mass (kilogram). Temperature is not actually part of the system. It is included here for convenience of comparing the more familiar units (English system and Fahrenheit scale) and less familiar units (metric system and Celsius scale). The abbreviation SI stands for Système Internationale, in French.

Units of Measurement

> This bottle of juice has a volume of 1 liter.

> That is a little more than 1 quart.

> She can walk 20 meters in 5 seconds.

> That means her speed is 4 meters per second.

Table of Measurements

International System of Units (SI)	English System of Units
Temperature Water freezes at 0°C and boils at 100°C.	**Temperature** Water freezes at 32°F and boils at 212°F.
Length and Distance 1,000 meters (m) = 1 kilometer (km) 100 centimeters (cm) = 1 meter 10 millimeters (mm) = 1 centimeter	**Length and Distance** 5,280 feet = 1 mile 3 feet = 1 yard 12 inches = 1 foot
Volume 1,000 milliliters (mL) = 1 liter (L) 1 cubic centimeter (cm³) = 1 milliliter	**Volume of Fluids** 4 quarts = 1 gallon 2 pints = 1 quart 2 cups = 1 pint 8 fluid ounces = 1 cup
Mass 1,000 grams (g) = 1 kilogram (kg)	**Weight** 2,000 pounds = 1 ton 16 ounces = 1 pound

R 3

Using the Illustrations

Have students study the table of measurements. Ask:

- **What are two systems used to report measurements?** (the SI or metric system; the English or customary system)

- **What kind of information can you find in a table of measurement?** (different units of measure; ways of converting between different units)

- **Where can you find tables of measurement?** (Possible answers: in the back of a math or science textbook; in a large dictionary; in an encyclopedia)

WRITING LINK

Students may write about their experiences using at least two different kinds of measuring instruments.

Informal Assessment

Write these words on the board: *distance, mass, temperature,* and *capacity.* Ask:

- **For each word, name a tool used to measure each quantity. Then name at least two units of measure.** (Distance: ruler, tape measure, meterstick; meter, centimeter, inch, foot. Mass: balance; kilograms, grams. Temperature: thermometer; degrees Celsius, degrees Fahrenheit. Capacity: calibrated beaker, graduated cylinder; liters, milliliters, cubic centimeters.)

- **What units can you use to report the speed of a moving object? Give both metric and English system examples.** (Metric: kilometers per hour, meters per second, kilometers per minute. English: miles per hour, feet per second, miles per minute.)

Math | MiniLesson

Metric Conversions

Develop An aquarium is 132 millimeters (mm) wide. Will this width fit on a table that is 15 centimeters (cm) wide?

To solve this problem, change 132 millimeters to centimeters. To change between metric units, you multiply or divide by powers of ten.

132 mm = ■ cm
Think: 10 mm = 1 cm
Divide to change from smaller to larger units.
132 ÷ 10 = 13.2

132 mm = 13.2 cm
13.2 < 15
The aquarium will fit.

2.51 km = ■ meters
Think: 1 km = 1,000 m
To change from larger to smaller units, multiply.
2.51 × 1,000 = 2,150 meters

Practice Complete.
1. 35 cm = ■ m (0.35 m)
2. 6.25 L = ■ mL (6,250 mL)
3. 1.75 kg = ■ g (1,750 g)
4. 58 mm = ■ cm (5.8 cm)

Use a Hand Lens and a Microscope

Objective

■ Practice collecting data using hand lenses and microscopes.

Build on Prior Knowledge

Display a hand lens and a microscope. Have students share past experiences using these tools. Ask:

■ **How are these tools like a pair of eyeglasses?** (Both use lenses to help a person see better.)

■ **How are these tools alike? How are they different?** (They both magnify objects. Differences include: the microscope is more powerful, more expensive, and more difficult to learn to use.)

Exploring the Main Idea

For the two activities on page R4, provide each group with the needed materials. Have groups read all the directions before they begin working. After students have drawn their pictures of the cereal, allow time for them to examine other objects with the lenses. When they are finished, ask:

■ **How do you know how close the hand lens should be to the object?** (You don't; you must experiment until the object looks clear and not blurred.)

Have students complete the activity with the radish seeds. (Sprouting times will vary.)

Use a Hand Lens

You use a hand lens to magnify an object, or make the object look larger. With a hand lens, you can see details that would be hard to see without the hand lens.

Magnify a Piece of Cereal

1. Place a piece of your favorite cereal on a flat surface. Look at the cereal carefully. Draw a picture of it.
2. Look at the cereal through the large lens of a hand lens. Move the lens toward or away from the cereal until it looks larger and in focus. Draw a picture of the cereal as you see it through the hand lens. Fill in details that you did not see before.
3. Look at the cereal through the smaller lens, which will magnify the cereal even more. If you notice more details, add them to your drawing.
4. Repeat this activity using objects you are studying in science. It might be a rock, some soil, or a seed.

Observe Seeds in a Petri Dish

Can you observe a seed as it sprouts? You can if it's in a petri dish. A petri dish is a shallow, clear, round dish with a cover.

1. Line the sides and bottom of a petri dish with a double layer of filter paper or paper towel. You may have to cut the paper to make it fit.
2. Sprinkle water on the paper to wet it.
3. Place three or four radish seeds on the wet paper in different areas of the dish. Put the lid on the dish, and keep it in a warm place.
4. Observe the seeds every day for a week. Use a hand lens to look for a tiny root pushing through the seed. Record how long it takes each seed to sprout.

R 4

Science Background

Hand Lenses and Microscopes

A hand lens consists of a convergent lens of short focal length. Most hand lenses have a magnifying power of about 5 times actual size. To examine objects too small for a hand lens, a microscope can be used. Like a telescope, a microscope is based on two lenses in a tube that can be focused by changing the length of the tube.

Use a Microscope

Hand lenses make objects look several times larger. A microscope, however, can magnify an object to look hundreds of times larger.

Examine Salt Grains

1. Look at the photograph to learn the different parts of your microscope.
2. Place the microscope on a flat surface. Always carry a microscope with both hands. Hold the arm with one hand, and put your other hand beneath the base.
3. Move the mirror so that it reflects light up toward the stage. Never point the mirror directly at the Sun or a bright light. Bright light can cause permanent eye damage.
4. Place a few grains of salt on the slide. Put the slide under the stage clips. Be sure that the salt grains you are going to examine are over the hole in the stage.
5. Look through the eyepiece. Turn the focusing knob slowly until the salt grains come into focus.
6. Draw what the grains look like through the microscope.
7. Look at other objects through the microscope. Try a piece of leaf, a human hair, or a pencil mark.

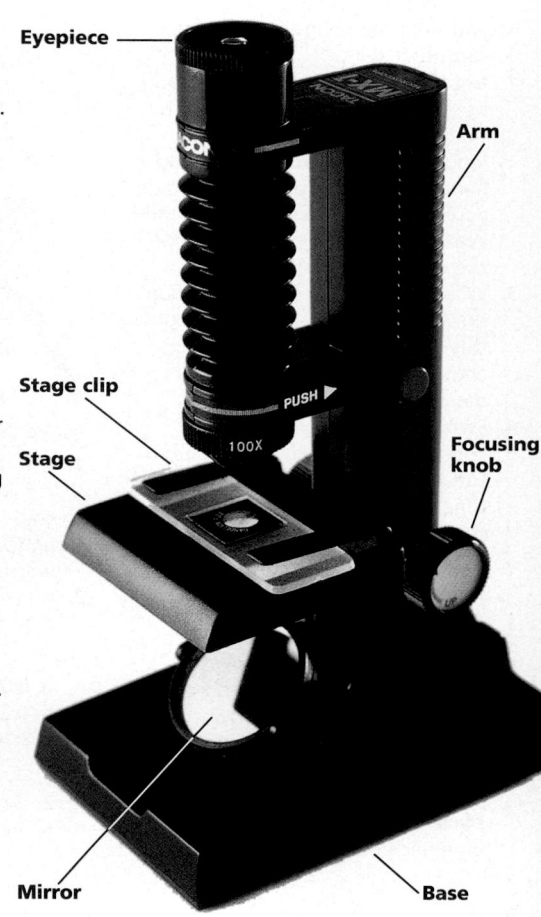

Eyepiece

Arm

Stage clip

Stage

Focusing knob

Mirror

Base

R 5

SCIENCE • HANDBOOK

Using the Illustrations
Ask students to study the diagram on page R5 showing the parts of a microscope. Have them use the diagram to find corresponding parts of a real microscope.

Exploring the Main Idea
Many students will need help when first using a microscope. Try to group students so that they can help each other learn. You may need to first teach a small group of students how to use the microscope and then have those students work with others until everyone has learned the skill.

Have students work through the steps. Demonstrate how to hold and carry a microscope. Stress the need for never pointing the mirror directly at the Sun or another bright light.

WRITING LINK
Students may write about objects they would like to examine with a hand lens or a microscope.

Informal Assessment
Have students choose a flower or the skin of a fruit. Have them draw what they see without using a hand lens. Then have them look at the object through the hand lens and add more detail to their drawings. Ask:

■ **Why are lenses and microscopes important in scientific work?** (Possible answer: Scientists can learn more about objects by finding out what they look like when highly magnified.)

Inclusion

One Eye, Two Eyes
As students begin to use a microscope, they may tend to close the eye that is not looking into the eyepiece. Have them practice viewing specimens with both eyes open and explain if there is any difference. (No. They are still seeing a 1-dimensional view of the specimen.) Having both eyes open allows them to keep a specimen under view while they attempt to draw their observations. **Kinesthetic; Spatial**

Measure Time

Objective

- Use clocks and stopwatches to measure elapsed time.

Build on Prior Knowledge

Ask students to describe different kinds of clocks and watches. Ask:

- **What are some units we use to measure time?** (days, hours, minutes, seconds)

Using the Illustrations

Have students look at the picture of the stopwatch. Ask:

- **How many seconds are shown on the stopwatch?** (25.75 seconds)

Exploring the Main Idea

Tell students that the first part of the page will give them practice in measuring time. When students have finished activities 1–6, ask:

- **Did you get exactly the same time in both experiments?** (No. There is some measurement error in any measurement activity.)

WRITING LINK

Students may write about measuring time.

Informal Assessment

Ask:

- **What are some advantages in using a stopwatch?** (With the stopwatch, you don't have to subtract one time from another; a stopwatch is probably more precise.)

Make Measurements

Measure Time

You use timing devices to measure how long something takes to happen. Some timing devices you use in science are a clock with a second hand and a stopwatch. Which one is more accurate?

Comparing a Clock and Stopwatch

1. Look at a clock with a second hand. The second hand is the hand that you can see moving. It measures seconds.
2. Get an egg timer with falling sand or some device like a wind-up toy that runs down after a certain length of time. When the second hand of the clock points to 12, tell your partner to start the egg timer. Watch the clock while the sand in the egg timer is falling.
3. When the sand stops falling, count how many seconds it took. Record this measurement. Repeat the activity, and compare the two measurements.
4. Switch roles with your partner.
5. Look at a stopwatch. Click the button on the top right. This starts the time. Click the button again. This stops the time. Click the button on the top left. This sets the stopwatch back to zero. Notice that the stopwatch tells time in minutes, seconds, and hundredths of a second.
6. Repeat the activity in steps 1–3, using the stopwatch instead of a clock. Make sure the stopwatch is set to zero. Click the top right button to start timing the reading. Click it again when the sand stops falling. Make sure you and your partner time each other twice.

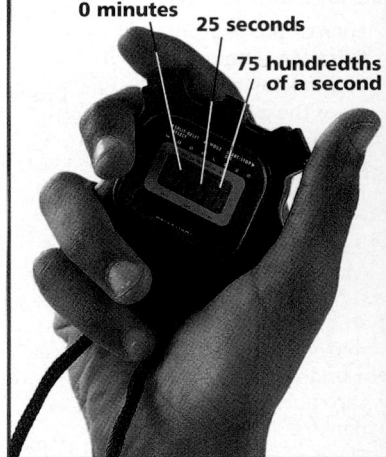

0 minutes   25 seconds   75 hundredths of a second

More About Time

1. Use the stopwatch to time how long it takes an ice cube to melt under cold running water. How long does an ice cube take to melt under warm running water?
2. Match each of these times with the action you think took that amount of time.

   a. 0:00:14:55
   b. 0:24:39:45
   c. 2:10:23:00

   1. A Little League baseball game
   2. Saying the Pledge of Allegiance
   3. Recess

R 6

 **Inclusion**

Clocks

A standard, or analog, clock shows the time by the movement of hands. A digital clock displays time in numbers. A stopwatch can measure time to the nearest hundredth of a second. Have students discuss another kind of clock, the sundial. Have them explain how it tells time and give its limitations. (not useful at night or on very cloudy days) **Linguistic**

Measure Length

Find Length with a Ruler

1. Look at this section of a ruler. Each centimeter is divided into 10 millimeters. How long is the paper clip?
2. The length of the paper clip is 3 centimeters plus 2 millimeters. You can write this length as 3.2 centimeters.
3. Place the ruler on your desk. Lay a pencil against the ruler so that one end of the pencil lines up with the left edge of the ruler. Record the length of the pencil.
4. Trade your pencil with a classmate. Measure and record the length of each other's pencil. Compare your answers.

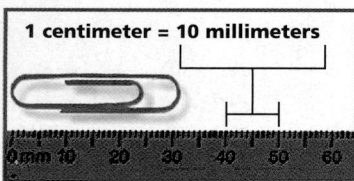

1 centimeter = 10 millimeters

Measuring Area

Area is the amount of surface something covers. To find the area of a rectangle, multiply the rectangle's length by its width. For example, the rectangle here is 3 centimeters long and 2 centimeters wide. Its area is 3 cm x 2 cm = 6 square centimeters. You write the area as 6 cm².

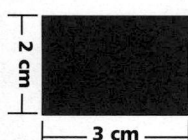

2 cm

3 cm

1. Find the area of your science book. Measure the book's length to the nearest centimeter. Measure its width.
2. Multiply the book's length by its width. Remember to put the answer in cm².

Find Length with a Meterstick

1. Line up the meterstick with the left edge of the chalkboard. Make a chalk mark on the board at the right end of the meterstick.
2. Move the meterstick so that the left edge lines up with the chalk mark. Keep the stick level. Make another mark on the board at the right end of the meterstick.
3. Continue to move the meterstick and make chalk marks until the meterstick meets or overlaps the right edge of the board.
4. Record the length of the chalkboard in centimeters by adding all the measurements you've made. Remember, a meterstick has 100 centimeters.

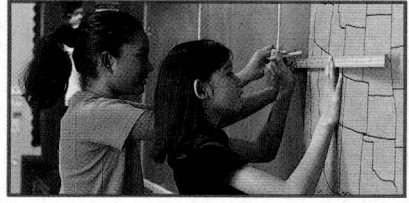

Estimating Length

Try estimating the length of objects in the room. Then measure the length, and compare the estimation with the measurement.

SCIENCE FOR ALL

Inclusion

Rulers

Rulers measure length and distance. In contrast to length, area is usually calculated rather than measured. However as an activity, students can use centimeter graph paper to draw the outline of small objects that have a flat side—such as blocks or small books. They can count the number of boxes on the graph paper to find the area.
Spatial

Measure Length

Objective

■ Use centimeter rulers to measure length and multiply to calculate area.

Build on Prior Knowledge

Hold up a ruler or a pencil that is about 10 centimeters long. Ask:

■ **This object is 10 centimeters long. Find some objects that are more and some that are less than 10 centimeters long.** (More: desk, table, door, book. Less: crayon, scissors.)

■ **One meter equals 100 centimeters. Find things that are about 1 meter long.** (height of a door knob, width of a desk)

Using the Illustrations
Ask:

■ **How long is the paper clip in the diagram?** (32 millimeters or 3.2 centimeters)

■ **What are two ways to represent the same length?** (32 mm; 3.2 cm)

Developing the Main Idea
Draw a rectangle on the board and label its sides 8 cm and 3 cm. Ask:

■ **How can you find the area of a rectangle?** (Multiply the length times the width.)

■ **What is the area of this rectangle?** (24 square centimeters, or 24 cm²)

Check that students have labeled their areas using the symbol cm².

WRITING LINK

Students may write about giving examples of lengths and areas they might use in a science experiment.

Informal Assessment
Have students draw a rectangle. Have them measure the length and width to the nearest tenth of a centimeter, then find the area.

Measure Mass

Build on Prior Knowledge

Ask students if they have ever used a scale to find their weight. Then show them a pan balance. Ask:

- **How is this balance like a scale? Different?** (They both are instruments used to measure. The scale gives a number for a weight; the balance compares two different masses.)

Developing the Main Idea

Explain to students that grams are used for small masses and kilograms for more massive objects. The prefix *kilo-* means thousand. So 1 kilogram equals 1,000 grams.

Using the Illustrations

Ask:

- **How can you tell when the pans hold equal masses?** (The pointer must point exactly to the middle mark on the scale.)

WRITING LINK

Students may write about using a pan balance, including directions on how to use this tool.

Informal Assessment

Have students choose three light objects and find the mass of each in grams. Have them estimate how many crayons equal a mass of 1 kilogram. Then have them use a balance to check their estimate.

Answers

1. 1.97 kilograms (1,970 grams)
2. Have students name combinations of the mass that exceed 1 kilogram: such as 2 of the 500 g mass plus any of the smaller masses.

Measure Mass

Mass is the amount of matter an object has. You use a balance to measure mass. To find the mass of an object, you balance it with objects whose masses you know. Let's find the mass of a box of crayons.

Measure the Mass of a Box of Crayons

1. Place the balance on a flat, level surface. Check that the two pans are empty and clean.
2. Make sure the empty pans are balanced with each other. The pointer should point to the middle mark. If it does not, move the slider a little to the right or left to balance the pans.
3. Gently place a box of crayons on the left pan. This pan will drop lower.
4. Add masses to the right pan until the pans are balanced.
5. Add the numbers on the masses that are in the right pan. The total is the mass of the box of crayons, in grams. Record this number. After the number write a *g* for "grams."

Estimating Mass

Once you become familiar with the mass of objects, you can try estimating the masses of objects. Then you can compare the estimation with the actual mass.

More About Mass

The mass of your crayons was probably less than 100 grams. You may not have enough masses to balance a pineapple. It has a mass of about 1,000 grams. That's the same as 1 kilogram, because *kilo* means "1,000."

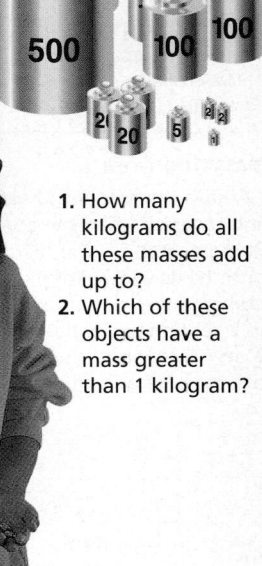

1. How many kilograms do all these masses add up to?
2. Which of these objects have a mass greater than 1 kilogram?

R 8

Science Background

Mass

Mass is the amount of material in an object. In the metric system, mass is measured in units such as grams, kilograms, and milligrams. A pan balance is used to compare masses. A scale measures weight, the pull of gravity on an object.

Measure Volume

Volume is the amount of space something takes up. In science you usually measure the volume of liquids by using beakers and graduated cylinders. These containers are marked in milliliters (mL).

Measure the Volume of a Liquid

1. Look at the beaker and at the graduated cylinder. The beaker has marks for each 25 mL up to 200 mL. The graduated cylinder has marks for each 1 mL up to 100 mL.
2. The surface of the water in the graduated cylinder curves up at the sides. You measure the volume by reading the height of the water at the flat part. What is the volume of water in the graduated cylinder? How much water is in the beaker? They both contain 75 mL of water.
3. Pour 50 mL of water from a pitcher into a beaker.
4. Now pour the 50 mL of water into a graduated cylinder.

Find the Volume of a Solid

Here's a way to find the volume of a solid, such as a rock.

1. Start with 50 mL of water in a graduated cylinder.
2. Place a small rock in the water. The water level rises.
3. Measure the new water level. Subtract 50 mL from the new reading. The difference is the volume of the rock. Record the volume in cm^3.

Estimating Volume

Once you become familiar with the volumes of liquids and solids, you can estimate volumes. Estimate the amount of liquid in a glass or can. Estimate the volume of an eraser.

Inclusion

Units of Volume

The basic unit for measuring the volume of a liquid in the metric system is the liter. (Students will use milliliters more frequently.) There are 1,000 milliliters in 1 liter. The volume of a solid can be measured in cubic centimeters. One cubic centimeter equals 1 milliliter. Have students practice converting from milliliters to liters by dividing by 1,000; and from liters to milliliters by multiplying by 1,000. **Logical**

Measure Volume

Objective

- Use beakers and graduated cylinders to measure volume.

Build on Prior Knowledge

Hold up a graduated cylinder marked in milliliters. Ask:

- **What do the marks mean on this tool?** (Each mark shows one milliliter.)
- **What is the symbol for liter?** (L)
- **What is the symbol for milliliter?** (mL)

Using the Illustrations

Ask the following about the illustration:

- **How is using a beaker different from using a graduated cylinder?** (With the beaker, the liquid is flatter. With the graduated cylinder, it curves up at the sides.)

Exploring the Main Idea

Have students practice steps 3 and 4 of "Measure the Volume of a Liquid," using other equal volumes, to visualize the same volume in two different containers.

Have students "Find the Volume of a Solid" by the displacement of water. Ask:

- **How can you measure the volume of a marble?** (Measure an amount of water in a graduated cylinder. Place the marble in the cylinder. Measure the new water level. Subtract the water level with the marble from the water level without the marble to find the marble's volume.)

WRITING LINK

Students may write about what they have learned about measuring volume.

Informal Assessment

Tell students to pour about 200 mL of water into an unmarked cup without measuring. Then have them measure to find out how close their estimate was. (Students should measure volumes to the nearest milliliter.)

Measure Weight/Force

Build on Prior Knowledge
Ask students if they have ever used a bathroom scale.

■ **What unit of measure is used on a bathroom scale?** (pounds or kilograms)

Developing the Main Idea
Explain that a spring scale measures weight in newtons (N). There are about 4.5 N in 1 pound.

Exploring the Main Idea
Ask students if they could find their weight with a spring scale like this one? (No, the scale can only be used for objects up to 20 newtons, or about 5 pounds.)

WRITING LINK

Students may write about weighing objects using a spring scale.

Informal Assessment
Ask:

■ **How is a spring scale like a pan balance? How are they different?** (They are both measurement tools; the pan balance compares two masses; the spring scale gives weight as a number.)

Make Measurements

Measure Weight/Force

You use a spring scale to measure weight. An object has weight because the force of gravity pulls down on the object. Therefore, weight is a force. Weight is measured in newtons (N) like all forces.

Measure the Weight of an Object

1. Look at your spring scale to see how many newtons it measures. See how the measurements are divided. The spring scale shown here measures up to 5 N. It has a mark for every 0.1 N.
2. Hold the spring scale by the top loop. Put the object to be measured on the bottom hook. If the object will not stay on the hook, place it in a net bag. Then hang the bag from the hook.
3. Let go of the object slowly. It will pull down on a spring inside the scale. The spring is connected to a pointer. The pointer on the spring scale shown here is a small bar.
4. Wait for the pointer to stop moving. Read the number of newtons next to the pointer. This is the object's weight. The mug in the picture weighs 4 N.

More About Spring Scales

You probably weigh yourself by standing on a bathroom scale. This is a spring scale. The force of your body stretches a spring inside the scale. The dial on the scale is probably marked in pounds—the English unit of weight. One pound is equal to about 4.5 newtons.

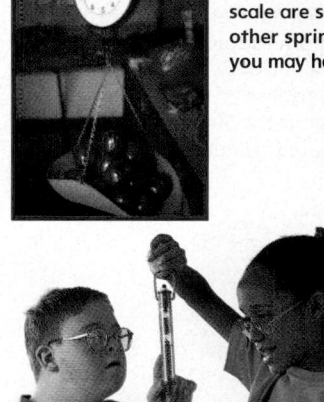

A bathroom scale, a grocery scale, and a kitchen scale are some other spring scales you may have seen.

Science Background

Weight

Weight is the pull of gravity on an object. Mass and weight are connected, in that we can measure weight to find mass. The newton is a derived unit in the metric system: one newton equals the force required to give one kilogram an acceleration of one meter per second. Students might practice converting familiar pound measures to newtons by multiplying by 4.5.

Make Measurements

Measure Temperature

You use a thermometer to measure temperature—how hot or cold something is. A thermometer is made of a thin tube with colored liquid inside. When the liquid gets warmer, it expands and moves up the tube. When the liquid gets cooler, it contracts and moves down the tube. You may have seen most temperatures measured in degrees Fahrenheit (°F). Scientists measure temperature in degrees Celsius (°C).

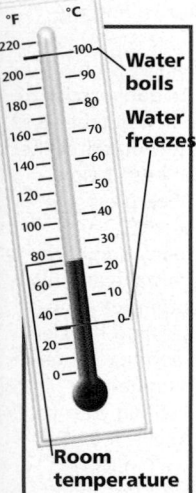

Water boils
Water freezes
Room temperature

Read a Thermometer

1. Look at the thermometer shown here. It has two scales—a Fahrenheit scale and a Celsius scale.
2. What is the temperature shown on the thermometer? At what temperature does water freeze?

What Is Convection?

1. Fill a large beaker about two-thirds full of cool water. Find the temperature of the water by holding a thermometer in the water. Do not let the bulb at the bottom of the thermometer touch the sides or bottom of the beaker.
2. Keep the thermometer in the water until the liquid in the tube stops moving—about 1 minute. Read and record the temperature in °C.
3. Sprinkle a little fish food on the surface of the water in the beaker. Do not knock the beaker, and most of the food will stay on top.
4. Carefully place the beaker on a hot plate. A hot plate is a small electric stove. Plug in the hot plate, and turn the control knob to a middle setting.
5. After 1 minute measure the temperature of water near the bottom of the beaker. At the same time, a classmate should measure the temperature of water near the top of the beaker. Record these temperatures. Is water near the bottom of the beaker heating up faster than near the top?
6. As the water heats up, notice what happens to the fish food. How do you know that warmer water at the bottom of the beaker rises and cooler water at the top sinks?

Science Background

Temperature Scales

Two common scales for measuring temperature are the Fahrenheit and Celsius scales. In the Celsius scale, each degree is $\frac{1}{100}$ of the difference between the temperature of melting ice and boiling water. In the Fahrenheit scale, each degree is $\frac{1}{180}$ of this difference.

Measure Temperature

Measure Temperature

Objective

- Use thermometers to measure temperature.

Build on Prior Knowledge

Ask students what the outside temperature is. What tool is used to measure temperature? (a thermometer)

Developing the Main Idea

Point out that there are two scales on the thermometer, one for Fahrenheit and one for Celsius.

Using the Illustrations

Have students look at the diagram of the thermometer. Ask:

- **At what temperature does water boil?** (212°F, 100°C)
- **At what temperature does water freeze?** (32°F, 0°C)

Exploring the Main Idea

As students do the convection activity, they will find that at first, in step 5, the water is heated faster at the bottom. In minutes, however, that is, in step 6, they will see the fish food spread out and move down to the bottom and then rise in a continuous current. The heated water rises, cools at the surface and sinks, bring the fish food along.

WRITING LINK

Students may write about measuring temperature.

Informal Assessment

Ask:

- **A student measured a temperature and reported it was 35 degrees. Why is this not a complete measurement?** (The student must record whether the temperature was in Fahrenheit or Celsius.)

Use Calculators

■ Use calculators to analyze collected data.

Build on Prior Knowledge

Have students share experiences using calculators. Ask:

■ **Why do you sometimes get the wrong answer when using a calculator?** (The numbers are not entered correctly; the wrong operation was chosen.)

Developing the Main Idea

Explain that students will practice using a calculator, first, to add a list of numbers, and second, to find the average or mean.

Ask students to read the left column on page R12. Ask:

■ **How can you find the total amount of rain that fell over the 11 weeks?** (Add the numbers in the second column.)

Exploring the Main Idea

Have students work in pairs to complete the steps of the "Find the Mean" activity. One student can read off the numbers while the other enters them. Before they do step 4, the division, they might estimate what the average rainfall per week might be (by scanning through the numbers in the Rain column of the table).

Ask students to generalize a method that they could use to find the mean of any set of numbers. (Find the total of a set of numbers. Divide the total by the number of members of the set.)

Use Calculators

Sometimes after you make measurements, you have to analyze your data to see what it means. This might involve doing calculations with your data. A calculator helps you do time-consuming calculations.

Find an Average

After you collect a set of measurements, you may want to get an idea of a typical measurement in that set. What if, for example, you are doing a weather project? As part of the project, you are studying rainfall data of a nearby town. The table shows how much rain fell in that town each week during the summer.

Week	Rain (cm)
1	2.0
2	1.4
3	0.0
4	0.5
5	1.2
6	2.5
7	1.8
8	1.4
9	2.4
10	8.6
11	7.5

What if you want to get an idea of how much rain fell during a typical week in the summer? In other words, you want to find the average for the set of data. There are three kinds of averages—mean, median, and mode. Does it matter which one you use?

Find the Mean

The mean is what most people think of when they hear the word *average*. You can use a calculator to find the mean.

1. Make sure the calculator is on.
2. Add the numbers. To add a series of numbers, enter the first number and press ⊞. Repeat until you enter the last number. See the hints below. After your last number, press ⊟. Your total should be 29.3.
3. While entering so many numbers, it's easy to make a mistake and hit the wrong key. If you make a mistake, correct it by pressing the clear entry key, CE. Then continue entering the rest of the numbers.
4. Find the mean by dividing your total by the number of weeks. If 29.3 is displayed, press ⊟ 1 1 ⊟. Rounded up to one decimal point, your mean should be 2.7.

Hints:
• If the only number to the right of the decimal point is 0, you don't have to enter it into the calculator. To enter 2.0, just press 2.
• If the only number to the left of the decimal point is 0, you don't have to enter it into the calculator. To enter 0.5, just press . 5.

Inclusion

Calculators

Calculators are used in scientific work to perform basic computation. They are particularly useful with long lists of quantitative data. They can help analyze data to find averages (means) and percents of totals. Means that students might look for as they study science include mean number of corn kernels of different colors; mean number of students with attached or unattached earlobes; mean lengths of leaves of a given tree when studying variation; mean magnitude of earthquakes in a given area; mean time it takes water to seep through a soil sample; mean distance or time measured when studying speed or acceleration. Have students measure and tabulate student heights and find the mean, medium, and mode. **Logical**

Use Technology

Find the Median

The median is the middle number when the numbers are arranged in order of size. When the rainfall measurements are arranged in order of size, they look like this.

0.0
0.5
1.2
1.4
1.4
1.8 ——— The median is 1.8. This number is in the middle; there are five numbers above it and five numbers below it.
2.0
2.4
2.5
7.5
8.6

Find the Mode

The mode is the number that occurs most frequently. From the ranked set of data above, you can see that the most frequent number is 1.4. It occurs twice. Here are your three different averages from the same set of data.

Average Weekly Rainfall (cm)

Mean	2.7
Median	1.8
Mode	1.4

Why is the mean so much higher than the median or mode? The mean is affected greatly by the last two weeks when it rained a lot. A typical week for that summer was much drier than either of those last two weeks. The median or mode gives a better idea of rainfall for a typical week.

Find the Mean, Median, and Mode

The table shows the length of 15 peanuts. Find the mean, median, and mode for this set of data. Which do you think best represents a typical peanut?

Peanut	Length (mm)
1	32
2	29
3	30
4	31
5	33
6	26
7	28
8	27
9	29
10	29
11	32
12	31
13	23
14	36
15	31

Find the Percent

Sometimes numbers are given as percents (%). *Percent* literally means "per hundred." For example, 28% means 28 out of 100. What if there are about 14,000 trees in the forest and 28% are over 50 years old? How many of them are over 50 years old? Use your calculator. You want to find 28% of 14,000. Press 1 4 0 0 0 × 2 8 %. The answer should be 3,920.

R 13

Inclusion

Range

Another way to analyze data is to find the range, the difference between the greatest and least numbers in a set. Students can use calculators to find the range of the rainfall data on page R12 and the peanut lengths on page R13. Point out that ordering the numbers helps to find the greatest and least numbers. (rainfall = 8.6 − 0.0 = 8.6; peanut length = 36 − 23 = 13)

Logical

Developing the Main Idea

Have students read "Find the Median". Explain that this is not a calculator activity, but is another way of finding the "center" of the data. Ask:

■ **How is this list of numbers like or unlike the rainfall numbers listed on page R12?** (They are the same numbers, but listed in order from least to greatest, top to bottom.)

Exploring the Main Idea

Have students generalize a method for finding the median. (List a set of numbers in order. If there is an odd number of numbers, the middle number is the median. If there is an even number of numbers, the median is the average (mean) of the two middle numbers.)

Developing the Main Idea

Have students read "Find the Mode". Point out again that this is not a calculator activity.

■ **Does every set of numbers have a mode?** (No; for example, if every number appears once in a set, there is no mode.)

Have students read "Find the Mean, Median, and Mode" and discuss how to find each number and note which can be found by using a calculator. (finding the mean) Have them read "Find the Percent". Point out that another way to do the calculation is to express 28% as a decimal (0.28) and multiply 14,000 × 0.28 with the calculator.

WRITING LINK

Students may write about their experiences using a calculator.

Informal Assessment

Have students do "Find the Mean, Median, and Mode" on page R13. (mean = 29.8, median = 30, mode = 29)

Use Computers

It is recommended that students of this age access the Internet with adult supervision.

Build on Prior Knowledge
Have students share computer experiences such as using various application programs and writing or getting e-mail. Ask:

■ **How is using a computer like going to the library?** (Both are ways to find information.)

Developing the Main Idea
Explain that in this lesson students will learn about some different ways they can use computers to learn science.

Using the Illustrations
Have students read the top of page R14 and study the two photographs. Explain that a table on a computer can be created with a spreadsheet program. Ask:

■ **What kinds of information are these students putting into the computer?** (measurements they have made about the weather)

Use Technology

Use Computers

A computer has many uses. The Internet connects your computer to many other computers around the world, so you can collect all kinds of information. You can use a computer to show this information and write reports. Best of all you can use a computer to explore, discover, and learn.

You can also get information from CD-ROMs. They are computer disks that can hold large amounts of information. You can fit a whole encyclopedia on one CD-ROM.

Use Computers for a Project
Here is how one group of students uses computers as they work on a weather project.

1. The students use instruments to measure temperature, wind speed, wind direction, and other parts of the weather. They input this information, or data, into the computer. The students keep the data in a table. This helps them compare the data from one day to the next.

R 14

Inclusion

Using the Computer
Computer applications such as word processing and spreadsheets are useful in organizing scientific observations. Internet access is a relatively new tool for research. Have students discuss how they or their families use computers every day.
(Families use them in their cars, for banking, for doing many jobs at the workplace; students use them to find books at the library, and so on.) **Linguistic**

Use Technology

2. The teacher finds out that another group of students in a town 200 kilometers to the west is also doing a weather project. The two groups use the Internet to talk to each other and share data. When a storm happens in the town to the west, that group tells the other group that it's coming their way.

3. The students want to find out more. They decide to stay on the Internet and send questions to a local TV weather forecaster. She has a Web site and answers questions from students every day.

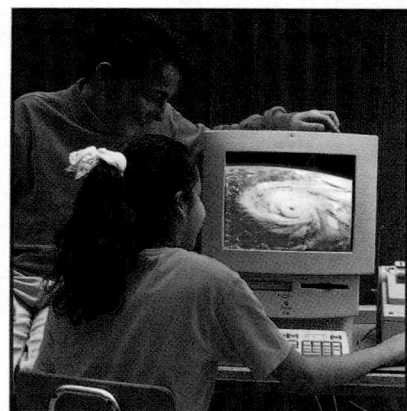

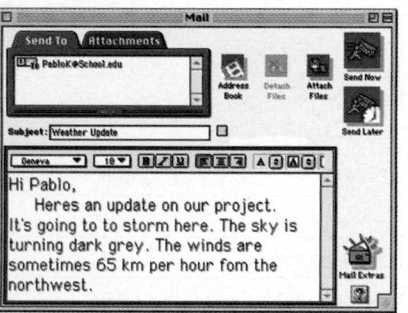

4. Meanwhile some students go to the library to gather more information from a CD-ROM. The CD-ROM has an encyclopedia that includes movie clips. The clips give examples of different kinds of storms.

5. The students have kept all their information in a folder called Weather Project. Now they use that information to write a report about the weather. On the computer they can move around paragraphs, add words, take out words, put in diagrams, and draw weather maps. Then they print the report in color.

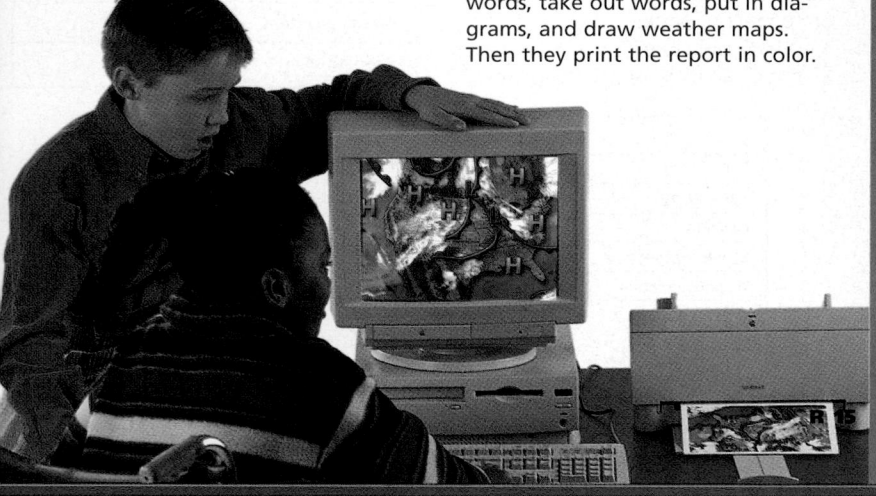

Inclusion

Birthdate Weather

Work with students to use the Internet to research weather patterns from the year and month they were born. Demonstrate to students how to perform keyword searches. They may want to narrow their searches as they research sites.

Linguistic

Using the Illustrations

Have students read page R15 and look at the illustration about e-mail. Ask:

■ **What is e-mail?** (a message you write or read that is sent from one computer to another computer)

■ **Why does a computer need to be hooked up to a telephone line for someone to get e-mail?** (The e-mail messages travel over the telephone lines from one place to another. Many newer e-mail systems do not require the use of telephone lines.)

Developing the Main Idea

Explain that using an on-line encyclopedia or looking for information on the Internet requires the use of key words. Ask:

■ **What key words would you use for a project about last year's weather in Virginia?** (Virginia and weather and the specific date)

WRITING LINK

Students may write about their experiences receiving and sending e-mail or using a computer for a school project.

Informal Assessment

Ask students to describe how a computer can be used to organize facts or to gather information for a project. (The computer can be used to make tables and graphs; a word processor can be used to write a report; an on-line encyclopedia or a Web-page search can provide facts and pictures.)

Make Graphs to Organize Data

Objective

- Compare graphs and choose one type to represent a set of data.

Build on Prior Knowledge

Take a class tally on favorite pizza toppings—students can vote only once—mushrooms, peppers, olives, or onions. Discuss different ways to collect and display the data, including graphs, posters, tables.

Using the Illustrations

Have students read page R16 and study the bar graph. Ask:

- **What are the parts of a bar graph?** (the bars, the two scales, the title, the labels on the two scales)

- **What do you do if a bar doesn't exactly meet one of the lines on a bar graph?** (Estimate the number the bar shows.)

Developing the Main Idea

Have students read the section about pictographs. Ask:

- **How is a pictograph different from a bar graph?** (A pictograph uses symbols; a bar graph uses bars.)

- **Why is the key important on a pictograph?** (It tells what each symbol on the graph stands for.)

Have students answer the questions in the text. (Bar graphs: 3 clips with 20 coils, 9 clips with 50 coils Pictographs: 1. Washing clothes; 2. Drinking)

Represent Data

Make Graphs to Organize Data

When you do an experiment in science, you collect information. To find out what your information means, you can organize it into graphs. There are many kinds of graphs.

Bar Graphs

A bar graph uses bars to show information. For example, what if you do an experiment by wrapping wire around a nail and connecting the ends of the wire to a battery? The nail then becomes a magnet that can pick up paper clips. The graph shows that the more you wrap the wire around the nail, the more paper clips it picks up. How many paper clips did the nail with 20 coils pick up? With 50 coils?

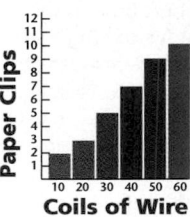

Pictographs

A pictograph uses symbols, or pictures, to show information. What if you collect information about how much water your family uses each day? The table shows what you find.

You can organize this information into the pictograph shown here. The pictograph has to explain what the symbol on the graph means. In this case each bottle means 20 liters of water. A half bottle means half of 20, or 10 liters of water.

1. Which activity uses the most water?
2. Which activity uses the least water?

Activity	Water Used Each Day (L)
Drinking	10
Showering	180
Bathing	240
Brushing teeth	80
Washing dishes	140
Washing hands	30
Washing clothes	280
Flushing toilet	90

A Family's Daily Use of Water — = 20 liters of water

Drinking	
Showering	
Bathing	
Brushing teeth	
Washing dishes	
Washing hands	
Washing clothes	
Flushing toilet	

R 16

Science Background

Graphs

Graphs are visual ways of representing quantitative data. Students can use graphs to identify relationships, make comparisons, and predict future occurrences. Often, more than one kind of graph can be used to display the same set of data. Different kinds of graphs can be used for different kinds of emphasis—such as to compare amounts or to show change over time.

Represent Data

Circle Graphs

A circle graph is helpful to show how a complete set of data is divided into parts. The circle graph here shows how water is used in the United States. What is the single largest use of water?

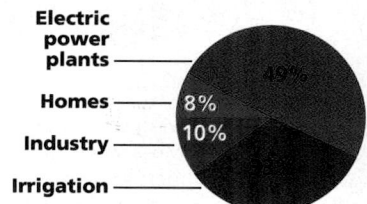

Electric power plants — 49%
Homes — 8%
Industry — 10%
Irrigation —

Line Graphs

A line graph shows information by connecting dots plotted on the graph. It shows change over time. For example, what if you measure the temperature out of doors every hour starting at 6 A.M.? The table shows what you find.

You can organize this information into a line graph. Follow these steps.

Time	Temperature (°C)
6 A.M.	10
7 A.M.	12
8 A.M.	14
9 A.M.	16
10 A.M.	18
11 A.M.	20

1. Make a scale along the bottom and side of the graph. The scales should include all the numbers in the chart. Label the scales.
2. Plot points on the graph. For example, place your finger at the "6 A.M." on the bottom line. Place a finger from your other hand on the "10" on the left line. Move your "6 A.M." finger up and your "10" finger to the right until they meet, and make a pencil point. Plot the other points in this way.
3. Connect the points with a line.

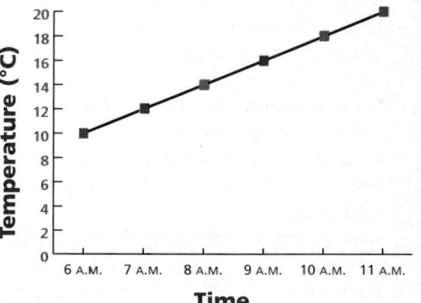

The line graph to the right organizes measurements you collected so that you can easily compare them.

1. Between which two weeks did the plant grow most?
2. When did plant growth begin to level off?

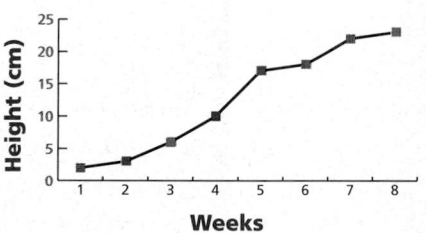

R 17

Developing the Main Idea

Read the circle graph information together. Point out that all the values can be represented as either fractions, decimals, or percents—that is, the individual pieces of data are converted to "parts of a whole", which are gotten by dividing one piece of data by the sum of all the data. The parts of the graph total 100% (or 1) The single largest use of water is electric power plants, 49%.

Exploring the Main Idea

Read the first line graph data together. Students may conclude that this kind of graph shows how one kind of data changes over time, such as weeks. Have students answer the questions. (1. Growth was greatest where the line is steepest, between weeks 4 and 5. 2. Growth levels off after week 7.)

WRITING LINK

Students may write about graphs they may have seen in newspapers or magazines.

Informal Assessment

Have students use the data from the pictograph section, "Water Used Each Day, " to make another kind of graph — circle, bar, or line. (Converting these data to percents is difficult since there is a wide range from small to large numbers and the total is 1,050. A bar graph can show the data as they are without converting them. Since there is no change over time involved, a line graph is inappropriate.)

SCIENCE FOR ALL

Inclusion

Graph It

This table sums up some of the medal winning countries at the 25th Summer Olympic Games:

Country	Number of Medals
Cuba	31
Hungary	30
South Korea	29
France	29
Australia	27
Spain	22

Have students choose a type of graph and make a graph of this information. **Logical; Spatial**

Make Maps to Show Information

Objective

- Read and make geographical maps and idea maps.

Build on Prior Knowledge

Have students share experiences about using road maps, then ask:

- **How is a road map like the area it represents? Different?** (Both show key features such as streets and important buildings. The map is smaller and not as detailed.)

Developing the Main Idea

Explain that students will use two kinds of maps. The first is like a road map. The second type of map is a way to show how ideas are related.

Using the Illustrations

Ask:

- **How can you indicate the location of the red building?** (Put your finger on the red building. Then move the finger *up* or *down* to the closest side of the map. Record the number. Then put your finger on the building again. Move the finger *across* to the closest side of the map. Record the letter.)

Exploring the Main Idea

Have students work in small groups to complete the first three exercises. (**1.** red; **2.** D1; **3.** Answers will vary.) Then have them look at the idea map about rocks. Explain that this kind of diagram can also be called a "map."

WRITING LINK

Students may write about how coordinates are used to locate places on road maps.

Informal Assessment

Have students make a map showing how to get to school from home. (Maps should include written instructions as well as sketches of major streets and buildings.)

Represent Data

Make Maps to Show Information

Locate Places

A map is a drawing that shows an area from above. Most maps have coordinates—numbers and letters along the top and side. Coordinates help you find places easily. For example, what if you wanted to find the library on the map? It is located at B4. Place a finger on the letter B along the side of the map, and another finger on the number 4 at the top. Then move your fingers straight across and down the map until they meet. The library is located where the coordinates B and 4 meet, or very nearby.

1. What color building is located at F6?
2. The hospital is located three blocks north and two blocks east of the library. What are its coordinates?
3. Make a map of an area in your community. It might be a park or the area between your home and school. Include coordinates. Use a compass to find north, and mark north on your map. Exchange maps with classmates, and answer each other's questions.

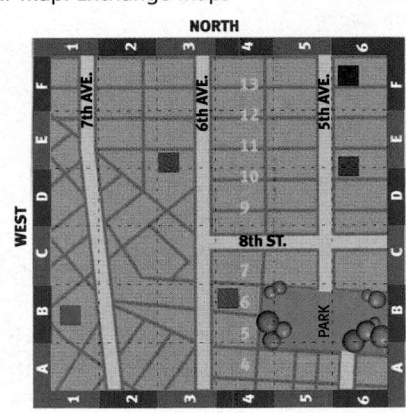

Idea Maps

The map below shows how places are connected to each other. Idea maps, on the other hand, show how ideas are connected to each other. Idea maps help you organize information about a topic.

The idea map above connects ideas about rocks. This map shows that there are three major types of rock—igneous, sedimentary, and metamorphic. Connections to each rock type provide further information. For example, this map reminds you that igneous rocks are classified into those that form at Earth's surface and far beneath it.

Make an idea map about a topic you are learning in science. Your map can include words, phrases, or even sentences. Arrange your map in a way that makes sense to you and helps you understand the ideas.

R 18

Advanced Learners

Maps

Explain that geographical maps are used to show key features of geographical areas. They can present other information, such as elevation. Have students locate countries on a world map and give coordinates of cities, using longitude in degrees East and West of the prime meridian and latitude in degrees North and South of the equator. **Spatial**

Make Tables and Charts to Organize Information

Tables help you organize data during experiments. Most tables have columns that run up and down, and rows that run across. The columns and rows have headings that tell you what kind of data goes in each part of the table.

A Sample Table

What if you are going to do an experiment to find out how long different kinds of seeds take to sprout? Before you begin the experiment, you should set up your table. Follow these steps.

1. In this experiment you will plant 20 radish seeds, 20 bean seeds, and 20 corn seeds. Your table must show how many radish seeds, bean seeds, and corn seeds sprouted on days 1, 2, 3, 4, and 5.

2. Make your table with columns, rows, and headings. You might use a computer to make a table. Some computer programs let you build a table with just the click of a mouse. You can delete or add columns and rows if you need to.
3. Give your table a title. Your table could look like the one here.

Make a Table

Now what if you are going to do an experiment to find out how temperature affects the sprouting of seeds? You will plant 20 bean seeds in each of two trays. You will keep each tray at a different temperature, as shown below, and observe the trays for seven days. Make a table you can use for this experiment.

Make a Chart

A chart is simply a table with pictures as well as words to label the rows or columns.

R19

Make Tables and Charts to Organize Information

Objective

■ Read and make tables and charts.

Build on Prior Knowledge

Write *cat*, *dog*, *fish*, *other* vertically on the board. Ask for three volunteers who have at least two pets. Write the students' names horizontally and use the data to make a simple table. Ask:

■ **How can you find how many dogs a particular student has?** (Find the number listed under the word dog next to the student's name in the table.)

Using the Illustrations

Have students read the first column on page R19 and study the sample table on the computer screen. Ask:

■ **What do the columns of this table show?** (number of seeds that sprout; Day 1, Day 2, Day 3, Day 4, Day 5)
■ **What do the rows show?** (radish seeds, bean seeds, corn seeds)
■ **How can you show that 12 corn seeds sprouted on the third day?** (Enter the number 12 in the corn seeds row under Day 3.)

Exploring the Main Idea

Have students carry out the "Make a Table" activity, the experiment with the 20 bean seeds. Ask:

■ **What will the columns in your table show?** (Answers will vary.)
■ **What will the rows show?** (Answers will vary.)

WRITING LINK

Students can write a description of information given in a table they find.

Informal Assessment

Ask:

■ **A student recorded the temperature for 5 days. Can the student make a table with these data?** (Yes, but the table will have only one row or column. Most tables have more.)

The Skeletal System - Joints

Objectives

- Explore the structure, function, and care of the skeleton and bones.
- Distinguish among three kinds of joints.

Build on Prior Knowledge

Have students discuss what they know about the parts of the body that support it and help it move. Ask:

- **What supports or holds up a building?** (steel or wood frame, concrete walls)
- **What supports your body?** (bones)
- **What happens if a bone is broken?** (It can't support the weight of the body around it.)
- **What do we call the place where bones meet, like at your elbow or knee?** (joint)

Developing the Main Idea

Invite students to suggest how their lives would be different if their bodies had no bones. (They wouldn't be able to sit, stand, or move and they'd have nothing to protect their hearts, lungs, or other organs inside their bodies.)

Using the Illustrations

Ask:

- **What is the name of the long bone at the top of the arm?** (humerus)
- **What is the long bone at the top of the leg?** (femur)
- **What is the name of the shoulder bone?** (clavicle)
- **What is the large bone that covers the head?** (skull)
- **What is the set of bones that goes up the back of the body?** (vertebrae)

HEALTH Handbook

The Skeletal System

The body has a supporting frame, called a skeleton, which is made up of bones. The skeleton has several jobs.

- It gives the body its shape.
- It protects organs in the body.
- It works with muscles to move the body.

Each of the 206 bones of the skeleton is the size and shape best fitted to do its job. For example, long and strong leg bones support the body's weight.

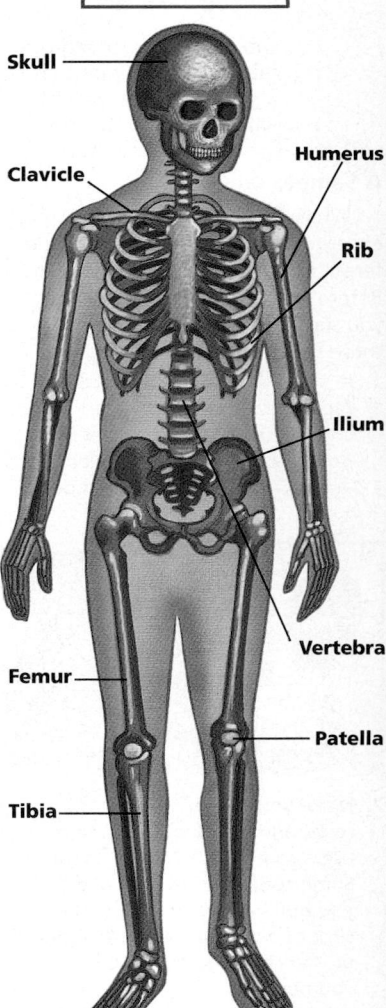

The Skeleton

Skull · Clavicle · Humerus · Rib · Ilium · Vertebra · Femur · Patella · Tibia

CARE!

- Exercise to keep your skeletal system in good shape.
- Don't overextend your joints.
- Eat foods rich in vitamins and minerals. Your bones need the minerals calcium and phosphorus to grow strong.

R 20

Science Background

Internal Skeletons

A skeleton gives a body shape, allows it to move, and protects its internal organs. Animals with internal skeletons and a backbone are called *vertebrates*. The group consists of mammals, birds, reptiles, amphibians, and fish. *Invertebrates* are animals without backbones. Some invertebrates, such as crustaceans and insects, have *exoskeletons,* or outer skeletons. Hard plates support the animals' bodies and protect the organs inside.

Joints

The skeleton has different types of joints. A joint is a place where two or more bones meet. Joints can be classified into three major groups— immovable joints, partly movable joints, and movable joints.

Types of Joints

Immovable Joints

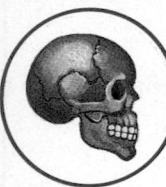

Head

Immovable joints are places where bones fit together too tightly to move. Nearly all the 29 bones in the skull meet at immovable joints. Only the lower jaw can move.

Partly Movable Joints

Partly movable joints are places where bones can move only a little. Ribs are connected to the breastbone with these joints.

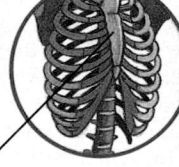

Breastbone

Ribs

Movable Joints

Movable joints are places where bones can move easily.

Gliding joint

Hand and wrist

Small bones in the wrists and ankles meet at gliding joints. The bones can slide against one another. These joints allow some movement in all directions.

Ball-and-socket joint

The hips are examples of ball-and-socket joints. The ball of one bone fits into the socket, or cup, of another bone. These joints allow bones to move back and forth, in a circle, and side to side.

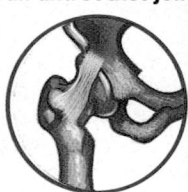

Hip

Hinge joint

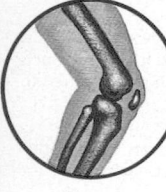

Knee

The knees are hinge joints. A hinge joint is similar to a door hinge. It allows bones to move back and forth in one direction.

Pivot joint

The joint between the skull and neck is a pivot joint. It allows the head to move up and down, and side to side.

Neck

R 21

Using the Illustrations
Ask:

- **What are the three kinds of joints?** (immovable, partly movable, movable)

- **Why are some joints immovable?** (bones fit together too tightly)

- **What kind of joints connect the ribs to the breastbone?** (partly movable)

- **What are the four different kinds of movable joints?** (gliding, ball-and-socket, hinge, pivot)

- **Which kind of movable joint do you think your elbow is?** (hinge) **your shoulder?** (ball-and-socket)

WRITING LINK

Have students write a description of how their bones and joints help them as they go to lunch, sit down, and eat.

Informal Assessment

Ask students to draw a skeleton showing a body in motion, then label as many bones and joints as possible without looking back at the illustrations on pages R20 and R21. Then, if necessary, allow students to complete their labeling using information from the diagrams.

Math MiniLesson

Measure the Angle

Develop Make a large circle-protractor to measure the motion of a joint. Tie a pencil to one end of a 20-cm length of string. Press the free end of the string with your thumb onto the center of a large piece of posterboard and draw a circle with the pencil by holding the string taut. Draw a straight line through the center of your circle. Use a small protractor to divide the large circle into 12 equal "pie pieces." Each piece = 30°.

To measure motion of the shoulder, one student ("the measurer") holds the large circle protractor with the center at a partner's shoulder. The partner moves the arm as far back as possible without straining or stretching. The measurer lines up a radius line on the protractor with the arm. Then the partner moves the arm forward and back as much as possible, without straining. The measurer notes how many pie pieces on the protractor are covered by the motion.

Inclusion

Angle Practice

Multiply the number of pie pieces by 30° and add any estimated portion of a pie piece, if the arm moved into part of a pie piece.

Find ways to measure the motion of each movable joint using the large circle protractor. Compare the amounts. (shoulder: 360°; hip: 50°-100°; elbow bending: 180°; elbow twisting: 250°-270°; head: 160°-180°; knee: 160°) **Spatial**

The Muscular System

Objective

- Explore the three kinds of muscles in the body: skeletal, cardiac, and smooth.

Build on Prior Knowledge

Discuss with students what they know about their muscles and how to take care of them. Ask:

- **How do muscles help you move?** (pull on bones in the skeleton)

- **Why are warm-up and cool-down exercises important?** (protect muscles from being over-stretched or being strained)

Developing the Main Idea

Invite students to discuss activities that their muscles help them perform and how they think muscles work to move bones. Ask a volunteer to use muscles that move body parts other than bones. (blinking eye, smiling mouth, wrinkling nose, and so on) Then ask:

- **What important muscle keeps blood pumping through your body?** (heart)

Using the Illustrations

Ask:

- **What are the names of the muscles in the upper arm?** (biceps and triceps)

- **What happens when a muscle contracts?** (It becomes shorter and thicker; it pulls on the bone it's attached to.)

WRITING LINK

Have students write detailed plans indicating how they'll care for their muscles, including kinds of exercise, food choices, and sleep and rest times.

Informal Assessment

Ask students to hold a book in one hand and hold that arm straight out in front of them. Have them put their other hands on the muscle of that upper arm (biceps). Discuss how the muscle feels, then have students lift their books up toward their shoulders. Ask:

- **What did you feel?** (Muscles shorten and bunch up.)

The Muscular System

Three types of muscles make up the body—skeletal muscle, cardiac muscle, and smooth muscle.

The muscles that are attached to and move bones are called skeletal muscles. These muscles are attached to bones by a tough cord called a tendon. Skeletal muscles pull bones to move them. Muscles do not push bones.

Cardiac muscles are found in only one place in the body—the heart. The walls of the heart are made of strong cardiac muscles. When cardiac muscles contract, they squeeze blood out of the heart. When cardiac muscles relax, the heart fills with more blood.

Smooth muscles make up internal organs and blood vessels. Smooth muscles in the lungs help a person breathe. Those in the blood vessels help control blood flow around the body.

CARE!

- Exercise to strengthen your muscles.
- Eat the right foods.
- Get plenty of rest.
- Never take steroids unless your doctor tells you to.

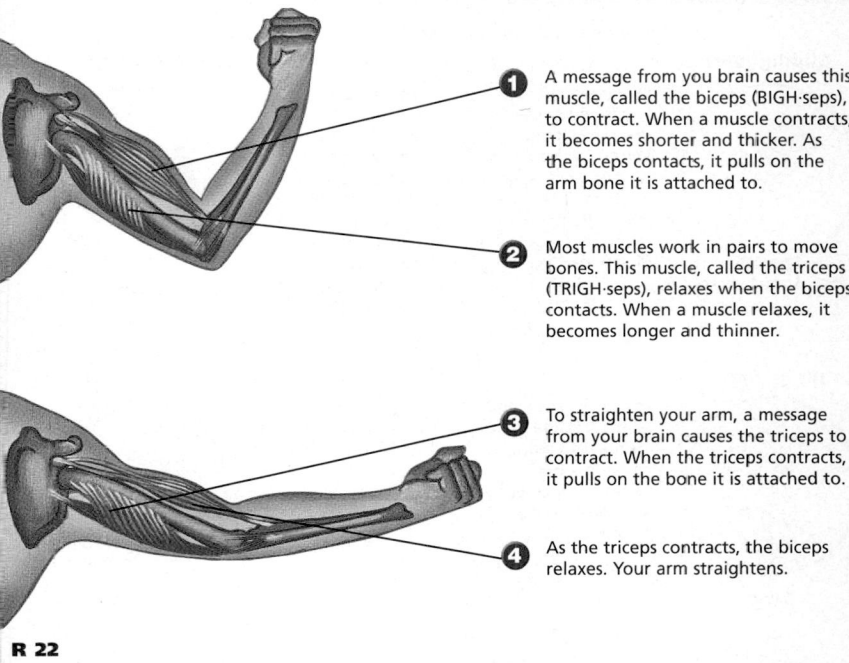

1 A message from you brain causes this muscle, called the biceps (BIGH-seps), to contract. When a muscle contracts, it becomes shorter and thicker. As the biceps contacts, it pulls on the arm bone it is attached to.

2 Most muscles work in pairs to move bones. This muscle, called the triceps (TRIGH-seps), relaxes when the biceps contacts. When a muscle relaxes, it becomes longer and thinner.

3 To straighten your arm, a message from your brain causes the triceps to contract. When the triceps contracts, it pulls on the bone it is attached to.

4 As the triceps contracts, the biceps relaxes. Your arm straightens.

R 22

 Science Background

Muscles

Most skeletal muscles move in pairs. As one muscle in a pair contracts, the other relaxes. The contracting muscle pulls on the bone to which it's attached by a tendon. Cardiac muscles pump blood, and smooth muscles make up our internal organs. We sit on the largest muscle in the body, the *gluteus maximus*, which also helps us run, jump, and climb. The smallest muscle, the *stapedius,* is inside the ear. It protects our ears from loud sounds.

The Circulatory System

The circulatory system consists of the heart, blood vessels, and blood. Circulation is the flow of blood through the body. Blood is a liquid that contains red blood cells, white blood cells, and platelets. Red blood cells carry oxygen and nutrients to cells. White blood cells work to fight germs that enter the body. Platelets are cell fragments that make the blood clot.

The heart is a muscular organ about the size of a fist. It beats about 70 to 90 times a minute, pumping blood through the blood vessels. Arteries carry blood away from the heart. Some arteries carry blood to the lungs, where the cells pick up oxygen. Other arteries carry oxygen-rich blood from the lungs to all other parts of the body. Veins carry blood from other parts of the body back to the heart. Blood in most veins carries the wastes released by cells and has little oxygen. Blood flows from arteries to veins through narrow vessels called capillaries.

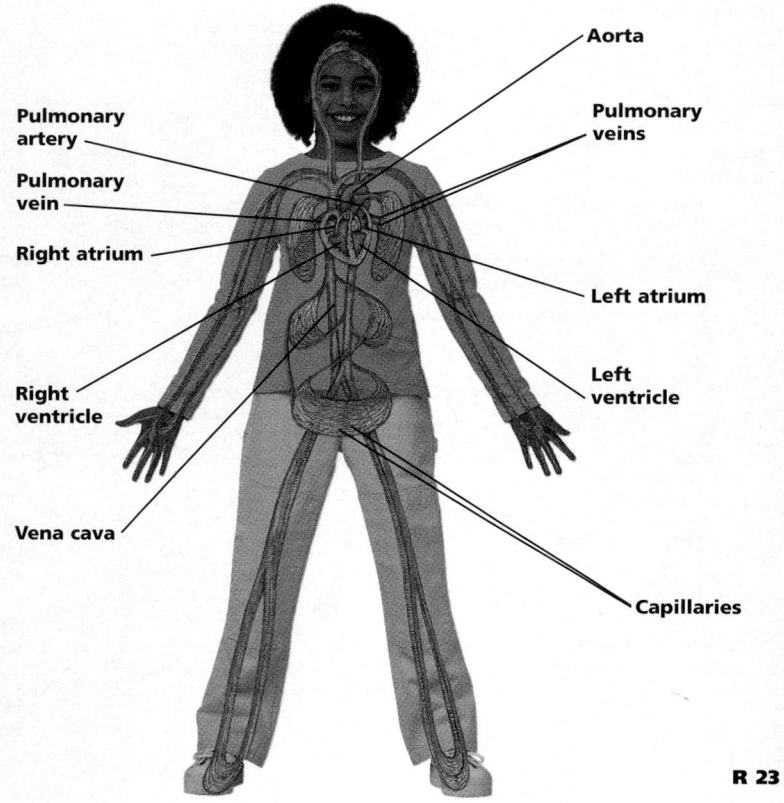

Aorta

Pulmonary artery

Pulmonary vein

Right atrium

Pulmonary veins

Left atrium

Left ventricle

Right ventricle

Vena cava

Capillaries

R 23

Science Background

The Circulatory System

The circulatory system includes the heart, blood, and blood vessels. Blood is made of red and white blood cells and platelets, or cell fragments. These platelets collect at a point where there is a wound and form a clot. White blood cells that fight germs also come to the wound site to fight infection. Blood flows from and back to the heart through arteries, veins, and capillaries. Red blood cells follow the flow, bringing oxygen and nutrients to cells in the body.

The Circulatory System

Objective

- Explore the circulatory system, including the heart and the parts of and functions of blood.

Build on Prior Knowledge
Have students discuss what they know about how blood moves throughout their bodies. Ask:

- **What is the muscle that pumps blood through your body?** (heart) **How big do you think the heart is?** (about the size of a fist)

Have students examine the veins in the backs of their hands. Point out that these blood vessels are returning blood *to* the heart. Then have students locate the blood vessel on the wrist that's used to check the pulse. Stress that this blood vessel carries blood *from* the heart.

Developing the Main Idea
Ask:

- **What's in blood?** (red and white blood cells, platelets)

- **How often does the heart beat?** (about 70-90 times per minute)

- **Which blood vessels carry blood away from the heart?** (arteries)

- **What are capillaries?** (narrow vessels that connect arteries and veins)

Using the Illustrations
Discuss with students the various parts of the diagram. Ask:

- **What does the diagram show?** (part of the circulatory system)

- **What are the tubelike parts in the circulatory system?** (blood vessels)

Continue the lesson on p. R24.

The Heart

Developing the Main Idea

This discussion of the heart continues the lesson on the circulatory system from p. R23. Ask:

- **What separates the two sides of the heart?** (wall of thick muscle)

- **Where does the pulmonary artery carry blood?** (to the lungs)

- **How does the nicotine in tobacco affect the heart?** (makes the heart beat faster and work harder to pump blood)

Using the Illustrations

When students read the labels, they have to place the book onto their chests so that "right" will be on their right side and "left" will be on their left side. Ask:

- **What is the upper right chamber called?** (right atrium)

- **What is the lower left chamber called?** (left ventricle)

- **What are the two veins near the top of the heart called?** (pulmonary veins)

- **Where do they lead?** (from the lungs to the heart)

WRITING LINK

Invite students to imagine they are a drop of blood and describe their trip through the heart, out an artery, and back again through a vein.

Informal Assessment

Ask students to describe in their own words, or draw and label a sketch to show, how blood circulates through the body.

Technology

- **Science Newsroom CD-ROM** Have students use *We Got the Beat* to learn more about the heart and the circulatory system.

The Heart

The heart has two sides, right and left, separated by a thick muscular wall. Each side has two chambers for blood. The upper chamber is the atrium. The lower chamber is the ventricle. Blood enters the heart through the vena cava. It leaves the heart through the aorta.

The pulmonary artery carries blood from the body into the lungs. Here carbon dioxide leaves the blood to be exhaled by the lungs. Fresh oxygen enters the blood to be carried to every cell in the body. Blood returns from the lungs to the heart through the pulmonary veins.

CARE!

- Don't smoke. The nicotine in tobacco makes the heart beat faster and work harder to pump blood.

- Never take illegal drugs, such as cocaine or heroin. They can damage the heart and cause heart failure.

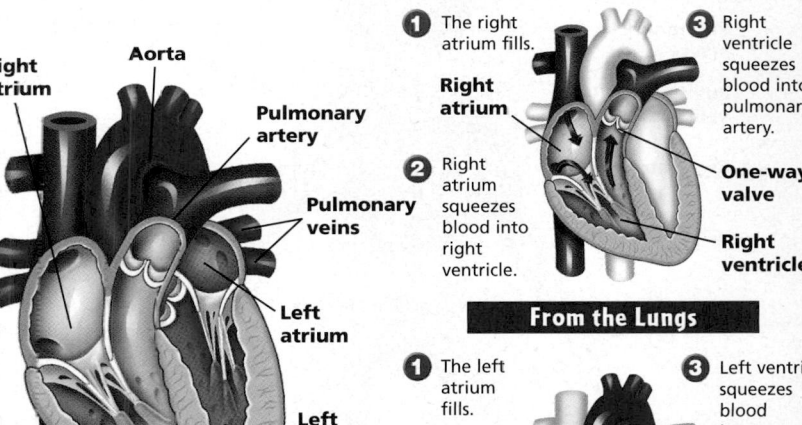

How the Heart Works

- Right atrium
- Aorta
- Pulmonary artery
- Pulmonary veins
- Left atrium
- Left ventricle
- Vena cava
- Right ventricle
- Muscle wall

To the Lungs

1. The right atrium fills.
2. Right atrium squeezes blood into right ventricle.
3. Right ventricle squeezes blood into pulmonary artery.
- Right atrium
- One-way valve
- Right ventricle

From the Lungs

1. The left atrium fills.
2. Left atrium squeezes blood into left ventricle.
3. Left ventricle squeezes blood into aorta.
- Left atrium
- One-way valve
- Left ventricle

R 24

Science Background

The Heart

The human heart is a four-chambered double pump that circulates blood. The top two chambers, the atria, receive blood. The bottom two chambers, or ventricles, pump blood out of the heart. Blood loaded with carbon dioxide arrives in the right atrium from all parts of the body. From there it flows to the right ventricle and is pumped to the lungs, where the carbon dioxide is exchanged for oxygen. Then the oxygen-rich blood returns to the left atrium of the heart, flows to the left ventricle, and is pumped to all parts of the body. The "thump-thump" we hear when our hearts beat is the sound of closing valves. The first noise is made when valves close between the atria and the ventricles; the second is the sound of valves closing between the ventricles and the great vessels.

The Respiratory System

The process of getting and using oxygen in the body is called respiration. When a person inhales, air is pulled into the nose or mouth. The air travels down into the trachea. In the chest the trachea divides into two bronchial tubes. One bronchial tube enters each lung. Each bronchial tube branches into smaller tubes called bronchioles.

At the end of each bronchiole are tiny air sacs called alveoli. The alveoli exchange carbon dioxide for oxygen.

Oxygen comes from the air a person breathes. Two main muscles control breathing. One is located between the ribs. The other is a dome-shaped sheet of muscle called the diaphragm.

To inhale, the diaphragm contracts and pulls down. Other muscles pull the ribs up and out. This makes more room in the chest. Air rushes into the lungs and fills the space.

To exhale, the diaphragm relaxes and returns to its dome shape. The lungs get smaller and force the air out.

CARE!

- Don't smoke. Smoking damages your respiratory system.
- Exercise to strengthen your breathing muscles.
- If you ever have trouble breathing, tell an adult at once.

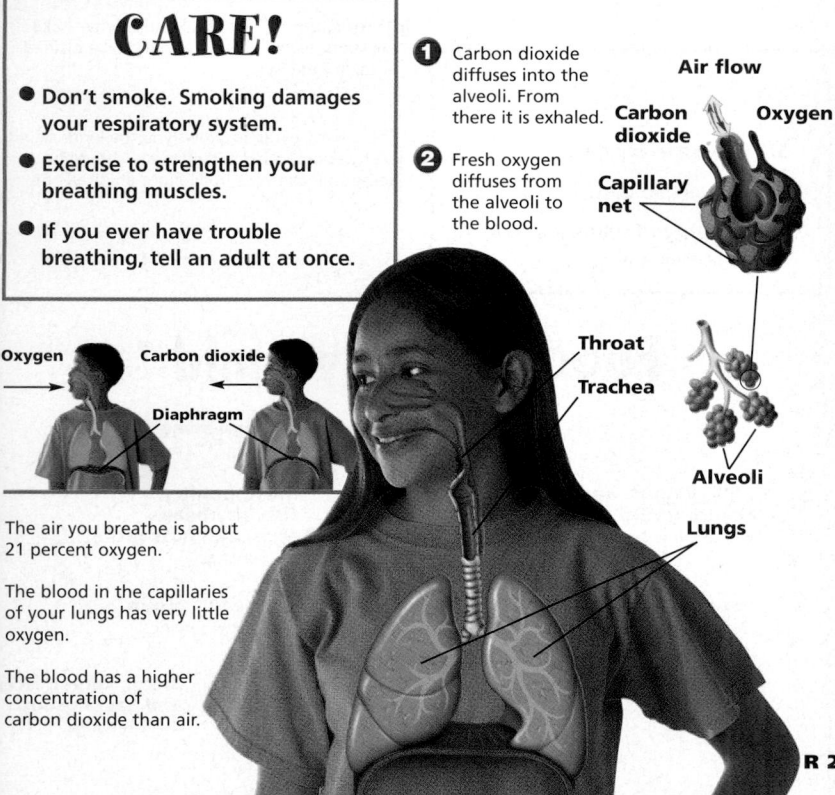

① Carbon dioxide diffuses into the alveoli. From there it is exhaled.

② Fresh oxygen diffuses from the alveoli to the blood.

Air flow

Carbon dioxide

Oxygen

Capillary net

Throat

Trachea

Alveoli

Lungs

Oxygen   Carbon dioxide

Diaphragm

The air you breathe is about 21 percent oxygen.

The blood in the capillaries of your lungs has very little oxygen.

The blood has a higher concentration of carbon dioxide than air.

R 25

Science Background

Breathing

The respiratory system includes the nose, mouth, trachea, bronchial tubes, alveoli, lungs, and the diaphragm, a sheet of muscle that's below the chest cavity, under the lungs, and above the abdomen. It's in the alveoli that carbon dioxide is exchanged for oxygen. Each lung has about 300 million alveoli that, if flattened out, would cover about 600 to 1,000 square feet (56 to 93 square meters). The lungs' total surface area is about 25 times that of the skin covering the body.

The Respiratory System

Objective

- Explore the parts of the respiratory system and what happens when we breathe.

Build on Prior Knowledge
Have students discuss what they know about breathing and why humans need to breathe.

Developing the Main Idea
Ask students to hold their breaths as long as possible, then ask:

- **Why did you finally have to take a breath?** (need oxygen)
- **How did the oxygen from the air get into your body?** (through nose or mouth)
- **What is the diaphragm?** (sheet of muscle)
- **What happens when the diaphragm relaxes?** (lungs get smaller; air forced out)

Using the Illustrations
Ask:

- **What parts of the respiratory system are shown in the diagrams?** (throat, trachea, lungs, alveoli, diaphragm)
- **Where's the diaphragm located?** (under the lungs)
- **What kind of gas comes out when you exhale?** (carbon dioxide)

WRITING LINK

Have students write public service announcements that would convince people not to smoke because it's harmful to their respiratory systems.

Informal Assessment
Ask students to use the diagrams on page R25 to describe in their own words how humans breathe.

Technology

- **Science Newsroom CD-ROM** Have students use *A Breath of Fresh Air* to learn more about the lungs.

Activity Pyramid
Food Guide Pyramid

Build on Prior Knowledge
Have students discuss what they know about how physical activities and food affect their health.

Developing the Main Idea
Have students list exercises and activities that build physical fitness. Invite them to jump in place, to discover how it affects their heart rates. Ask:

- **How does this help the body?** (Heart and lungs bring oxygen to the muscles and get rid of carbon dioxide.)

- **What kind of food might you eat to get energy to exercise?** (food high in vitamins; fruit; nuts)

Using the Illustrations
Ask:

- **What kind of activities should you only do occasionally?** (inactive ones)

- **What kind should you do 3-5 times a week?** (aerobic activities)

- **What kinds of foods should you eat most?** (bread, cereal, rice, and pasta) **least?** (fats, oils, and sweets)

- **In which group does carrots belong?** (Vegetable) **Where does candy belong?** (fats, oils, and sweets)

WRITING LINK

Ask students to plan a physically-fit day that includes different exercises and healthful foods. Suggest they prepare their plans as daily schedules and menus.

Informal Assessment
Ask each student what activities and foods he or she did or ate yesterday and how each contributes to physical fitness.

Activity Pyramid

Physical fitness is the condition in which the body is healthy and works the best it can. It involves working the skeletal muscles, bones, joints, heart, and respiratory system.

Occasionally Inactive pastimes such as watching TV, playing board games, talking on the phone

2–3 times a week Leisure activities such as gardening, golf, softball

3–5 times a week Aerobic activities such as swimming, biking, climbing; sports activities such as basketball, handball

Daily Substitute activity for inactivity—take the stairs, walk instead of riding, bike instead of taking the bus

The activity pyramid shows you the kinds of exercises and other activities you should be doing to make your body more physically fit.

CARE!

- Stay active every day.
- Eat a balanced diet.
- Drink plenty of water—6 to 8 large glasses a day.

Food Guide Pyramid

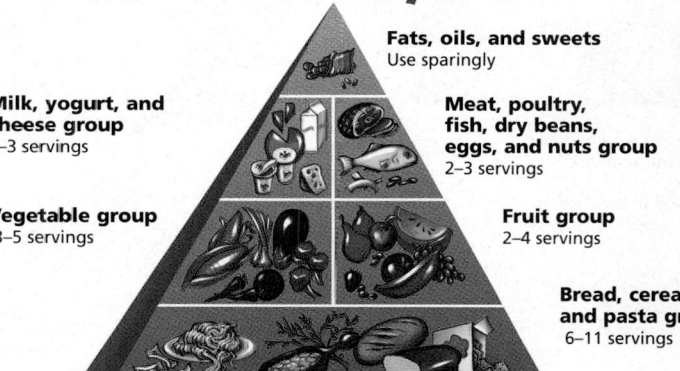

Fats, oils, and sweets Use sparingly

Milk, yogurt, and cheese group 2–3 servings

Meat, poultry, fish, dry beans, eggs, and nuts group 2–3 servings

Vegetable group 3–5 servings

Fruit group 2–4 servings

Bread, cereal, rice, and pasta group 6–11 servings

R 26

Science Background

Physical Fitness

In order to function optimally, a person needs a balance of exercise, rest, and a steady supply of food and water. Regular exercise and proper diet can delay the loss of muscle strength and the thinning of bones that come with age. The USDA Food Pyramid illustrates the amounts of different kinds of foods that we should eat daily. The higher an edible is on the food pyramid, the less of it we should eat. The higher a pastime is on the activity pyramid, the less we should do it!

The Digestive System

Digestion is the process of breaking down food into simple substances the body can use. Digestion begins when a person chews food. Chewing breaks the food down into smaller pieces and moistens it with saliva. Saliva is produced by the salivary glands.

Digested food is absorbed in the small intestine. The walls of the small intestine are lined with villi. Villi are tiny fingerlike projections that absorb digested food. From the villi the blood transports nutrients to every part of the body.

The shape of the small intestine's villi increases the amount of nutrients that can be absorbed from the food.

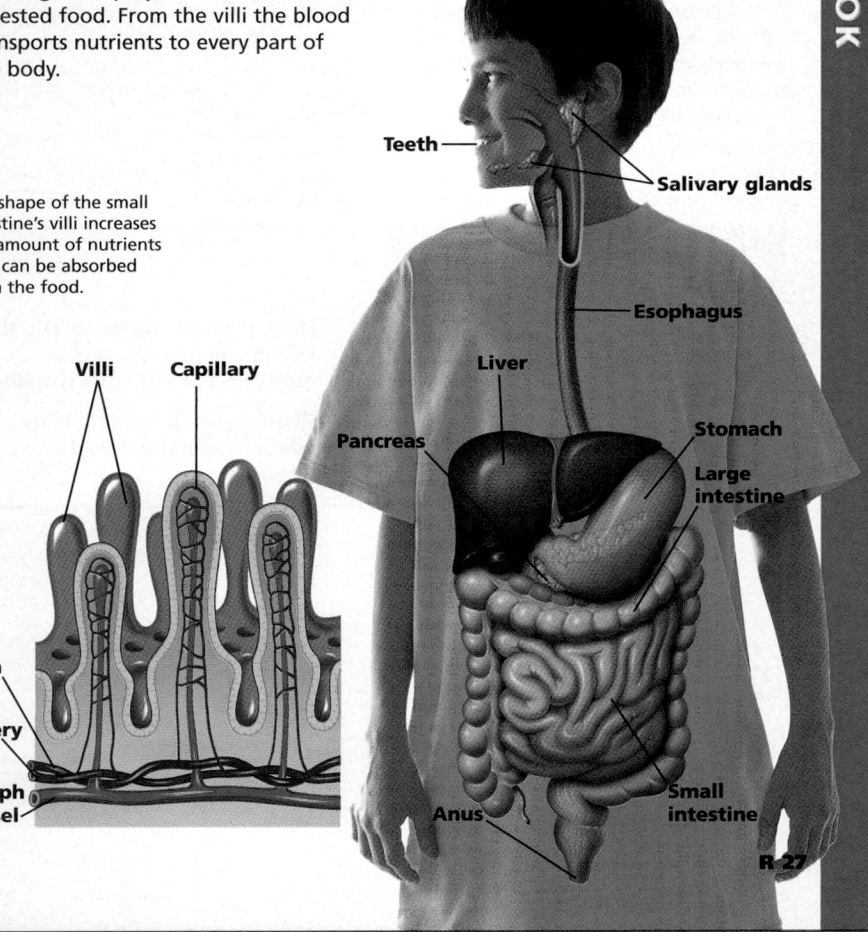

Teeth
Salivary glands
Esophagus
Liver
Pancreas
Stomach
Large intestine
Small intestine
Anus

Villi
Capillary
Vein
Artery
Lymph vessel

R-27

Science Background

Saliva and Digestion

Digestion, the process of breaking down food, begins in the mouth, where food is bitten, chewed, and softened by saliva. The saliva flows through tiny tubes into the mouth from glands under the tongue, in the lower jaw, and in the mouth below the ears. Sour, dry, and hard foods stimulate the flow of saliva and bitter foods make it thicker. Enzymes in saliva begin to break complex carbohydrates, such as those in a cracker, into simple sugars, thus changing the taste of the cracker.

The Digestive System

Objective

■ Explore how the digestive system breaks down food so that our bodies can use it.

Build on Prior Knowledge
Ask:

■ **What gives your body energy?** (food)

■ **Does food give you energy as soon as you put it into your mouth?** (No, it must be broken down so the body can use it.)

■ **How do your teeth help break down food?** (cut or mash large pieces into smaller bits)

Developing the Main Idea
Have students feel their teeth, then ask:

■ **Which teeth are shaped for biting or tearing off food? Which are shaped for mashing food?** (front, incisors; molars)

Using the Illustrations
Ask:

■ **What two things in the mouth start the digestive process?** (teeth and saliva)

■ **What is the tube that leads from the mouth to the stomach?** (esophagus)

■ **How does the absorbed digested food get from the villi to the rest of the body?** (through blood vessels)

WRITING LINK

Have students describe how life would change if they had no teeth or gums with which to chew or mash food to start the digestive process.

Informal Assessment
Ask students to explain in their own words what happens to food once it enters the mouth.

The Excretory System

Objective

- Explore how the body gets rid of wastes.

Build on Prior Knowledge

Ask:

- **What would happen if we never threw anything away?** (trash would pile up; have no room to live)

- **What kind of gas do we breathe out?** (carbon dioxide)

- **Is this one way our bodies get rid of waste?** (Yes.)

- **How else might our bodies get rid of wastes?** (through sweat, through the kidneys, through the intestine)

Developing the Main Idea

Remind students that during the digestive process the body takes what it needs from food and sends what it doesn't need to the intestines.

Using the Illustrations

Ask:

- **How does blood enter the kidneys?** (through an artery)

- **What do nephrons do?** (sort out wastes from useful nutrients)

- **What happens to the useful nutrients?** (flow back through veins)

- **Where is urine stored?** (in the bladder)

- **What are the small holes in skin called?** (pores)

WRITING LINK

Have students write about a very hot day that causes people to sweat a lot. Remind students to tell how people replace the lost moisture.

Informal Assessment

Ask students to explain in their own words what people should do to care for their excretory systems. (Drink plenty of water; keep the body clean.)

The Excretory System

Excretion is the process of removing waste products from the body. The liver filters wastes from the blood and converts them into urea. Urea is then carried to the kidneys for excretion. Each kidney contains more than a million nephrons. Nephrons are structures in the kidneys that filter blood.

The skin takes part in excretion when a person sweats. Glands in the inner layer of the skin produce sweat. Sweat is mostly water. Sweat tastes salty because it contains mineral salts the body doesn't need. There is also a tiny amount of urea in sweat.

Sweat is excreted by the sweat glands onto the outer layer of the skin. There it evaporates into the air. Evaporation takes place in part because of body heat. When sweat evaporates, a person feels cooler. On hot days or when exercising, a person sweats more to keep the body from overheating.

How You Sweat

Glands under your skin push sweat up to the surface, where it collects.

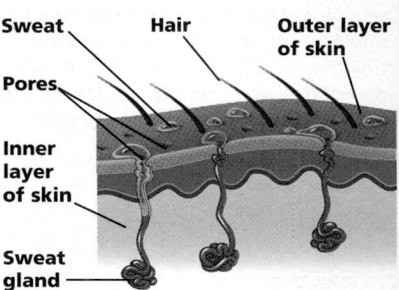

Sweat — Hair — Outer layer of skin

Pores

Inner layer of skin

Sweat gland

How Your Kidneys Work

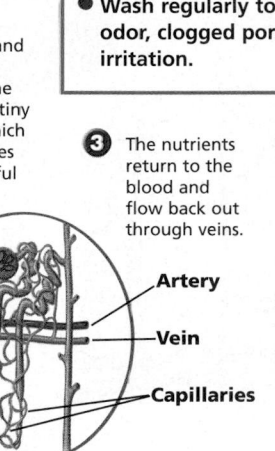

Kidneys

Ureters

Bladder

Urethra

R 28

1. Blood enters the kidney through an artery and flows into capillaries.

2. Sugars, salts, water, urea, and other wastes move from the capillaries to tiny nephrons, which sort out wastes from the useful nutrients.

3. The nutrients return to the blood and flow back out through veins.

4. Urea and other wastes become urine, which flows down the ureters.

5. Urine is stored in the bladder and excreted through the urethra.

Artery

Vein

Capillaries

CARE!

- Drink plenty of water to help the kidneys do their job and to replace water loss from sweating.

- Wash regularly to avoid body odor, clogged pores, and skin irritation.

Science Background

Water and the Body

The human body is mostly water that can be lost to sweat, respiration, and urine. The kidneys filter blood and separate out materials, recycling some back to the blood and turning others into urine. We must constantly replace the water to help our kidneys keep wastes moving out of our bodies. Our skin excretes wastes in the form of sweat. Sweat glands are found all over the body, but are concentrated in the armpits, palms of the hands, and soles of the feet.

The Nervous System

The nervous system has two parts. The brain and the spinal cord are the central nervous system. All other nerves are the outer, or peripheral, nervous system.

The largest part of the brain is the cerebrum. A deep groove separates the right half, or hemisphere, of the cerebrum from the left half. Both the right and left hemispheres of the cerebrum contain control centers for the senses.

The cerebellum lies below the cerebrum. It coordinates the skeletal muscles so they work smoothly together. It also helps in keeping balance.

The brain stem connects to the spinal cord. The lowest part of the brain stem is the medulla. It controls heartbeat, breathing, blood pressure, and the muscles in the digestive system.

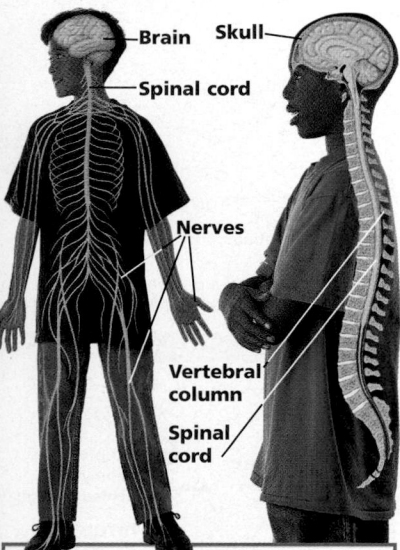

Brain — Skull
Spinal cord
Nerves
Vertebral column
Spinal cord

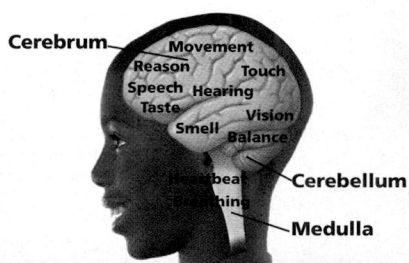

Cerebrum — Movement, Touch, Reason, Speech, Hearing, Taste, Vision, Smell, Balance, Heartbeat, Breathing
Cerebellum
Medulla

Parts of a Neuron

The nerves in the nervous system are made up of nerve cells called neurons. Each neuron has three main parts—a cell body, dendrites, and an axon. Dendrites are branching nerve fibers that carry impulses, or electrical signals, toward the cell body. An axon is a nerve fiber that carries impulses away from the cell body.

When an impulse reaches the tip of an axon, it must cross a tiny gap to reach the next neuron. This gap between neurons is called a synapse.

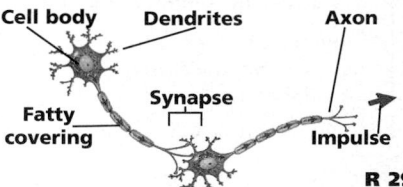

Cell body   Dendrites   Axon
Synapse
Fatty covering   Impulse

R 29

CARE!

- Wear protective headgear when you play sports or exercise.
- Stay away from drugs, such as stimulants, which can speed up the nervous system.
- Stay away from alcohol, which is a depressant and slows down the nervous system.

The Nervous System

Objective

- Explore the nature and care of the body's nervous system.

Build on Prior Knowledge
Ask:

- **What part of your body helps you know and understand things?** (brain)
- **How could your brain make your leg move?** (by sending a message along nerves to the leg muscles)

Developing the Main Idea
Explain to students that in this section they'll discover that their bodies actually produce electricity—electrical signals that relay messages between the brain and other body parts. Then ask:

- **What are the parts of the central nervous system?** (brain, spinal cord)
- **What are neurons?** (nerve cells)
- **What is the gap between neurons?** (synapse)

Using the Illustrations
Ask:

- **What protects the spinal cord?** (vertebral column)
- **Which part of the brain controls the five senses—taste, smell, touch, hearing, vision?** (cerebrum)
- **What are the long fibers between nerve cells?** (axons)

WRITING LINK

Have students make a flowchart showing how the nervous system gets a message to the brain. (Receptor cells send signals to the brain where they are interpreted and an action taken.)

Informal Assessment
Ask students to name the parts of the central nervous system.

Science Background

Nerves

Electrical signals (impulses) travel between the body and the brain along neurons, each having a cell body, dendrites, and an axon. The three types of neurons are sensory, associative, and motor. For example if you stub your toe, sensory neurons immediately send a message to associative neurons in your spinal cord and brain, where the message is interpreted and conveyed to motor neurons that make you hop on one foot and say "Ow!"

The Senses

Objective

- Explore the workings and care of the five senses.

Build on Prior Knowledge

You may wish to review the nervous system on p. R29. Ask:

- **What are the five senses?** (see, hear, touch, taste, smell)

- **How does your body let you know if something is hot to the touch?** (Nerve endings in your fingers send a message to your brain.)

Developing the Main Idea

Explain to students that in this section they'll discover just how their five senses work to give them information. Add that the senses involve nerves that relay messages to the brain.

Read page R30 with students, then ask:

- **Where are the receptor cells in the eye?** (on the retina)

- **How do signals from the receptor cells get to the brain?** (along the optic nerve)

- **What is the nerve in the ear that carries impulses to the brain?** (auditory nerve)

- **How can you protect your eyes and ears?** (Avoid eye strain from watching too much TV, sitting too close to the TV or computer screen, or reading in an area that's not well lighted. Avoid loud noises, protect ears with headphones and listen to music with volume turned down.)

Using the Illustrations

Ask:

- **What are the six parts of the eye?** (cornea, pupil, lens, iris, retina, optic nerve)

- **Why does your eye bend light?** (so it will hit the retina)

- **Where does the optic nerve take the impulses?** (the seeing center of the brain)

- **What are the three tiny ear bones that vibrate?** (hammer, anvil, stirrup)

- **To which part of the ear is the auditory nerve connected?** (cochlea)

- **Where does the auditory nerve send the impulses?** (the hearing center of the brain)

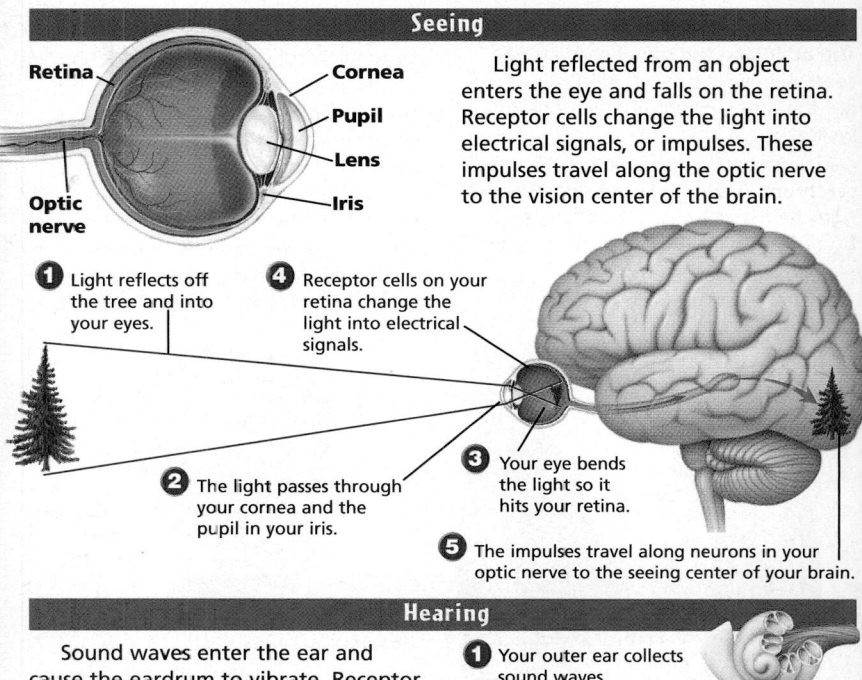

The Senses

Seeing

Retina, Cornea, Pupil, Lens, Optic nerve, Iris

Light reflected from an object enters the eye and falls on the retina. Receptor cells change the light into electrical signals, or impulses. These impulses travel along the optic nerve to the vision center of the brain.

1. Light reflects off the tree and into your eyes.
2. The light passes through your cornea and the pupil in your iris.
3. Your eye bends the light so it hits your retina.
4. Receptor cells on your retina change the light into electrical signals.
5. The impulses travel along neurons in your optic nerve to the seeing center of your brain.

Hearing

Sound waves enter the ear and cause the eardrum to vibrate. Receptor cells in the ear change the sound waves into impulses that travel along the auditory nerve to the hearing center of the brain.

Hammer, Anvil, Stirrup, Cochlea, Auditory nerve, Semicircular canals

1. Your outer ear collects sound waves.
2. They are funneled down your ear canal.
3. The eardrum vibrates.
4. Three tiny ear bones vibrate.
5. The cochlea vibrates.
6. Receptor cells inside your cochlea change.
7. The impulses travel along your auditory nerve to the brain's hearing center.

CARE!

- To avoid straining your eye muscles, don't sit too close to the TV screen or computer monitor.
- Avoid loud music. Turn down the volume when wearing headphones.

R 30

Science Background

Seeing and Hearing

Each sensory organ contains receptors that convert stimuli from the environment into electrical impulses that are carried to specific regions of the brain, where they are interpreted. The visual cortex, or sight center, of the brain interprets shapes and colors to help us identify things we see. The auditory cortex, or hearing center, of the brain receives sounds and identifies them by comparing them with sound patterns in our memory banks.

The Senses

Smelling

The sense of smell is really the ability to detect chemicals in the air. When a person breathes, chemicals dissolve in mucus in the upper part of the nose. When the chemicals come in contact with receptor cells, the cells send impulses along the olfactory nerve to the smelling center of the brain.

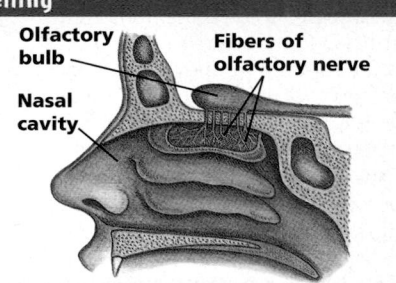

Olfactory bulb
Fibers of olfactory nerve
Nasal cavity

Tasting

When a person eats, chemicals in food dissolve in saliva. Saliva carries the chemicals to taste buds on the tongue. Inside each taste bud are receptors that can sense the four main tastes—sweet, sour, salty, and bitter. The receptors send impulses along a nerve to the taste center of the brain. The brain identifies the taste of the food, which is usually a combination of the four main tastes.

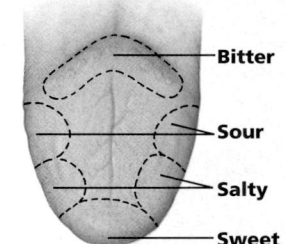

Bitter
Sour
Salty
Sweet

Touching

Receptor cells in the skin help a person tell hot from cold, wet from dry, and the light touch of a feather from the pressure of stepping on a stone. Each receptor cell sends impulses along sensory nerves to the spinal cord. The spinal cord then sends the impulses to the touch center of the brain.

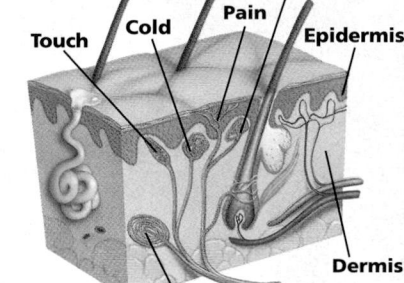

Touch   Cold   Pain   Heat
Epidermis
Dermis
Pressure

CARE!

● To prevent the spread of germs, always cover your mouth and nose when you cough or sneeze.

R 31

Science Background

Smell, Taste, and Touch

Our bodies are constantly collecting information from external stimuli. When we smell something, chemicals dissolved in mucus contact the nose's receptor cells that send a message to the brain's smelling center for interpretation. When we eat, food chemicals stimulate receptors in taste buds that contact the taste center of the brain. When we feel something, receptors in the skin send impulses to the spinal cord, which relays the message to the brain's touch center.

Developing the Main Idea
Ask:

■ **What does the sense of smell help you detect in the air?** (chemicals)

■ **What sends messages to the brain's smelling center?** (olfactory nerve)

■ **What are the receptors on the tongue?** (taste buds)

■ **What helps you know if something is cold?** (receptor cells in the skin)

Using the Illustrations
Ask:

■ **What is the name of sensory nerve in the nose?** (olfactory nerve)

■ **What are the four main tastes the tongue can identify?** (sweet, salty, sour, bitter)

■ **Where is the bitter taste bud located?** (at the back of the tongue)

■ **What four things do the skin's receptor cells help you feel?** (touch, cold, pain, heat)

WRITING LINK

Have students describe a cookout or picnic using sensory words so that a reader would see, hear, smell, feel, and taste what the writer saw, heard, smelled, felt, and tasted.

Informal Assessment

Ask students to make a flowchart to show how a message is transmitted to either the vision, hearing, smell, touch, or taste center of the brain.

Technology

■ **Science Newsroom CD-ROM** Have students use *You Have Some Nerve* to learn more about nerves and the nervous system.

The Immune System

Objective

- Explore the structure, function, and care of the immune system.

Build on Prior Knowledge
Ask:

- **What does an immunization shot do?** (Helps the body fight off that disease.)

Developing the Main Idea
Explain to students that they'll learn how the immune system helps the body fight off diseases. Add that if the immune system is not working properly, the body is defenseless against many diseases.

Read page R32 with students, then ask:

- **What is the soft tissue inside some bones?** (red marrow) **How does it help the body?** (makes new red blood cells, platelets, and germ-fighting white cells)

- **What is lymph?** (straw-colored fluid around cells) **How do lymph nodes help fight disease?** (filter out harmful materials; produce white blood cells)

Using the Illustrations
Ask:

- **Where is red marrow located?** (in spaces of spongy bone)

- **What covers the outside of a bone?** (thin, tough membrane)

- **What do lymph vessels do?** (collect fluid and return it to bloodstream)

- **How are lymph vessels like blood vessels?** (both carry fluid through body)

WRITING LINK

Have students write a PSA (public service announcement) stressing the importance of immunizations against diseases such as polio, measles, or the flu.

Informal Assessment
Ask students to explain in their own words how the immune system helps when a person is cut.

The Immune System

The immune system helps the body fight disease. Inside some bones is a soft tissue known as red marrow that fills the spaces in spongy bone. Red marrow makes new red blood cells, platelets that stop a cut from bleeding, and germ-fighting white blood cells.

There are white blood cells in the blood vessels and in the lymph vessels. Lymph vessels are similar to blood vessels. Instead of blood, they carry lymph. Lymph is a straw-colored fluid surrounding body cells.

Lymph nodes filter out harmful materials in lymph. Like red marrow, they also produce white blood cells to fight infections. Swollen lymph nodes in the neck are a clue that the body is fighting germs.

CARE!

- Be sure to get immunized against common diseases.
- Keep cuts clean to prevent infection.

1. A bone is covered with a tough but thin membrane that has many small blood vessels. The blood vessels bring nutrients and oxygen to the living parts of the bone and remove wastes.

2. Inside some bones is a soft tissue known as marrow. Yellow marrow is made mostly of fat cells and is one of the body's energy reserves. It is usually found in the long, hollow spaces of long bones.

3. Part of the bone is compact, or solid. It is made up of living bone cells and nonliving materials. The nonliving part is made up of layers of hardened minerals such as calcium and phosphorus. In between the mineral layers are living bone cells.

4. Red marrow fills the spaces in spongy bone. Red marrow makes new red blood cells, germ-fighting white blood cells, and cell fragments that stop a cut from bleeding.

5. Part of the bone is made of bone tissue that looks like a dry sponge. It is made of strong, hard tubes. It is also found in the middle of short, flat bones.

Lymph vessels   Lymph nodes   Lymph node   Lymph vessels

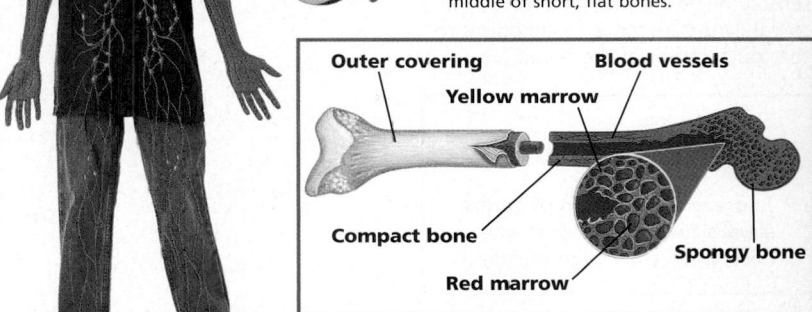

Outer covering   Blood vessels
Yellow marrow
Compact bone
Red marrow   Spongy bone

R 32

The Endocrine System

Hormones are chemicals that control body functions. A gland that produces hormones is called an endocrine gland. Sweat from sweat glands flows out of tubes called ducts. Endocrine glands have no ducts.

The endocrine glands are scattered around the body. Each gland makes one or more hormones. Every hormone seeks out a target organ, the place in the body where the hormone acts.

CARE!

● Doctors can treat many diseases, such as diabetes, caused by endocrine glands that produce too little or too much of a hormone.

Some Glands in the Endocrine System

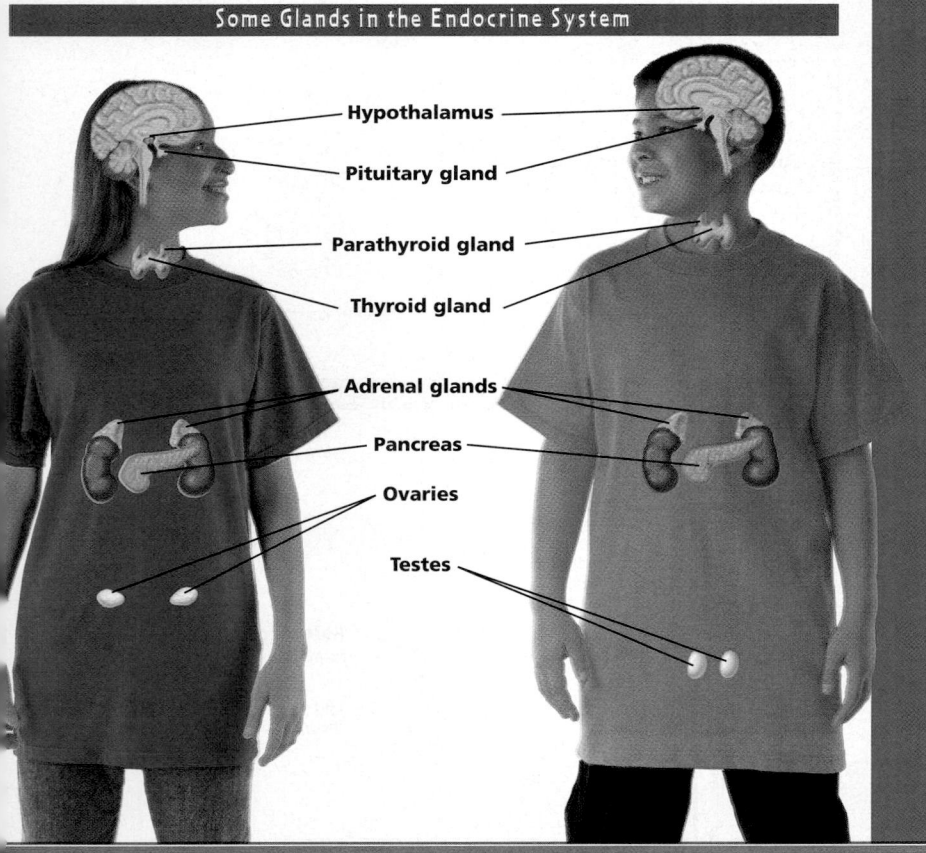

- Hypothalamus
- Pituitary gland
- Parathyroid gland
- Thyroid gland
- Adrenal glands
- Pancreas
- Ovaries
- Testes

Science Background

Jobs of the Endocrine Glands

Hypothalamus: produces hormones that tell the pituitary gland which of its hormones to start or stop producing

Pituitary gland: produces many hormones that control day-to-day body functions and long-term growth

Parathyroid glands: produce a hormone that controls the amount of calcium in the blood

Thyroid gland: produces hormones that affect the rate at which cells use oxygen to

release energy from foods

Adrenal glands: produces hormones that control how much salt is in the blood, how much water is in the body, how well a person fights disease, and how quickly person can handle emergencies

Pancreas controls the amount of sugar in the bloodstream

Ovaries/Testes produce sex hormones that result in physical changes between the ages of 9 and 14

The Endocrine System

Objective

■ Explore the glands of the endocrine system.

Build on Prior Knowledge
Have students discuss changes in their sleep patterns, energy level, or weight. Ask:

■ **How do you think the body "knows" when it's time to grow or sleep or get more energy?** (Something in the body tells it; chemicals signal changes to start.)

Developing the Main Idea
Explain to students that the prefix *endo-* comes from the Latin for "inside." Add that in this lesson, they'll learn about the endocrine system in their bodies that helps to control body functions. Explain that chemicals made in one part of the body and carried in the bloodstream to a target site can change the way the body functions. Such chemicals, or hormones, can affect growth, sleep, energy, and weight.

Using the Illustrations
Ask:

■ **What are the names of some glands in the endocrine system?** (hypothalamus, pituitary, parathyroid, thyroid, adrenal, pancreas, ovaries, testes)

■ **Which endocrine glands are in the throat?** (parathyroid, thyroid)

WRITING LINK
Invite students to write about a time when they were very frightened or had a sudden burst of energy. Explain that these effects are due to hormones produced by the endocrine system.

Informal Assessment
Ask students to explain what a hormone is and where it is produced. (chemical; in an endocrine gland)

The Reproductive System

Objective

- Describe the male and female reproductive systems.

Build on Prior Knowledge

Ask:

- **What is puberty?** (teen years when a boy or girl matures into a man or woman) **What are some changes that take place?** (growth of body hair, change of body shape and size, and so on)

Developing the Main Idea

Explain to students that the reproductive system allows the human species to continue.

Read page R34 with students, then ask:

- **What are testes?** (male reproductive organs)
- **What do the female reproductive organs contain?** (eggs)
- **What is the only way to avoid sexually-transmitted diseases?** (abstinence)
- **What does abstinence mean?** (avoiding, not taking part in)

WRITING LINK

Encourage students to write about their feelings as they look forward to or are entering puberty. Help them build self-esteem by reminding them to feel proud about all the things they do that makes them special.

Informal Assessment

Ask students to compare and contrast the female and male reproductive systems. (both produce hormones and sex cells, but differ in location and structure)

The Reproductive System

The testes are the male reproductive organs. At puberty the testes begin to produce sperm. Sperm move through sperm ducts, where they mix with fluid from endocrine glands.

The ovaries are the female reproductive organs, which contain eggs. After puberty one mature egg is released about once every 28 days. The egg moves to the oviduct, a narrow tube leading from the ovary.

CARE!

- Abstinence is the only sure way to avoid sexually transmitted diseases.

The Male Reproductive System

Sperm move from the testes through sperm ducts, where they mix with fluid from the glands. The sperm and fluid move through the urethra, a tube that leads out through the penis.

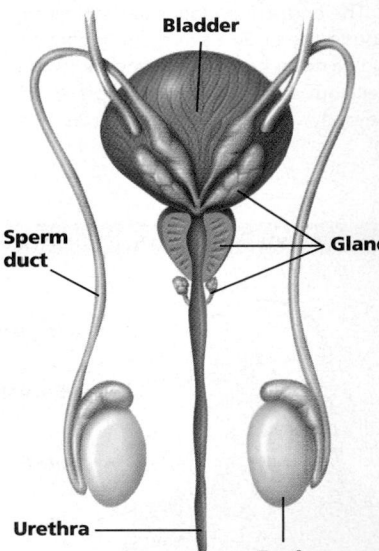

Bladder

Sperm duct

Glands

Urethra

Testis

The Female Reproductive System

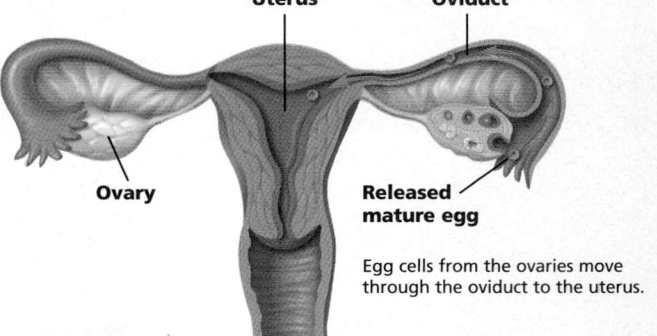

Uterus

Oviduct

Ovary

Released mature egg

Egg cells from the ovaries move through the oviduct to the uterus.

R 34

Science Background

Puberty

During the natural transition from childhood to adulthood, puberty, youngsters go through many physical, mental, and social changes. Girls usually enter puberty at a younger age than boys. Once this was at about age 11, but today girls as young as 9 may begin the transition. The first sign of physical change for girls is usually developing breasts; for boys, it's a growth spurt. Changes are essentially due to hormones in the reproductive organs that are suddenly released into the young person's body.

Glossary

This Glossary will help you to pronounce and understand the meanings of the Science Words introduced in this book. The page number at the end of the definition tells where the word appears.

A

abiotic factor (ā′bī ot′ik fak′tər) A nonliving part of an ecosystem. (p. B6)

absorption (əb sôrp′shən) The disappearance of a sound wave into a surface. (p. F66)

abyssal plain (ə bis′əl plān) The vast flat lands beyond the continental shelf that cover almost half of the deep ocean floor. (p. C90)

acceleration (ak sel′ə rā′shən) Change in velocity with respect to time. (pp. F13, F22)

acid (as′id) A substance that tastes sour and turns blue litmus paper red. (p. E82)

acid rain (as′id rān) Moisture that falls to Earth after being mixed with wastes from burned fossil fuels. (p. C65)

acidity (ə sid′ə tē) The strength of an acid. (p. E86)

action (ak′shən) The force one object applies to a second, as in Newton's third law of motion, which states, "For every action, there is an equal but opposite reaction." *See* **reaction**. (p. F24)

adaptation (ad′əp tā′shən) A characteristic that enables a living thing to survive in its environment. (pp. A82, A106, B52)

aerial root (âr′ē əl rüt) A root that never touches the ground but can take in moisture from the air. (p. A21)

aerosol (âr′ə sōl′) A type of colloid in which liquid drops or solid particles are spread throughout a gas. (p. E60)

air mass (âr mas) A large region of the atmosphere where the air has similar properties throughout. (p. D54)

air pressure (âr presh′ər) The force put on a given area by the weight of the air above it. (p. D11)

alkalinity (al′kə lin′i tē) The strength of a base. (p. E86)

alternation of generations (ôl′tər nā′shən uv jen′ə rā′shənz) The process in which offspring are reproduced sexually, their offspring are reproduced asexually, and so on. (p. A53)

alternative energy source (ōl tûr′nə tiv en′ər jē sôrs) A source of energy other than the burning of a fossil fuel. (p. C104)

PRONUNCIATION KEY

The following symbols are used throughout the McGraw-Hill Science 2002 Glossaries.

a	at	e	end	o	hot	u	up	hw	white	ə about
ā	ape	ē	me	ō	old	ū	use	ng	song	taken
ä	far	i	it	ôr	fork	ü	rule	th	thin	pencil
âr	care	ī	ice	oi	oil	ù	pull	<u>th</u>	this	lemon
ô	law	îr	pierce	ou	out	ûr	turn	zh	measure	circus

′ = primary accent; shows which syllable takes the main stress, such as **kil** in **kilogram** (kil′ə gram′).

′ = secondary accent; shows which syllables take lighter stresses, such as **gram** in **kilogram**.

R 35

ammonia (ə mōn′yə) A compound that contains the element nitrogen and is used as a fertilizer. (p. B34)

anemometer (an′ə mom′ĭ tər) A device that measures wind speed. (p. D44)

aneroid barometer (an′ə roid bə rom′i tər) A spring enclosed in a pleated metal can that expands or contracts to indicate changes in air pressure. (p. D12)

angiosperm (an′jē ə spûrm′) A seed plant that produces flowers. *See* **gymnosperm**. (p. A58)

aquifer (ak′wə fər) An underground layer of rock or soil filled with water. (p. C75)

asexual reproduction (a sek′shü əl rē′prō duk′shən) The production of a new organism from only one cell. (p. A52)

atmosphere (at′məs fîr′) The blanket of gases that surrounds Earth. (pp. C12, D10)

atom (at′əm) The smallest unit of an element that retains the properties of that element. *See* **molecule**. (p. E26)

aurora (ə rôr′ə) The northern or southern lights that appear in the night sky, especially in polar regions. (p. D10)

aurum (ôr′əm) The Latin word for *gold*. (p. E23)

B

bacterium (bak tîr′ē əm) *sing., n. pl.* **bacteria** (-ē ə) A member of either of two kingdoms of one-celled living things that have no nucleus, or center, in their cell body. (p. A15)

balanced forces (bal′ənst fôrs′əz) Forces that cancel each other out when acting together on a single object. (p. F21)

barometer (bə rom′i tər) A device for measuring air pressure. (p. D12)

base (bās) A substance that tastes bitter and turns red litmus paper blue. (p. E82)

basin (bās′in) The floor of an ocean, containing mountains, valleys, and plains. (p. C84)

Beaufort scale (bō′fərt skāl) A system for measuring wind speed by observing its effect on the surface of the sea, using a scale of 0 (low) to 12 (high) for each effect. (p. D44)

bench mark (bench′märk′) A plaque left by surveyors to tell the exact location and elevation of a place. (p. C18)

benthos (ben′thos) Organisms that live on the bottom in aquatic ecosystems. (p. B72)

biomass (bī′ō mas′) Energy from plant matter or animal waste. (p. C106)

biome (bī′ōm) One of Earth's large ecosystems, with its own kind of climate, soil, plants, and animals. (p. B64)

biotic factor (bī ot′ik fak′tər) A living part of an ecosystem. (p. B7)

boiling point (boil′ing point) The particular temperature for each substance at which it changes state from a liquid to a gas. (p. E37)

buoyancy (boi′ən sē) The upward push of a liquid on an object placed in it. (p. E12)

C

cambium (kam′bē əm) The layer in plants that separates the xylem from the phloem. (p. A21)

camouflage (kam′ə fläzh′) An adaptation in which an animal protects itself against predators by blending in with the environment. (p. A108)

carbon cycle (kär′bən sī′kəl) The continuous exchange of carbon dioxide and oxygen among living things. (p. B37)

carnivore (kär′nə vôr′) An animal that eats another animal. (p. B20)

chemical change (kem′i kəl chānj) A change of matter that occurs when atoms link together in a new way, creating a new substance different from the original substances. (p. E71)

chemical formula (kəm'i kəl fôr'myə lə) A way to write a compound's name using symbols. The letters tell what elements are in the compound, and the subscripts tell the number of particles in the compound. (p. E25)

chemical reaction (kem'i kəl rē ak'shən) Another name for chemical change. (p. E71)

chemosynthesis (kē'mō sin'thə sis) In tube worms the process by which bacteria create nutrients from hydrogen sulfide and oxygen, using chemical reactions rather than light. (p. C93)

chlorophyll (klôr'ə fil') A green chemical in plant cells that allows plants to use the Sun's energy for making food. (pp. A6, A32)

chloroplast (klôr'ə plast') The part of a plant cell containing chlorophyll, the green substance that enables the plant to produce food. (p. A24)

cirrus cloud (sir'əs kloud) A high-altitude cloud with a featherlike shape, made of ice crystals. (p. D24)

classification (klas'ə fi kā'shən) The science of finding patterns among living things. (p. A8)

classification key (klas'ə fi kā'shən kē) A series of paired choices describing organisms that is arranged in a way that leads to the identity of a given organism. (p. A100)

classify (klas'ə fi) To place things that share properties together in groups. (p. S7)

cleavage (klē'vij) The tendency of a mineral to break along flat surfaces. (p. C34)

climate (klī'mit) The average weather pattern of a region. (p. D82)

climate zone (klī mat' zōn) A region that has similar weather patterns based on temperature, precipitation, wind, distance from a coast, mountain ranges, ocean currents, and vegetation. (p. D82)

climax community (klī'maks kə mū'ni tē) The final stage of succession in an area, unless a major change happens. (p. B84)

cold front (kōld frunt) A front where cold air moves in under a warm air mass. (p. D56)

colloid (kol'oid) A special type of mixture in which the particles of one material are scattered through another and block the passage of light without settling out. (pp. E54, E60)

commensalism (kə men'sə liz'əm) A relationship between two kinds of organisms that benefits one without harming the other. (p. B57)

communicate (kə mū'ni kāt') To share information. (p. S7)

community (kə mū'ni tē) All the living things in an ecosystem. (p. B10)

complete flower (kəm plēt' flou'ər) A flower that has sepals, petals, stamens, and pistils. (p. A70)

compound (kom'pound) Any substance that is formed by the chemical combination of two or more elements and acts like a single substance. (p. E24)

compression (kəm presh'ən) 1. The part of a sound wave where molecules are crowded together. (p. F51) 2. A movement of plates that presses together or squeezes Earth's crust. (p. C20)

concave lens (kon kāv' lenz) A lens that is thicker at the edges than at the middle. As it curves inward, it spreads light rays apart, making images appear smaller. (p. F100)

PRONUNCIATION KEY

a **at**; ā **ape**; ä **far**; âr **care**; ô **law**; e **end**; ē **me**; i **it**; ī **ice**; îr **pierce**; o **hot**; ō **old**; ôr **fork**; oi **oil**; ou **out**; u **up**; ū **use**; ü **rule**; ů **pull**; ûr **turn**; hw **white**; ng **song**; th **thin**; th **this**; zh **measure**; ə **about, taken, pencil, lemon, circus**

concave mirror (kon kāv′ mir′ər) A mirror that curves in on the shiny side. (p. F88)

condensation (kon′den sā′shən) *n.* The changing of a gas into a liquid. (pp. B32, D17) —**condense** (kən dens′) *v.* (p. E37)

conduction (kən duk′shən) *n.* The passing of heat through a material while the material itself stays in place. (p. E97) —**conduct** (kən dukt′) *v.* (p. E14)

conifer (kon′ə fər) Any of a group of gymnosperms that produce seeds in cones and have needlelike leaves. (p. A59)

conserve (kən′sûrv′) To save, protect, or use resources wisely. (p. C39)

constellation (kon′stə lā′shən) Any of the patterns formed by groups of stars in the night sky. To people in the past, these patterns looked like pictures of animals or people. (p. C14)

consumer (kən sü′mər) Any animal that eats plants or eats other plant-eating animals. (pp. B7, B20)

continental rise (kon′tə nen′təl rīz) A buildup of sediment on the sea floor at the bottom of the continental slope. It is a zone of sand and mud that stretches from the slope down to the deep-sea floor. (p. C90)

continental shelf (kon′tə nen′təl shelf) The underwater edge of a continent. (p. C90)

continental slope (kon′tə nen′təl slōp) The steep slope leading down from the continental shelf toward the sea floor. (p. C90)

contour plowing (kon′tür plou′ing) Preventing erosion by plowing across rather than up and down a slope. (p. C51)

contract (*v.*, kən trakt′) To shrink, as when a material gets colder. (p. E41)

convection (kən vek′shən) The flow of heat through a liquid or a gas, causing hot parts to rise and cooler parts to sink. (p. E97)

convection cell (kən vek′shən sel) A circular pattern of air rising, air sinking, and wind. (p. D38)

convex lens (kon veks′ lenz) A lens that is thicker at the middle than at the edges. As it curves outward, it brings light together, making images appear larger. (p. F100)

convex mirror (kon veks′ mir′ər) A mirror that curves out on the shiny side. (p. F88)

coquina (kō kē′nə) A sedimentary rock formed from seashell fragments. (p. C44)

Coriolis effect (kôr′ē ō′lis i fekt′) The curving of the path of a moving object caused by Earth's rotation. (p. D40)

cortex (kôr′teks) The layer of tissue just inside the epidermis of a plant's roots and stems. (p. A20)

cotyledon (ko′tə lē′dən) A tiny leaflike structure, also called a seedleaf, inside the seed of an angiosperm. (p. A62)

crop rotation (krop rō tā′shən) Growing different crops each year so that the soil does not use up the same kinds of minerals year after year. (p. C51)

crossbreeding (krôs′brēd′ing) Producing offspring by mating individuals from two distinct breeds or varieties of the same species. (p. A112)

cross-pollination (krôs′pol′ə nā′shən) The transfer of pollen from one flower to another. (p. A72)

crust (krust) The rocky surface that makes up the top of the lithosphere and includes the continents and the ocean floor. (p. C12)

crystal (kris′təl) The geometric shape a mineral forms when its atoms and molecules get into fixed patterns. (p. C32)

cumulus cloud (kū′myə ləs kloud) A puffy cloud that appears to rise up from a flat bottom. (p. D24)

current (kûr′ənt) An ocean movement; a large stream of water that flows in the ocean. (p. C86)

cycad (sī′kad) One of the evergreen gymnosperms that resemble palms and have seed-bearing cones. (p. A59)

D

decibel (dB) (des′ə bel′) A unit that measures loudness. (p. F58)

deciduous (di sij′ü əs) Said of a plant that loses its leaves each fall. *See* **evergreen**. (pp. A59, B70)

deciduous forest (di si′jə wəs fôr′ist) A forest biome with many kinds of trees that lose their leaves each autumn. (p. B70)

decomposer (dē′kəm pōz′ər) Any of the fungi or bacteria that break down dead plants and animals into useful things like minerals and rich soil. (pp. B7, B21, B34)

define based on observations (di fīn′ bāst ôn ob′zər vā′shənz) To put together a description that relies on examination and experience. (p. S7)

density (den′si tē) A measure of how tightly packed the matter in an object is. (pp. C35, E8)

deposition (dep′ə zish′ən) The dropping off of bits of eroded rock. (p. C25)

desalination (dē sal′ə nā′shən) Getting fresh water from seawater. (p. C73)

desert (dez′ərt) A sandy or rocky biome, with little precipitation and little plant life. (p. B69)

dicot (dī′kot′) An angiosperm with two cotyledons in each seed. *See* **monocot**. (p. A62)

dinoflagellate (din′ə flaj′ə lāt′) A protist containing chlorophyll that has two flagella for motion. When they overreproduce, they can cause "red tides." (p. A14)

distillation (dis′tə lā′shən) The process of separating the parts of a mixture by evaporation and condensation. (p. E64)

diversity (di vûr′si tē) A wide variety of traits in individuals from the same population. (p. A114)

Doppler effect (dop′lər i fekt′) The change in frequency (and pitch) as a source of sound moves toward or away from you. (p. F71)

downdraft (doun′draft′) A downward rush of air caused by the falling of rain during a thunderstorm. (pp. D38, D67)

E

echo (e′kō) A reflected sound wave. (p. F68)

echolocation (ek′ō lō kā′shən) Finding an object by using reflected sound. (p. F70)

ecological succession (ek′ə loj′i kəl sək sesh′ən) The gradual replacement of one community by another. (p. B82)

ecology (ē kol′ə jē) The study of how living and nonliving things interact. (p. B6)

ecosystem (ek′ō sis′təm) All the living and nonliving things in an environment, including their interactions with each other. (p. B6)

electromagnetic spectrum (i lek′trō mag net′ik spek′trəm) All the wavelengths of visible and invisible light in order, from short (gamma rays) to long (radio). (p. F119)

electromagnetism (i lek′trō mag′ni tiz′əm) The production of magnetism by electricity (and the production of electricity by magnets). (p. F118)

electron (i lek′tron) A particle in the space outside the nucleus of an atom that carries one unit of negative electric charge. (p. E27)

element (el′ə mənt) A pure substance that cannot be broken down into any simpler substances. (p. E22)

PRONUNCIATION KEY

a **at**; ā **ape**; ä **far**; âr **care**; ô **law**; e **end**; ē **me**; i **it**; ī **ice**; îr **pierce**; o **hot**; ō **old**; ôr **fork**; oi **oil**; ou **out**; u **up**; ū **use**; ü **rule**; u̇ **pull**; ûr **turn**; hw **white**; ng **song**; th **thin**; <u>th</u> **this**; zh measure; ə **a**bout, tak**e**n, penc**i**l, lem**o**n, circ**u**s

R 39

elevation (el′ə vā′shən) The height of a place above sea level. (p. C18)

embryo (em′brē ō′) The immature plant inside a seed. (p. A74)

emulsion (i mul′shən) A type of colloid in which one liquid is spread throughout another. (p. E60)

epidermis (ep′i dûr′mis) An outermost layer of such plant parts as roots and leaves. (p. A20)

erosion (i rō′zhən) The picking up and carrying away of pieces of rocks. (p. C22)

evaporation (i vap′ə rā′shən) The slow changing of a liquid into a gas. (pp. B32, D16, E38)

evergreen (ev′ər grēn′) Said of a gymnosperm that keeps its leaves for at least a few years. *See* **deciduous.** (p. A59)

expand (ek spand′) To spread out, as when a material gets hotter. (p. E41)

experiment (ek sper′ə ment′) To perform a test to support or disprove a hypothesis. (p. S7)

F

fault (fôlt) A crack in Earth's crust whose sides show evidence of motion. (p. C18)

fault-block mountain (fôlt blok moun′tən) A mountain formed by blocks of Earth's crust moving along a fault. (p. C21)

fertilization (fûr′tə lə zā′shən) The joining of a sperm cell with an egg cell to make one new cell, a fertilized egg. (pp. A52, A73)

fertilizer (fûr′tə lī′zər) A substance used to add minerals to the soil. (p. B34)

fibrous root (fī′brəs rüt) One of the many hairy branching roots that some plants have. (p. A21)

filament (fil′ə mənt) The wire in a light bulb that gives off light and heat. (p. E92)

foam (fōm) A type of colloid in which a gas is spread throughout a liquid. (p. E60)

fog (fôg) A cloud that forms at ground level. (p. D24)

fold mountain (fōld moun′tən) A mountain made up mostly of rock layers folded by being squeezed together. (p. C20)

food chain (füd chān) The path of the energy in food from one organism to another. (p. B18)

food web (füd web) The overlapping food chains in an ecosystem. (p. B20)

force (fôrs) A push or pull exerted by one object on another, causing a change in motion. (p. F6)

form a hypothesis (fôrm ə hī poth′ə sis) To make a statement that can be tested to answer a question. (p. S7)

fossil (fos′əl) Any remains or imprint of living things of the past. (p. C45)

fossil fuel (fos′əl fū′əl) A fuel formed from the decay of ancient forms of life. (p. C64)

fracture (frak′chər) The characteristic way some minerals break in uneven patterns. (p. C35)

freezing point (frēz′ing point) Another name for *melting point,* that temperature at which a substance changes state, either from a liquid to a solid or from solid to liquid. (p. E37)

frequency (frē′kwən sē) The number of times an object vibrates per second. (p. F57)

friction (frik′ shen′) A force that opposes the motion of one object moving past another. (p. F8)

frond (frond) The leaf of a fern. (p. A51)

front (frunt) A boundary between air masses with different temperatures. (p. D55)

fruit (früt) The ripened ovary of a flowering seed plant. (p. A75)

fundamental frequency (fun′də men′təl frē′kwən sē) The lowest frequency at which an object vibrates. (p. F72)

fungus (fung′gəs) *n.,* **fungi** (fun′jī) *pl.* Members of a kingdom that contains one-celled and many-celled living things that absorb food from their environment. (p. A13)

gas (gas) A form of matter that does not take up a definite amount of space and has no definite shape. (p. E36)

gel (jel) A type of colloid in which a solid is spread throughout a liquid. (p. E60)

gem (jem) A mineral valued for being rare and beautiful. (p. C38)

geologist (jē ol′ə jist) A scientist who studies rocks to tell how they formed and to predict when an earthquake may occur. (p. C18)

geothermal energy (jē′ō thûr′məl en′ər jē) Earth's internal energy. (p. C104)

germination (jûr′mə nā′shən) The sprouting of a seed into a new plant. (p. A75)

ginkgo (ging′kō) *n., pl.* **ginkgoes** A large gymnosperm with fan-shaped leaves. (p. A59)

gnetophyte (ne′tō fīt′) One of the gymnosperms that are closely related to flowering plants and live in both deserts and the tropics. (p. A59)

grassland (gras′land′) A biome where grasses, not trees, are the main plant life. Prairies are one kind of grassland region. (p. B66)

gravitropism (grav′ī trō′pi′zəm) The response of a plant to gravity. (p. A80)

gravity (grav′i tē) A force of attraction, or pull, between any object and any other objects around it. Gravity is a property of all matter. (pp. C8, F35)

greenhouse effect (grēn′hous′ i fekt′) The ability of the atmosphere to let in sunlight but not to let heat escape. (p. D87)

groundwater (ground wô′tər) Precipitation that seeps into the ground and is stored in tiny holes, or pores, in soil and rocks. (pp. B33, C74, D28)

gymnosperm (jim′nə spûrm′) A seed plant that does not produce flowers. *See* **angiosperm**. (p. A58)

habitat (hab′i tat) The place where a plant or animal naturally lives and grows. (p. B11)

hail (hāl) Pellets made of ice and snow. (p. D27)

hardness (härd′nis) How well a mineral resists scratching. (p. C34)

herbivore (hûr′bə vôr′) An animal that eats plants, algae, and other producers. (p. B20)

heredity (hə red′i tē) The passing down of inherited traits from parents to offspring. (p. A110)

hertz (Hz) (hûrts) A unit for measuring frequency. One hertz equals a frequency of one vibration per second. (p. F57)

heterogeneous (het′ər ə jē′nē əs) Differing in kind or nature; dissimilar; not homogeneous. (p. E54)

high-pressure system (hī′presh′ər sis′təm) A pattern surrounding a high pressure center, from which winds blow outward. In the Northern Hemisphere these winds curve to the right in a clockwise pattern. (p. D42)

host (hōst) The organism a parasite lives in or on and is harmed by. (p. B56)

humidity (hū mid′i tē) The amount of water vapor in the air. (p. D16)

humus (hū′məs) Decayed plant or animal material in soil. (pp. B14, C49)

hurricane (hûr′i kān′) A very large, swirling storm with very low pressure at the center. (p. D70)

PRONUNCIATION KEY

a **at**; ā **ape**; ä **far**; âr **care**; ô **law**; e **end**; ē **me**; i **it**; ī **ice**; îr **pierce**; o **hot**; ō **old**; ôr **fork**; oi **oil**; ou **out**; u **up**; ū **use**; ü **rule**; ù **pull**; ûr **turn**; hw **white**; ng **song**; th **thin**; <u>th</u> **this**; zh **measure**; ə **about, taken, pencil, lemon, circus**

hybrid (hī′brid) An organism produced by the crossing of parents that have different forms of the same trait. (p. A112)

hydrocarbon (hī′drə kär′bən) Any of the large group of compounds made solely from hydrogen and carbon atoms. (p. E32)

hydroelectric plant (hī′drō i lek′trik plant) A factory where running or falling water spins a generator to make electricity. (p. C104)

hydrosphere (hī′drə sfîr′) Earth's water, found in continents and oceans, including the fresh water in ice, lakes, rivers, and underground water. (p. C12)

hydrotropism (hī drot′rə piz′əm) The response of a plant to a nearby source of water. (p. A81)

hyperthermia (hī′pər thûr′mē ə) The overheating of the body that can be caused by overexposure in a hot, dry climate. (p. D90)

hypothesis (hī poth′ə sis) A guess or *if . . . then* statement that can be answered clearly in an experiment. (p. A35)

I

ice age (īs āj) Any period when glaciers and ice sheets covered much of Earth's surface. (p. B58)

igneous rock (ig′nē əs rok) A rock formed when melted rock material cools and hardens (p. C43)

image (im′ij) A "picture" of the light source that light rays make in bouncing off a polished, shiny surface. (p. F89)

imperfect flower (im pûr′fikt flou′ər) A flower with either a stamen or a pistil, but not both. (p. A70)

incomplete flower (in′kəm plēt′ flou′ər) A flower that lacks sepals, petals, stamens or pistils. (p. A70)

indicator (in′di kā′tər) A substance such as litmus paper whose color changes when it is mixed with an acid or a base. (p. E84)

inertia (i nûr′shə) The tendency of a moving object to keep moving in a straight line or of any object to resist a change in motion. (pp. C9, F7)

inexhaustible resource (in′eg zôs′tə bəl rē′sôrs′) A resource that cannot be depleted or used up easily. (p. B40)

infer (in fûr′) To form an idea from facts or observations. (p. S7)

inherited trait (in her′i təd trāt) A characteristic that is passed from parents to offspring. (p. A110)

insolation (in′sə lā′shən) The amount of the Sun's energy that reaches Earth at a given time and place. *Insolation* is short for *in*coming *sol*ar radi*ation*. (p. D6)

instinct (in′stingkt′) An inherited behavior, one that is not learned but is done automatically. (p. A110)

insulate (in′sə lāt′) To prevent heat from passing through. (p. E14)

interpret data (in tûr′prit dā′tə) To use the information that has been gathered to answer questions or solve a problem. (p. S7)

intertidal zone (in′tər tī′dəl zōn) The shallowest section of the marine, or ocean, ecosystem, where the ocean floor is covered and uncovered as the tide goes in and out. (p. B73)

invertebrate (in vûr′tə brit) An animal that does not have a backbone. (p. A95)

ionized (ī′ə nīzd′) Electrically charged by radiation, as gas particles of auroras in the night sky. (p. D10)

isobar (ī′sə bär′) A line on a weather map connecting places with equal air pressure. (p. D42)

K

kinetic energy (ki net′ik en′ər jē) The energy of any moving object. (p. E95)

L

land breeze (land brēz) Wind that blows from land to sea. (p. D39)

laser (lā′zər) A device that produces a thin stream of light of just a few close wavelengths. (p. F122)

lava (lä′və) Magma that reaches Earth's surface. (pp. C21, C43)

law of reflection (lô uv ri flek′shən) The angle between an incoming light ray and a surface equals the angle between the reflected light ray and the surface. (p. F87)

light ray (līt rā) A straight-line beam of light as it travels outward from its source. (p. F85)

lightning (līt′ning) One of the huge electric sparks that leap from clouds to the ground in thunderstorms. (p. D66)

limiting factor (lim′ə ting fak′tər) Anything that controls the growth or survival of a population. (p. B50)

liquid (lik′wid) A form of matter that takes up a definite amount of space and has no definite shape. (p. E36)

lithosphere (lith′ə sfîr′) The hard outer layer of Earth, about 100 km thick. (p. C12)

long-day plant (lông′dā plant) A plant that blooms when there is much more daylight than darkness. (p. A82)

low-pressure system (lō′presh′ər sis′təm) A pattern surrounding a low-pressure center, in which winds blow in toward the center. In the Northern Hemisphere, these winds blow to the right in a counterclockwise pattern. (p. D42)

luster (lus′tər) The way light bounces off a mineral's surface. (p. C33)

M

magma (mag′mə) Hot, molten rock deep below Earth's surface. (p. C21)

magnetic (mag net′ik) The property of a material like iron in which the particles line up pole to pole, causing it to be attracted or repelled by a magnet. (p. E15)

make a model (māk ə mod′əl) To make something to represent an object or event. (p. S7)

mare (mär′ā) *n., pl.* **maria** (mär′ē ə) Dark-colored land on the Moon that is dry and flat and is surrounded by mountains and ridges. (p. C13)

mass (mas) A measure of the amount of matter in an object. (p. E6)

matter (ma′tər) Anything that has mass and takes up space. (pp. E6, F51)

measure (mezh′ər) To find the size, volume, area, mass, weight, or temperature of an object, or how long an event occurs. (p. S7)

melting point (melt′ing point) The particular temperature for each substance at which it changes state from a solid to a liquid. (p. E37)

membrane (mem′brān) A thin envelope surrounding the nucleus of a cell. (p. A14)

metal (met′əl) Any of a group of elements found in the ground that conducts heat and electricity. (p. C38)

metamorphic rock (met′ə môr′fik rok) A rock formed under heat and pressure from another kind of rock. (p. C46)

meteorite (mē′tē ə rīt′) A chunk of rock from space that strikes the surface of Earth or the Moon. (p. C26)

mid-ocean ridge (mid ō′shun rij) Chain of mountains that wind along all the world's major oceans. (p. C91)

PRONUNCIATION KEY

a **at**; ā **ape**; ä **far**; âr **care**; ô **law**; e **end**; ē **me**; i **it**; ī **ice**; îr **pierce**; o **hot**; ō **old**; ôr **fork**; oi **oil**; ou **out**; u **up**; ū **use**;
ü **rule**; u̇ **pull**; ûr **turn**; hw **white**; ng **song**; th **thin**; <u>th</u> **this**; zh measure; ə **a**bout, tak**e**n, penc**i**l, lem**o**n, circ**u**s

R 43

mimicry (mim′i krē) An adaptation in which an animal is protected against predators by its resemblance to another, unpleasant animal. (p. A106)

mineral (min′ə rəl) A solid material of Earth's crust with a definite composition. (p. C32)

mixture (miks′chər) A physical combination of two or more substances that are blended together without forming new substances. (p. E52)

molecule (mol′ə kūl′) A particle that contains more than one atom joined together. (p. E30) *See* **atom**. (p. E26)

monocot (mon′ə kot′) An angiosperm with one cotyledon in each seed. *See* **dicot**. (p. A62)

mountain breeze (moun′tən brēz) A cool night wind that blows down a mountain slope to replace the warmer air in the valley. (p. D39)

mutualism (mū′chü ə liz′əm) A relationship between two kinds of organisms that benefits both. (p. B54)

N

neap tide (nēp tīd) The slightest changes from high to low tide that occur when the Sun, the Moon, and Earth form a right angle or are perpendicular to each other. (p. C89)

nekton (nek′tən) Organisms that swim through the water in aquatic ecosystems. (p. B72)

neutral (nü′trəl) Neither acid nor base. (p. E82)

neutron (nü′tron) A particle in the nucleus of an atom that has no net electric charge. (p. E27)

newton (nü′tən) A basic unit measuring the amount of pull or push a force such as gravity produces between two masses. (pp. E7, F20)

NEXRAD (neks′rad′) A new form of Doppler radar that is used to track storms. The word stands for *NEXt generation of weather RADar*. (p. D77)

niche (nich) The role of an organism in a community. (p. B11)

nitrogen cycle (nī′trə jən sī′kəl) The continuous trapping of nitrogen gas into compounds in the soil and its return to the air. (p. B38)

nonrenewable resource (non′ri nü′ə bəl rē′sôrs′) A resource that cannot be replaced within a short period of time or at all. (pp. B40, C64)

nonvascular (non vas′kyə lər) Containing no plant tissue through which water and food move. (p. A9)

nucleus (nü′klē əs) **1.** A dense structure inside the cell. (p. A14) **2.** One of the airborne dust particles around which water condenses as droplets or ice crystals before falling as precipitation. (p. D26) **3.** An atom's dense center, where most of its mass is. (p. E27)

O

observe (əb sûrv′) To use one or more of the senses to identify or learn about an object or event. (p. S7)

occluded front (ə klüd′id frunt) A front formed where a warm front and a cold front meet. (p. D56)

omnivore (om′nə vôr′) An animal that eats both plants and animals. (p. B21)

opaque (ō pāk′) Completely blocking light from passing through it. (p. F96)

orbit (ôr′bit) The path of a planet traveling around a star. (p. C6)

ore (ôr) A mineral containing a useful substance. (p. C38)

organ (ôr′gən) A group of tissues that work together to do a certain job. (p. A94)

organism (ôr′gə niz′əm) Any living thing that can carry out its life on its own. (p. B6)

ovary (ō′və rē) A structure containing egg cells; the base of a pistil in a flower. (p. A70)

overtone (ō′vər tōn′) One of a series of pitches that blend to give a sound its quality. (p. F72)

ozone layer (ō′zōn lā′ər) A layer of ozone gas in the atmosphere that screens out much of the Sun's UV (ultraviolet) rays. (p. C63)

P

parasitism (par′ə sī tiz′əm) A relationship in which one organism lives in or on another organism and benefits from that relationship while the other organism may be harmed by it. (p. B56) —**parasite** (par′ə sīt′) (p. A61)

perfect flower (pûr′fikt flou′ər) A flower with both male and female parts, that is, both a stamen and a pistil. (p. A70)

permafrost (pûr′mə frôst′) A layer of permanently frozen soil found in arctic and antarctic regions. (p. B68)

pH (pē′aitch′) The scale that tells how acidic or basic a solution is. (p. E86)

phloem (flō′em) The tissue through which food from the leaves moves down through the rest of a plant. (p. A21)

photon (fō′ton) The tiny bundles of energy by means of which light travels. (p. F119)

photoperiodism (fō′tō pîr′ē ə diz′əm) The flowering response of a plant to changing periods of daylight and darkness. (p. A82)

photosynthesis (fō′tə sin′thə sis) The food-making process in green plants that uses sunlight. (p. A32)

phototropism (fō tot′rə piz′əm) The response of a plant to changes in light. (p. A80)

phylum (fī′ləm) *n., pl.* **phyla** (-lə) One of the large groups in the animal kingdom. (p. A12)

physical change (fiz′i kəl chānj) A change of matter in size, shape, or state without any change in identity. (p. E70)

pioneer community (pī′ə nîr′ kə mū′ni tē) The first community thriving in a once lifeless area. (p. B83)

pioneer species (pī′ə nîr′ spē′shēz) The first species living in an otherwise lifeless area. (p. B83)

pitch (pich) How high or low a sound is. (p. F56)

planet (plan′it) Any of the nine objects that travel around the Sun and shine by reflecting its light. (p. C6)

plankton (plangk′tən) Organisms that float on the water in aquatic ecosystems. (p. B72)

plate (plāt) One of the moving pieces of Earth's crust that has been broken by upward pressure from the mantle. (p. C19)

plate tectonics (plāt tek ton′iks) A scientific theory that Earth's crust is made of moving plates. (p. C19)

polarization (pō′lər ə zā′shən) Allowing light vibrations to pass through in only one direction. (p. F97)

pollen (pol′ən) Dustlike grains in the flower of a plant that contain its male sex cells. (p. A64)

pollination (pol′ə nā′shən) The transfer of a pollen grain to the egg-producing part of a plant. (p. A72)

pollute (pə lüt′) *v.* To add unnatural substances to Earth's land, water, or air. (p. C50) —**pollutant** (pə lü′tənt) *n.* Something that pollutes. (p. C50) —**pollution** (pə lü′shən) *n.* A polluted condition. (p. C50)

PRONUNCIATION KEY

a **at**; ā **ape**; ä **far**; âr **care**; ô **law**; e **end**; ē **me**; i **it**; ī **ice**; îr **pierce**; o **hot**; ō **old**; ôr **fork**; oi **oil**; ou **out**; u **up**; ū **use**; ū **rule**; ù **pull**; ûr **turn**; hw **white**; ng **song**; th **thin**; <u>th</u> **this**; zh **measure**; ə **about, taken, pencil, lemon, circus**

population – reflection

population (pop'yə lā'shən) All the members of one species in an area. (p. B10)

potential energy (pə ten'shəl en'ər jē) Stored energy. (p. E95)

precipitation (pri sip'i tā'shən) Any form of water particles that falls from the atmosphere and reaches the ground. (pp. B33, D26)

predator (pred'ə tər) An animal that hunts other anmals for food. (pp. A106, B21)

predict (pri dikt') To state possible results of an event or experiment. (p. S7)

prey (prā) A living thing that is hunted for food. (p. B21)

primary color (prī'mer'ē kul'ər) Red, green, or blue. Mixing these colors can produce all the colors of the spectrum. (p. F110)

primary pigment (prī'mer'ē pig'mənt) Magenta, cyan, or yellow. Materials with any of these colors absorb one primary color of light and reflect the other two. (p. F112)

primary succession (prī'mer'ē sək sesh'ən) The beginning of a community where few, if any, living things exist, or where earlier communities were wiped out. (p. B82)

prism (priz'əm) A cut piece of clear glass (or plastic) with two opposite sides in the shape of a triangle or other geometric shape. (p. F108)

producer (prə dü'sər) Any of the plants and algae that produce oxygen and food that animals need. (p. B7)

product (prod'ukt) A new substance produced by a chemical change. (p. E71)

prop root (prop rüt) One of the roots that grow out of a plant's stemlike main roots and help prop up the plant. (p. A21)

property (prop'ər tē) A characteristic of matter that can be observed, such as mass, volume, weight, or density. (pp. E6, E24)

protective coloration (prə tek'tiv kul'ə rā'shən) A type of camouflage in which the color of an animal blends in with its background, protecting it against predators. (p. A109)

protein (prō'tēn) A substance rich in nitrogen that the body uses for growth and the repair of cells. (p. B38)

protist (prō'tist) A member of a kingdom that contains one-celled and many-celled living things, some that make food and some that hunt for food. (p. A14)

proton (prō'ton) A particle in the nucleus of an atom that carries one unit of positive electric charge. (p. E27)

Q

quality (kwol'i tē) The difference you hear between two sounds of the same loudness and pitch. (p. F72)

R

radar (rā'där) A device for tracking the position and path of a distant moving object. It works by sending out radio waves and recording their echoes. The word stands for *RAdio Detecting And Ranging*. (p. D76)

radiation (rā'dē a'shən) The transfer of heat through electromagnetic rays. (p. E97)

radiative balance (rā'dē a'tiv bal'əns) A balance between energy lost and energy gained. (p. D86)

rarefaction (râr'ə fak'shən) The part of a sound wave where molecules are spread apart. (p. F51)

raw material (râ mə tîr'ē əl) Material not yet refined, manufactured, or processed. (p. B40)

reactant (rē ak'tənt) An original substance at the beginning of a chemical reaction. (p. E71)

reaction (rē ak'shən) The force with which an object responds to an action, as in Newton's third law of motion, which states, "For every action, there is an equal but opposite reaction." *See* **action**. (p. F24)

reflection (ri flek'shən) The bouncing of a sound wave off a surface. (p. F66)

refraction (ri frak′shən) The bending of light rays as they pass from one substance into another. (p. F98)

relative humidity (rel′ə tiv hū mid′i tē) A comparison between how much water vapor is in the air and how much the air could hold at a given temperature if it were full, or saturated. (p. D18)

renewable resource (ri nü′ə bəl rē′sôrs′) A resource that can be replaced in a short period of time. (pp. B40, C62)

reservoir (rez′ər vwär′) A storage area for fresh water supplies. (p. C75)

resonance (rez′ə nəns) In an instrument or object, a unique blend of the fundamental frequency and its overtones. When an external force vibrates at the same frequency, a buildup of that resonance can occur. (p. F72)

resource (rē′sôrs′) Any material that helps support life on Earth. (p. C12)

respiration (res′pə rā′shən) The release of energy in plants and animals from food (sugar). (p. A33)

response (ri spons′) What a living thing does as a result of a stimulus. (p. A80)

rhizoid (rī′zoid) One of the hairlike fibers that anchor a moss to the soil and take in water from the soil. (p. A48)

rhizome (rī′zōm) The underground stem of a fern. (p. A51)

rock (rok) A naturally formed solid in the crust made up of one or more minerals. (p. C42)

rock cycle (rok sī′kəl) Rocks changing from one into another in a never-ending series of processes. (p. C52)

root cap (rüt kap) A thin covering made up of cells that protect the root tip of a plant as it grows into the soil. (p. A20)

root hair (rüt hâr) Any of the threadlike projections from a plant root that absorb water and dissolved minerals from the soil. (p. A20)

rotate (rō′tāt) To make a complete spin on an axis, causing one day on a planet. A day differs in length from planet to planet. (p. C10)

runoff (run′ôf) Precipitation that flows across the land's surface or falls into rivers and streams. (pp. B33, D28)

S

savanna (sə van′ə) A tropical grassland with some trees and shrubs. (p. B66)

scanning tunneling microscope (scan′ing tun′əl ing mī′krə skōp′) A device that uses electric current flowing through a needle to trace the contours of atoms and magnify them as much as 30 million times. (p. E26)

scavenger (skav′ən jər) A meat-eating animal that feeds on the remains of dead animals. (p. B21)

sea breeze (sē brēz) Wind that blows from sea to land. (p. D39)

sea-floor vent (sē′flôr′ vent) An opening in a mid-ocean ridge where mineral-saturated water boils up from the seafloor crust. (p. C93)

seamount (sē′mount′) A huge underwater volcanic mountain that may emerge from the ocean surface as an island. (p. C90)

secondary succession (sek′ən der′ē sək sesh′ən) The beginning of a new community where an earlier community already exists. (p. B82)

sedimentary rock (sed′ə men′tə rē rok) A rock made of bits of matter joined together. (p. C44)

PRONUNCIATION KEY

a at; ā ape; ä far; âr care; ô law; e end; ē me; i it; ī ice; îr pierce; o hot; ō old; ôr fork; oi oil; ou out; u up; ū use; ü rule; ů pull; ûr turn; hw white; ng song; th thin; <u>th</u> this; zh measure; ə about, taken, pencil, lemon, circus

R 47

seed (sēd) An undeveloped plant with stored food sealed in a protective covering. (p. A58)

seed coat (sēd kōt) The outer covering of a seed. (p. A74)

seed dispersal (sēd di spûr'səl) The movement of a seed from the flower to a place where it can sprout. (p. A75)

self-pollination (self'pol'ə nā'shən) The transfer of pollen from an anther to a stigma in the same plant. (p. A72)

sexual reproduction (sek'shü əl rē'prō duk'shən) The production of a new organism from a female sex cell and a male sex cell. (p. A52)

shear (shîr) A movement of plates that twists, tears, or pushes one part of Earth's crust past another. (p. C20)

short-day plant (shôrt'dā plant) A plant that blooms when there is more darkness and less daylight. (p. A82)

smog (smog) A mixture of smoke and fog. (p. C64)

solar system (sō'lər sis'təm) The Sun and the objects that are traveling around it. (p. C6)

solid (sol'id) A form of matter that has a definite shape and takes up a definite amount of space. (p. E36)

solubility (sol'yə bil'i tē) The ability of a substance to be dissolved by another substance. (p. E58)

solute (sol'ūt) A substance that is dissolved by another substance to form a solution. (p. E57)

solution (sə lü'shən) A mixture of substances that are blended so completely that the mixture looks the same everywhere. (p. E54)

solvent (sol'vənt) A substance that dissolves one or more other substances to form a solution. (p. E57)

sound wave (sound wāv) A vibration that spreads away from a vibrating object. (p. F51)

spectrum (spek'trəm) A band of colors produced when light goes through a prism. (p. F108)

speed (spēd) How fast an object's position changes with time at any given moment. (p. F11)

spore (spôr) Cells in seedless plants that grow into new organisms. (p. A48)

spring (spring) A place where groundwater seeps out of the ground. (p. C75)

spring tide (spring tīd) The greatest changes from high to low tide that occur when the Sun, the Moon, and Earth are lined up. (p. C89)

state of matter (stāt uv mat'ər) One of the three forms that matter can take—solid, liquid, or gas. (p. E36)

stationary front (stā'shə ner ē frunt) An unmoving front where a cold air mass and a warm air mass meet. (p. D57)

statistical forecasting (stə tis'ti kəl fôr'kas'ting) Predicting weather by using past weather records, based on the chances of a pattern repeating itself. (p. D60)

stimulus (stim'yə ləs), *n., pl.* **stimuli** (-lî) Something in the environment that causes a living thing to react. (p. A80)

stomata (stō'mə tə) *pl. n., sing.* **stoma** Pores in the bottom of leaves that open and close to let in air or give off water vapor. (p. A24)

storm surge (stôrm sûrj) A great rise of the sea along a shore caused by low pressure clouds. (p. D72)

stratus cloud (strā'təs kloud) A cloud that forms in a blanketlike layer. (p. D24)

streak (strēk) The color of the powder left when a mineral is rubbed against a hard, rough surface. (p. C34)

strip farming (strip fär'ming) Trapping runoff by alternating tightly growing grasses with more widely spaced plants. (p. C51)

subscript (sub'skript') A number in a chemical formula that tells the number of atoms in the compound. (p. E25)

surveyor (sər vā′ər) A specialist who makes accurate measurements of Earth's crust. (p. C18)

suspension (sə spen′shən) A mixture in which suspended particles can easily be seen. (p. E59)

symbiosis (sim′bē ō′sis) A relationship between two kinds of organisms that lasts over time. (p. B54)

synoptic weather map (si nop′tik weth′ər map) A type of map showing a summary of the weather using station models. (p. D60)

system (sis′təm) A group of organs that work together to carry on life functions. (p. A94)

T

taiga (tī′gə) A cool forest biome of conifers in the upper Northern Hemisphere. (p. B67)

taproot (tap′rüt′) A root that has few hairy branches and grows deep into the ground. (p. A21)

temperate (tem′pər it) Free from extremes of temperature. (p. B66)

tension (ten′shən) A movement of plates that stretches or pulls apart Earth's crust. (p. C20)

terracing (ter′is ing) Shaping hillsides into steps so that runoff and eroded soil get trapped on the steps. (p. C51)

texture (teks′chər) An identifying quality of a rock based on how coarse, fine, or glassy it is and on how angular or rounded it is. (p. C42)

thunder (thun′dər) The noise caused by lightning-heated air during a thunderstorm. (p. D66)

thunderhead (thun′dər hed′) A cumulonimbus cloud in which a thunderstorm forms. (p. D66)

thunderstorm (thun′dər stôrm′) The most common severe storm, formed in cumulonimbus clouds. (p. D66)

tissue (tish′ü) A group of similar cells that work together at the same job. (pp. A7, A94)

topsoil (top′soil′) The dark, top layer of soil, rich in humus and minerals, in which many tiny organisms live and most plants grow. (p. B14)

tornado (tôr nā′dō) A violent whirling wind that moves across the ground in a narrow path. (p. D68)

trade wind (trād wind) A belt of winds around Earth moving from high pressure zones toward the low pressure at the equator. (p. D41)

translucent (trans lü′sənt) Letting only some light through, so that objects on the other side appear blurry. (p. F96)

transparent (trans pâr′ənt) Letting all light through, so that objects on the other side can be seen clearly. (p. F96)

transpiration (tran′spə rā′shən) The loss of water through a plant's leaves, which draws water up through the plant to replace it. (pp. A25, D17)

trench (trench) A deep valley in the sea floor. (p. C91)

tropical rain forest (trop′i kəl rān fôr′ist) A hot, humid biome near the equator, with much rainfall and a wide variety of life. (p. B71)

tropism (trō′piz′əm) A growth response of a plant toward or away from a stimulus. (p. A80)

troposphere (trop′ə sfîr′) The layer of the atmosphere closest to Earth's surface. (p. D10)

PRONUNCIATION KEY

a **at**; ā **ape**; ä **far**; âr **care**; ô **law**; e **end**; ē **me**; i **it**; ī **ice**; îr **pierce**; o **hot**; ō **old**; ôr **fork**; oi **oil**; ou **out**; u **up**; ū **use**; ü **rule**; ù **pull**; ûr **turn**; hw **white**; ng **song**; th **thin**; <u>th</u> **this**; zh **measure**; ə **about, taken, pencil, lemon, circus**

tube worm (tüb wûrm) Large wormlike animals that live near sea floor vents and obtain their food through bacterial chemosynthesis. (p. C93)

tundra (tun'dra) Large, treeless plain in the arctic regions, where the ground is frozen all year. (p. B68)

ultrasonic (ul'trə son'ik) Said of a sound with a frequency too high to be heard by humans. (p. F57)

unbalanced forces (un bal'ənst fôrs'əz) Forces that do not cancel each other out when acting together on a single object. (p. F21)

updraft (up'draft') An upward rush of heated air during a thunderstorm. (pp. D38, D66)

use numbers (ūz num'bərz) To order, count, add, subtract, multiply, and divide to explain data. (p. S7)

use variables (ūz vâr'ē ə bəlz) To identify and separate things in an experiment that can be changed or controlled. (p. S7)

V

vacuum (vak'ū əm) A space through which sound waves cannot travel because it contains no matter. (p. F116)

valley breeze (val'ē brēz) A cool wind that blows up a mountain slope and replaces the slope's rising Sun-warmed air. (p. D39)

variable (vâr'ē ə bəl) One of the changes in a situation that may affect the outcome of an experiment. (p. A35)

vascular (vas'kyə lər) Containing plant tissue through which water moves up and food moves down. (p. A9)

velocity (və los'i tē) The speed and direction of a moving object. (p. F12)

vertebrate (vûr'tə brit) An animal that has a backbone. (p. A95)

vibration (vī brā'shən) A back-and-forth motion. (p. F50)

volume (vol'ūm) **1.** A measure of how much space an object takes up. (p. E6) **2.** The loudness or softness of a sound. (p. F58)

W

warm front (wôrm frunt) A front where warm air moves in over a cold air mass. (p. D56)

water cycle (wô'tər sī'kəl) The continuous movement of water between Earth's surface and the air, changing from liquid to gas to liquid. (pp. B33, C74, D29)

water table (wô'tər tā'bəl) The top of the water-filled spaces in the ground. (p. C75)

water vapor (wô'tər vā'pər) Water in the form of a gas. (pp. B32, D16)

waterspout (wô'tər spout') A tornado that forms over water. (p. D69)

weather (weth'ər) What the lower atmosphere is like at any given place and time. (p. D12)

weather vane (weth'ər vān) A device that indicates wind direction. (p. D44)

weathering (weth'ər ing) Breaking down rocks into smaller pieces. (p. C22)

weight (wāt) The force of gravity between Earth and an object. (pp. E7, F36)

well (wel) A hole dug below the water table that water seeps into. (p. C75)

wind (wind) Air that moves horizontally. (p. D38)

xylem (zī'ləm) The tissue through which water and minerals move up through a plant. (p. A20)

year (yîr) The time it takes a planet to orbit the Sun. A *year* is different from planet to planet. (p. C7)

Index

A

Abiotic factors, B6–7
Absorption, of sound, F66–67
Abyssal plain, C90
Acceleration, F13, F18, F26–27
  calculation of, F20
  force and, F18
  mass and, F19, F20
  of falling objects, F36
  of the Moon, F37
Acidity, E86
Acid rain, C23, C65
Acids, C65*
  identifying, E81*–82, E84–85
  reactivity of, E83
  strength of, E86–87
  uses of, E88
Action, F24
Adaptation, A78–89, A104–109
  camouflage as, A108–109
  chemical, A84
  competition as, A83*, B23
  in sow bugs, A105*
  in taste, A107
  mimicry as, A106
  root growth as, A79*
  thorns as, A107
  to harsh environments, B52–53
  tropisms, A80–81
Aerial roots, A21
Aerogels, E16
Aerosol, E60
Agnatha, A98
Air, C62–63
  as solution, E56
  cleaning up, C66
  composition of, D11
  cooling of, D20
  dirty, C61*
  dust in, D11
  nitrogen in, B38
  pollution of, C64, C67
Air masses, D54–55
Air pressure
  altitude and, D11

changes in, D35*–37
  convection cells and, D38
  isobars, D42
  measuring, D12
  storm surges and, D72
Air resistance, F34
Air sac (swim bladder), A98
Air temperature
  altitude and, D10
  mean, D6
  measuring, D12
  relative humidity and, D19
  Sun's angle and, D5*–7*
Algae, B24, B73
  as producers, B7
  blooms, B26
  green, A14, A54
Alkalinity, E86
Alloys, E56
Alternation of generations, A53
Alternative energy sources, C104–105, C106
Altitude
  air pressure and, D11, D36
  air temperature and, D10
  climate and, D85
Aluminum, C38, E23
Alvin (submersible), C92, C96–97
AM, F120
Amazon rain forest, B76–77
Ammeter, E93
Ammonia, B34, B38, B39, E83
Amphibia, A98
Amphibians, A12
Amplifier, F60
"Ancient" bacteria kingdom, A15
Anemometer, D44
Anemones, A12, A96, B57
Aneroid barometer, D12
Angiosperms, A11, A54, A58, A59, A60–61, A60–65
  aromatic flowers, A64
  cotyledons, A62–63*, A74
Animals, A12, A92–120. *See also* Populations.
  adaptation of, A104–109
    camouflage, A108–109

    mimicry, A106
    sow bugs, A105*
    taste, A107
    thorns, A107
  as consumers, B7
  carbon cycle and, B37
  classification of, A93*–101
    invertebrates, A95–97
    traits used for, A94–95
    vertebrates, A95, A98–99
  crossbreeds, A112–113
  diversity among, A114–15
  habitat change and, B12
  hoofed, B66
  hybrids, A112, A113*
  in deciduous forests, B70
  inherited vs. learned traits in, A110–111
  in nitrogen cycle, B39
  in prairie ecosystem, B8–9
  in tropical rain forests, B71
  plants vs., A12
  water cycle and, B33
Annelida (segmented worms), A97
Antacids, E88
Anther, A70, A72
Anthracite (hard coal), C47
Aquifer, C75
Arica, Chile, B69
Aristotle, D62, E22, F35
Armadillo, B9
Arthropoda, A12, A97
Asexual reproduction, A52
Atacama Desert, B69
Atmosphere, C12, C60–67, D10
  acid rain and, C65
  greenhouse effect and, D87
  living things' need for, C62–63
  of other planets, C68–69
  radiative balance and, D86
  weather and, D12
Atoms, E26–27
Auroras, D10
Auxin, A81
Aves (birds), A12, A99

---

* Indicates an activity related to this topic.

R 51

*Indicates an activity related to this topic.

*Indicates an activity related to this topic.

*Indicates an activity related to this topic.

*Indicates an activity related to this topic.

*Indicates an activity related to this topic.

*Indicates an activity related to this topic.

Teacher's Notes

Credits

Page placement key: (t) top, (tr) top right, (tc) top center, (tl) top left, (tml) top middle left, (tmr) top middle right, (ml) middle left, (m) middle, (mr) middle right, (umr) upper middle right, (uml) upper middle left, (bmr) bottom middle right, (bml) bottom middle left, (l) left, (r) right, (b) bottom, (br) bottom right, (bl) bottom left, (bc) bottom center, (bg) background, (i) inset.

Cover Design and Illustration: Robert Brook Allen

Cover Photos: ©Tim Flach/Stone; (bg) ©Darrell Gulin/Natural Selection; (i) ©PhotoSpin 2000.

Illustrations: Kenneth Batelman: pp. C9, C89, F24, F35, F37, F39; Denny Bond: p. A32, B38; Ka Botzis: pp. B20, B21; Drew-Brook-Cormack: pp. D20, D25; Susan Carlson: p. A12; Karen Carr: p. S1; Andrea Champlin: p. F31; Barbara Cousins: pp. B28 R24, R26, R27, R28; Marie Dauenheimer: pp. A6, A7; John Edwards: pp. C6, E7, E10, E12, F70, F84, F85, F89, F90, F100; Peter Fasolino: pp. E43, E61; Robert Frank: p. B36; Function Thru Form: pp. A32, A62, A117, B18, B20, B21, B24, B25, B27, B40, B51, C7, C8, C31, C33, C37, C39, C46, C50, C65, C72, C76, C103, D6, D7, D8, D10, D11, D16, D17, D25, D26, D30, D35, D38, D39, D41, D43, D51, D53, D69, D81, D85, D86, D89, D93, E15, E26, E27, E29, E30, E31, E32, E36, E37, E39, E46, E69, E82, ,E86, E92, E97, F6, F7, F10, F11, F12, F18, F19, F20, F21, F22, F23, F36, F38, F51, F55, F57, F59, F60, F61, F66, F69, F76, F108, F110, F112, F117, F119, F124, F125; Thomas Gagliano: pp. D36, D37, D39; Greg Harris: pp. B73, D55; Carlyn Iverson: pp. B32, B80, B81; Sidney Jablonski: p. C86; John Karapelou: pp. R29, R30, R31; Virge Kask: pp. A12, A70, A72, A73, A74, A76, B18, B24, B25; George Kelvin: pp. A24, A35, A52, A53, A54, A79, A81, A82, C12, C14, C19, C20, C25, C47, C49, C62, C63, C74, C75, C88, C90, C91, C102, C103, F27, F85, F101, F118; Katie Lee: pp. A102, B6, B7, B84; Tom Leonard: pp. F102, F20, R21, R22, R32; Rebecca Merrilees: pp. A20, A21, A22, A37, A38, A51; Dave Merrill: pp. B9, B52, B54, C21, D85; Mowry Graphics: pp. D28, D54, D89; Steve Oh: pp. A94, F3, F14, F22, F25, F26, F27, F34, R25, R27, R28, R29, R32, R33, R34; Chris Porter: pp. B7, C14; Saul Rosenbaum: pp. D8, D9, D27, D38, D56, D57, D66, D67, D87, F99, F116, F117; Wendy Smith: pp. A8, A10, A11, A60, A62, F112; Steve Stankiewicz: pp. B64, B77, B89, C32, C52, C73, C78, C100, D18, D40, D53, D60, D69, D89, E38, E42, E92, E94, F74, F86, F93, F101, F104, F105, F110, F122, R8, R9, R12, R13; Art Thompson: pp. C10, C11, D7, D42, D70, D82, D84, E12, E62, E63, E64; Patricia Wynne: pp. R23, R31.

Photography Credits: All photographs are by the Macmillan/McGraw-Hill School Division (MMSD) and Dan Howell for MMSD except as noted below.

Contents: iv: ©Norbert Wu. v: ©Tim Flach/Stone. vi: l ©Jules Cowan/Index Stock Imagery; b ©Joyce Photographics/Photo Researchers, Inc; r ©A.J. Copley/VU. vii: l ©NOAA, colored by John Wells/Science Photo Library/Photo Researchers, Inc; r ©Runk/Schoenberger/Grant Heilman. viii: l ©Roger Ressmeyer/Corbis; b ©Science/VU; ix: ©Duomo/Corbis.

National Geographic Invitation to Science: S1: ©Gianni Tortoli/ Photo Researchers, Inc. S2: ©Tom Bean/Tom & Susan Bean Photography. S3: ©Chris Hondros/Liaison Agency Inc. S4: ©Carlos Munoz-Yague/ Eurelios/Science Photo Library/Photo Researchers, Inc. S5: ©Mark Pilkington/Geological Survey of Canada/Science Photo Library/Photo Researchers, Inc. S7: ©Richard Hutchings.

National Geographic Unit Opener A: A0 ©Kelvin Aitken/Peter Arnold,Inc;A1 ©Norbert Wu; A1 ©Kelvin Aitken/Peter Arnold,Inc. **Unit A:** A2: ©William Waterfall/The Stock Market. A4: ©Ted Levin/Animals Animals/Earth Scenes. A5: ©Richard Hutchings. A6: ©Peter Miller/Photo Researchers, Inc. A7: ©Dick Thomas/VU. A9: ©Rob Hadlow/Bruce Coleman, Inc. A13: (bc) ©Doug Sokell/VU; (br) ©R.M. Meadows/Peter Arnold, Inc.; (bl) ©Veronika Burmeister/VU. A14: (tr) ©Cabisco/VU; (bl) ©Gilbert S. Grant/Photo Researchers, Inc.; (tl) ©Patrick W. Grace/Science Source/Photo Researchers, Inc.; (br) ©R. Kessel-G. Shih/VU; (tc) ©Veronika Burmeister/VU. A15: (br) Blair Seitz/Photo Researchers, Inc.; (bmr) ©A. & F. Michler/Peter Arnold, Inc.; (bml) ©Telegraph Colour Library/FPG; (bl) R. Robinson/VU. A16: (b) ©Adam Jones/Dembinsky Photo Associates; (br) ©Arthur R. Hill/VU. A17: ©Manfred Kage/Peter Arnold, Inc. A18: ©Dominique Braud/Dembinsky Photo Associates. A19: ©Richard Hutchings. A23: (tl) ©George Bernard/Animals Animals/Earth Scenes; (tr) ©Robert Maier/Animals Animals/Earth Scenes; (br) ©Willard Clay/Dembinsky Photo Associates. A25: ©G.Buttner/OKAPIA/Photo Researchers, Inc. A26: (m) ©David S. Addison/VU; (tr) ©Tim Hauf/VU. A27: ©James R. Holland/National Geographic Society. A 28: (inset) Tom & Pat Leeson/Photo Researchers, Inc.; (bl) ©Michael J. Balick/Peter Arnold, Inc.; (br) ©Ray Pfortner/Peter Arnold, Inc. A29: ©J.C. Teyssier/ Publiphoto/Photo Researchers, Inc. A30: ©Robert Maier/Animals Animals/Earth Scenes. A31: ©Richard Hutchings. A32: ©PHOTODISC/ Gettyone. A34: ©Willard Clay/Dembinsky Photo Associates. A36: (t)

©Gerry Ellis/ENP Images; (bl, br) ©Jack M. Bostrack/VU. A37: ©Phil Degginger/Color-Pic. A40: ©Jim Olive/Pictor/Uniphoto. A41: (tl) ©courtesy of Katherine Banks/Prof. K. Banks; (tr) ©Hans Reinhard/ Bruce Coleman, Inc.; (r) ©WHM Bildarchiv/Peter Arnold, Inc. A43: ©Hans Reinhard/Bruce Coleman, Inc. A44: ©Bob Krist/Corbis. A46: ©Michael Fogden/Bruce Coleman, Inc. A47: ©Richard Hutchings. A48: (br) ©David Sieren/VU; (bml) ©Doug Sokell/VU; (bl) ©John Trager/VU. A49: (br) ©E.F.Anderson/ VU; (bl) ©Ed Reschke/Peter Arnold, Inc.; (bc) ©Mike Perry/Pictor/ Uniphoto. A50: (tl) ©Dan Suzio/Photo Researchers, Inc.; (br, tr) ©Richard Hutchings. A51: ©David Dennis/ Animals Animals/Earth Scenes. A54: ©Dick Keen/VU. A55: ©Ed Degginger/Color-Pic, Inc. A56: ©Michael Gadomski/Animals Animals/Earth Scenes. A57: ©Richard Hutchings. A58: (bl) ©Jim Hughes/VU; (br) ©V.P. Weinland/Photo Researchers, Inc.; (bc) ©W. Ormerod/VU. A59: (tr) ©Ed Degginger/ Bruce Coleman, Inc.; (br) ©E. Webber/VU; (bc) ©Gerald & Buff Corsi/VU;(ml) ©Jan Taylor/Bruce Coleman, Inc.; (l) ©John N. Trager/VU. A60: (b) ©Dick Keen/VU; (tr) ©V. McMillan/ VU. A61: (br) ©Bud Nielsen/VU; (t) ©E.F. Anderson/VU. A63: (br) ©Arthur R. Hill/VU; (r) ©Mark S. Skalny/VU. A64: (tr) ©Jerome Wexler/Photo Researchers, Inc.; (tl) ©John Gerlach/VU. A66: (br) ©Jeff Greenberg/ VU; (tr) ©Larry Lefever/Grant Heilman Photography, Inc. A67: ©Jim Sugar Photography/Bettmann/CORBIS. A68: ©Robert P. Carr/Bruce Coleman, Inc. A69: ©Richard Hutchings. A71: (b) ©Adam Jones/Photo Researchers, Inc.; (tl) ©Derrick Ditchburn/VU; (i) ©Doug Sokell/VU. A74: ©Henry T. Kaiser/ Pictor/Uniphoto. A75: (tl) ©Inga Spence/VU; (tr) ©Ken Wagner/VU; (br) ©Stephen J. Lang/VU. A76: ©Scott T. Smith. A78: ©Joel Harrington/VU. A80: ©David Newman/VU. A81: ©R. Calentine/VU. A83: (tr) ©Dick Keen/VU; (br) ©Richard Hutchings. A84: (b) ©Bill Beatty/VU; (tr) ©Parke H. John, Jr./VU. A85: ©Runk/ Schoenberger/ Grant Heilman Photography, Inc. A86: (bg) ©Brock May/Photo Researchers, Inc.; (tr) ©Joel Sartore/Grant Heilman Photography, Inc. A87: ©Catherine Karnow/CORBIS. A89: (b) ©Hans Reinhard/ Bruce Coleman, Inc.; (t) ©John McAnulty/CORBIS. A90: ©R&V Taylor/Bruce Coleman, Inc. A92: ©Frank Krahmer/Bruce Coleman, Inc. A95: (bl) ©BIOS Klein/Hubert/Peter Arnold, Inc.; (m) ©Joe McDonald/Bruce Coleman, Inc.; (tr) ©John Hyde/Bruce Coleman, Inc. A96: (mr, br) ©Ed Degginger/Color-Pic; (tr) ©Jeff Mondragon/ Mondragon Photography; (ml) ©Scott Johnson/Animals Animals/ Earth Scenes; (tl) ©Susan Blanchet/Dembinsky Photo Associates; (bl) ©Tom E. Adams/Peter Arnold, Inc. A97: (bl) © Breck P. Kent/ Animals Animals/Earth Scenes; (tr, br) ©Fred Bavendam/Peter Arnold, Inc.; (tl) ©Hans Pfletschinger/Peter Arnold, Inc.; (ml) ©Jeff J. Daly/Stock Boston; (mr) ©Pictor/Uniphoto; (m) ©Robert Lubeck/Animals Animals/ Earth Scenes. A98: (br) ©Gary Meszaros/ Bruce Coleman, Inc.; (mr) ©Marilyn Kazmers/Dembinsky Photo Associates; (ml) ©Norbert Wu/Peter Arnold, Inc.; (bl) ©Skip Moody/Dembinsky Photo Associates; (tr) ©Pictor/Uniphoto; (tl) ©Zig Leszczynski/Animals Animals/Earth Scenes. A99: (mr) ©Bob Cranston/Animals Animals/ Earth Scenes; (tl) ©Darrell Gulin/CORBIS; (m) ©Des & Jen Bartlett/ Bruce Coleman, Inc.; (ml) ©Ed Degginger/ Color-Pic; (tm) ©Michael Newman/PhotoEdit; (br) ©Rob Simpson/ Pictor/Uniphoto; (tr) ©Pictor/Uniphoto. A100: (tr) Mark Downey/Lucid Images/ Picturequest; (bm) ©Jim Roetzel/Dembinsky Photo Associates; (tl) ©John Cancalosi/Peter Arnold, Inc.; (br) ©John Shaw/Bruce Coleman, Inc.; (m) ©Skip Moody/Dembinsky Photo Associates. A101: ©Graham Pizzey/Bruce Coleman, Inc. A104: (bg) ©John Gerlach/Dembinsky Photo Associates; (m) ©Rolf Kopfle/ Bruce Coleman, Inc. A106: (tr) ©Stan W. Elems/VU; (bl) ©L. West/ Bruce Coleman, Inc.; (br) ©Stan W. Elems/VU. A107: (bl) ©Ed Degginger/Color-Pic; (br) ©Rod Planck/Dembinsky Photo Associates; (tl) ©Stan W. Elems/VU. A108: ©Steve Kaufman/Peter Arnold, Inc. A109: ©Kim Taylor/Bruce Coleman, Inc. A110: ©Ed Degginger/ Color-Pic. A111: (bl) ©D. Robert Franz/Bruce Coleman, Inc.; (br) ©Erwin & Peggy Bauer/Bruce Coleman, Inc.; (tc) ©John Shaw/Bruce Coleman, Inc.; (tl) ©John Snyder/Bruce Coleman, Inc.; (tr) ©Skip Moody/Dembinsky Photo Associates. A112: (ml, tr) ©Ed Degginger/Color-Pic; (tl) ©Randa Bishop/Pictor/Uniphoto. A113: (br) ©Fritz Prenzel/Animals Animals/Earth Scenes; (bm, bl) ©Hans Reinhard/Bruce Coleman, Inc. A114: ©Stan Osolinski/Dembinsky Photo Associates. A115: ©Gerard Lacz/Animals Animals/Earth Scenes. A118: ©Courtesy of HSWRI. A119: ©Courtesy of HSWRI.

National Geographic Unit Opener B: B0 ©Tim Flach/Stone; B1 ©Art Wolfe/Stone; B1 ©Tim Flach/Stone. **Unit B:** B2: ©Lee Rentz/Bruce Coleman, Inc. B4: ©Zig Leszczynski/Animals Animals/Earth Scenes. B5: ©Richard Hutchings. B8: (t) ©John Shaw/Bruce Coleman, Inc.; (br) ©John Shaw/Bruce Coleman, Inc. B9: (tc) ©David J. Sams/ Stock, Boston; (br) ©Joe McDonald/CORBIS; (bl) ©John Giustina/ Bruce Coleman, Inc. B10: ©Lee Rentz/Bruce Coleman, Inc. B11: (tr) ©Laura Riley/Bruce Coleman, Inc.; (br) ©Robert M. Balou/Animals Animals/ Earth Scenes. B12: (b) ©Bruce Coleman, Inc.; (tr) ©N.E. Swedberg/ Bruce Coleman, Inc. B13: ©Joe McDonald/Animals Animals/Earth Scenes. B14: ©John Shaw/Bruce Coleman, Inc. B16: ©Beverly Joubert/National Geographic Collection/GettyOne Images. B19:

R 66

©Richard Hutchings. D88: (bl) ©Science/VU (br) ©VU. D89: ©Jim Sugar Photography/CORBIS. D90: (tr) ©Don Smetzer/Stone; (br) ©Jeff Greenberg/PhotoEdit D91: ©Frost Fair on the Thames, Abraham Hondius, Museum of London, UK/The Bridgeman Art Library International Ltd. D93: ©Mark A. Schneider/Dembinsky Photo Associates. D94: (r) ©CORBIS; (bl) ©courtesy of Dr. Henry Diaz/Climate Diagnostics Ctr, NOAA. D95: ©Jim Sugar/CORBIS.

National Geographic Unit Opener E: E0, E1 ©Roger Ressmeyer/CORBIS. **Unit E:** E2: ©Christine Osborne/CORBIS. E4: ©Michael T. Sedam/CORBIS. E5: ©Richard Hutchings. E6: ©Ken Karp/McGraw-Hill School Division. E8: (m,bl,br) ©Ken Karp/McGraw-Hill School Division. E9: ©Richard Hutchings. E11: (tl) Klaus Guldbransen/Photo researchers, Inc.; (tr) George Bernard/Photo researchers, Inc.; (bl) ©Buddy Mays/Bettmann /CORBIS; (ml) ©The Purcell Team/Bettmann/CORBIS; (mr) ©Vaughan Fleming/ Science Photo Library/ Photo Researchers, Inc.; (br) ©Wolfgang Kaehler/ Bettmann/ CORBIS. E13: ©Walter Meayers Edwards. E14: (bl) ©Kim Sayer/ CORBIS; (tr) ©Phil Degginger/Color-Pic; (br) ©Phil Degginger/Color-Pic. E16: (m) ©IBM Research/Peter Arnold, Inc.; (tr) ©Lawrence Livermore National Laboratory/Science Photo Library/Photo Researchers, Inc.; (b) ©National Railway of Japan/PhotoTake. E18: ©Rod Plack/Photo Researchers, Inc. E20: ©NASA/Science Photo Library/Photo Researchers, Inc. E21: ©Richard Hutchings. E22: (m) ©Lowell Georgia /Photo Researchers, Inc.; (b) ©Rich Treptow/Photo Researchers, Inc. E23: (bl, mr, tr, br) Charles D. Winters/Photo Researchers, Inc.; (ml) ©Russ Lappa/ Science Source/Photo Researchers, Inc.; (tl) ©Science/VU. E24: (i) ©Bill Beatty/VU/ Visuals Unlimited.; (m) ©Charles D. Winters/Photo Researchers, Inc.; (br) ©1998 PhotoDisc, Inc.; (bl) ©Yoav Levy/PhotoTake. E25: (tl) ©David Taylor/Photo Researchers, Inc.; (tc) ©David Taylor/Photo Researchers, Inc.; (tr) ©David Taylor/Photo Researchers, Inc. E28: (bl) ©Charles D. Winters/Photo Researchers, Inc.; (tr, tl, bmr) ©Dr. E. R. Degginger/Color-Pic; (ml) ©George Bernard/Photo Researchers, Inc.; (m, mr) ©Klaus Guldbrandsen/ Science Photo Library/Photo Researchers, Inc.; (br) ©Russ Lappa/Photo Researchers, Inc. E32: (bl, ml) ©Christine Coscioni/CO2, Inc.; (tr) ©Leonard Lessin/Peter Arnold, Inc. E33: (r) ©The Image Bank/ GETTYONE. E34: ©W.Wisniewski/Okapia/Photo Researchers, Inc. E35: ©Richard Hutchings. E36: (bc) ©Clyde H. Smith/Peter Arnold, Inc.; (bl) ©Gordon Wiltsie/Peter Arnold, Inc.; (br) ©Jeff & Alexa Henry/Peter Arnold, Inc. E37: ©Cesar Llacuna. E40: (umr) ©Carolina Biological Supply/PhotoTake.; (tr) ©Cesar Llacuna; (br, bmr) ©Charles D. Winters/Photo Researchers, Inc.; (m) ©Christine L. Coscioni/CO2, Inc. E41: ©Richard Hutchings. E42: (bl) ©Jack Plekan/Fundamental Photographs; (tr) ©Richard Chung/Peter Arnold, Inc.; (br) ©Chris Rogers/The Stock Market. E44: (tr) ©Vic Bider/PhotoEdit. E45: (m) ©Charles Pefley/Stock Boston; (b) ©Deborah Davis/PhotoEdit; (tr) ©Hal Charms/PhotoEdit. E48: ©Paul A. Souders/CORBIS. E50: ©Nathan Benn/CORBIS. E51: ©Richard Hutchings. E52: (bl) ©Charles D. Winters/Photo Researchers, Inc.; (br) ©Jacana/Photo Researchers, Inc. E53: (m) ©Becky Luigart-Stayner/CORBIS; (bl,tr) ©Dr. Ed Degginger/Color-Pic; (tl,br) ©Phil Degginger/Color-Pic. E54: (bl, br) ©Phil Degginger/Color-Pic; (tr) ©Richard Hutchings. E55: (bmr) ©Adam Jones/Photo Researchers, Inc.; (m) ©Artville; (b) ©EyeWire/GETTYONE; (br, tr, umr) ©Phil Degginger/Color-Pic. E56: (tr) ©Charles D. Winters/Photo Researchers, Inc.; (bl) ©Phil Degginger/ Color-Pic. E57: (tc, tr) ©Richard Hutchings; (tl) ©Richard Megna/ Fundamental Photographs. E59: (tr) ©Joyce Photographics/Photo Researchers, Inc.; (bl, br) ©Richard Hutchings. E60: ©S. Strickland/ Naturescapes/VU. E61: (l) ©M.I. Walker/Photo Researchers, Inc.; (br) ©Richard Hutchings. E62: (bl) ©Richard Hutchings. E64: ©Mark E. Gibson/VU. E65: ©PhotoDisc. E66: ©Larry Lefever/Grant Heilman Photography, Inc. E67: (l) ©David R. Frazier/ Photo Researchers, Inc.; (br) ©David S. Addison/VU. E68: ©Nik Wheeler/CORBIS. E70: ©Richard Hutchings. E71: ©Richard Hutchings. E72: (bl) ©Ed Degginger/Color-Pic; (br) ©Richard Hutchings. E73: (br) ©Lee Snyder/Photo Researchers, Inc.; (tr, tl) ©Richard Hutchings; (bl) ©Richard Megna/Fundamental Photographs. E74: (l inset) ©Science/ VU; (tl) ©Christine L. Coscioni/CO2, Inc.; (tr, r inset) ©Leonard Lessin/Peter Arnold, Inc.; (br) ©NASA. E75: ©Richard Hutchings. E76: (tr) ©Cesar Llacuna; (br) ©Christine Coscioni/CO2, Inc. E78: (br) ©Henry Horenstein/Stock Boston; . E79: (bg) ©LSF OSF/ Animals Animals/Earth Scenes; (tl) ©Michael Newman/PhotoEdit. E80: ©Michael P. Gadomski/Photo Researchers, Inc. E82: (bmr) ©PhotoDisc; (br) ©Ed Degginger/Color-Pic; (bml) ©Ken Karp; (bl) ©Richard Megna/Fundamental Photographs. E83: ©Kristen Brochmann/ Fundamental Photographs. E84: (tl) ©John Cunningham/VU; (bl) ©Geoff Bryant/Photo Researchers Inc.; (br) ©Ken Karp. E85: ©Renee Lynn/Photo Researchers, Inc. E87: (b,m) ©Dan Howell; (tl) ©Ed Degginger/Color-Pic. E88: ©Paul Silverman/Fundamental

Photographs. E89: ©Tony Freeman/ PhotoEdit. E90: ©Denise Mattia/Denise Mattia Underwater Photography. E91: ©Richard Hutchings. E96: (bl) ©Andrew McClenaghan/Photo Researchers, Inc.; (r) ©Science/VU. E97: ©Michael Dalton/Fundamental Photographs. E98: ©Richard Hutchings. E99: ©Sheila Terry/Photo Researcher, Inc. E101: ©Craig Lovell/ Bettmann/ CORBIS. E102: (tr) ©Courtesy of Dr Mario Molina/MIT; (m) ©NASA/Science Photo Library/Photo Researchers, Inc. E103: (m) ©NASA/Photo Researchers, Inc.

National Geographic Unit Opener F: F0 ©Comstock; F1 ©Duomo/CORBIS. **Unit F:** F2: ©Photri/Tom Sanders/The Stock Market. F4: ©Annie Griffiths Belt/CORBIS. F7: ©Paul Silverman/Fundamental Photographs. F8: (m) ©NASA/Ed Degginger/Color-Pic; (b) ©Neil Rabinowitz/CORBIS. F9: (br) ©Duomo/Chris Trotman/Duomo Photography Inc.; (bl) ©Joe McDonald/CORBIS; (tl) 'Museum of Flight'/CORBIS. F10: ©Bill Aron/Photo Researchers, Inc. F11: ©Jerry Wachter/Photo Researchers, Inc. F12: ©Peter Turnley/CORBIS. F13: (b) ©George Lepp/CORBIS; (tr) ©Robert Mathena/Fundamental Photographs. F15: ©TSM/Photri/The Stock Market. F16: ©Ed Kashi/CORBIS. F20: (tr,lmr) ©Ed Degginger/Color-Pic; (umr,br) ©Tony Freeman/PhotoEdit. F21: (br) ©Ed Degginger/Color-Pic; (tr) ©Phil Degginger/Color-Pic. F22: ©LBJ Space Center/Nasa NASA. F28: (b) ©Kevin R. Morris/CORBIS; (tr) ©Paul A. Souders/CORBIS; (mr) ©Peter Turnley/CORBIS; (ml) ©Russ Schleipman/CORBIS. F30: (t) ©Barney McGrath/Science Photo Library/Photo Researchers, Inc.; (m) ©JPL/NASA; (b) ©MSSS/JPL/NASA/ Science Photo Library/ Photo Researchers, Inc. F32: ©Bettmann/CORBIS. F35: ©G.Sauvage/Vandystadt/Photo Researchers, Inc. F36: ©J-L Charmet/Science/ Photo Library/Photo Researchers, Inc. F40: (tr) ©Davis Barber/ PhotoEdit; (bl) ©Kevin R. Morris/CORBIS; (tl) ©The Image Bank/ Gettyone. F41: ©NASA/Media Dallas. F42: (bg) ©JSC/NASA; (bl) ©Zero/JSC/NASA. F45: ©NASA. F46: ©Miro/Vintoniv/Stock Boston F48: ©NASA/Galaxy Contact/Oxford Scientific Film and Photo Library. F49: ©Richard Hutchings. F50: (bl,bml,bmr) ©Artville; (br) ©Cartesia Software. F52: (tl) ©PhotoDisc; (b) ©Ken Fisher/Stone. F54: ©Ulrike Welsch. F55: ©Richard Hutchings. F56: ©Artville LLC 1997. F57: ©Tim Davis/Photo Researchers, Inc. F58: (bl) ©Courtesy Alexander Graham Bell/National Historic Park; (tr) ©William James Warren/CORBIS. F59: ©George Hall/CORBIS. F60: ©1998 PhotoDisc, Inc. F61: ©Dr. Jeremy Burgess/ Photo Researchers, Inc. F62: ©Brenda Tharp/Photo Researchers, Inc. F64: ©Kevin Fleming/CORBIS. F65: ©Richard Hutchings. F66: (br) Allsport/Brian Bahr/VU; (bl) ©Duomo/ CORBIS. F67: (tr) ©Marty Loken/Stone; (br) ©Museum der Stadt, Vienna/Austria Superstock. F68: (br) ©TSM/John M. Roberts/The Stock Market. F69: ©Wolfgang Kaehler/CORBIS. F72: (tr) ©Artville; (b) ©Joseph Schuyler/Stock Boston. F73: ©Luc Novovitch/Gamma Liaison Agency. F77: ©Artville. F78: ©VCG/FPG. F80: ©Richard Cummins/CORBIS. F81: ©Richard Hutchings. F82: (tr) ©Arthur Morris/VU; (b) ©Robert Holmgren/Peter Arnold, Inc. F83: (t) ©Barb Gerlach/VU; (mr) ©C.P. George/VU; (m) ©Rich Treptow/VU. F84: ©Richard Hutchings. F85: ©Image courtesy of Barry Luokkala, Department of Physics/Carnegie Mellon University. F86: (br) ©Richard Hutchings; (tl) ©PhotoDisc. F87: (tr) ©Paul Silverman/Fundamental Photographs; (bl, m) ©Richard Hutchings. F88: (mr,tr) ©Richard Hutchings; (bc, bl) ©Roger Ressmeyer/CORBIS. F90: ©Cesar Llacuna. F91: ©Dr. Ed Degginger/ Color-Pic. F92: (bc) ©North Wind Picture Archive/North Wind Pictures; (bl) ©Science Photo Library/Photo Researchers, Inc.; (r) ©Wolfgang Kaehler/ CORBIS. F93: (bl) ©The Queens Borough Public Library, Long Island Division, Latimer Family Papers/The Queens Borough Library; (bc) ©The Schenectady Museum. F94: ©Jack Plekan/Fundamental Photographs. F95: ©Richard Hutchings. F96: (m) ©Alfred Pasieka/ Science Photo Library/Photo Researchers, Inc.; (b) ©Richard Hutchings; (tr) ©Science/VU. F97: (tr) ©Jeff Greenberg/VU; (bl, br) ©Richard Hutchings. F98: (tr) ©Bill Beatty/VU; (bl, ml) ©Richard Hutchings. F99: ©Richard Hutchings. F100: (tl) ©PhotoDisc, 2000; (r,bc) ©Richard Hutchings. F103: ©James Webb/PhotoTake. F106: ©Jeremy Walker/Stone Gettyone. F107: ©Richard Hutchings. F109: ©Richard Hutchings. F113: ©Ed Degginger/Color-Pic. F114: ©NASA/ Media Dallas. F116: ©Richard Hutchings. F118: ©Bettmann/CORBIS. F119: ©Hewlitt Packard Fundamental Photographs. F120: (br) ©1998 PhotoDisc, Inc.; (i) ©Science/VU. F121: ©Carolyn A. McKeone/Photo Researchers, Inc. F122: ©Science/VU. F126: (t) ©Gary Gold/Rennsslaer Polytechnical Institute; (b) ©courtesy of Dr. Shirley Jackson/Rennsslaer Polytechnical Institute.

Science and Health Handbook: All photos ©Richard Hutchings with the following exceptions: R10: (m) ©Jim Harrison/Stock Boston/PNI. R14: (m) ©G.R. Roberts/Photo Researchers, Inc.

Teacher's Notes

Contents

Correlated to
National Science Education Content Standards
(Grades 5–8)

	Units of *McGraw-Hill Science:* Grade 5					
	UNIT A Structures of Plants/Animals	**UNIT B** Interactions of Living Things	**UNIT C** Earth and Its Resources	**UNIT D** Weather and Climate	**UNIT E** Properties of Matter/Energy	**UNIT F** Motion and Energy
Science as Inquiry						
Abilities necessary to do scientific inquiry	✔	✔	✔	✔	✔	✔
Understanding about scientific inquiry	✔	✔	✔	✔	✔	✔
Physical Science						
Properties and changes of properties in matter	✔	✔	✔	✔	✔	
Motion and forces			✔	✔		✔
Transfer of energy	✔	✔	✔	✔	✔	✔
Life Science						
Structure and function in living things	✔					
Reproduction and heredity	✔					
Regulation and behavior	✔	✔				
Populations and ecosystems	✔	✔				
Diversity and adaptations of organisms	✔	✔			✔	
Earth and Space Science						
Structure of the Earth system	✔	✔	✔	✔		✔
Earth's history	✔	✔	✔	✔		
Earth in the solar system			✔	✔		✔
Science and Technology						
Abilities of technological design	✔	✔	✔	✔	✔	✔
Understanding about science and technology	✔	✔	✔	✔	✔	✔
Science in Personal and Social Perspectives						
Personal health	✔	✔	✔	✔	✔	
Populations, resources, and environments	✔	✔	✔	✔		✔
Natural hazards	✔	✔	✔	✔		
Risks and benefits	✔	✔	✔	✔	✔	
Science and Technology in Society	✔	✔	✔	✔	✔	✔
Nature and History of Science						
Science as a human endeavor; Nature of science	✔	✔	✔	✔	✔	✔
History of science	✔			✔	✔	✔
Unifying Concepts and Processes						
Systems, order, and organization	✔	✔	✔	✔	✔	
Evidence, models, and explanation		✔	✔	✔	✔	✔
Change, constancy, measurement	✔	✔	✔	✔	✔	✔
Evolution and equilibrium		✔	✔			
Form and function	✔					

Correlated to
Benchmarks for Science Literacy
(Grades 3–5)

Benchmarks for Science Literacy (Grades 3–5)	Units of McGraw-Hill Science: Grade 5					
	UNIT A Structures of Plants and Animals	**UNIT B** Interactions of Living Things	**UNIT C** Earth and Its Resources	**UNIT D** Weather and Climate	**UNIT E** Properties of Matter and Energy	**UNIT F** Motion and Energy
The Nature of Science						
Scientific view of the world	✔	✔	✔	✔	✔	✔
Scientific inquiry	✔	✔	✔	✔	✔	✔
The scientific enterprise	✔	✔	✔	✔	✔	✔
The Nature of Technology						
Technology and science	✔		✔		✔	✔
Design and systems			✔	✔	✔	✔
Issues in technology	✔	✔	✔			✔
The Physical Setting						
The universe			✔	✔		✔
The Earth	✔		✔	✔		✔
Processes that shape Earth			✔			✔
Structure of Matter			✔	✔		
Energy transformations			✔	✔		
Motion			✔	✔		✔
Forces of nature	✔	✔	✔			✔
The Living Environment						
Diversity of life	✔	✔	✔		✔	✔
Heredity	✔	✔				
Cells	✔					
Interdependence of life	✔	✔				
Flow of matter and energy	✔	✔	✔			
Evolution of life	✔	✔				
The Human Organism						
Human identity	✔	✔		✔	✔	✔
Basic functions	✔	✔			✔	
Physical health	✔	✔			✔	✔
Common Themes						
Systems	✔	✔	✔	✔	✔	✔
Models		✔	✔	✔	✔	✔
Constancy and change	✔	✔	✔	✔	✔	✔
Scale	✔	✔			✔	✔

McGraw-Hill Curriculum Integration: Science and Reading

Correlation of *McGraw-Hill Science* with:
• *Spotlight on Literacy* • *McGraw-Hill Reading*

McGraw-Hill Science correlates with these reading programs by means of its content as well as of the Reading Skills highlighted in each unit.

McGraw-Hill Science Grade 5	Spotlight on Literacy selections with corresponding content or skills	McGraw-Hill Reading selections with corresponding content or skills
UNIT 1 STRUCTURES OF PLANTS AND ANIMALS **Topic Focus** • diversity of life • using sunlight to make food • survival, response • reproduction, life cycles **Process Skill Builders** • Experiment • Classify • Observe **Chapter Reading Skills** • Draw conclusions • Summarize • Compare and contrast	**Content** • The Gold Coin (farming, crops) • The Best Bad Thing (harvesting, crops) **Skills** *Draw conclusions* • The Voyage of the *Dawn Treader* • The Gold Coin *Compare and contrast* • Dive to the Coral Reefs • New Providence: A Changing Cityscape *Summarize* • Dive to the Coral Reefs • The News About Dinosaurs	**Content** • The Gold Coin (farming, crops) • Carlos and the Skunk • Tonweya and the Eagles **Skills** *Draw conclusions* • The Voyage of the *Dawn Treader* * • Hot on Lewis & Clark's Trail *Compare and contrast* • The Riddle * • Breaker's Bridge *Summarize* • The Marble Champ * • The Paper Dragon
UNIT 2 INTERACTIONS OF LIVING THINGS **Topic Focus** • ecosystems, roles of living things • cycles • biomes, oceans & land • change in ecosystems • environmental concerns **Process Skill Builders** • Use variables • Infer **Chapter Reading Skills** • Sequence of Events • Summarize	**Content** • Dive to the Coral Reefs (ocean ecosystems) • Human-Made Reef Relief • Grandma Essie's Covered Wagon (prairie) • The News About Dinosaurs (ancient ecosystems) **Skills** *Sequence of events* • It's Our World, Too! • Breaker's Bridge *Summarize* • Dive to the Coral Reefs • A Wave in Her Pocket	**Content** • Amazon Alert (rain forests) • An Island Scrapbook **Skills** *Sequence of events* • The Paper Dragon * • Amazon Alert! *Summarize* • The Marble Champ * • The Paper Dragon
UNIT 3 EARTH AND ITS RESOURCES **Topic Focus** • Earth in space • changes on Earth, landforms • minerals, rocks, soil • Earth's air, water, energy • environmental concerns **Process Skill Builders** • Define • Form a hypothesis **Chapter Reading Skills** • Sequence of events • Draw conclusions	**Content** • New Providence: A Changing Cityscape (human impact on land) • Identified Flying Objects (solar system) • It's Our World, Too! **Skills** *Sequence of events* • It's Our World, Too! • Breaker's Bridge *Draw conclusions* • The Voyage of the *Dawn Treader* • Einstein Anderson	**Content** • It's Our World, Too! • Cleaning Up America's Air **Skills** *Sequence of events* • The Paper Dragon * • Amazon Alert! *Draw conclusions* • The Voyage of the *Dawn Treader* * • Hot on Lewis & Clark's Trail

*Skill is introduced in McGraw-Hill Reading with a two-page lesson that accompanies the selection.

McGraw-Hill Science Grade 5	Spotlight on Literacy selections with corresponding content or skills	McGraw-Hill Reading selections with corresponding content or skills
UNIT D WEATHER AND CLIMATE **Topic Focus** • the Sun as energy source • water cycle, making clouds • weather conditions, storms • climate, past and present **Process Skill Builder:** • Interpret data • Measure **Chapter Reading Skills** • Find the main idea & supporting details • Sequence of events	**Content** • The Big Storm ***Main idea & supporting details*** • Dive to the Coral Reefs • The News About Dinosaurs ***Sequence of events*** • It's Our World, Too! • The Big Storm • Breaker's Bridge • Tonweya and the Eagles • Klondike Fever	**Content** • Tornado Watch: Tracking Storms • The Big Storm **Skills** ***Main idea & supporting details*** • It's Our World, Too! * • Rediscovering Jamestown ***Sequence of events*** • The Paper Dragon * • Grandma Essie's Covered Wagon
UNIT E PROPERTIES OF MATTER AND ENERGY **Topic Focus** • properties, atomic structure • solids, liquids, gases • mixtures, acids, bases • chemical changes, energy **Process Skill Builder** • Make a model • Experiment **Chapter Reading Skills** • Find the main idea & supporting details • Cause and effect	**Content** • Money, Money, Money (metals as money) • Klondike Fever (gold) **Skills:** ***Main idea & supporting details*** • Dive to the Coral Reefs • The News About Dinosaurs ***Cause and effect*** • Klondike Fever • The Wreck of the *Zephyr*	**Content** ***Main idea & supporting details*** • It's Our World, Too! * • Rediscovering Jamestown ***Cause and effect*** • Wilma Unlimited * • Sea Maidens of Japan
UNIT F MOTION AND ENERGY **Topic Focus** • Newton's Laws • nature of sound, properties of sound • visible light, mirrors, lenses, color • uses of invisible light • how scientists found out what light is **Process Skill Builder** • Use numbers • Communicate • Predict **Chapter Reading Skills** • Draw conclusions • Cause and effect • Compare and contrast	**Content** • How to Think Like a Scientist **Skills** ***Predict*** • The Talking Eggs • The Voyage of the *Dawn Treader* ***Draw conclusions*** • The Voyage of the *Dawn Treader* • Einstein Anderson ***Cause and effect*** • The Silent Lobby • The Wreck of the *Zephyr* ***Compare and contrast*** • Dive to the Coral Reefs • New Providence: A Changing Cityscape	**Content** • How to Think Like a Scientist • The Marble Champ **Skills** ***Predict*** • The Gold Coin * • Dear Mr. Henshaw ***Draw conclusions*** • The Voyage of the *Dawn Treader* * • Hot on Lewis & Clark's Trail ***Cause and effect*** • Wilma Unlimited * • Amazon Alert ***Compare and contrast*** • The Riddle * • Breaker's Bridge

Inch Graph Paper

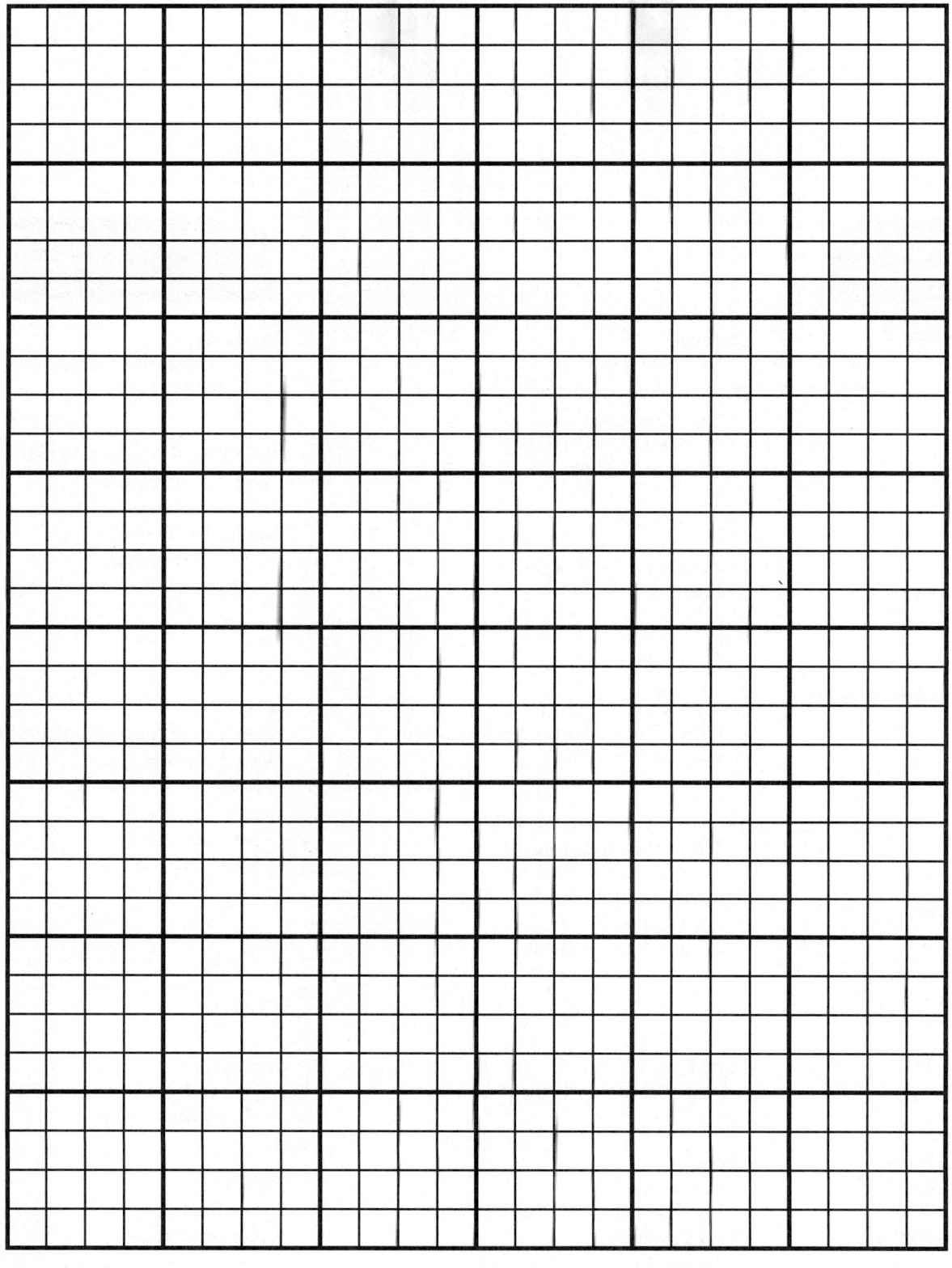

Macmillan/McGraw-Hill

Rulers: Inch, Centimeter

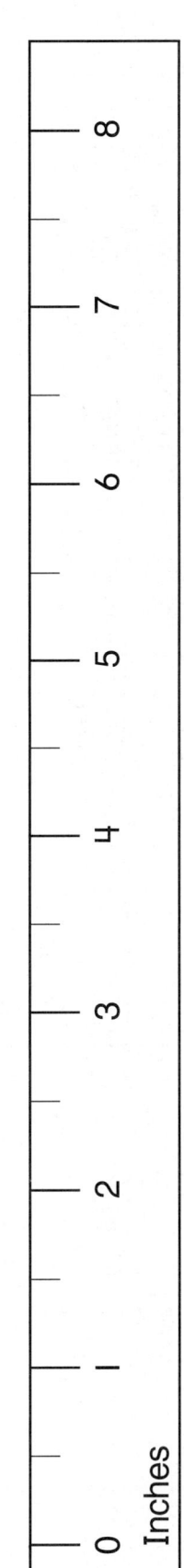

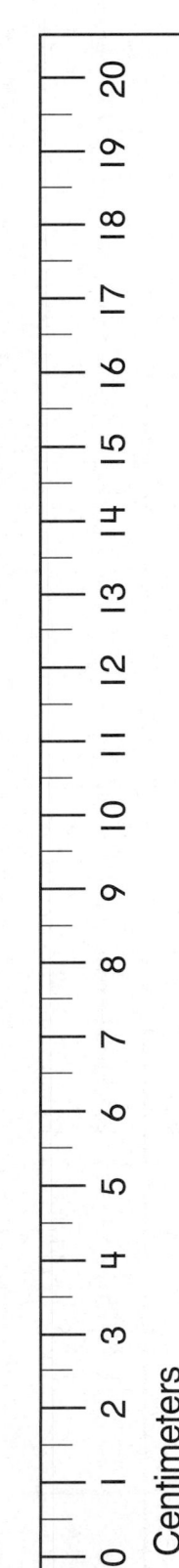

Map of United States

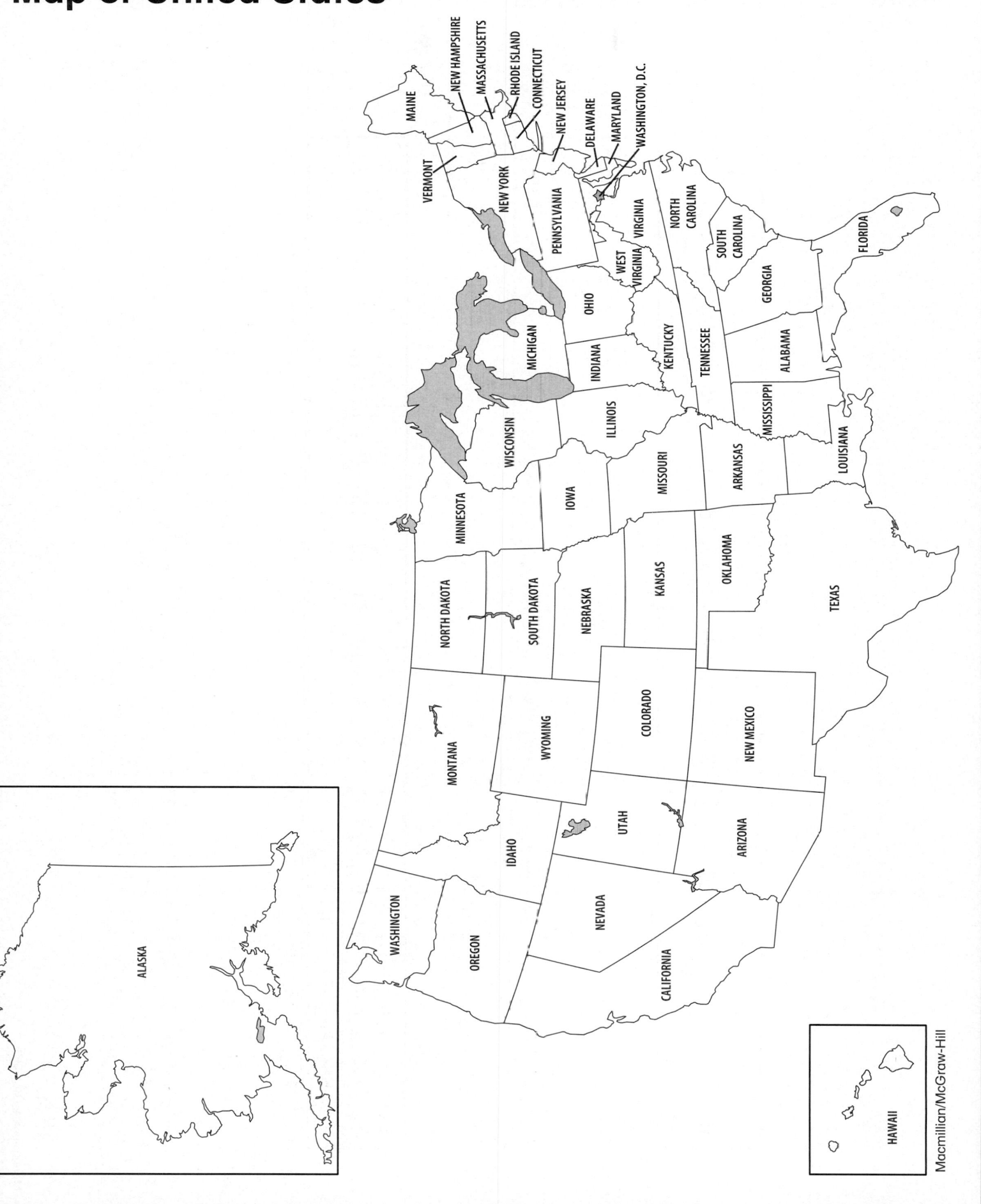

MAINE

NEW HAMPSHIRE

MASSACHUSETTS

RHODE ISLAND

CONNECTICUT

NEW JERSEY

DELAWARE

MARYLAND

WASHINGTON, D.C.

VERMONT

NEW YORK

PENNSYLVANIA

VIRGINIA

NORTH CAROLINA

SOUTH CAROLINA

FLORIDA

WEST VIRGINIA

OHIO

GEORGIA

MICHIGAN

INDIANA

KENTUCKY

TENNESSEE

ALABAMA

WISCONSIN

ILLINOIS

MISSISSIPPI

MISSOURI

ARKANSAS

LOUISIANA

MINNESOTA

IOWA

NORTH DAKOTA

SOUTH DAKOTA

NEBRASKA

KANSAS

OKLAHOMA

TEXAS

MONTANA

WYOMING

COLORADO

NEW MEXICO

IDAHO

UTAH

ARIZONA

WASHINGTON

OREGON

NEVADA

CALIFORNIA

ALASKA

HAWAII

Macmillian/McGraw-Hill

World Map

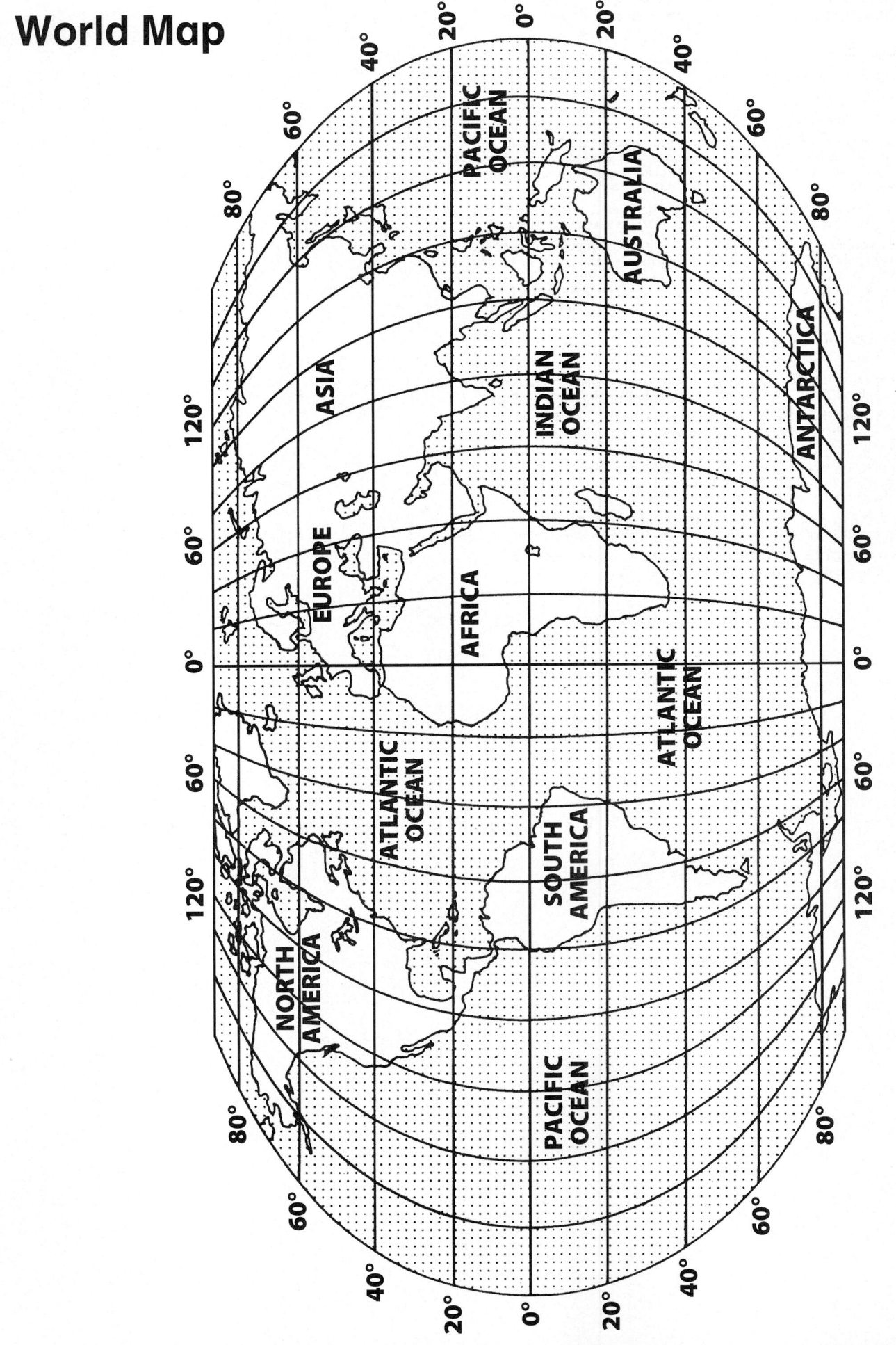

Credits for Teacher's Edition

Cover Design and Illustration: Robert Brook Allen

Cover Photos: ©Tim Flach/Stone; (bg) ©Darrell Gulin/Natural Selection; (i) ©PhotoSpin 2000.

Title Page: ©PhotoSpin 2000.

Cracked Earth Borders: ©PhotoSpin 2000.

Contents: iv: ©Norbert Wu. v: ©Tim Flach/Stone. vi: l ©Jules Cowan/Index Stock Imagery; b ©Joyce Photographics/Photo Researchers, Inc; r ©A.J. Copley/VU. vii: l ©NOAA, colored by John Wells/Science Photo Library/Photo Researchers, Inc; r ©Runk/Schoenberger/Grant Heilman. viii: l ©Roger Ressmeyer/Corbis; b ©Science/VU; ix: ©Duomo/Corbis.

p. Tvi: t.l. Siede Preis/ PhotoDisc; m.l. Clement Mok/ PhotoDisc; b.l. Siede Preis/ PhotoDisc. Tviii: t.l. Dan Howell for MHSD; t.r. Dan Howell for MHSD; (1/4) David Waitz for MHSD.

Invitation to Science: p. S1: (clockwise from upper left) Mark A. Madison; James L. Stanfield, National Geographic Image Collection; © Gianni Tortoli/ Photo Researchers, Inc.; © Chris Hondros/ Liaison Agency, Inc. p. S2: (clockwise from left) David Coleman, Stock • Boston; Roger Tulley, Tony Stone Images; Lawrence Migdale, Stock • Boston; Bob Daemmrich, Bob Daemmrich Photo Inc.; Bob Daemmrich, Bob Daemmrich Photo Inc.; Jim Cummins/FPG International.

National Geographic Tab A: Kelvin Aitken, Peter Arnold, Inc. **Unit A:** p. A1•a: © R&V Taylor/ Bruce Coleman, Inc.; p. A1•d: t.r. CMCD/ PhotoDisc; p. A1: ©Kelvin Aitken/Peter Arnold, Inc..

National Geographic Tab B: Stone/Tim Flach. **Unit B:** p. B1•a: © Kennan Ward/ The Stock Market; p. B1•d: t.r. CMCD/ PhotoDisc; p. B1: ©Art Wolfe/Stone; p. B1: ©Tim Flach/Stone.

National Geographic Tab C: Jules Cowan, Index Stock Imagery. **Unit C:** p. C1•a: © Peter French/ Bruce Coleman, Inc.; p. C1•d: t.r. Siede Preis/ PhotoDisc; p. C1: ©Jules Cowan/Index Stock Imagery.

National Geographic Tab D: NOAA, colored by John Wells/Science Photo Library, Photo Researchers, Inc. **Unit D:** p. D1•a: © Stephen Ingram/ Animals Animals/ Earth Scenes; p. D1•d: t.r. Siede Preis/ PhotoDisc; p. D1: © World Perspective/Stone.

National Geographic Tab E: © Roger Ressmeyer/CORBIS. **Unit E:** p. E1•a: © Christine Osborne/ CORBIS; p. E1•d: t.r. CD Squared/PhotoDisc; p. E1: ©Roger Ressmeyer/Corbis.

National Geographic Tab F: COMSTOCK, Inc. **Unit F:** p. F1•a: © Photri/ Tom Sanders/ The Stock Market; p. F1•d: t.r. CD Squared/PhotoDisc; p. F1: ©Duomo/Corbis.

Teacher's Notes

Teacher's Notes

Teacher's Notes

Teacher's Notes

Teacher's Notes

PERIODIC TABLE OF THE ELEMENTS

Key

6
C
Carbon

- Atomic number
- Element symbol
- Element name

Phase at 20° C

C	Solid
Br	Liquid
H	Gas

Metallic Properties

Li	Metal
B	Metalloid
C	Nonmetal

1	2	3	4	5	6	7	8	9	10	11	12	13	14	15	16	17	18
1 **H** Hydrogen																	2 **He** Helium
3 **Li** Lithium	4 **Be** Beryllium											5 **B** Boron	6 **C** Carbon	7 **N** Nitrogen	8 **O** Oxygen	9 **F** Fluorine	10 **Ne** Neon
11 **Na** Sodium	12 **Mg** Magnesium											13 **Al** Aluminum	14 **Si** Silicon	15 **P** Phosphorus	16 **S** Sulfur	17 **Cl** Chlorine	18 **Ar** Argon
19 **K** Potassium	20 **Ca** Calcium	21 **Sc** Scandium	22 **Ti** Titanium	23 **V** Vanadium	24 **Cr** Chromium	25 **Mn** Manganese	26 **Fe** Iron	27 **Co** Cobalt	28 **Ni** Nickel	29 **Cu** Copper	30 **Zn** Zinc	31 **Ga** Gallium	32 **Ge** Germanium	33 **As** Arsenic	34 **Se** Selenium	35 **Br** Bromine	36 **Kr** Krypton
37 **Rb** Rubidium	38 **Sr** Strontium	39 **Y** Yttrium	40 **Zr** Zirconium	41 **Nb** Niobium	42 **Mo** Molybdenum	43 **Tc** Technetium	44 **Ru** Ruthenium	45 **Rh** Rhodium	46 **Pd** Palladium	47 **Ag** Silver	48 **Cd** Cadmium	49 **In** Indium	50 **Sn** Tin	51 **Sb** Antimony	52 **Te** Tellurium	53 **I** Iodine	54 **Xe** Xenon
55 **Cs** Cesium	56 **Ba** Barium	71 **Lu** Lutetium	72 **Hf** Hafnium	73 **Ta** Tantalum	74 **W** Tungsten	75 **Re** Rhenium	76 **Os** Osmium	77 **Ir** Iridium	78 **Pt** Platinum	79 **Au** Gold	80 **Hg** Mercury	81 **Tl** Thallium	82 **Pb** Lead	83 **Bi** Bismuth	84 **Po** Polonium	85 **At** Astatine	86 **Rn** Radon
87 **Fr** Francium	88 **Ra** Radium	103 **Lr** Lawrencium	104 **Rf** Rutherfordium	105 **Db** Dubnium	106 **Sg** Seaborgium	107 **Bh** Bohrium	108 **Hs** Hassium	109 **Mt** Meitnerium	110	111	112	114		116		118	

Lanthanide Series

| 57 **La** Lanthanum | 58 **Ce** Cerium | 59 **Pr** Praseodymium | 60 **Nd** Neodymium | 61 **Pm** Promethium | 62 **Sm** Samarium | 63 **Eu** Europium | 64 **Gd** Gadolinium | 65 **Tb** Terbium | 66 **Dy** Dysprosium | 67 **Ho** Holmium | 68 **Er** Erbium | 69 **Tm** Thulium | 70 **Yb** Ytterbium |

Actinide Series

| 89 **Ac** Actinium | 90 **Th** Thorium | 91 **Pa** Protactinium | 92 **U** Uranium | 93 **Np** Neptunium | 94 **Pu** Plutonium | 95 **Am** Americium | 96 **Cm** Curium | 97 **Bk** Berkelium | 98 **Cf** Californium | 99 **Es** Einsteinium | 100 **Fm** Fermium | 101 **Md** Mendelevium | 102 **No** Nobelium |